Environmental Ethics

Environmental Ethics

Divergence and Convergence

THIRD EDITION

Susan J. Armstrong
Humboldt State University

Richard G. Botzler
Humboldt State University

Boston Burr Ridge, IL Dubuque, IA Madison, WI New York
San Francisco St. Louis Bangkok Bogotá Caracas Kuala Lumpur
Lisbon London Madrid Mexico City Milan Montreal New Delhi
Santiago Seoul Singapore Sydney Taipei Toronto

Higher Education

ENVIRONMENTAL ETHICS: DIVERGENCE AND CONVERGENCE, THIRD EDITION
Published by McGraw-Hill, a business unit of The McGraw-Hill Companies, Inc., 1221
Avenue of the Americas, New York, NY 10020. Copyright © 2004, 1998, 1993 by The
McGraw-Hill Companies, Inc. All rights reserved. No part of this publication may be
reproduced or distributed in any form or by any means, or stored in a database or retrieval
system, without the prior written consent of The McGraw-Hill Companies, Inc., including,
but not limited to, any network or other electronic storage or transmission, or broadcast for
distance learning.

Some ancillaries, including electronic and print components, may not be available to
customers outside the United States.

5 6 7 8 9 0 DOC/DOC 0

ISBN: 978-0-07-283845-9
MHID: 0-07-283845-0

Vice president and editor-in-chief: *Thalia Dorwick*
Publisher: *Chris Freitag*
Sponsoring editor: *Jon-David Hague*
Marketing manager: *Lisa Berry*
Production editor: *Holly Paulsen*
Manuscript editor: *Judith Brown*
Art director: *Jeanne M. Schreiber*
Design manager: *Cassandra Chu*
Cover designer: *Yvo Riezebos*
Interior designer: *Glenda King*
Art manager: *Robin Mouat*
Art editor: *Cristin Yancey*
Illustrator: *Precision Graphics*
Production supervisor: *Tandra Jorgensen*

The text was set in 10/11.5 Times by ColorType and printed on acid-free, 45# New Era
Matte by R. R. Donnelley, Crawfordsville.

Cover image: © Steve Satushek/Getty Images/The Image Bank

The text credits for this book begin on page 605, a continuation of the copyright page.

Library of Congress Cataloging-in-Publication Data
Environmental ethics : divergence and convergence / edited by Susan J. Armstrong,
  Richard G. Botzler. — 3rd ed.
    p. cm.
  Includes bibliographical references.
  ISBN 0-07-283845-0 (softcover)
  1. Environmental ethics. 2. Human ecology — History. I. Armstrong, Susan J. (Susan
Jean) II. Botzler, Richard George, 1942–

GF80.E585 2003
179'.1 — dc21

2003056100

www.mhhe.com

Dedicated to

My grandchildren
Mike, Bobby, Jessie, Shelby, and Gracie
SJA

Sally
RGB

About the Authors

SUSAN J. ARMSTRONG is professor of philosophy and women's studies at Humboldt State University. She received her Ph.D. in philosophy from Bryn Mawr College in 1976. During graduate school she was manager of the *Review of Metaphysics.* She is co-editor of *The Animal Ethics Reader* (2003). Her dissertation, "The Rights of Nonhuman Beings: a Whiteheadian Study" (1976), is considered to be the first dissertation written on environmental ethics (available online at www.humboldt.edu/~phil/susan.html). She has published articles in *Environmental Ethics,* the *Journal of Wildlife Diseases,* the *Trumpeter,* and *Process Studies.* She has contributed book chapters on Hegel and Kierkegaard, animal psi, and postmodern theology and is a member of the editorial review board of *Environmental Ethics.* She was nominated for outstanding professor in 1989 and 2002.

RICHARD G. BOTZLER is professor of wildlife at Humboldt State University. He received a Ph.D. in wildlife management from the University of Michigan in 1970. He served as a Fulbright Fellow to Germany in 1981–82 and as editor for the *Journal of Wildlife Diseases* from 1991 through 1996. He has authored over forty publications on wildlife diseases and environmental ethics and is co-editor with Susan of *The Animal Ethics Reader* (2003). He was selected as Humboldt State University's outstanding professor for 1991–92 and as 1992 outstanding professor for the twenty-campus California State University. He received the Wildlife Disease Association's distinguished service award in 1997. He enjoys hiking the backcountry of Humboldt County.

Preface to the Third Edition

The third edition of *Environmental Ethics: Divergence and Convergence* has been extensively revised. Over sixty percent of the readings are new. We have aimed at preserving the best features of earlier editions as well as incorporating readings that reflect the dynamic changes in the field of environmental ethics.

With this third edition, we believe each student will have the foundations necessary to develop her or his own environmental ethic. While working through this text, students will encounter all of the major approaches to environmental ethics in a way that allows them to evaluate both the strengths and the weaknesses of each approach.

As indicated by the subtitle, *Divergence and Convergence,* some of the current ethical perspectives converge on similar answers in practice. We believe it important to point this out where it occurs. Yet some approaches resist further unification and need to be understood and evaluated on their own.

It is our conviction that environmental issues *must* be approached in a multidisciplinary manner. The dominant mode of addressing these issues in Western society is through a combination of science and economics, partly because of the ease with which information can be quantified in these fields. We contend, however, that adequate solutions to environmental problems require the addition of well-informed ethical, aesthetic, and cultural perspectives.

The text is a comprehensive and balanced introduction to the field of environmental ethics for upper-division undergraduate students. It also may be useful for lower-division courses and for introductory courses at the graduate level. This text is appropriate for use in courses dealing with environmental ethics from a theoretical perspective. It also can serve as a foundation for courses that address specific environmental problems.

Both of us have been professionally involved in environmental ethics since the 1970s. Rick Botzler has taught environmental ethics courses since 1977. Susan Armstrong's dissertation *The Rights of Nonhuman Beings: A Whiteheadian Study* was copyrighted in 1976 and is considered to be the first dissertation on environmental ethics, though it emphasizes animals and plants. This book is based on our experience of team-teaching environmental ethics since 1983. All except the most recent articles have been tested in the classroom for effective use.

Environmental Ethics: Divergence and Convergence offers the instructor a number of features not available, or less prominent, in other texts:

- A multidisciplinary approach incorporating natural science, social science, aesthetic, ethical, and religious perspectives
- Non-Western as well as Western religious and cultural perspectives
- A structured and standardized terminology for this developing field

- Instructional aids for each chapter: chapter introductions and individual headnote introductions to each reading, discussion topics for each reading, a class exercise for each chapter, and annotated recommended readings
- Ecofeminist perspectives
- Editorship by both a scientist and a philosopher
- Focus on the students' development of their own environmental ethic. This goal is furthered by the solicitation of student perspectives, reactions, and experiences in the discussion topics, as well as by the selection of readings that are well-written and accessible to upper-division students

The *third edition* also includes:

- Thirty-nine new articles to include the best of recent material
- More emphasis on social issues and applications
- Updated chapter introductions and study questions
- Current topics such as land rights, biodiversity, management, environmental justice, and genetic engineering
- Cutting-edge articles in environmental ethical theory
- Contemporary perspectives on the environment from writers of Christian, Jewish, and Islamic faiths, as well as from various cultural groups
- Excellent coverage of the dominant approaches to the environment
- Five new case studies

Because the development of such a comprehensive text is beyond the abilities of one or even two editors, we gratefully acknowledge the help of many others. We thank those who helped us form the design of the text. We also thank the following reviewers who have contributed many valuable suggestions:

Joe Bowersox III, *Willamette University*

Rick Brown, *Humboldt State University*

Lowell Diller, *Simpson Timber Co.*

James Goetsch, Jr., *Eckerd College*

William Harger, *College of the Redwoods*

Valerie Luzadis, *SUNY College of Environmental Science and Forestry*

Daniel Primozic, *Elmhurst College*

Robert Snyder, *Humboldt State University*

Rick is particularly grateful to his wife, Sally, whose unflagging support, salient insights, and editorial skills helped make his contribution to this project a reality. Susan also wishes to thank those she is most closely associated with for their support: her children, Tom, Summer, Alex, and Emily, and her mother, Shirley.

We have benefited greatly from the criticism and suggestions of professional colleagues and students in the revision of this book. However, any errors herein are entirely our own.

In one sense, a book of this nature is never completed but must continually evolve to serve its users in this rapidly changing field. We invite you, both professional colleagues and students, to help enhance its value. Tell us what aspects you found helpful and what you believe could be improved. The topic of environmental ethics is of such importance, it deserves the best that each of us can bring to its development.

Susan J. Armstrong   sja3@humboldt.edu

Richard G. Botzler   rgb2@humboldt.edu

Contents

CHAPTER 3   Aesthetics   117

CHAPTER 4   Historical Context   158

PART TWO
FUNDAMENTAL WORLD VIEWS

CHAPTER 5   Religious and Cultural Perspectives   215

POLITICS

CASE STUDIES

INTRODUCTION

In the short essay "Unchopping a Tree" at the end of this introduction, W. S. Merwin gives us directions on reassembling a tree. In the essay, even if all goes well and the tree is reassembled, the tree is still dead. Yet Merwin ends with an imperative: "Everything is going to have to be put back."

How much easier not to chop down the tree in the first place! Yet we know that some trees must be chopped down, at least at present. Which ones, and how? These are urgent questions.

Human activities have profound impacts on our planet. How great are these impacts? One scientist has recently suggested that humans may now be the world's dominant evolutionary force.[1] A recent scientific article estimated that approximately forty percent of Earth's total plant growth or net primary production is appropriated by human beings for their own use.[2] According to some estimates humanity now exceeds by about thirty percent the planet's capacity to sustain its production of renewable resources.[3] As a consequence, the world is currently undergoing a very rapid loss of biodiversity.

For example, between 1970 and 2000, the Living Planet Index (LPI), a measure of the populations of hundreds of species, declined by about thirty-five percent. Within the past fifty years, tropical forests have shrunk by half, resulting in poor economic returns from the land that has been converted to croplands and ecological disaster in terms of species extinctions. Most accessible rivers are dammed and channeled. Fishing is the major threat to the oceans' biodiversity. Most major fish stocks are overfished.[4] While there are also positive changes, such as the facts that eighty-five percent of streams in the United States now meet human health standards, and land threatened by erosion has declined by a third since

---

[1]S. R. Palumbi, "Humans as the World's Greatest Evolutionary Force," *Science* 293 (2001): 1786–90.

[2]C. B. Field, "Sharing the Garden," *Science* 294 (2001): 2490–91.

[3]Living Planet Report, 2002, available at http://www.panda.org/news_facts/publications/general/livingplanet/index.cfm.

[4]S. L. Pimm, et al., "Can We Defy Nature's End?" *Science* 293 (2001): 2207–8.

1985,[5] overall, the many and growing human impacts on global ecosystems are resulting in a loss of resiliency (the ability to spring back to a former state). Recent studies have shown that a loss of resilience can pave the way for large-scale, catastrophic shifts in major ecosystems.[6]

Environmental ethics has emerged during the past thirty years as a response both to new information about the interconnectedness of life and to new experiences of environmental degradation. We believe that this discipline can contribute to meeting the challenges that face us.

WHAT IS ENVIRONMENTAL ETHICS?

Environmental ethics is the field of inquiry that addresses the ethical responsibilities of human beings for the natural environment. It is concerned with values: Does nature have value that extends beyond its obvious role of meeting human needs? Do some parts of nature have more value than others? What is the responsibility of humans toward nature and natural entities? While the field took its name from the 1979 creation of the journal *Environmental Ethics,* we recognize that this field is not limited to ethical inquiry but is also imbedded in a larger matrix of aesthetic, religious, scientific, economic, and political considerations.

Environmental Ethics Is a Developing Field

Environmental ethics encompasses a surprising richness and diversity of responses to the concerns raised by the environmental crisis. As a distinctive discipline, it probably did not develop much before 1970. Environmental ethics deals with a global subject matter in a world that is just beginning to develop the ability to engage in global cooperation. No single set of ideas has been persuasive in convincing the majority of environmentally aware scholars that it is the key to the right relationship to the environment. As such, the field is still in a stage of active growth and development and offers a variety of exciting ideas. In fact, the field has expanded so much since 1992, when we edited the first edition of this book, that it has been extremely difficult to canvass, analyze, and summarize even a portion of the significant and relevant work published since then. It is likely that the field will continue to grow exponentially in the years ahead.

Environmental Ethics Is Multidisciplinary

Because environmental ethics concerns the human relationship to the environment, it includes all of the major perspectives on this relationship: scientific, ethical, aesthetic, political, economic, and religious. One-sided or narrow perspectives simply do not address the subject matter in an adequate way.

Unfortunately, many policy decisions are currently based primarily on some combination of science and economics. These disciplines are attractive to decision makers in that they lend themselves to quantification and computerization. However, when relied on to resolve environmental problems, they can yield false, oversimplified answers. This restricted information base is further narrowed by the fact that throughout much of the twentieth century scientists have been trained to take a negative view of ethics and values, according to which values are "subjective, biased, emotional, and even irrational."[7]

Despite the anti-value orientation of many scientists and economists, people in general affirm a number of environmental values. David Bengston, an ecological economist with the U.S. Forest Service, has distinguished four types of values: economic/utilitarian, life support (or ecological value), aesthetic value, and moral/spiritual value.[8] His analysis

---

[5]B. Shouse, "Report Takes Stock of Knowns and Unknowns," *Science* 297 (27 Sept. 2002): 2191.

[6]M. Scheffer, et al., "Catastrophic Shifts in Ecosystems," *Nature* 413 (11 Oct. 2001): 591–96.

[7]Eugene Hargrove, "Science, Ethics and the Care of Ecosystems," in *Northern Protected Areas and Wilderness,* Juri Peepre and Bob Jickling, eds. (Whitehorse, Yukon: Canadian Parks and Wilderness Society, 1994). Hargrove provides an illuminating account of the development of the scientific attitude toward values. For a similar analysis and a description of the outcome for our treatment of animals, see Bernard E. Rollin, *The Unheeded Cry* (Oxford: Oxford University Press, 1990).

[8]David N. Bengston, "The Nature of Value and the Value of Nature," in *Foresters Together: Meeting Tomorrow's Challenges,* Proceedings of the 1993 Society of American Foresters National Convention, Indianapolis, Ind. (Bethesda, MD: Society of American Foresters Publication 94-01, 1994).

has disclosed a shift in public opinion in recent decades, such that the noneconomic values have become more important.[9]

Environmental policymakers, government officials, and ecological scientists are making value decisions in their work, whether they realize it or not. Their decisions may reflect a generally unarticulated and uncritical vision of life and value. In order to help remedy this situation, a central aim of this book is to equip the reader to articulate and examine his or her personal values as well as the collective values of society.

Environmental Ethics Is Multicultural

The environmental crisis is international. It is no longer possible for one society to live without having a significant impact on others. The political, economic, religious, moral, and aesthetic traditions, as well as institutional structures in both Western and non-Western societies, must be sympathetically addressed and understood to successfully develop a respectful, workable international environmental ethic. A multicultural perspective provides richer resources from which both Western and non-Western societies can draw to reframe and resolve environmental problems. Issues of justice in the distribution of resources, both between existing countries and between existing generations and those of the future, require attention and action.

Environmental Ethics Is Transformative

Because environmental ethics has emerged in response to global environmental crisis, many proposals address the need for a transformation of human experience. Traditional economic arrangements that ignore environmental consequences, traditional political arrangements that impose artificial territorial limits on continuous physical processes and systems, and traditional philosophic and religious theories that consider human beings in isolation from

their natural surroundings are all being examined and modified. The incorporation of environmental concerns into these traditional theories is not just a minor shift of emphasis but a substantial change in approach.

ENVIRONMENTAL ETHICS: DIVERGENCE AND CONVERGENCE

We have subtitled this book *Divergence and Convergence* because of its double aim. First, we want to offer readings that represent the major philosophical approaches to environmental ethics, including anthropocentrism, individualism, ecocentrism, ecofeminism, and several based on both Western and non-Western religious traditions. We believe that each of these approaches can be held by intellectually sincere people. We have sought to include the writings of those scholars that best help the reader evaluate the relative strengths and weaknesses of each position.

Second, we believe that some of these approaches have begun to converge in important ways. As you consider each chapter, we suggest that you keep this convergence in mind. Note that while theoretical approaches differ, the policy recommendations or conduct based on these approaches sometimes are relatively similar. This convergence is important because it indicates that similar constructive changes in the human treatment of the environment can result from more than one philosophical approach to environmental ethics.[10]

FEATURES OF THIS BOOK

We have edited this book as an aid to developing your own environmental ethic. To do so, we include essays encompassing the major approaches to environmental ethics. The chapter openers not only introduce specific readings but also provide brief orientations to the entire field addressed by the readings.

---

[9]Bengston has used a computer content analysis approach to examine shifts over time in the relative importance of the four categories of value from 1982 to 1993. Xu, Zhi, and David N. Bengston, "Trends in National Forest Values among Forestry Professionals, Environmentalists, and the News Media, 1982–1993," *Society and Natural Resources* 10, no. 1 (1997): 43–59.

[10]See Bryan G. Norton, *Toward Unity among Environmentalists* (New York: Oxford University Press, 1991), and Gary E. Varner, "The Prospects for Consensus and Convergence in the Animal Rights Debate," *Hastings Center Report* 24, no. 1 (1994): 24–28.

The suggestions for further reading at the end of each chapter include only a small portion of what is available, but they provide a good foundation in each area. Many of the books cited also contain valuable bibliographies for further reference. The discussion topics at the end of each reading will help you assess the strengths and weaknesses of the various philosophical approaches, as well as encourage you to evaluate the ideas presented. The class exercises suggested for a number of the chapters will help you confront some of the issues raised in the chapter while exchanging ideas with your classmates.

HOW TO USE THIS BOOK

We suggest that the book's introduction be read first. The introduction provides basic characterizations of the field of environmental ethics and also analyzes different approaches to values in environmental ethics.

Chapters 1 through 4 in Part I concern multidisciplinary perspectives and methodologies. Chapters 5 through 9 in Part II present distinct visions of or approaches to the human relationship to the environment. Chapter 10 presents social issues of landownership, economics, politics, law, policy, and management.

We strongly urge students to read each chapter introduction. These introductions are designed to

highlight important themes in each chapter

place the individual readings in perspective by comparison and contrast

introduce distinctions and concepts that supplement the chapter readings

provide additional insights and perspectives not developed elsewhere in the text

CHANGE HAPPENS
ONE PERSON AT A TIME

Deep, fundamental changes such as those described above originate in the minds and lives of individuals. It is important to realize the challenge and responsibility that each of us has. As you examine your own beliefs and conduct, you influence your friends and family. Your choice of courses, major, and career will influence educational institutions. Your conduct as a consumer will influence manufacturers and advertising firms. Your vote will influence the composition of planning commissions, city councils, county boards of supervisors, representatives, governors, and presidents. Your choices are crucial to formulating the direction your society takes in addressing the many significant problems it faces. Your choices are crucial to the lives of your children and their children, to wildlife, and to the health of forests and oceans. Your responsibility is indeed a heavy one, but its very weight and urgency, if accepted in a thoughtful spirit, can enrich your life and the lives of many others with greater meaning and value.

FOR FURTHER READING

Collett, Jonathan, and Stephen Karakashian. *Greening the College Curriculum: A Guide to Environmental Teaching in the Liberal Arts.* Washington, D.C.: Island Press, 1996. An excellent volume providing course plans and resources, arranged by discipline.

Davos, Climis A. "Harmonizing Environmental Facts and Values: A Call for Co-Determination," *Environmental Professional* 10 (1988): 46–53. An attempt to integrate facts and values in the context of hazardous waste management issues.

Kane, G. Stanley. "Restoration or Preservation? Reflections on a Clash of Environmental Philosophies," in *Beyond Preservation: Restoring and Inventing Landscapes,* ed. A. Dwight Baldwin, Jr., Judith DeLuce, and Carl Pletsch. Minneapolis: University of Minnesota Press, 1994. A clear statement of the deep disagreements concerning the meaning of nature and human knowledge that fuel the restoration–preservation arguments.

Lemons, John. "The Need to Integrate Values into Environmental Curricula," *Environmental Management* 13.2 (1989): 133–47. A thorough discussion of why and how to incorporate value and ethics into the training of environmental scientists, managers, and public-policy representatives.

Unchopping a Tree

W. S. Merwin

W. S. Merwin is the author of more than fifteen books of poetry and nearly twenty books of translation. He is a former chancellor of the Academy of American Poets and is currently judge of the Yale Series of Younger Poets. In the following essay, which appeared in A Forest of Voices *(2000), he describes an incredible project.*

Start with the leaves, the small twigs, and the nests that have been shaken, ripped, or broken off by the fall; these must be gathered and attached once again to their respective places. It is not arduous work, unless major limbs have been smashed or mutilated. If the fall was carefully and correctly planned, the chances of anything of the kind happening will have been reduced. Again, much depends upon the size, age, shape, and species of the tree. Still, you will be lucky if you can get through this stage without having to use machinery. Even in the best of circumstances it is a labor that will make you wish often that you had won the favor of the universe of ants, the empire of mice, or at least a local tribe of squirrels, and could enlist their labors and their talents. But no, they leave you to it. They have learned, with time. This is men's work. It goes without saying that if the tree was hollow in whole or in part, and contained old nests of bird or mammal or insect, or hoards of nuts or such structures as wasps or bees build for their survival, the contents will have to be repaired where necessary, and reassembled, insofar as possible, in their original order, including the shells of nuts already opened. With spiders' webs you must simply do the best you can. We do not have the spider's weaving equipment, nor any substitute for the leaf's living bond with its point of attachment and nourishment. It is even harder to simulate the latter when the leaves have once become dry—as they are bound to do, for this is not the labor of a moment. Also it hardly needs saying that this is the time for repairing any neighboring trees or bushes or other growth that may have been damaged by the fall. The same rules apply. Where neighboring trees were of the same species it is difficult not to waste time conveying a detached leaf back to the wrong tree. Practice, practice. Put your hope in that.

Now the tackle must be put into place, or the scaffolding, depending on the surroundings and the dimensions of the tree. It is ticklish work. Almost always it involves, in itself, further damage to the area, which will have to be corrected later. But as you've heard, it can't be helped. And care now is likely to save you considerable trouble later. Be careful to grind nothing into the ground.

At last the time comes for the erecting of the trunk. By now it will scarcely be necessary to remind you of the delicacy of this huge skeleton. Every motion of the tackle, every slight upward heave of the trunk, the branches, their elaborately re-assembled panoply of leaves (now dead) will draw from you an involuntary gasp. You will watch for a leaf or a twig to be snapped off yet again. You will listen for the nuts to shift in the hollow limb and you will hear whether they are indeed falling into place or are spilling in disorder—in which case, or in the event of anything else of the kind—operations will have to cease, of course, while you correct the matter. The raising itself is no small enterprise, from the moment when the chains tighten around the old bandages until the bole hangs vertical above the stump, splinter above splinter. Now the final straightening of the splinters themselves can take place (the preliminary work is best done while the wood is still green and soft, but at times when the splinters are not badly twisted most of the straightening is left until now, when the torn ends are face to face with each other). When the splinters are perfectly complementary the appropriate fixative is applied. Again we have no duplicate of the original substance. Ours is extremely strong, but it is rigid. It is limited to surfaces, and there is no play in it. However the core is not the part of the trunk that conducted life from the roots up into the branches and back again. It was relatively inert. The fixative for this part is not the same as the one for the outer layers and the bark, and if either of these is involved in the splintered section they must receive applications of the appropriate adhesives. Apart from being incorrect and probably ineffective, the core fixative would leave a scar on the bark.

When all is ready the splintered trunk is lowered onto the splinters of the stump. This, one might say, is only the skeleton of the resurrection. Now the chips must be gathered, and the sawdust, and returned to their former positions. The fixative for the wood layers will be applied to chips and sawdust consisting only of wood. Chips and sawdust consisting of several substances will receive applications of the correct adhesives. It is as well, where possible, to shelter the materials from the elements while working. Weathering makes it harder to identify the smaller fragments. Bark sawdust in particular the earth lays claim to very quickly. You must find your own ways of coping with this problem. There is a certain beauty, you will notice at moments, in the pattern of the chips as they are fitted back into place. You will wonder to what extent it should be described as natural, to what extent man-made. It will lead you on to speculations about the parentage of beauty itself, to which you will return.

The adhesive for the chips is translucent, and not so rigid as that for the splinters. That for the bark and its subcutaneous layers is transparent and runs into the fibers on either side, partially dissolving them into each other. It does not set the sap flowing again but it does pay a kind of tribute to the preoccupations of the ancient thoroughfares. You could not roll an egg over the joints but some of the mineshafts would still be passable, no doubt. For the first

exploring insect who raises its head in the tight echoless passages. The day comes when it is all restored, even to the moss (now dead) over the wound. You will sleep badly, thinking of the removal of the scaffolding that must begin the next morning. How you will hope for sun and a still day!

The removal of the scaffolding or tackle is not so dangerous, perhaps, to the surroundings, as its installation, but it presents problems. It should be taken from the spot piece by piece as it is detached, and stored at a distance. You have come to accept it there, around the tree. The sky begins to look naked as the chains and struts one by one vacate their positions. Finally the moment arrives when the last sustaining piece is removed and the tree stands again on its own. It is as though its weight for a moment stood on your heart. You listen for a thud of settlement, a warning creak deep in the intricate joinery. You cannot believe it will hold. How like something dreamed it is, standing there all by itself. How long will it stand there now? The first breeze that touches its dead leaves all seems to flow into your mouth. You are afraid the motion of the clouds will be enough to push it over. What more can you do? What more can you do?

But there is nothing more you can do.

Others are waiting.

Everything is going to have to be put back.

PART ONE

The Multidisciplinary Context of Environmental Ethics

CHAPTER ONE
The Role of Science

Science offers a perspective that strongly influences environmental decisions. In this chapter we define science and summarize the scientific method, clarifying some of the relationships of science to resource management and environmental decision making. Ethical issues concerning science and use of the scientific method to solve environmental problems are also explored.

SCIENCE AND THE SCIENTIFIC METHOD

Most environmental decisions depend on having accurate knowledge about the physical world, the choices available, and the consequences of making these various choices. The knowledge about the physical world falls in the realm of science. Thus, to make sound environmental judgments, one must have a basic understanding of science and the methods on which it is based.

The concept of science is described in such diverse ways that it is difficult to provide a simple definition. Etymologically, the word *science* is derived from the Latin *scientia,* meaning "knowledge," and *scire,* meaning "to know." The term *science* originally referred to the state or fact of knowing and was contrasted with the notions of intuition or belief (*Webster's New Twentieth Century Dictionary,* 2nd ed.).

The realm of science deals with the objects and events of the physical world. Conversely, science has traditionally avoided topics not open to concrete analysis, such as moral or aesthetic values, notions of divinity, and metaphysics in general. The goals of science are to discover knowledge about the world, to fit this knowledge into conceptual schemes, and to discover the relationships between these schemes so as to accurately describe, explain, and make predictions about the physical world.

Science can be divided into a variety of disciplines. One major division distinguishes empirical from nonempirical sciences. Nonempirical sciences begin with basic theorems or assumed truths and apply logic to develop new truths and insights. Examples include formal logic and some types of theoretical mathematics. In contrast, empirical sciences use observations and experiments, along with logic, to develop new insights.

Empirical sciences can be divided further into the natural and social sciences. Natural sciences include the physical, earth, and life sciences. Social sciences include economics, political science, sociology, and history, among others. Some disciplines, such as psychology, may be represented in both categories.

Numerous fields of study incorporate more than one branch of science (e.g., biophysics, geochemistry, etc.). Ecology, which can be defined as the study of how living things interact with each other and their environments, has strong roots in the life sciences but also draws on other natural sciences (e.g., geochemistry) and more recently has developed ties to the social sciences.

For many, the term *science* refers primarily to the organized body of knowledge describing the physical world. However, others maintain that a proper definition of science must include the methods by which this knowledge is gained. The scientific method provides a process for testing hypotheses about the physical world; the role of the scientific method often has more to do with correcting false ideas than establishing probable truth. Much of the work in science is directed to ruling out untenable ideas until a core of theories remain that are difficult or impossible to disprove. These persisting ideas form the foundation of our scientific perspectives—unless or until they too are disproven and replaced by theories that provide better descriptions, explanations, and predictions about the world. James Woodward and David Goodstein, in the following selection, explore some of the variations in how science is defined and practiced.

No standard description of the scientific method exists. And, as Woodward and Goodstein maintain, there are important reasons why all scientists should not follow some single, uniform method. The authors do offer valuable insights on the structure, application, and strengths and limitations of the scientific process.

For some, science is seen as approaching certain absolute truths. However, other scholars disagree with this perspective. Some argue that science progresses through a series of elaborate systems of theory and methodology based on predominantly subjective interpretations scientists make of new, paradigmatic experiments and insights. The process of changing systems entails subjective and political elements. In this view, newer systems may solve some problems better than previous ones did, but they are not necessarily more accurate in describing reality. See the work by Kuhn in the section "For Further Reading" at the end of this chapter for some additional insights on these ideas.

Ragnar Fjelland addresses the issue of uncertainty in relation to environmental problems. Because of the finite nature of the biosphere and the global character of some environmental problems (e.g., global warming, ozone layer), elements of scientific uncertainty cannot be ignored or simply sequestered in mathematical or probability models. Owing to their scale, these recent environmental issues are different kinds of problems from those that scientists and technologists are traditionally trained to address.

IS SCIENCE VALUE NEUTRAL?

Much of the confidence in the scientific method as a process for solving environmental problems is based on the assumption that researchers can address important issues without being biased by their own personal values. Is this a safe assumption?

Ideally, the scientist is said to be motivated by a love of truth for its own sake, unbiased by any personal preferences or cultural beliefs. Leslie Stevenson[1] challenges this image, arguing that scientific research cannot be value neutral because, as a human activity, it constantly involves choices of how to spend time, energy, money, and other resources. Since all of these resources are limited, the scientist's personal values contribute significantly to the choices made.

Using animal behavior as an example, Marlene Zuk challenges the image of the neutrality of science from a feminist perspective in her essay in this chapter. She notes that questions we ask of nature are shaped by our social contexts and that many questions are viewed differently when addressed through traditional male or through feminist scientific perspectives.

---

[1]Leslie Stevenson, "Is Scientific Research Value Neutral?" *Inquiry* 32 (1989): 213–22.

ETHICAL CONDUCT AMONG SCIENTISTS AND MANAGERS

Defining and addressing appropriate ethical conduct in scientific research has received increasing attention in the scientific community in recent years.[2] Woodward and Goodstein maintain that the most serious forms of misconduct among research scientists are those that require specialized expert judgment on the part of other scientists to be understood and assessed. These include fabricating or falsifying data and using the ideas of others without acknowledging due credit. However, Woodward and Goodstein also point out that many ethical norms that initially appear sound may not lead to the optimal and effective practice of science.

SCIENCE AND ENVIRONMENTAL POLICY

One difficult issue in contemporary society has been the application of scientific findings to the formula-

---

[2]Examples include R. G. Botzler and S. J. Armstrong-Buck, "Ethical Considerations in Research on Wildlife Diseases," *Journal of Wildlife Diseases* 21 (1985): 341–45; Elizabeth J. Farnsworth and Judy Rosovsky, "The Ethics of Ecological Field Experimentation," *Conservation Biology* 7 (1993): 463–72; Judith P. Swazey, Melissa S. Anderson, and Karen Seashore Lewis, "Ethical Problems in Academic Research," *American Scientist* 81 (1993): 542–53; as well as American Chemical Society, "Ethical Guidelines to Publication of Chemical Research," *Chemical Reviews* 95, 11A–13A (1985, 1989, 1995).

tion of environmental policies. In this chapter, Eric Freyfogle and Julianne Newton address the proper role of science in land management by focusing on two key distinctions. First, they consider the contrast between describing land in all of its functional complexity versus evaluating it normatively in human terms. Second, they address differences between the standards used to evaluate a landscape's "goodness" or "badness," and the various processes by which such standards are developed and then applied in the field to a given landscape.

Building on the new concerns associated with scientific uncertainty in global environmental problems, Fjelland proposes some changes in the application of science to policy. These include shifting the burden of proof in science, from those claiming to suffer environmental damage from the action of others to those asserting that their actions will cause no detrimental environmental effects. Other proposed changes include involving a greater variety of experts in developing and assessing environmental models and involving nonexperts in the traditional scientific community.

Edward O. Wilson addresses another emerging insight that might affect policy issues. Because of their size and obvious presence, vertebrates (animals with backbones) commonly are viewed as the most important group of species in the biosphere. Wilson points out how unimportant vertebrates generally are in the overall dynamics of the planet.

Conduct, Misconduct, and the Structure of Science

James Woodward and David Goodstein

James Woodward and David Goodstein are professors at the California Institute of Technology, Pasadena, California, where Woodward teaches philosophy and Goodstein teaches physics. Woodward has served Caltech as executive officer for the humanities; Goodstein serves as vice provost and is the Frank J. Gilloon Distinguished Teaching and Service Professor. They team-teach a course in research ethics.

In an article from American Scientist, *Woodward and Goodstein evaluate how science operates and identify many of the major motivations of scientists. They then use these perceptions to define and evaluate scientific misconduct.*

In recent years the difficult question "what constitutes scientific misconduct?" has troubled prominent ethicists and scientists and tied many a blue-ribbon panel in knots. In teaching an ethics class for graduate and undergraduate students over the past few years, we have identified what seems to be a necessary starting point for this debate: the clearest possible understanding of *how science actually works*. Without such an understanding, we believe, one can easily imagine formulating plausible-sounding ethical principles that would be unworkable or even damaging to the scientific enterprise.

Our approach may sound so obvious as to be simplistic, but actually it uncovers a fundamental problem, which we shall try to explore in this article. The nature of the problem can be glimpsed by considering the ethical implications of the earliest theory of the scientific method. Sir Francis Bacon, a contemporary of Galileo, thought the scientist must be a disinterested observer of nature, whose mind was cleansed of prejudices and preconceptions. As we shall see, the reality of science is radically different from this ideal. If we expect to find scientists who are disinterested observers of nature we are bound to be disappointed, not because scientists have failed to measure up to the appropriate standard of behavior, but because we have tried to apply the wrong standard of behavior. It can be worse: Rules or standards of conduct that seem intuitively appealing can turn out to have results that are both unexpected and destructive to the aims of scientific inquiry.

In drafting this article, we set out to examine the question of scientific ethics in light of what we know about science as a system and about the motivations of the scientists who take part in it. The reader will find that this exercise unearths contradictions that may be especially unpleasant for those who believe clear ethical principles derive directly from the principles of scientific practice. In fact, one can construct a wonderful list of plausible-sounding ethical principles, each of which might be damaging or unworkable according to our analysis of how science works.

IDEALS AND REALITIES

We can begin where Sir Francis left off. Here is a hypothetical set of principles, beginning with the Baconian ideal, for the conduct of science:

1. Scientists should always be disinterested, impartial and totally objective when gathering data.
2. A scientist should never be motivated to do science for personal gain, advancement or other rewards.
3. Every observation or experiment must be designed to falsify a hypothesis.
4. When an experiment or an observation gives a result contrary to the prediction of a certain theory, all ethical scientists must abandon that theory.
5. Scientists must never believe dogmatically in an idea nor use rhetorical exaggeration in promoting it.
6. Scientists must "lean over backward" (in the words of the late physicist Richard Feynman) to point out evidence that is contrary to their own hypotheses or that might weaken acceptance of their experimental results.
7. Conduct that seriously departs from that commonly accepted in the scientific community is unethical.
8. Scientists must report what they have done so fully that any other scientist can reproduce the

experiment or calculation. Science must be an open book, not an acquired skill.

9. Scientists should never permit their judgments to be affected by authority. For example, the reputation of a scientist making a given claim is irrelevant to the validity of the claim.

10. Each author of a multiple-author paper is fully responsible for every part of the paper.

11. The choice and order of authors on a multiple-author publication must strictly reflect the contributions of the authors to the work in question.

12. Financial support for doing science and access to scientific facilities should be shared democratically, not concentrated in the hands of a favored few.

13. There can never be too many scientists in the world.

14. No misleading or deceptive statement should ever appear in a scientific paper.

15. Decisions about the distribution of resources and publication of results must be guided by the judgment of scientific peers who are protected by anonymity.

Should the behavior of scientists be governed by rules of this sort? We shall argue that it should not. We first consider the general problems of motivation and the logical structure of science, then the question of how the community of scientists actually does its work, showing along the way why each of these principles is defective. At the end, we offer a positive suggestion of how scientific misconduct might be recognized.

MOTIVES AND CONSEQUENCES

Many of the provocative statements we have just made raise general questions of motivation related to the issue explicitly raised in principle 2, and it is worth dealing with these up front. We might begin with a parallel: the challenge of devising institutions, rules and standards to govern commerce. In economic life well-intentioned attempts to reduce the role of greed or speculation can turn out to have disastrous consequences. In fact, behavior that may seem at first glance morally unattractive, such as the aggressive pursuit of economic self-interest, can, in

a properly functioning system, produce results that are generally beneficial.

In the same way it might appear morally attractive to demand that scientists take no interest in obtaining credit for their achievements. Most scientists are motivated by the desire to discover important truths about nature and to help others to do so. But they also prefer that they (rather than their competitors) be the ones to make discoveries, and they want the recognition and the advantages that normally reward success in science. It is tempting to think that tolerating a desire for recognition is a concession to human frailty; ideally, scientists should be interested only in truth or other purely epistemic goals. But this way of looking at matters misses a number of crucial points.

For one thing, as the philosopher Philip Kitcher has noted, the fact that the first person to make a scientific discovery usually gets nearly all the credit encourages investigators to pursue a range of different lines of inquiry, including lines that are thought by most in the community to have a small probability of success. From the point of view of making scientific discoveries as quickly and efficiently as possible, this sort of diversification is extremely desirable; majority opinion turns out to be wrong with a fairly high frequency in science.

Another beneficial feature of the reward system is that it encourages scientists to make their discoveries public. As Noretta Koertge has observed, there have been many episodes in the history of early modern science in which scientists made important discoveries and kept them private, recording them only in notebooks or correspondence, or in cryptic announcements designed to be unintelligible to others. The numerous examples include Galileo, Newton, Cavendish and Lavoisier. It is easy to see how such behavior can lead to wasteful repetition of effort. The problem is solved by a system of rewards that appeals to scientists' self-interest. Finally, in a world of limited scientific resources, it makes sense to give more resources to those who are better at making important discoveries.

We need to be extremely careful, in designing institutions and regulations to discourage scientific misconduct, that we not introduce changes that disrupt the beneficial effects that competition and a concern for credit and reputation bring with them. It is frequently claimed that an important motive in a number of recent cases of data fabrication has been the desire to establish priority and to receive credit for a discovery, or that a great deal of fraud can be traced to the highly competitive nature of modern science. If these claims are correct, the question becomes, how can we reduce the incidence of fraud without removing the beneficial effects of competition and reward?

THE LOGICAL STRUCTURE OF SCIENCE

The question of how science works tends to be discussed in terms of two particularly influential theories of scientific method, *Baconian inductivism* and *Popperian falsification,* each of which yields a separate set of assumptions.

According to Bacon's view, scientific investigation begins with the careful recording of observations. These should be, insofar as is humanly possible, uninfluenced by any prior prejudice or theoretical preconception. When a large enough body of observations is accumulated, the investigator generalizes from these, via a process of induction, to some hypothesis or theory describing a pattern present in the observations. Thus, for example, an investigator might inductively infer, after observing a large number of black ravens, that all ravens are black. According to this theory good scientific conduct consists in recording all that one observes and not just some selected part of it, and in asserting only hypotheses that are strongly inductively supported by the evidence. The guiding ideal is to avoid any error that may slip in as a result of prejudice or preconception.

Historians, philosophers and those scientists who care are virtually unanimous in rejecting Baconian inductivism as a general characterization of good scientific method. The advice to record all that one observes is obviously unworkable if taken literally; some principle of selection or relevance is required. But decisions about what is relevant inevitably will be influenced heavily by background assumptions, and these, as many recent historical studies show, are often highly theoretical in character. The vocabulary we use to describe the results of measurements, and even the instruments we use to make the measurements, are highly dependent on theory. This

point is sometimes expressed by saying that all observation in science is "theory-laden" and that a "theoretically neutral" language for recording observations is impossible.

The idea that science proceeds only and always via inductive generalization from what is directly observed is also misguided. Theories in many different areas of science have to do with entities whose existence or function cannot be directly observed: forces, fields, subatomic particles, proteins and other large organic molecules, and so on. For this and many other reasons, no one has been able to formulate a defensible theory of inductive inference of the sort demanded by inductivist theories of science.

The difficulties facing inductivism as a general conception of scientific method are so well known that it is surprising to find authoritative characterizations of scientific misconduct that appear to be influenced by this conception. . . .

The idea that data selection and overinterpretation of data are forms of misconduct seems natural if one begins with [an inductive] view of scientific method. A less restrictive view would lead to a different set of conclusions about what activities constitute misconduct.

Although relatively few contemporary scientists espouse inductivism, there are many scientists who have been influenced by the falsificationist ideas of Karl Popper. According to falsificationists, we test a hypothesis by deducing from it a testable prediction. If this prediction turns out to be false, the hypothesis from which it is deduced is said to be falsified and must be rejected. For example, the observation of a single nonblack raven will falsify the hypothesis H: "All ravens are black." But if we set out to test H and observe a black raven or even a large number of such ravens we cannot, according to Popper, conclude that H is true or verified or even that it is more probable than it was before. All that we can conclude is that H has been tested and has not yet been falsified. There is thus an important asymmetry between the possibility of falsification and the possibility of verification; we can show conclusively that a hypothesis is false, but not that it is true.

Because of this asymmetry it is a mistake to think, as the inductivist does, that good science consists of hypotheses that are proved or made probable by observation, whereas bad science does not. Instead, according to Popper, good science requires hypotheses that might be falsified by some conceivable observation. For example, the general theory of relativity predicts that starlight passing sufficiently close to the sun will be deflected by a certain measurable amount E. General relativity is a falsifiable theory because observations of starlight deflection that differ substantially from E are certainly conceivable and had they been made, would have served to falsify general relativity. By contrast, writes Popper, Freudian psychology is unfalsifiable and hence unscientific. If, for example, a son behaves in a loving way toward his mother, this will be attributed to his Oedipus complex. If, on the contrary, he behaves in a hostile and destructive way, this will be attributed to the same Oedipus complex. No possible empirical observation constitutes a refutation of the hypothesis that the son's behavior is motivated by an Oedipus complex.

According to Popper, bad scientific behavior consists in refusing to announce in advance what sorts of evidence would lead one to give up a hypothesis, in ignoring or discarding evidence contrary to one's hypothesis or in introducing ad hoc, content-decreasing modifications in one's theories in order to protect them against refutation. Good scientific method consists in putting forward highly falsifiable hypotheses, specifying in advance what sorts of evidence would falsify these hypotheses, testing the hypotheses at exactly those points at which they seem most likely to break down and then giving them up should such evidence be observed. More generally (and moving somewhat beyond the letter of Popper's theory) we can say that to do science in a Popperian spirit is to hold to one's hypothesis in a tentative, nondogmatic fashion, to explore and draw to the attention of others various ways in which one's hypothesis might break down or one's experimental result may be invalid, to give up one's hypothesis willingly in the face of contrary evidence, to take seriously rather than to ignore or discard evidence that is contrary to it, and in general not to exaggerate or overstate the evidence for it or suppress problems that it faces. . . .

Although falsificationism has many limitations (see below), it introduces several corrections to in-ductivism that are useful in understanding how science works and how to characterize misconduct. To begin with, falsificationism rejects the idea that good scientific behavior consists in making observations without theoretical preconceptions. For Popper, scientific activity consists in attempting to falsify. Such testing requires that one have in mind a hypothesis that will indicate which observations are relevant or worth making. Rather than something to be avoided, theoretical preconceptions are essential to doing science.

Inductivists attach a great deal of weight to the complete avoidance of error. By contrast, falsificationists claim that the history of science shows us that all hypotheses are falsified sooner or later. In view of this fact, our aim should be to detect our errors quickly and to learn as efficiently as possible from them. Error in science thus plays a constructive role. Indeed, according to falsificationists, putting forward a speculative "bold conjecture" that goes well beyond available evidence and then trying vigorously to falsify it will be the strategy that enables us to progress as efficiently as possible. For science to advance, scientists must be free to be wrong.

Despite these advantages, there are also serious deficiencies in falsificationism, when it is taken as a general theory of method. One of the most important of these is sometimes called the Duhem-Quine problem. We claimed above that testing a hypothesis H involved deriving from it some observational consequence O. But in most realistic cases such observational consequences will not be derivable from H alone, but only from H in conjunction with a great many other assumptions A (auxiliary assumptions, as philosophers sometimes call them). For example, to derive an observational claim from a hypothesis about rates of evolution, one may need auxiliary assumptions about the processes by which the fossil record is laid down. Suppose one hypothesizes that a certain organism has undergone slow and continuous evolution and derives from this that one should see numerous intermediate forms in the fossil record. If such forms are absent it may mean H is false, but it may also be the case that H is true but fossils were preserved only in geological deposits that were laid down at widely separated times. It is possible that H is true and that the reason that O is false is that A is false.

One immediate result of this simple logical fact is that the logical asymmetry between falsification and verification disappears. It may be true, as Popper claims, that we cannot conclusively verify a hypothesis, but we cannot conclusively falsify it either. Thus, as a matter of method, it is sometimes a good strategy to hold onto a hypothesis even when it seems to imply an observational consequence that looks to be false. In fact, the history of science is full of examples in which such anti-Popperian behavior has succeeded in finding out important truths about nature when it looks as though more purely Popperian strategies would have been less successful.

Anti-Popperian strategies seem particularly prevalent in experiments. In doing an experiment one's concern is often to find or demonstrate an effect or to create conditions that will allow the effect to appear, rather than to refute the claim that the effect is real. Suppose a novel theory predicts some previously unobserved effect, and an experiment is undertaken to detect it. The experiment requires the construction of new instruments, perhaps operating at the very edge of what is technically possible, and the use of a novel experimental design, which will be infected with various unsuspected and difficult-to-detect sources of error. As historical studies have shown, in this kind of situation there will be a strong tendency on the part of many experimentalists to conclude that these problems have been overcome if and when the experiment produces results that the theory predicted. Such behavior certainly exhibits anti-Popperian dogmatism and theoretical "bias," but it may be the best way to discover a difficult-to-detect signal. Here again, it would be unwise to have codes of scientific conduct or systems of incentives that discourage such behavior.

SOCIAL STRUCTURE

Inductivism, falsificationism and many other traditional accounts of method are inadequate as theories of science. At bottom this is because they neglect the psychology of individual scientists and the social structure of science. These points are of crucial importance in understanding how science works and in characterizing scientific misconduct.

Let us begin with what Philip Kitcher has called the division of cognitive labor and the role of social interactions in scientific investigation. Both inductivism and falsificationism envision an individual investigator encountering nature and constructing and assessing hypotheses all alone. But science is carried out by a community of investigators. This fact has important implications for how we should think about the responsibilities of individual scientists.

Suppose a scientist who has invested a great deal of time and effort in developing a theory is faced with a decision about whether to continue to hold onto it given some body of evidence. As we have seen, good Popperian method requires that scientists act as skeptical critics of their own theories. But the social character of science suggests another possibility. Suppose that our scientist has a rival who has invested time and resources in developing an alternative theory. If additional resources, credit and other rewards will flow to the winner, perhaps we can reasonably expect that the rival will act as a severe Popperian critic of the theory, and vice versa. As long as others in the community will perform this function, failure to behave like a good Popperian need not be regarded as a violation of some canon of method.

There are also psychological facts to consider. In many areas of science it turns out to be very difficult, and to require a long-term commitment of time and resources, to develop even one hypothesis that respects most available theoretical constraints and is consistent with most available evidence. Scientists, like other human beings, find it difficult to sustain commitments to arduous, long-term projects if they spend too much time contemplating the various ways in which the project might turn out to be unsuccessful.

A certain tendency to exaggerate the merits of one's approach, and to neglect or play down, particularly in the early stages of a project, contrary evidence and other difficulties, may be a necessary condition for the success of many scientific projects. When people work very hard on something over a long period of time, they tend to become committed or attached to it; they strongly want it to be correct and find it increasingly difficult to envision the possibility that it might be false, a phenomenon related to what psychologists call *belief-perseverance*. Moreover, scientists like other people like to be right and to get credit and recognition from others for being right: The satisfaction of demolishing a theory one has laboriously constructed may be small in comparison with the satisfaction of seeing it vindicated. All things considered, it is extremely hard for most people to adopt a consistently Popperian attitude toward their own ideas.

Given these realistic observations about the psychology of scientists, an implicit code of conduct that encourages scientists to be a bit dogmatic and permits a certain measure of rhetorical exaggeration regarding the merits of their work, and that does not require an exhaustive discussion of its deficiencies, may be perfectly sensible. In many areas of science, if a scientist submits a paper that describes all of the various ways in which an idea or result might be defective, and draws detailed attention to the contrary results obtained by others, the paper is likely to be rejected. In fact, part of the intellectual responsibility of a scientist is to provide the best possible case for important ideas, leaving it to others to publicize their defects and limitations. Studies of both historical and contemporary science seem to show that this is just what most scientists do.

If this analysis is correct, there is a real danger that by following proposals . . . to include within the category of "out-of-bounds conduct" behavior such as overinterpretation of data, exaggeration of available evidence that supports one's conclusion or failure to report contrary data, one may be proscribing behavior that plays a functional role in science and that, for reasons rooted deep in human psychology, will be hard to eliminate. Moreover, such proscriptions may be unnecessary, because interactions between scientists and criticisms by rivals may by themselves be sufficient to remove the bad consequences at which the proscriptions are aimed. Standards that might be optimal for single, perfectly rational beings encountering nature all by themselves may be radically deficient when applied to actual scientific communities.

REWARDING USEFUL BEHAVIOR

From a Popperian perspective, discovering evidence that merely supports a hypothesis is easy to do and has little methodological value; therefore one might think it doesn't deserve much credit. It is striking that the actual distribution of reward and

credit in science reflects a very different view. Scientists receive Nobel prizes for finding new effects predicted by theories or for proposing important theories that are subsequently verified. It is only when a hypothesis or theory has become very well established that one receives significant credit for refuting it. Unquestionably, rewarding confirmations over refutations provides scientists with incentives to confirm theories rather than refute them and thus discourages giving up too quickly in the face of contrary experimental results. But, as we have been arguing, this is not necessarily bad for science.

Conventional accounts of scientific method . . . share the implicit assumption that all scientists in a community should adopt the same strategies. In fact, a number of government agencies now have rules that define as scientific misconduct "practices that seriously deviate from those that are commonly accepted within the scientific community . . ." (see principle 7). But rapid progress will be more likely if different scientists have quite different attitudes toward appropriate methodology. As noted above, one important consequence of the winner-takes-all (or nearly all) system by which credit and reward are allocated in science is that it encourages a variety of research programs and approaches. Other features of human cognitive psychology — such as the belief-perseverance phenomenon described above — probably have a similar consequence. It follows that attempts to characterize misconduct in terms of departures from practices or methods commonly accepted within the scientific community will be doubly misguided: Not only will such commonly accepted practices fail to exist in many cases, but it will be undesirable to try to enforce the uniformity of practice that such a characterization of misconduct would require. More generally, we can see why the classical methodologists have failed to discover "the" method by which science works. There are deep, systematic reasons why all scientists should not follow some single uniform method.

Our remarks so far have emphasized the undesirability of a set of rules that demand that all scientists believe the same things or behave in the same way, given a common body of evidence. This is not to say, however, that "anything goes." One very important distinction has to do with the difference between claims and behavior that are open to public assessment and those that are not. Exaggerations, omissions and misrepresentations that cannot be checked by other scientists should be regarded much more harshly than those that can, because they subvert the processes of public assessment and intellectual competition on which science rests. Thus, for example, a scientist who fabricates data must be judged far more harshly than one who does a series of experiments and accurately records the results but then extrapolates beyond the recorded data or insists on fitting some favored function to them. The difference is the fact that in the case in which there is no fabrication nothing has been done to obstruct the critical scrutiny of the work by peers; they can look at the data themselves and decide whether there is support for the conclusions. By contrast, other scientists will not be able to examine firsthand the process by which the data have been produced. They must take it on trust that the data resulted from an experiment of the sort described. Fabrication should thus be viewed as much more potentially damaging to the process of inquiry and should be more harshly punished than other forms of misrepresentation.

SCIENCE AS CRAFT

Contemporary scientific knowledge is so vast and complex that even a very talented and hardworking scientist will be able to master only an extremely small fragment well enough to expect to make contributions to it. In part for this reason scientists must rely heavily on the authority of other scientists who are experts in domains in which they are not. A striking example of this is provided by the sociologist Trevor Pinch's recent book, *Confronting Nature,* which is a study of a series of experiments that discovered in the solar-neutrino flux far fewer neutrinos than seemed to be predicted by accepted theory. Pinch found that what he called the "personal warrant" of the experimenters involved in this project played a large role in how other scientists assessed the experimental results. According to Pinch, other scientists often place at least as much weight on an experimentalist's general reputation for careful, painstaking work as on the technical details of the experiment in assessing whether the data constitute reliable evidence.

One reason why such appeals to personal warrant play a large role in science has to do with the specialized character of scientific knowledge. There is, however, another related reason which is of considerable importance in understanding how science works and how one should think about misconduct. This has to do with the fact that science in general — and especially experimentation — has a large "skill" or "craft" component.

Conducting an experiment in a way that produces reliable results is not a matter of following algorithmic rules that specify exactly what is to be done at each step. As Pinch put it, experimenters possess skills that "often enable the experimenter to get the apparatus to work without being able to formulate exactly or completely what has been done." For the same reason, assessing whether another investigator has produced reliable results requires a judgment of whether the experimenter has demonstrated the necessary skills in the past. These facts about the role of craft knowledge may be another reason why the general rules of method sought by the classical methodologists have proved so elusive.

The importance of craft in science is supported by empirical studies. For example, in a well-known study, Harry Collins investigated a number of experimental groups working in Britain to recreate a new kind of laser that had been successfully constructed elsewhere. Collins found that no group was able to reproduce a working laser simply on the basis of detailed written instructions. By far the most reliable method was to have someone from the original laboratory who had actually built a functioning laser go to the other laboratories and participate in the construction. The skills needed to make a working device could be acquired by practice *"without necessarily formulating, enumerating or understanding them."* Remarks on experimental work by working scientists themselves often express similar claims, notwithstanding principle 8 above. If claims of this sort are correct, it often will be very difficult for those who lack highly specific skills and knowledge to assess a particular line of experimental work. A better strategy may be to be guided at least in large part by the experimenter's general reputation for reliability.

These facts about specialization, skill and authority have a number of interesting consequences for understanding what is proper scientific conduct. For example, a substantial amount of conduct that may look to an outsider like nonrational deference to authority may have a serious epistemological rationale. When an experimentalist discards certain data on the basis of subtle clues in the behavior of the apparatus, and other scientists accept the experimentalist's judgment in this matter, we should not automatically attribute this to the operation of power relationships, as is implied by principle 9 in our list above.

A second important consequence has to do with the responsibility of scientists for the misconduct or sloppy research practices of collaborators. It is sometimes suggested that authors should not sign their names to joint papers unless they have personally examined the evidence and are prepared to vouch for the correctness of every claim in the paper (principle 10). However, many collaborations bring together scientists from quite different specializations who lack the expertise to evaluate one another's work directly. This is exactly why collaboration is necessary. Requiring that scientists not collaborate unless they are able to check the work of collaborators or setting up a general policy of holding scientists responsible for the misconduct of coauthors would discourage a great deal of valuable collaboration.

Understanding the social structure of science and the operation of the reward system within science also has important ethical implications. We consider three examples: the Matthew effect, the Ortega hypothesis and scientific publication.

MATTHEW VS. ORTEGA

The sociologist Robert K. Merton has observed that credit tends to go to those who are already famous, at the expense of those who are not. A paper signed by Nobody, Nobody and Somebody often will be casually referred to as "work done in Somebody's lab," and even sometimes cited (incorrectly) in the literature as due to "Somebody *et al.*" Does this practice serve and accurately depict science, or does the tendency to elitism distort and undermine the conduct of science?

It is arguable that what Merton called the Matthew Effect plays a useful role in the organization of sci-

ence; there are so many papers in so many journals that no scientist has time to read more than a tiny fraction of those in even a restricted area of science. Famous names tend to identify those works that are more likely to be worth noticing. In certain fields, particularly biomedical fields, it has become customary to make the head of the laboratory a coauthor, even if the head did not participate in the research. One reason for this practice is that by including the name of the famous head on the paper, chances are greatly improved that the paper will be accepted by a prestigious journal and noticed by its readers. Some people refer to this practice as "guest authorship" and regard it as unethical (as would be implied by principle 11 above). However, the practice may be functionally useful and may involve little deception, since conventions regarding authorship may be well understood by those who participate in a given area of science.

"In the cathedral of science," a famous scientist once said, "every brick is equally important." The remark (heard by one of the authors at a gathering at the speaker's Pasadena, California home) evokes a vivid metaphor of swarms of scientific workers under the guidance, perhaps, of a few master builders erecting a grand monument to scientific faith. The speaker was Max Delbrück, a Nobel laureate often called the father of molecular biology. The remark captures with some precision the scientists' ambivalent view of their craft. Delbrück never for an instant thought the bricks he laid were no better than anyone else's. If anything, he regarded himself as the keeper of the blueprints, and he had the fame and prestige to prove it. It was exactly his exalted position that made it obligatory that he make a ceremonial bow to the democratic ideal that many scientists espouse and few believe. In fact it is precisely the kind of recognition that Delbrück enjoyed that propels the scientific enterprise forward.

The view expressed by Delbrück has been called the Ortega Hypothesis. It is named after Jose Ortega y Gasset, who wrote in his classic book, *The Revolt of the Masses,* that

... it is necessary to insist upon this extraordinary but undeniable fact: experimental science has progressed thanks in great part to the work of men astoundingly mediocre. That is to say, modern science, the root and symbol of our actual civilization, finds a place for the intellectually commonplace man and allows him to work therein with success. In this way the majority of scientists help the general advance of science while shut up in the narrow cell of their laboratory like the bee in the cell of its hive, or the turnspit of its wheel.

This view (see principle 12) is probably based on the empirical observation that there are indeed, in each field of science, many ordinary scientists doing more or less routine work. It is also supported by the theoretical view that knowledge of the universe is a kind of limitless wilderness to be conquered by relentless hacking away of underbrush by many hands. An idea that is supported by both theory and observation always has a very firm standing in science.

The Ortega Hypothesis was named by Jonathan and Steven Cole when they set out to demolish it, an objective they pursued by tracing citations in physics journals. They concluded that the hypothesis is incorrect, stating:

> It seems, rather, that a relatively small number of physicists produce work that becomes the base for future discoveries in physics. We have found that even papers of relatively minor significance have used to a disproportionate degree the work of the eminent scientists. . . .

In other words, a small number of elite scientists produce the vast majority of scientific progress. Seen in this light, the reward system in science is a mechanism evolved for the purpose of identifying, promoting and rewarding the star performers.

One's view of the Ortega Hypothesis has important implications concerning how science ought to be organized. If the Ortega Hypothesis is correct, science is best served by producing as many scientists as possible, even if they are not all of the highest quality (principle 13). On the other hand, if the elitist view is right, then since science is largely financed by the public purse, it is best for science and best for society to restrict our production to fewer and better scientists. In any case, the question of whether to produce more or fewer scientists involves ethical issues (what is best for the common good?) as well as policy issues (how to reach the desired goal).

PEERS AND PUBLICATION

In a classic paper called "Is the Scientific Paper a Fraud?" Peter Medawar has argued that typical experimental papers intentionally misrepresent the actual sequence of events involved in the conduct of an experiment, the process of reasoning by which the experimenter reached various conclusions and so on. In general, experimentalists will make it look as if they had a much clearer idea of the ultimate result than was actually the case. Misunderstandings, blind alleys and mistakes of various sorts will fail to appear in the final written account.

Papers written this way are undoubtedly deceptive, at least to the uninitiated, and they certainly stand in contrast to Feynman's exhortation to "lean over backward." They also violate principle 14. Nevertheless, the practice is virtually universal, because it is a much more efficient means of transmitting results than an accurate historical account of the scientist's activities would be. Thus it is a simple fact that, contrary to normal belief, there are types of misrepresentation that are condoned and accepted in scientific publications, whereas other types are harshly condemned.

Nevertheless, scientific papers have an exalted reputation for integrity. That may be because the integrity of the scientific record is protected, above all, by the institution of peer review. Peer review has an almost mystical role in the community of scientists. Published results are considered dependable because they have been reviewed by peers, and unpublished data are considered not dependable because they have not been. Many regard peer review to be (as principle 15 would suggest) the ethical fulcrum of the whole scientific enterprise.

Peer review is used to help determine whether journals should publish articles submitted to them, and whether agencies should grant financial support to research projects. For most small projects and for nearly all journal articles, peer review is accomplished by sending the manuscript or proposal to referees whose identities will not be revealed to the authors.

Peer review conducted in this way is extremely unlikely to detect instances of intentional misconduct. But the process is very good at separating valid science from nonsense. Referees know the current thinking in a field, are aware of its laws, rules and conventions, and will quickly detect any unjustified attempt to depart from them. Of course, for precisely this reason peer review can occasionally delay a truly visionary or revolutionary idea, but that may be a price that we pay for conducting science in an orderly way.

Peer review is less useful for adjudicating an intense competition for scarce resources. The pages of prestigious journals and the funds distributed by government agencies have become very scarce resources in recent times. The fundamental problem in using peer review to decide how these resources are to be allocated is obvious enough: There is an intrinsic conflict of interest. The referees, chosen because they are among the few experts in the author's field, are often competitors with the author for those same resources.

A referee who receives a proposal or manuscript to judge is being asked to do an unpaid professional service for the editor or project officer. The editor or officer thus has a responsibility to protect the referee, both by protecting the referee's anonymity and by making sure that the referee is never held to account for what is written in the report. Without complete confidence in that protection, referees cannot be expected to perform their task. Moreover, editors and project officers are never held to account for their choice of referees, and they can be confident that, should anybody ask, their referees will have the proper credentials to withstand scrutiny.

Referees would have to have high ethical standards to fail to take personal advantage of their privileged anonymity and to make peer review function properly in spite of these conditions. Undoubtedly, most referees in most circumstances do manage to accomplish that. However, the fact is that many referees have themselves been victims of unfair reviews and this must sometimes influence their ability to judge competing proposals or papers fairly. Thus the institution of peer review seems to be suffering genuine distress.

Once again, this analysis shows that science is a complex enterprise that must be understood in some detail before ethical principles can be formulated to help guide it.

CONCLUSIONS

We have put forth arguments in this article that indicate why each of the principles listed above may be defective as a guide to the behavior of scientists. However, our repeated admonition that there are no universal rules of scientific conduct does not mean that it is impossible to recognize distinctive scientific misconduct. We would like to conclude with some thoughts on how scientific misconduct might be distinguished from other kinds of misconduct.

We propose that distinctively scientific forms of misconduct are those that require the expert judgment of a panel of scientists in order to be understood and assessed. Other forms of misconduct may take place in science, but they should not constitute scientific misconduct. For example, fabricating experimental data is scientific misconduct, but stealing scientific instruments is not. Similarly, misappropriation of scientific ideas is scientific misconduct, but plagiarism (copying someone else's words) is not. Stealing and plagiarism are serious misdeeds, but there are other well-established means for dealing with them, even when they are associated with science or committed by scientists. No special knowledge is required to recognize them.

On the other hand, only a panel of scientists can deal with matters such as data fabrication that require a detailed understanding of the nature of the experiments, the instruments used, accepted norms for presenting data and so on, to say nothing of the unique importance of experimental data in science. In a dispute over an allegation that a scientific idea has been misappropriated, the issues are likely to be so complex that it is difficult to imagine a lay judge or jury coming to understand the problem from testimony by expert witnesses or any other plausible means. Similarly, judgment will usually be required to determine whether an experimenter's procedures in selecting or discarding data constitute misconduct — the conventions governing this vary so much across different areas of science that judgments about what is reasonable will require a great deal of expert knowledge, rather than simply the application of some general rule that might be employed by non-scientists.

In the section on the logical structure of science, we drew a sharp distinction between advocacy, which is permitted or encouraged in science, and deception that is not open to public assessment, which is judged very harshly in science. Fabrication or covert and unwarranted manipulation of data is an example of the kind of deceptive practice that cannot be tolerated because it undermines the mutual trust essential to the system of science that we have described. Similarly, misappropriation of ideas undermines the reward system that helps motivate scientific progress. In both cases, a panel of scientists will be required to determine whether the deed occurred and, if so, whether it was done with intent to deceive or with reckless disregard for the truth. Should these latter conditions be true, the act may be judged to be not merely scientific misconduct but, in fact, scientific fraud.

BIBLIOGRAPHY

Cole, J., and S. Cole. 1972. The Ortega hypothesis. *Science* 178: 368–75.

Collins, H. 1974. The TEA-set: Tacit knowledge and scientific networks. *Science Studies* 4: 165–86.

Collins, H. 1975. The seven sexes: A study in the sociology of a phenomenon, or the replication of experiments in physics. *Sociology* 9: 205–24.

Duhem, P. 1962. *The Aim and Structure of Physical Theory.* New York: Athenaeum.

Feyerabend, P. 1975. *Against Method: Outline of an Anarchistic Theory of Knowledge.* London: New Left Books.

Feynman, R. 1985. *Surely You're Joking, Mr. Feynman.* New York: W. W. Norton.

Galison, P. 1987. *How Experiments End.* Chicago: University of Chicago Press.

Kitcher, P. 1990. The division of cognitive labor. *Journal of Philosophy* 87: 5–22.

Koertge, N. 1991. The function of credit in Hull's evolutionary model of science. *Proceedings of the Philosophy of Science Association* 2: 237–44.

Kuhn, T. 1970. *The Structure of Scientific Revolutions.* Chicago: University of Chicago Press.

Lakatos, I. 1974. Falsification and the methodology of scientific research programmes. In *Criticism and the Growth of Knowledge,* ed. I. Lakatos and A. Musgrave. Cambridge, U.K.: Cambridge University Press, pp. 91–196.

Medawar, P. 1963. Is the scientific paper a fraud? *The Listener* (12 September) 70: 377–78.

Merton, R. 1968. The Matthew Effect in science. *Science* 159: 56–63.

Ortega y Gasset, J. 1932. *The Revolt of the Masses.* New York: W. W. Norton.

Pinch, T. 1986. *Confronting Nature.* Dordrecht, Holland: P. Reidel.

Popper, K. 1968. *The Logic of Scientific Discovery.* New York: Harper and Row.

Popper, K. 1969. *Conjectures and Refutations.* London: Routledge and Kegan Paul.

Quine, W. V. O. 1961. *From a Logical Point of View.* New York: Harper and Row.

DISCUSSION TOPICS

1. Does the description of the scientific process provided by the authors align with your perceptions of science? How is it similar and how does it differ?

2. In the discussion of the Matthew Effect, the authors argue that there are circumstances in which adding a well-known name to a paper might be appropriate, even though that person did not contribute significantly to the study. Do you agree? Why or why not? Can you identify some circumstances where such a decision might be appropriate?

3. Based on your reading of Woodward and Goodstein, what general principles might you now identify as associated with the proper conduct of science?

Putting Science in Its Place

Eric T. Freyfogle and Julianne Lutz Newton

Eric Freyfogle is in the University of Illinois College of Law, Champaign. Julianne Lutz Newton is a member of the department of natural resources and environmental sciences, University of Illinois, Urbana.

In an article from Conservation Biology, *Freyfogle and Newton explore the role of science in the overall land management equation. They distinguish the substantive criteria used to make judgments about nature from the process by which these criteria are applied to make the judgments. They also clarify (1) when nature can be said to possess intrinsic value; (2) why it is proper for conservation biologists to include normative goals in their work; and (3) why arguments surrounding ecosystem management are often diverted into less fruitful arguments about science and process.*

INTRODUCTION

Land management is, in operation, a complex, human-guided enterprise. Policy factors are important to it, and so are good data and good science. Our aim is to clarify the proper roles of science in that enterprise: that is, to put science in its place. We do so by centering our analysis on two key distinctions: (1) description versus evaluation, which considers the contrasting functions of describing land in all its functional complexity and evaluating it normatively—deciding whether a given or proposed landscape is good or bad in human terms and (2) substance versus process, which attends to the differences between, on the one side, the substantive norms or standards used to evaluate a landscape's goodness or badness and, on the other, the various processes by which such standards are developed and then applied in the field to a given tract or landscape.

DESCRIPTION, EVALUATION, AND INTRINSIC VALUE

In the context of land, the aim of science is to describe nature and how it functions, rather than to pass normative judgment upon it. A description could focus on a single moment in time and space or on change over time or space, dwell on community composition, attend to causal mechanisms or relationships, or predict future events or conditions based on assumed conditions. In all cases, however, science's function is entirely descriptive in the sense that it merely states (or predicts) facts. Practitioners of science would accordingly describe a seriously eroding farm field much differently than they would a vegetatively covered field that builds soil, but they would have no purely scientific basis for claiming that one field was better than the other. They would describe a largely untouched forest in different terms than a monocultural pine plantation but could not say which landscape was more desirable. Pure description of this kind we refer to as "science." Those who produce it, when engaged solely in that task, we call "scientists."

Normative standards are needed to judge natural conditions; that is, to decide whether a condition or change in nature is qualitatively good or bad, absolutely or comparatively. Judgments of this type entail the application of chosen normative standards to particular natural conditions, a process we refer to as "evaluation." Normative standards can vary widely, depending on the aims of the people setting them. Does a field or landscape yield as much corn as possible? Does it provide good recreational opportunities for hikers and hunters? Does it provide good places to build homes? Does it provide food and habitat for particular desired wildlife species? Under applicable standards, a particular land parcel might be deemed good if completely paved with asphalt. It might also be deemed good if planted in tallgrass prairie plants and burned annually.

In drawing this sharp distinction, we are challenging widely held views about what science entails. Objections are easy to imagine. Is not clean water normatively better than polluted water? Is not a field that holds soil normatively better than one that is eroding? Is not a mixed-age, mixed-species forest better than an even-aged, monocultural plantation? And if the answers here are yes, might not a scientific appraisal of a landscape (or a comparison of two prospective conditions of a landscape) at least sometimes produce valid normative judgments?

Our answer is an unequivocal no. Consider, for instance, an old-growth forest versus a monocultural pine plantation. The old-growth forest would often be deemed better, but what if the pine plantation is the sole remaining home of an endangered species, the trees being harvested provide a critically needed medicine, or the plantation provides the most environmentally and economically sound way of meeting valid timber needs? In such cases, the pine plantation might, overall, be normatively better. Clean water, of course, is typically better than contaminated water, but again, what if the contamination is a high saline level that sustains an endangered pupfish? The point is that one cannot move from landscape facts to substantive judgment without drawing upon other considerations. And because these considerations can vary from setting to setting, so too can evaluations about the desirability of various land conditions. To be sure, one might propose a comparison between two alternative landscape conditions, one so obviously good and the other so horrid that no sane person would prefer it. But an instance would not, we believe, undercut our claim; it would merely highlight that substantive standards vary within a confined range and that a particular landscape might rate abysmally under all conceivable standards.

Although we are confident in claiming that science in this setting is purely descriptive (in the sense we have just explained), we do recognize (and set to the side as unimportant here) limits on the power of humans to engage in value-free description, whether because of Heisenberg's uncertainty principle, because values inevitably affect which questions are asked and which facts are selected, or for other reasons (Callicott 1999*a*). We also recognize that certain descriptive conditions, such as clean water and fertile soil, have powerful normative overtones in the sense that, absent unusual factors, such conditions would be viewed as normatively good. But unusual factors do arise, particularly in landscapes heavily used by humans, as our pine plantation example illustrates. Until substantive standards are brought into the picture, science alone merely describes.

Our distinction between description and evaluation can be illuminated by considering the claim sometimes made that nature merely "is": that, in other words, nature is neither good nor bad and that one therefore cannot jump from the "is" of nature to the "ought" of desired landscape. In what sense might this be true? If by nature one means the world as described by science, the statement is a simple tautology. Science is purely descriptive and makes no claim about the "ought." The statement's accuracy becomes debatable only when it is vested by the speaker or listener with a much different meaning, when the claim being made is that a natural area always lacks normative status or content.

Natural communities can plainly differ widely in their goodness and badness once they are subjected to evaluation. Not only can nature as evaluated be deemed normatively good or bad, but an evaluation could lead to the identification of a particular landscape as an ideal one — a long- and well-used pastoral landscape, for instance. Such a landscape might serve, as a consequence of this evaluation, as an example of the normative "ought," with land managers thereafter using it as a baseline by which to judge and manage other lands. Considered normatively, in short, nature can be highly value-laden.

Aside from any evaluation, however, the claim that nature just "is" is subject to an important challenge. Many people perceive a transcendent moral order in the universe, whether coming from God or elsewhere. One widespread belief based on a transcendent order is that humans have special moral value that distinguishes them from other life forms, value that does not rest on human convention alone (Baer 1971; Zizioulas 1998). A related common belief is that other life forms or collectives also possess certain value independent of any human action in recognizing it or creating it (Baer 1966). To the extent that a transcendent moral order does exist, some parts or conditions of nature might stand on their own (that is, prior to any evaluation) as the "ought" of moral goodness.

The moral value that arises by reason of a transcendent order is one type of what is commonly called *intrinsic value,* a term that typically comprises any moral value possessed by a thing that does not arise due to the thing's contribution to human utility. As thus defined, the term includes both objective value arising by reason of a transcendent moral order and all value, not based on utility, that humans create through moral reasoning and convention. Many philosophers, for instance, conclude that endangered species possess intrinsic value, but believe that such value exists only when morally guided humans are present to recognize it (Wenz 2001). Claims of intrinsic value not based on religion remain largely within the modernist world view, which requires the presence of a valuing human subject to confer or ascribe value (Callicott 1999d).

The matter of intrinsic value is worth considering in the context of land management because of the light it sheds on science's varied roles. Neither type of intrinsic value has any tangible existence, which means neither is amenable to direct study through empirical data collection and analysis. Because scientists rest their descriptions of nature on empirical data, they possess no tools with which to describe intrinsic value or even to comment meaningfully on it. Intrinsic value is not an issue of science (excluding, here as elsewhere, social-science studies of the human behavior involved).

Of the two types of intrinsic value, claims based on a transcendent moral order pose the greater difficulties for science. Science presumes that the world is a purely physical phenomenon and seeks to understand it as such. It rejects *ab initio* any claim that nonmaterial forces, processes, essences, or moral orders exist in the world. This presumption is pervasive and highly potent, so much so that scientists are prone to assume that science has disproved transcendent forms and values (Wilson 1998). In fact it has not. Science merely employs analytic methods that presume their nonexistence and seeks to describe all that it perceives without them (Berry 2000).

Three observations, useful to what follows, emerge from our consideration of intrinsic value: (1) Intrinsic-value claims are unscientific in the sense that science yields no clear proof to sustain them, but they are not unscientific in the sense of being falsified or otherwise disproved. (2) Because science has no tools with which to study intrinsic value, it has no legitimate role in assessing claims about it (although scientists, in their roles as citizens, certainly do). (3) The claim that we cannot shift from the "is" of nature to the "ought" of desired landscape outcomes is plainly true only if "na-

ture" refers to the detailed description generated by pure science. If "nature" means something other or more than that, the claim raises issues that go beyond science and that normatively might be false.

THE SUBSTANCE AND PROCESS OF EVALUATION

Evaluation and the Distinction between Substance and Process

Evaluation in the land-management setting is a matter of passing judgment on the goodness or badness of conditions or processes in nature. Put simply, evaluation is undertaken when identified people employ substantive criteria to make determinations of goodness or badness. This activity is usefully divided into two parts: (1) the substantive criteria used to judge (the substantive evaluation standards) and (2) the overall process by which the standards are applied and land-use practices are set (the evaluation process).

Substantive Evaluation Standards

Substantive evaluation standards properly reflect the full range of factors people might take into account in deciding whether a landscape is good or bad, from the most highly practical considerations to ones that are entirely aesthetic, moral, or religious. Is the land producing food, fuel, and fiber for humans in the way desired by those who set the standards? Is the land a beautiful, healthful place for people to live? Is adequate habitat provided for particular species or (if desired) all native species? Are adequate natural areas set aside for study, recreation, and other purposes? Do current and proposed land-use practices properly reflect moral duties to future generations and other life forms, all as determined by those who set the standards?

In thinking about standards, it is useful to break their constituent elements into three overlapping components: (1) *human utility,* with utility broadly conceived to include aesthetics and the full range of quality-of-life issues; (2) *respect* or *virtue,* drawing upon a wide range of moral and religious assessments of nature and of how humans ought to interact with it; (3) *humility* or *precaution,* which takes into account and seeks to accommodate the considerable limits on human knowledge and understanding.

Although these components are not difficult to grasp in broad terms, a few explanations may be helpful. A transcendent moral order, to the extent recognized, would likely enter the standards as part of component 2, as would other claims of intrinsic value. A sense of moral obligation to future human generations might also enter in to component 2, although it could also be deemed part of component 1. A perceived need to act cautiously toward the land might well fit within all of the components. It appears here separately because of the emphasis that it receives in many proposed schemes of evaluation standards (Ehrenfeld 1981; Freyfogle 1993, 1998; Raffensperger & Tickner 1999).

Plainly, these components can take a variety of forms, and much discussion today centers on them. Many proposed land-management goals or guidelines draw overtly on all three components. Others emphasize one or two. For our purposes it is chiefly important to note the three components and to recognize the diverse ways they can come together. It is not the case that standards fall into two distinct categories: those based only on human utility and those based on a "biocentric" perspective of the world. Real life is vastly more complex: various factors intermingle complexly, forming an undivided range.

The Evaluation Process and Its Importance

A number of questions and issues need to be raised and resolved—however deliberately—whenever a process for evaluating land is put in place. Who will the evaluators be? What spatial scale will be employed? What study will occur and what evidence will be deemed relevant? How frequently will evaluations be updated?

The way an evaluation process is structured and conducted can have considerable effect on the evaluation that results, which is to say that any given evaluation will be much influenced by the process that produces it and not just by the substantive evaluation standards that are employed. Who decides, upon what evidence, and in what setting can all considerably influence the ultimate evaluation. Processes can entail little or much study, little or much

expert scientific input, and little or much discussion and deliberation. All affect the outcome.

The effect of process on outcome is usefully illustrated by considering the methods available to gain public input on an issue of policy. One method, the standard opinion poll, seeks evaluations from people as isolated individuals without study or deliberation. It presumes that people know enough to make determinations, and it allows them to select the standards to use in doing so. The opinion-poll approach is usefully compared to its opposite: the courtroom process in which public jurors are called upon to make consensus evaluations. Courtroom jurors are deliberately screened to ensure that they have no prior knowledge of the dispute and no cause for bias. Carefully prepared evidence is presented to them, in a setting arranged to encourage reflection. Decisions are made by jurors acting collectively. The laws they apply (the evaluation standards) are established in advance and proffered when the time comes to judge.

Methods of gaining public input vary between these extremes, with the method chosen having considerable effect on the input received. In this way and many others, process can be as important as substantive standards in shaping ultimate decisions—as the legal profession for generations has known well.

Setting Standards—the Process

Substantive evaluation standards are themselves typically the products of a process—here termed the standard-setting process—one that also exerts considerable influence on what it yields. Such processes can be public and highly formal ones, as when the U.S. Congress enacts laws that are signed by the president or when a federal agency promulgates regulations after extensive study and hearings. On the other side, they can be casual, individual, and instantaneous, as when an individual landowner makes a snap land-use decision. Scholars, of course, commonly develop and propose their own substantive evaluation standards (conservation biologists and economists prominently among them), and a huge and useful literature on the subject exists. Collectively, the standards in a given setting can be viewed as the overall management goal, although the term *goal* might also be applied to a single standard in isolation, particularly if it is a standard that takes precedence over other applicable standards.

Complicating the matter of how standards arise is the fact that a standard-setting process can be intertwined with an evaluation process: that is, one process can both set standards and apply them. They are often intertwined when substantive evaluation standards are insufficiently detailed to apply to a given landscape, vesting evaluators with so much latitude that they are required in effect to complete the standards-setting work by putting flesh on incomplete standards. For instance, a substantive evaluation standard might call upon evaluators to make determinations as to what is "reasonable" or "feasible" or "cost-effective" under the circumstances. It might, alternatively, call for a determination as to whether a landscape produces the "highest sustained yield" of a resource or provides for the "maximum diversity" of plant and animal species. To varying degrees, such terms are sufficiently vague that those who apply them must give them meaning. As they do so, they engage both in setting standards (even if merely fine-tuning) and in evaluation.

Health as Metaphor

Our comments here are pertinent to the question of whether it is metaphorical to speak of land or an ecosystem as being healthy (Callicott 1992, 1999c; Ehrenfeld 1992). Our answer is simple: yes and no. Yes, if the question is one purely of science, and no, if the question refers to health as a substantive evaluation standard.

Although scientists are free to develop new terms and make new uses of old ones, they have so far used health solely to describe the functioning of individual organisms. Because an ecosystem is not an organism, it cannot literally possess health in this way. To speak of ecosytem health as science, therefore, is to use the term metaphorically — at least until such time as the term is assigned a broader meaning. On the other hand, the larger community apart from science does not limit the term *health* so narrowly but uses it in other ways, as when people speak of community health, public health, or the health of the economy. In such settings, all value-laced, health describes modes of functioning that are thriving, vigorous, and growing in desired ways. These are literal

uses of the word, and land can be healthy in the same literal way. In this regard, it is worth noting the claim of Wendell Berry (1995) that the well-being of an organism is so linked to surrounding life that it is misleading to speak of the health of an organism in isolation. The community "is the smallest unit of health," in his view, and "to speak of the health of an isolated individual is a contradiction in terms."

Leopold and Land Health

In similar manner, our approach sheds light on one of the most prominent proposed standards for land management, the goal of land health proposed by Aldo Leopold. Responding to what he viewed as an acute national need, Leopold proposed that the conservation community come together to embrace land health as its guiding aim. In a series of late writings (many, unfortunately, unpublished at his death) Leopold explained generally what land health means and listed the principal symptoms of land sickness. As he defined it, land health centers chiefly on the functioning of ecological processes and only indirectly on biological composition (Callicott 1992, 1999b; Freyfogle 2000).

Leopold did not offer *land health* as a term or statement of science, although he drew extensively upon science in formulating it. He offered it instead as what we call a substantive evaluation standard. His first requirement for healthy land was that the soil be retained and kept fertile. Eroding fields, he knew, could still sustain life, but they would do so over time at lower levels of productivity. Productivity, in turn, was a good thing in many ways, not the least because it promoted overall human utility. By including soil preservation as part of land health, Leopold drew upon all three component parts of substantive evaluation standards: (1) fertile soil contributed to long-term human utility; (2) soil conservation showed proper respect for what he viewed as the biotic right of other life forms to exist; and (3) conservation seemed a wise way to act cautiously in the face of our ignorance about community functioning. In similar ways, Leopold's other functional components of land health drew upon the various elements of substantive standards, while leaving open the possibility that, in given settings, other substantive standards would also have bearing.

Because it is best understood as a substantive evaluation standard, land health as Leopold defined it is properly challenged — as are other substantive evaluation standards only based upon a full assessment of the factors relevant to the setting of them. Accordingly, it is wrong to dismiss such a goal as bad science, although it would certainly be proper to argue that better science could improve it. It would also be wrong, given our comments on health as metaphor, to claim that such a goal presumes an outdated organismic understanding of ecosystem functioning. In Leopold's case, neither land health nor his now-famous land ethic, in which he used the term *stability* as a synonym for land health, was based on such an understanding (Callicott 1992; Freyfogle 2000).

THE ROLES OF SCIENCE

Having divided the land-management process into its central parts, it becomes easier to see the many ways science fits into the process and the full range of ways that scientists as such can contribute to it.

Setting Standards

Science plays a vital supporting role in the standards-setting process, chiefly with respect to two of the three components. Science has its slightest role in formulating the respect or virtue component of the standards, because this component addresses questions of moral and religious value that are largely detached from science. Science's main role here is likely to be indirect. By helping people learn about the natural world, it can stimulate their moral sentiments, prompting changes in what they value (Callicott 1989).

In terms of the humility or precautionary component of the standards, science is useful in highlighting limits on human knowledge and abilities and in emphasizing nature's indeterminacy and interdependencies. In the end, humility raises questions of value or virtue rather than science, but good science can help greatly in the exploration of such questions. Scientists would be remiss if they did not step out of their science roles and engage these issues.

Science's most prominent role lies in helping to gauge the many factors relating to human utility, particularly those pertaining to the land's carrying capacity and its long-term ability to satisfy diverse human needs. With respect to endangered species, for instance, science is needed to help estimate the direct and indirect utility of various species; similarly and even more so, science is needed to gauge the benefits of particular ecosystem processes. Still, even with respect to human utility, science must be interpreted in light of human needs, desires, and aspirations. Science has little to say about aesthetics, for instance, or about the functioning of the market economy. Thus, on this component as well, science needs to work in tandem with other considerations.

Evaluating Nature and Implementing Chosen Standards

Science becomes even more important during the evaluation process and thereafter, when land-use plans and decisions are developed and implemented (here termed *implementation*). A standards-setting process could lead to a determination, for instance, that farm fields should be used in ways that preserve the quantity and quality of the soil. Science would then be needed to study various land-use patterns, whether existing or hypothetical, to determine whether they satisfy this standard. Similarly, a chosen standard might call for the restoration of a native salmon population in a given river. Again, science would be needed to decide whether particular plans of action would or would not achieve that standard.

Formulating Processes Used to Set Standards, Evaluate, and Implement

Science can also provide valuable information when procedural issues are being resolved. Some processes will be far better than others in making good use of science. For instance, the spatial scale of a land-management effort presents an important process issue. The choice among possible scales is not itself a science issue, but science can help describe appropriate ecological boundaries such as watersheds or functional boundaries of ecosystems. Evaluation and implementation done on such a scale is more likely to incorporate good science than a similar effort undertaken on a less natural scale. This is particularly true, of course, in the conservation of biodiversity, which is most effectively done by managing ecosystems rather than individual species in isolation (Knight 1996). Scientists can provide useful advice on the issue of scale, as they can on many other process issues, in terms of timing, study methods, data drawn upon, deliberation modes, and monitoring and feedback mechanisms.

Conservation Biology, Values, and Advocacy

A process-centered approach to land management helps shed light on the issue of values and advocacy in conservation biology (Noss 1996). If conservation biology were nothing more than science, its aim might be simply to catalogue and describe the elements of biodiversity, currently and prospectively, along with their processes, functions, and interactions. It would produce no judgments or recommendations, and passion would not have a role in it.

Conservation biology, however, began with the postulate that biotic diversity has intrinsic value and deserves protection (Soulé 1985). That overarching goal still motivates the discipline (Meffe & Carroll 1997). Such a goal plainly reaches beyond science and is best understood (in our framework) as a substantive evaluation standard. To the extent that the embedded standard — protecting and restoring native biodiversity — is accepted, conservation biology is well grounded in established policy, but, when the embedded substantive standard is contested or rejected, the discipline is not.

The question commonly asked about conservation biology is whether it is in some way scientifically illegitimate because its practitioners embrace a particular standard and advocate on behalf of it. We think not. Conservation biology is hardly alone in seeking to promote established, widely shared policy aims (Meine & Meffe 1996). Human medicine offers a good comparison (Soulé 1985; Ehrenfeld 2000); it is premised on the similar non-science determination that it is good to preserve human life. Normative bases such as these, in fact, undergird much contemporary science. Soil scientists presume (and with good reason) that it is typically good to retain soil and keep it fertile; water-quality researchers presume (with equally good reason) that clean water is typically better than polluted. In the case of conservation biology, the normative bases are in fact well grounded in public sentiment (Kempton et al. 1995). In none of these instances is science establishing the normative bases

that undergird it; we do not mean here to say otherwise. And we must keep open, again, the possibility that, in particular physical settings, infertile soil or contaminated water or biological impoverishment might be normatively preferred, based on governing substantive standards. Science in these settings does not create its own normative bases; it accepts them and uses them to guide its efforts.

We see no problem with advocacy on the part of conservation biologists, so long as they remain clear about which aspects of their work are science (mere description) and which go beyond science to become advocacy for particular, biodiversity-enhancing standards. That is perhaps best done when scientists expressly state the normative presumptions upon which they work, particularly when those presumptions might be challenged. Clear expression serves many good purposes, not the least of which is to put pressure on opposing interests to make clear their own presumptions. Once normative presumptions are set forth — supported, when appropriate, with evidence from public opinion surveys, legislative determinations, and the like — conservation biologists can proceed with their science work, as objectively and responsibly as medical researchers and many other scientists.

Understanding Ecosystem Management

. . .

At its fullest, ecosystem management could provide the entire procedural and substantive framework for making decisions about a landscape — much as an individual landowner might do if completely unhindered by outside factors and constraints. To do the full job well, ecosystem management ought to cover all the steps: (1) prescribe the procedural rules for setting standards, including who sets them and how; (2) provide substantive guidance (as appropriate) for use in that process, including minimum requirements for the substantive evaluation standards that ultimately emerge; (3) set the governing procedural rules for the evaluation process, in terms of data collection, assessment, and study; and (4) explain the processes for implementation, including how responsibilities should be assigned and plans prepared.

A more limited form of ecosystem management would be one in which functions at one or both ends of the overall land-management sequence are omitted. Thus, an ecosystem management process might begin with some or all of the substantive evaluation standards already in place, perhaps set by law or by agency or landowner decision. At the other end, it might terminate earlier, at the stage of detailed evaluation, for instance, or early in implementation, leaving later steps for others to perform.

Ecosystem management efforts often become confused and contentious because the assigned functions are unclear and feuding interests have differing understandings of what is going on. A prime example of confused guidance appeared in the 1995 federal *Report of the Interagency Ecosystem Management Task Force,* which strongly endorsed the ecosystem approach for federal management efforts (Freyfogle 1997). At various places the report refers to ecosystem management as merely "a process," the neutral aim of which is to select and then achieve whatever "desired ecosystem outcome" is deemed appropriate in the collective view of the various participants. Language of this type suggests that the standards-setting and evaluation processes would be merged. At other places, however, the report states that ecosystem management is a "goal driven" enterprise; it is "a method for sustaining and restoring natural systems and their functions and values" with a predetermined goal of "restor[ing] and sustain[ing] the health, productivity, and biological diversity of ecosystems." Such language, sprinkled throughout the report, suggests that management processes are to begin with an important substantive evaluation standard already in place. The federal report, in short, pushes two ways, sowing confusion along the way.

Ecosystem management is a contested managerial approach. At least nominally, controversies around it largely involve such scientific issues as whether ecosystems exist, how they might be characterized, and whether their natural functioning is sufficiently orderly and persistent to serve as a management guide (Pickett & White 1985; Worster 1993, 1994; Pahl-Wostl 1995). We cannot elaborate here, but it is our sense that many such debates, ostensibly about science, are more aptly understood as disputes about other issues, disputes that would be more productive if the real issues were faced directly. The issue in a given debate, for instance, might really be about the best substantive evaluation standards to employ in a given evaluation process. Or it might be about matters of process, such as who the evaluators are or whether sound input is being gained from users of managed lands. Even the prominent debate about what, as a matter of science, characterizes an ecosystem is largely miscast when the true land-management issue is choosing the best spatial scale for management—a process-related issue that science informs but does not determine.

USING SCIENCE TERMS AS STANDARDS

No small amount of confusion arises in the land-management arena when terms developed by scientists to aid in science are borrowed and put to use as overall management goals. As tools useful in the descriptive work of science, such terms can become degraded. As substantive evaluation standards, they can be poorly cast. Beyond that, scientists can have a hard time keeping straight what is science and what is not when a single term is used in two ways—as both the descriptive *is* (or *will be*) and the normative *ought.* Nonscientists, predictably, risk even greater confusion. The practice of using terms in two ways, however, is not without potential benefits. How the costs and benefits compare is a matter that deserves more attention.

Ecological Integrity as a Goal

The much-discussed idea of ecological integrity illustrates this practice. As a science term, *ecological integrity* is used as a shorthand way of describing the functioning of particular ecosystems, typically ecosystems largely unaffected by humans (Karr 1990). It is used scientifically, too, as a benchmark by which to measure the extent to which humans have altered given landscapes (Angermeier 2000; Sagoff 2000). Like other science terms, ecological integrity might prove useful in managing land at any step in the overall effort where science is properly employed.

Ecological integrity, however, might also be used (and has been used quite prominently) as a normative idea, that is, as a shorthand way of identifying a key feature of a valued landscape. Or, to draw upon the above terminology, a standards-setting process could, in a given spatial setting, select ecological integrity as a substantive evaluation standard. (The standard, in such an instance, might be the only one chosen for the landscape, or it could be one of several chosen standards.) When this happens, ecological integrity shifts from being a tool used simply to describe nature to being part of a land-management goal, perhaps even the key standard that forms the goal.

When used as a tool to describe nature, ecological integrity is subject to challenge if and to the extent that it is poor science. Scientists could debate its utility in describing nature and measuring human-caused change, but their debate on that issue, being pure science, would carry no moral or normative overtones. Conversely, when ecological integrity is put to use in a substantive evaluation standard, it would not be subject to objection on this scientific basis, because substantive evaluation standards are by no means limited to valid scientific ideas. Standards can, and indeed normally should, draw upon many moral and prudential considerations. A substantive evaluation standard could legitimately (though perhaps unwisely) draw an idea from science and then proceed to modify the idea—based upon considerations of human utility, virtue or respect, and humility or precaution—yielding a revised version of the idea, quite distinct from pure science.

Plainly, a single term used in two ways can breed confusion. It is an obvious problem with an obvious solution: to find another term to fill one of the verbal roles. Given the obvious solution, why might science terms be put to normative uses when the result may be confusion and worse? One speculative answer is that scientists are unaware of what they are doing, or they are aware of it but underestimate the dangers. Another is simply that the terms are already familiar and conveniently at hand. Without discounting these answers, it is possible to propose another: scientists are well aware of what they are doing, and they mix verbal roles deliberately as a way to expand science's roles in land management, particularly in the vital step of setting standards.

To choose ecological integrity as a guiding standard is to promote one normative vision of land over others. The vision being promoted, it is important to note, is strongly slanted toward conservation,

and it is a vision in which scientists as such would play a dominant role in achieving it. One could phrase a strongly proconservation standard in other ways, using only nonscience terms. But standards phrased in nonscience terms would not similarly grant to scientists the influence they receive when a guiding standard uses terms that so obviously play to their expertise.

Our argument here is speculative, particularly to the extent that it requires proof of the motives driving individual scientists. Yet we are inclined to believe that such speculation is useful even without exploring motives. The fundamental reality is that a goal phrased in scientific terms is likely to augment the roles of science and scientists in efforts to promote it. Whether or not intended, such a phrasing entails a move to gain power. And it is, in the case of ecological integrity, a move to exercise that power sharply in favor of land conservation.

Friends of conservation might see much to like in any attempt to add strength to their cause. As for the legitimacy of such a move, other disciplines have done much the same and with great effect: witness the spectacular success of economics in elevating the descriptive term *efficiency* into an all-purpose normative goal. Even so, the dangers in seeking influence in this way are not modest.

When ecological integrity becomes an influential standard, its proponents might easily be prone to clarify or modify the term in ways that are simply not justified scientifically. Because substantive evaluation standards need not stand alone as science, their manipulations might well be proper as a normative matter. But it is easy to see how adjustments made to standards could quickly cross back to the science side and distort scientific conclusions. This is particularly true, we believe, given that the power gained by pushing ecological integrity as a standard depends upon the confusion generated by the term—much as the influence of economists is based on widespread confusion about efficiency. The more blurring that occurs between science and evaluation standards, the more power scientists acquire, yet the more likely it is too that the various components of standards (moral and precautionary factors, for instance, as well as estimates of overall utility) will permeate the science side and cause distortion.

As we see matters, though, the greater danger lurking in such a verbal sleight of hand is a different one: normative disagreements about the nonscience components of substantive evaluation standards will become, through confusion, disagreements instead about matters of science. Those who resist measures to promote integrity could well respond (as they already have responded) by claiming that they are bad science rather than by contesting their legitimacy as sound substantive evaluation standards. In the extreme, the entire scientific field that studies land functioning could turn into a political battleground, with disagreements framed as issues of science standing as surrogates for arguments that chiefly reflect differing perspectives on human utility, morals, and the wisdom of acting humbly.

Misplaced arguments of this type can easily crop up as disputes about how to define key scientific terms. For instance, does nature on its own operate as a "system?" The answer depends not only on nature but on how one defines the word *system.* When the question is purely one of science, cool heads might prevail and a consensus definition might emerge. But when more is riding on the question — when an affirmative answer to it will have vast effects on land-management practices — a consensus definition might prove elusive. Misgivings about the wisdom of conservation can take the form of technical arguments about the definition of *system* or *order* or *integrity* or *health.* Those who favor intensive land uses can bolster their policy preferences by defining a term such as system so that no natural community — and perhaps nothing short of a machine — possesses it. Those who oppose efforts to promote ecological integrity can easily define it, if they choose, so that no natural area ever has it.

We might illustrate today's predicament by imagining two scientists who independently study a particular, barely altered natural area. The scientists might both use the term integrity to describe how barely altered areas function, yet disagree factually as to how the particular area they study does function. Alternatively, they might agree entirely on how the particular area functions and yet disagree as to whether it is helpful to use the term integrity to describe that functioning, and if so how the term might be defined. Finally, they might agree that the natural area possesses integrity but disagree on whether the maintenance of that integrity is an appropriate aim for land-management efforts. Facts, definitions, policy factors: all are good matters to talk about, but it is hard to discuss them sensibly when they are mingled and confused.

Given these dangers (if not already realized costs) of employing science terms as land-management goals, we see considerable appeal in using an updated version of Leopold's land health as an alternative conservation goal. The term *land* is plainly not a scientific term; thus, is not subject to criticism in the ways a term such as *ecosystem* is (Callicott 1999c). As for the term *health,* it is less likely to draw criticism as bad science (Callicott 1999c), although we recognize that the term has sometimes been so attacked. Its virtue is that, apart from scientists and their quibbles about its metaphorical usage, health has strong, broad connotations (Karr 2000). It is not popularly viewed as a technical science term (although academics sometimes view it as such), and people will be more likely to sense (rightly) that many policy factors are relevant to it (Ehrenfeld 1992). At the same time, it promotes a vision of the land as a vigorous, productive operation, and no one can avoid recognizing the strong roles of science in understanding and managing that operation.

Ecology and Politics

Our probing here of the contentious intellectual terrain surrounding such terms as ecosystem, ecological integrity, and health leads us to conclude with more wide-ranging comments about the political context in which such debates take place, particularly debates among scientists. Nature is so interwoven and interdependent that those who seek evidence of structure and system can easily find it. Yet given the constancy of natural change, the variations among communities, and the various options as to scale of analysis, those who seek disorder can find that too. Is it possible that a scientist might be particularly inclined, for nonscience reasons, to look for one rather than another?

To argue that nature is random and disorderly above the organism level is the ultimate expression of classical liberalism, which sought to knock down traditional social restraints and maximize individual freedom. It is no surprise, then, that those who see chaos in nature sometimes turn for historical support to such influential liberal philosophers as John Stuart Mill, whose atomistic view of nature corresponded with his individualistic view of the human social condition (Sagoff 2000). How one views nature, as historian Donald Worster has speculated, may have more to do than we yet recognize with one's political and social leanings (Worster 1993, 1994).

A view of nature-as-chaos builds upon and carries forward the powerful force of American individualism. At the same time, it is easily associated with widespread hostility toward government constraints on liberty and to America's deep-seated love of the free market. It is easy to see why private industry prefers a view of nature as chaotic. With equal ease one can see why pro-liberty and pro-market think tanks offer unwavering support for the nature-as-chaos view. Their embrace of disequilibrium says much about them and little about the soundness of any relevant science.

But might it be true that independent scientists also have trouble keeping matters straight, whether they personally favor the chaos and competition of the market or instead see social welfare as dependent chiefly on healthy families, neighborhoods, schools, churches, and other communal structures? Is it irrelevant whether scientists believe humans ought to share, cooperate, and act humbly when dealing with one another or whether they are comfortable with the aggressive pursuit of self-chosen aims?

Communities in nature are not machines, and they are not organisms. Their closest analogue, it would seem, is the human social community, a fact Aldo Leopold recognized near the end of his life when he drew a parallel between ecology and sociology (Leopold 1946). In important ways, both disciplines deal with ultimate levels of organization, which leads one to wonder: rather than distance itself from social and political considerations, might ecology do better to embrace them more openly, not so as to bias research but to help improve it? Might ecology move ahead today by drawing more extensively on the wisdom of observers who have struggled to find sense in communal structures and who have attended in their prescriptions not to the parts in isolation but to their lasting and healthy interactions?

LITERATURE CITED

Angermeier, P. L. 2000. The natural imperative for biological conservation. Conservation Biology 14: 373–381.

Baer, R. A. 1966. Land misuse: a theological concern. The Christian Century 83 (October 12):1239–1241.

Baer, R. A. 1971. Ecology, religion, and the American dream. American Ecclesiastical Review 165 (September):46–47.

Berry, W. 1995. Health as membership. Pages 86–109 in W. Berry. Another turn of the crank. Counterpoint Press, Washington, D.C.

Berry, W. 2000. Life is a miracle: an essay against modern superstition. Counterpoint Press, Washington, D.C.

Callicott, J. B. 1989. In defense of the land ethic. State University of New York Press, Albany.

Callicott, J. B. 1992. Aldo Leopold's metaphor. Pages 42–56 in R. Costanza, B. Norton, B. D. Haskell, editors. Ecosystem health: new goals for environmental management. Island Press, Washington, D.C.

Callicott, J. B. 1999a. Just the facts, ma'am. Pages 79–97 in J. B. Callicott. Beyond the land ethic. State University of New York Press, Albany.

Callicott, J. B. 1999b. Do deconstructive ecology and sociobiology undermine the Leopold land ethic? Pages 117–139 in J. B. Callicott. Beyond the land ethic. State University of New York Press, Albany.

Callicott, J. B. 1999c. The value of ecosystem health. Pages 347–364 in J. B. Callicott. Beyond the land ethic. State University of New York Press, Albany.

Callicott, J. B. 1999d. Intrinsic value in nature: a metaethical analysis. Pages 239–261 in J. B. Callicott. Beyond the land ethic. State University of New York Press, Albany.

Ehrenfeld, D. 1981. The arrogance of humanism. Oxford University Press, New York.

Ehrenfeld, D. 1992. Ecosystem health and ecological theories. Pages 135–143 in R. Costanza, B. Norton, B. D. Haskell, editors. Ecosystem health: new goals for environmental management. Island Press, Washington, D.C.

Ehrenfeld, D. 2000. War and peace and conservation biology. Conservation Biology 14:105–112.

Freyfogle, E. T. 1993. Justice and the earth: images for our planetary survival. The Free Press, New York.

Freyfogle, E. T. 1997. Repairing the waters of the national parks: notes on long-term strategy. Denver University Law Review 74:815–846.

Freyfogle, E. T. 1998. Bounded people, boundless lands: envisioning a new land ethic. Island Press/Shearwater Books, Washington, D.C.

Freyfogle, E. T. 2000. *A Sand County Almanac* at 50: Leopold in the new century. Environmental Law Reporter 1-2000:10058–10068.

Karr, J. R. 1990. Biological integrity and the goal of environmental legislation: lessons for conservation biology. Conservation Biology 4:244–250.

Karr, J. R. 2000. Health, integrity, and biological assessment: the importance of measuring whole things. Pages 209–226 in D. Pimentel, L. Westra, and R. F. Noss, editors. Ecological integrity: integrating environment, conservation, and health. Island Press, Washington, D.C.

Kempton, W. J., S. Boster, and J. A. Hartley. 1995. Environmental values in American culture. MIT Press, Cambridge, Massachusetts.

Knight, R. L. 1996. Aldo Leopold, the land ethic, and ecosystem management. Journal of Wildlife Management 60:471–474.

Leopold, A. 1946. The land-health concept and conservation. Pages 218–226 in J. B. Callicott and E. T. Freyfogle, editors. 1999. Aldo Leopold, for the health of the land: unpublished essays and other writings. Island Press/Shearwater Books, Washington, D.C.

Meffe, G. K., and C. R. Carroll. 1997. Principles of conservation biology. Sinauer Associates, Sunderland, Massachusetts.

Meine, C., and G. K. Meffe, 1996. Conservation values, conservation science: a healthy tension. Conservation Biology 10:916–917.

Noss, R. F. 1996. Conservation biology, values, and advocacy. Conservation Biology 10:904.

Pahl-Wostl, C. 1995. The dynamic nature of ecosystems. Wiley, West Sussex, United Kingdom.

Pickett, S. T. A., and P. S. White, 1985. The ecology of natural disturbance and patch dynamics. Academic Press, Orlando.

Raffensperger, C., and J. Tickner, editors. 1999. Protecting public health and the environment: implementing the precautionary principle. Island Press, Washington, D.C.

Sagoff, M. 2000. Ecosystem design in historical and philosophical context. Pages 61–78 in D. Pimentel, L. Westra, and R. F. Noss, editors. Ecological integrity: integrating environment, conservation, and health. Island Press, Washington, D.C.

Soulé, M. E. 1985. What is conservation biology? BioScience 35:727–734.

Wenz, P. 2001. Environmental ethics today. Oxford University Press, New York.

Wilson, E. O. 1998. Consilience: the unity of knowledge. Alfred A. Knopf, New York.

Worster, D. 1993. The wealth of nature: environmental history and the ecological imagination. Oxford University Press, New York.

Worster D. 1994. Nature's economy: a history of ecological ideas. Cambridge University Press, Cambridge, United Kingdom.

Zizioulas, J. D. 1989. Preserving God's creation: three lectures on theology and ecology. King's Theological Review 12(2):41–45.

DISCUSSION TOPICS

1. How has your image of the role of science in the formation of land management policy changed in light of the authors' points?
2. In light of the authors' discussion, what role do you see for science in supporting or refuting intrinsic value among endangered species?
3. Based on the article, how do you believe science might be used to measure land health in biotic communities?

READING 3

Facing the Problem of Uncertainty

Ragnar Fjelland

Ragnar Fjelland is associated with the Center for the Study of the Sciences and the Humanities, University of Bergen, Norway.

In this excerpt of an article from the Journal of Agricultural and Environmental Ethics, *Fjelland argues that the global character of many environmental problems has become a genuinely new situation for scientists and technologists and that the problems of ignorance and uncertainty in science can no longer be minimized through application of probability theory or statistics. He proposes that the standard use of statistics has to be changed, that the traditional application of "burden of proof" must be reversed, and that science should not only draw on more and different kinds of expertise but also include greater public involvement.*

In this paper, I shall try to answer two questions: 1) Does uncertainty represent something genuinely new in science? 2) What are the implications of recognizing uncertainty for science and science policy?

THE PURSUIT OF CERTAINTY

Let me start with the first question. No doubt, one strong driving force in Western science and philosophy is the pursuit of certainty. This pursuit is motivated by a mathematical scientific ideal, and we can draw a line from Plato, via Galileo and Einstein, to Hawking and "theories of everything.". . .

The common denominator is mathematics. Plato's theory of knowledge was inspired by geometry as the paradigm of knowledge, and, according to Galileo, "the book of nature" is written in the language of mathematics. However, there is an important difference between Plato on the one side and Galileo and modern science on the other. Whereas Plato's reality was immaterial, Galileo's reality was material. Galileo called objective reality "primary sense qualities." Today we would rather use the term "matter." The essential property of matter is that it can be described mathematically. But this property presupposes another property that is one of the most important preconditions of modern science: Matter can be divided. Therefore, one of the most important characteristics of modern science is that complex objects are reduced to their parts, and in the last resort to simple elements. When the whole has been reduced to its parts, the parts may be put together again.

Galileo recognized that a mathematical description requires measurements, and that measurements require controlled laboratory experiments. The aim of the controlled laboratory experiment is to keep all or most factors constant. Only one or a few factors are varied at a time. These ideal conditions increase *certainty*. According to the traditional view, controlled experiments are merely simplification and purification of natural situations. We have to leave out some factors to make the problems manageable. Afterwards we "add back" the factors that were left out, and in this way we come closer to natural situations.

However, we do not only remove complicating factors. We *impose* artificial conditions on the object as well, because the ideal conditions are normally not realized in everyday life. Therefore, "adding back" may not be an easy task. There is an alternative, though. We may realize the ideal conditions through technology. From this point of view, technology is a way of reducing uncertainty. . . .

To put it simply: Technology to a large extent realizes the ideal conditions of the laboratory at a larger scale. We can see how this works in biotechnology by looking at the so-called "green revolution" of the 1960s as an example. It involved the development and introduction of new plant species that gave larger yields per acre than did the traditional species. This first happened with wheat in Mexico, and later with wheat and rice in Asia. The new "high-yielding varieties" could make better use of fertilizer with far higher concentrations than traditional varieties, and they had noticeably faster maturation rates. One crucial factor was that the plants receive the correct amount of watering at the correct time. They were also less resistant against a number of diseases and parasites. To summarize: If the new variants were to give higher yields, a *"technological package,"* in the form of the correct amounts of fertilizer, water, pesticides, and plant protection products was needed. If these things are not in place, the process can go wrong. The desired effects can in other words only be achieved if one also has control over the environment. What was needed to carry out the "green revolution," was to realize *controlled laboratory conditions in agriculture.*

UNCERTAINTY CANNOT BE IGNORED

Although we can control parts of nature in this way, the inescapable problem is, however, that there will always be something outside the system we control.

A factory is a typical example of a controlled system. However, the control is normally far from perfect. First, the production process itself is full of risks, for example the risk of explosions and chemical hazards. Second, there is the area around the factory. Traditionally this was heavily polluted. Although regulations have reduced local pollution, the problem is often moved to other places. In particular, heavily polluting production is often moved from the rich countries to third world countries, where regulations are absent or less strict. Third, we have the uses of the products and the disposal of the worn-out products, and so on. Therefore, when an area is subject to technical control, there is always a large area that escapes control. In what follows, I shall use the term "natural conditions" in contrast to the simplified and idealized conditions of the laboratory and the factory. However, the word "natural" does not imply that the conditions are prior to human intervention. . . .

The problem of "adding back" from the simplified and idealized conditions of the laboratory to natural conditions has been recognized by ecologists. Therefore, laboratory experiments have limited value in ecology because the artificial conditions sometimes prevent important natural effects from appearing and they may magnify incidental and trivial effects. . . .

If laboratory experiments fail, field experiments might do the job. They are something between a laboratory experiment and the natural system. Because they are closer to the natural systems, they are popular in ecology. However, it looks as if we get nothing for free. There is a trade-off between control of the conditions on the one hand and relevance to natural situations on the other: The better the field experiments, the less relevant they are.

The problem of uncertainty may also be formulated in the language of risk assessment. We must (at least) distinguish between two different situations: uncertainty and ignorance. When we have uncertainty, it means that we know what can go wrong (when we also know the probabilities, we are talking about risk). However, there are often situations where we have no idea of what can go wrong. These situations are characterized by *ignorance*. In risk assessment, it is desirable to reduce uncertainty to risk,

because it enables the application of the mathematical methods of risk analysis (probability theory, statistics, and the like). This requires simplification and idealization, either in the form of experiments as described earlier or by applying mathematical models. However, we have a similar problem as in the case of ecology: The reduction of uncertainty may increase ignorance (Wynne, 1992: 114).

Mathematically speaking, the problem is nonlinearity. The mathematical sciences have since the time of Galileo, largely concentrated on linear or approximately linear systems. One reason is that the analytical tools of mathematics can be used. However, when the interactions between the parts of a system or the factors determining a process are nonlinear, the situation is changed. This was first observed in chaos. Chaos is characterized by *sensitive dependence on initial conditions* (the "Butterfly effect"): Small uncertainties in the determination of the initial conditions of a system may increase exponentially until they are the same magnitude as the parameters of the system. In that case, "adding back" does not work, and predictions are limited. . . .

However, organic nature is in general not chaotic, but complex. Complexity and chaos are not the same. It is sometimes said that complexity arises at "the edge of chaos." But they do have non-linearity in common, rendering impossible both "adding back" and exact predictions.

Let me return to my first question, if uncertainty is genuinely new in science. The answer is simply "no." From the very beginning of philosophy and science there were alternative schools of thought that emphasized uncertainty. The contemporaries of Plato, the Sophists, and even Plato's own teacher, Socrates, stressed both uncertainty and ignorance. Therefore, we can draw an alternative line, from Socrates, via the Renaissance Humanism of Erasmus and Montaigne, and to the present situation (cf. Toulmin, 1990).

In a certain sense, the two aspects, certainty and uncertainty, are combined in the theories of probability and statistics. The birth of the mathematical theory of probability is usually dated to 1654, to a discussion between the two mathematicians Pascal and Fermat. Statistics was developed in the nineteenth century, and integrated in most empirical sciences during the twentieth century (Gigerenzer et al., 1989). Furthermore, the recognition of uncertainty is the very foundation of one of the most basic and influential theories of contemporary science, quantum mechanics. According to quantum mechanics, uncertainty cannot be eliminated for theoretical reasons.

However, what is genuinely new today is the recognition that uncertainty cannot be tamed or ignored. Previously, unintended side-effects of industrial production that were outside our control could to a large extent be ignored. However, the global character of some environmental problems has shown that there is no "outside": The biosphere is finite. Therefore, scientists and technologists have in many ways come into a new situation. The Chernobyl accident is a dramatic example. However, problems such as a possible greenhouse effect, a possible reduction of the ozone layer, and so on are all of the same type. These encompass totally different problems than scientists and technologists are traditionally trained to deal with (Funtowicz and Ravetz, 1993: 742).

SOME CONSEQUENCES OF RECOGNIZING UNCERTAINTY

I shall now address the second question, and elaborate some consequences of recognizing uncertainty.

Statistics

My first point concerns the uses of statistics. It is theoretically almost trivial, but important in practice. One of the standard methods for establishing causal connections is the use of significance tests. We compare one group that has been exposed to the alleged cause with a similar group that has not been exposed to the same cause. This is based on Mill's method of difference. However, if we do not have complete control of all the factors, we must have recourse to statistics. We start with a "null hypothesis": We assume that the observed difference between the two groups has come about by chance. Only if the probability of this happening by chance is lower than the significance level [do] we conclude that there is a real difference, and reject the null hypothesis.

We may make two kinds of error due to the statistical nature of the problem: A type I error is rejecting a true null hypothesis. This is equivalent to claiming that there is an effect that in reality does not exist ("false positive"). A type II error is accepting a false null hypothesis. This is equivalent to overlooking an effect that really exists ("false negative"). It is important to note that there is an asymmetry built into the standard uses of statistics concerning the two types of error. We can only claim that there is a significant difference when there is a high probability that the difference cannot be blamed on statistical chance. In all other cases, we must refrain from claiming that there is a difference. This is similar here to the burden of proof needed in criminal cases. There, it is such that the defendant is innocent until proven guilty. Doubt should benefit the defendant. When using statistical methods, we assume that there is no statistical difference until the opposite is proven. . . .

Although the relationship between a type I and a type II error depends on the specific problem, in general there is a trade-off between them: If we decrease the probability of one, the probability of the other increases. In traditional significance tests, the probability of a type I error is controlled (it is like the significance level), thus leaving the probability of a type II error open. If researchers inform us that they have not found a statistically significant difference, it would be important additional information if the probability of overlooking the difference is large. In statistics textbooks, it is therefore emphasized that the probability for a type II error should always be evaluated. However in practice this is different. We know that this rule is often violated.

The Canadian marine biologist R. M. Peterman examined a total of 400 articles in two journals during the period of 1987–1989. Of these, 160 contained at least one incidence where a null hypothesis was not rejected, that is, one had not proved a significant difference. Of these, 83 articles contained recommendations *as if the null hypothesis was true,* in spite of the fact that only one article had evaluated the probability for a type II error. Peterman shows that in examples within marine biology, the probability for a type II error can easily come up to 50%. This then implies that one gives recommendations about situations under the assumption that there is no difference, when, in fact, there may be a 50% likelihood that one has overlooked a difference (Peterman, 1990: 8).

Let us imagine that a group of researchers get the assignment to examine whether there is a difference in the incidence of illness between two groups, and they give the answer T_0: "We have not found any (statistically significant) difference." However, this information lacks something. Two possibilities come to mind here, either T_1: "We have not found any difference, and we most likely would have found it if it existed" or T_2: "We have not found any difference, but we most likely would not have found it even if it existed." Needless to say, T_0 would carry much more weight if the correct interpretation was T_1 than if it was T_2. Therefore, it is a serious problem when researchers answer T_0, the majority of politicians and others interpret it as T_1, and the correct interpretation is T_2. This was probably the case in many of the examples reported by Peterman. . . .

One possible reason for the neglect of type II errors is the fact that estimating a type II error is not just a matter of standard procedures. A type II error can only be calculated relative to an *alternative* hypothesis. An adequate estimate of a type II error should take several possible alternative hypotheses into consideration, and their plausibility and cost of possible errors should be discussed too. There is something healthy in this. To carry out these calculations, science has to be put into context. For example, what may be an acceptable cost of an error in one situation, may be unacceptable in a different situation.

To put the burden of proof on the one who asserts that there is an effect may be justified in basic science, but it turns out differently when used in applied science. In environmental questions, it is often the case that those affected by the pollution have the burden of proof, while those who pollute benefit from the question of doubt. The traditional approach of minimizing type I error favors the producer and puts the burden of proof on the consumer or victim of pollution. . . .

Some have argued that in such cases the burden of proof should be turned around. This is the basis for, among other things, the *precautionary principle:*

Where there are threats of serious or irreversible damage, lack of full scientific certainty shall not be used as a reason for postponing cost-effective measures to prevent environmental degradation (Rio Declaration, Principle 15).

. . .

Models

The use of statistics is the technical part of the problem. It is more difficult to come to terms with other kinds of uncertainty. . . . All application of statistics must be based on some kind of model. . . .

Experts trained in a field have a tendency to apply the kinds of models that conform with their field. . . .

. . . The problem is that it is not a part of professional training to learn about the limits of the models and methods of a field.

A serious obstacle to coming to terms with this problem is the fact that Thomas Kuhn's description of the scientific community is to a large extent valid. We do not have to accept the more controversial parts of Kuhn's theory in order to agree that scientists are trained within a "paradigm." Parts of the paradigm will be the tacit knowledge that is imperative to everyday scientific work. This kind of knowledge cannot be articulated as explicit rules. Kuhn himself uses Michael Polanyi's term "tacit knowledge" (Kuhn, 1970: 187). When experts deal with situations that fit into their paradigm, this works fine. But when confronted with situations that are not so easy to accommodate to the expert's paradigm, it is a source of error. Because experts in the same field are trained within the same paradigm, they are usually blind to many of their own tacit assumptions. However, experts from other fields may immediately be aware of some of the tacit assumptions of the field. Therefore, in cases involving complexity and uncertainty, it is imperative to draw on various kinds of expertise. . . .

In their important book *Uncertainty and Quality in Science for Policy* (1990), Silvio Funtowicz and Jerome Ravetz argue that science has to enter into a "post-normal" phase to adequately address problems where uncertainty and "decision stakes" are high. In the book, they develop a conceptual scheme to deal with the new challenges. I shall not go into technical details, but just mention one aspect of "post-normal" science that is relevant to my discussion: the uses of what they call "extended peer communities."

"Extended peer communities" implies an extension of the traditional scientific community to include non-experts as well. However, this does not mean that non-experts should invade the research laboratories and carry out research. It does mean, though, that non-experts should take part in discussions of priorities, evaluation of results, and policy debates. One reason for including non-experts is that they sometimes are closer to the problem.

For example, persons directly affected by an environmental problem will have a keener awareness of its symptoms, and a more pressing concern with the quality of official reassurances, than those in any other role. Thus they perform a function analogous to that of professional colleagues in the peer-review or refereeing process in traditional science, which otherwise might not occur in these new contexts (Funtowicz and Ravetz, 1993: 752).

The arguments in favor of extended peer communities are similar to Paul Feyerabend's arguments for a democratization of science. I regard it as a continuation of an important element in the Socratic tradition. We know that it was part of Socrates's strategy to pretend that he was more ignorant than he actually was. By asking apparently naive questions [of] an expert, one may reveal tacit assumptions that the expert himself is not aware of. Many scientists are skeptical [of] public debates about controversial scientific and technological questions, like nuclear power and genetically modified food, and allege that public opinion is often based on prejudices and lack of information. No doubt this is sometimes the case. But there are at least two reasons for not keeping these kinds of questions away from the public. First, non-experts may be wrong because they are prejudiced or lack the required information. But experts may also be wrong. Some of their errors may be corrected by bringing in non-experts. To put it simply: The public may be wrong because it is too far away from the technical problems, whereas experts may be wrong because they are too close. The "tunnel" vision of experts is at least as great a problem as the

ignorance of non-experts. The second reason is that common people are affected by the decisions that are made. The questions of global warming, the ozone layer, radioactive waste, and genetically modified food concerns everybody, experts as well as non-experts. These questions are too important to be left only to the experts.

CONCLUSION

In this paper, I have addressed two questions: 1) Does uncertainty represent something genuinely new in science? and 2) What are the implications of recognizing uncertainty for science and science policy? My answer to the first question was that although uncertainty has been recognized since the Greeks, the present situation is genuinely new in the sense that uncertainty has moved into focus. I pointed to two consequences of this recognition, one concerning the uses of statistics (and more generally the burden of proof) and one concerning the uses of models (in particular idealized models). I argued that in some cases the burden of proof should be reversed, one should draw on various kinds of expertise, and science should be "democratized."

It can be argued that these consequences do not influence science and "the scientific method," but only science policy. In a certain sense this is true, but it depends on what is meant by "the scientific method." What is affected, is not science per se, but a dominating ideal of what science should be, emphasizing measurements, mathematics, idealized models, laboratory experiments, exact predictions, and reductionism. When it is recognized that this scientific ideal is too narrow even for the mathematical (or "exact") sciences, the toxicologist or ecologist should have few reservations against doing the same.

However, one might take one step further and argue that the root of uncertainty is complexity. Therefore, to come to terms with the new situation, a new science of complexity is required. An increasing number of authors argue in this way (for a small selection, see Nicolis and Prigogine, 1989; Bak, 1997; Auyang, 1998). This is an important question, but it goes beyond the scope of this paper.

REFERENCES

Auyang, Sunny Y., *Foundations of Complex-System Theories* (Cambridge University Press, Cambridge, 1998).

Bak, Per, *How Nature Works. The Science of Self-Organized Criticality* (Oxford University Press, Oxford, 1997).

Funtowicz, Silvio and Jerome Ravetz, *Uncertainty and Quality in Science for Policy* (Kluwer, Dordrecht, 1990).

Funtowicz, Silvio and Jerome Ravetz, "Science for the Post-Normal Age," *Futures* (September, 1993), 739–755.

Gigerenzer, Gerd, Zeno Swijtink, Theodore Porter, Lorraine Daston, John Beatty, and Lorenz Krüger, *The Empire of Chance. How probability changed science and everyday life* (Cambridge University Press, Cambridge, 1989).

Kuhn, Thomas, "Postscript? 1969," *The Structure of Scientific Revolutions* (University of Chicago Press, Chicago, 1970).

Nicolis, Grégoire and Ilya Prigogine, *Exploring Complexity* (Freeman and Company, New York, 1989).

Peterman, Randall M., "Statistical Power Analysis Can Improve Fisheries Research and Management," *Can. J. Fish. Aquat. Sci.* 47 (1990), 1–15.

Toulmin, Stephen, *Cosmopolis. The Hidden Agenda of Modernity* (The Free Press, New York, 1990).

Wynne, Brian "Uncertainty and Environmental Learning," *Global Environmental Change* (June, 1992), 111–127.

DISCUSSION TOPICS

1. Give some advantages and disadvantages of reversing the "burden of proof" regarding a case of water pollution—that is, that those proposing a new mining operation must show that their operation will not cause significant damage from water pollution.

2. Explain how you might add public input to science-based policy decisions. Give some advantages and disadvantages of the plan you propose.

READING 4

Feminism and the Study of Animal Behavior

Marlene Zuk

Marlene Zuk is a member of the department of biology, University of California, Riverside. Her research interests include mate choice and sexual selection in animals. She has taught courses on women in science and maintains a long-standing interest in feminist issues in science.

In an article from BioScience, Zuk argues that social perspective has a substantial influence on what biologists choose to study, how they interpret their findings, and even how they interact with colleagues. She believes that being aware of such biases can help scientists recognize the need to listen to a variety of perspectives and, ultimately, will result in less biased and more productive science. In the context of animal behavior, Zuk gives a number of examples of how a feminist perspective has been influential in understanding and interpreting the natural world.

Although the importance of female choice, and therefore female behavior, was recognized as a force in sexual selection by Charles Darwin as early as 1871, its influence on evolution was largely dismissed almost until the last decade. Once recognized, however, the mechanism of female choice has been widely observed and is now thought to affect animal and perhaps even plant evolution. Why was female choice so long neglected? I argue that this neglect is an example of how social perspective influences what biologists choose to study and how we interpret our findings, as well as how we interact as colleagues. An awareness of such bias can help us recognize the need to listen to a variety of voices, which will ultimately result in less biased and more productive science.

I am a behavioral ecologist interested in sexual selection and mate choice. For the last several years, my research has focused on the evolution of male secondary sexual characters and on the basis for female preference of particular traits. When nonscientists eager for a succinct answer ask me what I do, I tell them I study the differences between males and females, how those differences came about, and what they mean in the lives of the animals. Virtually everyone can relate to this interest and thinks it is an important area of biology to examine.

I also am interested in relations between the sexes in my own species and how they affect my personal and political life. A long-standing struggle for social equality both inside and outside academia has led to my having a feminist perspective; . . . the idea that men and women deserve equally just treatment is really quite straightforward. Feminism is also basic to the many world views rooted in the concept of human rights.

It would seem, then, that these two perspectives of feminism and evolutionary biology would share some intellectual content, both being concerned with sex and gender differences, how they arose, and their consequences. Yet, the merging of them has been uneasy at best, both in my own mind and in the literature of both fields.

Feminists often decry behavioral biology, especially sociobiology, seeing an oppressive, deterministic view of human nature in its concepts that is perhaps best exemplified in the saying "biology [or anatomy] is destiny." In an effort to avoid association with the idea that having a vagina constrains one's career, many feminist writers have condemned — wrongfully, in my opinion — the ability of any scientific viewpoint to explain behavior, given the enormous contribution of culture, socialization, and learning to human development.

Similarly, many, though certainly not all, biologists eschew the notion that any cultural or political bias, however well-intentioned, influences their discipline. Nevertheless, several biologists have recently explored the relationship between feminism and behavioral sciences (Gowaty 1992, Smuts in press). I, too, believe the two perspectives have much to offer each other, and here I address biologists as a feminist, to explore ways that feminism can affect and hopefully improve the study of the evolution of behavior. In a complementary vein, Gowaty (1992) suggests ways in which feminists might profit from an evolutionary viewpoint.

As a behavioral biologist, I have found that a feminist perspective can influence what we choose to study and how we interpret our findings, how we use language to describe what we see, and how we behave toward each other and see ourselves while practicing science. . . . In this article, I discuss . . . our subjects, our language, and our interactions in turn, with the hopes of suggesting a broader perspective on the study of behavior and its evolution.

WHAT WE CHOOSE TO STUDY

Numerous philosophers of science have pointed out that the questions we ask of nature are shaped by the social context in which we live (Gould 1981, Keller 1985). Extreme examples of such cultural bias are easy to spot: research into the deleterious effects of higher education on female physiology reached its peak in the nineteenth century, when women were beginning to attend universities and colleges in substantial numbers. Attending such institutions was apparently convincingly linked to high rates of nervous disorders, low fertility, and inability to nurse if the student miraculously managed to both find a husband and conceive a child (Ehrenreich and English 1978). These studies were ostensibly done in the name of pure research, and our skepticism about the motives behind them comes only with the benefit of hindsight (Gould 1981).

The National Institutes of Health more recently has recognized a disturbing lack of data on the normal physiology and medicine of women. Even in studies of nonsexual systems such as the lungs or heart, subjects both in human and animal experiments have been predominately male. Sex differences in the functioning of these systems, both in health and in disease, are little known, despite the potential for valuable and perhaps lifesaving insights and also despite the resultant incompleteness of our understanding of human function.

Along lines more relevant to my purpose here, the primate behavior literature in the early part of the century up until perhaps the late 1960s was mainly concerned with dominance relationships and how aggression shaped monkey and ape — and often, by extension, human — societies (Devore 1965). Male hierarchies were thought to define troop movements, population growth, the ability of the group to fend off predators, and much more. Then, with the pioneering work of Jane Lancaster, Thelma Rowell, and other female primatologists (Fedigan 1982, Haraway 1989, Jolly 1985, Morell 1993), a somewhat different perspective on primate societies emerged. Female behavior was seen to influence mating patterns, and knowledge of the relationships among female relatives was crucial for understanding the structure of social groups.

More recently, Smuts (in press) stated that "Humans are an exception to the typical primate pattern of sexual egalitarianism; in humans, male interests usually predominate, so that most, if not all, human societies are characterized by male dominance over women. Why?" Both the categorization of most primates as egalitarian and the idea that male dominance in humans is an unusual attribute worth questioning are novel. Although I think it is not necessary for female researchers alone to provide this perspective, numerous behavioral biologists have noted the coincidence of women scientists and a more pluralistic viewpoint (e.g., Hrdy 1986, Morell 1993).

Similarly, female choice as a mechanism in sexual selection, though first proposed by Darwin, was largely ignored or even actively resisted (by his contemporary Alfred Russel Wallace, for instance) until students of animal behavior, many though certainly not all female, began accumulating evidence that females in many animal species are capable of distinguishing among males within a population and choosing only those individuals with certain desirable characteristics. Furthermore, female choice may be responsible for the evolution of many of the exaggerated male characters that make animals such as birds of paradise so distinctive (Bradbury and Andersson 1987, Kirkpatrick and Ryan 1992).

Yet, even when females are seen as important forces in evolution, the way in which this importance is manifested has been questioned; a recent article by Hrdy (1986) questions "the myth of the coy female." She suggests that Darwin's own Victorian stereotypes may have paved the way for an inaccurate image of females as sexually passive, when in fact breeding systems contain a much greater variety of female behavior than mere discrimination (Wasser 1983). In those plant species in which male-female interactions influence fertilization success (Lyons et al. 1989, Waser et al. 1987), some botanists are reluctant to ascribe the controlling role to

the female partner, arguing against the existence of "female choice" in non-animals. Consideration of the female point of view is implicitly feminist, because feminism attempts to embrace rather than ignore variation and to understand how social biases can channel our thinking.

Other examples of areas of research that may be influenced by a feminist perspective include the importance of variation (Gowaty 1992) and the role of male aggression and sexual coercion toward females, as well as the role of female resistance (Gowaty 1992, Smuts and Smuts in press). Both topics are certainly not predicated on feminism, but their exploration requires examining the world from a point of view that may not be that of the mainstream. This diversity of approach points to what I believe is the reason for the previous emphasis on males in primatology and the use of male rats in studies of physiology. It is not that people with two X chromosomes automatically have different ideas about areas of research than do people with one, but that in a male-dominated society, what males do is seen as the norm, whereas females are variations on the theme. . . .

From the male-dominated perspective, the cyclic nature of female reproduction in mammals, for instance, is then seen as unwanted "noise" obscuring a view of the "real" system. A more unbiased approach would have the female's function just as valid as the male's, with the reproductive cycle adding no more "noise" than the workings of the eye add to a study of other sense organs; no one would suggest that hearing would be better studied in the blind, even if the simultaneous operation of auditory and visual systems creates interactions between the two. I am not suggesting that audition or any other physiological function would not bear examination under a variety of circumstances; indeed, the recognition of diversity and its importance is one of the goals of feminism. The point is that female variation is no less valid than any other form of human variation. . . .

Perhaps the best illustration of this common perception of female as *other* comes from a study on mental health in humans conducted by Broverman and colleagues nearly a quarter century ago. Participants in the study were mental health clinicians given a sex-role stereotype questionnaire consisting of 122 bipolar items such as "not competitive . . . very competitive" and asked to describe a "healthy, mature, socially competent (a) adult, sex unspecified; (b) a man; or (c) a woman" (Broverman et al. 1970, p. 1). The results were, to my mind at least, distressing: although males and females were described differently, the description of a man was virtually identical to that of an adult, whereas women were seen as distinct from adults. Inescapably, then, women cannot be both feminine and mature human: if they behave as society expects them to if they are to fulfill ideals of femininity, they cannot fulfill the ideals of mental health for an adult human being. Expectations of female behavior have not changed sufficiently over the intervening years to invalidate these conclusions (Faludi 1991).

The relevance of the Broverman study to animal behavior is clear: scientists, like other people, may tend to view what males do as the norm and what females do as a variation on the theme, a subcategory. Even if this attitude does not make females less studied to begin with, it can make them seem less interesting or a special case that should only be dealt with after the important individuals have been described. To use primatology as an example again, the "female as other" assumption may be responsible for Hrdy's (1986) statement that "amazing as it sounds, only relatively recently have primatologists begun to examine [female] behaviors other than direct mother-infant interactions that affect the fates of infants" (p. 131). Female monkeys are thus often equated with mother monkeys, as if no other role could exist.

Ironically, a recent book on parental care (Clutton-Brock 1991) perpetuates this stereotype in a rather odd way. The book contains a chapter titled "Parental care in birds and mammals." Of the eight subheadings, only three (one of which is the summary) are not concerned with male behavior; the rest have titles such as "Why do males help in biparental species?" and "Why do males agree to polyandry?" This emphasis is puzzling, given the widespread and diverse distribution of maternal care in both of these vertebrate classes. The equation of females and mothers is so omnipresent that it is not even deemed worthy of discussion; we need only consider the exciting "exceptions." The political implications of this categorization of females and minor-

ity groups (such as homosexuals) into an "other" grouping have been discussed with regard to scientific objectivity (Halpin 1989).

LANGUAGE AND THE PRACTICE OF BIOLOGY

Nowhere is the perception of maleness as the norm so clear as in the words we use to describe what we see. The argument that the terms *man* and *mankind* are false generics has been made elsewhere (Miller and Swift 1980), and I shall not repeat it; because language reflects our beliefs, an awareness of language is an awareness of the potential for bias.

I used to regard the feminist concern over the use of terminology a form of fiddling while Rome burned — that is, women were being raped, underpaid, denied access to reasonable child care, and discriminated against in myriad other ways, and here were people spending their time trying to come up with a new word for manhole cover. . . .

After some time of listening to the debate, however, I changed my mind. One source of this change was research showing that we are indeed influenced by the terms we use; children, for example, asked to draw a fireman draw a male, whereas those asked to draw a firefighter may draw one of either sex (Eberhard 1976, Schneider and Hacker 1973). The other source was my own observation of the unrelenting maleness attributed to animals by my students and colleagues. Birds, mammals, reptiles, and insects were all called "he," and it is difficult to train oneself out of this generalization even when it should be obvious that males and females may behave differently in the field. Making prejudgments about the sex of an animal is risky. In the case of social insects such as ants or bees, for example, one can actually miss the pertinent biology, because in many species only females forage for the colony or perform other tasks best interpreted in light of their reproductive roles.

In addition, the issue of social bias in language was rearing its head within the biological literature. In 1981, an article appeared in the scientific mainstream journal *Animal Behaviour* called "The concept of rape in non-humans: a critique." In it, behavioral biologists Daniel Estep of Animal Behavior Associates in Littleton, Colorado, and Katherine

Bruce of the University of North Carolina in Wilmington, point out the emotional and moral connotations of the word *rape* and suggest a substitution of *resisted copulation* for description of the behavior in nonhumans. Their article was followed by one in 1982 by Patricia Gowaty, now at the University of Georgia in Athens, a biologist working on mating systems in bluebirds, which was titled "Sexual terms in sociobiology: emotionally evocative and, paradoxically, jargon." She generalized the objection to terms such as *cuckoldry, adultery,* and *homosexual,* all of which were in use for behaviors seen in nonhumans. Even further generalization appeared in 1983, when zoologist Robin Stuart, of the University of Vermont in Burlington, published "A note on terminology in animal behavior, with special reference to slavery in ants," which took issue with use of the term *slavery.*

Although specific criticisms of the use of these terms differ, many of the critics claim that certain terminology biases the observer of the behavior in animals, causing it to be seen in terms of human motivations and emotions, and might bolster the notion that such behavior in humans is natural. Furthermore, words such as *harem* are not operationally useful, and operational definitions have many advantages for all scientists, not just those concerned with the political misuse of scientific terms. Current usage includes *extra-pair copulations,* a term more general than *adultery* or *rape,* and indeed much recent research has focused on the way in which females engaging in such copulations might thereby control paternity of their offspring (e.g., Lifjeld and Robertson 1992). I believe that such an interpretation would have been more difficult had the biologists called the behavior *adultery* or *rape.*

Other examples include the categorization of mating systems: an article on a polyandrous bird referred to "wife-sharing" (Maynard Smith and Ridpath 1972), but I have never seen polygyny, the prevailing breeding system in many vertebrates, called "husband-sharing." In earlier writings on this topic, I called my discipline "sociobiology," meaning the study of social behavior from an evolutionary viewpoint. The word has acquired so many negative connotations, however, that I and many others in the field have largely dropped the name, and we

now call ourselves "behavioral ecologists." It is this awareness of the power of language that motivated me to examine how we speak about our field in a feminist context.

HOW WE BEHAVE TOWARD EACH OTHER

It is in the more personal arena that the schism between personal and professional interests in gender becomes most apparent. As a veritable barrage of studies attests, women are scarce in science; their absence is most acute in the physical sciences, but in 1988 women still only received about half as many doctorates in the life sciences as men did, and the problem grows more acute with advancement in the profession (Anderson 1989).

Academia is an overwhelmingly male bastion, and those of us who discuss and do research on sex differences and sexual behavior do so in an atmosphere that makes those differences extremely apparent. The atmosphere is often not conducive to women's success. As a result, my female colleagues and I sometimes find ourselves lecturing, in a place where no day care is available, about the evolution of animal maternal behavior patterns, or describing female control of paternity or female choice to an audience which, intentionally or not, discourages women from speaking. Several articles in the *Bulletin of the Ecological Society of America* have explored these social aspects of doing science, including male and female publication rates and the likelihood of men and women to be invited to present symposium papers at scientific meetings (Gurevitch 1988, Primack and O'Leary 1989).

It is not my goal here either to trace the origin of male oppression of women in academia or to suggest that we take our examples from some of the creatures we study and engage in overt physical battles over access to a podium. Rather, an understanding of the need to listen to a variety of voices has arisen from my feminism, as has an understanding of how the stifling of this variety can likewise stifle science.

A colleague of mine says she cannot teach the last chapter of a popular animal behavior text because it contains material on the evolution of human marriage and sexual preference patterns that she finds both personally offensive and scientifically false; her feminist viewpoint increased her sensitivity to what was ultimately scientific inaccuracy. Obviously, the right to object to material in a book on a personal level is not limited to feminists. But the feminist movement embraced the saying that "the personal is political," and if our political biases influence our science then our personal experiences do so as well.

Biochemist Marion Namenworth (1986), who was at the University of Wisconsin in Madison, in an article titled "Science seen through a feminist prism," said, "scientists firmly believe that any political movement, like feminism, that seeks to influence science would undermine the essential neutrality of the scientific enterprise . . . as long as they are not *conscious* of any bias or political agenda, they are neutral and objective, when in fact they are only unconscious" (p. 29, emphasis hers). This cautionary note does not tell us to simply give up on science as a way of knowing, nor that objectivity is an illusion. It does suggest that an awareness of bias can make us all better scientists.

REFERENCES CITED

Anderson, A. 1989. Still a soft female touch for doctorates. *Nature* 340: 417.

Bradbury, J. W., and M. S. Andersson, eds. 1987. *Sexual Selection: Testing the Alternatives.* John Wiley & Sons, New York.

Broverman, I. K., D. M. Broverman, and F. E. Clarkson. 1970. Sex-role stereotypes and clinical judgments of mental health. *J. Consult. Clin. Psych.* 34: 1–7.

Clutton-Brock, T. H. 1991. *The Evolution of Parental Care.* Princeton University Press, Princeton, N.J.

Devore, I., ed. 1965. *Primate Behavior: Field Studies of Monkeys and Apes.* Holt, Rinehart and Winston, New York.

Eberhard, O. M. Y. 1976. Elementary students' understanding of certain masculine and neutral generic nouns. Doctoral dissertation, Kansas State University.

Ehrenreich, B., and D. English. 1978. *For Her Own Good: 150 Years of the Experts' Advice to Women.* Doubleday, New York.

Estep, D. Q., and K. E. M. Bruce. 1981. The concept of rape in non-humans: a critique. *Anim. Behav.* 29: 1272–1273.

Faludi, S. 1991. *Backlash: The Undeclared War against American Women.* Crown Publ., New York.

Fedigan, L. M. 1982. *Primate Paradigms: Sex Roles and Social Bonds.* Eden Press, Montreal, Quebec, Canada.

Gould, S. J. 1981. *The Mismeasure of Man.* W. W. Norton, New York.

Gowaty, P. A. 1982. Sexual terms in sociobiology: emotionally evocative and, paradoxically, jargon. *Anim. Behav.* 30: 630–631.

———. 1992. Evolutionary biology and feminism. *Human Nature* 3: 217–249.

Gurevitch, J. 1988. Differences in the proportion of women to men invited to give seminars: is the old boy still kicking? *Bulletin of the Ecological Society of America* 69: 155–161.

Halpin, Z. T. 1989. Scientific objectivity and the concept of "the other." *Women's Studies International Forum* 12: 285–294.

Haraway, D. J. 1989. *Primate Visions.* Routledge, New York.

Hrdy, S. B. 1986. Empathy, polyandry, and the myth of the coy female. Pages 119–146 in R. Bleier, ed. *Feminist Approaches to Science.* Pergamon Press, New York.

Jolly, A. 1985. *The Evolution of Primate Behavior.* Macmillan, New York.

Keller, E. F. 1985. *Reflections on Gender and Science.* Yale University Press, New Haven, CT.

Kirkpatrick, M., and M. J. Ryan. 1992. The evolution of mating preferences and the paradox of the lek. *Nature* 350: 33–38.

Lifjeld, J. T. and R. J. Robertson. 1992. Female control of extra-pair fertilization in tree swallows. *Behav. Ecol. Sociobiol.* 31: 89–96.

Lyons, E. E., N. M. Waser, M. V. Price, J. Antonovics, and A. F. Motten. 1989. Sources of variation in plant reproductive success and implications for concepts of sexual selection. *Am. Nat.* 134: 409–433.

Maynard Smith, J., and Ridpath, M. G. 1972. Wife sharing in the Tasmanian native hen, *Tribonyx mortierii*: a case of kin selection? *Am. Nat.* 106: 447–452.

Miller, C., and K. Swift. 1980. *The Handbook of Nonsexist Writing.* Harper and Row, New York.

Morell, V. 1993. Seeing nature through the lens of gender. *Science* 260: 428–429.

Namenworth, M. 1986. Science seen through a feminist prism. Pages 18–41 in R. Bleier, ed. *Feminist Approaches to Science.* Pergamon Press, New York.

Primack, R. B., and V. O'Leary. 1989. Research productivity of men and women ecologists: a longitudinal study of former graduate students. *Bulletin of the Ecological Society of America* 70: 7–12.

Schneider, J. W., and S. L. Hacker. 1973. Sex role imagery and use of the generic "man" in introductory texts: a case in the sociology of sociology. *American Sociology* 8: 12–18.

Smuts, B. In press. The origins of patriarchy: an evolutionary perspective. In A. Zagarell, ed. *Origins of Gender Inequality*. New Issues Press, Kalamazoo, MI.

Smuts, B., and R. W. Smuts. In press. Male aggression and sexual coercion of females in nonhuman primates and other mammals: evidence and theoretical implications. *Adv. Study Behav.*

Stuart, R. 1983. A note on terminology in animal behavior, with special reference to slavery in ants. *Anim. Behav.* 31: 1259–1260.

Waser, N. M., M. V. Price, A. M. Montalvo, and R. N. Gray. 1987. Female mate choice in a perennial herbaceous wildflower, *Delphinium nelsonii*. *Evol. Trends Plants* 1: 29–33.

Wasser, S. C., ed. 1983. *The Social Behavior of Female Vertebrates*. Academic Press, New York.

DISCUSSION TOPICS

1. Give an example of an environmental problem that might be viewed differently from a traditional male, as opposed to a feminist, perspective.

2. What changes might you propose to make science in academia more welcoming to women?

3. Do you agree that "any political movement, like feminism, that seeks to influence science would undermine the essential neutrality of the scientific enterprise . . ."? Justify your answer.

The Little Things That Run the World

Edward O. Wilson

Edward O. Wilson is Pellegrino University Professor and curator of entomology at the Museum of Comparative Zoology, Harvard University, Cambridge, Massachusetts. His recent books include Biodiversity *(1988),* The Diversity of Life *(1992),* The Biophilia Hypothesis, *with Stephen R. Kellert (1993),* In Search of Nature *(1996), and* Consilence *(1998).*

Wilson challenges the common belief that vertebrate animals are the most important species on the planet. He acknowledges the significant impact of humans on the planet, but points out that, generally, invertebrates have a far greater impact on the planet than do nonhuman vertebrates. Finally, he emphasizes that the world could get on very well if all vertebrates, including humans, were to disappear. At least two insights emerge from Wilson's paper. One is that it might be valuable to place a greater emphasis on the conservation of invertebrates, a point that Wilson develops further in his reading. Another is that the human sense of self-importance may be greatly overrated; Wilson's perspectives give a more realistic view of the role of humans as a species and the human relationship with the biosphere.

On the occasion of the opening of the remarkable new invertebrate exhibit of the National Zoological Park, let me say a word on behalf of these little things that run the world. To start, there are vastly more kinds of invertebrates than of vertebrates. At the present time, on the basis of the tabulation that I have just completed (from the literature and with the help of specialists), I estimate that a total of 42,580 vertebrate species have been described, of which 6,300 are reptiles, 9,040 are birds, and 4,000 are mammals. In contrast, 990,000 species of invertebrates have been described, of which 290,000 alone are beetles—seven times the number of all the vertebrates together. Recent estimates have placed the number of invertebrates on the earth as high as 30 million, again mostly beetles—although many other taxonomically comparable groups of insects and other invertebrates also greatly outnumber vertebrates.

We don't know with certainty why invertebrates are so diverse, but a commonly held opinion is that the key trait is their small size. Their niches are correspondingly small, and they can therefore divide up the environment into many more little domains where specialists can coexist. One of my favorite examples of such specialists living in microniches are the mites that live on the bodies of army ants: one kind is found only on the mandibles of the soldier caste, where it sits and feeds from the mouth of its host; another kind is found only on the hind foot of the soldier caste, where it sucks blood for a living; and so on through various bizarre configurations.

Another possible cause of invertebrate diversity is the greater antiquity of these little animals, giving them more time to explore and fill the environment. The first invertebrates appeared well back into Precambrian times, at least 600 million years ago. Most invertebrate phyla were flourishing before the vertebrates arrived on the scene, some 500 million years ago.

Invertebrates also rule the earth by virtue of sheer body mass. For example, in tropical rain forest near Manaus, in the Brazilian Amazon, each hectare (or 2.5 acres) contains a few dozen birds and mammals but well over one billion invertebrates, of which the vast majority are not beetles this time but mites and springtails. There are about 200 kilograms dry weight of animal tissue in a hectare, of which 93 percent consists of invertebrates. The ants and termites alone compose one-third of this biomass. So when you walk through a tropical forest, or most other terrestrial habitats for that matter, or snorkel above a coral reef or some other marine or aquatic environment, vertebrates may catch your eye most of the time — biologists would say that your search image is for large animals — but you are visiting a primarily invertebrate world.

It is a common misconception that vertebrates are the movers and shakers of the world, tearing the vegetation down, cutting paths through the forest, and consuming most of the energy. That may be true in a few ecosystems such as the grasslands of Africa with their great herds of herbivorous mammals. It has certainly become true in the last few centuries in the case of our own species, which now appropriates in one form or other as much as 50 percent of the solar energy captured by plants. That circumstance is what makes us so dangerous to the fragile environment of the world. But it is otherwise more nearly true in most parts of the world of the invertebrates rather than the nonhuman vertebrates. The leafcutter ants, for example, rather than deer, or rodents, or birds, are the principal consumers of vegetation in Central and South America. A single colony contains over two million workers. It sends out columns of foragers a hundred meters or more in all directions to cut forest leaves, flower parts, and succulent stems. Each day a typical mature colony collects about 50 kilograms of this fresh vegetation, more than the average cow. Inside the nest, the ants shape the material into intricate sponge-like bodies on which they grow a symbiotic fungus. The fungus thrives as it breaks down and consumes the cellulose, while the ants thrive by eating the fungus.

The leafcutter ants excavate vertical galleries and living chambers as deep as 5 meters into the soil. They and other kinds of ants, as well as bacteria, fungi, termites, and mites, process most of the dead vegetation and return its nutrients to the plants to keep the great tropical forests alive.

Much the same situation exists in other parts of the world. The coral reefs are built out of the bodies of coelenterates. The most abundant animals of the open sea are copepods, tiny crustaceans forming part of the plankton. The mud of the deep sea is home to a vast array of mollusks, crustaceans, and other small creatures that subsist on the fragments of wood and dead animals that drift down from the lighted areas above, and on each other.

The truth is that we need invertebrates but they don't need us. If human beings were to disappear tomorrow, the world would go on with little change. Gaia, the totality of life on earth, would set about healing itself and return to the rich environmental states of a few thousand years ago. But if invertebrates were to disappear, I doubt that the human species could last more than a few months. Most of the fishes, amphibians, birds, and mammals would crash to extinction about the same time. Next would go the bulk of the flowering plants and with them the physical structure of the majority of the forests and other terrestrial habitats of the world. The earth would rot. As dead vegetation piled up and dried out, narrowing and closing the channels of the nutrient cycles, other complex forms of vegetation would die off, and with them the last remnants of the vertebrates. The remaining fungi, after enjoying a population explosion of stupendous proportions, would also perish. Within a few decades the world would return to the state of a billion years ago, composed primarily of bacteria, algae, and a few other very simple multicellular plants.

If humanity depends so completely on these little creatures that run the earth, they also provide us with an endless source of scientific exploration and naturalistic wonder. When you scoop up a double handful of earth almost anywhere except the most barren deserts, you will find thousands of invertebrate animals, ranging in size from clearly visible to microscopic, from ants and springtails to tardigrades and rotifers. The biology of most of the species you hold is unknown: we have only the vaguest idea of what they eat, what eats them, and the details of their life cycle, and probably nothing at all about their biochemistry and genetics. Some of the species might even lack scientific names. We have little concept of how important any of them are to our existence. Their study would certainly teach us new principles of science to the benefit of humanity. Each one is fascinating in its own right. If human beings were not so impressed by size alone, they would consider an ant more wonderful than a rhinoceros.

New emphasis should be placed on the conservation of invertebrates. Their staggering abundance and diversity should not lead us to think that they are indestructible. On the contrary, their species are just as subject to extinction due to human interference as are those of birds and mammals. When a valley in Peru or an island in the Pacific is stripped of the last of its native vegetation, the result is likely to be the extinction of several kinds of birds and some dozens of plant species. Of that tragedy we are painfully aware, but what is not perceived is that hundreds of invertebrate species also vanish.

The conservation movement is at last beginning to take recognition of the potential loss of invertebrate diversity. The International Union for the Conservation of Nature has an ongoing invertebrate program that has already published a Red Data Book of threatened and endangered species—although this catalog is obviously still woefully incomplete. The Xerces Society, named after an extinct California butterfly, was created in 1971 to further the protection of butterflies and other invertebrates. These two programs are designed to complement the much larger organized efforts of other organizations on behalf of vertebrates and plants. They will help to expand programs to encompass entire ecosystems instead of just selected star species. The new invertebrate exhibition of the National Zoological Park is one of the most promising means for raising public appreciation of invertebrates, and I hope such exhibits will come routinely to include rare and endangered species identified prominently as such.

Several themes can be profitably pursued in the new field of invertebrate conservation:

- It needs to be repeatedly stressed that invertebrates as a whole are even more important in the maintenance of ecosystems than are vertebrates.

- Reserves for invertebrate conservation are practicable and relatively inexpensive. Many species can be maintained in large, breeding populations in areas too small to sustain viable populations of vertebrates. A 10-ha plot is likely to be enough to sustain a butterfly or crustacean species indefinitely. The same is true for at least some plant species. Consequently, even if just a tiny remnant of natural habitat exists, and its native vertebrates have vanished, it is still worth setting aside for the plants and invertebrates it will save.

- The *ex situ* preservation of invertebrate species is also very cost-effective. A single pair of rare mammals typically costs hundreds or thousands of dollars yearly to maintain in a zoo (and worth every penny!). At the same time, large numbers of beautiful tree snails, butterflies, and other endangered invertebrates can be cultured in the laboratory, often in conjunction with public exhibits and educational programs, for the same price.

- It will be useful to concentrate biological research and public education on star species when these are available in threatened habitats, in the manner that has proved so successful in vertebrate conservation. Examples of such species include the tree snails of Moorea, Hawaii, and the Florida Keys; the Prairie sphinx moth of the Central States; the bird-wing butterflies of New Guinea; and the metallic blue and golden ants of Cuba.

• We need to launch a major effort to measure biodiversity, to create a complete inventory of all the species of organisms on Earth, and to assess their importance for the environment and humanity. Our museums, zoological parks, and arboreta deserve far more support than they are getting — for the future of our children.

A hundred years ago few people thought of saving any kind of animal or plant. The circle of concern has expanded steadily since, and it is just now beginning to encompass the invertebrates. For reasons that have to do with almost every facet of human welfare, we should welcome this new development.

DISCUSSION TOPICS

1. How might the general public be persuaded to more fully support invertebrate conservation? Give some examples. Assuming that there is a fixed amount of money available for species preservation, what reasons can you give for diverting more money from vertebrate species to aid invertebrates? What reasons might be used to advocate continuing to emphasize vertebrates? Which reasons are most persuasive, and why?

2. Wilson identifies several themes that might be pursued on behalf of invertebrate conservation. What others might you add? Are there some themes in the selection that you believe to be relatively unimportant? Justify your opinions.

CLASS EXERCISES

1. Some scholars consider the field of ecology to be a rich source of principles about how humans ought to relate to the natural world. It also has been argued that humans need to learn to trust nature more fully. Other scholars, however, believe that human moral values should be derived independently of nature; some philosophers maintain that ecology does not offer a coherent set of moral precepts. To what degree is it appropriate to use principles from the field of ecology as guidelines for human moral values? Support your opinions.

2. There is a proposal to dam a river for the purpose of generating electricity in your region. The dam will generate about 20 megawatts of electricity annually, with little pollution produced. The resulting 12,000 ha (30,000 acre) reservoir of water is estimated to bring in about 600,000 visitor-days and $25 million to the region annually from increased recreational use.

   What other scientific, social, ethical, and aesthetic values might need to be considered with this proposal? How would you rank these latter values in relation to each other? How would you rank them in relation to the identified economic and technical values of the project? How might your opinion be influenced if you had the opportunity to acquire ownership of a motel in that region? Support your reasoning.

OPTIONAL EXERCISE

Separate the class into groups of five to seven students each. Based on their reading of the selection by Woodward and Goodstein, each group should develop a set of general principles that they believe might now be identified with the proper conduct of science. When each group is ready, compare the principles to determine which are held in common among the student groups.

FOR FURTHER READING

American Chemical Society. "Ethical Guidelines to Publication of Chemical Research." *Chemical Reviews* 95, 11A–13A (1985, 1989, 1995). Summarizes the responsibilities of the editor, authors, and reviewers in the publication process for all journals published by the American Chemical Society.

Bella, David A. "Ethics and the Credibility of Applied Science," in *Ethical Questions for Resource Managers, ed.* Gordon Reeves, Daniel Bottom, and Martha Brookes. General Technical Report PNW-GTR-288, Washington D.C.: U.S. Forest Service, 1992. Argues that environmental impact reports are developed, sustained, and promoted by organizational systems that tend to selectively produce and sustain information favorable to those systems. He proposes means for addressing some of the problems resulting from these conditions.

Botzler, R. G., and S. J. Armstrong-Buck. "Ethical Considerations in Research on Wildlife Diseases." *Journal of Wildlife Diseases* 21 (1985): 341–45. Describes several conflicting positions in how society views the responsibilities of scientists toward the natural world and offers examples of how the Leopoldian land ethic might affect research in the area of wildlife diseases.

Cohen, Joel E., and David Tilman. "Biosphere 2 and Biodiversity: The Lessons So Far." *Science* 274 (1996): 1150–51. The authors conclude that there is no demonstrated alternative to support human life on earth.

Costanza, R. "Toward an Operational Definition of Ecosystem Health," In *Ecosystem Health,* ed. R. Costanza, B. Norton, and B. Haskell. Washington, D.C.: Island Press, 1992.

Crawford-Brown, Douglas J., and Neil E. Pearce. "Sufficient Proof in the Scientific Justification of Environmental Actions." *Environmental Ethics* 11 (1989): 153–67. The authors explore the points at which evidence is used to support inferences about environmental effects in environmental risk analysis, with the purpose of providing a framework for evaluating how evidence may provide a sufficient basis for ethical decisions for environmental actions.

Dobzhansky, Theodosius. *The Biology of Ultimate Concern, Perspectives in Humanism.* New York: New American Library, 1967. An evolutionary biologist seeks to examine some of the philosophical implications of biology and anthropology. He integrates the thoughts of Teilhard de Chardin.

Farnsworth, Elizabeth J., and Judy Rosovsky. "The Ethics of Ecological Field Experimentation." *Conservation Biology* 7 (1993): 463–72. The authors note that little information is available in the scientific literature on the impact of ecological studies on organisms and ecosystems, and propose that ethical considerations, conservation, and restoration measures compatible with sound scientific protocols be incorporated into field experiments.

Feyerabend, Paul. *Farewell to Reason.* New York: Verso, 1987. A series of essays addressing cultural diversity and cultural exchange. The author criticizes two ideas: the idea of objectivity and the idea of reason. The idea of objectivity is that a claim can be made that something is valid independent of human expectations, attitudes, and wishes. The idea of rationality is that there is one correct procedure.

"Gender and the Culture of Science; Women in Science." *Science* 260 (1993): 383–430. Twelve articles by a variety of experts on the role of women in science.

Graves, Jonathon, and Duncan Reavey. *Global Environmental Change: Plants, Animals, and Communities.* Essex, England: Longman, 1996. A summary of the effects of global environmental change on various components of the biosphere. Although a technical coverage, it is written for a broad range of readers.

Haught, John F. "The Emergent Environment and the Problem of Cosmic Purpose." *Environmental Ethics* 8 (1986): 139–50. The author questions whether scientific materialism can consistently sustain an environmental concern. He calls for a new vision based on Whitehead's integration of modern science, philosophy, and religion for a workable ethic.

Hempel, Carl G. *Aspects of Scientific Explanation.* New York: Free Press, 1965. A series of essays on the philosophy of science. The author provides an excellent overview of how science works. Sections include confirmation, induction, and rational belief; structure and function of scientific concepts and theories; and scientific explanations.

Kellert, Stephen R., and Edward O. Wilson (eds.). *The Biophilia Hypothesis.* Washington, D.C.: Island Press, 1993. Results of a meeting among scholars and scientists to address E. O. Wilson's idea of biophilia. The general argument in this volume is that the natural world is intrinsically valuable to the human psyche and spirit.

Kim, Ke Chung, and Robert D. Weaver (eds.). *Biodiversity and Landscapes.* Cambridge: Cambridge University Press, 1994. A collection of 22 papers by social and natural scientists on the relationship of biodiversity and human values and human-induced changes.

Kirkman, Robert. *Skeptical Environmentalism: The Limits of Philosophy and Science.* Bloomington: Indiana University Press, 2002. A critical overview of the speculative tendencies of academic environmental philosophy.

Kuhn, Thomas S. *Structure of Scientific Revolutions,* 2nd ed. Chicago: University of Chicago Press, 1970. The book that caused a major rethinking of the image of science and how it works.

Maddox, Brenda. *Rosalind Franklin: Dark Lady of DNA.* London and New York: HarperCollins, 2002. A careful, well-documented account of scientific practice and of the career of Rosalind Franklin, the only woman participating in the discovery of DNA's double helix. The book raises some important issues about science ethics.

McLaughlin, Andrew. "Images and Ethics of Nature." *Environmental Ethics* 7 (1985): 293–320. Challenges a common view in science that nature is devoid of meaning or value, and that, consequently, moral limits on human manipulation are irrational. Provides three alternative images of nature.

Moss, Ian S. "Foresters' Ethics." *Forestry Chronicle* 68 (1992): 340–41. Proposes a code of ethics as a foundation to unite foresters based, in part, on Paul Taylor's philosophy of Respect for Nature.

Murphy, Dennis D., and Barry R. Noon. "Coping with Uncertainty in Wildlife Biology." *Journal of Wildlife Management* 55 (1991): 773–82. To make science effective in the courtroom and in the arena of public controversies, the authors advocate that two factors are essential: the rigorous application of scientific methods and the development of clear operational definitions for terminology.

Nichols, James D. "Science, Population Ecology, and the Management of the American Black Duck." *Journal of Wildlife Management* 55 (1991): 790–99. The author addresses the value of the hypothetico-deductive method of science to population ecology and management of wildlife, using the American black duck as an example.

Norton, Bryan G. *Why Preserve Natural Variety?* Princeton, N.J.: Princeton University Press, 1987. The author provides a thoughtful presentation on reasons for preserving species. Written from the perspective of an anthropocentrist.

Norton, Bryan G., and Robert E. Ulanowicz. "Scale and Biodiversity Policy: A Hierarchical Approach." *Ambio* 21 (1992): 244–49. The authors use a hierarchical approach to natural systems, assuming that smaller subsystems change more rapidly than the larger systems of which they are a part; this differential rate of change with scale is used as a foundation for a policy on biodiversity.

Peepre, Juri, and Bob Jickling (eds.). *Northern Protected Areas and Wilderness: Proceedings of a Forum on Northern Protected Areas and Wilderness,* Whitehorse, Yukon: Canadian Parks and Wilderness Society–Yukon Chapter, 1994. Provides several articles on practical ethical issues by scientists and natural resources managers.

Reeves, Gordon, Daniel Bottom, and Martha Brooks (eds.). *Ethical Questions for Resource Managers.* General Technical Report PNW-GTR-288, Washington, D.C.: U.S. Forest Service, 1992.

Richards, Stewart. *Philosophy and Sociology of Science,* 2nd ed. New York: Basil Blackwell, 1987. Richards challenges the notion of the neutrality of science and contends that the quality and breadth of the education of scientists will have a marked effect on the quality of judgments they can later make.

Rolston, Holmes, III. "Science-Based versus Traditional Values," in *Ethics of Environment and Development: Global Challenge and International Response,* ed. J. Ronald Engel and Joan Gibb Engel. London: Belhaven Press, Pinter Publishers, 1990. Rolston addresses whether science-based values occupy a privileged position as criteria against which the traditional cultural values are to be tested and concludes there is no simple answer because of the pluralistic nature of both science-based and traditional values.

Ruse, Michael. *Taking Darwin Seriously: A Naturalistic Approach to Philosophy.* Oxford: Basil Blackwell, 1986. The author seeks to develop a consistent and satisfying philosophy founded on evolutionary biology. He questions whether ethics can be placed on an evolutionary foundation and argues that knowledge, including ethics, is shaped by the human evolutionary past. The book develops an evolutionary-based ethic patterned after Hume.

Sagoff, Mark. "Fact and Value in Ecological Science." *Environmental Ethics* 7 (1985): 99–116. Sagoff develops the roles that ecology can play in the human relationship with nature.

Schachmann, Howard K. "What Is Misconduct in Science?" *Science* 261 (1993): 148–49, 183. The author seeks to avoid open-ended definitions of misconduct in science by identifying those forms of scientific misconduct considered most significant; he proposes data fabrication, data falsification, and misappropriation of ideas of others.

Soskoine, Colin L., and Andrew Light. "Toward Ethics Guidelines for Environmental Epidemiologists." *Science of the Total Environment* 184 (Nos. 1–2), 1996. The authors reviewed the draft ethical guidelines for epidemiologists from several organizations and developed some common denominators.

Soulé, Michael. "The Social Siege of Nature," in *Reinventing Nature? Responses to Postmodern Deconstruction,* ed. M. Soulé and G. Lease. Washington, D.C.: Island Press, 1995. The author defends nature protection against those who view nature protection as interfering with the liberation of oppressed humans from oppressing social situations. He also contributes to the deconstruction of the notion that ecosystems are harmonious, integrated communities.

Stevenson, L. "Is Scientific Research Value-Neutral?" *Inquiry* 32:213–22. 1989.

Swazey, Judith P., Melissa S. Anderson, and Karen Seashore Lewis. "Ethical Problems in Academic Research." *American Scientist* 81 (1993): 542–53. The authors survey doctoral candidates and faculty in four scientific disciplines on their perceived exposure to misconduct among their peers and find that scientific misconduct, such as plagiarism and data falsification, takes place less frequently than other types of unethical or questionable behavior.

Tennekes, Henk. "The Limits of Science," in *Ecology, Technology and Culture,* ed. William Zeers and Jan J. Boersema. Cambridge: White Horse Press, 1994. Looks at the complexity and chaotic state of the natural world as an important limitation on the use of science to understand it.

Thomas, Jack Ward. "Integrity as Professionalism: Ethics and Leadership in Practice." Presented at the Society of American Foresters National Convention, Portland, Maine, 1992.

Toulmin, Stephen. *The Philosophy of Science.* London: Hutchinson, 1967. The types of arguments and methods scientists employ in actual practice are presented. Using examples, the author identifies what questions must be asked to most readily understand a scientific theory. The book includes chapters on discovery, laws of nature, theories and maps, and uniformity and determinism.

Van Fraassen, Bas C. *The Scientific Image.* Oxford: Oxford University Press, 1980. In developing an alternative to scientific realism, the author presents three theories: a theory of empirical import, a theory of scientific explanations, and a theory of the explication of probability as it occurs within physical theory.

Westra, Laura, and John Lemons (eds.). *Perspectives on Ecological Integrity.* London: Kluwer Academic, 1995. Provides a variety of perspectives to encourage discussion concerning the importance and consequences of ecological integrity for science, morality, and public policy.

Wildlife Disease Association. "Ethical Guidelines to Publication in the Journal of Wildlife Diseases." *Journal of Wildlife Diseases* 32 (1996): 163–67. Summarizes the responsibilities of the editor, authors, assistant editors, and reviewers in the publication process in the *Journal of Wildlife Diseases.*

CHAPTER TWO
Morality

In this chapter we discuss some central concepts in moral philosophy as they concern the environment, including what morality is, how to evaluate a moral argument, and the moral value of the environment.

Moral philosophy can be defined as the search for knowledge of the good life and of right conduct. Its subject matter is human conduct as it relates to the attainment of moral value, and its methodology is the systematic questioning and critical examination of our beliefs and values, including their consistency with each other and their implications for action.

Moral philosophy differs from the empirical sciences in both its subject matter and specific methodology. Moral philosophy is often characterized as prescriptive rather than descriptive; rather than describing human behavior as done in the social sciences, moral philosophers evaluate such behavior in the light of moral principles and norms. Moral philosophers' concern lies more with how human beings ought to act than with how human beings do act.

Moral philosophy encompasses two main levels: meta-ethics and normative ethics. *Meta-ethics* is concerned with the justification of moral judgments — in

other words, the correct method for answering moral questions, as well as a conceptual analysis of such morally crucial terms as *value* and *rights-holder*. Asking whether moral questions are ultimately to be answered by personal opinion or cultural bias is a meta-ethical inquiry. An appropriate meta-ethical question would be "What is meant by 'right'?" *Normative ethics* is concerned with practical questions such as "What should I do?" and "Is it right for anyone to steal in such a situation?" Normative ethics is based on some metaphysical vision of what is real and valuable, though this vision may only be implicitly assumed by the author rather than explicitly stated.

Several of the essays in this chapter are meta-ethical and pose questions about the nature of morality and moral theory. James Rachels discusses the three major approaches currently found in Western societies: social contract theory, utilitarianism, and Kantian ethics. He also points out that a philosophical theory is acceptable only if there are sound arguments in its favor. A sound argument has true premises and a conclusion that follows logically from them. In "Environmental Ethics as Environmental

Etiquette," Jim Cheney and Anthony Weston make the meta-ethical point that such traditional ethical approaches are inadequate for environmental ethics: they contend that the environment we live in arises out of our ethical practice, rather than vice versa. Peter Wenz in "Just Garbage" provides another important meta-ethical claim—that principles of distributive justice are the appropriate principles to use when we are making decisions concerning environmental hazards such as toxic wastes.

ARE MORAL JUDGMENTS UNIVERSAL?

A basic meta-ethical question is whether value judgments—particularly moral judgments—are universal or relative, objective or subjective. These terms are used in many different ways by different thinkers. Currently there seem to be four main approaches:

1. *Traditional relativism,* according to which the truth or falsity of moral judgments is relative to either the individual making the judgment or the culture of which he or she is a part.[1]
2. *Contextualism* differs from traditional relativism in that the truth or falsity of moral judgments is tied to the specific place (geographical and historical) in which the moral judgments occur. *(Narrative contextualism* is a form of contextualism emphasizing that moral terms cannot be abstracted or separated from their context but can only be adequately conveyed by means of stories.)
3. *Pluralism* is a perspective in which the truth or falsity of a moral judgment is decided by reference to a universal standard with limited applicability; different domains of life (e.g., environment, business, family) may have different moral frameworks. These different moral frameworks may exist side by side, each governing its own set of relationships, such as those with future generations, those with sentient creatures, and those with inanimate beings.[2]

4. *Universalism,* according to which the truth or falsity of moral judgments is decided by reference to a universal moral standard, applicable to all individuals and cultures.

The various theories sketched above differ partly because they involve different views of what reason is. What is the relationship of reason to the rest of human life? How important are the cultural milieu, geographical place, gender, ethnicity, and personality of the reasoner? Is reason capable of presenting us with universal truth, independent of context? Readings in this chapter present several different responses to these questions. Anna Peterson's essay affirms a form of contextualism, in which concepts of reason and value depend on various human practices and institutions. In contrast, James Rachels presents a traditional view of reason as requiring impartiality and consistency. In the second essay by Rachels, he tells us that "good reasons" for moral judgments are those that would be accepted by "any reasonable person." His view represents a form of universalism.

This monistic view has recently been challenged by Jim Cheney and Christopher Stone, who argue for moral pluralism and contextualism—approaches in which the goal of a single universal moral theory is rejected. Cheney understands environmental ethics as "bioregional narrative" or "ethical vernacular," inextricably linked to the place from which it was developed. Cheney believes that such bioregional narratives possess enough generality to allow for cross-cultural understanding.[3]

Christopher Stone[4] has raised the issue of pluralism in a different way. Stone agrees with Cheney that a universal moral theory is not achievable, not

---

[1]For a clear discussion of why traditional relativism in both its forms is unsatisfactory, see James Rachels, *The Elements of Moral Philosophy* (New York: McGraw-Hill, 1999), ch. 2 and 3.

[2]Christopher Stone states that, strictly speaking, moral pluralism is consistent with either relativism or moral realism. For the sake of displaying possible moral theories, pluralism is treated here as a form of moral realism. See Christopher Stone, *Earth and Other Ethics: The Case for Moral Pluralism* (New York: Harper & Row, 1987), pp. 246–47.

[3]Jim Cheney, "Postmodern Environmental Ethics: Ethics as Bioregional Narrative," *Environmental Ethics* 11 (1989): 117–34.

[4]Christopher D. Stone, "Moral Pluralism and the Course of Environmental Ethics," *Environmental Ethics* 10 (1989): 139–54.

because of the linkage between concepts and place, but because there are so many different domains of experience and such a variety of things (e.g., species, nations, individual organisms, unborn generations) to which morality must refer. Some moral theories are applicable to our dealings with the environment, for example, whereas others are appropriate to dealings with our immediate family. While Cheney's "local truth" might be thought of as cultural relativism because it is context dependent, Stone's view is not necessarily relativist. There may really be right answers, but the answers are limited in their applicability to certain types of things and experiences.[5] J. Baird Callicott criticizes Stone's pluralism on the grounds of incoherence, arguing that Stone is asking us to play musical chairs with our ideas of reality. While Callicott agrees that we have many different moral relationships, he stresses that they are all rooted in our moral sentiments.[6]

WHAT IS NATURAL?

One key difference between the various approaches to environmental ethics is found in the definition of *natural.* Three main definitions dominate the literature:

1. Independent of significant influence and control by human beings (e.g., Eric Katz, Henry David Thoreau, John Muir).
2. Anything done by any organism, including human beings (e.g., Frederick Turner).
3. Human actions that are in harmony with our evolutionary history (e.g., Holmes Rolston, J. Baird Callicott).

The definition of *natural* plays a key role in the following controversies: wilderness preservation, the meaning of biodiversity, environmental justice, genetic engineering of plants and animals, and ecological restoration.[7]

DOES THE NATURAL WORLD HAVE OBJECTIVE MORAL VALUE?

Several different kinds of natural value are affirmed in the essays in this and other chapters:

1. *Intrinsic value:* the value of an object that is independent of the presence of a valuer. For example, a planet consisting only of plants or even of rocks — a planet without sentient beings — might be said by some to have intrinsic value. Holmes Rolston argues for this position in his reading in this chapter.
2. *Inherent value:* value that requires the presence of a valuer who can appreciate the object or experience. A wilderness area can have inherent value only if there is a being who can recognize its value, though it is not necessary for the valuer to be present at that area to value it. J. Baird Callicott argues for this view in his reading in Chapter 8. Holmes Rolston suggests that a better term for Callicott's inherent value (sometimes termed *truncated intrinsic value*) is *extrinsic* value, with the

---

[5]James C. Anderson, "Moral Planes and Intrinsic Values," *Environmental Ethics* 13, no. 1 (1991), finds Stone's pluralism unsatisfactory because Anderson believes it leads to relativism.

[6]Peter Wenz agrees with Callicott's criticism of what Wenz terms the "extreme moral pluralism" of Stone, arguing that Stone does not consider the fact that moral judgments are ideally made only after all relevant matters have been considered. Moral behavior requires that one be responsive to all of one's roles and commitments, and thus moral behavior is integrative. However, Wenz goes on to maintain that Callicott's interpretation of Leopold's land ethic is itself moderately pluralistic in that it includes many moral principles, some of which are more important than others. Peter Wenz, "Minimal, Moderate, and Extreme Moral Pluralism," *Environmental Ethics* 15, no. 1 (1993): 61–74.

Wim J. van der Steen argues against Wenz that disunity of theories is common in both science and ethics and that such disunity is compatible with unity of practice. Normative ethics requires an empirical component and hence involves trade-offs. The resultant pluralism is not a matter of theoretical significance. Wim J. van der Steen, "The Demise of Monism and Pluralism in Environmental Ethics," *Environmental Ethics* 17, no. 2 (1995): 209–20.

---

[7]For a judicious discussion of the meanings of nature, restoration, and sustainable development in Katz, Sylvan, Callicott, and Rolston, see Robin Attfield, "Rehabilitating Nature and Making Nature Habitable," in *Philosophy and the Natural Environment,* Robin Attfield and Andrew Belsey, eds. (Cambridge: Cambridge University Press, 1994).

ex indicating the external, human-generated source of the value.[8]

3. *Instrumental value:* the value of an object or experience in serving as a means to accomplish a goal that has intrinsic or inherent value. For example, a human being might use a stand of timber as a source of money to increase the comfort and material quality of her life. The instrumental value of the timber allows the individual to attain an experience of well-being, and the experience of well-being for many is of inherent value. Thus, the stand of timber is said to serve an instrumental value.

In his reading in this chapter Holmes Rolston maintains that nature has intrinsic value. While individuals have a good of their own, species have more value as being goods of their kind. Ecosystems too have objective value. Value in nature is on a continuum from subjective to objective, individual to system. Rolston believes that this view accords well with our intuitive experience of natural value. However, according to Callicott, the only reasonable basis for natural value is found in valuers. Value is inherent — that is, produced by someone who values. Value is based on human moral sentiments.

The reading by Anna Peterson provides something of a middle position between Rolston and Callicott. With Callicott, she affirms that the human contribution to our assertions of natural value can never be removed. Yet she maintains that there is a "real world" shaped not only by the perspectives of humans but by the perspectives of all other organisms, a world that transcends human knowing.

An additional concept basic to the study of natural value is that of naturalistic fallacy, sometimes identified with the "is-ought dichotomy" discerned by prominent eighteenth-century Scottish philosopher David Hume (1711–1776).[9] The *naturalistic fallacy* consists of arguing from what is biologically or culturally "natural," from what "is," to what we "ought" to do.[10] In other words, a movement is made from what is descriptively true of the world to a prescriptive claim. Whether a thinker considers such an argument to be valid depends on the thinker's view of the relationship between morality and the world. Philosophers such as Plato and Kant see reason as having a transcendental or autonomous nature, upholding ideals of what we ought to do, regardless of what has been done in the past or is currently being done. They note that we are blamed or praised for our actions, whereas natural processes are not subject to moral praise and blame. Similarly, according to the great British philosopher Alfred North Whitehead (1851–1947), moral judgments are a contrast between what is and the apprehension of what ideally ought to be. In such theories, human beings are portrayed as not simply part of nature but as partaking of an ideal rational order, in terms of which what is natural might well be morally wrong. For example, it may be natural to have as many children as possible, but it may in fact be immoral to do so in today's overcrowded world.

However, there is an ancient and robust moral tradition of "natural law" and "natural order" in which it is argued that the only way to know what we should do is to understand what the world truly is. According to this approach, our deepest moral guidance comes from understanding nature and our natural place in it. The land ethic of Leopold and the deep ecology movement (Chapter 8) rely on a concept or intuition of what is "natural."[11]

HOW IS ENVIRONMENTAL ETHICS RELATED TO PRACTICE?

Eugene Hargrove, the editor of the journal *Environmental Ethics,* has commented that environmental ethics is a domain, not of specialists alone, but of all

---

[8]Holmes Rolston III, "Value in Nature and the Nature of Value," in *Philosophy and the Natural Environment,* Robin Attfield and Andrew Belsey, eds. (Cambridge: Cambridge University Press, 1994).

[9]Callicott and others argue that the naturalistic fallacy is a different issue and is most accurately associated with the ethics of G. E. Moore. See Callicott, "Hume's Is/Ought Dichotomy," *Environmental Ethics* 4 (1982): 163–74, especially pp. 166–67.

[10]In this sense Hume commits the naturalistic fallacy because he derives moral imperatives from the cultural traditions of his society, hence from how people do, in fact, act.

[11]For further discussion, see the exchange between J. Baird Callicott and Kristin Shrader-Frechette in *Between the Species* 6, no. 4 (Fall 1990): 185–96.

citizens. In order for environmental problems to be solved, more interaction is needed between those who make theories and those who make management decisions.[12] Bernard Rollin states that philosophers working in applied ethics must be prepared to help people put such an applied ethic into practice.[13] Accordingly, some environmental philosophers are directly involved in writing, interpreting, and applying theory to environmental decision making.

However, in a broader sense, good theorizing is itself a contribution to practice. J. Baird Callicott has noted that the power of Lynn White's essay (Chapter 5) is White's basic claim that what we do is dependent on what we think. We filter our experience through a conceptual framework; ideas shape our values.[14] Thus by rethinking the Western intellectual legacy concerning nature and by contributing to the development of a natural philosophy adequate to our own time and place, environmental philosophers help shape action.

---

[12]Eugene Hargrove, "Science, Ethics and the Care of Ecosystems," in *Northern Protected Areas and Wilderness,* Juri Peepre and Bob Jickling, eds. (Whitehorse, Yukon: Canadian Parks and Wilderness Society, 1994).

[13]Bernard Rollin, *Animal Rights and Human Morality* (Buffalo, NY: Prometheus Books, 1992), p.10.

[14]J. Baird Callicott, "Environmental Philosophy Is Environmental Activism: The Most Radical and Effective Kind," in *Environmental Philosophy and Environmental Activism,* Don E. Marietta, Jr. and Lester Embree, eds. (Lanham, MD: Rowman and Littlefield, 1995).

HOW IMPORTANT IS ENVIRONMENTAL JUSTICE?

Environmental justice has received increasing attention from environmentalists, as more information has been obtained about the unfair allocation of environmental risks and benefits. Often developing nations, as well as minorities and the poor within industrialized countries, have suffered disproportionately from environmental risks, such as nearby toxic waste dumps, incinerators, and nuclear reactors. Troy Hartley argues that while environmental justice does not present novel ideas to environmental ethics, it does emphasize the significance of the equal distribution of environmental quality.[15]

In his essay, Peter Wenz emphasizes that we usually assume those deriving benefits should accept the burdens that accompany such benefits. Yet currently the poor, and especially people of color, suffer the burdens of environmental hazards produced by activities that mainly benefit the rich. Wenz provides an approach designed to reduce these burdens.

---

[15]Troy W. Hartley, "Environmental Justice: An Environmental Civil Rights Value Acceptable to All World Views," *Environmental Ethics* 17, no. 3 (1995): 277–89.

Eugene Hargrove points out some of the historical and theoretical obstacles to an increased focus on justice within environmental ethics. See Eugene Hargrove, "Foreword," in *Faces of Environmental Racism: Confronting Issues of Global Justice,* Laura Westra and Peter S. Wenz, eds. (Lanham, MD: Rowman and Littlefield, 1995).

A Short Introduction to Moral Philosophy

James Rachels

James Rachels is University Professor of Philosophy at the University of Alabama in Birmingham. He is the author of The End of Life: Euthanasia and Morality *(1986),* Created from Animals: The Moral Implications of Darwinism *(1990), and* Can Ethics Provide Answers? And Other Essays in Moral Philosophy *(1997). The following selection is from* The Elements of Moral Philosophy *(1999). Rachels describes and evaluates the main moral theories in Western thought. He stresses the importance of impartiality, as well as the need to support one's views with good reasons.*

An ancient legend tells the story of Gyges, a poor shepherd who found a magic ring in a fissure opened by an earthquake. The ring would make its wearer invisible, so he could go anywhere and do anything undetected. Gyges was an unscrupulous fellow, and he quickly realized that the ring could be put to good advantage. We are told that he used its power to gain entry to the royal palace where he seduced the queen, murdered the king, and seized the throne. (It is not explained how invisibility helped him to seduce the queen — but let that pass.) In no time at all, he went from being a poor shepherd to being king of all the land.

This story is recounted in Book II of Plato's *Republic.* Like all of Plato's works, the *Republic* is written in the form of a dialogue between Socrates and his companions. Glaucon, who is having an argument with Socrates, uses the story of Gyges's ring to make a point.

Glaucon asks us to imagine that there are two such rings, one given to a man of virtue and the other given to a rogue. How might we expect them to behave? The rogue, of course, will do anything necessary to increase his own wealth and power. Since the cloak of invisibility will protect him from discovery, he can do anything he pleases without fear of being caught. Therefore, he will recognize no moral constraints on his conduct, and there will be no end to the mischief he will do.

But how will the so-called virtuous man behave? Glaucon suggests that he will do no better than the rogue:

> No one, it is commonly believed, would have such iron strength of mind as to stand fast in doing right or keep his hands off other men's goods, when he could go the market-place and fearlessly help himself to anything he wanted, enter houses and sleep with any woman he chose, set prisoners free and kill men at his pleasure, and in a word go about among men with the powers of a god. He would behave no better than the other; both would take the same course.

Moreover, Glaucon asks, why shouldn't he? Once he is freed from the fear of reprisal, why shouldn't a person simply do what he pleases, or what he thinks is best for himself? Why should he care at all about "morality"?

The *Republic,* written over 2,300 years ago, was one of the first great works of moral philosophy in Western history. Since then, philosophers have formulated theories to explain what morality is, why it is important, and why it has the peculiar hold on us that it does. What, if anything, justifies us in believing that we *morally ought* to act in one way rather than another?

RELATIVISM

Perhaps the oldest philosophical theory about morality is that right and wrong are relative to the customs of one's society — in this view, there is nothing behind the demands of morality except social convention. Herodotus, the first of the great Greek historians, lived at about the time of Socrates. His *History* is full of wonderful anecdotes that illustrate his belief that "right" and "wrong" are little more than names for social conventions. Of the Massagetae, for example, he writes:

> The following are some of their customs — Each man has but one wife, yet all the wives are held in common . . . Human life does not come to its natural close with these people; but when a man grows very old, all his kinsfolk collect together and offer him up in sacrifice; offering at the same time some cattle also. After the sacrifice they boil the flesh and

feast on it; and those who thus end their days are reckoned the happiest. If a man dies of disease they do not eat him, but bury him in the ground, bewailing his ill-fortune that he did not come to be sacrificed. They sow no grain, but live on their herds, and on fish, of which there is great plenty in the Araxes. Milk is what they chiefly drink. The only god they worship is the sun, and to him they offer the horse in sacrifice; under the notion of giving the swiftest of the gods the swiftest of all mortal creatures.

Herodotus did not think the Massagetae were to be criticized for such practices. Their customs were neither better nor worse than those of other peoples; they were merely different. The Greeks, who considered themselves more "civilized," may have thought that their customs were superior, but, Herodotus says, that is only because everyone believes the customs of his own society to be the best. The "truth" depends on one's point of view — that is, on the society in which one happens to have been raised.

Relativists think that Herodotus was obviously on to something and that those who believe in "objective" right and wrong are merely naive. Critics, however, object to the theory on a number of grounds. First, it is exceedingly conservative, in that the theory endorses whatever moral views happen to be current in a society. Consider our own society. Many people believe that our society's moral code is mistaken, at least on some points — for example, they may disagree with the dominant social view regarding capital punishment, or homosexuality, or the treatment of nonhuman animals. Must we conclude that these would-be reformers are wrong, merely because they oppose the majority view? Why must the majority always be right?

But there is a deeper problem with Relativism, emphasized by Socrates. Some social customs are, indeed, merely arbitrary, and when these customs are at issue it is fruitless to insist that one society's practices are better than another's. Funerary practices are a good example — it is neither better nor worse to bury the dead than to burn them. But it does not follow from this that *all* social practices are arbitrary in the same way. Some are, and some are not. The Greeks and the Callatians were free to accept whatever funerary practices they liked because

no objective reason could be given why one practice was superior to the other. In the case of other practices, however, there may be good reasons why some are superior. It is not hard, for example, to explain why honesty and respect for human life are socially desirable, and similarly it is not hard to explain why slavery and racism are undesirable. Because we can support our judgments about these matters with rational arguments, we do not have to regard those judgments as "merely" the expression of our particular society's moral code.

DIVINE COMMANDS

A second ancient idea, also familiar to Socrates, was that moral living consists in obedience to divine commands. If this were true, then we could easily answer the challenge of Gyges's ring — even if we had the power of invisibility, we would still be subject to divine retribution, so ultimately we could not "get away with" doing whatever we wanted.

But Socrates did not believe that right living could consist merely in trying to please the gods. In the *Euthyphro,* another of Plato's dialogues, Socrates is shown considering at some length whether "right" can be the same as "what the gods command." Now we may notice, to begin with, that there are considerable practical difficulties with this as a general theory of ethics. How, for example, are we supposed to *know* what the gods command? There are, of course, those who claim to have spoken with God about the matter and who therefore claim to be in a position to pass on his instructions to the rest of us. But people who claim to speak for God are not the most trustworthy folks — hearing voices can be a sign of schizophrenia or a megalomania just as easily as an instance of divine communication. Others, more modestly, rely on scripture or church tradition for guidance. But those sources are notoriously ambiguous — they give vague and often contradictory instructions — so, when people consult these authorities, they typically rely on whatever elements of scripture or church tradition support the moral views they are already inclined to agree with. Moreover, because scripture and church tradition have been handed down from earlier times, they provide little direct help in addressing distinctively contemporary problems: the problem of environmental preservation, for example, or the problem of how much our resources should be allocated to AIDS research as opposed to other worthy endeavors.

Still, it may be thought that God's commands provide the ultimate *authority* for ethics, and that is the issue Socrates addressed. Socrates accepted that the gods exist and that they may issue instructions. But he showed that this cannot be the ultimate basis of ethics. He points out that we have to distinguish two possibilities: Either the gods have some reason for the instructions they issue, or they do not. If they do not, then their commands are merely arbitrary — the gods are like petty tyrants who demand that we act in this way and that, even though there is no good reason for it. But this is an impious view that religious people will not want to accept. On the other hand, if we say that the gods do have good reasons for their instructions, then we have admitted that there is a standard of rightness independent of their commands — namely, the standard to which the gods themselves refer in deciding what to require of us.

It follows, then, that even if one accepts a religious picture of the world, the rightness or wrongness of actions cannot be understood merely in terms of their conformity to divine prescriptions. We may always ask why the gods command what they do, and the answer to *that* question will reveal why right actions are right and why wrong actions are wrong.

ARISTOTLE

Although Relativism and the Divine Command Theory have always had supporters, they have never been popular among serious students of moral philosophy. The first extended, systematic treatise on moral philosophy, produced two generations after Socrates, was Aristotle's *Nicomachean Ethics* (ca. 330 B.C.), and Aristotle wasted no time on such notions. Instead Aristotle offered a detailed account of the virtues — the qualities of character that people need to do well in life. The virtues include courage, prudence, generosity, honesty, and many more; Aristotle sought to explain what each one is and why it is important. His answer to the question of Gyges's ring was that virtue is necessary for human beings to achieve happiness; therefore, the man of virtue is ultimately better off because he is virtuous.

Aristotle's view of the virtuous life was connected with his overall way of understanding the world and our place in it. Aristotle's conception of what the world is like was enormously influential; it dominated Western thinking for over 1,700 years. A central feature of this conception was that *everything in nature exists for a purpose.* "Nature," Aristotle said, "belongs to the class of causes which act for the sake of something."

It seems obvious that artifacts such as knives and chariots have purposes, because we have their purposes in mind when we make them. But what about natural objects that we do not make? Do they have purposes too? Aristotle thought so. One of his examples was that we have teeth so that we can chew. Such biological examples are quite persuasive; the parts of our bodies do seem, intuitively, to have particular purposes — eyes are for seeing, the heart is for pumping blood, and so on. But Aristotle's thesis was not limited to organic beings. According to him, *everything* in nature has a purpose. He also thought, to take a different sort of example, that rain falls so that plants can grow. As odd as it may seem to a modern reader, Aristotle was perfectly serious about this. He considered other alternatives, such as that the rain falls "of necessity" and that this helps the plants only by "coincidence," and rejected them. His considered view was that plants and animals are what they are, and that the rain falls as it does, "because it is better so."

The world, therefore, is an orderly, rational system, with each thing having its own proper place and serving its own special purpose. There is a neat hierarchy: The rain exists for the sake of the plants, the plants exist for the sake of the animals, and the animals exist — of course — for the sake of people, whose well-being is the point of the whole arrangement. In the *Politics* he wrote:

> [We] must believe, first that plants exist for the sake of animals, second that all other animals exist for the sake of man, tame animals for the use he can make of them as well as for the food they provide; and as for wild animals, most though not all of these can be used for food or are useful in other ways; clothing and instruments can be made out of them. If then we are right in believing that nature makes nothing without some end in view, nothing

to no purpose, it must be that nature has made all things specifically for the sake of man.

It was a stunningly anthropocentric view. Aristotle may be forgiven, however, when we consider that virtually every important thinker in our history has entertained some such thought. Humans are a remarkably vain species.

NATURAL LAW

The Christian thinkers who came later found Aristotle's view of the world to be perfectly congenial. There was only one thing missing: The addition of God was required to make the picture complete. (Aristotle had denied that God was a necessary part of the picture. For him, the worldview we have outlined was not religious; it was simply a description of how things are.) Thus the Christian thinkers said that the rain falls to help the plants because *that is what the Creator intended,* and the animals are for human use because *that is what God made them for.* Values and purposes were, therefore, conceived to be a fundamental part of the nature of things, because the world was believed to have been created according to a divine plan.

This view of the world had a number of consequences for ethics. On the most general level, it affirmed the supreme value of human life and it explained why humans are entitled to do whatever they please with the rest of nature. The basic moral arrangement — human beings, whose lives are sacred, dominating a world made for their benefit — was enshrined as the Natural Order of Things.

At a more detailed level, a corollary of this outlook was that the "laws of nature" specify how things *ought to be* as well as describing how things *are.* In turn, knowing how things ought to be enables us to evaluate states-of-affairs as objectively good or bad. Things are as they ought to be when they are serving their natural purposes; when they do not or cannot serve those purposes, things have gone wrong. Thus, teeth that have decayed and cannot be used for chewing are defective; and drought, which deprives plants of the rain they need, is a natural, objective evil.

There are also implications for human action: In this view moral rules are one type of law of nature.

The key idea here is that some forms of human behavior are "natural" while others are not; and "unnatural" acts are said to be wrong. Beneficence, for example, is natural for us because God has made us as social creatures. We want and need the friendship of other people and we have natural affections for them; hence, behaving brutishly toward them is unnatural. Or to take a different sort of example, the purpose of the sex organs is procreation. Thus any use of them for other purposes is "contrary to nature" — which is why the Christian church has traditionally regarded any form of sexual activity that does not result in procreation, such as masturbation, gay sex, or the use of contraceptives, as impermissible.

This combination of ideas, together with others like them, formed the core of an outlook known as natural-law ethics. The Theory of Natural Law was developed most fully by Saint Thomas Aquinas (1225–1274), who lived at a time when the Aristotelian worldview was unchallenged. Aquinas was the foremost thinker among traditional Catholic theologians. Today natural-law theory still has adherents inside the Catholic church, but few outside. The reason is that the Aristotelian worldview, on which natural-law ethics depended, has been replaced by the outlook of modern science.

Galileo, Newton, and others developed ways of understanding natural phenomena that made no use of evaluative notions. In their way of thinking, the rain has no purpose. It does not fall in order to help the plants grow. Plants typically get the amount of water they need because each species has evolved, by natural selection, in the environment in which that amount of water is available. Natural selection produces an orderly arrangement that *appears* to have been designed, but that is only an illusion. To explain nature there is no need to assume teleological principles, neither Aristotle's "final causes" nor the Christians' God. This changed outlook was by far the most insidious feature of the new science; it is little wonder that the church's first response was to condemn it.

Modern science transformed people's view of what the world is like. But part of the transformation, inseparable from the rest, was an altered view of the nature of ethics. Right and wrong could no longer be deduced from the nature of things, for in the new view the natural world does not, in and of itself, manifest value and purpose. The *inhabitants* of the world may have needs and desires that generate values special to them, but that is all. The world apart from those inhabitants knows and cares nothing for their values, and it has no values of its own. A hundred and fifty years before Nietzsche declared that "There are no moral facts," the Scottish philosopher David Hume had come to the same conclusion. Hume summed up the moral implications of the new worldview in his *Treatise of Human Nature* (1739) when he wrote:

> Take any action allow'd to be vicious: Willful murder, for instance. Examine it in all lights, and see if you can find that matter of fact, or real existence, which you call *vice*. In whichever way you take it, you find only certain passions, motives, volitions and thoughts. There is no other matter of fact in the case.

To Aristotle's idea that "nature has made all things for the sake of man," Hume replied: "The life of a man is of no greater importance to the universe than that of an oyster."

THE SOCIAL CONTRACT

If there are no moral facts and no God, what becomes of morality? Ethics must somehow be understood as a purely human phenomenon—as the product of human needs, interests, and desires—and nothing else. Figuring out how to do this has been the basic project of moral philosophy from the 17th century on.

Thomas Hobbes, the foremost English philosopher of the 17th century, suggested one way in which ethics might be understood in purely human terms. Hobbes assumed that "good" and "bad" are just names we give to things we like and dislike. Thus, because we may like different things, we may disagree about what is good or bad. However, Hobbes said, in our fundamental psychological makeup we are all very much alike. We are all basically self-interested creatures who want to live and to live as well as possible. This is the key to understanding ethics. Ethics arises when people realize *what they must do* to live well.

Hobbes was the first important modern thinker to provide a secular, naturalistic basis for ethics. He pointed out that each of us is enormously better off living in a mutually cooperative society than we would be if we tried to make it on our own. The benefits of social living go far beyond companionship: Social cooperation makes possible schools, hospitals, and highways; houses with electricity and central heating; airplanes and telephones; newspapers and books; movies, opera, and bingo; science and agriculture. Without social cooperation we would lose these benefits and more. Therefore, it is to the advantage of each of us to do whatever is necessary to establish and maintain a cooperative society.

But it turns out that a mutually cooperative society can exist only if we adopt certain rules of behavior—rules that require telling the truth, keeping our promises, respecting one another's lives and property, and so on:

- Without the presumption that people will tell the truth, there would be no reason for people to pay any attention to what other people say. Communication would be impossible. And without communication among its members, society would collapse.
- Without the requirement that people keep their promises, there could be no division of labor—workers could not count on getting paid, retailers could not rely on their agreements with suppliers, and so on—and the economy would collapse. There could be no business, no building, no agriculture, no medicine.
- Without assurances against assault, murder, and theft, no one could feel secure; everyone would have to be constantly on guard against everyone else, and social cooperation would be impossible.

Thus, to obtain the benefits of social living, we must strike a bargain with one another, with each of us agreeing to obey these rules, provided others do likewise. (We must also establish mechanisms for enforcing these rules—such as legal sanctions and other, less formal methods of enforcement—so that we can *count on* one another to obey them.) This "social contract" is the basis of morality. Indeed, morality can be defined as nothing more or less than *the set of rules that rational people will agree to obey, for their mutual benefit, provided that other people will obey them as well.*

This way of understanding morality has a number of appealing features. First, it takes the mystery out of ethics and makes it a practical, down-to-earth business. Living morally is not a matter of blind obedience to the mysterious dictates of a supernatural being; nor is it a matter of fidelity to lofty but pointless abstract rules. Instead, it is a matter of doing what it takes to make social living possible.

Second, this theory makes it clear how morality can be rational and objective even if there are no moral facts. It is not merely a matter of opinion that the rule against murder must be a part of any workable social scheme or that rational people, to secure their own welfare, must agree to adopt such a rule. Nor is it merely a matter of opinion that rules requiring truthfulness and promise keeping are needed for people to flourish in a social setting. Even if there are no moral facts, the reasoning that leads to such conclusions is perfectly objective.

Third, the Social Contract Theory explains why we should *care* about ethics—it offers at least a partial response to the problem of Gyges's ring. If there is no God to punish us, why should we bother to do what is "right," especially when it is not to our advantage? The answer is that it *is* to our advantage to live in a society where people behave morally—thus, it is rational for us to accept moral restrictions on our conduct as part of a bargain we make with other people. We benefit directly from the ethical conduct of others, and our own compliance with the moral rules is the price we pay to secure their compliance.

Fourth, the Social Contract approach gives us a sensible and mature way of determining what our ethical duties really are. When "morality" is mentioned, the first thing that pops into many people's minds is an attempt to restrict their sex lives. It is unfortunate that the word *morals* has come to have such a connotation. The whole purpose of having a system of morality, according to Social Contract Theory, is to make it possible for people to live their individual lives in a setting of social cooperation—its purpose is not to tell people what kinds of lives they should live (except insofar as it is necessary to restrict conduct in the interests of maintaining social cooperation). Therefore, an ethic based on the Social Contract would have little interest in what people do in their bedrooms.

Finally, we may note again that Social Contract Theory assumes relatively little about human nature. It treats human beings as self-interested creatures and does not assume that they are naturally altruistic, even to the slightest degree. One of the theory's charms is that it can reach the conclusion that we ought, often, to *behave* altruistically, without assuming that we *are* naturally altruistic. We want to live as well as possible, and moral obligations are created as we band together with other people to form the cooperative societies that are necessary for us to achieve this fundamentally self-interested goal.

ALTRUISM AND SELF-INTEREST

Are people essentially self-interested? Although the Social Contract Theory continues to attract supporters, not many philosophers and psychologists today would accept Hobbes's egoistic view of human nature. It seems evident that humans have a least *some* altruistic feelings, if only for their family and friends. We have evolved as social creatures just as surely as we have evolved as creatures with legs—thus, caring for our kin and members of our local group is as natural for us as walking.

If humans do have some degree of natural altruism, does this have any significance for morals? David Hume thought so. Hume agreed with Hobbes that our moral opinions are expressions of our feelings. In 1739, when he invited his readers to consider "willful murder" and see if they could find that "matter of fact" called "vice," Hume concluded that:

> You can never find it, till you turn your reflexion into your own breast, and find a sentiment of disapprobation, which arises in you, towards this action. Here is a matter of fact; but 'tis the object of feeling . . . It lies in yourself, not in the object. So that when you pronounce any action or character to be vicious, you mean nothing, but that from the constitution of your nature you have a feeling or sentiment of blame from the contemplation of it.

And what, exactly, is "the constitution of our nature"? Of course, it is part of our nature to care about ourselves and our own welfare. But Hume added that we also have "*social* sentiments"—feelings that connect us with other people and make us concerned about their welfare. That is why, Hume said, we measure right and wrong by "the true interests of mankind":

> In all determinations of morality, this circumstance of public utility is ever principally in view; and wherever disputes arise, either in philosophy or common life, concerning the bounds of duty, the question cannot, by any means, be decided with greater certainty than be ascertaining, on any side, the true interests of mankind.

This view came to be known as Utilitarianism. In modern moral philosophy it is the chief alternative to the theory of the Social Contract.

UTILITARIANISM

Utilitarians hold that there is one principle that sums up all our moral duties. The ultimate moral principle is that *we should always do whatever will produce the greatest possible balance of happiness over unhappiness for everyone who will be affected by our action.* This "principle of utility" is deceptively simple. It is actually a combination of three ideas: First, in determining what to do, we should be guided by the expected consequences of our actions—we should do whatever will have the best consequences. Second, in determining which consequences are best, we should give the greatest possible weight to the happiness or unhappiness that would be caused—we should do whatever will cause the most happiness or the least unhappiness. And finally, the principle of utility assumes that each individual's happiness is equally as important as anyone else's.

Although Hume expressed the basic idea of Utilitarianism, two other philosophers elaborated it in greater detail. Jeremy Bentham, an Englishman who lived in the late 18th and early 19th centuries, was the leader of a group of philosophical radicals who aimed to reform the laws of Britain along Utilitarian lines. They were remarkably successful in advancing such causes as prison reform and restrictions on the use of child labor. John Stuart Mill, the son of one of Bentham's original followers, gave the theory its most popular and influential defense in his book *Utilitarianism,* published in 1861.

The Utilitarian movement attracted critics from the outset. It was an easy target because it ignored conventional religious notions. The point of morality, according to the Utilitarians, had nothing to do with obedience to God or gaining credit in Heaven. Rather, the point was just to make life in this world as comfortable and happy as possible. So some critics condemned Utilitarianism as a godless doctrine. To this Mill replied:

> the question depends upon what idea we have formed of the moral character of the Deity. If it be a true belief that God desires, above all things, the happiness of his creatures, and that this was his purpose in their creation, utility is not only not a godless doctrine, but more profoundly religious than any other.

Utilitarianism was also an easy target because it was (and still is) a *subversive* theory, in that it turned many traditional moral ideas upside down. Bentham argued, for example, that the purpose of the criminal justice system cannot be understood in the traditional way as "paying back" miscreants for their wicked deeds—that only piles misery upon misery. Instead, the social response to crime should be threefold: to identify and deal with the causes of criminal behavior; where possible, to reform individual lawbreakers and make them into productive citizens; and to "punish" people only insofar as it is necessary to deter others from committing similar crimes. (Today, of course, these are familiar ideas, but only because the Utilitarians' victory was so sweeping.) Or, to take a different example, by insisting that everyone's happiness is equally important, the Utilitarians offended various elitist notions of group superiority. According to the Utilitarian standard, neither race, sex, nor social class makes a difference to one's moral status. Mill himself wrote a book on *The Subjection of Women* that became a classic of the 19th-century suffragist movement.

Finally, Utilitarianism was controversial because it had no use for "absolute" moral rules. The Utilitarians regarded the traditional rules — against killing, lying, breaking one's promises, and so on — as "rules of thumb," useful because following them will generally be for the best. But they are not absolute — whenever breaking such a rule will have better results for everyone concerned, the rule should be broken. The rule against killing, for example, might be suspended in the case of voluntary euthanasia for someone dying of a painful illness. Moreover, the Utilitarians regarded some traditional rules as dubious, even as rules of thumb. For example, Christian moralists had traditionally said that masturbation is evil because it violates the Natural Law; but from the point of view of the Principle of Utility, it appears to be harmless. A more serious matter is the traditional religious condemnation of homosexuality, which has resulted in misery for countless people. Utilitarianism implies that if an activity makes people happy, without anyone being harmed, it cannot be wrong.

But it is one thing to describe a moral view; it is another thing to justify it. Utilitarianism says that our moral duty is to "promote the general happiness." Why should we do that? How can the challenge of Gyges's ring be answered? As Mill puts it,

> I feel that I am bound not to rob or murder, betray or deceive; but why am I bound to promote the general happiness? If my own happiness lies in something else, why may I not give that the preference?

Aside from the "external sanctions" of law and public opinion, Mill thinks there is only one possible reason for accepting this or any other moral standard. The "internal sanction" of morality must always be "a feeling in our minds," regardless of what sort of ethic this feeling endorses:

> The ultimate sanction, therefore, of all morality (external motives apart) being a subjective feeling in our own minds, I see nothing embarrassing to those whose standard is utility in the question, What is the sanction of that particular standard? We may answer, the same as all other moral standards — the conscientious feelings of mankind. Undoubtedly this

sanction has no binding efficacy on those who do not possess the feelings it appeals to; but neither will these persons be more obedient to any other moral principle than the utilitarian one.

The kind of morality we accept will, therefore, depend on the nature of our feelings: If human beings have "social feelings," then Mill says that utilitarian morality will be the natural standard for them.

> The firm foundation [of utilitarian morality] is that of the social feelings of mankind — the desire to be in unity with our fellow creatures, which is already a powerful principle in human nature, and happily one of those which tend to become stronger, even without express inculcation, from the influences of advancing civilization.

IMPARTIALITY

Utilitarianism, as we have seen, has implications that are at odds with traditional morality. Much the same could be said about Social Contract Theory. In most of the practical matters that have been mentioned — punishment, racial discrimination, women's rights, euthanasia, homosexuality — the two theories have similar implications. But there is one matter on which they differ dramatically. Utilitarians believe that we have a very extensive moral duty to help other people. Social Contract Theorists deny this.

Suppose, for example, you are thinking of spending $1,000 for a new living room carpet. Should you do this? What are the alternatives? One alternative is to give the money to an agency such as the United Nations Children's Fund. Each year between 10 and 20 million third-world children die of easily preventable diseases, because there isn't enough money to provide the vitamin-A capsules, antibiotics, and oral rehydration treatments they need. By giving the money to UNICEF, and making do a while longer with your old carpet, you could provide much-needed medical care for dozens of children. From the point of view of utility — seeking the best overall outcome for everyone concerned — there is no doubt you should give the money to UNICEF. Obviously, the medicine will help the kids a lot more than the new rug will help you.

But from the point of view of the Social Contract, things look very different. If morality rests on an agreement between people—remember, an agreement they enter into *to promote their own interests*—what would the agreement say about helping other people? Certainly, we would want the contract to impose a duty not to harm other people, even strangers. Each of us would obviously benefit from that. And it might be in our best interests to accept a mutual obligation to provide aid to others when it is easy and convenient to do so. But would rational people accept a general duty to provide virtually unlimited aid to strangers, even at great cost to themselves? From the standpoint of self-interest, that sounds crazy. Jan Narveson, a contract theorist who teaches philosophy at the University of Waterloo in Canada, writes in his book *Moral Matters* (1993):

> Morals, if they are to be rational, must amount to agreements among people—people of all kinds, each pursuing his or her own interests, which are various and do not necessarily include much concern for others and their interests. But people have minds, and apply information gleaned from observing the world around them to the task of promoting their interests, and they have a broad repertoire of powers including some that can make them exceedingly dangerous, as well as others that can make them very helpful. This gives us reason to agree with each other that we will refrain from harming others in the pursuit of our interests, to respect each other's property and grant extensive civil rights, but not necessarily to go very far out of our way to be very helpful to those we don't know and may not particularly care for. . . .
>
> It is reasonable, then, to arrive at a general understanding that we shall be ready to help when help is urgent and when giving it is not very onerous to us. But a general understanding that we shall help everyone as if they were our spouses or dearest friends is quite another matter.

Unlike many philosophers who prefer to keep things abstract, Narveson is good about spelling out the implications of his view in a way that leaves no room for misunderstanding:

> What about parting with the means for making your sweet little daughter's birthday party a memo-

rable one, in order to keep a dozen strangers alive on the other side of the world? Is this something you are morally required to do? Indeed not. She may well *matter* to you more than they. This illustrates again the fact that people do *not* "count equally" for most of us. Normal people care more about some people than others, and build their very lives around those carings.

Which view is correct? Do we have a moral duty to provide extensive aid to strangers, or not? Both views appeal ultimately to our emotions. A striking feature of Narveson's contractarian argument is its appeal to the fact that we *care more* for some people than others. This is certainly true: As he says, we care more for our own children than for "strangers on the other side of the world." But does this really mean that I may choose some trivial benefit for my children over the very lives of the strangers? Suppose there were two buttons on my desk at this moment, and by pressing button A, I can provide my son with a nice party; by pressing B, I can save the lives of a dozen strangers. Is it really all right for me to press A, just because I "care more" for my son? Mill agrees that the issue must be decided on the basis of feelings (how else could it be?), but for him it is not these small-scale personal feelings that have the final say. Instead, it is one's "conscientious feelings"—the feelings that prevail after everything has been thought through—that finally determine one's obligations. Mill assumes that we cannot, when we are thoughtful and reflective, approve of ourselves pushing button A.

However, some contemporary Utilitarians have argued that the matter need not be left to the vicissitudes of individual feeling. It may be true, they say, that we all care more for ourselves, our family, and our friends than we care for strangers. But we have rational capacities as well as feelings, and if we think objectively about the matter, we will realize that other people are no different. Others, even strangers, also care about themselves, their families, and their friends, in the same way that we do. Their needs and interests are comparable to our own. In fact, *there is nothing of this general sort that makes anyone different from anyone else*—and if we are in all relevant respects similar to one another, then there is no justification for anyone taking his or her own interests to be more important. Peter Singer, a utilitarian philosopher at Princeton University writes in his book *How Are We to Live?* (1995):

Reason makes it possible for us to see ourselves in this way . . . I am able to see that I am just one being among others, with interests and desires like others. I have a personal perspective on the world, from which my interests are at the front and centre of the stage, the interests of my family and friends are close behind, and the interests of strangers are pushed to the back and sides. But reason enables me to see that others have similarly subjective perspectives, and that from "the point of view of the universe" my perspective is no more privileged than theirs. Thus my ability to reason shows me the possibility of detaching myself from my own perspective, and shows me what the universe might look like if I had no personal perspective.

So, from an objective viewpoint, each of us must acknowledge that our own perspective — our own particular set of needs, interests, likes, and dislikes — is only one among many and has no special status.

KANT

The idea of impartiality is also central to the third major alternative in modern moral philosophy, the system of ethical ideas devised by the great German philosopher Immanuel Kant (1724–1804). Like the Social Contract Theorists and the Utilitarians, Kant sought to explain ethics without appealing to divine commands or "moral facts." Kant's solution was to see morality as a product of "pure reason." Just as we must do some things because of our *desires* — for example, because I desire to attend a concert, I must reserve a ticket — the moral law is binding on us because of our *reason.*

Like the Utilitarians, Kant believed that morality can be summed up in one ultimate principle, from which all our duties and obligations are derived. But his version of the "ultimate moral principle" was very different from the principle of utility, because Kant did not emphasize the outcomes of actions. What was important for him was "doing one's duty," and he held that a person's duty is not determined by calculating consequences.

Kant called his ultimate moral principle the "Categorical Imperative." But he gave this principle two very different formulations. The first version of the Categorical Imperative, as expressed in his *Fundamental Principles of the Metaphysics of Morals* (1785), goes like this:

Act only according to that maxim by which you can at the same time will that it should become a universal law.

Stated in this way, Kant's principle summarizes a procedure for deciding whether an act is morally permissible. When you are contemplating a particular action, you are to ask what rule you would be following if you were to do it. (This will be the "maxim" of the act.) Then you are to ask whether you would be willing for that rule to be followed by everyone all the time. (That would make it a "universal law" in the relevant sense.) If so, the rule may be followed, and the act is permissible. However, if you would not be willing for everyone to follow the rule, then you may not follow it, and the act is morally impermissible.

This explains why the moral law is binding on us simply by virtue of our rationality. The first requirement of rationality is that we be consistent, and it would not be consistent to act on a maxim that we could not want others to adopt as well. Kant believed, in addition, that consistency requires us to interpret moral rules as having no exceptions. For this reason, he endorsed a whole range of absolute prohibitions, covering everything from lying to suicide.

However, Kant also gave another formulation of the Categorical Imperative. Later in the same book, he said that the ultimate moral principle may be understood as saying:

So act that you treat humanity, whether in your own person or in that of another, always as an end and never as means only.

What does it mean to say that persons are to be treated as "ends" and never as "means"? Kant gives us this example: Suppose you need money, and so you want a "loan," but you know you could not repay it. In desperation, you consider making a false promise (to repay) in order to trick a friend into giving you the money. May you do this? Perhaps you need the money for a good purpose, so good, in fact, that you might convince yourself the lie would be justified. Nevertheless, if you lied to your friend, you would merely be manipulating him, and using him "as a means."

On the other hand, what would it be like to treat your friend "as an end"? Suppose you told the truth, that you need the money for a certain purpose, but could not repay it. Then your friend could make up his own mind about whether to let you have it. He could exercise his own powers of reason, consulting his own values and wishes, and make a free, autonomous choice. If he did decide to give the money for this purpose, he would be choosing to make that purpose his own. Thus you would not merely be using him as a means to achieving your goal. This is what Kant meant when he said, "rational beings . . . ought always be esteemed also as ends, that is, as beings who must be capable of containing in themselves the end of the very same action."

CONCLUSION

Our purpose here is not to reach any firm conclusion about which of these approaches, if any, is correct. But we may end with an observation about how that project might be undertaken.

Philosophical ideas are often very abstract, and it is difficult to see what sort of evidence counts for or against them. It is easy enough to appreciate, intuitively, the ideas behind each of these theories, but how do we determine which, if any, is correct? It is a daunting question. Faced with this problem, people are tempted to accept or reject philosophical ideas on the basis of their intuitive appeal—if any idea sounds good, one may embrace it; or if it rubs one the wrong way, it may be discarded. But this is hardly a satisfactory way to proceed if we want to discover the truth. How an idea strikes us is not a reliable guide, for our "intuitions" may be mistaken.

Happily, there is an alternative. An idea is no better than the arguments that support it. So, to evaluate a philosophical idea, we may examine the reasoning behind it. The great philosophers knew this very well: They did not simply announce their philosophical opinions; instead, they presented arguments in support of their views. The leading idea, from the time of Socrates to the present, has been that truth is discovered by considering the reasons for and against the various alternatives—the "correct" theory is the one that has the best arguments on its side. Thus, philosophical thinking consists, to a large extent, in formulating and assessing arguments. This is not the whole of philosophy, but it is a big part of it. It is what makes philosophy a rational enterprise, rather than an empty exercise in theory mongering.

DISCUSSION TOPICS

1. According to Rachels, what is the "deeper problem" with relativism? Do you agree with his view? Why or why not?
2. Rachels argues that, even if one accepts a religious view of the world, one should reject the divine command theory. What reasons does he give for his position? Do you find them convincing?
3. Modern science has replaced the world view of natural law, according to Rachels. In your view, are there ways to combine the idea of purpose in nature with current science? Explain your position.
4. Rachels finds many strengths in social contract theory. Explain and evaluate these strengths.
5. What does Rachels mean by characterizing utilitarianism as "subversive"? Explain why you agree or disagree.
6. Describe the aspects of Kant's theory that you believe to be correct. Are there any that you believe to be incorrect? Give your reasons.

READING 7

Some Basic Points about Arguments

James Rachels

James Rachels is University Professor of Philosophy at the University of Alabama in Birmingham. In this selection, drawn from his book The Elements of

Moral Philosophy (1999), Rachels presents some basic ideas concerning logical arguments. He illustrates these ideas by evaluating the argument that morality is a matter of opinion, which varies between cultures, and also the argument that moral judgments cannot be proved true or false. In his view both of these arguments are unsound.

Philosophy without argument would be a lifeless exercise. What good would it be to produce a theory, if there were no reasons for thinking it correct? And of what interest is the rejection of a theory, if there are no good reasons for thinking it incorrect? A philosophical idea is exactly as good as the arguments in its support.

Therefore, if we want to think clearly about philosophical matters, we have to learn something about the evaluation of arguments. We have to learn to distinguish the sound ones from the unsound ones. This can be a tedious business, but it is indispensable if we want to come within shouting distance of the truth.

ARGUMENTS

In ordinary English the word *argument* often means a quarrel, and there is a hint of acrimony in the word. That is not the way the word is used here. In the logician's sense, an argument is a chain of reasoning designed to prove something. It consists of one or more *premises* and a *conclusion,* together with the claim that the conclusion *follows from* the premises. Here is a simple argument. This example is not particularly interesting in itself, but it is short and clear and will help us grasp the main points we need to understand about the nature of arguments.

(1) All men are mortal.

 Socrates is a man.

 Therefore, Socrates is mortal.

The first two statements are the premises; the third statement is the conclusion; and it is claimed that the conclusion follows from the premises.

What does it mean to say that the conclusion "follows from" the premises? It means that a certain logical relation exists between the premises and the conclusion, namely, that *if* the premises are true, then the conclusion must be true also. (Another way to put the same point is: The conclusion follows from the premises if and only if it is impossible for the premises to be true, and the conclusion false, at the same time.) In example (1), we can see that the conclusion does follow from the premises. If it is true that all men are mortal, and Socrates is a man, then it must be true that Socrates is mortal. (Or, it is impossible for it to be true that all men are mortal, and for Socrates to be a man, and yet be false that Socrates is mortal.)

In example (1), the conclusion follows from the premises, *and* the premises are in fact true. However, the conclusion of an argument may follow from the premises even if the premises are not actually true. Consider this argument:

(2) All people from Georgia are famous.

 Jimmy Carter is from Georgia.

 Therefore, Jimmy Carter is famous.

Clearly, the conclusion of this argument does follow from the premises: *If* it were true that all Georgians were famous, and Jimmy Carter was from Georgia, then it follows that Jimmy Carter would be famous. This logical relation holds between the premises and conclusion even though one of the premises is in fact false.

At this point, logicians customarily introduce a bit of terminology. They say that an argument is *valid* just in case its conclusion follows from its premises. Both the examples given above are valid arguments, in this technical sense.

In order to be a *sound* argument, however, two things are necessary: The argument must be valid, *and* its premises must be true. Thus, the argument about Socrates is a sound argument, but the argument about Jimmy Carter is not sound, because even though it is valid, its premises are not all true.

It is important to notice that an argument may be unsound, even though its premises and conclusion are both true. Consider the following silly example:

(3) The earth has one moon.

 John F. Kennedy was assassinated.

 Therefore, snow is white.

The premises of this "argument" are both true, and the conclusion is true as well. Yet it is obviously a bad argument, because it is not valid — the conclusion does not follow from the premises. The point is that *when we ask whether an argument is valid, we are not asking whether the premises actually are true, or whether the conclusion actually is true. We are only asking whether,* if *the premises were true, the conclusion would really follow from them.*

So far, our examples have all been trivial. I have used these trivial examples because they permit us to make the essential logical points clearly and uncontroversially. But these points are applicable to the analysis of any argument, trivial or not. To illustrate, let us consider how these points can be used in analyzing a more important and controversial issue. We will look at the arguments for Moral Skepticism in some detail.

MORAL SKEPTICISM

Moral Skepticism is the idea that *there is no such thing as objective moral truth.* It is not merely the idea that we cannot *know* the truth about right and wrong. It is the more radical idea that, where ethics is concerned, "truth" does not exist. The essential point may be put in several different ways. It may be said that

> Morality is subjective; it is a matter of how we feel about things, not a matter of how things *are.*
>
> Morality is only a matter of opinion, and one person's opinion is just as good as another's.
>
> Values exist only in our minds, not in the world outside us.

However the point is put, the underlying thought is the same: The idea of "objective moral truth" is only a fiction; in reality, there is no such thing.

We want to know whether Moral Skepticism is correct. Is the idea of moral "truth" only an illusion? What arguments can be given in favor of this idea? In order to determine whether it is correct, we need to ask what arguments can be given for it and whether those arguments are sound.

The Cultural Differences Argument

One argument for Moral Skepticism might be based on the observation that in different cultures people have different ideas concerning right and wrong. For example, in traditional Eskimo society, infanticide was thought to be morally acceptable — if a family already had too many children, a new baby might have been left to die in the snow. (This was more likely to happen to girl babies than to boys.) In our own society, however, this would be considered wrong. There are many other examples of the same kind. Different cultures have different moral codes.

Reflecting on such facts, many people have concluded that there is no such thing as objective right and wrong. Thus they advance the following argument:

> (4) In some societies, such as among the Eskimos, infanticide is thought to be morally acceptable.
>
>   In other societies, such as our own, infanticide is thought to be morally odious.
>
>   Therefore, infanticide is neither objectively right nor objectively wrong; it is merely a matter of opinion that varies from culture to culture.

We may call this the "Cultural Differences Argument." This kind of argument has been tremendously influential; it has persuaded many people to be skeptical of the whole idea of moral "truth." But is it a sound argument? We may ask two questions about it: First, are the premises true, and second, does the conclusion really follow from them? If the answer to either question is "No," then the argument must be rejected. In this case, the premises seem to be correct — there have been many cultures in which infanticide was accepted. Therefore, our attention must focus on the second matter: Is the argument valid?

To figure this out, we may begin by noting that the premises concern *what people believe.* In some societies, people think infanticide is all right. In others, people believe it is immoral. The conclusion, however, concerns not what people believe, but whether infanticide *really is* immoral. The problem is that this sort of conclusion does not follow from this sort of premise. It does not follow, from the mere fact that people have different beliefs about something, that there is no "truth" in the matter. Therefore, the Cultural Differences Argument is not valid.

To make the point clearer, consider this analogous argument:

(5) In some societies, the world is thought to be flat.

In other societies, the world is thought to be round.

Therefore, objectively speaking, the world is neither flat nor round. It is merely a matter of opinion that varies from culture to culture.

Clearly, *this* argument is not valid. We cannot conclude that the world is shapeless, simply because not everyone agrees what shape it has. But exactly the same can be said about the Cultural Differences Argument: We cannot validly move from premises about what people *believe* to a conclusion about what is so, because people — even whole societies — may be wrong. The world has a definite shape, and those who think it is flat are mistaken. Similarly, infanticide might be objectively wrong (or not wrong), and those who think differently might be mistaken. Therefore, the Cultural Differences Argument is not valid, and so it provides no legitimate support for the idea that moral "truth" is only an illusion.

There are two common reactions to this analysis. These reactions illustrate traps that people often fall into.

1. The first reaction goes like this. Many people find the conclusion of the Cultural Differences Argument very appealing. This makes it hard for them to believe that the argument is invalid — when it is pointed out that the argument is fallacious, they tend to respond: "But right and wrong really *are* only matters of opinion!" They make the mistake of thinking that, if we reject an argument, we are somehow impugning the truth of its conclusion. But that is not so. Remember example (3) above; it illustrates how an argument may have a true conclusion and still be a bad argument. If an argument is unsound, then it fails to provide any reason for thinking the conclusion is true. The conclusion may still be true — that remains an open question — but the point is just that the unsound argument gives it no support.

2. It may be objected that is unfair to compare morality with an obviously objective matter like the shape of the earth, because we can prove what shape the earth has by scientific methods. Therefore, we know that the flat-earthers are simply wrong. But morality is different. There is no way to prove a moral opinion is true or false.

This objection misses the point. The Cultural Differences Argument tries to derive the skeptical conclusion about morality *from a certain set of facts,* namely, the facts about cultural disagreements. This objection suggests that the conclusion might be derived from a *different* set of facts, namely facts about what is and what is not provable. It suggests, in effect, a different argument, which might be formulated like this:

(6) If infanticide (or anything else, for that matter) is objectively right or wrong, then it should be possible to *prove* it right or wrong.

But it is not possible to prove infanticide right or wrong.

Therefore, infanticide is neither objectively right nor objectively wrong. It is merely a matter of opinion that varies from culture to culture.

This argument is fundamentally different from the Cultural Differences Argument, even though the two arguments have the same conclusion. They are different because they appeal to different considerations in trying to prove that conclusion — in other words, they have different premises. Therefore, the question of whether argument (6) is sound is separate from the question of whether the Cultural Differences Argument is sound. The Cultural Differences Argument is not valid, for the reason given above.

We should emphasize the importance of *keeping arguments separate.* It is easy to slide from one argument to another without realizing what one is doing. It is easy to think that, if moral judgments are "unprovable," then the Cultural Differences Argument is strengthened. But it is not. Argument (6) merely introduces a different set of issues. It is important to pin down an argument, and evaluate *it* as carefully as possible, before moving on to different considerations.

The Provability Argument

Now let us consider in more detail the question of whether it is possible to prove a moral judgment true or false. The following argument, which we might call the "Provability Argument," is a more general form of argument (6):

(7) If there were any such thing as objective truth in ethics, we should be able to prove that some moral opinions are true and others false.

But in fact we cannot prove which moral opinions are true and which are false.

Therefore, there is no such thing as objective truth in ethics.

Once again, we have an argument with a certain superficial appeal. But are the premises true? And does the conclusion really follow from them? It seems that the conclusion does follow. Therefore, the crucial question will be whether the premises are in fact true.

The general claim that moral judgments can't be proven *sounds* right: Anyone who has ever argued about a matter like abortion knows how frustrating it can be to try to "prove" that one's point of view is correct. However, if we inspect this claim more closely, it turns out to be dubious.

Suppose we consider a matter that is simpler than abortion. A student says that a test given by a teacher was unfair. This is clearly a moral judgment—fairness is a basic moral value. Can the student prove the test was unfair? She might point out that the test was so long that not even the best students could complete it in the time allowed (and the test was to be graded on the assumption that it should be completed). Moreover, the test covered trivial matters in detail, while ignoring matters the teacher had stressed as very important. And finally, the test included questions about some matters that were not covered in either the assigned readings or the class discussions.

Suppose all this is true. And further suppose that the teacher, when asked to explain, has no defense to offer. (In fact, the teacher, who is rather inexperienced, seems muddled about the whole thing and doesn't seem to have had any very clear idea of what he was doing.) Now, hasn't the student proved the test was unfair? What more in the way of proof could we possible want?

It is easy to think of other examples that make the same point:

Jones is a bad man. To prove this, one might point out that Jones is a habitual liar; he manipulates people; he cheats when he thinks he can get away with it; he is cruel to other people; and so on.

Dr. Smith is irresponsible. He bases his diagnoses on superficial considerations; he drinks before performing delicate surgery; he refuses to listen to other doctors' advice; and so on.

A certain used-car salesman is unethical. He conceals defects in his cars; he takes advantage of poor people by pressuring them into paying exorbitant prices for cars he knows to be defective; he runs false advertisements in any newspaper that will carry them; and so on.

The point is that we can, and often do, back up our ethical judgments with good reasons. Thus it does not seem right to say that they are all unprovable, as though they were nothing more than "mere opinions." If a person has good reasons for his judgments, then he is not *merely* giving "his opinion." On the contrary, he may be making a judgment with which any reasonable person would have to agree.

If we can sometimes give good reasons for our moral judgments, what accounts for the persistent impression that they are "unprovable"? There are two reasons why the Provability Argument appears to be more potent than it actually is.

First, there is a tendency to focus attention only on the most difficult moral issues. The question of abortion, for example, is an enormously difficult and complicated matter. If we think only of questions like *this,* it is easy to believe that "proof" in ethics is impossible. The same could be said of the sciences. There are many complicated matters that physicists cannot agree on; if we focused our attention entirely on *them,* we might conclude that there is no "proof" in physics. But of course, there are many simpler matters in physics that can be proven, and about which all competent physicists agree. Similarly, in ethics there are many matters far simpler than abortion, about which all reasonable people must agree.

Second, it is easy to confuse two matters that are really very different:

1. Proving an opinion to be correct.
2. Persuading someone to accept your proof.

Suppose you are having an argument with someone about some moral issue, and you have perfectly cogent reasons in support of your position, while they have no good reasons on their side. Still, they refuse to accept your logic and continue to insist they are right. This is a common, if frustrating, experience. You may be tempted to conclude that it is impossible to prove you are right. But this would be a mistake. Your proof may be impeccable; the trouble may be that the other person is being pig-headed. (Of course, that is not the *only* possible explanation of what is going on, but it is one possible explanation.) The same thing can happen in any sort of discussion. You may be arguing about creationism versus evolution, and the other person may be unreasonable. But that does not necessarily mean there is something wrong with your arguments. There may be something wrong with him.

CONCLUSION

We have examined two of the most important arguments in support of Moral Skepticism and seen that these arguments are no good. Moral Skepticism might still turn out to be true, but if so, then other, better arguments will have to be found. Provisionally, at least, we have to conclude that Moral Skepticism is not nearly as plausible as we might have thought.

The purpose of this exercise, however, was to illustrate the process of evaluating philosophical arguments. We may summarize what we have learned about evaluating arguments like this:

1. Arguments are offered to provide support for a theory or idea; a philosophical theory may be regarded as acceptable only if there are sound arguments in its favor.
2. An argument is sound only if its premises are true and the conclusion follows logically from them.

   (a) A conclusion "follows from" the premises just in case the following is so: *If* the premises were true, then the conclusion would have to be true also. (An alternative way of saying the same thing: A conclusion follows from the premises just in case it is impossible for the premises to be true and the conclusion false at the same time.)

   (b) A conclusion can follow from premises even if those premises are in fact false.

   (c) A conclusion can be true and yet not follow from a given set of premises.

3. Therefore, in evaluating an argument, we ask two *separate* questions: Are the premises true? And, does the conclusion follow from them?
4. It is important to avoid two common mistakes. We should be careful to keep arguments separate, and not slide from one to the other, confusing different issues. And, we should not think an argument stronger than it is simply because we happen to agree with its conclusion. Moreover, we should remember that, if an argument is unsound, that does not mean the conclusion must be false—it only means that *this* argument does nothing to show it is true.

DISCUSSION TOPICS

1. Construct an argument in which
   a. the premises are false but the conclusion is true.
   b. the premises are true but the conclusion is false.
   c. the conclusion is true but does not follow from the premises.
2. Explain Rachels' reasoning when he says that the Cultural Differences Argument is not valid. Do you agree with him? Why or why not?
3. Rachels states that a good reason is one with which "any reasonable person" would have to agree. Explain the strengths and weaknesses of his view.

Environmental Ethics: Values in and Duties to the Natural World

Holmes Rolston III

Holmes Rolston III is University Distinguished Professor of Philosophy at Colorado State University at Fort Collins, Colorado. A major creative force in the development of environmental ethics, he is the author of Philosophy Gone Wild: Essays in Environmental Ethics *(1989) and* Environmental Ethics: Duties to and Values in the Natural World *(1988) as well as other books and many articles. In the following essay he characterizes environmental ethics as an "invitation to moral development." Rolston believes anthropocentrism is too specialized an ethic, because it limits itself to the self-interest of just one species.*

To arrive at an adequate ethic, Rolston urges us to respect all life, sentient or insentient. Organisms are vital, spontaneous systems that have a good of their own and a good of their kind. Value is not anthropogenic (human-created) but is biogenic (life-created). Organisms are intrinsically valuable in themselves, as part of the web of life.

Environmental ethics stretches classical ethics to the breaking point. All ethics seeks an appropriate respect for life. But we do not need just a humanistic ethic applied to the environment as we have needed one for business, law, medicine, technology, international development, or nuclear disarmament. Respect for life does demand an ethic concerned about human welfare, an ethic like the others and now applied to the environment. But environmental ethics in a deeper sense stands on a frontier, as radically theoretical as it is applied. It alone asks whether there can be nonhuman objects of duty.

Neither theory nor practice elsewhere needs values outside of human subjects, but environmental ethics must be more biologically objective—nonanthropocentric. It challenges the separation of science and ethics, trying to reform a science that finds nature value-free and an ethics that assumes that only humans count morally. Environmental ethics seeks to escape relativism in ethics, to discover a way past culturally based ethics. However much

our worldviews, ethics included, are embedded in our cultural heritages, and thereby theory-laden and value-laden, all of us know that a natural world exists apart from human cultures. Humans interact with nature. Environmental ethics is the only ethics that breaks out of culture. It has to evaluate nature, both wild nature and the nature that mixes with culture, and to judge duty thereby. After accepting environmental ethics, you will no longer be the humanist you once were.

Environmental ethics requires risk. It explores poorly charted terrain, where one can easily get lost. One must hazard the kind of insight that first looks like foolishness. Some people approach environmental ethics with a smile—expecting chicken liberation and rights for rocks, misplaced concern for chipmunks and daisies. Elsewhere, they think, ethicists deal with sober concerns: medical ethics, business ethics, justice in public affairs, questions of life and death and of peace and war. But the questions here are no less serious: The degradation of the environment poses as great a threat to life as nuclear war, and a more probable tragedy.

HIGHER ANIMALS

Logically and psychologically, the best and easiest breakthrough past the traditional boundaries of interhuman ethics is made when confronting higher animals. Animals defend their lives; they have a good of their own and suffer pains and pleasures like ourselves. Human moral concern should at least cross over into the domain of animal experience. This boundary crossing is also dangerous because if made only psychologically and not biologically, the would-be environmental ethicist may be too disoriented to travel further. The promised environmental ethics will degenerate into a mammalian ethics. We certainly need an ethic for animals, but that is only one level of concern in a comprehensive environmental ethics.

One might expect classical ethics to have sifted well an ethics for animals. Our ancestors did not think about endangered species, ecosystems, acid rain, or the ozone layer, but they lived in closer association with wild and domestic animals than we do. Hunters track wounded deer; ranchers who let their horses starve are prosecuted. Still, until recently, the scientific, humanistic centuries since the so-called Enlightenment have not been sensitive ones for animals, owing to the Cartesian legacy. Animals were mindless, living matter; biology has been mechanistic. Even psychology, rather than defending animal experience, has been behaviorist. Philosophy has protested little, concerned instead with locating values in human experiences at the same time that it dispirited and devalued nature. Across several centuries of hard science and humanistic ethics there has been little compassion for animals.

The progress of science itself smeared the human-nonhuman boundary line. Animal anatomy, biochemistry, cognition, perception, experience, behavior, and evolutionary history are kin to our own. Animals have no immortal souls, but then persons may not either, or beings with souls may not be the only kind that count morally. Ethical progress further smeared the boundary. Sensual pleasures are a good thing; ethics should be egalitarian, nonarbitrary, nondiscriminatory. There are ample scientific grounds that animals enjoy pleasures and suffer pains; and ethically there are no grounds to value these sensations in humans and not in animals. So there has been a vigorous reassessment of human duties to sentient life. The world cheered in the fall of 1988 when humans rescued two whales from winter ice.

"Respect their right to life": A sign in Rocky Mountain National Park enjoins humans not to harass bighorn sheep. "The question is not, Can they reason, nor Can they talk? but, Can they suffer?" wrote Jeremy Bentham (1948 [1789]), insisting that animal welfare counts too. The Park Service sign and Bentham's question increase sensitivity by extending rights and hedonist goods to animals. The gain is a vital breakthrough past humans, and the first lesson in environmental ethics has been learned. But the risk is a moral extension that expands rights as far as mammals and not much further, a psychologically based ethic that counts only felt experience. We respect life in our nonhuman but near-human animal cousins, a semianthropic and still quite subjective ethics. Justice remains a concern for just-us subjects. There has, in fact, not been much of a theoretical breakthrough, no paradigm shift.

Lacking that, we are left with anomaly and conceptual strain. When we try to use culturally extended rights and psychologically based utilities to protect the flora or even the insentient fauna, to protect endangered species or ecosystems, we can only stammer. Indeed, we get lost trying to protect bighorns, because, in the wild, cougars are not respecting the rights or utilities of the sheep they slay, and, in culture, humans slay sheep and eat them regularly, while humans have every right not to be eaten by either humans or cougars. There are no rights in the wild, and nature is indifferent to the welfare of particular animals. A bison fell through the ice into a river in Yellowstone Park; the environmental ethic there, letting nature take its course, forbade would-be rescuers from either saving or killing the suffering animal to put it out of its misery. A drowning human would have been saved at once. Perhaps it was a mistake to save those whales.

The ethics by extension now seems too nondiscriminating; we are unable to separate an ethics for humans from an ethics for wildlife. To treat wild animals with compassion learned in culture does not appreciate their wildness. Man, said Socrates, is the political animal; humans maximally are what they are in culture, where the natural selection pressures (impressively productive in ecosystems) are relaxed without detriment to the species *Homo sapiens,* and indeed with great benefit to its member persons. Wild animals cannot enter culture; they do not have that capacity. They cannot acquire language at sufficient levels to take part in culture; they cannot make their clothing or build fires, much less read books or receive an education. Animals can, by human adoption, receive some of the protections of culture, which happens when we domesticate them, but neither pets nor food animals enter the culture that shelters them.

Worse, such cultural protection can work to their detriment; their wildness is made over into a human artifact as food or pet animal. A cow does not have the integrity of a deer, or a poodle that of a wolf. Culture is a good thing for humans but often a bad thing for animals. Their biology and ecology — neither justice nor charity, nor rights nor welfare — provide the benchmark for an ethics.

Culture does make a relevant ethical difference, and environmental ethics has different criteria from interhuman ethics. Can they talk? and, Can they reason? — indicating cultural capacities — are relevant questions; not just, Can they suffer? *Equality* is a positive word in ethics, *discriminatory* a pejorative one. On the other hand, simplistic reduction is a failing in the philosophy of science and epistemology; to be "discriminating" is desirable in logic and value theory. Something about treating humans as equals with bighorns and cougars seems to "reduce" humans to merely animal levels of value, a "no more than" counterpart in ethics of the "nothing but" fallacy often met in science. Humans are "nothing but" naked apes. Something about treating sheep and cougars as the equals of humans seems to elevate them unnaturally and not to value them for what they are. There is something insufficiently discriminating in such judgments; they are species-blind in a bad sense, blind to the real differences between species, valuational differences that do count morally. To the contrary, a discriminating ethicist will insist on preserving the differing richness of valuational complexity, wherever found. Compassionate respect for life in its suffering is only part of the analysis.

Two tests of discrimination are pains and diet. It might be thought that pain is a bad thing, whether in nature or culture. Perhaps when dealing with humans in culture, additional levels of value and utility must be protected by conferring rights that do not exist in the wild, but meanwhile we should at least minimize animal suffering. That is indeed a worthy imperative in culture where animals are removed from nature and bred, but it may be misguided where animals remain in ecosystems. When the bighorn sheep of Yellowstone caught pinkeye, they were blinded, injured, and starving as a result, and three hundred of them, more than half the herd, perished. Wildlife veterinarians wanted to treat the disease, as they would have in any domestic herd, and as they did with Colorado bighorns infected with an introduced lungworm, but the Yellowstone ethicists left the animals to suffer, seemingly not respecting their life.

Had those ethicists no mercy? They knew rather that, although intrinsic pain is a bad thing whether in humans or in sheep, pain in ecosystems is instrumental pain, through which the sheep are naturally selected for a more satisfactory adaptive fit. Pain in a medically skilled culture is pointless, once the alarm to health is sounded, but pain operates functionally in bighorns in their niche, even after it becomes no longer in the interests of the pained individual. To have interfered in the interests of the blinded sheep would have weakened the species. Even the question, Can they suffer? is not as simple as Bentham thought. What we ought to do depends on what is. The *is* of nature differs significantly from the *is* of culture, even when similar suffering is present in both.

At this point some ethicists will insist that at least in culture we can minimize animal pain, and that will constrain our diet. There is predation in nature; humans evolved as omnivores. But humans, the only moral animals, should refuse to participate in the meat-eating phase of their ecology, just as they refuse to play the game merely by the rules of natural selection. Humans do not look to the behavior of wild animals as an ethical guide in other matters (marriage, truth telling, promise keeping, justice, charity). Why should they justify their dietary habits by watching what animals do?

But the difference is that these other matters are affairs of culture; these are person-to-person events, not events at all in spontaneous nature. By contrast, eating is omnipresent in wild nature; humans eat because they are in nature, not because they are in culture. Eating animals is not an event between persons but a human-to-animal event; and the rules for this act come from the ecosystems in which humans evolved and have no duty to remake. Humans, then, can model their dietary habits from their ecosystems, though they cannot and should not so model their interpersonal justice or charity. When eating, they ought to minimize animal suffering, but they have no duty to revise trophic pyramids whether in nature or culture. The boundary between animals and humans has not been rubbed out after all; only what was a boundary line has been smeared into a boundary zone. We have discovered that animals count morally, though we have not yet solved the challenge of how to count them.

Animals enjoy psychological lives, subjective experiences, the satisfaction of felt interests — intrinsic values that count morally when humans encounter them. But the pains, pleasures, interests, and welfare of individual animals are only one of the considerations in a more complex environmental ethics that cannot be reached by conferring rights on them or by a hedonist calculus, however far extended. We have to travel further into a more biologically based ethics.

ORGANISMS

If we are to respect all life, we have still another boundary to cross, from zoology to botany, from sentient to insentient life. In Yosemite National Park for almost a century humans entertained themselves by driving through a tunnel cut in a giant sequoia. Two decades ago the Wawona tree, weakened by the cut, blew down in a storm. People said, "Cut us another drive-through sequoia." The Yosemite environmental ethic, deepening over the years, answered, "No. You ought not to mutilate majestic sequoias for amusement. Respect their life." Indeed, some ethicists count the value of redwoods so highly that they will spike redwoods, lest they be cut. In the Rawah Wilderness in alpine Colorado, old signs read, "Please leave the flowers for others to enjoy." When the signs rotted out, new signs urged a less humanist ethic: "Let the flowers live!"

But trees and flowers cannot care, so why should we? We are not considering animals that are close kin, nor can they suffer or experience anything. Plants are not valuers with preferences that can be satisfied or frustrated. It seems odd to assert that plants need our sympathy, odd to ask that we should consider their point of view. They have no subjective life, only objective life.

Perhaps the questions are wrong, because they are coming out of the old paradigm. We are at a critical divide. That is why I earlier warned that environmental ethicists who seek only to extend a humanistic ethic to mammalian cousins will get lost. Seeing no moral landmarks, those ethicists may turn back to more familiar terrain. Afraid of the naturalistic fallacy, they will say that people should enjoy letting flowers live or that it is silly to cut drive-through sequoias, that it is aesthetically more excellent for humans to appreciate both for what they are. But these ethically conservative reasons really do not understand what biological conservation is in the deepest sense.

It takes ethical courage to go on, to move past a hedonistic, humanistic logic to a bio-logic. Pains, pleasures, and psychological experience will no further be useful categories, but — lest some think that from here on I as a philosopher become illogical and lose all ethical sense — let us orient ourselves by extending logical, propositional, cognitive, and normative categories into biology. Nothing matters to a tree, but much is vital to it.

An organism is a spontaneous, self-maintaining system, sustaining and reproducing itself, executing its program, making a way through the world, checking against performance by means of responsive capacities with which to measure success. It can reckon with vicissitudes, opportunities, and adversities that the world presents. Something more than physical causes, even when less than sentience, is operating within every organism. There is information superintending the causes; without it, the organism would collapse into a sand heap. This information is a modern equivalent of what Aristotle called formal and final causes; it gives the organism a telos, or end, a kind of (nonfelt) goal. Organisms have ends, although not always ends in view.

All this cargo is carried by the DNA, essentially a linguistic molecule. By a serial reading of the DNA, a polypeptide chain is synthesized, such that its sequential structure determines the bioform into which it will fold. Ever-lengthening chains are organized into genes, as ever-longer sentences are organized into paragraphs and chapters. Diverse proteins, lipids, carbohydrates, enzymes — all the life structures — are written into the genetic library. The DNA is thus a logical set, no less than a biological set, and is informed as well as formed. Organisms use a sort of symbolic logic, using these molecular shapes as symbols of life. The novel resourcefulness lies in the epistemic content conserved, developed, and thrown forward to make biological resources out of the physicochemical sources. This executive steering core is cybernetic — partly a special kind of cause-and-effect system and partly something more. It is partly a historical information system discovering and evaluating ends so as to map and make a way through the world, and partly a system of significance attached to operations, pursuits, and resources. In this sense, the genome is a set of conservation molecules.

The genetic set is really a propositional set — to choose a provocative term — recalling that the Latin *propositum* is an assertion, a set task, a theme, a plan, a proposal, a project, as well as a cognitive statement. From this, it is also a motivational set, unlike human books, because these life motifs are set to drive the movement from genotypic potential to phenotypic expression. Given a chance, these molecules seek organic self-expression. They thus proclaim a lifeway; and with this an organism, unlike an inert rock, claims the environment as source and sink, from which to abstract energy and materials and into which to excrete them. It takes advantage of its environment. Life thus arises out of earthen sources (as do rocks), but life (unlike rocks) turns back on its sources to make resources out of them. An acorn becomes an oak; the oak stands on its own.

So far we have only description. We begin to pass to value when we recognize that the genetic set is a normative set; it distinguishes between what is and what ought to be. This does not mean that the organism is a moral system, for there are no moral agents in nature; but the organism is an axiological, evaluative system. So the oak grows, reproduces, repairs its wounds, and resists death. The physical state that the organism seeks, idealized in its programmatic form, is a valued state. Value is present in this achievement. *Vital* seems a better word here than *biological.* We are dealing not simply with another individual defending its solitary life but with an individual having situated fitness in an ecosystem. Still, we want to affirm that the living individual, taken as a point-experience in the web of interconnected life, is per se an intrinsic value.

A life is defended for what it is in itself, without necessary further contributory reference, although, given the structure of all ecosystems, such lives necessarily do have further contributory reference. The organism has something it is conserving, something for which it is standing: its life. Though organisms must fit into their niche, they have their own standards. They promote their own realization, at the same time that they track an environment. They have a technique, a know-how. Every organism has a good of its kind; it defends its own kind as a good kind. In that sense, as soon as one knows what a giant sequoia tree is, one knows the biological identity that is sought and conserved.

There seems no reason why such own-standing normative organisms are not morally significant. A moral agent deciding his or her behavior ought to take account of the consequences for other evaluative systems. Within the community of moral agents, one has not merely to ask whether x is a normative system but also, because the norms are at personal option, to judge the norm. But within the biotic community, organisms are amoral normative systems, and there are no cases in which an organism seeks a good of its own that is morally reprehensible. The distinction between having a good of its kind and being a good kind vanishes, so far as any faulting of the organism is concerned. To this extent, everything with a good of its kind is a good kind and thereby has intrinsic value.

One might say that an organism is a bad organism if, during the course of pressing its normative expression, it upsets the ecosystem or causes widespread disease. Remember, though, that an organism cannot be a good kind without situated environmental fitness. By natural selection the kind of goods to which it is genetically programmed must mesh with its ecosystemic role. In spite of the ecosystem as a perpetual contest of goods in dialectic and exchange, it is difficult to say that any organism is a bad kind in this instrumental sense either. The misfits are extinct, or soon will be. In spontaneous nature any species that preys upon, parasitizes, competes with, or crowds another will be a bad kind from the narrow perspective of its victim or competitor.

But if we enlarge that perspective, we typically have difficulty in saying that any species is a bad kind overall in the ecosystem. An "enemy" may even be good for the "victimized" species, though harmful to individual members of it, as when predation keeps the deer herd healthy. Beyond this, the "bad kinds" typically play useful roles in population control, in symbiotic relationships, or in providing opportunities for other species. The *Chlamydia* microbe is a bad kind from the perspective of the bighorns, but when one thing dies, something else lives. After the pinkeye outbreak among the bighorns, the golden eagle population in Yellowstone flourished, preying on the bighorn carcasses. For the eagles, *Chlamydia* is a good kind instrumentally.

Some biologist-philosophers will say that even though an organism evolves to have a situated environmental fitness, not all such situations are good arrangements; some can be clumsy or bad. True, the vicissitudes of historical evolution do sometimes result in ecological webs that are suboptimal solutions, within the biologically limited possibilities and powers of interacting organisms. Still, such systems have been selected over millennia for functional stability, and at least the burden of proof is on a human evaluator to say why any natural kind is a bad kind and ought not to call forth admiring respect. Something may be a good kind intrinsically but a bad kind instrumentally in the system; such cases will be anomalous however, with selection pressures against them. These assertions about good kinds do not say that things are perfect kinds or that there can be no better ones, only that natural kinds are good kinds until proven otherwise.

In fact, what is almost invariably meant by a bad kind is an organism that is instrumentally bad when judged from the viewpoint of human interests, often with the further complication that human interests have disrupted natural systems. *Bad* as so used is an anthropocentric word; there is nothing at all biological or ecological about it, and so it has no force in evaluating objective nature, however much humanistic force it may sometimes have.

A vital ethic respects all life, not just animal pains and pleasures, much less just human preferences. The old signs in the Rawah Wilderness — "Please leave the flowers for others to enjoy" — were application signs using an old, ethically conservative, humanistic ethic. The new ones invite a change of reference frame — a wilder ethic that is more logical because it is more biological, a radical ethic that goes down to the roots of life, that really is conservative because it understands biological conservation at depths. What the injunction "Let the flowers live!" means is this: "Daisies, marsh marigolds, geraniums, and larkspurs are evaluative systems that conserve goods of their kind and, in the absence of evidence to the contrary, are good kinds. There are trails here by which you may enjoy these flowers. Is there any reason why your human interests should not also conserve these good kinds?" A drive-through sequoia causes no suffering; it is not cruel. But it is callous and insensitive to the wonder of life.

SPECIES

Sensitivity to the wonder of life, however, can sometimes make an environmental ethicist seem callous. On San Clemente Island, the U.S. Fish and Wildlife Service and the Natural Resource Office of the U.S. Navy planned to shoot two thousand feral goats to save three endangered plant species (*Malacothamnus clementinus, Castilleja grisea,* and *Delphinium kinkiense*), of which the surviving individuals numbered only a few dozen. After a protest, some goats were trapped and relocated. But trapping all of them was impossible, and many thousands were killed. In this instance, the survival of plant species was counted more than the lives of individual mammals; a few plants counted more than many thousands of goats.

Those who wish to restore rare species of big cats to the wild have asked about killing genetically inbred, inferior cats presently held in zoos, in order to make space available for the cats needed to reconstruct and maintain a population that is genetically more likely to survive upon release. All the Siberian tigers in zoos in North America are descendants of seven animals; if these tigers were replaced by others nearer to the wild type and with more genetic variability, the species might be saved in the wild. When we move to the level of species, sometimes we decide to kill individuals for the good of their kind.

Or we might now refuse to let nature take its course. The Yellowstone ethicists let the bison drown, in spite of its suffering; they let the blinded bighorns die. But in the spring of 1984 a sow grizzly and her three cubs walked across the ice of Yellowstone Lake to Frank Island, two miles from shore. They stayed several days to feast on two elk carcasses, and the ice bridge melted. Soon afterward, they were starving on an island too small to support them. This time the Yellowstone ethicists promptly rescued the grizzlies and released them on the mainland, in order to protect an endangered species. They were not rescuing individual bears so much as saving the species.

Coloradans have declined to build the Two Forks Dam to supply urban Denver with water. Building the dam would require destroying a canyon and altering the Platte River flow, with many negative environmental consequences, including further endangering the whooping crane and endangering a butterfly, the Pawnee montane skipper. Elsewhere in the state, water development threatens several fish species, including the humpback chub, which requires the turbulent spring runoff stopped by dams. Environmental ethics doubts whether the good of humans who wish more water for development, both for industry and for bluegrass lawns, warrants endangering species of cranes, butterflies, and fish.

A species exists; a species ought to exist. An environmental ethics must make these assertions and move from biology to ethics with care. Species exist only instantiated in individuals, yet they are as real as individual plants or animals. The assertion that there are specific forms of life historically maintained in their environments over time seems as certain as anything else we believe about the empirical world. At times biologists revise the theories and taxa with which they map these forms, but species are not so much like lines of latitude and longitude as like mountains and rivers, phenomena objectively there to be mapped. The edges of these natural kinds will sometimes be fuzzy, to some extent discretionary. One species will slide into another over evolutionary time. But it does not follow from the fact that speciation is sometimes in progress that species are merely made up and not found as evolutionary lines with identity in time as well as space.

A consideration of species is revealing and challenging because it offers a biologically based counterexample to the focus on individuals—typically sentient and usually persons—so characteristic in classical ethics. In an evolutionary ecosystem, it is not mere individuality that counts; the species is also significant because it is a dynamic life-form maintained over time. The individual represents (re-presents) a species in each new generation. It is a token of a type, and the type is more important than the token.

A species lacks moral agency, reflective self-awareness, sentience, or organic individuality. The older, conservative ethic will be tempted to say that specific-level processes cannot count morally. Duties must attach to singular lives, most evidently those with a self, or some analogue to self. In an individual organism, the organs report to a center; the good of a whole is defended. The members of a species report to no center. A species has no self. It is not a bounded singular. There is no analogue to the nervous hookups or circulatory flows that characterize the organism.

But singularity, centeredness, selfhood, and individuality are not the only processes to which duty attaches. A more radically conservative ethic knows that having a biological identity reasserted genetically over time is as true of the species as of the individual. Identity need not attach solely to the centered organism; it can persist as a discrete pattern over time. From this way of thinking, it follows that the life the individual has is something passing through the individual as much as something it intrinsically possesses. The individual is subordinate to the species, not the other way around. The genetic set, in which is coded the telos, is as evidently the property of the species as of the individual through which it passes. A consideration of species strains any ethic fixed on individual organisms, much less on sentience or persons. But the result can be biologically sounder, though it revises what was formerly thought logically permissible or ethically binding. When ethics is informed by this kind of biology, it is appropriate to attach duty dynamically to the specific form of life.

The species line is the vital living system, the whole, of which individual organisms are the essential parts. The species too has its integrity, its individuality, its right to life (if we must use the rhetoric of rights); and it is more important to protect this vitality than to protect individual integrity. The right to life, biologically speaking, is an adaptive fit that is right for life, that survives over millennia. This idea generates at least a presumption that species in a niche are good right where they are, and therefore that it is right for humans to let them be, to let them evolve.

Processes of value that we earlier found in an organic individual reappear at the specific level: defending a particular form of life, pursuing a pathway through the world, resisting death (extinction), regenerating, maintaining a normative identity over time, expressing creative resilience by discovering survival skills. It is as logical to say that the individual is the species' way of propagating itself as to say that the embryo or egg is the individual's way of propagating itself. The dignity resides in the dynamic form; the individual inherits this form, exemplifies it, and passes it on. If, at the specific level, these processes are just as evident, or even more so, what prevents duties from arising at that level? The appropriate survival unit is the appropriate level of moral concern.

A shutdown of the life stream is the most destructive event possible. The wrong that humans are doing, or allowing to happen through carelessness, is stopping the historical vitality of life, the flow of natural kinds. Every extinction is an incremental decay in this stopping of life, no small thing. Every extinction is a kind of superkilling. It kills forms (species) beyond individuals. It kills essences beyond existences, the soul as well as the body. It kills collectively, not just distributively. It kills birth as well as death. Afterward nothing of that kind either lives or dies.

Ought species x to exist? is a distributive increment in the collective question, ought life on Earth to exist? Life on Earth cannot exist without its individuals, but a lost individual is always reproducible; a lost species is never reproducible. The answer to the species question is not always the same as the answer to the collective question, but because life on Earth is an aggregate of many species, the two are sufficiently related that the burden of proof lies with those who wish deliberately to extinguish a species and simultaneously to care for life on Earth.

One form of life has never endangered so many others. Never before has this level of question — superkilling by a superkiller — been deliberately faced. Humans have more understanding than ever of the natural world they inhabit and of the speciating processes, more predictive power to foresee the intended and unintended results of their actions, and more power to reverse the undesirable consequences. The duties that such power and vision generate no longer attach simply to individuals or persons but are emerging duties to specific forms of life. What is ethically callous is the maelstrom of killing and insensitivity to forms of life and the sources producing them. What is required is principled responsibility to the biospheric Earth.

Human activities seem misfit in the system. Although humans are maximizing their own species interests, and in this respect behaving as does each of the other species, they do not have any adaptive fitness. They are not really fitting into the evolutionary processes of ongoing biological conservation and elaboration. Their cultures are not really dynamically stable in their ecosystems. Such behavior is therefore not right. Yet humanistic ethical systems limp when they try to prescribe right conduct here. They seem misfits in the roles most recently demanded of them.

If, in this world of uncertain moral convictions, it makes any sense to assert that one ought not to kill individuals without justification, it makes more sense to assert that one ought not to superkill the species without superjustification. Several billion years' worth of creative toil, several million species of teeming life, have been handed over to the care of this late-coming species in which mind has flowered and morals have emerged. Ought not this sole moral species do something less self-interested than count all the produce of an evolutionary ecosystem as nothing but human resources? Such an attitude hardly seems biologically informed, much less ethically adequate. It is too provincial for intelligent humanity. Life on Earth is a many-splendored thing; extinction dims its luster. An ethics of respect for life is urgent at the level of species.

ECOSYSTEMS

A species is what it is where it is. No environmental ethics has found its way on Earth until it finds an ethic for the biotic communities in which all destinies are entwined. "A thing is right," urged Aldo Leopold (1968 [1949]), "when it tends to preserve the integrity, stability, and beauty of the biotic community. It is wrong when it tends otherwise." Again, we have two parts to the ethic: first, that ecosystems exist, both in the wild and in support of culture; second, that ecosystems ought to exist, both for what they are in themselves and as modified by culture. Again, we must move with care from the biological assertions to the ethical assertions.

Giant forest fires raged over Yellowstone National Park in the summer of 1988, consuming nearly a million acres despite the efforts of a thousand fire fighters. By far the largest ever known in the park, the fires seemed a disaster. But the Yellowstone land ethic enjoined: "Let nature take its course; let it burn." So the fires were not fought at first, but in midsummer, national authorities overrode that policy and ordered the fires put out. Even then, weeks later, fires continued to burn, partly because they were too big to control but partly too because Yellowstone personnel did not really want the fires put out. Despite the evident destruction of trees, shrubs, and wildlife, they believe that fires are a good thing—even when the elk and bison leave the park in search of food and are shot by hunters. Fires reset succession, release nutrients, recycle materials, and renew the biotic community. (Nearby, in the Teton wilderness, a storm blew down fifteen thousand acres of trees, and some people proposed that the area be declassified from wilderness to allow commercial salvage of the timber. But a similar environmental ethic said, "No, let it rot.")

Aspen are important in the Yellowstone ecosystem. Although some aspen stands are climax and self-renewing, many are seral and give way to conifers. Aspen groves support many birds and much wildlife, especially beavers, whose activities maintain the riparian zones. Aspen are rejuvenated after fires, and the Yellowstone land ethic wants the aspen for their critical role in the biotic community. Elk browse the young aspen stems. To a degree this is a good thing, because it provides the elk with critical nitrogen, but in excess it is a bad thing. The elk have no predators, because the wolves are gone, and as a result the elk overpopulate. Excess elk also destroy the willows, and that destruction in turn destroys the beavers. So, in addition to letting fires burn, rejuvenating the aspen might require park managers to cull hundreds of elk—for the sake of a healthy ecosystem.

The Yellowstone ethic wishes to restore wolves to the greater Yellowstone ecosystem. At the level of species, this change is desired because of what the wolf is in itself, but it is also desired because the greater Yellowstone ecosystem does not have its full integrity, stability, and beauty without this majestic animal at the top of the trophic pyramid. Restoring the wolf as a top predator would mean suffering and death for many elk, but that would be a good thing for the aspen and willows, the beavers, and the riparian habitat and would have mixed benefits for the bighorns and mule deer (the overpopulating elk consume their food, but the sheep and deer would also be consumed by the wolves). Restoration of wolves would be done over the protests of ranchers who worry about wolves eating their cattle; many of them also believe that the wolf is a bloodthirsty killer, a bad kind. Nevertheless, the Yellowstone ethic demands wolves, as it does fires, in appropriate respect for life in its ecosystem.

Letting nature take its ecosystemic course is why the Yellowstone ethic forbade rescuing the drowning bison but required rescuing the sow grizzly and her cubs, the latter case to insure that the big predators remain. After the bison drowned, coyotes, foxes, magpies, and ravens fed on the carcass. Later, even a grizzly bear fed on it. All this is a good thing because the system cycles on. On that account, rescuing the whales trapped in the winter ice seems less of a good thing, when we note that rescuers had to drive away polar bears that attempted to eat the dying whales.

Classical, humanistic ethics finds ecosystems to be unfamiliar territory. It is difficult to get the biology right and, superimposed on the biology, to get the ethics right. Fortunately, it is often evident that human welfare depends on ecosystemic support, and in this sense all our legislation about clean air, clean water, soil conservation, national and state forest policies, pollution controls, renewable resources, and so forth is concerned about ecosystem-level processes. Furthermore, humans find much of value in preserving wild ecosystems, and our wilderness and park system is impressive.

Still, a comprehensive environmental ethics needs the best, naturalistic reasons, as well as the good, humanistic ones, for respecting ecosystems. Ecosystems generate and support life, keep selection pressures high, enrich situated fitness, and allow congruent kinds to evolve in their places with sufficient containment. The ecologist finds that ecosystems are objectively satisfactory communities in the sense that organismic needs are sufficiently met for species to survive and flourish, and the critical ethicist finds (in a subjective judgment matching the objective process) that such ecosystems are satisfactory communities to which to attach duty. Our concern must be for the fundamental unit of survival.

An ecosystem, the conservative ethicist will say, is too low a level of organization to be respected intrinsically. Ecosystems can seem little more than random, statistical processes. A forest can seem a loose collection of externally related parts, the collection of fauna and flora a jumble, hardly a community. The plants and animals within an ecosystem have needs, but their interplay can seem simply a matter of distribution and abundance, birth rates and death rates, population densities, parasitism and predation, dispersion, checks and balances, and stochastic process. Much is not organic at all (rain, groundwater, rocks, soil particles, air), and some organic material is dead and decaying debris (fallen trees, scat, humus). These things have no organized needs. There is only catch-as-catch-can scrimmage for nutrients and energy, not really enough of an integrated process to call the whole a community.

Unlike higher animals, ecosystems have no experiences; they do not and cannot care. Unlike plants, an ecosystem has no organized center, no genome. It does not defend itself against injury or death. Unlike a species, there is no ongoing telos, no biological identity reinstantiated over time. The organismic parts are more complex than the community whole. More troublesome still, an ecosystem can seem a jungle where the fittest survive, a place of contest and conflict, beside which the organism is a model of cooperation. In animals the heart, liver, muscles, and brain are tightly integrated, as are the leaves, cambium, and roots in plants. But the so-called ecosystem community is pushing and shoving between rivals, each aggrandizing itself, or else seems to be all indifference and haphazard juxtaposition — nothing to call forth our admiration.

Environmental ethics must break through the boundary posted by disoriented ontological conservatives, who hold that only organisms are real, actually existing as entities, whereas ecosystems are nominal — just interacting individuals. Oak trees are real, but forests are nothing but collections of trees. But any level is real if it shapes behavior on the level below it. Thus the cell is real because that pattern shapes the behavior of amino acids; the organism, because that pattern coordinates the behavior of hearts and lungs. The biotic community is real because the niche shapes the morphology of the oak trees within it. Being real at the level of community requires only an organization that shapes the behavior of its members.

The challenge is to find a clear model of community and to discover an ethics for it: better biology for better ethics. Even before the rise of ecology, biologists began to conclude that the combative survival of the fittest distorts the truth. The more perceptive model is coaction in adapted fit. Predator and prey, parasite and host, grazer and grazed, are contending forces in dynamic process in which the well-being of each is bound up with the other — coordinated as much as heart and liver are coordinated organically. The ecosystem supplies the coordinates through which each organism moves, outside which the species cannot really be located.

The community connections are looser than the organism's internal interconnections but are not less significant. Admiring organic unity in organisms and stumbling over environmental looseness is like valuing mountains and despising valleys. The matrix that the organism requires to survive is the open, pluralistic ecological system. Internal complexity — heart, liver, muscles, brain — arises as a way of dealing with a complex, tricky environment. The skin-out processes are not just the support; they are the subtle source of the skin-in processes. In the complete picture, the outside is as vital as the inside. Had there been either simplicity or lockstep concentrated unity in the environment, no organismic unity could have evolved. Nor would it remain. There would be less elegance in life.

To look at one level for what is appropriate at another makes a mistake in categories. One should not look for a single center or program in ecosystems, much less for subjective experiences. Instead, one should look for a matrix, for interconnections between centers (individual plants and animals, dynamic lines of speciation), for creative stimulus and open-ended potential. Everything will be connected to many other things, sometimes by obligate associations but more often by partial and pliable dependencies, and, among other things, there will be no significant interactions. There will be functions in a communal sense: shunts and crisscrossing pathways, cybernetic subsystems and feedback loops. An order arises spontaneously and systematically when many self-concerned units jostle and seek to fulfill their own programs, each doing its own thing and forced into informed interaction.

An ecosystem is a productive, projective system. Organisms defend only their selves, with individuals defending their continuing survival and with species increasing the numbers of kinds. But the evolutionary ecosystem spins a bigger story, limiting each kind, locking it into the welfare of others, promoting new arrivals, increasing kinds and the integration of kinds. Species increase their kind, but ecosystems increase kinds, superposing the latter increase onto the former. Ecosystems are selective systems, as surely as organisms are selective systems. The natural selection comes out of the system and is imposed on the individual. The individual is programmed to make more of its kind, but more is going on systemically than that; the system is making more kinds.

Communal processes—the competition between organisms, statistically probable interactions, plant and animal successions, speciation over historical time—generate an ever-richer community. Hence the evolutionary toil, elaborating and diversifying the biota, that once began with no species and results today in five million species, increasing over time the quality of lives in the upper rungs of the trophic pyramids. One-celled organisms evolved into many-celled, highly integrated organisms. Photosynthesis evolved and came to support locomotion—swimming, walking, running, flight. Stimulus-response mechanisms became complex instinctive acts. Warm-blooded animals followed cold-blooded ones. Complex nervous systems, conditioned behavior, and learning emerged. Sentience appeared—sight, hearing, smell, taste, pleasure, pain. Brains coupled with hands. Consciousness and self-consciousness arose. Culture was superposed on nature.

These developments do not take place in all ecosystems or at every level. Microbes, plants, and lower animals remain, good for their kinds and, serving continuing roles, good for other kinds. The understories remain occupied. As a result, the quantity of life and its diverse qualities continue—from protozoans to primates to people. There is a push-up, lock-up ratchet effect that conserves the upstrokes and the outreaches. The later we go in time, the more accelerated are the forms at the top of the trophic pyramids, the more elaborated are the multiple trophic pyramids of Earth. There are upward arrows over evolutionary time.

The system is a game with loaded dice, but the loading is a pro-life tendency, not mere stochastic process. Though there is no Nature in the singular, the system has a nature, a loading that pluralizes, putting natures into diverse kinds: $nature_1$, $nature_2$, $nature_3 \ldots nature_n$. It does so using random elements (in both organisms and communities), but this is a secret of its fertility, producing steadily intensified interdependencies and options. An ecosystem has no head, but it heads toward species diversification, support, and richness. Though not a superorganism, it is a kind of vital field.

Instrumental value uses something as a means to an end; intrinsic value is worthwhile in itself. No warbler eats insects to become food for a falcon; the warbler defends its own life as an end in itself and makes more warblers as it can. A life is defended intrinsically, without further contributory reference. But neither of these traditional terms is satisfactory at the level of the ecosystem. Though it has value *in* itself, the system does not have any value *for* itself. Though it is a value producer, it is not a value owner. We are no longer confronting instrumental value, as though the system were of value instrumentally as a fountain of life. Nor is the question one of intrinsic value, as though the system defended some unified form of life for itself. We have reached something for which we need a third term: systemic value. Duties arise in encounters with the system that projects and protects these member components in biotic community.

Ethical conservatives, in the humanistic sense, will say that ecosystems are of value only because they contribute to human experiences. But that mistakes the last chapter for the whole story, one fruit for the whole plant. Humans count enough to have the right to flourish in ecosystems, but not so much that they have the right to degrade or shut down ecosystems, not at least without a burden of proof that there is an overriding cultural gain. Those who have traveled partway into environmental ethics will say that ecosystems are of value because they contribute to animal experiences or to organismic life. But the really conservative, radical view sees that the stability, integrity, and beauty of biotic communities are what are most fundamentally to be conserved. In a comprehensive ethics of respect for life, we ought to set ethics at the level of ecosystems alongside classical, humanistic ethics.

VALUE THEORY

In practice the ultimate challenge of environmental ethics is the conservation of life on Earth. In principle the ultimate challenge is a value theory profound enough to support that ethics. In nature there is negentropic construction in dialectic with entropic teardown, a process for which we hardly yet have an adequate scientific theory, much less a valuational theory. Yet this is nature's most striking feature, one that ultimately must be valued and of value. In one sense, nature is indifferent to mountains, rivers, fauna, flora, forests, and grasslands. But in another sense, nature has bent toward making and remaking these projects, millions of kinds, for several billion years.

These performances are worth noticing, are remarkable and memorable—and not just because of their tendencies to produce something else; certainly not merely because of their tendency to produce this noticing in certain recent subjects, our human selves. These events are loci of value as products of systemic nature in its formative processes. The splendors of Earth do not simply lie in their roles as human resources, supports of culture, or stimulators of experience. The most plausible account will find some programmatic evolution toward value, and not because it ignores Darwin but because it heeds his principle of natural selection and deploys it into a selection exploring new niches and elaborating kinds, even a selection upslope toward higher values, at least along some trends within some ecosystems. How do we humans come to be charged up with values, if there was and is nothing in nature charging us up so? A systematic environmental ethics does not wish to believe in the special creation of values or in their dumbfounding epigenesis. Let them evolve. Let nature carry value.

The notion that nature is a value carrier is ambiguous. Much depends on a thing's being more or less structurally congenial for the carriage. We value a thing and discover that we are under the sway of its valence, inducing our behavior. It has among its strengths (Latin: *valeo,* "be strong") this capacity to carry value. This potential cannot always be of the empty sort that a glass has for carrying water. It is often pregnant fullness. Some of the values that nature carries are up to us, our assignment. But fundamentally there are powers in nature that move to us and through us.

No value exists without an evaluator. So runs a well-entrenched dogma. Humans clearly evaluate their world; sentient animals may also. But plants cannot evaluate their environment; they have no options and make no choices. A fortiori, species and ecosystems, Earth and Nature, cannot be bona fide evaluators. One can always hang on to the assertion that value, like a tickle or remorse, must be felt to be there. Its *esse* is *percipi*. To be, it must be perceived. Nonsensed value is nonsense. There are no thoughts without a thinker, no percepts without a perceiver, no deeds without a doer, no targets without an aimer.

Such resolute subjectivists cannot be defeated by argument, although they can be driven toward analyticity. That theirs is a retreat to definition is difficult to expose, because they seem to cling so closely to inner experience. They are reporting, on this hand, how values always excite us. They are giving, on that hand, a stipulative definition. That is how they choose to use the word *value.*

If value arrives only with consciousness, experiences in which humans find value have to be dealt with as appearances of various sorts. The value has to be relocated in the valuing subject's creativity as a person meets a valueless world, or even a valuable one—one able to be valued but one that before the human bringing of valuableness contains only possibility and not any actual value. Value can only be extrinsic to nature, never intrinsic to it.

But the valuing subject in an otherwise valueless world is an insufficient premise for the experienced conclusions of those who respect all life. Conversion to a biological view seems truer to world experience and more logically compelling. Something from a world beyond the human mind, beyond human experience, is received into our mind, our experience, and the value of that something does not always arise with our evaluation of it. Here the order of knowing reverses, and also enhances the order of being. This too is a perspective but is ecologically better-informed. Science has been steadily showing how the consequents (life, mind) are built on their precedents (energy, matter), however much they overleap them. Life and mind appear where they did not before exist, and with them levels of value emerge that did not before exist. But that gives no reason to say that all value is an irreducible emergent at the human (or upper-animal) level. A comprehensive environmental ethics reallocates value across the whole continuum. Value increases in the emergent climax but is continuously present in the composing precedents. The system is value-able, able to produce value. Human evaluators are among its products.

Some value depends on subjectivity, yet all value is generated within the geosystemic and ecosystemic pyramid. Systemically, value fades from subjective to objective value but also fans out from the individual to its role and matrix. Things do not have their separate natures merely in and for themselves, but they face outward and co-fit into broader natures. Value-in-itself is smeared out to become value-in-togetherness. Value seeps out into the system, and we lose our capacity to identify the individual as the sole locus of value.

Intrinsic value, the value of an individual for what it is in itself, becomes problematic in a holistic web. True, the system produces such values more and more with its evolution of individuality and freedom. Yet to decouple this value from the biotic, communal system is to make value too internal and elementary; this decoupling forgets relatedness and externality. Every intrinsic value has leading and trailing *and*'s. Such value is coupled with value from which it comes and toward which it moves. Adapted fitness makes individualistic value too system-independent. Intrinsic value is a part in a whole and is not to be fragmented by valuing it in isolation.

Everything is good in a role, in a whole, although we can speak of objective intrinsic goodness wherever a point-event — a trillium, for example — defends a good (its life) in itself. We can speak of subjective intrinsic goodness when such an event registers as a point-experience, at which point humans pronounce both their experience and what it is to be good without need to enlarge their focus. Neither the trilliums nor the human judges of it require for their respective valuings any further contributory reference.

When eaten by foragers or in death resorbed into humus, the trillium has its value destroyed, transformed into instrumentality. The system is a value transformer where form and being, process and reality, fact and value, are inseparably joined. Intrinsic and instrumental values shuttle back and forth, parts-in-wholes and wholes-in-parts, local details of value embedded in global structures, gems in their settings, and their setting-situation a corporation where value cannot stand alone. Every good is in community.

In environmental ethics one's beliefs about nature, which are based upon but exceed science, have everything to do with beliefs about duty. The way the world is informs the way it ought to be. We always shape our values in significant measure in accord with our notion of the kind of universe that we live in, and this process drives our sense of duty. Our model of reality implies a model of conduct. Differing models sometimes imply similar conduct, but often they do not. A model in which nature has no value apart from human preferences will imply different conduct from one in which nature projects fundamental values, some objective and others that further require human subjectivity superimposed on objective nature.

This evaluation is not scientific description; hence it is not ecology per se but metaecology. No amount of research can verify that, environmentally, the right is the optimum biotic community. Yet ecological description generates this valuing of nature, endorsing the systemic rightness. The transition from *is* to *good* and thence to *ought* occurs here; we leave science to enter the domain of evaluation, from which an ethics follows.

What is ethically puzzling and exciting is that an *ought* is not so much derived from an *is* as discovered simultaneously with it. As we progress from descriptions of fauna and flora, of cycles and pyramids, of autotrophs coordinated with heterotrophs, of stability and dynamism, on to intricacy, planetary opulence and interdependence, unity and harmony with oppositions in counterpoint and synthesis, organisms evolved within and satisfactorily fitting their communities, and we arrive at length at beauty and goodness, we find that it is difficult to say where the natural facts leave off and where the natural values appear. For some people at least, the sharp *is-ought* dichotomy is gone; the values seem to be there as soon as the facts are fully in, and both values and facts seem to be alike properties of the system.

There is something overspecialized about an ethic, held by the dominant class of *Homo sapiens,* that regards the welfare of only one of several million species as an object and beneficiary of duty. If the remedy requires a paradigm change about the sorts of things to which duty can attach, so much the worse for those humanistic ethics no longer functioning in, or suited to, their changing environment. The anthropocentrism associated with them was fiction anyway. There is something Newtonian, not yet Einsteinian, besides something morally naive, about living in a reference frame in which one species takes itself as absolute and values everything else relative to its utility. If true to its specific epithet, which means wise, ought not *Homo sapiens* value this host of life as something that lays on us a claim to care for life in its own right?

Only the human species contains moral agents, but perhaps conscience on such an Earth ought not to be used to exempt every other form of life from consideration, with the resulting paradox that the sole moral species acts only in its collective self-interest toward all the rest. Is not the ultimate philosophical task the discovery of a whole great ethic that knows the human place under the sun?

DISCUSSION TOPICS

1. What reasons does Rolston provide for his assertion that nature has value independent of human consciousness? Is his view based on a claim of intuitive truth? Explain your answer.

2. Rolston maintains that eating meat is morally acceptable because it concerns diet, which is an affair of nature, not culture. Do you agree with him? Explain your reasoning.

3. Does Rolston's view deprive the individual of importance? Explain why or why not.

4. Explain Rolston's view that species are more important than individuals. Do you agree with his argument? Why or why not?

5. Rolston dismisses the naturalistic fallacy as itself a fallacy. What ramifications does his

view have for the relationship between science and ethics?

6. Describe the types of value discussed by Rolston and explain how they form a continuum. What is your evaluation of Rolston's perspective on natural value?

7. Rolston states that there are no "bad" organisms or species, because natural selection has bestowed "situated environmental fitness" on each organism and species. How might Rolston's view be used to evaluate genetically engineered plants and animals?

8. Do you agree with Rolston that human beings "do not have any adaptive fitness"? Explain your answer.

READING 9

Environmental Ethics and the Social Construction of Nature

Anna L. Peterson

Anna L. Peterson is University of Florida Research Foundation Professor and an affiliate of both the Center for Latin American Studies and the College of Natural Resources and the Environment. One of her major interests is the mutual shaping of religion and politics in Latin America. She has published a number of articles on social and environmental ethics, as well as Being Human: Ethics, Environment, and Our Place in the World *(2001).*

In this selection she discusses several versions of the claim that nature is socially constructed, emphasizing that such claims highlight the diversity of ways of viewing and living in nature. She agrees with Rolston that environmental ethics requires some concept of intrinsic value in the nonhuman world but affirms that we can have no unmediated apprehension of nature.

Nature can be viewed as socially constructed in two distinct, though not contradictory, ways. First, different individuals, times, and societies construct particular versions of nature insofar as they interpret it in different ways in and through cultural categories and values. Many scholars insist that this type of construction is universal and unavoidable: we cannot experience nature except through the lens of meanings assigned to it by particular cultures and periods. These meanings affect attitudes not only toward nature but toward humans, communities, politics, and much more. In Kate Soper's words, "Nature carries an immensely complex and contradictory symbolic load."[1] Or, as Raymond Williams noted years earlier, "the idea of nature contains, though often unnoticed, an extraordinary amount of human history."[2] Soper and Williams are making the important, though relatively modest, claim that ideas about nature are historically and culturally determined. There is no single, essential "nature" that all individuals in all places and times recognize as such or can access outside the mediations of human culture.

This argument builds on long-standing debates in Western philosophy about the social meaning and shaping of "reality." This discussion has roots in William of Ockham's nominalism, which highlights the lack of an intrinsic link between words and the objects or qualities to which they refer. What we call a "book" (or a *libro* or a *Buch*) is only such because a group of people has agreed to call it that. The same holds for natural objects such as trees and rivers: different cultures assign not only different words, but different meanings and valuations to these objects. For (a timeworn) example, the multiplicity of Eskimo words for snow suggests its centrality in that culture, while English covers the frozen white stuff quite well with one or at most a few terms, and many cultures, no doubt, find no need to name it at all. Nominalism, insofar as it makes clear the disjuncture between things and the terms we use to describe them, provides the crucial insight for theories of the social construction of nature (or anything else): there is no intrinsic, universal quality that is captured in the terms we use, but rather those terms are conventions of particular cultures and times, loaded with, and intelligible because of, the meanings and values of those cultures.

This basic insight has been elaborated and illustrated in contemporary ethnographic work on the different meanings given to "nature" in different cultures today. Extensive documentation emphasizes that modern Western notions about "nature" (which

are themselves complex and diverse) often make no sense outside the cultural contexts in which they arose. Philippe Descola identifies three main ways of "constructing" nature: totemism, in which nonhumans are treated as signs; animism, in which they are treated as the terms of a relation; and naturalism, which sees nature as an autonomous domain, essentially "other" to human culture.[3] The latter is clearly the dominant "construction" of nature in modern Western cultures. Equally clearly, it is not the only way to construct it. As Tim Ingold points out, non-Western and especially hunter-gatherer cultures "systematically reject the ontological dualism of that tradition of thought and science which—as a kind of shorthand—we call 'Western,' and of which the dichotomy between nature and culture is the prototypical instance."[4]. . .

These diverse ways of constructing nature might more accurately be described as ways of construing it. What is "constructed" in this sense is not the physical objects themselves—not the trees or animals or rivers—but their identities and worth in a particular context. In a second sense, however, nature is literally, physically constructed by human society. According to this view, not only do cultural concepts mediate our experience of it, but most of what we refer to as "nature," from city parks to rain forests, has in fact been shaped by human actions. Thus, very little of the world today remains "natural" if that means free of human intervention. Such intervention includes not only the obviously inhabited areas, but also many places commonly viewed as wilderness. . . .

This second understanding of the social construction of nature also carries important implications for ethics, environmental and other. First, acknowledging the human shaping of "wild" areas such as the Americas prior to European settlement or tropical forests today challenges the erasure of native peoples, whose "invisibility," evidenced by the apparent absence of marks of their habitation, helped (and helps) justify exploitation of the lands they occupied. (This erasure, of course, was effected by a European perspective that viewed indigenous peoples as part of a less than human nature.) Further, awareness of human impacts on the environment . . . is the first step to critical analysis of those impacts and their ethical implications. It is important for environmental ethicists, ecologists, and activists to know, for example, how global climate change is affecting particular ecosystems, or, more positively, if the careful work of generations of indigenous inhabitants has helped nurture the extraordinary diversity in a tropical forest.[5] Only with such knowledge can we reflect on our responsibilities in regard to what we call "nature" and its human and nonhuman residents. Finally, the recognition that even "wild" areas have often been inhabited by humans can inform an evaluation of the varying environmental impacts of different forms of life: from those that remain invisible to outsiders, such as the hunting, gathering, agriculture, and forestry practices by pre-Columbian peoples in much of North America, to those with obvious, and undeniably negative, consequences for both humans and nonhumans, like the paving, clear-cutting, and burning of modern industrial societies. People have lived in most parts of the world and have always affected the places they live, but the effects vary widely in environmental and human cost. This knowledge can help environmentalists avoid a blanket condemnation of all human practices and point to precedents for more or less positive ways of acting in nature. . . .

ETHICAL DANGERS AND POSSIBILITIES

The danger in social constructionism arises when it emphasizes not the mutual shaping of culture and nature, but a one-sided "invention" of nature by culture. In such a view, the natural, as that which is not humanly created, does not in fact exist, or it exists, paradoxically, only as a human construct. Expressing this view, Peter Dwyer argues that "in the domain of human affairs culture should be taken as prior, nature as emergent." The idea of "wilderness," Dwyer continues, is "no more than an attempt to represent an imaginary place as a concrete symbol. 'Nature' as Westerners know it is an invention, an artefact.[6] Along similar lines, Robert Harrison claims that culture is not an epiphenomenon of nature but is in an important sense more real than nature: "human beings, unlike other living species, live not in nature but in their relation to nature. Even the belief that we are part of nature is a mode of relating to it."[7] In this perspective, humans are first,

foremost, and perhaps only products of culture. We live in culture, which includes our ideas about nature, and there is no nature apart from those ideas. . . .

One danger of strong versions of social constructionism in regard to nature [is the implication that] if there is no "real" nature, if all nature is constituted by human interpretation or intervention, then we have no grounds on which to evaluate one environment as better or worse or to resist some forms of intervention and support others. This is, perhaps, a postmodern version of the old ethical dilemma of relativism. In its mildest form, it contends that since all interpretations of nature are relative, it is difficult, perhaps impossible, to judge among them. If nature means different things to different people, we cannot know who is behaving responsibly toward nature. Thus, James Proctor, in a discussion of the struggle over ancient forests in the Pacific Northwest, writes, "It could be that there exist an infinite possible number of environmentalisms, each with its own nature to save. If so, how are we to choose among them?"[8] The forests that some groups are working to protect "is as much a reflection of their own particular view of nature as it is some primeval ecosystem under siege by logging. Their ethic, their passionate sense of right and wrong, is only one of many possible ethics."[9] Proctor himself makes some qualitative distinctions among these ethics, but he points to the possibility, realized by others, of simply casting all the alternatives into a single heap, with no ultimately justifiable way of judging among them.

More pernicious, perhaps, than relativizing ethics or interpretations is the relativizing of practices. The latter can lead to an erasure of differences among ways of intervening in nature. William Cronon, for example, contends that wilderness "is quite profoundly a human creation" and "a product of civilization, and could hardly be contaminated by the very stuff of which it is made."[10] Because those areas we call natural or wild are shaped by human intervention, Cronon implies, anything goes. Because humans have already intervened, in this perspective, no human interference or practice can harm or "contaminate" wilderness. This view, however, ignores the crucial insight of a more restrained approach to the social construction of nature, which points precisely to the very significant differences among ways that people not only interpret, but also live in their environments. It would recognize, for example, that the hunter-gatherer transplanting native fruit trees in one part of the Amazon and the logger clear-cutting another part of the same forest are both intervening in nature, constructing a certain vision and reality of it. Guided by these constructionist insights, environmental ethics must acknowledge that neither of these human interventions in nature is completely "innocent." It must go on, further, to evaluate such interventions, to provide ethical guidelines for understanding the actions themselves and their consequences and differentiating between them. Instead of taking these steps, however, Cronon asks (rhetorically?) how we can accept one and not the other. . . .

The erasure of difference in which some social constructionists engage depends in part on their ability to set up straw men against whom they can argue. The preferred target is environmentalists, who are usually portrayed as naively or misanthropically trying to remove all human traces from nature and return to some pristine, essential wilderness. . . .

A favorite claim is that the environmentalists and others who argue for the preservation of wilderness areas live in isolation from nature. Cronon, for example, writes that "Only people whose relationship to the land was already alienated could hold up wilderness as a model for human life in nature. . . ."[11] (It is worth pointing out the incoherence of this argument in light of Cronon's own belief that there is no correct or essential way of relating to nature. How can any other way thus be "alienated"?) Environmentalists, Cronon asserts, are scornful or even hostile toward people who make their living from the land. The environmentalists want to preserve "wild" nature at the cost of both human well-being and accurate understandings of real human needs and their ecological impact. Similarly, Richard White claims that "Most environmentalists disdain and distrust those who most obviously work in nature,"[12] while he, on the other hand, "cannot see [his] labor as separate from the mountains, and [he knows] that [his] labor is not truly disembodied."[13] Along the same lines, Budiansky lauds the knowledge of hunters and farmers, "the few . . . whose daily work still brings them into contact with ani-

mals."[14] Those who work on the land and/or with nonhuman animals, these authors suggest, have a more legitimate right to make descriptive or prescriptive statements about the nonhuman world than do environmentalists or animal rights activists, who presumably spend their days in offices attacking those "in the field" who understand the inevitability — and thus, presumably, the benevolence — of human intervention in nature. . . .

Another common target of social constructionists is the supposed misanthropy of environmentalists, particularly those concerned with areas inhabited by indigenous groups in such places as Brazil. Thus, Cronon contends that rain forest activists in the U.S. and Europe want to protect the forests from the people who live there,[15] and Candace Slater writes that "It troubled me that many of my students, friends, and neighbors did not seem aware of anything beyond The Rain Forest or particularly interested in how environmental questions impinged not just on trees and animals but on countless human lives.[16] Like Cronon, Slater assumes that concern for the environment precludes any concern for humans, as a result of the environmentalists' false vision of nature as that which is apart from the human. This critique fails to acknowledge the countervailing evidence that many environmental activists, in groups ranging from the mainstream Nature Conservancy to the more radical Rainforest Action Network, have joined with native groups in the U.S., Latin America, and elsewhere in order to preserve both the wildlife and the cultures that inhabit threatened ecosystems. . . .

Slater's comments also imply that "trees and animals" inevitably matter less than human interests. This is a common underlying theme in many social constructionist critiques of environmentalists' ideas about nature. In the end, it is not just the supposed naiveté of the idea of a nature without humans that bothers the critics, but the idea that nature — anything — could have importance apart from human inhabitation or discourse. . . .

Some approaches to the social construction of nature, then, do not go far enough. In the end, they challenge only part of the dominant perspective that they set out to deconstruct. They attack some elements of Western culture — mainly assumptions of an intrinsic tie between ideas (or words) and reality — but take for granted other, more damaging assumptions. The multiplicity of perspectives and values upon which social constructionism insists ought to lead to serious consideration of alternative world views, not just as evidence of "diversity," but as more constructive or appropriate ways of seeing humans and their place in nature. This world view, in turn, might encourage critics to question not only the notion that there is a pristine nature "out there," but also other beliefs about nature, equally embedded in our culture and probably much more dangerous than romanticized visions of Yosemite or Yellowstone, such as the ideas that some essential quality (reason? naming? tool use?) separates humans absolutely from all other species or that nature is passive and other species are incapable of active intervention in their own environments.

Social constructionist arguments would be more valuable for environmental ethics if they considered alternative world views as sources not just of multiplicity but of actual knowledge about the world. Then we might see some indigenous cultures' identification of other animals as "persons" not just as proof that human culture is endlessly varied but as equally, or even more, accurate understandings of those animals. For example, in the Amazon, the Huaorani people use the same term for woolly monkey and human (Huaorani) social groups, not simply because they have "invented" a likeness, but because they have observed real similarities, not present in other animals.[17] The Huaorani can perceive (and not merely "construct") such similarities because they see other animals not just as ciphers on the opposite side of an unbridgeable us-them gap, but as active agents, sharing space, resources, and common traits. Similarly, Chewong people do not distinguish categorically between humans and animals or plants, but rather understand beings "on the basis of presence or absence of consciousness." Consciousness makes one a "personage" (*ruwai*), regardless of outer shape as animal, plant, or spirit.[18] Such views, based on close proximity to and observation of other species, challenge the predominant Western idea that some essential trait such as reason or consciousness distinguishes humans from all other species and natural objects. Most discussions

of the social construction of nature, however, fail to take up such challenges. Instead, they dismiss all ideas as equally "invented" — except, of course, for the idea that humans exist in a uniquely cultural, discursive realm from which they give meaning to all other possible realms. . . .

Against this "hard" version of social constructionism regarding nature, several writers have offered a qualified or "soft" realism. Soper, one of the most articulate advocates of this position, argues that while it is true that any distinction we make between the reality of nature and its cultural representation is itself conceptual, it does not follow that

> . . . there is no ontological distinction between the ideas we have of nature and what the ideas are about: that since nature is only signified in human discourse, inverted commas 'nature' is nature, and we should therefore remove the inverted commas.
>
> In short, it is not language that has a hole in its ozone layer; and the 'real' thing continues to be polluted and degraded even as we refine our deconstructive insights at the level of the signifier.[19]

Soper argues that there is a nature out there, although she remains agnostic about our capacity to "know" this nature. Holmes Rolston, III defends a "harder" realism regarding nature. While Rolston acknowledges that "All human knowing colours whatever people see, through our percepts and concepts,"[20] he believes that we can still know nature "out there" in a (relatively and locally) accurate manner. Thus, commenting on Neil Evernden's description of nature as "a category, a conceptual container,"[21] Rolston contends that we invent the category nature and put things into it because "there is a realm out there, labelled nature, into which things have been put before we arrive. . . . Nature is what is not constructed by the human mind. . . . 'Nature' is a generic word for these objects encountered and the forces and processes that produce them."[22] The word *nature* emerged, for Rolston, because of the need for a "container" to match the nonhuman "forces and processes" that existed before we arrived and continue to exist even when we are not paying attention. Although such terms as *nature* and *wilderness* are not historically or culturally universal, we should not conclude that they do not have real referents or that we cannot "know" those referents in a meaningful way.

It is true, Rolston admits, that we cannot escape our skins and our conceptual frameworks. However, "humans do not have to get out of their skins to reach what's really there; there are windows out and in — they are called eyes, ears, noses, hands. Life is a matter of transactions across semipermeable membranes."[23] Rolston's point is a vital corrective to the solipsism and paralysis encouraged by hard versions of social constructionism, which too often contend that our incapacity to "know" the nonhuman world, in any complete or final sense, absolves us of responsibility for learning about or caring for it. This position often is tied to a suggestion that our inability to avoid intervening in nature frees us from a duty to intervene in the least damaging ways possible.

The hard dimension of Rolston's realism, and one that even some critics of a hard constructionism might find problematic, is his insistence that our "transactions" with nature, at least in some cases, "are registering natural forms" rather than just perceiving one among many possible versions of them.[24] There are many ways to construe nature, in other words, but some are more accurate than others. As many postmodernists would be quick (and correct) to point out, the risk of absolutism, universalism, and ethnocentrism lurks in this assertion. However, so does the very possibility of making ethical claims. As Rolston puts it, "We cannot correctly value what we do not to some degree correctly know."[25] It is precisely the extreme constructionists' insistence that we cannot know nature that leads to their rejection of claims to intrinsic value in, for example, wilderness areas or nonhuman species. In Rolston's words, "We must release some realms of value from our subject-minds and locate these instead out there in the world."[26]

Advocates of a softer realism (or a softer constructionism), such as Soper's, might amend Rolston's point to emphasize both the potential dangers of a strong realist position and the potential contributions of a nuanced reading of social constructionism. Ultimately, however, more unites than separates the two positions, at least in relation to the hard constructionist position they both critique. Rolston's insistence that natural entities "out there in the world" have value of their own, apart from human subjectivity, echoes Soper's point about the danger of thinking of nature as only a human construct. If nature is just a construction, they both emphasize, then we can hardly be concerned about harm due to ozone holes or other physical phenomena.

What Soper and especially Rolston find threatening in extreme constructionism is the way it undermines arguments in favor of protecting nonhuman species or wilderness areas. The potential for social constructionism to weaken arguments for conservation is exemplified in Cronon's and White's attacks on [Bill] McKibben's lament for the end of nature. They contend that what has ended is merely an idea of nature (and ultimately a false idea, so good riddance to it). In criticizing McKibben's realism, they fail to recognize the possibility that something real is in fact ending and is, further, worth lamenting. Their deconstructions of environmentalist naiveté thus lead away from appreciation of the nonhuman world, in all its various meanings, and toward "the radiant emanations of cynicism" against which Donna Haraway warns.[27]

CONCLUSIONS

. . . In principle, social constructionist arguments hint at the possibility of deconstructing boundaries between humans and "a genuine Other" — nonhuman nature.[28] In practice, however, most constructionists shrink from that potential and instead enshrine discourse as something only humans can do. This enshrinement reinforces the division between humans "as ontologically privileged beings, set apart from, or even against, the rest of nature."[29]

In contrast, a naturalist position advocates an understanding of humans "as a species of natural being, as part of the order of nature."[30] This view makes possible ecological arguments based on our commonalities with other species or our need for healthy ecosystems, in which humans and nonhumans are materially interdependent. Ethics requires a naturalism of this sort, Ted Benton argues, to understand both the positive requirements of different species (including humans) and distortions of normal behavior. Such knowledge is necessary in order to know, for example, whether certain conditions meet basic needs or impose pain and, thus, to make ethical judgments. Rolston pushes the link between the descriptive and the normative even farther, arguing that the "genetic set" of every organism enables it to distinguish "between what is and what ought to be. The organism is an axiological, though not a moral, system. . . . Every organism has a good-of-its-kind; it defends its own kind as a good kind." For Rolston, "These are observations of values which are at the same time biological facts."[31]

Rolston and Benton correctly assert that extreme anti-naturalist or social constructionist approaches undermine efforts to attribute intrinsic value to nonhuman entities, places, or creatures. They are right, further, that environmental ethics requires some conception of intrinsic value in the nonhuman world. If language and culture not only interpret but somehow invent reality, then nothing can have value outside human attribution. In extreme versions of social constructionism, the initial insight that there is no essential relationship between signifier and signified degenerates into the claim that there is, in fact, nothing at all to be signified, merely an endless process of signification. This argument denies the reality of power which can harm things like human bodies, ozone layers, or nonhuman animals. . . .

The conceptual failures of extreme social constructionism and the ethical and political harm it causes lead some ethicists to dismiss all constructionist insights. Is such a rejection necessary? Put another way, can we achieve a balance between the social constructionist critique of the "naive" idea of an essential, universal nature, on the one hand, and a sense of the independent reality and value of nature, on the other? . . .

Answers are not easy to find or to construct. Perhaps the most promising approach, for environmental ethics, lies in Soper's and N. Katherine Hayles's call for the productive tension between realism and constructionism. Soper, following Benton, calls this approach a "non-reductive realism," while Hayles speaks of "constrained constructivism." This position strives to combine the constructionist insight that we can have no unmediated apprehension of nature with the realist claim that the world consists

of more than human mediations and, linked to this, the naturalist insistence on continuities between human and nonhuman nature. In this view, as Haraway summarizes, "The world neither speaks itself nor disappears in favour of a master decoder." The natural world does not exist in "pristine" form, but neither is it "raw material for humanization."[32]

The constructionism that Hayles advocates is "constrained" because it asserts the existence of an unmediated "real world." In another sense, though, it takes constructionism beyond its usual boundaries. Hayles contends that humans are not only the only beings who "construct" worlds: all subjects, including nonhuman animals, constitute different worlds through their embodied interactions with their environments, and every construction, from a mouse's to a philosopher's, is "positional and local, covering only a tiny fraction of the spectrum of possible embodied interactions."[33] This view calls us to respect, take seriously, and seek out the viewpoints and the worlds shaped and inhabited not just by other humans, but by a whole host of organisms sharing the planet. All these organisms are, like humans, embodied and embedded in the physical world. However, they are also all shapers of it, in various ways, active agents and not merely blank slates waiting for human symbols and discourse (and hoes and bulldozers) to make something of them. . . .

. . . We live in the midst of multiple worlds, not all of them human, not all of them open to us. Sometimes, however, our trajectories cross, and "a piece of the universe is revealed as if for the first time."[34] Hope lies in the possibility of this crossing, of glimpses into lives, and goods, that are both real and fragile.

NOTES

1. Kate Soper, *What Is Nature?* (Oxford: Blackwell, 1995), p. 2.
2. Raymond Williams, "Ideas of Nature," in *Problems in Materialism and Culture* (London: Verso, 1980), p. 67.
3. Philippe Descola, "Constructing Natures: Symbolic Ecology and Social Practice," in Philippe Descola and Gisli Palsson, eds.,

Nature and Society: Anthropological Perspectives (London and New York: Routledge, 1996), p. 88.

4. Tim Ingold, "Hunting and Gathering as Ways of Perceiving the Environment," in Roy Ellen and Katsuyoshi Fukui, eds., *Redefining Nature: Ecology, Culture, and Domestication* (Oxford and Washington: Berg, 1996), p. 117.

5. See Moran, "Nurturing the Forest," in Ellen and Fukui, *Redefining Nature,* pp. 531–55.

6. Peter Dwyer, "The Invention of Nature," in Ellen and Fukui, *Redefining Nature, p.* 157.

7. Robert P. Harrison, "Toward a Philosophy of Nature," in William Cronon, ed., *Uncommon Ground: Rethinking the Human Place in Nature* (New York: W. W. Norton, 1996), p. 426.

8. James D. Proctor, "Whose Nature? The Contested Moral Terrain of Ancient Forests," in Cronon, *Uncommon Ground,* p. 273.

9. Ibid., p. 288.

10. William Cronon, "The Trouble with Wilderness: or, Getting Back to the Wrong Nature," in Cronon, *Uncommon Ground,* p. 69.

11. Cronon, "The Trouble with Wilderness," p. 80.

12. Richard White, "Are You an Environmentalist, or Do You Work for a Living? Work and Nature," in Cronon, *Uncommon Ground,* p. 172.

13. Ibid., p. 184.

14. Budiansky, *The Covenant of the Wild* (New York: William Morrow and Co., 1992), p. 12. Budiansky ignores the obvious fact that hunting is "daily work" for very few people in contemporary Western societies.

15. Cronon, "The Trouble with Wilderness," p. 82.

16. Candace Slater, "Amazonia as Edenic Narrative," in Cronon, *Uncommon Ground,* p. 130.

17. Laura Rival, "Blowpipes and Spears: The Social Significance of Huaorani Technological Choices," in Descola and Palsson, *Nature and Society,* pp. 148–49, 150.

18. Howell, "Nature in Culture," in Descola and Palsson, *Nature and Society,* p. 131.

19. Soper, *What Is Nature?* (Oxford: Blackwell, 1995), p. 151.

20. Holmes Rolston, III, "Nature for Real: Is Nature a Social Construct?" in Timothy Chappell, ed., *The Philosophy of the Environment* (Edinburgh: Edinburgh University Press, 1997), p. 38.

21. Neil Evernden, *The Social Creation of Nature* (Baltimore and London: Johns Hopkins University Press, 1992), p. 89.

22. Rolston, "Nature for Real," p. 42.

23. Ibid., p. 55.

24. Ibid., pp. 53–54.

25. Ibid., p. 40.

26. Ibid., p. 62.

27. Donna J. Haraway, *Simians, Cyborgs, and Women: The Reinvention of Nature* (New York: Routledge, 1991), p. 184.

28. Snyder's phrase comes from this sentence: "For all the talk of 'the other' in everybody's theory these days, when confronted with a genuine Other, the nonhuman realm, the response of the come-lately anti-Nature intellectuals is to circle the wagons and declare that Nature is really part of culture" ("Is Nature Real?" p. 32).

29. Ted Benton, *Natural Relations: Ecology, Animal Rights, and Social Justice* (London: Verso, 1993), p. 17. See also Lynda Birke, *Feminism, Animals and Science: The Naming of the Shrew* (London and Buckingham, Pa.: Open University Press, 1994), p. 146.

30. Benton, *Natural Relations,* p. 17.

31. Rolston, "Nature for Real," p. 61.

32. Haraway, *Simians,* p. 198.

33. N. Katherine Hayles, "Searching for Common Ground," in Michael Soulé and Gary Lease, eds., *Reinventing Nature? Responses to Postmodern Deconstruction* (Washington, D.C. and Covelo, Calif.: Island Press, 1995), p. 58.

34. Adrienne Rich, "Woman and Bird," in *What Is Found There: Notebooks on Poetry and Politics* (New York: Quality Paperback Book Club, 1994), p. 8.

DISCUSSION TOPICS

1. According to Peterson, how does the dominant construction of nature in modern Western cultures differ from that found in non-Western hunter-gatherer cultures?

2. Explain some of the implications for ethics that result from what Peterson terms "strong versions" of constructionism. Do you agree with her that these implications are unacceptable? Why or why not?

3. Explain what Peterson means by saying that strong constructivism goes both too far and not far enough.
4. According to Peterson, what is the danger in Rolston's "realism" concerning nature? Do you agree? Explain your reasoning.
5. Explain the "constrained" constructionism that Peterson advocates at the end of her essay. Do you agree that this approach is the best one for environmental ethics? Why or why not?

READING 10

Environmental Ethics as Environmental Etiquette: Toward an Ethics-Based Epistemology

Jim Cheney and Anthony Weston

Jim Cheney is professor of philosophy at the University of Wisconsin-Waukesha. He is the author of over twenty articles on environmental philosophy. Anthony Weston is professor of philosophy at Elon College in North Carolina. He is the author of eight books on ethics and environmental philosophy, including An Invitation to Environmental Philosophy *(1999).*

In the following selection, drawn from an Environmental Ethics *article published in 1999, Cheney and Weston explain the contrast between an ethics-based epistemology and an epistemology-based ethics. They argue that the world we inhabit arises out of our ethical practice, rather than vice versa. The fundamental ethical failure of traditional ethical theory and practice is the failure to acknowledge ourselves as living and participating in a larger animate universe, of which we are not the center.*

I. INTRODUCTION

Environmental philosophers have long suspected that environmental ethics is much more than the mere extension of general ethical principles and methods to a new applied area. Accordingly, environmental philosophers have been especially intrigued by those ways in which environmental philosophy has

progressively called into question substantive and methodological assumptions about ethics itself: that ethics is an affair solely of humans, or even just rational or sentient beings; that standard ethical theories can be stretched to retrofit all new ethical insights; that ethical theories, standard or not, are what we should want at all. Each of these assumptions, and more, have been called into question.

It is our view, however, that environmental ethicists have not yet gotten to the bottom of things. We have not yet uncovered the most radical of challenges that environmental philosophy poses to traditional assumptions. Environmental philosophy is most radical, we think, because it calls into question basic assumptions concerning the relationship between epistemology and ethics and, hence, basic assumptions concerning ethics itself.

We do mean basic. For example, what if environmental philosophy finally must call into question the seemingly most obvious assumption of all, that the world consists of a collection of more or less given facts to which we must respond, responses which ethics then systematizes and unifies? What if the actual, necessary relation is the other way around? What if the world we inhabit arises most fundamentally out of our ethical practice, rather than vice versa?

II. TWO ETHICAL EPISTEMOLOGIES

Consider, very briefly, four features of the traditional view of the place of epistemology in ethics, what we call an "epistemology-based ethics."[1] (1) *Ethical action is a response to our knowledge of the world.* Knowledge comes first; then, and only then, practice. Ethical arguments presuppose or articulate some factual situation to which the question is what our appropriate response is to be. That natural ecosystems, for example, may show integrity, stability, or beauty, as a matter of fact, is supposed to be the basis upon which we can "consider" them ethically. That animals feel pain, or are self-conscious, or have expectations that can be violated, is supposed to be the basis upon which they might be attributed rights. Indeed, to speak of a "basis" in this way is only a way of underlining the necessity of some factual appeal, some empirical starting-point. Often an object's or system's alleged possession of "intrinsic value" is itself supposed to be a kind of fact to which ethical action responds. That even the "possession" of value itself is thereby treated as a kind of *fact* illustrates just how taken-for-granted the fact-based model of ethics currently is.

(2) *The world is readily knowable—at least to the extent required for ethical response.* Ethicists are confident about what it is we need to know in order to determine our ethical responsibilities, and are confident that this knowledge is attainable. We can understand ecosystems; we can know, even with precision, exactly what animals do or do not feel; we can even know what things have a special property called "intrinsic value," even though we cannot begin to cash out that notion ontologically or any other way. Even in cases where the relevant understanding is acknowledged to be far from complete, it is thought that we have enough to go on for ethical decision making—or else that the very incompleteness of our knowledge is itself a critical fact that determines ethical response. In any case, *we know what we need to know.*

(3) *Ethics is inherently an incremental and extensionist business.* If ethics is a response to the world, and the world is readily known, then ethics is likely to have a well-established core. Change and expansion are supposed to take place slowly, at the margins, and by extension from the (assumed) well-understood central models. Peter Singer's "expanding circle," for example, is quite explicitly *not* taken to be in any serious flux near its center: the whole idea is that we work out from the "given," from the reliable and established, to the less certain and more speculative. At the margins, of course, we ought to expect some surprises, but the common and given background against which any surprise must emerge is the stable and well-understood familiar world.

Even new experiences at the margins are interpreted and assimilated on the familiar models. Animals have rights, or we have duties to them, or "welfare" must be construed more broadly, or "no compromise" is now a principle to be asserted in a new area, and so on. The basic *patterns* of ethical relationship seem to be taken as "given," even at the margins.

These three assumptions lead in turn to a specific vision of the task of ethics. (4) *The task of ethics is to sort the world ethically—that is, to articulate the nature of things in ethical terms.* It is for this reason that the "considerability" question surfaces so early in the development of environmental ethics. Ethics thinks of itself as addressing the criteria for *mattering* ethically, for "counting," and these criteria are supposed to be articulated in terms of the relevant features of the things that "count." Of course, there is room for debate about just what features are relevant, but once again it is usually supposed that the problem is merely one of making careful distinctions. We are already supposed to understand the relevant criteria. People are in, bacteria and rocks are out, and animals might be in or not depending on how much like us, and unlike bacteria or rocks, they are.[2]

All manner of familiar consequences follow from this model. For example, the familiar kind of careful distinction making and legalistic principle articulation is already well in view after (4). A philosophy of language emerges: descriptive rather than expressive and performative functions of language are crucial. An account of ethical failure also follows. It follows directly from (1) that the great pitfalls of ethics—the primary ways in which we fail to be ethical—are inadequacies of *belief,* or have to do with the conformity of action to belief. We may be ignorant of, or blind to, the facts. We may resist acknowledging the facts: we may even, like the vivisectionists, cut animals' vocal cords so that we do not have to hear them scream. Or we may acknowledge the facts but fail to act on our knowledge (which is why weakness of will is a topic of such interest in contemporary ethics). Still we remain in the orbit of facts.

Alternative foundational assumptions might be offered, however, which differ from the traditional assumptions *on every point:* an ethics-based epistemology, rather than an epistemology-based ethics. (1a) *Ethical action is first and foremost an attempt to open up possibilities, to enrich the world.* It is not an attempt to respond to the world as *already* known. On the usual view, for example, we must first know what animals are capable of, then decide on that basis whether and how we are to consider them ethically. On the alternative view, we will have no idea of what other animals are actually capable—

we will not readily understand them—until we *already* have approached them ethically—that is, until we have offered them the space and time, the occasion, and the acknowledgment necessary to enter into relationship. Ethics must come *first*.

Consider the phenomenon of love in this regard. In terms of a traditional ethical epistemology, love is a difficult, embarrassing, marginal case: love is supposed to be blind, irrational, and "pathological." In terms of an alternative ethical epistemology, however, love is paradigmatic. Love is in fact a way of knowing, but its dynamics are the reverse of the usual models. Love comes first, and opens up possibilities. Without love people may never open up enough to reveal all that they can be. In this sense, lovers *do* see what others cannot see—but the *others* are the ones who are blind. Love in this sense is already an ethical relationship. It thus stands at the beginning, at the core, of ethics itself: a venture as well as an adventure—a risk, an attitude that may (*may,* for we cannot say for sure at the beginning) lead in time to more knowledge of someone or something, wholly wild possibilities.

(2a) *Hidden possibilities surround us at all times.* The world is *not* readily knowable. People who were previously dismissed as below notice, even if "respected" in the purely formal sense, might turn out to be quite fantastic companions, lovers, adversaries, or who knows what, if offered the "space," the invitation. Or perhaps they would choose to have nothing to do with us—a state of affairs from which we could also learn. We must *ask* them, however: we must venture something, expose ourselves too; and for any number of reasons the invitation may be declined.

The same goes for other animals and for the larger worlds beyond. There is a vast fund of experience in Midgleyan "mixed communities," for example, in which all manner of animals, from cats, dogs, and horses to cormorants, whales, raccoons, and bees have shown unexpected powers—while some of them too, no doubt, would rather have nothing to do with us. We are still only beginning to sense the communication going on all around us: whales singing to each other across whole oceans, elephants rumbling in infra-sound across the savannahs, bees dancing their comrades to new pollens.[3]

Even in the face of the staggering reduction of nature in modern times, wild possibilities abound. We have only begun to consider that all life on Earth might itself function in an integrated, maybe even organism-like way. Who knows what else we will yet discover? The world has barely unfolded for us.

(3a) *Ethics is pluralistic, dissonant, discontinuous—not incremental and extensionist.* If established knowledge and ethical relationships in no way exhaust the possibilities, then ethical *discovery* is always possible, including discoveries that may be unnerving and disruptive. We may discover that even values we thought long-established might have to be rethought and changed. Rather than emphasize the continuities (animal rights, for example, as an extension of human rights, from males to females to historically disadvantaged races and, finally, beyond the human species to, maybe, adult mammals . . .) the alternative notices that each of these revisions also upends the central and supposedly "given" models as well. If barbarians or females or even animals can have rights, then the meaning of rights holding and our understanding of rights holders themselves changes. Dissonance abounds.

A sense of familiarity and settledness characterize the tradition. The alternative needs a more uncertain and disruptive metaphor. Consider, for example, the experience of living in a foreign land. Here it is evident to us that a great deal is going on that is mysterious and perhaps must remain so. Melodies, smells, a certain tilt of the head, the line of the hills, or the way the rains start in the afternoons are all more intricate and complex than surface attention would suggest, even right next to us. In foreign lands, a certain bare courtesy is extended both ways, because both we and the natives know we are reaching across a distance. We need to be carefully attentive, always aware that there is much we do not understand, open to discovery and surprise.

This is not merely an analogy, though, but the actual state of things. We do live among different others, every day and all the time. Other humans, even those close to us, see the world their own way, have their own structures of meaning, different from our own. Even the most seemingly established relationships may have to be regularly reestablished. The analogy applies quite precisely to other animals. Recall Henry Beston's famous words:

> In a world older and more complete than ours, they move finished and complete, gifted with extensions of the senses we have lost or never attained, living by voices we shall never hear. They are not brethren, they are not underlings; they are other nations, caught with ourselves in the net of life, fellow prisoners of the splendor and travail of time.[4]

Other nations are beings with their own structures of meaning, which we conceivably could join or at least move in concert with, but not structures that we should expect to fit neatly or smoothly with our own. What is really asked of us is courtesy, openness to surprise.

Finally, the three assumptions just outlined lead in turn to a specific vision of the tasks of ethics: (4a) *The task of ethics is to explore and enrich the world.* Hidden possibilities surround us: the task of ethics is to call them forth. Rather than sorting relatively fixed-natured things into relatively well-established categories of considerability, thus not just ruling some potential consideranda *in* but also — and quite crucially for the traditional conception of things — ruling a great many potential consideranda *out,* what is asked of us, insofar as we can manage it, is an open-ended, nonexclusive consideration of everything: people, bacteria, rocks, animals, everything, insofar as we can.

Tom Birch calls this kind of consideration *universal consideration.* He offers an elegant and (it seems to us) unanswerable argument for its necessity. Because the self-proclaimed concern of ethics is to discover what things in the world demand practical respect, then we must *for that reason alone,* he says, "consider" them in the most fundamental way: by paying close, careful, and persistent attention. Thus, all things must be considerable in this basic and unavoidable sense. Indeed, rather than any new potential considerandum having to meet a burden of proof, universal consideration requires us to reverse the usual burden of proof as we approach others in the world. "Others are now taken as valuable, even though we may not yet know how or why, until they are proved otherwise."[5] Actually, even more deeply,

universal consideration requires us not merely to extend this kind of benefit of the doubt but actively to take up the case, so to speak, for beings so far excluded or devalued. Once again, ethics is primary: ethics opens the way to knowledge, epistemology is value-driven, not vice versa.

All manner of consequences follow from this alternative model. Once again, for example, philosophy of language emerges: rather than descriptive accuracy, the alternative will draw upon the evocative, expressive, and performative aspects of language. This theme is taken up in the next section. The alternative also has direct implications for the great pitfalls of ethics — the ways in which we fail to be ethical. On our view, these are inadequacies of *etiquette,* failures of *courtesy.* Blind to the possibilities right next to us, we may never know what we are missing, and we may close them down or even destroy them as a result.[6]

III. CEREMONIAL WORLDS

In this section, we examine in more detail the relationship between etiquette and epistemology in an ethics- or etiquette-based epistemology. Although we believe that *all* epistemologies are at least implicitly value- or ethics-based, we focus here on examples drawn from indigenous cultures, since the ethics-based nature of epistemology is more clearly exemplified in them.[7]

Referring to the work of the Canadian Inuit philosopher Gordon Christie, Leroy Meyer and Tony Ramirez argue that "one ought not to put too much stock in the word 'philosophy.'. . . [T]here are alternative ways of intelligently engaging the world. To construe one's thinking in terms of belief is characteristic of a particular kind of world view and it remains to be seen whether those who share an indigenous world view conceive of experience in such an overtly intellectualized manner."[8]

Walter Ong and others have linked the visual metaphor of knowing — as in the term *world view,* as used to refer to a people's fundamental *beliefs* about the world — with the advent of the written word. Whereas "sight presents surfaces," Ong says, "sound reveals interiors" and "signals the present use of power, since sound must be in active production in order to exist at all." In a sound-oriented culture, "the universe [is] something one respond[s] to, as to a voice, not something merely to be inspected."[9] Words on the page no longer reveal interiors, they no longer signal the present use of power. Words are not *objects;* they are inert, in themselves lifeless. They become signs, symbols of something else. Words come to refer primarily to beliefs, systems of thought. Sam Gill reports (as have many others) that nonliterate people are often highly critical of writing. He says, however, that he does

> . . . not believe that it is actually writing that is at the core of their criticism. The concern is with certain dimensions of behavior and modes of thought that writing tends to facilitate and encourage. And these dimensions are linked to the critical, semantical, encoding aspects of language. . . . We interpret texts to discern systems of thought and belief, propositional or historical contents, messages communicated. Put more generally, we seek the information in the text. We tend to emphasize code at the expense of behavior, message at the expense of the performance and usage contexts.[10]

The written word conspires with the visual metaphor to turn the world into a passive object for human knowledge and to focus our attention on language as a sign system primarily designed to encode beliefs.

In a number of articles, Sam Gill has attempted to reinstate the fundamental nature of the *performative* function of language, using Navajo prayer as a case study. Invariably, when he asks Navajo elders what prayers *mean,* they tell him "not what messages pray-ers carry, but what prayers *do.*" Further, "the person of knowledge in Navajo tradition holds that [theology, philosophy, and doctrine] are ordinarily to be discouraged. Such concerns are commonly understood by Navajos as evidence that one totally misunderstands the nature of Navajo religious traditions."[11]

Generalizing from his analysis of prayer acts to religious practice generally, Gill asserts that "the importance of religion as it is practiced by the great body of religious persons for whom religion is a way of life [is] a way of creating, discovering, and communicating worlds of meaning largely through ordinary and common actions and behavior."[12]

We would like to explore the possibility of generalizing even further, arguing that the performative dimension of language be understood as fundamental — not just in obviously religious settings, but *generally.* Perhaps then we can understand the full import of Myer and Ramirez's assertion that there are alternative ways of intelligently engaging the world, alternatives to construing one's thinking in terms of belief. We *do* things with words. Foremost among these performative functions is the creation of what we call the *ceremonial worlds* within which we live. Other performative functions of language are possible only within these ceremonial worlds — promise making, for instance, is possible only within an accepted set of social conventions, as is the progress achieved within science.[13]

Take, for example, Diamond Jenness's report of an unnamed Carrier Indian of the Bulkley River who says: "The white man writes everything down in a book so that it might not be forgotten; but our ancestors married the animals, learned their ways, and passed on the knowledge from one generation to another."[14] His ancestors passed down the means of creating, or recreating, the worlds, the ceremonial worlds, within which they lived — the stories, the ceremonies, the rituals, the daily practices. They passed down modes of action, which when written down come to be understood as information. Euro-Americans want to know what beliefs are encoded in the utterances of indigenous peoples; they want to treat these utterances as mirrors of indigenous worlds. In doing so, however, we may be asking the wrong question. In fact, these utterances function primarily to *produce* these worlds. Euro-Americans tend to be concerned with ontology, correct descriptions of indigenous worlds. Many indigenous people, on the other hand, are concerned with the right relationship to those beings that populate their worlds, they are concerned with mindfulness, "respect." It is this suggestion that we wish to explore in greater depth here.

N. Scott Momaday, in justly famous words, says: "It seems to me that in a sense we are all made of words; that our most essential being consists in language. It is the element in which we think and dream and act, in which we live our daily lives. There is no way in which we can exist apart from the morality of a verbal dimension."[15] Momaday is speaking not of sets of *beliefs* by which people constitute themselves, but more fundamentally of performance, enactment, the bringing into being of one's identity by means of action and practice, primarily *verbal*. It is the difference, for example, between the sacred as *object* of knowledge or belief (and, derivatively, of acts of faith and adoration) and sacramental *practice* — a matter of comportment, which brings into being a world, a ceremonial world, around it.

Ceremonial worlds are not fantasy worlds. We do, of course, experience the world. Experience is taken up into ceremonial worlds. It is part of the self-correcting feedback loop that makes it possible for the day-to-day activities of food gathering, child rearing, shelter building and so on to take place, to succeed, not only on the terms set by the world, but within the context of a richly textured ceremonial world. In such a world, as Paul Shepard has observed, "everyday life [is] inextricable from spiritual significance and encounter," "natural things are not only themselves but a speaking."[16]

If language is performative, and if we have our being and identity fundamentally within ceremonial worlds, then the coherence we should be listening for is not merely the logical coherence of one sentence with another, one belief with another, but something more like the harmonic coherence of one note with another. Practices, including linguistic practices, create ceremonial songs of the world, worlds of meaning, within ecological niches. Within these ceremonial songs of the world language is a mode of *interaction* with the world. As Henry Sharp has put it, "symbols, ideas, and language . . . are not passive ways of perceiving a determined positivist reality but a mode of interaction shared between [humans] and their environment."[17]

Sacramental *practice* is the key — not the *sacred* as understood by ontologists. Ceremonial practice defines the world in which we live and work. The ontology of one's world is a kind of residue from one's ethical practice and the modes of attaining knowledge associated with that practice. This residue is highly prized, and receives intense scrutiny, in Euro-American cultures, but etiquette is the fundamental dimension of our relationship to, and understanding of, the world. Ontology is a kind of picture, or metaphor, of ethical practice.

Moving away from epistemology-based ethics and toward an ethics-based epistemology, we move closer to an older sense of the word *knowledge:* knowledge as intimacy and reciprocity. Contrary to the emphasis some place on the *constructed* nature of the worlds we live in, reflected in the catch phrase "It's words all the way down," we suggest a very different emphasis: "It's *world* all the way *up*" — even into the language of the ceremonial worlds we have been discussing.

The poet Robert Bringhurst speaks of poetry as "knowing freed from the agenda of possession and control." He understands poetry as "knowing in the sense of stepping in tune with being, hearing and echoing the music and heartbeat of being."[18] A friend says of Indian Paintbrush — a plant we know well from the American West — that it "speaks the soil." Its palette, she says, varies with the mineral composition of the soil.[19] Similarly, language is most fundamentally an expression of the world — it "speaks the world." Language is rooted in being, rooted in the world as are we who speak forth that world in our language. Our language is a mode of interaction with, and hence a mode of knowing, that world. Knowing can take shape as a form of domination and control. It can also take shape as a way of "stepping in tune with being."

Though the epistemologies of modernism have detached themselves from the world — treating the nonhuman world and even the human world as objects of domination and control — and though the postmodern view of language and self (the self as solipsistic maker of worlds of words) to a large extent reflects this detachment, we and our languages are fundamentally *of* the world. Before they convey information, before they are assertions with "truth values," our words are a welling up of the world. The more-than-human world[20] bursts forth in multiple songs of the world — human songs in a more-than-human world, songs rooted in, and expressive of, that world. They carry the power and energy of that world.

Ceremonial worlds, then, embody *ethics-based epistemologies.* As a result, they have the potential to open up the hidden possibilities of the world, possibilities shut down by epistemologies driven by values of domination and control. Traditional epistemology-based ethics, as we have seen, tend to keep these hidden possibilities hidden, thereby effectively blocking any ethical relationship premised on them. In setting out criteria of moral considerability, contemporary epistemology-based environmental ethics is engaged (even if implicitly) at least as much in domination and control as it is in the liberation of heretofore ethically disenfranchised "citizens" of the land community.[21]

The centrality of the notion of "respect" for nature is pervasive in indigenous cultures and underscores the rich possibilities inherent in opting for an ethic that opens up the hidden possibilities of the world. To Euro-American ears, "respect" may have overtones of hierarchically structured relationships, or it might have a Kantian flavor of obedience to moral law. But to indigenous ears it points to an epistemological-ethical complex the central concept of which is *awareness* of all that is, an awareness that is simultaneously epistemological and ethical, as Carol Geddes explained in response to a question concerning the meaning of the indigenous notion of respect: "I asked a similar question of someone who knows the Tlingit language very well. Apparently it does not have a very precise definition in translation—the way it is used in English. It is more like awareness. It is more like knowledge and that is a very important distinction, because it is not like a moral law, it is more like something that is just a part of your whole awareness.[22]

The pluralistic, dissonant, and discontinuous (vs. incremental and extensionist) nature of such an ethic is also richly exemplified by indigenous cultures. Indigenous people not only acknowledge but *celebrate* the differences that exist among the various indigenous peoples in truly remarkable ways, ways that have inclined us to prefer the terms *ceremonial worlds* and *songs of the world* to *world views,* which suggests the idea of a set of *beliefs* about how the world actually *is.* Belief figures in indigenous worlds rather more obliquely than is suggested by the term *world view.* In indigenous worlds epistemology is, once again, *ethics-based,* and, given the notion of "respect" that underlies in-

digenous ceremonial worlds, a richly pluralistic set of worlds unfolds.

IV. REDUCTION AND INVITATION

In sections four and five, we pick out two aspects of our reconceived ethical epistemology for particular emphasis: invitation in this section and narrative in the next. Our aim in doing so is twofold. First, both themes illustrate and deepen the practical turn that the alternative ethical epistemology requires. Practice is no longer some application of ethical knowledge: it is now *constitutive of ethics itself,* our very mode of access to the world's possibilities. Second, conversely, the alternative epistemology also helps to ground these themes and practices themselves. These are not merely specific topics, disjunct from each other, but connected and central to the field as we reconceive it. These themes both exemplify an ethics-based epistemology and are highlighted and required by it.

"Etiquette" is a genuine means of *discovery.* As we said above, we oppose the usual view that puts knowledge of animals, for instance, before any possible (serious, intellectually respectable) ethical response to them. On our view, we can have no idea of what other animals are actually capable *until* we approach them ethically. Now we need to spell out this reversal more carefully.

To begin with, certain kinds of self-fulfilling prophecies turn out to be crucial in ethics. There is, in particular, a kind of self-fulfilling prophecy in which one of the main effects of the "prophecy" is to reduce someone or something in the world—to make that person or thing less than they or it are or could be, to diminish some part of the world's richness and depth and promise—and in which this reduction in turn feeds back not only to justify the original prophecy but also to perpetuate it. This process is therefore *self-validating* reduction. There are all too many examples. Animals reduced to pitiful or hostile vestiges of their former selves, whose incapacities and hostility are then taken to justify exploitation or further violence. The land itself, scourged, deliberately desacralized (Yahweh even commands the Israelites to destroy the ancient world's sacred groves), subdivided, ravaged, then of course has very little of the stability, integrity, or beauty that might give it any kind of noninstrumental value. Cut down the sacred groves and you succeed in driving the sacred out of this world.[23]

To break this cycle of "reduction," it is necessary to invoke a parallel cycle of "invitation"—indeed, quite precisely, self-validating invitation. Here the kind of practice asked of us is to venture something, to offer an invitation to, or to open a possibility toward, another being or some part of the world, and see what comes of it. We are called, in fact, to a kind of etiquette once again, but here in an experimental key: the task is to create the space within which a response can emerge or an exchange coevolve.

Trust, for example, is crucial. Think, for instance, of how we approach children, or students: already offering trust and love. This approach is what enables them to grow into it. We could even define a good teacher as someone who offers that kind of respect "up front," and for all of his or her charges (hence, it is also "universal," returning to Birch's notion of universal consideration).

Here, then, the reversal from an epistemology-based ethics to an ethics-based epistemology becomes most evident. "Invitation" in this sense is not an assessment of something's value based upon an inventory—even the most open-minded or objective inventory—of the thing's present characteristics. The point, once again, is that those present characteristics do not exhaust the thing's possibilities. Knowledge does not and cannot come first; first must come the invitation. Consequently, invitation cannot represent some formal kind of respect, but rather an experimental, open-ended and sometimes even personally risky kind of offering.

Birch's insistence that universal consideration "reverse the usual burden of proof" prefigures this same logic. We suggest that this reversal is not merely a matter of epistemological caution. It is a matter of setting the dynamics of relationship going in a different direction. For the very necessity to "prove oneself" may prove debilitating, may make its own satisfaction impossible. Precisely that demand already represents a way of closing ourselves off from the beings in question. Human beings trip over their own feet when treated with such distance and skepticism, when put into question this way, and there is no reason to expect other animals to do

any better, especially when many animals are exquisitely more sensitive to the affective environment than we are. Conversely, though it may seem paradoxical, removing the "burden" of proof may be precisely what is necessary if it is to be met. Once again, only in this way are we likely to discover what kind of relationship actually is possible. To "invite," then, is not merely to make a space for something, to let it in: it is, literally, bringing new possibilities to *life.* Without it, without venturing real-world invitations, we cannot begin to know what the real possibilities are.

There are many styles of invitation. Sometimes what we need most of all to do is to give a child or animal or plant or river *time:* time to grow to its natural lifespan, at its own tempo. "Invitation" in the case of non-sentient beings—rocks, for example—may have to move at their tempo: millions of years, perhaps. Or perhaps not. Indigenous traditions generally consider rocks rather tricky beings. Places, buildings, communities can be more or less inviting: we need to *plan* for what Mary Midgley calls the "mixed community." Considering—inviting—other animals in this sense, for example, partly means designing places and media where we can meet each other halfway. Sometimes it is as simple as designing places that they and we can safely share. . . .

. . . Certainly, self-conscious "niceness" is the *last* thing we need: better simply to be oblivious. Consider what things are like for the animal: what "communication," for example, would really be for a herring gull or a dolphin. Consider Jim Nollman jamming with orcas, using musical media which all cetaceans seem to prefer, paddling out to them in his floating rhythm section, thus in a way that allows them to decline encounter entirely or to break it off whenever they wish.[24] Could *this kind of courtesy* just possible be the environmental-philosophical challenge of the future?

V. SONGS OF THE EARTH

When indigenous peoples are presented with what Euro-Americans would call *beliefs* or *world views* different from their own, they tend to respond not with an inquiry into which are *true* but by saying that "they tell different stories than we do."[25] In this section, we focus on the *narrative* component of indigenous ceremonial worlds.

. . . In indigenous stories, knowledge follows upon correct behavior, proper etiquette; they clearly illustrate an ethics-based epistemology. Stories are *inviting*. They *invite* the telling of other stories, other songs of the world. They invite others into the stories—human and nonhuman, the whole land community.

Theory is not inconsistent with storied understanding of self, community, and world. Indeed, as philosophers and sociologists of science have amply demonstrated, theories are fully intelligible only when embedded in stories—at the very least, in stories that exemplify in actual cases the application of scientific concepts, laws, and theories (what Thomas Kuhn calls "paradigm applications"), but also, and more importantly for our purposes, in the wider cultural stories that define us as individuals and define the cultures within which we live and come to understand ourselves. The storied nature of indigenous knowledge shows clearly that indigenous knowledge is grounded in ethical practice, that indigenous epistemology is ethics-based. In general, it seems that stories provide a more nuanced, "ecological" understanding of our place in the world—including our *ethical* place. Stories are the real homes of so-called thick moral concepts, concepts in which evaluation and description are so intertwined as to be conceptually inseparable. They *exemplify* what theory cannot—namely, as Lee Hester says, that in addition to the "true" statements that can be made about things, things have their *own* truth.[26] To say that everything has its *own* truth (if we understand Hester correctly) is not so much a theoretical claim about the world as it is an expression of the thought that unless we extend a very basic courtesy to things in our attempts to understand them, we cannot arrive at an understanding of them *or* ourselves that makes *sense,* that makes sense of our lives, our cultures, our relationship to all that is.

As environmental ethicists, then, we might begin to explicitly discover and acknowledge the stories within which we think about environmental ethics. Although we know that theories are deeply shaped by personal and cultural values and that these values are deeply shaped by stories—that is, they are carried and propagated by the stories that define us—

this understanding is not often reflected in practice; nor is it reflected in our meta-level analyses of practice. Articles in environmental ethics literature, including this one,[27] do not first invoke worlds within which discussion might meaningfully proceed. The implicit assumption is that we can profitably discuss these matters without defining and locating the ceremonial worlds and stories within which our discussions proceed. We speak as though *from* no world at all; and we presumptuously speak *for* all worlds. . . .

. . . The landscapes that shape Euro-American identities are mostly human landscapes, landscapes of human culture and humanly transformed nature—broken landscapes that mirror our own brokenness. It has not always been so and is even now not so for perhaps most indigenous peoples. The *deepest* sources of personal and cultural identity are the ecological and geological landscapes that shape and sustain us. This identity, and our present loss, is given voice in what are surely Momaday's most memorable words:

> East of my grandmother's house the sun rises out of the plain. Once in his life a man ought to concentrate his mind upon the remembered earth, I believe. He ought to give himself up to a particular landscape in his experience, to look at it from as many angles as he can, to wonder about it, to dwell upon it. He ought to imagine that he touches it with his hands at every season and listens to the sounds that are made upon it. He ought to imagine the creatures there and all the faintest motions of the wind. He ought to recollect the glare of noon and all the colors of the dawn and dusk.[28]

These unbroken landscapes are characterized by their integrity. As Barry Lopez has put it, the "landscape is organized according to principles or laws or tendencies beyond human control. It is understood to contain an integrity that is beyond human analysis and unimpeachable.[29] It is this integrity, beyond human analysis and unimpeachable, that marks the land as sacred for most indigenous peoples. The "sacred" (for example, the Lakota *wakan tanka,* "great mysterious") is the more-than-human quality of *this* world, not a being transcendent to the world. A Lakota asked an older Lakota about the meaning and origin of the term *wakan tanka* and received this story as his answer:

> Way back many years ago, two men went walking. It was on the prairies. As they walked, they decided, "Let's go up the hill way towards the west; let's see what's over the hill."
>
> So they walked and they came to the top of this hill and they looked west and it was the same. Same thing as they saw before; there was nothing. They just kept going like that, all day and it was the same. They came to a big hill and there was another big hill further back. Finally they stopped and they said, "You know, this is Wakan Tanka."[30]

. . .

Euro-Americans, too, have stories that define us in relationship to the land. One such tale is Aldo Leopold's "Marshland Elegy," in his *A Sand County Almanac,* which ends:

> And so they live and have their being—these cranes—not in the constricted present, but in the wider reaches of evolutionary time. Their annual return is the ticking of the geologic clock. Upon the place of their return they confer a peculiar distinction. Amid the endless mediocrity of the commonplace, a crane marsh holds a paleontological patent of nobility, won in the march of eons. . . . The sadness discernible in some marshes arises, perhaps, from their once having harbored cranes. Now they stand humbled, adrift in history.[31]

"Marshland Elegy" helps define many who live in the upper Midwest in relationship to the geologic and ecosystemic legacy of the last Wisconsin Ice, as a prairie/wetland people. The elegy also haunts us—it is a story of loss that fits our cultural temper. It is a fair question whether our religions of loss and redemption are in some way tied to the mutual estrangement of the natural, the personal, and the sacred in Western culture. . . .

Swaggering, talking too loud, not knowing how to listen, this very (often innocent) clumsiness we now reconceive as *the* fundamental ethical failure: failure to acknowledge and understand ourselves as living in a larger animate universe, and failure too—crucially—to draw out, to co-participate with, that very universe. Instead, we drive it into silence, and then take that silence to confirm our own centrality, as if we really were the only ones with anything to say. . . .

NOTES

1. It is almost impossible to give citations for this model in general, since it is the common assumption of nearly all contemporary philosophical work recognized as ethics, and consequently is almost never explicitly articulated. It is both immediately familiar and never spelled out. J. Baird Callicott's recent *Earth's Insights: A Survey of Ecological Ethics from the Mediterranean Basin to the Australian Outback* (Berkeley: University of California Press, 1994) can perhaps be cited in this connection, particularly as his emphatically epistemology-based ethics does considerable disservice to the ethics-based epistemologies typical of indigenous philosophies that we examine below.

2. See Thomas H. Birch, "Moral Considerability and Universal Consideration," *Environmental Ethics* 15 (1993): 313–32.

3. See Anthony Weston, *Back to Earth: Tomorrow's Environmentalism* (Philadelphia: Temple University Press, 1994), chaps. 2 and 3.

4. Henry Beston, *The Outermost House* (New York: Viking, 1976), p. 25.

5. Birch, "Moral Considerability," p. 328.

6. This discussion is, of course, only the briefest sketch, and leaves many questions unaddressed. Could ethics-based epistemology and epistemology-based ethics each be appropriate at different times or in different spheres, for example? (Maybe.) Is "care" ethics closer to an ethics-based epistemology than traditional ethics? (Again, maybe: this strand does emerge in some care ethicists, although there is a strong strand of epistemology-based care ethics as well.) These are questions for another place.

7. The indigenous ideas on which we draw are filtered—indeed, double-filtered in cases where we work from secondary sources—through the conceptual lens of the Western-defined problematics in environmental ethics

that we address in this paper. We do not claim to understand indigenous thought as that thought lives in indigenous worlds. The *only* real authorities on indigenous thought are indigenous people themselves. We only claim that this thought *as we understand it* sheds light on current problems in environmental ethics.

8. Leroy N. Meyer and Tony Ramirez, "'Wakinyan Hotan' ('The Thunderbeings call out'): The Inscrutability of Lakota/Dakota Metaphysics," in Sylvia O'Meara and Douglas A. West, eds., *From Our Eyes: Learning from Indigenous People* (Toronto: Garamond Press, 1996), p. 104

9. Walter J. Ong, S.J., "World as View and World as Event," *American Anthropologist* 71 (1969): 63–67.

10. Sam Gill, "Holy Book in Nonliterate Traditions: Toward the Reinvention of Religion," in Sam Gill, *Native American Religious Action: A Performance Approach to Religion* (Columbia: University of South Carolina Press, 1987), pp. 139–40.

11. Sam Gill, "One, Two, Three: The Interpretation of Religious Action," in Gill, *Native American Religious Action,* pp. 162–163, 151.

12. Ibid., p. 162.

13. These examples make it clear, we hope, that the term *ceremonial worlds* is not intended to refer to ceremonies such as baptisms and sun dances that occur within cultures.

14. Diamond Jenness, "The Carrier Indians of the Bulkley River," *Bureau of American Ethnology Bulletin,* no. 133 (1943): 540.

15. N. Scott Momaday, "The Man Made of Words," in Sam Gill, *Native American Traditions: Sources and Interpretations* (Belmont, Calif.: Wadsworth Publishing Co., 1983), p. 44.

16. Paul Shepard, *Nature and Madness* (San Francisco: Sierra Club Books, 1982), pp. 6 and 9.

17. Henry S. Sharp, *The Transformation of Bigfoot: Maleness, Power, and Belief among the Chipewyan* (Washington, D.C.: Smithsonian Institution Press, 1988), p. 144.

18. Robert Bringhurst, "Everywhere Being Is Dancing, Knowing Is Known," *Chicago Review* 39 (1993): 138.

19. Irene Klaver (personal communication).

20. This term is from David Abram, *The Spell of the Sensuous: Perception and Language in a More-than-Human World* (New York: Pantheon Books, 1996). The term, as used here, has primary reference to the wider biological dimensions in which we are embedded.

21. This point is well-argued in Birch, "Moral Considerability."

22. Carol Geddes, panel discussion by Yukon First Nations people on the topic "What is a good way to teach children and young adults to respect the land?" transcript in Bob Jickling, ed., *Environment, Ethics, and Education: A Colloquium* (Whitehorse: Yukon College, 1996), p. 46.

23. See Anthony Weston, "Self-Validating Reduction: Toward a Theory of the Devaluation of Nature," *Environmental Ethics* 18 (1996): 115–32.

24. Jim Nollman, *Dolphin Dreamtime* (New York: Bantam Books, 1987).

25. Conversations with those involved in the Native Philosophy Project bear this out. See Geddes, panel discussion, in Jickling, *Environment, Ethics, and Education,* pp. 32–33.

26. In conversation at the Native Philosophy Project.

27. With this admission, we acknowledge that we speak of indigenous worlds from the quite different world of academic philosophy. One reviewer worried quite rightly about what he or she called "performative contradiction" in this regard. Fair enough. We are indeed trying to cross a formidable boundary here, to speak of things in an academic voice that truly calls for the voice of ceremony and song, a personal stance more than an intellectual attitude. We accept the awkwardness and clumsiness (indigenous people might see it as irony) of the attempt. Better this than the (at present) only alternative: silence. May those who come later find the way easier.

28. N. Scott Momaday, *The Way to Rainy Mountain* (New York: Ballantine Books, 1970), p. 113.

29. Barry Lopez, "Landscape and Narrative," in *Crossing Open Ground* (New York: Random House, 1988), p. 66.

30. Elaine Jahner, "The Spiritual Landscape," in D. M. Dooling and Paul Jordan-Smith, eds., *I Become Part of It: Sacred Dimensions in Native American Life* (San Francisco: Harper-Collins, 1992), p. 193.
31. Aldo Leopold, *A Sand County Almanac* (New York: Ballantine Books, 1970), pp. 101–03.

DISCUSSION TOPICS

1. Cheney and Weston identify four central features of traditional ethics. In your view, should we retain any or all of these features as we explore environmental ethics?
2. Explain how "universal consideration" conflicts with a human-centered, traditional approach to ethics. Which approach do you believe to be appropriate to environmental ethics? Give your reasoning.
3. What do Cheney and Weston mean by suggesting that the performative dimension of language is fundamental to all thought?
4. Provide an example from your own experience of discovering that how you approach something (a child, an animal, a river, a plant) is part of what that entity is.
5. What is the role of stories in our own and our culture's identities? What part of your identity (if any) is found in stories that include the land in which you grew up?

READING 11

Just Garbage:
Environmental Injustice

Peter S. Wenz

Peter S. Wenz is professor of philosophy and legal studies at Sangamon State University and adjunct professor of medical humanities at Southern Illinois School of Medicine, both in Springfield, Illinois. His books include Environmental Justice *(1988),* Nature's Keeper *(1996), and* Environmental Ethics Today *(2001).*

In this selection, published in Faces of Environmental Racism *(1995), Wenz examines current practices in the distribution of environmental hazards and concludes that many such practices discriminate against racial minorities and against the poor. He then examines theoretical justifications for such practices and concludes that distributive justice can best be achieved through the use of a system that assigns points to different types of locally undesirable land uses.*

Environmental racism is evident in practices that expose racial minorities in the United States, and people of color around the world, to disproportionate shares of environmental hazards.[1] These include toxic chemicals in factories, toxic herbicides and pesticides in agriculture, radiation from uranium mining, lead from paint on older buildings, toxic wastes illegally dumped, and toxic wastes legally stored. In this chapter, which concentrates on issues of toxic waste, both illegally dumped and legally stored, I will examine the justness of current practices as well as the arguments commonly given in their defense. I will then propose an alternative practice that is consistent with prevailing principles of justice.

A DEFENSE OF CURRENT PRACTICES

Defenders often claim that because economic, not racial, considerations account for disproportionate impacts on nonwhites, current practices are neither racist nor morally objectionable. Their reasoning recalls the Doctrine of Double Effect. According to that doctrine, an effect whose production is usually blameworthy becomes blameless when it is incidental to, although predictably conjoined with, the production of another effect whose production is morally justified. The classic case concerns a pregnant woman with uterine cancer. A common, acceptable treatment for uterine cancer is hysterectomy. This will predictably end the pregnancy, as would an abortion. However, Roman Catholic scholars who usually consider abortion blameworthy consider it blameless in this context because it is merely incidental to hysterectomy, which is morally justified to treat uterine cancer. The hysterectomy would be performed in the absence of pregnancy, so the abortion effect is produced neither as an end-in-itself, nor as a means to reach the desired end, which is the cure of cancer.

Defenders of practices that disproportionately disadvantage nonwhites seem to claim, in keeping with the Doctrine of Double Effect, that racial effects are blameless because they are sought neither as ends-in-themselves nor as means to reach a desired goal. They are merely predictable side effects of economic and political practices that disproportionately expose poor people to toxic substances. The argument is that burial of toxic wastes, and other locally undesirable land uses (LULUs), lower property values. People who can afford to move elsewhere do so. They are replaced by buyers (or renters) who are predominantly poor and cannot afford housing in more desirable areas. Law professor Vicki Been puts it this way: "As long as the market allows the existing distribution of wealth to allocate goods and services, it would be surprising indeed if, over the long run, LULUs did not impose a disproportionate burden upon the poor." People of color are disproportionately burdened due primarily to poverty, not racism.[2] This defense against charges of racism is important in the American context because racial discrimination is illegal in the United States in circumstances where economic discrimination is permitted.[3] Thus, legal remedies to disproportionate exposure of nonwhites to toxic wastes are available if racism is the cause, but not if people of color are exposed merely because they are poor.

There is strong evidence against claims of racial neutrality. Professor Been acknowledges that even if there is no racism in the process of siting LULUs, racism plays at least some part in the disproportionate exposure of African Americans to them. She cites evidence that "racial discrimination in the sale and rental of housing relegates people of color (especially African Americans) to the least desirable neighborhoods, regardless of their income level."[4]

Without acknowledging for a moment, then, that racism plays no part in the disproportionate exposure of nonwhites to toxic waste, I will ignore this issue to display a weakness in the argument that justice is served when economic discrimination alone is influential. I claim that even if the only discrimination is economic, justice requires redress and significant alteration of current practices. Recourse to

the Doctrine of Double Effect presupposes that the primary effect, with which a second effect is incidentally conjoined, is morally justifiable. In the classic case, abortion is justified only because hysterectomy is justified as treatment for uterine cancer. I argue that disproportionate impacts on poor people violate principles of distributive justice, and so are not morally justifiable in the first place. Thus, current practices disproportionately exposing nonwhites to toxic substances are not justifiable even if incidental to the exposure of poor people.

Alternate practices that comply with acceptable principles of distributive justice are suggested below. They would largely solve problems of environmental racism (disproportionate impacts on nonwhites) while ameliorating the injustice of disproportionately exposing poor people to toxic hazards. They would also discourage production of toxic substances, thereby reducing humanity's negative impact on the environment.

THE PRINCIPLE OF COMMENSURATE BURDENS AND BENEFIT

We usually assume that, other things being equal, those who derive benefits should sustain commensurate burdens. We typically associate the burden of work with the benefit of receiving money, and the burdens of monetary payment and tort liability with the benefits of ownership.

There are many exceptions. For example, people can inherit money without working, and be given ownership without purchase. Another exception, which dissociates the benefit of ownership from the burden of tort liability, is the use of tax money to protect the public from hazards associated with private property, as in Superfund legislation. Again, the benefit of money is dissociated from the burden of work when governments support people who are unemployed.

The fact that these exceptions require justification, however, indicates an abiding assumption that people who derive benefits should shoulder commensurate burdens. The ability to inherit without work is justified as a benefit owed to those who wish to bequeath their wealth (which someone in the line of inheritance is assumed to have shouldered burdens to acquire). The same reasoning applies to gifts.

Using tax money (public money) to protect the public from dangerous private property is justified as encouraging private industry and commerce, which are supposed to increase public wealth. The system also protects victims in case private owners become bankrupt as, for example, in Times Beach, Missouri, where the government bought homes made worthless due to dioxin pollution. The company responsible for the pollution was bankrupt.

Tax money is used to help people who are out of work to help them find a job, improve their credentials, or feed their children. This promotes economic growth and equal opportunity. These exceptions prove the rule by the fact that justification for any deviation from the commensuration of benefits and burdens is considered necessary.

Further indication of an abiding belief that benefits and burdens should be commensurate is grumbling that, for example, many professional athletes and corporate executives are overpaid. Although the athletes and executives shoulder the burden of work, the complaint is that their benefits are disproportionate to their burdens. People on welfare are sometimes criticized for receiving even modest amounts of taxpayer money without shouldering the burdens of work, hence recurrent calls for "welfare reform." Even though these calls are often justified as means to reducing government budget deficits, the moral issue is more basic than the economic. Welfare expenditures are minor compared to other programs, and alternatives that require poor people to work are often more expensive than welfare as we know it.

The principle of commensuration between benefits and burdens is not the only moral principle governing distributive justice, and may not be the most important, but it is basic. Practices can be justified by showing them to conform, all things considered, to this principle. Thus, there is no move to "reform" the receipt of moderate pay for ordinary work, because it exemplifies the principle. On the other hand, practices that do not conform are liable to attack and require alternate justification, as we have seen in the cases of inheritance, gifts, Superfund legislation, and welfare.

Applying the principle of commensuration between burdens and benefits to the issue at hand yields the following: In the absence of countervailing considerations, the burdens of ill health associated with toxic hazards should be related to benefits derived from processes and products that create these hazards.

TOXIC HAZARDS AND CONSUMERISM

In order to assess, in light of the principle of commensuration between benefits and burdens, the justice of current distributions of toxic hazards, the benefits of their generation must be considered. Toxic wastes result from many manufacturing processes, including those for a host of common items and materials, such as paint, solvents, plastics, and most petrochemical-based materials. These materials surround us in the paint on our houses, in our refrigerator containers, in our clothing, in our plumbing, in our garbage pails, and elsewhere.

Toxins are released into the environment in greater quantities now than ever before because we now have a consumer-oriented society where the acquisition, use, and disposal of individually owned items is greatly desired. We associate the numerical dollar value of the items at our disposal with our "standard of living," and assume that a higher standard is conducive to, if not identical with, a better life. So toxic wastes needing disposal are produced as by-products of the general pursuit of what our society defines as valuable, that is, the consumption of material goods.

Our economy requires increasing consumer demand to keep people working (to produce what is demanded). This is why there is concern each Christmas season, for example, that shoppers may not buy enough. If demand is insufficient, people may be put out of work. Demand must increase, not merely hold steady, because commercial competition improves labor efficiency in manufacture (and now in the service sector as well), so fewer workers can produce desired items. More items must be desired to forestall labor efficiency-induced unemployment, which is grave in a society where people depend primarily on wages to secure life's necessities.

Demand is kept high largely by convincing people that their lives require improvement, which consumer purchases will effect. When improvements are seen as needed, not merely desired, people purchase more readily. So our culture encourages economic expansion by blurring the distinction between wants and needs.

One way the distinction is blurred is through promotion of worry. If one feels insecure without the desired item or service, and so worries about life without it, then its provision is easily seen as a need. Commercials, and other shapers of social expectations, keep people worried by adjusting downward toward the trivial what people are expected to worry about. People worry about the provision of food, clothing, and housing without much inducement. When these basic needs are satisfied, however, attention shifts to indoor plumbing, for example, then to stylish indoor plumbing. The process continues with needs for a second or third bathroom, a kitchen disposal, and a refrigerator attached to the plumbing so that ice is made automatically in the freezer, and cold water can be obtained without even opening the refrigerator door. The same kind of progression results in cars with CD players, cellular phones, and automatic readouts of average fuel consumption per mile.

Abraham Maslow was not accurately describing people in our society when he claimed that after physiological, safety, love, and (self-) esteem needs are met, people work toward self-actualization, becoming increasingly their own unique selves by fully developing their talents. Maslow's Hierarchy of Needs describes people in our society less than Wenz's Lowerarchy of Worry. When one source of worry is put to rest by an appropriate purchase, some matter less inherently or obviously worrisome takes its place as the focus of concern. Such worry-substitution must be amenable to indefinite repetition in order to motivate purchases needed to keep the economy growing without inherent limit. If commercial society is supported by consumer demand, it is worry all the way down. Toxic wastes are produced in this context.

People tend to worry about ill health and early death without much inducement. These concerns are heightened in a society dependent upon the production of worry, so expenditure on health care consumes an increasing percentage of the gross domestic product. As knowledge of health impairment due to toxic substances increases, people are decreasingly tolerant of risks associated with their proximity. Thus, the same mindset of worry that elicits production

that generates toxic wastes, exacerbates reaction to their proximity. The result is a desire for their placement elsewhere, hence the NIMBY syndrome — Not In My Back Yard. On this account, NIMBYism is not aberrantly selfish behavior, but integral to the cultural value system required for great volumes of toxic waste to be generated in the first place.

Combined with the Principle of Commensurate Burdens and Benefits, that value system indicates who should suffer the burden of proximity to toxic wastes. Other things being equal, those who benefit most from the production of waste should shoulder the greatest share of burdens associated with its disposal. In our society, consumption of goods is valued highly and constitutes the principal benefit associated with the generation of toxic wastes. Such consumption is generally correlated with income and wealth. So other things being equal, justice requires that people's proximity to toxic wastes be related positively to their income and wealth. This is exactly opposite to the predominant tendency in our society, where poor people are more proximate to toxic wastes dumped illegally and stored legally.

REJECTED THEORIES OF JUSTICE

Proponents of some theories of distributive justice may claim that current practices are justified. In this section I will explore such claims.

A widely held view of justice is that all people deserve to have their interests given equal weight. John Rawls's popular thought experiment in which people choose principles of justice while ignorant of their personal identities dramatizes the importance of equal consideration of interests. Even selfish people behind the "veil of ignorance" in Rawls's "original position" would choose to accord equal consideration to everyone's interests because, they reason, they may themselves be the victims of any inequality. Equal consideration is a basic moral premise lacking serious challenge in our culture, so it is presupposed in what follows. Disagreement centers on application of the principle.

Libertarianism

Libertarians claim that each individual has an equal right to be free of interference from other people. All burdens imposed by other people are unjustified unless part of, or consequent upon, agreement by the party being burdened. So no individual who has not consented should be burdened by burial of toxic wastes (or the emission of air pollutants, or the use of agricultural pesticides, etc.) that may increase risks of disease, disablement, or death. Discussing the effects of air pollution, libertarian Murray Rothbard writes, "The remedy is simply to enjoin anyone from injecting pollutants into the air, and thereby invading the rights of persons and property. Period."[5] Libertarians John Hospers and Tibor R. Machan seem to endorse Rothbard's position.[6]

The problem is that implementation of this theory is impractical and unjust in the context of our civilization. Industrial life as we know it inevitably includes production of pollutants and toxic substances that threaten human life and health. It is impractical to secure the agreement of every individual to the placement, whether on land, in the air, or in water, of every chemical that may adversely affect the life or health of the individuals in question. After being duly informed of the hazard, someone potentially affected is bound to object, making the placement illegitimate by libertarian criteria.

In effect, libertarians give veto power to each individual over the continuation of industrial society. This seems a poor way to accord equal consideration to everyone's interests because the interest in physical safety of any one individual is allowed to override all other interests of all other individuals in the continuation of modern life. Whether or not such life is worth pursuing, it seems unjust to put the decision for everyone in the hands of any one person.

Utilitarianism

Utilitarians consider the interests of all individuals equally, and advocate pursuing courses of action that promise to produce results containing the greatest (net) sum of good. However, irrespective of how "good" is defined, problems with utilitarian accounts of justice are many and notorious.

Utilitarianism suffers in part because its direct interest is exclusively in the sum total of good, and in the future. Since the sum of good is all that counts in utilitarianism, there is no guarantee that the good of some will not be sacrificed for the greater good of others. Famous people could receive (justifiably according to utilitarians) particularly harsh sentences for criminal activity to effect general deterrence. Even when fame results from honest pursuits, a famous felon's sentence is likely to attract more attention than sentences in other cases of similar criminal activity. Because potential criminals are more likely to respond to sentences in such cases, harsh punishment is justified for utilitarian reasons on grounds that are unrelated to the crime.

Utilitarianism suffers in cases like this not only from its exclusive attention to the sum total of good, but also from its exclusive preoccupation with future consequences, which makes the relevance of past conduct indirect. This affects not only retribution, but also reciprocity and gratitude, which utilitarians endorse only to produce the greatest sum of future benefits. The direct relevance of past agreements and benefits, which common sense assumes, disappears in utilitarianism. So does direct application of the Principle of Commensurate Burdens and Benefits.

The merits of the utilitarian rejection of common sense morality need not be assessed, however, because utilitarianism seems impossible to put into practice. Utilitarian support for any particular conclusion is undermined by the inability of anyone actually to perform the kinds of calculations that utilitarians profess to use. Whether the good is identified with happiness or preference-satisfaction, the two leading contenders at the moment, utilitarians announce the conclusions of their calculations without ever being able to show the calculation itself.

When I was in school, math teachers suspected that students who could never show their work were copying answers from other students. I suspect similarly that utilitarians, whose "calculations" often support conclusions that others reach by recourse to principles of gratitude, retributive justice, commensuration between burdens and benefits, and so forth, reach conclusions on grounds of intuitions influenced predominantly by these very principles.

Utilitarians may claim that, contrary to superficial appearances, these principles are themselves supported by utilitarian calculations. But, again, no one has produced a relevant calculation. Some principles seem *prima facie* opposed to utilitarianism, such as the one prescribing special solicitude of parents for their own children. It would seem that in cold climates more good would be produced if people bought winter coats for needy children, instead of special dress coats and ski attire for their own children. But utilitarians defend the principle of special parental concern. They declare this principle consistent with utilitarianism by appeal to entirely untested, unsubstantiated assumptions about counterfactuals. It is a kind of "Just So" story that explains how good is maximized by adherence to current standards. There is no calculation at all.

Another indication that utilitarians cannot perform the calculations they profess to rely upon concerns principles whose worth is in genuine dispute. Utilitarians offer no calculations that help to settle the matter. For example, many people wonder today whether or not patriotism is a worthy moral principle. Detailed utilitarian calculations play no part in the discussion.

These are some of the reasons why utilitarianism provides no help to those deciding whether or not disproportionate exposure of poor people to toxic wastes is just.

Free Market Approach

Toxic wastes, a burden, could be placed where residents accept them in return for monetary payment, a benefit. Since market transactions often satisfactorily commensurate burdens and benefits, this approach may seem to honor the principle of commensuration between burdens and benefits.

Unlike many market transactions, however, whole communities, acting as corporate bodies, would have to contract with those seeking to bury wastes. Otherwise, any single individual in the community could veto the transaction, resulting in the impasse attending libertarian approaches.[7] Communities could receive money to improve such public facilities as schools, parks, and hospitals, in addition to obtaining tax revenues and jobs that result ordinarily from business expansion.

The major problem with this free market approach is that it fails to accord equal consideration to everyone's interests. Where basic or vital goods and services are at issue, we usually think equal consideration of interests requires ameliorating inequalities of distribution that markets tend to produce. For example, one reason, although not the only reason, for public education is to provide every child with the basic intellectual tools necessary for success in our society. A purely free market approach,

by contrast, would result in excellent education for children of wealthy parents and little or no education for children of the nation's poorest residents. Opportunities for children of poor parents would be so inferior that we would say the children's interests had not been given equal consideration.

The reasoning is similar where vital goods are concerned. The United States has the Medicaid program for poor people to supplement market transactions in health care precisely because equal consideration of interests requires that everyone be given access to health care. The 1994 health care debate in the United States was, ostensibly, about how to achieve universal coverage, not about whether or not justice required such coverage. With the exception of South Africa, every other industrialized country already has universal coverage for health care. Where vital needs are concerned, markets are supplemented or avoided in order to give equal consideration to everyone's interests.

Another example concerns military service in time of war. The United States employed conscription during the Civil War, both world wars, the Korean War, and the war in Vietnam. When the national interest requires placing many people in mortal danger, it is considered just that exposure be largely unrelated to income and market transactions.

The United States does not currently provide genuine equality in education or health care, nor did universal conscription (of males) put all men at equal risk in time of war. In all three areas, advantage accrues to those with greater income and wealth. (During the Civil War, paying for a substitute was legal in many cases.) Imperfection in practice, however, should not obscure general agreement in theory that justice requires equal consideration of interests, and that such equal consideration requires rejecting purely free market approaches where basic or vital needs are concerned.

Toxic substances affect basic and vital interests. Lead, arsenic, and cadmium in the vicinity of children's homes can result in mental retardation of the children.[8] Navaho teens exposed to radiation from uranium mine tailings have seventeen times the national average of reproductive organ cancer.[9] Environmental Protection Agency (EPA) officials estimate that toxic air pollution in areas of South Chicago increase cancer risks one hundred to one thousand times.[10] Pollution from Otis Air Force base in Massachusetts is associated with alarming increases in cancer rates.[11] Non-Hodgkin's Lymphoma is related to living near stone, clay, and glass industry facilities, and leukemia is related to living near chemical and petroleum plants.[12] In general, cancer rates are higher in the United States near industries that use toxic substances and discard them nearby.[13]

In sum, the placement of toxic wastes affects basic and vital interests just as do education, health care, and wartime military service. Exemption from market decisions is required to avoid unjust impositions on the poor, and to respect people's interests equally. A child dying of cancer receives little benefit from the community's new swimming pool.

Cost-Benefit Analysis (CBA)

CBA is an economist's version of utilitarianism, where the sum to be maximized is society's wealth, as measured in monetary units, instead of happiness or preference satisfaction. Society's wealth is computed by noting (and estimating where necessary) what people are willing to pay for goods and services. The more people are willing to pay for what exists in society, the better off society is, according to CBA.

CBA will characteristically require placement of toxic wastes near poor people. Such placement usually lowers land values (what people are willing to pay for property). Land that is already cheap, where poor people live, will not lose as much value as land that is currently expensive, where wealthier people live, so a smaller loss of social wealth attends placement of toxic wastes near poor people. This is just the opposite of what the Principle of Commensurate Burdens and Benefits requires.

The use of CBA also violates equal consideration of interests, operating much like free market approaches. Where a vital concern is at issue, equal consideration of interests requires that people be considered irrespective of income. The placement of toxic wastes affects vital interests. Yet CBA would have poor people exposed disproportionately to such wastes.[14]

In sum, libertarianism, utilitarianism, free market distribution, and cost-benefit analysis are inadequate principles and methodologies to guide the just distribution of toxic wastes.

LULU POINTS

An approach that avoids these difficulties assigns points to different types of locally undesirable land uses (LULUs) and requires that all communities earn LULU points.[15] In keeping with the Principle of Commensurate Benefits and Burdens, wealthy communities would be required to earn more LULU points than poorer ones. Communities would be identified by currently existing political divisions, such as villages, towns, city wards, cities, and counties.

Toxic waste dumps are only one kind of LULU. Others include prisons, half-way houses, municipal waste sites, low-income housing, and power plants, whether nuclear or coal fired. A large deposit of extremely toxic waste, for example, may be assigned twenty points when properly buried but fifty points when illegally dumped. A much smaller deposit of properly buried toxic waste may be assigned only ten points, as may a coal-fired power plant. A nuclear power plant may be assigned twenty-five points, while municipal waste sites are only five points, and one hundred units of low-income housing are eight points.

These numbers are only speculations. Points would be assigned by considering probable effects of different LULUs on basic needs, and responses to questionnaires investigating people's levels of discomfort with LULUs of various sorts. Once numbers are assigned, the total number of LULU points to be distributed in a given time period could be calculated by considering planned development and needs for prisons, power plants, low-income housing, and so on. One could also calculate points for a community's already existing LULUs. Communities could then be required to host LULUs in proportion to their income or wealth, with new allocation of LULUs (and associated points) correcting for currently existing deviations from the rule of proportionality.

Wherever significant differences of wealth or income exist between two areas, these areas should be considered part of different communities if there is any political division between them. Thus, a county with rich and poor areas would not be considered a single community for purposes of locating LULUs. Instead, villages or towns may be so considered. A city with rich and poor areas may similarly be reduced to its wards. The purpose of segregating areas of different income or wealth from one another is to permit the imposition of greater LULU burdens on wealthier communities. When wealthy and poor areas are considered as one larger community, there is the danger that the community will earn its LULU points by placing hazardous waste near its poorer members. This possibility is reduced when only relatively wealthy people live in a smaller community that must earn LULU points.

PRACTICAL IMPLICATIONS

Political strategy is beyond the scope of this chapter, so I will refrain from commenting on problems and prospects for securing passage and implementation of the foregoing proposal. I maintain that the proposal is just. In a society where injustice is common, it is no surprise that proposals for rectification meet stiff resistance.

Were the LULU points proposal implemented, environmental racism would be reduced enormously. To the extent that poor people exposed to environmental hazards are members of racial minorities, relieving the poor of disproportionate exposure would also relieve people of color.

This is not to say that environmental racism would be ended completely. Implementation of the proposal requires judgment in particular cases. Until racism is itself ended, such judgment will predictably be exercised at times to the disadvantage of minority populations. However, because most people of color currently burdened by environmental racism are relatively poor, implementing the proposal would remove 80 to 90 percent of the effects of environmental racism. While efforts to end racism at all levels should continue, reducing the burdens of racism is generally advantageous to people of color. Such reductions are especially worthy when integral to policies that improve distributive justice generally.

Besides improving distributive justice and reducing the burdens of environmental racism, implementing the LULU points proposal would benefit life on earth generally by reducing the generation of toxic hazards. When people of wealth, who exercise control of manufacturing processes, marketing campaigns, and media coverage, are themselves threatened disproportionately by toxic hazards, the culture

will evolve quickly to find their production largely unnecessary. It will be discovered, for example, that many plastic items can be made of wood, just as it was discovered in the late 1980s that the production of many ozone-destroying chemicals is unnecessary. Similarly, necessity being the mother of invention, it was discovered during World War II that many women could work in factories. When certain interests are threatened, the impossible does not even take longer.

The above approach to environmental injustice should, of course, be applied internationally and intranationally within all countries. The same considerations of justice condemn universally, all other things being equal, exposing poor people to vital dangers whose generation predominantly benefits the rich. This implies that rich countries should not ship their toxic wastes to poor countries. Since many poorer countries, such as those in Africa, are inhabited primarily by nonwhites, prohibiting shipments of toxic wastes to them would reduce significantly worldwide environmental racism. A prohibition on such shipments would also discourage production of dangerous wastes, as it would require people in rich countries to live with whatever dangers they create. If the principle of LULU points were applied in all countries, including poor ones, elites in those countries would lose interest in earning foreign currency credits through importation of waste, as they would be disproportionately exposed to imported toxins.

In sum, we could reduce environmental injustice considerably through a general program of distributive justice concerning environmental hazards. Pollution would not thereby be eliminated, since to live is to pollute. But such a program would motivate significant reduction in the generation of toxic wastes, and help the poor, especially people of color, as well as the environment.

NOTES

1. Laura Westra and Bill E. Lawson, "Introduction," *Faces of Environmental Racism* (Lanham, Md.: Rowman & Littlefield, 2001), xvii–xxvi.
2. Vicki Been, "Market Forces, Not Racist Practices, May Affect the Siting of Locally Undesirable Land Uses," in *At Issue: Environmental*

Justice, ed. by Jonathan Petrikin (San Diego, Calif.: Greenhaven Press, 1995), 41.

3. See *San Antonio Independent School District v. Rodriguez,* 411 R.S. 1 (1973) and *Village of Arlington Heights v. Metropolitan Housing Development Corporation,* 429 U.S. 252 (1977).

4. Been, 41.

5. Murray Rothbard, "The Great Ecology Issue," *The Individualist* 21, no. 2 (February 1970): 5.

6. See Peter S. Wenz, *Environmental Justice* (Albany, N.Y.: State University of New York Press, 1988), 65–67 and associated endnotes.

7. Christopher Boerner and Thomas Lambert, "Environmental Justice Can Be Achieved through Negotiated Compensation," in *At Issue: Environmental Justice.*

8. F. Diaz-Barriga et al., "Arsenic and Cadmium Exposure in Children Living Near to Both Zinc and Copper Smelters," summarized in *Archives of Environmental Health* 46, no. 2 (March/April 1991): 119.

9. Dick Russell, "Environmental Racism," *Amicus Journal* (Spring 1989): 22–32, 24.

10. Marianne Lavelle, "The Minorities Equation," *National Law Journal* 21 (September 1992): 3.

11. Christopher Hallowell, "Water Crisis on the Cape," *Audubon* (July/August 1991): 65–74, especially 66 and 70.

12. Athena Linos et al., "Leukemia and Non-Hodgkin's Lymphoma and Residential Proximity to Industrial Plants," *Archives of Environmental Health* 46, no. 2 (March/April 1991): 70–74.

13. L. W. Pickle et al., *Atlas of Cancer Mortality among Whites: 1950–1980,* HHS publication # (NIH) 87-2900 (Washington D.C.: U.S.

Department of Health and Human Services, Government Printing Office: 1987).

14. Wenz, 216–18.

15. The idea of LULU points comes to me from Frank J. Popper, "LULUs and Their Blockage," in *Confronting Regional Challenges: Approaches to LULUs, Growth, and Other Vexing Governance Problems,* ed. by Joseph DiMento and Le Roy Graymer (Los Angeles, Calif.: Lincoln Institute of Land Policy, 1991), 13–27, especially 24.

DISCUSSION TOPICS

1. Are you aware of any situations in your community or state in which poor people or racial minorities have borne the burden of toxic waste disposal?

2. Peter Wenz rejects the use of the Doctrine of Double Effect to justify disproportionate economic burdens on the poor. Explain his reasoning. Do you agree? Why or why not?

3. Based on the principle of commensuration between benefits and burdens, Wenz maintains that justice requires that the more wealth people have the closer they should live to toxic wastes. Do you agree with this view? Explain your reasoning.

4. Wenz dismisses libertarian, utilitarian, and free market approaches to the issue of toxic waste. Evaluate his reasoning.

5. Wenz proposes a system of LULU (locally undesirable land use) points as a remedy for injustice and suggests that the approach should be applied internationally. Do you agree? Why or why not?

CLASS EXERCISES

1. Consider a grove of alder trees in a remote watershed, which has never been (and never will be) observed by human beings. Do the trees have value? What kind? Give reasons for your answer.

2. Consider the moral judgment "It is wrong to cause the extinction of a species." What are some reasons for and against such a judgment? Classify your reasons according to whether they assume traditional relativism, universalism, contextualism, or pluralism.

3. Is there any connection between being good and being natural? For example, consider the following: the desire to have children, the desire to hunt animals, the desire for social approval.

4. Does environmental justice include duties toward future generations of human beings? If so, what might be some examples?

FOR FURTHER READING

Armstrong-Buck, Susan. "What Process Philosophy Can Contribute to the Land Ethic and Deep Ecology." *Trumpeter* 8, no. 1 (Winter 1991): 29–34. Discusses some weaknesses of Callicott's and Rolston's positions on value and presents a brief introduction to the advantages of process metaphysics in clarifying the concept of self in deep ecology.

Attfield, Robin, and Andrew Belsey, eds. *Philosophy and the Natural Environment.* Cambridge: Cambridge University Press, 1994. A fine collection of papers, with an illuminating introduction by Attfield. Dale Jamieson's paper "Global Environmental Justice" points out difficulties with treating the environment as a commodity to be justly distributed.

Bryan, Bunyan, ed. *Environmental Justice: Issues, Policies, and Solutions.* Washington, D.C.: Island Press, 1995. Useful essays for advanced students, particularly the essay by Frederick H. Buttel on international environmental policy. Buttel argues that the Third World debt crisis and the world monetary order are the key issues.

Callicott, J. Baird. "Rolston on Intrinsic Value: A Deconstruction." *Environmental Ethics* 14 (1992): 129–43. Callicott argues that Rolston's view is not well-grounded. For Callicott, all value is anthropogenic, or at least "vertebragenic" (produced by a vertebrate).

Ferré, Frederick, and Peter Hartel. *Ethics and Environmental Policy: Theory Meets Practice.* Athens: University of Georgia Press, 1994. Well-chosen essays speaking to the importance of context and illustrating that to theorize is to practice.

Light, Andrew. "Compatibilism in Political Ecology," in *Environmental Pragmatism,* ed. A. Light and E. Katz. London: Routledge, 1996. Light aims at resolving claims made by deep ecologists and materialists. For advanced students.

Macauley, David, ed. *Minding Nature: The Philosophers of Ecology.* New York: Guilford Press, 1996. Critical social theory, with articles on Hobbes, Heidegger, Arendt, Ernst Bloch, Hans Jonas, Marcuse, Mumford, Habermas, Bookchin, and others.

Monist 75 (1992). Special issue, edited by J. Baird Callicott, on natural value theory.

Norton, Bryan G. *Why Preserve Natural Variety?* Princeton, N.J.: Princeton University Press, 1987. A valuable discussion of types of values, including demand values, amenity values, and transformative values. Norton argues that preservation of habitats is the best way to preserve biodiversity.

———. "Biodiversity and Environmental Values: In Search of a Universal Earth Ethic." *Biology and Conservation* 9 (2000): 1029–44.

Oelschlaeger, Max, ed. *Postmodern Environmental Ethics.* Albany, N.Y.: SUNY Press, 1995. A useful collection of papers published in *Environmental Ethics.* Oelschlaeger describes the essays as forms of "effective discourse," working through language to promote a sustainable society.

Partridge, Ernest. "Why Care about the Future?" in *Responsibilities to Future Generations,* ed. Ernest Partridge. Buffalo, N.Y.: Prometheus Books, 1981. A persuasive argument to care about the future based on the need for self-transcendence.

———. "On the Rights of Future Generations," in *Upstream/Downstream: Issues in Environmental Ethics,* ed. Donald Scherer. Philadelphia: Temple University Press, 1993. Partridge demonstrates that future generations have rights and speculates on their content.

Rolston, Holmes, III. *Environmental Ethics.* Philadelphia: Temple University Press, 1988. The most complete account so far of the notion of intrinsic natural value. A subtle and complex study with ample use of biological examples.

Rowlands, Mark. *The Environmental Crisis: Understanding the Value of Nature.* New York: St. Martin's Press, 2000. Rowlands aims at breaking down the distinction between mind and world while retaining the independence of the world. For advanced students.

Soulé, Michael E., and Gary Lease, eds. *Reinventing Nature? Responses to Postmodern Deconstruction.* Washington, D.C.: Island Press, 1995. Thought-provoking responses to the attempted deconstruction of nature by certain postmodern social critics.

Stone, Christopher D. *Earth and Other Ethics: The Case for Moral Pluralism.* New York: Harper and Row, 1987. An important attack on moral monism; Stone explains the advantages of a more flexible approach.

Wenz, Peter. *Environmental Justice.* Albany, N.Y.: SUNY Press, 1988. Wenz develops a pluralist, concentric circle theory, where humans have differing kinds of obligations to different entities. For advanced students.

Westra, Laura, and Peter S. Wenz, eds. *Faces of Environmental Racism: Confronting Issues of Global Justice.* Lanham, MD: Rowman & Littlefield, 2001. Environmental racism is a major but largely unnoticed problem. This volume unmasks its presence in the United States and Africa.

CHAPTER THREE
Aesthetics

. . . [T]he ultimate historical foundations of nature preservation are aesthetic. . . .

—Eugene Hargrove
Foundations of Environmental Ethics, p. 168

In this chapter we discuss some characteristics of aesthetic experience. We also describe how the aesthetic experience of nature differs from the aesthetic experience of art objects. Finally we consider the experiences of nature as sacred and as wilderness.

CHARACTERISTICS OF AESTHETIC EXPERIENCE

Aesthetic[1] experience, like all experience, has both an objective aspect, determined by the characteristics of the object or event, and a subjective aspect, referring to the characteristics, states of mind, and interests of the subject or observer. Aesthetic experience, however, differs from other experience in important ways.[2] First, aesthetic experience in-

volves an attitude that is guided almost exclusively by the nature of the object or event, so that the object or event is valued for its own sake rather than for its potential use. Thus aesthetic experience is either intrinsically or inherently valuable, as discussed in the introduction to Chapter 2.

Second, aesthetic experience is a sympathetic, contemplative, receptive experience, in which the observer lets the object or event be itself. The observer seeks to understand or relate to the object on its own terms.

Third, aesthetic experience is centered in the present moment rather than in the past or future. The observer is concerned primarily with what an object or event is in itself rather than with what caused it or what consequences the object or event might have.

Fourth, aesthetic experience concerns a particular object or event, or a particular kind of object or event. Aesthetically, the observer does not engage the object (or kind of object) as merely an instance or example of a general principle, as would be the case in scientific inquiry. Rather, the focus is on the uniqueness of the object.

Fifth, aesthetic experience entails delight in harmony and complex unity. In aesthetic feeling, a goal

---

[1]A. G. Baumgarten coined the term in 1750; it is based on the Greek *aistheikos,* meaning "sense perception."

[2]The following discussion draws from Jerome Stolnitz, "The Aesthetic Attitude," in *Aesthetics and the Philosophy of Art Criticism* (New York: Houghton Mifflin, 1960) and from Allen Carlson, "Appreciating Art and Appreciating Nature," in *Landscape, Natural Beauty and the Arts,* Salim Kemal and Ivan Gaskell, eds. (Cambridge: Cambridge University Press, 1993).

is to avoid both discord (the lack of a unifying pattern) and monotony (a boring or repetitive pattern). The observer recognizes an organizing structure or pattern that unifies many parts.

Sixth, aesthetic experience can involve primarily the spontaneous feelings of the observer,[3] but it can also include a distinctly conceptual aspect.[4] The conceptual aspect may involve reflection upon the fruitfulness of that experience in leading to additional experiences of value. Recognition of both emotive and conceptual aspects of aesthetic experience allows the postulation that nonhuman sentient organisms may have aesthetic experiences. Examples include the paintings of captive chimpanzees and elephants, as well as the bowers, decorations, dances, and paintings of bower birds.[5]

Seventh, aesthetic experience can be of any object or event, as long as we encounter the object with sympathetic attention. There are no specific properties that an object or event must possess in order to be considered aesthetic. The object can be sensuous — perceived with the five senses — or intellectual — apprehended only with the mind. Because most cultures have considered the mind to be superior to the body, intellectual beauty such as that found in mathematical systems generally has been thought to be a higher form of beauty than is sensuous beauty. For example, Edna St. Vincent Millay wrote, "Euclid alone has looked upon beauty bare."[6]

THE BEAUTY OF NATURE

Although the aesthetic appreciation of art has been evident for millennia, in the West the appreciation of natural beauty has developed very slowly.[7] In medieval and Renaissance art, nature was only the background to human activity, and a symbolic one at that. Nature was either a source of the "mirror of God" or simply hard work and danger for human beings; nature was not something of interest in its own right. As Callicott points out in his essay "The Land Aesthetic," the enjoyment of natural beauty for its own sake developed from a tradition of landscape painting in the seventeenth century; its origin lies in the "picturesque" as formed by the history of painting.[8] So strong is that art historical influence that it has been claimed that only those areas deemed picturesque owing to having been painted by a notable artist have been given protected status as parks or wilderness areas.[9] In the eighteenth century, garden activities and games became popular, and cities began to include trees in their urban planning. In the mid-eighteenth to the mid-nineteenth centuries many people traveled to beautiful places, and enjoyed the emerging activities of landscape gardening and landscape architecture. In the nineteenth century the development of natural science contributed to the recognition of the scientifically "interesting" as an aesthetic category in addition to the traditional categories of the beautiful, the sublime, and the picturesque.[10]

How does an aesthetic experience of nature differ from one of human-made art? One essential

---

[3]Noël Carroll stresses the emotional responses involved in nature appreciation, and argues that the objectivity of nature appreciation is based partly on the appropriateness of such emotional responses. "On Being Moved by Nature: Between Religion and Natural History," in *Landscape, Natural Beauty and the Arts.* Salim Kemal and Ivan Gaskell, eds. (Cambridge: Cambridge University Press, 1993), pp. 244–66.

[4]Charles Hartshorne, *Born to Sing: An Interpretation and World Survey of Bird Song* (Bloomington: Indiana University Press, 1973).

[5]A. J. Marshall, *Bower-Birds: Their Displays and Breeding Cycles* (Oxford: Clarendon Press, 1954). Jared Diamond, "Art of the Wild," *Discover* (February 1991): 79–85, discusses chimp and elephant art. Elephant art is also extensively and perceptively discussed by David Gucwa and James Ehmann in *To Whom It May Concern: An Investigation of the Art of Elephants* (New York: W. W. Norton, 1985). See also John Terborgh, "Cracking the Bird Code," *New York Review of Books,* January 11, 1996: 40–44, a review of research into bird song, illustrating that there is no simple answer to why birds sing.

[6]Edna St. Vincent Millay, "Euclid Alone Has Looked upon Beauty Bare," in *Modern American Poetry,* Louis Untermeyer, ed. (New York: Harcourt Brace, 1942).

[7]In Japan and China the admiration of wild mountain landscapes has existed since ancient times.

[8]Marcia M. Eaton, *Aesthetics and the Good Life* (London: Fairleigh Dickinson University Press, 1989).

[9]Eugene Hargrove, *Foundations of Environmental Ethics* (Englewood Cliffs, N.J.: Prentice-Hall, 1989), p. 106, fn. 47.

[10]Hargrove, *Foundations of Environmental Ethics,* pp. 88–92.

difference is that of *participation.* Nature surrounds, involves all of our senses, and sustains us in a way no painting, poem, or sculpture can. In experiencing natural beauty the observer may experience himself or herself as a living creature dependent upon the soil, plants, water, air, and light. Some contemporary thinkers have suggested a "habitat" theory of landscape beauty, according to which we admire environments where we feel safe.[11] We like landscapes in which we have both vision (prospect) and protection. This participatory quality of our experience of nature might explain what Allen Carlson terms "positive aesthetics," in which our task is to understand why nature (undisturbed by human beings) is always beautiful.[12] Perhaps we experience untouched nature as beautiful because healthy natural cycles promote human well-being.

In addition, nature is *frameless.*[13] The experience of nature provides surprises, whereas art objects often have spatial and temporal boundaries. The aesthetic experience of nature requires an alertness to new experiences, arising from the dynamism of natural processes and from the fact that the observer can choose any point of observation. In his essay on Leopold's natural aesthetic, Callicott notes the aesthetic excitement of the noumena of the land — the hidden, unpredictable presence of wolves and bears, loons, and cutthroat trout.

These characteristics of participation and framelessness are evident in "earth art," in which natural objects are inseparable from the work of art and in which the art is often bound to its site. This kind of art began in the United States in the late 1960s,

though it is not limited to that country.[14] Early works pitched themselves against the elements, but more recently artists have been working in greater harmony with the earth. For example, "Roden Crater," the project envisaged by James Turrell, is an extinct cinder cone. Turrell has purchased the site and is building underground chambers to be aligned with the sun. Turrell's intention is that the spectator will become participant; the artwork will be the movement of natural forces undisturbed by artificial light. The work will surround the spectator and extend for hundreds of miles.[15] "Eco-art" has been used to refer to noninterventionist artworks that employ ecological processes such as water filtration and plant growth; eco-art may be a new form of activism.[16] Recently, striking images of the earth from the Landsat 7 satellite have been selected on the basis of aesthetic appeal and made available to the public online.[17]

Eugene Hargrove has pointed out that the *independent existence* of natural objects is crucial to the aesthetic experience of nature.[18] We value the self-creating, continuous history of natural objects.[19] We value the nonhuman origin, the "naturalness" of nature. David Johns points out that the term *wilderness* evolved from earlier Celtic words meaning "self-willed land."[20] Our delight at a stand of trees is changed into something else if we are informed that the trees are plastic. Gary Nabhan's essay "The

---

[11]Jay Appleton, *The Experience of Landscape* (London: John Wiley & Sons, 1975). Appleton reaffirms this theory in the more recent book by Nasar. (See "For Further Reading.")

[12]Allen Carlson, "Aesthetic Appreciation of the Natural Environment," in *Environmental Ethics,* R. Botzler and S. Armstrong, eds. (New York: McGraw-Hill, 1998) pp. 122–31.

[13]R. W. Hepburn, "Aesthetic Appreciation of Nature," in *Contemporary Aesthetics,* Matthew Lipman, ed. (Boston: Allyn & Bacon, 1973), pp. 340–54.

[14]Urjo Sepanmaa, in *The Beauty of Environment: A General Model for Environmental Aesthetics* (Denton, Tex.: Environmental Ethics Books, 1993), discusses the works of Christo and the Finnish artists Lanu and Lukkela.

[15]Craig Adcock, *James Turrell: The Art of Light and Space* (Berkeley: University of California Press, 1990). The Roden Crater is scheduled for public access in 2005 or later. See also J. Beardsley, *Earthworks and Beyond: Contemporary Art in the Landscape* (New York: Abbeville Press, 1989).

[16]Sue Chudley, "Art, Earth Art and Eco-Art," *Ecos* 16, no. 1 (1995): 11–18. See also Suzi Gablik, "Arts and the Earth: Making Art As If the World Mattered," *Orion* 14, no. 4 (1995): 44–53.

[17]See at http://landsat.gsfc.nasa.gov/earthasart.

[18]Hargrove, "The Ontological Argument for the Preservation of Nature," in *Foundations of Environmental Ethics.*

[19]Eric Katz stresses this point in order to exhibit what is wrong with ecological restoration. "The Big Lie," *Research in Philosophy and Technology,* 12 (1992).

[20]David Johns, "Wilderness and Human Habitation," in *Place of the Wild,* David Clarke Burks, ed. (Washington, D.C.: Island Press, 1994). See also Jay Hansford and C. Vest, "Will of the Land," *Environmental Review* (Winter 1985): 321–29.

Far Outside" stresses the importance of getting outside human self-preoccupation and learning the stories of other species.

Fundamental parts of our aesthetic experience of nature are the *connectedness and complexity* of natural systems. In "The Land Aesthetic," J. Baird Callicott illustrates how the understanding of ecology and evolutionary history can heighten our participation in nature.

Because of the connectedness within natural systems, an aesthetic experience of nature has a *normative* character based on the health of continuous, self-sufficient natural cycles. Qualities such as integrity, stability, and appropriateness of a part to the whole characterize natural systems.

Further, nature provides *transcendence* of ordinary experience. Nature has been interpreted not only as picturesque or beautiful, but as sublime, as inspiring feelings of awe and grandeur. Great storms at sea, waterfalls, and ranges of towering mountains often were considered sublime, particularly in the eighteenth and nineteenth centuries. Although the term is no longer much used, feelings of awe and grandeur appear in the contemporary appreciation of wilderness and the associated sense of nature as sacred. In wild places human experience is transcended. We can experience humility in the face of the nonhuman and a liberation from human planning and conventional human thinking. We apprehend something approaching a cosmic order and ultimate meaning. Examples of the transcendence of ordinary experience can be found in the earth art mentioned earlier. Maureen Korp points to the fact that earthworks are site specific and argues that some are of such high quality that they evoke the sacred in the sense of "an earth-centered reverence."[21]

The essays by the nineteenth-century American writers John Muir and Henry David Thoreau—"Walking" by Thoreau and Muir's "A Near View of the High Sierra"—exemplify a deep appreciation for wilderness and its revelations of what makes for a truly satisfying human life. David Abram, in "A More-Than-Human World," vividly represents those in the twenty-first century who continue to apprehend the magical and beautiful "otherness" of nonhuman nature, not only in wilderness areas but even in the activities of the insects that surround us.

---

[21]Maureen Korp, *Sacred Art of the Earth: Ancient and Contemporary Earthworks* (New York: Continuum, 1997), esp. ch. 5. Color photographs of a number of examples of earth art can be found in the summer 2001 edition of *Spirituality and Health.*

Walking

Henry David Thoreau

Henry David Thoreau (1817–1862) is generally considered the greatest American nature writer. His best-known work, Walden, *has influenced several generations through its call to a life of natural simplicity, harmony, and spiritual liberty. For Thoreau, nature teaches us how to wake up from our slothful, conventional everyday consciousness and to live out our own, original lives.*

Thoreau's essay "Walking" is one of the best expressions of his love for wilderness. The walking he speaks of occurs in two dimensions: that of country paths and that of spiritual paths. Thoreau tells the reader that a walk requires the readiness to leave familiar, ordinary life and to venture into the "springs of life."

I wish to speak a word for Nature, for absolute freedom and wildness, as contrasted with a freedom and culture merely civil—to regard man as an inhabitant, or a part and parcel of Nature, rather than a member of society. I wish to make an extreme statement, if so I may make an emphatic one, for there are enough champions of civilization: the minister and the school committee and every one of you will take care of that.

I have met with but one or two persons in the course of my life who understood the art of Walking, that is, of taking walks—who had a genius, so to speak, for *sauntering,* which word is beautifully derived "from idle people who roved about the country, in the Middle Ages, and asked charity, under pretense of going *à la Sainte Terre,*" to the Holy Land, till the children exclaimed, "There goes a *Sainte-Terrer,*" a Saunterer, a Holy-Lander. They who never go to the Holy Land in their walks, as they pretend, are indeed mere idlers and vagabonds; but they who do go there are saunterers in the good sense, such as I mean. Some, however, would derive the word from *sans terre,* without land or a home, which, therefore, in the good sense, will mean, having no particular home, but equally at home everywhere. For this is the secret of successful saunter-

ing. He who sits still in a house all the time may be the greatest vagrant of all; but the saunterer, in the good sense, is no more vagrant than the meandering river, which is all the while sedulously seeking the shortest course to the sea. But I prefer the first, which, indeed, is the most probable derivation. For every walk is a sort of crusade, preached by some Peter the Hermit in us, to go forth and reconquer this Holy Land from the hands of the Infidels.

It is true, we are but faint-hearted crusaders, even the walkers, nowadays, who undertake no persevering, never-ending enterprises. Our expeditions are but tours, and come round again at evening to the old hearth-side from which we set out. Half the walk is but retracing our steps. We should go forth on the shortest walk, perchance, in the spirit of undying adventure, never to return—prepared to send back our embalmed hearts only as relics to our desolate kingdoms. If you are ready to leave father and mother, and brother and sister, and wife and child and friends, and never see them again—if you have paid your debts, and made your will, and settled all your affairs, and are a free man, then you are ready for a walk. . . .

But the walking of which I speak has nothing in it akin to taking exercise, as it is called, as the sick take medicine at stated hours—as the swinging of dumb-bells or chairs; but is itself the enterprise and adventure of the day. If you would get exercise, go in search of the springs of life. Think of a man's swinging dumb-bells for his health, when those springs are bubbling up in far-off pastures unsought by him!

Moreover, you must walk like a camel, which is said to be the only beast which ruminates when walking. When a traveler asked Wordsworth's servant to show him her master's study, she answered, "Here is his library, but his study is out of doors."

Living much out of doors, in the sun and wind, will no doubt produce a certain roughness of character—will cause a thicker cuticle to grow over some of the finer qualities of our nature, as on the face and hands, or as severe manual labor robs the hands of some of their delicacy of touch. So staying in the house, on the other hand, may produce a softness and smoothness, not to say thinness of skin, accompanied by an increased sensibility to certain impressions. Perhaps we should be more susceptible to some influences important to our intellectual and moral growth, if the sun had shone and the wind blown on us a little less: and no doubt it is a nice matter to proportion rightly the thick and thin skin. But methinks that is a scurf that will fall off fast enough—that the natural remedy is to be found in the proportion which the night bears to the day, the winter to the summer, thought to experience. There will be so much the more air and sunshine in our thoughts. The callous palms of the laborer are conversant with finer tissues of self-respect and heroism, whose touch thrills the heart, than the languid fingers of idleness. That is mere sentimentality that lies abed by day and thinks itself white, far from the tan and callus of experience.

When we walk, we naturally go to the fields and woods: what would become of us, if we walked only in a garden or a mall? . . . Of course it is of no use to direct our steps to the woods, if they do not carry us thither. I am alarmed when it happens that I have walked a mile into the woods bodily, without getting there in spirit. In my afternoon walk I would fain forget all my morning occupations and my obligations to society. But it sometimes happens that I cannot easily shake off the village. The thought of some work will run in my head and I am not where my body is—I am out of my senses. In my walks I would fain return to my senses. What business have I in the woods, if I am thinking of something out of the woods? I suspect myself, and cannot help a shudder, when I find myself so implicated even in what are called good works—for this may sometimes happen.

My vicinity affords many good walks; and though for so many years I have walked almost every day, and sometimes for several days together, I have not yet exhausted them. An absolutely new prospect is a great happiness, and I can still get this any afternoon. Two or three hours' walking will carry me to as strange a country as I expect ever to see. A single farmhouse which I had not seen before is sometimes as good as the dominions of the King of Dahomey. There is in fact a sort of harmony discoverable between the capabilities of the landscape within a circle of ten miles' radius, or the limits of an afternoon walk, and the threescore years and ten of human life. It will never become quite familiar to you.

Nowadays almost all man's improvements, so called, as the building of houses and the cutting down of the forest and of all large trees, simply deform the landscape, and make it more and more tame and cheap. A people who would begin by burning the fences and let the forest stand! I saw the fences half consumed, their ends lost in the middle of the prairie, and some worldly miser with a surveyor looking after his bounds, while heaven had taken place around him, and he did not see the angels going to and fro, but was looking for an old post-hole in the midst of paradise. I looked again, and saw him standing in the middle of a boggy Stygian fen, surrounded by devils, and he had found his bounds without a doubt, three little stones, where a stake had been driven, and looking nearer, I saw that the Prince of Darkness was his surveyor.

I can easily walk ten, fifteen, twenty, any number of miles, commencing at my own door, without going by any house, without crossing a road except where the fox and the mink do: first along by the river, and then the brook, and then the meadow and the woodside. There are square miles in my vicinity which have no inhabitant. From many a hill I can see civilization and the abodes of man afar. The farmers and their works are scarcely more obvious than woodchucks and their burrows. Man and his affairs, church and state and school, trade and commerce, and manufactures and agriculture, even politics, the most alarming of them all—I am pleased to see how little space they occupy in the landscape. Politics is but a narrow field, and that still narrower highway yonder leads to it. I sometimes direct the traveler thither. If you would go to the political world, follow the great road—follow that marketman, keep his dust in your eyes, and it will lead you straight to it; for it, too, has its place merely, and does not occupy all space. I pass from it as from a bean-field into the forest, and it is forgotten. In one half-hour I can walk off to some portion of the earth's surface where a man does not stand from one year's end to another, and there, consequently, politics are not, for they are but as the cigar-smoke of a man. . . .

At present, in this vicinity, the best part of the land is not private property; the landscape is not owned, and the walker enjoys comparative freedom.

But possibly the day will come when it will be partitioned off into so-called pleasure-grounds, in which a few will take a narrow and exclusive pleasure only — when fences shall be multiplied, and man-traps and other engines invented to confine men to the *public* road, and walking over the surface of God's earth shall be construed to mean trespassing on some gentleman's grounds. To enjoy a thing exclusively is commonly to exclude yourself from the true enjoyment of it. Let us improve our opportunities, then, before the evil days come.

What is it that makes it so hard sometimes to determine whither we will walk? I believe that there is a subtle magnetism in Nature, which, if we unconsciously yield to it, will direct us aright. It is not indifferent to us which way we walk. There is a right way; but we are very liable from heedlessness and stupidity to take the wrong one. We would fain take that walk, never yet taken by us through this actual world, which is perfectly symbolical of the path which we love to travel in the interior and ideal world; and sometimes, no doubt, we find it difficult to choose our direction, because it does not yet exist distinctly in our idea.

When I go out of the house for a walk, uncertain as yet whither I will bend my steps, and submit myself to my instinct to decide for me, I find, strange and whimsical as it may seem, that I finally and inevitably settle southwest, toward some particular wood or meadow or deserted pasture or hill in that direction. My needle is slow to settle — varies a few degrees, and does not always point due southwest, it is true, and it has good authority for this variation, but it always settles between west and south-southwest. The future lies that way to me, and the earth seems more unexhausted and richer on that side. The outline which would bound my walks would be, not a circle, but a parabola, or rather like one of those cometary orbits which have been thought to be non-returning curves, in this case opening westward, in which my house occupies the place of the sun. I turn round and round irresolute sometimes for a quarter of an hour, until I decide, for a thousandth time, that I will walk into the southwest or west. Eastward I go only by force; but westward I go free. Thither no business leads me. It is hard for me to believe that I

shall find fair landscapes or sufficient wildness and freedom behind the eastern horizon. I am not excited by the prospect of a walk thither; but I believe that the forest which I see in the western horizon stretches uninterruptedly toward the setting sun, and there are no towns nor cities in it of enough consequence to disturb me. Let me live where I will, on this side is the city, on that the wilderness, and ever I am leaving the city more and more, and withdrawing into the wilderness. I should not lay so much stress on this fact, if I did not believe that something like this is the prevailing tendency of my countrymen. I must walk toward Oregon, and not toward Europe. And that way the nation is moving, and I may say that mankind progress from east to west. . . .

We go eastward to realize history and study the works of art and literature, retracing the steps of the race; we go westward as into the future, with a spirit of enterprise and adventure. The Atlantic is a Lethean stream, in our passage over which we have had an opportunity to forget the Old World and its institutions. If we do not succeed this time, there is perhaps one more chance for the race left before it arrives on the banks of the Styx; and that is in the Lethe of the Pacific, which is three times as wide. . . .

The West of which I speak is but another name for the Wild; and what I have been preparing to say is, that in Wildness is the preservation of the World. Every tree sends its fibres forth in search of the Wild. The cities import it at any price. Men plow and sail for it. From the forest and wilderness come the tonics and barks which brace mankind. Our ancestors were savages. The story of Romulus and Remus being suckled by a wolf is not a meaningless fable. The founders of every state which has risen to eminence have drawn their nourishment and vigor from a similar wild source. It was because the children of the Empire were not suckled by the wolf that they were conquered and displaced by the children of the northern forests who were. . . .

The African hunter Cumming tells us that the skin of the eland, as well as that of most other antelopes just killed, emits the most delicious perfume of trees and grass. I would have every man so much like a wild antelope, so much a part and parcel of nature, that his very person should thus sweetly advertise our senses of his presence, and remind us of those parts of nature which he most haunts. I feel no disposition to be satirical, when the trapper's coat emits the odor of musquash even; it is a sweeter scent to me than that which commonly exhales from the merchant's or the scholar's garments. When I go into their wardrobes and handle their vestments, I am reminded of no grassy plains and flowery meads which they have frequented, but of dusty merchants' exchanges and libraries rather.

A tanned skin is something more than respectable, and perhaps olive is a fitter color than white for a man—a denizen of the woods. "The pale white man!" I do not wonder that the African pitied him. Darwin the naturalist says, "A white man bathing by the side of a Tahitian was like a plant bleached by the gardener's art, compared with a fine, dark green one, growing vigorously in the open fields."

Ben Jonson exclaims,—

"How near to good is what is fair!"

So I would say,—

How near to good is what is *wild!*

Life consists with wildness. The most alive is the wildest. Not yet subdued to man, its presence refreshes him. One who pressed forward incessantly and never rested from his labors, who grew fast and made infinite demands on life, would always find himself in new country or wilderness, and surrounded by the raw material of life. He would be climbing over the prostrate stems of primitive forest-trees.

Hope and the future for me are not in lawns and cultivated fields, not in towns and cities, but in the impervious and quaking swamps. When, formerly, I have analyzed my partiality for some farm which I had contemplated purchasing, I have frequently found that I was attracted solely by a few square rods of impermeable and unfathomable bog—a natural sink in one corner of it. That was the jewel which dazzled me. I derive more of my subsistence from the swamps which surround my native town than from the cultivated gardens in the village. There are no richer parterres to my eyes than the dense beds of dwarf andromeda (*Cassandra calyculata*) which cover these tender places on the earth's surface. Botany cannot go farther than tell me the names of the shrubs which grow there—the high blueberry, panicled andromeda, lambkill, azalea, and rhodora—all standing in the quaking sphagnum. I often think that I should like to have my house front on this mass of dull red bushes, omitting other flower plots and borders, transplanted spruce and trim box, even graveled walks—to have this fertile spot under my windows, not a few imported barrowfuls of soil only to cover the sand which was thrown out in digging the cellar. Why not put my house, my parlor, behind this plot, instead of behind that meagre assemblage of curiosities, that poor apology for a Nature and Art, which I call my front yard? It is an effort to clear up and make a decent appearance when the carpenter and mason have departed, though done as much for the passer-by as the dweller within. The most tasteful front-yard fence was never an agreeable object of study to me; the most elaborate ornaments, acorn tops, or what not, soon wearied and disgusted me. Bring your sills up to the very edge of the swamp, then (though it may not be the best place for a dry cellar), so that there be no access on that side to citizens. Front yards are not made to walk in, but, at most, through, and you could go in the back way.

Yes, though you may think me perverse, if it were proposed to me to dwell in the neighborhood of the most beautiful garden that ever human art contrived, or else of a Dismal Swamp, I should certainly decide for the swamp. How vain, then, have been all your labors, citizens, for me!

My spirits infallibly rise in proportion to the outward dreariness. Give me the ocean, the desert, or the wilderness! In the desert, pure air and solitude compensate for want of moisture and fertility. The traveler Burton says of it: "Your *morale* improves; you become frank and cordial, hospitable and single-minded. . . . In the desert, spirituous liquors excite only disgust. There is a keen enjoyment in a mere animal existence." They who have been traveling long on the steppes of Tartary say, "On reentering cultivated lands, the agitation, perplexity, and turmoil of civilization oppressed and suffocated us; the air seemed to fail us, and we felt every moment as if about to die of asphyxia." When I would recreate myself, I seek the darkest wood, the thickest and most interminable and, to the citizen, most dismal, swamp. I enter a swamp as a sacred place, a *sanctum sanctorum.* There is the strength, the marrow, of Nature. The wildwood covers the virgin mould, and the same soil is good for men and for trees. A man's health requires as many acres of meadow to his prospect as his farm does loads of muck. There are the strong meats on which he feeds. A town is saved, not more by the righteous men in it than by the woods and swamps that surround it. A township where one primitive forest waves above while another primitive forest rots below — such a town is fitted to raise not only corn and potatoes, but poets and philosophers for the coming ages. In such a soil grew Homer and Confucius and the rest, and out of such a wilderness comes the Reformer eating locusts and wild honey.

To preserve wild animals implies generally the creation of a forest for them to dwell in or resort to. So it is with man. A hundred years ago they sold bark in our streets peeled from our own woods. In the very aspect of those primitive and rugged trees there was, methinks, a tanning principle which hardened and consolidated the fibres of men's thoughts. Ah! already I shudder for these comparatively degenerate days of my native village, when you cannot collect a load of bark of good thickness, and we no longer produce tar and turpentine.

The civilized nations — Greece, Rome, England — have been sustained by the primitive forests which anciently rotted where they stand. They survive as long as the soil is not exhausted. Alas for human culture! little is to be expected of a nation, when the vegetable mould is exhausted, and it is compelled to make manure of the bones of its fathers. There the poet sustains himself merely by his own superfluous fat, and the philosopher comes down on his marrowbones. . . .

In literature it is only the wild that attracts us. Dullness is but another name for tameness. It is the uncivilized free and wild thinking in Hamlet and the Iliad, in all the scriptures and mythologies, not learned in the schools, that delights us. As the wild duck is more swift and beautiful than the tame, so is the wild — the mallard — thought, which 'mid falling dews wings its way above the fens. A truly good book is something as natural, and as unexpectedly and unaccountably fair and perfect, as a wild-flower discovered on the prairies of the West or in the jungles of the East. Genius is a light which makes the darkness visible, like the lightning's flash, which perchance shatters the temple of knowledge itself — and not a taper lighted at the hearth-stone of the race, which pales before the light of common day.

English literature, from the days of the minstrels to the Lake Poets — Chaucer and Spenser and Milton, and even Shakespeare, included — breathes no quite fresh and, in this sense, wild strain. It is an essentially tame and civilized literature, reflecting Greece and Rome. Her wilderness is a greenwood, her wild man a Robin Hood. There is plenty of genial love of Nature, but not so much of Nature herself. Her chronicles inform us when her wild animals, but not when the wild man in her, became extinct.

The science of Humboldt is one thing, poetry is another thing. The poet today, notwithstanding all the discoveries of science, and the accumulated learning of mankind, enjoys no advantage over Homer.

Where is the literature which gives expression to Nature? He would be a poet who could impress the winds and streams into his service, to speak for him; who nailed words to their primitive senses, as farmers drive down stakes in the spring, which the frost has heaved; who derived his words as often as he used them — transplanted them to his page with earth adhering to their roots; whose words were so true and fresh and natural that they would appear to expand like the buds at the approach of spring, though they lay half smothered between two musty leaves in a library — aye, to bloom and bear fruit there, after their kind, annually, for the faithful reader, in sympathy with surrounding Nature.

I do not know of any poetry to quote which adequately expresses this yearning for the Wild. Approached from this side, the best poetry is tame. I do not know where to find in any literature, ancient or modern, any account which contents me of that Nature with which even I am acquainted. You will perceive that I demand something which no Augustan nor Elizabethan age, which no *culture,* in short, can give. Mythology comes nearer to it than anything. How much more fertile a Nature, at least, has Grecian mythology its root in than English literature!

Mythology is the crop which the Old World bore before its soil was exhausted, before the fancy and imagination were affected with blight; and which it still bears, wherever its pristine vigor is unabated. All other literatures endure only as the elms which overshadow our houses; but this is like the great dragontree of the Western Isles, as old as mankind, and, whether that does or not, will endure as long; for the decay of other literatures makes the soil in which it thrives.

The West is preparing to add its fables to those of the East. The valleys of the Ganges, the Nile, and the Rhine having yielded their crop, it remains to be seen what the valleys of the Amazon, the Plate, the Orinoco, the St. Lawrence, and the Mississippi will produce. Perchance, when, in the course of ages, American liberty has become a fiction of the past — as it is to some extent a fiction of the present — the poets of the world will be inspired by American mythology. . . .

In short, all good things are wild and free. There is something in a strain of music, whether produced by an instrument or by the human voice — take the sound of a bugle in a summer night, for instance — which by its wildness, to speak without satire, reminds me of the cries emitted by wild beasts in their native forests. It is so much of their wildness as I can understand. Give me for my friends and neighbors wild men, not tame ones. The wildness of the savage is but a faint symbol of the awful ferity with which good men and lovers meet.

I love even to see the domestic animals reassert their native rights — any evidence that they have not wholly lost their original wild habits and vigor; as when my neighbor's cow breaks out of her pasture early in the spring and boldly swims the river, a cold, gray tide, twenty-five or thirty rods wide, swollen by the melted snow. It is the buffalo crossing the Mississippi. This exploit confers some dignity on the herd in my eyes — already dignified. The seeds of instinct are preserved under the thick hides of cattle and horses, like seeds in the bowels of the earth, an indefinite period.

Any sportiveness in cattle is unexpected. I saw one day a herd of a dozen bullocks and cows running about and frisking in unwieldy sport, like huge rats, even like kittens. They shook their heads, raised their tails, and rushed up and down a hill, and I perceived by their horns, as well as by their activity, their relation to the deer tribe. But, alas! a sudden loud *Whoa!* would have damped their ardor at once, reduced them from venison to beef, and stiffened their sides and sinews like the locomotive. Who but the Evil One has cried "Whoa!" to mankind? Indeed, the life of cattle, like that of many men, is but a sort of locomotiveness; they move a side at a time, and man, by his machinery, is meeting the horse and the ox half-way. Whatever part the whip has touched is thenceforth palsied. Who would ever think of a *side* of any of the supple cat tribe, as we speak of a *side* of beef?

I rejoice that horses and steers have to be broken before they can be made the slaves of men, and that men themselves have some wild oats still left to sow before they become submissive members of society. Undoubtedly, all men are not equally fit subjects for civilization; and because the majority, like dogs and sheep, are tame by inherited disposition, this is no reason why the others should have their natures broken that they may be reduced to the same level. Men are in the main alike, but they were made several in order that they might be various. If a low use is to be served, one man will do nearly or quite as well as another; if a high one, individual excellence is to be regarded. Any man can stop a hole to keep the wind away, but no other man could serve so rare a use as the author of this illustration did. Confucius says, "The skins of the tiger and the leopard, when they are tanned, are as the skins of the dog and the sheep tanned." But it is not the part of a true culture to tame tigers, any more than it is to make sheep ferocious; and tanning their skins for shoes is not the best use to which they can be put. . . .

Here is this vast, savage, howling mother of ours, Nature, lying all around, with such beauty, and such affection for her children, as the leopard; and yet we are so early weaned from her breast to society, to that culture which is exclusively an interaction of man on man — a sort of breeding in and in, which produces at most a merely English nobility, a civilization destined to have a speedy limit. . . .

I would not have every man nor every part of a man cultivated, any more than I would have every acre of earth cultivated: part will be tillage, but the greater part will be meadow and forest, not only serving an immediate use, but preparing a mould against a distant future, by the annual decay of the vegetation which it supports. . . .

For my part, I feel that with regard to Nature I live a sort of border life, on the confines of a world into which I make occasional and transient forays only, and my patriotism and allegiance to the state into whose territories I seem to retreat are those of a moss-trooper. Unto a life which I call natural I would gladly follow even a will-o'-the-wisp through bogs and sloughs unimaginable, but no moon nor firefly has shown me the causeway to it. Nature is a personality so vast and universal that we have never seen one of her features. The walker in the familiar fields which stretch around my native town sometimes finds himself in another land than is described in their owners' deeds, as it were in some faraway field on the confines of the actual Concord, where her jurisdiction ceases, and the idea which the word Concord suggests ceases to be suggested. These farms which I have myself surveyed, these bounds which I have set up, appear dimly still as through a mist: but they have no chemistry to fix them; they fade from the surface of the glass, and the picture which the painter painted stands out dimly from beneath. The world with which we are commonly acquainted leaves no trace, and it will have no anniversary.

I took a walk on Spaulding's Farm the other afternoon. I saw the setting sun lighting up the opposite side of a stately pine wood. Its golden rays straggled into the aisles of the wood as into some noble hall. I was impressed as if some ancient and altogether admirable and shining family had settled there in that part of the land called Concord, unknown to me, — to whom the sun was servant, — who had not gone into society in the village, — who had not been called on. I saw their park, their pleasure-ground, beyond through the wood, in Spaulding's cranberry-meadow. The pines furnished them with gables as they grew. Their house was not obvious to vision, the trees grew through it. I do not know whether I heard the sounds of a suppressed hilarity or not. They seemed to recline on the sunbeams. They have sons and daughters. They are quite well. The farmer's cart-path, which leads directly through their hall, does not in the least put

them out, as the muddy bottom of a pool is sometimes seen through the reflected skies. They never heard of Spaulding, and do not know that he is their neighbor — notwithstanding I heard him whistle as he drove his team through the house. Nothing can equal the serenity of their lives. Their coat-of-arms is simply a lichen. I saw it painted on the pines and oaks. Their attics were in the tops of the trees. They are of no politics. There was no noise of labor. I did not perceive that they were weaving or spinning. Yet I did detect, when the wind lulled and hearing was done away, the finest imaginable sweet musical hum — as of a distant hive in May — which perchance was the sound of their thinking. They had no idle thoughts, and no one without could see their work, for their industry was not as in knots and excrescences embayed.

But I find it difficult to remember them. They fade irrevocably out of my mind even now while I speak, and endeavor to recall them and recollect myself. It is only after a long and serious effort to recollect my best thoughts that I become again aware of their cohabitancy. If it were not for such families as this, I think I should move out of Concord.

We are accustomed to say in New England that few and fewer pigeons visit us every year. Our forests furnish no mast for them. So, it would seem, few and fewer thoughts visit each growing man from year to year, for the grove in our minds is laid waste — sold to feed unnecessary fires of ambition, or sent to mill — and there is scarcely a twig left for them to perch on. They no longer build nor breed with us. In some more genial season, perchance, a faint shadow flits across the landscape of the mind, cast by the *wings* of some thought in its vernal or autumnal migration, but, looking up, we are unable to detect the substance of the thought itself. Our winged thoughts are turned to poultry. . . .

We hug the earth — how rarely we mount! Methinks we might elevate ourselves a little more. We might climb a tree, at least. I found my account in climbing a tree once. It was a tall white pine, on the top of a hill; and though I got well pitched, I was well paid for it, for I discovered new mountains in the horizon which I had never seen before — so much more of the earth and the heavens. I might have walked about the foot of the tree for threescore years and ten, and yet I certainly should never have seen them. But, above all, I discovered around me — it was near the end of June — on the ends of the topmost branches only, a few minute and delicate red conelike blossoms, the fertile flower of the white pine looking heavenward. I carried straightway to the village the topmost spire, and showed it to stranger jurymen who walked the streets — for it was court week — and to farmers and lumber-dealers and wood-choppers and hunters, and not one had ever seen the like before, but they wondered as at a star dropped down. Tell of ancient architects finishing their works on the tops of columns as perfectly as on the lower and more visible parts! Nature has from the first expanded the minute blossoms of the forest only toward the heavens, above men's heads and unobserved by them. We see only the flowers that are under our feet in the meadows. The pines have developed their delicate blossoms on the highest twigs of the wood every summer for ages, as well over the heads of Nature's red children as of her white ones; yet scarcely a farmer or hunter in the land has ever seen them.

Above all, we cannot afford not to live in the present. He is blessed over all mortals who loses no moment of the passing life in remembering the past. Unless our philosophy hears the cock crow in every barn-yard within our horizon, it is belated. That sound commonly reminds us that we are growing rusty and antique in our employments and habits of thought. His philosophy comes down to a more recent time than ours. There is something suggested by it that is a newer testament — the gospel according to this moment. He has not fallen astern; he has got up early and kept up early, and to be where he is to be in season, in the foremost rank of time. It is an expression of the health and soundness of Nature, a brag for all the world — healthiness as of a spring burst forth, a new fountain of the Muses, to celebrate this last instant of time. Where he lives no fugitive slave laws are passed. Who has not betrayed his master many times since last he heard that note?

The merit of this bird's strain is in its freedom from all plaintiveness. The singer can easily move us to tears or to laughter, but where is he who can excite in us a pure morning joy? When, in doleful dumps, breaking the awful stillness of our wooden sidewalk on a Sunday, or, perchance, a watcher in the house of mourning, I hear a cockerel crow far or near, I think to myself. "There is one of us well, at any rate," — and with a sudden gush return to my senses.

We had a remarkable sunset one day last November. I was walking in a meadow, the source of a small brook, when the sun at last, just before setting, after a cold, gray day, reached a clear stratum in the horizon, and the softest, brightest morning sunlight fell on the dry grass and on the stems of the trees in the opposite horizon and on the leaves of the shrub oaks on the hillside, while our shadows stretched long over the meadow eastward, as if we were the only motes in its beams. It was such a light as we could not have imagined a moment before, and the air also was so warm and serene that nothing was wanting to make a paradise of that meadow. When we reflected that this was not a solitary phenomenon, never to happen again, but that it would happen forever and ever, an infinite number of evenings, and cheer and reassure the latest child that walked there, it was more glorious still.

The sun sets on some retired meadow, where no house is visible, with all the glory and splendor that it lavishes on cities, and perchance as it has never set before — where there is but a solitary marsh hawk to have his wings gilded by it, or only a musquash looks out from his cabin, and there is some little blackveined brook in the midst of the marsh, just beginning to meander, winding slowly round a decaying stump. We walked in so pure and bright a light, gilding the withered grass and leaves, so softly and serenely bright. I thought I had never bathed in such a golden flood, without a ripple or a murmur to it. The west side of every wood and rising ground gleamed like the boundary of Elysium, and the sun on our backs seemed like a gentle herdsman driving us home at evening.

So we saunter toward the Holy Land, till one day the sun shall shine more brightly than ever he has done, shall perchance shine into our minds and hearts, and light up our whole lives with a great awakening light, as warm and serene and golden as on a bankside in autumn.

DISCUSSION TOPICS

1. What might Thoreau mean by saying "In my walks I would fair return to my senses"?
2. What might Thoreau mean by saying that "to enjoy a thing exclusively is commonly to exclude yourself from the true enjoyment of it"? Do you agree with him?
3. Thoreau states that "in Wildness is the preservation of the world." What reasoning does he present in support of this assertion?
4. Thoreau urges us to walk toward the Holy Land. What does he mean by "Holy Land"? Have you ever taken such a walk?
5. Who lives at Spaulding's Farm?

A Near View of the High Sierra

John Muir

Born in Scotland, John Muir (1838–1914) labored on a pioneer Wisconsin farm and wandered alone in the wilds of Canada, walked a thousand miles from Wisconsin to the Gulf of Mexico, and delighted in the glories of the Sierra Nevada mountains of California. For Muir the natural world was both a laboratory for scientific research and a temple for worship. Almost every step in the mountains brought him a fresh revelation. His writings for periodicals in the late nineteenth century had wide influence. He was a prime mover in the national park system and played a central role in preserving what is now Yosemite National Park. He was president of the Sierra Club from its founding in 1892 until his death. Muir's writings continue to inspire his readers to a deeper appreciation of what wilderness offers the solitary adventurer.

In "A Near View of the High Sierra" Muir provides a vivid description of the sensory and emotional richness of his mountaineering experience on the glacier-clad Mt. Ritter.

Early one bright morning in the middle of Indian summer, while the glacier meadows were still crisp with frost crystals, I set out from the foot of Mount Lyell, on my way down to Yosemite Valley, to replenish my exhausted store of bread and tea. I had spent the past summer, as many preceding ones, exploring the glaciers that lie on the head waters of the San Joaquin, Tuolumne, Merced, and Owen's rivers; measuring and studying their movements, trends, crevasses, moraines, etc., and the part they had played during the period of their greater extension in the creation and development of the landscapes of this alpine wonderland. . . .

To artists, few portions of the High Sierra are, strictly speaking, picturesque. The whole massive uplift of the range is one great picture, not clearly divisible into smaller ones; differing much in this respect from the older, and what may be called, riper mountains of the Coast Range. All the landscapes of the Sierra, as we have seen, were born again, remodeled from base to summit by the developing ice-floods of the last glacial winter. But all these new landscapes were not brought forth simultaneously; some of the highest, where the ice lingered longest, are tens of centuries younger than those of the warmer regions below them. In general, the younger the mountain landscapes—younger, I mean, with reference to the time of their emergence from the ice of the glacial period—the less separable are they into artistic bits capable of being made into warm, sympathetic, lovable pictures with appreciable humanity in them.

Here, however, on the head waters of the Tuolumne, is a group of wild peaks on which the geologist may say that the sun has but just begun to shine, which is yet in a high degree picturesque, and in its main features so regular and evenly balanced as almost to appear conventional—one somber cluster of snowladen peaks with gray pine-fringed granite bosses braided around its base, the whole surging free into the sky from the head of a magnificent valley, whose lofty walls are beveled away on both sides so as to embrace it all without admitting anything not strictly belonging to it. The foreground was now aflame with autumn colors, brown and purple and gold, ripe in the mellow sunshine; contrasting brightly with the deep, cobalt blue of the sky, and the black and gray, and pure, spiritual white of the rocks and glaciers. Down through the midst, the young Tuolumne was seen pouring from its crystal fountains, now resting in glassy pools as if changing back again into ice, now leaping in white cascades as if turning to snow; gliding right and left between granite bosses, then sweeping on through the smooth, meadowy levels of the valley, swaying pensively from side to side with calm, stately gestures past dipping willows and sedges, and around groves of arrowy pine; and throughout its whole eventful course, whether flowing fast or slow, singing loud or low, ever filling the landscape with spiritual animation, and manifesting the grandeur of its sources in every movement and tone.

Pursuing my lonely way down the valley, I turned again and again to gaze on the glorious picture, throwing up my arms to inclose it as in a frame. After long ages of growth in the darkness beneath the glaciers, through sunshine and storms, it seemed now to be ready and waiting for the elected artist, like yellow wheat for the reaper; and I could not help wishing that I might carry colors and brushes with me on my travels, and learn to paint. In the mean time I had to be content with photographs on my mind and sketches in my notebooks. At length, after I had rounded a precipitous headland that puts out from the west wall of the valley, every peak vanished from sight, and I pushed rapidly along the frozen meadows, over the divide between the waters of the Merced and Tuolumne, and down through the forests that clothe the slopes of Cloud's Rest, arriving in Yosemite in due time—which, with me, is *any* time. And, strange to say, among the first people I met here were two artists who, with letters of introduction, were awaiting my return. They inquired whether in the course of my explorations in the adjacent mountains I had ever come upon a landscape suitable for a large painting; whereupon I began a description of the one that had so lately excited my admiration. Then, as I went on further and further into details, their faces began to glow, and I offered to guide them to it, while they declared that they would gladly follow, far or near, whithersoever I could spare the time to lead them.

Since storms might come breaking down through the fine weather at any time, burying the colors in snow, and cutting off the artists' retreat, I advised getting ready at once.

I led them out of the valley by the Vernal and Nevada Falls, thence over the main dividing ridge to the Big Tuolumne Meadows, by the old Mono trail, and thence along the upper Tuolumne River to its head. This was my companions' first excursion into the High Sierra, and as I was almost always alone in my mountaineering, the way that the fresh beauty was reflected in their faces made for me a novel and interesting study. They naturally were affected most of all by the colors—the intense azure of the sky, the purplish grays of the granite, the red and browns of dry meadows, and the translucent purple and crimson of huckleberry bogs; the flaming yellow of aspen groves, the silvery flashing of the streams, and the bright green and blue of the glacier lakes. But the general expression of the scenery—rocky and savage—seemed sadly disappointing; and as they threaded the forest from ridge to ridge, eagerly scanning the landscapes as they were unfolded, they said: "All this is huge and sublime, but we see nothing as yet at all available for effective pictures. Art is long, and art is limited, you know; and here are foregrounds, middle-grounds, backgrounds, all alike; bare rock-waves, woods, groves, diminutive flecks of meadow, and strips of glittering water." "Never mind," I replied. "only bide a wee, and I will show you something you will like."

At length, toward the end of the second day, the Sierra Crown began to come into view, and when we had fairly rounded the projecting headland before mentioned, the whole picture stood revealed in the flush of the alpenglow. Their enthusiasm was excited beyond bounds, and the more impulsive of the two, a young Scotchman, dashed ahead, shouting and gesticulating and tossing his arms in the air like a madman. Here, at last, was a typical alpine landscape.

After feasting awhile on the view, I proceeded to make camp in a sheltered grove a little way back from the meadow, where pine-boughs could be obtained for beds, and where there was plenty of dry wood for fires, while the artists ran here and there, along the river-bends and up the sides of the cañon, choosing foregrounds for sketches. After dark, when our tea was made and a rousing fire had been built, we began to make our plans. They decided to remain several days, at the least, while I concluded to make an excursion in the meantime to the untouched summit of Ritter.

It was now about the middle of October, the springtime of snow-flowers. The first winter-clouds had already bloomed, and the peaks were strewn with fresh crystals, without, however, affecting the climbing to any dangerous extent. And as the weather was still profoundly calm, and the distance to the foot of the mountain only a little more than a day, I felt that I was running no great risk of being storm-bound.

Mount Ritter is king of the mountains of the middle portion of the High Sierra, as Shasta of the north and Whitney of the south sections. Moreover, as far as I know, it had never been climbed. I had explored the adjacent wilderness summer after summer; but my studies thus far had never drawn me to the top of it. Its height above sea-level is about 13,300 feet, and it is fenced round by steeply inclined glaciers, and cañons of tremendous depth and ruggedness, which render it almost inaccessible. But difficulties of this kind only exhilarate the mountaineer.

Next morning, the artists went heartily to their work and I to mine. Former experiences had given good reason to know that passionate storms, invisible as yet, might be brooding in the calm sun-gold; therefore, before bidding farewell, I warned the artists not to be alarmed should I fail to appear before a week or ten days, and advised them, in case a snow-storm should set in, to keep up big fires and shelter themselves as best they could, and on no account to become frightened and attempt to seek their way back to Yosemite alone through the drifts.

My general plan was simply this: to scale the cañon wall, cross over to the eastern flank of the range, and then make my way southward to the northern spurs of Mount Ritter in compliance with the intervening topography; for to push on directly southward from camp through the innumerable peaks and pinnacles that adorn this portion of the axis of the range, however interesting, would take too much time, besides being extremely difficult and dangerous at this time of year.

All my first day was pure pleasure; simply mountaineering indulgence, crossing the dry pathways of the ancient glaciers, tracing happy streams, and learning the habits of the birds and marmots in the groves

and rocks. Before I had gone a mile from camp, I came to the foot of a white cascade that beats its way down a rugged gorge in the cañon wall, from a height of about nine hundred feet, and pours its throbbing waters into the Tuolumne. I was acquainted with its fountains, which, fortunately, lay in my course. What a fine traveling companion it proved to be, what songs it sang, and how passionately it told the mountain's own joy! Gladly I climbed along its dashing border, absorbing its divine music, and bathing from time to time in waftings of irised spray. Climbing higher, higher, new beauty came streaming on the sight: painted meadows, late-blooming gardens, peaks of rare architecture, lakes here and there, shining like silver, and glimpses of the forested middle region and the yellow lowlands far in the west. Beyond the range I saw the so-called Mono Desert, lying dreamily silent in thick purple light — a desert of heavy sunglare beheld from a desert of ice-burnished granite. Here the waters divide, shouting in glorious enthusiasm, and falling eastward to vanish in the volcanic sands and dry sky of the Great Basin, or westward to the Great Valley of California, and thence through the Bay of San Francisco and the Golden Gate to the sea.

Passing a little way down over the summit until I had reached an elevation of about 10,000 feet, I pushed on southward toward a group of savage peaks that stand guard about Ritter on the north and west, groping my way; and dealing instinctively with every obstacle as it presented itself. . . .

. . . In so wild and so beautiful a region was spent my first day, every sight and sound inspiring, leading one far out of himself, yet feeding and building up his individuality.

Now came the solemn, silent evening. Long, blue, spiky shadows crept out across the snow-fields, while a rosy glow, at first scarce discernible, gradually deepened and suffused every mountain-top, flushing the glaciers and the harsh crags above them. This was the alpenglow, to me one of the most impressive of all the terrestrial manifestations of God. At the touch of this divine light, the mountains seemed to kindle to a rapt, religious consciousness, and stood hushed and waiting like devout worshipers. Just before the alpenglow began to fade, two crimson clouds came streaming across the summit like wings of flame, rendering the sublime scene yet more impressive; then came darkness and the stars. . . .

I made my bed in a nook of the pine-thicket, where the branches were pressed and crinkled overhead like a roof, and bent down around the sides. These are the best bedchambers the high mountains afford — snug as squirrel-nests, well ventilated, full of spicy odors, and with plenty of wind-played needles to sing one asleep. I little expected company, but, creeping in through a low side-door, I found five or six birds nestling among the tassels. The night-wind began to blow soon after dark; at first only a gentle breathing, but increasing toward midnight to a rough gale that fell upon my leafy roof in ragged surges like a cascade, bearing wild sounds from the crags overhead. The waterfall sang in chorus, filling the old ice-fountain with its solemn roar, and seeming to increase in power as the night advanced — fit voice for such a landscape. I had to creep out many times to the fire during the night, for it was biting cold and I had no blankets. Gladly I welcomed the morning star.

The dawn in the dry, wavering air of the desert was glorious. Everything encouraged my undertaking and betokened success. There was no cloud in the sky, no storm-tone in the wind. Breakfast of bread and tea was soon made. I fastened a hard, durable crust to my belt by way of provision, in case I should be compelled to pass a night on the mountain-top; then, securing the remainder of my little stock against wolves and wood-rats, I set forth free and hopeful.

How glorious a greeting the sun gives the mountains! To behold this alone is worth the pains of any excursion a thousand times over. The highest peaks burned like islands in a sea of liquid shade. Then the lower peaks and spires caught the glow, and long lances of light, streaming through many a notch and pass, fell thick on the frozen meadows. The majestic form of Ritter was full in sight, and I pushed rapidly on over rounded rock-bosses and pavements, my ironshod shoes making a clanking sound, suddenly hushed now and then in rugs of bryanthus, and sedgy lake-margins soft as moss. . . .

On the southern shore of a frozen lake, I encountered an extensive field of hard, granular snow, up which I scampered in fine tone, intending to follow it to its head, and cross the rocky spur against which it leans, hoping thus to come direct upon the base of the main Ritter peak. The surface was pitted with oval hollows, made by stones and drifted pine-needles that had melted themselves into the mass by the radiation of absorbed sun-heat. These afforded good footholds, but the surface curved more and more steeply at the head, and the pits became shallower and less abundant, until I found myself in danger of being shed off like avalanching snow. I persisted, however, creeping on all fours, and shuffling up the smoothest places on my back, as I had often done on burnished granite, until, after slipping several times, I was compelled to retrace my course to the bottom, and make my way around the west end of the lake, and thence up to the summit of the divide between the head waters of Rush Creek and the northernmost tributaries of the San Joaquin.

Arriving on the summit of this dividing crest, one of the most exciting pieces of pure wilderness was disclosed that I ever discovered in all my mountaineering. There, immediately in front, loomed the majestic mass of Mount Ritter, with a glacier swooping down its face nearly to my feet, then curving westward and pouring its frozen flood into a dark blue lake, whose shores were bound with precipices of crystalline snow; while a deep chasm drawn between the divide and the glacier separated the massive picture from everything else. I could see only the one sublime mountain, the one glacier, the one lake; the whole veiled with one blue shadow — rock, ice, and water close together without a single leaf or sign of life. After gazing spellbound, I began instinctively to scrutinize every notch and gorge and weathered buttress of the mountain, with reference to making the ascent. . . .

I could not distinctly hope to reach the summit from this side, yet I moved on across the glacier as if driven by fate. Contending with myself, the season is too far spent, I said, and even should I be successful, I might be storm-bound on the mountain; and in the cloud-darkness, with the cliffs and crevasses covered with snow, how could I escape! No; I must wait till next summer. I would only approach the mountain now, and inspect it, creep about its flanks, learn what I could of its history, holding myself ready to flee on the approach of the first storm-cloud. But we little know until tried how much of the uncontrollable there is in us, urging across glaciers and torrents, and up dangerous heights, let the judgment forbid as it may.

I succeeded in gaining the foot of the cliff on the eastern extremity of the glacier, and there discovered the mouth of a narrow avalanche gully, through which I began to climb, intending to follow it as far as possible, and at least obtain some fine wild views for my pains. . . .

I thus made my way into a wilderness of crumbling spires and battlements, built together in bewildering combinations, and glazed in many places with a thin coating of ice, which I had to hammer off with stones. The situation was becoming gradually more perilous; but, having passed several dangerous spots, I dared not think of descending; for, so steep was the entire ascent, one would inevitably fall to the glacier in case a single misstep were made. . . .

At length, after attaining an elevation of about 12,800 feet, I found myself at the foot of a sheer drop in the bed of the avalanche channel I was tracing, which seemed absolutely to bar further progress. It was only about forty-five or fifty feet high, and somewhat roughened by fissures and projections; but these seemed so slight and insecure, as footholds, that I tried hard to avoid the precipice altogether, by scaling the wall of the channel on either side. But, though less steep, the walls were smoother than the obstructing rock, and repeated efforts only showed that I must either go right ahead or turn back. The tried dangers beneath seemed even greater than that of the cliff in front; therefore, after scanning its face again and again, I began to scale it, picking my holds with intense caution. After gaining a point about half-way to the top, I was suddenly brought to a dead stop, with arms outspread, clinging close to the face of the rock, unable to move hand or foot either up or down. My doom appeared fixed. I *must* fall. There would be a moment of bewilderment, and then a lifeless rumble down the one general precipice to the glacier below.

When this final danger flashed upon me, I became nerve-shaken for the first time since setting foot on the mountains, and my mind seemed to fill with a stifling smoke. But this terrible eclipse lasted only a moment, when life blazed forth again with preternatural clearness. I seemed suddenly to become possessed of a new sense. The other self, bygone experiences, instinct, or Guardian Angel—

call it what you will—came forward and assumed control. Then my trembling muscles became firm again, every rift and flaw in the rock was seen as through a microscope, and my limbs moved with a positiveness and precision with which I seemed to have nothing at all to do. Had I been borne aloft upon wings, my deliverance could not have been more complete.

Above this memorable spot, the face of the mountain is still more savagely hacked and torn. It is a maze of yawning chasms and gullies, in the angles of which rise beetling crags and piles of detached boulders that seem to have been gotten ready to be launched below. But the strange influx of strength I had received seemed inexhaustible. I found a way without effort, and soon stood upon the topmost crag in the blessed light.

How truly glorious the landscape circled around this noble summit!—giant mountains, valleys innumerable, glaciers and meadows, rivers and lakes, with the wide blue sky bent tenderly over them all. But in my first hour of freedom from that terrible shadow, the sunlight in which I was laying seemed all in all.

Looking southward along the axis of the range, the eye is first caught by a row of exceedingly sharp and slender spires, which rise openly to a height of about a thousand feet, above a series of short, residual glaciers that lean back against their bases; their fantastic sculpture and the unrelieved sharpness with which they spring out of the ice renders them peculiarly wild and striking. These are "The Minarets." Beyond them you behold a sublime wilderness of mountains, their snowy summits towering together in crowded abundance, peak beyond peak, swelling higher, higher as they sweep on southward, until the culminating point of the range is reached on Mount Whitney, near the head of the Kern River, at an elevation of nearly 14,700 feet above the level of the sea. . . .

Could we have been here to observe during the glacial period, we should have overlooked a wrinkled ocean of ice as continuous as that now covering the landscapes of Greenland; filling every valley and cañon with only the tops of the mountain peaks rising darkly above the rock-encumbered ice-waves like islets in a stormy sea—those islets the only hints of the glorious landscape now smiling in the sun.

Standing here in the deep, brooding silence all the wilderness seems motionless, as if the work of creation were done. But in the midst of this outer steadfastness we know there is incessant motion and change. Ever and anon, avalanches are falling from yonder peaks. These cliff-bound glaciers, seemingly wedged and immovable, are flowing like water and grinding the rocks beneath them. The lakes are lapping their granite shores and wearing them away, and every one of these rills and young rivers is fretting the air into music, and carrying the mountains to the plains. Here are the roots of all the life of the valleys, and here more simply than elsewhere is the eternal flux of nature manifested. Ice changing to water, lakes to meadows, and mountains to plains. And while we thus contemplate Nature's methods of landscape creation, and, reading the records she has carved on the rocks, reconstruct, however imperfectly, the landscapes of the past, we also learn that as these we now behold have succeeded those of the preglacial age, so they in turn are withering and vanishing to be succeeded by others yet unborn.

But in the midst of these fine lessons and landscapes, I had to remember that the sun was wheeling far to the west, while a new way down the mountain had to be discovered to some point on the timber line where I could have a fire; for I had not even burdened myself with a coat. I first scanned the western spurs, hoping some way might appear through which I might reach the northern glacier, and cross its snout; or pass around the lake into which it flows, and thus strike my morning track. This route was soon sufficiently unfolded to show that, if practicable at all, it would require so much time that reaching camp that night would be out of the question. I therefore scrambled back eastward, descending the southern slopes obliquely at the same time. Here the crags seemed less formidable, and the head of a glacier that flows northeast came in sight, which I determined to follow as far as possible, hoping thus to make my way to the foot of the peak on the east side, and thence across the intervening cañons and ridges to camp.

The inclination of the glacier is quite moderate at the head, and, as the sun had softened the *névé,* I made safe and rapid progress, running and sliding, and keeping up a sharp outlook for crevasses. . . .

Night drew near before I reached the eastern base of the mountain, and my camp lay many a rugged mile to the north; but ultimate success was assured. It was now only a matter of endurance and ordinary mountain-craft. The sunset was, if possible, yet more beautiful than that of the day before. The Mono landscape seemed to be fairly saturated with warm, purple light. The peaks marshaled along the summit were in shadow, but through every notch and pass streamed vivid sunfire, soothing and irradiating their rough, black angles, while companies of small luminous clouds hovered above them like very angels of light. . . . I discovered the little pine thicket in which my nest was, and then I had a rest such as only a tired mountaineer may enjoy. After lying loose and lost for awhile, I made a sunrise fire, went down to the lake, dashed water on my head, and dipped a cupful for tea. The revival brought about by bread and tea was as complete as the exhaustion from excessive enjoyment and toil. Then I crept beneath the pine-tassels to bed. The wind was frosty and the fire burned low, but my sleep was none the less sound, and the evening constellations had swept far to the west before I awoke.

After thawing and resting in the morning sunshine, I sauntered home—that is, back to the Tuolumne camp—bearing away toward a cluster of peaks that hold the fountain snows of one of the north tributaries of Rush Creek. . . .

A loud whoop for the artists was answered again and again. Their camp-fire came in sight, and half an hour afterward I was with them. They seemed unreasonably glad to see me. I had been absent only three days; nevertheless, though the weather was fine, they had already been weighing chances as to whether I would ever return, and trying to decide whether they should wait longer or begin to seek their way back to the lowlands. Now their curious troubles were over. They packed their precious sketches, and next morning we set out homeward bound, and in two days entered the Yosemite Valley from the north by way of Indian Cañon.

DISCUSSION TOPICS

1. Muir's writing contains scientific observation, aesthetic delight, religious inspiration, and moral instruction. Find a passage in the

reading which illustrates each of the four perspectives.

2. Muir's anthropomorphism is out of fashion today. Find an example in the essay and consider its effect on the reader. In your view, does it add or detract from the vividness of his account?

3. Describe Muir's experience of danger on the cliff face. How did he react to the situation? How would you have reacted?

4. What process of change in perception does Muir describe regarding the "incomprehensible grandeur" of the view from the top of Mt. Ritter?

5. Why do you think Muir climbs Mt. Ritter without bringing a coat or blanket?

READING 14

The Land Aesthetic

J. Baird Callicott

J. Baird Callicott is a professor of philosophy at the University of North Texas, Denton. He is a major contributor to the field of environmental ethics. He has edited Companion to a Sand County Almanac *(1987), coedited with Susan Flader* The River of the Mother of God and Other Essays by Aldo Leopold *(1991), and is author of* Earth's Insights *(1994) and* Beyond the Land Ethic *(1999). In the following essay Callicott summarizes the Western aesthetic experience of nature as it emerged in landscape painting of the seventeenth century. Callicott argues that Leopold's ideas constitute the first autonomous natural aesthetic, based on evolutionary and ecological biology.*

Aldo Leopold is best known for the land ethic. He also developed an equally original and revolutionary "land aesthetic." Leopold's land aesthetic, however, has not enjoyed the same attention and celebrity as his land ethic, probably for two reasons. First, because — unlike the land ethic, which is concentrated in a single *Sand County Almanac* essay and labeled as such — the land aesthetic is scattered

throughout that book and Leopold's other writings, most of which, until recently, have been unavailable to all but the most dedicated scholars; and second, because aesthetics is usually regarded as an even less rigorous and certainly less important subject than ethics. While we earnestly debate matters of right and wrong, most of us have little to say about beauty, natural or artistic, except "ah" or "wow." And besides, what practical differences does aesthetic evaluation make? Such expressions as "to each his (or her) own" and "there's no accounting for taste" are not tolerated in the universe of ethical discourse, but they are virtual truisms in the realm of the aesthetic.

Aesthetics generally is a poor step-sister, a despised and neglected subject of theoretical discussion, in the general field of philosophy. Natural aesthetics is in even worse straits since what little aesthetic theory there is has centered almost entirely on art — painting, sculpture, architecture, drama, literature, dance, music, and more recently, cinema.[1] Indeed, during the twentieth century, "aesthetics" has become practically synonymous with "art criticism."

I suppose artifact aestheticians could make a persuasive case for the importance of artifactual aesthetics in the face of general neglect, but I can certainly say that natural aesthetic evaluation — albeit inarticulate and uncritical — has made a terrific difference to American conservation policy and land management. One of the main reasons that we have set aside certain natural areas as national, state, and county parks is because they are considered beautiful. In the conservation and resource management arena, historically, natural aesthetics has, indeed, been much more important than environmental ethics. Many more of our conservation and management decisions have been motivated by aesthetical rather than ethical values, by beauty instead of duty. What kinds of country we consider to be exceptionally beautiful makes a huge difference when we come to decide which places to save, which to restore or enhance, and which to allocate to other uses. Therefore, a sound natural aesthetics is crucial to sound conservation policy and land management.

Primarily, what I shall do here is assemble and juxtapose the scattered fragments of Leopold's land aesthetic in *A Sand County Almanac,* in *Round River,* and in the new collection of his literary and philosophical papers, *The River of the Mother of God and Other Essays by Aldo Leopold,* that Susan Flader and I have edited for the University of Wisconsin Press, and abstract from them a systematic theory of natural beauty and the criteria for its appreciation. One cannot, however, begin to comprehend the originality of Leopold's contribution to the appreciation of natural beauty without some knowledge of how prevailing conventional tastes in natural beauty came to be what they are.

First of all, I think that the appreciation of natural beauty, now as common as Sierra Club calendars, PBS television programs, and L. L. Bean catalogues, is a relatively recent cultural achievement in the West. A negative thesis like this would be hard to verify short of an exhaustive review of classical and Medieval art and literature. So I state it only as a hypothesis and hope some hapless graduate student will devote a dissertation to trying to prove me wrong.

One does not have to search very far, however, in the ancient and Medieval art and literature of China and Japan to find a rich tradition of landscape drawing and painting, nature poetry, and the attendant philosophical analysis of why misty mountains are so enthralling, cherry blossoms so heart-stopping, and rushing brooks so captivating.

But what does Homer have to say about the beauty of Ilium or the island of Circe? A little, but not much. Sappho is without peer in her description of feminine pulchritude, a form of natural beauty to be sure, but she scarcely notices the charms of her native Lesbos. Plato is as flipped out about the beauty of boys as Sappho of girls, but what does he have to say about why the Attic landscape or the Aegean coast are so special? Nothing at all. How about Aristotle? He wrote philosophy's first treatise on aesthetics. But it's all about poetry.

Read the Old Testament. Do you find any celebration or analysis of natural beauty? As in contemporaneous Greek literature, maybe some passing notice of it, here and there in the psalms, but no sustained celebration, and certainly no analysis or criticism. How about the New Testament—the Gospels, or Epistles, or Revelation? Forget it.

In the Church-dominated Middle Ages, sensitivity to natural beauty was, in fact, regarded as vaguely sinful or at best a worldly distraction from the soul's proper preoccupation with its spiritual pilgrimage. In Medieval painting the natural world is pictured as a symbolic backdrop for the artists' central religious motifs. Indeed, it seems that in Western civilization, prior to the seventeenth century, nature was simply not a source of much aesthetic experience. If true, this realization is monumental, even shocking, given the nearly universal susceptibility to natural beauty ambient today in Western culture.

In the West susceptibility to natural beauty was, as Christopher Hussey points out, ancillary to the representation of nature in the exciting new genre of painting for which the name "landscape" was coined: "It was not until Englishmen [as well as other Westerners] became familiar with the landscapes of Claude Lorraine and Salvatore Rosa, Ruysdael and Hobbema, that they were able to receive any [aesthetical] pleasure from their [natural] surroundings." Hence, cultivated Europeans began "viewing and criticizing nature as if it were an infinite series of more or less well composed subjects for painting."[2]

This, in short, is what seems to have happened in the strange history of natural beauty in the West. People saw landscape paintings in galleries, enjoyed an aesthetic experience, and so turned to the painters' motifs for a similar gratification. Natural beauty thus shone forth in the West, but, like the moon, by a borrowed light.

A device of the period, the Claude glass, named for the seventeenth-century French landscape artist, Claude Lorraine, tells the whole story. The new natural aesthetes carried the rectangular, slightly concave, tinted mirror with them into the countryside. Upon finding a suitably picturesque prospect, they turned their backs to it and rear-viewed its image in the Claude-glass. Thus framed, the natural landscape looked almost (but of course not quite) pretty as a picture.

European landscape painting itself, however, did not originate as a response to a sudden, spontaneous discovery of the beauty of nature on the part of a few inspired individuals. Rather, the painters were providing, some of them quite consciously, a concrete representation of the abstract picture of nature emerging in the scientific revolution taking place during that period. In the new science, nature was objectified, separated, and distanced from the subjective observer. And it was mathematized. Linear perspective in painting, the principal means by which artists achieved a realistic representation, is, formally speaking, an exercise in projective geometry. Linear perspective in landscape also creates an implied subject, an observer, who looks on, but is not personally situated or actively involved in the pictorial space.

The "picturesque" aesthetic, as the name suggests, self-consciously canonized as beautiful natural "scenes" or "landscapes" suitable as motifs for pictures. It was formulated in William Gilpin's *Three Essays on Picturesque Beauty* first published in 1792 and Uvedale Prince's *Essay on the Picturesque,* first published in 1794. The aesthetic analysis of nature was thus largely cast in terms of the colors, tones, textures, relative size, and arrangement or "composition" of topographical masses like mountains, valleys, lakes, woods, meadows, fields, streams, and so on. . . . We continue to admire and preserve primarily "landscapes," "scenery," and "views" according to essentially eighteenth century standards of taste inherited from Gilpin, Price, and their contemporaries. Our tastes in natural beauty may now be broader than the very specific canons demanded by Muir's two artists, but they still remain fixed on visual and formal properties.

The word "landscape," as I just pointed out, was first coined to refer to a genre of painting. But it soon began to be used derivatively to refer to the actual countryside. In English one can hardly begin to speak about the beauty of nature without lapsing into referring to the countryside as "the landscape." That we call the aesthetic management of nature "*landscape* architecture" continues, I suspect, insidiously to tether that discipline to the picturesque aesthetic or at least to a more general concern with the visual characteristics of a piece of land. I don't know, in this case, what's in a name — how much the name "landscape architecture" continues to affect the attitudes and values of the discipline; although, as I just admitted, I do have my suspicions. In classic landscape architecture, certainly, visual qualities were of predominant concern and design considerations could be expressed in such terms as vista, view, and scene — with foreground, middle ground, and background; subtle symmetry of side screening; tension of vertical and horizontal line, re-

lieved by arcs, curves, and diagonals; harmonious patterns of color; variety, movement, and so on. Today, significantly, the avant-garde wing of the discipline seems to be moving in the direction to which Leopold pointed at mid-century.

To sum up my historical review, Western appreciation of natural beauty is recent and derivative from art. The prevailing natural aesthetic, therefore, is not autonomous: it does not flow naturally from nature itself; it is not directly oriented to nature on nature's own terms; nor is it well informed by the ecological and evolutionary revolutions in natural history. It is superficial and narcissistic. In a word, it is trivial.

Naturally occurring scenic or picturesque "landscapes" are regarded, like the art they imitate, to be precious cultural resources and are stored, accordingly, in "museums" (the national parks) or private "collections" (the "landscaped" estates of the wealthy). They are visited and admired by patrons just like their originals deposited in the actual museums in urban centers. Nonscenic, nonpicturesque nonlandscapes are aesthetic nonresources and thus become available for less exalted uses. While land must be used, it is well within our means to save, restore, and aesthetically manage representative nonscenic, nonpicturesque nonlandscapes — swamps and bogs, dunes, scrub, prairie, bottoms, flats, deserts, and so on as aesthetic amenities — just as we preserve intact representative scenic ones. Aldo Leopold's land aesthetic provides a seminal autonomous natural aesthetic theory which may help to awaken our response to the potential of these aesthetically neglected communities.

Leopold shows us that an autonomous natural aesthetic could involve so much more than the visual appeal of natural environments. One is in the landscape, i.e., in the natural environment, as the mobile center of a three-dimensional, multisensuous experiential continuum. The appreciation of an environment's natural beauty could involve the ears (the sounds of rain, insects, birds, or silence itself), the surface of the skin (the warmth of the sun, the chill of the wind, the texture of grass, rock, sand, etc.), the nose and tongue (the fragrance of flowers, the odor of decay, the taste of saps and waters) — as well as the eyes. Most of all it could involve the mind, the faculty of cognition. For Leopold, as for his contemporaries in structural design, form follows function. The aesthetic appeal of country, in other words, should have less to do with its adventitious colors and shapes or its scenic expanses and picturesque proportions than with the integrity of its evolutionary heritage and ecological processes.

Leopold was, apparently, well aware of the primacy of artifactual aesthetics in Western civilization and thus, as an expository device, he approaches natural aesthetics via analogy with the more familiar branch.

He remarks, "our ability to perceive quality in nature begins, as in art, with the pretty" (exemplified by, for example, "landscaped" English gardens). "It proceeds through successive stages of the beautiful . . ." (exemplified by, say, the naturally "picturesque" Yosemite Valley, high Alpine "scenery," "sublime" sequoia groves, etc.), "to values as yet uncaptured by language."[3] Leopold then goes on to capture, in his own compact, descriptive prose, the subtler gamut of aesthetic quality in a nonlandscape which the conventional painting-mediated natural aesthetic finds plain, if not odious — a crane marsh.

Among gallery goers there are also those whose taste is limited to the pretty (to naive, realistic, still-life, and portraiture, for example). Then, there are those capable of appreciating successive stages of the beautiful present in "modern art" (Cezanne, Picasso, or Pollack), whether pretty or not. As in art, the capacity to actualize the aesthetic potentialities of land which go beyond the pretty and the picturesque requires some cultivation of sensibility. One must acquire "a refined taste in natural objects."[4]

> The taste for country displays the same diversity in esthetic competence among individuals as the taste for opera, or oils. There are those who are willing to be herded in droves through "scenic" places; who find mountains grand if they be proper mountains with waterfalls, cliffs, and lakes. To such the Kansas plains are tedious.[5]

For Leopold the Kansas plains are aesthetically exciting less for what is directly seen (or, indeed, otherwise sensuously experienced) than for what is known of their history and biology: "They see the endless corn, but not the heave and the grunt of ox teams breaking the prairie. . . . They look at the low

horizon, but they cannot see it, as de Vaca did, under the bellies of the buffalo."[6]

In "Marshland Elegy" Leopold beautifully illustrates the impact of an evolutionary biological literacy on perception. Wisconsin's first settlers called sandhill cranes "red shitepokes" for the rusty clay stain their "battleship gray" feathers acquire in summer.[7] The Wisconsin homesteaders saw red shitepokes as just large birds in the way of farm progress. But evolutionary literacy can alter and deepen perception:

> Our appreciation of the crane grows with the slow unraveling of earthly history. His tribe, we now know, stems out of the remote Eocene. The other members of the fauna in which he originated are long since entombed within the hills. When we hear his call we hear no mere bird. We hear the trumpet in the orchestra of evolution. He is the symbol of our untamable past, of that incredible sweep of millennia which underlies the daily affairs of birds and men.[8]

Ecology, as Leopold pictures it, is the biological science which runs at right angles to evolution.[9] Evolution lends to perception a certain depth, "that incredible sweep of millennia," while ecology provides it breadth: Wild things do not exist in isolation from one another. They are "interlocked in one humming community of cooperations and competitions, one biota."[10] Hence the crane, no mere bird, lends "a paleontological patent of nobility" to its marshy habitat.[11] We cannot love cranes and hate marshes. The marsh itself is now transformed by the presence of cranes from a "waste," "God-forsaken" mosquito swamp, into a thing of precious beauty.

The crane is also a species native to its marshy habitat. Many pretty plants and animals are not. From the point of view of the land aesthetic, the attractive purple flower of centauria or the vivid orange of hawkweed might actually spoil rather than enhance a field of (otherwise) native grasses and forbes. Leopold writes lovingly of draba, pasque-flowers, sylphium, and many other pretty and not-so-pretty native plants, but with undisguised contempt for peonies, downy chess or cheat grass, foxtail, and other European imports and stowaways. He takes delight in the sky dance of the native woodcock and the flight plan of a fleeing partridge, but not (hunter though he may have been) in, say, the evasive maneuvers of the imported oriental ring-necked pheasant.

In an (until just now) unpublished 1936 lecture entitled "Means and Ends in Wild Life Management," Leopold frankly declares that while "our tools are scientific . . . our output is weighed in aesthetic satisfaction rather than economic pounds or dollars."[12] Then he briefly sets out a few criteria for evaluating the aesthetic significance of wildlife species. One such criterion he denominates "artistic value," by which he seems to mean things like colorful plumage and musical songs of birds — the sorts of sensory qualities that wildlife and art might have in common. But that is the least important criterion for the aesthetic appraisal of wildlife. More important is "personality" or "character" which we perceive of the species, not the individual animal — the resourcefulness of the fox, the grace of the deer, and so on. Leopold identifies, further, "scarcity value" — both natural scarcity, as in the case of the badger, or humanly induced rarity as in the case of the Carolina parakeet — as a criterion of the natural aesthetics of wildlife. Further still, the wilder the animal, the less tolerant of man and his works — such as the grizzly bear as opposed to the black bear and the timber wolf as opposed to the coyote — the more aesthetically valuable. And of course the native species, once again, is to be prized over the exotic.

Ecology, history, paleontology, geology, biogeography — each forms of knowledge or cognition — penetrate the surface provided by direct sensory experience and supply substance to "scenery." Leopold was quite consciously aware of the profound transformation in general sensibility that he was calling for. In another (until now) unpublished piece from the 1930s, "Land Pathology," Leopold lampoons the conventional taste for "scenery" immured in the National Parks as "an epidemic of esthetic rickets."[13] In the almanac, similarly, he disparaged "that underaged brand of esthetics which limits the definition of 'scenery' to lakes and pine trees."[14] "In country," he writes, "a plain exterior often conceals hidden riches."[15] To get at these hidden riches takes more than a gaze at a scenic view through a car window or camera view finder. To promote appreciation of nature is "a job not of building roads into lovely country, but of building receptivity into the still unlovely human mind."[16]

Leopold's land aesthetic, like his land ethic, is self-consciously informed by evolutionary and ecological biology. It involves a subtle interplay between conceptual schemata and sensuous experience. Experience, as the British Empiricists insisted, informs thought. That is true and obvious to everyone. What is not so immediately apparent is that thought equally and reciprocally informs experience. The "world," as we drink it in through our senses, is first filtered, structured, and arranged by the conceptual framework or cognitive set we bring to it, prior, not necessarily to all, but to any articulate experience.

This was Kant's great and lasting contribution to philosophy, his self-styled "Copernican revolution" of philosophy. Kant believed that the cognitive conditions of experience were *a priori* — universal and necessary — but that proved to be a narrowly parochial judgment. The discovery by anthropologists of very different "cultural worlds" or "world views" and subsequent revolutionary changes in Western science affecting even the fundamental experiential parameters of space and time relativized Kant's transcendental "aesthetic" and "logic." His basic revolutionary idea, though, remains very much intact. What one experiences is as much a product of how one thinks as the condition of one's senses and the specific content of one's environment.

Leopold is quite consciously aware of the interplay between the creative or active cognitive component of experience and the receptive or passive sensory component. He imagines what Daniel Boone's experience of nature must have been like as an outdoorsman living before the advent of an evolutionary-ecological biology:

> Daniel Boone's reaction depended not only on the quality of what he saw, but on the quality of the mental eye with which he saw it. Ecological science has wrought a change in the mental eye. It has disclosed origins and functions for what to Boone were only facts. It has disclosed mechanisms for what to Boone were only attributes. We have no yardstick to measure this change, but we may safely say that, as compared with the competent ecologist of the present day, Boone saw only the surface of

things. The incredible intricacies of the plant and animal community—the intrinsic beauty of the organism called America, then in the full bloom of her maidenhood—were as invisible and incomprehensible to Daniel Boone as they are today to Babbitt. The only true development in American [aesthetic] resources is the development of the perceptive faculty in Americans. All of the other acts we grace by that name are, at best, attempts to retard or mask the process of dilution.[17]

Thus, while an autonomous natural aesthetic, as I earlier pointed out, must free itself from the prevailing visual bias and involve all sensory modalities, it is not enough to simply open the senses to natural stimuli and enjoy. A complete natural aesthetic, like a complete artifactual aesthetic, shapes and directs sensation, often in surprising ways. It is possible, in certain theoretical contexts, to enjoy and appreciate dissonance in music or the clash of color and distortion of eidetic form in painting. Similarly, in natural aesthetics, it is possible to appreciate and relish certain environmental experiences which are not literally pleasurable or sensuously delightful.

For example, I am acquainted with a certain northern bog which is distinguished from the others in its vicinity by the presence of pitcher plants, an endangered species of floral insectivore. I visit this bog at least once each season. The plants themselves are not, by garden standards, beautiful. They are a dark red in color, less brilliant than maple leaves in autumn, and humbly hug the low bog floor. They lie on a bed of sphagnum moss in the deep shade of fifty-foot, ruler-straight tamaracks. To reach the bog I must wade across its mucky moat, penetrate a dense thicket of tag alders and in summer fight off mosquitoes, black flies, and deer flies. My shoes and trousers get wet; my skin gets scratched and bitten. The experience is certainly not spectacular or, for that matter, particularly pleasant; but it is always somehow satisfying aesthetically. The moss bed on which the pitcher plants grow is actually floating. It undulates sensually as I walk through. I smell the sweet decay aroma of the peat and hear the whining insects (in season). I run my finger down and then up the vulva-shaped interior of a pitcher plant's leaf—turned insect trap—

to feel the grain of the fibers which keep the insects from crawling out again. It is silky smooth on the way in, bristled on the way out. I look through the trees, beyond, to the adjoining pond. I dig my hand into the moss and bring up a brown rotting mass. I sometimes see a blue heron lift itself off the shore into the air with a single silent stroke of its great wings or see the glint and splash of a northern pike out on the pond. I feel the living bark of the tamaracks, precariously anchored on a floating island. In spring and summer everything is drably green or brown except the sky, and the pitcher plants. Fall is the most colorful, the tamaracks are a "smoky gold." In winter everything shades from black to white. Yet there is a rare music in this place. It is orchestrated and deeply moving.

The beauty of this bog is not serial—an aggregate of interesting objects, like specimens displayed in cases in a natural history museum, nor is it phenomenological—a variety of sensory stimuli or "sense data"; rather its beauty is a function of the palpable organization and closure of the interconnected living components. The sphagnum moss and the chemical regime it imposes constitutes the basis of this small, tight community. The tamaracks are a second major factor. The flora and fauna of the stories between are characteristic of, and some like the pitcher plants are unique to, this sort of community. There is a sensible fittingness, a unity there, not unlike that of a good symphony or tragedy. But these connections and relations are not directly sensed in the aesthetic moment, they are *known* and *projected,* in this case by me. It is this conceptual act that completes the sensory experience and causes it to be distinctly aesthetic . . . instead of merely uncomfortable.

Given the Western heritage, it is, perhaps, impossible to express and analyze natural aesthetic experience except by analogy with artifactual aesthetic experience. Leopold's evolutionary-ecological aesthetic is, yielding to this expository necessity, perhaps more akin to aural aesthetics than to visual aesthetics. Few authors have expressed the sense of the familiar metaphor "harmony of nature" with more authority and grace than he:

The song of a river ordinarily means the tune that waters play on rock, root, and rapid. . . .

This song of the waters is audible to every ear, but there is other music in these hills, by no means audible to all. To hear even a few notes of it you must first live here for a long time, and you must know the speech of hills and rivers. Then on a still night, when the campfire is low and the Pleiades have climbed over rimrocks, sit quietly and listen for a wolf to howl, and think hard of everything you have seen and tried to understand. Then you may hear it—a vast pulsing harmony—its score inscribed on a thousand hills, its notes the lives and deaths of plants and animals, its rhythms spanning the seconds and the centuries.[18]

In 1935 Leopold traveled abroad for the first time, studying forestry and wildlife management in Germany. This experience inspired a piece entitled "Wilderness," which has now also been published for the first time in the new collection of his essays. As in the almanac's haunting "Marshland Elegy," Leopold fuses the evolutionary and ecological dimensions of informed perception. He expresses his displeasure with the intensively managed German "forest landscape deprived of a certain exuberance which arises from a rich variety of plants fighting with each other for a place in the sun."[19] Maintenance of an excessively high deer herd had resulted in "an illusive burglary of esthetic wealth . . . an unnatural simplicity and monotony in the vegetation of the forest floor, which is still further aggravated by the too-dense shade cast by the artificially crowded trees, and by the soil-sickness . . . arising from conifers."[20] But species diversity, the lack of which is discernible to the ecological eye, is an evolutionary legacy. "It is almost, he suggests, as if the geological clock had been set back to those dim ages when there were only pines and ferns."[21] And, as in the almanac's "Song of the Gavilan," he expresses his (this time negative) aesthetic response with an even more powerful musical metaphor: "I never realized before that the melodies of nature are music only when played against the undertones of evolutionary history. In the German forest one now hears only a dismal fugue out of the timeless reaches of the carboniferous."[22]

In addition to this general Kantian emphasis on the cognitive dimension of natural aesthetic experience, Leopold has formulated a quite specialized

and somewhat technical natural aesthetic category, "the noumenon," also ultimately inspired by the philosophy of Kant. To an academic historian of philosophy, Leopold may seem simply to have misappropriated Kant's term. By "noumenon" Kant meant a purely intelligible object, a thing-in-itself (*Ding an sich*) which was beyond human ken. Only phenomena are present to human consciousness, according to Kant. In Leopold's general sense of the term, however, the noumena of land are quite actual or physical (and therefore, strictly speaking, phenomenal). Nonetheless, in a metaphorical way, they constitute the "essence" of the countryside. In this sense Leopold's usage observes the spirit of Kant's definition, if not the letter. Here is how Leopold introduces the term, "noumenon" in *Sand County:*

> The physics of beauty is one department of natural science still in the Dark Ages. Not even the manipulators of bent space have tried to solve its equations. Everybody knows, for example, that the autumn landscape in the north woods is the land, plus a red maple, plus a ruffed grouse. In terms of conventional physics, the grouse represents only a millionth of either the mass or the energy of an acre. Yet subtract the grouse and the whole thing is dead. An enormous amount of some kind of motive power has been lost.
>
> It is easy to say that the loss is all in our mind's eye, but is there any sober ecologist who will agree? He knows full well that there has been an ecological death, the significance of which is inexpressible in terms of contemporary science. A philosopher has called this imponderable essence the *noumenon* of material things. It stands in contradistinction to *phenomenon,* which is ponderable and predictable, even to the tossings and turnings of the remotest star.
>
> The grouse is the noumenon of the north woods, the blue jay of the hickory groves, the whiskeyjack of the muskegs, the piñonero of the juniper foothills. . . .[23]

And we could go on: the cutthroat trout of high mountain streams, the sandhill crane of northern marshes, the pronghorn antelope of the high plains, the loon of glacial lakes, the alligator of southeastern swamps, etc., etc. We might call these noumena more precisely, though less arrestingly, "aesthetic indicator species." They supply the hallmark, the imprimatur, to their respective ecological communities. If they be missing, then the rosy glow of perfect health, as well as aesthetic excitement, is absent from the countryside. Like the elusive mountain lion and timber wolf, they need not be seen or heard to grace and enliven their respective habitats. It is enough merely to *know* that they are present.

In "Wilderness," Leopold expresses an aesthetic dissatisfaction not only with "what the geometrical mind has done to German rivers," but also with the decidedly picturesque German countryside, because "to the critical eye, there is something lacking that should not be."[24] In addition to much of the native flora, many species of native fauna, especially predators, had been extirpated from the German *Walder* by "cubistic forestry" and by the "misguided zeal of the game-keeper and herdsman." Leopold laments especially the absence of "the great owl or 'Uhu,'" more often heard than seen, "without whose vocal austerity the winter night becomes a mere blackness."[25] The Uhu, we realize, is, for Leopold, the noumenon of the German forests.

To sum up, the land aesthetic, desultorily and intermittently developed in *A Sand County Almanac*, in *Round River*, and now in *The River of the Mother of God* is a new natural aesthetic, the first, to my knowledge, to be informed by ecological and evolutionary natural history and thus the only genuinely autonomous natural aesthetic in Western philosophical literature: It does not treat natural beauty as subordinate to or derivative from artifactual beauty. However, because natural beauty has traditionally and historically been treated as a reflection of artifactual beauty, the land aesthetic is perforce developed by analogy with artifactual aesthetics. Though more analogous to an aesthetic of music, the land aesthetic is no more aurally biased than visually biased. It involves all sensory modalities equally and indiscriminately.

The popularly prevailing natural aesthetic, the scenic or picturesque aesthetic, frames nature, as it were, and deposits it in "galleries"—the national parks—for most ordinary folk, far from home. We herd in droves to Yellowstone, Yosemite, and the Smokies to gaze at natural beauty and, home again, despise the river bottoms, fallow fields, bogs, and ponds on the back forty. The land aesthetic enables us to mine the hidden riches of the ordinary; it ennobles the commonplace; it brings natural beauty literally home from the hills.

The land aesthetic is sophisticated and cognitive, not naive and hedonic; it delineates a refined taste in natural environments and a cultivated natural sensibility. The basis of such refinement or cultivation is natural history, and more especially, evolutionary and ecological biology. The crane, for example, is no mere bird because of its known, not directly sensed, phylogenetic antiquity and, thus, the experience of cranes is especially aesthetically satisfying only to those who have a paleontological dimension to their outlook. The experience of a marsh or bog is aesthetically satisfying less for what is literally sensed than what is known or schematically imagined of its ecology. Leopold enters a caveat, however, to the cognitive stress of the land aesthetic:

Let no man jump to the conclusion that Babbitt must take his Ph.D. in ecology before he can "see" his country. On the contrary, the Ph.D. may become as callous as an undertaker to the mysteries at which he officiates. Like all real treasures of the mind, perception can be split into infinitely small fractions without losing its quality. The weeds in a city lot convey the same lesson as the redwoods; the farmer may see in his cow-pasture what may not be vouchsafed to the scientist adventuring in the South Seas. Perception, in short, cannot be purchased with either learned degrees or dollars; it grows at home as well as abroad, and he who has a little may use it to as good advantage as he who has much. As a search for perception, the recreational stampede is footless and unnecessary.[26]

Finally and, practically speaking, more importantly, the land aesthetic is not biased in favor of some natural communities or some places and not others. Leopold in his discussion and I in mine have dwelt on wetlands (marshes and bogs) because they are characteristic of Wisconsin (where I also live) and also because, since they are so thoroughly unaesthetic, as measured by conventional canons of landscape beauty, they highlight certain contrasts between the picturesque aesthetic and the land aesthetic. But conventionally beautiful environments—alpine communities, for example—are, for that reason, not the less land aesthetically interesting. All biocoenoses from arctic tundra to tropical rainforest and from deserts to swamps can be aesthetically appealing upon the land aesthetic. Hence, no matter where one may live, one's environment holds the potential for natural aesthetic experience.

NOTES

1. Some recent exceptions include Marjorie Hope Nicholson, *Mountain Gloom, Mountain Glory: The Development of the Aesthetics of the Infinite* (Ithaca, NY: Cornell University Press, 1969); Ian McHarg, *Design with Nature* (Garden City, NY: Doubleday and Co., 1971); Paul Shepard, *Man in the Landscape: A Historic View of the Esthetics of Nature* (New York: Alfred Knopf, 1967); Yi-Fu Tuan, *Topophilia: A Study of Environmental Perception, Attitudes, and Values* (Englewood Cliffs, NJ: Prentice Hall, 1974); Mark Sagoff, "On Preserving the Natural Environment," *The Yale Law Journal* 84 (1974): 245–67; Ronald Rees, "The Taste for Mountain Scenery," *History Today* 25 (1975): 305–12; Eugene C. Hargrove, "The Historical Foundations of American Environmental Attitudes," *Environmental Ethics* 1 (1979): 209–40 and "Anglo-American Land Use Attitudes," *Environmental Ethics* 2 (1980): 121–48; Allen Carlson, "Appreciation and the Natural Environment," *Journal of Aesthetics and Art Criticism* 37 (1979): 267–75 and "Nature, Aesthetic Judgment, and Objectivity," *Journal of Aesthetics and Art Criticism* 40 (1981): 15–27 and "Nature and Positive Aesthetics," *Environmental Ethics* 6 (1984): 5–34; Barbara Novak, *Nature and Culture: American Landscape Painting 1825–1875* (New York: Oxford University Press, 1980); J. Baird Callicott, "Aldo Leopold's Land Aesthetic and Agrarian Land Use Values," *Journal of Soil and Water Conservation* 38 (1983): 329–32; Philip G. Terrie, *Forever Wild: Environmental Aesthetics and the Adirondack Forest Preserve* (Philadelphia: Temple University Press, 1985); Holmes Rolston, III, some essays in *Philosophy Gone Wild* (Buffalo, NY: Prometheus Books, 1986).

2. Christopher Hussey, *The Picturesque: Studies in a Point of View* (London: G. P. Putnam's Sons, 1927) pp. 1–2.

3. Aldo Leopold, *A Sand County Almanac: And Sketches Here and There* (New York: Oxford University Press, 1949), p. 96.

4. Aldo Leopold, *The Round River,* pp. 32–33.

5. Ibid., p. 33.

6. Leopold, *Sand County,* p. 99.

7. Ibid., p. 96.

8. Leopold, *Round River,* p. 159.

9. Ibid., p. 148.

10. Leopold, *Sand County,* p. 97.

11. Wetlands to those farmers wearing economic blinders (by no means all farmers) are, in my neck of the woods, regularly referred to as "waste" lands, because they are not in "production," i.e., not cultivated.

12. Aldo Leopold, "Means and Ends in Wildlife Management," in Susan L. Flader and J. Baird Callicott, eds., *The River of the Mother of God and Other Essays by Aldo Leopold* (Madison: University of Wisconsin Press, 1991), p. 236.

13. Aldo Leopold, "Land Pathology," in *The River of the Mother of God,* p. 216.

14. Leopold, *Sand County,* p. 191.

15. Leopold, *Round River,* p. 33.

16. Leopold, *Sand County,* p. 177.

17. Ibid., p. 174.

18. Ibid., p. 149.

19. Aldo Leopold, "Wilderness," in *The River of the Mother of God,* p. 229.

20. Ibid., p. 228.

21. Ibid., p. 229.

22. Ibid.

23. Leopold, *Sand County,* pp. 138–39.

24. Leopold, "Wilderness," pp. 226–27.

25. Ibid., p. 228.

26. Leopold, *Sand County,* p. 174.

DISCUSSION TOPICS

1. According to Leopold, what contributions to aesthetic experience can be made by "evolutionary literacy" in the observer? Give an example.

2. In your view, is the "picturesque" sense of natural beauty, which Callicott dates from the seventeenth century, still dominant in the

West? What role does the picturesque play in your own experience of natural beauty?

3. Explain Leopold's idea of the noumena of various ecological communities and give an example from your own geographical area.

4. Compare the overall tone of Leopold's land aesthetic with the essays of Thoreau, Muir, and Abrams. How prominent are the biological, moral, emotional, spiritual, and traditionally aesthetic perspectives in the various writers?

The Far Outside

Gary Paul Nabhan

Gary Nabhan is director of the Center for Sustainable Environments at Northern Arizona University. He has received the John Burroughs medal for nature writing and a MacArthur Award. In the following essay he emphasizes his sense that the world has its own reality, that its meaning does not depend upon human beings.

> *Any good poet, in our age at least, must begin with the scientific view of the world; and any scientist worth listening to must be something of a poet, must possess the ability to communicate to the rest of us his sense of love and wonder at what his work discovers.*
>
> Edward Abbey
> *The Journey Home*

I was in a small room in Alaska when I heard it. That was part of the trouble. I was supposed to be paying attention to what was being said in the room; after all, this was a nature writing symposium. But from where I sat I could hear ravens coming in to roost in the spruce trees above us, and wondered how their calls were different from those of the Chihuahuan ravens down where I live. I could look out the windows and see bald eagles swooping over the waters of the sound. Worse yet, I already had the stain and smell of salmonberries on my hands, and had been perplexed all morning as to why the ripe berries on two adjacent bushes were entirely different colors.

It was then that I heard it. A familiar warble came out of the well-educated, widely read humanist a few chairs away from me. She asserted a truism I had heard in one form or another for nearly thirty years:

"Each of us has to go *inside* before we can go *outside!* How can we give any meaning to the natural world until each individual finds out who he or she is as a human being, until each of us finds our own internal source of peace?"

Queasy, I immediately felt nauseous, indisposed. Something she said had stuck in my craw. Instantly, I was so out of sorts I had to leave the room. Our moderator followed me out to the porch, where I gasped for air.

"Are you *okay?*" she asked earnestly. "You looked *green* all of a sudden."

"I dunno." I breathed deeply and looked up at the crisp blue sky. "I must be . . . uh . . . under the weather a little. Let me see if some fresh air will help. . . . If you don't mind, I had better go for a walk."

As I ambled along, I wondered what had set me off. I wandered around on a rainforest trail, trying to spiral in on what in that room had disoriented me. First, I felt uncomfortable with the notion that we can give the natural world "its meaning." The plants and animals which I have observed most diligently over twenty years as a field biologist hardly seem to be waiting for me to give *them* meaning. Instead, most humans want to feel as though *we* are meaningful, and so we project *our* meanings upon the rest of the world. We read meaning into other species' behavior, but with few exceptions they are unlikely to do the same toward us.

Humans may, in fact, be rare even among primates in the attention we give to a wide range of other species' tracks, calls, and movements. To paraphrase one prominent primatologist: "If their inattention to their neighbors other than predators is any indication, most monkeys are extremely poor naturalists." The same can be said of many other wild animals which live in sight of, and in spite of, human habitations.

While it may somehow be good for *us* to think and write about plants and animals, I am reminded of John Daniel's humbling insight while hopping through a snake-laden boulder field: the snakes were not fazed by his thoughts, fears, or needs. As Daniel writes in *The Trail Home:* "The rattlesnakes beneath the boulders instructed me, in a way no book could have, that the natural world did not exist entirely for my comfort and pleasure; indeed, that it did not particularly care whether my small human life continued to exist at all."

Walking along, my restlessness increased as I considered the premise put forth in that room: the shortest road to wisdom and peace with the world is that which turns inward. I will not argue that meditation, psychotherapy, and philosophical reflection are unproductive, but I simply can't accept that inward is the only or best way for everyone to turn. The more disciplined practitioners of contemplative traditions can turn inward and still get beyond the self, but many others simply stumble into self-indulgence.

As Robinson Jeffers suggested over a half century ago, it may be just as valid to turn outward: "The whole human race spends too much emotion on itself. The happiest and freest man is the scientist investigating nature or the artist admiring it, the person who is interested in things that are not human. Or if he is interested in human beings, let him regard them objectively as a small part of the great music."

Finishing my walk among the great music of crashing waves and hermit thrushes, I conceded that the wisest, most inspired people I knew had all taken this second path, heading for what I call the Far Outside. It is the path found when one falls into "the naturalist's trance," the hunter's pursuit of wild game, the *curandera*'s search for hidden roots, the fisherman's casting of the net into the current, the water-witcher's trust of the forked willow branch, the rock climber's fixation on the slightest details of a cliff face. Oddly, it is hanging onto that cliff, beyond the reach of the safety net of civilization, where one may gain the deepest sense of what it is to be alive. As arctic writer and ethnographer Hugh Brody says of his predilection for working in the most remote human communities and wildest places he can find, "it is at the periphery that I can come to understand the central issues of living."

Unlike conditions within the metropolitan grid where it seems we have got nature surrounded, the Far Outside still offers the comic juxtapositions, the ones worthy of a Gary Larson cartoon. The flood suddenly looms large before Noah can get his family onto the ark full of animals; the bugs in the test tube have the last say about the entire experiment.

INWARD AND OUTWARD PATHS

When I returned home to the Stinkin Hot Desert, I had an urge to see how an elder from another culture might view this apparent dichotomy between inward and outward paths—or for that matter, the dichotomy between culture and nature. I drove a hundred miles across the desert to see a seventy-four-year-old O'odham farmer who had worked all his life "outdoors": tending native crops, chopping wood, driving teams of horses, gathering cactus fruit, hunting, and building ceremonial houses for his tribe's rain-bringing rites. He was consistently wise in ways that my brief bouts with Jungian analysis, *zazen* practice, and Franciscan prayer had not enabled me to be. And I knew that because he'd had a brush with death over the last year, he had been made sedentary and forced to be alone, and at home, for a longer time than ever before in his entire life. He sat outside on an old wooden bench, a crutch on either side of him, looking out at a small field which he would not be able to plant this year. I asked him what he had been working over in his mind the last couple months.

"I'd like to make a trip," he said nonchalantly for a man who had only traveled once beyond the limits of the desert—all the way to Gallup—and who now lived at the end of his life less than thirty miles from where he was born.

"Yes, before I die, I'd like to go over there to the ocean," he nodded to the southwest, where the Sea of Cortez lay a hundred miles away. It was a sacred place for the desert O'odham, where they used to go as pilgrims for salt and for songs. My elderly friend paused, then continued.

"Yes, I would like to hear the birds there in the sea. I would like to hear those ocean birds sing in my native language."

"In *O'odham ha-neoki?*" I asked. I must have looked surprised he felt the birds spoke in his language, for he then offered to explain his comment as if it had been scribbled in a shorthand indiscernible to me.

"Whenever my people used to walk over there to the ocean for salt, they would stand on the edge and listen to those birds sing. And they are in many of the songs we still sing today, even though we haven't walked or ridden horses there since the hoof-and-mouth quarantines in the forties. In the old days, they didn't start to sing those songs while they were still at the ocean. No, the people would go back home, and then some night, those ocean birds would begin singing in their dreams. That's where our songs come from. They would come to our medicine men, from the ocean, in their dreams. Maybe the ones who play the violin would hear them in their sleep, and their voices would turn up in their fiddle tunes. Maybe the *pascola* dancers would hear the way they flew, and it would end up in the way they sounded when they danced with their rattles. Those birds have ended up in our songs, and I want to hear them at the ocean before I die."

What struck me about my friend's last request was his desire to hear those birds for himself at the edge of the ocean. For a lifelong dweller in a riverless desert, the ocean must be a landscape wilder than the imagination, truly unfathomable. In the end, he sought to juxtapose his culture's aural imagery of ocean birds with what the birds themselves were saying. He desired to experience nature directly, as a measure of the cultural symbols and sounds he had carried with him most of his life.

My friend's songs and stories are conversant with and responsive to what we often refer to as "outer reality." This larger landscape is not superfluous or irrelevant to his culture's literature, music, or ways of healing. When I arrived at his home once, years ago, I saw him carrying into the kitchen a mockingbird which he had captured in a seed trap, killed, and carefully butchered, in order to cook the meat up and feed it to his grandson. Mockingbirds are not simply good mimics, they are irrepressibly loquacious; his grandson was not. In fact, the boy was nearly three years old and had not spoken a word. Concerned, my friend recalled the sympathetic ritual of his people for curing such difficulties: feed the mute one the songbird's flesh. He will have the best chance of being able to express himself if he ingests the wild world around him. In the O'odham language, the words for curing, wildness, and health come from the same root.

This is where "inner" and "outer" become not a duality but a dynamic—like every breath we take. We are *inspired* by what surrounds us; we take it into our bodies, and after some rumination we respond with *expression*. What we have inside us is, ultimately, always of the larger, wilder world. Nature is not just "out there," beyond the individual. The O'odham boy now has seed, bird, and O'odham history in his very muscles, in the cells of his tongue, in his reverberating voice box.

Lynn Margulis has recently pointed out that thousands of other such lives are literally inside each so-called human "individual." For every cell of our own genetic background that we embody, there are a thousand times more cells of other species within and on each of our bodies. It would be more fitting to imagine each human corpus as a diverse wildlife habitat than to persist with the illusion of the individual self. Or better, each of us is really a corpus of *stories:* bacteria duking it out for the final word in our mouths; fungi having clandestine affairs between our toes; other microbes collaborating to digest the world within our intestines; archetypal images from our evolutionary past roaming through our nerve synapses, testing our groin muscles against our brain tissue.

If I could distill what I have learned during a thousand and one nights working as a field biologist, waiting around campfires while mist-netting bats, running lines of live traps, or pressing plants, it would be this: each plant or animal has a story of some unique way of living in this world. By tracking their stories down to the finest detail, our own lives may somehow be informed, and perhaps enriched. The zoologist who radio-collars a mountain lion may call his research a range utilization analysis, but he is simply tracking that critter's odyssey. A botanist may refer to the adaptive strategy of a cactus, but only after carefully recording chapter and verse how the plant endures and prevails, despite droughts, freezes, or heat waves. An ecologist interested in the nutcracker's dispersal of pine seeds is slowly learning the language of the forest, and the birds are her newly found verbs.

Perhaps due to what Paul Ehrlich calls "physics envy," many biologists feel inclined to mask their recording of stories in shrouds of numbers, jargon, and theory. We find their remarkable insights buried beneath techno-babble about life histories, optimal foraging tests, or paleoecological reconstructions. Most of them, however, are merely tracing the trajectory of another life as it demonstrates ways to survive in the Far Outside. In *Writing Natural History,* two-time Pulitzer Prize winner E. O. Wilson tells of the struggle scientists have simply to be storytellers: "Scientists live and die by their ability to depart from the tribe and go out into an unknown terrain and bring back, like a carcass newly speared, some new discovery or new fact or theoretical insight and lay it in front of the tribe; and then they all gather and dance around it. Symposia are held in the National Academy of Sciences and prizes are given. There is fundamentally no difference from a Paleolithic campsite celebration. . . ."

In short, scientists too grapple with the challenge of telling the unheard-of stories which may move their tribes. And yet it is tragic to realize how few of these stories any of us will ever glimpse. In *The Diversity of Life,* it is E. O. Wilson again who reminds us that we have only the crudest of character sketches—let alone any understanding of the plots—involved with most of these floral and faunal narratives:

> Even though some 1.4 million species of organisms have been discovered (in the minimal sense of having specimens collected and formal scientific names attached), the total number alive on the earth is somewhere between 10 and 100 million. . . . Of the species given scientific names, fewer than 10 percent have been studied at a level deeper than gross anatomy. [Intensively studied species make up] . . . a still smaller fraction, including colon bacteria, corn, fruit flies, Norway rats, rhesus monkeys, and human beings, altogether comprising no more than a hundred species.

STORIES

Try to imagine the still-untold stories, the sudden flowerings, the cataclysmic extinctions, the episodic turnovers in dominance, the failed attempts at mutualistic relationships, and the climaxes which took hundreds of years to achieve. In every biotic community, there are story lines which fiction writers would give their eyeteeth for: Desert tortoises with allegiances to place that have lasted upward of forty thousand years, dwarfing any dynasty in Yoknapatawpha County. Fidelities between hummingbird and montane penstemon that make the fidelities in Port William, Kentucky, seem like puppy love. Dormancies of lotus seeds that outdistance Rip Van Winkle's longest nap. Promiscuities between neighboring oak trees which would make even Nabokov and his Lolita blush. Or all-female lizard species with reproductive habits more radical than anything in lesbian literature.

And yet, with the myriad stories around and within us, how many of them do we recognize as touching our lives in any way? Most natural history essays are so limited in their range of plot, character development, and emotive currents that Joyce Carol Oates has come to an erroneous, near-fatal assumption about nature itself. In her essay "Against Nature," Oates claims that nature "inspires a painfully limited set of responses in 'nature writers' . . . *reverence, awe, piety, mystical oneness.*"

Most environmental journalists offer an even more limited set of "news" stories: (1) that someone has momentarily succeeded in disrupting the plans of the bastards who are ruining the world; and (2) that the bastards are still ruining the world. Most newspaper and magazine journalists who ostensibly cover biological diversity tell the same doom and gloom story over and over, with virtually nothing substantial about the nonhuman lives embedded in that diversity. One week, "Paradise Lost" is told with the yew tree as the victim in the temperate rainforest; the next, the scene has shifted to peyote in the Chihuahuan desert; but the plot is still the same.

I believe that human existence is being degraded by our ignorance of these diverse stories. In stark contrast to the O'odham elder's dreams, fewer and fewer creatures are inhabiting the dreams of those in mainstream society. I know another elderly man who lives in the midst of metropolitan Phoenix. Although he is a few years younger than my friend the Indian farmer, he seems far closer to death; I can feel it every time I visit him. He too was formerly an outdoorsman and farmer, skilled with horses, hunting, building, and wood carving. But now he has emphysema and cannot even go outside and sit, the contaminated air of Phoenix is so vile. Yet that is not all that is killing him. Confined to a hermetically sealed tract house, he sits in front of a television all day long and hears just three stories repeated ad nauseam: (1) Saddam Hussein and other foreign despots are out to get us; (2) substance-abusing street gangs are out to get us; and (3) mutant microbes are out to get us. He seems drained of all resilience, a man without hope. He has lost all contact with the wildlife, the Far Outside, that had been his source of renewal most of his life.

Harking back to William Carlos Williams, we might say that society pays little attention to these myriad lives, but people die for lack of contact with them every day. As with our teeth, what we don't pay attention to is likely to disappear. By the end of this decade, twenty-five thousand species—twenty-five thousand distinctive ways of living in this world—are likely to be lost unless we begin to learn of these beings in ways that move us sufficiently to curtail our destructive habits.

And scientists cannot do the work by themselves. As E. O. Wilson admits, the capacity to tell of these vanishing lives in compelling ways is tightly constrained by the stylistic conventions of technical scientific journals. In *Writing Natural History* he argues that

the factual information that we get and the new metaphors created out of science somehow have to be translated into the language of the storyteller—by film, by speech, by literature, by any means that will make it meaningful and powerful for the human mind. . . . And the storyteller has always had this central role in societies: of translating that information in forms that played upon the great mythic themes and used the rhythms and the openings . . . the body . . . and the closures that make up literature.

Now, more urgently than ever before, we all need to come face to face with other lives in the Far Outside—not just with the Bali Mynah and the Furbish Lousewort, but with the fungi between our toes as well. Imagine what might happen if some of those who now turn inward, apprenticing themselves to all kinds of gurus, priests, therapists, and masters, would turn outward as apprentices to other species: Komodo Dragons, Marbled Murrelets, Desert Pupfish, Beer-Making Yeasts, Texas Wild Rice, or Okeechobee Gourds.

I can't help but wonder if the dilemma of our society is not unlike that of the mute child who needs to eat the songbird in order to speak. Unless we come to embody the songs from the Far Outside, we will be left dumb before an increasingly frightening world. But that is just the first step. Once we have begun to express in our own ways the stories inspired by those other lives, we may need to keep seeking them out, to constantly compare the images we have conjured up with the beings themselves.

It is time to leave this room and go Outside, farther than we have ever gone together before. It is time to hear the seabirds singing at the edge of the world and to bring them back, freshly, into our dreams.

DISCUSSION TOPICS

1. Nabhan believes that a scientist, in order to be worth listening to, must be something of a poet. What does he mean, and why is this important?
2. Does Nabhan's nausea at the idea that we first must go inside ourselves before we can go outside of ourselves seem like a reasonable response? Explain your reasoning.
3. Describe in your own words what Nabhan means by saying it is time "to hear the seabirds singing at the edge of the world and to bring them back, freshly, into our dreams."

READING 16

A More-Than-Human World

David Abram

David Abram is a magician and philosopher, and author of The Spell of the Sensuous (1996), *winner of the Lannan Prize for best nonfiction of 1996. In the following selection he describes his experiences in Bali, a place where he learned of the "multiple non-human sensibilities that animate the local landscape." These modes of intelligence, in insect or other form, are the more-than-human spirits of the place.*

Late one evening I stepped out of my little hut in the rice paddies of eastern Bali and found myself falling through space. Over my head the black sky was rippling with stars, densely clustered in some regions, almost blocking out the darkness between them, and more loosely scattered in other areas, pulsing and beckoning to each other. Behind them all streamed the great river of light with its several tributaries. Yet the Milky Way churned beneath me as well, for my hut was set in the middle of a large patchwork of rice paddies, separated from each other by narrow two-foot-high dikes, and these paddies were all filled with water. The surface of these pools, by day, reflected perfectly the blue sky, a reflection broken only by the thin, bright green tips of new rice. But by night the stars themselves glimmered from the surface of the paddies, and the river of light whirled through the darkness underfoot as well as above; there seemed no ground in front of my feet, only the abyss of star-studded space falling away forever. . . .

Fireflies! It was in Indonesia, you see, that I was first introduced to the world of insects, and there that I first learned of the great influence that insects — such diminutive entities — could have upon the human senses. I had traveled to Indonesia on a research grant to study magic — more precisely, to study the relation between magic and medicine, first among the traditional sorcerers, or *dukuns,* of the Indonesian archipelago, and later among the *dzankris,* the traditional shamans of Nepal. One aspect of the grant was somewhat unique: I was to journey into rural Asia not outwardly as an anthropologist or academic researcher, but as a magician in my own right, in hopes of gaining a more direct access to the local sorcerers. I had been a professional sleight-of-hand magician for five years back in the United States, helping to put myself through college by performing in clubs and restaurants throughout New England. I had, as well, taken a year off from my studies in the psychology of perception to travel as a street magician through Europe and, toward the end of that journey, had spent some months in London, England, exploring the use of sleight-of-hand magic in psychotherapy, as a means of engendering communication with distressed individuals largely unapproachable by clinical healers. The success of this work suggested to me that sleight-of-hand might

lend itself well to the curative arts, and I became, for the first time, interested in the relation, largely forgotten in the West, between folk medicine and magic. . . .

But the focus of my research gradually shifted from questions regarding the application of magical techniques in medicine and ritual curing toward a deeper pondering of the relation between traditional magic and the animate natural world. This broader concern seemed to hold the keys to the earlier questions. For none of the several island sorcerers that I came to know in Indonesia, nor any of the *dzankris* with whom I lived in Nepal, considered their work as ritual healers to be their major role or function within their communities. . . .

. . . For the magician's intelligence is not encompassed *within* the society; its place is at the edge of the community, mediating *between* the human community and the larger community of beings upon which the village depends for its nourishment and sustenance. This larger community includes, along with the humans, the multiple nonhuman entities that constitute the local landscape, from the diverse plants and the myriad animals — birds, mammals, fish, reptiles, insects — that inhabit or migrate through the region, to the particular winds and weather patterns that inform the local geography, as well as the various landforms — forests, rivers, caves, mountains — that lend their specific character to the surrounding earth. . . .

The primacy for the magician of nonhuman nature — the centrality of his relation to other species and to the earth — is not always evident to Western researchers. Countless anthropologists have managed to overlook the ecological dimension of the shaman's craft, while writing at great length of the shaman's rapport with "supernatural" entities. We can attribute much of this oversight to the modern, civilized assumption that the natural world is largely determinate and mechanical, and that that which is regarded as mysterious, powerful, and beyond human ken must therefore be of some other, nonphysical realm *above* nature, "supernatural." . . .

. . . We no longer describe the shamans' enigmatic spirit-helpers as the "superstitious claptrap of heathen primitives" — we have cleansed ourselves of at least *that* much ethnocentrism; yet we still refer to such enigmatic forces, respectfully now, as "supernatural"—for we are unable to shed the sense, so endemic to scientific civilization, of nature as a rather prosaic and predictable realm, unsuited to such mysteries. Nevertheless, that which is regarded with the greatest awe and wonder by indigenous, oral cultures is, I suggest, none other than what we view as nature itself. The deeply mysterious powers and entities with whom the shaman enters into a rapport are ultimately the same forces—the same plants, animals, forests, and winds—that to literate, "civilized" Europeans are just so much scenery, the pleasant backdrop of our more pressing human concerns.

The most sophisticated definition of "magic" that now circulates through the American counterculture is "the ability or power to alter one's consciousness at will." No mention is made of any *reason* for altering one's consciousness. Yet in tribal cultures that which we call "magic" takes its meaning from the fact that humans, in an indigenous and oral context, experience their own consciousness as simply one form of awareness among many others. The traditional magician cultivates an ability to shift out of his or her common state of consciousness precisely in order to make contact with the other organic forms of sensitivity and awareness with which human existence is entwined. Only by temporarily shedding the accepted perceptual logic of his culture can the sorcerer hope to enter into relation with other species on their own terms; only by altering the common organization of his senses will he be able to enter into a rapport with the multiple nonhuman sensibilities that animate the local landscape. It is this, we might say, that defines a shaman: the ability to readily slip out of the perceptual boundaries that demarcate his or her particular culture—boundaries reinforced by social customs, taboos, and most importantly, the common speech or language—in order to make contact with, and learn from, the other powers in the land. His magic is precisely this heightened receptivity to the meaningful solicitations—songs, cries, gestures—of the larger, more-than-human field.

Magic, then, in its perhaps most primordial sense, is the experience of existing in a world made up of multiple intelligences, the intuition that every form one perceives—from the swallow swooping overhead to the fly on a blade of grass, and indeed the blade of grass itself—is an *experiencing* form, an entity with its own predilections and sensations, albeit sensations that are very different from our own. . . .

But in genuinely oral, indigenous cultures, the sensuous world itself remains the dwelling place of the gods, of the numinous powers that can either sustain or extinguish human life. It is not by sending his awareness out beyond the natural world that the shaman makes contact with the purveyors of life and health, nor by journeying into his personal psyche; rather, it is by propelling his awareness laterally, outward into the depths of a landscape at once both sensuous and psychological, the living dream that we share with the soaring hawk, the spider, and the stone silently sprouting lichens on its coarse surface.

The magician's intimate relationship with nonhuman nature becomes most evident when we attend to the easily overlooked background of his or her practice—not just to the more visible tasks of curing and ritual aid to which she is called by individual clients, or to the larger ceremonies at which she presides and dances, but to the content of the prayers by which she prepares for such ceremonies, and to the countless ritual gestures that she enacts when alone, the daily propitiations and praise that flow from her toward the land and *its* many voices.

All this attention to nonhuman nature was, as I have mentioned, very far from my intended focus when I embarked on my research into the uses of magic and medicine in Indonesia, and it was only gradually that I became aware of this more subtle dimension of the native magician's craft. The first shift in my preconceptions came rather quietly, when I was staying for some days in the home of a young "balian," or magic practitioner, in the interior of Bali. I had been provided with a simple bed in a separate, one-room building in the balian's family compound (most compound homes, in Bali, are comprised of several separate small buildings, for sleeping and for cooking, set on a single enclosed plot of land), and early each morning the balian's wife came to bring me a small but delicious bowl of fruit, which I ate by myself, sitting on the ground outside, leaning against the wall of my hut and watching the sun slowly climb through the rustling palm leaves. I noticed, when she delivered the fruit, that my hostess was also balancing a tray containing many little green plates: actually, they were little boat-shaped platters, each woven simply and neatly from a freshly cut section of palm frond. The platters were two or three inches long, and within each was a little mound of white rice. After handing me my breakfast, the woman and the tray disappeared from view behind the other buildings, and when she came by some minutes later to pick up my empty bowl, the tray in her hands was empty as well.

The second time that I saw the array of tiny rice platters, I asked my hostess what they were for. Patiently, she explained to me that they were offerings for the household spirits. When I inquired about the Balinese term that she used for "spirit," she repeated the same explanation, now in Indonesian, that these were gifts for the spirits of the family compound, and I saw that I had understood her correctly. She handed me a bowl of sliced papaya and mango, and disappeared around the corner. I pondered for a minute, then set down the bowl, stepped to the side of my hut, and peered through the trees. At first unable to see her, I soon caught sight of her crouched low beside the corner of one of the other buildings, carefully setting what I presumed was one of the offerings on the ground at that spot. Then she stood up with the tray, walked to the other visible corner of the same building, and there slowly and carefully set another offering on the ground. I returned to my bowl of fruit and finished my breakfast. That afternoon, when the rest of the household was busy, I walked back behind the buildings where I had seen her set down the two offerings. There were the little green platters, resting neatly at the two rear corners of the building. But the mounds of rice that had been within them were gone.

The next morning I finished the sliced fruit, waited for my hostess to come by for the empty bowl, then quietly headed back behind the buildings. Two fresh palm-leaf offerings sat at the same spots where the others had been the day before. These were filled with rice. Yet as I gazed at one of these offerings, I abruptly realized, with a start, that one of the rice kernels was actually moving.

Only when I knelt down to look more closely did I notice a line of tiny black ants winding through the dirt to the offering. Peering still closer, I saw that two ants had already climbed onto the offering and were struggling with the uppermost kernel of rice; as I watched, one of them dragged the kernel down and off the leaf, then set off with it back along the line of ants advancing on the offering. The second ant took another kernel and climbed down with it, dragging and pushing, and fell over the edge of the leaf, then a third climbed onto the offering. The line of ants seemed to emerge from a thick clump of grass around a nearby palm tree. I walked over to the other offering and discovered another line of ants dragging away the white kernels. This line emerged from the top of a little mound of dirt, about fifteen feet away from the buildings. There was an offering on the ground by a corner of my building as well, and a nearly identical line of ants. I walked into my room chuckling to myself: the balian and his wife had gone to so much trouble to placate the household spirits with gifts, only to have their offerings stolen by little six-legged thieves. What a waste! But then a strange thought dawned on me: what if the ants were the very "household spirits" to whom the offerings were being made?

I soon began to discern the logic of this. The family compound, like most on this tropical island, had been constructed in the vicinity of several ant colonies. Since a great deal of cooking took place in the compound (which housed, along with the balian and his wife and children, various members of their extended family), and also much preparation of elaborate offerings of foodstuffs for various rituals and festivals in the surrounding villages, the grounds and the buildings at the compound were vulnerable to infestations by the sizable ant population. Such invasions could range from rare nuisances to a periodic or even constant siege. It became apparent that the daily palm-frond offerings served to preclude such an attack by the natural forces that surrounded (and underlay) the family's land. The daily gifts of rice kept the ant colonies occupied — and, presumably, satisfied. Placed in regular, repeated locations at the corners of various structures around the compound, the offerings seemed to establish certain boundaries between the human and ant communities;

by honoring this boundary with gifts, the humans apparently hoped to persuade the insects to respect the boundary and not enter the buildings.

Yet I remained puzzled by my hostess's assertion that these were gifts "for the spirits." . . . While the notion of "spirit" has come to have, for us in the West, a primarily anthropomorphic or human association, my encounter with the ants was the first of many experiences suggesting to me that the "spirits" of an indigenous culture are primarily those modes of intelligence or awareness that do *not* possess a human form. . . .

. . . [T]he other forms of experience that we encounter — whether ants, or willow trees, or clouds — are never absolutely alien to ourselves. Despite the obvious differences in shape, and ability, and style of being, they remain at least distantly familiar, even familial. It is, paradoxically, this perceived kinship or consanguinity that renders the difference, or otherness, so eerily potent.

Several months after my arrival in Bali, I left the village in which I was staying to visit one of the pre-Hindu sites on the island. I arrived on my bicycle early in the afternoon, after the bus carrying tourists from the coast had departed. A flight of steps took me down into a lush, emerald valley, lined by cliffs on either side, awash with the speech of the river and the sighing of the wind through high, unharvested grasses. On a small bridge crossing the river I met an old woman carrying a wide basket on her head and holding the hand of a little, shy child; the woman grinned at me with the red, toothless smile of a betel-nut chewer. On the far side of the river I stood in front of a great moss-covered complex of passageways, rooms, and courtyards carved by hand out of the black volcanic rock.

I noticed, at a bend in the canyon downstream, a further series of caves carved into the cliffs. These appeared more isolated and remote, unattended by any footpath I could discern. I set out through the grasses to explore them. This proved much more difficult than I anticipated, but after getting lost in the tall grasses, and fording the river three times, I at last found myself beneath the caves. A short scramble up the rock wall brought me to the mouth of one of them, and I entered on my hands and knees. It was a wide but low opening, perhaps only

four feet high, and the interior receded only about five or six feet into the cliff. The floor and walls were covered with mosses, painting the cave with green patterns and softening the harshness of the rock; the place, despite its small size — or perhaps because of it — had an air of great friendliness. I climbed to two other caves, each about the same size, but then felt drawn back to the first one, to sit cross-legged on the cushioning moss and gaze out across the emerald canyon. It was quiet inside, a kind of intimate sanctuary hewn into the stone. I began to explore the rich resonance of the enclosure, first just humming, then intoning a simple chant taught to me by a balian some days before. I was delighted by the overtones that the cave added to my voice, and sat there singing for a long while. I did not notice the change in the wind outside, or the cloud shadows darkening the valley, until the rains broke — suddenly and with great force. The first storm of the monsoon!

I had experienced only slight rains on the island before then, and was startled by the torrential downpour now sending stones tumbling along the cliffs, building puddles and then ponds in the green landscape below, swelling the river. There was no question of returning home — I would be unable to make my way back through the flood to the valley's entrance. And so, thankful for the shelter, I recrossed my legs to wait out the storm. Before long the rivulets falling along the cliff above gathered themselves into streams, and two small waterfalls cascaded across the cave's mouth. Soon I was looking into a solid curtain of water, thin in some places, where the canyon's image flickered unsteadily, and thickly rushing in others. My senses were all but overcome by the wild beauty of the cascade and by the roar of sound, my body trembling inwardly at the weird sense of being sealed into my hiding place.

And then, in the midst of all this tumult, I noticed a small, delicate activity. Just in front of me, and only an inch or two to my side of the torrent, a spider was climbing a thin thread stretched across the mouth of the cave. As I watched, it anchored another thread to the top of the opening, then slipped back along the first thread and joined the two at a point about midway between the roof and the floor.

I lost sight of the spider then, and for a while it seemed that it had vanished, thread and all, until my focus rediscovered it. Two more threads now radiated from the center to the floor, and then another; soon the spider began to swing between these as on a circular trellis, trailing an ever-lengthening thread which it affixed to each radiating run as it moved from one to the next, spiraling outward. The spider seemed wholly undaunted by the tumult of waters spilling past it, although every now and then it broke off its spiral dance and climbed to the roof or the floor to tug on the radii there, assuring the tautness of the threads, then crawled back to where it left off. Whenever I lost the correct focus, I waited to catch sight of the spinning arachnid, and then let its dancing form gradually draw the lineaments of the web back into visibility, tying my focus into each new knot of silk as it moved, weaving my gaze into the ever-deepening pattern.

And then, abruptly, my vision snagged on a strange incongruity: another thread slanted across the web, neither radiating nor spiraling from the central juncture, violating the symmetry. As I followed it with my eyes, pondering its purpose in the overall pattern, I began to realize that it was on a different plane from the rest of the web, for the web slipped out of focus whenever this new line became clearer. I soon saw that it led to its own center, about twelve inches to the right of the first, another nexus of forces from which several threads stretched to the floor and the ceiling. And then I saw that there was a *different* spider spinning this web, testing its tautness by dancing around it like the first, now setting the silken cross weaves around the nodal point and winding outward. The two spiders spun independently of each other, but to my eyes they wove a single intersecting pattern. This widening of my gaze soon disclosed yet another spider spiraling in the cave's mouth, and suddenly I realized that there were *many* overlapping webs coming into being, radiating out at different rhythms from myriad centers poised — some higher, some lower, some minutely closer to my eyes and some farther — between the stone above and the stone below.

I sat stunned and mesmerized before this ever-complexifying expanse of living patterns upon patterns, my gaze drawn like a breath into one converging group of lines, then breathed out into open space, then drawn down into another convergence. The curtain of water had become utterly silent — I tried at one point to hear it, but could not. My senses were entranced. I had the distinct impression that I was watching the universe being born, galaxy upon galaxy. . . .

I have never, since that time, been able to encounter a spider without feeling a great strangeness and awe. To be sure, insects and spiders are not the only powers, or even central presences, in the Indonesian universe. But they were *my* introduction to the spirits, to the magic afoot in the land. It was from them that I first learned of the intelligence that lurks in nonhuman nature, the ability that an alien form of sentience has to echo one's own, to instill a reverberation in oneself that temporarily shatters habitual ways of seeing and feeling, leaving one open to a world all alive, awake, and aware. It was from such small beings that my senses first learned of the countless worlds within worlds that spin in the depths of this world that we commonly inhabit, and from them that I learned that my body could, with practice, enter sensorially into these dimensions. The precise and minuscule craft of the spiders had so honed and focused my awareness that the very webwork of the universe, of which my own flesh was a part, seemed to be being spun by their arcane art. I have already spoken of the ants, and of the fireflies, whose sensory likeness to the lights in the night sky had taught me the fickleness of gravity. . . .

I had rarely before paid much attention to the natural world. But my exposure to traditional magicians and seers was shifting my senses; I became increasingly susceptible to the solicitations of nonhuman things. . . . My ears began to attend, in a new way, to the songs of birds — no longer just a melodic background to human speech, but meaningful speech in its own right, responding to and commenting on events in the surrounding earth. I became a student of subtle differences: the way a breeze may flutter a single leaf on a whole tree, leaving the other leaves silent and unmoved (had not that leaf, then, been brushed by a magic?); or the way the intensity of the sun's heat expresses itself in the precise rhythm of the crickets. Walking along the dirt paths, I learned to slow my pace in order to *feel* the difference between one nearby hill and the next, or to taste the presence of a particular field at a certain time of day when, as I had been told by a local *dukun,* the place had a special power and proffered unique gifts. . . .

And gradually, then, other animals began to intercept me in my wanderings, as if some quality in my posture or the rhythm of my breathing had disarmed their wariness; I would find myself face-to-face with monkeys, and with large lizards that did not slither away when I spoke, but leaned forward in apparent curiosity. In rural Java, I often noticed monkeys accompanying me in the branches overhead, and ravens walked toward me on the road, croaking. While at Pangandaran, a nature preserve on a peninsula jutting out from the south coast of Java ("a place of many spirits," I was told by nearby fishermen), I stepped out from a clutch of trees and found myself looking into the face of one of the rare and beautiful bison that exist only on that island. Our eyes locked. When it snorted, I snorted back; when it shifted its shoulders, I shifted my stance; when I tossed my head, it tossed *its* head in reply. I found myself caught in a nonverbal conversation with this Other, a gestural duet with which my conscious awareness had very little to do. It was as if my body in its actions was suddenly being motivated by a wisdom older than my thinking mind, as though it was held and moved by a logos, deeper than words, spoken by the Other's body, the trees, and the stony ground on which we stood. . . .

I returned to North America . . . excited by the new sensibilities that had stirred in me—my newfound awareness of a more-than-human world, of the great potency of the land, and particularly of the keen intelligence of other animals, large and small, whose lives and cultures interpenetrate our own. I startled neighbors by chattering with squirrels, who swiftly climbed down the trunks of their trees and across lawns to banter with me, or by gazing for hours on end at a heron fishing in a nearby estuary, or at gulls opening clams by dropping them from a height onto the rocks along the beach.

Yet, very gradually, I began to lose my sense of the animals' own awareness. The gulls' technique for breaking open the clams began to appear as a largely automatic behavior, and I could not easily feel the attention that they must bring to each new shell. Perhaps each shell was entirely the same as the last, and *no* spontaneous attention was really necessary. . . .

As the expressive and sentient landscape slowly faded behind my more exclusively human concerns, threatening to become little more than an illusion or fantasy, I began to feel—particularly in my chest and abdomen—as though I were being cut off from vital sources of nourishment. I was indeed reacclimating to my own culture, becoming more attuned to its styles of discourse and interaction, yet my bodily senses seemed to be losing their acuteness, becoming less awake to subtle changes and patterns. The thrumming of crickets, and even the songs of the local blackbirds, readily faded from my awareness after a few moments, and it was only by an effort of will that I could bring them back into the perceptual field. The flight of sparrows and of dragonflies no longer sustained my focus very long, if indeed they gained my attention at all. My skin quit registering the various changes in the breeze, and smells seemed to have faded from the world almost entirely, my nose waking up only once or twice a day, perhaps while cooking, or when taking out the garbage. . . .

Our bodies have formed themselves in delicate reciprocity with the manifold textures, sounds, and shapes of animate earth—our eyes have evolved in subtle interaction with *other* eyes, as our ears are attuned by their very structure to the howling of wolves and the honking of geese. To shut ourselves off from these other voices, to continue by our lifestyles to condemn these other sensibilities to the oblivion of extinction, is to rob our own senses of their integrity, and to rob our minds of their coherence. We are human only in contact, and conviviality, with what is not human. Only in reciprocity with what is Other do we begin to heal ourselves.

DISCUSSION TOPICS

1. Describe the difference between the Western perspective on the natural world and the perspective found in an indigenous and oral culture such as Bali.
2. What change of attitude does Abram undergo when he understands the purpose of the tiny rice platters?

3. Abram experienced the "magic afoot in the land" from his seeing the spinning of spiders at a cave entrance. What effect did this experience have on his perception of the natural world?

4. Cheney and Weston, in Chapter 2, speak of "invitation." Where in Abram's essay do you find illustrations of such a perspective?
5. What mental and physical changes did Abram note when he returned to North America?

CLASS EXERCISES

(For small-group discussion)

1. We suggest this activity be used after reading and discussion of the introduction to this chapter, but before assignment of individual authors.
   Procedure: Divide the class into groups of three to five students. Select at least four different kinds of situations that might give rise to aesthetic perceptions, several human-made and several natural.
   Suggestions:

   a football game

   a rock concert

   a familiar movie

   a dinner of several courses

   a solitary canoe trip on a wilderness lake

   a thunderstorm in a forest

   a spectacular sunset in the desert

   Ask each group to answer one or more of the following questions:

   a. What is the overall emotional tone, mood, or flavor of the experience? Name some feelings involved in the experience. Describe the sensory qualities: visual, auditory, touch, taste, odor. Are there imaginative qualities in the experience?
   b. What is the structure or pattern of the experience? How does it hang together? Are there distinct parts within the structure? If so, name them. Does the experience have a culmination or closure?
   c. Consider how biological, historical, or other knowledge would heighten or diminish the aesthetic experience.

2. What difference does wildness make to our appreciation of nature?
3. Consider the similarities and differences between the views of chapter authors on the relationship of human beings and nature. Which author do you think is most correct?
4. Suppose you are observing a stand of trees, and are then informed that the trees are made of plastic. In what respects would your perceptions of the trees change?

FOR FURTHER READING

Balmford, Andrew, et al. "Why Conservationists Should Heed Pokemon." *Science* 295 (29 March 2002): 2367. Children's interests are becoming redirected toward human artifacts.

Berleant, Arnold, ed. *The Aesthetics of Environment.* Philadelphia: Temple University Press, 1992. The natural world engages and assimilates us. Most important is mystery, awe, the ultimately ungraspable breadth of nature.

Burks, David Clarke, ed. *Place of the Wild.* Washington, D.C.: Island Press, 1994. A valuable collection of essays by advocates of the preservation and restoration of wildlands.

Carlson, Allen. "Aesthetic Appreciation of the Natural Environment," in *Environmental Ethics: Divergence and Convergence,* ed. R. Botzler and S. Armstrong. New York: McGraw-Hill, 1998, pp. 122–31.

———. *Aesthetics and the Environment: The Appreciation of Nature, Art, and Architecture.* London: Routledge, 2000. A collection of essays published over two decades.

Carroll, Noël. "On Being Moved by Nature: Between Religion and Natural History," in *Landscape, Natural Beauty and the Arts,* ed. S. Kemal and I. Gaskell. Cambridge: Cambridge University Press, 1993, pp. 244–66. Argues that Carlson's emphasis on nature appreciation needs to be supplemented by inclusion of emotional arousal.

Dillard, Annie C. *Pilgrim at Tinker Creek.* New York: Bantam Books, 1978. A prize-winning excursion into nature mysticism, in the tradition of American transcendentalism.

Eaton, Marcia Muelder. *Aesthetics and the Good Life.* London: Fairleigh Dickinson University Press, 1989. A defense of aesthetic experience as delight in the intrinsic features of objects or events as based on the history of values. Chapters 3 and 4 are concerned with environmental aesthetics.

Elliot, Robert. *Faking Nature: The Ethics of Environmental Restoration.* London: Routledge, 1997. An argument for the value of "naturalness" as based on the history of the thing or system in question.

Ellis, Gerry, and Karen Kane. *Wilderness Remembered.* Minocqua, Wis.: Northwood Press, 1995. Excerpts from earlier explorers of the wilderness, their diaries, journals, and other works. Accompanied by contemporary photographs.

Fudge, Robert S. "Imagination and the Science-Based Aesthetic Appreciation of Unscenic Nature." *Journal of Aesthetic and Art Criticism* 59.3 (2001): 275–85. Incorporation of the imagination into science-based aesthetic appreciation.

Godlovitch, Stan. "Icebreakers: Environmentalism and Natural Aesthetics." *Journal of Applied Philosophy* 2, no. 1 (1994): 15–30. Godlovitch develops an "acentric" environmentalism, whose subject is insensate (e.g., the far side of the moon). From this point of view we do not matter; Nature is aloof and the only fitting response is a sense of mystery.

———, ed. "Symposium: Natural Aesthetics." *Journal of Aesthetic Education* 33.3 (1999).

Hargrove, Eugene C. *Foundations of Environmental Ethics.* Englewood Cliffs, N.J.: Prentice-Hall, 1989. An important account of environmental ethics from the perspective of the history of ideas, emphasizing aesthetics.

Hartshorne, Charles. *Born to Sing: An Interpretation and World Survey of Bird Song.* Bloomington: Indiana University Press, 1973. An account of aesthetic phenomena with a focus on bird song by a foremost process philosopher.

Hepburn, R. W. "Aesthetic Appreciation of Nature," in *Contemporary Aesthetics,* ed. Matthew Lipman. Boston: Allyn & Bacon, 1973, pp. 340–54. Emphasizes similarities and differences between aesthetic experiences of human-made and natural objects.

Kellert, Stephen R. *Kinship to Mastery: Biophilia in Human Evolution and Development.* Washington,

D.C.: Island Press, 1997. Chapter 3 discusses the universality of the human aesthetic response to nature.

Kellert, Stephen R., and Edward O. Wilson, eds. *The Biophilia Hypothesis.* Washington, D.C.: Island Press, 1993. A valuable collection of essays stressing the human need for natural environments.

Kilham, Lawrence. "Instinct for Beauty and Love of Animals." *Defenders* 63, no. 3 (1988): 38–40. A brief, charming essay illustrating the "innateness" of the sense of beauty.

Nasar, Jack L., ed. *Environmental Aesthetics: Theory, Research, and Applications.* Cambridge: Cambridge University Press, 1988. Nasar's book notes the difficulties with integrating the normative-rational models of planners with aesthetics. Jay Appleton's essay usefully reiterates his groundbreaking work on prospect-refuge theory, but in general the papers are too abstract for instructional use. Includes an extensive bibliography.

Norton, Bryan G. "Thoreau's Insect Analogies: Or, Why Environmentalists Hate Mainstream Economists." *Environmental Ethics* 13, no. 3 (1991): 235–51. An interpretation of Thoreau's mature thought as recommending naturalistic observation as the key to perceptual and psychological transformation. Norton argues that neoclassical economists cannot capture this value of transforming preferences.

Oelschlaeger, Max, ed. *The Wilderness Condition: Essays on Environment and Civilization.* San Francisco: Sierra Club Books, 1992. An excellent collection of essays, discussing wilderness from a number of perspectives.

Rothenberg, David, ed. *Wild Ideas.* Minneapolis: University of Minneapolis Press, 1995. An exciting collection of essays.

Rolston, Holmes, III. "Does Aesthetic Appreciation of Landscapes Need to be Science-Based?" *British Journal of Aesthetics* 35, no. 4 (1995): 374–85. Rolston argues that a science-based landscape aesthetics is urgent, but it must also be a "science-transcending aesthetic of participatory experience."

Scharfstein, Ben-Ami. *Of Birds, Beasts, and Other Artists: An Essay on the Universality of Art.* New York: New York University Press, 1988. Scharfstein focuses on painting and sculpture as he discusses art as rooted in biology and in social life. He discusses bird song and bird display as well as primate art.

Sepanmaa, Yrjo. *The Beauty of Environment: A General Model for Environmental Aesthetics.* Denton, Tex.: Environmental Ethics Books, 1993. A groundbreaking, thorough consideration of the environment as an aesthetic object; Sepanmaa argues that ecology provides the norm for beauty in nature. The book's conceptual structure and sentence transitions are sometimes hard to follow. Comprehensive bibliography.

Shore, William H., ed. *The Nature of Nature: New Essays from America's Finest Writers on Nature.* New York: Harcourt Brace, 1994. Contains many fine essays, especially the beautifully written "The Emus" by Sy Montgomery.

Snyder, Robert A., ed. "Environmental Aesthetics." Theme issue of *Essays in Philosophy* 3.1 (2001). http://www.humboldt.edu/~essays/.

Stolnitz, Jerome. "The Aesthetic Attitude," in *Aesthetics and the Philosophy of Art Criticism.* Boston: Houghton Mifflin, 1960. A concise introduction to some important characteristics of aesthetic experience.

Thomas, John C. "Values, the Environment and the Creative Act." *Journal of Speculative Philosophy* 4, no. 4 (1990): 323–36. Thomas argues that human beings are essentially aesthetic and that overemphasis on moral value alienates human beings from natural being.

Tobias, Michael, and Georgianne Cowan, eds. *The Soul of Nature: Visions of a Living Earth.* New York: Continuum, 1994. Some fine nature writing, expressive of personal relationships.

Weintraub, Linda. *Art on the Edge and Over: Searching for Art's Meaning in Contemporary Society 1970s–1990s.* Litchfield, Conn.: Art Insights, 1996. Includes discussion of three artists with different approaches to nature as a theme.

CHAPTER FOUR

Historical Context

The major secular and religious historical ideas that have contributed to current Western attitudes toward the environment are identified in the readings of this chapter. Authors of several of the readings offer suggestions for approaching the current environmental crisis, based on their historical analyses.

HISTORICAL FOUNDATIONS FOR CURRENT WESTERN ENVIRONMENTAL PERSPECTIVES

In the first essay, "The Ancient Roots of Our Ecological Crisis," J. Donald Hughes proposes that the foundations for the attitude that nature is something to be conquered, used, and dominated lie deep within the ancient world and are based on the influences of animism, the transcendent monotheism of Israel, the Greek and Roman philosophies, and the emergence of Christianity. Hughes concludes that the modern ecological crisis can be traced to several sources, but that it was strongly influenced by the attitudes developed in ancient Greece and Rome.

Eugene Hargrove proposes in his essay, "Anglo-American Land Use Attitudes," that current attitudes in the United States that support the powerful position of landowners were influenced by several sources. The Germans and Saxons introduced pri-

mogeniture and taxation, which expedited the shift from a society with many small landholders to one with a few powerful landowners. County courts (moots) evolved from the freemen's custom of consulting with neighbors to settle disputes and still tend to favor the interests of landowners over the concerns of other citizens.

Thomas Jefferson was a strong advocate for establishing small freehold farmsteads (allodiums) held with little obligation to any governing authority. John Locke maintained that the right to own and use land was determined by a farmer's labor, and that society should have little or no role in managing a landowner's property. Hargrove concludes that these precedents still influence policies today.

J. Baird Callicott identifies three significant moral ideals in his essay, "Whither Conservation Ethics?" that were developed in the nineteenth and twentieth centuries in American conservation: the Romantic-Transcendental Preservation Ethic espoused by John Muir and others, the Progressive-Utilitarian Resource Conservation Ethic advocated by Gifford Pinchot, and the more recent Evolutionary-Ecological Land Ethic articulated by Aldo Leopold. Callicott proposes that these three themes are still represented, respectively, by some private conservation organizations, public resource agencies, and the conservation biology movement.

In his essay, "Wasty Ways," Alan Taylor proposes that early American settlers may have behaved harshly toward nature because they perceived that nature was often very hard on them. Fear may also have been an important influence along with any feelings of dominance and superiority over nature. Taylor combines insights on European culture, the North American environment, and ordinary human behavior to provide a more sympathetic interpretation of the often ecologically wasteful lives of early American settlers.

Neil Evernden asserts in his essay, "Nature in Industrial Society," that the term *nature* has many different connotations in industrial society; he analyzes how the concept has changed over time. In contrast to the themes presented by the other scholars in this chapter, Evernden suggests that there has been a recent shift in perspectives in Western society, from viewing nature as intrinsically valuable to viewing it primarily as a means for human survival. Evernden describes how this shift was influenced by the publication of Rachel Carson's *Silent Spring*.

Rachel Carson helped crystallize the environmental movement with *Silent Spring* (1962, Houghton Mifflin). In "Rachel Carson's Environmental Ethics," Philip Cafaro identifies some ethical themes influencing this ecologist/philosopher: her frequent criticisms of human attempts to dominate nature; a strong sense of compassion and caring for nature, which included a "reverence for life"; a commitment to humane treatment of animals; and a willingness to express her insights and values in her writing.

CONTRIBUTIONS OF RELIGIOUS AND SECULAR PHILOSOPHIES TO WESTERN ENVIRONMENTAL ATTITUDES

An issue stimulated by the Lynn White, Jr., debate (see White's reading in Chapter 5) is the relative contribution of Judaism and Christian religious beliefs to current Western attitudes toward the environment. With the exception of Hughes, the scholars in this chapter identify primarily secular ideas as contributing to current Western attitudes. Hughes identifies ideological precursors to contemporary views in Western society in the attitudes and practices of Judaism and Christianity; but he argues that as much or more can

be traced to ancient Greek and Roman perspectives. Callicott notes that Muir turned to religious language and ideas to address the intrinsic value of nature.

PERSPECTIVES REACHED FROM HISTORICAL ANALYSES

Based on his study of ancient civilizations, Hughes offers several recommendations to assist Western society in solving the current ecological crisis. He proposes an attitude of respect for the earth and for nature closer to that held by societies in the past; a concerted effort to better understand past and present ecological relationships, before more environmental damage occurs; use of technology so as to benefit both the human community and the environment; and acceptance of the limitations on human's exploitation of the natural world.

Callicott notes the dominant anthropocentric themes in the perspectives of both Pinchot and Muir, with Muir having some evidence for a budding ecocentric perspective. Callicott and Cafaro note that Leopold and Carson moved beyond traditional anthropocentric thinking to include ecocentric perspectives in the context of the American conservation movement. Cafaro also identifies themes of ecofeminism and individualism in the ethical perspectives of Rachel Carson. Evernden further assesses Carson's contributions to environmental concern among the general public.

Hargrove concludes that government regulation of individual private landowners has been ineffective because, from the beginning of American government, representation at state and federal levels has usually been based on land-ownership; this has assured control of the legislatures by the rural community. Public officials elected by landowners have not effectively regulated private landowners.

Evernden proposes that the view humans hold of nature will affect their idea of what constitutes proper behavior toward nature. In the modern industrial state, humans view nature primarily as composed of impersonal objects. Evernden provides two alternative perspectives that could enlarge this limited view. One is to extend a separate sense of selfhood to nature (nature-as-self); the other is to learn to appreciate the uncanny and unpredictable elements of nature (nature-as-miracle).

The Ancient Roots of Our Ecological Crisis

J. Donald Hughes

J. Donald Hughes is professor of history, University of Denver, Colorado. He has written extensively on the ecological perceptions and environmental impacts of ancient civilizations. This selection is taken from a chapter in his book, Ecology in Ancient Civilizations. *Hughes believes that a human community's relationship to the natural environment is influenced by numerous factors. He identifies animism, Judaism and Christianity, and Greek and Roman philosophies as the dominant factors influencing Western attitudes toward nature.*

The damaging changes being suffered today by the natural environment are far more rapid and widespread than anything known in ancient times. Today deforestation proceeds on a worldwide scale, the atmosphere becomes more turbid and opaque every year, the oceans are being polluted on a massive scale, species of animals and plants are being wiped out at a rate unmatched in history, and the earth is being plundered in many other ways. But although the peoples of ancient civilizations were unfamiliar with such recent discoveries as radioactivity, insecticides, and the internal combustion engine, they faced problems sometimes analogous to those the modern world faces, and we may look to the ancients in order to see the beginnings of many of our modern difficulties with an environment which is decaying because of human misuse.

A human community determines its relationship to the natural environment in many ways. Among the most important are its members' attitudes toward nature, the knowledge of nature and the understanding of its balance and structure which they attain, the technology they are able to use, and the social control the community can exert over its members to direct their actions which affect the environment. The ancient world shows us the roots of our present problems in each of these areas.

In a well-known and often reprinted article, "The Historical Roots of Our Ecologic Crisis,"[1] Lynn White traced modern Western attitudes toward the natural world back to the Middle Ages. But both medieval and modern attitudes have ancient roots. Greece and Rome, as well as Judaism and Christianity, helped to form our habitual ways of thinking about nature. And it is evident that the modern ecological crisis is to a great extent the result of attitudes which see nature as something to be freely conquered, used, and dominated without calculation of the resultant cost to mankind and the earth.

These attitudes stem from similar ideas which were held by the ancient peoples who have most influenced us. Animism, which saw the natural world as sharing human qualities and treated things and events in nature as sacred objects of respect or worship, was the dominant attitude in early antiquity and persisted almost everywhere in the Mediterranean world, but it gradually gave way to other ways of thinking. In Israel, transcendent monotheism replaced animism's "world full of gods." Instead of being divine in itself, nature was seen as a lower order of creation, given as a trust to mankind with accountability to God. But in the later history of that idea, people tended to take the command to have dominion over the earth as blanket permission to do what they wished to the environment, conveniently forgetting the part about accountability to God, or else interpreting most human activities as improvements in nature and therefore pleasing to God.

Perhaps even more important in the history of human attitudes toward nature was the departure from animism made by the Greek philosophers. Rejecting traditional mythological and religious explanations of the natural world, they insisted on the ability of the human mind to discover the truth about nature through the use of reason. Instead of a place filled with spiritual being, or beings, a theater of the gods, the environment was to them an object of thought and rational analysis. Worship of nature became mere ritual, supposedly replaced with philosophical understanding. Since, in the words of Protagoras, "man is the measure of all things,"[2] it followed that all things have usefulness to mankind as their reason for existence. This idea has persisted in Western thought in various forms until the present, for the belief that everything in nature must justify its existence by its purposeful relationship to mankind is firmly, though perhaps implicitly, held by most people.

What was for the Greeks a philosophical opinion became for the Romans a practical reality. Early Roman animism was overcome less by the ingestion of Greek ideas than by the Romans' own demonstrated ability to dominate and to turn most things to their own profit, but both Greek influence and Roman practicality helped the Romans to develop attitudes toward nature which are remarkably similar to those expressed and demonstrated today. The Romans treated the natural environment as if it were one of their conquered provinces. If they needed any justification of this beyond their own pragmatism and cupidity, they could find it in Greek philosophy, which reached them in a late, skeptical form that had removed the sacred from nature and made nature an object of manipulation in thought and, by extension, in action. Our Western attitudes can be traced most directly to the secular, businesslike Romans. Today the process of dominating the earth is seen not as a religious crusade following a biblical commandment but as a profitable venture seeking economic benefit. In this, we are closer to the Romans than to any other ancient people, and in this we demonstrate to a great extent our heritage from them.

Attitudes alone do not determine the way a human community will interact with the natural environment. People whose religion teaches them to treat the world as a sacred place may still manage to make their surroundings a scene of deforestation and erosion, because good intentions toward nature are not enough if they are not informed by accurate knowledge about nature and its workings.

The earlier civilizations of the Near East accumulated a vast amount of information about the world through trial and error, and the information was passed on through tradition. Some of what they thought they knew was correct and useful, and much was colorfully inaccurate, interwoven with myth and folk stories.

A few Greek thinkers were the first to approach the natural world in a consistently rational fashion, demanding that reasonable explanations be found for all natural phenomena. This enabled them to begin the process of gaining knowledge which eventually developed into what might be called the scientific method. Many of the Greek thinkers were also careful observers of nature and attempted to check their ideas against what could be observed, but all of them held rational thought to be superior to what could be seen in the world and assumed that the inner workings of the human mind are congruent with the outer workings of the universe. This assumption, along with the antipathy of Greek thinkers toward work done with the hands, limited the range of their discoveries and led them into some fallacious speculations. Nonetheless, the discoveries of the Greek philosophers and scientists are many and impressive.

Unfortunately, research and discovery in this field gradually diminished under the Romans, who were collectors of older bits of information about the world of nature rather than discoverers of new knowledge. A few Greek scientists continued to work under the Roman Empire, but the Romans themselves produced few creative thinkers in this field. With the advent of Christianity, the situation worsened. Living in a world which they believed to be temporary, early Christians seemed to regard study of the things of this world to be irrelevant, if not a positive barrier on the way to salvation. "The wisdom of this world is foolishness,"[3] said Paul. He spoke in a somewhat different connection, but the Christians of the later Roman Empire, with very few outstanding exceptions, tended to look at all scientific inquiry in the spirit of that statement.

The modern world, having revived the works of the ancient Greeks, has gone beyond them in developing a rigorous methodology for gaining knowledge about the natural environment. The extent and accuracy of the understanding of nature that is available today is truly impressive, but far from complete. Much remains to be discovered about the circulation of the earth's atmosphere, weather, and the effects of pollution of various kinds on climate, for example. The behavior of species of animals and the interaction of all forms of life in an ecosystem are only imperfectly understood. Governments and institutions have not always seen the relevance of such knowledge, and support for research has been a sometime thing. At the same time, human activities are inexorably destroying the last few examples of relatively undisturbed ecosystems that remain on earth, so that soon they will no longer be available for study. Brazilians are proclaiming that the Amazon rain forest will be gone in thirty years, to give one example, and no one can accurately predict what effects that massive change will have on South America and the world. Careful study is still needed.

The speed, scope, and intensity of interaction with the natural environment are crucially determined by the level of technology available to a human community. Using human and animal motive power and the energy of water, wind, and fire with the relatively simple tools and machines that had been invented, the ancient peoples constructed huge monuments which still impress us, but their level of interaction with the natural environment was relatively low as compared with that of modern industrial society. The changes wrought in the environment by ancient civilizations are massive indeed, but involved centuries or millennia for their accomplishment. Today more significant changes take place in months or years — or even seconds, in the case of atomic explosions. While the real extent and nature of the impact of ancient technology must not be underestimated, what impresses us almost as much is the failure of the ancients to pursue inventions, and the slow rate of technological change that resulted. Of all ancient peoples, the Romans possessed the most highly developed technology, and in this respect they are closest to us. Their machines for war, construction, and industry foreshadowed some that are still in use today. The fact that ancient peoples absorbed and survived changes in the technology of war and peace cannot be of much comfort to us today, because the rapidity, size, and power of such changes today are of an entirely different order from anything experienced in ancient times.

Another factor determining the way a human community will interact with the natural environment is the degree of organization and social control the community possesses. This is true because environmental ends desired for the good of the community may involve sacrifices on the part of its individual members, sacrifices which they would not make without some degree of social encouragement or coercion. The early civilizations of the river valleys, for example, had to be able to call for large expenditures of human energy on the construction of canals which seemed to benefit the entire society. Ancient civilizations were able to exert a consider-

able degree of social control because the vast majority of ancient people regarded themselves primarily as parts of their societies, and only secondarily, if at all, as individuals. Each person had a place in the social hierarchy which was rigidly defined and rarely changed. This was true of the pharaonic autocracy of Egypt, perhaps the most marked example of social control in the ancient world. But Egypt suffered periodic breakdowns in social control, and no ancient civilization could have channeled the actions of its citizens with regard to the environment to the extent that is at least theoretically possible today.

All ancient societies depended to a large extent on slave labor, a fact which seems to indicate an extreme degree of social control, until it is remembered that the majority of slaves were owned by citizens, not by the state, and that citizens were to a surprising degree able to pursue their private goals, at least in Greece and Rome.

Greek and Roman governments established policies in the fields of agriculture, forestry, mining, and commerce, but citizens were allowed a wide latitude of choice within certain guidelines. Greek citizens had carefully defined duties to the community, but the city-states are noted for the freedom they allowed. The later Roman Empire tried to interfere in and control the lives of its citizens to an unusual extent; the edicts of Diocletian attempted to stabilize occupations, regulate prices, and control religion, while his secret police kept him informed of activities dangerous to the state. But no ancient autocracy remotely approached the ability of a modern industrial state to keep informed about its citizens and see that they performed their social duties. Greece operated without imprisonment as a punishment, and the Roman Empire supported itself financially without an income tax. The degree of control that can be exercised in the modern world by governments with electronic surveillance, computers, chemical and psychological methods, bureaucracies, police, deportations, and prisons is unmatched by anything seen before in world history. In democracies, environmental policies can be established only when widespread public support for them exists. Over the last few decades, such policies have in part been established even over the opposition of powerful pressure groups. Some needed measures have been blocked by the same groups or by the tendency of the public to prefer short-term personal gains to long-term benefit for society. Totalitarian states such as the former Soviet Union have also taken some steps to preserve the environment, but we have not yet seen a major government take all of the steps which seem called for in the present ecological dilemma. Neither in ancient times nor in modern times have human communities become fully aware of the role which their relationship to the natural environment plays in their long-term welfare and even survival.

One conclusion which seems clear to this author is that the modern ecological crisis grew out of roots which lie deep in the ancient world, particularly in Greece and Rome. The problems of human communities with the natural environment did not begin suddenly with the ecological awakening of the 1960s, nor indeed with the onset of the Industrial Revolution or the Christian Middle Ages. Mankind has been challenged to find a way of living with nature from the earliest times, and many of our habitual answers to that challenge received their first conscious formulation within ancient societies, especially the classical civilizations.

At this point, one might well ask whether this study of ancient civilizations has produced any insights which might be of use in meeting the present crisis. If our ecological crisis has ancient roots, it might also be possible to learn from some of the successes and failures of ancient civilizations as we look to the future.

First of all, it might be possible for people today to recover something like the attitude of respect for the earth and nature that was felt by many in ancient societies. This could come not as a renaissance of animism, or a revival of ancient religions which have lost their ability to infuse human minds, but as a new insight compatible with many religions and philosophies. Judaism and Christianity could expand their concepts of human stewardship to recapture the biblical inclusion of the whole created natural world within the responsibility of people to God. Islam has its own unique insights along similar lines. Others will be impressed by Albert Schweitzer's demonstration that the concept of reverence for life serves as a basis for philosophical ethics. Eastern philosophies, which have long contained attitudes toward nature which emphasize har-

mony, respect, and refusal to exploit, might find ways to realize their insights. Recent interest in the American Indian feeling for the land and its creatures reveals that the Native Americans had ecological wisdom which can be studied and emulated. Better attitudes toward the natural environment will have to develop in a pluralistic human community, as people of varying traditions and points of view come to see the necessity of caring for the earth in order to preserve life itself and improve the quality of life.

Second, a concentrated effort to study the natural environment in all of its facets and interrelationships is needed. This is particularly crucial at the present moment, before much of the evidence about nature is altered, marred, or erased by human activities. These activities themselves and their effects upon the natural environment must also be investigated thoroughly. No wise environmental policy can be based on ignorance of the workings of nature. So that we may learn from what mankind has experienced through millennia of interaction with nature, more research is needed into the ecological relationships of past human societies, to correct and fill out the broad outline which is presented here.

Third, each human community must seek a viable relationship with the natural environment at the level made possible by the technology available to it. A study of ancient civilizations should demonstrate that a rejection of modern technology or an attempt to turn back the clock would not in itself assure a proper balance with nature or prevent environmental degradation. Rather, we should find ways to use our technological abilities in order to minimize the destructive impact of our civilization upon the natural environment and to enhance our relationship with nature in ways which are beneficial both to people and to the environment. This would no doubt mean that some possible avenues of technological development ought to be abandoned, and that human population ought to be stabilized at some optimum size. No level of technology could support an unlimited increase of human numbers without catastrophic damage to the natural world and resultant crisis for mankind.

Finally, as human beings, we must be willing to accept freely certain limitations on our actions which affect the earth. In democracies, these limitations can be based on public awareness of the magnitude of environmental problems and of the options which exist to meet them. The alternatives to freely chosen environmental policies, consistently administered, are probably few. History does not provide us with an example of an ecologically aware dictatorship, willing to coerce its people to take the courses of action which it deems necessary for survival in balance with nature, but such a government is certainly a future possibility somewhere in the world, unpleasant as it may be to contemplate. History does, however, provide us with many examples of ancient peoples who failed to adapt themselves to live in harmony with the ecosystems within which they found themselves, who depleted their environment, exhausted their resources, and exist today only as ruins within eroded and desiccated landscapes. That fate might also await our own civilization, but this time on a global scale. Ancient history is a warning and a challenge to our attitudes, our ability to understand, our technological competence, and our willingness to make far-reaching decisions. The challenge will not go away, and the response we will make is not yet clear.

NOTES

1. Lynn White, "The Historical Roots of Our Ecologic Crisis," *Science* 155 (1967): 1203–7.
2. Plato, *Theaetetus* 160D (15).
3. 1 Cor. 3:19.

DISCUSSION TOPICS

1. How are our current attitudes toward the environment like those held by the ancient Romans? What are some of the implications of these similarities?
2. Hughes calls attention to the great increase in governmental control over citizens in modern Western society. In what ways do you believe that increasing or decreasing governmental control affects the quality of environmental policies in Western society?
3. How might one make a convincing argument that humans should accept limitations on their exploitation of the natural world, as Hughes proposes?

READING 18

Anglo-American Land Use Attitudes

Eugene C. Hargrove

Eugene C. Hargrove, professor of philosophy at the University of North Texas, Denton, has served as editor-in-chief of the journal Environmental Ethics *since its founding in 1979. He has also edited* Religion and Environmental Crisis, Beyond Spaceship Earth *(1986) and* The Animal Rights/Environmental Ethics Debate: The Environmental Perspective *(1992). Hargrove is the author of* Foundations of Environmental Ethics *(1989).*

In his article from Environmental Ethics, *Hargrove traces the philosophical strands underlying contemporary attitudes in the United States toward land and land use that account for the powerful position of landowners. He describes three major sources of influence: practices of German and Saxon freemen, Thomas Jefferson's theory of allodial rights, and John Locke's theory of property.*

Freemen among early German tribes set important precedents, including primogeniture and taxation. These practices ultimately resulted in a shift from a society in which there were many landholders to a society characterized by feudal conditions in which a few wealthy landholders held political and economic power. Saxon freemen developed county courts (moots) that were originally composed of the freemen themselves; their impact is still evident in U.S. courts.

Thomas Jefferson advocated the notion of allodial rights, in which landowners could own small freehold farmsteads with little or no obligation to governmental authority. John Locke believed that a farmer's labor determined his right to own and use land and that society should have little role in managing a landowner's property.

INTRODUCTION

Such protected areas as Yosemite, Yellowstone, and the Grand Canyon are often cited as great successes of the environmental movement in nature preservation and conservation. Yet, not all natural objects and areas worthy of special protection or management are of such national significance and these must be dealt with at state, regional, or local levels. In such cases, environmentalists almost always plead their cause before a county court, a local administrative political body, usually consisting of three judges elected by the rural community, who may or may not have legal backgrounds.

Here the environmentalists are probably in for a great shock. Inevitably, some rural landowner will defend his special property rights to the land in question. He will ask the court rhetorically, "What right do these outsiders, these so-called environmentalists, have to come in here and try to tell me what to do with my land?" and answering his own question, he will continue, "They don't have any right. I worked the land; it's my property, and no one has the right to tell me what to do with it!" The environmentalists may be surprised that the farmer does not bother to reply to any of their carefully made points, but the real shock comes at the end when the county court dismisses the environmental issues, ruling in favor of the landowner.

While the environmentalists may suspect corruption (and such dealings are not unlikely), usually both the judges and the landowner are honestly convinced that they have all acted properly. The property rights argument recited by the rural landowner is a very powerful defense, particularly when presented at this level of government. The argument is grounded in a political philosophy almost three centuries old as well as in land use practices which go back at least to Saxon and perhaps even to Celtic times in Europe and England. When the argument is presented to county court judges who share these beliefs and land use traditions, the outcome of the court decision is rarely in doubt. On the other hand, the tradition that natural objects and areas of special beauty or interest ought to be protected from landowners claiming special property rights, and from the practice of landowning in general, is of very recent origin, and without comparable historical and emotional foundations. . . .

My present purpose is to examine traditional land use attitudes. First, I examine the ancient land use practices which gave rise to these attitudes, second, the political activities and views of Thomas Jefferson which secured a place for them in Ameri-

can political and legal thought, and, finally, the political philosophy of John Locke which provided them with a philosophical foundation.

LANDHOLDING AMONG EARLY GERMAN AND SAXON FREEMEN

About two thousand years ago most of Europe was occupied by tribes of peoples known collectively as the Celts. At about that time, these peoples came under considerable pressure from the Romans moving up from the south and from Germanic tribes entering central Europe from the east. Five hundred years later, the Celts had either been subjugated by the German and Roman invaders or pushed back into Ireland and fringe areas of England. The Roman Empire, too, after asserting its presence as far north as England, was in decay. Roman influence would continue in the south, but in northern and central Europe as well as in most of England German influence would prevail.

The Germanic tribes which displaced the Celts and defeated the Romans were composed of four classes: a few nobles or earls, a very large class of freemen, a smaller class of slaves, and a very small class of semifree men or serfs. Freemen were the most common people in early German society. They recognized no religious or political authority over their own activities, except to a very limited degree. As *free* men, they could, if they desired, settle their accounts with their neighbors and move to another geographical location. Each freeman occupied a large amount of land, his freehold farmstead, on which he grazed animals and, with the help of his slaves, grew crops. When necessary, he joined together with other freemen for defense or, more often, for the conquest of new territories.[1]

Freemen were the key to German expansion. When overcrowding occurred in clan villages and little unoccupied land remained, freemen moved to the border and with other freemen defeated and drove away the neighboring people. Here they established for themselves their own freehold farmsteads. Their descendants then multiplied and occupied the vacant land between the original freehold estates. When land was no longer available, clan villages began to form again and many freemen moved on once more to the new borders to start new freehold farmsteads. In this way, the Germans slowly but surely moved onward across northern and central Europe with freemen leading the way until no more land was available.

Strictly speaking, a freeman did not own his land. The idea of landownership in the modern sense was still many centuries away. In England, for example, landowning did not become a political and legal reality until 1660 when feudal dues were finally abolished once and for all. Freemen, however, lived in prefeudal times. They usually made a yearly offering to the local noble or earl, but technically this offering was a gift rather than a feudal payment and had nothing to do with their right to their land. As the term *freehold* suggests, a freeman held his land freely without any forced obligations to an overlord or to his neighbors.

In early times, when land was readily available, each freeman occupied as much land as he needed. There was no set amount that a freeman ought to have and no limit on his holdings, except that he could not hold more land than he could use. Thus, in effect, his personal dominion was restricted only by the number of animals that he had available for grazing and the number of slaves he had for agricultural labor. Sometimes, when the land began to lose its fertility, he would abandon his holdings and move to some other unoccupied location nearby. The exact location of each holding was only vaguely determined, and when disputes arose about boundaries, they were settled with the help of the testimony of neighbors or, when that failed, by armed combat between the parties involved.

Much of the unoccupied land was held in common with other freemen in accordance with various local arrangements. Sometimes the use was regulated by establishing the number of cattle that each freeman could place on the land. In other cases, plots were used by different freemen every year on a rotational basis.

When occupied border lands were no longer available for new freemen to settle, the way of life of the freemen began to change. The primary problem was one of inheritance. In the beginning, land had never been divided; rather, it had always been "multiplied" as sons moved to adjacent areas and established new freehold farmsteads. Eventually, however, it became necessary for the sons to divide the land which had been held by their father. A serious problem then developed, for, if division took place too many times, then the holdings became so small that they had little economic value, and the family as a whole slipped into poverty.

The solution was *entail,* i.e., inheritance along selected family lines. The most common form of entail was *primogeniture,* according to which the eldest son inherited everything and the others little or nothing. In this way, the family head remained powerful by keeping his landholdings intact, but most of his brothers were condemned to the semifree and poverty-stricken life of serfdom. As a result of these new inheritance practices, the number of freemen became an increasingly smaller portion of the society as a whole as most of the rest of the population, relatives included, rapidly sank to the level of serfs.

Another problem affecting freemen was taxation. The custom of giving an offering to the local noble was gradually replaced by a tax, and once established, taxes often became large burdens on many of the poorer freemen who in many instances paid taxes while other richer landholders were exempted. In such circumstances, freemen often gave up their status and their lands to persons exempted from the taxes and paid a smaller sum in rent as tenants.

Germans thus made a transition from prefeudal to feudal conditions, and freemen ceased to be an important element in the community as a whole. While freemen never disappeared altogether, most lost the economic freedom that they had formerly had. Although theoretically free to move about as they pleased, they often lacked the economic means of settling their accounts, and so in most cases were little better off than the serfs.

These feudal conditions did not appear in England until long after they were firmly established in Europe. At the time of the conquest of England by William the Conqueror most Englishmen were freemen. Thus, in England, unlike in Germanic Europe, prefeudal conditions did not slip away gradually but were abruptly replaced by a feudal system imposed on much of the native population by the victorious Normans. Under such circumstances, freemen declined in numbers, but struggled as best they could to maintain their freeman status in opposition to Norman rule and as a part of their Saxon heritage.

As a result, freemen managed to maintain a presence in England no longer conceivable in Europe. Through them, memories of the heyday of the flamboyant Saxon freemen remained to shade political thought and to shape land use attitudes for centuries after the conquest. Ironically, the conquest drew attention to a class status which might otherwise have quietly passed away.

There were four major political divisions in Saxon England: the kingdom, the shire (called the *county* after the arrival of the Normans), the hundred, and the township, the last two being subdivisions of the shire or county. Throughout English history the exact nature of the government of the kingdom fluctuated, sometimes very radically. Changes occurred in the hundreds and the townships as the courts at these levels were gradually replaced by those of the local nobility, probably with the support of the government of the kingdom. The shire or county and its court or moot, however, persisted unchanged and continued to be one of the most important political units from the earliest Saxon times in England to the present day in both England and the United States.

The county court met to deal with cases not already handled by the hundred moots and with other business of common importance to the community. The meetings were conducted by three men: the alderman, representing the shire; the sheriff, representing the king; and the bishop, representing the church. All freemen in the county had the right to attend the court and participate in the decision process. Most of them, of course, were usually too busy to come except when personal interests were at stake.

There are only small differences between the county courts of Saxon and Norman times and those of modern rural America. The three judges, alderman, sheriff, and bishop, have been replaced by elected judges. Court procedure in most of these courts, however, remains as informal today as it was in pre-Norman England. In many, no record is kept by the court of its decisions and, in such cases, except for word of mouth and intermittent coverage by the news media, little is known of what goes on there. Court judges are primarily concerned with keeping the local landowners contented by resolving local differences and by providing the few community services under the administrative jurisdiction of the court, e.g., maintaining dirt or gravel roads. This casual form of government is replaced only when the county becomes urbanized, thereby enabling residents to incorporate it and enjoy extensive new administrative and legal powers and, of course, responsibilities.

The special considerations given to the local landowner by the modern rural county court reflects the relationship of Saxon freemen to the court at the time when such courts first came into existence. The court evolved out of the freeman's custom of consulting with his neighbors during local disputes as an alternative to physical combat between the parties involved. Thus, rather than being something imposed on the freemen from above, the court was created by them for their own convenience. Since the freemen gave up little or none of their personal power, the power of the court to enforce its decisions was really nothing more than the collective power of the freemen ultimately comprising the membership of the court. From the earliest times, freemen had had absolute control over all matters pertaining to their own landholdings. When county courts were formed, freemen retained this authority over what they considered to be their own personal affairs. This limitation on the power of the court was maintained for more than a thousand years as part of the traditional conception of what a county court is, and how it is supposed to function. Today, when a landowner demands to know what right the court or anyone else has to tell him what to do with his own land he is referring to the original limitations set on the authority of the county court, and is appealing to the rights which he has informally inherited from his political ancestors, Saxon or German freemen—specifically, the right to do as he pleases without considering any interests except his own.

A modern landowner's argument that he has the right to do as he wishes is normally composed of a set series of claims given in a specific order. First, he points out that he or his father or grandfather worked the land in question. Second, he asserts that his ownership of the land is based on the work or labor put into it. Finally, he proclaims the right of uncontrolled use as a result of his ownership claim. Not all of this argument is derived directly from the freemen's world view. The modern concept of ownership was unknown to freemen who were engaged in landholding rather than landowning. In other respects, however, there are strong similarities between the views of modern landowners and those of the freemen.

Landholding among German freemen was based on work. A freeman, like the nineteenth-century American homesteader, took possession of a tract of land by clearing it, building a house and barns, and dividing the land into fields for the grazing of animals and for the growing of crops. In this way, his initial work established his claim to continued use.

This emphasis on work as the basis for landholding is especially clear in connection with inheritance. When plenty of vacant land was available, landholdings were never divided among the sons, but the sons moved to unoccupied land nearby and started their own freehold farmsteads. Thus, inheritance in those early times was not the acquisition of land itself but rather the transferal of the right to acquire land through work. This distinction is reflected in the early German word for inheritance, *Arbi* in Gothic and *Erbi* in Old High German, both of which have the same root as the modern High German word *Arbeit,* meaning work.[2]

Thus freemen were interested in land use rather than landownership. The right to land was determined by their social status as freemen and not by the fact that they or their fathers had occupied or possessed a particular piece of ground. The specific landholdings, thus, were not of major importance to the early freemen. Conceivably, they might move several times to new landholdings abandoning the old without the size of their landholdings being affected in any way. As mentioned above, it was their ability to use their holdings, the number of grazing animals, and slave workers they owned, not some form of ownership, which determined the size of their landholdings at any particular time in their lives.

Of course, once unoccupied land ceased to be readily available, freemen started paying much more attention to their land as property, encouraging the development of the idea of landownership in the modern sense. When the inheritance of sons became only the right to work a portion of their father's holdings, the transition from landholding to landowning was well on its way.

Until the time when there were no more unoccupied lands to move to, there was really no reason for freemen to be concerned with proper use or management of their land or for them to worry about possible long-term problems for themselves or their neighbors resulting from misuse and abuse of particular pieces of land. When a freeman lost his mobility, however, he did start trying to take somewhat better care of his land, occasionally practicing crop rotation and planting trees to replace those he cut down, but apparently these new necessities had little influence on his general conviction that as a freeman he had the right to use and even abuse his land as he saw fit.

Today's rural landowner finds himself in a situation not unlike that of freemen in the days when inheritance became the division of land rather than the multiplication of it. In the late eighteenth century and during most of the nineteenth, American rural landowners led a way of life much like that of prefeudal German freemen; now modern landowners face the same limitations their freemen ancestors did as feudal conditions began to develop. Although willing to take some steps toward good land management, especially those which provide obvious short-term benefit, when faced with broader issues involving the welfare of their neighbors and the local community and the protection and the preservation of the environment as a whole, they claim ancient rights which have come down to them from German freemen, and take advantage of their special influence with the local county court, a political institution as eager to please them today as it was more than a thousand years ago.

THOMAS JEFFERSON AND THE ALLODIAL RIGHTS OF AMERICAN FARMERS

When British colonists arrived in North America, they brought with them the land laws and land practices that were current in England at that time. These included entail, primogeniture, and most other aspects of the feudal tenure system which had taken hold in England after the Norman Conquest. The American Revolution called into question the right of the king of England to lands in North America which in turn led to attempts to bring about major land reform — specifically, efforts to remove all elements of the feudal system from American law and practice and replace them with the older Saxon free-hold tenure system. At the forefront of this movement was a young Virginian lawyer named Thomas Jefferson, . . .

From the first moment that Jefferson began airing his land tenure opinions, however, he made it completely clear that they were based entirely on Saxon, and not on Norman, common law. Thus, he consistently spoke of allodial rights — *allodial* being the adjectival form of the Old English word *allodium* which refers to an estate held in absolute dominion without obligation to a superior — i.e., the early German and Saxon freehold farmstead. . . .

Noting the right of a Saxon freeman to settle his accounts and move to another realm at his own pleasure without obligation to the lord of his previous domain, Jefferson argues that this is also the case with the British citizens who moved to North America. According to his analogy, England has no more claim over residents of America than Germany has over residents of England. In accordance with Saxon tradition, the lands of North America belong to the people living there and not to the king of England.[3] . . .

It is not the king, Jefferson declares, but the individual members of a society collectively or their legislature that determine the legal status of land, and, if they fail to act, then, in accordance with the traditions of Saxon freemen, "each individual of the society may appropriate to himself such lands as he finds vacant, and occupancy will give him title."[4] . . . Jefferson, of course, did not succeed in refuting the claim of the king of England to all land in British America, but by arguing in terms of this old dispute, he gives his position a legal basis which would have strong appeal among Englishmen with Saxon backgrounds, assuring some political support of the American cause in England.

In 1776, Jefferson got the opportunity to try to turn his theory into practice. Although Jefferson is most famous for writing the *Declaration of Independence,* most of his time that year was spent working on his draft of the Virginia constitution and on the reform of various Virginia laws including the land reform laws. In his draft constitution, Jefferson included a provision which gave each person of full age the right to fifty acres of land "in full and absolute dominion." In addition, lands previ-

ously "holden of the crown in feesimple" and all other lands appropriated in the future were to be "holden in full and absolute dominion, of no superior whatever."[5] Although these provisions were deleted, and similar bills submitted to the legislature failed to pass, Jefferson, nevertheless, did succeed in getting the legislature to abolish the feudal inheritance laws, entail and primogeniture. . . .

As for the government selling the land, Jefferson was completely opposed. "I am against selling the land at all," he writes to Pendleton, "By selling the lands to them, you will disgust them, and cause an avulsion of them from the common union. They will settle the lands in spite of every body." This prediction proved to be remarkably correct as evidenced by the fact that the next eighty years of American history was cluttered with squatters illegally occupying government land and then demanding compensation for their "improvements" through special preemption laws.[6]

In 1784, when he was appointed to head the land committee in the Congress of the Confederacy, Jefferson had a second opportunity to reestablish the Saxon landholding system. Whether Jefferson tried to take advantage of this opportunity is not known because the report of the committee, called the Ordinance of 1784, contains nothing about allodial rights to land. In addition, it even contains recommendations for the selling of western lands as a source of revenue for the government. It should be noted, however, that in one respect at least the document still has a very definite Saxon ring to it. Jefferson managed to include in his report a recommendation that settlers be permitted to organize themselves into new states on an equal footing with the original colonies. This recommendation, which was retained in the Ordinance of 1787, a revised version of the earlier ordinance, not only created the political structure necessary to turn the thirteen colonies into a much larger union of states, but also provided future generations of Americans with an independence and mobility similar to that enjoyed by the early Saxon and German freemen. In his *Summary View* of 1774, as mentioned above, Jefferson had argued that just as the Saxons invading England had had the right to set up an independent government, so British Americans had the right to an independent government in North America. The

Ordinances of 1784 and 1787 extended this right to movement and self-determination of American settlers leaving the jurisdiction of established states and moving into the interior of the continent. In large measure, it is thanks to this provision that Americans today are able to move from state to state without any governmental control in the form of visas, passports, immigration quotas, or the like as unhassled by such details as were early German freemen.

The absence of any provisions specifically granting landowners full and absolute dominion over their land, however, does not mean that Jefferson abandoned this conception of landholding or ownership. Privately and in his published writings he continued to champion the right of Americans to small freehold farmsteads. The only major change seems to be that Jefferson stopped trying to justify his position in terms of historical precedents and instead began speaking in moral terms claiming that small independent landholders were the most virtuous citizens any state could ever hope to have. In a letter to John Jay in 1785, Jefferson writes:

> Cultivators of the earth are the most valuable citizens. They are the most vigorous, the most independent, the most virtuous, and they are tied to their country and wedded to its liberty and interests by the most lasting bands.[7]

In a letter to James Madison in the same year, he adds:

> Whenever there is in any country, uncultivated lands and unemployed poor, it is clear that the laws of property have been so far extended as to violate natural right. The earth is given as a common stock for man to labour and live on. If, for the encouragement of industry we allow it to be appropriated, we must take care that other employment be furnished to those excluded from that appropriation. If we do not the fundamental right to labour the earth returns to the unemployed. It is too soon yet in our country to say that every man who cannot find employment but who can find uncultivated land, shall be at liberty to cultivate it, paying a moderate rent. But it is not too soon to provide by every possible means that as few as possible shall be without a little portion of land. The small landholders are the most precious part of the state.[8]

. . . These remarks are probably . . . the basis for the position of rural landowners today when faced with environmental issues. They are defending the American moral virtues which they have always been told their style of life and independence represents.

Had Jefferson been alive in the late nineteenth century when his views were being cited in opposition to the preservation of Yellowstone or were he alive today to see his Saxon freemen busily sabotaging county planning and zoning, he might have become disillusioned with his faith in the virtues of independent rural landowners. Jefferson, after all, as a result of his purchase of the Natural Bridge, perhaps the first major act of nature preservation in North America, ranks as a very important figure in the history of the nature preservation movement. Unfortunately, however, Jefferson's homesteaders and their modern day descendants did not always retain his aesthetic interest in nature or his respect for sound agricultural management which he interwove with his Saxon land use attitudes to form a balanced land use philosophy.

In part, the callousness and indifference of most rural landowners to environmental matters reflects the insensitivity of ancient Saxon freemen who viewed land as something to be used for personal benefit and who, being semi-nomadic, were unconcerned about whether that use would result in irreparable damage to the particular piece of land that they held at any given point in their lives. In addition, however, it can also be traced back to the political philosophy and theory of property of John Locke, a seventeenth-century British philosopher, who had a major impact on the political views of Jefferson and most other American statesmen during the American Revolution and afterwards. This influence is the subject of the next section.

JOHN LOCKE'S THEORY OF PROPERTY

As noted above, German and Saxon freemen did not have a concept of landownership, but only of landholding. As long as there was plenty of land for everyone's use, they did not concern themselves with exact boundaries. Disputes arose only when two freemen wanted to use the same land at the same time. By the end of the Middle Ages, however, with land in short supply, landholders began enclosing their landholdings to help ensure exclusive use. Enclosure kept the grazing animals of others away and also provided a sign of the landholder's presence and authority. Although enclosure was only a small step toward the concept of landownership, it, nonetheless, proved useful as a pseudo-property concept in early seventeenth-century New England where Puritans were able to justify their occupation of Indian lands on the grounds that the lack of enclosures demonstrated that the lands were vacant. Landownership became an official legal distinction in England after 1660 with the abolishment of feudal dues. The concept of landownership was introduced into British social and political philosophy thirty years later as part of John Locke's theory of property. This theory was presented in detail in Locke's *Two Treatises of Government,* a major work in political philosophy first published in 1690.[9]

Jefferson had immense respect and admiration for Locke and his philosophical writings. On one occasion, he wrote to a friend that Locke was one of the three greatest men that had ever lived — Bacon and Newton being the other two. Jefferson's justification of the American Revolution in the *Declaration of Independence* was borrowed directly from the *Second Treatise.* Many of Jefferson's statements in the document are almost identical to remarks made by Locke. For example, when Jefferson speaks of "life, liberty, and the pursuit of happiness," he is closely paraphrasing Locke's own views. His version differs from Locke's in only one minor respect: Jefferson substitutes for Locke's "enjoyment of property" the more general phrase "the pursuit of happiness," a slight change made to recognize other enjoyments in addition to those derived from the ownership of property. . . .

In the *Second Treatise* Locke bases property rights on the labor of the individual:

> Though the Earth, and all inferior Creatures be common to all Men, yet, every Man has *property* in his own *Person.* This no Body has any Right to but himself. The *Labour* of his Body, and the *Work* of his Hands, we may say, are properly his. Whatsoever then he removes out of the State that Nature hath provided, and left in, he hath mixed his *Labour* with, and joyned to it something that is his own, and thereby makes it his *Property.*[10]

This theory of property served Locke's friends well since it made their property rights completely independent of all outside interest. According to Locke, property rights are established without reference to kings, governments, or even the collective rights of other people. If a man mixes his labor with a natural object, then the product is his. . . .

The relevance of Locke's labor theory to the American homestead land use philosophy becomes especially clear when he turns to the subject of land as property:

> But the *chief matter of Property* being now not the Fruits of the Earth, and the Beasts that subsist on it, but the *Earth it self* as that which takes in and carries with it all the rest; I think it is plain, that *Property* in that too is acquired as the former. *As much land* as a Man Tills, Plants, Improves, Cultivates, and can use the Product of, so much is his *Property.* He by his Labour does, as it were, inclose it from the Common. . . . God, when He gave the World in common to all Mankind, commanded Man also to labour, and the penury of his Condition required it of him. God and his Reason commanded him to subdue the Earth, *i.e.* improve it for the benefit of Life, and therein lay out something upon it that was his own, his labour. He that in Obedience to this Command of God, subdued, tilled, sowed any part of it, thereby annexed to it something that was his *Property,* which another had no Title to, nor could without injury take from him.[11]

In this passage, the right of use and ownership is determined by the farmer's labor. When he mixes his labor with the land, the results are *improvements,* the key term in homesteading days and even today in rural America where the presence of such improvements may qualify landowners for exemption from planning and zoning under a grandfather clause. Since property rights are established on an individual basis independent of a social context, Locke's theory of property also provides the foundation for the landowner's claim that society has little or no role in the management of his land, that nobody has the right to tell him what to do with his property.

Locke reenforces the property owner's independence from societal restraints with an account of the origins of society in which property rights are supposedly more fundamental than society itself.

According to Locke, the right to the enjoyment of property is a presocietal *natural right*. It is a natural right because it is a right which a person would have in a state of nature. Locke claims that there was once, at some time in the distant past, a true state of nature in which people possessed property as a result of their labor, but, nevertheless, did not yet have societal relations with one another. This state of nature disappeared when these ancient people decided to form a society, thereby giving up some of their previous powers and rights. They did not, however, Locke emphatically insists, relinquish any of their natural rights to their own property, and the original social contract establishing the society did not give society any authority at all over personal property. In fact, the main reason that society was formed, according to Locke's account, was to make it possible for individuals to enjoy their own property rights more safely and securely. Thus, society's primary task was and allegedly still is to protect private property rights, not to infringe on them. A government which attempts to interfere with an individual's natural and uncontrolled right to the enjoyment of his property, moreover, deserves to be overthrown and the citizens of the society are free to do so at their pleasure. In effect, Locke is arguing along lines completely compatible with the early Saxon and Jeffersonian doctrine that a landowner holds his property in full and absolute dominion without any obligation to a superior.

The similarity of Locke's position to this doctrine invites the conclusion that Locke, like Jefferson, was drawing inspiration from Saxon common law and that Locke's social contract was actually the establishment of the shire or county court by Saxon freemen. Curiously, however, Locke makes no mention of the Saxons in these contexts and, even more curiously, no political philosopher ever seems to have considered the possibility that Locke might have been referring to this period of English history. In his chapter on conquest, nevertheless, Locke does demonstrate (1) that he knew what a freeman was, (2) that he was aware of the legal conflicts resulting from the Norman Conquest, and (3) that he sided with the Saxons in that controversy. In the one paragraph where he mentions the Saxons by name, he flippantly remarks that, even if they did lose their rights as freemen at the time of the conquest, as a result of the subsequent six centuries of intermarriage all Englishmen of Locke's day could claim freeman status through some Norman ancestor and it would "be very hard to prove the contrary."[12] Locke may have chosen not to mention the specifics of Saxon history fearing that if he did so, his political philosophy might have been treated as nothing more than just another call for a return to Saxon legal precedents. It is hard to imagine, nonetheless, that Locke's readers in the seventeenth century were not aware of these unstated connections considering the ease with which Jefferson saw them eighty years later in colonial North America. It is also possible, of course, that Locke may have been ignorant of the details of Saxon common law and may have simply relied on the popular land use attitudes of his day without being aware of their Saxon origin. At any rate, however, the ultimate result would be the same — a political philosophy which provides philosophical foundations for the ancient Saxon land use attitudes and traditions. . . .

Not everyone in the first half of the nineteenth century shared Jefferson's enthusiasm for land reform based on Saxon common law modified by Locke's theory of property, and for a time the idea of landholding independent of landowning continued to be influential in American political and legal thought. Early versions of the homestead bill before the beginning of the Civil War, for example, often contained inalienability and reversion clauses. According to these, a homesteader had the right to use the land, but could not subdivide it, sell it, or pass it on to his children after his death. These limitations, however, were not compatible with the wishes of potential homesteaders who wanted to be landowners, not just landholders, and, as a result, they were not included in the Homestead Act of 1862. It is unlikely that homesteading based entirely on Saxon common law ever had much chance of passing Congress because early nineteenth-century settlers squatting illegally on Western lands and demanding the enactment of special preemption laws had always had landownership as their primary objective.[13]

Because it was probably Locke's theory of property as much as Saxon common law which encouraged American citizens and immigrants to move westward, both should be given a share of the credit for the rapid settlement of the American West which ultimately established a national claim to all the lands west of the Appalachians as far as the Pacific. This past benefit to the American people, nevertheless, should not be the only standard for evaluating this doctrine's continuing value. We must still ask just how well the position is suited to conditions in twentieth-century America.

MODERN DIFFICULTIES WITH LOCKE'S POSITION

One obvious problem with Locke's theory today is his claim that there is enough land for everyone.[14] This premise is of fundamental importance to Locke's argument because, if a present or future shortage of land can be established, then any appropriation of land past or present under the procedure Locke recommends, enclosure from the common through labor, is an injustice to those who must remain unpropertied. By Locke's own estimates there was twice as much land at the end of the seventeenth century as all the inhabitants of the Earth could use. To support these calculations Locke pointed to the "in-land, vacant places of America" — places which are now occupied.[15] Since Locke's argument depends on a premise which is now false, Locke would have great difficulty advancing and justifying his position today.

Another problem is Locke's general attitude toward uncultivated land. Locke places almost no value on such land before it is improved and after improvement he says the labor is still the chief factor in any value assessment:

> . . . when any one hath computed, he will then see, how much *labour makes the far greatest part of the value* of things we enjoy in this World: And the ground which produces the materials, is scarce to be reckon'd in, as any, or at most, but a very small part of it; So little, that even amongst us, Land that is left wholly to Nature, that hath no improvement of Pasturage, Tillage, or Planting, is called, as indeed it is, *waste* and we shall find the benefit of it amount to little more than nothing.

According to Locke's calculations, 99 to 99.9 percent of the value of land even after it is improved still re-

sults from the labor and not the land. Although these absurdly high figures helped strengthen Locke's claim that labor establishes property rights over land, by making it seem that it is primarily the individual's labor mixed with the land rather than the land itself which is owned, such estimates, if presented today, would be considered scientifically false and contrary to common sense.[16]

Locke's land-value attitudes reflect a general desire prevalent in Locke's time as well as today for maximum agricultural productivity. From Locke's point of view, it was inefficient to permit plants and animals to grow naturally on uncultivated land:

> . . . I aske whether in the wild woods and uncultivated waste of America left to Nature, without any improvement, tillage, or husbandry, a thousand acres will yield the needy and wretched inhabitants as many conveniences of life as ten acres of equally fertile land doe in Devonshire where they are well cultivated?[17]

The problem, however, is not just productivity and efficiency, but also a general contempt for the quality of the natural products of the Earth. Locke writes with great conviction that "*Bread* is more worth than Acorns, *Wine* than Water, and *Cloth* or *Silk* than Leaves, Skins or Moss."[18] Even though we might be inclined to agree with Locke's pronouncements in certain contexts, the last two hundred years of the American experience have provided us with new attitudes incompatible with those of Locke and his contemporaries, and apparently completely unknown to them, which place high value on trees, water, animals, and even land itself in a wholly natural and unimproved condition. Unlike Locke, we do not always consider wilderness land or uncultivated land synonymous with waste.

At the very core of Locke's land-value attitudes is his belief that "the Earth, and all that is therein, is given to Men for the Support and Comfort of their being." In one sense, this view is very old, derived from the biblical and Aristotelian claims that the Earth exists for the benefit and use of human beings. At the same time, it is very modern because of Locke's twin emphasis on labor and consumption. Both of these activities are of central importance in communistic and capitalistic political systems, and they became so important precisely because the founders and ideologists of each system originally took their ideas about labor and consumption from Locke's philosophy. In accordance with these ideas, the Earth is nothing more than raw materials waiting to be transformed by labor into consumable products. The Greeks and Romans would have objected to this view on the grounds that labor and consumption are too low and demeaning to be regarded as primary human activities.[19] From a twentieth-century standpoint, given the current emphasis on consumption, the neglect of the aesthetic and scientific (ecological) value of nature seems to be a more fundamental and serious objection to this exploitative view.

The worst result of Locke's property theory is the amoral or asocial attitude which has evolved out of it. Locke's arguments have encouraged landowners to behave in an antisocial manner and to claim that they have no moral obligation to the land itself, or even to the other people in the community who may be affected by what they do with their land. This amoral attitude, which has been noted with dismay by Aldo Leopold, Garrett Hardin, and others, can be traced directly to Locke's political philosophy, even though Locke himself may not have intended to create this effect. The reasons why this moral apathy developed are complex.

First, the divine rights of kings had just been abolished. In accordance with this doctrine, the king had had *ultimate* and *absolute* property rights over all the land in his dominion. He could do whatever he wanted with this land—give it away, take it back, use it himself, or even destroy it as he saw fit. Locke's new theory of property stripped the king of this power and authority and transferred these *ultimate* and *absolute* rights to each and every ordinary property owner. This transfer has been a moral disaster in large part because the king's rights involved moral elements which did not carry over to the new rights of the private landowner. As God's agent on Earth, the king was morally obligated to adhere to the highest standards of right and wrong. Furthermore, the king, as the ruler of the land, had a moral and political obligation to consider the general welfare of his entire kingdom whenever he acted. Of course, kings did not always behave as they should have, but, nevertheless, there were standards recognized by these kings and their subjects as to what constituted proper and kingly moral behavior. Private landowners, however, did not inherit these sorts of obligations. Because they were not instruments of church or state, the idea that they should have moral obligations limiting their actions with regard to their own property does not seem to have come up. The standard which landowners adopted to guide their actions was a purely selfish and egotistical one. Because it involved nothing more than the economic interest of the individual, it was devoid of moral obligation or moral responsibility. . . .

Theoretically, Locke's qualification of the right to destroy property is compatible with the American conception of checks and balances and it might have provided a *political* solution to the problem, though not a moral one. Unfortunately, however, it has not been carried over into our political and legal system as successfully as the right to destroy. A man certainly has a right in the United States to sue for damages in court after the fact, when the actions of others have clearly injured him or his property, but the right of the government to take preventive action before the damage is done has not been effectively established. It is this preventive action which private landowners are assailing when they assert their right to use and even destroy their land as they see fit without any outside interference. The success of landowners in this area is amply demonstrated by the great reluctance of most state legislatures to place waste management restrictions on small private *landowners* which have long governed the activities of rural land *developers*.

Government regulation of individual private landowners has been ineffective historically because, from the very beginnings of American government, representation at state and federal levels has nearly always been based on landownership, an approach which has usually assured rural control of the legislature even when most of the citizens in the state lived in urban population centers. Government leaders intent on acting primarily in the interests of landowners could hardly have been expected to play the preventive role which Locke recommends. The unwillingness of legislators to act in this way in the nineteenth century and most of the twentieth, moreover, further contributed to the amoral belief of rural landowners that they can do whatever they want without being concerned about the welfare or rights of others.

When Jefferson attempted to build American society on a Lockeian foundation of small landowners, he did so in large measure because he believed that small landowners would make the most virtuous citizens. He failed to foresee, however, that the independence provided by Locke's presocietal natural rights would discourage rather than encourage social responsibility, and, therefore, would contribute little to the development of moral character in American landowners. Since social responsibility is basic to our conception of morality today, the claim of landowners that their special rights relieve them of any obligation or responsibility to the community can be regarded only as both socially and morally reprehensible. The position of such rural landowners is analogous to that of a tyrannical king. Tyranny is always justified, when it is justified at all, by a claim that the tyrant has the *right* to do as he pleases regardless of the consequences. In practice, however, the impact of rural landowners more closely approaches anarchy than tyranny, but only because landowners, though sharing a common desire to preserve their special rights, do not always have common economic interests. As a result, landowners are usually more willing to promote the theoretical rights of their fellow property owners than their specific land use and development projects, which as members of society, they may find objectionable or even despicable—in spite of their Saxon and Lockeian heritage rather than because of it.

A landowner cannot justify his position morally except with the extravagant claim that his actions are completely independent and beyond any standard of right and wrong—a claim which Locke, Jefferson, and even Saxon freemen would probably have hesitated to make. Actually, there is only one precedent for such a claim. During the Middle Ages, church philosophers concluded that God was independent of all moral standards. They felt compelled to take this position because moral limitations of God's actions would have conflicted with His omnipotence. Therefore, they reasoned that God's actions created moral law—i.e., defined moral law—and that theoretically moral law could be radically changed at any moment. Descartes held this position in the seventeenth century, and in the

nineteenth and twentieth centuries some atheistic existential philosophers have argued that because God is dead each man is now forced to create his own values through his individual actions. Although this position could be adopted as a defense of the landowners' extraordinary amoral rights, it would probably be distasteful to most landowners. Without it, this aspect of the rural landowners' position may be indefensible.[20]

Today, of course, whenever Locke's theory of property and the heritage of the ancient Saxon freeman surface in county courts, at planning and zoning meetings, and at state and federal hearings on conservation and land management, they still remain a formidable obstacle to constructive political action. As they are normally presented, however, they are certainly not an all-purpose answer to our environmental problems or even a marginally adequate reply to environmental criticism. When a landowner voices a Lockeian argument he is consciously or unconsciously trying to evade the land management issues at hand and to shift attention instead to the dogmatic recitation of his special rights as a property owner.

Some of Locke's fundamental assumptions and attitudes are either demonstrably false or no longer generally held even among landowners. These difficulties need to be ironed out before the landowners can claim that they are really answering their environmental critics. Furthermore it is likely that, even if the position can be and is modernized, the moral issues will still be unresolved.

As it stands, the force of the rural landowners' arguments depends on their historical associations—their biblical trappings, the echoes of Locke's political philosophy, the Saxon common-law tradition, the feudal doctrine of the divine rights of kings, and the spirit of the nineteenth-century American land laws. Can they be modernized? That remains to be seen. Until they are, however, landowners, environmentalists, politicians, and ordinary citizens should regard them with some suspicion.

NOTES

1. The account given in this section is based most directly on Denman W. Ross, *The Early History of Land-Holding among the Germans*

(Boston: Soule and Bugbee, 1883), and Walter Phelps Hall, Robert Greenhalgh Albion, and Jennie Barnes Pope, *A History of England and the Empire-Commonwealth,* 4th ed. (Boston: Ginn and Company, 1961).

2. Ross, *Land-Holding,* p. 24.
3. Thomas Jefferson, "A Summary View of the Rights of British America," in *The Portable Thomas Jefferson,* ed. Merrill D. Peterson (New York: Viking Press, 1975), pp. 4–5.
4. Ibid., pp. 17–19.
5. Thomas Jefferson, "Draft Constitution for Virginia," in *Portable Jefferson,* p. 248.
6. Jefferson to Edmund Pendleton, 13 August 1776, in *Papers of Thomas Jefferson,* 1:492.
7. Jefferson to John Jay, 23 August 1785, in *Portable Jefferson,* p. 384.
8. Jefferson to James Madison, 28 October 1785, in *Portable Jefferson,* p. 397.
9. John Locke, *Two Treatises of Government,* ed. Thomas I. Cook (New York and London: Hafner Press, 1947).
10. Locke, *Second Treatise,* sec. 27.
11. Ibid., sec. 32.
12. Ibid., sec. 177.
13. Paul W. Gates, *History of Public Land Law Development* (Washington D.C.: Public Land Law Commission, 1968), pp. 390–93.
14. Locke, *Second Treatise,* sec. 33.
15. Ibid., sec. 36.
16. Ibid., secs. 42–43.
17. Ibid., sec. 37.
18. Ibid., sec. 42.
19. Ibid., sec. 26; for a full discussion of labor and consumption see Hannah Arendt, *The Human Condition* (Chicago and London: University of Chicago Press, 1958), chap. 3.
20. Jean-Paul Sartre, *Existentialism and Human Emotions* (New York: Philosophical Library, 1957), pp. 13–18.

DISCUSSION TOPICS

1. In what ways is the policy of primogeniture fair or unfair? What policy might be better?
2. How important should historical precedents be in determining the laws governing land use today? What other factors should be considered?

3. John Locke proposed that property rights should be based primarily on the investment of a person's labor. Is that philosophy still valid today? Explain. If not, what is a better approach?

READING 19

Whither Conservation Ethics?

J. Baird Callicott

J. Baird Callicott is a professor of philosophy at the University of North Texas, Denton, and has been president of the International Society for Environmental Ethics. He is the author of many books on the topic of environmental ethics and, in particular, has been a thoughtful contributor to the growing literature on ecocentrism and Leopold's land ethic.

In an article from Conservation Biology, *Callicott discusses historical insights into the development of environmental perspectives in the United States. He notes the contributions of Ralph Waldo Emerson, Henry David Thoreau, and John Muir in forming a Romantic-Transcendental Preservation Ethic that focused on aesthetic and spiritual benefits of nature — in contrast to the Resource Conservation Ethic of Gifford Pinchot that had a greater emphasis on long-term use and benefits of natural resources for the general population. Muir also developed a nonanthropocentric preservation ethic in a biblical context. More recently, Aldo Leopold articulated a nonanthropocentric ethic in evolutionary and ecological terms.*

Today we face an ever-deepening environmental crisis, global in scope. What values and ideals, what vision of biotic health and wholeness should guide our response? American conservation began as an essentially moral movement and has, ever since, orbited around several ethical foci. Here I briefly review the history of American conservation ethics as a context for exploring a moral paradigm for twenty-first century conservation biology.

Ralph Waldo Emerson and Henry David Thoreau were the first notable American thinkers to insist, a century and a half ago, that other uses might be made of nature than most of their fellow citizens had theretofore supposed (Nash 1989). Nature can be a temple, Emerson (1836) enthused, in which to draw near and commune with God (or the Oversoul) (Albanese 1990). Too much civilized refinement, Thoreau (1863) argued, can overripen the human spirit; just as too little can coarsen it. In wildness, he thought, lay the preservation of the world.

John Muir (1894, 1901) made the Romantic-Transcendental nature philosophy of Emerson and Thoreau the basis of a national, morally charged campaign for the appreciation and preservation of wild nature. The natural environment, especially in the New World, was vast enough and rich enough, he believed, to satisfy our deeper spiritual needs as well as our more manifest material needs. Amplifying Thoreau's countercultural theme, Muir strongly condemned prodigal destruction of nature in the service of profligate materialism and greed (Cohen 1984). In Muir's opinion, people going to forest groves, mountain scenery, and meandering streams for religious transcendence, aesthetic contemplation, and healing rest and relaxation put these resources to a "better" — i.e., morally superior — use than did the lumber barons, mineral kings, and captains of industry hell-bent upon little else than worshiping at the shrine of the Almighty Dollar and seizing the Main Chance (Fox 1981). . . .

At the turn of the century Gifford Pinchot, a younger contemporary of John Muir, formulated a resource conservation ethic reflecting the general tenets of Progressivism, an American social and political movement then coming into its own. America's vast biological capital had been notoriously plundered and squandered, not for the benefit of all its citizens, but for the profit of a few. Pinchot bluntly reduced the Romantic poets' and Transcendental philosophers' "Nature" to "natural resources." Indeed, he insisted that "there are just two things on this material earth — people and natural resources" (1947:325). Pinchot (1947:325–26) crystalized the Resource Conservation Ethic in a motto which he credits W. J. McGee with formulation: "the greatest good of the greatest number for the longest time" — without making direct reference to John Stuart Mill (1863), Bentham's Utilitarian protegé, whose summary moral maxim it echoes.

The first moral principle of the Resource Conservation Ethic is equity — the just or fair distribution of natural resources among present and also future generations of consumers and users. Its second moral principle, equal in importance to the first, is efficiency — a natural resource should not be wastefully exploited. Just slightly less obvious, the principle of efficient resource utilization involves the concepts of "best" or "highest use" and "multiple use."

The "gospel of efficiency," as Samuel Hays (1959) characterized the Resource Conservation Ethic, also implies a sound scientific foundation. The Resource Conservation Ethic thus became wedded to the eighteenth- and nineteenth-century scientific world view in which nature is conceived to be a collection of bits of matter, assembled into a hierarchy of externally related chemical and organismic aggregates, which can be understood and successfully manipulated by analytic and reductive methods.

The Resource Conservation Ethic is also wedded to the correlative social science of economics — the science of self-interested rational monads pursuing "preference satisfaction" in a free market. However, because the market, notoriously, does not take account of "externalities" — certain costs of doing business, such as soil erosion and environmental pollution — and because standard economic calculations discount the future dollar value of resources in comparison with present dollar value, the free market cannot be relied upon to achieve the most efficient, and certainly not the most prudent, use of natural resources. Pinchot (1947) persuasively argued, therefore, that government ownership or regulation of natural resources and resource exploitation is a necessary remedy. Federal and state bureaucracies, accordingly, were created to implement and administer conservation policy as the twentieth century advanced.

Since the Resource Conservation Ethic was based so squarely upon Progressive democratic social philosophy and was rhetorically associated with the modern secular ethic of choice — Utilitarianism — it triumphed politically and became institutionalized in the newly created government conservation agencies. The nonconsumptive use of nature by aesthetes, Transcendentalists, and wilderness recreationalists can be accommodated by assigning them a contingent market value or "shadow-price" (Krutilla & Fisher 1985). In some circumstances such uses may turn out to be the highest or most efficient allocation of a given "resource." Thus, an occasional otherwise worthless wild sop might be thrown to the genteel minority.

The celebrated schism in the traditional American conservation movement — the schism between the Conservationists proper and the Preservationists, associated with the legendary names of Pinchot and Muir, respectively — was thus in the final analysis a matter of differing moral (and metaphysical) philosophies. Both were essentially human-centered or "anthropocentric." Both, in other words, regarded human beings or human interests as the only legitimate ends and nonhuman natural entities and nature as a whole as means. In the now standard terminology of contemporary environmental ethics, for both Conservationists and Preservationists, only people possess *intrinsic* value; nature possesses merely instrumental value (Norton 1986). The primary difference is that the Preservationists posited a higher Transcendental reality above and beyond the physical world and pitted the psychospiritual use of nature against its material use. And they insisted that the one was incomparably superior to the other. The Conservationists were more materialistic and insisted, democratically, that all competing uses of resources should be weighed impartially and that the fruits of resource exploitation should be distributed broadly and equitably.

Although Muir's public campaign for the appreciation and preservation of nature was cast largely in terms of the putative superiority of the human spiritual values served by contact with undeveloped, wild nature, Muir also seems to have been the first American conservationist privately to ponder the proposition that nature itself possessed intrinsic value — value in and of itself — quite apart from its human utilities (no matter whether of the more spiritual or more material variety). To articulate this essentially nonanthropocentric intuition, Muir (1916) turned, ironically, to Biblical fundamentals for the rhetorical wherewithal. Very directly and plainly stated, God created man and all the other creatures. Each of His creatures — man included, but not man alone — and the creation as a whole are "good" in His eyes (i.e., in philosophical terms they have intrinsic value). Hence, to eradicate a species or to efface nature is to undo God's creative work, and to subtract so much divinely imbued inherent goodness from the world — a most impious and impertinent expression of human arrogance.

More radically than most contemporary exponents of the by-now familiar Judeo-Christian Stewardship Environmental Ethic, Muir insisted that people are just a part of nature on a par with other creatures and that all creatures (including ourselves) are valued equally by God, for the contribution we and they make to the whole of His creation — whether we can understand that contribution or not. . . .

. . . There was another mind set animating Muir's moral vision — an evolutionary and ecological world view. Darwin had unseated from his self-appointed throne the creature Muir sometimes sarcastically called "lord man" and reduced him to but a "small part" of creation, and the likes of H. C. Cowles, S. A. Forbes, and F. E. Clements would soon validate Muir's intuition that there exists a unity and completeness — if not in the cosmos or universe at large, certainly in terrestrial nature — to which each creature, no matter how small, functionally contributes (McIntosh 1985). This world view held a profound but murky moral import. It fell to Aldo Leopold to bring the ethical implications of the ripening evolutionary-ecological paradigm clearly and fully to light.

Leopold began his career as a professional conservationist trained in the utilitarian Pinchot philosophy of the wise use of natural resources, for the satisfaction of the broadest possible spectrum of human interest, over the longest time (Meine 1988). His ultimately successful struggle for a system of wilderness reserves in the national forests was consciously molded to the doctrine of highest use, and his new technique of game management essentially amounted to the direct transference of the principles of forestry from a standing crop of large plants to a standing crop of large animals (Leopold 1919, 1921). But Leopold gradually came to the conclusion that the Pinchot Resource Conservation Ethic was inadequate, because, in the last analysis, it was untrue.

The Resource Conservation Ethic's close alliance with science proved to be its undoing. Applied science cannot be thoroughly segregated from pure science. Knowledge of ecology is essential to efficient resource management, but ecology began to give shape to a radically different scientific paradigm than that which lay at the very foundations of Pinchot's philosophy. From an ecological perspective, nature is more than a collection of externally related useful, useless, and noxious species furnishing an elemental landscape of soils and waters. It is, rather, a vast, intricately organized and tightly integrated *system* of complex *processes.* It is less like a vast mechanism and more like a vast organism. Specimens are its cells and species its organs. . . .

Thus, we cannot remodel our natural *oikos* or household, as we do our artificial ones, without inducing unexpected disruptions. More especially, we cannot get rid of the Early American floral and faunal "furniture" (the prairie flora, bison, elk, wolves, bears) and randomly introduce exotic pieces (wheat, cattle, sheep, English sparrows, Chinese pheasants, German carp, and the like) that suit our fancy without inducing destructive ecological chain reactions.

Conservation, Leopold came to realize, must aim at something larger and more comprehensive than a maximum sustained flow of desirable products (like lumber and game) and experiences (like sport hunting and fishing, wilderness travel, and solitude) garnered from an impassive nature (Flader 1974). It must take care to ensure the continued function of natural processes and the integrity of natural systems. For it is upon these, ultimately, that human resources and human well-being depend.

The Pinchot Resource Conservation Ethic is also untrue on the human side of its bifurcation of people and natural resources. Human beings are not specially created and uniquely valuable demigods any more than nature itself is a vast emporium of goods and services, a mere pool of resources. We are, rather, very much a part of nature. Muir (1916) groped to express this bioegalitarian concept in theological terms. Leopold did so in more honest ecological terms. Human beings are "members of a biotic team," plain members and citizens of one humming biotic community (Leopold 1949:205). We and the other citizen-members of the biotic community sink or swim together. Leopold's affirmation that plants and animals, soils and waters are entitled to full citizenship as fellow members of the biotic community is tantamount to the recognition that they too have intrinsic, not just instrumental,

value. An evolutionary and ecological world view, in short, implies a land ethic.

In sum, then, examining a core sample of the ethical sediments in the philosophical bedrock of American conservation, one may clearly discern three principal strata of laterally coherent moral ideals. They are the Romantic-Transcendental Preservation Ethic, the Progressive-Utilitarian Resource Conservation Ethic, and the Evolutionary-Ecological Land Ethic. American conservation policy and the conservation profession reflect them all—thus giving rise to internal conflict and, from an external point of view, the appearance of confusion. The public agencies are still very much ruled by the turn-of-the-century Resource Conservation Ethic; some of the most powerful and influential private conservation organizations remain firmly rooted in the even older Romantic-Transcendental philosophy; while contemporary conservation biology is clearly inspired and governed by the Evolutionary-Ecological Land Ethic (Soulé 1985). . . .

LITERATURE CITED

Albanese, C. L. 1990. Nature religion in America: from the Algonkian Indians to the new age. University of Chicago Press, Chicago, Illinois.

Cohen, M. P. 1984. The pathless way: John Muir and the American wilderness. University of Wisconsin Press, Madison, Wisconsin.

Emerson, R. W. 1836. Nature. James Monroe and Co., Boston, Massachusetts.

Flader, S. L. 1974. Thinking like a mountain: Aldo Leopold and the evolution of an ecological attitude toward deer, wolves, and forests. University of Missouri Press, Columbia, Missouri.

Fox, S. 1981. John Muir and his legacy: the American conservation movement. Little, Brown and Co., Boston, Massachusetts.

Hays, S. P. 1959. Conservation and the gospel of efficiency: the progressive conservation movement. Harvard University Press, Cambridge, Massachusetts.

Krutilla, J., and A. Fisher. 1985. The economics of natural environments: studies in the valuation of commodity and amenity resources. Rev. ed. Resources for the Future, Washington, D.C.

Leopold, A. 1919. Forestry and game conservation. Journal of Forestry 16:404–11.

Leopold, A. 1921. The wilderness and its place in forest recreation policy. Journal of Forestry 19:718–21.

Leopold, A. 1949. A Sand County Almanac: and sketches here and there. Oxford University Press, New York.

McIntosh, R. P. 1985. The background of ecology: concept and theory. Cambridge University Press, Cambridge, England.

Meine, C. 1988. Aldo Leopold: his life and work. University of Wisconsin Press, Madison, Wisconsin.

Mill, J. S. 1863. Utilitarianism. Parker, Son and Brown, London, England.

Muir, J. 1894. The mountains of California. Century, New York.

Muir, J. 1901. Our national parks. Houghton Mifflin, Boston, Massachusetts.

Muir, J. 1916. A thousand mile walk to the gulf. Houghton Mifflin, Boston, Massachusetts.

Nash, R. F. 1989. The rights of nature: a history of environmental ethics. University of Wisconsin Press, Madison, Wisconsin.

Norton, B. G. 1986. Conservation and preservation: a conceptual rehabilitation. Environmental Ethics 8: 195–220.

Pinchot, G. 1947. Breaking new ground. Harcourt, Brace, and Co., New York.

Soulé, M. E. 1985. What is conservation biology? BioScience 35:727–733.

Thoreau, H. D. 1863. Excursions. Ticknor and Fields, Boston, Massachusetts.

DISCUSSION TOPICS

1. How might you propose a resolution to the differences in perspectives represented by John Muir and Gifford Pinchot? Explain your position.

2. In what ways do you believe the nonanthropocentric ethic of Leopold was similar and different from that of Muir? Give your reasoning.

"Wasty Ways": Stories of American Settlement

Alan Taylor

Alan Taylor teaches early American and western American history at the University of California, Davis. He is author of several books on early American history, including Frontier of the Early American Republic *(1995), which won the 1996 Bancroft, Beveridge, and Pulitzer Prizes in American history.*

In an article from Environmental History, *Taylor notes that environmental history is typically interpreted to show that we "live in an altered nature of diminished diversity and painful dilemmas that derive from the settlement past." While not disputing the often wasteful behavior of the settlers, Taylor argues for a fresh and more empathetic look at the impact of European settlement on the North American continent and an explanation of settler behavior that considers their often marginal position, suffering, and the considerable threats they regularly faced.*

In his 1823 novel *The Pioneers, or The Sources of the Susquehanna,* James Fenimore Cooper recalls his childhood world: Otsego County in central New York during the 1790s, when settlers remade the local forest into farms. Cooper depicts the settlers as possessed by an irrational, emotional lust to decimate nature. Their slaughter of the wild plants and animals exceeds all considerations of economic need and interest. In two especially vivid scenes, the settlers of Templeton (the fictional version of the Otsego village of Cooperstown) festively muster to massacre a flock of passenger pigeons and a school of Otsego bass. At the pigeon hunt, "None pretended to collect the game, which lay scattered over the fields in such profusion, as to cover the very ground with the fluttering victims." Similarly, the settlers are "Inflamed beyond the bounds of discretion" at "the sight of the immense piles of fish, that were slowly rolling over on the gravelly beach." They leave most to die and rot, unwanted and unneeded. Otsego's dominant landlord, Judge Marmaduke Temple (modeled on the novelist's father, Judge William Cooper) sadly assures his daughter, "The poor are always prodigal, my child, where there is plenty, and seldom think of a provision against the morrow." He especially laments the rapid decline of the local fish: "like all the other treasures of the wilderness, they already begin to disappear, before the wasteful extravagance of man." Another character, the canny old hunter Natty Bumppo, shares this distress: "I call it sinful and wasty to catch more than can be eat."[1]

Raised in wealth and comfort, Cooper offered an elitist explanation for settler profligacy with nature — abundance brought out the worst in the human nature of common folk. Incapable of restraint, the vulgar settlers despoiled nature as an unthinking sport. In contrast to explanations that emphasize the short-term rationality of profit maximization, Cooper insisted that the "profit" settlers sought was primarily psychic and emotional: the sheer thrill of killing and wasting. In the early American republic, where the unrestrained transformation of the wilderness was the essence of egalitarian opportunity, Cooper's argument was literally uncommon. But his distrust of the common man more often echoes in this century's writings by environmentalists and environmental historians appalled at the consequences of the settler past.[2]

Like Cooper, environmental historians write after the fact of transformation, and most cannot help but be impressed by the settlers' destructive mastery over nature, at least in the short term. Environmental historical narratives of North American settlement often open with a nostalgic description of a natural abundance now lost: towering forests, immense flocks of waterfowl, majestic game animals, a boundless, diverse tangle of wild plants, and native peoples who manage their environment with restraint (but never without effect). Then the powerful Euro-American settlers appear to attack and subdue the wild. Only later do their successors experience the harsh consequences, as a nature scorned counterattacks with severe erosion, dust storms, shrinking aquifers, and salinized soil. In sum, a tripartite structure characterizes the classic environmental histories: initial abundance, transforming settlers, and a legacy of diminished nature. Such narratives are powerful and persuasive because, from our contemporary vantage point, they convey a truth: we do live in an altered nature of diminished diversity and painful dilemmas that derive from the settlement past.[3]

By making so much of settlers' power over nature, however, our environmental narratives make too little of settlers' initial weakness and suffering. In fact, their eventual power derived from their initial pain. This essay locates the settlers' assault on the wild within their often harsh initial experiences with a new land and within the stories they told one another about the meaning of their experiences. The focus will be on Otsego County, the setting for *The Pioneers,* during its period of intense settlement and deforestation, from 1785 to 1820. This case study means to illuminate the general phenomenon of frontier settlement in the United States during the late eighteenth and early nineteenth centuries (prior to the rural introduction of industrial technologies).

The drastic consumption of nature had its roots in the prolonged and previous period when early settlers felt threatened and often overmatched by their new environmental setting. The forest's abundant and diverse plant and animal life was simultaneously alluring and threatening to new settlers coming from older communities. The "wilderness" contained both resources that were scarce at home *and* dangerous beings that had been exterminated further east. The vast forest was a valuable storehouse of firewood, potash, and lumber, *and* a haven for wild, dangerous predators, as well as an encumbrance that obstructed sunlight where settlers intended to plant crops. Pigeons and deer were windfall sources of food *and* a menace to newly planted crops. Settlers valued bears for their meat and hides, but dreaded their attacks on orchards and livestock. In settler experience, the abundance of nature was often either fleeting or complicated with hidden menace. The scenes of slaughter remembered by Cooper were particular moments of transition when settlers felt a new power to impose their will upon the wilderness — moments of perverse but joyous revenge. Only by restoring settlers' fears and sufferings can we adequately explain the excesses of their assault upon nature. This does not justify their actions, but it does render comprehensible patterns of behavior that modern sensibilities and perfect hindsight too easily dismiss as simple irrationality and greed.[4]

Settlers' behavior emerged from a dialectic between their experiences and their own environmental storytelling. They entered into the Otsego country informed by the stories heard at home and in childhood about their parents' and grandparents' struggles to make their own farms in a similar landscape of rocky soil, heavy timber, and howling wolves. Repeating the harsh experiences of their predecessors, Otsego's settlers added to a stock of stories about environmental conflict. On the one hand, their stories of endurance in the face of daunting hardships asserted that they were worthy heirs, replicating the environmental ordeals and triumphs of their venerable ancestors. On the other hand, their stories also built up an animus against the wild as the source of their pain and anxiety. Small wonder then that they could delight in opportunities to kill trees, birds, or fish by the thousands. Their stories shaped their behavior, which generated new experiences of both hardship and conquest. In turn, these became the substance of their own narratives, shaping the environmental expectations and behavior of the next generation, who tended to move westward to make their own farms in the forests and prairies of Michigan, Ohio, Illinois, Wisconsin, and Iowa.

HARDSHIPS

Upstate New York's settlers were farming people who ventured onto tracts recently wrested from the Iroquois during the American Revolution. Migrating primarily from western New England, these settlers quadrupled New York's population from 340,120 in 1790 to 1,372,812 in 1820. At the same time, the Iroquois population shrank under the pressures of disease, war, and dispossession to only about 3,500 in 1794. The victors confined the vanquished to shrinking reservations on fractions of their prewar domain.[5]

Compared to their Iroquois predecessors, the settlers used more land more intensively because they came in vastly greater numbers and because they sought a marketable surplus as well as family subsistence from their agriculture. The Indians had confined their horticulture to subsistence and had restricted their settlements to the fertile riverine floodplains, reserving the extensive uplands as a forest for hunting and gathering. After 1783, the victorious settlers seized the riverine villages of the Indians and expanded up onto the forested hills and ridges, pushing their multiplying farms into almost every corner of the new state. In contrast to the In-

dians, who obtained most of their meat from fishing and hunting, the settlers relied primarily on domesticated livestock kept as private property. While no Indian family owned any particular deer or bear until the animal had been killed, settlers regarded their living cattle, horses, sheep, and pigs as private, individual possessions. The newcomers hoped to render the landscape safe and productive for their livestock and for their more extensive fields of grain by clearing the forest and destroying most of the wild mammals. In their drive to create more property, to produce grains for external markets (as well as for their own subsistence), and to maximize the number of privately owned animals, settler families cleared and fenced much more land, and built more and larger buildings, than did the Indians.[6]

Disregarding the signs of prior Indian use, the new settlers called the forested uplands of New York a "wilderness" — by which they meant a landscape that they had not yet reworked to fit their needs and expectations. No romantics, the settlers did not celebrate the American forest as a paradise, as an escape from corrupt society into a presocial innocence. On the contrary, they regarded the wilderness as threatening and unproductive. The Otsego land speculator William Cooper contrasted "the frowning terrors of forest-crowned precipices" with "the cultivated abodes of industry and peace." The abundance of the wilderness was entirely wasted until harnessed to meet the needs of its conquerors. The best that could be said of the wilderness was that it tested and improved the victors.[7]

The settlers regarded their farm-building as "improvements" that refined the so-called "wilderness" into a more productive and secure version of nature. . . . Indeed, the settlers' leaders insisted that their transforming work fulfilled their God's intent. . . . Settlers meant to replace a nature that they called wilderness with another nature called pastoral.

During that long process of transformation, however, the settlers were vulnerable to natural forces beyond their control. At the end of the eighteenth century, upstate New York was abundantly endowed with the wild life that settlers needed to subdue. A heavy, tangled forest of large oak, beech, maple, chestnut, pine, and hemlock trees covered the hills and sheltered numerous carnivorous mammals — bears, panthers, and wolves — who threatened the domesticated livestock and plants introduced by the settlers. Remaking this dense forest into productive farms was a long, laborious process for people armed only with hand tools — axes and saws, hammers and hoes, guns and knives — and assisted by oxen and fire. . . . At first, nature seemed too powerful; the settlers appeared overmatched by the forest and its denizens. Consequently, new settlements meant severe hardships, intense labor, sudden dangers, and frequent hunger. In 1798, Isaac Lyman explained that his fellow settlers disliked missionaries: "They say they wish not to have them preach of Hell & Damnation, for let any Person come into a New Settlement & see how they fare, [he] will say the Inhabitants suffer all those torments of Hell and Damnation to a perfection."[8]

Poorer folk, with limited prospects at home in eastern New York and western New England, bore the shocks of early settlement in upstate New York. . . . Because prosperous people felt little pressure and less inducement to forsake the comforts of an old community for the rigors of a new settlement, most early settlers came from relatively poor families.[9]

Quantitative evidence supports the ubiquitous picture of frontier poverty found in the travelers' accounts and settler memoirs. Combining the 1790 federal census with a 1787 tax list permits a test of the relative poverty of the men who emigrated to Otsego from one township, Hoosick, in eastern New York on the Vermont boundary. Twenty-one men from the Hoosick tax list of 1787 left that town and reappeared in 1790 on the census return for Otsego township. The Hoosick tax list recorded the varying taxes assessed on the 360 heads of households, ranging from one shilling to £7.9.0, depending upon their relative wealth; the median tax was eight shillings and the mean twelve. Compared to the 241 householders who remained in Hoosick in 1790, the twenty-one migrants paid, on average, one-third less (9.5 versus 13.9 shillings). Most of the persisters had been assessed more than the township's median tax of eight shillings (134 of 241) versus only a third of the Otsego migrants (7 of 21). According to the data from Hoosick, settlers came from the poorer half of the town's population, evidence in accord with William Cooper's insistence that his first settlers belonged to "the poorest order of men."[10]

The early newcomers struggled with a vicious cycle: their initial poverty increased their vulnerability to hardships, and those hardships prolonged their poverty. . . . This interplay of prolonged poverty and frontier hardship was manifest in the grim experiences of the Beach family, who emigrated from Connecticut during the 1780s to settle beside the Susquehanna River in the Otsego country. Their grandson, Josiah Priest, reported that after two years of hard labor their new homestead produced a promising crop. It seemed "that the period of their privations was near its close." But on October 6, 1787, a heavy rainstorm drenched the hills, filled the creeks, and swelled the Susquehanna into a flood that carried away the newly cut harvest: sheaves of wheat and rye and heaps of pumpkins and flax. For want of capital, the family had not built a barn to store their crop. The following June, another flood swamped Timothy Beach's canoe, drowning him and sentencing his widow and children to "wretched poverty."[11]

During their first two years on the land, few Otsego settlers could clear and cultivate enough land to feed themselves. Hunger was common during the late spring and early summer, after the previous harvest had been consumed and before the next ripened. Near-famine conditions prevailed in localities where crop parasites or early frosts cut short the harvest in their small clearings. When shaded by the large, surrounding forest, grains, especially corn, might not ripen before the mid-September frost. And the settlers unwittingly brought "the blast" (or "black stem rust") with them from New England; this fungal parasite could destroy an entire field of wheat, or at least render the grain unpleasantly dark and moldy. . . . Even when the settlers could raise sufficient crops, they suffered from a lack of bridges and roads to carry produce to gristmills and to market. To make flour, isolated settlers had to pound their corn by hand with a mortar and pestle — long, tedious, back-numbing labor.[12]

Early settlers also had to fight an often losing battle to defend orchards, poultry, and livestock from marauding bears and wolves, and to protect grain and garden plants from pigeons, squirrels, and grasshoppers. . . .

When their produce ran short, settlers relied upon hunting, gathering, and fishing for sustenance.

Ironically, during the seasons of early hardship the settlers found relief by tapping the wild abundance that they were ultimately determined to conquer. . . .

Fishing was the primary recourse for starving settlers. In the spring of 1785, Priest's family "learned of the Indians how to catch fish. . . . Without this relief, they must have finally perished." Fish abounded in "those early times before the Susquehannah was interrupted by milldams, and its lucid waters beclouded with sawdust." Settlers caught fish, especially trout, with baited hooks or lured them within spearing range at night by placing a burning pine knot in an iron basket that projected from the bow of a boat or canoe. Thousands of fish — especially shad, herring, and Otsego bass — could be taken at once with a seine net set into the lake or river waters by a boat and drawn ashore by cooperating settlers. Settlers also learned from the Indians to build weirs, elaborate V-shaped traps of tightly interwoven branches held in place by stakes driven into the river bottom and extending from one bank to the other. Whether employing nets or weirs, cooperating settlers threw the trapped fish onto the dry beach to die and then formed them into equal-sized piles, one per fisherman. The piles were "cried off" to particular fishermen in a manner intended to ensure a fair distribution without wrangling. One settler stood or sat with his back to the fish and answered with a man's name the question posed by another who went from pile to pile: "Who shall have this [(heap)]?" Cooperative labor culminated in an egalitarian distribution of the fish as private property.[13]

DANGERS

In addition to their endemic poverty and seasonal hunger, the first settlers were also prone to sudden and violent accidents. The dangers emerged, in part, from the raw power of nature's extremes, but also in part from the inadequate contrivances the settlers made to try and contain that energy. By immigrating into the forest, settlers placed themselves in harm's way, gambling their subsistence and health on their eventual success in the arduous transformation of the forest into farms. In the short term, they compounded their vulnerability by entrusting their lives and livestock to hastily built dams, roads,

bridges, and barns that often collapsed with crippling and fatal consequences. By claiming the life or health of a laboring boy or man, an accident could deal a disastrous blow to a frontier family already struggling to make ends meet.

The expedients of settlers could prove more deadly than the hunger that impelled them. In gathering forest plants to relieve that hunger, settlers sometimes made hasty, fatal mistakes. Poisonous "muskrat root" (*Cicuta aquasa,* or water hemlock) grew along stream banks and bore a dangerous resemblance to the edible wild leek. The similarity occasionally claimed the lives of unwary settlers after a few hours of intense torment.[14]

Traveling could turn deadly in a land where the forest dwarfed the new clearings, the rivers flowed rapidly over hidden logs and rocks, and the roads, bridges, and ferries were few and precarious. Sometimes the winter ice gave way beneath traveling parties, and the dark, frigid waters swallowed sleighs, horses, oxen, and humans. Winter blizzards could trap and disorient travelers and hunters, bringing death from exposure. . . . In April 1796, a canoe carrying a settler family overturned in the Susquehanna River after striking a heavy log. The four adults struggled to safety on the banks, but the river swept away and drowned their four children.[15] . . .

Traveling overland became even more dangerous as settlers began to thin out the forest. Before the settlers had arrived, the dense forest buffered individual trees from direct gusts of wind, permitting tall, straight growth without deep roots. As settlers cut into the groves, remaining trees that were weakly anchored by shallow roots were exposed to wind storms that toppled trunks and branches onto cattle and people below. . . .

Lightning or careless settlers frequently caused extensive forest fires that imperiled their farms, lives, and livestock. These fires broke out in times of summer drought and fed upon all the dead, drying trunks, branches, and brush that littered the forest floor as the settlers cut into the wilderness. Consequently, fires that escaped from settler control produced more intense, widespread, and destructive blazes than the smaller fires that Indians had annually set to consume the underbrush. Unlike Indian fires, settler fires raged up into the forest canopy to consume mature trees.[16]

Settlers had to build all the infrastructure they had taken for granted in their former communities: stores, roads, bridges, mills, schools, and meetinghouses. Hastily and sloppily built by unskilled labor, these structures frequently failed, with catastrophic consequences. As with their partial clearings, the settlers' buildings increased, rather than reduced, their danger in the short term. . . .

Of course, the great majority of settlers survived the swirling blizzards, swollen rivers, falling trees, forest fires, poisonous plants, collapsing leach tubs and house frames, runaway wagons, bursting dams and grinding waterwheels. But such episodes were sufficiently common to remind frontier dwellers that they led a harsher and more unpredictable life than did their friends and relatives back home in old Connecticut and Massachusetts. And those who did not directly encounter danger felt its proximity as they heard hearthside stories of harsh environmental experience. . . . By dwelling on the grim and horrific, local stories and reportage magnified the impact of fatal or crippling accidents on settler minds.

Grim episodes and tales of a harsh and capricious nature promoted morbid reflections. After one fatal accident, *Otsego Herald* editor Elihu Phinney poetically noted the fragility of life:

> By what a slender thread,
> Our feeble frame's suspended;
> One moment free of pain —
> The next our life is ended.

George Peck had nearly died beneath a falling hemlock tree while traveling on a Sunday. He later recalled that "for weeks the affair harrowed up my soul. . . . The idea of being [nearly] killed in the act of breaking the Sabbath made my very bones shake, and many were the vows I made to lead a new life. Often did I fear to close my eyes at night until I had promised God that if he would spare me to see another day, I would do better." The terrifying tales of lurking dangers and sudden deaths led the young Henry Clarke Wright to associate "the Deity with soul-crushing mysteries."[17]

Some brooding settlers went beyond somber reflection to fatal melancholy. Three sudden accidents —a toppling tree, a raging river, and a fall from a cart—claimed three men who were the friends of Luther Peck of Middlefield. "These sad events, following each other in swift succession, deeply affected him," recalled his son George. Luther Peck experienced morbid dreams and dreaded that his own death was imminent. "Such was his mental distress that he wasted away under it, and his kind neighbors were alarmed lest he should lose his reason or die." Peck found relief through an evangelical rebirth as a devout Methodist. Abigail Beach of Unadilla was not so fortunate. Returning home after her father's death by drowning, young Deborah Beach found her mother Abigail afflicted by paralyzing grief. "She only gazed with a sort of vacant stare, not seeming to know me" because "a settled melancholy had seized her for its victim." Abigail Beach never fully recovered. On a Sunday in 1804, Uriah Luce of Cooperstown entered his barn to find twelve-year-old Timothy Johnson "hanging by a rope fastened to the great beam." The coroners ruled his death a suicide. "It is remarkable," Elihu Phinney noted, "that his father was killed suddenly about four years ago, by the falling of a limb of a tree, which fractured his skull, and that his mother died very suddenly soon after and that a sister a few years since fell into a well and was drowned."[18]

ENDURANCE

Given these often grim conditions, why did settler families venture into the forest to make farms? They persisted through hardships and dangers because they anticipated that their labor would ultimately prevail in the creation of a new nature that would provide a secure prosperity. Settlers were, in the words of one frontier missionary, "all under the influence of a hope of better times," if they could but endure the early hardships to make substantial farms. Through persistence, settlers meant to amass the property that endowed independence, with all its promises of material comfort, social respectability, and political rights. They also found encouragement in the precedent of their parents and grandparents, who had persevered through similar travails in order to build successful farms on an earlier frontier.[19]

The Otsego settlers also found inspiration in their Protestant Christian faith, which taught that conquering the forest and its wild animals was service to God. In 1797, Otsego schoolboy Robert Campbell wrote in his notebook that "If we take tradition or revelation for our guide the matter is plain that God made man lord of the works of his hands and put under him all the other creatures." . . . By transforming the forest into a landscape of farms, stores, roads, bridges, and churches, the settlers believed that they secured their eternal, as well as their temporal, interests.[20]

In addition to their hopes of future prosperity and salvation, settlers endured frontier hardships and dangers because some of their stories celebrated extraordinary exertions against the wild. Although some frontier stories promoted dread, and even a morbid resignation, others exhorted action by heroicizing the people (usually men, sometimes boys, occasionally women) who dared the most to confront and transform their dangerous world. The stories especially honored those who destroyed wolves, panthers, and bears. Men took great pride in these victories because the wild predators were difficult and dangerous foes adept at eluding pursuit and capable of crippling or killing their tormentors. Settlers eagerly told and heard fireside tales about those who outwitted and outfought especially wily, large, and deadly beasts. Accounts of battles with wild carnivores were second only to tales of heroism in fighting Indians. Settlers defined themselves as civilized by hating and killing all other carnivorous beings — human and nonhuman alike — who preyed upon the herbivores of the North American forest.[21] . . .

DEVASTATION

Encouraged by their expectations, faith, and stories — and empowered by their swelling numbers and sustained labor — settlers eventually gained the upper hand over the forest and its beasts. They then assailed the wild plant and animal life with a vengeance born, in part, from the memory of recent sufferings. The English traveler Isaac Weld marveled that Americans hated trees and "cut away all before them without mercy; not one is spared; all share . . . in the general havoc." . . . Settlers loved to tell, and travelers to record, an anecdote about the American who ventured to the notoriously barren coast of Ireland and broke out in exultation at the beauty of a land utterly without trees.

Coming from a continent where forests had become preciously rare, European visitors were horrified by the massive destruction of the trees in New York. . . . In 1794, English visitor William Strickland . . . characterized New York's settlers as "the most destructive race that ever disfigured and destroyed a beautiful and luxuriant country." The deforestation was so rapid and thorough that by 1800 leading New Yorkers worried about a looming fuel crisis in the Hudson River valley and began to call, in vain, for conservation measures.[22]

As they filled the land and felled the forest, the settlers also destroyed the larger mammals — beavers, deer, bears, panthers, and wolves. Most hunting was carried out by individuals or by pairs of men, but sometimes settlers in a neighborhood united in a group hunt. Hunting parties manifested the medley of the competitive and the communal, the laborious and the festive, that characterized rural culture. Hunters simultaneously worked together to drive game into a narrowing circle and competed with one another (or with a rival team) to kill the greatest number of animals. At a predetermined day and time, the men gathered, elected captains, strung themselves apart in a semicircle, then advanced to close the circle, trapping and killing the animals within. After counting up the dead and recognizing the victors, the hunters ended the day with festive eating and drinking. Such hunts protected crops and asserted humanity's supremacy over other life, sustained bonds between neighbors, established a local pecking order of male prowess, celebrated republican principles, and reaffirmed a male monopoly over weapons and public gatherings.[23]

Wolves and bears were the principal targets of group hunts held during the first years of a new settlement. But as the settlers wiped out the major predators who afflicted their livestock, they unwittingly exposed their grain crops to increased attacks from squirrels and chipmunks. Wild rodents proliferated as they were liberated from the predation of foxes, wolves, panthers, and bears, and as they found an increased food supply in the fields of grain that expanded at the forest's expense. . . .

The population of large wild mammals rapidly declined under the gunfire of the growing number of settlers, as well as from the transformed habitat wrought by deforestation. In 1850, an old hunter in upstate New York calculated that in his lifetime he had killed 77 panthers, 214 wolves, 219 bears, and 2,550 deer. Many hunters ignored with impunity the rarely enforced state law against killing deer in winter. James Macauley lamented that "In the winter the hunters in the new countries often avail themselves of crusts, when these animals break through, and are unable to fly, and destroy whole flocks. The destruction on these occasions, is wanton, since neither their meat nor skins are [then] worth much." . . . William Cooper estimated that settlers could count on harvesting deer only during the first ten years of a settlement. In 1791, just five years after his settlement began, Cooper boasted that wolves had already retreated from the vicinity of Cooperstown: "those Swamps that four years ago was a safe retreat for those devouring animals are now become plentiful Pastures." In 1790, his store in Cooperstown received 140 animal pelts (38 deer, 33 muskrat, 24 beaver, 15 marten, 10 bear, 10 raccoon, 3 otter, 2 fisher, 2 mink, 2 wolf, and 1 panther) worth £85.17.9. One year later, the store obtained only 14 pelts (9 deer, 3 bear, and 1 marten) worth a mere £9.9.4 — measures of the rapid decline of fur-bearing animals. By 1810, major mammals had virtually disappeared from Otsego County, save for a few in the mountains on the southern fringe.[24]

Edible fish also began to dwindle under the pressure of a growing settler population and the accompanying changes in the land and rivers. As James Fenimore Cooper noted in *The Pioneers,* overharvesting took a toll on the celebrated bass of Otsego Lake. . . . Mill dams built in the Susquehanna River obstructed the ascent of shad and herring from Chesapeake Bay to Lakes Otsego and Canadarago. In turn, the loss of this food supply undercut the trout and bass, already under relentless pressure from fishermen. The discharge of sawdust from mills and acids from tanneries into the streams and lakes reduced the oxygen in the waters, afflicting the fish. Deforestation along the streams exposed their waters to direct sunlight and to an increased burden of eroded soil, raising water temperatures and diminished clarity, all to the detriment of cold-water fishes. Because the forest canopy and roots combined to retain moisture in the soil, the local streams

had enjoyed a relatively constant flow through the year; deforestation meant greater springtime surges and a diminished flow in the summer drought, extremes that stressed the traditional fishes. The one species that adapted well to the changes, the pickerel, aggressively expanded at the expense of the more docile and fleshier fishes preferred by humans.[25]

Settlers' treatment of wild animals and plants derived from their anticipation of a future landscape deforested, depleted of wildlife, and dedicated to agriculture. Rather than seek an equilibrium with wild animal and plant populations, most settlers killed as much and as often as they could in order to claim the largest possible share in a bounty that they regarded as inevitably short-lived. Emigrating from districts already deforested and depleted of wildlife, the settlers considered the wilderness as a temporary place and condition where an unconquered nature imposed special hardships and compensated with unusual windfalls. By exploiting nature's bounty, settlers meant to transform the conditions that entailed their hardships. Destroying the forest and its denizens brought immediate excitement and sustenance while advancing development of the agricultural landscape necessary for long-term prosperity. Drawing upon the precedent of previous settlements, the Otsego settlers told themselves stories of a transformed land virtually stripped of wild animals. Acting upon those narratives, settlers effected their expectations by relentless hunting and fishing and by clearing away the forest habitat. Virtually no one envisioned a restraint that would preserve some of the wild plants and animals, because none of their forebears in previous settlements had restrained themselves.

William Cronon argues that narration is not simply the long-after-the-fact imposition of historians on a receding past. Narratives were woven into the fabric of settlers' lives. Stories shaped their self-image, framed their expectations, and motivated their actions. In turn, their own experiences revised and added to the stock of narratives passed on to their children. By telling tales of their endurance and heroism in the face of a cruel nature, Otsego's settlers ensured that their children would perpetuate, on new frontiers farther west, their way of life as relentless transformers of a forested land.[26]

EPILOGUE

Success in environmental transformation eventually altered the perception of nature by later generations who lived in Otsego County. By the mid-nineteenth century, they enjoyed more security and comfort because there was so little left that their predecessors had called wild. Some could even begin to regret that their ancestors had so thoroughly cleared the forest, exterminating locally the larger mammals and tastier fish. While they lamented the loss of those animals that seemed attractive and useful, like deer or Otsego bass, no one yet openly mourned for destroyed wolves and panthers.

In the late 1840s, Susan Fenimore Cooper, daughter of the novelist, told the revealing story of the last deer then surviving in the vicinity of Cooperstown. Kept in the village as the pet of a local woman (probably Susan's mother), this deer "became a great favorite, following the different members of the family about, caressed by the neighbors, and welcome everywhere." One morning the fawn was sunning itself upon the steps of a store when a stranger and his hound strode into the village. Spooked, the fawn bolted, with the hound and some village dogs in pursuit. The men of Cooperstown ran after their dogs, hoping to save the fawn. Alas, the deer swam across part of the nearby lake and plunged into a wood where a stray rabbit hunter — not privy to the animal's history and ownership — was so surprised to see a fawn that he reflexively shot it dead. Discovering a collar bearing the owner's name, the hunter hastened into the village to return the item to the grieving family. In honor of the dead deer, the villagers renamed the bay it had swum across as "Fawn Bay" and the site of its death as "Fawn Spring."[27]

The scramble to save the deer, and the mourning and memorialization that its death evoked, reveals how thoroughly the times and nature had changed in Otsego by the 1840s. In contrast to their settler grandfathers, who had competed to kill the largest number of deer, the villagers of the 1840s raced to rescue the last, local survivor of the species. As private property, the fawn had enjoyed protection from the guns and dogs of the other villagers. As a rarity, the fawn had attracted sentimental affection and nostalgic curiosity from the local people. They cherished the fawn as a symbol of the wild that had become newly precious because their grandparents had rendered it so scarce. Indeed, they anthropomorphized the fawn into a sort of neighbor and mourned when it died. Unwilling to let the deer go, they memorialized the fawn's last moments in place names. As the settlers' ordeal faded in time and memory, their heirs began to regret the conquest of the wild that had left them such a tamed landscape.

NOTES

1. James Fenimore Cooper, *The Pioneers, or The Sources of the Susquehanna* (crit. ed. of New York, 1823; reprint, Albany: State University of New York Press, 1980), 244–52, 259–66.

2. For the majority view on the early American republic, see Roderick Nash, *Wilderness and the American Mind* (New Haven: Yale University Press, 1982), 38–43; William Cronon, *Changes in the Land: Indians, Colonists, and the Ecology of New England* (New York: Hill & Wang, 1983), 159–70. For an attempt to redeem environmental rhetoric and history from elitism, see William Cronon, ed., *Uncommon Ground: Rethinking the Human Place in Nature* (New York: W. W. Norton & Co., 1996), especially the essays by Cronon and Richard White.

3. Leading examples of such environmental narratives include Cronon, *Changes in the Land;* Donald Worster, *Dust Bowl: The Southern Plains in the 1930s* (New York: Oxford University Press, 1979); Donald Worster, *Rivers of Empire: Water, Aridity, and the Growth of the American West* (New York: Pantheon, 1985); Timothy Silver, *A New Face on the Countryside: Indians, Colonists, and Slaves in South Atlantic Forests, 1500–1800* (New York: Cambridge University Press, 1990). For an analysis of narration in environmental history, see William Cronon, "A Place for Stories: Nature, History, and Narrative," *Journal of American History* 78 (1992): 1347–79. For an attempt to break the narrative orthodoxy, see Richard White, *The Organic Machine* (New York: Hill & Wang, 1995).

4. During the early twentieth century, environmental historians tended to dwell on the initial

weakness and difficulties of settlers, rather than on their power. Leading examples of this older perspective include Walter Prescott Webb, *The Great Plains* (Boston: Ginn, 1931); James C. Malin, *The Grassland of North America: Prolegomena to Its History* (Lawrence, Kans.: n.p., 1956). By focusing on the settlers' hardships in framing their behavior, I do not mean to deny the importance of larger ideological and structural considerations (for example, the settlers' Judeo-Christian and capitalist commitments to mastering and commodifying nature).

5. Anthony F. C. Wallace, *The Death and Rebirth of the Seneca* (New York: Alfred A. Knopf, 1970), 196; William Wyckoff, *The Developer's Frontier: The Making of the Western New York Landscape* (New Haven: Yale University Press, 1988), 104–5; Stuart Bruchey and Jim Potter, "Social and Economic Developments After the Revolution," in *The Blackwell Encyclopedia of the American Revolution,* ed. Jack P. Greene and J. R. Pole (Cambridge: Basil Blackwell, 1991), 566; David Paul Davenport, "The Yankee Settlement of New York, 1783–1820," *Genealogical Journal* 17 (1988–1989): 63–88; David Maldwyn Ellis, "The Rise of the Empire State, 1790–1820," *New York History* 56 (1975): 5–6; James Macauley, *The Natural, Statistical, and Civil History of the State of New York,* vol. 1 (New York: William Gould & Co., 1829), 417–18; Franklin B. Hough, ed., *The New York Civil List From 1777 to 1860* (Albany: Weed, Parsons, & Co., 1860), 2.

6. Susan Fenimore Cooper, *Rural Hours, By a Lady* (New York: Putnam, 1850), 190–91; Wallace, *Death and Rebirth of the Seneca,* 24; Carolyn Merchant, *Ecological Revolutions: Nature, Gender, and Science in New England* (Chapel Hill: University of North Carolina Press, 1989), 87.

7. William Cooper, *A Guide in the Wilderness; Or, the History of the First Settlements in the Western Counties of New York, with Useful Instructions to Future Settlers* (Dublin, 1810; reprint, Cooperstown: New York State Historical Association, 1986), 50; Nash, *Wilderness and the American Mind,* 23–41; Merchant,

Ecological Revolutions, 101–2; Lester H. Cohen, "Eden's Constitution: The Paradisiacal Dream and Enlightenment Values in Late Eighteenth-Century Literature of the American Frontier," *Prospects: An Annual of American Cultural Studies* 3 (1977): 83–109. For greater emphasis on the few promoters prone to Edenic description, see Henry Nash Smith, *Virgin Land: The American West as Symbol and Myth* (Cambridge: Harvard University Press, 1950), 146–50.

8. Isaac Lyman (who had moved to central New York), quoted in Chilton Williamson Jr., *Vermont in Quandary: 1763–1825* (Montpelier, Vt.: n.p., 1949), 256.

9. For testimony on the prevalence of poverty among upstate New York's early settlers, see Timothy Dwight, *Travels in New England and New York,* ed. Barbara Miller Solomon, vol. 2 (New Haven, Conn., 1821; reprint, Cambridge: Harvard University Press, 1969), 321; Levi Beardsley, *Reminiscences: Personal and Other Incidents; Early Settlement of Otsego County* (New York: Charles Vinten, 1852), 25; Helen L. Fairchild, ed., *Francis Adrian Van Der Kemp, 1752–1829: An Autobiography* (New York: G. P. Putnam & Sons, 1903), 86: David M. Ellis, *Landlords and Farmers in the Hudson-Mohawk Region, 1790–1850* (Ithaca: Cornell University Press, 1946), 67–68; William Cooper, *Guide in the Wilderness,* 17; Griffith Evans, "Journal of Griffith Evans, 1784–1785," *Pennsylvania Magazine of History and Biography* 65 (1941): 216.

10. "Tax List of Hosack District, Pursuant to the Tax Law of the 11th April 1787," Gilbert Lansing Papers, New York State Library, Albany; U.S. Bureau of the Census, *Heads of Families at the First Census of the United States Taken in the Year 1790, New York* (Washington, D.C., 1908; reprint, Baltimore: Genealogical Publishing Co., 1966), 30–31, 112–13; William Cooper, *Guide in the Wilderness,* 14. In 1790, Otsego township included all the lands west of Lake Otsego and the Susquehanna as far as the Unadilla (most of what would become Otsego County a year later). Apparently, the presence or absence of

kin within Hoosick also played a role in the decision to stay or go. Almost half of the Otsego migrants (10 of 21) were the only adults with their surname on the town's tax list. By contrast, almost three-fifths of the persisters bore the same surname as someone else in town. In addition to the 21 migrants and the 241 holdovers, the remaining 98 had either died or moved somewhere other than Otsego.

11. Henry Clarke Wright, *Human Life Illustrated in My Individual Experience as a Child, a Youth, and a Man* (Boston: Bela Marsh, 1849), 26; Priest, *Stories of Early Settlers,* 4, 16, 35, 38.

12. Willard V. Huntington, "Old Time Notes," New York State Historical Association, Cooperstown, N.Y. (hereafter NYSHA), 707; Priest, *Stories of the Early Settlers,* 36; Benjamin Gilbert to Daniel Gilbert, 18 July 1786, in *A Citizen-Soldier in the American Revolution: The Diary of Benjamin Gilbert in Massachusetts and New York,* ed. Rebecca D. Symmes (Cooperstown: NYSHA, 1980), 81; Benjamin Gilbert, "Diary," 12 May 1786, 18 May 1786, NYSHA. On the wheat blast, see also E. L. Jones, "Creative Disruptions in American Agriculture, 1620–1820," *Agricultural History* 48 (1974): 520–21.

13. Priest, *Stories of Early Settlers,* 20, 22–23, 35; Huntington, "Old Time Notes," 1064; J. F. Cooper, *The Pioneers,* 251–66, 274; Edmund E. Lynch, "Fishing on Otsego Lake" (master's thesis, State University of New York at Oneonta, 1965), 20; De Witt Clinton, *Account of the Salmo Otsego, Or the Otsego Basse, In a Letter to John W. Francis, M.D.* (New York: C. S. Van Winkle, 1822), 3–4.

14. William Cooper, *Guide in the Wilderness,* 16; *Otsego Herald,* 12 May 1796; 20 July 1815.

15. William Cooper to Henry Drinker, 11 February 1790, Correspondence Box 1741–1792, Henry Drinker Papers, Historical Society of Pennsylvania, Philadelphia; *Otsego Herald,* 17 April 1797; 4 May 1797.

16. Lorain, "Observations on the Comparative Value of Soils," 106–7; Priest, *Stories of Early Settlers,* 38; J. F. Cooper, *Pioneers,* 407–15,

425; Susan Fenimore Cooper, "Small Family Memories," in *Correspondence of James Fenimore Cooper,* ed. James Fenimore Cooper, vol. 1 (New Haven: Yale University Press, 1922), 18.

17. *Otsego Herald,* 10 April 1800; Peck, *Life and Times of Rev. George Peck,* 35; Wright, *Human Life,* 44.

18. Deborah Beach, quoted in Priest, *Stories of Early Settlers,* 27; Peck, *Life and Times of Rev. George Peck,* 24, 26; *Otsego Herald,* 27 September 1804.

19. Reverend John Taylor, quoted in Ellis, *Landlords and Farmers,* 17; William Strickland, *Journal of a Tour in the United States of America, 1794–1795* (New York: New York Historical Society, 1971), 96; Michel-Guillaume St. Jean de Crevecoeur, *Journey Into Northern Pennsylvania and the State of New York,* ed. Clarissa Spencer Bostelmann (Ann Arbor: University of Michigan Press, 1964), 486.

20. Robert Campbell, "School Notes," 1797–1799, Box 1, Robert Campbell Papers, NYSHA; Beardsley, *Reminiscences,* 42–45.

21. Beardsley, *Reminiscences,* 46–47; Wright, *Human Life,* 41–42.

22. Budka, "Journey to Niagara, 1805," 91; Strickland, *Journal of a Tour,* 138, 146, 170; Simon Desjardins, "Castorland Journal," trans. Franklin B. Hough, New York State Library, 46; Samuel L. Mitchell, "Address," Society for the Promotion of Agriculture, Arts, and Manufactures, Instituted in the State of New York, *Transactions,* vol. 1 (Albany, 1801) 213.

23. "Wolf Hunt!" *Otsego Herald,* 22 November 1798; Beardsley, *Reminiscences,* 45–47.

24. Jeptha R. Simms, *Trappers of New York, or a Biography of Nicholas Stoner & Nathaniel Foster* (Albany, N.Y.: J. Munsell, 1850), 255; Macauley, *The Natural . . . History of the State of New York,* vol. 1, 449; Strickland, *Journal of a Tour,* 147; William Cooper, *Guide in the Wilderness,* 44; William Cooper to Henry Drinker, 3 November 1791, Correspondence Box 1741–1792, Henry Drinker Papers, Historical Society of Pennsylvania, Philadelphia; William Cooper and Richard R. Smith,

"Storebooks," I and II, 1790–1792, William Cooper Papers, Hartwick College Archives, Oneonta, N.Y.; James Fenimore Cooper, *Notions of the Americans, Picked Up by a Travelling Bachelor,* vol. 1 (Philadelphia, 1828; reprint, New York: Frederick Ungar, 1963), 241.

25. Priest, *Stories of Early Settlers,* 23; Macauley, *The Natural . . . History of the State of New York,* vol. 1, 109; Clinton, *Account of the Salmo Otsego,* 4–5; Shaw T. Livermore, *A Condensed History of Cooperstown* (Albany, N.Y.: J. Munsell, 1862), 125; David Starr Jordan and Barton Warren Evermann, *The Fishes of North and Middle America* (Washington, D.C.: GPO, 1896), 465; Elihu Phinney, "Fish and Fishing in Otsego Lake," in *A Centennial Offering, Being a Brief History of Cooperstown,* ed. S. M. Shaw (Cooperstown, N.Y.: Freeman's Journal Press, 1886), 185; Jay Bloomfield, ed., *Lakes of New York State,* vol. 3 (New York: Academic Press, 1978–1980), 119–23; New York (State) Conservation Department, *A Biological Survey of the Delaware and Susquehanna Watersheds: Supplemental to the Twenty-Fifth Annual Report, 1935* (Albany: State of New York, 1936), 49–53, 113–18.

26. Cronon, "A Place for Stories," 1349–79; David Carr, "Narrative and the Real World: An Argument for Continuity," *History and Theory* 25 (1986): 117.

27. Susan Fenimore Cooper, *Rural Hours,* 240–44.

DISCUSSION TOPICS

1. How does Taylor's accounting of past history affect your view of settler responsibility for the damage to the North American environment? Give some examples.

2. Compare the notion of *wilderness* in the days of these settlers and in contemporary society. In light of both perspectives, does your personal view of *wilderness* change? If so, how? If not, why not? Give your reasoning.

3. Would you consider being a settler in light of this selection? Explain your perspective.

READING 21

Nature in Industrial Society

Neil Evernden

Lorne Leslie Neil Evernden is on the faculty of environmental studies, Department of Environmental Science, York University, Downsview, Ontario, Canada. He also has written The Natural Alien *(1985), a critique of the philosophies in the environmental movement.*

In a chapter from the book Cultural Politics in Contemporary America, *Evernden analyzes three definitions of nature. The perception of "nature-as-object" results in exploitation of nature. The view of "nature-as-self" implies the extension of a separate selfhood to nature; this view allows thinking about environmental ethics and rights of nature. The perception of "nature-as-miracle" emphasizes its uncanny and unpredictable characteristics. In contrast to traditional scientific conceptions of nature, Evernden proposes that the nature-as-miracle definition allows an understanding compatible with human experience.*

Nature, to all appearances, remains remarkably "popular" in America. It is part of everyone's vocabulary, something we all have knowledge of and opinions about, and something many are moved to defend. Nature is very much a part of "popular culture." But *which* nature?

The question seems nonsensical, of course. There is nature, and there is culture, separate and distinct from each other. But while we acknowledge that we do not all dwell in the same culture or subculture, it is seldom acknowledged that we might not all share the same nature or "subnature." So firmly embedded is the notion of nature as a unitary entity, entirely separate from or even antithetical to, culture, that it is very difficult to entertain the notion of there being more than one understanding of nature. (Arthur Lovejoy once listed 66 uses of the word "nature" in politics, ethics, and metaphysics, and another 20 as used in aesthetics.)[1] In colloquial usage, nature is often simply "the world as given," the force that determines the way things are as well as the clutter of objects that we see interspersed between the "developments" of civilization. In the latter sense, it is nearly synonymous with "environment," or at least with "natural environment," and the "environmental movement" is widely understood as a defense of nature. However, in recent years the very prominence of that movement has been the cause of some reflection on just what this "nature" is that is being defended. As a result, it is becoming increasingly clear that people do not always have the same thing in mind when they speak of nature. This might be most easily illustrated by reviewing one of the success stories of the environmental movement.

[The year] 1987 marks the anniversary of one of the most remarkable incidents in the history of nature preservation in America, and indeed the world. In 1962, a biologist named Rachel Carson made a brave and inspired decision to try a different means of defending nature. The result was a book called *Silent Spring,* which evoked a reaction that has never entirely subsided. To the surprise of many, the resulting "environmental movement" has endured remarkably well, and most people still rank environmental issues above all others in importance. Yet it is doubtful whether, twenty-five years ago, they would have been concerned at all. Rachel Carson changed all that when she challenged our collective right to manipulate nature at will. "Control of nature," she said, "is a phrase conceived in arrogance, born in the Neanderthal age of biology and philosophy, when it was supposed that nature exists for the convenience of man."[2] But isn't "control of nature" what our civilization is principally concerned with? Did Carson genuinely challenge that assumption? Or did she merely wish to?

Although Rachel Carson had spent her life in the defense of nature, she concentrated in *Silent Spring* on one problem only: the widespread and indiscriminate use of pesticides. Her challenge drew the inevitable response from those whose oxen were being gored, and she suffered considerably as a result. Her own integrity was impugned, her publisher was threatened with loss of textbook sales, and the popular media attempted to dismiss her out of hand. A sympathetic but patronizing review in *Time* magazine concluded that while many scientists might sympathize with her intentions, they "fear that her emotional and inaccurate outburst in *Silent Spring* may do harm by alarming the nontechnical public," who should be reassured that while some pesticides may be dangerous, many "are roughly as harmless as DDT"[3] (which is, of course, now banned in most industrial countries). The *Time* review now seems dated; Carson's book does not. People reading it for the first time today are struck by the fact that all that seems to have changed are the names of the poisons. Despite Carson's apparent effectiveness as an advocate, the problem she addresses remains a serious one. Was she actually successful, or did the attempt fail? Or did she, perhaps, accomplish something other than what she intended?

The American debate over the best uses of nature has been unique, and the tradition Rachel Carson represents, following the likes of Henry David Thoreau and John Muir, is a noble one. But because the defense mounted was usually very personal, the audience tended to be made up of those who shared, in some measure, the valued experience of nature that motivated these famous advocates. In other words, they spoke to a constituency of nature-lovers, and however many prestigious names might figure among them, it was still a minority interest. In contrast, everyone had a stake in the economic development of the nation, and everyone was therefore a partner in the quest for control of nature. It was Carson's acceptance of this simple, arithmetic fact—that there were more of "them" than of "us"—that led, however indirectly, to the revolution that was *Silent Spring.* Its success led to widespread concern, and from "Earth Day" in 1970 the environmental movement became a force to be reckoned with.

But Carson's book was revolutionary not because it challenged the indiscriminate use of pesticides. Others had sounded the warning long before she did, and it was common knowledge in "wildlife" circles that many species were being harmed by this practice. Carson's originality lay in the manner in which she chose to speak and the audience she chose to address. She did not try to appeal to nature-lovers alone: she addressed the entire adult population. She did not speak to the protection of particular organisms that most people had no experience of or concern for, but instead created an entirely new protagonist. Rachel Carson made "environment" the endangered entity, rather than a wildlife species.[4]

And since humans are similarly dependent on environment, on "ecosystems," she immediately got our collective attention. The endangered species of concern was not the peregrine falcon or the whooping crane: it was us.

This may seem no more than a tactical improvement on her part: by showing each of us "what's in it for me," she made environmental protection a cause with extremely wide support. The introduction of such legislation as the National Environmental Policy Act of 1969 indicates just how widely accepted it has become. But strangely enough, in order to bring about this widespread popularity Carson had effectively to redefine what she meant by "nature." She had to describe a nature that mattered to "the man in the street." *She had to make nature popular.*

Of course, to make something popular is to make it universally understandable and appealing. Accomplishing this usually entails using language that is already in circulation: to be understandable one must say what is already understood. In Carson's case, this meant abandoning the older rhetoric which presumed a kind of valuing of nature that was not widespread, and replacing it with a valuing that was. Rather than rely on the nature-lover's assumption of a personal nature that is intrinsically valuable and must be defended for its own sake, she asserted, albeit only implicitly, that *human beings* are intrinsically valuable and must be defended at all costs— even if that means restraining development so that we can continue to have clean air and water. The nature she defended, then, was the nature that provides a stockpile of essential objects for humans to utilize. Of course, by linking these to the somewhat mysterious concept of an ecosystem, in which all players are assumed to have an essential role, she was also to extract some measure of protection for her beloved wildlife at the same time: people were afraid to exterminate toads for fear the ecosystem might collapse. But despite whatever short-term protection this might have provided, the effect has been the reinforcing of a particular understanding of nature.

NATURE AS OBJECT

Nature—that is, nature-as-object—was now perceived to be vulnerable in a way few had imagined before. It was still perceived to be a collection of objects, but now it was a collection of *important* objects. The general understanding of nature was not challenged in any significant way. For that reason, the consequences of the environmental movement have been less dramatic than one might have predicted of such a broadly supported venture. To understand why this might be so, we have to bear in mind something about the understanding we all have of nature. It might help, as a first step, to imagine what would have happened if Rachel Carson had chosen to speak as a nature-lover, rather than as a resource conservationist.

One of the common means of dismissing a writer like Carson was to accuse her of being "emotional" (as the *Time* reviewer did), or of being "anthropomorphic": of acting as if animals or nature in general had human characteristics and could feel the harm done to them. In the view of many, even to suggest that there are human characteristics (feelings, intelligence, awareness) in other organisms is to be a victim of the "Bambi syndrome," and to be afflicted with emotional delusions about useful natural resources. Since this kind of criticism enjoys the reputation of being hard-nosed and "objective," it is dangerous for an author to expose herself to it. The consequence was that Carson and others like her were totally vulnerable whenever they allowed their feeling for nature to show through. The notion of a world containing "persons" of other species, or even of nature as a kind of extended self, was simply unacceptable. To encourage nature preservation, she had to speak instead of the nature that most of society understands: a small price to pay for credibility, one might think.

This much is quite understandable. But why is it that a person is so vulnerable to criticism when she implies that nature is in any way sensate, anything more than a collection of objects? The history of the understanding of nature would very nearly amount to a history of human society, since every social group has had a conception of nature which it uses in maintaining its own internal stability. Mary Douglas, the eminent anthropologist, once suggested that every "environment," that is, every understanding of the non-human world around us, is "a mask and support for a certain kind of society." Were we able to describe each of these conceptions, we would have a kind of cultural fingerprint with which to identify any society that has ever existed. Like us, they had a notion of the necessity of nature and of their vulnerability if it is damaged or "polluted." The pollution they encountered was not always of the "contamination of drinking water" variety, but of course the dictionary definition of pollution is somewhat wider than our colloquial usage: the destruction of the purity or sanctity of something. Anything that threatens the purity of the world around us, physically or conceptually, is an instance of pollution. And since polluters put the whole of society at risk, they must be made to mend their ways. The understanding of the vulnerability of nature is, therefore, also a means of social control, since it enables the group to argue against a particular action by one of its members. The consequence is that both the physical environment and the social beliefs of the group are maintained intact.

Given our understanding of nature as a collection of physical properties or objects, it is easy for us to understand the dangers of contaminating these. We have more trouble understanding some other kinds of pollution: the eating of "summer food" (caribou) in winter, for instance, which cost an Eskimo girl her life, or the participation of women in "male" ceremonies. Yet these can also threaten the purity of the social conception of nature, because as Mary Douglas argues,

> The deepest emotional investment of all is in the assumption that there is a rule-obeying universe, and that its rules are objective, independent of social validation. Hence the most odious pollutions are those which threaten to attack a system at its intellectual base.[5]

And we too have trouble with this kind of contamination, whether we recognize it or not. In fact, it may have been fear of just such contamination that made it impossible for Rachel Carson to talk about her own understanding of nature, which we might call "nature-as-self."

THE CONCEPTUAL POLLUTION OF NATURE

My suggestion that there was some conflict between Rachel Carson's personal understanding of nature

and the one she espoused publicly in *Silent Spring* is, of course, conjecture. But we can say with confidence that she exemplifies the plight of a great many people who have been faced with this dilemma, and she certainly serves as a useful illustration of the way cultural premises dictate the very mode of communication an individual must select if he or she wishes to be taken seriously. It is a very subtle form of censorship which all societies practice, although perhaps not so massively and effectively as is the case in western industrialized countries. Thanks to modern mass communications, all of us are given daily instruction in the acceptable range of belief and expression. If we wish to share our ideas, we must make our message adhere to the required format and presuppositions. Even if this was less dramatically true in Carson's day, it may well have been the circumstance that provoked her to the kind of discourse she finally chose in *Silent Spring* and that denied her the ability to state the message that she, as a nature-lover of long standing, would have wished to deliver.

I suggested earlier that one of the things that forced her decision was the fact that she would have been thought foolish had she been overtly emotional or anthropomorphic in putting her case. If someone claims to perceive feelings in nature, it is generally assumed to be because that person is "projecting" some of his or her inner feelings into nature. But it is too mild a statement to say that this is regarded as erroneous. At a deeper level, it is also sensed to be a dangerous act of pollution. Just how this could be so might be more apparent if we briefly consider the notion of "projection" before returning to our main issue, the kind of "nature" that exists in popular culture today.

J. H. van den Berg spoke of the phenomenon of projection in his classic book *The Changing Nature of Man.* Van den Berg is a Dutch psychiatrist who initiated a study of "historical psychology" to discover how humans and their understanding of reality have changed over time. One of the beliefs that is widely held today is that of projection, even though no one has ever successfully explained just how this phenomenon might work. It is essentially an explanatory mechanism to account for the fact that some people see something in the world that the rest of us do not believe to be there. Van den

Berg illustrates this with a number of examples from his psychiatric practice. When the patient claims to see a world that is different from our own, we assure him that it is "all in his head," that it is "not real" but merely "projected." And if the patient denies being aware of any such projecting activity, as he almost surely will, then we explain that he is doing it "subconsciously." We cannot, of course, prove a word of what we say. It is simply a means of explaining a discrepancy in worldview which is discomforting to both the patient and ourselves, and of dismissing the patient's version of reality. We could instead accept what the patient says at face value, and conclude that he is gifted with a different insight, that he can see aspects of the world that the rest of us cannot. Some societies have been quite willing to do so, and even to admire the ability of the "insane" to reveal these other faces of nature. But we do not. And, according to van den Berg, we dare not.

> . . . it is quite clear that the patient cannot be permitted a brick — or a street, house, city, train *or nature* — of his own. He must be projecting; *what he sees are his own personal impurities* . . . We smile reassuringly and say, "You are projecting, what you are seeing is within yourself." (emphasis added)[6]

The patient has contaminated the world with the impurities of his inner self — he has *polluted.* That is, he has threatened the sanctity of the world and, in doing so, has threatened us all in some degree. The same is true of the nature-lover for whom nature is what we are calling "nature-as-self" rather than the conventional "nature-as-object": he or she contaminates reality by finding the qualities of persons in the world of nature. Since our agreement is that only physical objects can be said to populate nature, then the assertion of personal qualities is a breach of the accord, and must be a consequence of illegal "projection" on the part of the polluter. But so what? Even if we find this silly, what harm does it do? Why must we ridicule such a person and conjure up the stereotype of the "little old lady in tennis shoes," implying mental incompetence, in order to dismiss the perception out of hand? Van den Berg's answer would be that we can't collectively *afford* to have society members constituting their own personal understandings of nature. With the rise of humanism and the notion that the individual human is the only authority and the only source of value and meaning, the belief of each individual is potentially critical. If each of us is an authority, then it is crucial that we *agree* on what is. And the basis of our agreement, our lowest common denominator of perception, is nature-as-object, a bare-bones nature with no subjectivity and no personal variables at all: just stuff. According to van den Berg, we need agreement on nature-as-object because that is virtually the only thing we can agree on, and therefore the only piece of "certainty" we can cling to for social cohesion.

These specifications for nature have been with us a long time now. Hans Jonas has argued that the rejection of projection, and specifically of anthropomorphism, has been a condition of the modern scientific worldview from its inception: a condition, not a conclusion. It was dismissed by Francis Bacon, without any real attempt to justify the exclusion. Jonas comments that Bacon and his successors succeeded

> in putting a severe ban on any transference of features of internal experience into the interpretation of the external world. . . . Anthropomorphism at all events, and even zoomorphism in general, became scientific high treason. It is in this dualistic setting that we meet the "nature of man" as a source of defilement for "philosophy" (natural science), and the objection to "final" explanation is that it is anthropomorphic.[7]

Again, we find the charge that it is a "defilement" — a pollution — to find any human properties in nature. Is it any wonder, then, that authors like Rachel Carson had to take great pains to make nature-as-object the center of their discourse? To do otherwise would be to risk instant dismissal, except among the small sector of society that shares an understanding of the world as nature-as-self.

NATURE AS SELF

However, the consequences of that decision are difficult to assess. To some, it would appear that Carson's decision was an inspired one, and that the popularity that environmental issues have enjoyed was a consequence of that choice. However, one has to question whether anything more than popularity was gained by this subterfuge. Has the natural environment enjoyed a significantly greater degree of protection as a result? We cannot "re-run the experiment," so to speak, and so can never know for sure. But the very fact that Carson's book still seems so relevant raises serious doubts. Nature is still at risk, still being polluted, still being encroached upon, still being driven to extinction piece by piece, species by species. It may be, some now feel, that more was lost than was gained in the rise to prominence, because the price paid for public attention was the ability to speak of what matters. We cannot know whether Carson would agree with this assessment, but some of her successors have certainly found this to be the case. So many, in fact, that alternate schools of environmentalism have arisen to attempt to repair the damage.

With the realization that the translation to technocratic respectability has enucleated the subject of concern, there have been a variety of attempts to speak in defense of nature without resorting to the language of nature-as-object. One such attempt which has enjoyed a certain vogue is known as "deep ecology," referring to the attempt to attend to the root assumptions that lead to environmental destruction rather than simply to the technical symptoms of that malaise.[8] Proponents of this approach differ from each other in some respects, but they tend to concur in their notion of nature as "extended self." That is, they resist the idea of an individual being entirely restricted to what R. D. Laing calls a "skin-encapsulated ego" and suggest instead that people have a field of concern which they experience as self. Consequently, the nature they perceive is, in some measure, a portion of themselves. The loss of nature is therefore also a loss of self, rather like an amputation of an appendage done without the patient's permission.

But the nature-as-self can also imply a slightly different understanding. Instead of being "extended self," it may instead imply an extension of self-hood to nature — an understanding of nature as "like-self" or as a community of selves, of persons, with whom one has relationships similar to those within human society.[9] It therefore makes sense to think of

rights and obligations within nature, or even of a morality of nature. The arguments are complex, but obviously they lead in quite a different direction than does the resourcism implicit in the nature-as-object conception. And they quite commonly lead to talk of environmental ethics and rights,[10] although not among all practitioners (some would argue that the idea of ethics and rights presumes discrete, atomistic individuals, the very kind of dualism they are seeking to avoid).[11] For our purposes, however, the significant point is simply that there is an alternative understanding of nature present in contemporary society which is apparently growing in popularity. And while it is certainly far from challenging the hegemony of nature-as-object, its expansion is significant. Obviously the understanding of nature we have will affect the kind of expectations we have, both of nature and of ourselves in relation to nature: what seems proper and appropriate behavior toward an object is not necessarily appropriate toward a "self." The question one asks of nature-as-object is "What's in it *for* me?"; whereas of nature-as-self one might ask "what is it *to* me?" The former implies simple exploitation, whether "well managed" or not, while the latter implies a concern with the relationship of humans and non-humans.

But while these may be the two contending understandings of nature that figure most prominently in popular culture at the moment, they probably do not exhaust the possibilities.

NATURE AS MIRACLE

We believe in facts, just the facts. We do not, generally speaking, believe in miracles. It is highly unlikely, therefore, that many of us would hold a conception of nature as "miracle." Many nature-lovers no doubt have had experiences that one might consider "miraculous," even though they would probably choose a more prudent adjective such as "aesthetic." But the possibility of regarding nature as uncanny and unpredictable needs to be mentioned here, even though it is not possible to do more than hint at its possible significance.

It is commonly understood that a miracle, were such to exist, would be something that runs contrary to the laws of nature. Given that, it would make little sense to speak of nature-as-miracle. However, whether something is "against nature" would depend on our definition of nature. Given that we believe we have discovered "laws" of nature, then of course anything that seems to break those laws would be, by definition, unnatural — if not absurd. But to treat the possibility of nature-as-miracle seriously, one would have to ask just where these "laws" come from and what they actually apply to, which is not a simple task.

One of the reasons that the miracle has largely disappeared from our lives is that we have come to know the world as homogeneous and continuous. That is to say, since it is composed of matter which is similar in composition and behaves in a consistent manner, we are able to predict the result of actions confidently. Of course, it has been understood for centuries that one cannot actually *prove* a causal relationship — it could change on the next trial — but we can nevertheless act as if that were so, since nature seems seldom to surprise us. It is interesting, however, where the initial assumption came from. Why did we decide that nature is sufficiently homogeneous and continuous for us to assume consistent causal relationships?

We find the assumption firmly entrenched by the late seventeenth century, when Gottfried Leibniz could assert that "nature does not leap" — "Tout va par degrés dans la nature et rien par saut."[12] And of course such "natural laws" made possible all sorts of revised understandings, the most obvious being Charles Lyell's theory of gradual geological change which in turn fed Charles Darwin's belief in continuous biological evolution. But as J. H. van den Berg observed, the real germ of this idea lies in the meditations of René Descartes, for whom it bore intellectual fruit almost immediately. Once he concluded that discontinuity is inconceivable, that nature never "jumps" or makes abrupt, unexpected changes, he felt assured that the "stuff" of nature is everywhere the same: there are no pockets of resistance, no surprises. Nature is homogeneous.

This expectation permitted Descartes to take a new turn in his reflections on reality, one which continues to affect each of our lives today. If nature is homogeneous, if it is all essentially the same, then all we need to be concerned with is what he called "extensiveness": an object occupies space. Furthermore, what has extensiveness can be subdivided and can be understood in terms of mathematical analysis, which was of course one of Descartes's intentions. In fact, the very notion of a law of continuity may have come from his mathematical theorizing in which he realized that "if the first two or three terms of any progression are known, it is not difficult to find the other terms."[13] Whatever differences there may be between objects must be the result of differences in motion. His success in arguing this conception laid the groundwork for what we now know as nature, and for the tools of analysis — science — which we regard as the only valid means of knowing nature.

Nothing above should come as any surprise, for we are all heirs of Descartes and we all know nature to be a continuous and predictable phenomenon. The "laws of nature" could not permit such rebelliousness. It comes as something of a surprise, therefore, to find a reputable author like van den Berg making such a description and then saying "Yet it is not true." He denies Descartes's assumption, the one we all take for granted.

> The reader who might think that I do not mean this seriously is mistaken. I *am* serious. The way Descartes treats objects is not fair. If science wants to consider objects as they are, in the form they have as objects, then it is not permitted to speak of objects which consist of nothing but extensiveness. There is no such thing — and there was no such thing. But Descartes' ideas have penetrated so deeply into reality that nobody knows where the idea ends and reality (or, if preferred, another idea of reality) begins.[14]

Van den Berg is simply pointing out that what Descartes did was make an assumption about the nature of reality, an assumption that we, henceforth, have taken as indisputable fact. Certainly it has had useful consequences. But it is, nevertheless, an assumption, and one which, like all assumptions, rules out all other possibilities. Van den Berg argues that much of value is lost in this exclusion, including an understanding of nature that is genuinely compatible with our own *experience* of it rather than with an abstract *conception* of it — we know pigeons and sunsets, but only believe in ecosystems. In order to believe in Descartes's nature, we had to expunge all the qualities we thought we knew, all the colors, smells, weights, and textures — "projection" is a crime, remember — and attend only to what the model requires be there. We had to withdraw ourselves and our senses from the understanding of nature altogether.

> Withdrawing from the things means dehumanizing them. Only if we withdraw, can we find the "laws of nature." These exist, however, only in a close unity, one which does not include us. As a rule, this condition of withdrawal is not mentioned, and therefore it seems that the laws of nature are always valid. But they are only valid in an artificial reality, a reality from which we are excluded. Only tautologies can make them seem valid in our world.[15]

So according to van den Berg (among others),[16] the understanding of nature which we take as obvious is in fact a rather complex and abstract one which we acquire in a lengthy cultural exercise in indoctrination. Without schooling, who could possibly conceive of it? Even in the 1920s, it was apparent that our educational system was firmly committed to its dissemination. Alfred North Whitehead commented that the view of nature as "a dull affair, soundless, scentless, colourless; merely the hurrying of material, endlessly, meaninglessly" was ubiquitous. Every university "organizes itself in accordance with it." And yet, he concluded, it is quite unbelievable. This conception of the universe is surely framed in terms of high abstractions, and the paradox only arises because we have "mistaken our abstraction for concrete realities."[17] We are persuaded by abstractions — "ecosystems" — in a way we seldom are by realities — frogs and mourning doves. We have become victims of the "fallacy of misplaced concreteness" which requires that we regard our abstractions about nature as actual objects of nature, while simultaneously dismissing as trivial or as "projections" our actual experiences of nature. But experience cannot be entirely suffocated by belief, and even extensive schooling cannot remove all vestiges of the direct experience of a nature from which we are *not* withdrawn and in which the "laws of nature" do not always apply. Heterogeneity cannot be entirely exercised, and the occasional miracle just might still occur.

The reason this may be significant is that the idiosyncratic experience of the world may actually transcend the cultural heritage that has given us an understanding of nature that entails the "environmental crisis" as its consequence. That is, if it is so that nature-as-object is the inevitable consequence of a series of cultural interpretations, it may be that the whole of our behavior, including that which leads to the abuse of nature that we now characterize as the environmental crisis, is a consequence of our belief in nature-as-object. The only long term possibility of alleviating that crisis would be to transcend the understanding of nature that gives rise to it. The alternative could be something like what we have been calling nature-as-self, since this at least entails a greater sense of life in nature and some measure of personal responsibility and obligation toward it. But it might also be that something like nature-as-miracle, some experience that transcends the normal understanding and holds it temporarily in abeyance so that the personal awareness of the living world is restored, is a prerequisite to any real change in the awareness of individuals and therefore also to a change in the conception of nature in popular culture.

I suggested earlier that an understanding of nature-as-object implies a stance toward the world that could only prompt one to ask "what's in it for me" — the very question Carson exploited by appearing to answer it. An understanding of nature-as-self involves the premise of persons in the world beyond the human community alone, and therefore entails a search for some understanding of our relationship to the others: the question asked is, "what is it *to* me." But the third nature, nature-as-miracle, does not prompt questions of control or even questions of kinship. The stance toward the world as miraculous, as awesome, or even as beautiful, could only prompt one to ask "what *is* it?" — a metaphysical question rather than an economic or a political one.

THE SOCIAL CONSTRUCTION OF NATURE

The sense of nature we have will obviously affect our idea of what constitutes proper behavior toward it. The nature that dominates popular culture today is one that is consistent with our humanistic and technocratic assumptions. Nature-as-object is the only understanding of the three that facilitates exploitation and the resourcist rhetoric that legitimizes and facilitates it. The rise of nature-as-self in popular culture is an interesting phenomenon which may or may not entail a substantial change. It seems more in keeping with Aldo Leopold's expectation that we will expand our range of moral responsibility (his famous "land ethic")[18] to include the non-human, than with Rachel Carson's public stance as the advocate of human well-being through the defense of ecosystemic integrity. As for nature-as-miracle, as long as it is limited to the experience of relatively few individuals, or even to rather minor experiences interpreted as merely "aesthetic" by a larger section of society, it is probably nothing more than a source of pleasure or puzzlement to the individuals involved. But it *may* be more widespread than we realize: perhaps the occasional experiences of wonder which we all enjoy are symptomatic evidence of the continued possibility of the miraculous. And should this possibility ever gain credence in a larger way, it is conceivable that it might challenge our fundamental perception of the way the world is. Nature-as-miracle challenges the "nothing-but-ness" of contemporary technocratic explanation. It challenges the assumptions of homogeneity and continuity that permit us to exclude the possibility of surprise and to assume confidently public acceptance of a "lowest common nature" that can never be challenged without villainy or "projection." It is, perhaps, the refugium in which alternative "natures" still reside.

There will always be "nature" in popular culture: nature is a hypothesis that every society needs. We all like to claim to be doing what is "natural," and like our ancestors we often admonish each other to "follow nature." However there is some hypocrisy in this, because we only want to follow if nature is willing to lead in our chosen direction. If we have a dog named "nature," we can cheerfully claim to be following it by walking a step or two behind. But to be confident the dog will not deny us this pleasure, we keep it on a leash, lest it take a turn not of our choosing. But our desire to have some sort of control over the direction nature leads us, even while

proclaiming to be followers only, is not a perversion unique to our society. In fact, it may be the rule of the day where humans are concerned. Marshall Sahlins described this tendency in his remarkably concise study, *The Use and Abuse of Biology,* in which he used the recent debate surrounding "sociobiology" to illustrate this tendency at work in contemporary society. But he also described the general and possibly essential propensity of human societies to invent the nature they desire or need, and then to use it to justify the social pattern they have developed. He concludes that

> We seem unable to escape from this perpetual movement, back and forth between the culturalization of nature and the naturalization of culture. It frustrates our understanding at once of society and of the organic world.[19]

The nature that functions in the lives of the majority, that functions as a vital part of popular culture, is inevitably a consequence of this pendular movement between the world of nature and human culture. Nature is never irrelevant. It is used habitually to justify and legitimate the actions we wish to regard as normal, and the behavior we choose to impose on each other. The fact that we are content to construe nature as an object at the moment is symptomatic of our desire to avoid any constraints and to have a free hand to manipulate the world into the forms suited to the exchanges of modern technocracy. The investment we have in the maintenance of this understanding of nature is enormous. And yet, it is not secure. Nature-as-self is also a contemporary reality. It is certainly not the norm, but it is credible enough to generate widespread discussion. And if we ever find that nature-as-miracle has found its way into the columns of *Time* magazine, we may begin to wonder whether nature, whatever it may be, is about to slip its leash.

NOTES

1. Cited by Majorie Hope Nicolson, *Mountain Gloom and Mountain Glory* (New York: W. W. Norton & Co., 1959), pp. 22–23. See also "Nature as Aesthetic Norm" in Arthur O.

Lovejoy, *Essays in the History of Ideas* (New York: G. P. Putnam's Sons, 1960), pp. 69–77.

2. Rachel Carson, *Silent Spring* (Boston: Houghton Mifflin Co., 1962), p. 297.

3. "Pesticides: The Price of Progress," *Time* (September 28, 1962), p. 45.

4. For further elaboration of this see Neil Evernden, *The Natural Alien* (Toronto: University of Toronto Press, 1985).

5. Mary Douglas, "Environments at Risk," in Jonathon Benthall, ed., *Ecology: The Shaping Enquiry* (London: Longman, 1972), p. 144.

6. J. H. van den Berg, *The Changing Nature of Man: Introduction to a Historical Psychology* (New York: Delta, 1975), pp. 225–26.

7. Hans Jonas, *The Phenomenon of Life* (Chicago: University of Chicago Press, 1966), pp. 35–36.

8. See Bill Devall and George Sessions, *Deep Ecology: Living as if Nature Mattered* (Salt Lake City: Peregrine Smith Books, 1985).

9. See Erazim Kohak, *The Embers and the Stars* (Chicago: University of Chicago Press, 1984).

10. See, for example, Peter Singer's *Animal Liberation* (New York: Avon Books, 1975).

11. Warwick Fox, *Deep Ecology: A Response to Richard Sylvan's Critique of Deep Ecology* (Hobart, Tasmania: University of Tasmania, Environmental Studies Occasional Paper #20, 1986).

12. Van den Berg, *Changing Nature,* p. 52.

13. Ibid., p. 53.

14. Ibid., p. 56.

15. Ibid., p. 125.

16. Similar arguments have been put by many writers. See for instance John Livingston, *One Cosmic Instant* (Toronto: McClelland, 1973); Morris Berman, *The Re-Enchantment of the World* (Ithaca: Cornell University Press, 1981); Theodore Roszak, *Where the Wasteland Ends* (New York: Doubleday, 1972); Neil Evernden, *The Natural Alien;* David Ehrenfeld, *The Arrogance of Humanism* (New York: Oxford University Press, 1978).

17. Alfred North Whitehead, *Science and the Modern World* (New York: The Free Press, 1925), pp. 54–55.

18. Aldo Leopold, *A Sand County Almanac* (New York: Oxford University Press, 1949), pp. 201–26.

19. Marshall Sahlins, *The Use and Abuse of Biology* (London: Tavistock Publishers, 1977), p. 105.

DISCUSSION TOPICS

1. To what extent do you agree with Evernden that there were conflicts between Rachel Carson's personal understanding of nature and the view she espoused in *Silent Spring?*

2. Do the assertions by others on the importance of nature for meeting practical human needs conflict with Evernden's contention that Rachel Carson caused a shift in thinking from nature as intrinsically valuable to nature as important for human well-being? Give reasons for your opinion.

3. What views of nature might be equally valid as those proposed by Evernden? What is your view of nature, and how does it compare to Evernden's view?

READING 22

Rachel Carson's Environmental Ethics

Philip Cafaro

Philip Cafaro is a member of the department of philosophy, Colorado State University, Fort Collins. He specializes in environmental ethics and ethical theory, and has published in numerous scholarly journals. He also has lobbied as a representative of the Sierra Club and the Wilderness Society.

In an article from Worldview, *Cafaro traces the environmental ethical themes of Rachel Carson, starting with some of the ideas found in* Silent Spring. *He notes that Carson valued science and personal, direct experience of nature as ways to better understand nature's stories and thus achieve a truer perspective of reality in the natural world. Cafaro also notes a strong sense of compassion and caring for nature in Carson, which included a "reverence for life" and a commitment to the humane treatment of animals. Carson was an advocate for wilderness and also had considerable integrity and a willingness to express her insights and values in her writing.*

INTRODUCTION

. . .

I believe Rachel Carson was not just a successful polemicist, but an important environmental thinker. . . . Meeting Carson the scientist and naturalist clarifies our understanding of the role knowledge can play in a larger relationship to nature. Studying her fifteen-year career as a U.S. Fish and Wildlife Service biologist gives valuable insight into her views on practical conservation issues. Carson's personal story teaches us much about humility and courage, as she triumphed over various setbacks and achieved great literary success, while faithfully discharging her many responsibilities to family, friends, and nature. Still, in order to best understand Carson's environmental ethics, the place to start is with her final work, *Silent Spring.*

SILENT SPRING

Silent Spring constitutes an extended argument for strictly limiting the use of pesticides, herbicides, and other dangerous agricultural and industrial chemicals, and for their careful application and safe disposal when such use is necessary. This argument rests on both factual and evaluative premises. Factually, *Silent Spring's* case rests on numerous scientific and anecdotal accounts of the abuse of these chemicals. It also rests on such easy-to-establish facts as companies' common failure to test products' effects on humans and non-humans, users' frequent negligence in following instructions for applying agricultural chemicals, and the weakness and lack of enforcement of government regulations. Carson's clear presentation of such facts, and of the basic science needed to understand the issues, gave her book its authority. Carson's scientific credentials had already been firmly established in earlier works which had popularized recent developments

in oceanography and marine biology. Without Carson's scientific credibility and impressive presentation of "the facts," *Silent Spring* would not have won such a large hearing.[1]

Nevertheless, evaluative or ethical premises were equally important to Carson's overall position. She avoided complicated ethical argument in *Silent Spring,* perhaps believing that the ethical issues really were quite simple. More likely, Carson reasoned that simple appeals to widely held values would be more convincing. In any case, *Silent Spring* is filled with short, emphatic ethical statements and arguments. Evaluatively (and somewhat schematically) its plea for restraint rests on a triple foundation of human health considerations, the moral considerability of non-human beings, and the value to humans of preserving wild nature and a diverse and varied landscape.

Doubtless most important for many readers were Carson's chapters on acute pesticide poisoning, and these chemicals' potential to cause cancer and human birth defects. For these readers Carson states the moral clearly: 'Man, however much he may like to pretend the contrary, is part of nature. [He cannot] escape a pollution that is now so thoroughly distributed throughout the world.'[2] Examples of human sicknesses and fatalities caused by inappropriate use of chemicals recur throughout the book.

Carson was acutely aware of the importance of good health, having suffered a variety of serious illnesses over the years. In fact, she was dying of cancer as she finished *Silent Spring.* . . .

Silent Spring clearly shows Rachel Carson's concern for all of life, human and non-human. Many of its arguments explicitly assert or implicitly rely on the moral considerability of non-human beings. For example, she recounts a massive dieldrin spraying program to eradicate Japanese beetles in and around Sheldon, Illinois. Robins, meadowlarks, pheasants and other birds were virtually wiped out; so were squirrels. Amazingly, ninety per cent of area farm cats were killed during the first season of spraying. "Incidents like the eastern Illinois spraying," Carson reflected:

raise a question that is not only scientific but moral. The question is whether any civilization can wage relentless war on life without destroying itself, and without losing the right to be called civilized . . . These creatures [wild and domestic] are innocent of any harm to man. Indeed, by their very existence they and their fellows make his life more pleasant. Yet he rewards them with a death that is not only sudden but horrible.

. . .

In another section, Carson fights the common prejudice against insects by explaining to her readers the important role of honeybees, wild bees and other pollinators in natural and human economies. "These insects," she concludes: "so essential to our agriculture and indeed to our landscape as we know it, *deserve something better from us* than the senseless destruction of their habitat."[3] Here again, the notion of desert clearly implies moral considerability. Similar examples could be multiplied many times. . . .

Our interests and their interests largely coincide — for two reasons. First, we inhabit the same environment. Hence we cannot poison other animals without poisoning ourselves. Second, preserving wild nature helps promote human happiness and flourishing. Carson approvingly quotes ecologist Paul Shepard and U.S. Supreme Court Justice William O. Douglas on the aesthetic value and intellectual stimulation provided by wildlife, wild places, and a diverse and varied landscape.[4] . . . Pleasure, adventure, beauty, grace, even meaning — all these may be driven from our world along with the "target organisms," impoverishing our own lives. A silent spring is a season of loss to us and to them, the losses inseparably linked. . . .

What is the relative importance of these three main evaluative premises — preserve human health! respect the moral considerability of non-human beings! promote human happiness and flourishing! — in *Silent Spring?* I see no evidence that one was any more important than another to Carson's main argument. . . .

. . . Many critics argued that DDT was necessary to prevent mosquito borne diseases and increase harvests in developing nations.[5] . . . Carson generally steered clear of the ethical question of how to balance human and non-human interests. She probably believed that she stood a better chance of moving society toward safer, reduced pesticide use by emphasizing the common dangers pesticides posed to humans and non-humans. In her own life, however, she often went considerably out of her way to avoid harming non-human beings, carefully returning microscopic tidepool specimens to the ocean after studying them, for example.[6]

Similarly, Carson criticized the increasing simplification and sterility of modern farm and suburban landscapes, pointing out a *human* cost to such dullness. Her opponents countered that this was the cost of progress and prosperity, in effect arguing that increased wealth and productivity were more important than the merely aesthetic values appreciated by birdwatchers. "We can live without birds and animals," reflected one correspondent, "but, as the current market slump shows, we cannot live without business."[7] Once again, Carson preferred to argue that the choice — birds or business — was a false one, in most cases. But she also stood up strongly for the importance of non-economic values in a truly human life; particularly the appreciation of beauty, the search for knowledge, and the achievement of wisdom.[8] Such values were important to many of her readers, she believed, and if they weren't, they should be. As for herself, she found birds more essential than banknotes to her happiness.[9]

In general, Carson (and legions of environmentalists to come) emphasized the complementarity in the great majority of cases of the three basic goals of protecting human health, preserving non-human life, and promoting human flourishing. She shone a spotlight on the selfishness and short-sightedness which so often undermined all three goals. Meanwhile, in trying to move her society toward greater recognition of non-human interests and higher human interests, Carson developed an environmental ethic with both non-anthropocentric and enlightened anthropocentric elements. While *Silent Spring* shows how these two aspects may "converge" regarding an important public policy issue, Carson's own life, dedicated to knowing and appreciating nature, shows how they converge at the personal level.[10] Recognition of the intrinsic value of non-human beings provides benefits that outweigh the restrictions such recognition places upon us. So too, a nobler view of human life — one focused on friendship, the pursuit of knowledge and a rich experience, rather than on getting and spending—should lead to less environmentally destructive lifestyles. The lives of the great naturalists—including Rachel Carson's—suggest that we really will live better lives when we do right by nature.[11]

Philosophers may be inclined to ask: what are the "foundations" of Rachel Carson's environmental ethics? Otherwise put: how does she justify her three main evaluative premises (or her two controversial ones, concern for human health presumably needing no justification)? Clearly, meta-ethical reflection would have been out of place in a popular work like *Silent Spring,* but I have found little evidence that Carson gave sustained attention to this issue elsewhere. . . .

In *Silent Spring* Carson describes poisoned ground squirrels whose attitudes in death—backs bowed, mouths filled with dirt from biting the ground—suggest they died in agony. She adds the simple reflection that causing such suffering diminishes us as human beings. She pictures a varied and beautiful roadside filled with bright flowers and buzzing insects, then the same after spraying, a dull, sere, silent wasteland. Now, she writes, it is "something to be traversed quickly, a sight to be endured with one's mind closed to thoughts of the sterile and hideous world we are letting our technicians make."[12] Carson could paint such pictures and draw such obvious morals for her readers. In her earlier natural history writings, she helped hundreds of thousands of people to recognize new plants and animals and appreciate what they were seeing. She could create or enhance a mood before nature of wonder, appreciation, or reverence. But more than that she could not do. Without a personal experience of these things, there is no *is* from which to move to the moral *ought.* With such experience, the movement from *is* to *ought* is typically accomplished. Let the philosopher who can better explain this process do so!

Another intriguing question remains at the foundational level: the role that religion or spirituality played in grounding Carson's personal environmental ethic. *Silent Spring* is dedicated to Albert Schweitzer and Carson's biographer, Linda Lear, reports that a handwritten letter and inscribed portrait from Schweitzer were Carson's most prized possessions in her last years. In her foreword to Ruth

Harrison's *Animal Machines,* a pioneering work in the animal welfare movement, Carson wrote of the need for a "Schweitzerian ethic that embraces decent consideration for all living creatures—a true reverence for life." Carson's previous best-seller *The Edge of the Sea* shows flashes of a genuine if unobtrusive spiritual sensibility; particularly in its final, stirring paean to "the enduring sea" and "the ultimate mystery of life," but also in its appreciation of the "fragile beauty" of small, transient, individual life-forms.[13] Paul Brooks, Carson's friend and long-time editor, wrote that Carson "felt a spiritual as well as physical closeness to the individual creatures about whom she wrote" and asserted that "her attitude toward the natural world was that of a deeply religious person."[14]

Still, I think the importance of religion and spirituality to Carson's environmental ethics can be exaggerated. She clearly had moments of spiritual epiphany, but Carson's more usual posture before nature, in her books and in her life, seems to have been appreciation and interest. Reverence, respect, and appreciation are not three names for the same thing. Appeals to a proper reverence may have strong rhetorical and logical force, when addressed to believers, but Carson uses them sparingly in her books. Carson did write to a friend that the "Reverence-for-Life philosophy is of course somewhat like my own," and other approving references to Schweitzer are scattered throughout her writings and correspondence.[15] But it could be that for her, the word "reverence" captures an ascription of high value or intrinsic value, rather than an essentially religious view of the world. Carson always puts the emphasis on *life* rather than on any putative creator. She certainly had little interest in orthodox religious doctrine. . . .

Perhaps it is most accurate to say that Rachel Carson embraced nature in all its manifestations, from the small to the grand and from the scientific to the mystical. These experiences and interactions seem to have motivated her own powerful concern and effective action on behalf of nature. Ultimately, I think, her ethical foundation is experiential. Aesthetic, intellectual, sensual, imaginative, *personal* experience grounds ethical judgments and action. In the main, Carson's writings are concerned to facilitate such experiences, rather than to argue for particular ethical positions. They certainly do not argue for particular religious beliefs.[16]

Three further themes round out the ethical argument of *Silent Spring*. First, Carson's disapproval of economism—the overvaluation or exclusive focus on economic goals and pursuits. Second, her criticisms of a human "war on nature." Third, her warnings concerning the increased artificiality and simplification of the landscape.

Carson criticized the age as one "in which the right to make a dollar at whatever cost is seldom challenged." . . . Worst of all, people lose the ability to see the land and its natural communities for what they are, to learn their stories and appreciate their beauty and complexity. Instead nature is reduced to natural resources—both in our minds and on the ground—which humans may fully engross or utterly change, without compunction. Carson believed that conservation had to take economic reality into account, including the need to feed and protect growing numbers of human beings; hence her many suggestions for alternatives to chemical control and safer means of applying chemicals, when necessary. But she also saw the failure to recognize non-economic realities as a denial of our full humanity. Like the failure to prevent unnecessary suffering, the failure to understand and appreciate nature lessened our stature as human beings.

Carson was equally uncompromising in her criticism of what she saw as a "needless war" on nature. Again and again, she decries the desire for domination behind much of the use of agricultural chemicals.[17] She saw a revelling in power for its own sake and a will to simplify the landscape in order to control it. . . . Carson doubted that human beings would find peace among themselves without first making peace with nature.[18]

Finally, Carson spoke out against artificiality and simplification: on farms, forests and rangelands, as well as towns, suburbs and highway margins. . . . Carson insists that all native species have a right to persist in their environments—not just the ones human beings find attractive or useful. And while we must manage and change much of the landscape to suit our needs, some areas should be left wild, free from human artifice and control.[19] . . .

. . . Carson does not provide elaborate arguments to justify the moral considerability of these wild species and natural communities, or the value, to us, of knowing and appreciating them. A true teacher, she knows that she cannot prove the superiority of knowledge over ignorance. But she can make the pursuit of knowledge attractive. Once her readers know and experience that of which she speaks, she is convinced, they will value it. "The natural landscape is eloquent of the interplay of forces that have created it," Carson writes. "It is spread before us like the pages of an open book in which we can read why the land is what it is, and why we should preserve its integrity. But the pages lie unread."[20] *That* is the problem. Before we can appreciate ethical arguments for its preservation, we must appreciate wild nature itself, and we cannot appreciate what we have not seen, experienced, or at least imagined. Like a long line of naturalist/conservationists before her, then, Rachel Carson worked to teach us to read in the book of nature. In turning to her earlier natural history writings, we gain a fuller understanding of her environmental ethics.

NON-ANTHROPOCENTRISM

Today Rachel Carson is primarily known for *Silent Spring*. But that was her fourth book to make the *New York Times* best-seller list. Carson's natural history writings—*Under the Sea-Wind* (1941), the number one best-seller *The Sea Around Us* (1951/1961) and *The Edge of the Sea* (1955)—explored the astounding diversity of littoral and marine ecosystems. She took readers to some of the wildest and hardest to imagine places on earth: Arctic tundra in the grip of winter; the weird, dark depths of the ocean; microscopic planktonic worlds. Just as surely, Carson uncovered the many details of nature close to hand: the fishing techniques of herons and skimmers; the fine structures and hidden beauties of jellyfish. She was also a great explainer of relationships and connections. "It is now clear that in the sea nothing lives to itself," she wrote, and what holds true in the sea holds true throughout the biosphere.[21]

This oft-repeated message resounds somewhat ominously in *Silent Spring,* but even here Carson's clear message is that life's complexity and interconnections are cause for appreciation and celebration, if also for restraint. . . . Carson never doubted that increased knowledge was more precious than increased material wealth, or that a more widespread knowledge of nature would motivate people to protect it.[22] And knowledge, for her, was not simply learned, but lived and experienced, engaging and developing the senses and emotions as well as the mind, our imaginations as much as our analytic abilities.

Non-anthropocentrism is a main theme in the natural history works. We have already seen that Carson's ethics were non-anthropocentric: she recognized the moral considerability of non-human beings. But Carson's work reminds us that non-anthropocentrism is both an ethical position and an intellectual task, and the latter demands as much from us as the former. In particular, it demands repeated attention to the non-human world: the setting aside of our works and purposes and a concentration on *nature's* own stories and realities.[23] Experienced often enough and set within the proper intellectual frameworks, we may, we hope, see ourselves truly as parts of a more-than-human whole. Carson is convinced that such non-anthropocentrism is a part of wisdom.

. . . Carson worked back from what she knew of each animal's natural history, to try to imagine how it might perceive its environment and its varied interactions with other creatures. *Under the Sea-Wind* is a fascinating attempt to marry an imaginative, phenomenological exploration of other consciousnesses with the latest researches in scientific natural history.

Even in this first book, Carson's imagination took her beyond a focus on individual animals to the larger forces which shape their lives. "I very soon realized," she wrote . . . : "that the central character of the book was the ocean itself. The smell of the sea's edge, the feeling of vast movements of water, the sound of waves, crept into every page, and over all was the ocean as the force dominating all its creatures."[24]

How to make the ocean a character without inappropriate personification thus became a delicate task. Like other serious interpreters of nature, she struggled to avoid bogus personification and the pathetic fallacy, on the one hand, and an unjustified reductionism and simplification of nature's complexity, on the other.[25]

Carson's next book, which gave her fame, also took non-anthropocentrism as a key intellectual goal. *The Sea Around Us* synthesized recent discoveries in oceanography and marine biology. . . . She repeatedly invokes the ocean's radical non-humanity, asking readers to imagine underwater "tides so vast they are invisible and uncomprehended by the senses of man," or lights traveling over the water "that flash and fade away, lights that come and go for reasons meaningless to man," though "man, in his vanity, subconsciously attributes a human origin" to them.[26] This ocean wilderness teaches humility and wisdom, she believes. . . .

Achieving such a perspective involves both knowledge and imagination. From such a perspective, non-anthropocentric value judgments will tend to follow, along with a truer sense of the importance of our own problems. . . .

Non-anthropocentrism is thus a key to Rachel Carson's ethical philosophy, which contains the three complementary and equally challenging injunctions: "Respect nature!" "Know nature!" and "Place yourself in proper perspective!" We mistake the nature of ethics, and Carson's ethics in particular, if we separate the intellectual from the ethical challenge here, or fail to acknowledge an ethical force behind all three injunctions. For Carson, arrogance is both an intellectual and a moral failing, while ignorance is as culpable as wrong action.

Because she placed such a strong emphasis on knowing nature and transcending our habitual focus on people, science was a key human activity for Carson. "The aim of science is to discover and illuminate truth," she said in a speech accepting the National Book Award. Ideally, that illumination should inform the everyday lives of common people: not by creating more wealth or new consumer products, but by creating people who better know the earth which they inhabit and which has created them. . . .

Carson clearly believed in science. She earned an MA in marine biology from Johns Hopkins University, worked as a government scientist for the U.S. Fish and Wildlife Service, kept up with the latest developments in a wide variety of fields, and made her name as a scientific popularizer. Yet she also saw many of science's limitations. In contrast to common scientific practice, Carson emphasized direct appreciation of individual organisms. Personal connections to particular places, such as her beloved Maine coast, were very important to her. She rejected a purely objective outlook; her own writings often sought to create an emotional response to nature, which she believed would help further conservation.[27]

Many of Carson's critics, including some scientists, accused her of "emotionalism" after the publication of *Silent Spring,* usually making more or less explicit reference to her gender.[28] . . .

In response, Carson suggested that there was something wrong with people who felt no emotion in response to nature or nature's destruction. Emotional attachment, aesthetic appreciation, and a personal connection to particular places should complement the pursuit of rigorous science, she believed, since these all furthered our understanding and appreciation of nature, which in turn improved our lives. . . . In an earlier article, she assured parents with a limited knowledge of nature that they could still help their children appreciate it, since "it is not half so important to *know* as to *feel.*" Furthermore, she wrote, "it is possible to compile extensive lists of creatures seen and identified without ever once having caught a breath-taking glimpse of the wonder of life."[29]

Carson reflected long and hard on the proper role of science in human society. Just as it called into question the haphazard, unregulated use of pesticides and herbicides, *Silent Spring* touched off a heated debate, among scientists, on the proper ends of science: whether to control, dominate and change nature for human purposes, or to preserve, protect and further our understanding of it, as is. Obviously, this debate continues and has lost none of its urgency, as witnessed by the recent growth of both conservation biology and a massive biotechnology industry. Rachel Carson is properly seen as one of our first and greatest conservation biologists, who popularized the wild worlds of sea and shore and incited people to work to protect all of nature.[30]

Carson valued science and the personal experience of nature because they helped her to understand nature's stories and thus achieve a larger, truer, non-anthropocentric point of view. She was also a self-proclaimed *realist,* and this seems to have played an important role in her environmental ethics. Science can achieve truth and thus illuminate our lives, she believed. It teaches us, for instance, that we are kin, however distant, to all the life with which we share the Earth. As she expressed it in *The Edge of the Sea,* a scientifically informed personal experience gets us in touch with "the realities of ex-

istence," with "elemental realities."[31] Carson was aware of the great gulfs of ignorance surrounding so many scientific questions in her day; her revisions to new editions of her books reminded her of the provisional nature of scientific knowledge. As a natural *historian,* she was also aware of the shifting, evolutionary nature of nature. She wrote in *The Edge of the Sea's* conclusion of "coastal forms merging and blending in a shifting, kaleidoscopic pattern in which there is no finality, no ultimate and fixed reality — earth becoming fluid as the sea itself." What holds for the earth and sea obviously holds for organic nature, as the nature and meaning of life "haunts and ever eludes" the seeker after knowledge.[32] This passage suggests a Peircean limit concept of truth and reality, as the ever elusive goals of an endless process.

Nevertheless, it is a process to which Carson is passionately committed. As a scientist, she needs the concept of reality to make sense of scientific progress. As a naturalist, she values knowledge over ignorance and personal acquaintance with nature over casual disregard. As a mystic and nature lover, she speaks of "enchanted" experiences when the "realities" of nature "possessed my mind."[33] As a conservationist, she wants to protect "The Real World Around Us" — as she titled one talk — from humanity's relentless pressure to replace *the* creation with our creations.[34] Only a belief in reality, and in the possibility and sweetness of knowing and connecting to reality, can make sense of the goals Rachel Carson pursued throughout her life. . . . Environmentalists need to offer some positive alternative to gross economic consumption and the trivial pleasures offered by our destructive modern economy. With Carson, I can think of no alternative superior to a physical and intellectual engagement with the natural world. Away with all epistemological cavilling which would deny such realities! Away with all post-modernist literary maunderings which would substitute clever wordplay for knowledge and experience of what Carson elsewhere calls "the great realities."[35] The alternative to such realism is solipsism and the ever more exclusive focus on artificial worlds and virtual realities of our own creation.

Reading *Silent Spring* reminds us that it was not sophisticated post-modern deconstructionists but naive realist birdwatchers who provided much of the evidence about the dangers of pesticides that Rachel Carson laid before the public. Carson herself mentions how easy it is for people to destroy wild things when they do not even know they exist.[36] So we need to know "the real world around us" for its own sake. But we need to know it for our sakes, as well. "I have had the privilege of receiving many letters from people who, like myself, have been steadied and reassured by contemplating the long history of the earth and sea, and the deeper meanings of the world of nature," Carson wrote. "In contemplating 'the exceeding beauty of the earth' these people have found calmness and courage."[37]

Carson needed such calm fortitude throughout her life: to meet her many family obligations, to stand up to the personal and professional attacks levelled against her after *Silent Spring* was published; to persevere through difficult health problems during her last decade. She finished *Silent Spring* racing the cancer that she knew would shortly end her life. . . .

CONCLUSION

I'd like to end by noting several respects in which Rachel Carson's life and work might point the way forward for environmental ethics. First, Carson's frequent criticisms of human attempts to dominate nature suggest important parallels with contemporary ecofeminism. Consider also the roles compassion and caring seem to have played in her environmental ethics; also, her emphasis on the importance of direct experience. Finally, there were her pioneering efforts in the primarily male worlds of science, government service and conservation — and the misogynistic tone of many of her critics. All this suggests that Carson may be an important resource for ecofeminist reflection.

Second, Carson's philosophy of "reverence for life" seems to support the whole spectrum of environmental activism. . . . A recent collection of Carson's shorter and occasional pieces, titled *Lost Woods,* perhaps gives us a fuller picture of her conservation interests than we have had previously. Several pieces highlight her advocacy for wilderness, including "The Real World Around Us" and "Our Ever Changing Shore." The latter includes a moving plea for the preservation of wild beachlands. . . . Other articles show a concern for the beauty and health of more developed landscapes.

Lost Woods also contains Carson's prefaces to the U.S. Animal Welfare Institute's educational booklet "Humane Biology Projects" and to Ruth Harrison's *Animal Machines.* These indicate her commitment to the humane treatment of animals. "I am glad to see Ruth Harrison raises the question of how far man has a moral right to go in his domination of other life," she writes: "Has he the right, as in these examples [of intensive farming], to reduce life to a bare existence that is scarcely life at all? Has he the further right to terminate these wretched lives by means that are wantonly cruel? My own answer is an unqualified no."[38]

In her biography, Linda Lear shows that Carson muted her animal welfare advocacy, out of concern that it would undermine her case against the misuse of pesticides. Nevertheless, while writing *Silent Spring,* she wrote to a confidante that "I wish I could find time to turn my pen against the Fish and Wildlife Service's [her own former agency's] despicable poisoning activities [of predators and "vermin" such as prairie dogs] . . . it is all part of the same black picture."[39] What are the similarities between sacrificing a wild beach for condominium development and sacrificing the happiness of a veal calf for the pleasure of a gourmand? In both cases, human interests come first, no matter how trivial. In both cases, we dominate or deny nature and create new anthropocentric realities. In both cases, profit trumps a true humanity. This is the "black picture" which commands misery or disappearance for so much that is "not us." Carson's example suggests that a philosophy of love and appreciation for all nature and its creatures can bridge the gaps between environmental ethics and animal welfare ethics, and between anthropocentric urban environmentalists and biocentric advocates of wildlands.

This indicates a final way in which Rachel Carson might point a route forward for environmental ethics: through her example of personal commitment and activism. Carson was a woman of great character who balanced her personal, professional and political responsibilities with utter integrity. She did not relish controversy, but she did not retreat from it, when necessary. No one else, she realized, had the combination of literary skill and scientific knowledge to write

Silent Spring. Her struggle to synthesize a mountain of current scientific work and write one final book that was both accurate and compelling, in the face of family tragedy and failing health, provides one of the heroic stories in conservation history. One cannot read about it without being deeply moved. When Carson writes to a friend that it is "a privilege as well as a duty to have the opportunity to speak out — to many thousands of people — on something so important," we know she means it and love her for it.[40]

Here knowledge and respect for nature, and personal humility and commitment to nature, go hand in hand. Such an ethics is certainly demanding. Yet reading of Carson's life, one learns how much she received in return for living up to it. Perhaps we too may hope that Nature will repay us for our attentiveness and efforts on her behalf. As inspiration and provocation, then, Rachel Carson's life and writings also hold great potential for environmental philosophy.

NOTES

1. Lear, 1997, pp. 396–456.
2. Carson, 1962, p. 169.
3. Carson, 1962.
4. Ibid., pp. 22, 77.
5. Quoted in Lear, 1997, pp. 433–437.
6. Brooks, 1972, p. 8. Rachel Carson learned this respectful attitude from her mother, who, according to Carson's brother, "would put spiders and other insects out of the house, rather than kill them" (Gartner, 1983, p. 7).
7. Lear, 1997, p. 409.
8. Brooks, 1972, pp. 324–326.
9. Gartner, 1983, p. 8.
10. The "convergence thesis" is the idea that convincing, properly formulated anthropocentric and non-anthropocentric ethics will largely converge in their practical environmental recommendations. See Norton, 1991.
11. I discuss this convergence and develop the idea of an environmental virtue ethics grounded in our enlightened self-interest in Cafaro, 2001.
12. Carson, 1962, pp. 96, 71.
13. Lear, 1997, pp. 322, 438, 440. Harrison, 1964, p. viii. Carson, 1955, pp. 196, 215–216.
14. Brooks, 1972, pp. 8–9.
15. Freeman, 1995, p. 62; Brooks, 1972, p. 242.
16. Readers should know that Carson's biographer Linda Lear believes that she was a more spiritual person than my essay implies. Lear thinks that the concept of "material immortality," treated in *Under the Sea-Wind* and latter writings, is key to Carson's religion, and that her environmental ethics is grounded in this religious sensibility (Lear, 2001; see also Freeman, 1995, pp. 446–447).
17. Carson, 1962, pp. 118, 64, 83. Recent environmental historiography confirms the importance of an ideology of conquest and domination in the growth of modern industrial agriculture. See Feige, 1999, pp. 171–181.
18. See Carson, 1998, p. 196, and Lear, 1997, p. 407. In a commencement address delivered two years before her death, Carson explicitly linked human domination of nature to "the Jewish-Christian concept of man's relation to nature" (Gartner, 1983, p. 120).
19. Carson, 1962, p. 78. See also Carson, 1998, p. 194.
20. Carson, 1962, p. 65. Note the quick move from *is* to *ought.*
21. Carson, 1955, p. 39.
22. Carson, 1962, p. 118.
23. See Saito, 1998, pp. 135–149.
24. Carson, 1998, pp. 55–56.
25. Gartner, 1983, pp. 35–36; Lear, 1997, pp. 90–91.
26. Carson, 1951/1961, pp. 106, 45.
27. Gartner, 1983, p. 3.
28. Lear, 1997, pp. 430, 461.
29. Gartner, 1983, p. 118.
30. Lear, 1997, pp. 428–440.
31. Carson, 1955, pp. 13–14.
32. Ibid., pp. 215–216.
33. Ibid., p. 13.
34. Carson, 1998, pp. 147–163.
35. Ibid., p. 92.
36. Carson, 1962, pp. 110–115, 118.
37. Brooks, 1972, pp. 325–326.
38. Carson, 1998, p. 196.
39. Lear, 1997, p. 352. For more on Carson's views and actions on behalf of animal welfare see Brooks, 1972, pp. 314–317; Gartner, 1983, pp. 6–7, 26–27.
40. Lear, 1997, p. 328.

REFERENCES

Brooks, Paul. 1972. *The House of Life: Rachel Carson at Work*. Boston: Houghton Mifflin.

Cafaro, Philip. 2001. "Thoreau, Leopold, and Carson; Toward an Environmental Virtue Ethics," *Environmental Ethics* 23: 3–17.

Carson, Rachel. 1951/1961. *The Sea Around Us*. Revised ed. New York: Signet.

———. 1955. *The Edge of the Sea*. Boston: Houghton Mifflin.

———. 1962. *Silent Spring*. New York: Fawcett World Library

———. 1998. *Lost Woods: The Discovered Writing of Rachel Carson*. Linda Lear, ed. Boston: Beacon Press.

Feige, Mark. 1999. *Irrigated Eden: The Making of an Agricultural Landscape in the American West*. Seattle: University of Washington Press.

Freeman, Martha. (ed.) 1995. *Always, Rachel: The Letters of Rachel Carson and Dorothy Freeman, 1952–1964*. Boston: Beacon Press.

Gartner, Carol. 1983. *Rachel Carson*. New York: Frederick Ungar.

Harrison, Ruth. 1964. *Animal Machines: The New Factory Farming Industry*. London: Vincent Stuart.

Lear, Linda. 1997. *Rachel Carson: Witness for Nature*. New York: Henry Holt.

———. 2001. Personal communication.

Norton, Bryan. 1991. *Toward Unity Among Environmentalists*. New York: Oxford University Press.

Saito, Yuriko. 1998. "Appreciating Nature on Its Own Terms," *Environmental Ethics* 20: 135–149.

DISCUSSION TOPICS

1. How are the ideas of Rachel Carson as presented here similar to and different from those of Muir, Thoreau, and Leopold? Explain your perspectives.

2. How are the ideas of Rachel Carson similar to and different from those of contemporary ecofeminism? Explain your perspective.

3. What roles do aesthetics and emotion have in our valuing nature? Give examples to support your position.

CLASS EXERCISE

It has been proposed that twenty-five percent of all lands designated as wilderness would be reclassified as "sacred space." These lands would be closed to virtually all human visitation, including wilderness hiking, ecological monitoring, fire fighting, law enforcement, or activities related to public health; they would be open to indigenous native people for such spiritual purposes as vision quests, meditation, and art production.

Using the debating techniques outlined in Appendix A, debate the merits of this plan. What arguments and strategies were used by each side? Which were persuasive?

FOR FURTHER READING

Bilsky, Lester J. *Historical Ecology: Essays on Environment and Social Change*. Port Washington, N.Y.: Kennikat Press, 1980. A series of essays by eleven scholars on past environmental crises and past human relationships with nature, starting from prehistoric times. Most attention is focused on Europe, but some information is presented about China and other parts of the world.

Boyden, Stephen. *Biohistory: The Interplay between Human Society and the Biosphere*. Man and the Biosphere Series, vol. 8. Park Ridge, N.J.: Parthenon, 1992. The author presents an overview of the interactions of humans with the biosphere from the beginning of life to contemporary times. Twelve chapters cover such aspects as farming, war, urbanization, and disease.

Conviser, Richard. "Toward Agricultures of Context." *Environmental Ethics* 6 (1984): 71–85. The author explores origins of agricultural organization, particularly the movements toward scientism and capitalism. Forms of agriculture consistent with holism and localism, are recommended as better alternatives.

Crosby, Alfred W. *Germs, Seeds, & Animals: Studies in Ecological History*. London: M. E. Sharpe, 1994. The author evaluates human impact on North America, starting from the arrival of Columbus.

Crumley, Carole L., ed. *Historical Ecology: Cultural Knowledge and Changing Landscapes*. Santa Fe,

N.M.: School of American Research Press, 1994. The editor integrates ten chapters by a variety of authors, offering insights from environmental history, anthropology, and geography in evaluating the relationship of past human activities with environmental changes.

Dewey, Scott. "Working for the Environment: Organized Labor and the Origins of Environmentalism in the United States." *Environmental History* 3, 1 (1998): 45–63.

Environmental History Review (formerly *Environmental Review*) is a publication of the American Society for Environmental History. Established in 1976, the focus of the journal is on scholarly research into past environmental change.

Evernden, Neil. *The Natural Alien.* Toronto: University of Toronto Press, 1985. An insightful and thought-provoking perspective on the deficiencies inherent in the environmental movement's ideology. Evernden maintains that humans become alienated from the richness of nature and life when viewing the world primarily in terms of its technological value.

Flader, Susan. "Citizenry and the State in the Shaping of Environmental Policy." *Environmental History* 3(1) (1998): 8–24.

Hargrove, Eugene C. "The Historical Foundations of American Environmental Attitudes." *Environmental Ethics* 1 (1979): 209–40. Hargrove claims that American environmental attitudes developed from an interplay of Western science and art over the past three centuries. He views these attitudes as part of broad scientific and aesthetic changes that will probably become a permanent part of Western values.

Hughes, J. Donald. "Effects of Classical Cities on the Mediterranean Landscape." *Ekistics* 42, 253 (1976): 332–42. Practices in ancient cities resulted in environmental problems similar to those experienced in modern cities, including air, water, and noise pollution. Land use and urban planning decisions also were difficult during ancient times.

———. "The Environmental Ethics of the Pythagoreans." *Environmental Ethics* 2 (1980): 195–213. Identifies two conflicting perspectives among the Pythagoreans: a sense of reverence for nature and kinship with all life, and a doctrine of separability of soul and body that devalued the body and the external world of which it is a part.

———. "How the Ancients Viewed Deforestation." *Journal of Field Archeology* 10 (1983): 437–45. Hughes evaluates the causes and effects of defor-estation in ancient lands. He describes how the demands of human use superseded traditional values supporting the preservation of forested lands.

———. "Pan: Environmental Ethics in Classical Polytheism," in *Religion and Environmental Crisis,* ed. Eugene C. Hargrove. Athens, Ga.: University of Georgia Press, 1986, pp. 7–24. Provides a perspective on the role the Great Pan played in ancient times as an all-pervasive spiritual power and the universal god of nature. Notes that the death of Pan occurred when Christianity arose. Probes the role that these ancient ideas may have played in the development of an explicit environmental ethic.

Hughes, J. Donald, and Jim Swan. "How Much of the Earth Is Sacred Space?" *Environmental Review* 10 (Winter, 1986): 247–59. The authors trace the notion of sacred space as it has been presented in Native American and European cultures.

McGurty, Eileen Maura. "From NIMBY to Civil Rights: The Origins of the Environmental Justice Movement." *Environmental History* 2, 3 (1997): 301–23.

McPhee, Ross D. W., ed. *Extinctions in Near Time: Causes, Contexts, and Consequences.* New York: Plenum Publishers, 1999. Human effects have been especially disruptive on islands, and the contributors believe human presence on continents has often been almost as bad, although climate change complicates the evidence.

Merchant, Carolyn. *Ecological Revolution: Nature, Gender and Science in New England.* Chapel Hill: University of North Carolina Press, 1989. Merchant analyzes the colonial and capitalist revolutions in New England as an example of "ecological revolutions" in the relation between humans and nonhumans in nature. She covers the ecological and social transformations in New England from the seventeenth century to the present. Extensive notes and bibliography.

Nash, Roderick F. *The Rights of Nature: A History of Environmental Ethics.* Madison: University of Wisconsin Press, 1989. An interesting tracing of the ideas that led some in our society away from simple anthropocentrism to the belief that nature has rights that must be respected.

Norton, Bryan, G. *Toward Unity among Environmentalists.* Oxford: Oxford University Press, 1991. The author provides a useful overview of environmental history and a vision for unification among environmental philosophers.

Oelschlager, Max. *The Idea of Wilderness: From Prehistory to the Age of Ecology.* New Haven, Conn.: Yale University Press, 1991. A thoughtful and scholarly look at the history of ideas focusing on the notion of wilderness.

Roberts, Neil. *The Holocene: An Environmental History.* Oxford: Basil Blackwell, 1989. The author summarizes the history of human impact on the worldwide environment, from the Pleistocene to contemporary times. Well-documented scientific work.

Roosevelt, Theodore. "Forestry and Foresters." *Proceedings of the Society of American Foresters* 1, 1 (1905): 3–9. (Reprinted in the *Journal of Forestry* 98, 11 (2002): 4–5.) An important historical perspective from a founder of the Doctrine of Conservation in the United States.

Shabecoff, Philip. *Earth Rising: American Environmentalism in the 21st Century.* Washington, D.C.: Island Press, 2000. Using almost 100 interviews as well as a literature review, Shabecoff calls for the environmental movement to take a more active role in creating social change.

Shepherd, Paul. *The Tender Carnivore and the Sacred Game.* New York: Charles Scribner's Sons, 1973. A thoughtful look at the human place in the natural world and its historical foundations. Addresses fundamental assumptions in the relationship of Western society to nature, including human-nature dualism.

Simmons, I. G. *Changing the Face of the Earth: Culture, Environment, History.* Oxford: Basil Blackwell Ltd., 1989. The author follows human history from the origins of fire, through hunting, agriculture, industrialism, and the nuclear age. Provides a good summary of literature on related topics.

Stoll, M. "Green versus Green: Religions, Ethics, and the Bookchin-Foreman Dispute." *Environmental History* 6, 3 (2001): 412–27.

Vest, Jay H. "Nature Awe: Historical Views of Nature." *Western Wildlands* 1 (1983): 39–43. An interesting and insightful look at the relationships ancient Celts had with nature, and the foundation this culture had for some Western practices and perceptions.

Worster, Donald. *Nature's Economy: The Roots of Ecology.* San Francisco: Sierra Club Books, 1977. The author presents a history of ideas in the field of ecology. Three of the chapters in the final part of the text lead into a general discussion of the ethical implications of ecology.

———. "History as Natural History: An Essay on Theory and Method." *Pacific Historical Review* 53 (1984): 1–19. Analyzes the contributions of an ecological perspective to the study of human history. Reviews several American historians and anthropologists who have adopted an ecological perspective. Suggests that historians can add specificity to the generalizations of ecological analysis.

———. *The Ends of the Earth: Perspectives on Modern Environmental History.* Cambridge: Cambridge University Press, 1988.

PART TWO
Fundamental World Views

CHAPTER FIVE

Religious and Cultural Perspectives

In the process of developing principles of environmental ethics, many believe it is of great value to consider diverse religious and cultural perspectives. Different cultural groups have world views that collectively could aid contemporary societies in better reframing the issues of the environmental crisis and in seeking more satisfying solutions to ecological problems. The insights of diverse religious and cultural groups have been tested and refined over long periods of human history and yet have resulted in strikingly different perspectives. To reject or discount the perspectives of other groups not only reflects a parochial and elitist outlook but also severely limits the potential resources of any one society for effectively dealing with environmental problems.

It is also increasingly recognized that environmental decisions made in any one society have the potential of affecting other societies as well. Knowledge and respect for other members of the global community are essential if humans are to develop effective strategies for solving common environmental problems.

MONOTHEISM: JUDAISM, CHRISTIANITY, ISLAM

Judaism, Christianity, and Islam are the three monotheistic faiths that trace their origins to Abraham and the patriarchs, as outlined in the Hebrew Bible. Judaism and Christianity have strongly influenced philosophical perspectives in contemporary Western society, even among those who are not religious adherents. It is difficult, if not impossible, to evaluate Western values and behaviors without assessing the historical contributions of these pervasive and powerful traditions. Similarly, Islam has had an enormous impact in the Middle East, much of Africa, and parts of Asia and Eastern Europe. Although Judaism, Christianity, and Islam are distinct religious traditions, all are founded on a common Abrahamic tradition; also, there is significant overlap in environmental perspectives among some members of each tradition toward the natural world. Based on the selection by Izzi Deen in this chapter, and an article by Zaidi,[1] Islam promulgates a dualism similar to that reflected in Judaism and Christianity.

The Relation of God to Nature in the Monotheistic Traditions

The three monotheistic traditions contain a rich variety of perspectives about God's relationship to nature. A few preliminary definitions may help clarify some of these perspectives. The terms *deism* and *theism* signify different views of God's role in the universe. Proponents of deism believe that after creation God exerted no further control over the universe, including in the lives of human beings. In contrast, proponents of theism believe that God continues to care about and exert some control over the universe, the natural world, and humans. Also, theists believe that God is known through revelation, both through divine interaction with humans in history and through increasing knowledge and insight about the natural world (creation). Most authors in this chapter advocate or address some form of theism.

Transcendent monotheism is the traditional perspective of the Abrahamic tradition. Proponents of this view affirm that God existed prior to the universe, created it, and rules over it. God is separate from and superior to the creation (nature).

A view generally rejected in Judaism, Christianity, and Islam, and which offers a striking contrast to transcendent monotheism, is pantheism. *Pantheism* is the doctrine that God is everything and that everything collectively is God. In pantheism, the universe and God are considered to be the same. Harold Wood has proposed pantheism as a basis for an environmental ethic.[2]

In contrast to pantheism, an alternative to transcendent monotheism that is generally acceptable to Judaism and Christianity is *panentheism*—the perspective that God includes the world, but the world is not the whole of God's being. Thus, God is not identical with nature, but is both immanent in and transcendent to nature. In this chapter, Lawrence Troster presents an environmental ethic with a panentheistic perspective.

A Monotheistic Environmental Ethic

One concern in recent years is the charge that the tenets of Christianity and Judaism, in particular, may be among the principal causes of the environmental crisis. Lynn White, Jr., presents an articulate summary of this charge. While numerous writers have echoed White's charges, many others have opposed it; representatives of both perspectives are included in a selection of references at the end of this chapter. Hargrove argues that it is time to move beyond this debate and seek new directions. He proposes evaluating how the major religions can best respond to the environmental crisis.[3]

In addressing the potential of these monotheistic traditions to provide such a foundation, some may question whether they have enough of substance to say about environmental ethics in contemporary societies. Writers in the Bible and Qur'an were primarily concerned about understanding the proper relationship between God and humanity and secondarily about understanding the proper relationships among human beings. Insights about human responsibility toward the land, wildlife, and ecosystems seem, at best, distant considerations. Indeed, many ecological concepts that underlie contemporary environmental perspectives were not part of the world view of these earlier writers. However, others may argue that there are enough examples on attitudes toward the land in agricultural contexts, in related insights drawn from the historical narratives, and in careful interpretation of the language used in these sacred texts. Lawrence Troster and Holmes Rolston believe that a thoughtful interpretation of their sacred literature, and a careful reevaluation of their respective contemporary religious insights in

---

[1]Iqtidar H. Zaidi, "On the Ethics of Man's Interaction with the Environment: An Islamic Approach," *Environmental Ethics* 3 (1981): 35–47.

[2]Harold W. Wood, "Modern Pantheism as an Approach to Environmental Ethics," *Environmental Ethics* 7 (1985): 151–63.

[3]Eugene C. Hargrove, *Religion and Environmental Crisis* (Athens: University of Georgia Press, 1986), pp. ix–xix.

light of emerging knowledge of environmental problems, can provide a firm foundation for an environmental ethic. Troster addresses how Judaism and the Gaia hypothesis might be made compatible through the perspective of panentheism. Rolston provides a thoughtful account of how Christians might approach a contemporary ecocentric ethic.

At least three ideas can serve as a foundation for an environmental ethic in monotheism. One notion is that the world is God's creation. Another is that God is pleased with the results of this creative handiwork. Also, God values all of the creation — the individual members of creation as well as the underlying processes and relations among them. These three ideas support the view that each part of nature is something precious to God. It follows readily that to honor God, one must honor the creation that God loves.

COMPARING WESTERN AND NON-WESTERN PERSPECTIVES AS POSSIBLE SOURCES OF ECOLOGICAL WISDOM

In this chapter, the readings by Winona LaDuke and by Ramachandra Guha and J. Martinez-Alier compare and contrast the environmental perspectives and actions of local peoples to those of Western industrial societies. They conclude that the perspectives and approaches of these local peoples have much to offer Western industrial societies. LaDuke contrasts at least five perspectives commonly distinguishing Native American peoples from Western industrial people and provides some insights on valuable perspectives to incorporate into an environmental ethic. Guha and Martinez-Alier provide a vocabulary of protest in describing differences between local "ecosystem people" and "omnivores." They go on to describe two kinds of environmentalism distinguishing northern and southern countries.

Thich Nhat Hanh provides a thoughtful and articulate perspective of how Buddhism can provide insights on environmental ethics. Yi-Fu Tuan argues that while Buddhism and Taoism may have precepts that, in theory, promote respectful attitudes toward nature, those precepts did not prevent the Chinese from engaging in a long history of environmental changes and destruction.[4] In contrast, Hargrove points out that environmental values are the ideals for how people ought to live, rather than a description of how they always behave.[5] In any society, there is a broad range of responses in the thoroughness with which its members accept and follow prescribed societal values. Hargrove also points out that the gradual environmental degradation in the East may have resulted from empirical ignorance; he notes that empirical ignorance also may explain some of the problems in the West. Thus, the environmental problems observed in non-Western societies may very well be due to causes other than a lack of wisdom about the proper human relationship to the natural environment.

FINDING COMMON ELEMENTS AMONG VARIOUS RELIGIOUS AND CULTURAL PERSPECTIVES

In attempting to identify common elements among these varied perspectives, we must first consider the variety within individual perspectives. No one tradition can be said to represent "the Christian perspective," "the Native American perspective," or any other perspective. Making generalizations about diverse perspectives does not allow proper acknowledgment of the richness and variation of values found within each tradition.

All of these perspectives differ in many ways from each other. For example, the monotheistic religions recognize a supreme being; other perspectives may recognize a supreme being, but also lesser figures, in their cosmology. Native American belief systems commonly include numerous varied gods and spirits. Buddhism focuses primarily on human suffering and probably cannot be considered a theistic religion. Thus, the probability of

---

[4]Yi-Fu Tuan, "Discrepancies between Environmental Attitude and Behaviour. Examples from Europe and China," *Canadian Geographer* 13 (1968): 176–91.

[5]Eugene C. Hargrove, "Forward," in *Nature in Asian Traditions of Thought*, J. Baird Callicott and Roger T. Ames, eds. (Albany: State University of New York Press, 1989), pp. xiii–xxi.

identifying common elements among such diverse perspectives is limited.

Further, each of these perspectives is dynamic, changing over time. Some changes take place gradually, following the inevitable growth and evolution of a philosophy as its scholars study and probe its limits in a changing society. Some changes occur in violent episodes and rapid succession, as when Native American groups were invaded by Europeans.

Among some non-Western perspectives discussed in this chapter we can find two common elements: the absence of a strong monotheistic doctrine and a deemphasis on dualism between humans and the rest of nature. Rather, there is a greater sense of human connectedness with the natural world. In this chapter, Thich Nhat Hanh and Winona LaDuke each give distinct and articulate voices to that relationship.

The Historical Roots of Our Ecologic Crisis

Lynn T. White, Jr.

Lynn T. White, Jr., (1907–1987) was an internationally known medieval scholar who taught at Princeton and Stanford Universities, was president of Mills College (Oakland, California) for fifteen years, and then taught at the University of California, Los Angeles (UCLA), from 1958 until his retirement in 1974. He founded and directed the Center for Medieval and Renaissance Studies at UCLA.

In a classic paper in Science, *White argues that the ecological crisis of Western society is rooted in Christianity. He further cites Christianity as being the most anthropocentric religion of the world. By destroying pagan animism and the acceptance of guardian spirits found in nature, Christianity removed the old inhibitions against exploiting the natural world. White calls for a greater consideration of moving toward St. Francis's perspective of equality among all creatures, including humans, as a foundation for rethinking the human position and destiny.*

. . . All forms of life modify their contexts. The most spectacular and benign instance is doubtless the coral polyp. By serving its own ends, it has created a vast undersea world favorable to thousands of other kinds of animals and plants. Ever since man became a numerous species he has affected his environment notably. The hypothesis that his fire-drive method of hunting created the world's great grasslands and helped to exterminate the monster mammals of the Pleistocene from much of the globe is plausible, if not proved. For six millennia at least, the banks of the lower Nile have been a human artifact rather than the swampy African jungle which nature, apart from man, would have made it. . . . Quite unintentionally, changes in human ways often affect nonhuman nature. It has been noted, for example, that the advent of the automobile eliminated huge flocks of sparrows that once fed on the horse manure littering every street.

The history of ecologic change is still so rudimentary that we know little about what really happened, or what the results were. The extinction of the European aurochs as late as 1627 would seem to have been a simple case of overenthusiastic hunting. On more intricate matters it often is impossible to find solid information. . . .

People, then, have often been a dynamic element in their own environment, but in the present state of historical scholarship we usually do not know exactly when, where, or with what effects man-induced changes came. . . . It was not until about four generations ago that Western Europe and North America arranged a marriage between science and technology, a union of the theoretical and the empirical approaches to our natural environment. The emergence in widespread practice of the Baconian creed that scientific knowledge means technological power over nature can scarcely be dated before about 1850, save in the chemical industries, where it is anticipated in the 18th century. Its acceptance as a normal pattern of action may mark the greatest event in human history since the invention of agriculture, and perhaps in nonhuman terrestrial history as well.

Almost at once the new situation forced the crystallization of the novel concept of ecology; indeed, the word *ecology* first appeared in the English language in 1873. Today, less than a century later, the impact of our race upon the environment has so increased in force that it has changed in essence. . . . With the population explosion, the carcinoma of planless urbanism, the now geological deposits of sewage and garbage, surely no creature other than man has ever managed to foul its nest in such short order. . . .

What shall we do? No one yet knows. Unless we think about fundamentals, our specific measures may produce new backlashes more serious than those they are designed to remedy.

As a beginning we should try to clarify our thinking by looking, in some historical depth, at the presuppositions that underlie modern technology and science. Science was traditionally aristocratic, speculative, intellectual in intent; technology was lower-class, empirical, action-oriented. The quite sudden fusion of these two toward the middle of the 19th century, is surely related to the slightly prior and contemporary democratic revolutions which, by reducing social barriers, tended to assert a functional unity of brain and hand. Our ecologic crisis is the product of an emerging, entirely novel, democratic culture. The issue is whether a democratized world can survive its own implications. Presumably we cannot unless we rethink our axioms.

THE WESTERN TRADITIONS OF TECHNOLOGY AND SCIENCE

One thing is so certain that it seems stupid to verbalize it: both modern technology and modern science are distinctively *Occidental.* Our technology has absorbed elements from all over the world, notably from China; yet everywhere today, whether in Japan or in Nigeria, successful technology is Western. Our science is the heir to all the sciences of the past, especially perhaps to the work of the great Islamic scientists of the Middle Ages, who so often outdid the ancient Greeks in skill and perspicacity: al-Rāzī in medicine, for example; or ibn-al-Haytham in optics; or Omar Khayyám in mathematics. Indeed, not a few works of such geniuses seem to have vanished in the original Arabic and to survive only in medieval Latin translations that helped to lay the foundations for later Western developments. Today, around the globe, all significant science is Western in style and method, whatever the pigmentation or language of the scientists.

A second pair of facts is less well recognized because they result from quite recent historical scholarship. The leadership of the West, both in technology and in science, is far older than the so-called Scientific Revolution of the 17th century or the so-called Industrial Revolution of the 18th century. These terms are in fact out-moded and obscure the true nature of what they try to describe — significant stages in two long and separate developments. By A.D. 1000 at the latest — and perhaps, feebly, as much as 200 years earlier — the West began to apply water power to industrial processes other than milling grain. This was followed in the late 12th century by the harnessing of wind power. From simple beginnings, but with remarkable consistency of style, the West rapidly expanded its skills in the development of power machinery, labor-saving devices, and automation. . . .

. . . The distinctive Western tradition of science, in fact, began in the late 11th century with a massive movement of translation of Arabic and Greek scientific works into Latin. A few notable books — Theophrastus, for example — escaped the West's avid new appetite for science, but within less than 200 years effectively the entire corpus of Greek and Muslim science was available in Latin, and was being eagerly read and criticized in the new European universities. Out of criticism arose new observation, speculation, and increasing distrust of ancient authorities. By the late 13th century Europe had seized global scientific leadership from the faltering hands of Islam. It would be as absurd to deny the profound originality of Newton, Galileo, or Copernicus as to deny that of the 14th century scholastic scientists like Buridan or Oresme on whose work they built. Before the 11th century, science scarcely existed in the Latin West, even in Roman times. From the 11th century onward, the scientific sector of Occidental culture has increased in a steady crescendo.

Since both our technological and our scientific movements got their start, acquired their character, and achieved world dominance in the Middle Ages, it would seem that we cannot understand their nature or their present impact upon ecology without examining fundamental medieval assumptions and developments.

MEDIEVAL VIEW OF MAN AND NATURE

Until recently, agriculture has been the chief occupation even in "advanced" societies; hence, any change in methods of tillage has much importance. Early plows, drawn by two oxen, did not normally turn the sod but merely scratched it. Thus, cross-plowing was needed and fields tended to be squarish. In the fairly light soils and semiarid climates of the Near East and Mediterranean, this worked well. But such a plow was inappropriate to the wet climate and often sticky soils of northern Europe. By the latter part of the 7th century after Christ, however, following obscure beginnings, certain northern peasants were using an entirely new kind of plow, equipped with a vertical knife to cut the line of the furrow, a horizontal share to slice under the sod, and a moldboard to turn it over. The friction of this plow with the soil was so great that it normally required not two but eight oxen. It attacked the land with such violence that cross-plowing was not needed, and fields tended to be shaped in long strips.

In the days of the scratch-plow, fields were distributed generally in units capable of supporting a single family. Subsistence farming was the presupposition. But no peasant owned eight oxen: to use the new and more efficient plow, peasants pooled their oxen to form large plow-teams, originally receiving (it would appear) plowed strips in proportion to their contribution. Thus, distribution of land was based no longer on the needs of a family but, rather, on the capacity of a power machine to till the earth. Man's relation to the soil was profoundly changed. Formerly man had been part of nature; now he was the exploiter of nature. Nowhere else in the world did farmers develop any analogous agricultural implement. Is it coincidence that modern technology, with its ruthlessness toward nature, has so largely been produced by descendants of these peasants of northern Europe?

This same exploitive attitude appears slightly before A.D. 830 in Western illustrated calendars. In older calendars the months were shown as passive personifications. The new Frankish calendars, which set the style for the Middle Ages, are very different: they show men coercing the world around them — plowing, harvesting, chopping trees, butchering pigs. Man and nature are two things, and man is master.

These novelties seem to be in harmony with larger intellectual patterns. What people do about their ecology depends on what they think about themselves in relation to things around them. Human ecology is deeply conditioned by beliefs about our nature and destiny — that is, by religion. To Western eyes this is very evident in, say, India or Ceylon. It is equally true of ourselves and of our medieval ancestors.

The victory of Christianity over paganism was the greatest psychic revolution in the history of our culture. . . . We continue today to live, as we have lived for about 1700 years, very largely in a context of Christian axioms.

What did Christianity tell people about their relations with the environment?

While many of the world's mythologies provide stories of creation, Greco-Roman mythology was singularly incoherent in this respect. Like Aristotle, the intellectuals of the ancient West denied that the visible world had had a beginning. Indeed, the idea of a beginning was impossible in the framework of their cyclical notion of time. In sharp contrast, Christianity inherited from Judaism not only a concept of time as nonrepetitive and linear but also a striking story of creation. By gradual stages a loving and all-powerful God had created light and darkness, the heavenly bodies, the earth and all its plants, animals, birds, and fishes. Finally, God had created Adam and, as an afterthought, Eve to keep man from being lonely. Man named all the animals, thus establishing his dominance over them. God planned all of this explicitly for man's benefit and rule: no item in the physical creation had any purpose save to serve man's purposes. And, although man's body is made of clay, he is not simply part of nature: he is made in God's image.

Especially in its Western form, Christianity is the most anthropocentric religion the world has seen. As early as the 2nd century both Tertullian and Saint Irenaeus of Lyons were insisting that when God shaped Adam he was foreshadowing the image of the incarnate Christ, the Second Adam. Man shares, in great measure, God's transcendence of nature. Christianity, in absolute contrast to ancient paganism and Asia's religions (except, perhaps, Zoroastrianism), not only established a dualism of man and nature but also insisted that it is God's will that man exploit nature for his proper ends.

At the level of the common people this worked out in an interesting way. In antiquity every tree, every spring, every stream, every hill had its own *genius loci,* its guardian spirit. These spirits were accessible to men, but were very unlike men; centaurs, fauns, and mermaids show their ambivalence. Before one cut a tree, mined a mountain, or dammed a brook, it was important to placate the spirit in charge of that particular situation, and to keep it placated. By destroying pagan animism, Christianity made it possible to exploit nature in a mood of indifference to the feelings of natural objects.

. . . The spirits *in* natural objects, which formerly had protected nature from man, evaporated. Man's effective monopoly on spirit in this world was confirmed, and the old inhibitions to the exploitation of nature crumbled.

When one speaks in such sweeping terms, a note of caution is in order. Christianity is a complex faith, and its consequences differ in differing contexts. What I have said may well apply to the medieval West, where in fact technology made spectacular advances. But the Greek East, a highly civilized realm of equal Christian devotion, seems to have produced no marked technological innovation after the late 7th century, when Greek fire was invented. The key to the contrast may perhaps be found in a difference in the tonality of piety and thought which students of comparative theology find between the Greek and the Latin churches. The Greeks believed that sin was intellectual blindness, and that salvation was found in illumination, orthodoxy — that is, clear thinking. The Latins, on the other hand, felt that sin was moral evil, and that salvation was to be found in right conduct. Eastern theology has been intellectualist. Western theology has been voluntarist. The Greek saint contemplates; the Western saint acts. The implications of Christianity for the conquest of nature would emerge more easily in the Western atmosphere.

The Christian dogma of creation, which is found in the first clause of all the Creeds, has another meaning for our comprehension of today's ecologic crisis. By revelation, God had given man the Bible, the Book of Scripture. But since God had made nature, nature also must reveal the divine mentality. The religious study of nature for the better understanding of God was known as natural theology. In the early Church, and always in the Greek East, nature was conceived primarily as a symbolic system through which God speaks to men: the ant is a sermon to sluggards; rising flames are the symbol of the soul's aspiration. This view of nature was essentially artistic rather than scientific. While Byzantium preserved and copied great numbers of ancient Greek scientific texts, science as we conceive it could scarcely flourish in such an ambience.

However, in the Latin West by the early 13th century natural theology was following a very different bent. It was ceasing to be the decoding of the physical symbols of God's communication with man and was becoming the effort to understand God's mind by discovering how his creation operates. The rainbow was no longer simply a symbol of hope first sent to Noah after the Deluge: Robert Gorsseteste, Friar Roger Bacon, and Theodoric of Freiberg produced startlingly sophisticated work on the optics of the rainbow, but they did it as a venture in religious understanding. From the 13th century onward, up to and including Leibnitz and Newton, every major scientist, in effect, explained his motivation in religious terms. Indeed, if Galileo had not been so expert an amateur theologian he would have got into far less trouble: the professionals resented his intrusion. And Newton seems to have regarded himself more as a theologian than as a scientist. It was not until the late 18th century that the hypothesis of God became unnecessary to many scientists.

It is often hard for the historian to judge, when men explain why they are doing what they want to do, whether they are offering real reasons or merely culturally acceptable reasons. The consistency with which scientists during the long formative centuries of Western science said that the task and the reward of the scientist was "to think God's thoughts after him" leads one to believe that this was their real motivation. If so, then modern Western science was cast in a matrix of Christian theology. The dynamism of religious devotion, shaped by the Judeo-Christian dogma of creation, gave it impetus.

AN ALTERNATIVE CHRISTIAN VIEW

We would seem to be headed toward conclusions unpalatable to many Christians. Since both *science* and *technology* are blessed words in our contemporary vocabulary, some may be happy at the notions, first, that, viewed historically, modern science is an extrapolation of natural theology and, second, that modern technology is at least partly to be explained as an Occidental, voluntarist realization of the Christian dogma of man's transcendence of, and rightful mastery over, nature. But, as we now recognize, somewhat over a century ago science and technology — hitherto quite separate activities — joined to give humankind powers which, to judge by many of the ecologic effects, are out of control. If so, Christianity bears a huge burden of guilt.

I personally doubt that disastrous ecologic back-lash can be avoided simply by applying to our problems more science and more technology. Our science and technology have grown out of Christian attitudes toward man's relation to nature which are almost universally held not only by Christians and neo-Christians but also by those who fondly regard themselves as post-Christians. Despite Copernicus, all the cosmos rotates around our little globe. Despite Darwin, we are *not,* in our hearts, part of the natural process. We are superior to nature, contemptuous of it, willing to use it for our slightest whim. The newly elected Governor of California, like myself a churchman but less troubled than I, spoke for the Christian tradition when he said (as is alleged), "when you've seen one redwood tree, you've seen them all." To a Christian a tree can be no more than a physical fact. The whole concept of the sacred grove is alien to Christianity and to the ethos of the West. For nearly 2 millennia Christian missionaries have been chopping down sacred groves, which are idolatrous because they assume spirit in nature.

What we do about ecology depends on our ideas of the man-nature relationship. More science and more technology are not going to get us out of the present ecologic crisis until we find a new religion, or rethink our old one. The beatniks, who are the basic revolutionaries of our time, show a sound instinct in their affinity for Zen Buddhism, which conceives of the man-nature relationship as very nearly the mirror image of the Christian view. Zen, however, is as deeply conditioned by Asian history as Christianity is by the experience of the West, and I am dubious of its viability among us.

Possibly we should ponder the greatest radical in Christian history since Christ: Saint Francis of Assisi. The prime miracle of Saint Francis is the fact that he did not end at the stake, as many of his left-wing followers did. He was so clearly heretical that a General of the Franciscan Order, Saint Bonaventura, a great and perceptive Christian, tried to suppress the early accounts of Franciscanism. The key to an understanding of Francis is his belief in the virtue of humility—not merely for the individual but for man as a species. Francis tried to depose man from his monarchy over creation and set up a democracy of all God's creatures. With him the ant is no longer simply a homily for the lazy, flames a sign of the thrust of the soul toward union with God; now they are Brother Ant and Sister Fire, praising the Creator in their own ways as Brother Man does in his.

Later commentators have said that Francis preached to the birds as a rebuke to men who would not listen. The records do not read so: he urged the little birds to praise God, and in spiritual ecstasy they flapped their wings and chirped rejoicing. Legends of saints, especially the Irish saints, had long told of their dealings with animals but always, I believe, to show their human dominance over creatures. With Francis it is different. The land around Gubbio in the Apennines was being ravaged by a fierce wolf. Saint Francis, says the legend, talked to the wolf and persuaded him of the error of his ways. The wolf repented, died in the odor of sanctity, and was buried in consecrated ground.

What Sir Steven Ruciman calls "the Franciscan doctrine of the animal soul" was quickly stamped out. Quite possibly it was in part inspired, consciously or unconsciously, by the belief in reincarnation held by the Cathar heretics who at that time teemed in Italy and southern France, and who presumably had got it originally from India. It is significant that at just the same moment, about 1200, traces of metempsychosis are found also in western Judaism, in the Provençal *Cabbala.* But Francis held neither to transmigration of souls nor to pantheism. His view of nature and of man rested on a unique sort of pan-psychism of all things animate and inanimate, designed for the glorification of their transcendent Creator, who, in the ultimate gesture of cosmic humility, assumed flesh, lay helpless in a manger, and hung dying on a scaffold.

I am not suggesting that many contemporary Americans who are concerned about our ecologic crisis will be either able or willing to counsel with wolves or exhort birds. However, the present increasing disruption of the global environment is the product of a dynamic technology and science which were originating in the Western medieval world against which Saint Francis was rebelling in so original a way. Their growth cannot be understood historically apart from distinctive attitudes toward nature which are deeply grounded in Christian dogma. The fact that most people do not think of these attitudes as Christian is irrelevant. No new set of basic values has been accepted in our society to displace those of Christianity. Hence we shall continue to have a worsening ecologic crisis until we reject the Christian axiom that nature has no reason for existence save to serve man.

The greatest spiritual revolutionary in Western history, Saint Francis, proposed what he thought was an alternative Christian view of nature and man's relation to it: he tried to substitute the idea of the equality of all creatures, including man, for the idea of man's limitless rule of creation. He failed. Both our present science and our present technology are so tinctured with orthodox Christian arrogance toward nature that no solution for our ecologic crisis can be expected from them alone. Since the roots of our trouble are so largely religious, the remedy must also be essentially religious, whether we call it that or not. We must rethink and refeel our nature and destiny. The profoundly religious, but heretical, sense of the primitive Franciscans for the spiritual autonomy of all parts of nature may point a direction. I propose Francis as a patron saint for ecologists.

DISCUSSION TOPICS

1. White points out that all forms of life modify their environments. If humans are considered a part of nature, as White implies, why should humans be subject to any more criticism than another species when they modify their environments? Justify your answer.
2. Do you believe it would be possible to replace Christianity with a more ecologically sensitive religion? Why or why not? If yes, what religion might be a good candidate? Explain your reasoning.
3. White claims that acceptance of the idea that scientific knowledge results in technological power over nature may mark the greatest event in human history since the invention of agriculture, and perhaps in nonhuman terrestrial history as well. Do you agree? Explain your answer. What other events, if any, might be more significant?

READING 24

Created in the Image of God: Humanity and Divinity in an Age of Environmentalism

Lawrence Troster

Lawrence Troster is rabbi at Congregation Beth Israel, Bergenfield, New Jersey. In this selection from his paper originally published in Conservative Judaism, *Lawrence Troster seeks to find common ground between contemporary Judaism and the more radical Gaia movement through panentheism—the notion that God is both part of nature and separate from the universe. James Lovelock, founder of the Gaia concept, notes that humans are a partner with this Gaian entity, that this Gaian entity has a divine aspect (God), and that these insights call for a more active relationship with Gaia than implied by the notion of stewardship (benign management) of the earth. Troster further proposes that seeing God as a transcendent deity encourages humans to preserve their obligation to care for the earth. Seeing God as part of the earth (Gaia) encourages continued sensitivity to nonhuman life and our own physical/animal qualities.*

Humanity was created in the image of God. Modern environmentalism poses many challenges to this Biblical concept. Some authorities consider their differences to be irreconcilable. We shall examine a reconciliation of these positions through three interpretations and a synthesis with the Gaia theory, which conceives of the earth as a living, self-sustaining and self-regulating organism.

IN THE IMAGE OF GOD

And God said, "Let us make humanity in our image, after our likeness. They shall rule the fish of the sea, the birds of the sky, the cattle, the whole earth, and all creeping things that creep on earth." And God created humanity in His image, in the image of God He created him, male and female He created them. (Genesis 1:26–27)

References to humanity's being created in the image, or likeness, of God (*betzelem Elohim*)[1] have been some of the most influential Biblical verses in the history of both the Jewish and the Christian traditions. . . . It expresses the enormous value of a human life, and the inherent dignity and respect required in all interpersonal relationships. Modern Jewish writers on ethics have given an expanded meaning to this concept to include all aspects of the moral life. . . . For Seymour Siegel this value expresses our ability to be godlike but not God. Indeed, for both Siegel and David S. Shapiro, the concept of the "image of God" points both to the enormous potential and the inherent limitations of humanity.[2]

AGAINST THE IMAGE OF GOD

Since the sixteenth century, the development of modern secular culture can almost be encapsulated in challenges to the traditional religious status of humanity as derived from the "image of God" metaphor. These challenges began with the shift from the earth-centered worldview, first articulated by Ptolemy, to the heliocentric view of Copernicus. Earth and humanity were no longer viewed as the center of the universe. The Copernican cosmology asserted that the earth and, by extension, humanity do not occupy a privileged position in the universe.[3] There followed what might be called the evolution critique, which, since Darwin, has asserted that humanity also occupies no special place in nature. Humanity is not an intentionally created species, but is rather, in the words of biologist Stephen Jay Gould, a "happy accident,"[4] the result of a long series of evolutionary accidents stimulated by random large scale environmental changes. Indeed, Gould has asserted that if one were to "rewind the tape" of evolution and "replay it," it is highly unlikely that a conscious species like humanity would again emerge.

These paradigm shifts in worldview, plus the growing awareness of the damage done to the environment by humanity, have led to a radical environmental critique of humanity's place in nature. This critique seems to put environmental ethics in direct conflict with Judaism's view of the image of God in humanity.

These radical critiques emerge from the "deep ecologists"—those ecologists who assert that humanity has no special status as a species. This is in contrast to the "shallow ecologists," who favor a conservationist approach to environmental problems. Deep ecology is rooted in biocentrism (as opposed to anthropocentrism, or the more awkward and unfortunate term "speciesism," the biological form of racism). Biocentrism asserts that:

1. The needs, desires, interests, and goals of humans are not privileged.
2. The human species should not change the ecology of the planet.
3. The world ecological system is too complex for human beings ever to understand.
4. The ultimate goal, good, and joy of humankind is contemplative understanding of Nature.
5. Nature is a holistic system of parts (in which man is merely one among many equals), all of which are internally interrelated in dynamic, harmonious, ecological equilibrium.[5]

From this perspective, Judaism and Christianity are sources of the anthropocentric idea which asserts that humans have a special God-given status that separates them from nature and allows them to exercise unbridled domination over creation. From this perspective, God, as transcendent Creator, is also seen as separate from nature, thus desacralizing the environment and furthering humanity's alienation from nature.[6] The solution, according to some biocentrists, lies in a return to a pantheistic conception of god, nature, and humanity. . . .

Philosophers Steven S. Schwarzschild and Richard A. Watson have both subjected the philosophical basis of biocentrism to a thorough "critique."[7] According to this critique, biocentrism displays anthropocentric features by postulating a human moral concern for nature and by sacralizing the environment. . . . In other words, by postulating a human moral stance towards nature instead of an unrestrained competition with other species, biocentrism is also asserting a special status for humanity in nature.

The biocentric thesis also erroneously interprets the specific text (Genesis 1:28) used to "prove" Judaism's anti-ecological foundations, as Jeremy Cohen has shown.[8] This thesis also ignores the Jewish doctrine of humanity's responsibilities to the earth.[9] Judaism always has valued the prohibition of the wanton destruction of nature, as concretized in *halakhah*.[10] Nonetheless, the "image of God" concept does assert that human beings have a unique and dominant role in the world,[11] even if it is as stewards and protectors of the earth.

From an environmental perspective, however, there are problematic aspects of Judaism's regarding the relationship of human beings, divinity, and the earth. Indeed, human beings often are called "partners with God in the Work of Creation." In this view, the world is unfinished, and human beings are empowered by God to complete God's work. Jewish tradition asserts that the world was created essentially for human benefit. Judaism does have an anthropocentric view of the world, its relation to humanity and to God. Nature is identified with the divine, and its chief "value lies in its serviceability to man and God."[12] From this perspective, Jewish concern for the environment is fundamentally utilitarian: human beings must preserve, protect, and not squander the environment, in striving to attain the goal of creating the Kingdom of God upon earth. Nature is precious as a creation of God; it is not sacred in and of itself.

Humanity's relationship to the earth also reflects its primary concern with morality among humans or between humans and God, rather than our "ecological" morality with the earth. . . .

Indeed, throughout the Bible the earth is often the vehicle for a reflection of human morality. Earth seems to have a moral sensitivity regarding the way humans behave with respect to one another as well as with respect to God. There is no Biblical idea of humanity's relationship to the earth as an independent sacred covenant. Only within the covenant with God are humans bound to the earth. This picture of humanity, God, and the earth is an interesting counterpoint to much of the biocentric spirituality that is current in many environmental and some Jewish circles.

The "image of God" concept is basic for Jewish morality. To eliminate it, as some have proposed,[13]

would radically alter Judaism's basis for its moral code. Nonetheless, modern society's alienation from nature and our disregard for the environment is a serious religious concern.

MOTHER GAIA AND (SOME OF) HER CHILDREN

Human alienation from nature has been confronted by the British chemist James Lovelock in his two books describing the Gaia theory,[14] which asserts that the earth is one living self-sustaining and self-regulating organism. This organism he calls Gaia, after the Greek goddess of the earth.

His theory resulted from the attempt to evaluate life-detecting equipment for NASA's Mars probes in the 1970s. Lovelock decided that one possible way of knowing whether there is life on Mars was first to establish what makes it obvious that there is life on Earth. Comparing Earth to Venus and Mars, the other similar planets in our system, Lovelock stated that the obvious difference lies in the makeup of their respective atmospheres.

Venus and Mars have atmospheres in equilibrium, atmospheres made up of a stable combination of mostly carbon dioxide, some nitrogen, and traces of oxygen and argon. Earth, on the other hand, has an unusual and unstable atmosphere in a state of disequilibrium. It is unstable because the combination of gases that make up the earth's atmosphere (79% nitrogen, 21% oxygen, 0.03% carbon dioxide, 1% argon) react with one another to form byproducts which, left to their own devices, would eventually form an atmosphere much like Mars or Venus — one that is in equilibrium. Therefore, said Lovelock, Mars cannot have life, since a living planet is characterized by having an atmosphere in disequilibrium. What sustains this atmosphere of disequilibrium? Something must be regulating the earth's atmosphere to constantly maintain the proper ratios of gases.

This regulation also controls the surface temperature of the planet. Lovelock found that, despite the fluctuation of solar energy over the last three and one-half billion years, the surface temperature of the earth has remained fairly constant. What regulates the atmosphere of earth? Indeed, what created the unlikely atmosphere of earth so amenable for the development of life?

Lovelock's answer is that life itself created and sustained the atmosphere of earth. . . . The earth is one living organism, says Lovelock, in which the various individual species are like the bodily organs of a larger evolving whole. While Lovelock has not definitively "proven" this theory, much current research suggests he is right. His original analysis is being tested, new "Gaian" factors are being discovered, and what was first seen as a crackpot idea is now seriously debated in scientific circles.

What is the status of humanity in this living organism of Gaia? What is our place in this intricate web of life? How much are we part of this system, and how much are we outside of it? Lovelock sees humans as the "brain cells" of Gaia, since humanity is the only species on this planet with cognitive anticipation, the ability to consciously anticipate needs and then to act on them.[15] . . . Lovelock suggests that human cooperation and consciousness mean that Gaia has extended her perception beyond her own surface into outer space, not only that Gaia has a possible better way of managing her own environment. In other words, "She is now, through us, awake and aware of herself.[16]

Lovelock also states, however, that we must stop viewing Gaia as a farm for human management. "The Gaia hypothesis implies that the stable state of our planet includes man as part of, or partner in, a very democratic entity."[17] If we do not recognize this fact, then humanity, not Gaia, might be doomed to extinction from environmental change. For Gaia, the extinction of humanity as a result of the "greenhouse effect" would be only a temporary bump in the long road of life. Life would adjust to our passing and continue without us. Given the lifespan of Gaia, however, it is highly unlikely that another self-conscious species would evolve if humanity became extinct.

As a result of many religious responses to his first book, Lovelock devotes a chapter of his second book to the theological implications of Gaia and God. While admitting that he is an agnostic, Lovelock feels that Gaia is as close to divinity as we can possibly get. The origin of life and whether or not the universe was created for the purpose of the emergence of Gaia, Lovelock considers to be "ineffable questions," which are interesting but which serve no real purpose. Gaia, on the other hand, is a "religious as well as scientific concept, and in both spheres it is manageable."[18] For Lovelock, both Gaia and God are concepts for ways to view the relationship of the universe, the earth, and humanity with other living things. Since Gaia is one-fourth as old as the universe, "she" (and Lovelock is very much concerned with the return of the feminine element to the nature of the divine) is as close to immortality as we can experience. We are part of her and she is part of God.

Our concepts of God lack the element of Gaia because of our alienation from the environment. Since most of us dwell in cities, we are away from and out of touch with nature. Lovelock claims that this alienation has led to an extremely reductionist view of life in the sciences which prefers to analyze the parts with little or no reference to the whole. This trend also distances us from the earth. According to Lovelock, the Gaia concept, which was known intuitively by humanity through nature worship and earth goddess religions, has been difficult for science to accept. A more holistic approach to all forms of human knowledge is now showing that Gaia is real. A similar approach to the whole cosmos declares that the universe itself may be "living" in the sense that it is a self-organizing structure. In such a universe, the evolution of life is inevitable.

Can a Gaian, or biocentric, approach be incorporated within a Jewish perspective on the environment? The Gaia concept appears to show a dichotomy between the biblical concept of stewardship, or benign management of the earth with God, as compared with the Gaian concept of the partnership or "partnership of humanity" with the earth which is God. If humans are a part of Gaia, then must we act towards the earth with a kind of moral behavior as we would with another being/creature/ourselves? "Gaian morality" says that we must move beyond the concept of benign utilitarian management of life on earth.

Let us now examine three interpretations[19] of the term "in the image of God" (*betzelem Elohim*), and a synthesis of these interpretations with the Gaia metaphor which will attempt to harmonize both Jewish and ecological positions.

IN THE IMAGE: *PESHAT*

The Hebrew term for "image" (*tzelem*) has a cognate word in Old Akkadian and Old Babylonian that throws significant light upon the original nuance of the term used in Genesis. The cognate word (*tzalmu*) can mean a statue, a bodily shape, a figurine, or a relief drawing. The term sometimes refers to a statue or an image of the king, which is placed in a captured city or elsewhere in the kingdom as an extension of the king's presence and the king's law. In other words, it is as if the king were present wherever the king's *tzalmu* is placed. The king rules wherever his *tzalmu* stands.[20]

Seen in this light, humanity is the *tzalmu* of God. Wherever humans are, the presence of God is reflected. This cannot be said of any other creature. Indeed, the command to multiply and spread over the earth is none other than a desire to spread the presence of God and to actualize God's power throughout Creation, rather than a desire for mere numerical increase.[21] It is as if God could not function in the world without humanity. "While he (a human being) is not divine, his very existence bears witness to the activity of God in the life of the world."[22] This is certainly in accord with the Rabbinic idea of human beings as "partners of God in the work of Creation,"[23] necessary witnesses attesting to God's existence.[24] Heschel uses this idea in his concepts of the Divine Pathos and the interdependence of God and humanity.[25] Thus the term *tzelem,* in its plain meaning (*peshat*), connects humanity with God as rulers of the earth, and gives humanity the divine mandate to be stewards of creation. The immanence of God in the world is to be found in the physical presence of human beings.[26]

IN THE IMAGE: *DERASH*

He [God] created him with four attributes of the higher beings [i.e., angels] and four attributes of the lower beings [i.e., beasts]. [The four attributes of] the higher beings are: he stands upright, like the ministering angels; he speaks, like the ministering angels; he understands, like the ministering angels; and he sees, like the ministering angels. Yet, does not a dumb animal see?! But this one [man] can see from the side [i.e., with peripheral vision]. He has four attributes of the lower beings: he eats and drinks, like an animal; he procreates, like an animal; he excretes, like an animal; and he dies, like an animal.[27]

For the authors of this midrash, human beings "are situated on a cosmic frontier, between supernal and terrestrial realms of existence."[28] The divine characteristics specified are uniquely human, separating humanity from other creatures, while the characteristics shared with the lower beings bind humanity to nature. Speech and understanding are the attributes which produce human culture and, hence, ethical choice. In other Rabbinic texts,[29] human beings are given the choice to actualize their higher or lower attributes, which determines their ability to be the dominant species on earth. But the midrash reflects the dual nature of human beings, composed of both the earthly (*adamah*) and the divine (*tzelem*). Humans may choose not to actualize the divine *tzalmu,* but they cannot escape being earthly (*adamah*). Possessing the "higher" attributes makes humanity the conscious link between God and nature.

IN THE IMAGE: *REMEZ*

. . .

For Maimonides, what is unique about human beings is their intellectual apprehension—or, as we might term it, the human consciousness[30] and therefore what follows from human consciousness: moral choice and apprehension of the divine. For him this is the meaning of *tzelem.* Consciousness, which does not depend necessarily on sense perception, is what humanity shares with a noncorporeal God. Maimonides identifies this quality with the soul, and as a link between humanity and the angels.[31] Thus humanity shares with the "higher beings" an immortal element that is not tied to the natural world. In a modern context, we know that consciousness is a function of our brain, but the extent to which it is dependent on the brain is a matter of much debate.[32] Whether or not other animals have a form of consciousness is also a matter of great debate.[33] For Maimonides, however, consciousness is the great divide between humanity and the rest of the natural world. Even with this divide, Maimonides recognizes the strong link between the body and the soul, and knows that the health of one can influence the health of the other.[34] Nonetheless, it is consciousness that is our unique link to God, and the source of our ability to receive prophecy.

IN THE IMAGE: SYNTHESIS

These three interpretations of *tzelem* present a composite portrait of humanity as a nexus between God and the natural word. As the *tzalmu* of God, humanity if the physical extension of God's power and presence on earth. Having characteristics of both "higher" and "lower" creatures, we are aware of our connection to God, and to other living beings, and of our earthly origin and limitations as well. Finally, our consciousness provides us with the self-awareness to realize our responsibilities to God and to the earth which we tend.

This portrait of humanity as the link between God and the earth is not in conflict with the Gaia theory if we continue to reflect on our images of God. If we continue to look at God only as a transcendent deity separate from nature, then we preserve our morality, and our moral obligation not to waste the earth. However, we still may remain insensitive to nonhuman life and our own creaturely character. If we see God only from the perspective of pantheism, then all is God, and nature is intrinsically sacred; but we cannot have a human ethical system in the usual sense that Judaism has known it.

We should, instead, think of God as both Being and Becoming — what is called a panentheistic deity. Panentheism assumes that the universe and everything in it is part of God, and that God is also more than the universe. "God is all reality but not all reality is God."[35] Gaia is part of God, but not all of God. Therefore, the immanence of God is displayed in nature (through order, cooperation, and relationships) and we are part of and thus part of God. But God is more than nature, and also stands outside of nature as Creator. We are part of this nature and bound to the laws of nature and Gaia, but we are also the "brain cells" of Gaia. And as the *tzelem* (image) of God, we have the mandate for the cognitive anticipation of Gaia's needs, which ultimately are our own needs. The brain is the locus of consciousness and in control of the body, both in the autonomic nervous system and in conscious choices. But the brain is also dependent upon the body for

survival, and is significantly influenced by changes in the body.[36]

If the earth does reflect our morality, then certainly it is humanity's "environmental debt" that is growing each year. Life is posed on a delicate balance. We must end the "war against nature" that governs so many of our attitudes towards the earth. Perhaps our newfound environmental awareness is the "real" awakening of Gaia, an awakening that will lead us out of our childhood into the divine image that awaits us.[37]

NOTES

1. Cf. Gen. 5:1–2, 9:6.
2. David S. Shapiro. "The Doctrine of the Image of God and Imitatio Dei," in *Contemporary Jewish Ethics,* ed. Menachem Marc Keller, (New York: Sanhedrin Press, 1979).
3. Cf. John D. Barrow and Frank J. Tipler, *The Anthropic Cosmological Principle* (Oxford: Clarendon Press, 1986), 27–122; Ian G. Barbour, *Issues in Science and Religion* (New York: Harper Torchbooks, 1971), 15–22; and George Gale, "The Anthropic Principle," in *Scientific American,* 245.6 (December, 1981): 154–71.
4. Stephen Jay Gould, *The Flamingo's Smile* (New York: Norton, 1985), 13–14, 292–93.
5. Richard A. Watson, "A Critique of Anti-Anthropocentric Biocentrism." *Environmental Ethics* 5 (1983): 251. Cf. also Paul W. Taylor, "In Defense of Biocentrism," *Environmental Ethics* 5 (1983): 237–43.
6. Lynn White, "The Historic Roots of Our Ecological Crisis," *Science* 155 (1967): 1203–1207.
7. Watson, 247; Steven S. Schwarzschild, "The Unnatural Jew" [in Martin D. Yaffe, ed., *Judaism and Environmental Ethics,* (Lanham, Md.: Lexington Books, 2001), 265–82]. Schwarzschild goes a little too far in asserting that any form of immanentism is a form of Jewish heresy, in which he includes Kabbalah, Christianity, Spinoza, Marx, and Zionism.
8. Jeremy Cohen, *"Be Fruitful and Increase, Fill the Earth and Master It"* (Ithaca: Cornell University Press, 1989).
9. David Ehrenfeld and Phillip J. Bentley, "Judaism and the Practice of Stewardship" [in Yaffe, ed.,

Judaism and Environmental Ethics, 125–35]; David Ehrenfeld and Joan G. Ehrenfeld, "Some Thoughts on Nature and Judaism" [in Yaffe, ed., *Judaism and Environmental Ethics,* 283–85].

10. Deut. 20:19–20; Moses Maimonides, *Hilkhot Melakhim* 6:8–10.

11. Cf. Ps. 8:4–9.

12. Schwarzschild [in Yaffe, ed., *Judaism and Environmental Ethics,* 270].

13. Cf., for example, Judith Plaskow, *Standing Again at Sinai* (New York: Harper and Row, 1990), 144–45, 155.

14. James E. Lovelock, *Gaia: A New Look at Life on Earth* (Oxford: Oxford University Press, 1982); *The Ages of Gaia* (New York: W. W. Norton and Company, 1988).

15. Lovelock, *The Ages of Gaia,* 147.

16. Lovelock, *The Ages of Gaia,* 148.

17. Lovelock, *The Ages of Gaia,* 145.

18. Lovelock, *The Ages of Gaia,* 206.

19. This follows the traditional Jewish interpretive system of *PaRDeS: Peshat,* the plain meaning; *Remez,* the symbolic meaning; *Derash,* the homiletical meaning; and *Sod,* the mystical meaning.

20. Cf. Ignace J. Gelb, Benno Landsberger, and A. Leo Oppenheim, *The Assryrian Dictionary of the Oriental Institute of the University of Chicago* (Chicago: Oriental Institute, 1962), vol. 16, 78–85, s.v. *Salmu.* I would like to thank Professor Ted Lutz of the Near Eastern Studies Department of the University of Toronto for this interpretation of *tzalmu.*

21. Cf. Cohen, 20–23.

22. Nahum M. Sarna, *The JPS Torah Commentary Genesis* (Philadelphia: Jewish Publication Society of America, 1989), 12.

23. *Shabbat* 119b.

24. *Sifrei Deuteronomy* 346. Cf. also *Bereishit Rabbah* 17:4 on God's needing Adam to name the animals and Himself.

25. Abraham J. Heschel, *Man Is Not Alone* (New York: Octagon Books, 1972), 241–45.

26. Cf. Jon D. Levenson, *Creation and the Persistence of Evil* (San Francisco: Harper and Row, 1988). Levenson views the Biblical covenant as the partnership of humanity and God needed to maintain order over the forces of chaos.

27. *Midrash, Bereishit Rabbah* to Genesis 1:27. Translation adapted from H. Freedman, *Midrash Rabbah:* Genesis (London: Soncino Press, 1983), 61–62.

28. Jeremy Cohen, "On Classical Judaism and Environmental Crisis: [in Yaffe, ed., *Judaism and Environmental Ethics,* 71–79].

29. E.g., *Bereishit Rabbah* 8:11 (second half) and 8:12.

30. My thanks to Dr. David Bakan for this interpretation of Maimonides's concept of intellectual apprehension. Cf. David Bakan, *Maimonides on Prophecy* (Northvale, N.J.: Jason Aronson, 1991).

31. *Mishneh Torah, Hilkhot Yesodei Ha-Torah* 4:8–9.

32. Cf. Douglas B. Hofstadter and Daniel C. Dennett, *The Mind's Eye* (New York: Bantam Books, 1982); Roger Penrose, *The Emperor's New Mind* (New York: Vintage, 1989), 526–27.

33. Penrose, *The Emperor's New Mind.* 526–27.

34. Cf. Maimonides, *Eight Chapters.*

35. Moses Cordovero, quoted in Gershom G. Scholem, *Major Trends, in Jewish Mysticism* (New York: Schocken Books, 1954), 252–53.

36. Cf. Maimonides, *Guide of the Perplexed* I 72 (trans. Pines, 184–94), where the universe is compared to a single living organism.

37. Cf. Lawrence Troster, "The Love of God and the Anthropic Principle," *Conservative Judaism,* 40 (1987–88): 45, 49, on John A. Wheeler's version of the Strong Anthropic Principle. Cf. also Karl E. Peters, "Humanity in Nature: Conserving Yet Creating," *Zygon* 24 (1989). This article is a brilliant statement of the relationship between humanity and nature.

DISCUSSION TOPICS

1. Do you believe Troster makes a convincing case that Judaism and the Gaia hypothesis may be compatible ideas? Give your reasoning.

2. Make a list of questions you would ask to explore and understand the author's perspectives.

3. What similarities and differences do you find in the perspectives of Troster and Turner (Chapter 6)? Give your reasoning.

READING 25

Environmental Ethics: Some Challenges for Christians

Holmes Rolston III

Holmes Rolston III is professor of philosophy at Colorado State University, Fort Collins. He has been a significant contributor to the emergence of the field of environmental ethics as a discipline and has authored numerous books and articles exploring both religious and secular insights on the issues, especially on topics of ecocentric ethics.

Rolston acknowledges the importance of Christians having an environmental ethic and addresses whether there is a primary Christian environmental ethic that might have direct concern for individual animals, plants, species, ecosystems, and perhaps even for the planet as a whole. In the process, he discusses the role of Christian caring and compassion in the realm of environmental ethics in a variety of conflicting situations. Rolston finds the world to have beauty, perpetual renewal of life in death, uniqueness, and wondrous creativity; such qualities reflect the Spirit of God.

There is no doubt, we should notice at once, that Christians can and ought to have an ethic concerning the use of the environment. Humans are helped or hurt by the condition of their environment, and if there are duties to humans at all, there will be applications of these duties to environmental issues. No one can love neighbor, or do to others as one would be treated oneself, in disregard of that neighbor's life-support system in the natural world. That much, however, is only concern for the environment as contributory to human welfare; the environment is secondary and instrumental to human goods. Is there a primary Christian environmental ethic, one with a direct concern for animals, plants, species, ecosystems, perhaps even for the planet?

I. ANIMALS

It might seem easy enough to extend the Christian ethic to animal neighbors. But, on further reflection, just to treat animals like people is not very discrim-

inating. In some ways they are our cousins, in other ways not. . . .

The rescue of individual animals—a couple of whales, a bison, a few deer—is humane enough and does not seem to have any detrimental effects, but that may not be the end of moral considerations, which ought to act on principles that can be universalized. Perhaps it brings these duties into clearer focus to consider populations, herds with hundreds of animals. The bighorn sheep of Yellowstone caught pinkeye (conjunctivitis) in the winter of 1981–82. On craggy slopes, partial blindness can be fatal. A sheep misses a jump, feeds poorly, and is soon injured and starving. More than 300 bighorns, over 60 percent of the herd, perished.

Wildlife veterinarians wanted to treat the disease, as they would have in any domestic herd, but, again, the Yellowstone ethicists left the sheep to suffer, seemingly not respecting their life. Their decision was that the disease was natural, and should be left to run its course. A Christian may protest, "Where's the mercy? How inhumane! Where is the good shepherd caring for his sheep?" But perhaps mercy and humanity are not the criteria for decision here.

The ethic of compassion must be set in a bigger picture of animal welfare, recognizing the function of pain in the wild. The Yellowstone ethicists knew that, while intrinsic pain is a bad thing whether in humans or in sheep, pain in ecosystems is instrumental pain, through which the sheep are naturally selected for a more satisfactory adaptive fit. To have interfered in the interests of the blinded sheep would have weakened the species. Simply to ask whether they suffer is not enough. We must ask whether they suffer with a beneficial effect on the wild population.

. . . The welfare of the sheep still lies under the rigors of natural selection. As a result of the park ethic, those sheep that were genetically more fit, able to cope with the disease, survived; and this coping is now coded in the survivors. Caring for these sheep does not mean bringing them safely into the fold; it means caring that they stay wild and free.

What we *ought* to do depends on what *is*. The *is* of nature differs significantly from the *is* of culture, even when similar suffering is present. A human being in a frozen river would be rescued at once; a human attacked by a wolverine would be flown by helicopter to the hospital. Bison and deer are not humans and we cannot give them identical treatment; still, if suffering is a bad thing for humans, who seek to eliminate it, why is suffering not also a bad thing for bison? We cannot give medical treatment to all wild animals; we should not interrupt a predator killing its prey. But when we happen upon an opportunity to rescue an animal with the pull of a rope, or mercy-kill it lest it suffer, why not? If we can treat a herd of blinded sheep, why not? If we can feed the deer, starving in the winter, why not? That seems to be what human nature urges, and why not let human nature take its course? That seems to be what Jesus urges, doing to others as you would have them do to you, and why not follow the golden rule?

The answer is that both these compassionate feelings innate in us and also as the imperatives urged by our Christian education are misplaced when they are transferred to the wilds. A bison in a wild ecosystem is not a person in a culture. Pain in any culture ought to be compassionately relieved where it can be with an interest in the welfare of the sufferers. But pain in the wild ought not to be relieved if and when it interrupts the ecosystemic processes on which the welfare of these animals depends.

Sometimes it seems that an environmental ethic takes us nearer than we wish toward a tragic view of life. Perhaps Jesus came that nature should not take its course, but we also have it on his authority that the birds of the air need not be anxious and that God notices the sparrows that fall. . . .

. . . Letting wild animals "go free" provides a general orientation for the ethical treatment of wild animals; mercy or compassion do not. Beyond that, Christianity has no particular expertise in wildlife management, and many of the questions faced in environmental ethics have not been addressed by Christian thought.

II. PLANTS

. . .

Trees might not seem something that we can be ethical about, not directly. Where people have a stake in their trees, the trees count because people count them as fuel, timber, watershed, shade trees, scenery. What counts for people, counts morally. But there is more to it than that. How to count trees, or, collectively, forests, is a critical issue in environmental policy today. The larger issue is an appropriate respect for forests, not simply for what they are for people, but for what they are in themselves. . . .

The old-growth timber controversy is the principal public issue in the Pacific Northwest. Indeed, some environmentalists count the value of trees, especially the cathedral old-growth trees, so highly that they will spike these trees, lest they be cut. They are willing to risk civil disobedience, protesting that the forest service is itself disobeying the law, and citing as evidence the mounting dissension within the ranks of the Forest Service. Several thousand foresters have joined a protest organization, the Association of Forest Service Employees for Environmental Ethics. And the Society of American Foresters, by a three-to-one vote, has revised its canon of ethics, to include a land ethic. Foresters now say that an ethic "demonstrates our respect for the land."[1] The Society has issued a policy statement, an ethical statement, that sustainable forestry is not enough if that means only timber production; forestry must consider optimizing and conserving all the values carried by forests as natural ecosystems.[2] That is, if you like, an ecosystem ethic, to which we will be turning, but it all began with the cutting of trees, and a growing conviction that what a people do to forests is a moral matter.

Is all this outside the province of Christian ethics? It can seem so; nothing about Christianity gives one any expertise in forestry, any more than elsewhere in botany or zoology. The skills ethics has forged for people hardly seem relevant. Trying to make trees moral objects seems strange. They do not suffer pains and pleasures, so we cannot be compassionate toward them. Trees are not valuers with preferences that can be satisfied or frustrated, so we cannot practice the golden rule on them. It seems odd to claim that trees need our sympathy, odd to ask that we should consider their point of view. They do not need justice or fairness.

These are, as we might say, just resource questions, about which Christians can say that resources should be justly and charitably used, and little more. We can say that there should be stewardship. The Society of American Foresters say, in their new code of ethics, "Stewardship of the land is the cornerstone of the forestry profession,"[3] and Christians entirely concur, because they believe in the stewardship of everything. But after that, they have nothing more to say about making this forest ethic operational.

. . . In common with churches, forests invite transcending the human world and experiencing a comprehensive, embracing realm.

Forests can serve as a more provocative, perennial sign of this than many of the traditional, often outworn, symbols devised by the churches. Such experiences Christians should welcome and seek to preserve. [John] Muir continued, "The clearest way into the Universe is through a forest wilderness."[4] . . .

Being among the archetypes, a forest is about as near to ultimacy as we can come in the natural world—a vast scene of sprouting, budding, flowering, fruiting, passing away, passing life on. The planet has produced forests wherever on the globe soil and climate permit, and has done so for many millions of years. . . . A forest wilderness is a sacred space. There Christians recognize God's creation, and others may find the Ultimate Reality or a Nature sacred in itself. A forest wilderness elicits cosmic questions, differently from town. Christians have a particular interest in preserving wild places as sanctuaries for religious experiences, both for Christians and others inspired there.

III. SPECIES

Some of these animals and plants in these forests are endangered species, and that forces us to a new level of ethical and theological challenge. When the United States Congress lamented the loss of species, Congress declared that species have "esthetic, ecological, educational, historical, recreational and scientific value to the Nation and its people."[5] Religious value is missing from this list. Perhaps Congress would have overstepped its authority to declare that species carry religious value. But for many Americans this is the most important value. . . .

In the practical conservation of biodiversity on landscapes, concerned with habitat, breeding populations, DDT in food chains, or minimum water flows to maintain fish species, it might seem that God is the ultimate irrelevancy. In fact, when one is conserving life, ultimacy is always nearby. The practical urgency of on-the-ground conservation is based in a deeper respect for life. Extinction is forever; and, when danger is ultimate, absolutes become relevant. The motivation to save endangered species can and ought to be pragmatic, economic, political, and scientific; deeper down it is moral, philosophical, and religious. Or perhaps we should say that the first set of reasons is moral only for humanistic reasons; the second set of reasons extends moral concern into a reverence for nonhuman life based on intrinsic value found in such life for what it is in itself.

The Bible records the first Endangered Species Project—Noah and his ark! The story is quaint and archaic, as much parable as history, teaching how God wills for each species on Earth to continue, despite the disruptions introduced by humans. Although individual animals perish catastrophically, God has an "adequate concern and conservation" for species. On the Ark, the species come through. . . .

As with the treatment of animals before, we may first think that the endangered species question is easy. Noah settles that; we should not cause any species to go extinct.[6] But, once again, the going gets tough in actual decisions, and sensitivity to life at the level of species can sometimes make an environmental ethicist seem callous. San Clemente Island is far enough off the coast of California for endemic species to have evolved in the isolation there. The island also has a population of feral goats. After the passage of the Endangered Species Act, botanists resurveyed the island and found some additional populations of endangered plants. But goats do not much care whether they are eating endangered species. So the U.S. Fish and Wildlife Service and the U.S. Navy, which owns the island, planned to shoot thousands of feral goats to save three endangered plant species, *Malacothamnus clementinus, Castilleja grisea, Delphinium kinkiense,* of which the surviving individuals numbered only a few dozens. . . .

Is it inhumane to count plant species more than mammal lives, a few plants more than thousands of goats? An ethic of compassion and the Golden Rule may say that animals count but plants do not, because the goats can enjoy life and they suffer when shot, but the plants are insentient and do not feel anything at all. But perhaps we move to a new level of principle, where duties to species override duties to individuals. On Noah's ark, God did not seem much concerned with individuals, but rather greatly concerned for species. That principle holds even when the endangered species are plants. A population of plants, evolved as an adapted fit in an ecosystem, is of more value than a population of feral goats, who are misfits in their ecosystem. . . .

Duties to wildlife are not simply at the level of individuals; they are also to species. Our human nature shapes us for culture, not a wild but an "unnatural" environment, that is, an environment where the creative evolutionary and ecological forces are superimposed by emergent, humane forces. Conscience evolves to generate that respect for persons without which there can be no high quality of human life. But when conscience turns to address the high quality of wild life, our human instincts and the imperatives of our ethical traditions need to be rethought. We have a duty to conserve all the wildness, species in their wild ecosystems, not just individual animal welfare.

An ethic here has to take the word *genesis* seriously, and that seems plausible when we talk of divine creation, but it can become difficult when this creation is wild nature. In the Hebrew stories, the "days" (events) of creation are a series of divine imperatives that empower Earth with vitality. "And God said, 'Let there be . . .'" (Gn 1.2–3). "Let the earth put forth vegetation." "Let the earth bring forth living things according to their kinds" (Gn 1.11, 24). "Let the waters bring forth swarms of living creatures" (Gn 1.20). "Swarms" is, if you wish, the biblical word for biodiversity.

A prolific Earth generates teeming life, urged by God. The Spirit of God is brooding, animating the Earth, and Earth gives birth. As we would say now, Earth speciates. When Jesus looks out over the fields of Galilee, he recalls how "the earth produces of itself" (Mk 4.28, Greek: "automatically") or spontaneously. God reviews this display of life, finds it "very good," and bids it continue. "Be fruitful and multiply and fill the waters in the seas, and let birds multiply on the earth" (Gn 1.22). In current scientific vocabulary, there is dispersal, conservation by survival over generations, and niche saturation up to

carrying capacity. Adam's first task was to name this swarm of creatures, a project in taxonomy.

The Endangered Species Act and the God Committee are contemporary events, and it can be jarring to set beside them these archaic stories. But the stories are not only archaic in being couched in outmoded thought forms; they are archaic in that they are about aboriginal truths. The Noah story is an antiquated genre, but the Noah threat is imminent today and still lies at the foundations. The story is a myth teaching a perennial reverence for life. If there is a word of God here, lingering out of the primordial past, it is "Keep them alive with you" (Gn 6.19).

Indeed, these primitive stories sometimes exceed the recent legislation in the depths of their insights. Noah is not told to save just those species that are of "esthetic, ecological, educational, historical, recreational and scientific value" to people. He is commanded to save them all. These swarms of species are often useful to humans, and on the Ark clean species were given more protection than others. But Noah was not simply conserving global stock. The Noah story teaches sensitivity to forms of life and the biological and theological forces producing them. What is required is not human prudence but principled responsibility to the biospheric Earth, to God.

Today, preservation of species is routinely defended in terms of medical, agricultural, and industrial benefits. Other species may be indirectly useful for the resilience and stability they provide in ecosystems. High quality human life requires a high diversity of species. But such humanistic justifications, although correct and required as part of the endangered species policy, fall short of Noah's environmental ethics. These humanistic reasons are relevant, but they do not value these species for what they are in themselves, under God. These reasons are inadequate for either Hebrew or Christian faith, neither of which is simply humanistic about species. The value of species, though intrinsic, need not be absolute, of course; there is ample biblical justification for humans to make responsible uses of plants and animals, capturing their values in pursuit of their cultural goods. Still, facing the next century, turning the millennium, there is growing conviction among theologians that theology has been too anthropocentric. Valuable though humans may be, the nonhuman world too is a vital part of Earth's story.

Biology and theology are not always easy disciplines to join. One conviction they do share is that the Earth is prolific. Seen from the side of biology, this is called speciation, biodiversity, selective pressures for adapted fit, maximizing offspring in the next generation, niche diversification, species packing, and carrying capacity. Seen from the side of theology this trend toward diversity is a good thing, a godly thing. This fertility is sacred. Endangered species raise the "God" question because they are one place we come near the ultimacy in biological life. This genesis is, in biological perspective, "of itself," spontaneous, autonomous; and biologists find nature to be prolific, even before the God question is raised. Afterward, theologians wish to add that in such a prolific world, explanations may not be over until one detects God in, with, and under it all.

IV. ECOSYSTEMS

Biblical faith began with a land ethic, a covenanted promised land; but sometimes in the subsequent centuries both Jews and Christians have thought that their faith superseded any geography. These were faiths for any people any place, universal faiths true all over the planet, indeed all over the universe, should there prove to be extraterrestrial life. But another way to interpret this is that all peoples dwell on promised lands, that is, lands that are gifts of God and that ought to be used with justice and charity. . . .

But that, too, turns out, as with animals, plants, and species before, to be more challenging than first appears. Land use patterns as they affect the health and integrity of ecosystems are among the most intense environmental concerns that we now face, as we have already illustrated with the controversies over forests. Biodiversity depends on ecosystem integrity. . . .

There are two tensions here: one is whether humans are using their land resources intelligently, retaining enough ecosystem health not to degrade the resource; and the other is whether humans ought to manage land as nothing but resource for themselves and neighbors, or ought rather to see the integrity of ecosystems as a moral issue, loving the whole biotic community. . . .

Consider wilderness designation. About 96% of the contiguous United States is developed, farmed, grazed, timbered, designated for multiple use. Only about 2% has been designated as wilderness; another 2% might be suitable for wilderness or semi-wild status—cut-over forests that have reverted to the wild or areas as yet little developed. The wise use people say absolutely no more wilderness, and they would like to redesignate and open up much that we have already designated; the environmentalists press hard for more wilderness. The wise use people say that the Endangered Species Act, if not repealed, should be revised to decide whether to save species on an economic cost-benefit calculus. Environmentalists want the Act strengthened; they want ecosystem conservation as the basis of endangered species preservation. . . .

The natural world inescapably surrounds us, wherever we reside and work, and yet the built environment, necessary for culture, also is increasingly difficult to escape. Culture is and ought to be superimposed on the landscape, but not so as to extinguish the integrity of creation. This duty arises because of human welfare. Humans need, in differing degrees, elements of the natural to make and keep life human. Life in completely artificial environments, without options for experiencing natural environments, is undesirable. A society attuned to artifact forgets creation. Life without access to the divine creation is ungodly. And yet we can go too far in thinking that we want land health only for our human excellence. . . .

Another problem is that ecosystems can seem ungodly, or at least that the creative processes there can be challenging. For nature can seem chaotic and disordered. Giant forest fires raged over Yellowstone National park in the summer of 1988, consuming nearly a million acres, despite the efforts of a thousand fire fighters. By far the largest fires ever known in the park, the fires seemed a disaster. And we had put out fires for over a century. But now there was a new ethic, which enjoined: Let nature take its course. Let it burn! So the fires were not fought at first. In midsummer national authorities switched their ethics again, overrode that policy and ordered the fires put out.

Even then, weeks later, fires continued to burn, partly because they were too big to control, but partly too because Yellowstone personnel did not altogether want the fires put out. Despite the evident destruction of trees, shrubs, and wildlife, they believe that fires are a good thing. Fires reset succession, release nutrients, recycle materials, renew the biotic community. Nearby, in the Teton wilderness, a storm blew down 15,000 acres of trees, and some proposed that the area be de-classified as wilderness for commercial salvage of the timber. But a similar environmental ethics said: No, let it rot.

Let it burn! Let it rot! At first these do not seem to be any more Christian than: Let it suffer. But maybe there is something here that Christians can appreciate after all, for they are not unfamiliar with life destroyed and life regenerated. To the contrary, that theme is right at the center of Christian faith. There are sorts of creation that cannot occur without death, and these include the highest created goods. Death can be meaningfully put into the biological processes as a necessary counterpart to the advancing of life. Something is always dying, and something is always living on. For all the struggle, violence, and transition, there is abiding value.

"Conserved" is the biological word here, and we ought to conserve in nature those processes that conserve life. These are radical regenerative processes. For we must be careful here. It is not simply the experience of divine design, of architectural perfection, that has generated the Christian hypothesis of God. Experiences of the power of survival, of new life rising out of the old, of the transformative character of suffering, of good resurrected out of evil, are even more forcefully those for which the theory of God has come to provide the most plausible hypothesis. That governs the Christian ethic, an ethic for the most part directed toward human coping in the world, but an ethic also for understanding the creative processes that conserve and regenerate life throughout the natural world.

From this perspective, Christians can join with Aldo Leopold and his land ethic. "A thing is right when it tends to preserve the integrity, stability, and beauty of the biotic community. It is wrong when it tends otherwise."[7] That does not put human dignity or wise use first, though it can hardly result in undignified humans or unwise use. Those who wish to reside in a promised land must promise to preserve its integrity, stability, and beauty. "That land as a community is the basic concept of ecology, but that land is to be loved and respected as an extension of ethics."[8] If so, we cannot inherit our promised lands until we extend Christian ethics into ecology. "The land which you are going over to possess is a land of hills and valleys, which drinks water by the rain from heaven, a land which the Lord your God cares for; the eyes of the Lord your God are always upon it, from the beginning of the year to the end of the year" (Dt 11.11–12).

V. EARTH

Bible writers, though in a promised land, hardly knew they lived on Earth; they did not know earth was Earth. The twentieth century has been the century of seeing Earth whole, the home planet. . . .

That finds value in Earth as a precious place, and enjoins loving that place with the moral intensity with which we love neighbors, perhaps even God. . . . Earth is a precious thing in itself because it is home for us all; Earth is to be loved, as we do a neighbor, for an intrinsic integrity, which generates this world community in which we reside. In an environmental ethic, our argument and our duty is not complete until we have moved to the global level, to an Earth ethic. The center of focus is Earth, the planet.

But valuing the whole Earth and responsibilities to it are unfamiliar and need philosophical analysis. At first appearance, this can seem to be godly enough; but then again, we may seem to be going to extremes. Earth is not divinity, nor is dirt to be loved like God and neighbor. . . . Is there a legitimate and commanding duty to Earth?

This has been the century in which environmental issues have become global. Anyone who has looked at a graph of the escalating human population growth realizes that humans threaten the planet, and if one couples population growth with escalating consumption, only the blind can deny that the planet is headed for crisis. We do not now have sustainable development, either in First or Third World, North or South. The unity and community of the home planet is our global responsibility, and we live on what, in light of our recently gained human powers, is a fragile planet. . . . We need to form ethical and value judgments at the appropriate level. Earlier the challenge was to take into our ethical concern such things as persons, animals, plants, species, ecosystems; but environmental ethics is not over until we have risen to the planetary level. Earth is really the relevant survival unit.

Ought implies can, and we do not construct an ethics for things that lie outside our powers. Ethics is sometimes a question of scale. The late-coming, moral species, *Homo sapiens,* has still more lately gained startling powers for the rebuilding and modification, including the degradation, of this home planet. That does put ethics on a new scale. The value issues are so bigscale that the current events have to be interpreted as a fundamental contextual change altering the critical determinants of the history of the planet.

Only in the last century, Darwin's century more or less, have we learned the depth of historical change on this planet, life continuing over billions of years. Now, facing the next century, we humans have the understanding and the power to alter the history of the planet on global ecological scales. The future cannot be like the past. . . . Indeed, on most of our continent, the development pace in the next century cannot be like that of the last. All this brings urgent new duties. . . .

If we humans are true to our species epithet, "the wise species" needs to behave with appropriate respect for life. That will involve an interhuman ethics. It will involve an interspecific ethics, where the only moral species discovers that all the others, though not moral agents, are morally considerable. Also, finally, most ultimately, it will involve an Earth ethics, one that discovers a global sense of obligation to this whole inhabited planet, the only such biosphere we know.

Christian ethics has been almost entirely interhuman ethics, persons finding a way to relate morally to other persons—loving our neighbors. Ethics seeks to find a satisfactory fit for humans in their communities, and this has meant that ethics has often dwelt on justice, fairness, love, forgiveness, rights, peace, an ethics troubled about personal relations.

But ethics too is now anxious about the troubled planet. Can we have duties *concerning* the Earth, even duties *to* the Earth? Earth is, after all, just earth. Many will think that it is absurd to think we can have duties to dirt. Earth is, in a way, a big rockpile like the moon, only one on which the rocks are watered and illuminated in such a way that they support life. So maybe it is really the life we value and not the Earth, except as instrumental to life. We do not have duties to rocks, air, ocean, dirt, or Earth; we have duties to people, or living things. We must not confuse duties to the home with duties to the inhabitants.

But what if we see this home biosphere as the sphere of divinity? Consider all the complexity and diversity, integrity, richness, natural history and cultural history—the whole storied natural and cultural history of our planet. Really, the story is little short of a series of "miracles," wondrous, fortuitous events, unfolding of potential; and when Earth's most complex product, *Homo sapiens,* becomes intelligent enough to reflect over this cosmic wonderland, everyone is left stuttering about the mixtures of accident and necessity out of which we have evolved. Nobody has much doubt that this is a precious place, a pearl in a sea of black mystery. For Christians the black mystery will be numinous and signal transcendence. We reach a scale question again. On an everyday scale, earth, dirt, seems to be passive, inert, an unsuitable object of moral concern. But on a global scale? Earth could be the ultimate object of duty, short of God. Now we do begin to get absolute about natural values, about as absolute as we can ever get on Earth. For what absolutely must not happen is that the Earth be destroyed by human hands.

The scale changes nothing, a critic may protest, the changes are only quantitative. Earth too is a big rockpile, only one that happens to support life. It is no doubt precious as a means of life support, but it is not precious in itself. To add a new imperative, loving Earth, to the classical ones of loving neighbor and God, is to make a category mistake. Neighbors and God are persons, ends in themselves, who respond to love. God is Absolute. But Earth is just earth, dirt. . . .

. . . But another way of looking at this is that it is all dirt, only we find revealed what dirt can do when it is self-organizing under suitable conditions with water and solar illumination. That is pretty spectacular dirt. We can, if we insist on being anthropocentrists, say that it is all valueless except as our human resource, though quite valuable in that respect. But we will not be valuing Earth objectively until we appreciate this marvelous natural history. This really is a superb planet. In that light, moving from earth to Earth, duties to Earth do not seem like a *reductio ad absurdum* of duties at all; to the contrary, a duty to Earth is the most important duty of all. The valuable Earth is absolutely fundamental.

At this scale of vision, if we ask what is principally to be protected, the value of life arising as a creative process on Earth seems a better description than Earth as a human resource, and a more comprehensive category. Humans who see nature only as resource for their human development are not yet true to their Earth. Human "responsibility" on Earth is as good a word as human "dominion" over Earth, indeed a better one, for it captures what dominion originally meant in the famous Genesis charge to Adam and Eve, or what it ought to mean, a stewardship or trusteeship over something entrusted into one's care, the prolific Earth with its swarms of creatures brought forth under divine inspiration of such dirt and found to be very good.

Land is not where we *make* a living; it is where we *live,* and this can be seen if we enlarge the scope from earth to Earth, [which is] not just where we *make* a living; it *is* where we live. Our responsibility to Earth might be thought the most remote of our responsibilities; it seems so grandiose and vague beside our concrete responsibilities to our children or next door neighbors. But not so: the other way round, it is the most fundamental, the most comprehensive of our responsibilities. Though foreshadowed in the past by the sense of belonging that many peoples have had on their landscapes, loyalty to the planet is the newest demand in ethics, a new possibility that could also prove the highest level of duty.

VI. NATURE AND GRACE

So a task of Christian ethics is to discover again what it means to say that God so loved this world that God sent a son to come where he already was, to save it, and what kind of Christian conduct in the world this entails. In a planetary, environmental age, this requires combining nature and grace at new levels of insight and intensity. Nature is grace, whatever more grace may also be. The geophysical and biological laws, the evolutionary and ecological history, the creativity within the natural system we inherit, and the values these generate, are the ground of our being, not just the ground under our feet. This is the Earth in which we live and move and have our being and we owe this Earth system the highest allegiance of which we are capable, under God, in whom also we live and move and have our being.

Every animal, every plant has to seek resources, but life persists because it is provided for in the system. Earth is a kind of providing ground. Life is a struggle, which, seen from an earthy side, can seem to be indifference and chance, but seen from a godward side, is divine imperative and creativity. Each species is a bit of brilliance, a bit of endurance, a moment of truth, animated, spirited inventiveness. The swarms of creatures are not so much an ungodly jungle as a garden Earth. Design is not the right word; it is a word borrowed from mechanics and their machines, watchmakers and their clocks. An organism is not a machine, nor a clock. Genesis is the word we want; it is a word with "genes" in it, with the gift of autonomy and self-creation. Organisms must live story lines, and that epic is life lived on in the midst of its perpetual perishing, life arriving and struggling through to something higher. That Earth story has continued for several billion years; such an Earthen providing ground is, in the theological perspective, providential.

Ultimately, there is a kind of creativity in nature demanding either that we spell nature with a capital N, or pass beyond nature to nature's God. Biologists today are not inclined, nor should they be as biologists, to look for explanations in supernature, but biologists nevertheless find a nature that is super! Superb! Science teaches us to eliminate from nature any suggestions of teleology, but it is not so easy for science to talk us out of genesis. What has managed to happen on Earth is startling by any criteria. Biologists may doubt whether there is a Creator, but no biologist can doubt genesis. Life is a kind of gift, and whatever we may think of nature elsewhere in the universe, earthen nature is right for life.

The nature that is grace is also cruciform. Life is a table prepared in the midst of our enemies, green pastures in the valley of the shadow of death. For Christianity seeks to draw the harshness of nature into the concept of God, as it seeks by a doctrine of providence to draw all affliction into the divine will. Nature is intelligible, gracious, superb, a wonderland. But the world is not a paradise of hedonistic ease, rather the secret of life is that it is a passion play. Things perish in tragedy. The religions knew that full well, before biology arose to reconfirm it. But things perish with a passing over in which the sacrificed individual flows in the river of life. As we said when beginning, sometimes it seems that an environmental ethic takes us nearer than we wish toward a tragic view of life.

The enigmatic symbol of this is the cross, a symbol Christians adopt for God, and for an extrahistorical miracle in the atonement of Christ, but one which, more than they have known, is a parable of all natural and cultural history. There can be little doubt that life has flourished on Earth. The Bible writers experienced that exuberance of life, and biology since has expanded and further justified this claim. But even in the Garden Earth life has to be redeemed in the midst of its perpetual perishing. The Garden Earth forebodes the Garden of Gethsemane. Creation is cruciform.

When J. B. S. Haldane found himself in conversation with some theologians and was asked whether he had concluded anything about the character of God from his long studies in biology, he replied that God had an inordinate fondness for beetles. God must have loved beetles, he made so many of them. But species counts are only one indication of diversity, and perhaps the fuller response is that God must have loved life, God animated such a prolific Earth. Haldane went on to say that the marks of biological nature were its "beauty," "tragedy," and "inexhaustible queerness."[9]

This beauty approaches the sublime; the tragedy is perpetually redeemed with the renewal of life, and the inexhaustible queerness recomposes as the numinous. If anything at all on Earth is sacred, it must be this enthralling creativity that characterizes our home planet. If anywhere, here is the brooding Spirit of God. If there is any holy ground, any land of promise, this promising Earth is it.

NOTES

1. Ray Craig, "Land Ethic Canon Proposal: A Report from the Task Force," *Journal of Forestry* 90, no. 8 (1992): 40–41.
2. Society of American Foresters, *Sustaining Long-term Forest Health and Productivity* (Bethesda, MD: Society of American Foresters, 1993).
3. Craig, "Land Ethic Canon Proposal," 40
4. Linnie Marsh Wolfe, ed., *John of the Mountains: The Unpublished Journals of John Muir* (Boston: Houghton-Mifflin, 1938), 313.
5. Endangered Species Act of 1973, sec. 2a. 87 Stat. 884.
6. Noah knew nothing of natural extinction and respeciation over evolutionary time. Even the Endangered Species Act does not seek to prevent natural extinctions, when species that are no longer adapted fits go extinct, to be replaced by other species that evolve as better fits in the changing environment.
7. Aldo Leopold, *A Sand County Almanac* (New York: Oxford University Press, 1968), 224–25.
8. Ibid., foreword.
9. J. B. S. Haldane, *The Causes of Evolution* (Ithaca: Cornell University Press, 1932, 1966), 167–169.

DISCUSSION TOPICS

1. What aspects of Rolston's insights do you believe are applicable beyond the Christian community? Which aspects would be primarily or wholly applicable to Christians? Explain your position.
2. Rolston discusses duties toward nature. How might you justify duties toward nature in a secular sense? Explain your answer.
3. Do you agree, as Rolston implies, that biology and theology can be joined? If so, give some examples of how they can be joined. If not, explain why not.

Islamic Environmental Ethics, Law, and Society

Mawil Y. Izzi Deen (Samarrai)

Mawil Y. Izzi Deen (Samarrai) is a professor at King Abdul Aziz University, Jeddah, Saudi Arabia. Izzi Deen is also consultant to the Saudi Arabian Center for Science and Technology and coauthor of Islamic Principles for the Conservation of the Natural Environment *(1983).*

In this chapter from Ethics of Environment and Development: Global Challenge, International Response *(1990), Izzi Deen asserts that environmental protection in the Islamic faith is founded on the religious principle that all aspects of the natural world were created by God, with different functions that were determined and balanced by God. The role of humans is to enjoy, use, and benefit from the environment. This involves subjugation, use, construction, and development. It also includes meditation, contemplation, and enjoyment of the earth's beauty. Since the earth is also a source of beauty and a place to worship God, humans must intervene to protect it. Islamic responsibilities include the protection of certain zones (ḥimā) for the welfare of the people; establishment of certain inviolable zones (ḥarīm) often associated with wells, springs, or waterways; and the development of environmental projects.*

Islamic environmental ethics, like all other forms of ethics in Islam, is based on clear-cut legal foundations which Muslims hold to be formulated by God. Thus, in Islam, an acceptance of what is legal and what is ethical has not involved the same processes as in cultures which base their laws on humanistic philosophies.

Muslim scholars have found it difficult to accept the term "Islamic Law," since "law" implies a rigidity and dryness alien to Islam. They prefer the Arabic word *Sharī'aḥ* (Shariah) which literally means the "source of water." The Shariah is the source of life in that it contains both legal rules and ethical principles. This is indicated by the division of the Shariah relevant to human action into the categories of: obligatory actions (*wājib*)—those which a Mus-

lim is required to perform; devotional and ethical virtues (*mandūb*)—those actions a Muslim is encouraged to perform, the non-observance of which, however, incurs no liability; permissible actions (*mubāh*)—those in which a Muslim is given complete freedom of choice; abominable actions (*makrūh*)—those which are morally but not legally wrong; and prohibited actions (*ḥaram*)—all those practices forbidden by Islam.

A complete separation into the two elements, law and ethics, is thus unnecessary in Islam. For a Muslim is obliged to obey whatever God has ordered, his philosophical questions having been answered before he became a follower of the faith.

THE FOUNDATION OF ENVIRONMENTAL PROTECTION

In Islam, the conservation of the environment is based on the principle that all the individual components of the environment were created by God, and that all living things were created with different functions, functions carefully measured and meticulously balanced by the Almighty Creator. Although the various components of the natural environment serve humanity as one of their functions, this does not imply that human use is the sole reason for their creation. The comments of the medieval Muslim scholar, Ibn Taymīyah, on those verses of the Holy Qur'ān which state God created the various parts of the environment to serve humanity, are relevant here:

> In considering all these verses it must be remembered that Allah in His wisdom created these creatures for reasons other than serving man, for in these verses He only explains the benefits of these creatures [to man].[1]

The legal and ethical reasons for protecting the environment can be summarized as follows:[2] First, the environment is God's creation and to protect it is to preserve its values as a sign of the Creator. To assume that the environment's benefits to human beings are the sole reason for its protection may lead to environmental misuse or destruction.

Second, the component parts of nature are entities in continuous praise of their Creator. Humans may not be able to understand the form or nature of this praise, but the fact that the Qur'ān describes it is an additional reason for environmental preservation:

> The seven heavens and the earth and all that is therein praise Him, and there is not such a thing but hymneth his praise; but ye understand not their praise. Lo! He is ever Clement, Forgiving (Sūrah 17:44).[3]

Third, all the laws of nature are laws made by the Creator and based on the concept of the absolute continuity of existence. Although God may sometimes wish otherwise, what happens, happens according to the natural law of God (*sunnah*), and human beings must accept this as the will of the Creator. Attempts to break the law of God must be prevented. As the Qur'ān states:

> Hast thou not seen that unto Allah payeth adoration whosoever is in the heavens and whosoever is in the earth, and the sun, and the moon, and the stars, and the hills, and the trees, and the beasts, and many of mankind (Sūrah 22:18).

Fourth, the Qur'ān's acknowledgment that humankind is not the only community to live in this world — "There is not an animal in the earth, nor a flying creature flying on two wings, but they are peoples like unto you" (Sūrah 6:38) — means that while humans may currently have the upper hand over other "peoples," these other creatures are beings and, like us, are worthy of respect and protection. The Prophet Muḥammad (peace be upon him) considered all living creatures worthy of protection (*hurmah*) and kind treatment. He was once asked whether there will be a reward from God for charity shown to animals. His reply was very explicit: "For [charity shown to] each creature which has a wet heart there is a reward."[4] Ibn Hajar comments further upon this tradition, explaining that wetness is an indication of life (and so charity extends to all creatures), although human beings are more worthy of the charity if a choice must be made.[5]

Fifth, Islamic environmental ethics is based on the concept that all human relationships are established on justice (*'adl*) and equity (*iḥsān*): "Lo! Allah enjoineth justice and kindness" (Sūrah 16:90). The prophetic tradition limits benefits derived at the cost of animal suffering. The Prophet Muḥammad instructed: "Verily Allah has prescribed equity (*iḥsān*) in all things. Thus if you kill, kill well, and if you slaughter, slaughter well. Let each of you sharpen his blade and let him spare suffering to the animal he slaughters."

Sixth, the balance of the universe created by God must also be preserved. For "Everything with Him is measured" (Sūrah 13:8). Also, "There is not a thing but with Us are the stores thereof. And We send it not down save in appointed measure" (Sūrah 15:21).

Seventh, the environment is not in the service of the present generation alone. Rather, it is the gift of God to all ages, past, present, and future. This can be understood from the general meaning of Sūrah 2:29: "He it is Who created for you all that is in the earth." The word "you" as used here refers to all persons with no limit as to time or place.

Finally, no other creature is able to perform the task of protecting the environment. God entrusted humans with the duty of viceregency, a duty so onerous and burdensome that no other creature would accept it: "Lo! We offered the trust unto the heavens and the earth and the hills, but they shrank from bearing it and were afraid of it. And man assumed it" (Sūrah 33:72).

THE COMPREHENSIVE NATURE OF ISLAMIC ETHICS

Islamic ethics is founded on two principles — human nature, and religious and legal grounds. The first principle, natural instinct (*fitrah*), was imprinted in the human soul by God at the time of creation (Sūrah 91:7–8). Having natural instinct, the ordinary individual can, at least to some extent, distinguish not only between good and bad, but also between these and that which is neutral, neither good nor bad.[6] However, an ethical conscience is not a sufficient personal guide. Due to the complexities of life an ethical conscience alone cannot define the correct attitude to every problem. Moreover, a person does not live in a vacuum, but is affected by outside influences which may corrupt the ability to choose between good and evil. Outside influences include customs, personal interests, and prevailing concepts concerning one's surroundings.[7]

The religious and legal grounds upon which Islamic ethics is founded were presented by the messengers of God. These messengers were possessed of a special nature, and since they were inspired by God, they were able to avoid the outside influences which may affect other individuals.

Legal instructions in Islam are not negative in the sense of forcing the conscience to obey. On the contrary, legal instructions have been revealed in such a way that the conscience approves and acknowledges them to be correct. Thus the law itself becomes a part of human conscience, thereby guaranteeing its application and its success.

An imported, alien law cannot work because, while it may be possible to make it legally binding, it cannot be made morally binding upon Muslims. Muslims willingly pay the poor-tax (*zakāh*) because they know that if they fail to do so they will be legally and ethically responsible. Managing to avoid the legal consequences of failure to pay what is due will not help them to avoid the ethical consequences, and they are aware of this. Although a Muslim poacher may be able to shoot elephants and avoid park game wardens, if a framework based on Islamic principles for the protection of the environment has been published, he knows that he will not be able to avoid the everwatchful divine Warden. The Muslim knows that Islamic values are all based on what God loves and wants: "And when he turns away [from thee] his effort in the land is to make mischief therein and to destroy the crops and the cattle; and Allah loveth not mischief" (Sūrah 2:205).

When the Prophet Solomon and his army were about to destroy a nest of ants, one ant warned the rest of the colony of the coming destruction. When Solomon heard this he begged God for the wisdom to do the good thing which God wanted him to do. Solomon was obviously facing an environmental problem and needed an ethical decision; he begged God for guidance:

> Till, when they reached the Valley of the Ants, an ant exclaimed: O, ants! Enter your dwellings lest Solomon and his armies crush you, unperceiving.
> And [Solomon] smiled, laughing at her speech, and said: My Lord, arouse me to be thankful for Thy favor wherewith Thou hast favored me and my parents, and to do good that shall be pleasing unto Thee, and include me among [the number of] Thy righteous slaves (Sūrah 27:18–19).

Ethics in Islam is not based on a variety of separate scattered virtues, with each virtue, such as honesty or truth, standing isolated from others. Rather virtue in Islam is a part of a total, comprehensive way of life which serves to guide and control all human activity.[8] Truthfulness is an ethical value, as are protecting life, conserving the environment, and sustaining its development within the confines of what God has ordered. When 'Āisha, the wife of the Prophet Muhammad, was asked about his ethics she replied: "His ethics are the whole Qur'ān." The Qur'ān does not contain separate scattered ethical values. Rather it contains the instructions for a complete way of life. There are political, social and economic principles side by side with instructions for the construction and preservation of the earth.

Islamic ethical values are based not on human reasoning, as Aristotle claimed values to be, nor on what society imposes on the individual, as Durkheim thought, nor on the interests of a certain class, as Marxists maintain. In each of these claims values are affected by circumstances. In Islam, ethical values are held to be based on an accurate scale which is unalterable as to time and place.[9] Islam's values are those without which neither persons nor the natural environment can be sustained.

THE HUMAN-ENVIRONMENT RELATIONSHIP

As we have seen, within the Islamic faith, an individual's relationship with the environment is governed by certain moral precepts. These originate with God's creation of humans and the role they were given upon the Earth. Our universe, with all its diverse component elements was created by God and the human being in an essential part of His Measured and Balanced Creation. The role of humans, however, is not only to enjoy, use and benefit from their surroundings. They are expected to preserve, protect and promote their fellow creatures. The Prophet Muhammad (peace be upon him) said: "All creatures are God's dependents and the best among them is the one who is most useful to God's dependents."[10] The Prophet of Islam looked upon himself as responsible for the trees and the animals and all natural elements. He also said: "The only reasons that God does not cause his punishment to pour over you are the elderly, the suckling babes, and the animals which graze upon your land."[11] Muḥammad prayed for rain when he was reminded that water was short, the trees suffering from drought, and animals dying. He begged God's mercy to fall upon his creatures.[12]

The relationship between human beings and their environment includes many features in addition to subjugation and utilization. Construction and development are primary but our relationship to nature also includes meditation, contemplation and enjoyment of its beauties. The most perfect Muslim was the Prophet Muḥammad who was reported by Ibn 'Abbās to have enjoyed gazing at greenery and running water.[13]

When reading verses about the Earth in the Holy Qur'ān, we find strong indications that the Earth was originally a place of peace and rest for humans:

Is not He [best] Who made the earth a fixed abode, and placed rivers in the folds thereof, and placed firm hills therein, and hath set a barrier between the two seas? Is there any God beside Allah? Nay, but most of them know not! (Sūrah 27:61)

The Earth is important to the concept of interrelation. Human beings are made from two components of the Earth — dust and water.

And Allah hath caused you to grow as a growth from the earth. And afterward He maketh you return thereto, and He will bring you forth again, a [new] forthbringing. And Allah hath made the earth a wide expanse for you that ye may thread the valleyways thereof (Sūrah 71:1720).

The word earth (*arḍ*) is mentioned twice in this short quotation and in the Qur'ān the word occurs a total of 485 times, a simple measure of its importance.

The Earth is described as being subservient to humans: "He it is Who hath made the earth sub-

servient unto you, so walk in the paths thereof and eat of His providence" (Sūrah 67:15). The Earth is also described as a receptacle: "Have we not made the earth a receptacle both for the living and the dead" (Sūrah 77:25–26).[14] Even more importantly, the Earth is considered by Islam to be a source of purity and a place for the worship of God. The Prophet Muḥammad said: "The earth is made for me [and Muslims] as a prayer place (*masjid*) and as a purifier." This means that the Earth is to be used to cleanse oneself before prayer if water is unobtainable.[15] Ibn "Umar reported that the Prophet of Islam said: 'God is beautiful and loves everything beautiful. He is generous and loves generosity and is clean and loves cleanliness.'"[16]

Thus it is not surprising that the Islamic position with regard to the environment is that humans must intervene in order to protect the Earth. They may not stand back while it is destroyed. "He brought you forth from the earth and hath made you husband it" (Sūrah 11:61). For, finally, the Earth is a source of blessedness. And the Prophet Muḥammad said: "Some trees are as blessed as the Muslim himself, especially palm."[17]

THE SUSTAINABLE CARE OF NATURE

Islam permits the utilization of the natural environment but this utilization should not involve unnecessary destruction. Squandering is rejected by God: "O Children of Adam! Look to your adornment at every place of worship, and eat and drink, but be not prodigal. Lo! He loveth not the prodigals" (Sūrah 7:31). In this Qur'ānic passage, eating and drinking refer to the utilization of the sources of life. Such utilization is not without controls. The component elements of life have to be protected so that their utilization may continue in a sustainable way. Yet even this preservation must be undertaken in an altruistic fashion, and not merely for its benefit to human beings. The Prophet Muḥammad said: "Act in your life as though you are living forever and act for the Hereafter as if you are dying tomorrow."[18]

These actions must not be restricted to those which will derive direct benefits. Even if doomsday were expected imminently, humans would be expected to continue their good behaviour, for Muḥammad said, "When doomsday comes if someone has a palm shoot in his hand he should plant it."[19] This *hadīth* encapsulates the principles of Islamic environmental ethics. Even when all hope is lost, planting should continue for planting is good in itself. The planting of the palm shoot continues the process of development and will sustain life even if one does not anticipate any benefit from it. In this, the Muslim is like the soldier who fights to the last bullet.

A theory of the sustainable utilization of the ecosystem may be deduced from Islam's assertion that life is maintained with due balance in everything: "Allah knoweth that which every female beareth and that which the wombs absorb and that which they grow. And everything with Him is measured" (Sūrah 13:8). Also: "He unto Whom belongeth the sovereignty of the heavens and the earth, He hath chosen no son nor hath He any partner in the sovereignty. He hath created everything and hath meted out for it a measure" (Sūrah 25:2).

Humans are not the owners, but the maintainers of the due balance and measure which God provided for them and for the animals that live with them.

And after that He spread the earth,
And produced therefrom water thereof and the
  pasture thereof,
And He made fast the hills,
A provision for you and for your cattle (Sūrah
  79:30–33).

The Qur'ān goes on to say:

But when the great disaster cometh,
The day when man will call to mind his [whole]
  endeavor (Sūrah 79:34–35).

Humans will have a different home (*ma' wā*) or place of abode, different from the Earth and what it contains. The word *ma' wā* is the same word used in modern Arabic for "environment." One cannot help but wonder if these verses are an elaboration on the concept of sustainable development, a task that humans will undertake until their home is changed.

Sayyid Quṭb, commenting on these verses, observes that the Qur'ān, in referring to the origin of ultimate truth, used many correspondences (*muwāfaqāt*) — such as building the heavens, darkening the night, bringing forth human beings, spreading the earth, producing water and plants, and making the mountains fast. All these were provided for human beings and their animals as providence, and are direct signs which constitute proof as to the reality of God's measurement and calculation. Finally, Sayyid Quṭb observes that every part of God's creation was carefully made to fit into the general system, a system that testifies to the Creator's existence and the existence of a day of reward and punishment.

At this point, one must ask whether it is not a person's duty to preserve the proof of the Creator's existence while developing it. Wouldn't the wholesale destruction of the environment be the destruction of much which testifies to the greatness of God?

The concept of the sustained care of all aspects of the environment also fits into Islam's concept of charity, for charity is not only for the present generation but also for those in the future. A story is told of 'Umar ibn al-Khaṭṭab, the famous companion of the Prophet. He once saw that an old man, Khuzaymah ibn Thābit, had neglected his land. 'Umar asked what was preventing him from cultivating it. Khuzaymah explained that he was old and could be expected to die soon. Whereupon, 'Umar insisted that he should plant it. 'Khuzaymah's son, who narrated the story, added that his father and 'Umar planted the uncultivated land together.[20]

This incident demonstrates how strongly Islam encourages the sustained cultivation of the land. Land should not be used and then abandoned just because the cultivator expects no personal benefit.

In Islam, law and ethics constitute the two interconnected elements of a unified world view. When considering the environment and its protection, this Islamic attitude may constitute a useful foundation for the formulation of a strategy throughout, at least, the Muslim world. Muslims who inhabit so much of the developing world may vary in local habits and customs but they are remarkably united in faith and in their attitude to life.

Islam is a religion of submission to God, master of all worlds. The Earth and all its inhabitants were created and are dominated by God. All Muslims begin their prayers five times a day with the same words from the Holy Qur'ān: "Praise be to Allah, Lord of the Worlds" (Sūrah 1:1). These opening words of the Qur'ān have become not only the most repeated but also the most loved and respected words for Muslims everywhere. Ibn Kathīr, like many other Qur'ān commentators, considers that the word "worlds" (ālamīn) means the different kinds of creatures that inhabit the sky, the land, and the sea. Muslims submit themselves to the Creator who made them and who made all other worlds. The same author mentions that Muslims also submit themselves to the signs of the existence of the Creator and His unity. This secondary meaning exists because "worlds" comes from the same root as signs; thus the worlds are signs of the Creator.[21]

A Muslim, therefore, has a very special relationship with those worlds which in modern times have come to be known as the environment. Indeed, that these worlds exist and that they were made by the same Creator means that they are united and interdependent, each a part of the perfect system of creation. No conflict should exist between them; they should exist in harmony as different parts of the whole. Their coexistence could be likened to an architectural masterpiece in which every detail has been added to complete and complement the structure. Thus the details of creation serve to testify to the wisdom and perfection of the Creator.

THE PRACTICE OF ISLAMIC ENVIRONMENTAL ETHICS

Islam has always had a great influence on the formation of individual Muslim communities and the policy making of Muslim states. Environmental policy has been influenced by Islam and this influence has remained the same throughout the history of the Islamic faith.

The concept of *ḥimā* (protection of certain zones) has existed since the time of the Prophet Muḥammad. *Ḥimā* involved the ruler or government's protection of specific unused areas. No one may build on them or develop them in any way. The Mālikī school of Islamic law described the requirements of *ḥimā* to be the following.[22] First, the need of the Muslim public for the maintenance of land in an unused state. Protection is not granted to satisfy

an influential individual unless there is a public need. Second, the protected area should be limited in order to avoid inconvenience to the public. Third, the protected area should not be built on or cultivated. And fourth, the aim of protection (Zuhaylī 5:574) is the welfare of the people, for example, the protected area may be used for some restricted grazing by the animals of the poor.

The concept of *ḥimā* can still be seen in many Muslim countries, such as Saudi Arabia, where it is practised by the government to protect wildlife. In a less formal way it is still practised by some bedouin tribes as a custom or tradition inherited from their ancestors.

The *ḥarīm* is another ancient institution which can be traced back to the time of the Prophet Muḥammad. It is an inviolable zone which may not be used or developed, save with the specific permission of the state. The *ḥarīm* is usually found in association with wells, natural springs, underground water channels, rivers and trees planted on barren land or *mawāt*.[23] There is careful administration of the *ḥarīm* zones based on the practice of the Prophet Muḥammad and the precedent of his companions as recorded in the sources of Islamic law.

At present the role of Islam in environmental protection can be seen in the formation of different Islamic organizations and the emphasis given to Islam as a motive for the protection of the environment.

Saudi Arabia has keenly sought to implement a number of projects aimed at the protection of various aspects of the environment, for example, the late King Khalid's patronage of efforts to save the Arabian oryx from extinction.

The Meteorology and Environmental Protection Administration (MEPA) of Saudi Arabia actively promotes the principles of Islamic environmental protection. In 1983 MEPA and the International Union for the Conservation of Nature and Natural Resources commissioned a basic paper on the Islamic principles for the conservation of natural environment.[24]

The Islamic faith has great impact on environmental issues throughout the Arab and Muslim world. The first Arab Ministerial Conference took as its theme "The Environmental Aspects of Development" and one of the topics considered was the Islamic faith and its values.[25] The Amir of Kuwait emphasized the fundamental importance of Islam when he addressed the General Assembly of the United Nations in 1988. He explained that Islam was the basis for justice, mercy, and cooperation between all humankind; and he called for an increase in scientific and technological assistance from the North to help conserve natural and human resources, combat pollution and support sustainable development projects.

Finally, it is imperative to acknowledge that the new morality required to conserve the environment which the World Conservation Strategy (Section 13.1) emphasizes, needs to be based on a more solid foundation. It is not only necessary to involve the public in conservation policy but also to improve its morals and alter its attitudes. In Muslim countries such changes should be brought about by identifying environmental policies with Islamic teachings. To do this, the public education system will have to supplement the scientific approach to environmental education with serious attention to Islamic belief and environmental awareness.

NOTES

1. Aḥmad Ibn Taymīyah, *Majamū 'Fatawā* (Rabat: Saudi Educational Attaché, n.d.), 11:96–97.

2. Mawil Y. Izzi Deen (Samarrai), "Environmental Protection and Islam," *Journal of the Faculty of Arts and Humanities, King Abdulaziz University* 5 (1985).

3. All references to the Holy Qur'ān are from *The Meaning of the Glorious Koran,* trans. Mohammed M. Pickthall, (New York: Mentor, n.d.).

4. Ibn Hajar al-'Asqalānī, *Fatḥ al-Bārībi-Shārḥ Ṣaḥīḥ al-Bukhārī,* edited by M. F. 'Abd al-Bāqī, M. al-Khāṭib, and A.B. Bāz, 1959; 1970 (Beirut: Dār al-Ma'rifah, 195; 197), 5:40.

5. Ibid., 5:42.

6. Muḥammad 'Abd Allah Draz, *La Morale du Koran,* trans. into Arabic by A. Shahin and S. M. Badāwī (Kuwait: Dār al-Risālah, 1973), 28.

7. Ibid.

8. Sayyid Quṭb, *Muqāwamāt al-Tasawwur al-Islāmī* (Cairo: Dār al-Shurūq, 1985), 289.

9. Ibid., 290.

10. Ismā'il Ibn Muḥammad al-'Ajlūnī, *Kashf al-Khafā' wa Muzīl al-Ilbās,* edited by A. al-Qallash (Damascus: Mu'assasat al-Risālah, 1983), 1:458.

11. Ibid., 1:213.

12. Ibn Ḥajar, *Fatḥ al Bārī,* 2:512.

13. 'Ajlūnī, *Kash al-Khafā',* 1:387.

14. N. J. Dawood, trans., *The Koran* (New York: Penguin, 1974): 54.

15. Muḥammad Ibn Ismā'īl al-Bukhāri, *Ṣaḥīḥ al-Bukhāri* (Istanbul: Dār al-Ṭiba'ah al-Amīrah, 1897), 1:86.

16. Ajlūnī, *Kashf al-Khafā',* 1:260.

17. Bukhā ri, *Ṣaḥ īḥ al-Bukhārī,* 1:22, 6:211.

18. Aḥmad Ibn al-Ḥusayn al-Bayhāqī, *Sunan al-Bayhaqī al-Kubrā* (Hyderabad, India: n.d.), 3:19.

19. Ibid., 3:184.

20. Soūti, *al-Jāmi 'al-Kabīr,* manuscript (Egyptian General Committee for Publication, n.d.).

21. M. A. al-Sabunī, *Mukhtaṣar Tafsīr Ibn Kathīr* (Beirut: Dār al-Qur'ān al-Karīm, 1981), 1:21.

22. Wahbah Muṣtafa Zuḥayli, *al-Fiqh al-Islāmīwa 'Adilatuhu* (Damascus: Mu'assasat al-Risālah, 1985).

23. Ibid., 5:574.

24. A. H. Bakader, A. T. al-Sabbagh, M. A. al-Gelinid, and M. Y. Izzi Deen (Samarrai), *Islamic Principles for the Conservation of the Natural Environment* (Gland, Switzerland: International Union for the Conservation of Nature and MEPA, 1983).

25. *Habitat and the Environment* (Tunis: Economic Affairs Department of the Directorate of the Arab League, 1986).

DISCUSSION TOPICS

1. What similarities and differences are there between the Islamic view and the views presented by Rolston?

2. What particular insights from Islam might be applicable in developing a more judicious environmental ethic in Western society? Justify your position.

Voices from White Earth

Winona LaDuke

Winona LaDuke is a graduate of Harvard and an environmental activist. She was a U.S. vice-presidential candidate on the Green Party ticket for both 1996 and 2000 and was named one of Ms *magazine's women of the year in 1997. She is author of* Last Standing Woman *(1997), an attack on oppression of Native Americans, and is a member of the Anishinabeg community, who live on the White Earth Reservation in Mississippi.*

In this chapter from A Forest of Voices: Conversations in Ecology *(2nd ed., 2000), LaDuke notes that perspectives of indigenous people often differ from those of the dominant society in the United States. She describes at least five differences between what she perceives as indigenous thinking and "industrial thinking." These include the notions of natural law versus human domination; thinking of time as cyclical rather than linear; appreciating the natural and wild rather than emphasizing taming and civilizing; seeing nature as having animate qualities rather than inanimate; and emphasizing satisfaction with what one has and sharing rather than continuous accumulation (capitalism). She then illustrates these differences through examples of Native American practices and past U.S. federal government treatment of Native Americans.*

. . . I would like to talk about *keewaydahn,* which means "going home" in the Anishinabeg language. . . .

Anishinabeg is our name for ourselves in our own language; it means "people." We are called Ojibways in Canada and Chippewas in the United States. Our aboriginal territory, and where we live today, is in the northern part of five American states and the southern part of four Canadian provinces. . . .

There are about seven hundred different native communities in North America. Roughly one hundred are Ojibway or Anishinabeg communities, but we're different bands. . . .

Now, if you look at the United States, about 4 percent of the land is held by Indian people. That is

the extent of today's Indian reservations. The Southwest has the largest native population, and there's a significant population on the Great Plains. In northern Minnesota there are seven big reservations, all Ojibway or Anishinabeg. But if you go to Canada, about 85 percent of the population north of the fiftieth parallel is native. So if you look at it in terms of land occupancy and geography, in about two-thirds of Canada the majority of the population is native. I'm not even including Nunevat, which is an Inuit-controlled area the size of India in what used to be called the Northwest Territories.

If you look at the whole of North America, you find that the majority of the population is native in about a third of the continent. Within this larger area, indigenous people maintain their own ways of living and their cultural practices. This is our view of the continent, and it is different from the view of most other North Americans. When *we* look at the United States and Canada, we see our reservations and reserves as islands in the continent. When Indian people talk about their travels, they often mention reservations rather than cities: "I went to Rosebud, and then I went over to North Cheyenne." This is the indigenous view of North America.

Going beyond North America, I want to talk about the Western Hemisphere and the world from an indigenous perspective. My intent is to present you with an indigenous worldview and our perception of the world. There are a number of countries in the Western Hemisphere in which native peoples are the majority of the population: in Guatemala, Ecuador, Peru, Bolivia. In some South American countries we control as much as 22 to 40 percent of the land. Overall, the Western Hemisphere is not predominantly white. Indigenous people continue their ways of living based on generations and generations of knowledge and practice on the land.

On a worldwide scale there are about five thousand nations and a hundred and seventy states. Nations are groups of indigenous peoples who share common language, culture, history, territory, and government institutions. That is how international law defines a nation. And that is who *we* are: nations of people who have existed for thousands of years. There are about a hundred and seventy — maybe more now, about a hundred and eighty-five — states that are recognized by the United Nations. For the most part, these states are the result of colonial empires or colonial demarcations. And whereas indigenous nations have existed for thousands of years, many of these states in existence at the end of the twentieth century have been around only since World War II. That is a big difference. Yet the dominant worldview of industrial society is determined by these young states, not by the five thousand ancient nations.

The estimated number of indigenous people in the world depends on how you define indigenous people. It is said that there are currently about five hundred million of us in the world today, including such peoples as the Tibetans, the Masai, the Wara Wara, and the Quechua. I define indigenous peoples as those who have continued their way of living for thousands of years according to their original instructions.

That is a quick background on indigenous people. It should help you understand that my perspective, the perspective of indigenous peoples, is entirely different from that of the dominant society in this country.

Indigenous peoples believe fundamentally in natural law and a state of balance. We believe that all societies and cultural practices must exist in accordance with natural law in order to be sustainable. We also believe that cultural diversity is as essential as biological diversity to maintaining sustainable societies. Indigenous peoples have lived on earth sustainably for thousands of years, and I suggest to you that indigenous ways of living are the only sustainable ways of living. Because of that, I believe there is something to be learned from indigenous thinking and indigenous ways. I don't think many of you would argue that industrial society is sustainable. I think that in two or three hundred years this society will be extinct because a society based on conquest cannot survive when there's nothing left to conquer.

Indigenous people have taken great care to fashion their societies in accordance with natural law, which is the highest law. It is superior to the laws made by nations, states, and municipalities. It is the law to which we are all accountable. There are no Twelve Commandments of natural law, but there are

some things that I believe to be true about natural law. And this is my experience from listening to a lot of our older people. What I am telling you is not really my opinion; it's based on what has happened in our community, on what I've heard people say, and on their knowledge. We have noticed that much in nature is cyclical: the movements of moons, the tides, the seasons, our bodies. Time itself, in most indigenous worldviews, is cyclical. We also have experienced and believe that it is our essential nature and our need always to keep a balance in nature. Most indigenous ceremonies, if you look to their essence, are about the restoration of balance in nature. That is our intent: to restore, and then to retain, balance. Nature itself continually tries to balance, to equalize.

According to our way of living and our way of looking at the world, most of the world is animate. This is reflected in our language, Anishinabemowin, in which most nouns are animate. *Mandamin,* the word from corn, is animate; *mitig,* the word for tree, is animate; so is the word for rice, *manomin,* and the word for rock or stone, *asin.* Looking at the world and seeing that most things are alive, we have come to believe, based on this perception, that they have spirit. They have standing on their own. Therefore, when I harvest wild rice on our reservation up north, I always offer *asemah,* tobacco, because when you take something, you must always give thanks to its spirit for giving itself to you, for it has a choice whether to give itself to you or not. In our cultural practice, for instance, it is not because of skill that a hunter can harvest a deer or a caribou; it is because he or she has been honorable and has given *asemah.* That is how you are able to harvest, not because you are a good hunter but because the animal gives itself to you. That is our perception.

And so we are always very careful when we harvest. Anthropologists call this reciprocity, which means something anthropological, I guess. But from our perspective it means that when you take, you always give. This is about balance and equalness. We also say that when you take, you must take only what you need and leave the rest. Because if you take more than you need, that means you are greedy. You have brought about imbalance, you have been selfish. To do this in our community is a very big disgrace. It is a violation of natural law, and it leaves you with no guarantee that you will be able to continue harvesting.

We have a word in our language that describes the practice of living in harmony with natural law: *minobimaatisiiwin.* This word describes how you live your life according to natural law, how you behave as an individual in relationship with other individuals and in relationship with the land and all the things that are animate on the land. *Minobimaatisiiwin* is our cultural practice; it is what you strive towards as an individual as well as collectively as a society.

We have tried to retain this way of living and of thinking in spite of all that has happened to us over the centuries. I believe we do retain most of these practices to a great extent in many of our societies. In our community they are overshadowed at times by industrialism, but they still exist.

I would like to contrast what I've told you about indigenous thinking with what I call "industrial thinking." I think the Lakota have the best term to describe it. It actually refers to white people, although they are not the only ones who think this way. Indigenous peoples have interesting terms for white people: they are usually not just words, they are descriptions encapsulated in a word. I will tell you about one: the Lakota word for a white person is *wasichu.* It derives from the first time the Lakota ever saw a white person. There was a white man out in the prairie in the Black Hills, and he was starving. He came into a Lakota camp in the middle of the night, and the Lakota of course were astonished to see him. They began to watch him to see what he was doing. He went over to the food, took something, and ran away. A little while later, the Lakota looked to see what he had taken: he had stolen a large amount of fat. So the Lakota word for a white person, *wasichu,* means "he who steals the fat." Now, that is a description that doesn't necessarily have to do with white people, but taking more than you need has to do with industrial society. He who steals the fat. That's what I'm talking about when I refer to the industrial worldview.

Industrial thinking is characterized by several ideas that run counter to indigenous ideas. First, instead of believing that natural law is preeminent, in-

dustrial society believes that humans are entitled to full dominion over nature. It believes that man—and it *is* usually man of course—has some God-given right to all that is around him, that he has been created superior to the rest.

Second, instead of modeling itself on the cyclical structure of nature, this society is patterned on linear thinking. I went all the way through its school system, and I remember how time, for example, is taught in this society. It's taught on a timeline, usually one that begins around 1492. It has some dates on it that were important to someone, although I could never figure out to whom. The timeline is a clear representation of this society's linear way of thinking. And certain values permeate this way of thinking, such as the concept of progress. Industrial society wants to keep making progress as it moves down the timeline, progress defined by things like technological advancement and economic growth. This value accompanies linear thinking.

Third, there is the attitude toward what is wild as opposed to what is cultivated or "tame." This society believes it must tame the wilderness. It also believes in the superiority of civilized over primitive peoples, a belief that also follows a linear model: that somehow, over time, people will become more civilized. Also related of course is the idea behind colonialism: that some people have the *right* to civilize other people. My experience is that people who are viewed as "primitive" are generally people of color, and people who are viewed as "civilized" are those of European descent. This prejudice still permeates industrial society and in fact even permeates "progressive" thinking. It holds that somehow people of European descent are smarter—they have some better knowledge of the world than the rest of us. I suggest that this is perhaps a racist worldview and that it has racist implications. That is, in fact, our experience.

Fourth, industrial society speaks a language of inanimate nouns. Even words for the land are becoming inanimate. . . . Industrial language has changed things from being animate, alive, and having spirit to being inanimate, mere objects and commodities of society. When things are inanimate, "man" can view them as his God-given right. He can take them, commodify them, and manipulate them in society. This behavior is also related to the linear way of thinking.

Fifth, the last aspect on industrial thinking I'm going to talk about (although it's always unpopular to question it in America) is the idea of capitalism itself. In this country we are taught that capitalism is a system that combines labor, capital, and resources for the purpose of accumulation. The capitalist goal is to use the least labor, capital, and resources to accumulate the most profit. The intent of capitalism is accumulation. So the capitalist's method is always to take more than needed. Therefore, from an indigenous point of view capitalism is inherently out of harmony with natural law.

Based on this goal of accumulation, industrial society practices conspicuous consumption. Indigenous societies, on the other hand, practice what I would call "conspicuous distribution." We focus on the potlatch, the giveaway, an event that carries much more honor than accumulation does. In fact, the more you give away, the greater your honor. We make a great deal of these giveaways, and industrial society has something to learn from them.

Over the past five hundred years the indigenous experience has been one of conflict between the indigenous and the industrial worldviews. This conflict has manifested itself as holocaust. That is our experience. Indigenous people understand clearly that this society, which has caused the extinction of more species in the past hundred and fifty years than the total species extinction from the Ice Age to the mid-nineteenth century, is the same society that has caused the extinction of about two thousand different indigenous peoples in the Western Hemisphere alone. We understand intimately the relationship between extinction of species and extinction of peoples, because we experience both. And the extinction continues. Last year alone the Bureau of Indian Affairs, which has legal responsibility for people like myself — legally, I'm a ward of the federal government — declared nineteen different indigenous nations in North America extinct. The rate of extinction in the Amazon rainforest, for example, has been one indigenous people per year since 1900. And if you look at world maps showing cultural and biological distribution, you find that where there is the most cultural diversity, there is also the most biological diversity. A direct relationship exists between the two. That is why we argue that cultural diversity is as important to a sustainable global society as biological diversity.

Our greatest problem with all of this in America is that there has been no recognition of the cultural extinction, no owning up to it, no atonement for what happened, and no education about it. . . . Nobody admits that the holocaust took place. This is because the white settlers believed they had a God-given right to the continent, and anyone with this right wouldn't recognize what happened as holocaust. Yet it was a holocaust of unparalleled proportions: Bartholomew de las Casas and other contemporaries of Columbus estimated that fifty million indigenous people in the Western Hemisphere perished in a sixty-year period. In terms of millions of people, this was probably the largest holocaust in world history.

Now, it is not appropriate for me to say that my holocaust was worse than someone else's. But it is absolutely correct for me to demand that my holocaust be recognized. And that has not happened in America. . . . In this society we do not exist as full human beings with human rights, with the same rights to self-determination, to dignity, and to land — to territorial integrity — that other people have.

The challenge that people of conscience in this country face is to undo and debunk the mythology, to come clean, become honest, understand the validity of our demands, and recognize our demands. People must see the interlocking interests between their own ability to survive and indigenous peoples' continuing cultural sustainability. Indigenous peoples have lived sustainably in this land for thousands of years. I am absolutely sure that our societies could live without yours, but I'm not so sure that your society can continue to live without ours. This is why indigenous people need to be recognized now and included in the discussion of the issues affecting this country's future.

I'd like to tell you now about indigenous peoples' efforts to protect our land and restore our communities. . . . I could tell you many stories of these different struggles, but I'll use my own community as an example. Here is our story.

The White Earth Reservation, located at the headwaters of the Mississippi, is thirty-six by thirty-six miles square, which is about 837,000 acres. It is very good land. A treaty reserved it for our people in 1867 in return for relinquishing a much larger area of northern Minnesota. Of all our territory, we chose this land for its richness and diversity. There are forty-seven lakes on the reservation. There's maple sugar; there are hardwoods and all the different medicine plants my people use — our reservation is called "the medicine chest of the Ojibways." We have wild rice; we have deer; we have beaver; we have fish — every food we need. On the eastern part of the reservation there are stands of white pine. On the part farthest west there used to be buffalo, but this area is now farmland, situated in the Red River Valley. That is our area, the land reserved to us under treaty.

Our traditional forms of land use and ownership are similar to those of a community land trust. The land is owned collectively, and we have individual or, more often, family-based usufruct rights: each family has traditional areas where it fishes and hunts. In our language the words *Anishinabeg aking* describe the concept of land ownership. They translate as "the land of the people," which doesn't infer that we own our land but that we belong on it. Our definition doesn't stand up well in court, unfortunately, because this country's legal system upholds the concept of private property.

Our community enforces its traditional practices by adhering to *minobimaatisiiwin.* Historically, this involved punishing people who transgressed these rules. For instance, in our community the worst punishment historically — we didn't have jails — was banishment. That still exists in our community to a certain extent. Just imagine if the worst punishment in industrial society were banishment! With us, each person wants to be part of the community.

We have also maintained our practices by means of careful management and observation. For example, we have "hunting bosses" and "rice chiefs," who make sure that resources are used sustainably in each region. Hunting bosses oversee trap-line rotation, a system by which people trap in an area for two years and then move to a different area to let the land rest. Rice chiefs coordinate wild rice harvesting. The rice on each lake is unique: each has its own taste and ripens at its own time. We also have a "tally man," who makes sure there are enough animals for each family in a given area. If a family

can't sustain itself, the tally man moves them to a new place where animals are more plentiful. These practices are sustainable.

My children's grandfather, who is a trapper, lives on wild animals in the wintertime. When he intends to trap beavers, he reaches his hand into a beaver house and counts how many beavers are in there. (Beavers are not carnivorous; they won't bite.) By counting, he knows how many beavers he can take. Of course, he has to count only if he hasn't already been observing that beaver house for a long time. This is a very sustainable way to trap, one based on a kind of thorough observation that can come only with residency. Further, I suggest that this man knows more about his ecosystem than any Ph.D. scholar who studies it from the university.

As I have indicated, the White Earth Reservation is a rich place. And it is our experience that industrial society is not content to leave other peoples' riches alone. Wealth attracts colonialism: the more a native people has, the more colonizers are apt to covet that wealth and take it away — whether it is gold or, as in our case, pine stands and Red River Valley farmland. A Latin American scholar named Eduardo Galeano has written about colonialism in communities like mine. He says: "In the colonial to neo-colonial alchemy, gold changes to scrap metal and food to poison. We have become painfully aware of the mortality of wealth, which nature bestows and imperialism appropriates." For us, our wealth was the source of our poverty: industrial society could not leave us be.

Our reservation was created by treaty in 1867: in 1887 the General Allotment Act was passed on the national level, not only to teach Indians the concept of private property but also to facilitate the removal of more land from Indian Nations. The federal government divided our reservation into eighty-acre parcels of land and allotted each parcel to an individual Indian, hoping that through this change we would somehow become yeoman farmers, adopt the notion of progress, and become civilized. But the allotment system had no connection to our traditional land tenure patterns. In our society a person harvested rice in one place, trapped in another place, got medicines in a third place, and picked berries in a fourth. These locations depended on the ecosystem; they were not necessarily contiguous.

But the government said to each Indian, "Here are your eighty acres; this is where you'll live." Then, after each Indian had received an allotment, the rest of the land was declared "surplus" and given to white people to homestead. On our reservation almost the entire land base was allotted except for some pinelands that were annexed by the state of Minnesota and sold to timber companies. What happened to my reservation happened to reservations all across the country.

The federal government was legally responsible for this; they turned our land into individual eighty-acre parcels, and then they looked the other way and let the state of Minnesota take some of our land and tax what was left. When the Indians couldn't pay the taxes, the state confiscated the land. . . .

. . . It exemplifies the process by which native peoples were dispossessed of their land. The White Earth Reservation lost two hundred and fifty thousand acres to the state of Minnesota because of unpaid taxes. And this was done to native peoples across the country: on a national average reservations lost a full two-thirds of their land this way.

By 1920, 99 percent of original White Earth Reservation lands were in non-Indian hands. By 1930 many of our people had died from tuberculosis and other diseases, and half of our remaining population lived off-reservation. Three generations of our people were forced into poverty, chased off our land, and made refugees in this society. Now a lot of our people live in Minneapolis. Of twenty thousand tribal members only four or five thousand live on reservation. That's because we're refugees, not unlike other people in this society.

Our struggle is to get our land back. That's what we've been trying to do for a hundred years. By 1980, 93 percent of our reservation was still held by non-Indians. That's the circumstance we are in at the end of the twentieth century. We have exhausted all legal recourse for getting back our land. . . .

The federal, state, and county governments are the largest landholders on the reservation. It is good land still, rich in many things; however, when you do not control your land, you do not control your destiny. That's our experience. What has happened is that two-thirds of the deer taken in our reservation are taken by non-Indians, mostly by sports hunters

from Minneapolis. In the Tamarac National Wildlife Refuge nine times as many deer are taken by non-Indians as by Indians, because that's where sports hunters from Minneapolis come to hunt. Ninety percent of the fish taken on our reservation is taken by white people, and most of them are taken by people from Minneapolis who come to their summer cabins and fish on our reservation. Each year in our region, about ten thousand acres are being clear cut for paper and pulp in one county alone, mostly by the Potlatch Timber Company. We are watching the destruction of our ecosystem and the theft of our resources; in not controlling our land we are unable to control what is happening to our ecosystem. So we are struggling to regain control through the White Earth Land Recovery Project.

Our project is like several others in Indian communities. We are not trying to displace people who have settled there. A third of our land is held by the federal, state, and county governments. That land should just be returned to us. It certainly would not displace anyone. And then we have to ask the question about absentee land ownership. It is an ethical question that should be asked in this country. A third of the *privately* held land on our reservation is held by absentee landholders: they do not see that land, do not know it, and do not even know where it is. We ask these people how they feel about owning land on a reservation, hoping we can persuade them to return it.

Approximately sixty years ago in India the Gramdan movement dealt with similar issues. Some million acres were placed in a village trust as a result of the moral influence of Vinoba Bhave. The whole issue of absentee land ownership needs to be addressed—particularly in America, where the idea of private property is so sacred, where somehow it is ethical to hold land that you never see. As Vinoba said, "It is highly inconsistent that those who possess land should not till it themselves, and those who cultivate should possess no land to do so."

Our project also acquires land. It owns about nine hundred acres right now. We bought some land as a site for a roundhouse, a building that holds one of our ceremonial drums. We bought back our burial grounds, which were on private land, because we believe that we should hold the land our ancestors lived on. These are all small parcels of land. . . . It is a very slow process, but our strategy is based on this recovery of the land and of our cultural and economic practices.

We are a poor community. People look at our reservation and comment on the 85 percent unemployment—they do not realize what we do with our time. They have no way of valuing our cultural practices. For instance, 85 percent of our people hunt, taking at least one or two deer annually, probably in violation of federal game laws; 75 percent of our people hunt for small game and geese; 50 percent of our people fish by net; 50 percent of our people sugarbush and garden on our reservation. About the same percentage harvest wild rice, not just for themselves; they harvest it to sell. About half of our people produce handcrafts. There is no way to quantify this in America. It is called the "invisible economy" or the "domestic economy." Society views us as unemployed Indians who need wage-earning jobs. That is not how we view ourselves. . . .

Our strategy is to strengthen our own traditional economy (thereby strengthening our traditional culture as well) so that we can produce 50 percent or more of our own food, which we then won't need to buy elsewhere, and can eventually produce enough surplus to sell. In our case most of our surplus is in wild rice. We are rich in terms of wild rice. The Creator, Gitchi Manitu, gave us wild rice—said we should eat it and should share it; we have traded it for thousands of years. . . .

We've been working for several years now to increase the price of the rice we gather from fifty cents per pound to a dollar per pound, green. We are trying to market our rice ourselves. We try to capture the "value added" in our community by selling it ourselves. We went from about five thousand pounds of production on our reservation to about fifty thousand pounds last year. This is our strategy for economic recovery.

Other parts of our strategy include language immersion programs to restore our language and revival of drum ceremonies to restore our cultural practices. These are part of an integrated restoration process that is focused on the full human being.

In the larger picture, in Wisconsin and Minnesota our community is working hard to exercise specific treaty rights. Under the 1847 treaty, we have reserved-use rights to a much larger area than just our reservations. These are called extra-territorial treaty rights. We didn't say we were going to live there, we just said we wanted to keep the right to use that land in our usual and accustomed ways. This has led us to a larger political strategy, for although our harvesting practices are sustainable, they require an almost pristine ecosystem in order to take as much fish and grow as much rice as we need. To achieve this condition the tribes are entering into a co-management agreement in northern Wisconsin and northern Minnesota to prevent further environmental degradation as a first step toward preserving an extra-territorial area in accordance with treaty rights.

There are many similar stories all across North America. A lot can be learned from these stories, and we can share a great deal in terms of your strategies and what you're trying to do in your own communities. I see this as a relationship among people who share common issues, common ground, and common agendas. It is absolutely crucial, however, that our struggle for territorial integrity and economic and political control of our lands not be regarded as a threat by this society. . . .

. . . Our stories are about people with a great deal of tenacity and courage, people who have been resisting for centuries. We are sure that if we do not resist, we will not survive. Our resistance will guarantee our children a future. In our society we think ahead to the seventh generation; however, we know that the ability of the seventh generation to sustain itself will be dependent on our ability to resist now.

Another important consideration is that traditional ecological knowledge is unheard knowledge in this country's institutions. Nor is it something an anthropologist can extract by mere research. Traditional ecological knowledge is passed from generation to generation; it is not an appropriate subject for a Ph.D. dissertation. We who live by this knowledge have the intellectual property rights to it, and we have the right to tell our stories ourselves. There is a lot to be learned from our knowledge, but you need us in order to learn it, whether it is the story of my children's grandfather reaching his hand into that beaver house or of the Haida up on the Northwest coast, who make totem poles and plank houses. . . .

Traditional ecological knowledge is absolutely essential for the future. Crafting a relationship between us is absolutely essential. Native people are not quite at the table in the environmental movement—for example, in the management of the Great Plains. Environmental groups and state governors sat down and talked about how to manage the Great Plains, and nobody asked the Indians to come to the table. Nobody even noticed that there are about fifty million acres of Indian land out there in the middle of the Great Plains, land that according to history and law has never yet had a drink of water—that is, reservations have been denied water all these years because of water diversion projects. When water allocations are being discussed, someone needs to talk about how the tribes need a drink.

One proposal for the Great Plains is a Buffalo Commons, which would include one hundred and ten prairie counties that are now financially bankrupt and are continuing to lose people. The intent is to restore these lands ecologically, bringing back the buffalo, the perennial crops, and indigenous prairie grasses that Wes Jackson is experimenting with. I think we need to broaden the idea, though, because I don't think it should be just a Buffalo Commons; I think it should be an Indigenous Commons. If you look at the 1993 population in the area, you'll find that the majority are indigenous peoples who already hold at least fifty million acres of the land. We know this land of our ancestors, and we should rightly be part of a sustainable future for it.

Another thing I want to touch on is the necessity of shifting our perception. There is no such thing as sustainable development. Community is the only thing in my experience that is sustainable. We all need to be involved in building sustainable communities. We can each do that in our own way—whether it is European-American communities or Dené communities or Anishinabeg communities—returning to and restoring the way of life that is based on the land. To achieve this restoration we need to reintegrate with cultural traditions informed by the land. That is something I don't know how to tell you to do, but it is something you're going to need to do. Garrett Hardin and others are saying that

the only way you can manage a commons is if you share enough cultural experiences and cultural values so that you can keep your practices in order and in check: *minobimaatisiiwin*. The reason we have remained sustainable for all these centuries is that we are cohesive communities. A common set of values is needed to live together sustainably on the land.

Finally, I believe the issues deep in this society that need to be addressed are structural. This is a society that continues to consume too much of the world's resources. You know, when you consume this much in resources, it means constant intervention in other peoples' land and countries, whether it is mine or whether it is the Crees' up in James Bay or someone else's. It is meaningless to talk about human rights unless you talk about consumption. And that's a structural change we all need to address. It is clear that in order for native communities to live, the dominant society must change, because if this society continues in the direction it is going, our reservations and our way of life will continue to bear the consequences. This society has to be changed! We have to be able to put aside its cultural baggage, which is industrial baggage. It's not sustainable. Do not be afraid of discarding it. That's the only way we're going to make peace between the settler and the native.

Miigwech. I want to thank you for your time. *Keewaydahn.* It's our way home.

— 1993

DISCUSSION TOPICS

1. Which ideas espoused by LaDuke do you believe would be applicable to an environmental ethic in Western industrial societies? Which ones might not? Clarify your reasoning for each.

2. Which other reading(s) do you believe have the most in common with LaDuke's perspectives? Which have the least in common? Justify your answers.

3. Which of LaDuke's ideas do you believe are most readily incorporated into your own environmental ethic? Which ones seem less applicable? Explain your position.

READING 28

The Sun My Heart

Thich Nhat Hanh

Thich Nhat Hanh is a Vietnamese Buddhist monk, poet, and peace activist. Thich *is a title meaning "reverend," while* Nhat Hanh *means "one action." He has published over seventy-five books, is the founder of Van Hanh University, and acquired international recognition during the Vietnam War as a Buddhist committed to peace and the end of political oppression. He was nominated for the 1967 Nobel Peace Prize by Martin Luther King, Jr.*

In this chapter from Love in Action: Writings on Nonviolent Social Change *(1993), Thich Nhat Hanh develops an ethic of deep ecology based on the principles of Buddhism. He emphasizes the true oneness of the universe, with all phenomena connected in the unity of existence. Reality involves dissolving boundaries between self and other selves, human and nonhuman creatures, living and inanimate nature, and distinct life spans and an ongoing cycle of birth and death. He believes that our oneness with the universe will instill respect, humility, mindfulness, love, and compassion toward all other beings.*

. . . We have to remember that our body is not limited to what lies within the boundary of our skin. Our body is much more immense. We know that if our heart stops beating, the flow of our life will stop, but we do not take the time to notice the many things outside of our bodies that are equally essential for survival. If the ozone layer around our Earth were to disappear for even an instant, we would die. If the sun were to stop shining, the flow of our life would stop. The sun is our second heart, our heart outside of our body. It gives all life on earth the warmth necessary for existence. Plants live thanks to the sun. Their leaves absorb the sun's energy, along with carbon dioxide from the air, to produce food for the tree, the flower, the plankton. And thanks to plants, we and other animals can live. All of us — people, animals, plants, and minerals — "consume" the sun directly and indirectly. We can-

not begin to describe all the effects of the sun, the great heart outside of our body. . . .

There is no phenomenon in the universe that does not intimately concern us, from a pebble resting at the bottom of the ocean, to the movement of a galaxy millions of light years away. Walt Whitman said, "I believe a blade of grass is no less than the journey-work of stars . . ." These words are not philosophy. They come from the depths of his soul. He also said, "I am large, I contain multitudes."

This might be called a meditation on "interbeing endlessly interwoven." All phenomena are interdependent. When we think of a speck of dust, a flower, or a human being, our thinking cannot break loose from the idea of unity, of one, of calculation. We see a line drawn between one and many, one and not one. But if we truly realize the interdependent nature of the dust, the flower, and the human being, we see that unity cannot exist without diversity. Unity and diversity interpenetrate each other freely. Unity is diversity, and diversity is unity. This is the principle of interbeing.

If you are a mountain climber or someone who enjoys the countryside or the forest, you know that forests are our lungs outside of our bodies. Yet we have been acting in a way that has allowed millions of square miles of land to be deforested, and we have also destroyed the air, the rivers, and parts of the ozone layer. We are imprisoned in our small selves, thinking only of some comfortable conditions for this small self, while we destroy our large self. If we want to change the situation, we must begin by being our true selves. To be our true selves means we have to *be* the forest, the river, and the ozone layer. If we visualize ourselves as the forest, we will experience the hopes and fears of the trees. If we don't do this, the forests will die, and we will lose our chance for peace. When we understand that we inter-are with the trees, we will know that it is up to us to make an effort to keep the trees alive. In the last twenty years, our automobiles and factories have created acid rain that has destroyed so many trees. Because we inter-are with the trees, we know that if they do not live, we too will disappear very soon.

We humans think we are smart, but an orchid, for example knows how to produce noble, symmetrical flowers, and a snail knows how to make a beautiful, well-proportioned shell. Compared with their knowledge, ours is not worth much at all. We should bow deeply before the orchid and the snail and join our palms reverently before the monarch butterfly and the magnolia tree. The feeling of respect for all species will help us recognize the noblest nature in ourselves.

An oak tree is an oak tree. That is all an oak tree needs to do. If an oak tree is less than an oak tree, we will all be in trouble. In our former lives, we were rocks, clouds, and trees. We have also been an oak tree. This is not just Buddhist: it is scientific. We humans are a young species. We were plants, we were trees, and now we have become humans. We have to remember our past existences and be humble. We can learn a lot from an oak tree.

All life is impermanent. We are all children of the Earth, and, at the same time, she will take us back to herself again. We are continually arising from Mother Earth, being nurtured by her, and then returning to her. Like us, plants are born, live for a period of time, and then return to the Earth. When they decompose, they fertilize our gardens. Living vegetables and decomposing vegetables are part of the same reality. Without one, the other cannot be. After six months, compost becomes fresh vegetables again. Plants and the Earth rely on each other. Whether the earth is fresh, beautiful, and green, or arid and parched depends on the plants.

It also depends on us. Our way of walking on the Earth has great influence on animals and plants. We have killed so many animals and plants and destroyed their environment. Many are now extinct. In turn, our environment is now harming us. We are like sleepwalkers, not knowing what we are doing or where we are heading. Whether we can wake up or not depends on whether we can walk mindfully on our Mother Earth. The future of all life including our own, depends on our mindful steps.

Birds' songs express joy, beauty, and purity, and evoke in us vitality and love. So many beings in the universe love us unconditionally. The trees, the water, and the air don't ask anything of us; they just love us. Even though we need this kind of love, we continue to destroy them. By destroying the animals, the air, and the trees, we are destroying ourselves. We must learn to practice unconditional love for all

beings so that the animals, the air, the trees, and the minerals can continue to be themselves. . . .

Our ecology should be a deep ecology — not only deep, but universal. . . .

If we change our daily lives — the way we think, speak, and act — we change the world. The best way to take care of the environment is to take care of the environmentalist.

Many Buddhist teachings help us understand our interconnectedness with our Mother, the Earth. One of the deepest is the *Diamond Sutra,* which is written in the form of a dialogue between Buddha and his senior disciple Subhuti. It begins with this question by Subhuti: "If daughters and sons of good families wish to give rise to the highest, most fulfilled, awakened mind, what should they rely on and what should they do to master their thinking?" This is the same thing as asking, "If I want to use my whole being to protect life, what methods and principles should I use?

The Buddha answers, "We have to do our best to help every living being cross the ocean of suffering. But after all beings have arrived at the shore of liberation, no being at all has been carried to the other shore. If you are still caught up in the idea of a self, a person, a living being, or a life span, you are not an authentic bodhisattva." Self, person, living being, and life span are four notions that prevent us from seeing reality.

Life is one. We do not need to slice it into pieces and call this or that piece a "self." What we call a self is made only of non-self elements. When we look at a flower, for example, we may think that it is different from "non-flower" things. But when we look more deeply, we see that everything in the cosmos is in that flower. Without all of the non-flower elements — sunshine, clouds, earth, minerals, heat, rivers, and consciousness — a flower cannot be. That is why the Buddha teaches that the self does not exist. We have to discard all distinctions between self and non-self. How can anyone work to protect the environment without this insight?

The second notion that prevents us from seeing reality is the notion of a person, a human being. We usually discriminate between humans and non-humans, thinking that we are more important than other species. But since we humans are made of non-human elements, to protect ourselves we have to protect all of the non-human elements. There is no other way. If you think, "God created man in His own image and He created other things for man to use," you are already making the discrimination that man is more important than other things. When we see that humans have no self, we see that to take care of the environment (the non-human elements) is to take care of humanity. The best way to take good care of men and women so that they can be truly healthy and happy is to take care of the environment.

I know ecologists who are not happy in their families. They work hard to improve the environment, partly to escape family life. If someone is not happy within himself, how can he help the environment? That is why the Buddha teaches that to protect the non-human elements is to protect humans, and to protect humans is to protect non-human elements.

The third notion we have to break through is the notion of a living being. We think that we living beings are different from inanimate objects, but according to the principle of interbeing, living beings are comprised of non-living-being elements. When we look into ourselves, we see minerals and all other non-living-being elements. Why discriminate against what we call inanimate? To protect living beings, we must protect the stones, the soil, and the oceans. . . . Atoms are always moving. Electrons move at nearly the speed of light. According to the teachings of Buddhism, these atoms and stones are consciousness itself. That is why discrimination by living beings against non-living beings should be discarded.

The last notion is that of a life span. We think that we have been alive since a certain point in time and that prior to that moment, our life did not exist. This distinction between life and non-life is not correct. Life is made of death, and death is made of life. We have to accept death; it makes life possible. The cells in our body are dying every day, but we never think to organize funerals for them. The death of one cell allows for the birth of another. Life and death are two aspects of the same reality. We must learn to die peacefully so that others may live. This deep meditation brings forth non-fear, non-anger, and non-despair, the strengths we need for our work. With non-fear, even when we see that a problem is huge, we will not burn out. We will know how to make small, steady steps. If those who work to pro-

tect the environment contemplate these four notions, they will know how to be and how to act.

In another Buddhist text, the *Avatamsaka ("Adorning the Buddha with Flowers") Sutra,* the Buddha further elaborates his insights concerning our "interpenetration" with our environment. Please meditate with me on the "Ten Penetrations":

The first is, "All worlds penetrate a single pore. A single pore penetrates all worlds." Look deeply at a flower. It may be tiny, but the sun, the clouds, and everything else in the cosmos penetrates it. Nuclear physicists say very much the same thing: one electron is made by all electrons; one electron is in all electrons.

The second penetration is, "All living beings penetrate one body. One body penetrates all living beings." When you kill a living being, you kill yourself and everyone else as well.

The third is, "Infinite time penetrates one second. One second penetrates infinite time." A *ksana* is the shortest period of time, actually much shorter than a second.

The fourth penetration is, "All Buddhist teachings penetrate one teaching. One teaching penetrates all Buddhist teaching." As a young monk, I had the opportunity to learn that Buddhism is made of non-Buddhist elements. So, whenever I study Christianity or Judaism, I find the Buddhist elements in them, and vice versa. I always respect non-Buddhist teachings. All Buddhist teachings penetrate one teaching, and one teaching penetrates all Buddhist teaching. We are free.

The fifth penetration is, "Innumerable spheres enter one sphere. One sphere enters innumerable spheres." A sphere is a geographical space. Innumerable spheres penetrate into one particular area, and one particular area enters into innumerable spheres. It means every time you destroy one area, you destroy every area. When you save one area, you save all areas. A student asked me "Thây, there are so many urgent problems, what should I do?" I said, "Take one thing and do it very deeply and carefully, and you will be doing everything at the same time."

The sixth penetration is, "All sense organs penetrate one organ. One organ penetrates all sense organ" — eye, ear, nose, tongue, body, and mind. To take care of one means to take care of many. To take care of your eyes means to take care of the eyes of innumerable living beings.

The seventh penetration is, "All sense organs penetrate non-sense organs. Non-sense organs penetrate all sense organs." Not only do non-sense organs penetrate sense organs, they also penetrate non-sense organs. There is no discrimination. Sense organs are made of non-sense-organ elements. That is why they penetrate non-sense organs. This helps us remember the teaching of the *Diamond Sutra.*

The eighth penetration is, "One perception penetrates all perceptions. All perceptions penetrate one perception." If your perception is not accurate, it will influence all other perceptions in yourself and others. Suppose a bus driver has an incorrect perception. We know what may happen. One perception penetrates all perceptions.

The ninth penetration is, "Every sound penetrates one sound. One sound penetrates every sound." This is a very deep teaching. If we understand one sound or one word, we can understand all.

The tenth penetration is, "All times penetrate one time. One time penetrates all times—past, present, and future." In one second, you can find the past, present, and future. In the past, you can see the present and the future. In the present, you can find the past and future. In the future, you can find the past and present. They "inter-contain" each other. Space contains time, time contains space. In the teaching of interpenetration, one determines the other, the other determines this one. When we realize our nature of interbeing, we will stop blaming and killing, because we know that we inter-are.

Interpenetration is an important teaching, but it still suggests that things outside of one another penetrate into each other. Interbeing is a step forward. We are already inside, so we don't have to enter. In contemporary nuclear physics, people talk about implicit order and explicit order. In the explicit order, things exist outside of each other—the table outside of the flower, the sunshine outside of the cypress tree. In the implicit order, we see that they are inside each other—the sunshine inside the cypress tree. Interbeing is the implicit order. To practice mindfulness and to look deeply into the nature of things is to discover the true nature of interbeing. There we find peace and develop the strength to be in touch with everything. With this understanding, we can easily sustain the work of loving and caring for the Earth and for each other for a long time.

DISCUSSION TOPICS

1. What changes in attitudes does Thich Nhat Hanh's philosophy call for you to make personally? Which of these are feasible changes for you?
2. With which other writer in this chapter do you find the greatest similarity to the perspectives of Thich Nhat Hanh? What are some key similarities and differences?

READING 29

The Environmentalism of the Poor

Ramachandra Guha and Juan Martinez-Alier

Ramachandra Guha is a journalist working in India. He has been a Professorial Fellow at the Nehru Memorial Museum and Library, New Delhi. He has written numerous articles and books on the topic of environmentalism, particularly as related to India and other indigenous cultures.

Juan Martinez-Alier is in the Department of Economics and Economic History, Universitat Autonoma de Barcelona, Spain.

Guha and Martinez-Alier frame many environmental conflicts in India as taking place between the needs of "ecosystem people" and "omnivores." The former are heavily dependent on natural resources in their own locality; the latter are individuals and groups with the social power to capture, transform, and use natural resources from a much wider region—in fact, sometimes globally. Thus the "environmentalism of the poor" can be framed as the resistance of ecosystem people to the resource capture practiced by omnivores.

THE ORIGINS OF CONFLICT

. . .

The "Indian environmental movement" is an umbrella term that covers a multitude of these local conflicts, initiatives and struggles. The movement's origins can be dated to the Chipko movement, which started in the Garhwal Himalaya in April 1973. Between 1973 and 1980, over a dozen instances were recorded where, through an innovative technique of protest, illiterate peasants — men, women and children — threatened to hug forest trees rather than allow them to be logged for export. Notably the peasants were not interested in saving the trees *per se,* but in using their produce for agricultural and household requirements. In later years, however, the movement turned its attention to broader ecological concerns, such as the collective protection and management of forests, and the diffusion of renewable energy technologies.[1]

The Chipko movement was the forerunner of and in some cases the direct inspiration for a series of popular movements in defence of community rights to natural resources. Sometimes these struggles revolved around forests; in other instances, around the control and use of pasture, and mineral or fish resources. Most of these conflicts have pitted rich against poor: logging companies against hill villagers, dam builders against forest tribal communities, multinational corporations deploying trawlers against traditional fisherfolk in small boats. Here one party (e.g. loggers or trawlers) seeks to step up the pace of resource exploitation to service an expanding commercial–industrial economy, a process which often involves the partial or total dispossession of those communities who earlier had control over the resource in question, and whose own patterns of utilisation were (and are) less destructive of the environment.

More often than not, the agents of resource-intensification are given preferential treatment by the state, through the grant of generous long leases over mineral or fish stocks, for example, or the provision of raw material at an enormously subsidized price. With the injustice so compounded, local communities at the receiving end of this process have no recourse except direct action, resisting both the state and outside exploiters through a variety of protest techniques. These struggles might perhaps be seen as a manifestation of a new kind of class conflict. Where "traditional" class conflicts were fought in the cultivated field or in the factory, these new struggles are waged over gifts of nature such as forests and water, gifts that are coveted by all but increasingly monopolised by a few.

There is, then, an unmistakable material context to the upsurge of environmental conflict in India: the shortages of, threats to and struggles over natural resources. No one could even suggest, with regard to India, what two distinguished scholars claimed some years ago with regard to American environmentalism, namely that it had exaggerated or imagined the risk posed by ecological degradation.[2] All the same, the environmentalism of the poor is neither universal nor pre-given — there are many parts of India (and the South more generally) where the destruction of the environment has generated little or no popular response. To understand where, how and in what manner environmental conflict articulates itself requires the kind of location-specific work, bounded in time and space, that social scientists have thus far reserved for studies of worker and peasant struggles.

. . .

On 14 November 1984, the government of Karnataka entered into an agreement with Harihar Polyfibres, a rayon-producing unit located in the north of the state; the company forms part of the great Indian industrial conglomerate owned by the Birla family. By this agreement a new company was formed, called the Karnataka Pulpwoods Limited (KPL), in which the government had a holding of 51 per cent and Harihar Polyfibres held 49 per cent. KPL was charged with growing eucalyptus and other fast-growing species of trees for the use by Harihar Polyfibres. For this purpose, the state had identified 30,000 hectares of common land, spread over four districts in the northern part of Karnataka. This land was nominally owned by the state (following precedents set under British colonial rule, when the state had arbitrarily asserted its rights of ownership over non-cultivated land all over India), but the grass, trees, and shrubs standing on it were extensively used in surrounding villages for fuel, fodder and other materials.[3]

The land was granted by the state to KPL on a long lease of 40 years, and for a ridiculously low annual rent of one rupee per acre. As much as 87.5 per cent of the produce was to go directly to Harihar Polyfibres; the private sector company also had the option of buying the remaining 12.5 per cent. All in all, this was an extraordinarily advantageous arrangement for the Birla-owned firm. The government of

Karnataka was even willing to stand guarantee for the loans that were to finance KPL's operations: loans to be obtained from several nationalised banks, one of which was, ironically, the National Bank of Agriculture and Rural Development. . . .

. . . The formation of KPL seemed a clearly partisan move in favour of industry, as the lands it took over constituted a vital, and often irreplaceable, source of biomass for small peasants, herdsmen and wood-working artisans. Within months of its establishment, the new company became the object of severe criticism. . . .

In the forefront of the movement against KPL was the Samaj Parivartan Samudaya (Association for Social Change, SPS), a voluntary organisation working in the Dharwad district of Karnataka. The SPS had in fact cut its teeth in a previous campaign against Harihar Polyfibres. It had organised a movement against the pollution of the Tungabhadra river by the rayon factory, whose untreated effluents were killing fish and undermining the health and livelihood of villagers living downstream. . . .

. . . With public opinion and the central government arrayed against it, and possibly anticipating an adverse final judgement in the Supreme Court, the government of Karnataka decided to wind up KPL. The company's closure was formally announced at a board meeting on 27 September 1990, but by then KPL had already ceased operations. In its report for the previous financial year (April 1989 to March 1990) the company complained that "during the year the plantation activity has practically come to a standstill, excepting raising 449 hectares of plantations"—a tiny fraction of the 30,000 hectares of common land it had once hoped to capture for its exclusive use.

A VOCABULARY OF PROTEST

The struggle against KPL had as its mass base, so to speak, the peasants, pastoralists, and fisherfolk directly affected by environmental abuse. Yet key leadership roles were assumed by activists who, although they came from the region, were not themselves directly engaged in production. Of the SPS activists involved more or less full-time in the movement, one had been a labour organiser, a second a social worker and progressive farmer, a third a biology PhD and

former college lecturer, and a fourth an engineer who had returned to India after working for years in the United States. Crucial support was also provided by intellectuals more distant from the action. . . .

This unity, of communities at the receiving end of ecological degradation and of social activists with the experience and education to negotiate the politics of protest, has been characteristic of environmental struggles in India. In other respects, too, the SPS-led struggle was quite typical. For underlying the KPL controversy were a series of oppositions that frame most such conflicts in India: rich versus poor, urban versus rural, nature for profit versus nature for subsistence, the state versus the people. However the KPL case was atypical in one telling respect, for environmental movements of the poor only rarely end in emphatic victory.

To put it in more explicitly ecological terms, these conflicts pit "ecosystem people"—that is, those communities which depend very heavily on the natural resources of their own locality—against "omnivores," individuals and groups with the social power to capture, transform and use natural resources from a much wider catchment area; sometimes, indeed, the whole world. The first category of ecosystem people includes the bulk of India's rural population: small peasants, landless laborers, tribals, pastoralists, and artisans. The category of omnivores comprises industrialists, professionals, politicians, and government officials—all of whom are based in the towns and cities—as well as a small but significant fraction of the rural élite, the prosperous farmers in tracts of heavily irrigated, chemically fertilised Green Revolution agriculture. The history of development in independent India can then be interpreted as being, in essence, a process of resource capture by the omnivores at the expense of ecosystem people. This has in turn created a third major ecological class: that of "ecological refugees," peasants-turned-slum dwellers, who eke out a living in the cities on the leavings of omnivore prosperity.[4]

In this framework, the "environmentalism of the poor" might be understood as the resistance offered by ecosystem people to the process of resource capture by omnivores: as embodied in movements against large dams by tribal communities to be displaced by them, or struggles by peasants against the diversion of forest and grazing land to industry. In recent years, the most important such struggle has been the Narmada Bachao Andolan (NBA), the movement representing the ecosystem people who face imminent displacement by a huge dam on the Narmada river in central India. The movement has been led by the forty-year-old Medha Patkar, a woman of courage and character once described by a journalist as an "ecological Joan of Arc."

A detailed analysis of the origins and development of the Narmada conflict cannot be provided here,[5] but there is one aspect of the movement that is of particular relevance . . . ; namely, its flexible and wide-ranging vocabulary of protest.

The term "vocabulary of protest" is offered as an alternative to Charles Tilly's well-known concept of the "repertoire of contention." Tilly and his associates have done pioneering work on the study of dissent and direct action. Their work has focused on the techniques most characteristic of different societies, social groups or historical periods. Tilly's own understanding of direct action tends to be a narrowly instrumental one, with participants drawing on, from a broader repertoire of contention, those techniques which most effectively defend or advance their economic and political interests.[6] But in fact techniques of direct action have at the same time an utilitarian and an expressive dimension. In adopting a particular strategy, social protesters are both trying to defend their interests *and* passing judgement on the prevailing social arrangements. The latter, so to say, ideological dimension of social protest needs to be inferred even when it is not formally articulated — the fact that protesting peasants do not distribute a printed manifesto does not mean that they do not have developed notions of right and wrong. In field or factory, ghetto or grazing ground, struggles over resources, even when they have tangible material origins, have always also been struggles over meaning. Thus my preference for the term "vocabulary of protest" — for "vocabulary" more than "repertoire," and "protest" more than "contention" — helps to clarify the notion that most forms of direct action, even if unaccompanied by a written manifesto, are both statements of purpose and of belief. In the act of doing, protesters are saying something too. Thus the Kithiko-Hachiko *satyagraha* was not simply an affirmation of peasant claims over disputed property: as a strategy of protest, its aim was not merely to insist, "This land is ours," but also, and equally significantly, to ask, "What are trees for?"

To return to the Narmada Bachao Andolan. Like the anti-KPL struggle, the Narmada movement has operated simultaneously on several flanks: a strong media campaign, court petitions, and the lobbying of key players such as the World Bank, which was to fund a part of the dam project. Most effectively, though, it has deployed a dazzlingly varied vocabulary of protest, in defence of the rights of the peasants and tribal communities which were to be displaced by the dam.

These strategies of direct action might be classified under four broad headings. First, there is the collective *show of strength,* as embodied in demonstrations (Hindi: *pradarshan*) organized in towns and cities. Mobilising as many people as they can, protesters march through the town, shouting slogans, singing songs, winding their way to a public meeting that marks the procession's culmination. The aim here is to assert a presence in the city, which is the locus of local, provincial or national power. The demonstrators carry a message that is at once threatening and imploring: in effect, telling the rulers (and city people in general), "do not forget us, the dispossessed in the countryside. We can make trouble, but not if you hand out justice."

Second, there is the *disruption of economic life* through more militant acts of protest. One such tactic is the *hartal* or *bandh* (shut-down strike), wherein shops are forced to down shutters and buses to pull off the roads, bringing normal life to a standstill. A variation of this is the *rasta roko* (road blockade), through which traffic on an important highway is blocked by squatting protesters, sometimes for days on end. These techniques are rather more coercive than persuasive, spotlighting the economic costs to the state (or to other sections of the public) if they do not yield to the dissenters.

Whereas the *hartal* or *rasta roko* aim at disrupting economic activity across a wide area, a third type of action is more sharply focused on an individual target. For instance, the *dharna* or sit-down strike is used to stop work at a specific dam site or mine. Sometimes the target is a figure of authority rather than a site of production; thus protesting peasants might *gherao* (surround) a high public official, allowing him to move only after he has heard their grievances and promised to act upon them.

The fourth generic strategy of direct action aims at putting moral pressure on the state as a whole, not merely on one of its functionaries. Preeminent here is the *bhook hartal,* the indefinite hunger strike undertaken by the charismatic leader of a popular movement. This technique was once used successfully by Sunderlal Bahuguna of the Chipko movement; in recent years, it has been resorted to on several occasions by Medha Patkar, the remarkable leader of the Narmada Bachao Andolan. In the *bhook hartal,* the courage and self-sacrifice of the individual leader is directly counterposed to the claims to legitimacy of the state. The fast is usually carried out in a public place, and closely reported in the media. As the days drag on, and the leader's health perilously declines, the state is forced into a gesture of submission — if only the constitution of a fresh committee to review the case in contention.

The *bhook hartal* is most often the preserve of a single, heroic, exemplary figure. A sister technique, also aimed at *shaming the state,* is more of a collective undertaking. This is the *jail bharo andolan* (literally, "movement to fill the jails"), in which protesters peacefully and deliberately court arrest by violating the law, hoping the government would lose face by putting behind bars large numbers of its own citizens. The law most often breached is Section 144 of the Criminal Procedure Code, invoked, in anticipation of social tension, to prohibit gatherings of more than five people.

The *pradarshan, hartal, rasta roko, dharna, gherao, bhook hartal* and *jail bharo andolan* are some of the techniques which make up the environmental movement's vocabulary of protest. This is a vocabulary shared across the spectrum of protesting groups, but new situations constantly call for new innovations. In the 1970's peasants in Garhwal developed the idiosyncratic but truly effective Chipko technique; in the 1980s, the SPS in Dharwad opposing eucalyptus plantations, thought up the Kithiko-Hachiko *satyagraha;* and now, in the 1990s, the Narmada Bachao Andolan has threatened a *jal samadhi* (water burial), saying its cadres would refuse to move from the villages scheduled for submergence even after the dam's sluice gates are closed and the waters start rising.

The techniques of direct action itemised above have, of course, deep and honourable origins. They were first forged, in India's long struggle for freedom from British rule, by Mohandas Karamchand "Mahatma" Gandhi. In developing and refining this vocabulary of protest, Gandhi drew on Western theories of civil disobedience as well as traditions of peasant resistance within India itself.[7]

In fact, Mahatma Gandhi provides the environmental movement with both a vocabulary of protest and an ideological critique of development in independent India. . . . That movement commanded a mass base among the peasantry, assiduously developed by Gandhi himself, and freedom promised a new deal for rural India. And yet, after 1947 the political élite has worked to ensure that the benefits of planned economic development have flown primarily to the urban-industrial complex.

The KPL case illustrates this paradox as well as any other. On one side were the peasants and pastoralists of north Karnataka; on the other, an insensitive state government in league with the second largest business conglomerate in the country. . . .

The environmental movement's return to Gandhi is then also a return to his vision for free India: a vision of a "village-centered economic order" that has been so completely disregarded in practice. Perhaps it is more accurate to see this as a rhetoric of betrayal *and* of affirmation, as symbolised in the dates most often chosen to launch (or end) programmes of direct action. These dates are 2 October, Gandhi's birth anniversary; 15 August, Indian Independence Day; and most poignantly, 8 August, on which day in 1942 Gandhi's last great anti-colonial campaign was launched, the Quit India movement — in invoking this environmentalists are asking the state and the capitalists, the rulers of today, to "quit" their control over forests and water.

TWO KINDS OF ENVIRONMENTALISM

In the preceding sections of this chapter, the KPL controversy has been used to outline the origins, trajectory and rhetoric of the environmental movement in India. In conclusion, let us broaden the discussion by briefly contrasting the "environmentalism of the poor" with the more closely studied phenomenon of First World environmentalism. This analysis derives, for the most part, from my own research on the United States and India, two countries, ecologically and culturally diverse, but at very different "stages" of economic development. These are the countries and environmental movements I know best, and yet, because of their size and importance, they might be taken as representative, more generally, of the North and the South.[8]

I begin with the origins of the environmental impulse in the two contexts. Environmental movements in the North have, I think, been convincingly related to the emergence of a post-materialist or post-industrial society. The creation of a mass consumer society has not only enlarged opportunities for leisure but also provided the means to put this time off work to the most diverse uses. Nature is made accessible through the car, now no longer a monopoly of the élite but an artifact in almost everyone's possession. It is the car which, more than anything else, opens up a new world, of the wild, that is refreshingly different from the worlds of the city and the factory. In a curious paradox, this "most modern creation of industry" becomes the vehicle of anti-industrial impulses, taking one to distant adventures. . . . Here lies the source of popular support for the protection of wilderness in the United States — namely, that nature is no longer restricted to the privileged few, but available to all.

In India, still dominantly a nation of villages, environmentalism has emerged at a relatively early stage in the industrial process. Nature-based conflicts, it must be pointed out once again, are at the root of the environmental movement in countries such as India. These conflicts have their root in a lopsided, iniquitous and environmentally destructive process of development in independent India. They are played out against a backdrop of visible ecological degradation, the drying up of springs, the decimation of forests, the erosion of the land. The sheer immediacy of resource shortages means that direct action has been, from the beginning, a vital component of environmental action. Techniques of direct action often rely on traditional networks of organisation, the village and the tribe, and traditional forms of protest, the *dharna* and the *bhook hartal*.

Northern environmentalism, in contrast, relies rather more heavily on the "social movement organisation" — such as the Sierra Club or the Friends of the Earth — with its own cadre, leadership and

properly audited sources of funds. This organisation then draws on the methods of redressal available in what are, after all, more complete democracies — methods such as the court case, the lobbying of legislators and ministers, the exposure on television or in the newspaper. But the experience of recent years somewhat qualifies this contrast between militant protest in the one sphere and lobbying and litigation in the other. Indian environmentalists (as with the KPL case) are turning increasingly to the courts as a supplement to popular protest, while in America, radicals disaffected by the gentle, incremental lobbying of mainstream groups have taken to direct action — the spiking of trees, for example — to protect threatened wilderness.

In both the North and the South, however, environmentalism has been, in good measure, a response to the failure of politicians to mobilise effectively on the issue of, as the case may be, the destruction of the wilderness or the dispossession of peasants by a large dam. In India, for instance, the environmental movement has drawn on the struggles of marginal populations — hill peasants, tribal communities, fishermen, people displaced by construction of dams — neglected by the existing political parties. And as a "new social movement," environmentalism in the North emerged, in the first instance, outside the party process. Some environmentalists considered themselves as neither left nor right, representing a constituency that was anti-class or, more accurately, post-class.[9] However, over time the environmental constituency became part of the democratic process, sometimes through the formation of Green parties that fight, and even occasionally win, elections.

Origins and political styles notwithstanding, the two varieties of environmentalism perhaps differ most markedly in their ideologies. The environmentalism of the poor originates as a clash over productive resources: a third kind of class conflict, so to speak, but one with deep ecological implications. Red on the outside, but green on the inside. In Southern movements, issues of ecology are often interlinked with questions of human rights, ethnicity and distributive justice. These struggles, of peasants, tribals and so on, are in a sense deeply conservative (in the best sense of the word), refusing to exchange a world they know, and are in partial control over, for an uncertain and insecure future. They are a defence of the locality and the local community against the nation. At the same time, the sharper edge to environmental conflict, and its close connections to subsistence and survival, have also prompted a thoroughgoing critique of consumerism and of uncontrolled economic development.

In contrast, the wilderness movement in the North originates outside the production process. It is in this respect more of a single-issue movement, calling for a change in attitudes (towards the natural world) rather than a change in systems of production or distribution. Especially in the United States, environmentalism has, by and large, run parallel to the consumer society without questioning its socioecological basis, its enormous dependence on the lands, peoples and resources of other parts of the globe. It is absorbed not so much with relations within human society, as with relations between humans and other species. Here the claims of national sovereignty are challenged not from the vantage point of the locality, but from the perspective of the biosphere as a whole. This is a movement whose self-perception is that of a vanguard, moving from an "ethical present" where we are concerned only with nation, region and race to an "ethical future" where our moral development moves from a concern with plants and animals to ecosystems and the planet itself.[10]

In the preceding paragraphs, I have sketched a broad-brush comparison between two movements, in two different parts of the world, each carrying the prefix "environmental." One must, of course, qualify this picture by acknowledging the diversity of ideologies and of forms of action within each of these two trends. In the United States, anti-pollution struggles form a tradition of environmental action which has a different focus from the "wilderness crusade." Such, for instance, is the movement for environmental justice in the United States, the struggles of low-class, often black communities against the incinerators and toxic waste dumps that, by accident and frequently by design, come to be sited near them (and away from affluent neighborhoods). One American commentator, Ruth Rosen, has nicely captured the contrast between the environmental justice movement and the wilderness lovers. "At best," she writes, "the large, mainstream environmental groups

focus on the health of the planet—the wilderness, forests and oceans that cannot protect themselves. In contrast, the movement for environmental justice, led by the poor, is not concerned with overabundance, but with the environmental hazards and social and economic inequalities that ravage their communities."[11]

Likewise, the Northern wilderness crusade has its representatives in the Third World, who spearhead the constitution of vast areas as national parks and sanctuaries, strictly protected from "human interference." Southern lovers of the wilderness come typically from patrician backgrounds, and have shown little regard for the fate of the human communities who, after parkland is designated as "protected," are abruptly displaced without compensation from territory that they have lived on for generations and come to regard as their own.[12]

These caveats notwithstanding, there remains, on the whole, a clear distinction, in terms of origins and forms of articulation, between how environmental action characteristically expresses itself in the North and in the South. . . .

. . . "No Humanity without Nature," the epitaph of the Northern environmentalist, is here answered by the equally compelling slogan "No Nature without Social Justice!"[13]

NOTES

1. The development of the Chipko movement is discussed in Ramachandra Guha, *The Unquiet Woods: Ecological Change and Peasant Resistance in the Himalaya* (New Delhi: Oxford University Press and Berkeley: University of California Press, 1989).
2. See Mary Douglas and Aaron Wildavsky, *Risk and Culture: An Essay on the Selection of Technical and Environmental Dangers* (Berkeley: University of California Press, 1982).
3. Aside from specific sources cited later, this discussion of the KPL case also draws on numerous unpublished and locally printed documents, as well as on my own fieldwork and interviews in the region.
4. For a fuller definition and application of these categories, see Madhav Gadgil and Ramachan-

dra Guha, *Ecology and Equity: the Use and Abuse of Nature in Contemporary India* (London: Routledge, 1995).

5. The interested reader is referred to, among other works, Bradford Morse, et. al. *The Sardar Sarovar Project: The Report of the Independent Review* (Washington: The World Bank, 1993); Amita Baviskar, *In the Belly of the River: Adivasi Battles over Nature in the Narmada Valley* (New Delhi: Oxford University, 1995); Gadgil and Guha, *Ecology and Equity,* Chapter 3.

6. Tilly's works include *From Mobilization to Revolution* (Reading, MA: Addison-Wesley, 1978) and *The Contentious French* (Cambridge, MA: Harvard University Press, 1986). Cf. also the Tilly-inspired two-part special section entitled "Historical Perspectives on Social Movements." *Social Science History,* volume 17, numbers 2 and 3, Summer and Fall 1993.

7. In contemporary India these "Gandhian" techniques are by no means the sole preserve of the environmental movement. They are used in all sorts of ways by all sorts of social struggles: by farmers wanting higher fertiliser subsidies, hospital workers wanting greater security of tenure, or ethnic minorities fighting for a separate province.

8. Important studies of American environmentalism include, to select from a vast and ever proliferating literature, W. R. Burch, Jr. *Daydreams and Nightmares: A Sociological Essay on the American Environment* (New York: Harper & Row, 1971); Donald Fleming, "Roots of the New Conservation Movement," in Fleming and Bernard Bailyn, eds., *Perspectives in American History, Volume VI* (Cambridge, MA: Charles Warren Center for Studies in American History, 1972); Linda Graber, *Wilderness as Sacred Space* (Washington, DC: Association of American Geographers, 1976); Roderick Nash, *Wilderness and the American Mind* (3rd ed., New Haven, CT: Yale University Press, 1983); Alfred Runte, *National Parks: The American Experience* (Lincoln: University of Nebraska Press, 1984); Stephen Fox, *The American Conservation Movement:*

John Muir and His Legacy (Madison: University of Wisconsin Press, 1985); Samuel P. Hays, *Beauty, Health and Permanence: Environmental Politics in the United States, 1955–1985* (New York: Cambridge University Press, 1987); and, most recently, Philip Shabecoff, *A Fierce Green Fire: The American Environmental Movement* (New York: Hill & Wang, 1993). We cite influential books, without taking notice of a huge outcrop of journal and magazine articles. There is nothing like this profusion of work with regard to the environmental movement in India. Useful overviews are provided in Anil Agarwal, "Human-Nature Interactions in a Third World Country," *The Environmentalist,* volume 6, number 3, 1987 and in Bina Agarwal, "The Gender and Environment Debate: Lessons from India," *Feminist Studies,* volume 18, number 1, 1992. Other relevant writings include Guha, *The Unquiet Woods;* Vandana Shiva, with J. Bandyopadhyay, P. Hegde, B. V. Krishnamurthy, J. Kurien, G. Narendranath, V. Ramprasad and S. T. S. Reddy, *Ecology and the Politics of Survival* (New Delhi: Sage, 1991); Madhav Gadgil and Ramachandra Guha, "Ecological Conflicts and the Environmental Movement in India," *Development and Change,* volume 25, number 1, 1994; *Baviskar, In the Belly of the River* (New Delhi: Oxford University Press, 1995).

9. A point first made by the British sociologist Stephen Cotgrove in his book *Catastrophe or Cornucopia?* (Chichester: Wiley, 1982).

10. Cf. Roderick Nash, *The Rights of Nature: A History of Environmental Ethics* (Madison: University of Wisconsin Press, 1989).

11. Ruth Rosen, "Who Gets Polluted: The Movement for Environmental Justice," *Dissent* (New York), Spring 1994, p. 229. Cf. also Andrew Szasz, *Ecopopulism: Toxic Waste and the Movement for Environmental Justice* (Minneapolis: University of Minnesota Press, 1994); Bunyan Bryant, ed., *Environmental Justice: Issues, Policies and Solutions* (Washington D.C.: Island Press, 1995).

12. Cf. . . . Patrick C. West and Steven R. Brechin, eds., *Resident Peoples and National Parks:*

Social Dilemmas and Strategies in International Conservation (Tucson: The University of Arizona Press, 1991).
13. Smitu Kothari and Pramod Parajuli, "No Nature without Social Justice: a Plea for Ecological and Cultural Pluralism in India," in Wolfgang Sachs, ed., *Global Ecology: A New Arena of Political Conflict* (London: Zed Books, 1993).

DISCUSSION TOPICS

1. How might Northern (First World) environmentalists respond to Guha and Martinez-Alier's position? Explain your reasoning.
2. What aspects of Southern environmentalism do you believe could be adapted to the First World?

CLASS EXERCISE

Many scholars have addressed the question of whether religious values, such as Judaism and Christianity, or secular values, such as Greek philosophy, have been most responsible for the contemporary destructive environmental values found in Western society.

Using the guidelines presented in the appendix, debate the two sides of this issue. Which arguments were appealed to by each side? Which were most compelling?

FOR FURTHER READING

Abram, David. "The Ecology of Magic." *Orion* 10.3 (1991): 28–43. An essay on animism and the ecological role of the shaman in traditional cultures, arguing that animistic beliefs ensure a participatory, nonanthropocentric relationship to animals and plants and to the land itself.

Anderson, Bernhard W. *From Creation to New Creation: Old Testament Perspectives.* Minneapolis: Augsburg Fortress, 1994. Anderson interprets creation doctrine within the context of worship and as part of a larger narrative context within the Bible.

Badiner, Allan H., ed. *Dharman Gaia: A Harvest of Essays in Buddhism and Ecology.* Berkeley: Parallax Press, 1990. Contemporary essays by philosophers, and Buddhist scholars and practitioners.

Bakken, Peter W., Joan Gibb Engel, and J. Ronald Engel. *Ecology, Justice, and Christian Faith.* Westport, Conn.: Greenwood Press, 1995. Annotated references dealing with the issues of ecology, justice, and the Christian faith.

Batchelor, Martine, and Kerry Brown, eds. *Buddhism and Ecology.* London: Bassel, 1992. Ten chapters by a variety of authors, including the Dalai Lama, explore the relationship of Buddhism to ecology.

Benzoni, Francisco. "Rolston's Theological Ethic." *Environmental Ethics* 18 (1996): 339–52. Evaluates the objective value theory of Holmes Rolston III, which the author argues is grounded in the divine. Benzoni believes that Rolston would benefit from a richer, more fully developed, theological anthropology in his ethic.

Berkes, Fikret. *Sacred Ecology: Traditional Ecological Knowledge and Resource Management.* London: Taylor and Francis, 1999. Berkes approaches traditional ecological knowledge as a knowledge-practice complex involving local knowledge, resource management systems, social institutions, and world view.

Bernstein, Ellen, ed. *Ecology, the Jewish Spirit: Where Nature and the Sacred Meet.* Woodstock, Vt.: Jewish Lights Publishing, 1998. A variety of perspectives on the Jewish relationship to the natural world.

Berry, Wendell. *Another Turn of the Crank.* Washington, D.C.: Counterpoint, 1995. Argues against a global economy because of its undermining of regional economic viability and the viability of private individuals and farm families. Written from a well-grounded Christian perspective.

Booth, Annie L., and Harvey M. Jacobs. "Ties That Bind: Native American Beliefs as a Foundation for Environmental Consciousness." *Environmental Ethics* 12 (1990): 27–43. An interpretation of Native American beliefs through the lens of deep ecology.

Bratton, Susan P. "Loving Nature: Eros or Agape?" *Environmental Ethics* 14 (1992): 3–26. Bratton argues that God's love for nature has the same qualities as God's love for humans. Because agape is self-giving, it is preferable to eros in relationships with the environment.

Brown, Joseph Epes, ed. *The Sacred Pipe.* New York: Penguin Books, 1973. A sense of the connectedness between Sioux Indians and the earth clearly emerges in this fascinating account of the seven rites of the Oglala Sioux, as reported by Black Elk.

Bruun, Ole, and Arne Kallard, eds. *Asian Perceptions of Nature: A Critical Approach.* Richmond, England: Curzon Press, 1995. The contributors address the creativity and richness in the Asian perceptions of nature, as well as unique aspects each attaches to its relation between humans and the environment.

Burnet, G. W., and Kamuyu wa Kang'ethe. "Wilderness and the Bantu Mind." *Environmental Ethics* 16 (1994): 145–60. The authors point out that wilderness is viewed as an extension of human living space, but it is viewed as fearsome and hostile; thus it cannot provide inspiration or self-actualization. Wildlife is unnatural and alienated from human society, which is considered natural.

Callicott, J. Baird. "The Search for an Environmental Ethic," in *Matters of Life and Death,* ed. T. Regan. Prospect Heights, Ill.: Waveland Press, 1990, pp. 381–424. Offers a thoughtful and critical look at the environmental ethics derived from the Judeo-Christian tradition.

————. *Earth's Insights: A Survey of Ecological Ethics from the Mediterranean Basin to the Australian Outback.* Berkeley: University of California Press, 1994. An important work in which the author brings together the environmental perspectives of many cultural groups throughout the world. A comprehensive and thoughtful treatment.

Cromartie, Michael, ed. *Creation at Risk? Religion, Science, and Environmentalism.* Grand Rapids, Mich.: Eerdmans, 1995. Ten scholars and activists explore and disagree over a variety of scientific, religious, ethical, philosophical, economic, and political claims of contemporary environmentalists.

Deloria, Vine, Jr. *Red Earth, White Lies: Native Americans and the Myth of Scientific Fact.* New York: Charles Scribners and Sons, 1995. Deloria claims that Native American oral traditions may actually provide better explanations of evolution, planetary history, the origin of humans, natural disasters, and population than those provided by white European scientists. He disputes the claim that Native Americans caused extinctions of animal species in the Pleistocene.

DeSilva, Lily. "The Buddhist Attitude toward Nature," in *Buddhist Perspectives on the Ecocrisis,* ed. K. Sandell. Kandy, Sri Lanka: Buddhist Publication Society, 1987, pp. 9–29. A thoughtful interpretation of Buddhist attitudes toward the natural world.

Engel, J. Ronald, and Joan Gibb Engel, eds. *Ethics of Environment and Development: Global Challenge, International Response.* Tucson: University of Arizona Press, 1990. A collection of twenty-one papers focusing on the ethical principles at stake in the concept of sustainable development. Presents perspectives from Western Europe and North America, Eastern Europe and the Soviet Union, South and Central America, Africa and the Middle East, and Asia, including the experiences of women.

Fo Guang Shan. "Protecting the Environment." Translated from Chinese and edited by Jayde Lin Robert, Amy Lam, and Brenda Bolinger. Hacienda Heights, Calif.: Buddha's Light International Association, 2000. Addresses the Buddha as a forerunner of environmental protection, the Buddhist tradition of protecting the environment, and steps that can be taken to protect the environment.

Forward, Martin, and Mohamed Alam. "Islam," in *Attitudes to Nature,* ed. Jean Holm. London: Pinter, 1994. The Islamic view toward nature and the natural world. The Qur'an addresses the role of God in the creation, the spirit-world, humans as God's viceregents, the place of science, the role of animals, and environmental perspectives in Islam.

Fox, Michael W. "Animism, Empathy, and Human Development." *Between the Species* (Summer/Fall, 1995): 130–40. Animism and the practice of becoming more human and humane.

Gadgil, Madhav, and Ramachandra Guha. *Ecology and Equity: The Use and Abuse of Nature in Contemporary India.* London: Routledge, 1995. Initially the authors present an original theoretical framework for describing Indian society from an ecological point of view. Then they argue for a new environment-friendly agenda for development, which they believe would be in the interest of most Indians.

Gardiner, Robert W. "Between Two Worlds: Humans in Nature and Culture." *Environmental Ethics* 12 (1990): 339–52. The author identifies some of the tensions and paradoxes implicit in the view that humans live simultaneously in two worlds: the world of nature and the world of culture.

Giradot, N. H., James Miller, and Liu Xiaogan. *Daoism and Ecology: Ways within a Cosmic Landscape.* Cambridge, Mass.: Center for the Study of World Religions and Harvard University Press, 2001. Articles on Daoism and ecology, largely the views of scholars of religion and Daoism. Bibliography on Daoism and ecology.

Gordis, Robert. "Judaism and the Environment." *Congress Monthly* (September/October, 1990): 7–10. A summary of Jewish attitudes toward the environment. The author addresses the concern in the Talmud for the welfare of living creatures and protection of the nonliving environment. God asserts ownership of the land; humans are only temporary custodians.

Grim, John A. *Indigenous Traditions and Ecology: The Interbeing of Cosmology and Community.* Cambridge, Mass.: Center for the Study of World Religions and Harvard University Press, 2001. Grim discusses pressures threatening indigenous peoples and ways of life; their modes of resistance and regeneration by which these communities maintain a spiritual balance with larger cosmological forces while creatively accommodating current environmental, social, economic, and political changes.

Hadsell, Heidi. "Environmental Ethics and Health/Wholeness." *Council of Societies for the Study of Religion* 24 (1995): 67–71. Addresses human attitudes that contribute to the current environmental problems, including denial, the strong focus on individual rights and freedoms, materialism, and collective egoism.

Hallman, David G., ed. *Ecotheology: Voices from South and North.* Geneva: Orbis Books, 1994. Covers religious aspects of human ecology, including Christianity, as well as the moral and ethical aspects of environmental protection in the Western world and developing countries. Some discussion of the attitudes among indigenous people.

Hamilton, Lawrence S., ed. *Ethics, Religion and Biodiversity.* Isle of Harris, Scotland: White Horse Press, 1993. Provides environmental perspectives on a number of different cultural and religious groups.

Hessel, Dieter T., ed. *Theology for Earth Community: A Field Guide.* Maryknoll, N.Y.: Orbis Books, 1996. Essays evaluating recent scholarship on ecologically oriented Christian theology.

Holm, Jean, ed. *Attitudes to Nature.* London: Pinter, 1994. A selection of eight religious perspectives, including Judaism, Christianity, and Islam.

Hope, Marjorie, and James Young. *Voices of Hope in the Struggle to Save the Planet.* Croton-on-Hudson, N.Y.: Apex Press, 2000. Chronicles the lives and works of a wide range of religiously based groups. Leaders and activists drawn from Judaism, Western and Eastern Christianity, Islam, Buddhism, Taoism, Shinto, and the faiths of indigenous peoples.

Hou, Wenhui. "Reflections on Chinese Traditional Ideas of Nature." *Environmental History* 2, 4 (1997): 482–93.

Hughes, J. Donald. "Francis of Assisi and the Diversity of Creation." *Environmental Ethics* 18 (1996): 311–20. Hughes argues that St. Francis saw the diversity of life as an expression of God's creativity and benevolence and attempted to carry out that vision in ethical behavior.

Ingold, Tim. "Hunting and Gathering as Ways of Perceiving the Environment," in *Redefining Nature: Ecology, Culture and Domestication,* ed. Roy Ellen and Katsuyoshi. Oxford: Berg, 1996, pp. 117–55. Advocates following the lead of hunter-gatherers to have a sense of dwelling-in the world rather than a sense of a mind detached from the world.

Ip, Po-Keung. "Taoism and the Foundations of Environmental Ethics." *Environmental Ethics* 5, 4 (1983): 335–43. A careful analysis of Taoism and the relationship of humans to nature.

Johns, David M. "Relevance of Deep Ecology to the Third World: Some Preliminary Comments." *Environmental Ethics* 12 (1990): 233–52. Challenges Guha's criticisms of deep ecology. Argues that deep ecology's distinction between anthropocentrism and biocentrism is useful in dealing with the two critical problems Guha mentions: overconsumption and militarism.

Journal of Buddhist Ethics. Has included a number of articles on Buddhist environmental ethics in recent years.

Journal of Dharma 16, 3 (July/September, 1991). This special issue of an international quarterly of world religions contains eight articles centered on the theme Ahimsa and Ecology, written by scholars from India, Finland, Canada, and the United States.

Kelbessa, Workeneh. "Indigenous and Modern Environmental Ethics: A Study of the Indigenous Oromo Environmental Ethic and Oromo Environmental

Ethics in the Light of Modern Issues of Environment and Development." Ph.D. dissertation, University of Wales, Cardiff, 2001. The Oromo are a minority, traditionally pastoralist, people in southwest Ethiopia, making up some thirty percent of the Ethiopian population. They have developed complex systems of agriculture and intensive soil, water, vegetation, and wildlife management that have survived over time and the vagaries of the environment.

Martin, Calvin Luther. *In the Spirit of the Earth: Rethinking History and Time.* Baltimore, Md.: Johns Hopkins Press, 1992. Martin reflects on the philosophical power of Native American narratives and presents a thoughtful and insightful coverage of American Indians and their ethical perspectives.

Massanari, Ronald L. "A Problematic in Environmental Ethics: Western and Eastern Styles." *Buddhist-Christian Studies* 18 (1998): 37–61. Compares Buddhist and Christian approaches to questions surrounding the relationships among individuals, including humans and nature.

May, John D'Arcy. "Zen with Teeth: The Contributions of Buddhists and Christians to Preserving the Earth." *Buddhist-Christian Studies* 18 (1998): 213–15. Assessment of a Christian and Buddhist conference on spiritual practice.

McDaniel, Jay B. *Earth, Sky, Gods and Mortals.* Mystic, Conn.: Twenty-third Publications, 1990. A thoughtful look at living the life of a mature, reflective, ecological Christian, based on process theology.

———. *Living from the Center: Spirituality in an Age of Consumerism.* St. Louis, Mo.: Chalice Press, 2000. Ten healing alternatives to the temptations of consumerism.

Meltonian Journal: Issues and Themes in Jewish Education. Number 24 (Spring 1991). A special issue of this periodical focused on Judaism and ecology — our earth and our tradition.

Momaday, N. Scott. "A First American's View." *National Geographic* 150 (1976): 13–18. A personal reflection on the Native American relationship to the natural world.

Neihardt, John. G. *Black Elk Speaks.* New York: Simon and Schuster, 1972. The biography of a holy man of the Oglala Sioux. Information and insights about the relationship of this man and society to the natural world are infused throughout the text.

Oelschlaeger, Max. *Caring for Creation: An Ecumenical Approach to the Environmental Crisis.* New Haven, Conn.: Yale University Press, 1994. The author argues that religious belief is essential for resolution of the environmental crisis.

Patterson, John. "Maori Environmental Virtues." *Environmental Ethics* 16 (1994): 397–410. Traditional narratives are the standard sources for Maori ethics. These narratives depict a common ancestry for all natural entities and thus call for respect and responsibility.

Peerenboom, R. P. "Beyond Naturalism: A Reconstruction of Daoist Environmental Ethics." *Environmental Ethics* 13 (1991): 3–22. Offers an alternative interpretation of Taoism and concludes that it is no better than Western philosophies in dealing with the environmental crisis.

Peet, Richard, and Michael Watts, eds. *Liberation Ecologies: Environment, Development, Social Movements.* London: Routledge, 1996. Focuses on the interrelations of development, social movements, and the environment in "the South" — Latin America, Africa, and Asia.

Reichenback, Bruce R., and V. Elving Anderson, *On Behalf of God: A Christian Ethic for Biology.* Grand Rapids, Mich.: W. B. Eerdmans, 1995. The authors advocate an ethic that includes limiting population growth, enhancing the well-being of the disenfranchised rural poor, and limiting the Western world's exploitation of the world's resources.

Rolston, Holmes, III. "Wildlife and Wildlands: A Christian Perspective." *Church and Society* 80 (1990): 16–40. Addresses values, aesthetic features, and ethics about the natural world from a Christian perspective.

———. "Creation: God and Endangered Species," in *Biodiversity and Landscapes: A Paradox of Humanity,* ed. Ke Chung Kim and Robert D. Weaver. Cambridge: Cambridge University Press, 1994, pp. 47–60. Looks at endangered species and a wide variety of biological and religious issues from a Christian perspective, including the massive creativity and proliferation of life on earth, the degree to which life is an accident versus an expected product of the universe, the apparent random cruelty of life, and a basis for love, respect, and a protective sense for life on earth.

———. "Does Nature Need to Be Redeemed?" *Zygon* 29 (1994): 205–29. Rolston seeks to show that biological knowledge helps to clarify some of the theological issues considered, and theology gives a context to view the biological issues.

Santmire, H. Paul. "Is Christianity Ecologically Bankrupt? The View from Asylum Hill," in *An Ecology of the Spirit: Religious Reflections and Environmental Consciousness,* ed. Michael Barnes. Annual Publication of the College Theology Society, Vol. 36 (1990), University Press of America, Lanham, Md. Santmire argues for an Augustinian theology celebrating God's presence in nature, but still advocating a theology of fall and redemption.

———. "Healing the Protestant Mind: Beyond the Theology of Human Dominion," in *After Nature's Revolt: "Eco-Justice and Theology,* ed. Dieter T. Hessel. Minneapolis: Augsburg Fortress, 1992. Santmire proposes a new ecological paradigm in which the divine purpose is to initiate and shepherd a cosmic history and bring it to fulfillment.

Schwarzschild, Steven S. "The Unnatural Jew." *Environmental Ethics* 6 (1984): 347–62. Presents a scholarly discussion of the separateness of nature and ethics in Jewish history and culture. Argues that from a traditional Jewish standpoint, nature remains subject to human ends.

Steffen, Lloyd H. "In Defense of Dominion." *Environmental Ethics* 14 (1992): 63–80. Argues that the term *dominion* is meant in an ideal of human-divine intimacy and peacefulness and as an ideal of responsible action; dominion could promote interreligious dialogue on environmental issues.

Taylor, Bron Raymond, ed. *Ecological Resistance Movements: The Global Emergence of Radical and Popular Environmentalism.* Albany: State University of New York Press, 1995. A collection of articles on popular ecological resistance movements in various parts of the world, with a focus on North and South America, Asia and the Pacific, Africa, and Europe. Includes chapters on earth religion as well as an assessment of the effectiveness of radical environmentalism throughout the world.

Williams, Hugh. "What Is Good Forestry? An Ethical Examination of Forest Policy and Practice in New Brunswick." *Environmental Ethics* 18 (1996): 391–410. Williams presents a neoclassical theistic moral theory that affirms the existence of a public good that is understood teleologically as an objective purpose to be pursued.

Yaffe, Martin, D., ed. *Judaism and Environmental Ethics: A Reader.* Lanham, Md.: Lexington Books, 2001. Yaffe explores the ethical and philosophical questions underlying environmental dilemmas from a Jewish perspective.

CHAPTER SIX
Anthropocentrism

In this chapter we first define anthropocentrism, identify two major types (strong anthropocentrism and weak anthropocentrism), and then focus on some ethical issues within the context of an anthropocentric world view.

CONCEPTUAL FRAMEWORK

Anthropocentrism is the philosophical perspective that ethical principles apply to humans only and that human needs and interests are of highest, and even exclusive, value and importance. Thus, concern for nonhuman entities is limited to those entities having value to humans.

In contemporary Western society, anthropocentrism often serves as a default ethic — a position assumed without careful consideration of alternative world views. However, anthropocentrism is a position also held by many thoughtful and reflective people as the most morally correct perspective to advocate. It is this latter position that we describe and analyze in this chapter.

Roots of anthropocentrism in Western society can be found both in religious and secular philoso-

phies. Since the persuasiveness of a religious-based ethic depends on sharing a common faith and world view, those who are not adherents are less likely to find its tenets compelling. Therefore, many contemporary scholars have appealed to the more universal secular themes first developed among ancient Greek philosophers.

Bryan G. Norton[1] argues that there are two types of anthropocentrism prevalent in Western society. One type, strong anthropocentrism, is characterized by the notion that nonhuman species and natural objects have value only to the extent that they satisfy a "felt preference." A felt preference is any fulfillable human desire — whether or not it is based on thought and reflection. The reading from René Descartes and James Skidmore's assessment of Immanuel Kant in this chapter generally illustrate this perspective.

The other type, weak anthropocentrism, is distinguished by the affirmation that nonhumans and

---

[1]Bryan G. Norton, "Environmental Ethics and Weak Anthropocentrism and Nonanthropocentrism," *Environmental Ethics* 6 (1984): 131–48.

natural objects can satisfy "considered preferences" as well as felt preferences. A considered preference is a human desire or need based on careful deliberation and is compatible with a rationally adopted world view, incorporating sound metaphysics, scientific theories, aesthetic values, and moral ideals. Thus, weak anthropocentrists value nonhuman entities for more than their use in meeting unreflective human needs: They value them for enriching the human experience. In this chapter, William H. Murdy, Stephen Jay Gould, and Frederick Turner present positions more closely allied with weak anthropocentrism. Keep in mind, however, that strong and weak anthropocentrism are not always sharply distinguished. Anthropocentric positions can fall anywhere on a continuum between strong and weak.

LIMITING MORAL CONCERN TO HUMAN BEINGS

Clarifying the moral responsibility of humans to the rest of nature is one of the most difficult and controversial tasks in formulating an environmental ethic. Anthropocentrists restrict the object of our moral concern largely or exclusively to human beings, who are viewed as superior to other creatures and to nature. Anthropocentrists commonly justify their position by citing unique characteristics that emphasize the importance of the human species. For example, the human capacity to reason plays a central role in the arguments of Descartes and Kant. Descartes and Kant also stress the development and use of language in maintaining that moral concern be extended only to humans.

Kant asserts that only rational beings merit moral concern. He believes that for a rational being, rationality has intrinsic value and thus is a goal worth seeking in itself. Since rationality is the same for all rational beings, all rational beings work for a common goal, which is to achieve a rational world. Kant argues that rational beings cannot achieve a rational world if they compete with or hinder each other for personal gain such as wealth or power. Thus, morally correct behavior for rational beings entails helping other rational beings, because this contributes to their common goal of achieving a rational world. Kant asserts that *only* rational beings contribute directly to achieving the intrinsic good of a rational world. He maintains that because nonrational beings do not contribute directly, their treatment by rational beings does not affect the effort to achieve a rational world. Consequently, it is proper for nonrational beings to be used as means to an end (i.e., a rational world).

Kant defines rationality as the ability to universalize details into broader, general, concepts. He recognizes that many animals can communicate by signs, but believes that animals do not use symbols. Since the symbolic structure of language is necessary to express general concepts, beings without language cannot express general concepts and hence are not rational. Since nonhuman animals and natural entities are not rational, they do not merit moral concern. Kant concludes that human beings have little or no responsibility toward animals or the natural world.

In Skidmore's essay, "Duties to Animals: The Failure of Kant's Moral Theory," the author concludes that only rational beings (i.e., humans) have unconditional worth (intrinsic value) in Kant's philosophy and that rational beings have no direct duties to nonrational (nonhuman) creatures.

Some anthropocentrists, such as Murdy, base their positions on the observed power and biological superiority of humans in the natural world. Murdy also argues for the evolutionary necessity of taking this philosophic position.

In contrast, those who oppose anthropocentrism believe that a moral system restricted to humans is arbitrary, unjust, and illogical.[2] For example, in many well-established ethical systems, moral worth is extended not only to nonhuman animals, but to spiritual beings and sacred places as well. Some scholars point to the many similarities between humans and other animals, especially mammals, in arguing that any ethic that includes all humans and excludes all nonhumans is unjust since there are no morally relevant characteristics (e.g., rationality, consciousness, language) that all humans possess and no nonhumans possess. If all humans qualify for moral concern, then any objective criteria would require that some nonhuman entities also qualify.

---

[2]Bernard E. Rollin, *Animal Rights and Human Morality* (Buffalo, N.Y.: Prometheus Books, 1981), pp. 3–22.

Because of the controversy surrounding the issue of who ought to be accorded moral concern, the readings in this chapter offer varying perspectives on the moral limits that should be sanctioned in human treatment of nonhumans and the environment. Descartes suggests that nonhumans are little more than intricate machines lacking a soul and does not place any clear limits on how humans ought to treat them. Skidmore notes that Kant refers to indirect duties toward nonhumans based on our duties to humans. Murdy and Turner both advocate philosophies that they believe to be compatible with the position that nature has intrinsic value; however, both accept and encourage expression of human domination over nature.

ENLIGHTENED SELF-INTEREST

A central question that merits careful consideration is "Will anthropocentrism eventually lead the human species to self-destruction and perhaps to the destruction of many other species as well?" As an essentially self-serving ethic, anthropocentrism may lack the necessary safeguards to protect the planet from the effects of the human species' steadily increasing numbers and demands on world resources. The response of anthropocentrists to this question is built largely on the notion of "enlightened self-interest." From this perspective, many anthropocentrists acknowledge the human potential for environmental destruction and recognize that long-term human existence and well-being depend on the health and stability of the planet's ecological support system. They argue that humans must take responsibility for maintaining this support system in a healthy, useful condition.

This point of view is found most commonly among weak anthropocentrists. For example, Murdy acknowledges human superiority and maintains that human survival and well-being depend on the health and stability of the whole ecological support system. Murdy stresses the great destructive potential exhibited by humans and points out that dependence on the ecological support system must lead humans to be careful not to destroy this fragile planet. In Murdy's view, humans should ascribe value to nonhumans and the rest of the natural world in accordance with how these entities benefit humanity. Gould discounts the notion of the earth as a fragile planet but argues that an enlightened self-interest makes it prudent for humans to treat nature more gently than they have in the past. In a step further, Turner expresses little specific concern about the earth as a fragile planet and advocates moving toward a creative manipulation and experimentation with nature, including ecological niches, species, and ecosystems. He also predicts eventual expansion of such activities to other planets.

Animals Are Machines

René Descartes

René Descartes (1596–1650), often called "the father of modern philosophy," shaped the view that humans are distinctly different from other animals and the rest of the natural world. In Descartes's view, language and reason are the features that set humans apart from all other species. Using the principle of parsimony, in which one must always begin with the simplest explanation of observed phenomena, Descartes argues that the observed behaviors of all nonhuman creatures can be explained without ascribing minds and consciousness to them. He concludes that nonhuman animals can be viewed as no more than machines with parts assembled in intricate ways. Based on Descartes's rationale, humans have little responsibility to other animals or the natural world, unless the treatment of them affects other humans.

I

I had explained all these matters in some detail in the Treatise which I formerly intended to publish. And afterwards I had shown there, what must be the fabric of the nerves and muscles of the human body in order that the animal spirits therein contained should have the power to move the members, just as the heads of animals, a little while after decapitation, are still observed to move and bite the earth, notwithstanding that they are no longer animate; what changes are necessary in the brain to cause wakefulness, sleep and dreams; how light, sounds, smells, tastes, heat and all other qualities pertaining to external objects are able to imprint on it various ideas by the intervention of the senses; how hunger, thirst and other internal affections can also convey their impressions upon it; what should be regarded as the "common sense" by which these ideas are received, and what is meant by the memory which retains them, by the fancy which can change them in diverse ways and out of them constitute new ideas, and which, by the same means, distributing the ani-

mal spirits through the muscles, can cause the members of such a body to move in as many diverse ways, and in a manner as suitable to the objects which present themselves to its senses and to its internal passions, as can happen in our own case apart from the direction of our free will. And this will not seem strange to those, who, knowing how many different *automata* or moving machines can be made by the industry of man, without employing in so doing more than a very few parts in comparison with the great multitude of bones, muscles, nerves, arteries, veins, or other parts that are found in the body of each animal. From this aspect the body is regarded as a machine which, having been made by the hands of God, is incomparably better arranged, and possesses in itself movements which are much more admirable, than any of those which can be invented by man. Here I specially stopped to show that if there had been such machines, possessing the organs and outward form of a monkey or some other animal without reason, we should not have had any means of ascertaining that they were not of the same nature as those animals. On the other hand, if there were machines which bore a resemblance to our body and imitated our actions as far as it was morally possible to do so, we should always have two very certain tests by which to recognise that, for all that, they were not real men. The first is, that they could never use speech or other signs as we do when placing our thoughts on record for the benefit of others. For we can easily understand a machine's being constituted so that it can utter words, and even emit some responses to action on it of a corporeal kind, which brings about a change in its organs; for instance, if it is touched in a particular part it may ask what we wish to say to it; if in another part it may exclaim that it is being hurt, and so on. But it never happens that it arranges its speech in various ways, in order to reply appropriately to everything that may be said in its presence, as even the lowest type of man can do. And the second difference is, that although machines can perform certain things as well as or perhaps better than any of us can do, they infallibly fall short in others, by the which means we may discover that they did not act from knowledge, but only from the disposition of their organs. For while reason is a universal instrument which can serve for all contingencies, these organs have need of some special adaptation for every particular action. From this it follows that it is morally impossible that there should be sufficient diversity in any machine to allow it to act in all the events of life in the same way as our reason causes us to act.

By these two methods we may also recognise the difference that exists between men and brutes. For it is a very remarkable fact that there are none so depraved and stupid, without even excepting idiots, that they cannot arrange different words together, forming of them a statement by which they make known their thoughts; while, on the other hand, there is no other animal, however perfect and fortunately circumstanced it may be, which can do the same. It is not the want of organs that brings this to pass, for it is evident that magpies and parrots are able to utter words just like ourselves, and yet they cannot speak as we do, that is, so as to give evidence that they think of what they say. On the other hand, men who, being born deaf and dumb, are in the same degree, or even more than the brutes, destitute of the organs which serve the others for talking, are in the habit of themselves inventing certain signs by which they make themselves understood by those who, being usually in their company, have leisure to learn their language. And this does not merely show that the brutes have less reason than men, but that they have none at all, since it is clear that very little is required in order to be able to talk. And when we notice the inequality that exists between animals of the same species, as well as between men, and observe that some are more capable of receiving instructions than others, it is not credible that a monkey or a parrot, selected as the most perfect of its species, should not in these matters equal the stupidest child to be found, or at least a child whose mind is clouded, unless in the case of the brute the soul were of an entirely different nature from ours. And we ought not to confound speech with natural movements which betray passions and may be imitated by machines as well as be manifested by animals; nor must we think, as did some of the ancients, that brutes talk, although we do not understand their language. For if this were true, since they have many organs which are allied to our own, they could communicate their thoughts to us just as easily as to those of their own race. It is also a very remarkable fact that although there are many animals which exhibit more dexterity than we do in some of their actions, we at the same time observe that they do not manifest any dexterity at all in many others. Hence the fact that they do better than we do, does not prove that they are endowed with mind, for in this case they would have more reason than any of us, and would surpass us in all other things. It rather shows that they have no reason at all, and that it is nature which acts in them according to the disposition of their organs, just as a clock, which is only composed of wheels and weights is able to tell the hours and measure the time more correctly than we can do with all our wisdom.

I had described after this the rational soul and shown that it could not be in any way derived from the power of matter, like the other things of which I had spoken, but that it must be expressly created. I showed, too, that it is not sufficient that it should be lodged in the human body like a pilot in his ship, unless perhaps for the moving of its members, but that it is necessary that it should also be joined and united more closely to the body in order to have sensations and appetites similar to our own, and thus to form a true man. In conclusion, I have here enlarged a little on the subject of the soul, because it is one of the greatest importance. For next to the error of those who deny God, which I think I have already sufficiently refuted, there is none which is more effectual in leading feeble spirits from the straight path of virtue, than to imagine that the soul of the brute is of the same nature as our own, and that in consequence, after this life we have nothing to fear or to hope for, any more than the flies and ants. As a matter of fact, when one comes to know how greatly they differ, we understand much better the reasons which go to prove that our soul is in its nature entirely independent of the body, and in consequence that it is not liable to die with it. And then, inasmuch as we observe no other causes capable of destroying it, we are naturally inclined to judge that it is immortal.

II

I cannot share the opinion of Montaigne and others who attribute understanding or thought to animals. I am not worried that people say that men have an absolute empire over all the other animals; because

I agree that some of them are stronger than us, and believe that there may also be some who have an instinctive cunning capable of deceiving the shrewdest human beings. But I observe that they only imitate or surpass us in those of our actions which are not guided by our thoughts. It often happens that we walk or eat without thinking at all about what we are doing; and similarly, without using our reason, we reject things which are harmful for us, and parry the blows aimed at us. Indeed, even if we expressly willed not to put our hands in front of our head when we fall, we could not prevent ourselves. I think also that if we had no thought we would eat, as the animals do, without having to learn to; and it is said that those who walk in their sleep sometimes swim across streams in which they would drown if they were awake. As for the movements of our passions, even though in us they are accompanied with thought because we have the faculty of thinking, it is none the less very clear that they do not depend on thought, because they often occur in spite of us. Consequently they can also occur in animals, even more violently than they do in human beings, without our being able to conclude from that that they have thoughts.

In fact, none of our external actions can show anyone who examines them that our body is not just a self-moving machine but contains a soul with thoughts, with the exception of words, or other signs that are relevant to particular topics without expressing any passion. I say words or other signs, because deaf-mutes use signs as we use spoken words; and I say that these signs must be relevant, to exclude the speech of parrots, without excluding the speech of madmen, which is relevant to particular topics even though it does not follow reason. I add also that these words or signs must not express any passion, to rule out not only cries of joy or sadness and the like, but also whatever can be taught by training to animals. If you teach a magpie to say good-day to its mistress, when it sees her approach, this can only be by making the utterance of this word the expression of one of its passions. For instance it will be an expression of the hope of eating, if it has always been given a titbit when it says it. Similarly, all the things which dogs, horses, and monkeys are taught to perform are only expressions of their fear, their hope, or their joy; and consequently they can be performed without any thought. Now it seems to me very striking that the use of words, so defined, is something peculiar to human beings. Montaigne and Charron may have said that there is more difference between one human being and another than between a human being and an animal; but there has never been known an animal so perfect as to use a sign to make other animals understand something which expressed no passion; and there is no human being so imperfect as not to do so, since even deaf-mutes invent special signs to express their thoughts. This seems to me a very strong argument to prove that the reason why animals do not speak as we do is not that they lack the organs but that they have no thoughts. It cannot be said that they speak to each other and that we cannot understand them; because since dogs and some other animals express their passions to us, they would express their thoughts also if they had any.

I know that animals do many things better than we do, but this does not surprise me. It can even be used to prove they act naturally and mechanically, like a clock which tells the time better than our judgement does. Doubtless when the swallows come in spring, they operate like clocks. The actions of honeybees are of the same nature, and the discipline of cranes in flight, and of apes in fighting, if it is true that they keep discipline. Their instinct to bury their dead is no stranger than that of dogs and cats who scratch the earth for the purpose of burying their excrement; they hardly ever actually bury it, which shows that they act only by instinct and without thinking. The most that one can say is that though the animals do not perform any action which shows us that they think, still, since the organs of their body are not very different from ours, it may be conjectured that there is attached to those organs some thoughts such as we experience in ourselves, but of a very much less perfect kind. To which I have nothing to reply except that if they thought as we do, they would have an immortal soul like us. This is unlikely, because there is no reason to believe it of some animals without believing it of all, and many of them such as oysters and sponges are too imperfect for this to be credible. But I am afraid of boring you with this discussion, and my only desire is to show you that I am, etc.

III

But there is no prejudice to which we are all more accustomed from our earliest years than the belief that dumb animals think. Our only reasons for this belief is the fact that we see that many of the organs of animals are not very different from ours in shape and movement. Since we believe that there is a single principle within us which causes these motions — namely the soul, which both moves the body and thinks — we do not doubt that some such soul is to be found in animals also. I came to realize, however, that there are two different principles causing our motions: one is purely mechanical and corporeal and depends solely on the force of the spirits and the construction of our organs, and can be called the corporeal soul; the other is the incorporeal mind, the soul which I have defined as a thinking substance. Thereupon I investigated more carefully whether the motions of animals originated from both these principles or from one only. I soon saw clearly that they could all originate from the corporeal and mechanical principle, and I thenceforward regarded it as certain and established that we cannot at all prove the presence of a thinking soul in animals. I am not disturbed by the astuteness and cunning of dogs and foxes, or all the things which animals do for the sake of food, sex, and fear; I claim that I can easily explain the origin of all of them from the constitution of their organs.

But though I regard it as established that we cannot prove there is any thought in animals, I do not think it is thereby proved that there is not, since the human mind does not reach into their hearts. But when I investigate what is most probable in this matter, I see no argument for animals having thoughts except the fact that since they have eyes, ears, tongues, and other sense-organs like ours, it seems likely that they have sensation like us; and since thought is included in our mode of sensation, similar thought seems to be attributable to them. This argument, which is very obvious, has taken possession of the minds of all men from their earliest age. But there are other arguments, stronger and more

numerous, but not so obvious to everyone, which strongly urge the opposite. One is that it is more probable that worms and flies and caterpillars move mechanically than that they all have immortal souls.

It is certain that in the bodies of animals, as in ours, there are bones, nerves, muscles, animal spirits, and other organs so disposed that they can by themselves, without any thought, give rise to all animals the motions we observe. This is very clear in convulsive movements when the machine of the body moves despite the soul, and sometimes more violently and in a more varied manner than when it is moved by the will.

Second, it seems reasonable, since art copies nature, and men can make various automata which move without thought, that nature should produce its own automata, much more splendid than artificial ones. These natural automata are the animals. This is especially likely since we have no reason to believe that thought always accompanies the disposition of organs which we find in animals. It is much more wonderful that a mind should be found in every human body than that one should be lacking in every animal.

But in my opinion the main reason which suggests that the beasts lack thought is the following. Within a single species some of them are more perfect than others, as men are too. This can be seen in horses and dogs, some of whom learn what they are taught much better than others. Yet, although all animals easily communicate to us, by voice or bodily movement, their natural impulses of anger, fear, hunger and so on, it has never yet been observed that any brute animal reached the stage of using real speech, that is to say, of indicating by word or sign something pertaining to pure thought and not to natural impulse. Such speech is the only certain sign of thought hidden in a body. All men use it, however stupid and insane they may be, and though they may lack tongue and organs of voice; but no animals do. Consequently it can be taken as a real specific difference between men and dumb animals.

For brevity's sake I here omit the other reasons for denying thought to animals. Please note that I am speaking of thought, and not of life or sensation. I do not deny life to animals, since I regard it as consisting simply in the beat of the heart; and I do not deny sensation, in so far as it depends on a bodily organ. Thus my opinion is not so much cruel to animals as indulgent to men — at least to those who are not given to the superstitions of Pythagoras — since it absolves them from the suspicion of crime when they eat or kill animals.

Perhaps I have written at too great length for the sharpness of your intelligence; but I wished to show you that very few people have yet sent me objections which were as agreeable as yours. Your kindness and candour has made you a friend of that most respectful admirer of all who seek true wisdom, etc.

DISCUSSION TOPICS

1. What major differences does Descartes use to distinguish humans from other animals?
2. Descartes believed that there was no proof that animals think. Do you think he might believe otherwise today? Justify your position.
3. What arguments do you believe would be most persuasive in countering Descartes's position that nonhuman animals can be described as complicated machinery?

READING 31

Duties to Animals: The Failure of Kant's Moral Theory

James Skidmore

James R. Skidmore is a member of the Department of English and Philosophy, Idaho State University, Pocatello.

In this article from the Journal of Value Inquiry, *Skidmore questions whether Kant can be interpreted to ascribe unconditional (intrinsic) worth to nonhuman animals or nature. He looks at each of two formulations of Kant's categorical imperative. Skidmore interprets Kant as asserting that only rational beings (persons) have unconditional worth. Nonrational be-ings have only conditional worth and thus may be treated merely as means. Thus, he interprets Kant as concluding that there are no direct duties to animals.*

. . . Kant is well known, by now, for insisting that our duties to animals are merely "indirect duties towards humanity."[1] In short, he argues that if we develop a habit of treating animals cruelly this will damage our character and ultimately lead to inappropriate treatment of other human beings. . . .

The question that provides the challenge to a Kantian is clear: Can we separate Kant's conclusions regarding animals from his theory in the way some philosophers have argued that we can separate his conclusions regarding lying, suicide, or punishment? Even a brief look at his development of the categorical imperative in the *Groundwork for the Metaphysics of Morals* suggests that the task is difficult. His conclusions regarding animals seem much more obviously to be a straightforward application of the categorical imperative in at least two of its formulations.

Consider the formulation that commands us to act "in such a way that you treat humanity, whether in your own person or in the person of another, always at the same time as an end and never simply as a means."[2] Questions have been raised as to just what Kant means by "humanity" or *Menschheit.* While some philosophers have suggested that this formulation simply commands us to treat human beings as ends and never merely as means, most agree that with "humanity" Kant refers not to human beings as such, but to a particular feature of them, rational agency.[3] Meanwhile, no one has supposed that the term "humanity" refers also to animals lacking rationality. It has been taken for granted that a command to treat the humanity in persons as an end has no direct application to non-human animals.[4] Thus, this formulation of the categorical imperative appears simply to ignore all or most non-human animals, those that cannot plausibly be said to possess rational nature in Kant's sense.

This is made particularly clear in the discussion leading up to this formulation. Kant establishes first that if there were a moral imperative, it would have to command categorically. He then argues that the possibility of such a categorical imperative depends on the existence of ends whose value is absolute or unconditional:

> But let us suppose that there were something whose existence has in itself absolute worth, something which as an end in itself could be a ground of determinate laws. In it, and in it alone, would there be the ground of a possible categorical imperative.[5]

Why does a categorical imperative need an unconditional end? Since Kant argues that all action involves the pursuit of an end which is taken to be good, the possibility of an imperative that commands action unconditionally depends upon an end whose value is likewise unconditional. In this way, a categorical imperative exists if and only if an end of unconditional worth exists as well.[6]

Kant immediately goes on to argue that there is such an unconditional end, and it is none other than "man, and in general every rational being."[7] It is a person's existence as a rational being which has unconditional worth. This leads swiftly to the second formulation of the categorical imperative, namely, the command to treat the rational agency in a person for what it is, an end in itself. Kant concludes that all other beings have only a conditional worth. He says that beings "whose existence depends not on our will but on nature have, nevertheless, if they are not rational beings, only a relative value as means and are therefore called things."[8]

It seems clear that Kant's development of the second formulation of the categorical imperative divides living beings into two groups for the purposes of morality. First, there are rational beings, or persons, who have an unconditional worth which he calls dignity, and as such they must be treated as ends in themselves. Second, there are all other beings, non-rational beings who have only conditional worth and thus take on the moral status of things that may be treated merely as means. This suggests that Kant's later conclusion that there are no direct duties to animals can be seen as a simple and direct application of the formula of humanity and the reasoning that leads up to it.

The same can be said of the formulation of the categorical imperative that appeals to a kingdom of ends. Kant claims that "all maxims proceeding from (an agent's) own legislation ought to harmonize with a possible kingdom of ends as a kingdom of nature."[9] Two features of the ideal kingdom are crucial. First, according to Kant, members of such kingdom are rational agents and only rational agents: "A rational being belongs to the kingdom of ends as a member when he legislates in it universal laws while also being himself subject to these laws."[10] Second, Kant maintains: "In the kingdom of ends everything has either a price or a dignity."[11] Only the legislating members in such a kingdom have the incomparable worth of dignity. All other beings have only conditional worth, worth as a means to some end, and are thus accorded not dignity but price.

This brief look at two of Kant's formulations of the categorical imperative suggests that Kant's later conclusions regarding animals may prove difficult to disentangle from the theory itself. The claim that we have no direct duties to animals seems to follow immediately from the system of value that is present in the two formulations and the reasoning behind them. It is a system in which the source of all value is rational agency itself. It is rational agency, and only rational agency, which possesses the incomparable worth of dignity; and it is the ends of such agency that determine the price of everything else. Thus, as Christine Korsgaard says, on "Kant's view it is human beings, with our capacity for valuing things, that bring to the world such value as it has."[12] Indeed, he can claim later that without "men the whole creation would be a mere waste, in vain, and without final purpose."[13] It is this conception of value from which his later skeptical conclusions regarding duties to animals seem to follow so clearly. Far from mere prejudices, they appear to be a simple and direct application of his categorical imperative and the system of value that accompanies it.

NOTES

1. Immanuel Kant, *Lectures on Ethics,* Louis Infield, trans. (New York: Harper and Row, 1963), p. 373.
2. Immanuel Kant, *Grounding for the Metaphysics of Morals* (Indianapolis: Hackett Publishing, 1981), p. 429.

3. See Thomas Hill, "Humanity as an End in Itself," *Dignity and Practical Reason in Kant's Moral Theory*, p. 39, and Christine Korsgaard, "Formula of Humanity," *Creating the Kingdom of Ends* (Cambridge, England: Cambridge University Press, 1996) p. 110.
4. See William Wright, "Treating Animals as Ends," *Journal of Value Inquiry* 27 (1993).
5. Kant, *Grounding for the Metaphysics of Morals*, p. 428.
6. See Korsgaard, op. cit., pp. 114–19.
7. Kant, *Grounding for the Metaphysics of Morals* p. 428.
8. Ibid.
9. Ibid., p. 436.
10. Ibid., p. 433.
11. Ibid., p. 434.
12. Korsgaard, op. cit., p. 131.
13. Ibid.

DISCUSSION TOPICS

1. Do you believe that humans are the only rational beings? Explain your perspective.
2. What are the benefits of viewing rationality as having unconditional (intrinsic) worth? What are the possible problems?

█ R E A D I N G 3 2 █

Anthropocentrism: A Modern Version

William H. Murdy

A representative of weak anthropocentrism, William H. Murdy, a retired dean at Emory University and botanist specializing in genetics and reproductive biology, builds on the notion that concern for our own species has a strong evolutionary precedent. Murdy asserts that all species exist as ends for themselves; in biological terms, they seek to maximize their own reproductive success. Thus it is natural for humans to value other humans more highly than the rest of nature; in fact, it would be logical for members of any species to view themselves as most valuable. Murdy acknowledges, however, that human survival and well-being depend on the health and stability of our whole ecological support system. From an enlightened self-interest perspective, he maintains that humans should ascribe value to all elements of the natural world.

The capacity of man to affect the environment beyond himself is an evolutionary emergent, continuous with the much more limited ability of other organisms to affect the environment beyond themselves. It enables man to modify environments to suit his needs, which is a root cause of both his biological success and ecological problems. It also enables man to enhance values beyond himself, and this is a major feature of the new anthropocentrism expressed in this article.

PRE-DARWINIAN ANTHROPOCENTRISM

Socrates, in a dialogue with Euthydemus,[1] is reported to have said:

> Tell me, Euthydemus, has it ever occurred to you to reflect on the care the gods have taken to furnish man with what he needs?... Now, seeing that we need food, think how they make the earth to yield it, and provide to that end appropriate seasons which furnish in abundance the diverse things that minister not only to our wants but to our enjoyment.

The idea that nature was created to benefit man was a popular belief throughout Western history and was still very much alive in the 19th century. Cuvier, "father" of comparative anatomy and paleontology, "could think of no better reason for the existence of fishes . . . than that they provided food for man,"[2] and Lyell, a leading geologist of the 19th century, in his early years believed that domestic animals had been expressly designed for man's use. He writes:[3]

> The power bestowed on the horse, the dog, the ox, the sheep, the cat, and many species of domestic fowls, of supporting almost every climate, was given expressly to enable them to follow man throughout

all parts of the globe in order that we might obtain their services, and they our protection.

DARWINIAN ANTHROPOCENTRISM

Charles Darwin, in *The Origin of Species,* provided sufficient evidence to finally counter the idea that nature exists to serve man. According to William Paley, 18th-century exponent of natural theology, the rattlesnake's rattle was expressly designed to give warning to its prey. Darwin[4] asserts that "natural selection cannot possibly produce any modification in a species exclusively for the good of another species" and makes the following declaration:

If it could be proved that any part of the structure of any one species had been formed for the exclusive good of another species it would annihilate my theory, for such could not have been produced through natural selection. (p. 196)

Species exist as ends in themselves. They do not exist for the exclusive benefit of any other species. The purpose of a species, in biological terms, is to survive to reproduce. Potter[5] writes: "all successful living organisms behave purposefully in terms of their own or their species survival" (p. 16). Species that failed to do so became extinct.

A MODERN VIEW OF ANTHROPOCENTRISM

To be anthropocentric is to affirm that mankind is to be valued more highly than other things in nature — by man. By the same logic, spiders are to be valued more highly than other things in nature — by spiders. It is proper for men to be anthropocentric and for spiders to be arachnocentric. This goes for all other living species. The following statement by Simpson[6] expresses the modern version of anthropocentrism:

Man is the highest animal. The fact that he alone is capable of making such judgment is in itself part of the evidence that this decision is correct. And even if he were the lowest animal, the anthropocentric point of view would still be manifestly the only proper one to adopt for consideration of his place in the scheme of things and when seeking a guide on which to base his actions and his evaluations of them.

Anthropocentrism is a pejorative in many of the articles which deal with the so-called ecological crisis. Lynn White,[7] in his widely quoted article, "The Historical Roots of Our Ecological Crisis," upbraids Christianity for being the most anthropocentric religion the world has seen:

Christianity, in absolute contrast to ancient paganism and Asia's religions (except perhaps Zoroastrianism), not only established a dualism of man and nature but also insisted that it is God's will that man exploit nature for his proper ends.

White is right to remind us of how tragically myopic has been our exploitation of nature. However, he is wrong to infer that it is somehow wrong for man to exploit nature for "his proper ends." We must exploit nature to live. The problem lies in our difficulty to distinguish between "proper ends," which are progressive and promote human values, and "improper ends," which are retrogressive and destructive of human values.

Another attitude toward nature that eschews anthropocentrism is the "Franciscan" belief in the fundamental equality of all life. In this view, man is merely one of several million different species comprising a "democracy of all God's creatures."[7] Jordan[8] states: "The time will come when civilized man will feel that the rights of all living creatures on earth are as sacred as his own." Julian Huxley[9] expresses a similar opinion: "In ethical terms, the golden rule applies to man's relations with nature as well as to relations between human beings."

If we affirm that all species have "equal rights," or, that the rights of man are not of greater value than the rights of other species, how should it affect our behavior toward nature? The golden rule, "As ye would that men should do to you, do ye to them likewise," is a moral axiom which requires reciprocity among ethicizing beings. How does such a principle apply to nonethicizing forms of life which cannot reciprocate? The callous, wanton destruction of life is surely not a proper end for man, but what about our destruction of pathogenic bacteria, in order that we might remain healthy, or our destruction of plant and animal life, in order that we might be nourished? To affirm that men, dogs, and cats have more rights than plants, insects, and bacteria is a belief that species do not have equal rights. If, however, we believe in the equality of all species, none should be genetically manipulated or killed for the exclusive benefit of another.

To ascribe value to things of nature as they benefit man is to regard them as instruments to man's survival or well-being. This is an anthropocentric point of view. As knowledge of our dependent relationships with nature grows, we place instrumental value on an ever greater variety of things. Phytoplankton of the oceans becomes valuable when we recognize the key role of these organisms in providing the earth's free oxygen. Continued growth of knowledge may lead to an awareness that no event in nature is without some effect on the whole of which we are a part and therefore we should value all items in nature. Basic to the kind of anthropocentrism expounded in this article is the recognition that an individual's well-being depends on the well-being of both its social group and ecological support system.

Birch contends that to evaluate things of nature in terms of instrumental value, regardless of how enlightened our evaluation might be, will not provide us with a "valid ethic of nature." He writes:[10] "Conservation will rest on very uncertain foundations unless it comes to be based on a view that living creatures besides man have intrinsic worth. Unless they have, there seems no sound reason for conservation other than to suit the purposes of man, and these change from time to time and place to place." To have a "valid ethic of nature," according to Birch, we must affirm "the intrinsic value of every item in creation."

An anthropocentric attitude toward nature does not require that man be the source of all value, nor does it exclude a belief that things of nature have intrinsic value. According to Laszlo:[11] "There is nothing in all the realms of natural systems which would be value-free when looked at from the vantage point of the systems themselves" (p. 105). Whitehead[12] writes: "The element of value, of being valuable, of having value, of being an end in itself, of being something which is for its own sake, must not be

omitted in any account of an event as the most concrete actual something" (p. 93).

I may affirm that every species has intrinsic value, but I will behave as though I value my own survival and that of my species more highly than the survival of other animals or plants. I may assert that a lettuce plant has intrinsic value, yet I will eat it before it has reproduced itself because I value my own nutritional well-being above the survival of the lettuce plant. Birch[10] writes: "Man left only with his self-interest, however enlightened, will not provide sufficient motivation for ecological survival." Even this statement can be interpreted in terms of instructional value, that is, man should acknowledge the intrinsic value of things; otherwise he will not have sufficient motivation for ecological survival, which I assume includes human survival individually and as a species.

MAN'S PLACE IN NATURE

Whitehead[12] writes:

> That which endures is limited, obstructive, intolerant, infecting its environment with its own aspects. But it is not self-sufficient. The aspects of all things enter into its very nature. It is only itself as drawing together into its own limitation the larger whole in which it find itself. Conversely it is only itself by lending its aspects to this same environment in which it finds itself. (p. 94)

Ecologists have a saying: "You cannot do just one thing." Many of our actions, motivated by a desire to improve the quality of human life, have, to our detriment, caused unexpected consequences because we failed to recognize the essential interrelatedness of all things. "Man's first realization that he was not identical with nature" was a crucial step in evolution, writes Bohm,[13] "because it made possible a kind of autonomy in his thinking, which allowed him to go beyond the immediately given limits of nature, first in his imagination, and ultimately in his practical work." Realization that our freedom of choice is "bounded by the limits of compatibility with the dynamic structure of the whole" (p. 75)[11] and must "remain within the limits of natural systems values" (p. 107)[11] is yet another crucial step in evolution. "Not until man accepts his dependency on nature and puts himself in place as part of it," writes Iltis,[14] "not until then does man put man first. This is the greatest paradox of human ecology."

A human being is both a hierarchical system (composed of subsystems such as organs, cells, and enzyme systems) and a component of supra-individual, hierarchical systems (populations, species, ecosystems, cultural systems). Man is therefore a set within a hierarchical system of sets. "In hierarchies a given set must be described not only for itself but in terms both of what is within it, and what it is within."[15] Because science up to now has been strongly reductionist, we know more about the systems that make up our bodies and our cells than we do about those that transcend our individual lives — the evolutionary, ecologic, and social "wholes" of which we are "parts."

In an evolutionary sense, the life that animates us has existed in an unbroken line of descent, in numerous forms adapted to myriad environments, since life first appeared on earth some 3 billion years ago. Beside life, our ancestry extends back through billions of years of molecular change to the nuclei of former stars. Here the elements necessary for life were built up from hydrogen, the simplest and most abundant element in the universe. Beyond primordial hydrogen, our ancestral roots become lost in a profound mystery — the beginning of things, the origin of the universe of matter, energy, space, and time.

In an ecologic sense, our existence depends upon the proper functioning of the earth's present ecosystem. In the course of cosmic evolution the forces of matter and energy produced a planet fit to support life. In the course of biologic evolution, the activities of living things produced an environment fit to support human life. The day-to-day maintenance of our "life-support system" depends on the functional interaction of countless interdependent biotic and physiochemical factors. The movement of ocean currents and the activity of soil microbes are as essential to our existence as the oxygen we breathe.

In a social sense, we are as much a product of our culture as of our genes. "We are not ourselves only," writes Wells,[16] "We are also part of human experience and thought." We possess no greater innate intelligence, artistic skill, or emotional feeling than

did our prehistoric predecessors, who painted vivid images on cave walls over 30,000 years ago. We are different from Cro-Magnon man because we are heirs to a greater store of knowledge collected by the human species over thousands of years of cultural evolution. In large measure, our personalities are determined by a collective consciousness which we can contribute to and which is itself evolving.

CULTURE, KNOWLEDGE, AND POWER

Once the evolutionary process produced a species with culture, it was inevitable that knowledge of nature would accrue to such a species at an accelerating pace. Culture represents a unique way of acquiring, storing, and transmitting knowledge about the world. Knowledge acquired by one generation may be transmitted to succeeding generations by the agency of social learning. While each newborn person must acquire cultural knowledge anew, the amount of cultural knowledge available to the social group tends to grow in a cumulative fashion. "Culture may die," writes Hawkins,[17] "as cells may; but death is not built into them, as it is into multicellular animals. And through cultures learning becomes cumulative, evolutionary."

A species that can learn from the experiences of its predecessors can, potentially, build new knowledge upon an ever-expanding base. Cumulative knowledge provides man, the cultural species, with ever-increasing power to exploit nature and, as a result, he is a great biological success. The human species successfully occupies a greater variety of habitats, over a greater geographic range, with greater numbers, than any other species. Man is recognized as the latest dominant type in a succession of dominant types which emerged during the process of evolution, and represents the first time a species, and not a group of species, has achieved world dominance.

In acquiring his present position of dominance, the human species has radically reshaped the face of nature. "Whole landscapes are now occupied by man-dominated (and in part man-created) faunas and floras."[18] For the first time in earth's evolution, one species can genetically manipulate other species to their detriment, but to its own advantage. Darwin (p. 46) remarks:

One of the most remarkable features in our domesticated races is that we see in them adaptation, not indeed to the animal's or plant's own good, but to man's use or fancy.[4]

Maize (*Zea mays*) is a species which was molded into an artifact by our prehistoric ancestors. It is unable to survive in nature without man's intervention. Maize was the agricultural base of the great pre-Columbian civilizations of the New World. European colonists encountered it almost everywhere in America, but they found it only in cultivation. The "ear" or pistillate inflorescence of maize was modified by prehistoric man into a botanical monstrosity. There is "no natural way by which the grains can be detached from the cob, escape from the husks, and be dispersed." When the entire ear falls to the ground, "the germinating grains produce a compact cluster of seedlings, none of which has much chance to survive."[19]

Man's ability to exploit nature has been limited by the amount of energy available to the species. For most of human history, energy for man's activities came exclusively from the consumption of plants and animals. "The earliest culture systems developed techniques of hunting, fishing, trapping, collecting, gathering, etc. as means of exploiting the plant and animal resources of nature" (p. 371).[20] The first quantum jump in the energy resources for culture building took place with the domestication of plants and animals. White asserts that a few thousand years after this event, "the great civilizations of antiquity . . . came quickly into being." The second quantum jump in the amount of energy available to man was the tapping of fossil fuel deposits of coal, oil, and natural gas. "The consequences of the fuel revolution," writes White (p. 373), "were in general much like those of the agricultural revolution: an increase in population, larger political units, bigger cities, an accumulation of wealth, a rapid development of the arts and sciences, in short, a rapid and extensive advance of culture as a whole."[20]

Creation of the Cathedral of Chartres or the Declaration of Independence required the existence of civilizations based on artificial ecosystems. Natural ecosystems have intrinsic value, but the realization of value in human evolution, a proper end for man, has depended upon their replacement by artificial systems, which produce more energy.

INEVITABLE CRISIS IN CULTURAL EVOLUTION

Aristotle[21] began his *Metaphysica* with the sentence: "All men by nature desire to know." Throughout history, in spite of prophetic warnings that "knowledge increaseth sorrow," the fund of knowledge available to the human species has continued to expand. Major milestones in this process of knowledge accumulation include the invention of writing and the emergence of modern science.

Scientific knowledge has given us power to do miraculous things as well as monstrous things. We can eliminate diseases, transplant organs, explore the moon, while at the same time we can poison the earth's life-support system or engage in chemical, biological, and nuclear warfare. Nineteenth-century scientists saw the growth and application of scientific knowledge "leading infallibly upward to an empyrean noon hour for mankind," writes Monod,[22] "whereas what we see opening before us today is an abyss of darkness."

We live at a time in human history when the knowledge crisis has become acute. Our current knowledge enables us to "move mountains," but we are still ignorant about whether to do so would be in our best interest. Our collective knowledge of nature has outgrown our collective wisdom, which Potter (p. 1) defines as the "knowledge of how to use knowledge for man's survival and for improvement in the quality of life."[5]

In our frustration we sometimes blame science and technology or a particular ideology for our problems, or we wish that evolution had taken a different direction. If, however, modern society were wiped out and we were to begin again with our paleolithic ancestors, cultural evolution would inevitably lead to a similar knowledge crisis even though its course and time of development would be different. The knowledge crisis is one that every cultural species on every inhabitable planet in the universe must surmount at a point in its evolution, or become extinct. George Wald once remarked in a lecture that it took the planet earth 4.5 billion years to discover that it was 4.5 billion years old and he added: "Having got to that point . . . have we got much longer?"

MAN'S THREAT TO HIS OWN SURVIVAL

Whitehead[12] writes:

The key to the mechanism of evolution is the necessity for the evolution of a favorable environment, conjointly with the evolution of any specific type of enduring organisms of great permanence. Any physical object which by its influence deteriorates its environment, commits suicide. (p. 109)

Darwin[4] states in *The Origin of Species* (p. 78): "Never forget that every single organic being may be said to be striving to the utmost to increase its numbers," and Bertrand Russell[23] writes: "Every living thing is a sort of imperialist, seeking to transform as much as possible of its environment into itself and its seed." Man's unprecedented power to exploit nature has been used in part to improve the quality of human life, but also in part to transform as much as possible of the environment into ever more human beings. The latter process in our time threatens to undermine the former. George Wald[24] supposes that "man is the first living species, animal or plant, on this planet that has ever been threatened by its own reproductive success."

The maximization of reproductive potential is, from the biological point of view, in the best interest of most species. This was true for man throughout most of his history. In a world with small human populations at the mercy of environmental vicissitudes, with vast areas of unoccupied space and great stores of untapped resources, the biblical injunction, "Be fruitful and multiply and subdue the earth," had adaptive value and was in the species' best interest, but in the modern world such an injunction is an anachronism.

Negative feedback from the environment has done more to convince us of the essential interrelatedness of things than the prophetic preachments of philosophers ever could do. Unlimited growth of human numbers and human activities within the earth's limited ecosystem is a root cause of our ecological problems. The planet earth, except for a continuous input of solar energy, is essentially a closed system. Its supply of space, air, water, and other natural resources is definitely limited. Widespread pollution, scarcity of resources, and overcrowding are telltale signs that man is becoming maladapted to his niche.

Sinnott[25] writes: "Organisms often fail to act in such a way as to favor their survival." The production of ever more human biomass at the expense of ever greater environmental degradation is anti-anthropocentric in that it is maladaptive for the species. Sinnott continues: "Natural selection . . . preserves individuals which tend to react in a favorable way, which have 'purposes' that are conducive to successful life and survival, which 'want' the right things." The same could be said for populations, species, and cultures.

In order to survive as individuals and as a species we must choose to do the things which will preserve our "life-support system." However, to be anthropocentric is not to seek merely for biological survival. Man is not only an evolving biological entity, but an evolving cultural one as well. Eisenberg[26] asks: "Is mere perpetuation of the species, without concern for the quality of life, a sufficient criterion for man, even if it has been so for nature?" Our greatest danger is not that the human species will become extinct, which is unlikely to occur in the foreseeable future, but that the cultural values that make us human will become extinct.

The "ecological crisis" is basically a crisis in human evolution. Modern man stands at a crossroads. Continued geometric growth in human numbers, consumption of resources, and pollution of environments will propel mankind down a road of diminished options. A short way down this road, a point will be reached where the only alternative to extinction will be the regimented ant-heap. This is a process of evolutionary retrogression in which higher, emergent values are destroyed on behalf of the fundamental value of biological survival.

It is anthropocentric to value the factors that make us uniquely human, to seek to preserve and enhance such factors and to counter antihuman forces which threaten to diminish or destroy them. Nature outside of man will not act to preserve human values: it is our responsibility alone.

PARTICIPATION IN OUR OWN EVOLUTION

If all of man's actions were determined, he could not hope to constructively affect the course of human evolution by conscious intent, even if he were to conclude that its direction is inimical to personal freedom and human values. He could only hope to "fathom the direction of the process" in order to "make it less painful by accepting it rather than fighting it" (p. 355).[20] In this view, since man cannot direct change toward human purposes, his only recourse is to endlessly adjust human purposes to accommodate purposeless change.

The dismal portrayal of man as a passive entity in an evolutionary drama totally dominated by the environment is only one side of the evolutionary process. Evolution is more than the molding of entities by their surroundings. It also involves the ability of entities to interact with, adapt to, and change environments in creative, intelligent, and novel ways.

Man, because of his power of projection, has greater potential for affecting his own evolution than any other species. He is the only species, as far as is known, with the capacity to project purposes (goal-ideas), which arise in his mind from hopes, fantasies, and dreams about the future, and then proceed to work toward their realization. Birch[27] writes: "Possibilities are unseen realities. So far as our human lives are concerned they are potent causes that guide and transform our lives." Thus, the image of the future that man adopts is not merely an illusion, but an element in the chain of causality.

Birth, death, and reproduction are common to all life, but man, because he is capable of reflection and of planning his own actions, does not blindly respond to nature like other organisms: he assimilates and transforms nature and invests it with a meaning and intelligible moral value (p. 40).[28] "We cannot recapture the animal security of instinct," writes Teilhard de Chardin (p. 44).[28] "Because, in becoming men, we have acquired the power of looking to the future and assessing the value of things. We cannot

do nothing, since our very refusal to decide is a decision in itself."

FAITH IN THE POTENTIALITIES OF MANKIND

Man is not the measure of all things. He is not the center of the universe, nor the source of all value, nor the culmination of terrestrial evolution. Nevertheless, he is "the present crest of the evolutionary wave" (p. 237),[28] the entity in which the evolutionary trends of greater organizational complexity and greater consciousness have their most advanced development. It is in human evolution that the higher values of truth, justice, love, and beauty have their greatest expression. Further progress toward the realization of higher states of these values, if it is to occur at all, must develop in and through man. He is the key not only to his own survival, but to the survival and furtherance of values of cosmic significance.

In order to influence evolution in wise and responsible ways, we must strive for an ever fuller understanding of our relationship to greater wholes — society, nature, and ultimately to the primary source of order and value in the world. Personal identification with greater wholes is essential to the discovery of our own wholeness. An entity is only itself, according to Whitehead, "as drawing together into its own limitation the larger whole in which it finds itself. Conversely it is only itself by lending its aspects to this same environment in which it finds itself" (p. 94).[12]

Effective participation in our own evolution requires not only that we establish a harmonious relationship to larger wholes, but, in addition, that we affirm the human phenomenon to be a vitally significant process in its own right and our individual selves to be holistic centers "of spontaneity and self-creation contributing distinctively to the world."[29]

Teilhard de Chardin (p. 296) saw, as a possibility, "mankind falling suddenly out of love with its own destiny. This disenchantment would be conceivable, and indeed inevitable," he writes, "if as a result of growing reflection we came to believe that our end could only be collective death in an hermetically sealed world."[28] Boulding[30] concurs: "An ideology which states that the world is essentially meaningless but that we ought to strive, suffer and fight for it is unlikely to be powerful because of the essential contradictions among its components. If an interpretation of history says the world is meaningless, then our value system is likely to be pure hedonism— 'Eat, drink and be merry, for tomorrow we die'—or else one of apathy or stoic resignation."

Unbridled self-indulgence on the part of one generation without regard to future ones is the modus operandi of biological evolution and may be regarded as rational behavior. Heilbroner[31] asks: "On what private, 'rational' considerations, after all, should we make sacrifices now to ease the lot of generations whom we will never live to see?" If man, with his extraordinary power to multiply, consume, and pollute, seeks only to maximize short-term gain, global disaster will result in the very near future. The only possible answer to the above question, according to Heilbroner, "lies in our capacity to form a collective bond of identity with future generations." To do so is to affirm that the human enterprise has value which transcends our individual lives.

An anthropocentric faith in mankind affirms that we are not isolated monads acting out absurd roles within a meaningless context, but that we are essential elements of a meaningful whole and that our individual acts are vitally significant to the self-actualization of the process of human evolution itself and to the enhancement of value in the world.

SUMMARY

Anthropocentrism is proposed as a valid and necessary point of view for mankind to adopt for consideration of his place in nature. Our current ecological problems do not stem from an anthropocentric attitude per se, but from one too narrowly conceived. Anthropocentrism is consistent with a philosophy that affirms the essential interrelatedness of things and that values all items in nature since no event is without some effect on wholes of which we are parts. The ecological crisis is viewed as an inevitable crisis in human evolution. Through cultures knowledge becomes cumulative. A crisis occurs when our knowledge of nature, which determines our power to exploit nature, exceeds our knowledge of how to use

knowledge for our own survival and for improvement in the quality of our lives. An anthropocentric belief in the value, meaningfulness, and creative potential of the human phenomenon is considered a necessary motivating factor to participatory evolution which, in turn, may be requisite to the future survival of the human species and its cultural values.

NOTES

1. Xenophon, *Memorabilia and Oeconomicus* (Harvard University Press, Cambridge, MA, 1959), p. 299.
2. G. G. Simpson, *This View of Life* (Harcourt, Brace & World, New York, 1964), p. 101.
3. C. Lyell, *Principles of Geology* (Kay, Jun, and Brother, Philadelphia, 1837), vol. 1, p. 512.
4. C. Darwin, *The Origin of Species* (Doubleday, Garden City, NY, 1872 ed.).
5. V. R. Potter, *Bioethics* (Prentice Hall, Englewood Cliffs, NJ, 1971).
6. G. G. Simpson, *The Meaning of Evolution* (Yale University Press, New Haven, CT, 1949), p. 286.
7. L. White, Jr., *Science* 155, 1203–07 (1967).
8. D. S. Jordan, quoted in H. M. Smith, *Biologist* 52, 56 (1970).
9. J. Huxley, *The Human Crisis* (University of Washington Press, Seattle, 1963), p. 24.
10. C. Birch, *Zygon* 8, 255 (1973).
11. E. Laszlo, *The Systems View of the World* (Braziller, New York, 1972).
12. A. N. Whitehead, *Science and the Modern World* (Macmillan, New York, 1925).
13. D. Bohm, *The Van Leer Jerusalem Foundation Series* (Humanities Press, New York, 1973), p. 18.
14. H. H. Iltis, *BioScience* 20, 820 (1970).
15. C. Grobstein, in *Hierarchy Theory,* H. H. Pattee, ed. (Braziller, New York, 1973), p. 31.
16. H. G. Wells, in *Living Philosophies* (Simon & Schuster, New York, 1931), p. 83.
17. D. Hawkins, *The Language of Nature* (Freeman, San Francisco, 1964), p. 276.
18. E. Anderson, *Smithson. Inst. Annu. Rep.* (1956), p. 461.
19. P. Weatherwax, *Indian Corn in Old America* (Macmillan, New York, 1954), p. 179.

20. L. White, *The Science of Culture* (Farrar & Straus, New York, 1949), pp. 371–73.

21. Aristotle, *The Works of Aristotle,* vol. 8. *Metaphysica,* W. D. Ross, transl. (Clarendon, Oxford, ed. 2, 1928), p. 980a.

22. J. Monod, *Chance and Necessity* (Knopf, New York, 1971), p. 170.

23. B. Russell, *Philosophy* (Norton, New York, 1927), p. 27.

24. G. Wald, *Zygon* 5, 168 (1970).

25. E. W. Sinnott, *Cell and Psyche* (Harper & Row, New York, 1961), pp. 82–83.

26. L. Eisenberg, *Science* 176, 126 (1972).

27. C. Birch, *J. Am. Acad. Rel.* 40, 158 (1972).

28. P. Teilhard de Chardin, *The Future of Man* (Harper & Row, New York, 1964).

29. I. G. Barbour, *Issues in Science and Religion* (Prentice Hall, Englewood Cliffs, NJ, 1966), p. 131.

30. K. E. Boulding, *The Meaning of the Twentieth Century* (Harper & Row, New York, 1965), p. 163.

31. R. L. Heilbroner, *An Inquiry into the Human Prospect* (Norton, New York, 1974), p. 115.

DISCUSSION TOPICS

1. Summarize the reasoning Murdy uses to support his position that the only reasonable environmental ethic is an enlightened self-interest in which we affirm human value, work for its good, and plan for its future and long-term survival.

2. Murdy claims that all species behave purposefully in terms of their own or their species' survival and that those that have failed to do so have become extinct. Do you agree with this idea? Explain your reasoning.

3. Some might argue that Murdy's position is more concerned with the practical issue of human survival than with questions of moral right and wrong. Do you agree? Can you and, if so, how would you separate these issues? Explain your reasoning.

4. Do you agree with Murdy that survival of such higher values as truth, justice, beauty, and love justifies doing what is necessary to ensure human survival? Explain your reasoning.

READING 33

The Golden Rule — A Proper Scale for Our Environmental Crisis

Stephen Jay Gould

Stephen Jay Gould (1941–2002) was an evolutionary biologist at Harvard University. He and Niles Eldredge proposed the idea of punctuated equilibrium, a modification of the theory of evolution, which holds that most new species arise relatively quickly (over geological time), rather than through the slow, gradual accumulation of modifications.

In an article from Natural History, *Gould disputes two linked arguments: that humans live in a fragile world at serious risk to disruption from human impacts, and that we must learn to become stewards of the planet to prevent further destruction. He argues that human impact is greatly overrated, particularly on a geological time scale, and that humans have much less importance as a species than we would like to think. However, Gould acknowledges that over the short term, humans could be quite self-destructive. Rather than stewardship, Gould advocates an environmental ethic based on enlightened self-interest and patterned after the Golden Rule: He believes that humans ought to treat nature as they would want to be treated by nature.*

Patience enjoys a long pedigree of favor. Chaucer pronounced it "an heigh vertu, certeyn" ("The Franklin's Tale"), while the New Testament had already made a motto of the Old Testament's most famous embodiment: "Ye have heard of the patience of Job" (James 5:11). Yet some cases seem so extended in diligence and time that another factor beyond sheer endurance must lie behind the wait. When Alberich, having lost the Ring of the Nibelungen fully three operas ago, shows up in act 2 of *Götterdämmerung* to advise his son Hagen on strategies for recovery, we can hardly suppress a flicker of admiration for this otherwise unlovable character. (I happen to adore Wagner, but I do recognize that a wait through nearly all the *Ring* cycle would be, to certain unenlightened folks, the very definition of eternity in Hades.)

Patience of this magnitude usually involves a deep understanding of a fundamental principle, central to my own profession of geology but all too rarely grasped in daily life—the effects of scale. Phenomena unfold on their own appropriate scales of space and time and may be invisible in our myopic world of dimensions assessed by comparison with human height and times metered by human life spans. So much of the accumulating importance at earthly scales—the results of geological erosion, evolutionary changes in lineages—is invisible by the measuring rod of a human life. So much that matters to particles in the microscopic world of molecules—the history of a dust grain subject to Brownian motion, the fate of shrunken people in *Fantastic Voyage* or *Inner Space*—either averages out to stability at our scale or simply stands below our limits of perception.

It takes a particular kind of genius or deep understanding to transcend this most pervasive of all conceptual biases and to capture a phenomenon by grasping a proper scale beyond the measuring rods of our own world. Alberich and Wotan know that pursuit of the Ring is dynastic or generational, not personal. William of Baskerville (in Umberto Eco's *Name of the Rose*) solves his medieval mystery because he alone understands that, in the perspective of centuries, the convulsive events of his own day (the dispute between papacies of Rome and Avignon) will be forgotten, while the only surviving copy of a book by Aristotle may influence millennia. Architects of medieval cathedrals had to frame satisfaction on scales beyond their own existence, for they could not live to witness the completion of their designs.

May I indulge in a personal anecdote on the subject of scale? As a child, I loved to memorize facts but rebelled at those I deemed unimportant (baseball stats were in, popes of Rome and kings of England out). In sixth grade, I had to memorize the sequence of land acquisitions that built America. I could see the rationale for learning about the Louisiana Purchase and the Mexican Cession—since they added big chunks to our totality. But I remember balking, and publicly challenging the long-suffering Ms. Stack, at the Gadsden Purchase of 1853. Why did I have to know about a sliver of southern Arizona and New Mexico?

Now I am finally hoist by my own petard (blown up by my own noxious charge, according to the etymologies). After a lifetime of complete nonimpact by the Gadsden Purchase, I have become unwittingly embroiled in a controversy about a tiny bit of territory within this smallest of American growing points. A little bit of a little bit; so much for effects of scale and the penalties of blithe ignorance.

The case is a classic representative of a genre (environmentalists versus developers) made familiar in recent struggles to save endangered populations—the snail darter of a few years back, the northern spotted owl versus timber interests (decided, properly in my view, for the birds on the day that I write this essay, June 2, 1990). The University of Arizona, with the backing of an international consortium of astronomers, wishes to build a complex of telescopes atop Mount Graham in southeastern Arizona (part of the Gadsden Purchase). But the old-growth spruce-fir habitat on the mountaintop forms the heart of the range for *Tamiasciurus hudonicus grahamensis,* the Mount Graham red squirrel—a distinct subspecies that lives nowhere else and that forms the southernmost population of the entire species. The population has already been reduced to some 100 survivors, and destruction of several acres of spruce-fir growth (to build the telescopes) within the 700 or so remaining acres of best habitat might well administer a *coup de grâce* to this fragile population.

I cannot state an expert opinion on details of this controversy (I have already confessed my ignorance about everything involving the Gadsden Purchase and its legacy). Many questions need to be answered. Is the population already too small to survive in any case? If not, could the population, with proper management, coexist with the telescopes in the remaining habitat? (Environmentalists fear change of microclimate as much or more than loss of acreage. Reduction of forest canopy will increase wind and sun, producing a drop in humidity. The squirrels survive winter by storing unopened cones in food caches beside trees. If humidity falls, cones may dry out and open, causing loss of seeds and destruction of food.)

I do not think that, practically or morally, we can defend a policy of saving every distinct local population of organisms. I can cite a good rationale for the preservation of species — for each species is a unique and separate natural object that, once lost, can never be reconstituted. But subspecies are distinct local populations of species with broader geographical ranges. Subspecies are dynamic, interbreedable, and constantly changing; what then are we saving by declaring them all inviolate? Thus, I confess that I do not agree with all arguments advanced by defenders of the Mount Graham red squirrel. One leaflet, for example, argues: "The population has been recently shown to have a fixed, homozygous allele which is unique in Western North America." Sorry folks. I will stoutly defend species, but we cannot ask for the preservation of every distinctive gene, unless we find a way to abolish death itself (for many organisms carry unique mutations).

No, I think that for local populations of species with broader ranges, the brief for preservation must be made on a case by case basis, not a general principle of preservation (lest the environmental movement ultimately lose popular support for trying to freeze a dynamic evolutionary world in *status quo*). On this proper basis of individual merit, I am entirely persuaded that the Mount Graham red squirrel should be protected and the astronomical observatory built elsewhere — and for two reasons.

First, the red squirrel itself: the Mount Graham red is an unusually interesting local population within an important species. It is isolated from all other populations and forms the southernmost extreme of the species' range. Such peripheral populations, living in marginal habitats, are of special interest to students of evolution.

Second, the habitat: environmentalists continually face the political reality that support and funding can be won for soft, cuddly, and "attractive" animals, but not for slimy, grubby, and ugly creatures (of potentially greater evolutionary interest and practical significance) or for habitats. This situation has led to the practical concept of "umbrella" or "indicator" species — surrogates for a larger ecological entity worthy of preservation. Thus, the giant panda (really quite a boring and ornery creature despite its good looks) raises money to save the remaining bamboo forests of China (and a plethora of other endangered creatures with no political clout);

the northern spotted owl has just rescued some magnificent stands of old-growth giant cedars, Douglas fir, and redwoods (and I say hosanna); and the Mount Graham red squirrel may save a rare and precious habitat of extraordinary evolutionary interest.

The Pinaleno Mountains, reaching 10,720 feet at Mount Graham, are an isolated fault-block range separated from others by alluvial and desert valleys that dip to less than 3,000 feet in elevation. The high peaks of the Pinalenos contain an important and unusual fauna for two reasons. First, they harbor a junction of two biogeographic provinces: the Nearctic, or northern, by way of the Colorado Plateau, and the Neotropical, or southern, via the Mexican Plateau. The Mount Graham red squirrel (a northern species) can live this far south because high elevations reproduce the climate and habitat found near sea level in the more congenial north. Second, and more important to evolutionists, the old-growth spruce-fir habitats on the high peaks of the Pinalenos are isolated "sky islands" — 10,000-year-old remnants of a habitat more widely spread over the region of the Gadsden Purchase during the height of the last Ice Age. In evolutionary terms, these isolated pieces of habitat are true islands — patches of more northern microclimate surrounded by southern desert. They are functionally equivalent to bits of land in the ocean. Consider the role that islands (like the Galápagos) have played both in developing the concepts of evolutionary theory and in acting as cradles of origin (through isolation) or vestiges of preservation for biological novelties.

Thus, whether or not the telescopes will drive the Mount Graham red squirrel to extinction (an unsettled question well outside my area of expertise), the sky islands of the Pinalenos are precious habitats that should not be compromised. Let the Mount Graham red squirrel, so worthy of preservation in its own right, also serve as an indicator species for the unique and fragile habitat that it occupies.

But why should I, a confirmed eastern urbanite who has already disclaimed all concern for the Gadsden Purchase, choose to involve myself in the case of the Mount Graham red squirrel? The answer, unsurprisingly, is that I have been enlisted — involuntarily, unawares, and on the wrong side to boot. I am simply fighting mad, and fighting back.

The June 7, 1990, *Wall Street Journal* ran a pro-development, antisquirrel opinion piece by Michael D. Copeland (identified as "executive director of the Political Economy Research Center in Bozeman, Montana") under the patently absurd title: "No Red Squirrels? Mother Nature May Be Better Off." (I can at least grasp, while still rejecting, the claim that nature would be no worse off if the squirrel died, but I am utterly befuddled at how anyone could argue that the squirrels inflict a positive harm upon the mother of us all!) In any case, Copeland misunderstood my writings in formulating a supposedly scientific argument for his position.

Now, scarcely a day goes by when I do not read a misrepresentation of my views (usually by creationists, racists, or football fans, in order of frequency). My response to nearly all misquotation is the effective retort of preference: utter silence. (Honorable intellectual disagreement should always be addressed; misquotation should be ignored, when possible and politically practical.) I make an exception in this case because Copeland cited me in the service of a classic false argument—indeed, the standard, almost canonical misuse of my profession of paleontology in debates about extinction. Paleontologists have been enlisted again and again, in opposition to our actual opinions and in support of attitudes that most of us regard as anathema, to uphold arguments by developers about the irrelevance (or even, in this case, the benevolence) of modern anthropogenic extinction. This standard error is a classic example of failure to understand the importance of scale—thus I return to the premise and structure of my introductory paragraphs (did you really think that I waffled on so long about scale only so that I could talk about the Gadsden Purchase?).

Paleontologists do discuss the inevitability of extinction for all species—in the long run and on the broad scale of geological time. We are fond of saying that 99 percent or more of all species that ever lived are now extinct. (My colleague Dave Raup often opens talks on extinction with a zinging one-liner: "To a first approximation, all species are extinct.") We do therefore identify extinction as the normal fate of species. We also talk a lot—more of late since new data have made the field so exciting—about the mass extinctions that punctuate the

history of life from time to time. We do discuss the issue of eventual "recovery" from these extinctions, in the sense that life does rebuild or surpass its former diversity after several million years. Finally, we do allow that mass extinctions break up stable faunas and, in this sense, permit or even foster evolutionary innovations well down the road (including the dominance of mammals and the eventual origin of humans, following the death of dinosaurs).

From this set of statements about extinction in the fullness of geological time (on scales of millions of years), some apologists for development have argued that extinction at any scale (even of local populations within years or decades) poses no biological worry but, on the contrary, must be viewed as a comfortable part of an inevitable natural order. Or so Copeland states:

> Suppose we lost a species. How devastating would that be? "Mass extinctions have been recorded since the dawn of paleontology," writes Harvard paleontologist Stephen Gould . . . the most severe of these occurred approximately 250 million years ago . . . with an estimated 96 percent extinction of species, says Mr. Gould. . . . There is general agreement among scientists that today's species represent a small proportion of all those that have ever existed—probably less than 1 percent. This means that more than 99 percent of all species ever living have become extinct.

From these facts, largely irrelevant to red squirrels on Mount Graham, Copeland makes inferences about the benevolence of extinction in general (although the argument applies only to geological scales):

> Yet, in spite of these extinctions, both Mr. Gould and University of Chicago paleontologist Jack Sepkoski say that the actual number of living species has probably increased over time. [True, but not as a result of mass extinctions, despite Copeland's next sentence.] The "niches" created by extinctions provide an opportunity for a vigorous development of new species. . . . Thus, evolutionary history appears to have been characterized by millions of species extinctions and subsequent increases in species numbers. Indeed, by attempting to preserve

species living on the brink of extinction, we may be wasting time, effort and money on animals that will disappear over time, regardless of our efforts.

But all will "disappear over time, regardless of our efforts"—millions of years from now for most species if we don't interfere. The mean life span of marine invertebrate species lies between 5 and 10 million years; terrestrial vertebrate species turn over more rapidly, but still average in the millions. By contrast, *Homo sapiens* may be only 250,000 years old or so and may enjoy a considerable future if we don't self-destruct. Similarly, recovery from mass extinction takes its natural measure in millions of years—as much as 10 million or more for fully rekindled diversity after major catastrophic events.

These are the natural time scales of evolution and geology on our planet. But what can such vastness possibly mean for our legitimately parochial interest in ourselves, our ethnic groups, our nations, our cultural traditions, our bloodlines? Of what conceivable significance to us is the prospect of recovery from mass extinction 10 million years down the road if our entire species, not to mention our personal family lineage, has so little prospect of surviving that long?

Capacity for recovery at geological scales has no bearing whatever upon the meaning of extinction today. We are not protecting Mount Graham red squirrels because we fear for global stability in a distant future not likely to include us. We are trying to preserve populations and environments because the comfort and decency of our present lives, and those of fellow species that share our planet, depend upon such stability. Mass extinctions may not threaten distant futures, but they are decidedly unpleasant for species in the throes of their power (particularly if triggered by such truly catastrophic events as extraterrestrial impact). At the appropriate scale of our lives, we are just a species in the midst of such a moment. And to say that we should let the squirrels go (at our immediate scale) because all species eventually die (at geological scales) makes about as much sense as arguing that we shouldn't treat an easily curable childhood infection because all humans are ultimately and inevitably mortal. I love geological time—a wondrous and expansive notion that sets the foundation of my chosen profession, but such immensity is not the proper scale of my personal life.

The same issue of scale underlies the main contributions that my profession of paleontology might make to our larger search for an environmental ethic. This decade, a prelude to the millennium, is widely and correctly viewed as a turning point that will lead either to environmental perdition or stabilization. We have fouled local nests before and driven regional faunas to extinction, but we have never been able to unleash planetary effects before our current concern with ozone holes and putative global warming. In this context, we are searching for proper themes and language to express our environmental worries.

I don't know that paleontology has a great deal to offer, but I would advance one geological insight to combat a well-meaning, but seriously flawed (and all too common), position and to focus attention on the right issue at the proper scale. Two linked arguments are often promoted as a basis for an environmental ethic:

1. That we live on a fragile planet now subject to permanent derailment and disruption by human intervention;
2. That humans must learn to act as stewards for this threatened world.

Such views, however well intentioned, are rooted in the old sin of pride and exaggerated self-importance. We are one among millions of species, stewards of nothing. By what argument could we, arising just a geological microsecond ago, become responsible for the affairs of a world 4.5 billion years old, teeming with life that has been evolving and diversifying for at least three-quarters of that immense span? Nature does not exist for us, had no idea we were coming, and doesn't give a damn about us. Omar Khayyám was right in all but his crimped view of the earth as battered when he made his brilliant comparison of our world to an eastern hotel:

> Think, in this battered Caravanserai
>   Whose Portals are alternate
>   Night and Day,
> How Sultan after Sultan with his Pomp
>   Abode his destined Hour, and
>   went his way.

This assertion of ultimate impotence could be countered if we, despite our late arrival, now held power over the planet's future (argument number one above). But we don't, despite popular misperception of our might. We are virtually powerless over the earth at our planet's own geological time scale. All the megatonnage in our nuclear arsenals yield but one ten-thousandth the power of the asteroid that might have triggered the Cretaceous mass extinction. Yet the earth survived that larger shock and, in wiping out dinosaurs, paved the road for the evolution of large mammals, including humans. We fear global warming, yet even the most radical model yields an earth far cooler than many happy and prosperous times of a prehuman past. We can surely destroy ourselves, and take many other species with us, but we can barely dent bacterial diversity and will surely not remove many million species of insects and mites. On geological scales, our planet will take good care of itself and let time clear the impact of any human malfeasance. The earth need never seek a henchman to wreak Henry's vengeance upon Thomas à Becket: "Who will free me from this turbulent priest?" Our planet simply waits.

People who do not appreciate the fundamental principle of appropriate scales often misread such an argument as a claim that we may therefore cease to worry about environmental deterioration — just as Copeland argued falsely that we need not fret about extinction. But I raise the same counterargument. We cannot threaten at geological scales, but such vastness is entirely inappropriate. We have a legitimately parochial interest in our own lives, the happiness and prosperity of our children, the suffering of our fellows. The planet will recover from nuclear holocaust, but we will be killed and maimed by the billions, and our cultures will perish. The earth will prosper if polar icecaps melt under a global greenhouse, but most of our major cities, built at sea level as ports and harbors, will founder, and changing agricultural patterns will uproot our populations.

We must squarely face an unpleasant historical fact. The conservation movement was born, in large part, as an elitist attempt by wealthy social leaders to preserve wilderness as a domain for patrician leisure and contemplation (against the image, so to speak, of poor immigrants traipsing in hordes through the woods with their Sunday picnic bas-

kets). We have never entirely shaken this legacy of environmentalism as something opposed to immediate human needs, particularly of the impoverished and unfortunate. But the Third World expands and contains most of the pristine habitat that we yearn to preserve. Environmental movements cannot prevail until they convince people that clean air and water, solar power, recycling, and reforestation are best solutions (as they are) for human needs at human scales — and not for impossibly distant planetary futures.

I have a decidedly unradical suggestion to make about an appropriate environmental ethic — one rooted, with this entire essay, in the issue of appropriate human scale versus the majesty, but irrelevance, of geological time. I have never been much attracted to the Kantian categorical imperative in searching for an ethic — to moral laws that are absolute and unconditional and do not involve any ulterior motive or end. The world is too complex and sloppy for such uncompromising attitudes (and God help us if we embrace the wrong principle, and then fight wars, kill, and maim in our absolute certainty). I prefer the messier "hypothetical imperatives" that invoke desire, negotiation, and reciprocity. Of these "lesser," but altogether wiser and deeper, principles, one has stood out for its independent derivation, with different words but to the same effect, in culture after culture. I imagine that our various societies grope toward this principle because structural stability, and basic decency necessary for any tolerable life, demand such a maxim. Christians call this principle the "Golden Rule"; Plato, Hillel, and Confucius knew the same maxim by other names. I cannot think of a better principle based on enlightened self-interest. If we all treated others as we wish to be treated ourselves, then decency and stability would have to prevail.

I suggest that we execute such a pact with our planet. She holds all the cards and has immense power over us — so such a compact, which we desperately need but she does not at her own time scale, would be a blessing for us, and an indulgence for her. We had better sign the papers while she is still willing to make a deal. If we treat her nicely, she will keep us going for a while. If we scratch her, she will bleed, kick us out, bandage up, and go about her business at her planetary scale. Poor Richard told us that "necessity never made a good bargain," but the earth is kinder than human agents in the "art of the deal." She will uphold her end; we must now go and do likewise.

DISCUSSION TOPICS

1. How does Gould make the argument that we should not let a species (e.g., the Mount Graham red squirrel) become extinct, in light of the fact that over ninety-nine percent of all species have become extinct and all are expected to eventually do so?

2. Do you believe Gould is correct in his view that humans have much less importance over a long-term (geological) time scale than we would like to think? What reasons would you give to support or reject this position?

3. Will a "Golden Rule" relationship with our planet work if only one side (humans) can consciously agree to the terms? Explain your reasoning.

READING 34

The Invented Landscape

Frederick Turner

Frederick Turner is a poet, writer, and philosopher of science. He is a founding professor of the School of Arts and Humanities at the University of Texas at Dallas. Turner was awarded the Levinson Poetry Prize; his recent books include The Culture of Hope *(1995),* Rebirth of Value *(1991), and* Beauty: The Value of Values *(1991).*

In a chapter from Beyond Preservation: Restoring and Inventing Landscapes *(1994), Turner defines four main currents of thought in the contemporary environmental movement: conservationism, preservationism, restorationism, and inventionism. He likens the tenets of traditional environmentalism to those of a theistic religion and proposes that contemporary environmentalism has unspoken principles of an ecological religion. Turner then develops a new, alterna-*

tive, natural philosophy (theology): inventionist ecology. He presents ten axioms he believes are a logical part of such a new philosophy. Finally, he challenges the reader to consider the notion of expanding such an inventionist ecology to other, dead planets, as human technology expands.

ENVIRONMENTALISM CLASSIFIED

Four main currents of thought can be detected within the ecology movement at the present time: the conservationist, the preservationist, the restorationist, and what might be called the inventionist. The first two are very familiar, the third less so, and the fourth is so unrecognized that it does not have a fixed name—perhaps this book will help to give it one.

Conservation sees nature as a vast resource, physical and spiritual, that must be wisely husbanded so that it may continue to yield a rich harvest for human beings. Preservation sees nature as of intrinsic value, the greater for being untouched by humankind, and seeks to keep it inviolate and unpolluted. Restoration, which I believe is presently the most intellectually exciting organized field of ecological philosophy, seeks to reconstruct classical ecosystems, and is based on an assumption that to do so is not only possible, given nature's own easy-going and flexible standards, but also an important part of the human role within nature.

The restorationist philosophy is not necessarily at odds with the goals of conservation or preservation. But its purpose is different from conservation inasmuch as, for the restorationist, nature is of intrinsic worth as well as being valuable for human uses. Though they agree on nature's intrinsic value, the restorationist's definition of nature is different from that of the preservationist: restoration holds that a restored landscape is no less natural—and may even be more natural in some senses—than an "untouched" one. All landscapes, as restorationists know by experience, are always already touched—if not by earlier human beings, then by the world-transforming activities of the species that constitute them, or by other natural interventions such as volcanic eruptions and meteor strikes. Nature is the process of everything interfering with—touching—everything else. Human beings, another natural species, are part of this process of irreversible change, but it is quite possible that termites have transformed the planet at least as much as have humans (they have had more time to do so, however). Because the evolutionary mechanism of life is reproduction with differences in each generation (in other words, a system of imperfect copying), there is nothing unnatural about a copy of prairie, if accurate enough. . . .

This essay has a task to sketch the outlines of a nascent ecological philosophy, one that for lack of a better name we have dubbed "inventionist.". . .

Inventionist ecology, to give a crude definition, maintains that it is both possible and desirable not only to conserve natural resources, preserve natural ecosystems, and restore natural landscapes, but also, when the occasion warrants and the knowledge is sufficient, to *create* new ecosystems, new landscapes, perhaps even new species. Inventionist ecology does not contradict the goals of conservation, preservation, and restoration: far from it. Conservation is simply rational common sense and the solid foundation for any human activity, though insufficient by itself either practically or philosophically. Preservation is necessary at least to maintain the library of genetic richness from which our work can grow; only when the librarians seek to stop the public from touching the books must we gently dissuade them. Restoration is totally in harmony with invention, and indeed invention cannot happen without the tools and understanding provided by restoration. Moreover, it could well be argued that restoration is a special form of invention, a form whose aesthetic, like that of Aristotelian drama, is imitative or mimetic.

Potentially at least, human civilization can be the restorer, propagator, and even creator of natural diversity, as well as its protector and preserver. This will come about as biological science and technology are perfected, and as the traditional ecological wisdoms embodied in ancient gardening and husbandry are rediscovered through the practice of ecological restoration, or "earth-keeping," as it is known. Thus we will go from being a net destroyer of biological information and a (larger) net creator of cultural information to being a net creator of both. The dream of inventionist ecology is that eventually we will propagate life into presently dead regions of the universe, and even assist in the development of entirely new species.

This formulation dictates the main questions of this essay. How can the creation of new landscapes and species be ethically justified? What occasions might warrant it? Are human beings capable of such an invention? How much knowledge is sufficient? What guides exist? Has it ever been done before?

In order to address these issues, first the rudiments of a comprehensive environmental philosophy must be developed. But environmentalism, dealing with the whole cosmos and the human place in it, is more than a philosophy; given the definition of the divine as ultimate concern, it is also a theology. Thus this essay will question the contemporary environmental theology, which is hostile to invention in such matters, and replace it with one that permits and even mandates inventionist ecology.

TENETS OF TRADITIONAL ENVIRONMENTALISM

If asked to state the goal of the environmental movement, a contemporary participant would probably say something like, "to promote a sustainable relationship between human beings and Nature." How could one object to such a formulation? Yet hidden in it is a set of assumptions that may paradoxically lie at the root of our present environmental crisis.

There is a close resemblance between this stated goal and a much older idea from the rationalistic theology of the modern West: that the goal of the moral life is to promote a sustainable relationship between human beings and God. Just replace God with Nature, and much of the environmental movement looks very like a church, though without the disadvantage of being separated by law from the state.

A brief digression into theology may help to make this point clear. The God of Christian theism is eternal, transcendent, perfect, and unchanging. Obedience to Him is true happiness. We human beings are inherently fallen and wicked in part, and thus a caste of priests is necessary, themselves under the control of an ecclesiastical organization, to discipline the population in the correct beliefs and religious practices. . . .

The environmentalist ethic has in effect replaced God with Nature; and the God it replaced was the

God of modern theism, the abstract, unchanging, emotionless, moralistic authority who dwells outside the universe and who, knowing all in advance, can never be surprised, or grow, or have a story. Very often the environmentalist's idea of nature retains these characteristics of the transcendent God. As the phrase goes, "It's not nice to fool Mother Nature." James Lovelock's Gaia hypothesis, which argues plausibly that in some sense the planet Earth is a sort of superorganism, perhaps like a giant polyp or colonial animal or coral reef, maintaining its own atmosphere, climate, and chemical environment, has supplied its more religious followers with a personal name for the new deity: Gaia. But the fact that the name and sex of the deity have changed does not mean that the new environmentalism is any less a religion.

I would like to make clear before I go any further that I believe that religion is a unique means of apprehending profound truths, values, and beauties in our experience that cannot be captured in any other way. I also am deeply sympathetic to many of the goals of contemporary environmentalism, and work for them myself. However, I believe that some fundamental errors in the new naturalistic religion can be corrected if we recognize the implications of a theology that places the divine within, rather than outside, the natural universe.

Many contemporary environmentalists would probably accept without much question certain assumptions that are essentially religious, though not yet recognized as such. These concepts already function in public policy, demonstrating possible exceptions to the separation of church and state, and would include the following—what we might call the unspoken principles of the ecological religion.

- The basic feature of Nature is homeostasis; there is a natural balance that is restored when it is disturbed, and a natural harmony. Nature in this view has an ideal state, which is perfect and should not be tampered with. (This is an unpacking of the central term "sustainable.")
- Happiness is doing the will of Nature. Human beings are evil and distorted creatures, filled with greed and the desire to dominate, an unnatural presence in the universe. If they are con-

verted, however, then they will find true happiness in going back to nature, in humble service to the environment. (This feature of the environmental movement is much like the doctrine of original sin and salvation.)
- Happiness for human beings is fundamentally stasis, an unchanging and secure state in which the future is more or less predictable. Change, especially swift change, is evil.
- Humans are different and separate from, and subordinate to, a transcendent Nature. (Here the environmentalist religion ignores the central scientific principle of evolution, which treats humans as a part of nature, though contemporary environmentalism is quite happy to use scientific research if it seems to prove the point of human destructiveness.)
- Human beings are no better and no more important than any other species. (The Christian doctrine of the equality of souls before God has been translated into a doctrine of the equality of species before Nature.) In a sense, this principle contradicts the previous one, in which human beings are uniquely wicked among species, and separate from Nature. The contradiction can be partly resolved by saying that in a state of nature, human beings are just another animal species; where we went wrong—where we "fell"—was in thinking ourselves better than the others. But the problem remains: why shouldn't it be natural for us to think ourselves better—and why shouldn't it be true?!
- An (unelected) community of environmentally conscious, morally refined, sober, devout, humble, and self-denying ecological Brahmins should interpret to the masses the will of Nature and direct them accordingly, chastising the merchant/industrial caste, humbling the warrior caste, and disciplining the farmer caste.

CRITIQUE OF THE TRADITIONAL FAITH

This creed stands or falls on whether nature really is as its believers maintain—eternal, unchanging, and so on—and whether human beings are indeed as the theory says they are. As far as I can make out, there are four main problems with what we might call the "ecotheist" creed.

The first is that nature is not and has not ever been static and unchanging. It is easy to demonstrate that nature is a process of irreversible changes at every level of the microcosm and the macrocosm, both in the world of living organisms and in the world in general.

Let us start with the world of life. Since life appeared on Earth about four billion years ago, the number of species has pretty steadily increased, with occasional episodes of mass extinctions. . . . It is not just the number of species that has increased over the lifetime of this planet, however; so too has the complexity, hierarchical organization, and neural development of the most highly organized species. Though many very primitive and simple species still exist, the range of development among the species is now much greater than in the past. Thus the ecotheist principle that nature is homeostatic is false for living creatures.

It is false also for the inanimate parts of nature. The universe at large has experienced a steady and irreversible increase in several crucial measures, including its size (it has been expanding since the Big Bang) and its age. . . . The complexity, sensitivity, and degree of freedom of even inanimate objects has increased: the definition of time required to describe a photon (which preexisted all the more complex forms of matter) is much simpler than that required to describe an atom, a molecule, a crystal, a bacterium, an animal, or a human being, each of which inhabits a more complex temporal environment than its predecessors. The amount of feedback or self-reference in the universe has increased irreversibly. The amount of information in the universe has increased. The universe has cooled down irreversibly and will continue to do so. Even the *rate* of all these changes has been changing irreversibly, and for some of them also unpredictably. . . .

Life is full of such processes; collectively they are called evolution. The air of the Earth was the result of catastrophic changes brought about by the evolution of photosynthetic organisms, which gradually "poisoned" the early terrestrial atmosphere with oxygen so that the ancient prokaryotic inhabitants of the planet could no longer survive and had to give up their places to new, more adaptable organisms that were our ancestors. The natural disasters that have punctuated the Earth's history, whether the result of gigantic volcanoes or meteor strikes, may well have speeded up the process of evolution. It is entirely possible that the increase in carbon dioxide in our atmosphere will cause an increase in plant metabolism and world precipitation, and lead to an age of unparalleled natural fertility and species proliferation rather than an age of ecological catastrophe. Only the faulty assumption that any change is unnatural makes us conclude that the greenhouse effect will be bad for the planet.

Thus the idea of "sustainability" and general homeostasis is a profoundly unnatural goal. The universe does not, except in certain temporary periods and places, sustain or maintain: it changes, improves, complexifies, sometimes destroys. Sexual reproduction, to take a good example, consists of a sophisticated and powerful mechanism to ensure that the genetic inheritance of a species changes irreversibly: it is a system to subvert and disrupt sustainability and maintainability. Organisms that clone themselves, and play it safe, are opting for sustainability; but it is the more advanced, sexually reproducing organisms, which allow their genetic codes to be reshuffled every generation, that have driven evolution. We human beings may still want the security of sustainability, but we should not invoke the authority of Nature to bring it about.

The philosophical error of assuming that nature is essentially unchanging has led to actual damage to ecosystems managed by well-meaning believers in natural homeostasis. The ecological scientist Daniel Botkin cites many examples in his book *Discordant Harmonies,* including the reduction of huge fertile nature preserves in Africa to semi-deserts by exploding elephant populations, managed by preservationist true believers who could not face the necessity to cull the elephant population. Another example is the way in which various different but equally erroneous notions of natural balance led to the recent destruction of large areas of Yellowstone National Park. Wiser managers of prairie preserves in the Midwest, like those William Jordan describes, have learned that a good prairie needs to be burned from time to time; fire, the destructive element, must be wielded by human beings if we would keep nature in the same state. A similar philosophical puzzle confronts the managers of Niagara Falls, who may need to turn the falls off for a time, while the natural undermining of the rocky scarp over which it flows is repaired with concrete!

Another problem with the idea of sustainability derives from the axiom that humans are happiest when in harmony with an unchanging natural world. But it is surely naive to assume that human happiness can consist in stasis and obedience. Elementary psychology tells us that we are sensation-seeking animals, and that our brains work upon a principle of habituation and fatigue; if we encounter the same stimulus for a period of time (say, a ticking clock) we very quickly discount it and cease to notice it. It is our nature—and the nature of many higher animals—to seek out new stimuli. Stasis is thus sensory deprivation, which is the most subtle and severe form of torture we know. Human happiness cannot consist of lack of change. . . .

A more sophisticated version of the environmentalist position has recently abandoned the usual praise of natural homeostasis and asserted that only in the wild, the wilderness areas, can Nature find its true freedom to evolve and develop, in its naturally irreversible and unpredictable way. This argument reverses the usual complaint against human culture, that it changes things too fast, and declares that human culture, by taming and domesticating Nature, robs it of its creative powers of metamorphosis. This is a serious and interesting position, and clearly holds some truth that should be incorporated into the wiser environmentalism that is the goal of this essay. Its imagination is limited, however. For is not the disturbing, horrifying, unpredictable, dangerous, and protean character of human culture and technology, like Max in Maurice Sendak's fable, the wildest thing of all, the true wilderness that lies beyond the edge of the tamer, more serene, and self-maintaining fields of the terrestrial ecology? Is not human culture, as compared to the rest of nature, like a sexually reproducing species surrounded by an ecology of clones?

This reflection leads us to the second major objection to the ecotheist cliché, that is serving us so usefully as a straw man: the distinction it draws between the human and the natural is patently false.

We are descended in a direct evolutionary line from natural animal species, and are ourselves a natural species. Our nature, certainly optimistic, transformative, activist, and bent on propagating itself, is not unlike that of other species, only more so. We are what nature has always been trying to be, so to speak. Nor can it be objected that the *speed* at which we transform ourselves and the world around us is unnatural. Higher animals evolve faster than do more primitive organisms, as these in turn do so faster than nonliving systems. If we take flexibility, complexity, hierarchical organization, and self-referentiality as the measure, we may define nature as acceleration. For us to slow down would, if we take nature to *date* as the model of what is natural, be unnatural.

Likewise, the greater self-awareness of human beings compared to other species must be seen in a context in which the other higher animals are more self-aware than lower animals and plants, life is more self-aware than matter (in that it contains a record and blueprint of its own structure in the sequence of its DNA), and matter is more "self-aware" than energy, as matter is energy bound to itself rather than flying off radially from itself at the speed of light. Thus humans also appear to be the closest approximation nature has found to its own direction and tendency. If human beings are what nature comes up with given the freest play of development and the richest and stablest environment of complexity and available energy, then we might rightly assume that if we want to know what nature is *really* like, we should look at ourselves.

Not that I am necessarily advocating a continuous indiscriminate acceleration of our activities; but any moratorium we call cannot honestly be claimed to be in the name of Nature. Nor am I denying the human fact of evil actions, both against other human beings and against the rest of nature. In the old religion that serves as the tacit model for some aspects of current environmentalism, that evil was explained by the Fall. But in that religion there was also a wisdom that called the Fall a *felix culpa,* a happy fault. The good of knowledge, freedom, and possibility of divine redemption came with the darker lapsarian [i.e., after the fall] consequences of death, guilt, and the propensity to sin. My claim is that nature itself, like ourselves, is fallen, is falling, and has always been falling, outward into the future from the initial explosion of the Big Bang; onward into more and more conscious, beautiful, tragic, complex, and conflicted forms of existence, away from the divine simplicities and stupor of the primal energy field.

Thus for good and ill we are in solidarity with the rest of nature; and though there may be a vaguely good moral intention to the injunction that humankind should live in harmony with nature, the idea is essentially incoherent. Perhaps one might take it as a slightly stretched metaphor, as a doctor might advise living in harmony with one's kidney or liver, or that our brain should live in harmony with our body.

The third objection that might be raised against the "ecotheist" position is that the notion of universal species equality is, on analysis, inconsistent. It should not really be necessary to argue whether a human being or an AIDS virus is more valuable, but we are forced to such measures by the assertions of some of the more extreme deep ecologists, who question our right to consider ourselves more important and valuable than other species, and thus to affect their destiny. This point looks reasonable if we think about whales, bears, and other animals with whom we can easily identify, but it leads to deep absurdities. . . .

One of the fundamental principles of nature is hierarchy, as the food chain, the delegation of control down the nervous system, and the branched subordination of functions within a given living organism amply illustrate. Though interdependence is another basic principle, it does not imply equality. A fox will bite off its own leg to escape a trap, choosing against the living cells of its leg and for the rest of its body. The brain and the kidney may be interdependent, but any deep ecologist would rightly insist that his own kidney is subordinate to and less valuable than his brain, and would rightly demand of his surgeon that she sacrifice a kidney if necessary to save even a small piece of his brain.

Although the combination of ideas can cause cognitive dissonance in some minds, we humans are both part of nature, and superior to and more valuable than any other part; at the same time we are essentially dependent on the rest of nature, and the loss of any of its unique and beautiful forms is an absolute loss to us.

Our final objection is political. Any attempt by an ecological elite to impose Brahmanic control over the masses — over the merchant, warrior, and farmer castes, so to speak — is doomed to failure. In Eastern Europe the Communist party was just such an enlightened and refined elite, and indeed, as we are finding, it did help to keep down such atavistic tendencies as ethnic hatred. But all over the world those masses have sacrificed themselves, suffered, and died, to escape or overthrow this new form of priestly control. Moreover, the best-intentioned Brahmanic bureaucracy can be ecologically disastrous, as we have seen in the devastation left by iron-curtain industry in Poland and East Germany. Even the mild forms of state control over natural resources that we in the West have instituted can, especially when energized by ideology and the urge toward bureaucratic survival, paradoxically produce serious ecological damage, as in the case of the Forest Service and the public rangelands. There are more miles of Forest Service roads (which determine the service's budget) than of interstate highways.

To sum up, the formula "a sustainable relationship between human beings and Nature" is profoundly misleading. Nature does not sustain, but changes cumulatively, sometimes preserving earlier states while inventing new ones, and integrating old and new together in a more reflexive and self-observing way. There is no "between" the human and the natural, unless there can be a special relationship, not between one thing and another, but between the most characteristic and quintessential part of a whole, and the whole of which it is the privileged part — privileged because it is the most developed product of its own evolutionary process. Human beings are not equal to, but superior to, other species. The complete injunction to the sustainable relationship as formulated is politically impossible to enforce and often counterproductive when enforced.

A NEW ENVIRONMENTAL THEOLOGY

Nevertheless, there is a residual wisdom in the call for the sustainable relationship, and it might be worth our while to try to reformulate and rescue this goal by providing a sounder philosophical (and theological) basis for it. Cutting our theology to fit our environmental ethics may seem odd, but, in a playful spirit, let us do so anyway. Perhaps afterward we can see whether the result makes sense philosophically and morally, and discover if it has any significant continuity with the best of our religious traditions. If contemporary environmentalism is a new religion based upon a faulty idea of nature, how would it differ if we corrected its errors? What would a religion faithful to natural science look like?

Let us begin by following the Gaia hypothesis in its theological implications that the divine is present within the world, not detached from it. This is not necessarily to adopt a pantheist position—that is, that the world *is* God. If, by analogy, we assert that the mind and soul are present in a brain and body rather than detachable from them, we are not committed to believing that the mind and soul are only the brain and body. Thus the first axiom of a natural theology would be: *The divine is in nature.*

If the divine is *in* nature, how might we discover the nature of the divine? Surely by examining and listening to nature itself, just as we find out about man's or woman's personality by examining what they physically do and listening to what they physically say. That is, we should pay attention to the process, the *story,* of nature, if we wish to know its divine soul. Nature, as we have already seen, includes us as its acme and quintessence, so we must look especially at ourselves, the most characteristic part of God's natural body. The way we find out, the process of knowing, the attempt to come to know the story of things, is called science. Our second axiom might be: *We know the divine by means of the scientific understanding of nature and ourselves.*

A story is an irreversible process of events that are unpredictable beforehand but apparently inevitable and obvious once they have happened. If you are reading a good novel, the pleasure is partly that the next twist in the story can't be predicted. . . .

The possibility of story implies that time is asymmetrical, that truth can be different prospectively from what it is retrospectively. There are fixed truths, such as the laws of gravitation and thermodynamics, or we would have no points of reference by which to know. The newly emergent truths, however, include most of what we consider valuable, good, and beautiful: all the exquisite forms of matter, life, and mind that have evolved over the history

of the universe. If nature has no story, then we can conclude that the divine being is fixed and eternal, forever unsurprised and undisturbed. But nature manifestly and emphatically does have a story (or many stories), so we must conclude that the divine being has one, too. The third axiom of our natural theology would be: *The divine changes; the divine has a story.*

If we examine nature and ourselves we discover underlying unities in the variety of things (the mathematical forms, the constants of physics) but also that nature is an evolutionary drama, a competitive/cooperative dialogue among its parts, species, levels, and principles. If nature is the body of the divine, we may infer a fourth axiom: *The divine is both one and many.* It is one in its most remote, abstract, timeless, impersonal, simple-minded, and passive aspects, and many in its most immediate, concrete, changing, personal, intelligent, and active aspects. In deference to our own monotheistic tradition I shall from here on refer to the divine as "God," but with the understanding that the polytheistic and pluralist description of the divine as "the gods" is also intellectually attractive.

The transformations of this natural god of change are not exclusively random, reversible, and meaningless; as we have seen, the evolution of the universe is progressive, irrevocable, and dramatically meaningful. There is a one-way process of increasing feedback, reflexivity, self-organization, and freedom as the world evolves. Elementary particles have polarity but no shape. Atoms, more complex and self-referential than particles, have simple geometrical shapes that are symmetrical in many dimensions. With molecules, which could not exist until the universe had cooled enough to permit them, we see the first asymmetrical shapes and the birth of individuality. Molecules have complex feedback systems, many degrees of freedom, and the capacity to organize in periodic structures such as crystals. Living organisms are even more asymmetrical, free, and capable of organization, and they contain a recording of their own structure in the DNA language. Mind continues this story into the most complex forms of consciousness, self-determination, and communication. Thus the fifth axiom: *The story of God is one of increasing individuality, meaning, and freedom.* Progress is not a human invention, but a divine one.

If the universe is God's body, then we — and by "we" I mean all the intelligent species in the universe — are the most sensitive, most aware, most self-organizing of its parts. Though we are not the whole, we are that which increasingly has some knowledge of and control over the whole. The most sensitive and aware and controlling parts of a living body are its nervous system. Thus the sixth axiom: *We are the nervous system of God.*

This nervous system is still very rudimentary, and has penetrated and innervated only a tiny portion of the universe to date. It is like the nervous system of an unborn child. We stand at the first trembling moment of the history of the universe, the flash of a dawn that is a mere twenty billion years old, the beginning of a day that lasts ten trillion years. The universe is still only in its gestation; it is not yet fully developed. We bear some of the responsibility to complete that development, to increase our awareness and control over the rest of the universe, to extend the nerves of science and art into the inanimate and insentient parts of the world. Thus a seventh axiom: *God is still only a fetus.* Nature has not died, as some recent commentators have complained. It is only now awakening, and we are its eyes, its ears, and its tongue. From this follows an eighth axiom: *We serve God by helping him or her toward greater self-awareness.*

As organisms evolve, they develop more and more complex chemical, electrical, and mechanical systems, known as bodies, in order to control and be controlled by their environment — to act and to sense. All bodies are prostheses, that is, the matter of which they are made is not at first part of the living organism itself, but pressed artificially into service by that organism. For instance, the carbon atoms that my body uses to construct its protein and enzyme factories are exactly the same as they were before I commandeered them by eating them in my asparagus. . . . All living organisms do this at the atomic and molecular levels, even the crudest microorganisms; the more advanced an organism is, the larger and more organized in themselves are the outside structures that it is able to use and transform into its synthetic body.

Artificial systems of investigation, control, and communication, as these are, have a name: technology. The body of a living organism is its technology; the technology of an organism is its body. Our life is, after all, only the pattern of information spelled out in our genes: a pattern that survives any given atom in our bodies, except for the ones we have not yet metabolized at our death. Our own technology is an extension of our bodies, but our bodies are nothing more than such cumulative extensions. Biological evolution, and arguably even prebiological evolution, are in this sense precisely the increase in the complexity and power of technology. Nature is technology, then, and if nature is the body of God we may formulate a surprising ninth axiom: *God is the process of increasing technology.*

If our moral function is to serve God, then it is to help God change from a fetus into a fully developed being, to realize God's future growth and self-awareness. The way to do this is to continue to innervate the universe by knowledge and control, thereby extending our own bodies, the region of our own technology, throughout the universe. Thus the tenth axiom: *To serve God is to increase the scope, power, beauty, and depth of technology.*

Our logic has brought us to an astonishing and perhaps shocking conclusion, utterly at odds with the prevailing mood of our culture. How can we redeem this statement, and make it fit what we feel about our role in the world?

The answer must involve a thorough reevaluation of what technology is and what we mean by the term. We know there is such a thing as bad technology, but the theological implications we have discovered require that we define good technology, because without good technology we cannot adequately serve God, if God is conceived of as being within nature. It will no longer be sufficient for us to attempt to get away from or to dissolve our technology; even if this were possible, it would be to deny our divine duty and commit a sin against the spirit of nature. Our investigation of what good technology is may have the virtue of clarifying what is bad technology, bad service of God, and thus may constitute a powerful if gentle critique of society.

Good technology, first of all, increases and does not decrease the organized complexity of the world. . . . Good technology respects the existing technology of nature, and even when adding to it does not destroy the complex order and beauty that helped it evolve and upon which it is based. Bad technology is technology that destroys technology, whether in the form of the bodies of animals and plants, or in the form of our own rich material and mental culture.

As a direct implication of the injunction to increase the organized complexity of the world, good technology preserves earlier stages and products of its own process. It will, therefore, pay special attention to the preservation of chemical complexity, to the preservation of the richness and variety of life, to the preservation of the higher organisms in particular, and to the care and reverence of human life. This is the natural order of our increasing concern, because life, higher organisms, and human beings are closer and closer approximations to the emerging nervous system of God. Likewise, within an organism we give preference to the higher functions, especially the nervous system, over lower vegetative functions. This hierarchy is really common sense; it is the automatic assumption of any good surgeon or any animal caught in a trap in making decisions about which part must be sacrificed to save the rest. Indeed, it will be necessary to replace certain environmentally unsound technologies with the more efficient, elegant, and benign ones that the new science is making possible. We will need to isolate fine examples of ancient and unique ecosystems in "wilderness areas"—however misleading the term may be—from the natural interference of other, highly competitive species, such as ourselves and the pantropic weeds, in order to promote the richer evolution of the rest. This is exactly what some environmental radicals have demanded, though on other grounds, but we do not have to yield to an antihuman and antitechnological ideology to make such choices.

The theology outlined here would suggest that we embrace an activist, restorationist environmentalism that goes with, not against, the natural inclination of humanity toward greater experience, self-awareness, mutual feedback, and technical power. Our job is not to leave nature alone or to coexist peacefully with it; we *are* it, we are its future, its promise, its purpose. Its future landscapes are partly up to us.

CREATING THE LANDSCAPES OF THE FUTURE: INNATE RESOURCES

The creation of landscape is a special kind of human activity. To do it well, and especially to teach it to others, a sound working theory of the human capacities and talents involved might be valuable. Are we even capable of such an enterprise?

We can begin to answer this question by asking another: what other human activities would ecological invention resemble? Science, certainly; but science is normally considered a method of analysis, and ecological creation is a process of synthesis, of performance. Ecological creation would indeed be guided by analysis; it would serve as a test of the analysis it relies on and be richly suggestive of new analytic models, new hypotheses. But this fertility of hypotheses is called into being by the imperative of successful and positive action. Unlike science, which professes to understand the world by external observation and measurement, ecological creation must understand the object of its study from the inside.

. . . What ecological creation is challenged to do is to create an ecology that is indistinguishable from a natural reality, though the first of its kind.

But if ecological creation is not exactly a science, neither is it only a technology, in the traditional sense of the word, for its goal is not a product but a process. One could say that the biological "machine" the creative ecologist produces must first attend to its own ordered reproduction. Like the natural technology of animals and plants, its work is itself. Technology cannot guide itself; our earlier, crucial distinction between bad technology and good technology needs criteria that cannot be found within technique alone. Nor is ecological creation quite like a craft, in which the boundaries are clearly established and the criteria of productivity can be easily measured. In some ways it is almost more like play, a serious kind of play that submits itself to high and demanding canons of perfection, and which is not embarked on only for its own sake.

In fact the activity that inventionist ecology most resembles is art. First we must know what we mean by "art." A simple definition may be best: art is the creation of beauty. But what is beauty? Here, oddly enough, the perspective of the biologist may be more instructive than that of the aesthetician. Recent work in the biological foundation of aesthetics (which I have summarized and explored in my books *Natural Classicism: Essays on Literature and Science; Rebirth of Value: Meditations on Beauty, Ecology, Religion, and Education;* and *Beauty: The Value of Values*) suggests that the aesthetic capacity is an inherited and sophisticated competence. It is given specific form by culture, as is our predisposition to speech, but its deep syntax, as it were, is wired into our neural hardware. Obviously, then, aesthetic perception is designed for some very important function, and was selected for and refined by evolutionary mechanisms; we share this capacity with other animals, but in us it is enormously more developed, flexible, and variable in application.

Recent research suggests that the aesthetic sense is a capacity to organize and recognize meaning in very large quantities of ill-defined information, to detect and create complex relationships and feedback systems, to take into account multiple contexts and frames of reference, and to perceive harmonies and regularities that add up to a deep unity — a unity that generates predictions of the future and can act as a sound basis for future action. The new understanding of the vigorous constructive activity of the sensory cortex suggests that we do not passively receive the world of vision, but actively create it (see David Marr, *Vision*). The aesthetic capacity is to perception as perception is to mere sensation, or as sensation is to the mechanical effect of some outside event upon an inanimate object. In other words, the unities that the sense of beauty appreciates are a higher, more integrated version of the enduring solid objects in space and time that the sensory cortex constructs for our use out of the storm of disparate information that hits our sensors. A complex unity like an ecosystem is perceived by the aesthetic sense as a solid object in space is perceived by sight. The exercise of the aesthetic capacity is rewarded and reinforced by the brain's own self-reward system, which we feel as aesthetic pleasure.

A new generation of scientists, including Ilya Prigogine, Mitchell Feigenbaum, and Benoit Mandelbrot, has recognized the importance in nature of dissipative, nonlinear feedback systems, in which causality is not one-way but rather mutually circulated among all of the system's components or turned recursively back upon itself. The popular term for this new science is "Chaos," though more accurately it deals with the order in chaos and the chaos that can arise out of deterministic order. Much of this work is summarized in James Gleick's important book *Chaos: Making a New Science.* "Chaotic" systems have the peculiar characteristics of unpredictability and self-organization, and seem to be drawn toward "strange attractors," outcomes whose graphic representation is immediately recognizable as beautiful. Chaotic attractors exhibit the characteristics of self-similarity (their patterns are repeated, often with variations, at an infinite variety of scales) and fractal discontinuity (they never fill space homogeneously with straight lines or flat planes or solid volumes, but instead are always frilled or braided or pitted or interpenetrated with empty space, though they can, paradoxically, approach infinitely close to filling the available space as they are plotted). Such forms denote the feedback processes — of which biological evolution is one — that created the universe as we know it. There is good reason to believe that those forms appear beautiful to us because we have inherited from our own evolution a capacity to recognize, and to participate in, the creative processes of nature. We find a healthy and ecologically rich landscape beautiful because it embodies, as living attractors, the forms that are generated by self-organizing feedback systems. Thus our innate aesthetic abilities are a reliable rule of thumb when we wish to judge the ecological viability of a natural landscape.

What capacity could be better adapted than our aesthetic sense to the complex, context-rich work of ecological invention, which must harmonize into a higher unity large masses of mutually dependent information? Our destiny as a species now appears to be bound up with the success of our attempts to reconstruct our living environment (not only on this planet, perhaps). The sense of beauty tells us what is relevant, what is likely, what is proper, what is fruitful. We would be in a desperate case if the only capacity we could rely on was our logical ability to put two and two together; there is not enough time to work everything out in that fashion, and there is simply too much information, and too many possible consequences, to do so without those higher integrative abilities. Aldo Leopold suggested the existence of a human natural aesthetic; ecological invention may now with some justification call upon a human aesthetic capacity that is not a merely passive appreciation and in which the artificial and the natural cannot be distinguished. Indeed, one of our problems is this distinction: true gardeners of the planet will no longer need it.

CREATING THE LANDSCAPES OF THE FUTURE: HISTORICAL RESOURCES

Every major art form exists within a tradition, a context of prior practice that serves as the inspiration and raw material of the artist's conceptions. On what tradition can the environmental artist call?

We have at our disposal — though we have used it very little — a rich storehouse of theory and recorded experience in the field of art and nature: Renaissance aesthetics. The Renaissance already knew, for instance, that the simple recursive algorithm or feedback process that generates the Fibonacci series (add the two previous terms in the series to get the next) could be used both to predict the demographic future of a naturally reproducing population of animals, and to generate what might be called the simplest of all fractal curves, the beautiful Fibonacci spiral. That spiral can be found in seashells and sunflower heads and throughout nature in general. . . .

The Renaissance poet Sir Philip Sidney, author of the *Arcadia,* defines art as the imitation of nature. He does not mean that the artist imitates what nature merely *is,* as a photograph or a diorama copies the visual externals of a scene, but rather imitates what nature *does,* that is, generate a living and self-developing order. Human art, he maintains, can better the current productions of nature, but precisely because human art is a natural process. Shakespeare says the same in *The Winter's Tale.* The shepherdess Perdita has just declared that she won't have carnations or "streak'd gillyvors" in her garden because, like some American environmentalists, she disapproves of the fact that they have been bred and hybridized by genetic technology. . . .

Renaissance art gave rise to good science; its effort to imitate nature had profound heuristic value. The famous discoveries of Leonardo da Vinci in anatomy, aerodynamics, hydrostatics, and mechanics grew out of his attempt to imitate nature in drawing, painting, sculpture, and architecture. Brunelleschi, in his endeavor to imitate the natural phenomenon of visual perspective (whose discovery he — perhaps erroneously — attributed to the ancient Romans), invented pictorial perspective, and in so doing made large advances in the science of projective geometry. . . . If good science comes out of the artistic imitation of nature, we have a warrant that such art is itself an extension of the work of nature. The Elizabethans thought that we know by doing, and the best and highest thing we can do is imitate the creative activity of nature.

Our assessment of the human resources that can be deployed for the work of environmental invention presents us with some curious but suggestive conclusions. First, we must look to the artistic and aesthetic capacity, and learn more about its roots in our biology and evolution; the peculiar kind of art and aesthetics involved are those of the imitation of nature. Next, we may call on Renaissance aesthetics for the nucleus of a sound body of theory about the artistic imitation of nature. We can extend that body of theory by the study of chaotic self-organizing feedback systems. Finally, we may find in the practice of art the heuristic value of imitation: the attempt to reproduce accurately the functions of nature forces the artist not only to increasingly close observation, but beyond, to increasingly stringent experimental tests of ideas. This labor is not merely analytical, but creative, and its natural reward is beauty.

ARCADIAS, TERRESTRIAL AND EXTRATERRESTRIAL

If the artistic/scientific imitation of nature to create new landscapes were a new project, we might have cause to be anxious, on the grounds that though our theory might be sound, the stakes — the health of the planet — are too high. Two arguments address this reasonable objection.

The first is that human beings have in fact been creating new ecosystems for thousands of years.

The arcadian tradition of the farmed *rus* or country-side (*rus* is the Latin root of "rural" and "rustic") is an ancient library of techniques by which humans can live harmoniously in a landscape they have partly created. Genetically tailored species such as wheat, grapes, cattle, and fruit trees are interspersed with husbanded forests, wild game, and carefully managed rivers and streams. Examples of this arcadian landscape exist all over the world — in the wine countries of Tuscany and Provence, in the rice paddies of Java and Bali, in the English Cotswolds, and in the ancient farms of China.

This folk art has risen at various times and places into the status of a high art, with conscious canons and some abandonment of purely utilitarian criteria of success: the art of the garden. We can trace its tradition in the history of Chinese, Korean, and Japanese gardens, and in the West we note the great lineage that runs from the hanging gardens of Babylon, through the Greek garden as described by Homer in his mythical isle of Phaiakia, the Roman gardens of Virgil, Horace, and Cicero, on into the Renaissance gardens of Italy and France, the English neoclassical gardens (Stourhead, for instance), and the gardens planted by Capability Brown and Gertrude Jekyll, to the impressionist gardens, Monet's Clos Normand at Giverny and Vita Sackville-West's Sissinghurst in Kent, and across the Atlantic to the American gardens of Longwood and Dumbarton Oaks. These gardens are part of the aesthetic education of the creator of ecosystems; they are epitomes of the arcadian landscape. If we can sensibly combine our new scientific knowledge of ecology and genetics with the old empirical wisdom of the peasants and farmers and gardeners, and the influence of our existing garden aesthetics, there is no reason why the Earth should not under human care end up with an even greater richness and variety of ecosystems than it now possesses.

The other reason why we should not be too anxious about the idea of the created landscape is that we will not stay on this planet forever. We must conserve and preserve the life of the Earth, but there are also dead planets out there that might be brought to life without risk. NASA is already seriously researching the proposition.

Of course, we need to know much more about how ecologies work before we take any irreversible steps in this direction. We particularly need a better bacteriology and a better understanding of the subtle interplay of plant, animal, and human societies, gene pools, and the climatological and geological feedback loops. Evolutionists and ecologists, who sometimes do not seem to talk to each other, need to come together for a grand synthesis. The best way to do this is through the practical craft of ecological restoration. We learn how ecologies work by recreating them, and in the process of recreating ecologies we will create a community of scientists and restorationists who will devise the arts of seeding life on other planets.

We also need to know much more about genetic inheritance and genetic expression. It is beginning to look as if the 95 percent of the genome that is not expressed is actually a jumbled but fairly complete archive of a given organism's entire evolutionary history. As with certain big old business computer programs, which have been patched and augmented so many times that the programmers no longer know what might still be useful, it is simply too expensive to clean out all the old material and really very inexpensive to store it in a dormant state. Further, the bacteria and viruses of the world constitute a huge lending library of past genetic diversity from all other living species. Using recombinant DNA techniques (as bacteria do all the time) it may be possible one day to reconstruct and resurrect extinct species from this "fossil" DNA. We may thus eventually be able to undo the damage we have already done to species diversity, and perhaps even to restore whole ecosystems that existed before the advent of humankind.

Eventually we may modify existing species by gene tailoring, and even develop new species adapted to new ecological niches. Sooner or later we will leave the confines of this planet. When we do we may carry with us the seeds of earthly life, hardened and redesigned to thrive in alien environments and perhaps to transform those environments, as primitive life did on this planet, into a habitat for other more advanced earthly lifeforms. In this work we may become the seed-vectors and pollinators of the universe, carrying life beyond the fragile eggshell of this planet, so exposed to sterilization by a stray asteroid strike or an extra-large comet. We will eventually be in the business of the ecotransformation of planets—in fact we already are, with this one. We need to start thinking in these terms, and I have called for a commitment by our civilization to an eventual transformation of the dead planet Mars into a living ecosystem. We should do this not only because it is a noble thing to do in itself, but also because we will not ever know with any confidence how our own planetary ecosystem works until we ourselves have created one on another planet. . . .

REFERENCES

Botkin, Daniel. 1990. *Discordant Harmonies: A New Ecology for the Twenty-First Century.* New York: Oxford University Press.

Gleick, James. 1988. *Chaos: Making a New Science.* New York: Viking.

Le Guin, Ursula. 1983. *The Left Hand of Darkness.* New York: Ace Books.

Marr, David. 1982. *Vision.* New York: Freeman.

Turner, Frederick. 1988. *Genesis, an Epic Poem.* Dallas: Saybrook Publishing Company.

———. 1991. *Rebirth of Value: Meditations on Beauty, Ecology, Religion, and Education.* Albany: State University of New York Press.

———. 1992. *Natural Classicism: Essays on Literature and Science.* Charlottesville: University Press of Virginia.

———. 1992. *Beauty: The Value of Values.* Charlottesville: University Press of Virginia.

DISCUSSION TOPICS

1. Turner makes an analogy between the current environmental movement and a theistic religion. What other similarities between the two can you find that are not mentioned by Turner? What significant differences between the current environmental movement and theistic religions can you identify? Overall, do you agree with Turner's analogy? Justify your answer.

2. Do you believe that humans will eventually colonize other planets? Would you like to participate in such a colonization? Why or why not?

3. What is your opinion of the proposal that humans eventually should actively attempt to alter nature, such as by developing new species or wholly new ecosystems? Give reasons for your perspective.

CLASS EXERCISES

1. With which of the authors in this chapter do you find yourself in closest agreement, and at greatest odds? What are the decisive points made by each respective author that most influenced your decision?

2. The proposal to purchase a 40,000-hectare parcel of private timberland and form a national park is estimated to cost about 1300 local jobs over the next eight years in a community of 55,000 people. Using the debating guidelines presented in the appendix, have the class debate the wisdom of this proposal on the basis of anthropocentric considerations only. Thus, economics, aesthetic considerations, impacts on people now and in the future would be acceptable arguments, whereas arguments based on extending moral consideration to animals or the natural environment itself would not be.

   Which human concerns and values were appealed to by each side? Which were most persuasive?

FOR FURTHER READING

Cothern, C. Richard, ed. *Handbook for Environmental Risk Decisionmaking.* Boca Raton, Fla.: CRC Press, 1995. The editor argues that values and ethics should be included in environmental decision making because they are already a major component, many problems result from ignoring them, and it is the right thing to do.

Deardon, Phillip. "Park Literacy and Conservation." *Conservation Biology* 9 (1995): 1654–56. Develops the notion that parks play social roles as museums, art galleries, zoos, playgrounds, theaters, cathedrals, and generators of income, as well as ecological roles as banks, reservoirs, laboratories, and schoolrooms. Argues that these anthropocentric perspectives are strong arguments to many people for preserving parks.

Dommelen, Ad van, ed. *Coping with Deliberate Release: The Limits of Risk Assessment.* Tilburg, Netherlands: International Centre for Human and Public Affairs, 1996. Contributors evaluate the emerging social and political aspects of modern biotechnology. The limits of risk assessment in relation to the deliberate release of genetically modified organisms are addressed.

Durnil, Gordon K. *The Making of a Conservative Environmentalist.* Bloomington: Indiana University Press, 1995. The author, a conservative Republican politician, lawyer, and environmentalist, maintains that greater knowledge of how current environmental decisions will affect future generations will lead to greater action and support for environmentalism by everyone, including the conservative community.

Ferré, Frederick. *Philosophy of Technology.* Englewood Cliffs, N.J.: Prentice-Hall, 1988. Ferré provides an insightful look at the relationship of technology to intelligence, modern existence, ethics, religion and metaphysics, and life in general.

Hardin, G. *Living within Limits: Ecology, Economics, and Population Taboos.* Oxford: Oxford University Press, 1993. The author stresses the need for rich nations to close their borders to immigration from poor (and rapidly reproducing) nations and to limit their own populations, if they wish to survive. Argues against universal human rights as a policy.

Hughes, J. Donald. *Ecology in Ancient Civilization.* Albuquerque: University of New Mexico Press, 1975. Hughes presents an environmental history from the ancient world through Jewish, Greek, Roman, and Christian cultures, to gain insights on attitudes found in modern Western societies.

Kant, Immanuel. "Fundamental Principles of the Metaphysic of Morals," trans. T. K. Abbot. Indianapolis: Bobbs-Merrill, 1949.

McCloskey, A. J. *Ecological Ethics and Politics.* Totowa, N.J.: Rowman and Littlefield, 1983. An argument for an enlightened self-interest. Author adopts a liberal "ecologically informed" position in rejecting the "preservationist authoritarian" approach. He welcomes increased technological management of nature.

Nash, Roderick F. *American Environmentalism: Readings in Conservation History,* 3rd ed. New York: McGraw-Hill, 1990. Readings from leaders in the American environmentalist movement, 1832 to 1988. Several provide insights on the role of anthropocentrism in the environmental impacts of humans.

Norton, Bryan G. "Environmental Ethics and Weak Anthropocentrism and Nonanthropocentrism." *Environmental Ethics* 6 (1984): 131–48. Author distinguishes between strong and weak anthropocentrism and argues that weak anthropocentrism is adequate to serve as the basis for an environmental ethic.

———. *Why Preserve Natural Diversity.* Princeton, N.J.: Princeton University Press, 1987, pp. 3–22. Provides a clarification and taxonomy of anthropocentrism in the introductory chapter.

Parton, Glenn. "Humans-in-the-Wilderness." *Trumpeter* 12 (1995): 185–90. The author argues that civilization is a story that includes errors as well as good choices. Parton believes that the errors should be discarded and an emphasis placed on retaining the positive achievements.

Partridge, Ernest. "On the Rights of Future Generations," in *Upstream/Downstream,* ed. Donald Scherer. Philadelphia: Temple University Press, 1990, pp. 40–66. Thoughtfully evaluates five arguments used to discount extending moral concern to future human generations and finds all of them lacking.

Rollin, Bernard E. *Animal Rights and Human Morality,* 2nd ed. Buffalo, N.Y.: Prometheus Books, 1989. A clear, articulate account of anthropocentrism developed as part of his larger theme of justifying moral concern for nonhuman animals.

Schomberg, Ren von, ed. *Contested Technology Ethics, Risk and Public Debate.* Tilburg, Netherlands: International Centre for Human and Public Affairs, 1996. The papers in this volume address the social and philosophical dimensions of contested technology, public debate and technological innovation, ethics of risk assessment, and implications for the legal system. Includes new procedures for technology assessment.

Serres, Michel. *The Natural Contract.* Ann Arbor: University of Michigan Press, 1995. The author argues that ethical considerations are essential in the human relationship to nature.

Shrader-Frechette, K. S., and E. D. McCoy. *Method in Ecology: Strategies for Conservation.* Cambridge:

Cambridge University Press, 1993. The authors evaluate the issue of the degree to which general ecological theory can provide the necessary foundations needed for the development of environmental ethics and policies.

Soskolne, Colin, and Roberto Bertollini. Special issue of *Science of the Total Environment* 184, 1–2 (May 1996) on "Ethical and Philosophical Issues in Environmental Epidemiology." The articles cover an important aspect of human health and well-being; authors include Holmes Rolston III, Laura Westra, Dale Jamieson, Earl R. Winkler, and Andrew Light.

Thompson, Gary L., Fred M. Shelley, and Chand Wije, eds. *Geography, Environment, and American Law.* Niwot: University Press of Colorado, 1996. Evaluates the relation between geography and the American legal system to resolve such problems as land use, water resources, and mineral development. Uses geography as a framework for evaluating human and environmental problems.

Turpin, Jennifer, and Lois Ann Lorentzen, eds. *The Gendered New World Order: Militarism, the Environment, and Development.* New York: Routledge, 1996. The authors address the issue of gender within the global problems of militarism, underdevelopment, and environmental decay, assessing connections between refugees, water pollution, bombed villages, massive dam projects, starving children, deforestation, nuclear arms buildup, and the rights of women.

Tyson, C. B., and T. E. Worthley. "Managing Forests within a Watershed: The Importance of Stewardship." *Journal of Forestry* 99, 8 (2001): 4–10.

Varner, Gary E. *In Nature's Interests.* Oxford: Oxford University Press, 1998. Offers an anthropocentric perspective on many environmental issues.

Westra, Laura. *An Environmental Proposal for Ethics.* Lanham, Md.: Rowman and Littlefield, 1994. Proposes that biological integrity be used as a foundation for environmental ethics building on the work of Leopold and Naess. Has both anthropocentric and ecocentric aspects.

———. "Environmental Integrity, Racism, and Health." *Science of the Total Environment* 184 (1996): 57–66. Considering climate change and global warming, food production, and global equity, Westra notes relationships between protection of ecosystem integrity and wilderness, and human health.

Westra, Laura, and John Lemons, eds. *Perspectives on Ecological Integrity.* Boston: Kluwer Academic, 2001. The authors provide perspectives on the importance and consequences of ecological integrity for science, morality, and public policy. Builds on Westra's theme of integrity as a foundation for environmental ethics.

Wheale, Peter, ed. *The Social Management of Biotechnology: Workshop Proceedings.* Tilburg, Netherlands: International Centre for Human and Public Affairs, 1996. Topics include the ethics of genetic experimentation on animals, the controversy on patenting genetic material and transgenic animals, and the moral aspects of engineering transgenic animals for organ transplants to humans.

CHAPTER SEVEN
Individualism

In this chapter we discuss several perspectives that affirm the moral standing of nonhuman as well as human individuals. We identify what these approaches have in common and the differences between those views that include only individual animals and those that include individual plants as well.[1]

THE REJECTION OF HOLISM

The authors in this chapter affirm that only individuals[2] can be meaningfully said to have moral value in and of themselves.[3] Neither species nor ecosystems embody moral value. For example, Tom Regan points out in his essay, "The Case for Animal Rights," that individuals are the paradigmatic holders of rights, since it is individuals who are conscious, who feel and make decisions, who care about what happens to them, who are centers of life. He maintains that it is unclear what could be meant by attributing rights to *collections* of individuals.

Peter Singer's position, addressed in his essay "Equality for Animals?" is equally individualistic, although he talks in terms of interests rather than of rights. Singer follows the utilitarian lead of Jeremy Bentham in locating moral good and bad in

---

[1]For a comprehensive collection of readings on many aspects of animal ethics, see Susan J. Armstrong and Richard G. Botzler, eds., *The Animal Ethics Reader* (London: Routledge, 2003).

[2]Paul Taylor has extended his theory to encompass species, biotic communities, and ecosystems but has not yet (to the editors' knowledge) published his formulation of this extension (private correspondence, 1996). He now endorses the modifications suggested by James Sterba in "From Biocentric Individualism to Biocentric Pluralism," *Environmental Ethics* 17, 2 (Summer 1995): 191–207.

---

[3]This position is often called "extensionism," indicating that it is simply an extension of traditional ethics to cover nonhumans. However, while Regan's and Singer's views can be considered extensions of deontological theory and of utilitarian theory, Schweitzer's reverence for life and Taylor's *telos* view are not simply extensions of traditional ethics, because they urge respect for organic life itself. Also, the term extensionism has a somewhat dismissive tone.

the happiness or unhappiness of sentient individuals (those individuals capable of feeling pleasure and pain). Utilitarianism is an aggregative ethic. Thus, to arrive at the best moral choice, a moral agent must consider the probable consequences issuing from his or her actions for all of the sentient individuals affected by the action. The moral agent then sums these positive and negative consequences to decide whether to engage in the proposed action. Bentham tells us that in this summation each one counts for one, and no one counts for more than one.

In his article "Environmental Values," Singer argues that an individualist ethic can adequately justify wilderness preservation. Singer also seeks to demonstrate that views extending ethical consideration beyond sentient beings fail to give us direction as to what is the right thing to do. In addition, holistic views fail to show that species and ecosystems have morally significant interests.

Dale Jamieson, in "Animal Liberation Is an Environmental Ethic," states that sentient beings are of primary value. Nonsentient entities are of derivative value because "they do not have a perspective from which their lives go better or worse." There is no value independent of a mind, human or nonhuman. Nevertheless, the value of nonsentient entities such as plants, as well as of works of art, can be very great.

Paul Taylor, in an excerpt from *Respect for Nature,* tries to account for the relationships between individuals in an ecosystem while retaining the moral locus within the individual. He proposes that while the good of an individual is the full development of its biological powers, the good of a population of individuals is arrived at by assessing the optimal *average* good of individuals in that population. Thus even though "good" primarily applies to the welfare of individuals, we can speak of the "statistical good" of a species or a population.[4]

The focus on individual organisms accords well with the views of those conservation biologists who point out that defining species can be difficult. The species represents a level of evolutionary discontinuity, but it is somewhat controversial how discontinuous two populations or individuals must be in order to be of different species.[5] Some claim that only individuals or local interbreeding populations are biologically real and that species classifications are mainly political devices.[6] Similarly, Jane Goodall justifies her work with orphaned chimpanzees by maintaining that "individual animals make up the species, and that's been my life's work — recognizing the value of the individual."[7] (See the discussion of transgenic animals for more considerations concerning the nature of species.)

THE CONCERN WITH HUMAN-CAUSED SUFFERING

Individualism widens the concern with well-being to all those to whom suffering can be said to matter. A number of scholars have explored animal suffering, including physiological and psychological stress, particularly in confinement due to laboratory experiments and intensive food production.[8] Over 140 million experiments on animals are performed annually.[9] One important recent finding is that animals with a less elaborate nervous system may not be able to cope with a noxious stimulus as well as animals with a more complex nervous system, such as adult human beings. Also, a number of scientists argue that pain is not exclusively a neural event.[10] While many research scientists have resisted the

---

[4]Paul Taylor, *Respect for Nature: A Theory of Environmental Ethics* (Princeton, N.J.: Princeton University Press, 1986), pp. 69–71.

[5]G. Meffe and C. R. Carroll, "The Species in Conservation" in *Principles of Conservation Biology,* (Sunderland, Mass.: Sivauer, 1994).

[6]R. I. M. Dunbar, "What's in a Classification?" in *The Great Ape Project: Equality beyond Humanity,* Peter Singer and Paola Cavalieri, eds. (New York: St. Martin's Press, 1993).

[7]Virginia Morell, "Lost Chimps," *International Wildlife* (September/October 1996): 14–20.

[8]See Bernard Rollin and Marian Dawkins in "For Further Reading" at the end of this chapter. Also see Tim R. Kuchel, Margaret Rose, and Judith Burrell, eds., *Animal Pain: Ethical and Scientific Perspectives.* (Glen Osmond, Australia: Anzccart, 1995).

[9]Raymond Wacks, "Sacrificed for Science," in *Changing Nature's Course: The Ethical Challenge of Biotechnology,* Gerhold K. Becker and James P. Buchanan, eds. (Hong Kong: Hong Kong University Press, 1996).

[10]*Animal Pain,* p. 67.

moral concerns of individualism (as expressed in animal experimentation ethics committees, for example), recently some have stated that ethical considerations have in fact improved the quality of scientific research due to the careful reflection given to the research design.[11] Whatever the context, individualism points out the wrongness of unnecessary suffering imposed by human beings.[12]

TRANSGENIC ANIMALS

Growth-hormone-boosted, super milk-producing cows; leaner, faster-growing, but arthritis-ridden Beltsville pigs; the possibility of fish engineered to grow faster; Oncomouse, Cystic Fibrosis mouse, and Memory mouse, fashioned to chart significant human diseases or basic biological processes . Mice, goats, and sheep bioengineered to produce human insulin or other biologically active products in their milk.

The concern for the individual organism must now include concern for the well-being of *transgenic animals,* animals into whom foreign genetic material, usually from another species, has been introduced. More broadly, the term means the "purposeful amplification, spread, or dissemination of a gene within a species at a rate much faster than would have occurred in the absence of artificial interventions."[13] The ethical challenges of animal biotechnology include not only the moral status of individual animals but also the meaning of life itself and thus deserve far more extensive treatment than this chapter can provide.

Recent innovations in technique now allow the manipulation of genetic information between virtually any plants or animals. These novel genetic capabilities may or may not cause injury to the recipient organisms. Thus one concern relates to the potential

pain or suffering that the animal must undergo.[14] On a positive note, Bernard Rollin has argued that if carefully regulated, animals used in research and food production might be engineered so that they have a different nature, or *telos,* one that results in less pain or suffering.[15] Rollin proposes the "Principle of the Conservation of Welfare," according to which genetically engineered animals should be no worse off than they would be if they were not engineered and ideally should be better off (e.g., through having disease resistance). However, this position accepts a hitherto unattained degree of human exploitation and control of other animals in accepting the violation of animal integrity. Also, the issue of animal well-being becomes more complex: How can researchers promote well-being if the animal has been created with altered and perhaps unprecedented behavioral habits?

Also, the economic commodification of animals, already present in intensive agriculture, becomes heightened when animals are patented. Their status as living beings is changed to mere configurations of living matter at the disposal of human beings for their own self-interested purposes.

Another concern involves bridging "species barriers." The modern notion of species can be defined as "a reproductive community of populations (reproductively isolated from each other) that occupies a specific niche in nature."[16] The concept assumes that populations of organisms in ecological niches are evolutionarily derived. Species "are the things that evolve."[17] From an anthropocentric perspective,

---

[11]Ibid., pp. 54, 69.

[12]The *New Scientist* published a series on scientific experiments on animals in spring 1992. See particularly Patrick Bateson, "Do Animals Feel Pain?" *New Scientist* 25, April 1992: 30–33.

[13]Strachan Donnelley, Charles R. McCarthy, and Rivers Singleton, Jr., "The Brave New World of Animal Biotechnology," *Hastings Center Report* (January/February, 1994): S1–S31.

[14]Van der Meer, Baumans, and van Zutphen point out that the process of transgenesis itself may cause welfare problems beyond those found in selective breeding methods. They note that currently there have been very few studies made on the well-being of transgenic animals. M. van der Meer, V. Baumans, and L. F. M. van Zutphen, "Transgenic Animals: What about Their Well-Being?" *Scandinavian Journal of Laboratory Animal Science* 1, 23 (1996): 287–90.

[15]Bernard E. Rollin, *The Frankenstein Syndrome: Ethical and Social Issues in the Genetic Engineering of Animals* (Cambridge: Cambridge University Press, 1995).

[16]Ernst Mayr, *The Growth of Biological Thought* (Cambridge, Mass.: Harvard University Press, 1982), p. 273.

[17]D. Hull, *Science as a Process: An Evolutionary Account of the Social and Conceptual Development of Science* (Chicago: University of Chicago Press, 1988), p. 96.

one might argue that human beings have always altered the biological world and indeed that "tinkering with nature" is part of our human character. Therefore it might be argued that we have an ethical responsibility to pursue the knowledge that biotechnology makes attainable. (See Turner, Chapter 6.) While this argument might be applicable in laboratory environments, outside the laboratory species barriers may have greater moral significance. A transgenic organism might disrupt a subtle natural systemic balance. By "practicing transgenesis in the wild," are we not breaking into natural processes that are intrinsically good and that are of ultimate significance for many of us?[18] A further concern (particularly from an ecocentric perspective) is the possible ecological damage or loss of species integrity or even loss of natural species arising from intentional or unintentional release of transgenic organisms. According to a report by the National Research Council, the biggest risk of genetically modified animals, particularly fish and insects, is that they might change the environment in unpredictable ways.[19] Readings in Chapter 10 address some of these environmental concerns.

TAKING EQUALITY SERIOUSLY

Both Peter Singer and Tom Regan have developed theories building on the principle of equality. Singer argues that equality means the equal consideration of the interests of individuals rather than equal treatment of individuals.[20] He maintains that any individual with interest or with sentience must be morally considered. The species membership of the individual is irrelevant to this consideration.[21]

Singer's advocacy of equal consideration of interests has led him, together with Paola Cavalieri, to

argue that the complex interests of the great apes require special moral and legal recognition. Singer and Cavalieri maintain that "collective manumission" (freedom from slavery) for the great apes is a reasonable goal, given that equality for all nonhuman animals is not feasible at this time.[22] The "Declaration on the Great Apes" affirms the right to life, liberty, and freedom from torture for great apes. The moral status of great apes is of particular urgency since all great apes are now endangered or critically endangered in the wild, due largely to illegal logging and the sale of ape meat. Bonobos, perhaps the most mentally advanced, are predicted to go extinct within a decade.[23]

Similarly, Anthony D'Amato and Sudhir K. Chopra discuss the gradual emergence over the past four centuries of an international consensus that whales are morally considerable, based on their special capacities.[24] D'Amato and Chopra argue that whales are entitled to legally enforceable "humanist rights," the most important being the right to life. However, Frans de Waal has criticized Singer and Cavalieri's proposal (and might also criticize the position taken by D'Amato and Chopra) as anthropocentric. That is, these proposals take human capacities as the ultimate standard, rather than appreciating nonhuman animals for their different capacities.[25]

Regan bases his argument for animal rights on the notion of the equality of inherent value. Inherent value is used by Regan to mean what we termed intrinsic value in the introduction to Chapter 2.[26] This value is possessed by all individuals who are "subjects-of-a-life." Subjects-of-a-life have some sense of the past and anticipation of the future, as

[18]"The Brave New World of Animal Biotechnology," p. S20.

[19]E. Stokstad, "Animal Biotechnology: Environmental Impact Seen as Biggest Risk," *Science* 297 (23 Aug. 2002): 1257.

[20]Recently David DeGrazia has attempted to spell out in some detail what "equal consideration" means regarding nonhuman beings. David DeGrazia, *Taking Animals Seriously: Mental Life and Moral Status* (Cambridge: Cambridge University Press, 1996), ch. 8 and 9.

[21]Singer has made it clear that he is not arguing for animal rights in the revised (1990) edition of *Animal Liberation*.

[22]Peter Singer and Paola Cavalieri, eds., *The Great Ape Project* (New York: St. Martin's Press, 1993), pp. 308–11.

[23]John Bohamon, "An Eleventh Hour Rescue for Great Apes?" *Science* 297 (27 Sept. 2002): 2203.

[24]Anthony D'Amato and Sudhir K. Chopra, "Whales: Their Emerging Right to Life," *American Journal of International Law* 85 (1995): 21–62.

[25]Frans de Waal, *Good-Natured: The Origins of Right and Wrong in Humans and Other Animals.* (Cambridge, Mass.: Harvard University Press, 1996).

[26]Dale Jamieson has argued that Regan's theory should be revised in the direction of utilitarianism. See Dale Jamieson, "Rights, Justice, and Duties to Provide Assistance: A Critique of Regan's Theory of Rights," *Ethics* (January 1990): 349–62.

value in the case of moral agents and recognize the need to view *their* possession of it as being equal, then we will be rationally obliged to do the same in the case of moral patients. *All* who have inherent value thus have it equally, whether they be moral agents or moral patients. All animals *are* equal, when the notions of "animal" and "equality" are properly understood, "animal" referring to all (terrestrial, at least) moral agents and patients, and "equality" referring to their equal possession of inherent value.[1] Inherent value is thus a *categorical* concept. One either has it, or one does not. There are no in-betweens. Moreover, all those who have it, have it equally. It does not come in degrees. . . .

INHERENT VALUE AND THE SUBJECT-OF-A LIFE CRITERION

. . . To be the subject-of-a-life, in the sense in which this expression will be used, involves more than merely being alive and more than merely being conscious. . . . [I]ndividuals are subjects-of-a-life if they have beliefs and desires; perception, memory, and a sense of the future, including their own future; an emotional life together with feelings of pleasure and pain; preference- and welfare-interests; the ability to initiate action in pursuit of their desires and goals; a psychophysical identity over time; and an individual welfare in the sense that their experiential life fares well or ill for them, logically independently of their utility for others and logically independently of their being the object of anyone else's interests. Those who satisfy the subject-of-a-life criterion themselves have a distinctive kind of value—inherent value—and are not to be viewed or treated as mere receptacles. . . .

The subject-of-a-life criterion identifies a similarity that holds between moral agents and patients. Is this similarity a relevant similarity, one that makes viewing them as inherently valuable intelligible and nonarbitrary? The grounds for replying affirmatively are as follows: (1) A relevant similarity among all those who are postulated to have equal inherent value must mark a characteristic shared by all those moral agents and patients who are here viewed as having such value. The subject-of-a-life criterion satisfies this requirement. *All* moral agents and *all* those moral patients with whom we are concerned *are*

subjects of a life that is better or worse for them, in the sense explained, logically independently of the utility they have for others and logically independently of their being the object of the interests of others. (2) Since inherent value is conceived to be a categorical value, admitting of no degrees, any supposed relevant similarity must itself be categorical. The subject-of-a-life criterion satisfies this requirement. This criterion does not assert or imply that those who meet it have the status of subject-of-a-life to a greater or lesser degree, depending on the degree to which they have or lack some favored ability or virtue (e.g., the ability for higher mathematics or those virtues associated with artistic excellence). One either *is* a subject-of-a-life, in the sense explained, or one *is not*. All those who are, are so equally. The subject-of-a-life criterion thus demarcates a categorical status shared by all moral agents and those moral patients with whom we are concerned. (3) A relevant similarity between moral agents and patients must go some way toward illuminating why we have direct duties to both and why we have less reason to believe that we have direct duties to individuals who are neither moral agents nor patients, even including those who, like moral agents and those patients we have in mind, are alive. This requirement also is satisfied by the subject-of-a-life criterion. Not all living things are subjects-of-a-life, in the sense explained; thus not all living things are to be viewed as having the same moral status, given this criterion, and the differences concerning our confidence about having direct duties to some (those who are subjects) and our not having direct duties to others (those who are not subjects) can be at least partially illuminated because the former meet, while the latter fail to meet, the subject-of-a-life criterion. For these reasons, the subject-of-a-life criterion can be defended as citing a relevant similarity between moral agents and patients, one that makes the attribution of equal inherent value to them both intelligible and nonarbitrary. . . .

If individuals have equal inherent value, then any principle that declares what treatment is due them as a matter of justice must take their equal value into account. The following principle (*the respect principle*) does this: *We are to treat those individuals who have inherent value in ways that respect their inherent value. . . .* The principle does not apply only to how we are to treat some individuals having inherent value (e.g., those with artistic or intellectual virtues). It enjoins us to treat *all* those individuals having inherent value in ways that respect their value, and thus it requires respectful treatment of all who satisfy the subject-of-a-life criterion. Whether they are moral agents or patients, we must treat them in ways that respect their equal inherent value. . . .

It is not an act of kindness to treat animals respectfully. It is an act of justice. It is not "the sentimental interests" of moral agents that grounds our duties of justice to children, the retarded, the senile, or other moral patients, including animals. It is respect for their inherent value. The myth of the privileged moral status of moral agents has no clothes.

THE MINIRIDE AND WORSE-OFF PRINCIPLES

. . . If the rights view is to have any claim on our rational assent, it must be able to provide guidance in precisely those sorts of cases where . . . we are required to choose between harming the few or harming the many who are innocent. The rights view recognized two principles that apply to such cases, both of which are derivable from the respect principle. To prepare the grounds for this derivation requires recalling some of the results of [an] earlier analysis of harm.

Comparable Harm

In that earlier analysis a distinction was drawn between those harms that are inflictions and those that are deprivations. Harms that are deprivations deny an individual opportunities for doing what will bring satisfaction, when it is in that individual's interest to do this. Harms that are inflictions diminish the quality of an individual's life, not just if or as they deprive that individual of opportunities for satisfaction, though they usually will do this, but because they detract directly from the individual's overall welfare. . . .

. . . Two harms are comparable when they detract equally from an individual's welfare, or from the welfare of two or more individuals. For example, separate episodes of suffering of a certain kind and intensity are comparable harms if they cause an equal diminution in the welfare of the same indi-

vidual at different times, or in two different individuals at the same or different times. And death is a comparable harm if the loss of opportunities it marks are equal in any two cases. . . .

The Miniride Principle

By making use of the notion of comparable harm, the rights view can formulate two principles that can be appealed to in order to make decisions in prevention cases. The first principle (*the minimize overriding principle,* or *the miniride principle*) states the following:

> Special considerations aside, when we must choose between overriding the rights of many who are innocent or the rights of few who are innocent, and when each affected individual will be harmed in a prima facie comparable way, then we ought to choose to override the rights of the few in preference to overriding the rights of the many.

This principle is derivable from the respect principle. This latter principle entails that all moral agents and patients are directly owed the prima facie duty not to be harmed and that all those who are owed this duty have an equally valid claim, and thus an equal prima facie moral right, against being harmed. Now, *precisely because* this right is equal, no one individual's right can count for any more than any other's, when the harm that might befall either is prima facie comparable. Thus, A's right cannot count for more than B's, or C's, or D's. However, when we are faced with choosing between options, one of which will harm A, the other of which will harm B, C, and D, and the third of which will harm them all, and when the foreseeable harm involved for each individual is prima facie comparable, then numbers count. *Precisely because* each is to count for one, no one for more than one, we cannot count choosing to override the rights of B, C, and D as neither better nor worse than choosing to override A's right alone. Three are more than one, and when the four individuals have an equal prima facie right not to be harmed, when the harm they face is prima facie comparable, and when there are no special considerations at hand, then showing equal respect for the equal rights of the individuals involved requires that we override the right of A (the few) rather than the rights of the many (B, C, D). To choose to override the rights of the many in this case would be to override an equal right three times (i.e., in the case of three different individuals) when we could choose to override such a right only once, and *that* cannot be consistent with showing equal respect for the equal rights of all the individuals involved.

To favor overriding the rights of the few in no way contravenes the requirement that each is to count for one, no one for more than one; on the contrary, special considerations apart, to choose to override the rights of the many rather than those of the few would be to count A's right for more than one — that is, as being equal to overriding the rights of three relevantly similar individuals. Accordingly, because we must not allow any one individual a greater voice in the determination of what ought to be done than any other relevantly similar individual, what we ought to do in prevention cases of the sort under consideration is choose to override the rights of the fewest innocents rather than override the rights of the many. And since this is precisely what the miniride principle enjoins, that principle is derivable from the respect principle.

The Worse-off Principle

. . . Recall the earlier prevention case where we are called upon to choose between harming A quite radically (–125), or harming a thousand individuals modestly (–1 each), or doing nothing. . . .

. . . The miniride principle, since it applies *only* in prevention cases where harms are prima facie comparable, cannot be relied on in cases, such as this one, where the harm all the innocents face is not prima facie comparable. The rights view thus requires a second principle, distinct from but consistent with the miniride principle, and one that is distinct from and not reducible to the minimize harm principle. The following principle (*the worse-off principle*) meets these requirements. . . .

> Special considerations aside, when we must decide to override the rights of the many or the rights of the few who are innocent, and when the harm faced by the few would make them worse-off than any of the many would be if any other option were chosen, then we ought to override the rights of the many. . . .

UNFINISHED BUSINESS

[An issue] deferred in earlier discussions may now be addressed: the lifeboat case. Recall the situation. There are five survivors: four normal adults and a dog. The boat has room enough only for four. Someone must go or else all will perish. Who should it be? Our initial belief is: the dog. Can the rights view illuminate and justify this prereflective intuition? The preceding discussion of prevention cases shows how it can. All on board have equal inherent value and an equal prima facie right not to be harmed. Now, the harm that death is, is a function of the opportunities for satisfaction it forecloses, and no reasonable person would deny that the death of any of the four humans would be a greater prima facie loss, and thus a greater prima facie harm, than would be true in the case of the dog. Death for the dog, in short, though a harm, is not comparable to the harm that death would be for any of the humans. To throw any one of the humans overboard, to face certain death, would be to make that individual worse-off (i.e., would cause *that* individual a greater harm) than the harm that would be done to the dog if the animal was thrown overboard. Our belief that it is the dog who should be killed is justified by appeal to the worse-off principle. . . .

WHY HUNTING AND TRAPPING ARE WRONG

Since animals can pose innocent threats and because we are sometimes justified in overriding their rights when they do, one cannot assume that all hunting or trapping must be wrong. If rabid foxes have bitten some children and are known to be in the neighboring woods, and if the circumstances of their lives assume future attacks if nothing is done, then the rights view sanctions nullifying the threat posed by these animals. When we turn from cases where we protect ourselves against the innocent threats wild animals pose, to the activities of hunting and trapping, whether for commercial profit or "sport," the rights view takes a dim view indeed. Standard justifications of the "sport" of hunting — that those who engage in it get exercise, take pleasure in communion with nature, enjoy the camaraderie of their friends, or take satisfaction in a shot well aimed—are lame, given the rights view. All these pleasures are obtainable by engaging in activities that do not result in killing any animal (walking through the woods with friends and a camera substitutes nicely), and the aggregate of the pleasures hunters derive from hunting could only override the rights of these animals if we viewed them as mere receptacles, which, on the rights view, they are not.

The appeal to tradition—an appeal one finds, for example, in support of fox hunting in Great Britain—has no more force in the case of hunting than it does in the case of any other customary abuse of animals—or humans. All that appeals to tradition signal in this case, and all they signify in related contexts, is that it is traditional to view animals as mere receptacles or as renewable resources. These appeals to tradition, in other words, are themselves symptomatic of an impoverished view of the value animals have in their own right and thus can play no legitimate role in defending a practice that harms them. Such appeals are as deficient in Great Britain, when made in behalf of the "sport" of fox hunting, as they are when made in Japan or Russia in defense of commercial whaling,[2] or in Canada in defense of the annual slaughter of seals. To allow these practices to continue, if certain quotas are not exceeded, is wrong, given the rights view, for reasons that will become clearer as we proceed.

Of course, those who hunt and trap sometimes rest their case on other considerations. It is not *their* pleasure that justifies what they do; rather, it is the humane service they perform for *the animals* that does. The situation we are enjoined to believe is this: If a certain number of animals are not hunted or trapped, there will be too many animals belonging to a given species for a given habitat to support. That being so, some of these animals will die of starvation because of their inability to compete successfully with the other animals in the habitat. To cull or harvest a certain number of these animals thus has the humane purpose and achieves the humane goal of sparing these animals the ordeal of death by starvation. How can the rights view, or any other view that is sensitive to the welfare of animals, find fault with that?

The rights view finds fault with this defense of hunting and trapping on several counts. First, the defense assumes that the death endured by hunted and trapped animals is always better (i.e., always involves less suffering) than the death these animals would endure as a result of starvation. This is far from credible. Not all hunters are expert shots, and not all trappers tend their traps responsibly or use traps that exhibit their "humane" concern for animals, the infamous leg-hold trap being perhaps the most notorious example to the contrary. Is it obvious that animals who experience a slow, agonizing death as a result of a hunter's poor shot or a poorly tended trap have a "better death" than those who die from starvation? One looks for an argument here and finds none. Unless or until one does, the defense of hunting and trapping on the grounds that they kill "more humanely" is specious.

Second, appeals to "humane concern" are dramatically at odds with the philosophy of current hunting and trapping practices, as well as with wildlife management generally. This philosophy, or the creed of maximum sustainable yield, applies to hunting and trapping in the following way. Those who hunt and trap are legally permitted, within specified seasons, to "harvest" or "crop" a certain number of wildlife of various species, the quota for that season, both collectively and for each individual hunter, to be fixed by determining whether, together with the best estimates of natural mortality, those who hunt and trap will be able to "harvest" the same number next season, and the next, and so on. In this way the maximum sustainable yield is established. If this philosophy is applied successfully, hunters and trappers will be legally licensed to do the same thing in future seasons as others were licensed to do in the past—namely, kill up to a certain number (a certain quota) of animals. If, that is, restraint is exercised in each season, the *total* number of animals that can be harvested over time will be larger, or, to put the point in its simplest, starkest terms, if fewer animals are killed now, future generations of hunters will be able to kill a larger (aggregate) number of animals in the future, which will be better. This implication of the creed of maximum sustainable yield unmasks the rhetoric about "humane service" to animals. It must be a perverse distortion of the ideal of humane service to accept or engage in practices the explicit goal of which is to ensure that there will be a larger, rather than a smaller, number of animals to kill! With "humane friends" like that, wild animals certainly do not need any enemies.

Essentially the same point can be made regarding the aggregate amount of suffering animals will endure if the creed of maximum sustainable yield is successful. If successful, the total number of animals who will die an agonizing death as a result of the poor shooting of hunters, plus those who die in similar agony as a result of poorly tended "humane" traps, plus those who die by natural causes will be larger than if other options were adopted. It is a moral smokescreen, therefore, to defend sport hunting and trapping by appeal to their humane service. The actions allowed by the philosophy of maximum sustainable yield speak louder than the lofty words uttered in its defense. The success of this philosophy would guarantee that more, not fewer, animals will be killed, and that more, not fewer, animals will die horrible deaths, either at the hands of humans or in the course of nature.

But it is not only the inconsistency between what it proclaims and what it implies that marks the undoing of the creed of maximum sustainable yield. That approach to decision making regarding wildlife management policies profoundly fails to recognize or respect the rights of wild animals. No approach to wildlife can be morally acceptable if it assumes that policy decisions should be made on the basis of aggregating harms and benefits. In particular, these decisions should not be made by appeal to the minimize harm principle. That principle sets before us what seems to be a laudatory goal — namely, to minimize the total amount of harm in general and suffering in particular. But that principle lacks the moral wherewithal to place any limits on how this laudatory goal is to be achieved; it lacks the means to assess the means used to achieve this end. If the rights of individuals are violated, that simply does not compute morally, given the minimize harm principle, if violating these rights is instrumental in achieving the goal of minimizing total harm. The rights view categorically denies the propriety of this approach to decision making. Policies that lessen the total amount of harm at the cost of violating the rights of individuals, whether these individuals are moral agents or patients, and, if the latter, human or animal, are wrong. Even if it were true, which it is not, that the philosophy of maximum sustainable yield would lead to a reduction in the total amount of death and suffering for undomesticated animals, it

still would not follow that we should accept that philosophy. As it systematically ignores the rights of wild animals, so does it systematically violate them.

The rights view categorically condemns sport hunting and trapping. Though those who participate in it need not be cruel or evil people, what they do is wrong. And what they do is wrong because they are parties to a practice that treats animals as if they were a naturally recurring renewable resource, the value of which is to be measured by, and managed by reference to, human recreational, gustatory, aesthetic, social, and other interests. Animals do renew themselves. Normally, they do not require human assistance to reproduce, any more than do trees, for example; but wild animals are not natural resources *here for us*. They have value apart from human interests, and their value is not reducible to their utility relative to our interests. To make a sport of hunting or trapping them is to do what is wrong because it is to fail to treat them with the respect they are due as a matter of strict justice.

Shorn of their appeal to their "humane concern" for wildlife, defenders of hunting and trapping are likely to protest that what they do is no different in kind from what other animals do in the state of nature. Animals routinely kill members of other (though only infrequently members of their own) species, and the death they suffer at the hands of other animals is gruesome enough to make even the most hardened heart wince. When it comes to interspecies relations, nature *is* red in tooth and claw. If the rights view professes to condemn sport hunting and trapping, it might be claimed, then it should do the same when it comes to the fatal interaction between animals themselves.

The rights view rejects this argument. Animals are not moral agents and so have none of the same duties moral agents have, including the duty to respect the rights of other animals. The wolves who eat the caribou do no moral wrong, though the harm they cause is real enough. So it is that, according to the rights view, the overarching goal of wildlife management should not be to ensure maximum sustainable yield; it should be to protect wild animals from those who would violate their rights — namely, sport hunters and trappers, commercial developers who destroy or despoil their natural habitat in the name of economic interest, and the like. *It is, in short, human wrongs that need managing, not the "crop" of animals.* Put affirmatively, the goal of wildlife management should be to defend wild animals in the possession of their rights, providing them with the opportunity to live their own life, by their own lights, as best they can, spared that human predation that goes by the name of "sport." . . .

When we move from sport to the commercial exploitation of wildlife, the moral scene is the same, only worse because the number of animals involved is greater. The rights view condemns the business of killing wild animals. Even if it is true that those whose present quality of life is tied to commerce in wild animals would be made worse-off if their business failed, that is no reason why we should continue to allow it. Like anyone else who enters the world of business, those whose business it is to kill wild animals must understand that they waive their right not to be made worse-off if their business fails. We have no duty to buy their products, and they have no right to require that we keep either their business or their present quality of life afloat. To appeal to the risk of diminished welfare in the case of their dependents is as lame in the present case as it was in the case of animal agriculture, as a defense in support of those whose business it is to kill wild animals. Moreover, while those in this business, like the rest of us, have the right to do what they can to avoid being made worse-off, they, like the rest of us, exceed this right when what they do violates the rights of others. And the commercial exploitation of wildlife does this — with a vengeance. Animals in the wild are treated as renewable resources, as if they had value only relative to the economic interests of those who feed off their dead carcasses. The rights view categorically condemns the commercial harvesting of wild animals, not because those embarked on this business are, or must be, cruel or evil people, but because what they do is wrong. Justice will be done when, and only when, we refuse to allow these commercial ventures to continue.

One can imagine someone accepting the letter but not the spirit of the foregoing. For there are, after all, many nonhumans who are killed, either for sport or commerce, who are not animals in the limited sense in which this word has been used throughout this [discussion] — who are not, that is, normal mammalian animals, aged one year or more. A voice might be heard in support of duck hunting, for example, or in defense of the commercial exploitation of baby seals. Because similar protests might be raised in different contexts (for example, one might claim that what one does to nonmammals in science or to poultry in agriculture should not be covered by the same principles that apply to what is done to mammals), a review of this defense . . . will be deferred. . . . [See *The Case for Animal Rights,* p. 358 — eds.]

Here it will suffice to raise a simple question. Let us assume that newly born *wild mammalian animals* (e.g., baby seals) do not yet meet the subject-of-a-life criterion; still, they clearly have the potential to do so. Why, then, should the moral standards that apply to how they may be treated differ in any way from those that apply to how human infants should be? The rights view denies that there is a non-arbitrary difference one could cite to justify treating the two differently. Unless one would be willing to approve of harming human infants in pursuit of sport or profit, one cannot approve of the similar treatment of infant mammalian animals.

No even partial assessment of hunting and trapping could be adequate if it failed to mention the matter of predator control. Sheep farmers in the southwestern United States, for example, are troubled by predatory animals, most notably coyotes, who attack grazing sheep, sometimes killing more than they need to subsist. The economic loss suffered by these farmers occasions their public outcry, and they have taken steps, with the assistance of federal funds and personnel, to control these predators.

Those who accept the rights view must work to bring an end to such predator control programs. The official justification of these programs assumes that the predators cause losses to persons engaged in a justified enterprise — namely, the animal industry. Since the rights view denies that this industry's treatment of animals is morally justified, the harm done to predatory animals in the name of minimizing the financial losses of those engaged in this industry is morally to be condemned. In the struggle between those involved in the animal industry and those predatory animals who inhabit the lands used in the name of this industry, it is the industry, not the predators, that ought to go. And if in response those in this industry appeal to their legal rights to the land and their legal ownership of the animals in their business, those who accept the rights view should reply, first, that the appeal to legal rights by itself never settles any moral question and, second, that the present legal status of farm animals, as owned property, is itself one of the traditions the rights view seeks to change.

HOW TO WORRY ABOUT ENDANGERED SPECIES

The rights view is a view about the moral rights of individuals. Species are not individuals, and the rights view does not recognize the moral rights of species to anything, including survival. What it recognizes is the prima facie right of individuals not to be harmed, and thus the prima facie right of individuals not to be killed. That an individual animal is among the last remaining members of a species confers no further right on that animal, and its right not to be harmed must be weighed equitably with the rights of any others who have this right. If, in a prevention situation, we had to choose between saving the last two members of an endangered species or saving another individual who belonged to a species that was plentiful but whose death would be a greater prima facie harm to that individual than the harm that death would be to the two, then the rights view requires that we save that individual. Moreover, numbers make no difference in such a case. If the choice were between saving the last thousand or million members of the species to which the two belong, that would make no moral difference. The aggregate of their lesser harms does not harm any individual in a way that is prima facie comparable to the harm that would be done to this solitary individual. Nor would aggregating the losses of other interested parties (e.g., human aesthetic or scientific interests) make any difference. The sum of these losses harms no individual in a way that is prima facie comparable to the harm that would be done to the single individual if we chose to override his right.

The rights view is not opposed to efforts to save endangered species. It only insists that we be clear about the reasons for doing so. On the rights view, the reason we ought to save the members of endangered species of animals is not because the species is endangered but because the individual animals have valid claims and thus rights against those who would destroy their natural habitat, for example, or who would make a living off their dead carcasses through poaching and traffic in exotic animals, practices that unjustifiably override the rights of these animals. But though the rights view must look with favor on any attempt to protect the rights of any animal, and so supports efforts to protect the members of endangered species, these very efforts, aimed specifically at protecting the members of species that are endangered, can foster a mentality that is antagonistic to the implications of the rights view. If people are encouraged to believe that the harm done to animals matters morally *only when* these animals belong to endangered species, then these same people will be encouraged to regard the harm done to *other* animals as morally acceptable. . . .

Though said before, it bears repeating: *the rights view is not indifferent to efforts to save endangered species. It supports these efforts.* It supports them, however, not because these animals are few in number; primarily it supports them because they are equal in value to all who have inherent value, ourselves included, sharing with us the fundamental right to be treated with respect. Since they are not mere receptacles or renewable resources placed here for our use, the harm done to them as individuals cannot be justified merely by aggregating the disparate benefits derived by commercial developers, poachers, and other interested third parties. That is what makes the commercial exploitation of endangered species wrong, not that the species are endangered. On the rights view, the same principles apply to the moral assessment of rare or endangered animals as apply to those that are plentiful, and the same principles apply whether the animals in question are wild or domesticated.

The rights view does not deny, nor is it antagonistic to recognizing, the importance of human aesthetic, scientific, sacramental, and other interests in rare and endangered species or in wild animals generally. What it denies is that (1) the value of these animals is reducible to, or is interchangeable with, the aggregate satisfaction of these human interests, and that (2) the determination of how these animals should be treated, including whether they should be saved in preference to more plentiful animals, is to be fixed by the yardstick of such human interests, either taken individually or aggregatively. Both points cut both ways, concerning, as they do, both how animals may and how they may not be treated. In particular, any and all harm done to rare or endangered animals, done in the name of aggregated human interests, is wrong, according to the rights view, because it violates the individual animal's right to respectful treatment. With regard to wild animals, the general policy recommended by the rights view is: *let them be!* Since this will require increased human intervention in *human* practices that threaten rare or endangered species (e.g., halting the destruction of natural habitat and closer surveillance of poaching, with much stiffer fines and longer prison sentences), the rights view sanctions this intervention, assuming that those humans involved are treated with the respect they are due. Too little is not enough.

RIGHTS AND ENVIRONMENTAL ETHICS: AN ASIDE

The difficulties and implications of developing a rights-based environmental ethic should be abundantly clear by now and deserve brief comment before moving on. The difficulties include reconciling the *individualistic* nature of moral rights with the more *holistic* view of nature emphasized by many of the leading environmental thinkers. Aldo Leopold is illustrative of this latter tendency. "A thing is right," he states, "when it tends to preserve the integrity, stability, and beauty of the biotic community. It is wrong when it tends otherwise."[3] The implications of this view include the clear prospect that the individual may be sacrificed for the greater biotic good, in the name of "the integrity, stability, and beauty of the biotic community." It is difficult to see how the notion of the rights of the individual could find a home within a view that, emotive connotations to one side, might be fairly dubbed "environmental fascism." To use Leopold's telling phrase, man is *"only* a member of the biotic team,"[4] and as such has the same moral standing as any other "member" of "the team." If, to take an extreme, fanciful but, it is hoped, not unfair example, the situation we faced was either to kill a rare wildflower or a (plentiful) human being, and if the wildflower, as a "team member," would contribute more to "the integrity, stability, and beauty of the biotic commu-

nity" than the human, then presumably we would not be doing wrong if we killed the human and saved the wildflower. The rights view cannot abide this position, not because the rights view categorically denies that inanimate objects can have rights (more on this momentarily) but because it denies the propriety of deciding what should be done to individuals who have rights by appeal to aggregative considerations, including, therefore, computations about what will or will not maximally "contribute to the integrity, stability, and beauty of the biotic community." Individual rights are not to be outweighed by such considerations (which is not to say that they are never to be outweighed). Environmental fascism and the rights view are like oil and water: they don't mix.

The rights view does not deny the possibility that collections or systems of natural objects might have inherent value — that is, might have a kind of value that is not the same as, is not reducible to, and is incommensurate with any one individual's pleasures, preference-satisfactions, and the like, or with the sum of such goods for any number of individuals. The beauty of an undisturbed, ecologically balanced forest, for example, might be conceived to have value of this kind. The point is certainly arguable. What is far from certain is how moral rights could be meaningfully attributed to the *collection* of trees or the ecosystem. Since neither is an individual, it is unclear how the notion of moral rights can be meaningfully applied. Perhaps this difficulty can be surmounted. It is fair to say, however, that no one writing in this important area of ethics has yet done so.[5]

Because paradigmatic right-holders are individuals, and because the dominant thrust of contemporary environmental efforts (e.g., wilderness preservation) is to focus on the whole rather than on the part (i.e., the individual), there is an understandable reluctance on the part of environmentalists to "take rights seriously," or at least a reluctance to take them as seriously as the rights view contends we should. But this may be a case of environmentalists not seeing the forest for the trees — or, more accurately, of not seeing the trees for the forest. The implications of the successful development of a rights-based environmental ethic, one that made the case that individual inanimate natural objects (e.g., *this* redwood) have inherent value and a basic moral right to treatment respectful of that value, should be welcomed by environmentalists. If individual trees have inherent value, they have a kind of value that is not the same as, is not reducible to, and is incommensurate with the intrinsic values of the pleasures, preference-satisfactions, and the like, of others, and since the rights of the individual never are to be overridden merely on the grounds of aggregating such values for all those affected by the outcome, a rights-based environmental ethic would bar the door to those who would uproot wilderness in the name of "human progress," whether this progress be aggregated economic, educational, recreational, or other human interests. On the rights view, assuming this could be successfully extended to inanimate natural objects, our general policy regarding wilderness would be precisely what the preservationists want — namely, let it be! Before those who favor such preservation dismiss the rights view in favor of the holistic view more commonly voiced in environmental circles, they might think twice about the implications of the two. There is the danger that the baby will be thrown out with the bath water. A rights-based environmental ethic remains a live option, one that, though far from being established, merits continued exploration. It ought not to be dismissed out of hand by environmentalists as being in principle antagonistic to the goals for which they work. It isn't. Were we to show proper respect for the rights of the individuals who make up the biotic community, would not the *community* be preserved? And is not that what the more holistic, systems-minded environmentalists want? . . .

NOTES

1. The equality Singer has in mind ["Equality for Animals?" following] is the equality set forth in his equality principle and thus concerns counting equal interests equally. The equality of individuals — their having equal inherent value in their own right — is not what Singer means when he says "all animals are equal." It is what I mean here.
2. A fuller argument critical of commercial whaling is contained in my "Why Whaling Is Wrong," in Tom Regan, *All That Dwell Therein* (Berkeley: University of California Press, 1982).

3. Aldo Leopold, *A Sand County Almanac* (New York: Oxford University Press, 1949), p. 217.
4. Ibid., p. 209, emphasis added.
5. For further remarks on these matters, see my "What Sorts of Beings Can Have Rights?" and "The Nature and Possibility of an Environmental Ethic," both in Tom Regan, *All That Dwell Therein*.

DISCUSSION TOPICS

1. Do you find Regan's postulation of inherent value in individuals who are subjects-of-a-life to be convincing? Why or why not?
2. Do you agree with Regan that ecocentrism is environmental fascism? How do you think Leopold would respond to Regan's charge? (See Chapter 8.)
3. Is Regan correct that protection of individual animals will protect the biotic community? Give an example supporting your position.
4. Explain and evaluate Regan's theory by applying it to endangered species of plants, plants harmful to animals, and plants beneficial to animals.
5. You are a member of your state's fish and game commission. If you applied Regan's theories, what would be the outcome concerning
   a. Sport hunting of a deer population that is too large for its habitat.
   b. Control of coyote predation on domestic sheep. Do you agree with Regan's position?

READING 36

Equality for Animals?

Peter Singer

Peter Singer was born in Australia. Since 1999 he has been the DeCamp Professor of Bioethics in the University Center for Human Values at Princeton University. His book Animal Liberation *(1975) is widely credited with beginning the movement for animal rights. In the following selection from* Practical Ethics *(1993) Singer argues that it is immoral to discriminate against an individual simply because he or she is not a member of one's own species. Any sentient individual has interests that must be given moral consideration. In the concluding section, Singer discusses his controversial "replaceability" argument.*

RACISM AND SPECIESISM

In the previous chapter I gave reasons for believing that the fundamental principle of equality, on which the equality of all human beings rests, is the principle of equal consideration of interests. Only a basic moral principle of this kind can allow us to defend a form of equality which embraces all human beings, with all the differences that exist between them. I shall now contend that while this principle does provide an adequate basis for human equality, it provides a basis which cannot be limited to humans. In other words I shall suggest that, having accepted the principle of equality as a sound moral basis for relations with others of our own species, we are also committed to accepting it as a sound moral basis for relations with those outside our own species — the nonhuman animals.

This suggestion may at first seem bizarre. We are used to regarding the oppression of blacks and women as among the most important moral and political issues facing the world today. These are serious matters, worthy of the time and energy of any concerned persons. But animals? Surely the welfare of animals is in a different category altogether, a matter for old ladies in tennis shoes to worry about. How can anyone waste their time on equality for animals when so many humans are denied real equality?

This attitude reflects a popular prejudice against taking the interests of animals seriously — a prejudice no better founded than the prejudice of white slaveowners against taking the interests of blacks seriously. It is easy for us to criticize the prejudices of our grandfathers, from which our fathers freed themselves. It is more difficult to distance ourselves from our own beliefs, so that we can dispassionately search for prejudices among them. What is needed now is a willingness to follow the arguments where they lead, without a prior assumption that the issue is not worth attending to.

The argument for extending the principle of equality beyond our own species is simple, so simple that it amounts to no more than a clear understanding of the nature of the principle of equal consideration of interests. We have seen that this principle implies that our concern for others ought not to depend on what they are like, or what abilities they possess (although precisely what this concern requires us to do may vary according to the characteristics of those affected by what we do). It is on this basis that we are able to say that the fact that some people are not members of our race does not entitle us to exploit them, and similarly the fact that some people are less intelligent than others does not mean that their interests may be disregarded. But the principle also implies that the fact that beings are not members of our species does not entitle us to exploit them, and similarly the fact that other animals are less intelligent than we are does not mean that their interests may be disregarded.

. . . [M]any philosophers have advocated equal consideration of interests, in some form or other, as a basic moral principle. Few recognized that the principle has applications beyond our own species. One of the few who did was Jeremy Bentham, the founding father of modern utilitarianism. In a forward-looking passage, written at a time when black slaves in the British dominions were still being treated much as we now treat nonhuman animals, Bentham wrote:

> The day *may* come when the rest of the animal creation may acquire those rights which never could have been withholden from them but by the hand of tyranny. The French have already discovered that the blackness of the skin is no reason why a human being should be abandoned without redress to the caprice of a tormentor. It may one day come to be recognised that the number of the legs, the villosity of the skin, or the termination of the *os sacrum,* are reasons equally insufficient for abandoning a sensitive being to the same fate. What else is it that should trace the insuperable line? Is it the faculty of reason, or perhaps the faculty of discourse? But a full-grown horse or dog is beyond comparison a more rational, as well as a more conversable animal, than an infant of a day, or a week, or even a month, old. But suppose they were otherwise, what

would it avail? The question is not, Can they reason? nor Can they *talk?* but, *Can they suffer?*[1]

In this passage Bentham points to the capacity for suffering as the vital characteristic that entitles a being to equal consideration. The capacity for suffering—or more strictly, for suffering and/or enjoyment or happiness—is not just another characteristic like the capacity for language, or for higher mathematics. Bentham is not saying that those who try to mark "the insuperable line" that determines whether the interests of a being should be considered happen to have selected the wrong characteristic. The capacity for suffering and enjoying things is a prerequisite for having interests at all, a condition that must be satisfied before we can speak of interests in any meaningful way. It would be nonsense to say that it was not in the interests of a stone to be kicked along the road by a schoolboy. A stone does not have interests because it cannot suffer. Nothing that we can do to it could possibly make any difference to its welfare. A mouse, on the other hand, does have an interest in not being tormented, because it will suffer if it is.

If a being suffers, there can be no moral justification for refusing to take that suffering into consideration. No matter what the nature of the being, the principle of equality requires that its suffering be counted equally with the like suffering—insofar as rough comparisons can be made—of any other being. If a being is not capable of suffering, or of experiencing enjoyment or happiness, there is nothing to be taken into account. This is why the limit of sentience (using the term as a convenient, if not strictly accurate, shorthand for the capacity to suffer or experience enjoyment or happiness) is the only defensible boundary of concern for the interests of others. To mark this boundary by some characteristic like intelligence or rationality would be to mark it in an arbitrary way. Why not choose some other characteristic, like skin colour?

Racists violate the principle of equality by giving greater weight to the interests of members of their own race when there is a clash between their interests and the interests of those of another race. White racists do not accept that pain is as bad when it is felt by blacks as when it is felt by whites. Similarly those I would call "speciesists" give greater weight to the interests of members of their own species when there is a clash between their interests and the interests of those of other species. Human speciesists do not accept that pain is as bad when it is felt by pigs or mice as when it is felt by humans.

That, then, is really the whole of the argument for extending the principle of equality to nonhuman animals; but there may be some doubts about what this equality amounts to in practice. In particular, the last sentence of the previous paragraph may prompt some people to reply: "Surely pain felt by a mouse just is not as bad as pain felt by a human. Humans have much greater awareness of what is happening to them, and this makes their suffering worse. You can't equate the suffering of, say, a person dying slowly from cancer, and a laboratory mouse undergoing the same fate."

I fully accept that in the case described the human cancer victim normally suffers more than the non-human cancer victim. This in no way undermines the extension of equal consideration of interests to nonhumans. It means, rather, that we must take care when we compare the interests of different species. In some situations a member of one species will suffer more than a member of another species. In this case we should still apply the principle of equal consideration of interests but the result of so doing is, of course, to give priority to relieving the greater suffering. A simpler case may help to make this clear.

If I give a horse a hard slap across its rump with my open hand, the horse may start, but it presumably feels little pain. Its skin is thick enough to protect it against a mere slap. If I slap a baby in the same way, however, the baby will cry and presumably does feel pain, for its skin is more sensitive. So it is worse to slap a baby than a horse, if both slaps are administered with equal force. But there must be some kind of blow—I don't know exactly what it would be, but perhaps a blow with a heavy stick—that would cause the horse as much pain as we cause a baby by slapping it with our hand. That is what I mean by "the same amount of pain" and if we consider it wrong to inflict that much pain on a baby for no good reason then we must, unless we are speciesists, consider it equally wrong to inflict the same amount of pain on a horse for no good reason.

There are other differences between humans and animals that cause other complications. Normal adult human beings have mental capacities which will, in certain circumstances, lead them to suffer more than animals would in the same circumstances. If, for instance, we decided to perform extremely painful or lethal scientific experiments on normal adult humans, kidnapped at random from public parks for this purpose, adults who entered parks would become fearful that they would be kidnapped. The resultant terror would be a form of suffering additional to the pain of the experiment. The same experiments performed on nonhuman animals would cause less suffering since the animals would not have the anticipatory dread of being kidnapped and experimented upon. This does not mean, of course, that it would be *right* to perform the experiment on animals, but only that there is a reason, which is not speciesist, for preferring to use animals rather than normal adult humans, if the experiment is to be done at all. It should be noted, however, that this same argument gives us a reason for preferring to use human infants — orphans perhaps — or retarded humans for experiments, rather than adults, since infants and retarded humans would also have no idea of what was going to happen to them. So far as this argument is concerned nonhuman animals and infants and retarded humans are in the same category; and if we use this argument to justify experiments on nonhuman animals we have to ask ourselves whether we are also prepared to allow experiments on human infants and retarded adults. If we make a distinction between animals and these humans, how can we do it, other than on the basis of a morally indefensible preference for members of our own species?

There are many areas in which the superior mental powers of normal adult humans make a difference: anticipation, more detailed memory, greater knowledge of what is happening, and so on. These differences explain why a human dying from cancer is likely to suffer more than a mouse. It is the mental anguish which makes the human's position so much harder to bear. Yet these differences do not all point to greater suffering on the part of the normal human being. Sometimes animals may suffer *more* because of their more limited understanding. If, for instance, we are taking prisoners in wartime we can explain to them that while they must submit to capture, search, and confinement they will not otherwise be harmed and will be set free at the conclusion of hostilities. If we capture a wild animal, however, we cannot explain that we are not threatening its life. A wild animal cannot distinguish an attempt to overpower and confine from an attempt to kill; the one causes as much terror as the other.

It may be objected that comparisons of the sufferings of different species are impossible to make, and that for this reason when the interests of animals and humans clash the principle of equality gives no guidance. It is probably true that comparisons of suffering between members of different species cannot be made precisely. Nor, for that matter, can comparisons of suffering between different human beings be made precisely. Precision is not essential. As we shall see shortly, even if we were to prevent the infliction of suffering on animals only when the interests of humans will not be affected to anything like the extent that animals are affected, we would be forced to make radical changes in our treatment of animals that would involve our diet, the farming methods we use, experimental procedures in many fields of science, our approach to wildlife and to hunting, trapping and the wearing of furs, and areas of entertainment like circuses, rodeos, and zoos. As a result, a vast amount of suffering would be avoided.

So far I have said a lot about the infliction of suffering on animals, but nothing about killing them. This omission has been deliberate. The application of the principle of equality to the infliction of suffering is, in theory at least, fairly straightforward. Pain and suffering are bad and should be prevented or minimized, irrespective of the race, sex, or species of the being that suffers. How bad a pain is depends on how intense it is and how long it lasts, but pains of the same intensity and duration are equally bad, whether felt by humans or animals. When we come to consider the value of life, we cannot say quite so confidently that a life is a life, and equally valuable, whether it is a human life or an animal life. It would not be speciesist to hold that the life of a self-aware being, capable of abstract thought, of planning for the future, of complex acts of communication, and so on, is more valuable than the life of a being without these capacities. (I am not saying whether this view is justifiable or not; only that it cannot simply be rejected as speciesist, because it is not on the basis of species itself that one life is held to be more valuable than another.) The value of life is a notoriously difficult ethical question, and we can only arrive at a reasoned conclusion about the comparative value of human and animal life after we have discussed the value of life in general. . . . Meanwhile there are important conclusions to be derived from the extension beyond our own species of the principle of equal consideration of interests, irrespective of our conclusions about the value of life. . . .

SOME OBJECTIONS

Despite the increasing acceptance of many aspects of the case for animal liberation, and the slow but tangible progress made on behalf of animals, a variety of objections have emerged, some straightforward and predictable, some more subtle and unexpected. In this final section of the chapter I shall attempt to answer the most important of these objections. I shall begin with the more straightforward ones.

How Do We Know That
Animals Can Feel Pain?

We can never directly experience the pain of another being, whether that being is human or not. When I see my daughter fall and scrape her knee, I know that she feels pain because of the way she behaves — she cries, she tells me her knee hurts, she rubs the sore spot, and so on. I know that I myself behave in a somewhat similar — if more inhibited — way when I feel pain, and so I accept that my daughter feels something like what I feel when I scrape my knee.

The basis of my belief that animals can feel pain is similar to the basis of my belief that my daughter can feel pain. Animals in pain behave in much the same way as humans do, and their behaviour is sufficient justification for the belief that they feel pain. It is true that, with the exception of those apes who have been taught to communicate by sign language, they cannot actually say that they are feeling pain — but then when my daughter was a little younger she could not talk either. She found other ways to make her inner states apparent, however, so demonstrating that we can be sure that a being is feeling pain even if the being cannot use language.

To back up our inference from animal behaviour, we can point to the fact that the nervous systems of all vertebrates, and especially of birds and mammals, are fundamentally similar. Those parts of the human nervous system that are concerned with feeling pain are relatively old, in evolutionary terms. Unlike the cerebral cortex, which developed only after our ancestors diverged from other mammals, the basic nervous system evolved in more distant ancestors common to ourselves and the other "higher" animals. This anatomical parallel makes it likely that the capacity of animals to feel is similar to our own.

It is significant that none of the grounds we have for believing that animals feel pain hold for plants. We cannot observe behaviour suggesting pain — sensational claims to the contrary have not been substantiated — and plants do not have a centrally organized nervous system like ours.

Animals Eat Each Other, So Why
Shouldn't We Eat Them?

This might be called the Benjamin Franklin Objection. Franklin recounts in his *Autobiography* that he was for a time a vegetarian but his abstinence from animal flesh came to an end when he was watching some friends prepare to fry a fish they had just caught. When the fish was cut open, it was found to have a smaller fish in its stomach. "Well," Franklin said to himself, "if you eat one another, I don't see why we may not eat you" and he proceeded to do so.[2]

Franklin was at least honest. In telling this story, he confesses that he convinced himself of the validity of the objection only after the fish was already in the frying pan and smelling "admirably well"; and he remarks that one of the advantages of being a "reasonable creature" is that one can find a reason for whatever one wants to do. The replies that can be made to this objection are so obvious that Franklin's acceptance of it does testify more to his love of fried fish than his powers of reason. For a start, most animals that kill for food would not be able to survive if they did not, whereas we have no need to eat animal flesh. Next, it is odd that humans, who normally think of the behavior of animals as "beastly" should, when it suits them, use an argument that implies we ought to look to animals for moral guidance. The decisive point, however, is that nonhuman animals are not capable of considering the alternatives open to them or of reflecting on the ethics of their diet. Hence it is impossible to hold the animals responsible for what they do, or to judge that because of their killing they "deserve" to be treated in a similar way. Those who read these lines, on the other hand, must consider the justifiability of their dietary habits. You cannot evade responsibility by imitating beings who are incapable of making a choice.

Sometimes people point to the fact that animals eat each other in order to make a slightly different point. This fact suggests, they think, not that animals deserve to be eaten, but rather that there is a natural law according to which the stronger prey upon the weaker, a kind of Darwinian "survival of the fittest" in which by eating animals we are merely playing our part.

This interpretation of the objection makes two basic mistakes, one a mistake of fact and the other an error of reasoning. The factual mistake lies in the assumption that our own consumption of animals is part of the natural evolutionary process. This might be true of a few primitive cultures which still hunt for food, but it has nothing to do with the mass production of domestic animals in factory farms.

Suppose that we did hunt for our food, though, and this was part of some natural evolutionary process. There would still be an error of reasoning in the assumption that because this process is natural it is right. It is, no doubt, "natural" for women to produce an infant every year or two from puberty to menopause, but this does not mean that it is wrong to interfere with this process. We need to know the natural laws which affect us in order to estimate the consequences of what we do; but we do not have to assume that the natural way of doing something is incapable of improvement. . . .

Ethics and Reciprocity

. . . [I]f the basis of ethics is that I refrain from doing nasty things to others as long as they don't do nasty things to me, I have no reason against doing nasty things to those who are incapable of appreciating my restraint and controlling their conduct towards me accordingly. Animals, by and large, are in this category. When I am surfing far out from shore and a shark attacks, my concern for animals will not help; I am as likely to be eaten as the next

surfer, though he may spend every Sunday afternoon taking potshots at sharks from a boat. Since animals cannot reciprocate, they are, in this view, outside the limits of the ethical contract. . . .

When we turn to the question of justification, we can see that contractual accounts of ethics have many problems. Clearly, such accounts exclude from the ethical sphere a lot more than nonhuman animals. Since severely intellectually disabled humans are equally incapable of reciprocating, they must also be excluded. The same goes for infants and very young children; but the problems of the contractual view are not limited to these special cases. The ultimate reason for entering into the ethical contract is, on this view, self-interest. Unless some additional universal element is brought in, one group of people has no reason to deal ethically with another if it is not in their interest to do so. If we take this seriously we shall have to revise our ethical judgments drastically. For instance, the white slave traders who transported African slaves to America had no self-interested reason for treating Africans any better than they did. The Africans had no way of retaliating. If they had only been contractualists, the slave traders could have rebutted the abolitionists by explaining to them that ethics stops at the boundaries of the community, and since Africans are not part of their community they have no duties to them.

Nor is it only past practices that would be affected by taking the contractual model seriously. Though people often speak of the world today as a single community, there is no doubt that the power of people in, say, Chad, to reciprocate either good or evil that is done to them by, say, citizens of the United States is limited. Hence it does not seem that the contract view provides for any obligations on the part of wealthy nations to poorer nations.

Most striking of all is the impact of the contract model on our attitude to future generations. "Why should I do anything for posterity? What has posterity ever done for me?" would be the view we ought to take if only those who can reciprocate are within the bounds of ethics. There is no way in which those who will be alive in the year 2100 can do anything to make our lives better or worse. Hence if obligations only exist where there can be reciprocity, we need have no worries about problems like the disposal of nuclear waste. True, some nuclear wastes will still be deadly for a quarter of a million years; but as long as we put it in containers that will keep it away from us for 100 years, we have done all that ethics demands of us.

These examples should suffice to show that, whatever its origin, the ethics we have now does go beyond a tacit understanding between beings capable of reciprocity. The prospect of returning to such a basis will, I trust, not be appealing. Since no account of the origin of morality compels us to base our morality on reciprocity, and since no other arguments in favor of this conclusion have been offered, we should reject this view of ethics. . . .

KILLING OTHER ANIMALS

Arguments against killing based on the capacity to see oneself as an individual existing over time apply to some nonhuman animals, but there are others who, though presumably conscious, cannot plausibly be said to be persons. Of those animals that humans regularly kill in large numbers, fish appear to be the clearest case of animals who are conscious but not persons. The rightness or wrongness of killing these animals seems to rest on utilitarian considerations, for they are not autonomous and . . . do not qualify for a right to life.

Before we discuss the utilitarian approach to killing itself, we should remind ourselves that a wide variety of indirect reasons will figure in the utilitarian's calculations. Many modes of killing used on animals do not inflict an instantaneous death, so there is pain in the process of dying. There is also the effect of the death of one animal on his or her mate or other members of the animal's social group. There are many species of birds in which the bond between male and female lasts for a lifetime. The death of one member of this pair presumably causes distress, and a sense of loss and sorrow for the survivor. The mother-child relationship in mammals can be a source of intense suffering if either is killed or taken away. (Dairy farmers routinely remove calves from their mothers at an early age, so that the milk will be available for humans; anyone who has lived on a dairy farm will know that, for days after the calves have gone, the cows keep calling for them.) In some species the death of one animal may be felt by a larger group — as the behavior of wolves

and elephants suggests. All these factors would lead the utilitarian to oppose a lot of killing of animals, whether or not the animals are persons. These factors would not, however, be reasons for opposing killing nonpersons in itself, apart from the pain and suffering it may cause.

The utilitarian verdict on killing that is painless and causes no loss to others is more complicated, because it depends on how we choose between the two versions of utilitarianism [outlined in the previous chapter]. If we take what I called the "prior existence" view, we shall hold that it is wrong to kill any being whose life is likely to contain, or can be brought to contain, more pleasure than pain. This view implies that it is normally wrong to kill animals for food, since usually we could bring it about that these animals had a few pleasant months or even years before they died — and the pleasure we get from eating them would not outweigh this.

The other version of utilitarianism — the "total" view — can lead to a different outcome that has been used to justify meat-eating. The nineteenth-century British political philosopher Leslie Stephen once wrote:

> Of all the arguments for Vegetarianism none is so weak as the argument from humanity. The pig has a stronger interest than anyone in the demand for bacon. If all the world were Jewish, there would be no pigs at all.

Stephen views animals as if they were replaceable, and with this those who accept the total view must agree. The total version of utilitarianism regards sentient beings as valuable only in so far as they make possible the existence of intrinsically valuable experiences like pleasure. It is as if sentient beings are receptacles of something valuable and it does not matter if a receptacle gets broken, so long as there is another receptacle to which the contents can be transferred without any getting split. (This metaphor should not be taken too seriously, however; unlike precious liquids, experiences like pleasure cannot exist independently from a conscious being, and so even on the total view, sentient beings cannot properly be thought of merely as receptacles.) Stephen's argument is that although meat-eaters are responsible for the death of the animal they eat and for the loss of pleasure experienced by that animal, they are also responsible for the creation of more animals, since if no one ate meat there would be no more animals bred for fattening. The loss meat-eaters inflict on one animal is thus balanced, on the total view, by the benefit they confer on the next. We may call this "the replaceability argument."

The first point to note about the replaceability argument is that even if it is valid when the animals in question have a pleasant life it would not justify eating the flesh of animals reared in modern factory farms, where the animals are so crowded together and restricted in their movements that their lives seem to be more of a burden than a benefit to them.

A second point is that if it is good to create happy life, then presumably it is good for there to be as many happy beings on our planet as it can possibly hold. Defenders of meat-eating had better hope that they can find a reason why it is better for there to be happy people rather than just the maximum possible number of happy beings, because otherwise the argument might imply that we should eliminate almost all human beings in order to make way for much larger numbers of smaller happy animals. If, however, the defenders of meat-eating do come up with a reason for preferring the creation of happy people to, say, happy mice, then their argument will not support meat-eating at all. For with the possible exception of arid areas suitable only for pasture, the surface of our globe can support more people if we grow plant foods than if we raise animals.

These two points greatly weaken the replaceability argument as a defense of meat-eating, but they do not go to the heart of the matter. Are some sentient beings really replaceable? The response to the first edition of this book suggests that the replaceability argument is probably the most controversial, and widely criticized, argument in this book. Unfortunately none of the critics have offered satisfactory alternative solutions to the underlying problems to which replaceability offers one—if not very congenial—answer.

NOTES

1. Jeremy Bentham, *An Introduction to the Principles of Morals and Legislation, Works,* XIX (New York: Russell and Russell, 1962), sec. 1, footnote to paragraph 4.

2. Benjamin Franklin, *Autobiography* (New Haven and London: Yale University Press, 1964), pp. 87–88.

DISCUSSION TOPICS

1. Do you find Singer's arguments against speciesism convincing? Why or why not?

2. Do you accept Singer's distinction between causing suffering and killing? Does Singer's argument allow the "putting to sleep" of homeless dogs?

3. Singer argues that the pain suffered by a mouse generally is morally equivalent to that suffered by a human being in a similar situation. Do you agree? Why or why not?

4. Provide your own example of a situation in which a human being might experience more suffering than an animal in a comparable situation. In what situation might the human being suffer less than an animal?

5. Assuming you are restricted to using utilitarian theory, which do you find more correct: "prior existence" or "total" view utilitarianism? Explain your choice.

6. What do you find convincing about Singer's arguments against objections to his theory? Identify which of his arguments you believe to be the strongest and which the weakest.

READING 37

Environmental Values

Peter Singer

Peter Singer is DeCamp Professor of Bioethics in the University Center for Human Values at Princeton University. The following essay is from The Environmental Challenge *(edited by Ian Marsh, 1991). In it, Singer argues against views such as those of Schweitzer, Taylor, and Leopold, which would extend moral value to nonsentient living things. He maintains that arguments grounded in the interests of hu-*

man beings and sentient nonhumans are sufficient to show the value of preserving wilderness.

A river tumbles through steep wooded valleys and rocky gorges towards the sea. The state hydro-electricity commission sees the falling water as untapped energy. Building a dam across one of the gorges would provide three years of employment for a thousand people, and longer term employment for twenty or thirty. The dam would store enough water to ensure that the state could economically meet its energy needs for the next decade. This would encourage the establishment of energy-intensive industry in the state, thus further contributing to employment and economic growth.

The rough terrain of the river valley makes it accessible only to the reasonably fit, but it is nevertheless a favoured spot for bushwalking. The river itself attracts the more daring whitewater rafters. Deep in the sheltered valleys are stands of Huon pine, thousands of years old. The valleys and gorges are home to many birds and animals, including an endangered species of marsupial mouse found in only one other place in Australia. There may be other rare plants and animals as well, but no one knows, for scientists are yet to investigate the region fully.

Should the dam be built? This is one example of a situation in which we must choose between very different sets of values. . . .

A human-centred ethic can be the basis of powerful arguments for what we may call "environmental values." Even from the perspective of such an ethic, economic growth based on the exploitation of irreplaceable resources can be seen as something that brings gains to the present generation, and possibly the next generation or two, at a price that will be paid by every generation to come. The price to be paid by future human beings is too high. But should we limit ourselves to a human-centred ethic? We now need to consider more fundamental challenges to this traditional Western approach to environmental issues.

IS THERE VALUE BEYOND THE HUMAN SPECIES?

Although some debates about significant environmental issues can be conducted by appealing only to the long-term interests of our own species, in any serious exploration of environmental values a central issue will be whether there is anything of intrinsic value beyond human beings. To explore this question we first need to understand the notion of "intrinsic value." Something is of intrinsic value if it is good or desirable in itself; the contrast is with instrumental value, that is value as a means to some other end or purpose. Our own happiness, for example, is of intrinsic value, at least to most of us, in that we desire it for its own sake. Money, on the other hand, is only of instrumental value to us. We want it because of the things we can buy with it, but if we were marooned on a desert island, we would not want it (whereas happiness would be just as important to us on a desert island as anywhere else).

Now consider again for a moment the issue of damming the river described at the beginning of this chapter. Should the decision be made on the basis of human interests alone? If we say that it should, we shall balance the economic benefits for Tasmanians of building the dam against the loss for bushwalkers, scientists and others, now and in the future, who value the preservation of the river in its natural state. We have already seen that because this calculation includes an indefinite number of future generations, the loss of the wild river is a much greater cost than we might at first imagine. Even so, if we are justified in arguing that the decision whether to dam the river should be made on the basis of values that include, but are not limited to, the interests of human beings, we may have much more to set against the economic benefits for Tasmanians of building the dam. We may take into account the interests of the animals who will die if the valley is drowned; we may give weight to the fact that a species may be lost, that trees that have stood for thousands of years will die, and that an entire local ecosystem will be destroyed; and we may give the preservation of the animals, the species, the trees and the ecosystems a weight that is independent of the interests of human beings — whether economic, recreational or scientific — in their preservation.

Here we have a fundamental moral disagreement: a disagreement about what kinds of beings ought to be considered in our moral deliberations. Many people think that once we reach a disagreement of this kind, argument must cease. As I have already briefly indicated, I am more optimistic about the scope of rational argument in ethics. In ethics, even at a fundamental level, there are arguments that should convince any rational person. . . .

. . . In keeping with the dominant Western tradition, many people still hold that all the non-human natural world has value only or predominantly insofar as it benefits human beings. A powerful objection to the dominant Western tradition turns [on the fact that] many non-human animals are also capable of feeling pain, as humans are; they can certainly be miserable, and perhaps in some cases their lives could also be described as joyful; and members of many mammalian species can suffer from separation from their family group. Is it not therefore a blot on human civilisation that we brush aside these needs of non-human animals to satisfy minor needs of our own?

Pain is pain, and the extent to which it is intrinsically bad depends on factors like its duration and intensity, not on the species of the being who experiences it. Hence there is no justifiable basis for drawing the boundary of value around our own species. To do so is to give preference to the interests of members of one's own species, simply because they are members of one's own species. This is speciesism, a moral failing that is parallel to racism, because it attempts to put a morally crucial divide in a place that is not justified on any basis other than a preference for "us" over "them." To put it another way, if we are prepared to defend practices based on disregarding the interests of members of other species because they are not members of our own group, how are we to object to those who wish to disregard the interests of members of other races because they are also not members of our own group? I shall not here go further into this argument, because I have developed it elsewhere at some length.[1] The argument shows that the dominant Western tradition is untenable, at least in regard to creatures capable of suffering.

Rejecting the dominant Western tradition in this way makes a radical difference to the value basis on which we should consider environmental policy. Into the calculations about damming the river must now go the interests of all the non-human animals who live in the area that will be flooded. A few may be able to move to a neighbouring area that is suitable, but wilderness is not full of suitable niches awaiting an occupant; if there is territory that can sustain a native animal, it is most likely already occupied. Thus most of them will die: either they will be drowned, or they will starve.

Neither drowning nor starvation is an easy way to die, and the suffering involved in these deaths should, as we have seen, be given no less weight than we would give to an equivalent amount of suffering experienced by human beings. That, in itself, may be enough to swing the balance against building the dam. What of the fact that the animals will die, apart from the suffering that will occur in the course of dying? Are we also to weigh the deaths of non-human animals as equivalent to the deaths of a similar number of human beings? If so, it would seem that almost no development of any area can be justified; even industrial wastelands provide habitat for rodents who will die if the land is built upon. But the argument presented above does not require us to regard the death of a non-human animal as morally equivalent to the death of a human being, since humans are capable of foresight and forward planning in ways that non-human animals are not. This is surely relevant to the seriousness of death which, in the case of a human being capable of planning for the future, will thwart these plans, and which thus causes a loss that is different in kind from the loss that death causes to beings incapable even of understanding that they exist over time and have a future. It is also entirely legitimate to take into account the greater sense of loss that humans feel when people close to them die; whether non-human animals will feel a sense of loss at the death of another animal will depend on the social habits of the species, but in most cases it is unlikely to be as prolonged, and perhaps not as deep, as the grief that humans feel. These differences between causing death to human beings and to non-human animals do not mean that the death of a non-human animal should be treated as being of no account. On the contrary, death still inflicts a loss on the animal — the loss of all its future existence, and the experiences that that future life would have contained. When a proposed dam would flood a valley and kill thousands, perhaps millions, of sentient creatures, these deaths should be given great importance in any assessment of the costs and benefits of building the dam.

Let us summarise the conclusions reached so far. We have seen that the dominant Western tradition would restrict environmental values to human interests; but this tradition is based on an indefensible prejudice in favour of the interests of our own species. We share our planet with members of other species who are also capable of feeling pain, of suffering, and of having their lives go well or badly. We are justified in regarding their experiences as having the same kind of value as our own similar experiences. The infliction of suffering on other sentient creatures should be given as much weight as we would give to the infliction of suffering on human beings. The deaths of non-human animals, considered independently from the suffering that often accompanies death, should also count, although not as much as the deaths of human beings.

IS THERE VALUE BEYOND SENTIENT BEINGS?

Reverence for Life

The position we have now reached extends the ethic of the dominant Western tradition, but in other respects is recognisably of the same type. It draws the boundary of moral consideration around all sentient creatures, but leaves other living things outside that boundary. This means that if a valley is to be flooded, we should give weight to the interests of human beings, both present and future, and to the interests of the wallabies, possums, marsupial mice and birds living there; but the drowning of the ancient forests, the possible loss of an entire species, the destruction of several complex ecosystems, and the blockage of the wild river itself and the loss of those rocky gorges, are factors to be taken into account only insofar as they adversely affect sentient creatures. Is a more radical break with the traditional position possible? Can some or all of these aspects of the flooding of the valley be shown to have intrinsic value, so that they must be taken into account independently of their effects on human beings or non-human animals?

To extend an ethic in a plausible way beyond sentient beings is a difficult task. An ethic based on the interests of sentient creatures is on recognisable ground. Sentient creatures have wants and desires. They prefer some states to others. We can therefore, though with much imaginative effort and no guarantee of success, form an idea of what it might be like to be that creature under particular conditions. (The question "What is it like to be a possum drowning?" at least makes sense, even if it is impossible for us to give a more precise answer than "It must be awful.") In reaching moral decisions affecting sentient creatures, we can attempt to add up the effects of different actions on all the sentient creatures affected by the alternative actions open to us. This provides us with at least some rough guide to what might be the right thing to do. But there is *nothing* that corresponds to what it is like to be a tree dying because its roots have been flooded. Once we abandon the interests of sentient creatures as our source of value, where do we find value? What is good or bad for non-sentient creatures, and why does it matter?

It might be thought that as long as we limit ourselves to living things, the answer is not too difficult to find. After all, we know what is good or bad for the plants in our garden: water, sunlight and compost are good; extremes of heat or cold are bad. The same applies to plants in any forest or wilderness, so why can we not regard their flourishing as good in itself, independently of its usefulness to sentient creatures?

One problem here is that without conscious interests to guide us, we have no way of assessing the relative weights to be given to the flourishing of different forms of life. Is a two-thousand-year-old Huon pine more worthy of preservation than a tussock of grass? Most people will say that it is, but such a judgement seems to have more to do with our feelings of awe for the age, size and beauty of the tree, or with the length of time it would take to replace it, than with our perception of some intrinsic value in the flourishing of an old tree that is not possessed by a young grass tussock.

If we cease talking in terms of sentience, the boundary between living and inanimate natural objects becomes more difficult to defend. Would it really be worse to cut down an old tree than to destroy a beautiful stalactite that has taken even longer to grow? On what grounds could such a judgement be made? Probably the best known defence of an ethic that draws the boundaries of ethics around all living things is that of Albert Schweitzer. The phrase he used, "reverence for life," is often quoted; the arguments he offered in support of such a position are less well-known. Here is one of the few passages in which he defended his ethic:

> Just as in my own will-to-live there is a yearning for more life, and for that mysterious exaltation of the will which is called pleasure, and terror in face of annihilation and that injury to the will-to-live which is called pain; so the same obtains in all the will-to-live around me, equally whether it can express itself to my comprehension or whether it remains unvoiced.
>
> Ethics thus consists in this, that I experience the necessity of practising the same reverence for life toward all will-to-live, as toward my own. Therein I have already the needed fundamental principle of morality. It is *good* to maintain and cherish life; it is *evil* to destroy and to check life.[2]

A similar view has been defended recently by the contemporary American philosopher Paul Taylor. In his book *Respect for Nature,* Taylor argues that every living thing is "pursuing its own good in its own unique way." Once we see this, we can see all living things "as we see ourselves" and therefore "we are ready to place the same value on their existence as we do on our own."[3]

The problem with the defences offered by both Schweitzer and Taylor for their ethical views is that they use language metaphorically and then argue as if what they had said was literally true. We may often talk about plants "seeking" water or light so that they can survive, and this way of thinking about plants makes it easier to accept talk of their "will to live," or of them "pursuing" their own good. Once we stop, however, to reflect on the fact that plants are not conscious and cannot engage in any intentional behaviour, it is clear that all this language is metaphorical; one might just as well say that a river is pursuing its own good and striving to reach the sea, or that the "good" of a guided missile is to blow itself up along with its target. It is misleading of Schweitzer to attempt to sway us towards an ethic of reverence for all life by referring to "yearning," "exaltation," "pleasure" and "terror." Plants experience none of these.

Moreover, in the case of plants, rivers and guided missiles, it is possible to give a purely physical explanation of what is happening; and in the absence of consciousness, there is no good reason why we should have greater respect for the physical processes that govern the growth and decay of living things than we have for those that govern non-living things. This being so, it is at least not obvious why we should have greater reverence for a tree than for a stalactite, or for a single-celled organism than for a mountain; and we can pass silently by Taylor's even more extraordinary claim, that we should be ready not merely to respect every living thing, but that we should place the same value on the life of every living thing as we place on our own.

Deep Ecology

More than forty years ago the American ecologist Aldo Leopold wrote that there was a need for a "new ethic," an "ethic dealing with man's relation to land and to the animals and plants which grow upon it." His proposed "land ethic" would enlarge "the boundaries of the community to include soils, waters, plants, and animals, or collectively, the land."[4] The rise of ecological concern in the early 1970s led to a revival of this way of thinking. The Norwegian philosopher Arne Naess wrote a brief but influential article distinguishing between the "shallow" and "deep" forms of ecological thinking. Shallow ecological thinking was limited to the traditional moral framework; those who thought in this way were anxious to avoid pollution to our water supply so that we could have safe water to drink, and they sought to preserve wilderness so that people could continue to enjoy walking through it. Deep ecologists, on the other hand, wanted to preserve the integrity of the biosphere for its own sake, irrespective of the possible benefits to humans that might flow from so doing.[5] Subsequent writers who have attempted to develop some form of deep environmental theory include the Americans Bill Devall and George Sessions, and the Australians Lawrence Johnson, Val Plumwood and Richard Sylvan.[6]

Where the reverence for life ethic emphasises individual living organisms, proposals for deep ecology ethics tend to take something larger as the object of value: species, ecological systems, even the biosphere as a whole. Leopold summed up the basis of his new land ethic thus: "A thing is right when it tends to preserve the integrity, stability and beauty of the biotic community. It is wrong when it tends otherwise"[7] In a paper published in 1984, Arne Naess and George Sessions set out several principles for a deep ecological ethic, beginning with the following:

1. The well-being and flourishing of human and non-human Life on Earth have value in themselves (synonyms: intrinsic value, inherent value). These values are independent of the usefulness of the non-human world for human purposes.
2. Richness and diversity of life forms contribute to the realization of these values and are also values in themselves.
3. Humans have no right to reduce this richness and diversity except to satisfy *vital* needs.[8]

Although these principles refer only to life, in the same paper Naess and Sessions say that deep ecology uses the term "biosphere in a more comprehensive non-technical way to refer also to what biologists classify as 'non-living'; rivers (watersheds), landscapes, ecosystems." Sylvan and Plumwood also extend their ethic beyond living things, including in it an obligation "not to jeopardise the wellbeing of natural objects or systems without good reason."[9]

Behind this application of ethics not only to individuals, but also to species and ecosystems, lies some form of holism — some sense that the species or ecosystem is not just a collection of individuals, but really an entity in its own right. This holism is made explicit in Lawrence Johnson's *A Morally Deep World,* probably the most detailed and carefully argued statement of the case for an ethic of deep ecology yet to appear in print. Johnson is prepared to talk about the interests of a species in a sense that is distinct from the sum of the interests of each member of the species, and to argue that the interest of a species or an ecosystem ought to be taken into account, with individual interests, in our moral deliberations.

There is, of course, a real philosophical question about whether a species or an ecosystem can be considered as the sort of individual that can have interests; and even if it can, the deep ecology ethic will face problems similar to those we identified in considering the idea of the reverence for life ethic. For it is necessary, not merely that trees, species and ecosystems can properly be said to have interests, but that they have morally significant interests. We saw in discussing the ethic of reverence for life that one way of establishing that an interest is morally significant is to ask what it would be like for the entity affected to have that interest unsatisfied. This works for sentient beings, but it does not work for trees, species or ecosystems. There is nothing that corresponds to what it is like to be an ecosystem flooded by a dam. In this respect trees, ecosystems and species are more like rocks than they are like sentient beings; so the divide between sentient and non-sentient creatures is to that extent a firmer basis for a morally important boundary than the divide between living and non-living things or holistic entities.

If we were to adopt an ethic that attributed value to non-sentient living things, or to ecosystems as a whole, we would need to have a criterion of what made something more valuable than something else. Naess and Sessions, in common with many other deep ecologists, suggest "richness" and "diversity"; sometimes the term used is "complexity."[10] But what is it for something to be rich, diverse, or complex? Did the introduction of European birds into Australia make our birdlife richer and more diverse? If it could be shown that it did, would that make it a good thing? What if we should discover that allowing effluent from intensive farms to seep into our rivers greatly increases the number of microorganisms that live in them — thus giving rivers a different, but more diverse and more complex ecosystem than they had before they were polluted. Does that make the pollution desirable?

To seek intrinsic value in diversity or complexity is a mistake. The reason why we may feel more strongly about destruction of diverse and complex ecosystems than about simpler ones (such as a field of wheat) may be the same as the reason why we feel more strongly about preservation of the ceiling of the Sistine Chapel than we do about the preservation of the ceiling of the Lecture Theatre H3 at Monash University (which is painted a uniform white). To break up Michelangelo's fresco into handy-sized chunks for sale to tourists would be lucrative, and no doubt the Vatican could put the money to good use in fighting poverty (better use than that usually made of the returns from damming rivers or clearing forests); but would it be right to do so? The objection, in both cases, is to vandalism: the destruction, for short-term gain, of something that has enduring value to sentient beings, is easy to destroy but once destroyed can never exist again.

If the philosophical basis for a deep ecology ethic is difficult to sustain, this does not mean that the case for the preservation of wilderness is not strong. All it means is that one kind of argument — the argument for the intrinsic value of the plants, species or ecosystems — is, at best, problematic. We are on surer ground if we confine ourselves to arguments based on the interests of sentient creatures, present and future, human and non-human. In my view the arguments grounded on the interests of present and future human beings, and on the interests of the sentient non-humans who inhabit wilderness, are quite sufficient to show that, at least in a society where no one needs to destroy wilderness in order to survive, the value of preserving the remaining significant areas of wilderness greatly exceeds the values gained by its destruction.

NOTES

1. Peter Singer, *Animal Liberation,* New York Review of Books and Random House, New York, 2nd edn, 1990.
2. Albert Schweitzer, *Civilization and Ethics* (Part II of the *Philosophy of Civilization,* trans. T. T. Campion, London, 2nd edn, 1929, pp. 246–7).
3. Paul Taylor, *Respect for Nature,* Princeton, Princeton University Press, 1986, pp. 45, 128. My discussion draws on a fine critique of Taylor by Gerald Paske, "The Life Principle: A (Metaethical) Rejection," *Journal of Applied Philosophy* 6 (1989), pp. 219–25.
4. A. Leopold, *A Sand County Almanac,* Oxford University Press, New York, 1966 (first published 1949), pp. 219, 238.
5. A. Naess, "The Shallow and the Deep, Long-Range Ecology Movement," *Inquiry* 16 (1973), pp. 95–100.
6. See, for example, the following works: W. Devall & G. Sessions, *Deep Ecology: Living As If Nature Mattered,* Salt Lake City, Gibbs Smith, 1985; L. Johnson, *A Morally Deep World,* Cambridge, Cambridge University Press, 1990; V. Plumwood, "Ecofeminism: An Overview and Discussion of Positions and Arguments: Critical Review," *Australasian Journal of Philosophy* 64 (Supplement), 1986, pp. 120–38; R. Sylvan, "Three Essays Upon Deeper Environmental Ethics," *Discussion Papers in Environmental Philosophy* 13 (1986), published by the Australian National University, Canberra; and P. Taylor, op. cit.
7. Leopold, op. cit., p. 262.
8. A. Naess & G. Sessions, "Basic Principles of Deep Ecology," *Ecophilosophy* 6 (1984), pp. 3–7; quoted from D. Bennet & R. Sylvan, "Australian Perspectives on Environmental Ethics: A UNESCO Project," unpublished, 1989.
9. R. Routley [now R. Sylvan] & V. Routley [now V. Plumwood], "Human Chauvinism and Environmental Ethics" in D. Mannison, M. McRobbie & R. Routley (eds), *Environmental Philosophy,* Canberra, Australian National University Research School of Social Sciences, 1980.
10. For a useful survey of the value positions of deep ecologists, see R. Sylvan, "A Critique of Deep Ecology," *Discussion Papers in Environmental Philosophy* 12 (1985), 53, published by Australian National University, Canberra.

DISCUSSION TOPICS

1. Do you agree with Singer's argument that pain is intrinsically bad regardless of the species of the being who experiences it? Why or why not?

2. Consider a proposal to test military equipment by using powerful underwater sonar. First analyze the proposal using only the interests of present and future human beings, and then analyze the proposal including the interests of nonhuman sentient beings that communicate with sonar (whales and dolphins). Which analysis do you believe to be morally correct? Explain your reasoning.

3. Identify the reasons given by Singer for not considering the death of a nonhuman animal as morally equivalent to the death of a human being. Evaluate these reasons.
4. Singer provides several arguments against extending moral values to include nonsentient individuals such as plants, as well as species and ecosystems. Which of his arguments do you find to be the strongest? Which the weakest? Explain your responses.

Animal Liberation Is an Environmental Ethic

Dale Jamieson

Dale Jamieson is Henry R. Luce Professor in Human Dimensions of Global Change at Carleton College in Northfield, Minnesota. His most recent book is Morality's Progress: Essays on Humans, Other Animals, and the Rest of Nature *(2002). The following selection was published in* Environmental Values *in 1998. Jamieson argues that any plausible environmental ethic must address concerns about both animals and the environment. He goes on to clarify a number of distinctions in order to show that while only sentient beings are of primary value, nonsentient entities can also be intrinsically valued.*

ANIMAL LIBERATION AND THE VALUE OF NATURE

. . . In my view any plausible ethic must address concerns about both animals and the environment. (Indeed, I think that it is an embarrassment to philosophy that those who are most influential within the discipline typically ignore these issues or treat them as marginal.) Some issues that directly concern animals are obviously of great environmental import as well. The production and consumption of beef may well be the most important of them.[1] The addiction to beef that is characteristic of people in the industrialised countries is not only a moral atrocity for animals but also causes health problems for

consumers, reduces grain supplies for the poor, precipitates social divisions in developing countries, contributes to climate change, leads to the conversion of forests to pasture lands, is a causal factor in overgrazing, and is implicated in the destruction of native plants and animals. If there is one issue on which animal liberationists and environmentalists should speak with a single voice it is on this issue. To his credit Callicott appears to have recognised this, but many environmental philosophers have not.

In addition to there being clear issues on which animal liberationists and environmentalists should agree, it is also important to remember that nonhuman animals, like humans, live in environments. One reason to oppose the destruction of wilderness and the poisoning of nature is that these actions harm both human and nonhuman animals. I believe that one can go quite far towards protecting the environment solely on the basis of concern for animals.

Finally, and most importantly, environmental ethicists have no monopoly on valuing such collectives as species, ecosystems, and the community of the land. It has only seemed that they do because parties to the dispute have not attended to the proper distinctions.

One relevant distinction, noted by Callicott in different language, is between the source and content of values.[2] We can be sentientist with respect to the source of values, yet non-sentientist with respect to their content. Were there no sentient beings there would be no values but it doesn't follow from this that only sentient beings are valuable.[3]

The second important distinction is between primary and derivative value. Creatures who can suffer, take pleasure in their experiences, and whose lives go better or worse from their own point of view are of primary value. Failure to value them involves failures of objectivity or impartiality in our reasoning or sentiments.

Suppose that I recognise that I matter morally in virtue of instantiating some particular property, but I withhold the judgement that some other creature matters morally although I recognise that this other creature also instantiates this property. On the face of it, I hold inconsistent beliefs, though they can be made consistent by conceptual gerrymandering. Just as I can appear to assert P & –P but limit the interpretation of P to "then or there" and –P to "now or here," so I can say that a particular property is morally relevant only if it is instantiated in me or my close relatives. However such consistency is not worth having since it rests on an absurd view of how morally relevant properties function. Indeed, it seems to strip them of their significance. Contrary to what has been granted, what makes me morally significant in this case is not instantiating the property under consideration but rather instantiating the property of being me or my kin. Similar points apply with respect to the sentiments. If I fail to value a creature who instantiates a property in virtue of which I matter morally, then the reach and power of my sentiments are in some way defective. Whether it is reason or sentiment that is involved, in both cases I look out into the world and see creatures who instantiate properties that bestow moral value, yet I deny moral value to those who are not me or biologically close to me. It is natural to say about these cases that I lack objectivity or impartiality. . . .

Nonsentient entities are not of primary value because they do not have a perspective from which their lives go better or worse. Ultimately the value of nonsentient entities rests on how they fit into the lives of sentient beings. But although nonsentient entities are not of primary value, their value can be very great and urgent. In some cases their value may even trump the value of sentient entities. The distinction between primary and derivative value is not a distinction in degree of value, but rather in the ways different entities can be valuable.

A third distinction is that between intrinsic and non-intrinsic value. . . .

The distinction that I think is useful is that between intrinsically and non-intrinsically valuing something. I speak of "intrinsically valuing" rather than "intrinsic value" because it makes clear that the intended distinction is in the structure of valuing rather than in the sorts of things that are valued.[4] We intrinsically value something when we value it for its own sake. Making the distinction in this way also makes clear that one and the same entity can be valued both intrinsically and non-intrinsically at different times, in different contexts, by different valuers, or even by the same valuer at the same time. For example, I can intrinsically value Sean (i.e. value her for her own sake) yet non-intrinsically value her as

an efficient mail-delivering device (i.e. for how she conduces to my ends).

Collecting these distinctions we can entertain the possibility that the content of our values may include our intrinsically valuing an entity that is of derivative value, and that this valuing may be urgent and intense, even trumping something of primary value. The obvious candidates for satisfying this description are works of art. Many of us would say that the greatest works of art are very valuable indeed. We value them intrinsically, yet ultimately an account of their value devolves into understandings about their relations to people (e.g., artists, audiences, potential audiences, those who know of their existence, etc.).

During the second world war Churchill evacuated art from London to the countryside in order to protect it from the blitz. Resources devoted to this evacuation could have been allocated to life-saving. Although he may not have represented the decision in this way, Churchill made the judgement that evacuating the art was more important than saving some number of human lives. I don't know whether he was correct in his specific calculation, but he might well have been. Quantity of life is not the only thing that matters; quality of life matters too, and it is to this concern that Churchill's judgement was responsive.

A similar point could be made concerning the destruction of parts of the old city of Dubrovnik by Serbian gunners. I believe that over the course of human history the destruction of the old city would be a greater crime than some measure of death and destruction wrought upon the people of Dubrovnik. Indeed, I believe that some of the people of Dubrovnik share this view. This particular judgement need not be shared, however, in order to accept the basic point that I am making.

Nonsentient features of the environment are of derivative value, but they can be of extreme value and can be valued intrinsically. There are geological features of the Dolomites that are profoundly important to preserve. Rivers and forests can have the same degree of importance. Indeed, there may be features of the Italian natural environment that are as important to preserve as the city of Venice.

The main point I am making here is that many people have traditional evaluational outlooks yet value works of art intrinsically and intensely. There is no great puzzle about how they can both intrinsically value persons and works of art. Similarly, animal liberationists can value nature intrinsically and intensely, even though they believe that nonsentient nature is of derivative value. Because what is of derivative value can be valued intensely and intrinsically, animal liberationists can join environmental ethicists in fighting for the preservation of wild rivers and wilderness areas. Indeed, rightly understood, they can even agree with environmental ethicists that these natural features are valuable for their own sakes.

But at this point an objection may arise. The most that I have shown is that nonsentient entities can be intrinsically valued. I have not shown that they ought to be intrinsically valued. Canonical environmentalists can give a reason for intrinsically valuing nonsentient nature that animal liberationists cannot: Aspects of nonsentient nature are valuable independently of any conscious being.

The objection is correct in that environmental ethicists who believe in mind-independent value can appeal to normative high ground that is not available to those philosophers who do not believe in mind-independent value. However it should be noted that even if the value of nonsentient nature were mind-independent, it would not immediately follow that nonsentient nature should be valued intrinsically or that its value would be of greater urgency than that of other entities. But putting that point aside, the fundamental problem with this attempt to seize the normative heights is that they are a mirage. There is no mind-independent value, but none is required in order for nature to be valued intrinsically. Still, having said this, some account needs to be given of how my kind of environmental philosopher moves from the claim that wilderness can be intrinsically valued to the claim that wilderness ought to be intrinsically valued.

First, we should see that this question plunges us into the familiar if difficult problem of how first-order value claims can be defended and justified.[5] In order to give an account of this, very close attention would have to be paid to our everyday moral practices and our strategies of defence, offence, justification, and capitulation. I doubt that very much of general interest can be said about this. But as a first approximation, we might say that in order to see how environmentalist claims are justified, we should look at the practices of persuasion that environmentalists employ. Consider an example.

Many people think of deserts as horrible places that are not worth protecting. I disagree. I value deserts intrinsically and think you should too. How do I proceed? One thing I might do is take you camping with me. We might see the desert's nocturnal inhabitants, the plants that have adapted to these conditions, the shifting colours of the landscape as the day wears on, and the rising of the moon on stark features of the desert. Together we might experience the feel of the desert wind, hear the silence of the desert, and sense its solitude. You may become interested in how it is that this place was formed, what sustains it, how its plants and animals make a living. As you learn more about the desert, you may come to see it differently and to value it more. This may lead you to spend more time in the desert, seeing it in different seasons, watching the spring with its incredible array of flowers turn to the haunting stillness of summer. You might start reading some desert literature, from the monastic fathers of the church to Edward Abbey. Your appreciation would continue to grow.

But there is no guarantee that things will go this way. You may return from your time in the desert hot, dirty, hungry for a burger, thirsty for a beer, and ready to volunteer your services to the U.S. Army Corps of Engineers (whose *raison d'etre* seems to be to flood as much of the earth's surface as possible). Similarly, some people see Venice as a dysfunctional collection of dirty old buildings, find Kant boring and wrong, and hear Mahler as both excessively romantic and annoyingly dissonant. More experience only makes matters worse.

If someone fails to appreciate the desert, Venice, or Mahler, they need not have made any logical error. Our evaluative responses are not uniquely determined by our constitution or the world. This fact provokes anxiety in some philosophers. They fear that unless value is mind-independent, anything goes. Experience machines are as good as experience, Disney-desert is the same as the real thing, and the Spice Girls and Mahler are colleagues in the same business (one strikingly more successful than the other). Those who suffer this anxiety confuse a requirement for value with how value is constituted. Value is mind-dependent, but it is things in the world that are valuable or not. The fact that we draw attention to features of objects in our evaluative discourse is the common property of all theories of value.

These anxious philosophers also fail to appreciate how powerful psychological and cultural mechanisms can be in constituting objectivity. Culture, history, tradition, knowledge, and convention mediate our constitutions and the world. Culture, together with our constitutions and the world, determines our evaluative practices. Since the world and our constitutions alone are not sufficient for determining them, common values should be seen in part as cultural achievements rather than simply as true reports about the nature of things or expressions of what we are essentially. Evaluative practices are in the domain of negotiation and collective construction, as well as reflection and recognition. But the fact that these practices are in part constructed does not mean that they cannot be rigid and compelling. We can be brought to appreciate Venice, Mahler, or the desert by collectively and interactively educating our sensibilities, tastes and judgements, but such change often involves a deep reorientation of how we see the world. When I try to get you to appreciate the desert I direct your attention to objects in your visual field, but I am trying to change your way of seeing and thinking and your whole outlook towards nature. I am also trying to change our relationship from one of difference to one of solidarity. Similarly, when advocates of the enterprise society point to missed opportunities for profit and competitiveness, they are trying to educate our sensibilities as well as referring us to economic facts. Their descriptions of how economies work are to a great extent stories about the social world they want to construct.

What I have argued in this section is that animal liberationists can hold many of the same normative views as environmental ethicists. This is because many of our most important issues involve serious threats to both humans and animals as well as to the nonsentient environment; because animal liberationists can value nature as a home for sentient beings; and because animal liberationists can embrace environmental values as intensely as environmental ethicists, though they see them as derivative rather than primary values. What animal liberationists cannot do is claim the moral high ground of the mind-independent value of nature which, since the early days of the movement environmental ethicists have attempted to secure. But, as I have argued, this moral high ground is not there to be claimed anyway. Those who are deep green should not despair because some of our environmental values are to a great extent socially constructed. Constructivism is a story about how our practices come to be, not about how real, rigid or compelling they are.

Still, many will think that this is a flabby ethic that leans too far in the direction of subjectivism, relativism, constructivism or some other post-modern heresy. One way of making their point is to return to the distinction between primary and derivative value. Imagine two people: Robin, who thinks that trees are of primary value, and Ted, who denies that humans or gorillas are included in this class. What kind of a mistake are Robin and Ted making? If I say they are making a conceptual mistake then I will be dismissing some very influential views as non-starters; if I say they are making a normative mistake then my view of what has primary and derivative value will turn out to be just as subjective as my view that deserts are valuable, and therefore just as vulnerable to other people's lack of responsiveness to my concerns.

I want to reiterate that first-order value judgements can be both rigid and compelling, even though to some extent they are relative and socially constructed. But having said this, I want to reject the idea that Robin and Ted are making a logical or grammatical error. Robin, Ted, and I have a real normative dispute about how to determine what is of primary value. At the same time this dispute has a different feel to it than first-order normative disputes (e.g. the dispute about whether or not to value the desert). We can bring out this difference by saying as a first approximation that someone who fails to value deserts lacks sensitivity while someone who fails to value people or gorillas lacks objectivity. Although in both cases the dispute involves how we see ourselves in relation to the world, to a great extent different considerations are relevant in each case. Because questions about primary values are at the centre of how we take the world, abstract principles (e.g. those that concern objectivity and impartiality) are most relevant to settling these disputes. Differences about whether or not to value deserts, on the other hand, turn on a panoply of considerations, some of which I have already discussed.[6]

In this section I have argued that there is a great deal of theoretical convergence between animal liberationists and environmental ethicists. There is also a strong case for convergence at the practical and political level. The environmental movement has numbers and wealth while the animal liberation movement has personal commitment. Both environmental and animal issues figure in the choices people make in their daily lives, but they are so glaringly obvious in the case of animals that they cannot be evaded. Anyone who eats or dresses makes ethical choices that affect animals. Refraining from eating meat makes one part of a social movement: rather than being an abstainer, one is characterized positively as "a vegetarian." While other consumer choices also have profound environmental consequences, somehow they are less visible than the choice of whether to eat meat. This is part of the reason why self-identified environmentalists are often less motivated to save energy, reduce consumption, or refrain from purchasing toxic substances than animal liberationists are to seek out vegetarian alternatives.[7] Not only is animal liberation an environmental ethic, but animal liberation can also help to empower the environmental movement.

REMAINING CONUNDRUMS AND COMPLEXITIES

. . . [W]hat is important to see is that while animal liberationists and environmentalists may have different tendencies, the turf doesn't divide quite so neatly as some may think. Consider one example.

Gary Varner, who writes as an animal liberationist, has defended what he calls "therapeutic hunting" in some circumstances.[8] He defines "therapeutic hunting" as "hunting motivated by and designed to secure the aggregate welfare of the target species and/or the integrity of its ecosystem."[9] Varner goes on to argue that animal liberationists can support this kind of hunting and that this is the only kind of hunting that environmentalists are compelled to support. What might have appeared as a clear difference between the two groups turns out to be more complex.

In addition to such "convergence" arguments, it is important to recognize the diversity of views that exists within both the environmental and animal liberation movements. Differences between animal liberationists are obvious and on the table. At a practical level animal liberation groups are notorious for their sectarianism. At a philosophical level Tom Regan has spent much of the last fifteen years distinguishing his view from that of Peter Singer. . . . In recent years the same kind of divisions have broken out among environmental philosophers, with the rhetoric between Callicott and Rolston (and more recently Callicott and Norton) increasingly resembling that between Singer and Regan. Generally within the community of environmental philosophers there are disagreements about the nature and value of wilderness, the importance of biodiversity, and approaches to controlling population. At a practical level there are disagreements about the very goals of the movement. Some would say that preservation of nature's diversity is the ultimate goal; others would counter that it is the preservation of evolutionary processes that matters. Sometimes people assert both without appreciating that they can come into conflict.[10]

There are many practical issues on which neither animal liberationists nor environmentalists are of one mind. For example, South African, American, and German scientists working for the South African National Parks Board, with support from the Humane Society of the United States, are currently testing contraceptives on elephants in Kruger National Park as an alternative to "culling." The World Wide Fund for Nature is divided about the project, with its local branch opposing it.[11]

Part of the reason for the divisions within both the environmental and animal liberation movements is that contemporary western cultures have little by way of positive images of how to relate to animals and nature. Most of us know what is bad — wiping out songbird populations, polluting water ways, causing cats to suffer, contributing to smog, and so on. But when asked to provide a positive vision many people turn to the past, to their conception of what life is like for indigenous peoples, or what it is to be "natural." None of this will do. So long as we have a paucity of positive visions, different views, theories, and philosophies will compete for attention, with no obvious way of resolving some of the most profound disagreements.

These are early days for those who are sensitive to the interests of nature and animals. We are in the midst of a transition from a culture which sees nature as material for exploitation, to one which asserts the importance of living in harmony with nature. It will take a long time to understand exactly what are the terms of the debate. What is important to recognise now is that animal liberationists and environmental ethicists are on the same side in this transition. Animal liberation is not the only environmental ethic, but neither is it some alien ideology. Rather, as I have argued, animal liberation is an environmental ethic and should be welcomed back into the family.

NOTES

1. The case for this has been very convincingly argued by Jeremy Rifkin (1992).
2. John O'Neill (1993, ch.2) also makes a similar distinction.
3. Here we border on some important issues in philosophy of mind that cannot be discussed here. For present purposes I assume that sentience and consciousness determine the same class, and that there is something that it is like to be a "merely conscious" (as well as self-conscious) entity, although a "merely conscious" entity cannot reflect on what it is like to be itself. I say a little more about these matters in Jamieson 1983. See also various papers collected in Bekoff and Jamieson 1996.
4. This of course is not to deny that some things are better candidates for intrinsically valuing than others. For further discussion see Jamieson 1994.
5. I have discussed the relation between moral practice and moral theorising in Jamieson 1991. See also Weston 1985.
6. There is much more to say about these questions than I can say here. However it may help to locate my views if I invoke the Quinean image of the web of belief in which what is at the center of the web is defended in different ways than what is at the periphery, not because such beliefs enjoy some special epistemological status, but because of the density of their connections to other beliefs.

7. These and related issues are discussed in two reports to the United States Environmental Protection Agency (Jamieson and VanderWerf 1993, 1995). Both documents are available from the National Pollution Prevention Center at the University of Michigan, or the Center for Values and Social Policy at the University of Colorado.
8. Varner 1995.
9. Ibid., p. 257.
10. To some degree differences among environmentalists have been obscured by the rise of "managerialist" forms of environmentalism which are favoured by many scientists and are highly visible in the media. For a critique, see Jamieson 1990. For alternative forms of environmentalism, see Sachs 1993.
11. *New Scientist* 1996.

REFERENCES

Bekoff, Marc and Jamieson, Dale (eds) 1996. *Readings in Animal Cognition.* Cambridge MA: The MIT Press.

Callicott, J. Baird. 1992. "Rolston on Intrinsic Value: A Deconstruction," *Environmental Ethics* 14: 129–143.

Jamieson, Dale 1983. "Killing Persons and Other Beings," in H. Miller and W. Williams (eds), *Ethics and Animals.* Clifton NJ: Humana Publishing Company.

Jamieson, Dale 1990. "Managing the Future: Public Policy, Scientific Uncertainty, and Global Warming," in D. Scherer (ed.), *Upstream/Downstream: Essays in Environmental Ethics,* pp. 67–89. Philadelphia: Temple University Press.

Jamieson, Dale 1991. "Method and Moral Theory," in Peter Singer (ed.), *A Companion to Ethics,* pp. 473–487. Oxford: Basil Blackwell.

Jamieson, Dale 1994. "Ziff on Shooting an Elephant," in Dale Jamieson (ed.), *Language, Mind, and Art: Essays in Appreciation and Analysis, in Honor of Paul Ziff,* pp. 121–129. Dordrecht: Kluwer.

Jamieson, Dale and VanderWerf, Klasina 1993. *Cultural Barriers to Behavioral Change: General Recommendations and Resources for State Pollution Prevention Programs.* Report to US EPA.

Jamieson, Dale and VanderWerf, Klasina (eds, with the assistance of Sarah Goering) 1995. *Preventing Pollution: Perspectives on Cultural Barriers and Facilitators.* Report to US EPA.

New Scientist 1996. "Villagers slam 'Pill for elephants'," 30 November, p. 9.

O'Neill, John 1993. *Ecology, Policy and Politics: Human Well-Being and the Natural World.* London: Routledge.

Rifkin, Jeremy 1992. *Beyond Beef.* New York: Penguin Books, USA.

Sachs, Wolfgang (ed.) 1993. *Global Ecology: A New Arena of Political Conflict.* London: Zed Books.

Varner, Gary 1995. "Can Animal Rights Activists Be Environmentalists," in Christine Pierce and Donald VanDeVeer (eds), *People, Penguins, and Plastic Trees,* second edition, pp. 254–273. Belmont CA: Wadsworth.

Weston, Anthony 1985. "Beyond Intrinsic Value: Pragmatism in Environmental Ethics," *Environmental Ethics* 7: 321–339.

DISCUSSION TOPICS

1. Jamieson uses the example of Churchill evacuating art from London, using resources which could have been allocated to saving lives. What point is Jamieson making with this example?
2. Explain what Jamieson means by asserting that "value is mind-dependent, but it is things in the world that are valuable or not." Do you agree with his view? Why or why not?
3. Give an example of a normative dispute over what has primary value.
4. Do you agree with Jamieson's observation that the animal liberation movement has personal commitment, whereas the environmental movement has numbers and wealth? Explain your reasoning.

READING 39

From *Respect for Nature: A Theory of Environmental Ethics*

Paul W. Taylor

Paul Taylor is emeritus professor of philosophy at Brooklyn College, City University of New York. In Respect for Nature *(1986) he develops the view that human beings are members of the earth's living community but are not inherently superior to other living things. Each organism is a "teleological center of life" — a unique individual pursuing its own good in its own way.*

In order to resolve conflicting claims between human beings and wild living creatures, Taylor provides five principles: self-defense, proportionality, minimum harm, distributive justice, and restitutive justice.

THE BIOCENTRIC OUTLOOK AND THE ATTITUDE OF RESPECT FOR NATURE

. . . The beliefs that form the core of the biocentric outlook are four in number.

a. The belief that humans are members of the Earth's Community of Life in the same sense and on the same terms in which other living things are members of that Community.
b. The belief that the human species, along with all other species, are integral elements in a system of interdependence such that the survival of each living thing, as well as its chances of faring well or poorly, is determined not only by the physical conditions of its environment but also by its relations to other living things.
c. The belief that all organisms are teleological centers of life in the sense that each is a unique individual pursuing its own good in its own way.
d. The belief that humans are not inherently superior to other living things. . . .

INDIVIDUAL ORGANISMS AS TELEOLOGICAL CENTERS OF LIFE

So far the biocentric outlook has been presented as a belief-system that sets a framework for viewing ourselves in relation to other species and for understanding how we and they alike fit into the whole natural environment of our planet. The third component of that outlook, in contrast with the first two, focuses our attention on the lives of individual organisms. The biocentric outlook includes a certain way of conceiving of each entity that has a life of its own. To accept the outlook is to sharpen and deepen our awareness of what it means to be a particular living thing.

Our knowledge of individual organisms has expanded rapidly with advances in the biological and physical sciences in the past century. Organic chemistry and microbiology have brought us close to every cell and every molecule that make up the physical structure of the bodies of organisms. We have greatly increased our understanding of how living things function as physical and chemical systems. We are acquiring ever more accurate and complete explanations of why organisms behave as they do. As we thus come to know more about their life cycles, their interactions with other organisms and with the environment, we become increasingly aware of how each of them is carrying out its life functions according to the laws of its species-specific nature. But besides this, our increasing knowledge and understanding also enable us to grasp the uniqueness of each organism as an individual. Scientists who have made careful and detailed studies of particular plants and animals have often come to know their subjects as identifiable individuals. Close observation over extended periods, whether in the laboratory or in the field, has led them to an appreciation of the unique "personalities" of their subjects. Sometimes a scientist develops a special interest in a particular animal or plant, all the while remaining strictly objective in the gathering and recording of data.[1]

Nonscientists may likewise experience this development of interest when, as amateur naturalists, they make accurate observations over a sustained period of close acquaintance with a plant or animal. As one becomes more and more familiar with the organism being observed, one acquires a sharpened awareness of the particular way it is living its life. One may become fascinated by it and even get to be involved with its good and bad fortunes. The organism comes to mean something to one as a unique, irreplaceable individual. Finally one achieves a genuine understanding of its point of view. One can then imaginatively place oneself in the organism's situation and look at the world from its standpoint.

This progressive development from objective, detached knowledge to the recognition of individuality, and from the recognition of individuality to a full awareness of an organism's standpoint, is a process of heightening our consciousness of what it means to be an individual living thing.

. . . To say it is a teleological center of life is to say that its internal functioning as well as its external activities are all goal-oriented, having the constant tendency to maintain the organism's existence through time and to enable it successfully to perform those biological operations whereby it reproduces its kind and continually adapts to changing environmental events and conditions. It is the coherence and unity of these functions of an organism, all directed toward the realization of its good, that make it one teleological center of activity. Physically and chemically it is in the molecules of its cells that this activity occurs, but the organism as a whole is the unit that responds to its environment and so accomplishes (or tends to accomplish) the end of sustaining its life.[2]

Understanding individual organisms as teleological centers of life does not mean that we are falsely anthropomorphizing. It does not involve "reading into" them human characteristics. We need not, for example, consider them to have consciousness. That a particular tree is a teleological center of life does not entail that it is intentionally aiming at preserving its existence, that it is exerting efforts to avoid death, or that it even cares whether it lives or dies. As we saw [earlier], organisms like trees and one-celled protozoa do not have a conscious life. They are not aware of a world around them. They have no thoughts or feelings and hence no interest in anything that happens to them. Yet they have a good of their own around which their behavior is organized. All organisms, whether conscious or not, are teleological centers of life in the sense that each is a unified, coherently ordered system of goal-oriented activities that has a constant tendency to protect and maintain the organism's existence.

Under this conception of individual living things, each is seen to have a single, unique point of view. This point of view is determined by the organism's particular way of responding to its environment, interacting with other individual organisms, and undergoing the regular, lawlike transformations of the various stages of its species-specific life cycle. As it sustains its existence through time, it exemplifies all the functions and activities of its species in its own peculiar manner. When observed in detail, its way of existing is seen to be different from that of any other organism, including those of its species. To be aware of it not only as *a* center of life, but as *the* particular center of life that it is, is to be aware of its uniqueness and individuality. The organism is the individual it is precisely by virtue of its having its own idiosyncratic manner of carrying on its existence in the (not necessarily conscious) pursuit of its good.

This mode of understanding a particular individual is not possible with regard to inanimate objects. Although no two stones are exactly alike in their physical characteristics, stones do not have points of view. In pure fantasy, of course, we can play at performing the imaginative act of taking a stone's standpoint and looking at the world from its perspective. But we are then moving away from reality, not getting closer to it. The true reality of a stone's existence includes no point of view. This is not due to the fact that it lacks consciousness. As we have noted, plants and simple animal organisms also lack consciousness, but have points of view nonetheless. What makes our awareness of an individual stone fundamentally different from our awareness of a plant or animal is that the stone is not a teleological center of life, while the plant or animal is. The stone has no good of its own. We cannot benefit it by furthering its well-being or harm it by acting contrary to its well-being, since the concept of well-being simply does not apply to it.

This point holds even for those complex mechanisms (such as self-monitoring space satellites, chess-playing computers, and assembly-line "robots") that have been constructed by humans to function in a quasi-autonomous, self-regulating manner in the process of accomplishing certain purposes. Though such machines are understandable as teleological systems, they remain in actual fact inanimate objects. The ends they are programmed to accomplish are not purposes of their own, independent of the human purposes for which they were made. This is not to deny that in certain contexts it is perfectly proper to speak of what is good or bad for them. These would be conditions that add to or detract from their effectiveness as instruments for bringing

about the (human) ends they were made to serve. But it is precisely this fact that separates them from living things.

The goal-oriented operations of machines are not inherent to them as the goal-oriented behavior of organisms is inherent to *them.* To put it another way, the goals of a machine are derivative, whereas the goals of a living thing are original. The ends and purposes of machines are built into them by their human creators. It is the original purposes of humans that determine the structures and hence the teleological functions of those machines. Although they manifest goal-directed activities, the machines do not, as independent entities, have a good of their own. Their "good" is "furthered" only insofar as they are treated in such a way as to be an effective means to human ends.

A living plant or animal, on the other hand, has a good of its own in the same sense that a human being has a good of its own. It is, independently of anything else in the universe, itself a center of goal-oriented activity. What is good or bad for it can be understood by reference to its own survival, health, and well-being. As a living thing it seeks its own ends in a way that is not true of any teleologically structured mechanism. It is in terms of *its* goals that we can give teleological explanations of why it does what it does. We cannot do the same for machines, since any such explanation must ultimately refer to the goals their human producers had in mind when they made the machines.

I should add as a parenthetical note that this difference between mechanism and organism may no longer be maintainable with regard to those complex electronic devices now being developed under the name of artificial intelligence. Perhaps some day computer scientists and engineers will construct beings whose internal processes and electrical responses to their surroundings closely parallel the functions of the human brain and nervous system. Concerning such beings we may begin to speak of their having a good of their own independently of the purposes of their creators. At that point the distinction drawn above between living things and inanimate machines may break down. It is best, I think, to have an open mind about this. But for our present purposes we need not go into this matter. In working out a life-centered theory of environmental ethics that is applicable to the relations between humans and the natural world, we can use for practical purposes the distinction as it is made above. If mechanisms (organisms?) of artificial intelligence were ever to be produced, another system of ethics might have to be applied to the treatment of such entities by moral agents. . . .

THE DENIAL OF HUMAN SUPERIORITY

. . . [C]onsider one of the most frequently repeated assertions concerning the superiority of humans over nonhumans. This is the claim that we humans are *morally* superior beings because we possess, while animals and plants lack, the capacities that give us the status of moral agents. Such capacities as free will, accountability, deliberation, and practical reason, it is said, endow us with the special nobility and dignity that belong only to morally responsible beings. Because human existence has this moral dimension it exemplifies a higher grade of being than is to be found in the amoral, irresponsible existence of animals and plants. In traditional terms, it is freedom of the will and the moral responsibility that goes with it that together raise human life above the level of the beasts.

There is a serious confusion of thought in this line of reasoning if the conclusion drawn is understood as asserting that humans are morally superior to nonhumans. One cannot validly argue that humans are morally superior beings on the ground that they possess, while others lack, the capacities of a moral agent. The reason is that, as far as moral standards are concerned, only beings that have the capacities of a moral agent can meaningfully be said to be *either* morally good *or* morally bad. Only moral agents can be judged to be morally better or worse than others, and the others in question must be moral agents themselves. Judgments of moral superiority are based on the comparative merits or deficiencies of the entities being judged, and these merits and deficiencies are all moral ones, that is, ones determined by moral standards. One entity is correctly judged morally superior to another if it is the case that, when valid moral standards are applied to both entities, the first fulfills them to a greater degree than the second. Both entities, therefore, must fall within a

range of application of moral standards. This would not be the case, however, if humans were being judged superior to animals and plants, since the latter are not moral agents. Just as animals and plants can be neither good nor bad scientists, engineers, critics, or Supreme Court justices, so they can be neither good nor bad moral agents. More precisely, it is meaningless to speak of them as morally good or bad. Hence it is meaningless to say either that they are morally inferior to humans or that humans are morally superior to them. I conclude that it is not false but simply confused to assert that humans are the moral superiors of animals and plants. . . .

THE BASIC RULES OF CONDUCT

. . . I shall now set out and examine four rules of duty in the domain of environmental ethics. This is not supposed to provide an exhaustive account of every valid duty of the ethics of respect for nature. It is doubtful whether a complete specification of duties is possible in this realm. But however that may be, the duties to be listed here are intended to cover only the more important ones that typically arise in everyday life. I suggest later on, in connection with the discussion of priority principles, that in all situations not explicitly or clearly covered by these rules we should rely on the attitude of respect for nature and the biocentric outlook that together underlie the system as a whole and give it point. Right actions are always actions that express the attitude of respect, whether they are covered by the four rules or not. . . .

The four rules will be named (a) the Rule of Nonmaleficence, (b) the Rule of Noninterference, (c) the Rule of Fidelity, and (d) the Rule of Restitutive Justice.

(a) *The Rule of Nonmaleficence.* This is the duty not to do harm to any entity in the natural environment that has a good of its own. It includes the duty not to kill an organism and not to destroy a species-population or biotic community, as well as the duty to refrain from any action that would be seriously detrimental to the good of an organism, species-population, or life community. Perhaps the most fundamental wrong in the ethics of respect for nature is to harm something that does not harm us. . . .

(b) *The Rule of Noninterference.* Under this rule fall two sorts of negative duties, one requiring us to refrain from placing restrictions on the freedom of individual organisms, the other requiring a general "hands off" policy with regard to whole ecosystems and biotic communities, as well as to individual organisms. . . .

(c) *The Rule of Fidelity.* This rule applies only to human conduct in relation to individual animals that are in a wild state and are capable of being deceived or betrayed by moral agents. The duties imposed by the Rule of Fidelity, though of restricted range, are so frequently violated by so many people that this rule needs separate study as one of the basic principles of the ethics of respect for nature.

Under this rule fall the duties not to break a trust that a wild animal places in us (as shown by its behavior), not to deceive or mislead any animal capable of being deceived or misled, to uphold an animal's expectations, which it has formed on the basis of one's past actions with it, and to be true to one's intentions as made known to an animal when it has come to rely on one. Although we cannot make mutual agreements with wild animals, we can act in such a manner as to call forth their trust in us. The basic moral requirement imposed by the Rule of Fidelity is that we remain faithful to that trust.

The clearest and commonest examples of transgressions of the rule occur in hunting, trapping, and fishing. Indeed, the breaking of a trust is a key to good (that is, successful) hunting, trapping, and fishing. Deception with intent to harm is of the essence. . . .

(d) *The Rule of Restitutive Justice.* In its most general terms this rule imposes the duty to restore the balance of justice between a moral agent and a moral subject when the subject has been wronged by the agent. Common to all instances in which a duty of restitutive justice arises, an agent has broken a valid moral rule and by doing so has upset the balance of justice between himself or herself and a moral subject. To hold oneself accountable for having done such an act is to acknowledge a special duty one has taken upon oneself by that wrongdoing. This special duty is the duty of restitutive justice. It requires that one make amends to the moral subject by some form of compensation or reparation.

. . . It will be helpful to summarize our findings by taking an overall look at the priority relations holding among the four rules of duty. The general picture we then get shows the Rule of Nonmalefi-

cence to be at the top. Our most fundamental duty toward nature (putting aside possible conflicts with the duties of human ethics) is to do no harm to wild living things as far as this lies within our power. Our respect for nature primarily expresses itself in our adhering to this supreme rule.

With regard to the other three rules, we have found that it is usually possible to avoid violations of each of them by carefully choosing how we make restitution and when we set up the conditions that lead to the development of an animal's trust in us. But where conflicts cannot be avoided, the priority principles that generally hold are: (a) Fidelity and restitutive justice override noninterference when a great good is brought about and no creature is permanently harmed by the permitted interference. (b) Restitutive justice outweighs fidelity when a great good is brought about and no serious harm is done to a creature whose trust in us is broken.

It must be added that the two negative rules, to refrain from doing harm and to refrain from interfering in the natural world, are in ordinary circumstances almost always possible to comply with. We can usually find methods of making restitution that do not cause harm to or impose constraints upon living things. The same is true of developing in them the bonds of trust. The major modes of restitution are setting aside wilderness areas, protecting endangered and threatened species, restoring the quality of an environment that has been degraded, and aiding plants and animals to return to a healthy state when they have been weakened or injured by human causes. All of these measures can normally be taken without the necessity of breaking faith with or imposing restrictions upon the creatures of the wild. . . .

FIVE PRIORITY PRINCIPLES FOR THE FAIR RESOLUTION OF CONFLICTING CLAIMS

I shall now consider . . . five . . . principles, to be designated as follows:

a. The principle of self-defense.
b. The principle of proportionality.
c. The principle of minimum wrong.
d. The principle of distributive justice.
e. The principle of restitutive justice.

Although I believe these five principles cover all the major ways of adjudicating fairly among competing claims arising from clashes between the duties of human ethics and those of environmental ethics, I must emphasize at the outset that they do not yield a neat solution to every possible conflict situation. . . .

The Principle of Self-Defense

The principle of self-defense states that it is permissible for moral agents to protect themselves against dangerous or harmful organisms by destroying them. This holds, however, only when moral agents, using reasonable care, cannot avoid being exposed to such organisms and cannot prevent them from doing serious damage to the environmental conditions that make it possible for moral agents to exist and function as moral agents. Furthermore, the principle does not allow the use of just any means of self-protection, but only those means that will do the least possible harm to the organisms consistent with the purpose of preserving the existence and functioning of moral agents. There must be no available alternative that is known to be equally effective but to cause less harm to the "attacking" organisms.

The principle of self-defense permits actions that are absolutely required for maintaining the very existence of moral agents and for enabling them to exercise the capacities of moral agency. It does not permit actions that involve the destruction of organisms when those actions simply promote the interests or values which moral agents may have as persons. Self-defense is defense against *harmful* and *dangerous* organisms, and a harmful or dangerous organism in this context is understood to be one whose activities threaten the life or basic health of those entities which need normally functioning bodies to exist as moral agents.

. . . The principle of self-defense is formulated in such a way as to be species-blind. The statement of the principle refers only to moral agents and organisms (of whatever species) that are not moral agents. No mention is made of humans and nonhumans. Of course, in discussing various aspects and implications of the principle, one ordinarily refers to humans defending themselves against nonhumans as typical of situations in which the principle applies

to the practical circumstances of life. Strictly speaking, however, no reference to any species need be made. The fact that (most) humans are moral agents and (most) nonhumans are not is a contingent truth which the principle does not take to be morally relevant. Moral agents are permitted to defend themselves against harmful or dangerous organisms that are not moral agents. This is all the principle of self-defense allows. If there happen to be nonhuman moral agents whose existence as moral agents is endangered by the actions of humans who are not moral agents (such as the insane and the severely retarded), then the principle states that it is permissible for the nonhumans in question to kill those humans who endanger them, if this is required for the preservation of the nonhumans' status as moral agents and there is no alternative way to protect themselves. . . .

The Principle of Proportionality

Before considering in detail each of the four remaining priority principles, it is well to look at the way they are interrelated. First, all four principles apply to situations where the nonhuman organisms involved are *harmless*. If left alone their activities would not endanger or threaten human life and health. Thus all four principles apply to cases of conflict between humans and nonhumans that are not covered by the principle of self-defense.

Next we must make a distinction between basic and nonbasic interests.[3] Using this distinction, the arrangement of the four principles can be set out as follows. The principles of proportionality and minimum wrong apply to cases in which there is a conflict between the *basic* interests of animals or plants and the *nonbasic* interests of humans. The principle of distributive justice, on the other hand, covers conflicts where the interests of all parties involved are *basic*. Finally, the principle of restitutive justice applies only where, in the past, either the principle of minimum wrong or that of distributive justice has been used. Each of those principles creates situations where some form of compensation or reparation must be made to nonhuman organisms, and thus the idea of restitution becomes applicable. . . .

It is possible for us to make judgments of the comparative importance of interests of nonhuman animals and plants because, once we become factually enlightened about what protects or promotes their good, we can *take their standpoint* and judge what is, from their point of view, an important or unimportant event in their lives as far as their overall well-being is concerned. Thus we are able to make a reasonable estimate of how seriously they would be harmed or deprived of something good if a certain condition were absent from their lives.

What counts as a serious harm or deprivation will, of course, depend on the kind of organism concerned. If each organism has a good of its own, so that it makes sense to speak of its faring well or poorly to the extent that it is able or unable to live a life fitted for its species-specific nature, then we may consider a serious harm or deprivation as being whatever severely impairs its ability to live such a life or makes it totally unable to do so.

In the case of humans a serious harm or deprivation will be whatever takes away or greatly reduces their powers of rationality and autonomy, including conditions of mental or physical incapacity that make it impossible for them to live a meaningful life. Since properly functioning organs and the soundness and health of other components of one's body are essential to human well-being, whatever injures these parts of one's body is a harm. The seriousness of the harm depends on the extent and permanence of damage done to those parts and on their contribution to the ability of the organism as a whole to function in a healthy way. With regard to psychological aspects of a human being, a serious harm will include anything that causes insanity, severe emotional disorder, or mental retardation of a kind that prevents the development or exercise of the basic powers of rationality and autonomy.

I might note that with reference to humans, basic interests are what rational and factually enlightened people would value as an essential part of their very existence as *persons.* They are what people need if they are going to be able to pursue those goals and purposes that make life meaningful and worthwhile. Thus for human persons their basic interests are those interests which, when morally legitimate, they have a *right* to have fulfilled. . . . We do not have a right to whatever will make us happy or contribute to the realization of our value system; we do have a right to the necessary conditions for the maintenance and development of our personhood. These conditions include subsistence and security ("the right to life"), autonomy, and liberty. A violation of people's moral rights is the worst thing that can happen to them, since it deprives them of what is essential to their being able to live a meaningful and worthwhile life. And since the fundamental, necessary conditions for such a life are the same for everyone, our human rights have to do with universal values or primary goods. They are the entitlement we all have as persons to what makes us persons and preserves our existence as persons.

In contrast with these universal values or primary goods that constitute our basic interests, our nonbasic interests are the particular ends we consider worth seeking and the means we consider best for achieving them that make up our individual value systems. The nonbasic interests of humans thus vary from person to person, while their basic interests are common to all.

This discussion of basic and nonbasic interests has been presented to introduce the second and third priority principles on our list, proportionality and minimum wrong. Both principles employ the distinction between basic and nonbasic interests, so it was necessary to clarify this distinction before examining them.

The principles apply to two different kinds of conflicts among competing claims. In both cases we are dealing with situations in which the *basic* interests of animals and plants conflict with the *nonbasic* interests of humans. But each principle applies to a different type of nonbasic human interests. In order to differentiate between these types we must consider various ways in which the nonbasic interests of humans are related to the attitude of respect for nature.

First, there are nonbasic human interests which are *intrinsically incompatible with* the attitude of respect for nature. The pursuit of these interests would be given up by anyone who had respect for nature since the kind of actions and intentions involved in satisfying them directly embody or express an exploitative attitude toward nature. Such an attitude is incompatible with that of respect because it means that one considers wild creatures to have merely instrumental value for human ends. To satisfy nonbasic interests of this first kind is to deny the inherent worth of animals and plants in natural ecosystems. Examples of such interests and of actions performed to satisfy them are the following (all actually occur in the contemporary world):

Slaughtering elephants so the ivory of their tusks can be used to carve items for the tourist trade.

Killing rhinoceros so that their horns can be used as dagger handles.

Picking rare wildflowers, such as orchids and cactuses, for one's private collection.

Capturing tropical birds, for sale as caged pets.

Trapping and killing reptiles, such as snakes, crocodiles, alligators, and turtles, for their skins and shells to be used in making expensive shoes, handbags, and other "fashion" products.

Hunting and killing rare wild mammals, such as leopards and jaguars, for the luxury fur trade.

All hunting and fishing which is done as an enjoyable pastime (whether or not the animals killed are eaten), when such activities are not necessary to meet the basic interests of humans. This includes all sport hunting and recreational fishing.

The ends and purposes of these practices and the human interests that motivate them are inherently incompatible with the attitude of respect for nature in the following sense. If we consider the various practices along with their central purposes as representing a certain human attitude toward nature, this attitude can only be described as exploitative. Those who participate in such activities with the aim of accomplishing the various purposes that motivate and direct them, as well as those who enjoy or consume the products while knowing the methods by which they were obtained, cannot be said to have genuine respect for nature. For all such practices treat wild creatures as mere instruments to human ends, thus denying their inherent worth. Wild animals and plants are being valued only as a source of human pleasure or as things that can be manipulated and used to bring about human pleasure.

It is important to realize that the human interests that underlie these practices are nonbasic. Even when hunters and fishermen eat what they have killed, this is incidental to the central purpose and governing aim of their sport. (I am not at this point considering the very different case of subsistence hunting and fishing, where such activities are not done as enjoyable pastimes but out of necessity.) That eating what they kill is a matter of pleasure and hence serves only a nonbasic interest is shown by the fact that they would continue to hunt or fish even if, for some reason of health or convenience, they did not eat the mammal, bird, or fish they killed. They are not hunting or fishing in order to have enough food to live.

With reference to this and to all the other examples given, it should be noted that none of the actions violate human rights. Indeed, if we stay within the boundaries of human ethics alone, people have a moral right to do such things, since they have a freedom-right to pursue without interference their legitimate interests and, within those boundaries, an interest is "legitimate" if its pursuit does not involve doing any wrong *to another human being*.

It is only when the principles of environmental ethics are applied to such actions that the exercise of freedom-rights in these cases must be weighed against the demands of the ethics of respect for nature. We then find that the practices in question are wrong, *all things considered*. For if they were judged permissible, the basic interests of animals and plants would be assigned a lower value or importance than the nonbasic interests of humans, which no one who had the attitude of respect for nature (as well as the attitude of respect for persons) would find acceptable. After all, a human being can still live a good life even if he or she does not own caged wild birds, wear apparel made from furs and reptile skins, collect rare wildflowers, engage in hunting and fishing as recreational pastimes, buy ivory carvings, or use horn dagger handles. But every one of these practices treats wild animals and plants as if their very existence is something having no value at all, other than as means to the satisfaction of human preferences.

Let us now consider another type of nonbasic human interest that can come into conflict with the basic interests of wild animals and plants. These are human interests which, in contrast with those just considered, are not *in themselves* incompatible with respect for nature. Nevertheless, the pursuit of these interests has *consequences* that are undesirable from the perspective of respect for nature and should therefore be avoided if possible. Sometimes the nonbasic human interests concerned will not be valued highly enough to outweigh the bad consequences of fulfilling them. In that case a person who has respect for nature would willingly forego the pursuit of those interests. Other times the interests will be so highly valued that even those who genuinely respect nature will not be willing to forego the pursuit of the interests. In the latter case, although having and pursuing the interests do not embody or express the attitude of respect for nature, neither do they embody or express a purely exploitative attitude toward nature. Wild animals and plants are not being used or consumed as mere means to human ends, though the consequences of actions in which the interests are pursued are such that wild creatures suffer harm. Examples of nonbasic interests of this type are:

Building an art museum or library where natural habitat must be destroyed.

Constructing an airport, railroad, harbor, or highway involving the serious disturbance of a natural ecosystem.

Replacing a native forest with a timber plantation.

Damming a free-flowing river for a hydro-electric power project.

Landscaping a natural woodland in making a public park.

Whether people who have true respect for nature would give up the activities involved in these situations depends on the value they place on the various interests being furthered. This in turn would depend on people's total systems of value and on what alternatives were available — in particular, whether substitutes less damaging to the environment could be found and whether some or all of the interests could be satisfied in other ways.

Let us recapitulate this classification of nonbasic human interests, since it is crucial to the examination of the priority principles I will consider below. First there are interests that directly express an exploitative attitude toward nature; actions taken to satisfy such interests are intrinsically incompatible with respect for nature. Second, there are interests that do not exemplify in themselves an exploitative attitude toward nature, but in many practical circumstances the means taken to satisfy those interests bring about effects on the natural world which, in the eyes of those who have respect for nature, are to be avoided whenever possible. Among this second class of interests are those which are not important enough to (not so highly valued by) a person to make the gains of their pursuit outweigh the undesirable consequences for wildlife. Others are such that their value does outweigh the undesirable consequences, even when such weight is assigned by one who has full respect for nature.

This classification bears on the two priority principles we are now about to consider: the principle of proportionality and that of minimum wrong. Each of the two kinds of nonbasic human interests mentioned above determines the range of application of one of these principles. The principle of proportionality applies to situations of conflict between the basic interests of wild animals and plants and those nonbasic human interests that are intrinsically incompatible with respect for nature. The principle of minimum wrong, on the other hand, applies to conflicts between the basic interests of wild animals and plants and those nonbasic human interests that are so highly valued that even a person who has respect for nature would not be willing to abstain from pursuing them, knowing that the pursuit of such interests will bring about conditions detrimental to the natural world.

Figure 7-1 schematically represents the relations among the five priority principles and their ranges of application.

Putting aside consideration of the principle of minimum wrong until later, I shall now discuss that of proportionality. The central idea of the principle of proportionality is that, in a conflict between human values and the good of (harmless) wild animals and plants, greater weight is to be given to basic

FIGURE 7-1

RELATIONS AMONG PRIORITY PRINCIPLES

Wild Animals and Plants	Harmful to Humans	Harmless to Humans (Or: their harmfulness can reasonably be avoided)	
		Basic Interests	*Basic Interests*
. . . in conflict with . . .		. . . in conflict with . . .	. . . in conflict with . . .
Humans		*Nonbasic interests* Intrinsically incompatible with respect for nature. / Intrinsically compatible with respect for nature, but extrinsically detrimental to wildlife and natural ecosystems.	*Basic interests*
Priority Principles	(1) *Self-defense*	(2) *Proportionality* / (3) *Minimum wrong*	(4) *Distributive justice*
		. . . when (3) or (4) have been applied . . . (5) *Restitutive justice*	

than to nonbasic interests, no matter what species, human or other, the competing claims arise from. Within its proper range of application the principle prohibits us from allowing nonbasic interests to override basic ones, even if the nonbasic interests are those of humans and the basic are those of animals and plants. . . .

The Principle of Minimum Wrong

. . . The principle states that, when rational, informed, and autonomous persons *who have adopted the attitude of respect for nature* are nevertheless unwilling to forego the two sorts of values mentioned above, even though they are aware that the consequences of pursuing those values will involve harm to wild animals and plants, it is permissible for them to pursue those values only so long as doing so involves fewer wrongs (violations of duties) than any alternative way of pursuing those values. . . .

How does the principle of minimum wrong determine a fair resolution of competing claims in sit-

uations of that kind? The following considerations are the relevant ones to be taken into account. First we must ask ourselves whether the human values being furthered are really worth the extreme cost being imposed on wild creatures. In this connection we should reflect on our own value system and on the way of life of our community to see whether a modification in values or a shift in perspective could not be made, consistent with the most fundamental aspects of that system or way of life, which would obviate at least some of the direct killing of nonhumans. Secondly, we should examine carefully all alternative possibilities open to us with regard to the manner of pursuing our values and way of life. The principle of minimum wrong demands that we choose the alternative that either eliminates direct killing entirely or that involves the least numbers killed. Finally, our respect for nature makes us respond with abhorrence to whatever killing is done, and gives rise to the recognition of our duty to make reparation or some form of compensation for the harm we have done to living things in the natural world. . . .

We might say that the system of *intrinsically valued ends* shared by a whole society as the focus of its ways of life, along with those human creations and productions that are judged as *supremely inherently valuable* by rational and enlightened members of the society, determine the set of human interests that are to be weighed against the interests of animals and plants in the situations of conflict to which the principle of minimum wrong is applicable.

The Principle of Distributive Justice

This fourth priority principle applies to competing claims between humans and nonhumans under two conditions. First, the nonhuman organisms are not harming us, so the principle of self-defense does not apply. Secondly, the interests that give rise to the competing claims are on the same level of comparative importance, all being *basic* interests, so the principles of proportionality and of minimum wrong do not apply. The range of application of the fourth principle covers cases that do not fall under the first three.

This principle is called the principle of distributive justice because it provides the criteria for a just distribution of interest-fulfillment among all parties to a conflict when the interests are all basic and hence of equal importance to those involved. Being of equal importance, they are counted as having the same moral weight. This equality of weight must be preserved in the conflict-resolving decision if it is to be fair at all. The principle of distributive justice requires that when the interests of the parties are all basic ones and there exists a natural source of good that can be used for the benefit of any of the parties, each party must be allotted an equal share. A fair share in those circumstances is an equal share.

When we try to put this principle of distributive justice into practice, however, we find that even the fairest methods of distribution cannot guarantee perfect equality of treatment to each individual organism. Consequently we are under the moral requirement to supplement all decisions grounded on distributive justice with a further duty imposed by the fifth priority principle, that of restitutive justice. . . .

In working out the various methods by which the principle of distributive justice can be put into practice, we must keep in mind the fact that the wild animals and plants we are concerned with are not themselves harmful to us. Consequently we are not under any necessity to kill them in self-defense. Since they are not "attacking" us, we can try to avoid or eliminate situations where we are forced to choose between their survival and ours. Thus the principle of distributive justice requires us to devise ways of transforming situations of confrontation into situations of mutual accommodation whenever it is possible to do so. In this way we can share the beneficial resources of the Earth equally with other members of the Community of Life. Our aim is to make it possible for wild animals and plants to carry on their natural existence side by side with human cultures.

Sometimes, however, the clash between basic human interests and the equally basic interests of nonhumans cannot be avoided. Perhaps the most obvious case arises from the necessity of humans to consume nonhumans as food. Although it may be possible for most people to eat plants rather than animals, I shall point out in a moment that this is not true of all people. And why should eating plants be ethically more desirable than eating animals?

Let us first look at situations where, due to severe environmental conditions, humans must use wild animals as a source of food. In other words, they are situations where subsistence hunting and fishing are necessary for human survival. Consider, for example, the hunting of whales and seals in the Arctic, or the killing and eating of wild goats and sheep by those living at high altitudes in mountainous regions. In these cases it is impossible to raise enough domesticated animals to supply food for a culture's populace, and geographical conditions preclude dependence on plant life as a source of nutrition. The principle of distributive justice applies to circumstances of that kind. In such circumstances the principle entails that it is morally *permissible* for humans to kill wild animals for food. This follows from the equality of worth holding between humans and animals. For if humans refrained from eating animals in those circumstances they would in effect be sacrificing their lives for the sake of animals, and no requirement to do that is imposed by respect for nature. Animals are not of *greater* worth, so there is no obligation to further their interests at the cost of the basic interests of humans.

However, since it is always a prima facie duty of environmental ethics not to destroy whole ecosystems (the duties of nonmaleficence and noninterference), it follows that wherever possible the choice of animal food source and the methods used in hunting should be guided by the principle of minimum wrong. The impact on natural ecosystems of the practice of killing wild animals for food must not involve a greater number of wrongs than any available alternative.

The same considerations apply to the practice of culling wild animals for food (as is done with the Wildebeest and the Water Buffalo in Africa) where environmental conditions make it impossible to use domesticated animals or to grow edible plants for human survival. Here the morally right decision is determined, first by the permissibility of consuming wild animals under the principle of distributive justice, and second, by the obligation to choose the species of animal to be taken and the manner of taking them that entail least harm to all the wild living things in the area. Thus severe damage to nature ecosystems and whole biotic communities must be avoided wherever possible.

I turn now to the issue of meat-eating versus vegetarianism, at least as far as the principles of environmental ethics apply to it. There are two main points to be considered. The first is that, when we raise and slaughter animals for food, the wrong we do to them does not consist simply in our causing them pain. Even if it became possible for us to devise methods of killing them, as well as ways of treating them while alive, that involved little or no pain, we would still violate a prima facie duty in consuming them. They would still be treated as mere means to our ends and so would be wronged. Now, we see above that it is permissible to kill animals when this is necessary for our survival. But will not the very same be true of our killing plants, in the light of the fact that plants, just like animals, are our equals in inherent worth? Although no pain or conscious suffering to living things is involved here, we are nevertheless using plants wholly for our own purposes. They are therefore being wronged when we kill them to eat them. Yet it is permissible to do this, since we have no duty to sacrifice ourselves to them. Whether we are dealing with animals or with plants, then, the principle of distributive justice applies (and along with it, as we shall see later, the principle of restitutive justice).

Still, the factor of animal suffering does raise important considerations in practice even if no greater wrong is committed in eating animals than in eating plants. Granted that susceptibility to pain does not give animals a higher inherent worth; nevertheless any form of conscious suffering is an intrinsically bad occurrence in the life of a sentient creature. From the standpoint of the animals involved, a life without such experiences is better than a life that includes them. Such a being's good is not fully realized when it is caused to suffer in ways that are not contributory to its overall well-being. We know that this is so in our own case, and must therefore infer that it is so in their case.

Now, insofar as respect is due to sentient animals, moral consideration and concern for their well-being will accordingly include attempts to minimize intrinsic evils in their lives. So when there is a choice between killing plants or killing sentient animals, it will be less wrong to kill plants if animals are made to suffer when they are taken for food.

I consider now the main point regarding the relevance of the principles of environmental ethics to the issue of vegetarianism versus meat eating. It will become clear that, in the light of this second point, anyone who has respect for nature will be on the side of vegetarianism, even though plants and animals are regarded as having the same inherent worth. The point that is crucial here is the amount of arable land needed for raising grain and other plants as food for those animals that are in turn to be eaten by humans when compared with the amount of land needed for raising grain and other plants for direct human consumption. . . . We can drastically reduce the amount of cultivated land needed for human food production by changing from a meat-eating culture to a vegetarian culture. The land thus saved could be set aside as sanctuaries for wildlife. . . .

The Principle of Restitutive Justice

. . . As a priority principle in our present context, the principle of restitutive justice is applicable whenever the principles of minimum wrong and distributive justice have been followed. In both cases harm is done to animals and plants that are harmless, so some form of reparation or compensation is called for if our actions are to be fully consistent with the attitude of respect for nature. (In applying the minimum wrong and distributive justice principles, no harm is done to harmless *humans,* so there occurs an inequality of treatment between humans and nonhumans in these situations.) In its role as a priority principle for determining a fair way to resolve conflicts between humans and nonhumans, the principle of restitutive justice must therefore supplement those of minimum wrong and distributive justice.

What kinds of reparation or compensation are suitable? Two factors can guide us in this area. The first is the idea that the greater the harm done, the greater the compensation required. Any practice of promoting or protecting the good of animals and plants which is to serve to restore the balance of justice between humans and nonhumans must bring about an amount of good that is comparable (as far as can be reasonably estimated) to the amount of evil to be compensated for.

The second factor is to focus our concern on the soundness and health of whole ecosystems and their biotic communities, rather than on the good of particular individuals. As a practical measure this is the most effective means for furthering the good of the greatest number of organisms. Moreover, by setting aside certain natural habitats and by maintaining certain types of physical environments in their natural condition, compensation to wild creatures can be "paid" in an appropriate way. . . . To set aside habitat areas and protect environmental conditions in those areas so that wild communities of animals and plants can realize their good is the most appropriate way to restore the balance of justice with them, for it gives full expression to our respect for nature even when we have done harm to living things in order to benefit ourselves. We can, as it were, return the favor they do us by doing something for their sake. Thus we need not bear a burden of eternal guilt because we have used them—and will continue to use them—for our own ends. There is a way to make amends.

NOTES

1. It is nowadays standard practice for biologists conducting research in the field to study organisms not only by observing natural differences by which to identify particular individuals but also by tagging or marking individuals for purposes of ready recognition.

2. Three books have explored in depth the use of teleological concepts and explanations in biology. Although they are in sharp disagreement about the correct analysis to be made of such concepts and explanations, there is general acknowledgment that those concepts and explanations are integral to the biological sciences. See Michael Ruse, *The Philosophy of Biology* (London: J. M. Dent, 1973); Andrew Woodfield, *Teleology* (New York: Cambridge University Press, 1976); and Larry Wright, *Teleological Explanation* (Los Angeles: University of California Press, 1976).

3. In one of the few systematic studies of priority principles holding between humans and nonhumans, Donald VanDeVeer argues that the distinction between basic and "peripheral" (nonbasic) interests, which applies to all species that can be said to have interests, is a morally relevant difference; see VanDeVeer, "Interspecific Justice," *Inquiry* 22/1–2 (Summer 1979): 55–79. VanDeVeer would not, however, be likely to accept any of the priority principles I set out since he considers the psychological capacity to live a satisfying life a ground for counting the interests of beings possessing that capacity to be of greater weight than the equally basic interests of beings lacking it. His main reason for opposing pure egalitarianism among species seems to be that such a view is counterintuitive, being incompatible with "our deepest and strongest pre-theoretical convictions about specific cases" (p. 58; see also pp. 66 and 76).

VanDeVeer's position has recently been defended, with certain qualifications, by Robin Attfield in *The Ethics of Environmental Concern* (New York: Columbia University Press, 1983), chapter 9. Attfield holds that ". . . varying degrees of *intrinsic* value attach to lives in which different capacities are realized" (Attfield's italics, p. 176). This is a view similar to that of Louis G. Lombardi, which I critically examined in chapter three [of *Respect for Nature*]. Attfield's arguments, unlike

Lombardi's, are marred by a failure to distinguish the concept of intrinsic value from that of inherent worth. The utilitarianism Attfield espouses is not seen to be logically incompatible with the principle that each organism has inherent worth as an individual, a principle he also appears to hold. The incompatibility of these two ideas has been clearly explained by Tom Regan in *The Case for Animal Rights,* chapters 7 and 8.

DISCUSSION TOPICS

1. Give examples of your own of a plant and an animal having a good of its own. Do you agree with Taylor that a stone does not have a good of its own?
2. Taylor includes plants in his system of respect for nature, whereas Regan does not consider plants to have moral rights. Which author do you agree with? Why?
3. Apply Taylor's four duties to nature to the attempt to save the California condor with a captive breeding program. Is this program morally right?
4. Using Taylor's system of five priority principles, how would you decide
   a. whether to construct an airport, if you were a member of a board of supervisors in a rural area?
   b. whether to build a shelter for the homeless on land currently used as a wildlife refuge by your city, if you were mayor?

READING 40

Biocentric Individualism

Gary Varner

Gary Varner is associate professor of philosophy at Texas A & M University, College Station. He has written a number of significant articles as well as In Nature's Interests? Interests, Animal Rights, and En-

vironmental Ethics *(1998). In the following essay from* Environmental Ethics *(edited by D. Schmidtz and E. Willott, 2002), he defends biocentric individualism — the view that all living things have morally significant interests. Plants as well as human beings have biological interests in the fulfillment of their various biologically based needs. Varner develops a hierarchical theory of interests according to which it is good to save the life of plants and nonconscious animals when we can, but not at the expense of projects that give meaning to an individual's life.*

INTRODUCTION

As a boy, I often wandered in the woods near my home in central Ohio. One August day, I dug up a maple seedling from the woods and planted it in one of my mother's flowerbeds beside the house. Within hours, the seedling was terribly wilted. Convinced that I had mortally wounded the plant, I felt a wave of guilt and, wishing to hasten what I believed to be its inevitable and imminent demise, I pulled it up, broke its small stalk repeatedly, and stuffed it in the trash. When my mother later explained that the plant was only in temporary shock from being transplanted into full sun. I felt an even larger wave of guilt for having dispatched it unnecessarily.

Was I just a soft-headed lad? Even then, I did not think that the plant was conscious, and since childhood, I have not again tried to "euthanize" a doomed plant. I feel no guilt about weeding the garden, mowing the lawn, or driving over the plants which inevitably crowd the four wheel drive paths I gravitate towards while camping. Nevertheless, I now let "weeds" grow indiscriminately in my wooded backyard, I mow around the odd wildflower that pops up amid the Bermuda grass out front, and I sometimes swerve to avoid a plant when tracking solitude in my truck. I believe that insects are not conscious, that they are in the same category, morally speaking, as plants, yet I often carry cockroaches and wasps outside rather than kill them. I'll even pause while mowing to let a grasshopper jump to safety. My relative diffidence regarding insects could just be erring on the side of caution. I believe that insects *probably* are not conscious, whereas I am *cock-sure* that plants are not; so when I do dispatch an insect, I make a point of crushing it quite thoroughly, including its head. Similarly, my current plant-regarding decisions are doubtless inspired in part by aesthetic judgments rather than concern for their non-conscious well-being. The wildflowers in my front yard are just more interesting to look at than a continuous stretch of Bermuda grass and my unkempt backyard buffers me from my neighbors. Still, I believe it is better—*morally* better—that plants thrive rather than die, even if they do not benefit humans or other, conscious creatures. So if I was just soft-headed to feel bad about that maple seedling, then my gray matter hasn't quite firmed up yet.

But *am* I just soft-headed, or is there a rational case to be made for plants and other presumably non-conscious organisms? A few philosophers have thought so. The famous doctor and theologian, Albert Schweitzer, wrote:

> A man is truly ethical only when he obeys the compulsion to help all life which he is able to assist, and shrinks from injuring anything that lives. He does not ask how far this or that life deserves one's sympathy as being valuable, nor, beyond that, whether and to what degree it is capable of feeling. Life as such is sacred to him. He tears no leaf from a tree, plucks no flower, and takes care to crush no insect. If in summer he is working by lamplight, he prefers to keep the window shut and breathe a stuffy atmosphere rather than see one insect after another fall with singed wings upon his table.
>
> If he walks on the road after a shower and sees an earthworm which has strayed on it, . . . he lifts it from the deadly stone surface, and puts it on the grass. If he comes across an insect which has fallen into a puddle, he stops a moment in order to hold out a leaf or a stalk on which it can save itself. (Schweitzer 1955, p. 310)

And in the contemporary literature of environmental ethics, Paul Taylor's 1986 book, *Respect For Nature: A Theory of Environmental Ethics,* is a must-read for any serious student of the field. In it . . . Taylor argues that extending a Kantian ethic of respect to non-conscious individuals is plausible once one understands that organisms, "conscious or not, all are equally teleological centers of life in the sense that each is a unified system of goal-oriented activities directed toward their preservation and well-being," that each has a good of its own which is "prima facie worthy of being preserved or promoted as an end in itself and for the sake of the entity whose good it is" (Taylor 1981, pp. 210, 201 in original edition).

I call views like Schweitzer's and Taylor's *biocentric individualism,* because they attribute moral standing to all living things while denying that holistic entities like species or ecosystems have moral standing. Hence they are *bio*centric—rather than, say anthropocentric or sentientist—but they are still *individualist* views—rather than versions of holism.

Schweitzer's and Taylor's views differ in important ways. Perhaps most significantly, Schweitzer talks as if we incur guilt every time we harm a living thing, even when we do so to preserve human life. He writes:

> Whenever I in any way sacrifice or injure life, I am not within the sphere of the ethical, but I become guilty, whether it be egoistically guilty for the sake of maintaining my own existence or welfare, or unegoistically guilty for the sake of maintaining a greater number of other existences or their welfare. (Schweitzer 1955, p. 325).

In the '40s and '50s, Schweitzer was celebrated in the popular media for bringing modern hospital services to the heart of Africa. Yet he appears to have thought that he incurred guilt when he saved human lives by killing disease microbes, not to mention when he killed things to eat. By contrast, in his book, Taylor makes it clear that he believes we are justified in violating plants' (and some animals') most basic interests in a range of cases: certainly for the sake of surviving, but also for the sake of furthering non-basic, but culturally important, interests of humans. He does impose on this a requirement of "minimum wrong," that is, harming as few living things as possible in the process (Taylor 1986, p. 289), but Taylor, unlike Schweitzer, believes that we can prioritize interests in a way that justifies us in preserving our own lives and pursuing certain non-basic interests at the expense of plants' (and some animals') most basic interests.

I will return to this question of which interests take precedence in various cases of conflict later. That is certainly an important question for any biocentric individualist. After all, if you think that even disease microbes and radishes have moral standing, then you need an explanation of how your interests can override those of millions of plants and microbes which must be doomed in the course of living a full human life. Otherwise, you are left with Schweitzer's perpetual guilt. But if I wasn't just being a soft-headed lad when I regretted killing that maple seedling—if there is a rational case to be made for plants (and other non-conscious organisms) having moral standing—then the first question is: Why think this?

WHY THINK THAT PLANTS HAVE MORAL STANDING?

I have two basic arguments for the conclusion that they do. Before discussing these arguments, however, it is important to be more clear about what, specifically, is being asked.

As I use the terms, to say that an entity has moral standing is to say that it has interests, and to say that it has interests is to say that it has needs and/or desires, and that the satisfaction of those needs and/or desires creates intrinsic value. When I say that their satisfaction creates intrinsic value, I mean that it makes the world a better place, independent of the entity's relations to other things. . . . The term "intrinsic value" is a key one in environmental ethics, but it is also a very nuanced one. There certainly is a distinction to be drawn between valuing something because it is useful, and valuing it apart from its usefulness. One way of expressing the biocentric individualist stance, then, would be to describe it as the view that moral agents ought to value plants' lives intrinsically rather than merely instrumentally. However, putting it this way suggests that plants' flourishing might not be a good thing if there were no conscious valuers around to consider it, and one of my arguments for biocentric individualism purports to show that plants' flourishing is a good thing independent of there being any conscious valuers around

at all. So I define biocentric individualism in terms of plants having interests, the satisfaction of which creates intrinsic value as defined above, whether or not there are any conscious valuers around.

A second thing to be clear about is what I mean by "plants." For simplicity's sake, I will speak simply of "plants." But unless stated otherwise, what I mean by this is *all non-conscious organisms.* Later I will take up the question of which non-human animals lack consciousness. For now, suffice it to say that even after the taxonomic revisions of the 1970s, the animal kingdom includes a number of organisms that are poor candidates for consciousness, e.g. barnacles and sponges. Besides plants, the new taxonomy includes three whole kingdoms, the members of which are equally poor candidates. The fungi are just heterotrophic plants. Organisms in the new kingdoms monera and protista—single celled organisms like bacteria and amoebas (respectively)—were previously classified as animals. But in this essay, "plants" is a shorthand for all of these non-conscious organisms.

In summary, I assume the following definitions of these key terms:

> **Moral standing:** An entity has moral standing if and only if it has interests.
>
> **Interests:** An entity has interests if and only if the fulfillment of its needs and/or desires creates intrinsic value.
>
> **Intrinsic value:** Intrinsic value is the value something has independently of its relationships to other things. If a thing has intrinsic value, then its existence (flourishing, etc.) makes the world a better place, independently of its value to anything else or any other entity's awareness of it.
>
> **Plants:** Unless stated otherwise, "plants" refers to all non-conscious organisms, including (presumably) all members of the plant kingdom, but also all members of the kingdoms fungi, monera, and protista, as well as some members of the animal kingdom (to be specified later).

So the question is: Why think that all those "plants" have interests, the satisfaction of which creates intrinsic value, independently of any conscious organism's interest in them?

My first argument for this conclusion is developed in detail in my book, *In Nature's Interests?* (Varner 1998, chapter three). There I argue against the dominant, mental state theory of individual welfare (for short, the mental state theory). The dominant account of individual welfare in recent Western moral philosophy has identified what is in an individual's interests with what the individual actually desires, plus what the individual would desire if he or she were both adequately informed and impartial across phases of his or her life. This dominant account then identifies what is in an individual's *best* interests with the latter, with what he or she would desire under those idealized conditions. Formally:

The mental state theory of individual welfare: X is in an individual A's interest just in case:

1. A actually desires X, or
2. A would desire X if A were sufficiently informed and impartial across phases of his or her life; and
3. What is in A's *best* interests is defined in terms of clause (2).

Something like this theory is accepted by most contemporary moral and political philosophers.

My first argument for the moral standing of plants begins by pointing to an inadequacy of the mental state theory.

Argument 1: The mental state theory seem to provide an inadequate account of the interests of conscious individuals. If that is so, and if the way to fix it involves acknowledging that intrinsic value is created by the satisfaction of nonconscious, biologically based needs of such individuals, then it makes sense to attribute interests to plants. For although plants are incapable of having desires, they have biologically based needs just as do conscious individuals.

Here is an example that brings out the problem I see in the mental state theory:

Example 1: By the nineteenth century, British mariners were carrying citrus fruit on long sea voyages to prevent the debilitating disease of scurvy. It was not until this century that scientists discovered that we need about 10 milligrams of ascorbic acid a day, and that citrus fruits prevent scurvy because they contain large amounts of ascorbic acid.

To see how this raises a problem, consider what is meant by being "adequately informed" in the second clause of the mental state theory. Some authors limit "adequate information" to the best scientific knowledge of the day. But then it would be false that those mariners had any interest in getting 10 milligrams of ascorbic acid a day. This is because they did not in fact desire it (they did not even know it exists), and even having the best scientific knowledge of the day would not have led them to desire it because no one then knew about it. The problem is that it certainly seems wrong to say that getting 10 milligrams of ascorbic acid a day was not in their interests.

This problem is easily avoided by adding a clause about biologically based needs to our theory of individual welfare. Renamed appropriately, the theory would now be something like this:

The psycho-biological theory of individual welfare: X is in an individual A's interests just in case:

1. A actually desires X, or
2. A would desire X if A were sufficiently informed and impartial across phases of his or her life; or
3. X serves some biologically based need of A.

In my book (Varner 1998, pp. 64–71), I give a detailed analysis of the complex notion of a biologically based need, arguing that these can be determined by examining the evolutionary history of an organism. Here, I think it unnecessary to revisit that analysis. Ascorbic acid clearly served a biologically based need of sailors before modern scientists discovered it. So, on this psycho-biological theory, it was in those sailors' interest to get enough of it, even though no one knew anything about ascorbic acid at the time.

Note that this new theory says nothing about what is in one's *best* interests. I replaced clause (3) in the mental state theory rather than adding another clause because identifying what is in one's best interests with what one would desire under ideal motivational and informational conditions — clause (2) — faces similar problems. Other things being equal, it seems that getting enough ascorbic acid was in those mariners' best interests, even though they would still not have desired it even under the best motivational and informational conditions. So even after adding a clause about biologically based needs, it would still be a mistake to identify what is in one's best interests with clause (2).

One limitation of the nineteenth-century mariners example is that being "sufficiently informed" can be analyzed other than in terms of having "the best scientific knowledge of the day." We could, for instance, analyze it in terms of having all the scientific knowledge that humans will ever or could ever accumulate. I believe there are other problems with this analysis (see Varner 1998, pp. 58–60), but it would solve the problem raised by the above example. However, here is another example that brings out the same kind of problem with the mental state theory, and where the alternative analysis of "sufficiently informed" doesn't help:

> **Example 2:** Like many cat owners, I grapple with the question of whether and when to allow my cat, Nanci, to go outside. Cats find the outdoors endlessly fascinating, but they also encounter health risks outside, including exposure to feline leukemia virus (FeLV) and fleas (which Nanci happens to be allergic to).

I frankly do not know whether or not keeping Nanci indoors is in her best interests, all things considered. Nonetheless, it does seem clear that keeping her inside would serve some interests of hers, in at least some ways. For instance, it would prevent exposure to FeLV and fleas. Yet the mental state theory does not support this intuition because it is not clear that it even makes sense to talk about what an animal like Nanci would desire if she were "sufficiently in-

formed and impartial across phases of her life." I assume that Nanci is congenitally incapable of understanding the relevant information about FeLV and fleas. So on the mental state theory, what are we to say about her going outside? It looks like we have to conclude that, whenever she in fact wants to go out, she has no interest whatsoever in staying inside, because clause (2) is irrelevant in her case. It just doesn't make sense, in the case of animals like Nanci, to talk about what they would desire were they "sufficiently informed" (let alone "impartial across phases of their lives"). What is in their interests is whatever they happen to desire at any moment in time. This is another counter-intuitive implication of the mental state theory, and one which the psycho-biological theory avoids. Although the psycho-biological theory as formulated above is silent on the issue of what is in an individual's best interests, it at least supports the intuition that Nanci has some interest in staying inside (because doing so would serve her biologically based needs by preventing exposure to FeLV and fleas), even if she now desires to go outside and no sense can be made of what an animal like her would desire under ideal epistemological and motivational conditions.

The examples of Nanci and the nineteenth-century mariners together illustrate a general problem for the mental state theory. The theory ties all of our interests to what we desire, either actually or under ideal epistemological and motivational conditions, but not all of our interests are tied in this way to our conscious desires and beliefs. Most (maybe even all) of our desires are tied to our beliefs about the world, because as our beliefs change, our desires change. For instance, suppose that I desire to marry Melody, primarily because I believe that she is a fine fiddler. When I find out that my belief about her is false, my desire to marry her will presumably be extinguished. Similarly, if I do not desire to marry Melinda only because I believe that she is a lousy fiddler, when I find out that she is actually a virtuoso, I will presumably form a desire to marry her. My interest in marrying each woman comes and goes with my beliefs about her. However, nothing I could possibly believe about the world, whether true or false, could change the fact that I need about 10 milligrams a day of ascorbic acid to stay healthy, and no matter how strongly I might desire it, I will never be able to make it true that going without ascorbic acid is in my interest. My interest in ascorbic acid is determined by a biological need that exists wholly independent of my beliefs and desires. This is a central advantage of the psycho-biological theory over the mental state theory. Some things are only in our interests if we happen to desire them or have certain beliefs about the world, but other things are in our interests no matter what we desire or believe, or what we would desire and believe under ideal conditions. We can refer to the former as preference interests and to the latter as biological interests. The mental state theory errs by identifying all of our interests with our preference interests. The psycho-biological theory acknowledges these, but also accounts for biological interests that are wholly independent of our preference interests.

That being said, my first argument for the moral standing of plants is now complete. The above examples are intended to illustrate how the dominant, mental state theory of individual welfare is flawed, because it ties all of individuals' interests to their actual or hypothetical desires. An obvious way to fix this problem is to hold that individuals also have biological interests in the fulfillment of their various biologically based needs, whether they (like the nineteenth-century mariners) could only become aware of these needs under special circumstances, or they (like Nanci the cat) are congenitally incapable of desiring that those needs be fulfilled. But then, since plants too have biologically based needs, they too have interests, even though they are congenitally incapable of desiring anything at all.

I did not include my second argument for the view that plants have moral standing in my 1998 book because, frankly, I doubted that it would be persuasive to anyone not already essentially convinced. Nevertheless, I think that this second argument expresses very clearly the most basic value assumption of the biocentric individualist. It also ties in to famous thought experiments in ethical theory and environmental ethics, and so I include it here.

The argument is driven by a variant of a famous thought experiment that British philosopher G. E. Moore used to cast doubt on sentientism (the view that only sentient—that is conscious—organisms

have moral standing). Moore discussed the classical utilitarians (Jeremy Bentham, John Stuart Mill, and Henry Sidgwick, who were all sentientists) at length and in particular responded to Sidgwick's claim that "No one would consider it rational to aim at the production of beauty in external nature, apart from any possible contemplation of it by human beings." Moore responded:

Well, I may say at once, that I, for one, do consider this rational; and let us see if I cannot get any one to agree with me. Consider what this admission really means. It entitles us to put the following case. Let us imagine one world exceedingly beautiful. Imagine it as beautiful as you can; put into it whatever on this earth you most admire—mountains, rivers, the sea; trees, and sunsets, stars and moon. Imagine these all combined in the most exquisite proportions, so that no one thing jars against another, but each contributes to increase the beauty of the whole. And then imagine the ugliest world you can possibly conceive. Imagine it simply one heap of filth, containing everything that is most disgusting to us, for whatever reason, and the whole, as far as may be, without one redeeming feature. Such a pair of worlds we are entitled to compare: they fall within Prof. Sidgwick's meaning, and the comparison is highly relevant to it. The only thing we are not entitled to imagine is that any human being ever has or ever, by any possibility, *can,* live in either, can ever see and enjoy the beauty of the one or hate the foulness of the other. Well, even so, supposing them quite apart from any possible contemplation by human beings; still, is it irrational to hold that it is better that the beautiful world should exist, than the one which is ugly? Would it not be well, in any case, to do what we could to produce it rather than the other? (Moore 1903, p. 83)

Moore thought we would agree with him in answering yes. But then, he continued:

If it be once admitted that the beautiful world *in itself* is better than the ugly, then it follows, that however many beings may enjoy it, and however much better their enjoyment may be than it is itself, yet its mere existence adds *something* to the goodness of the whole . . . (Moore 1903, pp. 83–85; emphases in original)

That is, Moore concluded, the mere existence of beauty adds intrinsic value to the world.

I have always been unsure what to think about Moore's thought experiment, so apparently I am of two minds when it comes to saying that the mere existence of beauty adds intrinsic value to the world. However, I have always felt certain about my answer to an analogous question. Suppose that instead of choosing between creating a beautiful world and an ugly world, the choice were between creating a world devoid of life and a world brimming with living things, neither of which would ever evolve conscious life or even be visited or known about by any conscious organisms. If, like me, you believe that it matters which world is produced and that it would be better to produce the world chock-full of nonconscious life, then you seem to be committed to biocentric individualism. For you appear to believe that life — even non-conscious life — has intrinsic value. To paraphrase Moore:

> **Argument 2:** If we admit that a world of non-conscious living things is *in itself* better than a world devoid of all life, then it follows that however much better it is to be both conscious and alive, the mere existence of non-conscious life adds *something* to the goodness of the world. . . .

. . . If we agree that it matters which of my worlds is produced, and that it would be better to produce the plant-filled world, then we seem to agree that the lives of even the most mundane plants add intrinsic value to the world.

JUST WHAT ARE PLANTS' INTERESTS WORTH?

The next question has to be: *how valuable* are the interests of plants, in relation to those of humans and other animals? Moral hierarchies are unpopular in many quarters. In particular, feminist philosophers often condemn hierarchical views of beings' relative moral significance for being instruments of patriarchal oppression. . . . But as a biocentric individualist, I feel forced to endorse one. Otherwise,

how could I live with myself? I gleefully tear radishes from the garden for a snack, swatting mosquitoes all the while. I take antibiotics for a persistent sinus infection, and (at least when I'm not on antibiotics) I send countless intestinal bacteria on a deadly joyride into the city sewer system every morning. Unless I can give good reasons for thinking that my interests somehow trump those of microbes and plants (if not also animals), I am left with Albert Schweitzer's view, quoted above, that we "become guilty" whenever we "in any way sacrifice or injure life," even when fighting off disease organisms, eating, and defecating. In my book (Varner 1998, chapter four), I argue that a plausible assumption about what I call "hierarchically structured interests" does the trick, when coupled with empirical observations about certain broad categories of interests.

Here is what I mean by hierarchically structured interests:

> **Hierarchically structured interests:** Two interests are hierarchically structured when the satisfaction of one requires the satisfaction of the other, but not vice-versa.

Certain types of interests clearly stand in this relationship to other types of interests. For example, satisfying my desire to succeed professionally requires the satisfaction of innumerable more particular desires across decades, but not vice-versa. It takes years to succeed professionally, and therefore I have to satisfy innumerable day-to-day desires to eat this or that in the course of completing that long-term project. But each particular desire to eat can be satisfied without satisfying my long-term desire to succeed professionally. So my desires to eat and to succeed professionally are hierarchically structured in the above sense.

Generally, what the contemporary American philosopher Bernard Williams calls "ground projects" and "categorical desires" stand in this relationship to day-to-day desires for particular things. Here is how Williams defines these terms:

> **Ground projects and categorical desires:** A ground project is "a nexus of projects . . . which

are closely related to [one's] existence and which to a significant degree give a meaning to [one's] life," and a categorical desire is one that answers the question "Why is life worth living?" (Williams 1981, pp. 13, 12; 1973, pp. 85–86)

A person's ground project normally is a nexus of categorical desires, and generally, a ground project requires decades to complete. There are, of course, exceptions. It is conceivable that a person might have literally only one categorical desire, a desire which he or she could satisfy in one fell swoop. Perhaps a young gymnast aiming at a gold medal in the Olympics is a realistic approximation of this, but notice that even in the case of the gymnast: (1) satisfying the desire for a gold medal requires years of training, and (2) we would probably think it unhealthy and abnormal if the gymnast had no other ground project, if there were no other, longer-term desires that made her life worth living beyond the Olympics. So a ground project normally involves a host of very long-term desires, which bear the above kind of hierarchical relationship with the individual's day-to-day desires for this or that specific thing.

Here is a plausible assumption about interests that are clearly hierarchically structured:

Assumption: Generally speaking, ensuring the satisfaction of interests from similar levels in similar hierarchies of different individuals creates similar amounts of value, and the dooming of interests from similar levels in similar hierarchies of different individuals creates similar levels of disvalue.

In stating the assumption in this way, I do not mean to imply that we can make very fine-tuned judgments about which interests are more valuable than others.[1] All I claim is that interests from certain very broad categories *generally* bear this relationship to interests from other very broad categories. In particular, I argue that the following two principles are reasonable in light of the assumption:

Principle P1 (the priority of desires principle): Generally speaking, the death of an entity that has desires is a worse thing than the death of an entity that does not.

Principle P2′ (the priority of ground projects principle): Generally speaking, the satisfaction of ground projects is more important than the satisfaction of non-categorical desires.

Since I introduced the above assumption by discussing human ground projects, let me begin with principle P2′.

I call it P2′, rather than just P2, because in my book I first introduce, and dismiss, the principle:

Principle P2 (the priority of *human* desires principle): The satisfaction of the desires of humans is more important than the satisfaction of the desires of animals.

Principle P2 would solve the problem under discussion in this section., but it is transparently speciesist. It says that humans' desires are more important than any other organisms' simply because they are desires of *humans.* Principle P2′ compares ground projects to non-categorical desires without asserting that humans' desires are more important than any other organisms'. If it turns out that some non-human animals have ground projects, then Principle P2′ applies equally to theirs. Which animals, if any, have ground projects is an empirical question, as is the question of whether all human beings do. Surely some human beings do not. For instance, anencephalic babies and the permanently comatose clearly do not, and perhaps others, like the most profoundly retarded, or those who have lost the will to live, do not. Regarding animals, my hunch is that very few if any non-human animals have ground projects, but maybe some do (perhaps some great apes or cetaceans). The crucial thing to note is that principle P2′ is not speciesist. It does not say that humans' interests are more important *because they are humans' interests.* Principle P2′ only says that ground projects, wherever they occur, generally have more value than non-categorical desires. P2′ leaves the question of which beings have ground projects open for empirical investigation; it does not stipulate that only humans have this especially valuable kind of interest.

So why think that ground projects are more valuable than non-categorical desires? The reason is that, as we saw above, ground projects normally stand in a hierarchical relationship to day-to-day desires for particular things; satisfying a ground project requires the satisfaction of innumerable day-to-day desires for particular things, but not vice-versa. So under the above assumption (that various interests within each type generally have similar amounts of value), satisfying a ground project generally creates more value than satisfying any such day-to-day desire.

I will discuss the implications of P2′ in the next section, along with those of P1. First, however, let me discuss the justification of P1. Notice that P1 does not assert that just any desire trumps any biological need or set thereof. Some day-to-day desires for particular things are incredibly trivial and it would be implausible to say that these trivial desires trump seemingly important biological interests like one's biological interest in good cardiovascular health. But all that principle P1 states is that "Generally speaking, the death of an entity that has desires is a worse thing than the death of an entity that does not." This is plausible under the assumption stated above, given the following general fact: maintenance of the capacity to form and satisfy desires requires the on-going satisfaction of the lion's share of one's biological needs. Certainly not every biological need of a conscious organism must be fulfilled for it to go on forming desires. . . . One of the deep challenges to my position (as Vermont philosopher Bill Throop has driven home to me in conversation) is deciding how to individuate interests. Do I have just one biological interest in the continued functioning of my whole cardiovascular system? One interest in the functioning of my heart and another in the functioning of my vascular system? Or do I have myriad interests, in the functioning of my various ventricles, veins, arteries, and so on? This is a difficult issue, but however it gets sorted out, it seems plausible to say that just as satisfying a ground project requires the satisfaction of innumerable day-to-day desires for particular things, maintaining the general capacity to form and satisfy desires requires the on-going satisfaction of the lion's share of one's biological needs. As a conscious process, maintenance of the capacity to form and satisfy desires presumably requires maintenance of myriad biological organs and subsystems, including, at the very least, the respiratory and cardiovascular systems, and most of the central nervous system. The argument for principle P1, then, is this: The only interests plants have in common with conscious organisms are biological interests. The ability to form and satisfy desires stands in a hierarchical relationship to such biological interests. But if interests of these two types generally have similar value, then conscious animals' lives have more value than plants' lives, because animals satisfy both types of interests in the course of their lives, whereas plants satisfy only one type.

The question posed in this section has not been answered precisely. My argument has not shown precisely how much the interests of plants are worth, relative to the interests of humans or other animals. For reasons given in my book (Varner 1998, pp. 80–89), I think it is impossible to give such a precise answer to this question. However, if principle P1 is indeed justified by the principle of inclusiveness (coupled with the assumption articulated above), then it is plausible to conclude that the *lives* of plants are, generally, less valuable than the *lives* of desiring creatures, including yours and mine. And that goes a long way towards showing that biocentric individualism is a practicable view, although most environmental philosophers have doubted that it is.

IS BIOCENTRIC INDIVIDUALISM PRACTICABLE?

One reason for doubt would be that before Paul Taylor, the only well-known biocentric individualist was Albert Schweitzer, and as we have seen, he said flatly that we are guilty for merely keeping ourselves alive by eating and fighting disease. However, as the foregoing section shows, a biocentric individualist can reasonably endorse a hierarchy of interests and related principles showing why it is better that we do this than let ourselves perish. We can at least say that my view implies this rough hierarchy of value:

ground projects
non-categorical desires
biological interests

Principle P2′ states that the satisfaction of a ground project is better than (creates more value than) the satisfaction of any interest of the other two kinds. Thus killing an individual with a ground project robs the world of a special kind of value. According to principle P1, the lives of many non-human animals have more value than the lives of plants, because these conscious organisms have both biological interests and non-categorical desires, whereas plants have only biological interests. Thus killing an animal robs the world of more value than does killing a plant.

The second part of this value hierarchy focuses attention on questions about consciousness that were alluded to earlier: which animals are conscious, which ones have desires? These questions are related, but not equivalent. I assume that all "genuine" desires are conscious, or at least potentially conscious, just as pain is. However, the evidence for desires in non-human animals may not overlap the evidence for pain, because I also assume that desires require relatively sophisticated cognitive capacities, whereas the bare consciousness of pain may not. A detailed treatment of this issue is beyond the scope of this essay, but here is a summary of the conclusions I reach from the more detailed treatment in my book (Varner 1998, pp. 26–30). All normal, mature mammals and birds very probably *do* have desires, and there is a somewhat weaker case for saying that "herps" (reptiles and amphibians) do too. The case for saying that fish have desires is decisively weaker. However, the available evidence make it very likely that all vertebrates, including fish, can feel pain. This is a curious result—it sounds odd to say that fish could feel pain without desiring an end to it—and so I suspect that as more kinds of scientific studies are available than I considered in my book, the evidence for pain and for desire in the animal kingdom will converge. However, for the sake of discussion here, I assume that although mammals and birds have desires, fish and invertebrates do not.[2]

We can now spell out more specifically the implications of the principles defended in the preceding section. Principle P1 tells us that it is better to kill desireless organisms than desiring ones. This addresses Schweitzer's hyperbolic guilt, because it shows that it would be worse for a human being to kill herself than it would be for her to kill any plant or microbe for the sake of good nutrition or fighting off disease. However, in light of the above discussion of consciousness, this does not imply that vegetarian diets are better, since most invertebrates apparently lack consciousness, and even fish may lack desires. Also, since it is possible to obtain animal byproducts like eggs and dairy foods from animals without killing them, a lacto-ovo diet might be perfectly respectful of animals' intrinsic value. (There are other ethical considerations, of course, as well as complicated issues in human nutrition. For an overview, see the essays in Comstock 1994.)

I also suspect that Principle P2′ can be used to make a case for the humane killing of animals who clearly have (non-categorical) desires. My reasoning is as follows. To the extent that hunting and slaughter-based animal agriculture play an important role in sustainable human communities, the value of protecting the background conditions for satisfying humans' ground projects would seem to support the necessary killing, at least if the animals live good lives and are killed humanely. Obviously, various animals, including mammals and birds, played a very large role in both paleolithic hunting-gathering societies and in the emergence of agriculture. Domesticated mammals continue to have a crucial role in sustainable agricultural systems in so-called "developing" nations, where they provide not only food but draft power and fertilizer. But at present it is still unclear to me just how much killing of animals might be necessary in utopian sustainable communities of the future.

In light of these implications of Principles P1 and P2′, the biocentric individualist stance hardly looks unlivable in the way Schweitzer's talk of perpetual guilt would suggest. There is a deeper reason that many environmental philosophers dismiss the biocentric individualist stance, however. They fear that it somehow devalues nature and thus, even if it is not literally an unlivable ethic, it is "inadequate" as an *environmental* ethic. This charge of "inadequacy" takes at least two distinct forms, and the biocentric individualist response to each must be different.

First, it is often claimed that individualist theories in general (that is, anthropocentrism and sentientism in addition to biocentric individualism) have implications that do not comport with the environmentalist agenda, which includes things like endangered species programs, the elimination of exotic species from natural areas, and the whole emphasis on preserving remaining natural areas. The heart of this claim is that because they focus on individuals, such theories get the wrong answers in a range of cases. For instance, environmentalists are keenly interested in preserving remaining natural areas, but, so this objection goes, biocentric individualism cannot justify this emphasis. For if we compare a woods and a cultivated field, or an old growth forest and a managed timber lot, they may look equally valuable from a biocentric individualist stance. Simply put, if only biological interests are at stake, then a cultivated area supporting thousands of thriving plants creates just as much value as a wild area that supports the same number of plants. Similarly, the biological interests of common plants seem no more valuable than the biological interests of rare plants.

This first version of the "inadequacy" charge misfires precisely because there *is* more at stake than the biological interests of the plants involved. Environmentalists commonly claim that in order to preserve the ecological context in which humans can live healthy, productive, and innovative lives into the indefinite future, we must stop the current trend of species extinctions and preserve most remaining wild areas. Characterizing the environmentalists' claim as a general need to safeguard background biological diversity in our environment, my response to the first version of the inadequacy charge is this. Principle P2′ attaches preeminent importance to safeguarding humans' ability to satisfy their ground projects. But if safeguarding this ability requires safeguarding background biological diversity in our environment, then doing so is of preeminent importance, at least instrumentally, in my view. That is, to the extent that environmentalists are correct that their practical agenda safeguards long-term human interests, any version of biocentric individualism which, like mine, attributes preeminent importance to certain interests of humans can probably endorse their agenda.

At this point it is important to note that two senses of the term "anthropocentric" are sometimes conflated in discussions of environmental ethics. In one sense of the term, a view is anthropocentric just in case it denies that non-human nature has any intrinsic value whatsoever. Obviously, biocentric indi-

vidualism is not anthropocentric in this sense. But in another sense, a view is called anthropocentric if it gives pride of place to certain interests which only humans have. Schweitzer's version of biocentric individualism is not anthropocentric in this second sense, but because I doubt that any non-human animals have ground projects, mine is. For clarity's sake, I use the labels "valuational anthropocentrism" and "axiological anthropocentrism" to refer, respectively, to views that deny all intrinsic value to non-humans and to views that acknowledge the intrinsic value of some non-human beings but insist that only humans have certain preeminently important interests (Varner 1998, p. 121).

The other form of the "inadequacy" charge focuses on the fact that for the biocentric individualist, even if holistic entities like species and ecosystems have enormous value, this value is still only instrumental. Environmentalists, it is claimed, tend to think that such entities have intrinsic value rather than merely instrumental value, and thus environmentalists tend to think more like holists.

I think this version of the "inadequacy" charge misconstrues one of the central questions of environmental ethics. As environmental philosophers, we should not think of ourselves as focusing on the question: What do environmentalists *in fact* think has intrinsic value? Rather, we should be asking: What *should* we think has intrinsic value? Or, what do we *have good reasons* to think has intrinsic value? Defining an "adequate" environmental ethic as one that matches the pre-theoretic intuitions of self-professed environmentalists turns the discipline of environmental ethics into a kind of moral anthropology rather than a reasoned search for truth. In this essay, I have not developed a case against environmental holism, but the arguments of this section do show that biocentric individualism cannot be summarily dismissed as impracticable, either generally or in regard to environmental policy specifically.

CONCLUSION

My larger goal in this essay has been to show that one need not be soft-headed to think that it matters, morally speaking, how we treat plants. It would, in my judgment, be unreasonable to obsess on the microbes one's immune system is killing every day or on how one's dinner vegetables were dealt their death blows, but it is not irrational to think that it is good to save the life of plants and non-conscious animals when one can. Good arguments can be given for thinking this, and someone who thinks this can consistently live a good human life.

And, of course, if it is reasonable to think that plants' lives have intrinsic value, then it was not irrational for me to feel at least a little bit guilty about killing that maple seedling unnecessarily.

SOURCES CITED

Comstock, Gary. "Might Morality Require Veganism?" Special issue of *Journal of Agricultural and Environmental Ethics* 7, no. 1 (1994).

Moore, G. E. *Principia Ethics.* London: Cambridge University Press, 1903.

Schweitzer, Albert. *The Philosophy of Civilization.* New York: Macmillan, 1955.

Taylor, Paul. "The Ethics of Respect for Nature." *Environmental Ethics* 3 (1981): 197–218.

Taylor, Paul. *Respect for Nature: A Theory of Environmental Ethics.* Princeton: Princeton University Press, 1986.

Varner, Gary E. *In Nature's Interests? Interests, Animal Rights, and Environmental Ethics.* New York: Oxford University Press, 1998.

Williams, Bernard. *Problems of the Self.* Cambridge: Cambridge University Press, 1973.

Williams, Bernard. *Moral Luck.* Cambridge: Cambridge University Press, 1981.

NOTES

1. Strictly speaking, my view is that the *satisfaction* of interests creates intrinsic value, but in this essay I speak interchangeably of "the value of various interests," "the value of various interests' satisfaction," and "the value created by the satisfaction of various interests."

2. The issue is further complicated by the phenomenon of convergent evolution — some invertebrates could have evolved coping strategies that most other invertebrates have not. In particular, cephalopods (octopus, squid, and cuttlefish) may have evolved consciousness of pain and cognitive capacities that other invertebrates lack but most or all vertebrates have.

DISCUSSION TOPICS

1. Varner argues that the "mental state theory of individual welfare" is inadequate. Explain how his examples of nineteenth-century mariners and of his cat Nanci illustrate this inadequacy.

2. Do you agree with Varner's choice of a world with living things over a world without life? If so, are you convinced that this choice means that the lives of plants have intrinsic value? Explain your reasons for agreeing or disagreeing with Varner's view.

3. Give an example of your own of a "ground project" and a "categorical desire." Varner doubts that nonhuman beings have such projects. Do you agree? Explain your reasoning.

4. Explain the difference between Varner's principles P2 and P2′. Do you agree that P2 is not morally justifiable? Why or why not?

5. Varner maintains that biological interests are of less value than ground projects and categorical desires. What reasons does he give for this claim? Do you believe he is correct?

CLASS EXERCISES

1. At a conference held in Copenhagen, Denmark, in 1992, a panel of nonscientists concluded it is unethical to genetically engineer animals to adjust them to existing agricultural production methods (intensive confinement, "factory farming," etc.). The question seems to be: Should the animals' *telos* (genetic nature) be changed, or should agricultural methods be changed? Discuss the strengths and weaknesses of each view.

2. You have recently purchased a 100-acre forest. Assuming you are limited to the views presented in this chapter, which theory would

you use to guide your decisions in dealing with this forest? Would you choose a different theory if you were deciding how to raise a herd of dairy cows on a farm?

3. For debate (see the appendix for suggested procedure): The great apes and whales, due to their advanced mental capacities, should be accorded greater moral significance than other nonhuman animals, including the right to life, liberty, and freedom from torture.

FOR FURTHER READING

Adams, Carol J. *Neither Man nor Beast: Feminism and the Defense of Animals.* New York: Continuum, 1994. A valuable collection of Adams's essays that challenges the ideology of animals as usable.

Armstrong, Susan J. "Souls in Process: A Theoretical Inquiry into Animal Psi," in *Critical Reflections on the Paranormal,* ed. Michael Stoeber and Hugo Meynell. Albany: SUNY, 1996. Integrates empirical evidence of animal psi, a process philosophy view of animal souls, and animal immortality in the Christian tradition.

Armstrong-Buck, Susan. "Nonhuman Experience: A Whiteheadian Analysis." *Process Studies* 18, 1 (1989): 1–18. An analysis of recent findings concerning non-human experience, in particular primate experience. Includes a proposed typology of self-consciousness.

Barad, Judith A. *Aquinas on the Nature and Treatment of Animals.* Bethesda, Md.: International Scholars Publications, 1995. The first extensive study of the tension between Aquinas's view of evolutionary concepts and the status of animals.

Botzler, R. G., and S. B. Armstrong-Buck. "Ethical Considerations in Research on Wildlife Diseases." *Journal of Wildlife Diseases* 21 (1985): 341–54. Suggests guidelines for use of animals in wildlife research.

Cheney, Dorothy L., and Robert M. Seyforth. *How Monkeys See the World: Inside the Mind of Another Species.* Chicago: University of Chicago Press, 1990. A thorough and sophisticated study of wild vervets and captive primates, coauthored by an anthropologist and a psychologist. The book examines the communicative and cognitive abilities of primates living under natural conditions, emphasizing their social interactions. Extensive bibliography.

Clark, Stephen R. L. *The Nature of the Beast: Are Animals Moral?* Oxford: Oxford University Press, 1984. A perceptive, Aristotelian discussion.

Dawkins, Marian Stamp. *Animal Suffering: The Science of Animal Welfare.* London: Chapman and Hall, 1980. An important study that discusses the assessment of animal suffering in captivity.

DeGrazia, David. *Taking Animals Seriously: Mental Life and Moral Status.* Cambridge: Cambridge University Press, 1996. Integrates animal rights and mentality, using much empirical documentation.

de Waal, Frans. *Good Natured: The Origins of Right and Wrong in Humans and Other Animals.* Cambridge, Mass.: Harvard University Press, 1996. A significant account of many years of observation of primates. De Waal persuasively exhibits presence of elements of morality, such as sympathy, peace-making, reciprocity, and norm-related characteristics.

Dombrowski, Daniel A. *The Philosophy of Vegetarianism.* Amherst: University of Massachusetts Press, 1984. A well-written study emphasizing ancient Greek philosophy. Contains an extensive annotated bibliography.

———. *Hartshorne and the Metaphysics of Animal Rights.* Albany: SUNY, 1988. A perceptive study of Hartshorne's theory of God and Hartshorne's thoughts on animals, including the aesthetics of birdsong.

Donovan, Josephine, and Carol J. Adams, eds. *Beyond Animal Rights: A Feminist Caring Ethic for the Treatment of Animals.* New York: Continuum, 1996. Extends the justice/care debate in moral philosophy to the question of animal well-being and emphasizes the emotional dimension of the human-animal relation.

Etica & Animali 8/96. A special issue, edited by Paoli Cavalieri, following up on *The Great Ape Project.* Contains significant essays by authors from different countries and disciplines, including the continental intellectual tradition, arguing for the inclusion of the nonhuman great apes in an expanded community of equals. Discussion of bicultural citizenship, moral space, and collective rights to resources. (Available from *Etica & Animali,* Corso Magenta 62, 20123 Milano, Italy.)

Fowler, Cary. *Unnatural Selection: Technology, Politics, and Plant Evolution.* Yverdon, Switzerland: Gordon and Breach, 1994. An analysis of the complex and changing social processes that have led to the patenting of biological materials. Useful appendixes.

Godlovitch, Stanley, and Roslind Godlovitch, eds. *Animals, Men, and Morals: An Enquiry into the Maltreatment of Non-Humans.* New York: Tapliner, 1972. The book, by philosophers and sociologists, which arguably began the contemporary animal rights movement.

Gorilla. The journal of the Gorilla Foundation. An excellent nonprofit source of photos and conversations with Koko and Michael, and gorilla-related news. (P.O. Box 620–530, Woodside, CA 94062. ISSN #09768129.)

Griffin, Donald R. *Animal Minds.* Chicago: University of Chicago Press, 1994. A persuasive argument based on extensive empirical information that animal consciousness is the simplest explanation of much animal behavior. Valuable bibliography.

Hargrove, Eugene, ed. *The Animal Rights/Environmental Ethics Debate.* Albany: SUNY, 1992. An excellent collection that chronicles the debate, beginning with Richard Watson's 1979 article and ending with a 1988 article by J. Baird Callicott. Hargrove's preface provides an incisive commentary.

Hill, John Lawrence. *The Case for Vegetarianism: Philosophy for a Small Planet.* Lanham, Md.: Rowman and Littlefield, 1995. A good book for university courses. Includes global ecology and world hunger issues.

Howard, Walter E. *Animal Rights vs. Nature.* Davis, Calif.: W. E. Howard, 1990. A highly polemical argument against animal rights by a zoologist.

Linzey, Andrew. *Animal Theology.* Urbana: University of Illinois Press, 1995. An important book by an Anglican priest who holds a seat in animal welfare at Oxford University. Linzey argues that the generosity of God and a creative living of the Scriptures both point to theocentric rights for animals.

Lorenz, Konrad. *Man Meets Dog.* Middlesex, England: Penguin, 1953. A classic by a distinguished ethologist, describing the complexity of the human-dog relationship and the depth of canine personalities he has known.

Maclean, Norman. *Animals with Novel Genes.* Cambridge, Mass.: Cambridge University Press, 1994. A good introduction to the scientific aspects of transgenic animals, containing essays by ten internationally known molecular biologists. Animals are described by the editor as "living test tubes" whose new genetic traits will prove useful.

Mitchell, Robert W., and Nicholas S. Thompson, eds. *Deception: Perspectives on Human and Non-human Deceit.* Albany: SUNY, 1986. A fine collection of essays dealing with many aspects of deception.

Mitchell, Robert W., Nicholas S. Thompson, and H. Lyn Miles, eds. *Anthropomorphism, Anecdotes, and Animals.* Albany: SUNY, 1996. The first book to evaluate the significance of anthropomorphism and anecdotes for understanding animals. Includes essays from diverse perspectives.

Norton, Bryan G., Michael Hutchins, Elizabeth E. Stevens, and Terry L. Maple, eds. *Ethics on the Ark: Zoos, Animal Welfare, and Wildlife Conservation.* Washington, D.C.: Smithsonian Institution Press, 1995. A collection of valuable essays (some too brief), including captive breeding, culling of "surplus animals." Good appendix.

Pluhar, Evelyn B. *Beyond Prejudice: The Moral Significance of Human and Nonhuman Animals.* Durham, N.C.: Duke University Press, 1995. Pluhar defends the view that any sentient conative being, one capable of caring about what happens to him or herself, is morally significant. She confronts traditional and contemporary arguments in a thorough and sophisticated manner.

Preece, Rod, and Lorna Chamberlain. *Animal Welfare and Human Values.* Ontario, Canada: Wilfrid Laurier University Press, 1993. A discussion aiming at fairness to all sides. Useful historical summaries, including Canadian traditions.

Radner, Daisie, and Michael Radner. *Animal Consciousness.* Buffalo, N.Y.: Prometheus Books, 1989. A valuable analysis of the Cartesian concept of consciousness as involving reflective and nonreflective consciousness. The Radners argue that granting animals moral status requires recognizing species-specific interests.

Reed, Edward S. *Encountering the World: Toward an Ecological Psychology.* Oxford: Oxford University Press, 1996. Reed describes ecological psychology as a multidisciplinary field focusing on "an animal's encounters with its surroundings." For advanced students.

Regan, Tom, ed. *Animal Sacrifices: Religious Perspectives on the Use of Animals in Science.* Philadelphia: Temple University Press, 1986. Contains articles on animal experimentation from Western and non-Western religious views.

Regan, Tom, and Peter Singer, eds. *Animal Rights and Human Obligations.* Englewood Cliffs, N.J.: Prentice-Hall, 1989. A useful collection of contemporary and historical essays within the Western tradition. Includes some essays on wildlife.

Rollin, Bernard E. *The Unheeded Cry: Animal Consciousness, Animal Pain, and Science.* Oxford: Oxford University Press, 1990. A thoroughly researched study. Rollin discusses the attitude toward animal consciousness, beginning with George Romanes and Charles Darwin in the nineteenth century and including both American and European views. A powerful critique of the current scientific ideology. Extensive bibliography from 1879 to the present.

————. *Animal Rights and Human Morality.* Buffalo, N.Y.: Prometheus Books, 1992. A lucid and critical assessment of the Western view of animals, utilizing the concept of *telos.* Contains thoughtful chapters on experimentation on animals in laboratories and schools, and our obligations to pet animals.

————. *The Frankenstein Syndrome: Ethical and Social Issues in the Genetic Engineering of Animals.* Cambridge: Cambridge University Press, 1995. Rollin argues that genetic engineering can work to the benefit of animals if properly regulated and urges a five-year moratorium on animal patenting to allow democratic participation in the formulation of these rules.

Sapontzis, S. F. *Morals, Reason, and Animals.* Philadelphia: Temple University Press, 1987. A clearly and carefully written case for including animals in the moral community, critiquing some of the "first generation" theorists.

Savage-Rumbaugh, E. Sue. *Kanzi: The Ape at the Brink of the Human Mind.* New York: John Wiley & Sons, 1994. One of the foremost researchers chronicles the remarkable development of Kanzi, a bonobo (pygmy chimpanzee).

Shuldiner, Alan R. "Molecular Medicine: Transgenic Animals." *Molecular Medicine* 334, 10 (1996): 653–55. Provides a basic summary of the technology.

Singer, Peter. *Practical Ethics,* 2nd ed. Cambridge: Cambridge University Press, 1993. A well-written book which further develops his 1975 *Animal Liberation.* Addresses hunger, abortion, and euthanasia.

————. *Animal Liberation,* rev. ed. New York: Avon, 1992. A strong utilitarian argument for considering the interests of animals equally with those of any other sentient being. The 1975 book was crucial in jump-starting the animal rights movement.

Singer, Peter, and Paola Cavilieri, eds. *The Great Ape Project.* New York: St. Martin's Press, 1993. A selection of impressive essays arguing for the recognition of moral and legal rights for the great apes.

CHAPTER EIGHT
Ecocentrism

Ecocentrism is based on the philosophical premise that the natural world has inherent or intrinsic value. In this chapter we distinguish two major forms, the land ethic and deep ecology, and address several ethical issues that emerge from an ecocentric world view.

Proponents of the land ethic advocate human responsibility toward the natural world. Although the roots of the land ethic can be traced to many different cultures, its expression in Western philosophical thought is relatively recent, and it was first clearly articulated by Aldo Leopold in the late 1940s.

In contrast to anthropocentrists and individualists, proponents of the land ethic advocate an environmental ethic that values nature in and of itself, rather than only in relation to its significance for the survival and well-being of humans or other select species. The land ethic implies human responsibility for natural communities. In "The Land Ethic," Aldo Leopold asserts that "a thing is right when it tends to preserve the integrity, stability, and beauty of the biotic community. It is wrong when it tends otherwise." In Leopold's view, adherence to the land ethic results in a change of human self-perception: Humans cease to see themselves as conquerors or as members of a superior species on the planet, but rather as plain members and participating citizens of the land community. In "Aldo Leopold's Concept of Ecosystem Health," J. Baird Callicott gives an in-depth analysis of how ecosystem health might be understood as one applies Leopold's ethic to the land.

Deep ecology is a more recent ecocentric philosophy. The term *deep ecology* was coined in 1973 by Arne Naess, a Norwegian philosopher, to contrast with the notion of shallow ecology, which focuses on superficial, short-term reforms to solve such environmental problems as pollution and resource depletion. Deep ecology involves an intensive questioning of the values and lifestyles that originally led to serious environmental problems.

In his essay, "The Deep, Long-Range Ecology Movement" (DEM), Bill Devall notes that some radical environmentalists argue that deep changes in society require a paradigm shift, from the modern industrial paradigm to a new ecological paradigm. Many supporters of the DEM call for a transformation of the fundamental principles guiding a long-term relationship with the environment. These principles may include living a life that is simple in means but rich in ends; honoring the right of all life-forms to live and flourish; empathizing with other life-forms; maximizing the diversity of human and nonhuman life; and maximizing long-range universal self-realization. Deep ecologists share a commitment to a new vision of the world. They advocate an ecological wisdom, or *ecosophy,* that is defined as a philosophy of ecological harmony or equilibrium.

JUSTIFICATIONS FOR AN ECOCENTRIC PERSPECTIVE

All of the authors in this chapter state or imply that the natural world has inherent or intrinsic value, and most provide at least some rationale for their perspectives. However, Leopold explicitly articulates only a limited justification for the land ethic. In evaluating influences on Leopold, Callicott argues that human ethics originally evolved out of moral feelings or social sentiments.[1] He notes that this perspective originally was developed by Adam Smith and David Hume, that it later served as a basis for Darwin's views on the evolution of ethics, and that Leopold built the land ethic on this philosophical foundation. Callicott further proposes that a justification of the land ethic can be grounded on three scientific cornerstones: evolution, ecology, and Copernican astronomy.

Using the Aristotelian notion of *telos,* Rodman argues that moral consideration ought to be extended to anything that is autonomous and has the capacity for self-direction or self-regulation. In a radical proposal, Rodman extends the notion of *telos* to characterize, not only individual living entities, but also natural systems.[2] This application of the notion of *telos* to ecosystems has provoked controversy.[3]

In "The Land Ethic at the Turn of the Millennium," Holmes Rolston III evaluates some key qualities of ecosystems. For example, he points out that ecosystems generate a spontaneous order that envelopes all the richness, beauty, integrity, and stability among the living organisms observed in nature. He reminds us that ecosystem properties are intriguingly complex and go beyond the properties of the component species or individual organisms. He concludes that Leopold's respect and ethical concerns for ecosystems in the land ethic are well justified.

DOES A LAND ETHIC ASCRIBE RIGHTS OR RESPECT TO THE BIOTIC COMMUNITY?

Many traditional ethical systems incorporate the notion that certain rights are ascribed to those members falling under moral concern. Callicott addresses the matter of Leopold's views on preservation and argues that the notion of respect is a more appropriate perspective than rights with regard to the natural world.[4] Leopold implies the notion of respect when he points out that moral consideration for the land does not prevent the alteration, use, or management of biotic communities but does affirm their right to a continued existence and, at least in some places, their continued existence in a natural state. In "Whither Conservation Ethics?" Callicott asserts that Leopold was committed to active land management, not just a more passive preservation.

THE RELATIONSHIP OF HUMANS TO NATURE

One concern related to the land ethic is how to resolve the conflicting needs that exist between humans and nature. For example, Heffernan points out that feeding starving people through intense agriculture may lead to the disruption of healthy ecosystems but that ceasing these agricultural efforts may lead to immoral consequences.[5]

---

[1]J. Baird Callicott, "The Conceptual Foundations of the Land Ethic," in *Companion to a Sand County Almanac: Interpretive and Critical Essays,* J. Baird Callicott (Madison: University of Wisconsin Press, 1987), pp. 186–217.

[2]John Rodman, "Four Forms of Ecological Consciousness Reconsidered: Ecological Sensibility," in *Ethics and the Environment,* D. Scherer and T. Attig, eds. (Englewood Cliffs, N.J.: Prentice-Hall, 1983).

[3]H. Cahen, "Against the Moral Considerability of Ecosystems," *Environmental Ethics* 10 (1988): 195–216. S. N. Salthe and B. M. Salthe, "Ecosystem Moral Considerability: A Reply to Cahen," *Environmental Ethics* 11 (1989): 355–61. Also see L. E. Johnson, "Toward the Moral Considerability of Species and Ecosystems," *Environmental Ethics* 14 (1992): 145–57.

[4]Callicott, "Conceptual Foundations of the Land Ethic."

[5]J. D. Heffernan, "The Land Ethic: A Critical Appraisal," *Environmental Ethics* 4 (1982): 235–47.

The concern that ecocentrism may be a totalitarian rather than humanistic philosophy is addressed by Don Marietta, Jr.[6] He points out that there are several versions of holism (ecocentrism), each having several forms ranging from modest to extreme. In Marietta's view, only the extreme forms of ecocentrism that subordinate the interests and rights of individuals to the good of the natural world might justify the claim of critics that ecocentrism is a totalitarian position.

Most land ethic philosophers view the land ethic as an additional rule to a primary duty to humans. Callicott argues that land ethic values do not replace or preempt previous moral responsibilities toward humans; rather, they enhance them.[7] Callicott draws on parallel concepts among Native American groups, such as maintaining an attitude of respect toward individual creatures whether using them or allowing them their natural fates.

Guha (see also the reading by Guha and Martinez-Alier in Chapter 5) argues that ecocentrism, particularly the DEM, is not an appropriate philosophy to guide Third World countries because it places less emphasis on significant issues, such as growing militarism, overconsumption and materialism, human rights, problems related to ethnicity, and distributive justice.[8] In this chapter, Devall argues that the DEM is appropriate for Third World countries because of its emphasis on long-range sustainability of natural systems within which humans and all other species must dwell.

CHALLENGES TO ECOCENTRISM

In recent years, ecocentrism has often been interpreted as being based on an image of nature as a balanced homeostatic system in the absence of human disturbance; this view also has served as a model for how humans should live in relation to nature. However, according to Worster, the current theoretical framework of ecology is undergoing some sweeping changes.[9] Earlier views of holistic natural communities working in stable associations are being replaced by images of nature as fundamentally erratic, discontinuous, chaotic, and unpredictable. These images do not support the vision of a peaceful union between humans and nature. If correct, this shift in perspective could have a powerful impact on the validity of ecocentrism. However, this newer perspective has been challenged itself.[10] In this chapter, Callicott further applies the notion of ecosystem health in a way that accommodates the many changes that biotic communities undergo. Also in this chapter, Rolston carefully analyzes Leopold's land ethic in the context of these concerns. He concludes that while ecosystems can undergo substantial fluctuations over time, there is a dynamic stability/sustainability and order at larger scales that are often not evident at smaller spatial scales and time spans.

---

[6]Don E. Marietta, Jr., "Ethical Holism and Individualism," in *For People and the Planet: Holism and Humanism in Environmental Ethics* (Philadelphia: Temple University Press, 1995).

[7]Callicott, "Conceptual Foundations of the Land Ethic."

[8]Ramachandra Guha, "Radical American Environmentalism and Wilderness Preservation: A Third World Critique," *Environmental Ethics* 11 (1989): 71–83.

[9]D. Worster, "The Ecology of Order and Chaos," *Environmental Review* 14 (1990): 1–18.

[10]J. Baird Callicott, "Do Deconstructive Ecology and Sociobiology Undermine Leopold's Land Ethic?" *Environmental Ethics* 18 (1996): 353–72.

The Land Ethic

Aldo Leopold

Aldo Leopold (1887–1948), one of the earliest and most influential voices among Western scholars elucidating an ecocentric perspective, was a forester, wildlife manager, and creative thinker. Leopold graduated from the Yale School of Forestry and worked several years for the U.S. Forest Service. Later, Leopold was instrumental in establishing wildlife management as a profession.

In this chapter from his book, A Sand County Almanac, *Leopold expresses great concern over the detrimental effects of humans on the land and particularly the rapid deterioration of the environment in the southwestern United States. Leopold argued that the biotic world and natural environment themselves have intrinsic value and clarified the notion of human moral responsibility to the natural environment. He believed that humans should see themselves as "plain members and citizens" of the biotic community.*

When god-like Odysseus returned from the wars in Troy, he hanged all on one rope a dozen slave-girls of his household whom he suspected of misbehavior during his absence.

This hanging involved no question of propriety. The girls were property. The disposal of property was then, as now, a matter of expediency, not of right and wrong.

Concepts of right and wrong were not lacking from Odysseus' Greece: witness the fidelity of his wife through the long years before at last his black-prowed galleys clove the wine-dark seas for home. The ethical structure of that day covered wives, but had not yet been extended to human chattels. During the three thousand years which have since elapsed, ethical criteria have been extended to many fields of conduct, with corresponding shrinkages in those judged by expediency only.

THE ETHICAL SEQUENCE

This extension of ethics, so far studied only by philosophers, is actually a process in ecological evolution. Its sequences may be described in ecological as well as in philosophical terms. An ethic, ecologically, is a limitation on freedom of action in the struggle for existence. An ethic, philosophically, is a differentiation of social from antisocial conduct. These are two definitions of one thing. The thing has its origin in the tendency of interdependent individuals or groups to evolve modes of cooperation. The ecologist calls these symbioses. Politics and economics are advanced symbioses in which the original free-for-all competition has been replaced, in part, by cooperative mechanisms with an ethical content.

The complexity of cooperative mechanisms has increased with population density, and with the efficiency of tools. It was simpler, for example, to define the antisocial uses of sticks and stones in the days of the mastodons than of bullets and billboards in the age of motors.

The first ethics dealt with the relation between individuals; the Mosaic Decalogue is an example. Later accretions dealt with the relation between the individual and society. The Golden Rule tries to integrate the individual to society; democracy to integrate social organization to the individual.

There is as yet no ethic dealing with man's relation to land and to the animals and plants which grow upon it. Land, like Odysseus' slave-girls, is still property. The land relation is still strictly economic, entailing privileges but not obligations.

The extension of ethics to this third element in human environment is, if I read the evidence correctly, an evolutionary possibility and an ecological necessity. It is the third step in a sequence. The first two have already been taken. Individual thinkers since the days of Ezekiel and Isaiah have asserted that the despoliation of land is not only inexpedient but wrong. Society, however, has not yet affirmed their belief. I regard the present conservation movement as the embryo of such an affirmation.

An ethic may be regarded as a mode of guidance for meeting ecological situations so new or intricate, or involving such deferred reactions, that the path of social expediency is not discernible to the average individual. Animal instincts are modes of guidance for the individual in meeting such situations. Ethics are possibly a kind of community instinct in-the-making.

THE COMMUNITY CONCEPT

All ethics so far evolved rest upon a single premise: that the individual is a member of a community of interdependent parts. His instincts prompt him to compete for his place in that community, but his ethics prompt him also to cooperate (perhaps in order that there may be a place to compete for).

The land ethic simply enlarges the boundaries of the community to include soils, waters, plants, and animals, or collectively: the land.

This sounds simple: do we not already sing our love for and obligation to the land of the free and the home of the brave? Yes, but just what and whom do we love? Certainly not the soil, which we are sending helter-skelter downriver. Certainly not the waters, which we assume have no function except to turn turbines, float barges, and carry off sewage. Certainly not the plants, of which we exterminate whole communities without batting an eye. Certainly not the animals, of which we have already extirpated many of the largest and most beautiful species. A land ethic of course cannot prevent the alteration, management, and use of these "resources," but it does affirm their right to continued existence, and, at least in spots, their continued existence in a natural state.

In short, a land ethic changes the role of *Homo sapiens* from conqueror of the land-community to plain member and citizen of it. It implies respect for his fellow members, and also respect for the community as such.

In human history, we have learned (I hope) that the conqueror role is eventually self-defeating. Why? Because it is implicit in such a role that the conqueror knows, *ex cathedra,* just what makes the community clock tick, and just what and who is valuable, and what and who is worthless, in community life. It always turns out that he knows neither, and this is why his conquests eventually defeat themselves.

In the biotic community, a parallel situation exists. Abraham knew exactly what the land was for: it was to drip milk and honey into Abraham's mouth. At the present moment, the assurance with which we

regard this assumption is inverse to the degree of our education.

The ordinary citizen today assumes that science knows what makes the community clock tick; the scientist is equally sure that he does not. He knows that the biotic mechanism is so complex that its workings may never be fully understood.

That man is, in fact, only a member of a biotic team is shown by an ecological interpretation of history. Many historical events, hitherto explained solely in terms of human enterprise, were actually biotic interactions between people and land. The characteristics of the land determined the facts quite as potently as the characteristics of the men who lived on it.

Consider, for example, the settlement of the Mississippi Valley. In the years following the Revolution, three groups were contending for its control: the native Indian, the French and English traders, and the American settlers. Historians wonder what would have happened if the English at Detroit had thrown a little more weight into the Indian side of those tipsy scales which decided the outcome of the colonial migration into the canelands of Kentucky. It is time now to ponder the fact that the canelands, when subjected to the particular mixture of forces represented by the cow, plow, fire, and axe of the pioneer, became bluegrass. What if the plant succession inherent in this dark and bloody ground had, under the impact of these forces, given us some worthless sedge, shrub, or weed? Would Boone and Kenton have held out? Would there have been any overflow into Ohio, Indiana, Illinois, and Missouri? Any Louisiana Purchase? Any transcontinental union of new states? Any Civil War?

Kentucky was one sentence in the drama of history. We are commonly told what the human actors in this drama tried to do, but we are seldom told that their success, or the lack of it, hung in large degree on the reaction of particular soils to the impact of the particular forces exerted by their occupancy. In the case of Kentucky, we do not even know where the bluegrass came from—whether it is a native species, or a stowaway from Europe.

Contrast the canelands with what hindsight tells us about the Southwest, where the pioneers were equally brave, resourceful, and persevering. The impact of occupancy here brought no bluegrass, or other plant fitted to withstand the bumps and buffetings of hard use. This region, when grazed by livestock, reverted through a series of more and more worthless grasses, shrubs, and weeds to a condition of unstable equilibrium. Each recession of plant types bred erosion; each increment to erosion bred a further recession of plants. The result today is a progressive and mutual deterioration, not only of plants and soils, but of the animal community subsisting thereon. The early settlers did not expect this: on the ciénegas of New Mexico some even cut ditches to hasten it. So subtle has been its progress that few residents of the region are aware of it. It is quite invisible to the tourist who finds this wrecked landscape colorful and charming (as indeed it is, but it bears scant resemblance to what it was in 1848).

This same landscape was "developed" once before, but with quite different results. The Pueblo Indians settled the Southwest in pre-Columbian times, but they happened *not* to be equipped with range livestock. Their civilization expired, but not because their land expired.

In India, regions devoid of any sod-forming grass have been settled, apparently without wrecking the land, by the simple expedient of carrying the grass to the cow, rather than vice versa. (Was this the result of some deep wisdom, or was it just good luck? I do not know.)

In short, the plant succession steered the course of history; the pioneer simply demonstrated, for good or ill, what successions inhered in the land. Is history taught in this spirit? It will be, once the concept of land as a community really penetrates our intellectual life.

THE ECOLOGICAL CONSCIENCE

Conservation is a state of harmony between man and land. Despite nearly a century of propaganda, conservation still proceeds at a snail's pace; progress still consists largely of letterhead pieties and convention oratory. On the back forty we still slip two steps backward for each forward stride.

The usual answer to this dilemma is "more conservation education." No one will debate this, but is it certain that only the *volume* of education needs stepping up? Is something lacking in the *content* as well?

It is difficult to give a fair summary of its content in brief form, but, as I understand it, the content is substantially this: obey the law, vote right, join some organizations, and practice what conservation is profitable on your own land; the government will do the rest.

Is not this formula too easy to accomplish anything worthwhile? It defines no right or wrong, assigns no obligation, calls for no sacrifice, implies no change in the current philosophy of values. In respect of land-use, it urges only enlightened self-interest. Just how far will such education take us? An example will perhaps yield a partial answer.

By 1930 it had become clear to all except the ecologically blind that southwestern Wisconsin's topsoil was slipping seaward. In 1933 the farmers were told that if they would adopt certain remedial practices for five years, the public would donate CCC labor to install them, plus the necessary machinery and materials. The offer was widely accepted, but the practices were widely forgotten when the five-year contract period was up. The farmers continued only those practices that yielded an immediate and visible economic gain for themselves.

This led to the idea that maybe farmers would learn more quickly if they themselves wrote the rules. Accordingly the Wisconsin Legislature in 1937 passed the Soil Conservation District Law. This said to farmers, in effect: *We, the public, will furnish you free technical service and loan you specialized machinery, if you will write your own rules for land-use. Each county may write its own rules, and these will have the force of law.* Nearly all the counties promptly organized to accept the proferred help, but after a decade of operation, *no county has yet written a single rule.* There has been visible progress in such practices as strip-cropping, pasture renovation, and soil liming, but none in fencing woodlots against grazing, and none in excluding plow and cow from steep slopes. The farmers, in short, have selected those remedial practices which were profitable anyhow, and ignored those which were profitable to the community, but not clearly profitable to themselves.

When one asks why no rules have been written, one is told that the community is not yet ready to support them; education must precede rules. But the education actually in progress makes no mention of obligations to land over and above those dictated by self-interest. The net result is that we have more ed-ucation but less soil, fewer healthy woods, and as many floods as in 1937.

The puzzling aspect of such situations is that the existence of obligations over and above self-interest is taken for granted in such rural community enter-prises as the betterment of roads, schools, churches, and baseball teams. Their existence is not taken for granted, nor as yet seriously discussed, in bettering the behavior of the water that falls on the land, or in the preserving of the beauty or diversity of the farm landscape. Land-use ethics are still governed wholly by economic self-interest, just as social ethics were a century ago.

To sum up: we asked the farmer to do what he conveniently could to save his soil, and he has done just that, and only that. The farmer who clears the woods off a 75 percent slope, turns his cows into the clearing, and dumps its rainfall, rocks, and soil into the community creek, is still (if otherwise decent) a respected member of society. If he puts lime on his fields and plants his crops on contour, he is still en-titled to all the privileges and emoluments of his Soil Conservation District. The District is a beauti-ful piece of social machinery, but it is coughing along on two cylinders because we have been too timid, and too anxious for quick success, to tell the farmer the true magnitude of his obligations. Obli-gations have no meaning without conscience, and the problem we face is the extension of the social conscience from people to land.

No important change in ethics was ever accom-plished without an internal change in our intellec-tual emphasis, loyalties, affections, and convictions. The proof that conservation has not yet touched these foundations of conduct lies in the fact that philosophy and religion have not yet heard of it. In our attempt to make conservation easy, we have made it trivial.

SUBSTITUTES FOR A LAND ETHIC

When the logic of history hungers for bread and we hand out a stone, we are at pains to explain how much the stone resembles bread. I now describe some of the stones which serve in lieu of a land ethic.

One basic weakness in a conservation system based wholly on economic motives is that most members of the land community have no economic value. Wildflowers and songbirds are examples. Of the 22,000 higher plants and animals native to Wis-consin, it is doubtful whether more than 5 percent can be sold, fed, eaten, or otherwise put to economic use. Yet these creatures are members of the biotic community, and if (as I believe) its stability depends on its integrity, they are entitled to continuance.

When one of these noneconomic categories is threatened, and if we happen to love it, we invent subterfuges to give it economic importance. At the beginning of the century songbirds were supposed to be disappearing. Ornithologists jumped to the res-cue with some distinctly shaky evidence to the ef-fect that insects would eat us up if birds failed to control them. The evidence had to be economic in order to be valid.

It is painful to read these circumlocutions to-day. We have no land ethic yet, but we have at least drawn nearer the point of admitting that birds should continue as a matter of biotic right, regard-less of the presence or absence of economic advan-tage to us.

A parallel situation exists in respect of predatory mammals, raptorial birds, and fish-eating birds. Time was when biologists somewhat overworked the evidence that these creatures preserve the health of game by killing weaklings, or that they control rodents for the farmer, or that they prey only on "worthless" species. Here again, the evidence had to be economic in order to be valid. It is only in re-cent years that we hear the more honest argument that predators are members of the community, and that no special interest has the right to exterminate them for the sake of a benefit, real or fancied, to it-self. Unfortunately this enlightened view is still in the talk stage. In the field the extermination of pred-ators goes merrily on: witness the impending era-sure of the timber wolf by fiat of Congress, the Con-servation Bureaus, and many state legislatures.

Some species of trees have been "read out of the party" by economics-minded foresters because they grow too slowly, or have too low a sale value to pay as timber crops: white cedar, tamarack, cypress, beech, and hemlock are examples. In Europe, where forestry is ecologically more advanced, the non-commercial tree species are recognized as members of the native forest community, to be preserved as such, within reason. Moreover some (like beech) have been found to have a valuable function in building up soil fertility. The interdependence of the forest and its constituent tree species, ground flora, and fauna is taken for granted.

Lack of economic value is sometimes a character not only of species or groups, but of entire biotic communities: marshes, bogs, dunes, and "deserts" are examples. Our formula in such cases is to relegate their conservation to government as refuges, monuments, or parks. The difficulty is that these communities are usually interspersed with more valuable private lands; the government cannot possibly own or control such scattered parcels. The net effect is that we have relegated some of them to ultimate extinction over large areas. If the private owner were ecologically minded, he would be proud to be the custodian of a reasonable proportion of such areas, which add diversity and beauty to his farm and to his community.

In some instances, the assumed lack of profit in these "waste" areas has proved to be wrong, but only after most of them had been done away with. The present scramble to reflood muskrat marshes is a case in point.

There is a clear tendency in American conservation to relegate to government all necessary jobs that private landowners fail to perform. Government ownership, operation, subsidy, or regulation is now widely prevalent in forestry, range management, soil and watershed management, park and wilderness conservation, fisheries management, and migratory bird management, with more to come. Most of this growth in governmental conservation is proper and logical, some of it is inevitable. That I imply no disapproval of it is implicit in the fact that I have spent most of my life working for it. Nevertheless the question arises: What is the ultimate magnitude of the enterprise? Will the tax base carry its eventual ramifications? At what point will governmental conservation, like the mastodon, become handicapped by its own dimensions? The answer, if there is any, seems to be in a land ethic, or some other force which assigns more obligation to the private landowner.

Industrial landowners and users, especially lumbermen and stockmen, are inclined to wail long and loudly about the extension of government ownership and regulation to land, but (with notable exceptions) they show little disposition to develop the only visible alternative: the voluntary practice of conservation on their own lands.

When the private landowner is asked to perform some unprofitable act for the good of the community, he today assents only with outstretched palm. If the act costs him cash this is fair and proper, but when it costs only forethought, open-mindedness, or time, the issue is at least debatable. The overwhelming growth of land-use subsidies in recent years must be ascribed, in large part, to the government's own agencies for conservation education: the land bureaus, the agricultural colleges, and the extension services. As far as I can detect, no ethical obligation toward land is taught in these institutions.

To sum up: a system of conservation based solely on economic self-interest is hopelessly lopsided. It tends to ignore, and thus eventually to eliminate, many elements in the land community that lack commercial value, but that are (as far as we know) essential to its healthy functioning. It assumes, falsely, I think, that the economic parts of the biotic clock will function without the uneconomic parts. It tends to relegate to government many functions eventually too large, too complex, or too widely dispersed to be performed by government.

An ethical obligation on the part of the private owner is the only visible remedy for these situations.

THE LAND PYRAMID

An ethic to supplement and guide the economic relation to land presupposes the existence of some mental image of land as a biotic mechanism. We can be ethical only in relation to something we can see, feel, understand, love, or otherwise have faith in.

The image commonly employed in conservation education is "the balance of nature." For reasons too lengthy to detail here, this figure of speech fails to describe accurately what little we know about the land mechanism. A much truer image is the one employed in ecology: the biotic pyramid. I shall first sketch the pyramid as a symbol of land, and later develop some of its implications in terms of land-use.

Plants absorb energy from the sun. This energy flows through a circuit called the biota, which may be represented by a pyramid consisting of layers. The bottom layer is the soil. A plant layer rests on the soil, an insect layer on the plants, a bird and rodent layer on the insects, and so on up through various animal groups to the apex layer, which consists of the large carnivores.

The species of a layer are alike not in where they came from, or in what they look like, but rather in what they eat. Each successive layer depends on those below it for food and often for other services, and each in turn furnishes food and services to those above. Proceeding upward, each successive layer decreases in numerical abundance. Thus, for every carnivore there are hundreds of his prey, thousands of their prey, millions of insects, uncountable plants. The pyramidal form of the system reflects this numerical progression from apex to base. Man shares an intermediate layer with the bears, raccoons, and squirrels which eat both meat and vegetables.

The lines of dependency for food and other services are called food chains. Thus soil-oak-deer-Indian is a chain that has now been largely converted to soil-corn-cow-farmer. Each species, including ourselves, is a link in many chains. The deer eats a hundred plants other than oak, and the cow a hundred plants other than corn. Both, then, are links in a hundred chains. The pyramid is a tangle of chains so complex as to seem disorderly, yet the stability of the system proves it to be a highly organized structure. Its functioning depends on the cooperation and competition of its diverse parts.

In the beginning, the pyramid of life was low and squat; the food chains short and simple. Evolution has added layer after layer, link after link. Man is one of thousands of accretions to the height and complexity of the pyramid. Science has given us many doubts, but it has given us at least one certainty: the trend of evolution is to elaborate and diversify the biota.

Land, then, is not merely soil; it is a fountain of energy flowing through a circuit of soils, plants, and animals. Food chains are the living channels which conduct energy upward; death and decay return it to the soil. The circuit is not closed; some energy is dissipated in decay, some is added by absorption from the air, some is stored in soils, peats, and long-lived forests; but it is a sustained circuit, like a slowly augmented revolving fund of life. There is always a net loss by downhill wash, but this is normally small and offset by the decay of rocks. It is deposited in the ocean and, in the course of geological time, raised to form new lands and new pyramids.

The velocity and character of the upward flow of energy depend on the complex structure of the plant and animal community, much as the upward flow of sap in a tree depends on its complex cellular organization. Without this complexity, normal circulation would presumably not occur. Structure means the characteristic numbers, as well as the characteristic kinds and functions, of the component species. This interdependence between the complex structure of the land and its smooth functioning as an energy unit is one of its basic attributes.

When a change occurs in one part of the circuit, many other parts must adjust themselves to it. Change does not necessarily obstruct or divert the flow of energy; evolution is a longer series of self-induced changes, the net result of which has been to elaborate the flow mechanism and to lengthen the circuit. Evolutionary changes, however, are usually slow and local. Man's invention of tools has enabled him to make changes of unprecedented violence, rapidity, and scope.

One change is in the composition of floras and faunas. The larger predators are lopped off the apex of the pyramid; food chains, for the first time in history, become shorter rather than longer. Domesticated species from other lands are substituted for wild ones, and wild ones are moved to new habitats. In this worldwide pooling of faunas and floras, some species get out of bounds as pests and diseases, others are extinguished. Such effects are seldom intended or foreseen; they represent unpredicted and often untraceable readjustments in the structure. Agricultural science is largely a race between the emergence of new pests and the emergence of new techniques for their control.

Another change touches the flow of energy through plants and animals and its return to the soil. Fertility is the ability of soil to receive, store, and release energy. Agriculture, by overdrafts on the soil, or by too radical a substitution of domestic for native species in the superstructure, may derange the channels of flow or deplete storage. Soils depleted of their storage, or of the organic matter which anchors it, wash away faster than they form. This is erosion.

Waters, like soil, are part of the energy circuit. Industry, by polluting waters or obstructing them with dams, may exclude the plants and animals necessary to keep energy in circulation.

Transportation brings about another basic change: the plants or animals grown in one region are now consumed and returned to the soil in another. Transportation taps the energy stored in rocks, and in the air, and uses it elsewhere; thus we fertilize the garden with nitrogen gleaned by the guano birds from the fishes of seas on the other side of the Equator. Thus the formerly localized and self-contained circuits are pooled on a worldwide scale.

The process of altering the pyramid for human occupation releases stored energy, and this often gives rise, during the pioneering period, to a deceptive exuberance of plant and animal life, both wild and tame. These releases of biotic capital tend to becloud or postpone the penalties of violence.

This thumbnail sketch of land as an energy circuit conveys three basic ideas:

1. That land is not merely soil.
2. That the native plants and animals kept the energy circuit open; others may or may not.
3. That man-made changes are of a different order than evolutionary changes, and have effects more comprehensive than is intended or foreseen.

These ideas, collectively, raise two basic issues: Can the land adjust itself to the new order? Can the desired alterations be accomplished with less violence?

Biotas seem to differ in their capacity to sustain violent conversion. Western Europe, for example, carries a far different pyramid than Caesar found there. Some large animals are lost; swampy forests have become meadows or plowland; many new plants and animals are introduced, some of which escape as pests; the remaining natives are greatly changed in distribution and abundance. Yet the soil is still there and, with the help of imported nutri-

ents, still fertile; the waters flow normally; the new structure seems to function and to persist. There is no visible stoppage or derangement of the circuit.

Western Europe, then, has a resistant biota. Its inner processes are tough, elastic, resistant to strain. No matter how violent the alterations, the pyramid, so far, has developed some new *modus vivendi* which preserves its habitability for man, and for most of the other natives.

Japan seems to present another instance of radical conversion without disorganization.

Most other civilized regions, and some as yet barely touched by civilization, display various stages of disorganization, varying from initial symptoms to advanced wastage. In Asia Minor and North Africa diagnosis is confused by climatic changes, which may have been either the cause or the effect of advanced wastage. In the United States the degree of disorganization varies locally; it is worst in the Southwest, the Ozarks, and parts of the South, and least in New England and the Northwest. Better land-uses may still arrest it in the less advanced regions. In parts of Mexico, South America, South Africa, and Australia a violent and accelerating wastage is in progress, but I cannot assess the prospects.

This almost worldwide display of disorganization in the land seems to be similar to disease in an animal, except that it never culminates in complete disorganization or death. The land recovers, but at some reduced level of complexity, and with a reduced carrying capacity for people, plants, and animals. Many biotas currently regarded as "lands of opportunity" are in fact already subsisting on exploitative agriculture, i.e., they have already exceeded their sustained carrying capacity. Most of South America is overpopulated in this sense.

In arid regions we attempt to offset the process of wastage by reclamation, but it is only too evident that the prospective longevity of reclamation projects is often short. In our own West, the best of them may not last a century.

The combined evidence of history and ecology seems to support one general deduction: the less violent the man-made changes, the greater the probability of successful readjustment in the pyramid. Violence, in turn, varies with human population density; a dense population requires a more violent conversion. In this respect, North America has a better chance for permanence than Europe, if she can contrive to limit her density.

This deduction runs counter to our current philosophy, which assumes that because a small increase in density enriched human life, that an indefinite increase will enrich it indefinitely. Ecology knows of no density relationship that holds for indefinitely wide limits. All gains from density are subject to a law of diminishing returns.

Whatever may be the equation for men and land, it is improbable that we as yet know all its terms. Recent discoveries in mineral and vitamin nutrition reveal unsuspected dependencies in the up-circuit: incredibly minute quantities of certain substances determine the value of soils to plants, of plants to animals. What of the down-circuit? What of the vanishing species, the preservation of which we now regard as an esthetic luxury? They helped build the soil; in what unsuspected ways may they be essential to its maintenance? Professor Weaver proposes that we use prairie flowers to reflocculate the wasting soils of the dust bowl; who knows for what purpose cranes and condors, otters and grizzlies may some day be used?

LAND HEALTH AND THE A-B CLEAVAGE

A land ethic, then, reflects the existence of an ecological conscience, and this in turn reflects a conviction of individual responsibility for the health of the land. Health is the capacity of the land for self-renewal. Conservation is our effort to understand and preserve this capacity.

Conservationists are notorious for their dissensions. Superficially these seem to add up to mere confusion, but a more careful scrutiny reveals a single plane of cleavage common to many specialized fields. In each field one group (A) regards the land as soil, and its function as commodity-production; another group (B) regards the land as a biota, and its function as something broader. How much broader is admittedly in a state of doubt and confusion.

In my own field, forestry, group A is quite content to grow trees like cabbages, with cellulose as the basic forest commodity. It feels no inhibition against violence; its ideology is agronomic. Group B, on the other hand, sees forestry as fundamentally different from agronomy because it employs natural species, and manages a natural environment rather than creating an artificial one. Group B prefers natural reproduction on principle. It worries on biotic as well as economic grounds about the loss of species like chestnut, and the threatened loss of the white pines. It worries about a whole series of secondary forest functions: wildlife, recreation, watersheds, wilderness areas. To my mind, Group B feels the stirrings of an ecological conscience.

In the wildlife field, a parallel cleavage exists. For Group A the basic commodities are sport and meat; the yardsticks of production are ciphers of take in pheasants and trout. Artificial propagation is acceptable as a permanent as well as a temporary recourse — if its unit costs permit. Group B, on the other hand, worries about a whole series of biotic side-issues. What is the cost in predators of producing a game crop? Should we have further recourse to exotics? How can management restore the shrinking species, like prairie grouse, already hopeless as shootable game? How can management restore the threatened rarities, like trumpeter swan and whooping crane? Can management principles be extended to wildflowers? Here again it is clear to me that we have the same A-B cleavage as in forestry.

In the larger field of agriculture I am less competent to speak, but there seem to be somewhat parallel cleavages. Scientific agriculture was actively developing before ecology was born, hence a slower penetration of ecological concepts might be expected. Moreover the farmer, by the very nature of his techniques, must modify the biota more radically than the forester or the wildlife manager. Nevertheless, there are many discontents in agriculture which seem to add up to a new vision of "biotic farming."

Perhaps the most important of these is the new evidence that poundage or tonnage is no measure of the food value of farm crops; the products of fertile soil may be qualitatively as well as quantitatively superior. We can bolster poundage from depleted soils by pouring on imported fertility, but we are not necessarily bolstering food value. The possible ultimate ramifications of this idea are so immense that I must leave their exposition to abler pens.

The discontent that labels itself "organic farming," while bearing some of the earmarks of a cult, is nevertheless biotic in its direction, particularly in its insistence on the importance of soil flora and fauna.

The ecological fundamentals of agriculture are just as poorly known to the public as in other fields of land-use. For example, few educated people realize that the marvelous advances in technique made during recent decades are improvements in the pump, rather than the well. Acre for acre, they have barely sufficed to offset the sinking level of fertility.

In all of these cleavages, we see repeated the same basic paradoxes: man the conqueror *versus* man the biotic citizen; science the sharpener of his sword *versus* science the searchlight on his universe; land the slave and servant *versus* land the collective organism. Robinson's injunction to Tristram may well be applied, at this juncture, to *Homo sapiens* as a species in geological time:

> Whether you will or not
> You are a King, Tristram, for you are one
> Of the time-tested few that leave the world,
> When they are gone, not the same place it was.
> Mark what you leave.

THE OUTLOOK

It is inconceivable to me that an ethical relation to land can exist without love, respect, and admiration for land, and a high regard for its value. By value, I of course mean something far broader than mere economic value; I mean value in the philosophical sense.

Perhaps the most serious obstacle impeding the evolution of a land ethic is the fact that our educational and economic system is headed away from, rather than toward, an intense consciousness of land. Your true modern is separated from the land by many middlemen, and by innumerable physical gadgets. He has no vital relation to it; to him it is the space between cities on which crops grow. Turn him loose for a day on the land, and if the spot does not happen to be a golf links or a "scenic" area, he is bored stiff. If crops could be raised by hydroponics instead of farming, it would suit him very well. Synthetic substitutes for wood, leather, wool, and other natural land products suit him better than the originals. In short, land is something he has "outgrown."

Almost equally serious as an obstacle to a land ethic is the attitude of the farmer for whom the land is still an adversary, or a taskmaster that keeps him in slavery. Theoretically, the mechanization of farming ought to cut the farmer's chains, but whether it really does is debatable.

One of the requisites for an ecological comprehension of land is an understanding of ecology, and this is by no means coextensive with "education"; in fact, much higher education seems deliberately to avoid ecological concepts. An understanding of ecology does not necessarily originate in courses bearing ecological labels; it is quite as likely to be labeled geography, botany, agronomy, history, or economics. This is as it should be, but whatever the label, ecological training is scarce.

The case for a land ethic would appear hopeless but for the minority which is in obvious revolt against these "modern" trends.

The "key-log" which must be moved to release the evolutionary process for an ethic is simply this: quit thinking about decent land-use as solely an economic problem. Examine each question in terms of what is ethically and esthetically right, as well as what is economically expedient. A thing is right when it tends to preserve the integrity, stability, and beauty of the biotic community. It is wrong when it tends otherwise.

It of course goes without saying that economic feasibility limits the tether of what can or cannot be done for land. It always has and it always will. The fallacy the economic determinists have tied around our collective neck, and which we now need to cast off, is the belief that economics determines *all* land-use. This is simply not true. An innumerable host of actions and attitudes, comprising perhaps the bulk of all land relations, is determined by the land-user's tastes and predilections, rather than by his purse. The bulk of all land relations hinges on investments of time, forethought, skill, and faith rather than on investments of cash. As a land-user thinketh, so is he.

I have purposely presented the land ethic as a product of social evolution because nothing so important as an ethic is ever "written." Only the most superficial student of history supposes that Moses "wrote" the Decalogue; it evolved in the minds of a thinking community, and Moses wrote a tentative summary of it for a "seminar." I say tentative because evolution never stops.

The evolution of a land ethic is an intellectual as well as emotional process. Conservation is paved with good intentions which prove to be futile, or even dangerous, because they are devoid of critical understanding either of the land, or of economic land-use. I think it is a truism that as the ethical frontier advances from the individual to the community, its intellectual content increases.

The mechanism of operation is the same for any ethic: social approbation for right actions, social disapproval for wrong actions.

By and large, our present problem is one of attitudes and implements. We are remodeling the Alhambra with a steam-shovel, and we are proud of our yardage. We shall hardly relinquish the shovel, which after all has many good points, but we are in need of gentler and more objective criteria for its successful use.

DISCUSSION TOPICS

1. Is there a specifically *new* environmental ethic presented by Leopold? Explain why you do or do not believe so.
2. Give two weaknesses you perceive in Leopold's land ethic.
3. What contemporary organizations in society (political, commercial, environmental) might you identify with the Group A or Group B of the A-B cleavage Leopold discusses? What specific characteristics did you use to assign each organization to Group A or B? What (if any) characteristics do these same organizations have that might be associated with the opposite group?

READING 42

Whither Conservation Ethics?

J. Baird Callicott

J. Baird Callicott is a professor of philosophy at the University of North Texas, Denton.

In a continuation of this reading from Chapter 4, Callicott elaborates further on Leopold's land ethic and notes that Leopold advocated active land management rather than a passive preservation of

wilderness. Callicott stresses the importance of conservation values accommodating both economically productive and ecologically healthy ecosystems. Callicott further argues that there is a need to develop criteria for ecological health and integrity in an ever-changing, human-impacted natural world.

Since Leopold's Land Ethic is fully informed by and firmly grounded in evolutionary and ecological biology, it ought to supplant its nineteenth-century antecedents as our moral anchor in the face of the second wave of the environmental crisis looming threateningly on the horizon—but we need to be very clear about its implications.

The word "preserve" in Leopold's (1949:224–225) famous summary moral maxim—"A thing is right when it tends to preserve the integrity, stability, and beauty of the biotic community. It is wrong when it tends otherwise"—is unfortunate because it seems to ally Leopold and the Land Ethic with the Preservationists in the century-old Preservation versus Conservation conflict. . . . Bryan Norton (1989), however, has persuasively argued that Leopold was from first to last committed to active land management, not passive preservation. A review of Leopold's unpublished papers and published but long-forgotten articles confirms Norton's analysis. Leopold's vision went beyond the *either* efficiently develop *or* lock up and reserve dilemma of modern conservation. Leopold was primarily concerned, on the ground as well as in theory, with integrating an optimal mix of wildlife—both floral and faunal—with human habitation and economic exploitation of land. . . .

In [an] essay entitled "The Farmer as a Conservationist," Leopold (1939) regales his reader with a rustic idyll in which the wild and domesticated floral and faunal denizens of a Wisconsin farmscape are feathered into one another to create a harmonious whole. In addition to cash and the usual supply of vegetables and meat, lumber and fuel wood, Leopold's envisioned farmstead affords its farm family venison, quail and other small game, and a variety of fruit and nuts from its woodlot, wetlands, and fallow fields; its pond and stream yield pan fish and trout. It also affords intangibles—songbirds, wildflowers, the hoot of owls, the bugle of cranes, and intellectual adventures aplenty in natural history.

To obtain this bounty, the farm family must do more than permanently set aside acreage, fence woodlots, and leave wetlands undrained. They must sow food and cover patches, plant trees, stock the stream and pond, and generally thoughtfully conceive and skillfully execute scores of other modifications, large and small, of the biota that they inhabit.

The pressure of growing human numbers and rapid development, especially in the Third World, implies, I think, that a global conservation strategy focused primarily on "wilderness" preservation and the establishment of nature reserves represents a holding action at best—and a losing proposition at last. I support wilderness and nature reserves—categorically—with my purse as well as my pen. But faced with the sobering realities of the coming century, the only viable philosophy of conservation is, I submit, a generalized version of Leopold's vision of a mutually beneficial and enhancing integration of the human economy with the economy of nature—in addition to holding on to as much untrammeled wilderness as we can.

Lack of theoretical justification complements the present sheer impracticability of conserving biodiversity solely by excluding man and his works (Botkin 1990). Change—not only evolutionary change, but climatic, successional, seasonal, and stochastic change—is natural. And "man" is a part of nature. Therefore, it will no longer do to say, simply, that what existed before the agricultural-industrial variety of *Homo sapiens* evolved or arrived, as the case may be, is the ecological norm in comparison with which all anthropogenic modifications are degradations. To define environmental quality—the integrity, stability, and beauty of the biotic community—dynamically and positively, not statically and negatively, is part of the intellectual challenge that contemporary conservation biology confronts.

Happily, Leopold's conservation ideal of ecosystems that are at once productive and healthy is capable of generalization beyond the well-watered temperate latitudes and pastoral lifestyles characteristic of the upper Midwest. Charles M. Peters, Alwyn H. Gentry, and Robert O. Mendelsohn (1989) . . . conclude that "without question, the sustainable exploitation of non-wood forest resources represents the most immediate and profitable method for integrating the use and conservation of Amazonian forests" (Peters et al. 1989:656). Arturo Gomez-Pompa (1988) has argued that the greater incidence of trees bearing edible fruits than would occur naturally in the extant remnants of Central American rainforest suggests that these "pristine" habitats may once actually have been part of an extensive Maya permaculture.

Of course we must remember David Ehrenfeld's (1976) classic warning that we not put all our conservation eggs in the economic basket. It is too much to hope that a standard benefit-cost comparison will, in every case, indicate that the sustainable alternative to destructive development is more profitable. Certainly I am not here urging an unregenerate return to the economic determinism of the resource Conservation Ethic. Rather, I am simply pointing out that it is often possible for people to make a good living—and, in some instances, even the best living to be had—coexisting with rather than converting the indigenous biotic community. And I am urging that we strive to reconcile and integrate human economic activities with biological conservation. Expressed in the vernacular, I am urging that we think in terms of "win-win" rather than "zero-sum." Further, I would like explicitly to state—and thereby invite critical discussion of—Leopold's more heretical, from the Preservationist point of view, implied corollary proposition, viz., that human economic activities may not only coexist with healthy ecosystems, but that they may actually enhance them. . . . Ehrenfeld concludes that "the presence of people may enhance the species richness of an area, rather than exert the effect that is more familiar to us." Is species richness a measure of ecological health? What other standards of biological integrity can be formulated? How do these norms all fit together to form models of fit environments? Can we succeed . . . in enriching the environment as we enrich ourselves?

LITERATURE CITED

Botkin, D. 1990. Discordant harmonies. Oxford University Press, New York, New York.

Ehrenfeld, D. W. 1976. The conservation of non-resources. American Scientist 64:647–55.

Gomez-Pompa, A., and A. Kaus. 1988. Conservation by Traditional Cultures in the Tropics. In Vance Martin, editor. For the Conservation of Earth. Fulcrum Inc., Golden, Colorado.

Leopold, A. 1939. The farmer as a conservationist. American Forests 45:294–99, 316, 323.

Leopold, A. 1949. A Sand County Almanac: and sketches here and there. Oxford University Press, New York.

Norton, B. G. 1989. Operationalizing the land ethic: toward an integrated theory of environmental management. In W. Stout and P. B. Thompson, editors. Beyond the large farm. Manuscript submitted for publication.

Peters, C. M., A. H. Gentry, and R. O. Mendelsohn. 1989. Valuation of an Amazonian rainforest. Nature 339:655–56.

DISCUSSION TOPICS

1. What place do you think wilderness should play in overall environmental strategies? Give your reasoning.
2. What role do you believe economic productivity has in understanding ecosystem health? Explain your position.

READING 43

Aldo Leopold's Concept of Ecosystem Health

J. Baird Callicott

J. Baird Callicott is a professor of philosophy at the University of North Texas, Denton.

In this reading from Ecosystem Health: New Goals for Environmental Management *(1992), Callicott recalls Leopold's definition that land health is nature's capacity for self-renewal and notes that it carries both dynamic and functional rather than merely static and strictly structural connotations. Callicott proposes that in assessing ecosystem health, one can view change as natural, including change generated by humans; he also argues that some*

changes are better than others—whether caused by humans or nonhumans. Callicott concludes that both manipulative management and economic development are compatible with Leopold's general concept of land health; however, it is essential that human activities or impacts do not disrupt ecosystem functions.

WHY THE HEALTH METAPHOR

The concept of ecosystem health is metaphorical. "Health" in the literal, nonfigurative sense characterizes only a state or condition of an organism. . . .

The concept of health, in both its literal and figurative senses, is at once descriptive and prescriptive, objective and normative. Health, literally, is an objective condition of an organism capable of more or less precise empirical description. But it is also an intrinsically valuable state of being. Except under the most unusual circumstances, it is never better to be sick than well. For Plato, health is the good of the body, its appropriate condition of internal order or organization. Similarly, Plato argues, virtue is the good of the soul, *its* appropriate condition of internal order or organization. And, further extending the same metaphor, justice is the intrinsically good, healthy state of the body politic. Today, we could add the ecosystem to Plato's series of analogies. Ecosystem health is a condition of internal order and organization in ecosystems that—no less than analogous conditions of body, soul, and society—is both intrinsically good and objective (and specifiable in principle).

Echoing Plato, Peter Miller (1981, 194) explains why ecosystem health is a good candidate for intrinsic valuation: "[I]t wears the appearance of (a) a value, a basic ingredient in living well or thriving, which (b) characterizes nonhuman and even nonconscious living [systems] (c) independently of human utilities.". . .

. . . Bodily health is a paradigm case of something that is intrinsically as well as instrumentally valuable; it is good in and of itself, as well as a necessary condition for getting on with our projects. So is virtue and a healthy body politic, Plato would argue; and had the concept of an ecosystem been current in Plato's day, doubtless he would have also argued that ecosystem health too is something valuable for its own sake as well as for its utility. We have a reasonably clear, detailed scientific description of bodily health. The problem for science is to articulate objective norms of ecosystem health. Like the medical norms of bodily health, the norms of ecosystem health would be simultaneously descriptive and prescriptive, objective and nomothetic, instrumentally and intrinsically valuable.

If the concept of ecosystem health turns out to be plausible and persuasive and if the norms and indices of ecosystem health can be specified, the cause of biological conservation may be bolstered. Presently it is being undermined by an insidious skepticism within the scientific community. The erstwhile benchmarks of biological conservation are under withering attack.

THE CRUMBLING CORNERSTONES OF BIOLOGICAL CONSERVATION

Formerly, one could argue for biodiversity because it was believed to be causally related to ecological stability. The "diversity-stability hypothesis," however, has been severely criticized (May 1973; Goodman 1975) — how decisively, I am not competent to judge. But the mandate for the conservation of biodiversity will be put at risk to the extent that one of its mainstay rationales is suspect.

Wilderness once served as a gross standard of conservation. Wilderness was imagined to be a pristine environment, defined by an Act of the United States Congress as "in contrast to those areas where man and his own works dominate the landscape, an area where the earth and its community of life are untrammeled by man, where man himself is a visitor who does not remain" (Nash 1967, 5). But wilderness preservation, so understood, assumes a pre-Darwinian religious and metaphysical separation of *Homo sapiens* from the rest of nature. After Darwin, we cannot suppose that "man" is anything but a precocious primate, a denizen of "the earth" and a member of its "community of life." "His own works," therefore, are as natural as those of termites or beavers. Biological conservation via wilderness preservation is also vitiated by ethnocentrism. To suggest that, prior to being "discovered" only half a

millennium ago by the European subspecies of *Homo sapiens,* any landscape in North or South America was "untrammeled by man, where man himself is a visitor," implies either that large portions of North and South America were uninhabited or that the aboriginal inhabitants of the New World had no significant intentional or even unintentional effect upon their lands. Or, worse, it could imply that American Indians were not truly human, were not "man." But, by 1492, all of North and South America were fully if not densely populated (Dobyns 1966). And the effects of more than ten thousand years of human inhabitation of the Western Hemisphere have been profound and, upon the eve of European encroachment, were ongoing (Denevan 1992). After the arrival of *Homo sapiens* in the Western Hemisphere, some ten thousand or more years ago, the only large land area fitting Congress's description of wilderness was Antarctica (and now a good bit of that continent, and the atmosphere above it, have been thoroughly trammeled). When an area's aboriginal human inhabitants are removed, in order to create a wilderness, the ecologic conditions that existed at the time of their removal, presumably the conditions to be preserved in their "virgin" state, are put at jeopardy (Bonnicksen 1990). Biologic conservation via wilderness preservation thus proves to be based upon an incoherent idea, the wilderness idea (Callicott 1991).

Further, whether a "natural" area has been dominated by *Homo sapiens* or not, over time it will nevertheless change. The fourth dimension of ecosystems has recently been emphasized by Daniel Botkin (1990). Nature is dynamic. Change at every frequency — diurnal, meteorological, seasonal, successional, climatic, evolutionary, geological, astronomical — is inevitable. According to Botkin, the concept of succession in ecology culminating in a climax community that will perpetuate itself generation after generation until reset by wind, fire, chain saw, plow, or some other disturbance is suspect. While accounting for change, the concept of succession-to-climax, he argues, posits — like Aristotle's physics — rest or a static state as the "natural" condition of ecosystems. . . .

These recent developments — the impeachment of the diversity-stability hypothesis, the evaporation of the wilderness idea, the diminishing credibility of the Clementsian holistic paradigm and the corresponding ascendency of the Gleasonian individualistic paradigm in theoretical ecology, the impeachment of the community succession-to-climax model and even the typological community, and the emphasis, in general, on change rather than continuity (a kind of neocatastrophism, as it were, supplanting uniformitarianism)—all give aid and comfort to the foes of biological conservation. If change is a fundamental feature of nature; if man is a part of nature and anthropogenic changes are as natural as any other; if, for more than 10,000 years, there have been no large-scale, pristine, untouched terrestrial wilderness environments (outside Antarctica); if species in communities can mix and match as they always have to form novel associations; if diversity is not necessarily necessary to stability; then how can anyone express more than a personal subjective preference in declaring any change whatever that human beings may impose on landscapes to be bad? What's wrong, objectively wrong, with urban sprawl, oil slicks, global warming, or, for that matter, abrupt, massive, anthropogenic species extinction—other than that these things offend the quaint tastes of a few natural antiquarians? Most people prefer shopping malls and dog tracks to wetlands and old growth forests. Why shouldn't their tastes, however vulgar, prevail in a free market and democratic polity? Kristin Shrader-Frechette has explicitly brought us to this omega point:

> Ecosystems regularly change and regularly eliminate species. How would one . . . argue that humans should not modify ecosystems or even wipe out species, for example, when nature does this itself through natural disasters, such as volcanic eruptions and climate changes like those that destroyed the dinosaurs? . . . One cannot obviously claim that it is wrong on *ecological grounds* for humans to do what nature does—wipe out species. (Shrader-Frechette 1989, 76, emphasis in original)

The concept of ecosystem health to the rescue. Yes, change is natural, human beings are a part of nature, and anthropogenic changes are no different from other natural changes. But, quite irrespective of the vagaries of taste, we may still argue that some are bad and others good, if we can specify objective norms of ecologic health against which we may evaluate human modifications of the landscape. By the same criteria of course we might evaluate the changes wrought by any other species.

LAND HEALTH

I leave to ecologists the task of determining whether or not the concept of ecosystem health makes scientific sense and, if it does, what the general characteristics and indices of ecosystem health might be. As Plato provides a locus classicus for turning the metaphorical concepts of psychological and political health to moral advantage, Aldo Leopold provides a locus classicus for turning the metaphorical concept of ecosystem health (or "land health," as he more simply denominated it) to conservation advantage. That so distinguished and prescient a conservationist as Leopold thought that the concept had promise, and envisioned its scientific articulation, may be taken as prima facie evidence that the notion is at least worth a close look.

During the last decade of his life, 1938–48, Leopold frequently employed the concept of land health in his sundry writings, including several of the essays in *A Sand County Almanac*. In two of his papers from this period, Leopold provides a sustained discussion of the concept of land health.

Ironically, in view of the foregoing remarks, the first is "Wilderness as a Land Laboratory," in which Leopold offers a novel argument for wilderness preservation. Here he suggests that wilderness may serve as "a base-datum for land-health" and defines "land health" as nature's capacity for "self-renewal," a definition which he reiterates in subsequent usages and a definition that carries, importantly, both dynamic and functional rather than static and structural connotations (Leopold 1941, 3). Though not invoking Clements's organismic ecological paradigm in any strict or specific sense, Leopold here, as he will elsewhere, closely associates the concept of "land health" with an organic image of nature: "There are two organisms in which the unconscious automatic processes of self-renewal have been supplemented by conscious interference and control. One of these is man himself (medicine and public health) and the other is land (agriculture and conservation)" (Leopold 1941, 3).

That Leopold introduces the concept of land health, not as a casual rhetorical device, but as a serious scientific project, is suggested by the way he explores the analogy that he here draws to medicine. In the field of medicine, the symptoms of disease are manifest and doctoring is an ancient art, but medical science is relatively young and still incomplete. Analogously, "the art of land doctoring is being practiced with vigor," he comments, "but the science of land health is a job for the future" (Leopold 1941, 3). In 1941 ecology was not capable of specifying the norms of land health. On the other hand, the "symptoms" of "land-sickness" were all too evident to the discerning conservationist. Among such symptoms, Leopold (1941) mentions soil erosion and loss of fertility, hydrologic abnormalities, and the occasional irruptions of some species and the mysterious local extinctions of others.

While he argues that the most perfect "base-datum of normality" is wilderness, Leopold does not argue that the only way for land to stay healthy is to stay in an untrammeled condition. One may find places "where land physiology remains largely normal despite centuries of human occupation" (Leopold 1941, 3). Such places he believed the well-watered regions of Europe to be. Indeed, the practical raison d'être for a science of land health is precisely to determine the ecologic parameters within which land may be humanly occupied without making it dysfunctional, just as the whole point—or at least the only point that Leopold makes in this paper—of wilderness preservation is to provide a land laboratory in which such a science might be explored.

Leopold's uncritical belief in the existence of wilderness is traceable, I surmise, to the unconscious ethnocentrism that he shared with most of his contemporaries. In a paper written during the same year, he remarks that "the characteristic number of Indians in virgin America was small" (Leopold 1991b, 282). And in a paper published four years earlier he rhetorically reduces one group of American Indians, "the predatory Apache," to a form of less-than-fully-human indigenous wildlife (Leopold

1937, 118). But of course, North America, no less than temperate Europe, had also been subjected to "centuries of human occupation," indeed, more than 100 centuries.

Leopold's other sustained discussion of "land health" is found in an (until now) unpublished 1944 report, "Conservation: In Whole or in Part?" In it, he defines conservation as "a state of health in the land" and land health, once again, "as a state of vigorous self-renewal" (Leopold 1991a, 310). Here Leopold expressly draws out the functional connotation of this definition: "Such collective functioning of interdependent parts for the maintenance of the whole is characteristic of an organism. In this sense land is an organism, and conservation deals with its functional integrity, or health" (Leopold 1991a, 310). The maintenance of land health, therefore, is not necessarily the same thing as maintenance of existing community structures with their historical complement of species. Exotics may immigrate on their own or be deliberately introduced (cautiously) and evaluated, not xenophobically, but on the basis of their impact on the functional integrity of the host community. They may be pathologic, they may be benign, or, conceivably, they may actually enhance ecosystem functions.

In "Conservation: In Whole or in Part?" Leopold affirms the importance of diversity for ecologic function. Referring to the postglacial upper Midwest he writes, "The net trend of the original community was thus toward more and more diversity of native forms, and more and more complex relations between them" (Leopold 1991a, 312). He then draws the classic, but presently impugned, connection between diversity and stability: "Stability or health was associated with, and perhaps caused by this diversity and complexity" (Leopold 1991a, 312). It is a tribute to Leopold's scientific sensibilities that he carefully avoids stating dogmatically that stability was caused by diversity. Indeed, he registers an express caveat: "To assert a causal relation would imply that we understand the mechanism. . . ." But, absent thorough understanding, he argues that "The circumstantial evidence is that stability and diversity in the native community were associated for 20,000 years, and presumably depended on each other. Both now are partly lost, presumably because the original community has been partly lost and greatly altered. Presumably, the greater the losses and alterations, the greater the risks of impairments and disorganizations" (Leopold 1991a, 315).

As the science of land health is, for Leopold in the 1940s, only envisioned, only programmatic, he suggests that the art of land doctoring can only proceed on such circumstantial evidence and err on the side of caution. The "'rule of thumb'" for "ecological conservation" then should be, he thinks, that "the land should retain as much of its original membership as is compatible with human land-use [and] should be modified as gently and as little as possible" (Leopold 1991a, 315). But, again, it does not take a well-developed science of land health to notice the symptoms of land illness. In addition to those already mentioned in his earlier paper, Leopold here adds the qualitative deterioration in farm and forest products, the outbreak of pests and disease epidemics, and boom-and-bust wildlife population cycles.

Further to a governing philosophy of ecological conservation, Leopold suggests something similar to what is known today as holistic and preventive, as opposed to reductive and invasive, medicine: "This difference between gentle and restrained, as compared with violent and unrestrained, modification of the land is the difference between organic and mustard-plaster therapeutics in the field of land-health" (Leopold 1991a, 315). Leopold then goes on to outline a unified and holistic conservation strategy, as the title of his paper would indicate.

DISCUSSION

The contemporary ecologist looking for substantive norms of ecosystem health—in addition to substantive symptoms of ecosystem illness—which might serve as objective criteria for the evaluation of human modifications of historical ecologic conditions will find a review of Leopold's remarks about land health unrewarding. Leopold's scientific scruples preempted any impulse he may have had speculatively to detail them in the absence of basic ecological research. In general, he closely associates land health with both integrity—which he seems to understand primarily structurally—and stability. Leopold equates the integrity of land with the conti-

nuity of stable communities over long periods of time. Such integrity and stability, he cautiously suggests, depends upon species diversity and the complexity of relations between native species. . . .

. . . There exists a notion in contemporary biology cognate with Leopold's idea of "land health," the concept of "autopoiêsis." Leopold's concept of land health and the concept of autopoiêsis may indeed be mutually reinforcing: The imprimatur of Leopold's enormous reputation could attract greater attention to and exploration of the concept of autopoiêsis and the concept of autopoiêsis could update and more fully and abstractly express what Leopold was groping for with his notion of "land health" characterized as the "capacity of land for self-renewal."

Autopoiêsis is transliterated from two combined Greek words, (αυτο) and (ποιησισ); and, translated from Greek, means self-making. It was coined in 1972 by the Chilean biologists Humberto Maturana and Francisco Varela (1980) to characterize living systems more inclusive than organisms. Thus an organism is autopoiêtic, but so are other biological "entities." Instead of assimilating supraorganic biological systems to organisms, and implausibly attributing to them all sorts of similar characteristics, à la Clements, the concept of autopoiêsis permits a more limited comparison between organisms proper and larger living systems.

Explicitly assimilating Leopold's informal notion of land health with the contemporary formal concept of autopoiêsis could, therefore, rescue the former from guilt by association with the discredited organismic ecological paradigm. Though Leopold, for rhetorical effect, will sometimes say that "land *is* an organism," just as Clements had said that a plant formation *is* an organism, in trying more precisely to articulate what he means by "land health," Leopold focuses on the capacity of land for self-renewal and more carefully says that *"in this sense* land is an organism." Ecosystems and organisms, in other words, are very different and—it here seems that Leopold may have been aware—one would be mistaken to think that the former are just larger and more diffuse versions of the latter. Rather, Leopold thinks, they have one very fundamental, not to say essential, characteristic in common—the capacity

for self-organization and self-renewal. More technically expressed, organisms and ecosystems are both
autopoiêtic, self-organizing and self-recreating.

The concept of autopoiêsis wears its dynamism
on its sleeve, since "poiêsis" is a verb. "Health," on
the other hand, is a noun and may therefore suggest
a static condition in both organisms and ecosystems. But health, despite the grammar of its name,
actually is very much a process, a process of self-
maintenance and self-regeneration. In a healthy multicellular organism there is a constant turn-over of
cells. Further, while there is continuity in the organization of transient cells, over a lifetime there is
dramatic ontogeny: from zygote to embryo to fetus
to infant; then growth, maturation, reproduction;
and finally, decline and senescence. Or, even more
dramatically: from egg to larva to pupa to imago.
Today, ecologists emphasize that ecosystems also
change over time, but, as in healthy organisms,
healthy ecosystems maintain a certain continuity
and order in the midst of change. Thus radical and
discontinuous change is as destructive of autopoiêtic ecosystems as of autopoiêtic organisms.

All the symptoms of land illness that Leopold
notes are failures of ecologic function, not merely
alterations in composition. While Leopold believed
that the compositional integrity of biotic communities guaranteed their continued ecologic function,
he acknowledged that functional continuity could
be maintained in the midst of gradual and orderly
compositional change. According to Maturana and
Varela an autopoiêtic system, though by definition
a system whose whole and sole business is to regenerate itself, ordinarily undergoes structural changes.
But those changes must be orderly and, especially
if imposed from outside the system (what they call
"deformations"), limited: "Any structural changes
that a living system may undergo maintaining its
identity must take place in a manner determined by
and subordinate to its defining autopoiêsis; hence
in a living system loss of autopoiêsis is disintegra-
tion as a unity and loss of identity, that is death"
(Maturana and Varela, 1980, 112). Hence, human
inhabitation and transformation of ecosystems is
not, in principle, incompatible with their health —
that is, with their autopoiêsis or capacity for self-
renewal. Objectively good anthropogenic change is
change that benefits people and maintains land

health. Objectively bad anthropogenic change is
change that results in land sickness or worse in the
death of ecosystems. The overgrazed, eroded and
unrestorable erstwhile grasslands of the American
Southwest are very sick. The barren, laterized soil
of an erstwhile tropical rain forest is dead.

Leopold bought into the wilderness myth. Indeed, he was one of the most outspoken advocates
of wilderness preservation and one of the architects
of the North American wilderness movement. Nevertheless, unlike a Muir or a Murie, he devoted himself primarily to the conservation of humanly occupied and used ecosystems — "a more important and
complex task," as he put it (Leopold 1991c, 227).
And Leopold certainly acknowledged that long and
densely populated and heavily used land could be
healthy. In "A Biotic View of Land," he writes,
"Western Europe, for example, carries a far different pyramid than Caesar found there. Some large
animals are lost; many new plants and animals are
introduced, some of which escape as pests; the remaining natives are greatly changed in distribution
and abundance. Yet the soil is still fertile, the waters
flow normally, the new structure seems to function
and persist" (Leopold, 1939, 729).

Susan L. Flader (1974) observes that during the
1930s Leopold underwent a fairly sudden and dramatic shift of attitude toward land management.
From the reductive, Cartesian method, set out in
Game Management, of identifying and manipulating "factors" affecting wildlife populations — such
as food, cover, and predation — Leopold shifted to
a more holistic, organic approach. Eugene C. Hargrove (1989) compares his new attitude to "therapeutic nihilism" in medicine. This nineteenth-
century school of medicine frankly acknowledged
that doctors then did not know enough about the
physiology of the human organism to be confident
that any medical manipulation, invasion, or prescription would do more good than harm. So, they
argued, doctors should err on the side of caution, do
nothing, and hope their patients would recover on
their own. Leopold, similarly, believed that the contemporaneous state of ecological knowledge was so
incomplete that any humanly imposed changes on
land were altogether unpredictable. Hence, he coun-
seled caution and argued that the functioning of ecosystems could best be assured by preserving, and,

where practicable, restoring, their historic structural compositional integrity.

CONCLUSION

I have no idea how much more confident we can be today in the state of ecological knowledge. I can say with assurance, however, that neither manipulative management nor economic development are incompatible, in principle, with Leopold's general concept of land health. Human economic activities and the presence of domestic or exotic species are not inconsistent with land health, as Leopold conceived it, *provided that they do not disrupt ecosystem functions,* as indicated by the incidence or absence of the symptoms (some of which Leopold enumerates) of land-illness.

Of course, Leopold's land ethic may provide other reasons for exercising caution and more stringent constraints on human economic activities. If ecology, for example, could assure us that replacing golden trout with brown in California waters would have no adverse impact on the health of affected aquatic ecosystems, the "biotic right" of species to continuation, advocated by Leopold in "The Land Ethic," might still constitute a compelling reason not to do so. One can imagine all sorts of unnecessary and disfiguring operations that an unscrupulous doctor might perform on an unwitting patient, none of which ultimately compromised the patient's health, to satisfy the doctor's own whims or economic interests. But such operations would certainly compromise the patient's dignity and would violate the patient's rights. Human economic activities should certainly be constrained by considerations of land health. The observance of such constraints is as much a matter of morality as of prudence, since health — personal, social, and ecological — is an intrinsic value. But they should also be constrained by additional ethical and aesthetical considerations — by the "biotic right" of species to continuance and by the beauty of historic biotic communities.

BIBLIOGRAPHY

Bonnicksen, T. M. 1990. "Restoring Biodiversity in Park and Wilderness Areas: An Assessment of the Yellowstone Wildfires." In *Wilderness Areas: Their Impacts,* edited by A. Rasmussen, 25–32. Logan: Utah State University Cooperative Extension Service.

Botkin, D. 1990. *Discordant Harmonies: A New Ecology for the Twenty-first Century.* New York: Oxford University Press.

Callicott, J. B. 1991. "The Wilderness Idea Revisited: The Sustainable Development Alternative." *Environmental Professional* 13:235–47.

Denevan, W. 1992. "The Pristine Myth: The Landscape of the Americas in 1492." *Annals of the Association of American Geographers* 82:369–85.

Dobyns, H. F. 1966. "Estimating Aboriginal American Population: An Appraisal of Techniques with a New Hemispheric Estimate." *Current Anthropology* 7:395–412.

Flader, S. 1974. *Thinking Like a Mountain: Aldo Leopold and the Evolution of an Ecological Attitude toward Deer, Wolves, and Forests.* Columbia: University of Missouri Press.

Goodman, D. 1975. "The Theory of Diversity-Stability Relationships in Ecology." *Quarterly Review of Biology* 30:237–66.

Hargrove, E. C. 1989. *Foundations of Environmental Ethics.* Englewood Cliffs, N.J.: Prentice-Hall.

Leopold, A. 1937. "Conservationist in Mexico." *American Forests* 43:118–20.

———. 1939. "A Biotic View of Land." *Journal of Forestry* 37:727–30.

———. 1941. "Wilderness as a Land Laboratory." *The Living Wilderness* 6 (July): 3.

———. 1949. *"A Sand County Almanac" and "Sketches Here and There."* New York: Oxford University Press.

———. 1991a. "Conservation: In Whole or in Part?" In *The River of the Mother of God and Other Essays by Aldo Leopold,* edited by S. L. Flader and J. B. Callicott, 310–19. Madison: University of Wisconsin Press.

———. 1991b. "Means and Ends in Wildlife Management." In *The River of the Mother of God and Other Essays by Aldo Leopold,* 235–38.

———. 1991c. "Ecology and Politics." In *The River of the Mother of God and Other Essays by Aldo Leopold,* 281–86.

Maturana, H. R., and F. J. Varela, 1980. "Autopoiesis: The Organization of the Living." In *Autopoiesis and Cognition,* 59–140. Boston: D. Reidel.

May, R. M. 1973. *Stability and Complexity in Model Ecosystems.* Princeton: Princeton University Press.

Miller, P. 1981. Is Health an Anthropocentric Value? *Nature and System* 3:193–207.

Nash, R. F. 1967. *Wilderness and the American Mind.* New Haven: Yale University Press.

Shrader-Frechette, K. S. 1989. "Ecological Theories and Ethical Imperatives: Can Ecology Provide a Scientific Justification for the Ethics of Environmental Protection?" In *Scientists and Their Responsibility,* edited by W. R. Shea and B. Sitter, 73–104. Canton, Mass.: Watson Publishing International.

DISCUSSION TOPICS

1. To what extent do you believe "ecosystem health" can be defined? Do you find that Leopold's definition is usable? (See also Freyfogle and Newton's discussion, Chapter 1.)

2. Do you agree with Callicott that economic development is compatible with land health? Clarify your position on this.

3. Callicott's interpretations that "anthropogenic" (human-induced) changes should be perceived differently from "natural" changes go against the perspectives of some environmentalists and resource managers. What is your perspective on this? Give your reasoning.

READING 44

The Land Ethic at the Turn of the Millennium

Holmes Rolston III

Holmes Rolston is a professor of philosophy, Colorado State University, Fort Collins. In this article from Biodiversity and Conservation, *Rolston notes that Leopold's land ethic is concerned in both theory and practice with appropriate values carried by the natural world as well as human responsibilities for sustaining these values. Rolston argues that a blending of anthropocentric and biocentric values continues to be vital. He believes any plausible environmental policy must be based on realistic accounts of ecosystems and a sustainable biosphere. Rolston assesses some of the challenges to respecting nature, such as the notions that ecosystems do not exist as concrete entities that can be valued or that they are merely aggregations of individuals with more concrete problems. In response he argues that such positions do not fully account for the unique characteristics and qualities of ecosystems. He sees the future of the planet as intertwined with other critical problems that humans face.*

Fifty years ago, near mid-century, Aldo Leopold lamented, "There is as yet no ethic dealing with man's relation to land and to the animals and plants which grow upon it. . . ." (Leopold 1949(1968): 203). . . .

If someone had been attempting to foresee the future of philosophy at mid-century, when Leopold wrote, perhaps the two most surprising developments would have been the rise of environmental philosophy and the novel perspectives introduced by the feminists, including the ecofeminists. The next two surprising developments might well be the interest in animal welfare and in international development ethics and sustainability, both with ties to environmental philosophy. Someone attempting to foresee future concerns in religion would have been just as surprised: the prevalent neo-orthodoxy denied natural theology, had little use for a theology of nature, and was dominantly anthropocentric. . . .

Leopold insisted that ethics goes further, although prudential natural resource use is important. This new ethic enlarges traditional ideas about what is of moral concern to include animals, plants, endangered species, ecosystems, and (today) even Earth as a whole. Such ethics is unique in moving outside the sector of human interests, including our interests in this larger community of life. Leopold gave us, famously, a new commandment: "A thing is right when it tends to preserve the integrity, stability, and beauty of the biotic community. It is wrong when it tends otherwise" (Leopold 1949 (1968): 224–225). Entering the new millennium, I doubt that any philosopher or theologian in the Western world has not heard of environmental ethics. The land ethic has even gone global, as we shall see. All this would have both surprised and pleased Leopold.

Somewhat ironically, just when humans, with their increasing industry and technology, seemed further and further from nature, having more knowledge about natural processes and more power to manage them, just when humans were more and more rebuilding their environments, the natural world emerged as a focus of ethical concern. . . .

ETHICS TOWARD NATURE

Environmental ethics is theory and practice about appropriate concern for, values in, and duties to the natural world. Since humans are helped or hurt by the condition of their environment, this is a concern for what humans have at stake—benefits, costs, and their just distribution, risks, pollution levels, rights and torts, needs of future generations. But environmental ethics goes further. A naturalistic ethics is reached when humans ask about appropriate respect toward those who are other than human, such as the wildlife or the trees. This might be termed biocentric ethics, centering on a respect for life, rather than exclusively centering on humans. Environmental ethics applies ethics to the environment, analogously to ethics applied to business, medicine, engineering, law and technology. But the latter are still human-focused applications. Environmental ethics is more radical, more inclusive—so many claim. Whales slaughtered, wolves extirpated, whooping cranes and their habitats disrupted, ancient forests cut, Earth threatened by global warming—these are ethical questions intrinsically, owing to values destroyed in nature, as well as also instrumentally, owing to human resources jeopardized. Humans need to include nature in their ethics; humans need to include themselves in nature. . . .

We ought to love "the land," as Leopold terms it, "the natural processes by which the land and the living things upon it have achieved their characteristic form (evolution) and by which they maintain their existence (ecology)." "That land is a community is the basic concept of ecology, but that land is to be loved and respected is an extension of ethics" (Leopold (1949)1968: 173, 224–225). People still count, but this ecosystemic level in which people and all other organisms are embedded also counts morally. The appropriate units for moral concern are the fundamental units of development and survival. Those have been, over the millennia, evolutionary ecosystems—at least until humans began so drastically to introduce their cultural and agricultural changes. Even yet, natural systems remain fundamental to our support. We co-inhabit Earth with five or ten million other species, and we and they depend on these biotic communities of life.

The challenge to ethical respect toward nature is partly scientific and partly philosophical. Perhaps ecosystems do not exist—or exist in too loose a way to count morally. They are nothing but aggregations of their more real members, like a forest is (some say) nothing more than a collection of trees. An ethicist will have trouble valuing what does not really exist. One needs ecology to discover what biotic community means as an organizational mode. Then we can reflect philosophically to discover values there that might command our moral respect.

Ecosystems can seem little more than stochastic processes. A seashore, a tundra is a loose collection of externally related parts. Much of the environment is not organic at all (rain, groundwater, rocks, non-biotic soil particles, air). Some is dead and decaying debris (fallen trees, scat, humus). An ecosystem has no brain, no genome, no skin, no self-identification, no telos, no unified program. It does not defend itself against injury or death. It is not irritable. The parts (foxes, sedges) are more centrally integrated than the wholes (forests, grasslands). So it can seem as if an ecosystem is too low a level of organization to be the direct focus of moral concern. Ecosystems do not and cannot care; they have no interests about which they or we can care. There is really not enough centered process to call community.

But this is to misunderstand ecosystems, to make a category mistake. To doubt communities because they are not organismic individuals is to look at one level for what is appropriate at another. One should look for a matrix of interconnections between centers, for creative stimulus and open-ended potential. Everything will be connected to many other things, sometimes by obligate associations, more often by partial and pliable dependencies; and, among other components, there will be no significant interactions. There will be shunts and criss-crossing pathways, cybernetic subsystems and feedback loops.

One looks for selection pressures and adaptive fit, not for irritability or repair of injury, for speciation and life support, not for resisting death. We must think more systemically, and less organismically.

An ecosystem generates a spontaneous order that envelopes the richness, beauty, integrity, and dynamic stability of the component parts. One should not in an undiscriminating way extrapolate criteria of significance from organism to biotic community, any more than from person to animal or from animal to plant. Rather, one should discriminate the criteria appropriate to this level. The selective forces in ecosystems at once transcend and produce the lives of individual plants and animals. In evolutionary ecosystems over geological time the numbers of species on Earth have increased from zero to five million or more. Whittaker (1972) found that on continental scales and for most groups "increase of species diversity . . . is a self-augmenting evolutionary process without any evident limit." There is a tendency toward what he called "species packing."

Organisms defend only their own selves or kinds, but the system spins a bigger story. Organisms defend their continuing survival; ecosystems promote new arrivals. Species increase their kinds, but ecosystems increase kinds, and increase the integration of kinds. The system is a kind of field with characteristics as vital for life as any property contained within particular organisms. The organismic kind of creativity (regenerating a species, pushing to increase to a world-encompassing maximum) is used to produce, and is checked by, another kind of creativity (speciating that produces new kinds, interlocking kinds with adaptive fit, plus individuality and openness to future development). The collective order can be more complex than the behaviors of any of the individual parts. Ecosystemic order is a comprehensive, complex, fertile order just because it integrates (with some openness) the know-how of many diverse organisms and species; it is not an order built on the achievements of any one kind of thing. In result there are diversity, unity, dynamic stability, novelty, spontaneity, a life-support system, the wonderland of natural history.

Ethicists, sometimes encouraged by biologists, may think ecosystems are just epiphenomenal aggregations. This is a confusion. . . . Being real

requires an organization that shapes the existence and the behavior of member/parts. A complex system, such as an ecosystem, is one whose properties are not fully explained by an understanding of its components.

If we are concerned about what is value-able, able to sustain value on our landscapes, why not say that it is the productivity of such ecosystems? The products are valuable, able to be valued by the humans who come late in the process; but why not say that the process is what is really valuable, that is, able to produce these values in biodiversity? It would be foolish to value golden eggs and disvalue the goose that lays them. It would be a mistake to value the goose only instrumentally and not for what it is in itself. How much more so an ecosystem that generates myriads of species, or even an Earth that produces billions of species, ourselves included. Evolutionary history is past; we are not responsible for that. But the resulting life communities continue, and they have become our responsibility. Viewed in depth, these ecosystems remain today the source and support of individual and species alike. Such a perspective begins to naturalize ethics, an ethic for what Leopold called "the land."

ECOSYSTEM INTEGRITY VERSUS EVOLUTIONARY DYNAMISM?

Although Leopold became prophetic in the 1970s and early 1980s, there have been, in the latter 1980s and the 1990s, still further vigorous challenges to his vision of ecosystem integrity and stability as the fundamental principles of a land ethic. These challenges are, again, both scientific and philosophical. Ecosystems have proved more complex, subtle, and confusing than Leopold thought. We need to reconsider their integrity and dynamic historical changes.

Ecologists, Leopold included, always knew that there is disturbance in the orderly succession of their ecosystems, producing a patchwork landscape. Ecosystems have various kinds of resilience, but if the disturbances become amplified enough, the order gets swamped in disorder. Botkin (1990) finds, at best, "discordant harmonies." "Wherever we seek to find constancy we discover change. . . . Nature undisturbed is not constant in form, structure, or proportion, but changes at every scale of time and space." Pickett et al. (1992: 84) claim: "The classical paradigm in ecology, with its emphasis on the stable state, its suggestion of natural systems as closed and self-regulating, and its resonance with the nonscientific idea of the balance of nature, can no longer serve as an adequate foundation for conservation. The new paradigm, with its recognition of episodic events, openness of ecological systems and multiplicity of locus and kind of regulation, is in fact a more realistic basis."

... Soulé (1995), although ardent in his conservation biology, says, "Certainly the idea that species live in integrated communities is a myth. ... Living nature is not equilibrial. ... Nature at the level of local biotic assemblages has never been homeostatic." "So-called biotic communities" is "a misleading term." If so, perhaps the land ethic preserving biotic communities is also a myth. Natural history is fractured into undefinable and indefinite assemblages that defy generalization, the loose associations feared above, only now in chaotic flux. Much less are such random, chaotic collections worth preserving for any beauty, integrity or stability they might have.

Leopold does need to be revisited, even revised. But, with a second look, he proves to be surprisingly sophisticated (Callicott 1996). ...

Over the decades, ecosystems are not static but have dynamic stability, recurrent processes and patterns; over the millennia, this passes into evolutionary development. Leopold was well aware that North America has undergone ice ages, climatic changes, speciation and extinctions of fauna and flora, and respeciation. "Evolution has added layer after layer, link after link." "The trend of evolution is to elaborate and diversify the biota" (Leopold (1949)1968: 216). This is more true than static balance.

Meanwhile, we do have three and a half billion years of life on Earth, generated and regenerated; and the matrix of such speciation is always ecosystems. An ecosystem is a spontaneously organizing system of interrelated parts, simultaneously persisting and evolving through changes over decades and centuries. An ecosystem is a vital and dynamic collection of organisms, each with its capabilities and limits, each species selected over evolutionary history to do rather well in the niche it inhabits, an adapted fit, and with some capacities for adapting to changes in its altering environment. In these ecosystems qualities emerge that are corporate or holistic (such as trophic pyramids or tendencies to succession), not the qualities of any individual parts (such as metabolism or death). The result is the richness of biodiversity over the geological millennia.

There are ordered regularities (seasons returning, the hydrologic cycle, acorns making oak trees, squirrels feeding on the acorns) mixed with episodic irregularities (droughts, fires, lightning killing an oak, mutations in the acorns). The rains come; leaves photosynthesize; insects and birds go their way; earthworms work the soil; bacteria break down wastes that are recycled; coyotes find dens, have their pups, and hunt rabbits; and on and on. Ecosystems contain as cybernetic subsystems the species lineages reproduced generation after generation. The half-life, on average, of many species is something like 5 million years. Lions have lived on the Serengeti plains for a long time, as have the zebras they eat. Over longer scales there are climate changes, respeciation, new niches generated and occupied. This dynamic stability does not preclude but rather includes variation and change.

Philosophers of biology doubt whether there are laws anywhere in biology, as law is generally understood in physics and chemistry, owing to the historical, earthbound nature of biology. Life depends on unique information discovered and transmitted in genes and DNA. But it does not follow that biology is without dependable, repeatable regularities. ... Such regularities typically continue when evolutionary novelties are introduced. There are degrees of regularity and of contingency within both evolutionary history and landscape ecology, as there are also within genetics and molecular biology (Cooper 1998).

That an ecosystem is "stable," as Leopold put it, is related to the contemporary idea that an ecosystem is "sustainable." Natural systems were often "sustained" in the past for long periods of time, even while they gradually modified. The Ecological Society of America has warned that humans ought to preserve their "sustainable biosphere" (Lubchenco et al. 1991). But that presupposes that these biospheric ecosystems were once, before human disruptions, ongoing systems over time and that they can and will, with intelligent human uses of them, continue far into the future. Worries about global warming, for example, assume that characteristically (though not invariantly) climate does not change so rapidly that the fauna and flora cannot track those changes, sustaining the ecosystem through modifications.

Equilibrium theory and non-equilibrium theory represent two ends of a spectrum with real ecosystems somewhere in between equilibrium and non-equilibrium, and whether one sees one or the other can depend on the level and scale of analysis. If density or community structure as a whole is studied, equilibria may appear never to be reached. However, at population levels, species diversity, or community compositions, ecosystems can show more predictable patterns, and even approach steady states on restricted ranges (Koetsier et al. 1990). . . .

Perhaps there are no equilibria reached and kept, but ecosystems are equilibrating systems composed of co-evolving organisms, with checks and balances pulsing over time. Population growth is constantly checked by food supply, predation, disease, or habitat availability, for example. There are autotrophs, heterotrophs, predators and prey, herbivores, omnivores, carnivores, trophic pyramids. There are succession (often interrupted), competition, symbiosis, energy flow, carrying capacity, niches, co-evolution, and often density dependent regulation, as well as density independent factors. Many general characteristics are repeated; many local details vary. Patterns of growth and development are orderly and predictable enough to make ecological science possible — and also to make possible an environmental ethics respecting these dynamic, creative, vital processes.

There is a kind of order that arises spontaneously and systematically when many self-actualizing units jostle and seek their own programs, each doing its own thing and forced into informed interaction with other units. In culture, the logic of language or the integrated connections of the market are examples. . . .

Government too is at various scales: legislative, executive, and judicial checks and balances, at federal, state, county, and municipal levels. Cultural heritages are generally like this, and we may legitimately respect Judaism or Christianity, or democracy or science, none of which are centrally controlled processes, all of which mix elements of integrity and dependability with dynamic change, even surprise and unpredictability. We might wish for "beauty, integrity, and stability" in democracy or science, without denying the elements of pluralism, historical development, and novel discoveries.

Natural selection means changes, but natural selection fails without order, without enough stability in ecosystems to make the mutations selected for dependably good for the time being. There is variation, more or less contingent, but without relative stability in environments, sustained patterns of evolutionary change cannot occur. A rabbit with a lucky genetic mutation that enables it to run a little faster has no survival advantage to be selected for, unless there are foxes and coyotes reliably present to remove the slower rabbits. Ecosystems have to be more or less integrated (in their food pyramids, for example), relatively stable (with more or less dependable food supplies, grass growing again each spring for the rabbits), and with persistent patterns (the hydrologic cycle watering the grass), or nothing can be an adapted fit, nor can adaptations evolve. Various changes in evolutionary history may result from "drift," and therefore be contingent, but species lineage cannot drift through a world too chaotic to provide reliable life support.

Some events are more infrequent, such as extreme droughts or storms. Coded in the genetics and expressed in the coping behaviors of its member species, ecosystems will have some capacities to adjust to interruptions that come often enough to be remembered in the genetic memory of member species. Lodgepole pines can make serotinous cones, for example, and the forest replaces itself. Some species become adapted for rapid reproduction in disturbed habitats (*r*-selected), some adapted for sustained replacement in settled habitats (K-selected), because suitable habitats for such species recur. Provided that climatic changes or novel species invasions are not too overwhelming, ecosystems that have long persisted will probably persist longer.

Leopold knew well enough that there is dynamic change, through time yielding historical development. Integrity in ecosystems includes the capacity to evolve. Stability, and nothing more, would squelch this creativity. On a big enough scale, ecology meets evolution. Or, perhaps one should say, the evolution going on all the time becomes evident. Ecology is always a time slice out of evolution.

Botkin (1990: 62) finds little stability in ecosystems, but he amply finds order: "Nature undisturbed by human influence seems more like a symphony whose harmonies arise from variation and change over every interval of time. We see a landscape that is always in flux, changing over many scales of time and space." An ecosystem is "a certain kind of system composed of many individuals of different species . . . and their environment, making together a network of living and nonliving parts that can maintain the flow of energy and the cycling of chemical elements that, in turn, support life" (Botkin 1990: 7). Botkin is often able to computer model these systems, else ecosystem management is impossible.

That, if you like, revises Leopold, but it retains relatively ordered ecosystems, making ecosystem science possible. If these ecosystems are rather like "symphonies," that order has enough beauty to make environmental ethics a responsibility. Thankfully, ecosystems are proving more complex, and correspondingly more interesting and valuable than even Leopold knew.

Generally ecosystemic nature, out there independently of humans though it may be, is today under threat owing to human disruptions. This threat is variously described as a threat to ecosystem function, health, integrity, or quality. Such ecosystem functions are both objective features of the world (the hydrological cycles, the nutrient flows) at the same time that they are affected for better or worse by human activities (acid rain killing trees and fish). The processes and products originally in place will with high probability have been those for which organisms are naturally selected for their adaptive fits, since misfits go extinct and easily disrupted ecosystems collapse and are replaced by more stable ones. Ecosystems get tested over thousands of years for their resilience.

This is true even though ecosystems are continually changing and though from time to time natural systems are upset (when volcanoes erupt, tsunamis destroy whole regions, or catastrophic epidemics break out). Then organisms have to adapt to altered circumstances and, as new interdependencies and networks appear, the integrity of ecosystems have to become re-established. Natural systems are typically places of adapted fit, as evolutionary and ecology theory both teach.

Even if natural ecosystems have characteristically settled into rather predictable patterns only slowly modified over evolutionary time, it seems likely that such systems, already quite complex, will be destabilized by human modifications, since these are often drastically different (bulldozers scraping off soil, synthetic pesticides, exotic weeds from another continent, acid rain). The fauna and flora have no genetic memory of such disruptions. Reliable predictions of these novel upsets will be beyond the capacities of ecosystem science with its presently available models and theories. An ecosystem might have naturally evolved certain checks and balances, feedback loops, but little follows from this to what will happen with human-introduced innovations (when the Europeans move to Hawaii, for instance, where the flightless birds have no evolutionary experience with ground predators). On the scale of human duties in conservation, preservation, and land-use planning, many find that Leopold's land ethic is still wise advice. We cannot predict how the next millennium will end, but we can work to sustain the biosphere in the first century of that millennium.

EARTH ETHICS BEYOND THE LAND ETHIC

Leopold was onto something bigger than he knew, as prophets often are. He never faced many issues now paramount in environmental ethics. Here we reach another scale question. Leopold forged his ethic in the sand counties of Wisconsin, though he was quite aware that persons around the globe need a land ethic. He also wrote of New Mexico, of Iowa, lamented the lack of wilderness in Germany and hoped it could be saved in the Carpathian Mountains of central Europe, or in Siberia. But Leopold did not face the global issues now novel and developing in environmental ethics; he wrote little about the future of Earth as a planet. In that sense, environmental ethics has become more millenarian, eschatological.

Leopold knew nothing of the hole in the ozone layer, of global warming. He did not face issues of sustainable development in Africa or the Amazon. Nor did he ask questions about environmental justice. These arise where the poor bear disproportionately the burdens of environmental degradation, or where developed nations, with one-fifth of the world's population consume four-fifths of its resources, with four-fifths of the world in developing nations limited to one-fifth of the world's production. Ecofeminism did not exist in his lifetime; so he never faced its strident claims that the domination of women is inextricably linked with the domination of nature and both problems must be solved together. He does not deal with escalating populations in the Third World, nor with the consumer culture being produced by global capitalism. He does not mention the World Bank, or The North American Free Trade Agreement (NAFTA), or the World Trade Organization (WTO), with their environmental policies, or lack thereof. Nor does he ask who owns genetic resources in tropical rainforests, who can patent their use, nor whether ivory should be sold or banned in order best to protect elephants. He does not worry about the rights of indigenous peoples, or about the release of genetically engineered organisms into natural environments. Leopold's land ethic can seem simplistic, almost parochial before the urgency and complexity of these global issues.

Since Leopold wrote, the United Nations Conference on Environment and Development (UNCED) at Rio de Janeiro in 1992 brought together the largest number of world leaders that have ever assembled to address any one issue, coupling sustainable development with a sustainable biosphere, and finding both urgent. That conference drew 118 heads of state and government, delegations from 178 nations, virtually every nation in the world, 7000 diplomatic bureaucrats, 30,000 advocates of environmental causes, and 7000 journalists. The results of the Summit have been less effective than many hoped, but at least ethics was always on the agenda, and environmental values were fundamental to every topic discussed. Even where the Summit failed to act, the failure indicated how much of value was at stake in the issues negotiated. The Summit was symbolically important, and this has become increasingly evident as we turn the millennium. The issues that coalesced there have been gathering over the last five hundred years, and they will be with us for another 500. Agenda 21 is probably the most complex and comprehensive international document ever attempted.

Ethics in the modern West has been almost entirely interhuman ethics, persons finding a way to relate morally to other persons — loving our neighbors. Ethics seeks to find a satisfactory fit for humans in their communities, and this has meant that ethics has often dwelt on justice, fairness, love, rights, or peace, settling the disputes of right and wrong that arise among us. But ethics now is anxious also about the troubled planet, its fauna, flora, species, and ecosystems. The two great marvels of our planet are life and mind, both among the rarest things in the universe. In the global picture, the late-coming, moral species, *Homo sapiens,* arising a few hundred thousand years ago, has, still more lately in this century, gained startling powers for the rebuilding and modification, including the degradation, of this home planet.

Environmental ethics, started by a forester spending his weekends in a shack in the rural sand counties, will be taken by some, even yet, to be peripheral concern about chipmunks and daisies, extrapolated to rocks and dirt. But not so. The four most critical issues that humans currently face are peace, population, development, and environment. All are entwined. Human desires for maximum development drive population increases, escalate exploitation of the environment, and fuel the forces of war. Those who are not at peace with one another find it difficult to be at peace with nature, and vice versa. Those who exploit persons will typically exploit nature as or more readily — animals, plants, species, ecosystems, and Earth itself.

One can, if one wishes, say that concern for the environment is only enlightened human self-interest; one can, if one wishes, say that concern for justice and equitable distribution of resources is only enlightened self-interest. We do all benefit from sustainable development in a sustainable biosphere, as we do from justice and fair resource distribution.

Still, a perspective with more depth sees entwined destinies, people with other people, people with their planet, responsible caring in human and biotic communities. Environmental ethics is the elevation to ultimacy of an urgent world vision.

We are searching for an ethics adequate to respect life on this Earth, the only planet yet known with an ecology. On Earth, home to several million species, humans are the only species who can reflect about their land ethic, about the future of the planet. Earth is the planet "right (suitable) for life," and ethics asks about the (moral) "right to life" on such a planet. Certainly it seems "right" that life should continue here, a matter of "biotic right," as Leopold ((1949) 1968: 204, 211) put it. Life is, in the deepest sense, the most valuable phenomenon of all. Death has to be figured into the life process, with life regenerated. Life has to be sacrificed for the support of life, on which principle ecosystems are founded. Life might be sacrificed to support more abundant life. Still, these long-continuing life processes are the miracle of Earth, and have become, as never before as we humans turn our millennium, our evolutionary and ecological responsibility.

Nature has equipped *Homo sapiens,* the wise species, with a conscience to direct the fearful power of the brain and hand. Perhaps conscience is less wisely used than it ought to be when, as in classical Enlightenment ethics, it exempts the global community of life from consideration, with the resulting paradox that the self-consciously moral species acts only in its collective self-interest toward all the rest. Among the remarkable developments on Earth with which we have to reckon, there is the long-standing ingenuity of the myriads of species that compose natural history; there is the recent, explosive human development; and there ought to be, and is, a developing environmental ethic that optimizes natural values in complement to human concerns.

We are not so enlightened as we supposed, not until we reach this Earth ethics. This is the biology of ultimate concern. This is seeing further than Leopold, but we see so far because we stand on this giant's shoulders. We are traveling deeper into ethics than ever before, unfolding a worldview that Leopold began to envision, an urgent call as we turn the millennium. The land ethic has become Earth ethics.

REFERENCES

Botkin D (1990) Discordant Harmonies: A New Ecology for the Twenty-first Century. Oxford University Press, New York

Callicott JB (1996) Do deconstructive ecology and sociobiology undermine Leopold's land ethic? Environmental Ethics 18: 353–372

Cooper G (1998) Generalizations in ecology: a philosophical taxonomy. Biology and Philosophy 13: 555–586

Koetsier P, Dey P, Mladenka G and Check J (1990) Rejecting equilibrium theory: a cautionary note. Bulletin of the Ecological Society of America 71: 229–230

Leopold A ((1949)1968) A Sand County Almanac. Oxford University Press, New York

Lubchenco J et al. (1991) The sustainable biosphere initiative: an ecological research agenda. A report from the Ecological Society of America. Ecology 72: 371–412

Pickett STA, Parker VT and Fiedler PL (1992) The new paradigm in ecology: implications for conservation biology above the species level. In: Fiedler PL and Jain SK (eds) Conservation Biology, pp 65–88. Chapman & Hall, New York

Soulé ME (1995) The social siege of nature. In: Soulé ME and Lease G (eds) Reinventing Nature? Responses to Postmodern Deconstruction, pp 137–170. Island Press, Washington, DC

Whittaker R (1972) Evolution and measurement of species diversity. Taxon 21: 213–251

DISCUSSION TOPICS

1. How might someone make a "category mistake" in their assessment of ecosystems? Give two examples.
2. What are some qualities and characteristics of ecosystems (if any) that you believe go beyond features found among their components? Justify your position.
3. In what ways do you believe that Leopold's land ethic and the Deep Ecology Movement could change to accommodate our greater understanding of planetary ecology and the human relationship with nature?

The Deep, Long-Range Ecology Movement: 1960–2000—A Review

Bill Devall

Bill Devall is an emeritus professor of sociology at Humboldt State University, Arcata, California. He has been a prolific contributor to the deep ecology movement (DEM); his works include Simple in Means, Rich in Ends *(1988),* Living Richly in an Age of Limits *(1993), and numerous published papers.*

Devall outlines the DEM's general platform and shows how the movement was articulated and developed in the United States and in world conferences over the past forty years. Defining ecosophy *as a philosophy of ecological harmony, Devall believes the DEM can make significant contributions to political policies and actions because its supporters commonly have ecosophies with deep total views that include awareness of the ecological crisis as well as issues of social justice, war, and organized violence. He describes the development of an "ecological self" as an important step for effectively translating values into action.*

Professor Arne Naess of the University of Oslo catalyzed discussion of two streams of environmental philosophy when he articulated the distinction between "shallow ecology" and the "deep, long-range ecology movement" (DEM) in a short paper published in 1973. He characterized the shallow ecology movement as "Fight against pollution and resource depletion. Central objective: the health and affluence of people in the developed countries" (Naess 1973).

When Naess outlined principles of the deep, long-range ecology perspective, he included "fight against pollution and resource depletion," but he went beyond that statement to include principles that are not part of the dominant social paradigm. These included "ecocentrism," "wide sustainability," "complexity, not complication," and "rejection of man-in-environment image in favor of a relational, total-field image" (Naess 1973). Naess made it socially acceptable for academics to be activists on conservation issues by relating reflection to action. He also showed how people can move from denial to creative, nonviolent direct action based on their core values.[1]

When Naess wrote his original essay on deep ecology, he knew there was limited scientific data available on the impact of industrial civilization on free nature. That is why he was inspired by both the science and the feelings for free nature expressed by Rachel Carson in Silent Spring.[2]

The wave of enthusiasm for the environment that began with Earthday 1970 was reaching a climax in the United States with the passage of the federal Endangered Species Act. Many supporters of deep ecology in the U.S. consider the federal Endangered Species Act to be the most ecocentric environmental legislation because the underlying premise of the act is that humans have no right to willfully cause the extinction of other species, regardless of their value, or lack of value, for humans. . . .

Many researchers have documented the recurring, anthropogenic-caused collapse of natural systems at the regional or landscape level since modern humans began spreading across the planet approximately 35,000 years ago. However, the contemporary environmental crisis is the first planetary-wide anthropogenically caused extinction crisis (Wilson 1992; Bright 1998) and environmental crisis.

Much of the scientific research advanced during the 1970s, which had been proclaimed the "decade of the environment" by President Richard Nixon, is summarized in a report authorized by President Jimmy Carter and published in 1980, The Global 2000 Report to the President: Entering the Twenty-First Century (CEQ 1980). . . .

A convergence of various trends has led to what is frequently called the "environmental crisis." On a finite planet there is no "new land" available for expansion of industrial civilization. Yet human population has continued to grow; per capita consumption has increased; and technology has been applied on a grand scale. Demographers proclaimed that the six billionth human was born in October 1999. While some people believe that humans will find solutions to many problems through technology, the pace of technological change continues to disrupt the lives of hundreds of millions of people. . . .

In the face of a crisis of planetary scale, some radical environmentalists argue that mild reforms in public policy and practices are basically useless. Deep changes in society require a "paradigm shift" from the dominant modern paradigm of industrial civilization to a "new environmental paradigm" or "new ecological paradigm" (Catton 1980b; Drengson 1980).

THE ROLE OF THE DEEP, LONG-RANGE ECOLOGY MOVEMENT IN PROMOTING SOCIAL CHANGE

. . .

In 1984, while camping together in the California desert, Arne Naess and George Sessions compiled the platform for the deep, long-range ecology movement. . . .

Naess said his purpose in developing this "platform" was "modest," that is, to develop a set of very general principles or statements upon which supporters of deep ecology could comment and discuss. Naess's goal is to help people articulate their own deep ecological total view. The deep ecology "platform" therefore is a pedagogical tool to assist people in the process of developing their own statement of ecosophy and as a device to stimulate dialogue between supporters of and critics of the DEM.

Platform of Deep Ecology

1. The well-being and flourishing of human and nonhuman life on Earth have value in themselves (synonyms: inherent worth; intrinsic value, inherent value). These values are independent of the usefulness of the nonhuman world for human purposes.
2. Richness and diversity of life forms contribute to the realization of these values and are also values in themselves.
3. Humans have no right to reduce this richness and diversity except to satisfy vital needs.
4. The flourishing of human life and cultures is compatible with a substantial decrease of the human population. The flourishing of nonhuman life requires such a decrease.
5. Present human interference with the nonhuman world is excessive, and the situation is rapidly worsening.
6. Policies must therefore be changed. The changes in policies affect basic economic,

technological, and ideological structures. The resulting state of affairs will be deeply different from the present.
7. The ideological change is mainly that of appreciating life quality (dwelling in situations of inherent worth) rather than adhering to an increasingly higher standard of living. There will be a profound awareness of the difference between big and great.
8. Those who subscribe to the foregoing points have an obligation directly or indirectly to participate in the attempt to implement the necessary changes (this version of the deep ecology "platform" is found in Devall 1988).

The DEM is based on radical pluralism in "foundational" beliefs. Buddhists, Christians, Jews, Moslems, pantheists, agnostics, and materialists can come to a kind of deep ecology position or perspective both from their own experience (which Naess calls "the intuition of deep ecology") and from historic philosophic and religious traditions (Naess 1989).

Naess defines ecosophy as ". . . a philosophy of ecological harmony or equilibrium. A philosophy as a kind of sofia (or) wisdom, is openly normative, it contains both norms, rules, postulates, value priority announcements and hypotheses concerning the state of affairs of our universe. Wisdom is policy wisdom, prescription, not only scientific description and prediction. The details of an ecosophy will show many variations due to significant differences concerning not only the 'fact' of pollution, resources, population, etc., but also value priorities" (in Sessions 1995a).

Thus, when individuals and communities articulate their own authentic ecosophy they provide an intellectual and emotional basis for their practice of deep ecology. Arne Naess calls his version "ecosophy T." His philosophical reflection on his own ecosophy is based on his experiences in a mountain hut in Norway where he has worked for many decades. . . .

The slogan, "simple in means, rich in ends," emphasizes that the DEM encourages rich experiences, and rich experience includes experiences in free nature. As modern life continues to encroach on our daily lives, millions and millions of people are less and less able to have rich experiences in free nature. The importance of such experience is emphasized in the growing field of ecopsychology.

For Naess, rich experiences in free nature contributes to a sense of maturity. Both Dolores La-Chapelle (1988) and Paul Shepard (1973, 1998) have contributed thoughtful commentary on the usefulness of looking at other cultures, especially primal cultures, for models of appropriate experiences that encourage greater human maturity. . . .

Naess concludes that the DEM has a special role in political life. "For one, it rejects the monopoly of narrowly human and short-term argumentation patterns in favor of life-centered long-term arguments. It also rejects the human-in-environment metaphor in favor of a more realistic human-in-ecosystems and politics-in-ecosystems one. It generalizes most ecopolitical issues: from 'resources' to 'resources for . . .'; from 'life quality' to 'life quality for . . .'; from 'consumption' to 'consumption for . . .'; where 'for . . .' is, we insert 'not only humans, but other living beings'. Supporters of the DEM have, as a main source of motivation and perseverance, a philosophical/ecological total view (an ecosophy) that includes beliefs concerning fundamental goals and values in life which it applies to political argumentation. That is, it uses not only arguments of the usual rather narrow kind, but also arguments from the level of a deep total view and with the ecological crisis in mind. But supporters of the DEM do not consider the ecological crisis to be the only global crisis; there are also crises of social justice, and of war and organized violence. And there are, of course, political problems which are only distantly related to ecology. Nevertheless, the supporters of the DEM have something important to contribute to the solution of these crises: they provide an example of the nonviolent activism needed in the years to come" (in Sessions 1995a, 452). . . .

The translation of values and the "intuition" of deep ecology into action in the midst of industrial civilization requires purposeful, collective action and attention to "ecological self." The "ecological self," defined by Naess as "broad identification" with nature, whether based on biophilia or on experiences in the "wilderness" of nature, has stimulated some of the most provocative theories developed

from a deep ecology perspective (see for example Mathews 1991; Evernden 1993; Macy 1991; Fox 1990). When people have gone from denial to despair, how do they recatalyze energy to respond effectively and creatively to the environmental crisis? Teachers such as John Seed and Joanna Macy have pioneered in developing experimental workshops where participants are invited to explore "broader identification" through a "council of all beings" (Seed 1988). At least one researcher has concluded that experiences individuals have during a "council of all beings" can assist in helping participants engage in nonviolent direct action based on their awareness of their "ecological self" as part of an unfolding, interdependent "net" of relationships (Bragg 1995).

Joanna Macy, and other teachers who are supporters of the DEM, have demonstrated that participation in the "council of all beings" and other rituals and exercises designed to explore the "ecological self," is effective cross-culturally. Macy herself has led such exercises in Russia, Australia, several European nations, as well as in the United States with participants from culturally diverse backgrounds.[3] . . .

Naess asserts that there are three great social movements of the 20th century—the ecology movement, the peace movement, and the social justice movement. These three movements speak to our yearning for liberation and can be compatible with each other in specific political campaigns. However, in situations of conflict, priorities must be established.

Soon after Earthday 1970, commentators were warning of possible conflicts between environment and civil rights (Hutchins 1976) and between economic growth and environmental quality (Heller 1973). As the deep ecology perspective became more widely discussed during the 1980s, critics from postmodern schools of thought, feminism, and social ecology argued strenuously for nonessentialist, anthropocentric approaches to environmental ethics. Supporters of the DEM demonstrated that there are parallels between ecofeminism and deep ecology (Fox 1989; Plumwood 1992).

Some critics assume that the DEM is inappropriate for the Third World because the Third World must address problems of militarism, poverty, food supply, and demands for gender equality (Guha 1989). On the contrary, supporters of the DEM conclude it is most appropriate for the Third World because of its emphasis on long-range sustainability of natural systems within which humans as well as all other species must dwell (Naess 1995; Cafaro 1998). . . .

Supporters of the DEM recognize the need to address the great disparity between the opportunities of people living in the Third World to sustain their vital needs and people living in Japan, the United States, Canada, and the European Union. Much effort has been given by supporters of the DEM to addressing issues of environmental justice raised by a globalizing economy and the impact of free trade treaties such as NAFTA (and the WTO) on our ability to speak for the protection of wild species and their habitat, as well as the impact that global financial structures have on the lives of ordinary people around the world (Mander 1991).

When the demands for redistribution of money, power, and wealth, in the short-term, between more wealthy and less wealthy societies, between genders, between age groups, between politically defined ethnic groups, and so forth, become the primary agenda of social activists, there is a danger, as George Sessions has concluded, of "the demise of the ecology movement" because social justice concerns frequently replace concern for the ecological integrity of the Earth (Sessions 1995b, 1995c). While many social issues can be addressed simultaneously, even if a utopian social justice society could be established, it may be on a planet that is rapidly losing biodiversity, primary forests, and free nature.

WARNINGS TO HUMANITY

Before the Rio Summit on Development and the Environment in 1992, the Union of Concerned Scientists circulated the World Scientists' Warning to Humanity, signed by over 1,700 scientists, including 104 Nobel laureates. The Warning stated, in part, "Human beings and the natural world are on a collision course . . . A great change in our steward-

ship of the earth and the life on it is required, if vast human misery is to be avoided and our global home on the planet is not to be irretrievably mutilated . . . No more than one or a few decades remain before the chance to avert the threats we now confront will be lost" (Ehrlich 1996, Appendix B). . . .

It is widely accepted that reform environmentalism is now part of the political agenda of most nations. Politicians are expected to include "the environment" as part of their campaign promises and public policy objectives. Many governments of developing nations are willing to participate in conservation programs—if they are given cash in exchange for their participation, such as the "debt for nature" agreements reached with some nations in South America. Findings from cross-cultural surveys indicate that even in poor nations, there is widespread awareness of and concern with environmental issues (Brechin 1994). Radical grassroots environmental movements have developed in many Third World nations (Taylor 1995). Whether or not motivated by deep ecology or reform environmental perspective or demands for tribal or First Nations sovereignty from national governments, grassroots movements have irritated governments, some corporations, and other economic and political interest groups who ignited a backlash against radical environmentalism both in the United States and in many developing nations. Campaigns of suppression, detention, and even murder of grassroots radical environmentalists have been extensively documented (Rowell 1996).

Leaders of all the major world religions including Native American pantheism, Orthodox Christianity, Roman Catholic, Buddhism, Islam, and Judaism have presented statements that echo the World Scientists' Warning to Humanity. Religious leaders have presented statements affirming that conservation is part of their ethical teachings and that humans have no right to destroy the integrity of natural systems (Oelschlaeger 1994).

In 1982, the United Nations General Assembly passed the World Charter for Nature, sponsored by a Third World nation—Zaire—with only one dissenting vote, the United States. The World Charter contains significant deep ecology statements including,

1. Nature shall be respected and its essential processes shall not be disrupted.
2. The genetic viability on the earth shall not be compromised; the population level of all life forms, wild and domesticated, must be at least sufficient for their survival, and to this end necessary habitats shall be maintained.
3. All areas, both land and sea, shall be subject to these principles of conservation; special protection shall be given to unique areas, representative samples of all ecosystems and the habitats of rare and endangered species.
4. Ecosystems and organisms, as well as land, marine and atmospheric resources which are utilized by man shall be managed to achieve and maintain optimum sustainable productivity, but not in such a way as to endanger the integrity of those other ecosystems or species with which they coexist.
5. Nature shall be secured against degradation caused by warfare or other hostile activities.

The Charter challenges national and local governments to select the appropriate mix of social, political, and economic methods to achieve their goals (Wood 1985). However, the major world environmental conferences held during the 1990s, including the Rio Summit on Development and the Environment (1992) and the Kyoto Conference on Global Warming (1998), presented documents that retreated from deep ecological statements found in the World Charter for Nature.

Even by their own anthropocentric criteria, the world environmental conferences of the 1990s have had limited success. Five years after the Rio summit, the United Nations Environment Programme issued a report, The Global Environmental Outlook. The report concludes that "significant progress has been made in confronting environmental challenges. Nevertheless, the environment has continued to degrade in nations of all regions. Progress toward a sustainable future has simply been too slow" (UNEP 1997). . . .

With the prospect of a conscious, collective movement of rapid social turnaround fading, some supporters of the DEM suggest that the human species has exceeded the limits of natural systems

to respond to anthropogenic changes, and that radical changes in human society will occur during the 21st century because "nature bats last" (Catton 1980a; Meadows et al. 1992).

In his 1971 book, The Closing Circle, Barry Commoner summarized these "laws" of ecology: Nature is more complex than we know, and probably more complex than we can know. Everything has to go somewhere. There is no such thing as a free lunch. And, the most controversial "law," Nature knows best. Some commentators conclude that humans in industrial civilization have become like a cancer on the planet, killing the host organism.

Other visionary writers hypothesize that as a species *Homo sapiens* is evolving toward a planetary civilization that ". . . will come from the synergy of the collective experience and wisdom of the entire human family — the entire species. The world has become so interdependent that we must make it together, transcending differences of race, ethnicity, geography, religion, politics, and gender. It is the human species that must learn to live together as a civilized and mutually supportive community. To focus on the development of civility among the human species is not to inflate unduly the importance of humanity within the ecosystem of life on Earth; rather it is to recognize how dangerous the human race is to the viability of the Earth's ecosystem. Humanity must begin consciously to develop a planetary-scale, species-civilization that is able to live in a harmonious relationship with the rest of the web of life" (Elgin 1993, 14).

Philosopher Thomas Berry calls this project the "great work" of humans. Berry concludes that humans live in a "moment of grace" as we move into the 21st century which enables humanity to "be present to the planet in a mutually beneficial way" (Berry 1999). Others believe that Gaia herself, a conscious, self-organizing system, will regulate such an unruly species as *Homo sapiens*. The Gaia hypothesis has stimulated not only controversy among scientists but also has stimulated numerous religious, mystical, and feminist responses that indicate a yearning for integration with the "Earth Mother."[4]

The resurgence of interest in bioregionalism, restoration, locally based agriculture, and new initiatives to establish huge nature reserves in many nations indicates that supporters of the DEM will continue to be leaders in developing new agendas for the conservation movement as we move into the 21st century. For example, there is a growing number of alliances between conservation groups and tribal or First Nation peoples (a designation most commonly used in Canada) with the objective of assisting traditional cultures and protecting wilderness. From Ecuador to British Columbia, numerous NGOs continue to implement projects with tribal and First Nation peoples.[5]. . .

CONCLUSION

. . .

The continuing collective efforts to change human behavior to forestall global warming indicates that some attempts at effective political action in the face of a "global environmental crisis" are being made (Depledge 1999). Deep ecology perspectives and the DEM have contributed to the development of ecophilosophy, ecopsychology, and intellectual discussions of these issues over the past four decades, in particular by helping people articulate and develop their own ecosophy both individually and as part of a community (Glasser 1996). However, how the planet as an interdependent ecosystem, subject to increasing and generally negative human interventions, will fare in the 21st century remains an open question.

There are those who see hope for the future of *Homo sapiens* living in harmony with the rest of nature. They maintain that *Homo sapiens* have the capacity to develop into mature human beings both as individuals and collectively if humanity practices CPR on the earth — conservation, preservation, restoration (Brower 1995). Others, seeing that even small populations of *Homo sapiens* armed with simple but very effective technology of fire and stone arrowhead have, over the past 35,000 years, had immense impact on landscapes of whole continents (such as Australia), and conclude that at best *Homo sapiens* can be seen as an auto immune disease on the world system, on Gaia, or as a cancer on the world system that at this time has begun to destroy the vital organs of the planet. . . .

We are left to contemplate the question asked by John Muir, considered by many historians to be the founder of the American conservation movement, in 1875. Returning to the Central Valley of California, after spending another summer meditating in the Sierra Nevada, Muir wrote in his journal:

> Every sense is satisfied. For us there is no past, no future — we live only in the present and are full. No room for hungry hopes — none for regrets — none for exaltation — none for fears.
>
> Enlarge sphere of ideas. The mind invigorated by the acquisition of new ideas. Flexibility, elasticity.
>
> I often wonder what men will do with the mountains. That is, with their utilizable, destructable garments. Will he cut down all, and make ships and houses with the trees? If so, what will be the final and far upshot? Will human destruction, like those of Nature — fire, flood, and avalanche — work out a higher good, a finer beauty? Will a better civilization come, in accord with obvious nature, and all this wild beauty be set to human poetry? Another outpouring of lava or the coming of the glacial period could scarce wipe out the flowers and flowering shrubs more effectively than do the sheep. And what then is coming — what is the human part of the mountain's destiny? (Engberg and Wesling 1980, 162)

NOTES

1. The Selected Works of Arne Naess, edited by Harold Glasser and published by Kluwer Academic Publishers, will be available in early 2001. Information concerning the current status of this project is available from the Foundation for Deep Ecology, Building 1062, Ft. Cronkhite, Sausalito, CA 94965.
2. Naess frequently uses the term "free nature" to refer to landscapes that are relatively unmodified by human activities. Other supporters of the DEM frequently use the term "wild nature" to refer to landscapes that may contain human communities such as tribal societies, but are relatively untrammeled by industrial civilization, agriculture, roads, cattle, or sheep grazing. Henry David Thoreau expressed one of the central axioms of the modern conservation

movement when he wrote "in wildness is the preservation of the world."

Virtually all regions of the planet are currently impacted by planetary industrial civilization as witnessed by "global warming," the "hole in the ozone layer," and massive deforestation of all the primary forests on the planet (World Commission on Forests 1999).

3. Recent educational material on the deep, long-range ecology movement includes the 13-part radio series, "Deep Ecology for the 21st Century," available from New Dimensions Broadcasting Network, P.O. Box 569, Ukiah, CA 95482. Two videos highlight the work of Arne Naess in articulating deep ecology; "Crossing the Stones," produced by Norwegian Broadcasting Corporation in 1992 and available in the United States from Bullfrog Films, Oley, PA; and "The Call of the Mountain," produced by ReRun Produkties in 1997, distributed in the United States by the Foundation for Deep Ecology, Building 1062, Ft. Cronkhite, Sausalito, CA 94965.

4. When James Lovelock and Lynn Margulis presented the Gaia Hypothesis, it was embraced by the broader public before it was embraced by the community of scientists (Lovelock 1987). Surfing through Amazon.com, I found more than 120 books that use the word Gaia in titles published after 1988. These included "a guided meditation for vibrational medicine cards and Gaia matrix oracle," "from eros to Gaia," "Gaia and God: an ecofeminist theology of earth healing," "gay and Gaia, ethics, ecology, and the erotic," and "the goddess in the office: a personal energy guide for the spiritual warrior at work."

5. The agenda of the DEM now includes "rewilding," a term not yet found in the dictionaries. According to Michael Soulé, author of numerous books on biodiversity and president of The Wildlands Project, rewilding means "the process of protecting Nature by putting all the ecological pieces back together and restoring the landscape to its full glory and building a network of conservation reserves—cores, corridors, and mixed-use buffers—with enough land to allow wolves, jaguars, bears and other large

carnivores to move freely and reclaim a part of their former range" (Soulé and Noss 1998).

REFERENCES

Berry, Thomas. 1999. The Great Work: Our Way Into the Future. New York: Bell Tower.

Bragg, Elizabeth. 1995. "Towards Ecological Self: Individual and Shared Understandings of the Relationship Between Self and Environment." Dissertation. North Queensland: James Cook University.

Brechin, Steven R. and Willett Kempton. 1994. "Global Environmentalism: A Challenge to the Postmaterialism Thesis?" Social Science Quarterly 75 (2): 245–69.

Bright, Chris. 1998. Life Out of Bounds: Bioinvasions in a Borderless World. New York: W. W. Norton.

Brower, David. 1995. Let the Mountains Talk, Let the Rivers Run. San Francisco: Harper/Collins West.

Cafaro, Philip and Monish Verma. 1998. "For Indian Wilderness." Terra Nova (3): 53–58.

Catton, William R. Jr. 1980a. Overshoot: The Ecological Basis of Revolutionary Change. Urbana: University of Illinois Press.

Catton, William R. Jr. and Riley E. Dunlap. 1980b. "A New Ecological Paradigm for Post-Exuberant Sociology." American Behavioral Scientist 24 (1): 15–47.

Council on Environmental Quality (CEQ). 1980. The Global 2000 Report to the President: Entering the Twenty-First Century. Washington, D.C.: U.S. Government Printing Office.

Depledge, Joanna. 1999. "Coming of Age at Buenos Aires: The Climate Change Regime After Kyoto." Environment 41 (7) (September): 15.

Devall, Bill. 1988. Simple in Means, Rich in Ends: Practicing Deep Ecology. Salt Lake City, Utah: Peregrine Smith Books.

———. 1993. Living Richly in an Age of Limits. Salt Lake City: Peregrine Smith Books.

Drengson, Alan. 1980. "Shifting Paradigms: From the Technocratic to the Person-Planetary." Environmental Ethics 2 (3): 221–40.

Ehrlich, Paul and Anne Ehrlich. 1996. The Betrayal of Science and Reason: How Anti-environmental Rhetoric Threatens Our Future. Washington, D.C.: Island Press.

Elgin, Duane. 1993. Awakening Earth: Exploring the Evolution of Human Culture and Consciousness. New York: William Morrow.

Engberg, Robert and Donald Wesling, eds. 1980. To Yosemite and Beyond, Writings from the Years 1863 to 1875. Madison: University of Wisconsin Press.

Evernden, Neil. 1993. The Natural Alien, 2nd edition. Toronto: University of Toronto Press.

Fox, Warwick. 1989. "The Deep Ecology-Ecofeminism Debate and Its Parallels." Environmental Ethics 11 (1): 5–26.

———. 1990. Toward a Transpersonal Ecology. Boston: Shambhala.

Glasser, Harold. 1996. "Naess's Deep Ecology Approach and Environmental Policy." Inquiry 39: 157–87.

Guha, Ramachandra. 1989. "Radical American Environmentalism and Wilderness Preservation: A Third World Critique." Environmental Ethics 11 (1): 71–83.

Heller, Walter. 1973. "Economic Growth and Environmental Quality: Collision or Co-Existence," reprint. Morristown, N.J.: General Learning Press.

Hutchins, Robert M. 1976. "Environment and Civil Rights." The Center Magazine (January): 2–5.

LaChapelle, Dolores. 1988. Sacred Land, Sacred Sex: Rapture of the Deep. Durango, Colo.: Kivaki Press.

Lovelock, James. 1987. A New Look at Life on Earth. New York: Oxford University Press.

Macy, Joanne. 1991. World as Lover, World as Self. Berkeley, Calif.: Parallax Press.

Mander, Jerry. 1991. In the Absence of the Sacred: The Failure of Technology and the Survival of the Indian Nations. San Francisco: Sierra Club Books.

Mathews, Freya. 1991. The Ecological Self. Savage, Md.: Barnes and Noble.

Meadows, Donella, Dennis Meadows, and Jorgen Randers. 1992. Beyond the Limits: Confronting Global Collapse: Envisioning a Sustainable Future. Post Mills, Vt.: Chelsea Green.

Naess, Arne. 1973. "The Shallow and the Deep, Long-Range Ecology Movements: A Summary." Inquiry (16): 95–100.

———. 1989. Ecology, Community and Lifestyle, trans. and rev. by David Rothenberg. New York: Cambridge University Press.

———. 1995. "The Third World, Wilderness, and Deep Ecology." In George Sessions, ed. Deep Ecology for the 21st Century. Boston: Shambhala, 397–407.

Oelschlaeger, Max. 1994. Caring for Creation: An Ecumenical Approach to the Environmental Crisis. New Haven: Yale University Press.

Plumwood, Val. 1992. Gender and Ecology: Feminism and the Mastery of Nature. London: Routledge.

Rowell, Andrew. 1996. Green Backlash: Global Subversion of the Environmental Movement. New York: Routledge.

Seed, John, Joanne Macy, Pat Fleming, and Arne Naess. 1988. Thinking Like a Mountain: Towards a Council of All Beings. Santa Cruz, Calif.: New Society Publishers.

Sessions, George, ed. 1995a. Deep Ecology for the 21st Century: Readings on the Philosophy and Practice of the New Environmentalism. Boston: Shambhala.

———. 1995b. "Postmodernism and Environmental Justice: The Demise of the Ecology Movement?" The Trumpeter 12 (3): 150–154.

———. 1995c. "Political Correctness, Ecological Realities and the Future of the Ecology Movement." The Trumpeter 12 (4): 191–96.

Shepard, Paul. 1973. The Tender Carnivore and the Sacred Game. New York: Scribner's.

———. 1998. Coming Home to the Pleistocene. Washington, D.C.: Island Press.

Soulé, Michael and Reed Noss. 1998. "Rewilding and Biodiversity: Complementary Goals for Continental Conservation." Wild Earth 8 (3).

Taylor, Bron Raymond, ed. 1995. Ecological Resistance Movements: The Global Emergence of Radical and Popular Environmentalism. Ithaca, N.Y.: State University of New York Press.

United Nations Environment Programme. Global Environment Outlook. 1997. New York: Oxford University Press.

Wilson, Edward O. 1992. The Diversity of Life. Cambridge, Mass.: Harvard University Press.

Wood, Harold W., Jr. 1985. "The United Nations World Charter for Nature: The Developing Nations' Initiative to Establish Protections for the Environment." Ecology Law Quarterly 12: 977–96.

DISCUSSION TOPICS

1. What role do you see for DEM in addressing Third World countries' concerns? Do you agree with Devall's response to the Third World concerns raised?

2. Have you developed an ecosophy? If so, what are some of its features? If not, how might you begin one? Elaborate on your ideas.

3. What do you believe the DEM has done particularly well as a supporter of the environmental movement? What recommendations might you make to the DEM on how to become more effective in supporting environmental perspectives?

CLASS EXERCISES

1. Small Group Discussions
   a. How does the land ethic differ from the predominant ethics of Western society?
   b. How do the ecocentric ethics presented in this chapter differ from the perceptions held by Native American groups with which you are familiar?
   c. What sort of ecocentric ethic, if any, might be applicable in food-poor countries such as Bangladesh or countries found in sub-Saharan Africa?
   d. To what degree do Leopold, Callicott, and Rolston share perspectives with deep ecology?
   e. What morally relevant features may be missing from Leopold's land ethic or the deep ecology perspective presented by Devall? Explain.
   f. All things considered, how might you improve Leopold's statement of the land ethic or Devall's vision of deep ecology?

2. Class Debate

   A plan has been proposed to reintroduce peregrine falcons to a 308,000-hectare national forest in which they formerly lived. However, the horned lark, a common prey species for the peregrine, has been at a low population in that forest for several years. It is estimated that while the peregrine would readily survive on alternate prey species, there is about a ten percent risk that peregrines could drive the lark population to extinction.

   Using the techniques outlined in the appendix, debate the merits of this plan on the basis of ecocentric arguments only. Thus, anthropocentric arguments such as economics or impacts on current or future humans are excluded, as are arguments based on concern for individual animals. Arguments based on intrinsic or inherent values in nature are acceptable. Which arguments did each side use? Which were most effective?

FOR FURTHER READING

Armstrong-Buck, Susan. "What Process Philosophy Can Contribute to the Land Ethic and Deep Ecology." *Trumpeter* 8 (1991): 29–34. A summary of Callicott's and Rolston's positions on value, as well as a brief discussion of self in deep ecology from a process perspective.

Attfield, Robin. "Methods of Ecological Ethics." *Metaphilosophy* 14 (1983): 195–208. A criticism of the position that one should ascribe value to nature, as advocated by John Rodman and J. Baird Callicott.

Callicott, J. Baird. "Non-Anthropocentric Value Theory and Environmental Ethics." *American Philosophical Quarterly* 21 (1984): 299–309. A thoughtful and critical review of various nonanthropocentric value theories in environmental ethics.

———. "The Conceptual Foundations of the Land Ethic." *Companion to a Sand County Almanac: Interpretive and Critical Essays.* Madison: University of Wisconsin Press, 1987. A thoughtful evaluation of the ideas underlying Aldo Leopold's land ethic.

———. "Do Deconstructive Ecology and Sociobiology Undermine Leopold's Land Ethic?" *Environmental Ethics* 18 (1996): 353–72. Callicott argues that, if updated and revised, Leopold's land ethic is still viable in light of deconstructive developments in ecology.

———. *Beyond the Land Ethic: More Essays in Environmental Philosophy.* Albany: State University of New York Press, 1999. Covers a wide variety of topics central to the field of environmental ethics from an ecocentric perspective.

Devall, Bill. *Simple in Means, Rich in Ends: Practicing Deep Ecology.* Salt Lake City: Peregrine Smith Books, 1988. The author discusses practicing deep ecology at all levels, whether through inner clarification and insight, development of intellectual arguments to respect and protect nature, or political action.

————. *Living Richly in an Age of Limits.* Salt Lake City: Peregrine Smith Books, 1993.

Devall, William, and George Sessions. *Deep Ecology: Living as if Nature Mattered.* Salt Lake City: Gibbs M. Smith, 1985. A book designed to help raise ecological consciousness. Calls for a rejection of most current values of Western society in favor of biospheric egalitarianism. Favors low energy, low technology, and small decentralized communities.

Erman, Don C., and Edwin P. Pister. "Ethics and the Environmental Biologist." *Fisheries* 14, 2 (1989): 4–7. Addresses the responsibilities of resource managers and environmental biologists.

Ferré, Frederick. "Obstacles on the Path to Organismic Ethics." *Environmental Ethics* 11 (1989): 231–41. Advocates an organismic viewpoint over the more traditional mechanistic consciousness. Addresses some of the criticisms of organicism and proposes a form of personalistic organicism as the foundation for an environmental ethic.

Foreman, Dave. "Putting the Earth First," in *Confessions of an Eco-Warrior,* Dave Foreman. New York: Harmony Books, 1991. Environmental ethics through the eyes of a radical, and thoughtful, environmentalist.

Fox, Warwick. *Toward a Transpersonal Ecology: Developing New Foundations for Environmentalism.* Boston: Shambhala, 1990. Provides an excellent foundation for deep ecology. The author seeks to interest others in ecophilosophical issues and in the kinds of lifestyles and political actions that flow from the adoption of an ecocentric outlook.

French, William C. "Against Biospherical Egalitarianism." *Environmental Ethics* 17 (1995): 39–57. Argues against the notion of species equality and proposes that species ranking is best viewed as a justified articulation of vulnerability and need, rooted in their relative range of capacities and interests.

Golley, Frank B. "Deep Ecology from the Perspective of Environmental Science." *Environmental Ethics* 9 (1987): 45–55. Concludes that two norms of deep ecology — self-realization and biocentric equality — can be compatibly interpreted through the perspective of scientific ecology.

Guha, Ramachandra. "Radical American Environmentalism and Wilderness Preservation: A Third World Critique." *Environmental Ethics* 11 (1989): 71–83. A critical assessment of deep ecology as a solution for Third World environmental issues.

Hadsell, Heidi. "Environmental Ethics and Health/Wholeness." *Council of Societies for the Study of Religion Bulletin* 24 (1995): 67–71. Assesses the relationship of environmental health to human health.

Johnson, Lawrence E. "Toward the Moral Considerability of Species and Ecosystems." *Environmental Ethics* 14 (1992): 145–57. Argues that species and ecosystems are living entities with morally significant interests in their own right, and that it is possible to individuate such entities. Thus, species and ecosystems can meaningfully be said to have moral standing.

Lauer, D. W. "Arne Naess on Deep Ecology and Ethics." *Journal of Value Inquiry* 36 (2002): 109–15. Results of Lauer's interview of Naess in 1999.

Leopold, Aldo. "Standards of Conservation." *Conservation Biology* 4, 3 (1990): 227–32.

Light, Andrew, and David Rothenberg. "Arne Naess's Environmental Thought." *Inquiry* 39 (1996). A special issue on Arne Naess, with a wide variety of contributors.

List, Peter. *Radical Environmentalism: Philosophy and Tactics.* Belmont, Calif.: Wadsworth, 1993. A selection of papers demonstrating how radical ideas can ground radical action. Good selection on civil disobedience. Also addresses the relative merits of ecosabotage.

Livingston, John A. "Moral Concern and the Ecosphere." *Alternatives* 12 (1985): 3–9. A review of several philosophies that address the human:nature relationship.

MacCleery, Douglas W. "Aldo Leopold's Land Ethic: Is It Only Half a Loaf?" *Journal of Forestry* 98, 10 (2002): 5–7. Addresses the role of consumption in environmental ethics.

Marietta, Don E., Jr. *For People and the Planet.* Philadelphia: Temple University Press, 1995. The author describes changes in Western society indicating movement away from the concept of humans as separate from nature and toward a more holistic model of environmental ethics in which humans are perceived as a part of nature. Thoughtfully presented.

Martin, Michael. "Ecosabotage and Civil Disobedience." *Environmental Ethics* 12 (1990): 291–310. Argues that ecosabotage is not a form of civil disobedience but that both of these phenomena are special cases of a more general notion of conscientious wrongdoing. Evaluates two possible justifications of ecosabotage and concludes that utilitarian arguments could justify some forms of ecosabotage.

McIntosh, Robert P. "The Myth of Community as Organism." *Perspectives in Biology and Medicine* 41, 3 (1998): 426–39. Argues that ecological evidence does not support the belief that nature has the properties of a super-organism.

Merchant, Carolyn. *Radical Ecology: The Search for a Livable World.* New York: Routledge, Chapman & Hall, 1992. Merchant advocates new social, economic, scientific, and spiritual approaches to transform human relationships with nature.

Moline, Jon N. "Aldo Leopold and the Moral Community." *Environmental Ethics* 8 (1986): 47–58. Moline provides an interpretation of Leopold that avoids the problems of extreme holism and extreme individualism.

Naess, Arne. "A Defence of the Deep Ecology Movement." *Environmental Ethics* 6 (1984): 265–70. Responds to Watson's criticisms that a deep ecology perspective requires that humans be set apart from nature. Rather, deep ecologists insist that life on earth has intrinsic value and that human behavior must change drastically.

———. "The Deep Ecological Movement: Some Philosophical Aspects. *Philosophical Inquiry* 8, 1–2 (1987): 10–13. A thoughtful description and exposition of the deep ecology movement.

———. *Ecology, Community and Lifestyle: Outline of an Ecosophy.* Cambridge: Cambridge University Press, 1989. Includes Naess's own system of reasoning that led to his personal philosophy, Ecosophy T. Naess encourages readers to develop their own personal systems rather than having one standard system.

Nash, Roderick F. *The Rights of Nature: A History of Environmental Ethics.* Madison: University of Wisconsin Press, 1989. Provides an in-depth history of the idea that ethical standing should include the natural world.

———. *American Environmentalism: Readings in Conservation History,* 3rd ed. New York: McGraw-Hill, 1990. An annotated collection of many of the most pertinent writings in the development of environmental philosophy, including several by biocentric thinkers.

Ouderkirk, Wayne, and Mim Hill, eds. *Land, Value, Community: Callicott and Environmental Philosophy.* Albany: State University of New York Press, 2002. An anthology devoted to the work of J. Baird Callicott and the land ethic.

Rodman, John. "Four Forms of Ecological Consciousness Reconsidered: Ecological Sensibility," in *Ethics and the Environment,* eds. D. Scherer and T. Attig. Englewood Cliffs, N.J.: Prentice-Hall, 1983. A classic paper combining elements of Leopold's land ethic and deep ecology.

Rolston, Holmes, III. *Philosophy Gone Wild: Essays in Environmental Ethics.* Buffalo, N.Y.: Prometheus Books, 1986. A collection of fifteen essays in which a leading thinker in the field of environmental ethics addresses the problems of defining and justifying the values found in nature and of defining an ecocentric ethic.

———. *Environmental Ethics: Duties to and Values in the Natural World.* Philadelphia: Temple University Press, 1987. Rolston presents a philosophy of nature encompassing a theory of objective natural value — a view of how humans ought to fit into the natural world. He offers recommendations for environmental decision making.

———. "In Defense of Ecosystems." *Garden (New York Botanical Garden)* 12 (1988): 2–5, 32. A nontechnical introduction to ecosystems and the basis for valuing them and to ecocentric ethics.

———. "Value in Nature and the Nature of Value," in *Philosophy and the Natural Environment,* eds. R. Attfield and A. Belsey. Royal Institute of Philosophy Supplement 36 (1994): 13–30. Cambridge: Cambridge University Press. Looks at the value of humans, other creatures, and the natural world.

———. "Feeding People Versus Saving Nature," in *World Hunger and Morality,* 2nd ed., eds. W. Aiken and H. LaFollette, pp. 248–67. Englewood Cliffs, N.J.: Prentice-Hall, 1996. Addresses caring for the environment and caring for humans when the environment and humans come in conflict.

Rolston, Holmes, III, and James Coufall. "A Forest Ethic and Multivalue Forest Management." *Journal of Forestry* 89 (1991): 35–40. The integrity of forests and of foresters are bound together.

Salleh, Ariel. "Class, Race, and Gender Discourse in the Ecofeminism/Deep Ecology Debate." *Environmental Ethics* 15 (1993): 225–44. Argues that deep ecology is constrained by political attitudes meaningful to white, male, middle-class professionals whose thought is not grounded in the labor of daily maintenance and survival.

Scarce, R. *Eco-warriors.* Chicago: Noble Press, 1990. An overview of radical environmentalism, including some of the philosophical foundations, major players, and some of the practices.

Sessions, George. "The Deep Ecological Movement: A Review." *Environmental Review* 11 (1987): 105–25. A history of the deep ecology movement by the major bibliographer of the movement.

Stevenson, Brian K. "Ecocentrism and Ecological Modeling." *Environmental Ethics* 16 (1994): 71–88. Stevenson maintains that the assumption that humanity and nonhuman nature are essentially integrated into communal arrangements is crucial to ecocentric theories. He believes this claim generally is false and, even if it were true, would lead to some implausible moral considerations.

Sylvan, Richard. "A Critique of Deep Ecology." *Radical Philosophy* 40 (1985): 2–12, 41. Criticizes deep ecology as too vague and inconsistent, in part based on its deemphasis of rational argument.

Taylor, Bron Raymond, ed. *Ecological Resistance Movements: The Global Emergence of Radical and Popular Environmentalism.* Albany: State University of New York Press, 1995. Provides a rich overview of many resistance movements, primarily organized on a regional basis: the Americas, Asia and the Pacific, Africa, and Europe.

Varner, Gary E. "A Critique of Environmental Holism," in *In Nature's Interests? Interests, Animal Rights, and Environmental Ethics,* Gary Varner, pp. 10–25. New York: Oxford University Press, 1998. Assesses some of the strengths and weaknesses of ecocentrism.

Wildlife Society Bulletin 26, 4 (1998): 695–766. Includes a series of twelve articles on Aldo Leopold and his book *A Sand County Almanac.*

Zimmerman, Michael E. "Feminism, Deep Ecology and Environmental Ethics." *Environmental Ethics* 9 (1987): 21–44. Evaluates the ecofeminist criticism that patriarchy has played a crucial role in shaping the attitudes of Western society toward nature for both reform environmentalism and deep ecology.

———. "Rethinking the Heidegger-Deep Ecology Relationship." *Environmental Ethics* 15 (1993): 195–224. Despite some similarities, Heidegger's thought is generally incompatible with deep ecology, partly because deep ecologists generally support a "progressive" idea of human evolution.

———. "The Threat of Ecofascism." *Social Theory and Practice* 21, 2 (1995): 207–38. A critical review of some ecocentric perspectives.

CHAPTER NINE
Ecofeminism

One need never be lonely mid beautiful trees.

—Elizabeth Cady Stanton[1]
*Eighty Years and More:
Reminiscences 1815–1897,* p. 325

In this chapter we define *ecofeminism,* delineate its challenge to other forms of environmental ethics, and identify several central issues within ecofeminism.

Exactly where the term "ecofeminism" originated is disputed, but it first began to appear in the mid-1970s.[2] Since then there have been many ecofeminist political events, conferences, and publications. Although they adopt various approaches, ecofeminists agree that the dominance of nature is linked in inescapable ways with the dominance of women and that any analysis that comes to terms with the subordination of one must come to terms with the subordination of the other.

Ecofeminism can be considered a subsidiary branch of feminism or as the form that feminism as a whole should take. One fundamental purpose of feminist theory is to analyze the concept of gender in its many forms.[3] Feminism is a dynamic, broad-based philosophic perspective with a number of distinct theoretical approaches.[4]

As Karen Warren points out in her analysis of the "logic of domination" in her essay, "Quilting Ecofeminist Philosophies," the subordination of one group by another generally requires a conceptual dichotomy in which the first group is seen not only as different but as inferior to the other. In rejecting such value-laden, dualistic patterns of thinking, ecofeminism is transformational rather than merely reformist. Ecofeminists believe that social and political institutions must be radically restructured to eliminate such pernicious dualisms as the superior male versus the inferior female, or superior human

---

[1]Elizabeth Cady Stanton, together with her colleague and friend Susan B. Anthony, was a leader in the women's rights movement.

[2]Greta Gaard, *Ecological Politics: Ecofeminists and the Greens* (Philadelphia: Temple University Press, 1998) pp. 12–15.

[3]Jane Flax, "Postmodern and Gender Relations in Feminist Theory," *Signs* 12 (1987): 621–43.

[4]Feminism can be differentiated into such categories as Marxist, socialist, radical, liberal, postmodern, and spiritual feminism. For essays illustrating the first four types, see Alison M. Jaggar and Paula S. Rothenberg, eds., *Feminist Frameworks: Alternative Theoretical Accounts of the Relations between Women and Men* (New York: McGraw-Hill, 1993). For a treatment of postmodern feminism as well as psychoanalytic feminism, and existentialist feminism, see Rosemarie Tong, *Feminist Thought: A More Comprehensive Introduction,* 2nd edition (Boulder, Colo.: Westview Press, 1998). *Hypatia* 3, 3 (1989) is a special issue on French feminist philosophy, edited by Nancy Fraser and Sandra Bartky.

beings versus the rest of nature. Ecofeminism is nonhierarchical, egalitarian, and nonviolent.

WHY MUST ENVIRONMENTAL ETHICS BE FEMINIST?

Patriarchy—the systematic, institutional dominance of women by men—has characterized most historical societies. It is important to note, however, that *patriarchy* and *male* are not synonymous. Female patriarchs can be just as domineering as males. Like their male counterparts, they seek control over others, over themselves, and over nature.[5] Patriarchy characterizes Western science and Western ethics, including, to some extent, environmental ethics.[6] Feminists point out that contemporary science is still often practiced from a "masculine," reductivist, and domineering attitude toward nature as a resource for human beings.[7] Western ethics has often insisted on the supreme value of human "reason," as exclusive of sensation, feeling, intuition, and relatedness.

Patriarchy has not yet been significantly affected by the feminist movement, as indicated by the information collected during and since the United Nations Decade for Women (1975–1985).[8] Given the persistence of patriarchy, any theory of

environmental ethics that ignores the linking of women and nature is, as Warren states, historically inaccurate, as well as conceptually and morally inadequate.

However, analyses of the relations between women and their environments in the developing world indicate that there are multiple understandings of gender evident among independent local cultures. A simple opposition between women/nature on the one hand and global patriarchal capitalism on the other hand is inadequate to encompass this variation.[9]

THE CAUSES OF PATRIARCHY

One of the important debates among ecofeminist theorists concerns the origins of patriarchy and the concomitant attempts to dominate women and nature. One view, associated with the archaeological research of Marija Gimbutas (1921–1994),[10] is that such domination first manifested itself around 4500 B.C.E.[11] with the invasion of Old Europe (geographically from the Atlantic Ocean to the Dnieper River, 7000 to 3500 B.C.E.) by cattle-herding Indo-European tribes, which she refers to as the Kurgan culture.[12] These tribes, with domesticated horses and lethal weapons, emerged in the Volga River basin of south Russia. By the middle of the fifth millennium, even cultures west of the Black Sea had become patriarchal.

---

[5]Marion Woodman and Elinor Dickson, *Dancing in the Flames: The Dark Goddess in the Transformation of Consciousness* (Boston: Shambhala, 1996), p. 4.

[6]Ariel Kay Salleh, "Deeper than Deep Ecology: The Ecofeminist Connection," *Environmental Ethics* 6 (1984): 339–45. See also Marti Kheel, "From Heroic to Holistic Ethics: The Ecofeminist Challenge," in *Ecofeminism: Women, Animals, Nature*, Greta Gaard, ed. (Philadelphia: Temple University Press, 1993).

[7]Evelyn Fox Keller, *Reflections on Gender and Science* (New Haven, Conn.: Yale University Press, 1985), 4, 5, 6, and 9.

[8]Despite the increasing participation of women in society, the status of women is still universally regarded as secondary to that of men. Women experience high illiteracy rates, low educational and economic levels, and devaluation of their productive and reproductive roles. The major media in every country continue to stereotype women. For a discussion, see Arvonne S. Fraser, *The U.N. Decade for Women: Documents and Dialogue* (Boulder, Colo.: Westview Press, 1987), pp. 159–75; Rebecca J. Cook, ed., *Human Rights of Women: National and International Perspectives* (Philadelphia: University of Pennsylvania Press, 1994); Robert Engelman, Brian Halweil, and Danielle Nierenberg, "Rethinking Population, Improving Lives," in *State of the World 2002*, The Worldwatch Institute (New York: Norton, 2002), p. 133.

[9]See for example Deirdre McKay, "Gender and Ecology: Alternative Interpretations from the Southeast Asian Periphery," Northwest Regional Consortium for Southeast Asian Studies, 1994; A. Tsing, *In the Realm of the Diamond Queen: Marginality in an Out-of-the-Way Place* (Princeton, N.J.: Princeton University Press, 1993).

[10]Marija Gimbutas authored a number of books, including *Gods and Goddesses of Old Europe* (Berkeley: University of California, 1974) and *The Civilization of the Goddess* (New York: HarperCollins, 1989).

[11] "B.C.E." (Before the Common Era) and "C.E." (the Common Era) are increasingly used by both Christian and non-Christian scholars (although not by Gimbutas herself) to avoid dating world history according to an exclusively Christian framework.

[12]*Kurgan* means "barrow" in Russian. These peoples buried their dead in round barrows that covered the mortuary houses of important males. See Gimbutas, *The Language of the Goddess*, (New York: HarperCollins, 1989) p. xx.

According to Gimbutas, the earlier Old European cultures were goddess-centered "gylanies,"[13] in which women were heads of clans or queen-priestesses. These peaceful, earth-centered, nonpatriarchal, and nonmatriarchal social systems were destroyed by the invasions of the Kurgan people, which changed them from gylanic to androcratic and from matrilineal to patrilineal.[14]

Some ecofeminists, however, reject such a theory as a "Neolithic mystique" that is politically naive and irrelevant to the current situation.[15] Theorists such as Carolyn Merchant concentrate on the analysis of more recent historical periods and conclude that the concepts of nature and women are more recent social constructions.[16] Still others, such as the historian Gilda Lerner, locate the origins of patriarchy in the division of labor necessitated by child bearing and lactation.[17]

ARE WOMEN CLOSER TO NATURE THAN MEN?

One of the major differences among ecofeminist thinkers is found in their view of the relationship of women to nature. Theorists such as Karen Warren reject biologically based gender roles. Warren argues that the claim of women being closer to nature than men ignores the role of cultural conditioning over the centuries, in which women have been "lumped together" with nature, children, and indigenous peoples as more "primitive" and simpler than men. Thus once this cultural conditioning is changed, no special relationship between women and nature will remain.

Thinkers such as Charlene Spretnak, however, maintain that women's physical experiences of menstruation, pregnancy, birthgiving, and lactation do provide women with a biologically based, special closeness to natural processes, a closeness which is to be recognized and honored, as she espouses in her essay in this chapter, "States of Grace."[18]

The relationship of women to nonhuman animals is receiving new attention. The prominence of women in primatology,[19] their historical affinity with nonhuman animals, and the sense of emotional bonding with nonhuman animals in the work of women animal rights theorists all attest to this relationship. Carol Adams argues that ecofeminists should be vegetarians.[20] An ethic that requires a fundamental respect for nonhuman life-forms, grounded in an emotional and spiritual conversation with them rather than in the rationalist traditions exemplified by Tom Regan and Peter Singer, may well be the basis for a feminist ethic for the treatment of animals.[21]

IS THE EARTH OUR MOTHER?

Disagreements similar to those mentioned above also surround the sex typing of the planet.[22] Some thinkers are concerned that personifying the earth as female nurturer will tend to solidify oppressive gender stereotypes; these thinkers also argue that if the

[13]Gimbutas adopts Riana Eisler's term *gylany* for the social structure in which the sexes had equal status. See Riana Eisler, *The Chalice and the Blade: Our History Our Future* (San Francisco: Harper & Row, 1987), pp. 105–6. Gimbutas marshals archeological-mythical evidence for her claim that the paleolithic people of Old Europe (40,000 to 22,000 B.C.E.) worshiped nature and its mysteries in various forms of the "Great Goddess."

[14]*Matrilineal* and *patrilineal* refer to how power and property are inherited, through the female and male line, respectively.

[15]Janet Biehl, *Rethinking Ecofeminist Politics* (Boston: South End Press, 1991), pp. 29–56.

[16]Carolyn Merchant, *The Death of Nature: Women, Ecology, and the Scientific Revolution* (San Francisco: Harper & Row, 1989), especially ch. 1.

[17]Lerner states that the feminist critique of patriarchy, together with changes in women's reproductive lives, health, and education, are helping to build a truly human world, free of dominance and hierarchy. See her book, *The Creation of Patriarchy* (New York: Oxford University Press, 1986).

[18]Starhawk develops an earth-based religion that builds on these womanly experiences in *The Spiral Dance: Rebirth of the Ancient Religion of the Goddess* (San Francisco: Harper & Row, 1979).

[19]Marlene Zuk, "Feminism and the Study of Animal Behavior," *Bioscience* 43, no. 11 (December 1993): 774–78.

[20]Carol Adams, "Ecofeminism and the Eating of Animals," *Hypatia* 6.1 (1991): 125–45.

[21]See Josephine Donovan, "Animal Rights and Feminist Theory," in *Ecofeminism: Women, Animals, Nature*, Greta Gaard, ed. (Philadelphia: Temple University Press, 1993) for an excellent discussion of these points.

[22]Patrick Murphy, "Sex-Typing the Planet," *Environmental Ethics* 10 (1988): 155–68.

earth is identified as the mother of human beings, the powerful human projections involved in "mother" will tend to obscure the independence and rich diversity of nonhuman life. These theorists recommend that the same sentiments of respect and love for our earth home can and should be expressed in gender-neutral symbolism.

However, many ecofeminists value the numinous symbol of earth mother.[23] In "Introduction to *Ecofeminism*," Vandana Shiva and Maria Mies argue that Third World women have a direct awareness of Mother Earth as life sustainer.

CONNECTIONS BETWEEN THEORY AND PRACTICE

Ecofeminism is a call to thoughtful integration of what has been separated: nature and culture, mind and body, male and female, reason and feeling, theory and practice. Ecofeminists affirm the intimate relationship of theory and practice. In her essay, Spretnak stresses the importance of practice and commends the creation of equitable and ecologically sound lifestyles and communities. The two-

year long "treesit" by Julia "Butterfly" Hill exemplifies the ecofeminist commitment to practicing what one preaches. In the selection from *The Legacy of Luna* Hill describes her spiritually based nonviolent action on behalf of an ancient redwood tree.

IMPORTANCE OF THE INDIVIDUAL

Ecofeminist theorists stress the importance of individuals and their relationships, as well as the appreciation of genuine differences between peoples, organisms, and individual human beings. Marti Kheel has pointed out that some writers have defended hunting as an opportunity for their own merging with nature and thereby overlook the significance of the loss of life of individual animals.[24] In this respect the insights of ecofeminism parallel those of individualism, in which the standpoint of the individual animal is honored. In her essay, Karen Warren calls attention to the importance for ecofeminism of the relationships between particular people, as well as the affirmation of differences both between individual people and between groups of humans and nonhumans.

---

[23]See, for example, Julia Scofield Russell, "The Evolution of an Ecofeminist" as well as other essays in *Reweaving the World: The Emergence of Ecofeminism*. Irene Diamond and Gloria Feman Orenstein, eds. (San Francisco: Sierra Club Books, 1990). See also L. Teal Willoughby, "Ecofeminist Consciousness and the Transforming Power of Symbols" in *Ecofeminism and the Sacred*. Carol J. Adams, ed. (New York: Continuum, 1993).

[24]Marti Kheel, "Ecofeminism and Deep Ecology: Reflections on Identity and Difference," in *Reweaving the World: The Emergence of Ecofeminism*, Irene Diamond and Gloria Feman Orenstein, eds. (San Francisco: Sierra Club Books, 1990), pp. 128–37. For a brief critique of deep ecology's inclusive self, see Susan Armstrong-Buck, "What Process Philosophy Can Contribute to the Land Ethic and Deep Ecology," *Trumpeter* 8 (1991): 29–35.

Quilting Ecofeminist Philosophy

Karen J. Warren

Karen J. Warren is a professor of philosophy at Macalester College in St. Paul, Minnesota. She has published extensively on feminism, environmental ethics, critical thinking, and applied ethics. Her most recent book is Ecofeminist Philosophy *(2000), from which this selection is taken. Warren analyzes the "logic of domination" and indicates how an exaggerated emphasis on reason and rationality has functioned historically to sanction the inferiority of women and nature. Warren is careful to distinguish the roles of women and nature in primal (aboriginal) versus nonprimal societies, as well as the roles of dominant men versus the roles of subordinate men.*

Five basic claims characterize the version of ecofeminist philosophy I am defending in this book: (1) There are important interconnections among the unjustified dominations of women, other human Others [inferiorized groups], and nonhuman nature; (2) understanding the nature of these interconnections is important to an adequate understanding of and solutions to these unjustified dominations; (3) feminist philosophy should include ecofeminist insights into women–other human Others–nature interconnections; (4) solutions to gender issues should include ecofeminist insights into women–other human Others–nature connections; and (5) solutions to environmental problems should include ecofeminist insights into women–other human Others–nature interconnections.

The version of ecofeminist philosophy I defend grows out of and is responsive to the intersection of three overlapping areas of concern: feminism (and all the issues feminism raises concerning women and other human Others); nature (the natural environment), science (especially scientific ecology), development, and technology; and local or indigenous perspectives.[1] It might be visualized as in Figure 1. This Venn diagram provides a broad-stroke picture of the kinds of overlapping factors that are important as input and solution to interconnecting women–other

human Others–nature issues. It does so by showing that any policies or practices that fall outside the overlapping three areas demarcated by the asterisk will be prima facie ("other things being equal") inadequate or unacceptable from the ecofeminist philosophical perspective I am defending.

A casual perusal of this diagram serves as a visual suggestion of the sorts of policies and practices that will be prima facie unacceptable from the ecofeminist philosophical perspective I am defending. For example, policies or practices that destroy the current ability of rural women in India to maintain domestic economies by replacing indigenous forests with monoculture eucalyptus plantations falls outside the asterisk area: They fail to sufficiently accommodate the concerns of feminist or local Indian women who, as managers of domestic economies, rely on indigenous forests for survival. Or, any First World development and technology projects imposed on Third World communities that make it difficult for local communities to maintain sustainable agricultural practices will fall outside the asterisk area: They fail to sufficiently include local perspectives and expertise in the decision-making or to accommodate feminist and local concerns about the continued survival of those communities. Or, any policy or practice which causes or permits clear-cutting in the Amazonian rainforest will fall outside the asterisk area: It fails to sufficiently accommodate ecological and environmental concerns about the destruction of the rainforest ecosystem.

The qualification "prima facie" here is important. Appeal to the diagram suggests that patriarchal domination, opposed in principle by any feminism, will fall outside the asterisk area and, thus, will not be supported by ecofeminist philosophy. But sometimes the present-day socioeconomic realities of patriarchal domination are such that a decision one makes to ensure the survival of women (which has ecofeminist support) may also keep intact patriarchal structures (which, in principle, does not have ecofeminist support). For example, a decision to provide women with the means to maintain domestic economies may ensure the survival of women and women-headed households while also contributing to the survival of domestic economies, which are themselves patriarchal and exploitative of the

FIGURE 1

A VISUALIZATION OF ECOFEMINIST PHILOSOPHY

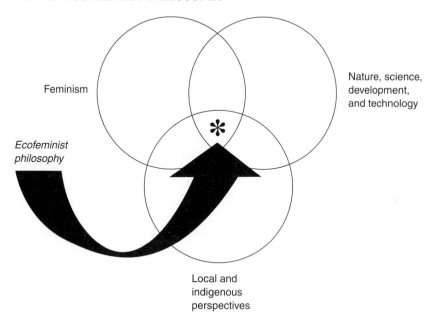

labor of women. Other things are *not* equal in such a case.

What should one do in such cases? Given the current socioeconomic realities of patriarchy, often the best a person currently can do is not a perfect or ideal solution. Often other things simply are *not* equal. Within contemporary patriarchal structures, there will be very real trade-offs between values one holds dear. For example, one may actively lobby for mass transit even though one currently drives a car to work. One may support organic farming even though one cannot currently afford organically raised foods. One may argue for decreased levels of energy consumption by North Americans even though one currently enjoys the benefits of airconditioned buildings. One may argue against the replacement of indigenous forests by eucalyptus plantations on the grounds that the eucalyptus plantations exacerbate the daily difficulties women in the Southern Hemisphere face in managing domestic economies, even though those domestic economies are themselves patriarchal.

My point is this: One simply cannot make ecologically perfect decisions or lead an ecologically perfect lifestyle within current institutional structures characterized by unequal distributions of wealth, consumption of energy, and gendered divisions of labor. When institutional structures themselves are unjust, it is often difficult to make truly just decisions within them. . . . Sometimes, the best one can do in the prefeminist present is to support policies and practices that ensure that present-day women are able to maintain a daily livelihood, while also challenging the very structures that keep intact the unjustified domination of women by men. The diagram of ecofeminist philosophy (above) shows *what to aim for* in one's ecofeminist philosophical understanding of and solutions to a gender or an environmental issue.

THE IMPORTANCE OF OPPRESSIVE CONCEPTUAL FRAMEWORKS

I have characterized ecofeminist philosophy as being concerned with *conceptual analysis* and *argumentative proof* about women–other human Others–nature interconnections. There is no more basic place to start to understand and appreciate this dimension of ecofeminist philosophy than with an analysis of the "conceptual frameworks" that have functioned historically to maintain, perpetuate, and "justify" the dominations of women, other subordinated humans, and nonhuman nature.

A *conceptual framework* is a set of basic beliefs, values, attitudes, and assumptions which shape and reflect how one views oneself and one's world. A conceptual framework functions as a socially constructed *lens* through which one perceives reality. It is affected and shaped by such factors as sex-gender, race/ethnicity, class, age, affectional orientation, marital status, religion, nationality, colonial influences, and culture.

Some conceptual frameworks are *oppressive*. An oppressive conceptual framework is one that functions to explain, maintain, and "justify" relationships of unjustified domination and subordination. When an oppressive conceptual framework is *patriarchal*, it functions to justify the subordination of women by men.

There are five common features of an oppressive conceptual framework. First, an oppressive conceptual framework involves *value-hierarchical thinking*, that is, "Up-Down" thinking, which attributes greater value to that which is higher, or Up, than to that which is lower, or Down. It may put men Up and women Down, whites Up and people of color Down, culture Up and nature Down, minds Up and bodies Down. By attributing greater value to that which is higher, the Up-Down organization of reality serves to legitimate inequality "when, in fact, prior to the metaphor of Up-Down one would have said only that there existed diversity."[2]

Second, an oppressive conceptual framework encourages *oppositional value dualisms*, that is, disjunctive pairs in which the disjuncts are seen as exclusive (rather than inclusive) and oppositional (rather than complementary) and that places higher value (status, prestige) on one disjunct than the other. Examples include value dualisms that give higher status to that which has historically been identified as "male," "white," "rational," and "culture" than to that which has historically been identified as "female," "black," "emotional," and "nature" (or "natural"). According to these value dualisms, it

is better to be male, white, or rational, than female, black, or emotional.

The third characteristic of an oppressive conceptual framework is that *power* is conceived (and exercised) as "power-over" power. There are many types of power. . . . In oppressive systems, power typically is conceived and exercised as power of Ups over Downs. The power of parents over their young children, of judges over defendants, of tyrants over citizens, of rapists over their victims are all examples of power-over. Some of these are justified cases of power-over power; others are not. When power-over power serves to reinforce the power of Ups as Ups in ways that keep Downs unjustifiably subordinated (which not all cases of power-over do), such conceptions and practices of power are unjustified.

The fourth characteristic of an oppressive conceptual framework is that it creates, maintains, or perpetuates a conception and practice of *privilege* as belonging to Ups and not to Downs. The privileges of driving a car, taking out a home equity loan, living in high-income housing areas, or attending a college of one's choice should belong to those who qualify. Sometimes small privileges are given to Downs (e.g., to house slaves or middle-class housewives) to keep them from challenging the power and privilege of Ups.[3] When the privilege of Ups functions to keep intact dominant-subordinate Up-Down relationships which systematically advantage Ups over Downs, they are part of an oppressive conceptual framework and set of practices.

The fifth and philosophically most important characteristic of an oppressive conceptual framework is that it sanctions a *logic of domination*, that is, a logical structure of argumentation that "justifies" domination and subordination. A logic of domination assumes that superiority justifies subordination. A logic of domination is offered as the moral stamp of approval for subordination, since, if accepted, it provides a justification for keeping Downs down. Typically this justification takes the form that the Up has some characteristic (e.g., in the Western philosophical tradition, the favored trait is "mind," reason, or rationality) that the Down lacks and by virtue of which the subordination of the Down by the Up is justified.

Contrary to what many feminists and ecofeminists have claimed, there may be nothing inherently problematic about hierarchical thinking (even value-hierarchical thinking), value dualisms, and conceptions and relations of power and privilege, which advantage the Ups, *in contexts other than oppression*. Hierarchical thinking is important for classifying data, comparing information, and organizing material. Taxonomies (e.g., plant taxonomies) and biological nomenclature seem to require some form of hierarchical thinking. Even value-hierarchical thinking may be quite acceptable in some contexts (e.g., in assessing the qualities of contestants or in rank-ordering participants in a contest). Responsible parents may exercise legitimate power and privilege (as Ups) over their infants (as Downs), be assigned higher prestige or value than their infants for some purposes (e.g., as logical reasoners), and yet not thereby be involved in any type of oppressive parent-child relationship. Up-Down parent-child relationships are only oppressive if the all-important logic of domination is in place; it is what "justifies" the unjustified domination of children by parents. The problem with value-hierarchical thinking, value dualisms, and conceptions of power and privilege that systematically advantage Ups over Downs, is the way in which each of these has functioned historically in oppressive conceptual frameworks to establish the inferiority of Downs and to justify the subordination of Downs by Ups. The logic of domination is what provides that alleged justification of subordination.

This last point raises the issue of justified and unjustified domination. If one describes healthy, morally permissible relationships (say between parents and infants) as relationships of domination, then unjustified domination occurs only where the logic of domination is in place. That is, the logic of domination falsely justifies the power and privilege of Ups over Downs in a way which keeps intact unjustified domination-subordination relationships. Child abuse is a case of unjustified domination; a parent exercising her power and privilege by forcibly removing a child's hand from a hot burning stove is not. So, if one claims that domination can be either justified or unjustified, then it is cases of unjustified domination that are of interest to ecofeminist philosophy. For purposes of this book, my discussion of domination refers to "unjustified domination."

WHY THE LOGIC OF DOMINATION IS EXPLANATORILY BASIC

Since it is the logic of domination that provides the moral premise for ethically justifying the subordination of Downs by Ups in Up-Down relationships of domination and subordination, the logic of domination is explanatorily basic to oppression and oppressive conceptual frameworks. That a logic of domination is explanatorily basic is important for four reasons.

First, since a logic of domination functions both to explain and to justify domination-subordination relationships, it is more than simply a logical structure; it also involves a substantive value system. This value system is what is needed to generate an allegedly morally relevant distinction between Ups and Downs (e.g., that Ups are rational and Downs are not), which, in turn, is used to sanction the justified subordination of what is Down. That value system is embedded in the logic of domination in the form of a moral premise — *Superiority justifies subordination* (or Whatever is Up is justified in being Up and in dominating whatever is Down). The logic of domination thereby operates both as a premise and as a process whereby others are constructed (or thought of) as inferior — that is, as Others. As Lori Gruen claims, in white patriarchal culture, the logic of domination "constructs inferior others and uses this inferiority to justify their oppression."[4]

This construction of inferiority can take many forms, depending on historical and social contexts. It may not be consciously, knowingly, or even intentionally maintained. Habit, custom, and prejudice (and not just consciously developed and endorsed ideologies) affect the social constructions of inferiority. Familiar expressions of these claims of inferiority are that the Ups are better than, stronger than, more powerful than, smarter than, older than, wiser than, more rational than, closer to the divine than, Downs. The logic of domination then functions to sanction the conclusion that Ups are justified in subordination (dominating, treating as inferior, enslaving) Downs.

The second reason a logic of domination is explanatorily basic is that without it, a description of similarities and differences would be just that—a description of similarities and differences. In order for differences to make a moral difference in how a group is treated or in the opportunities available to it, other moral premises (such as the logic of domination) must be accepted. The logic of domination is necessary both to turn diversity (or difference) into domination and to justify that domination.

To illustrate how differences are turned into justified domination by a logic of domination, let us suppose (even if it turns out to be contrary to fact) that what is unique about humans is our conscious capacity to radically reshape our social environments to meet self-determined ends, as Murray Bookchin suggests.[5] Then one could claim that humans are better equipped to radically reshape their environments in consciously self-determined ways than are rocks or plants—a value-hierarchical way of speaking—without thereby sanctioning any domination or exploitation of the nonhuman environment. To justify such domination, one needs a *logic of domination*—a moral premise that specifies that the superiority of humans as Ups (here, their superior ability to radically alter their environment in consciously self-determined ways) justifies the domination of nonhuman natural others as Others, as Downs (here, rocks or plants that do not have this ability).

It is helpful to formalize such reasoning, so that we can see clearly how the derivation of the conclusion about the justified domination of nonhuman nature rests on acceptance of two important claims: a claim about the moral superiority of humans over nonhuman entities on the basis of some ability humans have that nonhuman entities lack (premise 2 below), and the claim that superiority justifies subordination—the "logic of domination" (premise 4 below):

(A)   (1) Humans do, and plants and rocks do not, have the capacity to consciously and radically change the communities in which they live in self-determined ways.

(2) Whatever has the capacity to consciously and radically change the community in which it lives in self-determined ways is morally superior to whatever lacks this capacity.

Thus, (3) Humans are morally superior to plants and rocks.

(4) For any X and Y, if X is morally superior to Y, then X is morally justified in subordinating (dominating) Y.

Thus, (5) Humans are morally justified in subordinating (dominating) plants and rocks.

Notice that premise 2 might well be true; that is a topic debated in environmental philosophy. But even if 2 is true, without the logic of domination, 4, all one has are differences (even if morally relevant differences) between humans and some nonhumans. The moral superiority of humans over nonhuman natural beings, if it exists, does not *by itself* justify domination. In fact, one could argue that such moral superiority imposes on humans extraordinary responsibilities toward (rather than unjustified domination over) others less capable. . . . So, it is the logic of domination, 4, that is the bottom-line (necessary but not sufficient condition) in justifications of domination.

A third reason the logic of domination is so important is that historically, at least in Western societies, the oppressive conceptual frameworks that have justified the dominations of women and nonhuman nature have been patriarchal. Environmental historian Carolyn Merchant was among the first to argue for these historical interconnections between the twin dominations of women and nature in her book *The Death of Nature*. Merchant argues that historically, at least in Western societies, women have been identified in art, literature, and philosophy with nature, body, and the realm of the physical, while men have been identified with culture, reason, and the realm of the mental. These associations occur within a patriarchal conceptual framework that then functions to justify the subordination of women. It does so, for example, by associating the "public" realm of culture, politics, and business with the activities associated with men, and the inferior "private" realm of the home, the family, and personal relationships with women (e.g., childbearing and child rearing), and then justifying the unequal and inferior status of women in terms of women's "natural" childbearing and child raising roles.

Historically in Western culture, the justified inferiority of women and other inferiorized groups (other Others) often turns on claims that women and Others were not rational. Ecofeminist philosophers show how an exaggerated emphasis on reason and rationality, and the attendant "hyperseparation" of reason from emotion,[6] has functioned historically to sanction both the feminization of nature and the naturalization of women in ways that make women and nature inferior to male-gender identified culture. If this is correct, then both traditional feminism (concerned with eliminating sexism) and environmental ethics (concerned with eliminating the unjustified domination of nonhuman nature, or "naturism") ought to incorporate these ecofeminist philosophical insights into their analyses and practices.

Again, by formalizing such reasoning, we can see clearly through argument B how patriarchal conceptual frameworks have functioned historically to sanction sexism and naturism.[7]

(B) (1) At least in Western societies, whenever a group is historically identified with nonhuman nature and the realm of the physical, it is conceptualized as morally inferior to whatever group is historically identified with culture and the realm of the mental.

   (2) At least in Western societies, women as a group historically have been identified with nonhuman nature and the realm of the physical, while at least dominant men have been historically identified with culture and the realm of the mental.

Thus, (3) At least in Western societies, women as a group are conceptualized as morally inferior to at least dominant men.

   (4) For any X and Y, if X is conceptualized as morally inferior to Y, then Y is justified in subordinating (or dominating) X.

Thus, (5) At least in Western societies, dominant men are justified in subordinating (or dominating) both women and nonhuman nature.

Argument B represents the historically favored position, at least in Western societies, on the justified dominations of women and nonhuman nature. But argument B is unsound, since premise 4 — the logic of domination — is false as a prescriptive claim. (It may be true as a descriptive claim about how women, men, and nonhuman nature have been conceptualized and treated historically in Western cultures.) So, one ought to reject argument B.

Are there other premises of argument B besides (4) that are false or problematic? Ecofeminist philosophers argue that 1 and 2 are true — where 1 and 2 are properly understood as *historical* claims (i.e., as claims about how women, nature, and men historically have been viewed in the Western tradition), though not as claims about how women, nature, and men ought to be viewed. Establishing their truths as historical facts is, as Merchant has stated, an important ecofeminist project.

It is important to be clear about what is *not* asserted by premises 1 and 2. They do not assert that women are, in fact, closer to nature than men or that all women and all men are always and everywhere associated with inferior nature (in the case of women) and superior culture (in the case of men). The issue of women's closeness with nature was addressed by Sherry Ortner in her essay, "Is Female to Male as Nature Is to Culture?" Ortner claims that women are universally devalued and subordinated because they are "seen as closer to nature than men, men being seen as more unequivocally occupying the high ground of culture." According to Ortner, because "culture's job is to control nature," men are accorded the right to control women.[8]

But anthropologist Peggy Sanday disagrees with Ortner. Sanday argues that women's subordination is neither universal nor always associated with an inferior nature. Sanday's evidence is based on her studies of 150 tribal societies. She states:

In societies where the forces of nature are sacralized, . . . there is a reciprocal flow between the power of nature and the power inherent in women. The control and manipulation of these forces is left to women and to sacred natural symbols; men are largely extraneous to this domain and must be careful lest they antagonize earthly representatives of nature's power (namely, women).

Sanday concludes that,

Men are not universally aligned so unequivocally with the realm Ortner calls culture, "culture being minimally defined as the transcendence, by means of systems of thought and technology, of the natural givens of existence." On the contrary, in many cases men are inextricably locked into such natural givens as death, destruction, and animality.[9]

According to Sanday, "generally speaking, when men dominate, women play an inconsequential role in the sacred and secular domains. Almost always in male-dominated societies, the godhead is defined in exclusively masculine terms."[10] If Sanday is correct, then the truth of premises 1 and 2 turns on their being claims about Up men in nonprimal (e.g., Western) societies. That is why premises 1 and 2 are stated as they are in argument B (i.e., as claims about Western societies).

But there is another reason for stating premises 1 and 2 as they are stated in argument B. Historically, just as not all groups of men have occupied Up positions of power and privilege (e.g., African American men in the United States), some groups of women have occupied Up positions, especially vis-à-vis other women. In Europe and North America, for example, white, wealthy, aristocratic women (e.g., Rose Kennedy) and women heads of state (e.g., Margaret Thatcher) sometimes have been in uncontested Up positions or in Up positions relative to other women (e.g., white women-headed households that employ women of color as domestic servants). These differences among women are reflected in the way premises 1 and 2 are stated: 1 is a historical claim about those societies *in which* and *when* there is a marked separation between the realms of culture and nature (e.g., Western societies), and 2 is a historical claim about those societies *in which* and *when* there is an association of "Up" men with superior culture and women as a group with inferior nature.

However, even Western women who seem to be an exception by occupying Up positions of power and privilege in male-dominated Up-Down societies are often portrayed in ambiguous gender terms: They tended to be seen either as not really women (they "think like a man," have "masculine" characteristics, or "are manly") or as women who have higher status or value relative to other women but lower status or value relative to dominant men (e.g., "pure," "chaste," "untainted," white "virgins" who are placed precariously "on a pedestal"; "exceptional women" who have superior — because man-like — intelligence and reasoning powers, ambition and fortitude, courage and conviction). In such cases, their status as Ups is achieved by varying degrees of separation (or distancing) both from other groups of women and from the inferior realm of contaminated body, the physical and nonhuman nature.

The classic Broverman study in 1970 illustrates this point for U.S. women. One hundred psychiatrists, psychiatric social workers, and psychologists were asked to describe a normal man, a normal woman, and a normal human. The normal man and the normal human turned out to be the same; only the normal woman was different. As philosopher Elizabeth Minnick puts it, "That means that a woman can be *either* a 'normal' human and an 'abnormal' woman *or* a 'normal' woman and an 'abnormal' human — not both. Man is what human IS; woman is deviant."[11]

What about the status of premise 3, namely, the premise that at least in Western societies, women as a group are conceptualized as morally inferior to at least dominant men? All ecofeminist philosophers to date agree that women have been falsely *conceptualized* as inferior to men. This historical conceptualization of women as inferior has been based on any of three faulty assumptions: biological determinism, conceptual essentialism, and universalism. Biological determinism (popularized by the slogan "biology is destiny") incorrectly locates women as biologically "closer to nature than men" (typically because of women's reproductive capacities) or assumes a biological essence to women (a biological "women's nature"). Conceptual essentialism incorrectly assumes that the concept of women is a univocal, meaningful concept that captures some cross-culturally valid or essential (i.e., necessary and sufficient) conditions of women, womanhood, or femaleness.[12] Universalism incorrectly assumes that, as women, all women share a set of experiences in virtue of the fact that we are women.

Of course, even if all ecofeminist philosophers to date have been unanimous in a rejection of these three assumptions, it does not follow that all ecofeminist philosophers agree about what such a rejection means or implies. Some ecofeminist philosophers have argued, for example, that a rejection of biological determinism and universalism also involves a rejection of notions of "the female" or "the feminine." For example, in her article "Is Ecofeminism Feminist?" Victoria Davion argues that appeals to "the female" or "the feminine" are anti-feminist, since they uncritically valorize women's experiences and present them as universal and biologically grounded. Davion calls such positions *ecofeminine,* not *ecofeminist.* She states that "views which uncritically embrace unified or one-stance views of feminine sides of gender dichotomies are not feminist; they are better understood as ecofeminine, not ecofeminist. They are, in fact, dangerous views from a genuinely feminist perspective."[13]

Ecofeminist philosopher Chris Cuomo agrees with Davion's distinction between ecofeminine and ecofeminist. Because ecofeminism sometimes includes positions that Davion and Cuomo see as ecofeminine (not properly ecofeminist), Cuomo introduces a further distinction between *ecofeminism* and *ecological feminism,* identifying ecofeminist philosophy with ecological feminism. In this way Cuomo attempts to distance ecological feminist philosophy from spiritual approaches to ecofeminism ("which zoom in on women") and from ecofeminist approaches that appeal to problematic notions of the female and femininity, construe women's corporeality as naturally or essentially linked to nature, or which characterize women as radically separate from culture.[14] (Note that, unlike Cuomo, I have chosen throughout this book to use the expressions ecofeminist philosophy and ecological feminist philosophy interchangeably.)

Similarly, ecofeminist philosopher Val Plumwood criticizes ecofeminists who assert, on biologically determinist grounds, that women are naturally closer to nature and are "earth mothers":

This type of ecofeminism should be clearly distinguished from other types, and is open to serious objection . . . Such a position is difficult to sustain in any thorough way, because it depends upon not really examining the polarities or the reasons why a hierarchical and sexist division of labour is established to begin with.[15]

So, it is an important project of ecofeminist philosophy to determine which ecofeminist positions presuppose biological determinism, conceptual essentialism, or universalism, and which do not.

Having clarified what the logic of domination asserts, it is important to clarify what the logic of domination does *not* assert. It does not assert that there are no relevant differences between groups (whether between or among groups of humans or nonhumans) that may make some groups superior or inferior in some relevant respect. Race-car drivers *as* race-car drivers may be superior to ordinary drivers with regard to their ability to drive cars, but nothing follows morally from that fact about who deserves what sort of treatment. Rational humans *as* rational beings may be superior, even morally superior, to any nonrational animals without that by itself implying anything about what humans are morally permitted to do with regard to nonhuman animals. To get such implications, one needs the logic of domination.

A rejection of the logic of domination also does not specify what Downs may be justified in doing to end their domination by Ups (e.g., whether Downs are justified in using violence to end their oppression by Ups). Additional premises are needed to justify exercises of power by Downs against Ups.[16]

To summarize what has been said so far, the logic of domination is explanatorily basic and ought to be rejected for three reasons: First, a rejection of the logic of domination asserts that superiority, even moral superiority, does not by itself justify subordination; second, difference by itself does not justify domination; and third, historically, at least in Western societies, the oppressive conceptual frameworks that have justified the dominations of women and nonhuman nature have been patriarchal. A rejection of the logic of domination thereby challenges the historically favored view in Western societies (at least) that an identification of a human group with the realm of the physical and nonhuman nature justifies dominating both that human group and nonhuman nature. It also rules out a moral justification of relationships of domination and subordination on grounds of the alleged superiority of the Ups over the Downs.

But there is an additional, fourth reason the "logic of domination" is explanatorily basic, one that turns on an important distinction between "oppression" and "domination." This reason is that premise 4, the logic of domination, links *dominations* of women, other human Others, and nature, even if it also links the *oppression* of women, other human Others, and (some) nonhuman animals. That is, the logic of domination is about "domination"; its role in linking oppressions is unspecified. What does this mean, and why is this distinction between domination and oppression important?

Oppression consists in institutional structures, strategies, and processes whereby some groups (Downs) are limited, inhibited, coerced, or prevented from mobilizing resources for self-determined goals by limiting their choices and options. Oppressive institutions use various tools of subjugation (e.g., violence, threats, exploitation, colonization, exclusion) to reinforce the power and privilege of Ups in oppressive systems and to enforce the subordination or domination of Downs.[17] Domination is one such tool of subjugation: It reinforces the power and privileges of Ups over Downs in Up-Down relationships of domination and subordination. All oppression involves domination.

By contrast, not all domination involves oppression. This is basically because oppression limits choices and options. So it is only beings who can meaningfully be spoken of as "having options" who also can meaningfully be said to be oppressed. Since I assume that from a Western philosophical perspective trees, rivers, mountains, communities of flora and fauna, species, and ecosystems are not the sort of things that make choices or have options, I assume that they cannot be oppressed. But they can be dominated.

This terminological distinction between oppression and domination is important in other ways to the particular ecofeminist philosophy I defend in this book. I have defined an oppressive conceptual framework as a set of basic beliefs, values, attitudes, and assumptions that explains, justifies, and maintains relationships of domination and subordination. These conceptual frameworks are oppressive, not dominating conceptual frameworks; they maintain relationships of domination and subordination, not relationships of oppression.[18] The unjustified domination of nonhuman animals and nature is described in terms of relationships of domination and subordination, not in terms of relationships of oppression. I have argued that oppressive conceptual frameworks turn on a logic of domination, not a logic of oppression.

The choice of these terms was deliberate.[19] Persons have conceptual frameworks. In Western contexts, nonhuman natural entities such as rocks, plants, and rivers typically are not considered persons. Conceptual frameworks can and do function in ways that reflect, maintain, and reinforce both the *oppression* and *domination* of others. One can meaningfully speak of the historical, economic, social, legal, political, and psychological causes of oppression, domination, exploitation, and violence. And one can meaningfully speak of the conceptual links between "isms of domination," whether or not those "isms" are also "isms of oppression." But because oppression is linked to oppressive (not simply dominating) conceptual frameworks, it is entities who have conceptual frameworks who can be oppressors and oppressed. In at least Western contexts, this typically is a smaller group than the potential group of entities who/that can be dominated.

This brings us to the fourth reason the logic of domination is explanatorily basic to ecofeminist philosophy. The logic of domination links the *dominations* of women, other human Others, and nature, even if, in addition, it links the *oppression* of women, other human Others, and (some) nonhuman animals. Since, in Western cultural contexts, it is presumed that rocks and rivers do not have the capacity to make choices or entertain options, in these contexts it is a logic of domination, not a logic of oppression, that is key. . . .

CONCEPT OF PATRIARCHY

Ecofeminist philosophy is often focused on claims about patriarchy. As I use the term, "patriarchy" is the systematic domination of women by men through *institutions* (including policies, practices, offices, positions, roles), *behaviors,* and *ways of thinking* (conceptual frameworks), which assigns higher value, privilege, and power to men (or to what historically is male-gender identified) than to that given to women (or to what historically is female-gender identified). . . .

Anthropologist Ernestine Friedl claims that patriarchy (or, male dominance) is "a situation in which men have highly preferential access, although not always exclusive rights, to those activities to which the society accords the greatest value, and the exercise of which permits a measure of control over others.[20] Anthropologist Peggy Sanday agrees, arguing further that male dominance consists in two general types of behaviors:

First, there is the exclusion of women from political and economic decision making. Second, there is male aggression against women, which is measured here by the following five traits: the expectations that males should be tough, brave, and aggressive; the presense of men's houses or specific places where only men congregate; frequent quarreling, fighting, or wife beating; the institutionalisation or regular occurrence of rape; and raiding other groups for wives. The presence of all five in a society indicates a high degree of male aggression; the absense of all five indicates that male aggression is weakly developed.[21]

What characterizes the position of women under patriarchy is not that women have no power, valued status, prestige, or privilege; they do. Women in India who have responsibilities for water collection and distribution have some power and privilege, and lack other power and privilege. What characterizes women's position is the varying degrees and ways women, as a group, are excluded from political and economic institutions of power and privilege. While the specific forms that male dominance takes will vary, depending largely on the different material realities of women located in historically specific contexts, what women under patriarchy have in common, as a group, is less institutional power and privilege than men.

This focus on "institutional power and privilege" is relevant to a proper understanding of my ecofeminist philosophical critique of patriarchy and "isms of domination." The expression "white skin power and privilege" emphasizes that the benefits white people receive in a white racist society are inherited at birth by virtue of their having white skin or being white. Analogously, the expression "male power and privilege" emphasizes that the benefits males receive in a patriarchal society are inherited at birth by virtue of their being male. Because these benefits are received at birth, the sort of power and privilege that whites or males receive in such societies is not based on individual merit, ability, effort, or need; hence, they are not something for which individuals deserve praise or blame. Rather, these benefits are institutionally created, maintained, and sanctioned; they reflect the power and privilege of Ups in unjustified Up-Down systems. And such Up-Down systems create, maintain, or perpetuate unjustified "isms of domination" such as sexism, racism, classism, heterosexism, ethnocentrism, and colonialism.

This focus on institutional (rather than individual or personal) power and privilege is important here for three reasons. First, it provides a way of understanding why ecofeminist philosophy is neither inherently anti-male nor inherently pro-female. Ecofeminist philosophy is about institutional structures of power and privilege, not about praise or blame for what individuals (e.g., individual men, women, white people, upper-class people) do or do not do. It does not assume that all and only males are "the problem," or that all and only females are "the solution." The focus of ecofeminist philosophy is unjustified Up-Down systems of power and privilege, particularly patriarchal Up-Down systems, as well as on the actual social contexts in which Ups are beneficiaries of such unjustified Up-Down systems.

Second, although Ups cannot help receiving whatever institutional power and privilege benefits they receive as Ups in unjustified Up-Down social systems, nonetheless Ups are accountable for perpetuating unjustified Up-Down systems through their behaviors (including language) and thought-worlds. This is true even if individual Ups do not want the power and privilege they receive as Ups. That is why ecofeminist philosophy is about both theory and practice,[22] about not only understanding and analyzing but also about both Ups and Downs taking personal and political action against Up-Down systems of domination.

Third, since systems of domination are interrelated, the institutional power and privileges Ups receive will differ depending on the racial/ethnic, class, sexual orientation, age, ability, geographic location, religion, and nationality of those Ups. Different groups of Ups have different degrees of power and privilege in different cultural contexts. Ecofeminist philosophy recognizes these important differences among Ups and Downs in Up-Down systems, while also recognizing commonalities among Ups and Downs where those commonalities exist.

THEORIZING AS QUILTING

. . .

The version of ecofeminist philosophy I defend rejects [the] notion of theory as a set of necessary and sufficient conditions. This means that I assume that "ethical theory," for example is not about specifying a set of necessary and sufficient conditions that all and only right acts share in common. Nonetheless, I consider myself and other ecofeminist philosophers theorists. I assume that ecofeminist philosophy is engaged in theorizing, and that the theorizing it engages in is "feminist." How can that be?

The conception of theory that I propose is this: There are some necessary conditions of feminist theory. If there were not, there would be no grounds for calling the theory "a theory," for calling a feminist theory "feminist," or for calling an ecofeminist theory "ecofeminist." But one cannot specify, ahead of time, so to speak, what the "sufficient conditions" of right acts or morally acceptable human conduct is. For that one needs to know things about the historical, material, and social contexts. That is why, on my view of theory, theorizing is not about identifying a set of essential properties — necessary and sufficient conditions.

The metaphor I use for the conception of theory I endorse is that of a quilt: Theories are like quilts. The "necessary conditions" of a theory (say, ecofeminist philosophical theory) are like the borders of a quilt: They delimit the boundary conditions of the theory without dictating beforehand what the interior (the design, the actual patterns) of the quilt does or must look like. The actual design of the quilt will emerge from the diversity of perspectives of quilters

who contribute, over time, to the making of the quilt. Theory is not something static, preordained, or carved in stone; it is always *theory-in-process*.

The theorizing-as-quilting metaphor initially came to me as I reflected on the Names Project Quilt. This quilt is a patchwork of 10,500 panels of individual quilt-patches that record and commemorate human lives lost to AIDS — lives that collectively represent different ages, ethnicities, affectional orientations, race and gender identities, and class backgrounds. While each patch is unique, what the patches have in common is what constitutes the necessary condition for inclusion on the Names Project Quilt — each patch commemorates a life lost to AIDS. This necessary condition of having a patch qualify for the Names Project Quilt was clearly identified before the quilt was begun. What was not and could not be known at that time was what the interior design of the completed quilt would look like.

It seems to me that the same is true of ecofeminist philosophical theory and theorizing. Given the characterization of ecofeminist philosophy provided in this chapter, nothing that is knowingly, intentionally, or consciously naturist, sexist, racist, or classist — which reinforces or maintains "isms of domination" — belongs on the quilt. Nor does anything that is not, in some way, about nonhuman nature or human-nature relationships. An ecofeminist philosophical quilt will be made up of different "patches," constructed by quilters in particular social, historical, and material contexts, which express some aspect of that quilter's perspective on women–other human Others–nature interconnections. One cannot know, beforehand, what the actual interior of the quilt will look like. . . .

For me, there are three features of quilts and quilting that make it an especially apt metaphor for theory and theorizing. First, quilts are highly contextual; they grow out of and reflect specific historical, social, economic, and political influences. A Hmong quilt may reflect important cultural influences not captured on a Texan or Iowan farm woman's quilt in the United States. The Pentagon Peace Quilt, Judy Chicago's "The Birth Project," Jesse Jackson's Rainbow Coalition Quilt, North American slave quilts, and the millions of quilts that serve as a repository of "women's history" are also highly contextual. What makes them the quilts they are is that they satisfy some necessary (border) conditions, typically articulated in terms of some shared experience, beliefs, vision, or purposes known to the quilters. The point of these quilts is not to have one image or one story, based on one and only one view of reality; it is to have a *variety of images or stories.* There images/stories emerge out of the life experience and visions of people located in different historical circumstances. So, too, with ecofeminist philosophical theory and theorizing as I understand each.

Second, the quilt metaphor helps one visualize the role of generalizations in theory. Like any theory, ecofeminist theory is based on some generalizations. For example, it is a generalization to say that U.S. women, on the average, earn less than men for comparable work. This generalization about commonalities among U.S. women is true, even though it is also true that there are striking differences between what white Anglo-European women, African American women, and American Indian women earn. The quilt metaphor helps illustrate the role these generalizations play in theory in a way traditional theory (as a set of necessary and sufficient conditions) does not: The border conditions of the quilt, which express generalizations based on commonalities, provide the necessary conditions for a patch to become part of the quilt (theory). But they do not specify the sufficient conditions (what the interior looks like); that is provided by the diversity of quilt patches made by different quilters (theorists and practitioners) over time.

Third, quilting is historically a women-identified activity. Dismissed in the nineteenth century as a "minor art" (largely because quilt-making was practiced by women), quilting has reemerged in the latter part of the twentieth century as an important art form that has several functions. Quilts are a form of discourse; they tell stories, record people's lives, provide portraits of the quilters who make them, and often give shape and form to the experiences of those whose stories are not told in literal discourse. Quilts are practical; they are "comforters" that provide warmth, are an integral part of domestic production, and often provide an important source of income for the women who quilt them. Quilts are histori-

cal records; they capture diverse or distinct cultural traditions and thereby serve collectively to help preserve the past and create the future. Quilts are aesthetic; they can be very exciting visually, with precise, varied, and vibrant designs, bold color combinations, and exuberant displays of individual and community identities. Quilts are political statements; they can tell the story of the history of a people's migration (e.g., Hmong quilts), raise awareness about politically sensitive issues (e.g., the Names Project Quilt), or promote a particular vision or point of view (e.g., the Pentagon Peace Quilt). Ecofeminist philosophy grows out of and reflects just such forms of discourse. . . .

NOTES

1. "Local" perspectives may or may not be those of indigenous peoples in a community. Inclusion of local perspectives is intended to ensure that grassroots and citizen input be considered in the analysis of and solutions to environmental and gender issues.
2. Elizabeth Dodson Gray, *Green Paradise Lost* (Wellesley, Mass.: Roundtable Press, 1981), 20.
3. Bruce Nordstrom-Loeb made these comments on an earlier draft of this manuscript.
4. Lori Gruen, "On the Oppression of Women and Animals," *Environmental Ethics* 18, no. 4 (Winter 1996), 442.
5. Murray Bookchin, "Social Ecology versus 'Deep Ecology,'" in *Green Perspectives: Newsletter of the Green Program Project* (Summer 1987), 9.
6. See Val Plumwood, *Feminism and the Mastery of Nature* (New York: Routledge, 1993).
7. See Gray, *Green Paradise Lost;* Susan Griffin, *Woman and Nature: The Roaring Inside Her* (New York: Harper and Row, 1978); Carolyn Merchant, *The Death of Nature: Women, Ecology, and the Scientific Revolution* (San Francisco: Harper and Row, 1980); Rosemary Radford Ruether, *Women Healing Earth: Third World Women on Ecology, Feminism, and Religion* (Maryknoll, N.Y.: Orbis, 1996); Val Plumwood, "Ecofeminism: An Overview and Discussion of Positions and Arguments," *Australasian Journal of Philosophy* 64, Supplement

on Women and Philosophy (June 1986), 120–39.

8. Sherry B. Ortner, "Is Female to Male as Nature Is to Culture?" in *Women, Culture, and Society,* ed. M. Z. Rosaldo and L. Lamphere (Stanford, Calif.: Stanford University Press, 1974), 83–84. It may be that in contemporary Western society, which is so thoroughly structured by categories of gender, race, class, age, and affectional preference, there simply is no meaningful notion of "value-hierarchical thinking" that does not function in an oppressive context. For purpose of this book, I leave that question open.

9. Peggy Sanday, *Female Power and Male Dominance: On the Origins of Sexual Inequality* (New York: Cambridge University Press, 1981), 5.

10. Sanday, *Female Power,* 6.

11. Elizabeth Minnick, *Conceptual Errors Across the Curriculum: Toward a Transformation of the Curriculum* (Memphis: Research Clearinghouse and Curriculum Integration Project, at the Center for Research on Women, Memphis State University, 1986), 5.

12. I am making a distinction here between what I call "conceptual essentialism" and "strategic essentialism," understood as the claim that there are some material realities that form commonalities among women. Even with noteworthy differences among women, for reasons of political action and accurate descriptive theory, feminists are correct to call attention to these commonalities.

13. Victoria Davion, "Is Ecofeminism Feminist?" In *Ecological Feminism,* ed. Karen J. Warren (New York: Routledge, 1994), 17.

14. Chris Cuomo, *Feminism and Ecological Communities: An Ethic of Flourishing* (London: Routledge, 1998), 6.

15. Plumwood, "Ecofeminism: An Overview," 133–34.

16. . . . One might argue, for example, that Downs in an Up-Down hierarchy of power and privilege are justified in using whatever means are necessary to get their legitimate needs met (a twist on the familiar "just war" doctrine).

17. In her book *Justice and the Politics of Difference* (Princeton, N.J.: Princeton University Press, 1990), Iris Marion Young identifies exploitation, marginalization, powerlessness, cultural imperialism, and violence as five "faces" or "correlates of oppression."

18. Of course, for some dominated beings, relationships of domination and subordination may also be relationships of oppression.

19. Chris Crittenden has articulated and defended my position on the "logic of domination" and the underlying distinction between oppression and domination in his article, "Subordinate and Oppressive Conceptual Frameworks: A Defense of Ecofeminist Perspectives," *Environmental Ethics* 20, no. 3 (Fall 1998), 247–63.

20. Ernestine Friedl, *Women and Men: An Anthropologist's View* (New York: Holt, Rinehart and Winston, 1975), 7.

21. Sanday, *Female Power,* 164.

22. The reference to "theory and practice" is not intended to suggest that theorizing is not a practice or that engaging in practice is somehow "opposed" to theorizing.

DISCUSSION TOPICS

1. Warren acknowledges that we are in a prefeminist period of history and therefore we cannot make truly just decisions. What relevance does this point have for your choices as a consumer?

2. Identify the five features of an oppressive conceptual framework as presented by Warren, giving an example of your own.

3. Explain what is meant by biological determinism, conceptual essentialism, and universalism. What is Warren's position on these terms?

4. How does Warren distinguish between domination and oppression? Do you find this distinction to be a useful one?

5. Do you agree with Warren that ecofeminism is not inherently anti-male or pro-female? Explain your answer.

6. What are the similarities between ecofeminist philosophy and a quilt, according to Warren? Does this analogy clarify the nature of ecofeminism? Why or why not?

Introduction to *Ecofeminism*

Maria Mies and Vandana Shiva

Maria Mies is a sociologist and author of several books, including Patriarchy and Accumulation on a World Scale *(Zed Books, 1986). After returning from many years in India, she is now professor of sociology at the Fachhochschule in Cologne, Germany. She is active in women's and environmental movements in Germany. Vandana Shiva is a physicist, philosopher, and feminist and is director of the Research Foundation for Science, Technology and Natural Resource Policy in Dehradun, India. She is a leading activist in India. Her most recent book is* Earthwork: Women and Environments *(2001).*

Mies and Shiva collaborate in this introduction in order to address the inequalities that allow the affluent industrialized societies of the North (the United States, Europe, and Japan) to dominate the underdeveloped societies of the South (Africa, South America, and Asia). These inequalities are based on a new world order that they term the capitalist patriarchal world system. This system maintains itself through the domination of women, "foreign" peoples and their lands, and nature.

WHY IS IT SO DIFFICULT TO SEE THIS COMMON GROUND?

. . . Some women, . . . particularly urban, middle-class women, find it difficult to perceive commonality both between their own liberation and the liberation of nature, and between themselves and "different" women in the world. This is because capitalist patriarchy or "modern" civilization is based on a cosmology and anthropology that structurally dichotomizes reality, and hierarchically opposes the two parts to each other: the one always considered superior, always thriving, and progressing at the expense of the other. Thus, nature is subordinated to man; woman to man; consumption to production; and the local to the global, and so on. Feminists have long criticized this dichotomy, particularly the structural division of man and nature, which is seen as analogous to that of man and woman.[1]

Rather than attempting to overcome this hierarchical dichotomy many women have simply upended it, and thus women are seen as superior to men, nature to culture, and so on. But the basic structure of the world-view remains as also does the basically antagonistic relationship that, at the surface, exists between the two divided and hierarchically ordered parts. Because this world-view sees the "other," the "object," not just as different, but as the "enemy"; as Sartre put it in *Huis Clos:* Hell is other people! In the resultant struggle one part will eventually survive by subordinating, and appropriating the "other." This is also the core of Hegelian and Marxian dialectics, of their concept of history and progress. Evolutionary theory too, is based on the concept of a constant struggle for survival, on an antagonistic principle of life. These concepts are integral to what, since the Enlightenment, constitutes the European project of so-called modernity or progress.

Since Hobbes' writings, society has been conceptualized as an assembly of social atoms, activated by antagonistic interests. Modern economic theory sees self-interest as the impulse of all economic activity. Later, Darwin "discovered" a similar principle in nature. Accordingly, the symbioses, the interconnections that nurture and sustain life are ignored, and both natural evolution and social dynamics are perceived as impelled by a constant struggle of the stronger against the weaker, by constant warfare. Such a world-view militates against an appreciation of the enriching potential of the diversity of life and cultures, which instead are experienced as divisive and threatening. Attempts to rejoin the atomized parts lead only to standardization and to homogenization by eliminating diversity and qualitative differences.

An ecofeminist perspective propounds the need for a new cosmology and a new anthropology which recognizes that life in nature (which includes human beings) is maintained by means of co-operation, and mutual care and love. Only in this way can we be enabled to respect and preserve the diversity of all life forms, including their cultural expressions, as true sources of our well-being and happiness. To this end ecofeminists use metaphors like "re-weaving the world," "healing the wounds," and re-connecting and interconnecting the "web."[2] This effort to create a holistic, all-life embracing cosmology and anthropology, must necessarily imply a concept of freedom different from that used since the Enlightenment.

FREEDOM VERSUS EMANCIPATION

This involves rejecting the notion that Man's freedom and happiness depend *on an ongoing process of emancipation from nature,* on independence from, and dominance over natural processes by the power of reason and rationality. Socialist utopias were also informed by a concept of freedom that saw man's destiny in his historic march from the "realm of necessity" (the realm of nature), to the "realm of freedom" — the "real" human realm — which entailed transforming nature and natural forces into what was called a "second nature," or culture. According to scientific socialism, the limits of both nature and society are dialectically transcended in this process.

Most feminists also shared this concept of freedom and emancipation, until the beginning of the ecology movement. But the more people began to reflect upon and question why the application of modern science and technology, which have been celebrated as humanity's great liberators, had succeeded only in procuring increasing ecological degradation, the more acutely aware they became of the contradiction between the enlightenment logic of emancipation and the eco-logic of preserving and nurturing natural cycles of regeneration. In 1987, at the congress "Women and Ecology" in Cologne (Germany), Angelika Birk and Irene Stoehr spelt out this contradiction, particularly as it applied to the women's movement which, like many other movements inspired by the Enlightenment ideas, had fastened its hopes on the progress of science and technology, particularly in the area of reproduction, but also of house- and other work. Irene Stoehr pointed out that this concept of emancipation necessarily implied dominance over nature, including human, female nature; and, that ultimately, this dominance relationship was responsible for the ecological destruction we now face. How, then, could women hope to reach both their own and nature's "emancipation" by way of the same logic?[3]

To "catch-up" with the men in their society, as many women still see as the main goal of the feminist movement, particularly those who promote a policy of equalization, implies a demand for a greater, or equal share of what, in the existing paradigm, men take from nature. This, indeed, has to a large extent happened in Western society: modern chemistry, household technology, and pharmacy were proclaimed as women's saviours, because they would "emancipate" them from household drudgery. Today we realize that much environmental pollution and destruction is causally linked to modern household technology. Therefore, can the concept of emancipation be compatible with a concept of preserving the earth as our life base? . . .

Within a limited planet, there can be no escape from necessity. To find freedom does not involve subjugating or transcending the "realm of necessity," but rather focusing on developing a vision of freedom, happiness, the "good life" within the limits of necessity, of nature. We call this vision the subsistence perspective, because to "transcend" nature can no longer be justified; instead, nature's subsistence potential in all its dimensions and manifestations must be nurtured and conserved. Freedom *within* the realm of necessity can be universalized to all; freedom *from* necessity can be available to only a few.

THE GLOBAL VERSUS THE LOCAL

The "global" versus the "local" now figures widely in many ecological and development discourses. A closer examination of these reveals that the interest groups that seek free access to all natural resources as well as to human labour and markets, often present themselves as guardians of the "world community," "global peace," "global ecology" or of universal human rights and the free world market. The implicit promise of this globalism is that a "free world market" will lead to world peace and justice. In the name of common or global goals, which de facto acknowledge the fact that we all are dependent on the same planet, they nevertheless claim the right to exploit local ecology, communities, cultures and so on. The victims are always local, for example, as is manifest in the aftermath of the [first] Gulf War — a war justified by the apparently universal or global principle of justice, in the name of the "world community," represented by the United Nations. The world was called upon to feel responsibility for liberating Kuwait from Iraqi occupation. But, it is clear that the victims of this "liberation" are local: Iraqi and Kuwaiti women and children, the Kurds, and the Gulf region's environment.

The new "globalism" which emerged after the Gulf War — the "New World Order" — was propagated by U.S. President George Bush. With the end of the old superpower confrontation this New World Order is projected as a harbinger of world peace and harmony. But it is simply the Old World Order in a different garb.

. . . The "global" in the global order means simply the global domination of local and particular interests, by means of subsuming the multiple diversities of economies, cultures and of nature under the control of a few multinational corporations (MNCs), and the superpowers that assist them in their global reach through "free" trade, structural adjustment programmes and, increasingly, conflicts, military and otherwise. In unified Germany, there are now racist attacks on immigrants, there are civil wars in the erstwhile Soviet Union and Eastern European countries recently "integrated" in the world market, and ethnic conflicts in Sri Lanka, India and Africa — all of which point to new divisions and closed borders for the people, whereas for MNCs' investments and markets all borders are erased, in order to facilitate the grand design of a "New World Order," of "global integration."

In the dominant discourse the "global" is the political space in which the dominant local seeks global control, and frees itself of any local and national control. But, contrary to what it suggests, the global does not represent universal human interest but a particular local and parochial interest which has been globalized through its reach and control. The G-7, the group of the world's seven most powerful countries, dictate global affairs, but the interests that guide them remain parochial. The World Bank does not really serve the interests of all the

world's communities, but is an institution in which decisions are based on voting, weighted by the economic and political power of the donors. In this decision-making, the communities who pay the real price, the real donors (such as the tribals of Narmada Valley), have no voice.

The independence movements against colonialism had revealed the poverty and deprivation caused by economic drain from the colonies to the centres of economic power. The post-war world order which saw the emergence of independent political states in the South, also saw the emergence of the Bretton Woods institutions like the World Bank and the IMF which, in the name of underdevelopment and poverty, created a new colonialism based on development financing and debt burdens. The environment movement revealed the environmental and social costs generated by maldevelopment, conceived of and financed by these institutions. Protection of the environment now figures in the rhetoric and is cited as the reason for strengthening "global" institutions like the World Bank and extending their reach accordingly.

In addition to the legitimacy derived from co-opting the language of dissent is the legitimacy that derives from a false notion that the globalized "local" is some form of hierarchy that represents geographical and democratic spread, and lower order (local) hierarchies should somehow be subservient to the higher (global). Operationalizing undemocratic development projects was based on a similar false notion of the "national interest," and every local interest felt morally compelled to make sacrifices for what seemed the larger interest. This is the attitude with which each community made way for large dams in post-independent India. It was only during the 1980s when the different "local" interests met each other nationwide, that they realized that what was being projected as the "national interest" were the electoral and economic interests of a handful of politicians financed by a handful of contractors and industrialists who benefit from the construction of all dams such as Tehri and the Narmada Valley project. Against the narrow and selfish interest that had been elevated to the status of the "national" interest, the collective struggle of communities engaged in the resistance against large dams started to emerge as the real though subjugated common interest.

THE BREAKDOWN OF UNIVERSALIST (WESTERN) IDEOLOGIES AND THE EMERGENCE OF CULTURAL RELATIVISM

There are a number of people who interpret the end of the East-West confrontation as not only signalling the end of all socialist dreams and utopias but also of all universal ideologies based on a universal concept of human beings and their relation to nature and other human beings. These ideologies have been "deconstructed" as being eurocentric, egocentric and—according to some feminists—androcentric, and materialist.

The end of these ideologies is being proclaimed by post-modernist thinkers, who hold that the universalization of modernization—the European project of the Enlightenment—has failed. And there are environmentalists and developmentalists who argue that the emphasis on material or economic development and on emulation of the West's model of the industrial society has failed to appreciate that in most non-European societies culture plays a significant role. Moreover, they assert that the dualistic separation of economy and culture (or in Marxian terms of bases and superstructure) finds no resonance in most non-modern societies. They further criticize the Western development paradigm on the grounds that the modernization strategy has resulted in the destruction of cultural as well as biological diversity, to a homogenization of cultures on the U.S. Coca-Cola and fast-food model, on the one hand, and of life forms according to the demands of profit-oriented industries, on the other. We share much of the criticism directed to the West's paradigm of development; we reject the homogenization processes resulting from the world market and of capitalist production processes. We also criticize the dualistic division between superstructure or culture and the economy or base. In our view, the preservation of the earth's diversity of life forms and of human societies' cultures is a precondition for the maintenance of life on this planet.

But it is essential to beware of simply up-ending the dualistic structure by discounting the economy altogether and considering only culture or cultures. Furthermore, not all cultural traditions can be seen as of equal value; such a stance would simply replace eurocentric and androcentric and dogmatic ideological and ethical universalism with cultural relativism. This cultural relativism implies that we must accept even violence, and such patriarchal and exploitative institutions and customs as dowry, female genital mutilation, India's caste system and so on, because they are the cultural expressions and creations of particular people. For cultural relativists, traditions, expressed in language, religion, custom, food habits, and man-woman relations are always considered as particular, and beyond criticism. Taken to extremes the emphasis on "difference" could lead to losing sight of all commonalities, making even communication impossible. Obviously, cultural relativism, amounting to a suspension of value judgement, can be neither the solution nor the alternative to totalitarian and dogmatic ideological universalism. It is, in fact, the old coin reversed. It takes a liberal stance, but it should be remembered that European liberalism and individualism are rooted in colonialism, destruction of the commons, on wholesale privatization and on commodity production for profit. What must also be realized is that this new emphasis on the cultural, the local, and the difference, this cultural relativism, accords with MNCs' interests.

While intellectuals may concentrate on culture and on differences, international capital continues with its expansion of production and markets, insisting on free access to all natural resources and life forms and to localized cultures and traditions and their commodification. Local cultures are deemed to have "value" only when they have been fragmented and these fragments transformed into saleable goods for a world market. Only when food becomes "ethnic food," music "ethnic music," and traditional tales "folklore" and when skills are harnessed to the production of "ethnic" objects for the tourist industry, can the capital accumulation process benefit from these local cultures.

While local cultures are thus dissected and their fragments commodified, these atomized parts are then "re-unified" in the global supermarket, thereby procuring a standardization and homogenization of all cultural diversity. Cultural relativism is not only unaware of these processes but rather legitimizes them; and the feminist theory of difference ignores the working of the capitalist world system and its power to transform life into saleable commodities and cash.

To find a way out of cultural relativism, it is necessary to look not only for differences but for diversities and interconnectedness among women, among men and women, among human beings and other life forms, worldwide. The common ground for women's liberation and the preservation of life on earth is to be found in the activities of those women who have become the victims of the development process and who struggle to conserve their subsistence base: for example, the Chipko women in India, women and men who actively oppose mega dam construction, women who fight against nuclear power plants and against the irresponsible dumping of toxic wastes around the world, and many more worldwide.

In the dialogues with such grassroots women activists cultural relativism does not enter. These women spell out clearly what unites women worldwide, and what unites men and women with the multiplicity of life forms in nature. The universalism that stems from their efforts to preserve their subsistence — their life base — is different from the eurocentric universalism developed via the Enlightenment and the rise of capitalist patriarchy.

This universalism does not deal in abstract universal human "rights" but rather in common human needs which can be satisfied only if the life-sustaining networks and processes are kept intact and alive. These "symbioses or living interconnectedness" both in nature and in human society are the only guarantee that life in its fullest sense can continue on this planet. These fundamental needs: for food, shelter, clothing; for affection, care and love; for dignity and identity, for knowledge and freedom, leisure and joy, are common to all people, irrespective of culture, ideology, race, political and economic system and class.

In the usual development discourse these needs are divided into so-called basic needs (food, shelter, clothing, et al.) and so-called higher needs such as freedom and knowledge and so on. The ecofeminist

perspective as expressed by women activists recognizes no such division. Culture is very much part of their struggle for subsistence and life. They identify freedom with their loving interaction and productive work in co-operation with Mother Earth;[4] knowledge is the subsistence knowledge essential for their survival. For women in the affluent North or in the affluent classes of the South, such a concept of universalism or commonality is not easy to grasp. Survival is seen not as the ultimate goal of life but a banality — a fact that can be taken for granted. It is precisely the value of the everyday work for survival, for life, which has been eroded in the name of the so-called higher values.

ECOFEMINISM

Ecofeminism, "a new term for an ancient wisdom"[5] grew out of various social movements — the feminist, peace and the ecology movements — in the late 1970s and early 1980s. Though the term was first used by Francoise d'Eaubonne[6] it became popular only in the context of numerous protests and activities against environmental destruction, sparked-off initially by recurring ecological disasters. The meltdown at Three Mile Island prompted large numbers of women in the United States to come together in the first ecofeminist conference — "Women and Life on Earth: A Conference on Eco-Feminism in the Eighties" — in March 1980, at Amherst. At this conference the connections between feminism, militarization, healing and ecology were explored. As Ynestra King, one of the conference organizers, wrote:

> Ecofeminism is about connectedness and wholeness of theory and practice. It asserts the special strength and integrity of every living thing. For us the snail darter is to be considered side by side with a community's need for water, the porpoise side by side with appetite for tuna, and the creatures it may fall on with Skylab. We are a woman-identified movement and we believe we have a special work to do in these imperilled times. We see the devastation of the earth and her beings by the corporate warriors, and the threat of nuclear annihilation by the military warriors, as feminist concerns. It is the

same masculinist mentality which would deny us our right to our own bodies and our own sexuality, and which depends on multiple systems of dominance and state power to have its way.[7]

Wherever women acted against ecological destruction or/and the threat of atomic annihilation, they immediately became aware of the connection between patriarchal violence against women, other people and nature, and that: In defying this patriarchy we are loyal to future generations and to life and this planet itself. We have a deep and particular understanding of this both through our natures and our experience as women.[8] . . .

The new developments in biotechnology, genetic engineering and reproductive technology have made women acutely conscious of the gender bias of science and technology and that science's whole paradigm is characteristically patriarchal, anti-nature and colonial and aims to dispossess women of their generative capacity as it does the productive capacities of nature. The founding of the Feminist International Network of Resistance to Genetic and Reproductive Engineering (fiNR-RAGE) in 1984, was followed by a number of important congresses: 1985 in Sweden and in Bonn, 1988 in Bangladesh, and 1991 in Brazil. This movement reached far beyond the narrowly defined women's or feminist movement. In Germany women from trade unions, churches and universities, rural and urban women, workers and housewives mobilized against these technologies; their ethical, economic, and health implications continue to be hotly debated issues. This movement was instrumental in preventing the establishment of a "surrogate motherhood" agency in Frankfurt. The ecofeminist principle of looking for connections where capitalist patriarchy and its warrior science are engaged in disconnecting and dissecting what forms a living whole also informs this movement. Thus those involved look not only at the implications of these technologies for women, but also for animals, plants, for agriculture in the Third World as well as in the industrialized North. They understand that the liberation of women cannot be achieved in isolation, but only as part of a larger struggle for the preservation of life on this planet.

This movement also facilitates the creation of new connections and networks. An African woman at the Bangladesh congress, on hearing of these technologies exclaimed: "If that is progress, we do not want it. Keep it!"

"SPIRITUAL" OR "POLITICAL" ECOFEMINISM?

As women in various movements — ecology, peace, feminist and especially health — rediscovered the interdependence and connectedness of everything, they also rediscovered what was called the spiritual dimension of life — the realization of this interconnectedness was itself sometimes called spirituality. Capitalist and Marxist materialism, both of which saw the achievement of human happiness as basically conditional on the expansion of material goods' production, denied or denigrated this dimension. Feminists also began to realize the significance of the "witch hunts" at the beginning of our modern era insofar as patriarchal science and technology was developed only after these women (the witches) had been murdered and, concomitantly, their knowledge, wisdom and close relationship with nature had been destroyed.[9] The desire to recover, to regenerate this wisdom as a means to liberate women and nature from patriarchal destruction also motivated this turning towards spirituality. The term "spiritual" is ambiguous; it means different things to different people. For some it means a kind of religion, but not one based upon the continuation of the patriarchal, monotheistic religions of Christianity, Judaism or Islam, all of which are arguably hostile to women and to nature vis-à-vis their basic warrior traditions. Hence, some tried to revive or recreate a goddess-based religion; spirituality was defined as the Goddess.

Some call it the female principle, inhabiting and permeating all things — this spirituality is understood in a less "spiritual," that is, less idealistic way. Although the spirit was female, it was not apart from the material world, but seen as the life-force in everything and in every human being: it was indeed the connecting principle. Spirituality in these more material terms was akin to magic rather than to religion as it is commonly understood.[10] This interpretation of spirituality is also spelt out in the writings of Starhawk,[11] for whom spirituality is largely identical to women's sensuality, their sexual energy, their most precious life-force, which links them to each other, to other life forms and the elements. It is the energy that enables women to love and to celebrate life. This sensual or sexual spirituality, rather than "other-worldly" is centered on and thus abolishes the opposition between spirit and matter, transcendence and immanence. There is only immanence, but this immanence is not inert, passive matter devoid of subjectivity, life and spirit. The spirit is inherent in everything and particularly our sensuous experience, because we ourselves with our bodies cannot separate the material from the spiritual. The spiritual is the love without which no life can blossom; it is this magic which is contained within everything. The rediscovered ancient wisdom consisted of the old magic insight into the existence of these all-embracing connections and that through these, powerless women could therefore influence powerful men. This at least informed the thinking of the women who, in 1980, surrounded the Pentagon with their rituals and who formulated the first ecofeminist manifesto.[12]

The ecological relevance of this emphasis on "spirituality" lies in the rediscovery of the sacredness of life, according to which life on earth can be preserved only if people again begin to perceive all life forms as sacred and respect them as such. This quality is not located in an other-worldly deity, in a transcendence, but in everyday life, in our work, the things that surround us, in our immanence. And from time to time there should be celebrations of this sacredness in rituals, in dance and song.

This celebration of our dependence to Mother Earth is quite contrary to the attitude promoted by Francis Bacon and his followers, the fathers of modern science and technology. For them this dependence was an outrage, a mockery of man's right to freedom on his own terms and therefore had forcefully and violently to be abolished. Western rationality, the West's paradigm of science and concept of freedom are all based on overcoming and transcending this dependence, on the subordination of nature to the (male) will, and the disenchantment of all her forces. Spirituality in this context endeavors

to "heal Mother Earth" and to re-enchant the world. This means to undo the process of disenchantment, which Max Weber saw as the inevitable outcome of the European rationalization process.

Ecofeminists in the United States seemingly put greater emphasis on the "spiritual" than do those in Europe. For example, in Germany, particularly since the early 1980s, this tendency has often been criticized as escapism, as signifying a withdrawal from the political sphere into some kind of dream world, divorced from reality and thus leaving power in the hands of men. But the "spiritual" feminists argue that theirs is the politics of everyday life, the transformation of fundamental relationships, even if that takes place only in small communities. They consider that this politics is much more effective than countering the power games of men with similar games. In Germany, too, this debate has to be seen against the background of the emergence of the Greens, who participated in parliamentary politics since 1978. Many feminists joined the Green Party, less out of ecological than feminist concerns. The Greens, however, were keen to integrate these concerns too into their programmes and politics. The critique of the "spiritual" stand within the ecofeminist movement is voiced mainly by men and women from the left. Many women, particularly those who combine their critique of capitalism with a critique of patriarchy and still cling to some kind of "materialist" concept of history, do not easily accept spiritual ecofeminism, because it is obvious that capitalism can also co-opt the "spiritual" feminists' critique of "materialism."

This, indeed, is already happening. The New Age and esoteric movement have created a new market for esoterica, meditation, yoga, magic, alternative health practices, most of which are fragments taken out of the context of oriental, particularly Chinese and Indian, cultures. Now, after the material resources of the colonies have been looted, their spiritual and cultural resources are being transformed into commodities for the world market.

This interest in things spiritual is a manifestation of Western patriarchal capitalist civilization's deep crisis. While in the West the spiritual aspects of life (always segregated from the "material" world), have more and more been eroded, people now look towards the "East," towards pre-industrial traditions in the search for what has been destroyed in their own culture.

This search obviously stems from a deep human need for wholeness, but the fragmented and commodified way in which it takes place is to be criticized. Those interested in oriental spiritualism rarely know, or care to know, how people in, for example India, live or even the socio-economic and political contexts from which these fragments — such as yoga or tai-chi — have been taken. It is a kind of luxury spirituality. It is as Saral Sarkar put it,[13] the idealist icing on top of the material cake of the West's standard of living. Such luxury spiritualism cannot overcome the dichotomies between spirit and matter, economics and culture, because as long as it fails to integrate this search for wholeness into a critique of the existing exploitative world system and a search for a better society it can easily be co-opted and neutralized.

For Third World women who fight for the conservation of their survival base this spiritual icing-on-the-cake, the divorce of the spiritual from the material, is incomprehensible for them; the term Mother Earth does not need to be qualified by inverted commas, because they regard the earth as a living being which guarantees their own and all their fellow creatures' survival. They respect and celebrate Earth's sacredness and resist its transformation into dead, raw material for industrialism and commodity production. It follows, therefore, that they also respect both the diversity and the limits of nature which cannot be violated if they want to survive. It is this kind of materialism, this kind of immanence rooted in the everyday subsistence production of most of the world's women which is the basis of our ecofeminist position. This materialism is neither commodified capitalist nor mechanical Marxist materialism, both of which are based on the same concept of humanity's relationship to nature. But the ecofeminist spirituality as we understand it is not to be confused with a kind of other-worldly spirituality, that simply wants "food without sweat," not caring where it comes from or whose sweat it involves.

. . . Our basic understanding of ecofeminism is a perspective which starts from the fundamental necessities of life; we call this the subsistence per-

spective. Our opinion is that women are nearer to this perspective than men — women in the South working and living, fighting for their immediate survival are nearer to it than urban, middle-class women and men in the North. Yet all women and all men have a body which is directly affected by the destructions of the industrial system. Therefore, all women and finally also all men have a "material base" from which to analyse and change these processes. . . .

NOTES

1. Ortner, S., "Is Female to Male as Nature Is to Culture?" in Rosaldo, M. Z., and L. Lamphere, *Women, Culture and Society,* Stanford University Press, Stanford 1974.
2. Diamond, I., and G. F. Orenstein, *Reweaving the World: The Emergence of Ecofeminism.* Sierra Club Books, San Francisco 1990. Plant, J. *Healing the Wounds: The Promise of Ecofeminism,* New Society Publishers, Philadelphia and Santa Cruz, CA 1989. King, Y. "The Ecology of Feminism and the Feminism of Ecology," in Plant, op. cit., pp. 18–28.
3. Birk, A., and I. Stoehr, "Der Fortschritt entläßt seine Tochter," in Frauen and Ökologie. Gegen den Machbarkeitswahn, Volksblattverlag, Köln 1987.
4. This is based on an interview by Vandana Shiva; see Shiva 1987, op. cit.
5. Diamond and Orenstein, 1990, op. cit.
6. d'Eaubonne, F., "Feminism or Death," in Elaine Marks and Isabelle de Courtivron (eds.), *New French Feminisms, an Anthology,* Amherst University Press, Amherst 1980.
7. King, Y., "The Eco-Feminist Perspective," in Caldecott, L. and S. Leland (eds.), *Reclaiming the Earth: Women Speak out for Life on Earth.* The Women's Press, London 1983, p. 10.
8. Ibid., p. 11.
9. Merchant, C., *The Death of Nature: Women, Ecology and the Scientific Revolution,* Harper & Row, San Francisco 1983.
10. Mies, M., TANTRA, Magie oder Spiritualität? in: beitraege zur.
11. Starhawk, 1982.
12. Caldecott and Leland, op. cit., p. 15.

13. Sarkar, S., Die Bewegung und ihre Strategie. Ein Beitrag zum notwendigen Klärungsprozeß, in *Kommune,* Nr. Frankfurt 1987.

DISCUSSION TOPICS

1. In what ways is the "luxury spiritualism" described by Mies and Shiva different from what they call the "spiritual dimension of life"? Explain your evaluation of each.
2. In what ways do you agree and disagree with the critique of cultural relativism in this essay?
3. Give an example of a multinational corporation that is contributing to the standardization of local cultures. Are there any benefits to this process that Mies and Shiva do not note?
4. Mies and Shiva maintain that ecofeminism is more vital for Third World countries than for industrialized countries. Do you agree with this assessment? Are there subsistence issues in your local community that need attention?

From *States of Grace*

Charlene Spretnak

Charlene Spretnak has authored several books, including Lost Goddesses of Early Greece *(1981) and* The Resurgence of the Real *(1997). In the following essay, drawn from* States of Grace *(1991), she notes the lack of cultural support from a dualistic, anthropocentric culture for the experience of "ecocommunion," of our sacred oneness with the natural world. The experience of grace is the experience of ourselves as particular expressions of the cosmic body. Spretnak argues for the recognition of the reality of our larger self, as found in the bioregion of which we as individuals are a part. She speaks for those ecofeminists who experience nature in the form of the Goddess, one of whose names is "Gaia."**

---

*Gaia is the Greek Earth goddess whose name is often used to suggest that life on Earth functions as one organism. Anthony Weston, "Forms of Gaian Ethics," Environmental Ethics 9, 3 (1987): 217–30.

... To hone our awareness of the ecocommunity, most of us need to begin with basics, such as learning to recognize a dozen native plants, a dozen birds, and other local animals. Professional naturalists in city and regional parks can be of assistance, but it is also worth the effort to seek out the amateur naturalists in one's community. In both my former and present homes, I have enjoyed many half-day bird walks with white-haired ladies who were extremely knowledgeable and encouraging to novices. (All the naturalists I have known were good-natured and wore their knowledge lightly, perhaps because long periods of immersion in the larger reality have imbued them with an existential security that requires no grandstanding. In any case, getting out into nature seems to be good for the disposition, and even beginners find it nearly impossible to return home from birding in a negative mood.) Having a sense of one's bioregion may someday be considered as essential as knowing the local streets and highways. Newcomers might ask their neighbors, "On what day of the week is the local farmers' market held around here? What time of year is the all-species parade?[1] Oh, and who are the local naturalists—we don't want to remain know-nothings for long!"

As we begin to develop a sense of the ecocommunity in which we live, we grow to cherish it. Without much forethought we find ourselves creating personal rituals of communion—making visitations to a particular spot, suspending thought for a long moment at the beginning of the day to let the backyard bird song fill our mind/body, or feeling drawn to observe the daily progress of a budding tree. As our sensitivity increases, certain narrowly focused rituals within the human community seem to cry out for greater fullness. While saying grace before a meal, why not express gratitude not only for our food but for the presence of the animals, plants, landforms, and water? Participating in worship services, why not suggest various ways that the presence of the bioregion can be included? Celebrations of baptism, confirmation, Bar Mitzvah, Bat Mitzvah, and weddings could all include the ritual planting of a tree. Certainly the annual slaughter of millions of firs to celebrate the birth of Christ could be replaced with purchasing live firs, or better still, native trees, which could later be planted or donated to a regional park.

Beyond that, each of our religious rituals, those that mark the stages in an individual's spiritual life as well as those that are communal celebrations in the liturgical cycle, could be enriched by greater recognition of the cosmic web of life.[2] In this era of ecological awakening, the living presence of the ceremonies of native peoples—inspiring acts of regeneration of their sense of interrelatedness with the sacred whole—is a great gift. Perhaps the growing appreciation of their embodied wisdom will lead to an interfaith deepening of the spirituality of Earthlings.

While some people work to "cosmologize" organized religion, others have taken to grow-your-own ceremonies of cosmological celebration, especially at the solstices and equinoxes. The two days with the longest and shortest gift of light from our sun, plus the two days with light and darkness of equal length, plus the midpoint days between those four were celebrated in pre-Christian Europe as natural markers in the majestic cycles of Earth's body. Two of the midpoint holy days are preserved in modern times as May Day and All Saints Day (or All Hallows Day, preceded immediately by Hallows Eve, or "Halloween").[3] Today the solstices and equinoxes have become occasions for groups of friends and family to gather in celebration of the Earth community and to focus awareness on the particular turning of the season. With friends, I have given thanks at autumn equinox for the bountiful harvests of the soil and in our lives, turned inward on the long night of winter solstice to look directly at the dark, known regeneration at spring equinox as Earth's exuberance burst forth, and felt the fullness of fruition at summer solstice when Earth's day is long and sensuous.

Of all those images, the most beautiful that remains with me is the spring equinox ritual we evolved over time.[4] A group of some forty people in spring colors walk from our cars in procession to a gentle rise in a spacious park, carrying armfuls of flowers and greens, food and drink, and burning incense. Musicians among us play instruments as the children toss a trail of petals. We form a circle and place the flowers and greens at our feet, forming a huge garland for the Earth, one foot wide and half as high. In the center on colorful cloths we set baskets of food and objects of regeneration—feathers shed by eagles and other birds, a bowl of water, a small statue of a pregnant female, and several sprays of pink and white blossoms. We breathe together and plant our feet squarely on the warming earth, drawing up its procreative powers into our being. Working mindfully, we take some flowers and ivy from the Earth garland and make individual garlands with trailing ribbons for ourselves, then weave together the stems and greens in the grand garland. Standing, we call upon the presence of the East and the cleansing winds that clear our minds. We call upon the presence of the South and the fires of warmth and energy that enliven us. We call upon the presence of the West and the water that soothes and renews us. We call upon the presence of the North and the earth that grounds and feeds us. We sing, perhaps the Indian song "The Earth Is Our Mother." We seat ourselves around the garland and offer into the circle one-word poems about spring in our bioregion. Someone reads a favorite poem. A storyteller, accompanied by soft drumming and birdsong flute, tells an ancient tale of the meaning of spring. We sing a lilting song with her. A second storyteller tells another story of spring. We sing a rhythmic chant with him. The two bards put on masks they have made and dance and leap around the circle, sprung with vernal energies. In counterpoint, the men sing his song, the women hers. We rise and sway like saplings as we sing. We move as the spirit moves us, dancing, turning. When we come to rest, we sit, emptied of song, on the ground and let the flute song fill our bodies. We pass around a bowl of berries, each person taking one and offering into the circle thoughts of thanksgiving for particular gifts of spring. Brimming with love for the embodied wisdom of Gaia, we bid farewell to the presence of the four directions and break the circle. Then come feasting and visiting. Thus do we welcome spring.

THE ECOLOGICAL IMPERATIVE

. . . Our species is but one expression of the cosmos. We have always played an interactive role with the rest of the Earth community. There is no possibility that we could refrain from intervention; even walking down a street, we probably crush countless tiny creatures. Our bodies require food, warmth, clothing, and shelter — all of which we take from earthstuff. The *problem* is the denial of humility and care that marks the modern and ultra-modern revolutions against the integrity of Gaia, a dynamic unfolding that was well established long before our emergence. Our species' ethics should include the fulfilling of our vital needs with minimal damage to our cosmic relations. If that were our guideline, we would surely have to admit that our knowledge of the intricacies of Gaian life is so far from complete that we should make far-reaching changes in the ecosystems only with great caution.

Since the dominant culture continues to rush in the opposite direction — cleaning up a few production processes, for example, while still maintaining ravenous growth economies that devour habitats with dazzling efficiency — Gaian spirituality calls for "action prayers," activist engagement with those human systems that are furthering the gratuitous destruction of the Earth community. Much "green" activism in the industrialized nations as well as the Third and Fourth Worlds has been sustained by spiritual commitment.

Commitment, to be effective, must also be informed. Understanding basic principles of ecology — interdependence, diversity, resilience, adaptability, and limits — is necessary in opposing unwise human intervention.[5] People with untempered faith in the supposedly value-free, objective life of technology often insist that environmental dynamics are so complicated that the public should back off and let commissions of scientific experts make all decisions, which would then be enacted by government. If memory serves, that course of action gave us scores of dangerous nuclear power plants; numerous disastrous assaults on the ecological integrity of watersheds by the U.S. Army Corps of Engineers; approval of hundreds of toxic compounds for agricultural, industrial, and medical uses; and a flood of federal research funding for the development of genetically engineered animals, pesticides, and crops without adequate testing of *dynamic* interaction, such as will occur in a real ecosystem once a new microorganism leaves the lab. The burden of proof (of safety) should be on the people pushing for

novel, substantial change in the ecosystems, not on the citizens calling for caution.

Not only is it difficult for concerned citizens working through existing channels in modern technocracies to defend sustainability against destructive projects that will boost the GNP (a tally that includes costs of attempted environmental cleanup as if it were merely part of value-free production and services), but the voices of millions of other residents are not heard at all. In a parliament of all species, humans' expansionist schemes for industrial mastery of the biosphere would no doubt be hooted off the floor as too unbearably callous, greedy, and murderous to merit a formal vote. Because the existing governmental channels in societies with growth economies are not designed to welcome sustainable earth ethics in more than superficial ways, grassroots movements have had to mount direct, usually nonviolent, challenges to ecocide. Such campaigns demand much time and energy and often yield frustration. Yet, for increasing numbers of people worldwide, that work is experienced not merely as attempts to save enough of the biosphere for human survival, but as moral acts that embody our felt connection with the sacred whole. John Seed, a defender of the rain forests in Australia, has described the Gaian spiritual transformation he underwent in the course of his activism: "'I am protecting the rain forest' develops to 'I am part of the rain forest protecting myself. I am that part of the rain forest recently emerged into thinking.'" Through continuing engagement, he has found, one's Gaian memory improves.[6] . . .

CULTURAL FEMINISM AND THE HISTORY OF GODDESS SPIRITUALITY

Since the mid-seventies a movement of spiritual renewal that honors nature, the female, and the body has flourished in our society: the reclaiming of Goddess spirituality. The genesis of this recovery was part of the movement by many women from radical to cultural feminism, although there is still much overlap. In the initial burst of the current wave of feminism, the source of women's oppression was located in "male chauvinism" and "white males." Some feminists still cite the latter term as the cause of social ills. Many of us, however, came to focus attention on the dynamics of *acculturation* that maintained attitudes devaluing women. We located the problem in socialization rather than in oppressive types of supposedly inherent masculine behavior. Hence there is a good deal of common ground between cultural feminism and certain aspects of deconstructive-postmodern feminism.[7]

In my own life, I can recall the exact moment of the shift to a cultural analysis. I was traveling to a meditation retreat in 1974 in New Mexico from southern Illinois in a Volkswagen "Beetle" with two friends from our local women's center. Someone had recommended *The First Sex* by Elizabeth Gould Davis, which I had purchased and was reading in the backseat. Over the engine noise I would call out, "Amazing! Listen to this!" and read passage after passage. Davis revealed countless examples of how woman's cultural and legal status declined as Christianity gradually transformed the Celtic societies in France, England, Ireland, the Rhineland, and elsewhere. She also noted that Christian conversion succeeded in Celtic Europe only when the people agreed to accept "Mary" as a new name for the Goddess. As I read on with sustained astonishment, the fixed entity that had been taught to me as "history" disassembled along Interstate 40, and I saw for the first time that *patriarchy is a cultural construct* — although I did not conclude, as deconstructionists do, that there is *nothing but* cultural construction in human experience. (Even though I could see that Davis made a number of unwarranted leaps in her conclusions, I hope her memory will be honored as a catalyst for the more careful studies that followed.)

Cultural feminism has focused on prepatriarchal culture (such as Neolithic Old Europe), nonpatriarchal culture (such as the Hopi), dynamics of oppression in patriarchal culture, and creative possibilities for postpatriarchal culture. From this branch of feminism the terms "patriarchal culture," "patriarchal religion," and so forth have spread to the others. That the informing expressions of the prepatriarchal Neolithic era stood out in our readings, fixing the attention of women who had been raised in patriarchal religion, is not surprising. Feminist critiques of the Jewish and Christian traditions were

already in the air,[8] but they did not offer the spark of possibility that we found in poring over statues, symbols, and mythic narratives from the age of the Goddess. We discovered powerful female bodies of all sizes honored and revered; statues that were half bird and half female, linking humanity with the rest of nature; ritual figurines of female bodies incised with representations of life-giving water; symbols of the sacred pelvic triangle of the female; and sacred myths of the transformative powers of the Earth and the female celebrated in ecstatic dance and holy rite. Imagine our surprise.

During that period of awakening, I became engrossed with reconstructing the pre-Olympian myths of early Greece, the sacred stories and symbolism of the pre-Hellenic goddesses, whose artifacts, shrines, and other historic documentation long predate the arrival of the Indo-European thunderbolt god, Zeus, and his patriarchal soap opera on Mount Olympus.[9] The shift from the pre-Indo-European religion (centered on goddesses, who were enmeshed with people's daily experiencing of the energy forces in life and who were powerful sources of compassion and protection, as well as inspiration for divine wisdom and just law) to the Indo-Europeanized Greek religion (centered on a chieftain sky-god who was "up there" and remote, judgmental, warlike, and often involved in local strife) was well established. Yet I and other "spirituality feminists" were curious to know more about the societal transformation in which the disempowerment of the Goddess was embedded.

Over the years numerous studies have appeared documenting widespread occurrences of Goddess spirituality in Old Europe, the Middle East, Asia, Africa, and the Americas. It would be most interesting if an international task force of cultural historians were constituted to assemble and synthesize all the evidence regarding the myriad incidents of societal shift from Goddess to God, from matrifocal to patriarchal culture. (Most feminist cultural historians interested in the long era of the Goddess in various societies avoid the term "matriarchal," since the archaeological findings usually indicate a roughly gender-egalitarian society or are inconclusive regarding sex-role dominance — although many excavated sites clearly do reflect the centrality of women's social roles. Because "matriarchy" connotes the inverse of a power-over, male-dominant society, cultural feminists and several archaeologists prefer to use *matrifocal, matristic, matricentric, gynecentric,* and so forth, since the cultural artifacts demonstrate a focus on the transformative powers of the female regardless of whatever the exact form of government may have been.) Eventually, many matrifocal, matrilineal cultures were pressured to shift to patriarchal arrangements when they were confronted with dominant forces of Christianity, Islam, or Eurocentric colonialism.[10] Male-dominant cultures certainly existed before those powerful forces of social, economic, and religious conversion spread out over the world, but they did account for a sizable boost in the incidence of patriarchal societies. . . .

EARTHBODY AND PERSONAL BODY AS SACRED

The contemporary renaissance of Goddess spirituality draws on a growing body of knowledge about historical Goddess religion but is shaped and energized by the living practice, which is both personal and communal, ancient and spontaneous. The initial response to learning of the historical presence of Goddess religion, at least for myself, was wonder, followed by gratitude that the entire phenomenon, which had nearly been paved over by patriarchal culture, might now be known. That wonder was followed by puzzlement at what Goddess religion might mean to the spiritual lives of women in contemporary circumstances. Poring over the hundreds of photographs of Goddess figurines, bas-reliefs, and frescoes, one could not fail to grasp the centrality of the elemental power of the female body, jarring as that was to any reader raised under patriarchy.[11] Absorbing even a little of that orientation made it easy to see why our Neolithic, and probably even our Paleolithic, ancestors perceived the bountiful manifestations of the Earth as emanating from a fertile body—an immense female whose tides moved in rhythm with the moon, whose rivers sustained life, whose soil/flesh yielded food, whose caves offered ritual womb-rooms for ceremonies of sacred community within her body, whose vast subterranean womb received all humans in burial. It is not difficult to understand why they held Her sacred.

To even attempt to surmise the Neolithic thought processes that informed the artistic expressions of female forms and the ritual practices that must have surrounded them, however, was more difficult, even though Gimbutas's work has helped to sort the multiplicity of forms and focus on the recurring symbols of water, birth, regeneration, and so forth.[12] Stare as one might at, say, a small sculpted circle of ritual female dancers, one could not know, more than five thousand years later, what the actual and entire practice has been. Hence the contemporary expressions of Goddess spirituality, including its flowering in the arts,[13] are not simply attempts to replicate the extremely ancient religion that long preceded "the lost weekend" of patriarchal culture. Rather, they are creative spiritual practice, which is embedded in a profound historical tradition and, more fundamentally, in the female dimension of being.

Some forms of contemporary Goddess spirituality are entirely "free-form," creating practices by drawing directly on inspiration from the artifacts, myths, and other remnants of Goddess religion in early Greece, the biblical lands, Africa, Asia, and the pre-Columbian Americas. Other forms involved participation in mediating traditions, that is, systems of worship such as Goddess-centered "native European" witchcraft or the African-based folk religions of the Caribbean and Brazil. Some ancient traditions of Goddess spirituality, such as that of the Goddess Akonedi in Ghana, have spread to Europe and the Americas in recent decades through immigration. While there is great diversity within contemporary Goddess spirituality, the common threads among the forms that grew out of feminist renewal are the desire to honor the Earthbody and one's personal body via an ongoing birthing process of cosmological unfolding—the intention to articulate as deeply and fully as possible one's ontological potential as an embodied Earthbeing, a weaver of the cosmic web. . . .

The contemporary practice of Goddess spirituality includes creative participation in myth, symbol, and ritual. Because this spiritual orientation honors the elemental power of the female and its embeddedness in nature, it was perceived as regressive, embarrassing, or even horrifying to liberal and material/socialist feminists, who apparently accepted the patriarchal dualism of nature-versus-culture and had internalized the patriarchal rationalization that the reason women had traditionally been blocked from participation in culture was their bodily "plight" of being mired in the reproductive processes of nature. Investing their consciousness within such an orientation, it is quite understandable that "modern" feminists recoil (I use the present tense here because it still occurs today) when "spiritual feminists" celebrate our bodies and our elemental connectedness with nature. If one subscribes to the patriarchal view of culture as human endeavor pursued in opposition to nature, drawing attention to such connections automatically places women outside the realm of culture as "biological agents" *instead of* "cultural agents." The renewal of Goddess spirituality, however, rejected the patriarchal dualism from the outset. Like countless prepatriarchal and nonpatriarchal societies, we women who had drifted out of patriarchal religion[14] view culture not as a struggle in opposition to nature but as a potentially harmonious extension of nature, a human construction inclusive of creative tensions and reflective of our embeddedness in the Earthbody and the teachings of nature: diversity, subjectivity, adaptability, interrelatedness. Within such an orientation—let's call it ecological sanity—the bodily affinity of females and males with nature is respected and culturally honored, rather than denied and scorned.

The central understanding in contemporary Goddess spirituality is that the divine—creativity in the universe, or ultimate mystery—is laced throughout the cosmic manifestations in and around us. The divine is immanent, not concentrated in some distant seat of power, a transcendent sky-god. Instead of accepting the notion in patriarchal religion that one must spiritually transcend the body and nature, it is possible to apprehend divine transcendence as the sacred whole, or the infinite complexity of the universe. The Goddess, as a metaphor for divine immanence and the transcendent sacred whole, expresses ongoing regenerations with the cycles of her Earthbody and contains the mystery of diversity within unity: the extraordinary range of differentiation in forms of life on Earth issued from her dynamic form and are kin. A second aspect of con-

temporary Goddess spirituality is the empowerment experienced by people as they come to grasp their heritage and presence in terms of the cosmological self, the dimension of human existence that participates in the larger reality. Such empowerment is far different from a dominating "power-over," the binding force of social constructions in a patriarchal culture. Rather, it is a strengthening of one's capabilities of subjectivity and cosmic unfolding within a web of caring and solidarity that extends backward and forward in time, drawing one from the fragmentation and lonely atomization of modernity to the deepest levels of connectedness. A third aspect of Goddess spirituality is the perceptual shift from the death-based sense of existence that underlies patriarchal culture to a regeneration-based awareness, an embrace of life as a cycle of creative rebirths, a dynamic participation in the processes of infinity.

. . . Goddess spirituality celebrates the power of the erotic as the sparking of cosmic potential, rather than wrestling with the erotic as a process that potentially yields a new generation and hence the signal of one's approaching end. The erotic and the sensuous, expressed through the aesthetic, draw forth not only physical generation but unpredictably creative waves of spiritual, intellectual, and emotional renewal. . . .

NOTES

1. All-species parades are community celebrations of the animal citizens in the bioregion. Generally they feature children in costumes of local animals. Further information is available from the All-Species Project, 804 Apodaca Hill, Santa Fe, NM 85701.

2. For example, a tree-planting ceremony at home or on public land needing more vegetation could be part of rites of baptism, First Communion, marriage, and funerals. The liturgical language used in all of those ceremonies could be enriched by including awareness and appreciation of the creation.

   An example of moving in the other direction, that is, bringing rituals of blessing and thanksgiving to events of the natural world, is offered by Gertrude Mueller Nelson in "Blessing for First Fruits and Herbs," using Psalm 65 and derived from "the old ones found in the Roman Ritual" in her inspiring book *To Dance with God: Family Ritual and Community Celebration* (Mahwah, NJ: Paulist Press, 1986), 211.

3. People who observe all eight of the old "Earth holy days" usually consider themselves part of the neo-Pagan movement. "Pagan" means "country person."

4. The spring garland for the Earth in that ritual was the idea of the late Leslie Mahler, a creative and inspiring ritualist whose presence is deeply missed. Some of the other elements, including the songs, traveled from other ritual groups. A cassette tape of several widely used Earth-ritual songs, *Reclaiming Chants,* is available from the Reclaiming Collective, P.O. Box 14404, San Francisco, CA 94114.

5. A good textbook on ecology is *Living in the Environment* by G. Tyler Miller, Jr. (Belmont, CA: Wadsworth Publishing, 1982).

6. John Seed, "Beyond Anthropocentrism," in John Seed, Joanna Macy, Pat Fleming, and Arne Naess, *Thinking Like a Mountain: Towards A Council of All Beings* (Philadelphia and Santa Cruz: New Society Publishers, 1988), 36.

7. Two . . . expressions of cultural feminism are my "Naming the Cultural Forces that Push Us toward War" in *Exposing Nuclear Phallacies,* ed. Dianna E. H. Russell (New York: Pergamon Press, 1989) and my introduction to *The Politics of Women's Spirituality* (Garden City, NY: Doubleday, 1982), which proposes, among other things, that cultural power hoarded by males is a compensatory response to a fearful perception of the elemental power of the female, and that Jungian notions of the "eternal feminine" and the passive receptivity it entails are cultural constructions of patriarchy rather than universal truths about females.

8. See Mary Daly, *The Church and the Second Sex* (New York: Harper & Row, 1968) and Elizabeth Cady Stanton and the Revising Committee, *The Woman's Bible* (1895), republished as *The Original Feminist Attack on the Bible* (New York: Arno Press, 1974). Also available by then was Mary Daly's *Beyond God the Father: Toward a Philosophy of*

Women's Liberation (Boston: Beacon Press, 1973), which she refers to in the introduction as a sequel to *The Church and the Second Sex* and which advocated women's charting a post-patriarchal path.

It is important to note that Canaan was one of the last, not first, areas on the eastern Mediterranean region and southeastern Europe to "go patriarchal." The Yahwehists who migrated into Canaan definitely were not the sole cause of the destruction of all Goddess religion.

9. See Charlene Spretnak, *Lost Goddesses of Early Greece: A Collection of Pre-Hellenic Myths* (Boston: Beacon Press, 1981).

10. See, for example, Peggy Reeves Sanday, "The Decline of the Women's World: The Effect of Colonialism," chapter 7, in *Female Power and Male Dominance: On the Origins of Sexual Inequality* (Cambridge: Cambridge University Press, 1981).

11. For a thoughtful exploration of this experience, see Adrienne Rich, "Prepatriarchal Female/Goddess Images," in *The Politics of Women's Spirituality* (Garden City, NY: Doubleday, 1982), excerpted from her *Of Woman Born: Motherhood as Experience and Institution* (New York: W. W. Norton, 1976).

12. See Gimbutas, *Language of the Goddess.*

Skeptics sometimes accuse feminist cultural historians of "prettifying" the pre-Indo-European goddesses by ignoring the bloodthirsty, devouring ones, which they are certain must have existed. Actually, those forms seem to arise with the advent of patriarchal culture. The prepatriarchal goddesses represented the entire cycle of being—birth, maturation, death, regeneration—but apparently not as demonic forces. Even Kali, the devouring Hindu goddess, is believed by many scholars to be a revisited version of an indigenous Earth goddess who long predated the Aryan invasion; see the discussion by David R. Kinsley in chapter 3 of *The Sword and the Flute: Kali and Krsna* (Berkeley: University of California Press, 1975)

13. See Elinor W. Gadon, *The Once and Future Goddess* (San Francisco: Harper & Row, 1989) and Gloria Feman Orenstein, *The Reflowering*

of the Goddess (New York: Pergamon Press, 1990).

Also see Mary Beth Edelson, *Seven Cycles: Public Rituals; Seven Sites: Painting on Walls;* and *Shape Shifters: Seven Mediums* (all available from the artist: 110 Mercer St., New York, NY 10012).

Also see Janine Canan, ed., *She Rises Like the Sun: Invocations of the Goddess by Contemporary American Women Poets* (Freedom, CA: The Crossing Press, 1989).

14. Although the focus of this chapter is the renewal of Goddess spirituality by women who left institutional patriarchal religion, I do not mean to imply that only those women who left were feminist. A strong feminist movement exists today within both Judaism and Christianity. . . .

DISCUSSION TOPICS

1. Have you had experiences of oneness with nature? Have these experiences seemed remote from your daily life? Why do you believe that such experiences should (or should not) be cultivated?
2. Spretnak affirms that women have a special connection with the Earthbody. Do you agree with her? Why or why not?
3. Do you believe it is important to establish whether Earth Goddess–worshiping cultures have existed? What relevance, if any, would these have to environmental ethics? Explain.

READING 49

From *The Legacy of Luna*

Julia "Butterfly" Hill

Julia "Butterfly" Hill lived in a 200-foot redwood tree from December 10, 1997, to December 18, 1999, above the community of Stafford, California, about 230 miles north of San Francisco. The tree, over 1000 years old, is named Luna. As a result of her commitment, the

Pacific Lumber Company agreed to save Luna and a 200-foot buffer zone around the tree in exchange for her exit from the tree and $50,000 from her supporters, which Pacific Lumber would donate to Humboldt State University for forestry research. In 1999 Julia Hill created the Circle of Life Foundation. The selection that follows is drawn from The Legacy of Luna *(2000). Hill describes some of the physical and mental challenges she faced, as well as the power of a commitment to spiritually based, nonviolent civil disobedience.*

EMBODYING LOVE

The onslaught continued for twelve days. In an effort to terrorize us into coming down, Pacific Lumber's crew continued to cut dozens of trees around us, not just the two growing off Luna's trunk.

"Look, we're going through the trees, we're going through the trees," they taunted. "We're going through the big trunk next."

To make a tree fall in a certain direction, they drive a wedge into it. Since I was raised in a Christian background, driving that wedge into the tree reminded me of the crucifixion. Jesus, an amazing prophet of love, was crucified by others driving spikes through him into a fallen tree.

Once the wedge pushes through that final crack and just a few threads remain, the tree starts to rip. As its final shreds are broken, it makes this horrible scream before crashing into those trees near it, breaking any branches in its way. It's a bone-shattering sound all the way down, and then *wham!*, the ground shakes and the air hums and everything vibrates with this fallen warrior.

Then for a single breath, everything gets deathly quiet. I didn't recognize that brief moment of silence in the beginning; it took going through the cutting day after day to hear that space when everything falls silent as if paying due respect. Then a split second later, the noise returns. With the bigger trees the loggers whoop and holler, as if they had killed a deer with big antlers.

About a week and a half into our big sit, the loggers turned their chain saws on a big Douglas fir just west of Luna. They tend to cut the big ones uphill so they don't shatter upon impact, an all-too-frequent occurrence, because of high winds, that renders all the timber useless. That meant that this Douglas fir was being cut directly toward us.

One look told me that it would come close. I wanted to show people how recklessly these people were cutting — and how they were losing control of these trees — so I grabbed the video camera. Since loggers are paid per board feet instead of by the hour, they are pushed to cut bigger, better, and faster. So they work in conditions they shouldn't, and they take chances. But by choosing to cut such a big tree, so close to Luna, and in the day's high wind conditions, they chose to gamble with our lives. They — and I — nearly lost.

By now, I had gotten comfortable enough to do some climbing without a harness. Ironically, I preferred it that way. This time, though encumbered by my video camera, I had ventured pretty far out on a branch, determined to get the shot. The famous camera, however, didn't want to focus. As I tried to get it to work, I heard them slamming the wedge into our huge neighbor, *clank, clink, clank, clink.* I knew this was the final push before the tree went smashing into the ground. *Creaaaaaak, groan, snap, crash!* It started to fall while I was still trying to focus. As it thundered downward, the Douglas fir hit the outer branches of Luna.

Wham!

I dropped the camera and slid about two or three feet, until I managed to reach out and grab onto a nearby branch. With my legs tightened around one branch and my arms wrapped around another, I hung sideways over a hundred feet in the air.

"Oh, s..t!" I heard the logger yell. Those are words you don't want to hear from your surgeon, your haircutter, or your logger.

"You almost killed me, and that's all you have to say?" I yelled back.

Holding on as tightly as possible, I finally managed to regain my balance and pull myself back up. Only once I was safe did the reality that I'd almost dropped over a hundred feet hit me.

"I'm out in the middle of nowhere, surrounded by angry loggers with big chain saws, the winds are intense, and I'm in a tree," I finally acknowledged to myself. "If an accident happens this high up, I'm dead. Period."

That was a scary moment. But things were moving so quickly that I didn't focus on it very long. After a momentary shudder, I got back down to business. The loggers weren't stopping, so neither could we. We had to keep trying to get through to them.

They didn't stop until December 23. Instead of twelve days of Christmas, we had twelve days of chain saws, all day, every day. Each time a chain saw cut through those trees, I felt it cut through me as well. It was like watching my family being killed. And just as we lose a part of ourselves with the passing of a family member or friends, so did I lose a part of myself with each fallen tree.

My first reaction was to want to strike out like an animal that's hurt or afraid. I wanted to stop the violence, I wanted to stop the pain, I wanted to stop the suffering, I wanted to stop these men who were cutting this hillside in complete disregard for the forest and the people's lives in Stafford below. I had hate for everything. I even had hate for myself because I was disgusted that I was part of a race of people with such a lack of respect. I was angry with myself for having been part of such a society for so long.

But then I began to pray.

I knew that if I didn't find a way to deal with my anger and hate, they would overwhelm me and I would be swallowed up in the fear, sadness, and frustration. I knew that to hate and strike out was to be a part of the same violence I was trying to stop. And so I prayed.

"Please, Universal Spirit, please help me find a way to deal with this, because if I don't, it's going to consume me."

You see that a lot in activists. The intense negative forces that are oppressing and destroying the Earth wind up overcoming many of them. They get so absorbed by the hate and the anger that they become hollow. I knew I didn't want to go there. Instead, my hate had to turn to love — unconditional agape, love.

One day, through my prayers, an overwhelming amount of love started flowing into me, filling up the dark hole that threatened to consume me. I suddenly realized that what I was feeling was the love of the Earth, the love of Creation. Every day we, as a species, do so much to destroy Creation's ability to give us life. But that Creation continues to do everything in its power to give us life anyway. And that's true love.

If that beautiful source of Creation of which we're all a part could do that for us, I reasoned, then I had to find it within myself to have that feeling of unconditional love not only for the Earth as a planet, but also for humanity—even for those destroying the gift of life right in front of me.

But how to embody that philosophy? Somehow, I had to reach out on a personal level to the men cutting down the forest around me.

First, I tried reasoning with the loggers.

"What's the point in cutting at the rate you're cutting?" I asked. "Pretty soon all the trees will be gone. Then what will you do for work?"

I said whatever came to mind. I was emulating those activists who tried to talk issues with the loggers to slow them down. But I knew so little about the issues at that time, the loggers just blew me out of the water. They had been there, done that, heard it a billion times, and had an answer for everything.

So I started talking more on a human level. I always knew when I hit a good point, because they would immediately start up their chain saw or tell me, "F... you." Those were the standard responses when they weren't sure how to respond. I tried to get one guy to understand that old growth has a purpose, that Creation wouldn't have made things to grow old if they weren't meant to grow old.

"They're gonna fall over and die anyway, so what's your problem?" he responded.

I explained that it's important for the trees to fall over—it's part of the cycle, they become food for the Earth. I told him that we humans are supposed to become food for the Earth when we die, but we encase ourselves in coffins and other ways that will keep us from being part of the cycle.

Uninterested, he started up his chain saw. While he cut down yet another tree, I tried to figure out a way to get through to him. Suddenly, it hit me.

"Hey," I yelled once the chain saw grew silent.

"What!" he yelled back.

"You have any grandparents?"

"Yeah, so what?"

"Are they alive?"

"Yeah, what's it to ya?"

"Well, why don't we just kill them? They're just going to fall over and die anyway. So what good are they?"

"F... you!" he screamed, immediately pull-starting his saw.

I knew that if I continued to debate politics and science—and stayed in the mind instead of the heart and the spirit—it would always be about one side versus the other. We all understand love, however; we all understand respect, we all understand dignity, and we all understand compassion up to a certain point. But how could I convince the loggers to transfer those feelings that they might have for a human being to the forest? And how could I get them to let go of their stereotypes of me? Because in their mind, I was a tree-hugging, granola-eating, dirty, dreadlocked hippie *environmentalist*. They always managed to say this word with such disgust and disdain!

As I thought about this one afternoon, I remembered that I still had copies of one of the nicest snapshots ever taken of me, from my dear friend Kimberly's birthday just three months before I'd come up into the tree. I had sent them out to friends and family for Christmas, but I had a bunch left. Maybe seeing me made up and dressed in a silk suit and heels would shake up their stereotype of me!

Then I spied a canister in which we had stored some granola. I started laughing. I would show them that even "normal" people eat granola and that you didn't have to be a dirty, grungy, hairy, tree-hugging, leftist, extremist, radical *environmentalist* to like it. So I got a little plastic baggie, put in some granola and my photograph, sealed it off, and climbed down as low as I could. As usual, it was very cold and windy.

"Hey, buddy!" I said to the logger closest to the base of the tree. "I got something for ya."

"What?" he asked.

"I've got a gift for you. I want you to take a look at this. I've got a photograph of me, and I want you to see that I don't look like what you think I look like. Your preconceptions of me are wrong," I said, "and half the problem here is that you're dealing with me on the basis of your preconceptions. I'm trying to deal with you as a human being, and I'm not looking at you as some horrible logger. You won't do the same back, so I want you to see that I'm more human than you think I am. So I'm dropping this thing down on the ground."

"You *better* not drop anything on me!"

"Chill out, man. It's really small, it's a plastic baggie," I retorted. "It's got some granola in it. I figure you're probably hungry, and it's really good stuff. And it's got a photograph in it. Just take a look."

So I dropped it down on the ground and stayed seated on my branch. Though I didn't have a real clear view, I watched him pick the package up. After a few moments, he yelled up.

"You're lying! That's not you!"

"That was taken on September 13 of this year. That's me," I assured him. "Granted, my tan has faded, my hair's not quite as clean and styled, I'm not wearing makeup, and I'm not dressed in a suit, but that's me. I want you to see how silly our preconceptions of each other are. We gotta let go of that and get over it. Get over our appearances."

"Damn! You really look like this?"

"Yeah."

"Then what the hell you doing up in a tree?"

That exchange definitely broke some barriers and took the edge off for a long time. The loggers joked that I had climbed into a tree simply because I hadn't found the right guy. Finding him for me, they decided, would solve all our problems. They were still angry that I was up in a tree and in their way, but they definitely started connecting with me on more of a human level. I was no longer this preconceived idea. As I became more real, they grew nicer. They never did tell me if they ate the granola.

During this time, Almond, too, struggled with feelings of sadness and frustration. But whereas I experienced a transforming lesson of love and connection, Almond just seemed to sink deeper and deeper into despair and anger.

I love Almond a lot; I think he's a wonderful human being, and I'm really thankful for his friendships and insights. He taught me about the movement and about the history of activism while we were in the tree. Together we discussed strategy. He also impressed upon me the need for media outreach,

which we saw as the biggest failure with the Luna tree-sit. The whole point of a tree-sit, he repeated, was to draw public attention to the problem. His energy and his view of the world, however, were a lot darker than mine. I am the eternal optimist. But, even so, it was really tough to be the eternal optimist considering everything else I was going through.

I felt like I was being hit with wave after wave of negative feelings, and I was having to struggle day in and day out to transform those negative feelings into positive ones. I began to be very concerned about Almond. Day by day, he seemed to grow more drawn. His already deep-set eyes and his striking cheekbones and thick eyebrows were a part of him when I met him, but as the onslaught wore on, his cheeks and eyes sunk in more and more. He started looking like a skeleton, his skin stretched tight over the bones underneath. His life seemed to be draining away in front of my eyes.

"Why are you still up here?" I finally asked. "You're sinking away, you're struggling. This is obviously not a healthy place for you to be. You can't keep going like this. It's just too much."

Thankfully, Almond recognized that he was in a downward spiral that would be hard to shake in the tree. He needed to go somewhere safe, without the intensity of the wind and the loggers.

"But I don't want you to feel like I'm abandoning you," he announced. "I'm going to stick around. I'm going to try to help as much as I can."

Up to this time, Almond and I had been in this together and made Luna home. When we arrived in December, we had realized that the platform needed a lot of work. Basically it was falling apart. First, Almond set about fixing it up for the cold and the rain. Then he built a better water-catching system. The system I had devised, which was a tarp bowl out in the open, worked really well until the wind picked up and blew all the water out. So Almond created a better one, more protected and accessible from the inside, which allowed us to collect most, if not all, of the water we needed from our tarps.

Almond's choice for our platform renovation was duct tape. I would go out after the storms and gather branches that had broken off Luna during storms and haul them back up to the platform. Then he would use whatever rope, twine, or yarn we had up in the tree, along with his ever-present duct tape, to make a frame to hold the tarps up. By the time he was done, our whole fort was one big web of silver tape!

An unexpected two-week dry spell graced our construction phase. The wind, however, was a constant. It never stopped. Then came Christmas Eve and Christmas Day, and for once it was wonderfully quiet. The chain saws and loggers had taken a rest from ripping flesh from bone, trees from earth. The howling wind had slowed down as well. That was the best Christmas present Almond and I could have been given — the gift of peace! Though I didn't know it, I'd need those days of rejuvenation for what lay ahead.

Once our fort was resurrected, I began to settle into my new life. Certain basic details, like going to the bathroom, had almost become natural. *Almost* being the operative word.

After my first sit in Luna, I realized that this tree-sit hadn't been geared toward women. So I designed a more feminine toilet, consisting of a funnel with a hose. I changed this to a jar after wind kept ripping the funnel and hose.

I actually had two bathrooms. The first one consisted of the jar, which just got dumped overboard with each use. The wind would spread the urine over quite a large area in the time it took to fall a hundred and eighty feet. If Luna had been located in a dry forest, I wouldn't have been able to do that. The urine's acidity would have killed everything. But all the water in this forest made it okay.

The other bathroom was composed of a bucket lined with a heavy-duty trash bag. Nature had provided a storage space by striking Luna with lightning and burning out a huge cave. The bags were stored there until somebody offered to pack out the waste.

Cleaning up with our carefully rationed water also required a certain amount of ingenuity. My sponge baths were usually more like sponge dashes because of the cold. Once I had some privacy, I would heat water with a natural soap, strip from the waist down, and scrub like mad for all of about two minutes, if that, then grab a towel and dry off quickly before throwing my clothes back on. The tempera-tures and water and fuel rations just didn't allow for rinsing! Then I'd strip from the waist up and repeat the process. I washed my hair rarely, if at all. It took too much water and was usually so cold that if I got my head wet, I'd wind up sick.

In short, it wasn't easy. Whenever I'd get frustrated with these hygiene arrangements, however, I'd remember the seven families in Stafford who didn't even have homes, let alone a bathroom. That helped me readjust my focus back to what was important.

On the nesting front, I did what I could to make our small, wind-buffeted platform as cozy as possible. I added ambience and light by turning an extra little pot into a candleholder, which also doubled as a windscreen. For reading or writing during sleepless nights, I converted Almond's headlamp into a lantern. I had this only for the time that Almond was in the tree. The rest of the time, I had only candles.

It made me realize how little I really needed to get by and how much growing up poor helped on that front. I knew what it was like to eat oatmeal every day for breakfast for a month because that was all we had. But in Luna, I learned that there are things a lot more important than a gourmet meal — or even a real roof over one's head.

Actually, not having a solid roof or walls helped me notice details that otherwise would have completely escaped me. When the rain started up again following our short reprieve, for example, I noticed its musky scent, like the sweet sweat of the Earth. And I heard two different noises as it fell — the rain dripping through the branches, and the rain hitting the forest floor in the clearing below. Raindrops falling onto my tarps sounded like popcorn popping. It made me think of my father, who loves popcorn, and my childhood because we used to have it just about every night at home.

Living in Luna made me start to pay attention to things so much more. Everything in life is its own little world, but most of us have gotten so caught up in our narrow arenas that we've forgotten to realize the magic and the beauty that are in all the other little interconnected worlds, too. The magical world of Luna is just phenomenal, down to how these trees disperse the water that falls from the sky.

I was sitting in the fog one day, unable to see past Luna's branches, when I noticed that the needles at the top part of the tree are knobbier than the needles lower down. Up high they look like gnarled fingers raking in the moisture from the fog and the rain. The water, drip by drip, gathers until it starts swirling down the trunk to the ground, over the smooth bark at the tip of the tree toward the increasingly shaggy bark down below, which absorbs more and more of the meandering flow. Toward the bottom of the tree, the needles become flatter and smoother. I imagine that's because they don't need to gather as much moisture. Instead, they act like a sprinkler system for the forest floor.

Soon it was New Year's Eve, and the first anniversary of the Stafford slide. From up in Luna, Stafford looks like a miniature town. As I watched it from my perch on the hill, I was reminded of the place I visited in Chattanooga, Tennessee, as a little girl, with miniature trains, flying airplanes, hot-air balloons, and little towns with moving cars and people. Those memories, however, were quickly supplanted by the grim thought that a year after the slide, no material progress had been made toward protecting Stafford from another one. If anything, things had gotten worse.

"Okay," I told myself. "New Year's Eve is supposed to be about resolutions. So what are mine?"

I thought about it. Resolution is about resolve. My resolution, I decided, was to take a stand like the redwood tree and not back down.

Even after they've been chopped into the ground, redwoods don't give up. Instead, they try to sprout new life. If they're not coated with herbicide (used after a clear-cut to control the vegetation so it doesn't compete for sunlight with newly planted farmed trees) or burned with diesel fuel and napalm (a common cleanup practice), they manage to regenerate.

The redwoods would be my guide. I would stay in Luna no matter what. . . .

In Luna, the wind is a constant. And wind does something to you, something that rain doesn't. It makes your thoughts go wild. You can't focus. You can't read or write or paint or think. You feel disconnected and ungrounded. The sound of tarps whipping in the wind drives you crazy. You just sit here with a glaze, while your mind gets pummeled.

It was January, and gale-force winds, along with rain, sleet, and hail, had set in. I grew up with storms. I knew they passed. These didn't. This, as I later found out, was El Niño, one of the worst winters in recorded history in northern California. . . .

The storms were so loud and I was so cold so much of the time that I couldn't sleep. After six or seven of these sleepless nights, I started to break down. Suddenly, I couldn't stop crying. The intensity I had undergone over the preceding weeks had drained everything out of me. But without a decent night's rest, I was never able to recharge. I reached empty, and still I kept draining.

"I cannot survive any longer this way," I thought. "I cannot go one more night on no sleep, just hearing the howling of the wind and the sleet pelting me through the cracks. I can't do it anymore. I just can't." . . .

I tried to figure out what I was supposed to do. I didn't feel any need to play Superwoman, but I knew that I had given my word that I wasn't coming down until I had done everything I possibly could to protect this area. To come down because I was afraid of a storm would be to break my word, and I believe beyond a shadow of a doubt that we are only as good as our word. If our actions don't meet our words, our value as people is lessened. That's just the way I was raised.

Still, I was torn. My survival instinct was telling me to go down to the ground, that the Pacific Lumber people had all left, and that I could just climb back up in the morning and nobody would ever know. But that would mean breaking my word, and I just couldn't do it.

Before the storm ended, however, a promise would be the last thing on my mind. I would just be trying to stay alive — and not doing a very good job of it.

The moment the storm hit, I couldn't have climbed down if I had wanted to. To climb you have to be able to move, and my hands were frozen. Massive amounts of rain, sleet, and hail mixed together, and the winds blew so hard I might have been ripped off a branch.

The storm was every bit as strong as they said it would be. Actually, up here, it was even stronger. When a gust of wind would come through, it would flip the platform up into the air, bucking me all over the place.

"Boy! Whoaaah! Ooh! Whoa!"

The gust rolled me all the way up to the hammock. Only the rope that cuts an angle underneath it prevented me from slipping through the gap in the platform.

"I'm really ready for this storm to chill out. I'm duly impressed," I decided. "I've bowed and cowered once again before the great almighty gods of wind and rain and storm. I've paid my respects — and my dues — and I'd appreciate it if they got the heck out of here."

My thoughts seemed to anger the storm spirits.

"Whoa! Whoa!" I cried, as the raging wind flung my platform, straining the ropes that attached it.

"This is getting really intense! Oh, my God! Oh, my God! Okay, never mind, I take it back. Whoaaah!"

The biggest gust threw me close to three feet. I grabbed onto the branch of Luna that comes through the middle of the platform, and I prayed.

"I want to be strong for you, Luna. I want to be strong for the forest. I don't want to die, because I want to help make a difference. I want to be strong for the movement, but I can't even be strong for myself."

It seemed like it took all my will to stay alive. I was trying to hold onto life so hard that my teeth were clenched, my jaws were clenched, my muscles were clenched, my fists were clenched, everything in my body was clenched completely and totally tight.

I knew I was going to die.

The wind howled. It sounded like wild banshees, *rrahhh,* while the tarps added to the crazy cacophony of noise, *flap, flap, flap, bap, bap, flap, bap!* Had I remained tensed for the sixteen hours that the storm raged, I would have snapped. Instead, I grabbed onto Luna, hugging the branch that comes up through the platform, and prayed to her.

"I don't know what's happening here. I don't want to go down, because I made a pact with you. But I can't be strong now. I'm frightened out of my mind, Luna, I'm losing it. I'm going crazy!"

Maybe I was, maybe I wasn't, but in that moment I hear the voice of Luna speak to me.

"Julia, think of the trees in the storm."

And as I started to picture the trees in the storm, the answer began to dawn on me.

"The trees in the storm don't try to stand up straight and tall and erect. They allow themselves to bend and be blown with the wind. They understand the power of letting go," continued the voice. "Those trees and those branches that try too hard to stand up strong and straight are the ones that break. Now is not the time for you to be strong, Julia, or you, too, will break. Learn the power of the trees. Let it flow. Let it go. That is the way you are going to make it through this storm. And that is the way to make it through the storms of life."

I suddenly understood. So as I was getting chunked all over by the wind, tossed left and right, I just let it go. I let my muscles go. I let my jaw unlock. I let the wind blow and the craziness flow. I bent and flailed with it, just like the trees, which flail in the wind. I howled. I laughed. I whooped and cried and screamed and raged. I hollered and I jibbered and I jabbered. Whatever came through me, I just let it go.

"When my time comes, I'm going to die grinning," I yelled.

Everything around me was being ripped apart. My sanity felt like it was slipping through my fingers like a runaway rope. And I gave in.

"Fine. Take it. Take my life. Take my sanity. Take it all."

Once the storm ended, I realized that by letting go of all attachments, including my attachment to self, people no longer had any power over me. They could take my life if they felt the need, but I was no longer going to live my life out of fear, the way too many people do, jolted by our disconnected society. I was going to live my life guided from the higher source, the Creation source.

I couldn't have realized any of this without having been broken emotionally and spiritually and mentally and physically. I had to be pummeled by humankind. I had to be pummeled by Mother Nature. I had to be broken until I saw no hope, until I went crazy, until I finally let go. Only then could I be rebuilt; only then could I be filled back up with who I am meant to be. Only then could I become my higher self.

That's the message of the butterfly. I had come through darkness and storms and had been transformed. I was living proof of the power of metamorphosis.

A Year and Counting

. . .

The fact that my actions, increasingly spotlighted, affected so many more than me meant that I had to weigh the consequences of each word and deed. Everything we do ripples out and affects other people's lives. But what I did and said affected people's perceptions about the forest, environmentalism, and direct action. If I had made even the smallest mistake, the timber industry (and even corporate government) would have pounced and exploited it as much as they possibly could. And by discrediting me, they would have stripped other activists of their credibility. That was a huge weight.

As I settled into the rhythm of my second year, I felt drained, exhausted from my nerves being on edge all the time.

"Is this forever?" I wondered.

I wanted a shower so badly I could taste it. I could feel the hot water pouring over my body, into my pores and through my hair, which was in such bad need of cleaning. I wanted to be able to wake up at night and not have to pee over a bucket or a funnel if I needed to go to the bathroom. I wanted to sleep a full night through, not wondering if I would have to grab on tight when the wind picked up or whether I'd survive to hear the wind pick up the night after that.

Yet each time I started to feel that the fire inside me was just too weak to burn any longer and that I couldn't face another day, the great spirits of the universe would send something to fan those flames and burst them back into the bonfire I needed to renew my strength. Sometimes it would be a call from a friend. Other times it would involve a prayer being answered more quickly than I could have thought possible. Occasionally, even Pacific Lumber, however unwittingly, contributed to my resurgence of spirit.

On February 8, 1999, the same week that a wrongful-death suit was filed against the company for the loss of David Gypsy Chain's life, Pacific Lumber guards returned to post an eviction notice. The notice, which they hoped would protect them from future liability claims, said they were concerned with our safety and the safety of their employees, that we were engaged in an illegal activity, and that if we refused to leave their land, we would be subject to arrest under specific laws and codes, which they cited. It was all done very formally. They nailed a copy on Luna and the other trees with active tree-sits, and they published it in the legal notices of the *Times-Standard*.

I climbed out of the platform when I heard the *tap, tap* and felt the *thumk, thumk* of the hammer.

"We're posting a notice. Come down and read it," the men said when I asked what they were doing.

"You guys know I haven't been down in over a year," I retorted, adding that I didn't think that it was very fair for them to post an eviction notice on Luna, since she couldn't pick up and move.

"I'm sure she would if she could," I concluded. "The neighborhood has gone to pot since Charles Hurwitz moved in."

The pressure to come down wasn't limited to Pacific Lumber and Maxxam. A lot of people within the movement felt that I should leave Luna and help bring an important spotlight on other environmental battles. But the pressure other people put on me was nothing compared to the pressure I put on myself regarding this action. I cared about the forest, this planet, our world like I'd never cared about anything before in my life. So the question of whether to come down or not took on a whole new level of responsibility and a whole new level of reality. It even entered my dreams. I would toss and turn at night, anxious and confused about what I was supposed to do.

Under pressure, I have trouble hearing the guidance I live my life by. While I take other people's thoughts and concerns into account—I've never pretended to be a know-it-all—I get my ultimate guidance from prayer. That's why I pray every morning and every night. But though I prayed really hard about coming down, I remained trapped in this funky limbo state, torn about what to do next. As much as I would have loved to go down, I knew that the event would be a once-in-a-lifetime opportunity to get my message out.

I was feeling pulled in every direction. Part of the world wanted me up, part of the world wanted me down, another part of the world wanted me dead, and I had to try to figure out what to do. It was overwhelming, especially when I was trying to write a billion letters, conduct so many interviews, and fulfill speaking engagements.

At that point I reminded myself, as I have at many times in my life, to take my time and remember to breathe. This world is so fast, and there's so much pressure to move now, move quickly. But I knew that if I wasn't feeling clarity, I had to take the time to let the right thing happen. I couldn't let other people sway me just because I was unsure. That was part of the lesson that Luna had taught me: to be still and listen, even in the chaos of my life.

I knew prayer had taken me to the Lost Coast, prayer is what guided me to the redwood forest, and prayer is what led me to this tree and up this tree. Prayer is what had given me the strength to continue all this time. And someday, prayer would help guide me down. . . .

A year and a half in a tree! I found it difficult to believe I was still there. And yet I had lived in Luna so long I could hardly imagine living anywhere else. The tree had become part of me, or I her. I had grown a thick new muscle on the outer sides of my feet from gripping as I climbed and wrapping them around branches. My hands had also become a lot more muscular; their cracks from the weathering of my skin reminded me of Luna's swirling patterns. My fingers were stained brown from the bark and green from the lichen. Bits of Luna had been ground underneath my fingernails, while sap, with its embedded bits of bark and duff, speckled my arms and hands and feet. People even said that I smelled sweet, like a redwood.

The daily gifts that went along with living in Luna helped me continue giving everything I had in order to save her. Like the day a squirrel jumped on my knees while I spoke into a tape recorder, lifted its paws up in the air as it stood on its hind legs, and poked its nose up at me. Or watching the sun rise, orange and red and peach and gold, and shoot across the fog in the valley. Or having a black bear, searching for blackberries behind Luna, do a double take upon seeing me in the tree. . . .

I knew that the mainstream television media would want to talk with me when I finally came down from Luna, so I started scheduling interviews. One was for *The Late Show with David Letterman,* of all places! It was wild to imagine going from sitting in a tree to being a guest on a show that so many people I knew watched. I think the segment producer, however, was concerned that I might prove too serious a guest. She called to preinterview me.

"I'm going to have to ask you some questions," she cautioned.

"Like where do I go to the bathroom, how do I shower, and do I have a boyfriend?" I interjected.

"How did you know?" she asked in amazement.

"Well, I go to the bathroom like everyone else, but I use a bucket. I take sponge bathes using water that I collect in my tarp. And who needs a boyfriend? I have a tree." The segment producer was quiet for a second and then completely broke up.

So much for being too serious.

. . .

I wanted to protect Luna for her sake, for the sake of the hillside, and for the sake of the people in Stafford, whose voices I heard quivering as they described what it was like going to bed at night knowing that the hillside might at any minute give way and bury them in mud. I wanted to protect Luna for the thousands of people across the country and around the world for whom she had become a symbol of hope, a reminder that we can find peaceful, loving ways to solve our conflicts and that we can take care of our needs without destroying those needs to satisfy our greed. . . .

On December 18, 1999, a preservation agreement and deed of covenant to protect Luna and create a 200-foot buffer zone into perpetuity was documented and recorded.

I had kept up with the negotiations, but hadn't allowed myself to feel too hopeful. After all, things had fallen apart at the last minute before. So when the title officer called me on a speaker phone and said in a serious voice, "I have something to tell you," the first thought that ran through my head was, "Oh, they found something in the report that nullifies all this hard work!" But in the background, I could hear Tryphena, and there was something in her voice that betrayed her excitement. Then he said, "I have really good news for you. The document has been recorded. The Luna Preservation Agreement and Deed of Covenant is done."

"I think really good news is the understatement of the millennium!" I said but still did not feel much of anything. I think I was numb. But the moment I hung up the telephone, it hit me. I had been standing up, and I fell to the platform and cried. It was finally done. No more loopholes. No more stalls. Luna was protected. We did it.

Throughout the entire negotiation process, I hadn't allowed myself to feel anything. I had to act without attachment to what was going on. Otherwise, I would get too worn out riding my feelings up and down. But it was safe now. And the emotions hit me like a tidal wave.

What was wonderful was that when I received the news, my main support team was gathered at the base of Luna. I had asked Michael, my ground support coordinator, to bring some people up with him so that they could begin packing up things I had accumulated over two years. I was planning to hold on to my winter gear, but it was still time to clean out. So Michael, Spruce, Shunka (my dear friend from many years ago), and K.C. (who had been part of the first group who had assembled the first platform in Luna) were all there when I got the news, and it was phenomenal.

At last, it was time to go. During one of my last nightly climbs to the top platform to plug in a battery to the charging system, I climbed out onto one of my favorite branches of Luna and nestled in to her loving embrace. It was a gorgeous evening with the fog slowly rolling into the Eel River valley down below and a crystal clear sky above. The waxing moon brightly lit much of the sky and made the fog glow iridescently. A few stars shimmered at the edge of my view. It was a scene I had seen many times over the past two years—each time slightly different, each time breathtaking. As I sat there taking it all in, I realized that this was to be one of the last times I would ever look out at this view that had become as much a part of me as the experience had. I burst into tears.

Later that night I wrote, "I feel like I'm being separated from a part of myself—a piece of me—the essence of who I am. The woman I have become is being torn right now. I am beginning to feel the understanding—the never-ending lesson of letting

go. When I leave this tree, I will be leaving the best friend I've ever had. It is a pain I cannot describe, only feel . . . and be with. I am with it now, and it is only the beginning. I will be able to come back and be with Luna in her womb at her base, but never again will I perch in her branches viewing the world from this incredible perspective. I will do my best to live the rest of my life in honor of her and this experience—offering myself as the only gift I have to give. It is my prayer and my hope that I will always and only be an offering."

A few days later, as I prepared to descend Luna for the first time in 738 days, which would also be the last time, I began to sob once again. How would I be able to keep the focus, grounding, and truth that I had found in Luna? How would I be able to keep going when it felt like I was dying, having to leave this incredible living being? I prayed, and for the last time in her branches, Luna spoke to me and reminded me of something I had received in prayer nearly a year before: "Julia, all you have to do when you are afraid, lonely, worn out, or overwhelmed is touch your heart. Because it is there that I truly am, and it is there I will always be."

Editors' Note: Sadly, a year after Julia descended from Luna, someone attacked the tree with a chainsaw, cutting sixty percent of the trunk. Julia visited the tree shortly after the attack and stated that she felt that the saw was going right through her. An emergency rescue team immediately reinforced the tree with cable and steel bracing. Tree experts expect that much of Luna's canopy will die back, but that she will stand tall for many more years.

DISCUSSION TOPICS

1. Julia "Butterfly" Hill explains her change of attitude from arguing with the loggers to attempting to connect with them as human beings. In what situations do you think such an attitude is appropriate? Are there situations in which you believe it to be not appropriate? Explain your reasoning.
2. What was "the power of the trees" that she adopted?
3. Explain how "letting go" became decisive in Hill's experience with Luna.

Is Ecofeminism Feminist?

Victoria Davion

Victoria Davion is professor of philosophy at the University of Georgia in Athens. She specializes in feminist philosophy, ethical theory, applied ethics, and social and political philosophy. She is the editor of the journal Ethics and the Environment. *Davion agrees with Karen Warren that the patriarchal world view justifies both the domination of nature by human beings and of women by men. Thus ecofeminism must oppose patriarchy.*

... IMPORTANT ECOFEMINISM INSIGHTS

... In her ... article, "The Power and the Promise of Ecofeminism" (1990), Karen J. Warren explores some major conceptual connections between the domination of women by men and the domination of nature by humans. She argues that both depend on the "logic of domination." This logic always makes use of premises about morally significant differences between human beings and the rest of nature, along with a premise that asserts that these differences allow human beings to dominate nonhumans. ...

In "Nature, Self, and Gender: Feminism, Environmental Philosophy, and the Critique of Rationalism" (1991), Val Plumwood extends Warren's critique by examining rationalism from an ecofeminist perspective as the main conceptual underpinning of the twin dominations of women and nature. She argues that environmental ethicists who use a Kantian approach, in which reason is privileged over emotion and abstract universal principles are supposed to tell any rational agent what to do, and who assume that the human self is essentially the rational, morally valuable self, risk using rationality to separate human beings from the rest of nature.

Plumwood offers Paul Taylor's book *Respect for Nature* (1986) as an example of the approach discussed above. Taylor attempts to argue against the standard Western treatment of nature as having merely instrumental value for human well-being.

Taylor argues that living things are worthy of respect in their own right. However, he claims that "respect for nature" is moral respect only when it is universalizing and disinterested. ...

Plumwood's critique of this approach recognizes that it employs what Warren has named "the logic of domination," although Plumwood does not put the point quite this way. She points out Taylor's acceptance of the reason/emotion split, and his privileging of reason over emotion, which Plumwood argues has itself been used both to dominate women and to dominate nature within Western patriarchal ideologies. Thus, Plumwood argues that there is an inconsistency involved in employing a Western "rationalist" framework that has itself played such a major role in creating dualistic accounts of the human self as essentially rational, separated from the rest of nature.

... According to Plumwood, concepts of the self that separate human beings from the rest of nature inherit "the discontinuity problem," because they fail to see human beings as part of ("continuous with") nature, and reinforce the false human/nature dichotomy so prevalent in Western world views.

In attempting to deal with the discontinuity problem, deep ecologists have offered a concept of self that is "identified with nature." The term, often left vague, is used in at least three different ways, namely, what Plumwood calls the indistinguishable self, the expanded self, and the transcendence of self. Plumwood argues that none of these is acceptable from an ecofeminist standpoint.

The indistinguishability thesis, as discussed by deep ecologist Warwick Fox, is that "we can make no firm ontological divide in the field of existence . . . there is no bifurcation between the human and nonhuman realms" (Plumwood 1991:12). Thus, the self/other dichotomy is obliterated altogether. John Seed expresses this idea as follows: "I am protecting the rain forest" becomes "I am part of the rain forest protecting myself. I am that part of the rain forest recently emerged into thinking" (Plumwood 1991:12). Plumwood notes several problems with what she terms such "self merger theories." This picture of the indistinguishable self attempts to heal the discontinuity problem by denying that there are any morally relevant differences between self and other. The metaphysical claim is that everything is indistinguishable from everything else. According to Plumwood, this obliteration of all morally and metaphysically relevant distinctions is not the answer, since a recognition and respect of differences is important (more to be said on this later). Furthermore, Plumwood correctly notes that this obliteration of all distinctions between human and nonhuman nature will be equally true *regardless* of what relation humans stand in with the rest of nature. She writes,

> What John Seed seems to have in mind here is that once one has realized that one is indistinguishable from the rain forest, its needs would become one's own. But there is nothing to guarantee this—one could equally well take one's own needs for its. (Plumwood 1991:13)

According to both Plumwood and Warren, a failure to see oneself as distinct from others means an inability to separate the well-being of others from one's own well-being (see Warren 1990). This can easily lead to a failure to pay attention to, and care about, the needs of others, usually nonhuman natural "others."

According to Plumwood, the second concept, the "expanded self," has similar difficulties. Here, identification becomes not identity (as with the "indistinguishable self"), but something more like empathy. According to Arne Naess: "The self is as comprehensive as the totality of our identifications. . . . Our self is that with which we identify" (Plumwood 1991: 14). Plumwood's criticism is that the expanded self is *not* a critique of egoism; rather, it is simply another expression of it: instead of questioning the structures of possessive egoism and self-interest, it tries to expand the notion of self-interest to include more interests—nonhuman ones. Thus, we end up with a bigger atomistic nonrelational self, but an atomistic nonrelational self nonetheless. . . .

With the "transcended self," the suggestion is that we detach from the particular concerns of the individual human self in order to expand that self into a larger Self, one which overcomes the particular interests of any given individual self. We are to strive for impartial identification both with all particulars and with the cosmos, and to disregard our identifications with our own particular concerns, emotions, and attachments. . . . According to Plumwood, a commitment to a "transcended self" expresses a serious lack of concern for particular individuals and species—topics which are of concern to ecofeminists.

. . . Warren and Plumwood, like the majority of ecofeminist philosophers, notice that the feminine has been devalued within Western patriarchal ideological frameworks. I agree with them. However, in response to this, some ecofeminists (neither Warren nor Plumwood, however) have suggested that we embrace the feminine and femininity as a way of rejecting such oppressive patriarchal frameworks. In what follows I argue that to embrace the feminine side of the gender dichotomy uncritically is not a truly feminist solution to the problem.

FEMINISM

Feminism pays attention to women. Although there are many different kinds of feminism, virtually all feminists agree that sexist oppression is wrong, and therefore seek to overthrow patriarchy in its various forms. Thus, for an analysis to be feminist, it must include an analysis of sex and gender. It must look for the various ways that sexist oppression damages women, and seek alternatives to them. In looking at *how* patriarchy damages women, a feminist analysis must look closely at the roles women play in various patriarchies, the *feminine* roles. Insofar as these roles are damaging (to those who play them), they must be viewed with suspicion. If feminists fail to assert that at least some of the roles assigned to women under patriarchy are damaging, we fail to assert the very premise that makes feminism, the overthrowing of patriarchy, important. For, if sexist oppression is not damaging to women, women have no reason to resist it. If it does cause damage, we should expect to see this damage in traditionally assigned feminine roles. Thus, ecofeminist solutions which assert that feminine roles can provide an answer to the ecological crisis, without first examining how these roles presently are, or historically have been, damaging to those who play them, undermine the very conceptual significance and underpinnings of feminism that ecofeminist philosophers such as Warren and Plumwood assert.

Before continuing, I want to be clear about what I am *not* doing here. I am *not* claiming that there can be only one truly feminist perspective. There are many different kinds of feminism, including radical feminism, Marxist feminism, cultural feminism, and so forth. I am *not* attempting to distinguish between these approaches here. In my view, all of these can be feminist approaches as long as they have a critical analysis of sex, gender, and patriarchy. It is the *uncritical* acceptance of various aspects of sex, gender, and patriarchy that concerns me.

In what follows I examine five ecofeminist views which fail to critically examine femininity in its various forms. Each of them suggests that a more "feminine" perspective on the environment will help solve the ecological crisis. Because they all fail to consider that feminine perspectives are most likely damaged, and fail to explore just what this damage might be, they fail to explore the possible negative aspects of bringing more "feminine" perspectives to environmental ethics. They fail to notice that femininity may itself be a byproduct of patriarchy. In addition, several of these views imply that there is something that is *the* feminine role, that "the feminine perspective" is a unified perspective. However, if feminism is to be understood as a movement for the liberation of all women, we must understand that there is no one feminine voice. Rather, there are many different feminine voices, many "feminine" perspectives. Therefore, views which uncritically embrace unified or one-stance views of feminine sides of gender dichotomies are not feminist; when these views are linked with ecological perspectives, they are better understood as *ecofeminine* than *ecofeminist*. They are, in fact, dangerous views from a genuinely feminist perspective.

Five Ecofeminine Views

The first position I shall examine is presented by Ariel Kay Salleh in "Deeper than Deep Ecology: The Eco-Feminist Connection" (1984). Salleh says the following about women's lived experience under patriarchy:

> If women's lived experience were recognized as meaningful and were given legitimation in our culture, it would provide an immediate "living" social basis for alternative consciousness which the deep ecologist is trying to formulate and introduce as an abstract ethical construct. Women already, to borrow Devall's turn of phrase, "flow with the system of nature." (Salleh 1984:340)

According to Salleh, women do not need abstract ethical constructs to help create a consciousness of our connection with the rest of nature; women already have it. What women (and men) need to do is to recognize the value of women's experiences, something which patriarchal societies fail to do.

Salleh claims that while the masculine sense of self-worth in our culture has become entrenched in scientific habits of thought:

> Women, on the other hand, socialized as they are for a multiplicity of contingent tasks and practical labor functions in the home and out, do not experience the inhibiting constraints of status validation to the same extent. The traditional feminine role runs counter to the exploitative technical rationality which currently is the requisite masculine norm. In place of the disdain that the feminine role receives from all quarters, "the separate reality" of this role could well be taken seriously by ecologists and re-examined as a legitimate source of alternative values. As Snyder suggests, men should try out roles which are not highly valued in society, and one might add, particularly this one, for herein lies the basis of a genuinely grounded and nurturant environmentalism. (Salleh 1984:342)

Thus, according to Salleh, the problem is that "the traditional feminine role" is devalued. Salleh does not tell us exactly what "the traditional feminine role" is. However, she does imply that women under patriarchy are socialized into it. It is a role assigned to women under conditions of sexual oppression or patriarchy. She suggests that this role can provide the basis for a genuinely grounded and nurturant environmental ethic.

The arguments Salleh supplies omit some important facts about domination and submission that feminists must attend to. According to Salleh, because of the way women are socialized, we "do not experience the inhibiting constraints of status validation to the same extent" (Salleh 1984:342). However, in many contemporary societies the particular ways in which women seek validation are part of the feminine role. In contemporary American society validation is shown by such things as the high demand for cosmetics and other "beautifying" products, the increasing number of women opting for "elective" cosmetic surgery, and by the number of women who seek to become thin at the cost of their own well-being and health (e.g., through the development of eating disorders). Women may demonstrate the quest for social validation differently both from men and from each other, but such a quest is certainly an assigned, socialized part of many feminine ("female") roles. And, the industries supported by women playing out feminine roles are often responsible for gross environmental damage, e.g., the damage to the ozone layer by the use of aerosol hairspray cans, the cruel testing of cosmetics on animals. Finally, many women have sought validation by dominating other women and men through, for example, assertion of social status and use of power and privilege conferred by such factors as race and class. Thus, in seeking validation through playing out traditional feminine roles, women *may* be more concerned about the health of the environment than men, but that is neither a biological nor a social given; they also may perpetuate its destruction.

I find the reference to "the separate reality" of women disturbing as well. First, this implies that all women share the same reality. However, an important part of the history of feminist thought has been the lessons white middle class feminists have learned from being called on our racism and classism as we attempted to speak for all women. Because of this correct criticism, acknowledging such differences has come to be central to feminist projects. Many feminists now realize that if feminism is to be more than just a movement for the liberation of a particular group of women, and truly a movement for the liberation of *all* women, feminists must accept and address that there may be no unified experience of femininity (or womanhood). There are very deep differences among women which reflect diverse

social constructions and applications of notions of "women's femininity." The assumption that there is "a separate reality" experienced by all women must be examined and argued for, rather than simply assumed. For myself, I am deeply suspicious that any compelling argument can be given for its truth.

Another aspect of the "separate reality" claim I find troubling involves the idea that women's reality is separate from men's. In some very important ways, women do not live in a reality separate from men's. Men and women living under conditions of sexist oppression (patriarchy) live in a world inhabited by oppressors as well as by the oppressed. The reality of oppressed women is intimately connected to that of the oppressors. Women oppressed under a particular historically located patriarchy *may* share some experiences as members of the same group, and yet not share others as members of a different oppressed group (e.g., by race, class, or affectional orientation). Thus, to say that these experiences constitute a separate reality is not only to ignore important differences that other aspects of oppression bring to the situation (such as race or class oppression), but also to ignore the connections *to* oppressors that make women's oppression possible. Femininity makes sense only in relation to masculinity and vice versa. In an important sense, there is no separate reality because patriarchy *is* part of any woman's reality; and this — the pervasiveness of patriarchy — is the problem.

The idea that men could adopt the feminine role as a start to changing their attitude toward women and other men implies that the feminine role can be understood and adopted *ex nihilo,* without its masculine counterpart. However, because any traditional feminine role is a role of a dominated under conditions of sexist oppression, it makes no sense to speak of its existence independent of the masculine role; the role(s) of any dominated requires awareness and recognition of the role(s) assigned to the dominator. And, if feminists seek a society without domination and subordination as part of the solution to the present ecological crisis, the idea of a separate feminine reality cannot be part of that solution. "The feminine role" fails to provide a genuine grounding for anything other than the continued oppression of women. Besides, even if this role could provide something more positive, it still is important to think about the origins of this role, the possible damaging effects of playing it, and whether it makes sense to abstract it from patriarchy in the first place. We must look critically at femininity in its various forms.

A second so-called ecofeminist approach glorifies the feminine as a *principle* rather than a gender role. In "Development as a New Project of Western Patriarchy" (1990), Vandana Shiva discusses the concept of development from the perspective of Western patriarchy. She concludes that this so-called development actually breeds poverty in the areas that are developed, and therefore is properly called "maldevelopment." Shiva's argument for this is convincing. However, her discussion of the problem includes endorsement of the ideas of gender complementarity and the "feminine principle." Shiva writes:

> The Western development model based on the neglect of nature's work and women's work has become a source of deprivation of basic needs.
>
> In practice this reductionist, dualist perspective gives rise to the violation of the integrity and harmony between men and women. It ruptures the cooperative unity of the masculine and feminine, and puts men, deprived of the feminine principle, above and thus separated from nature and women. The violence to nature as symptomized by the current ecological crisis, and the violence to women as symptomized by women's subjugation and exploitation arise from the subjugation of the feminine principle. (Shiva 1990:193)

Shiva does not supply a definition of the feminine principle; however, she associates it with conservation and nurturing. She states of the Western patriarchal concept of development, "Such development becomes maldevelopment—deprived of the feminine, the conserving, the ecological principle" (Shiva 1990:191).

This analysis implies several questionable assumptions. One is some sort of natural gender complementarity. The suggestion is that gender roles are not the problem; rather, the devaluation of the feminine role is. This must be shown rather than assumed. A vital tradition in feminist critique has long

argued that gender roles cannot exist without domination and subordination. It is dangerous for feminists to assume that there is something "natural" or good in gender complementarity because that presupposes that there is some "natural" way for the sexes to relate to each other, that there is a "natural" division of labor, and that problems emerge from the devaluation of the feminine side. References to the integrity and harmony between men and women, the idea that the Western patriarchal concept of development "ruptures the cooperative unity between the masculine and the feminine" (Shiva 1990:191), make such assumptions. To simply accept uncritically gender complementarity is to ignore a large amount of feminist scholarship which claims that gender roles are part of *the means of* domination and subordination in patriarchy. It thus ignores questions about gender central to feminist analysis.

Shiva refers to "the" feminist principle as if there is one and only one principle that is feminine. It is not clear what is meant by this. However, as in the previous discussion of Salleh's analysis, it does seem to assume that "the feminine" is one thing, and that it generates a principle relevant to solving the ecological crisis. Again, for an analysis to be feminist, it is crucial that any talk of the liberating power of "the feminine" acknowledge how "the feminine" is shaped by patriarchy and that it is not necessarily an independent category but may be a cluster of various traits emerging out of oppression. There is great danger in abstracting "the feminine" from patriarchy, and a great danger in assuming it is one thing, given the importance of differences among women.

A third ecofemin*ine* approach within ecofemin*ist* literature assumes women have some special understanding of nature, even if there is unclarity about the source of this special understanding. It is interesting to note that although I have so far discussed only the views of *women* ecofeminists, a number of men are also now identifying with ecofeminism, often along this third, epistemological orientation. In "How to Cure a Frontal Lobotomy" (1990), Brian Swimme says the following in praise of women's intuition, using Starhawk as an example:

> Starhawk intuits effortlessly what remained beyond the group of the scientists. Our universe is quite

clearly a great swelling and birthing event, but why was this hidden from the very discoverers of the primeval birth? The further truth of the universe was closed to them because central regions of the mind were closed. . . . [T]his sentience is awake in Starhawk because of her life as a woman, as one who has the power to give birth herself, and because of her work as a scholar. . . . Women are beings who know from the inside out what it is like to weave the earth into a new human being. Given that experience and the congruent sensitivities seething within body and mind, it would be utterly shocking if ecofeminists did not bring forth meanings to the scientific data that were hidden from the scientists themselves. (Swimme 1990:19)

Swimme claims that there is some truth to the idea that the earth is a birthing process, but that this truth can only be seen, in fact "intuited effortlessly," by women. Swimme seems unsure whether women's epistemic privilege is the result of biology, socialization, or both. He refers both to Starhawk's life (socialization?) as a woman, and to the fact that she is a being who can give birth (biology?). Perhaps Swimme wants to deny any distinction between biology and socialization as an untenable dualism. It just is not clear what the source of this epistemic privilege is for Swimme. Yet, the description of the source of this so-called privilege is of vital importance to any feminist analysis. If this special understanding is the result of oppression, we should expect it to be skewed. Even if it is not skewed, we must ask whether there are other ways to get it. This is a crucial question because if there is no other way to get it, we risk saying that women's oppression is necessary to create the opportunity to gain knowledge needed to solve the ecological crisis — clearly an untenable *feminist* position. Once again, such crucial questions concerning sex and gender are left vague, and, problematically, women's roles under patriarchy are glorified.[1]

Along with literature assuming that the feminine offers an understanding of human connections to the earth comes literature praising Goddess worship. Much of this literature suggests that cultures that worshipped the Goddess instead of God, cultures in which the feminine was valued, were *peace-*

ful cultures in which human connection to non-human nature was understood. A fourth, allegedly ecofeminist, position is an example of this. In "The Gaia Tradition and the Partnership Future" (1990), Riane Eisler discusses societies that worshipped the Goddess and argues that they were more like the kind of society we need today to solve the ecological crisis. She says:

> Prehistoric societies worshiped the Goddess of nature and spirituality, our great Mother, the giver of life and creator of us all. But even more fascinating is that these ancient societies were structured very much like the more peaceful and just society we are now trying to construct.
>
> In short, they were societies which had what we today call an ecological consciousness: the awareness that the Earth must be treated with reverence and respect. And this reverence for life-giving and life-sustained powers of the Earth was rooted in a social structure where women and "feminine" values such as caring, compassion, and non-violence were not subordinate to men and the so-called masculine values of conquest and domination. Rather, the life-giving powers incarnated in women's bodies were given the highest social value. (Eisler 1990:23–4)

Eisler calls upon us to value these so-called feminine values once more:

> Let us reaffirm our ancient covenant, our sacred bond with our Mother, the Goddess of nature and spirituality. Let us renounce the worship of angry gods wielding thunderbolts or swords. Let us once again honor the chalice, the ancient symbol of the power to create and enhance life — and let us understand that this power is not woman's alone but also man's. (Eisler 1990:24)

Thus, Eisler claims that the problem with patriarchy lies in the devaluing of what she calls "feminine values" (e.g., caring, compassion, and nonviolence). By reaffirming such values we can better form the ecological conscience needed to deal with our destructive tendencies.

It is extremely important to examine history for ideas to help solve current problems. In this respect, Eisler's work is interesting and instructive. What is problematic is her use of the gender terms "masculine" and "feminine" in her historical analysis. Eisler uses the terms "masculine" and "feminine" to refer to kinds of values in her analysis. She maintains that traits now associated with the term feminine were highly valued during the time period she discusses.

However, this sort of historical work can easily be taken as an uncritical glorification of the feminine. Whether or not we should refer to these values as feminine is problematic. If patriarchy is necessary for femininity as we now understand it, then if these ancient cultures were not patriarchal or descended from patriarchies, they could not have feminine gender roles. It may be true that some of the respected values in those cultures are devalued in our culture, and that they are considered feminine now. But this is very different from asserting that there was anything "feminine" that was respected. My worry is that Eisler refers to "feminine" values without questioning what it means to call anything "feminine" in an (allegedly) nonpatriarchal culture or context. She thereby implies that femininity can exist without patriarchy, a worrisome assumption indeed.

The final view I shall discuss is offered by Marti Kheel in "Ecofeminism and Deep Ecology" (1990). Kheel argues that ecofeminists and deep ecologists have very different perspectives regarding the kinds of connection to be endorsed in an ecological ethic. As has been shown in connection with the discussion of Plumwood's position, many deep ecologists support developing a sense of oneself ("the expanded self") that is expanded to include all of nature. They argue that the concept of the self as a static individual with clear ego boundaries is a major factor in the ecological crisis. Moreover, hunting is often praised in the literature. Many deep ecologists believe that this sense of self can be developed through activities that involve killing. Kheel quotes philosopher/biologist Randall Eaton to exemplify this deep ecological perspective:

> To hunt is to experience extreme oneness with nature. . . . The hunter imitates his prey to the point of identity . . . [H]unting connects a man completely with the earth more deeply and profoundly than any other human enterprise. (Kheel 1990:131)

According to Kheel, this experience of connection is not the type that ecofeminists should support. In contrast, she argues that women feel a sense of connection in a very different way:

> It is out of women's unique, felt sense of connection to the natural world that an ecofeminist philosophy must be forged. Identification may, in fact, enter into this philosophy, but only to the extent that it flows from an *existing* connection with individual lives. Individual beings must not be used in a kind of psychological instrumentalism to help establish a *feeling* of connection that in fact does not exist. Our sense of oneness with nature must be connected with concrete, loving actions. (Kheel 1990:137)

If Kheel is right, much more needs to be said. Not all women feel connected to nature. Furthermore, some men may feel this more than many women. Hence, we should not assume that (1) all women feel this connection with nature or (2) the connections women do feel are healthy. By doing either, we fail once again to recognize important differences between women, and uncritically glorify women's experiences without critically examining them.

CONCLUSION

. . . While ecofeminists are correct in challenging dualisms such as human/nature, reason/emotion, and masculinity/femininity, the solution does not lie in simply valuing the side of the dichotomy that has been devalued in Western patriarchal frameworks. Rather, traits associated with both sides of these false dichotomies need to be reconceived and reconsidered; if these traits are to be retained, totally new ways of thinking about them in a nonpatriarchal context are needed. Simply beginning to value the devalued side reinforces the harmful dichotomies ecofeminism must overcome. Consequently, I encourage the future projects of ecofeminists to involve a reconceptualization of knowledge, reality, and ethics, so that these current dichotomous ways of conceptualizing the reality literally make no sense.

Part of such a reconceptualization will involve generating approaches to environmental ethics that recognize both the value of connections between particular individuals and the value of "nature" or "the environment" conceived of as both material entities and abstractions. However, in doing this, care will have to be taken to define which kinds of connections are ethically valuable and which are not, as a failure to make such distinctions would be to ignore the fact that oppression and exploitation themselves require connections between individuals. Thus, if we fail to assess particular connections, we risk entrenching the logic of domination rather than overthrowing it. I believe that a conceptual understanding of how the logic of domination works places ecofeminists in an excellent position among feminists and environmentalists to generate these much-needed alternative approaches.

NOTE

An earlier version of this piece appears under the title "How Feminist Is Ecofeminism?" in C. Pierce and D. VanDeVeer (eds.), *The Environmental Ethics and Policy Book,* Belmont, CA (Wadsworth, 1993). I owe a special thanks to Karen J. Warren for her extensive help on both versions, and for her contributions to my understanding of the complexity and importance of ecological feminism.

(1) For an interesting discussion of epistemic privilege, see U. Narayan, "Working Together Across Difference: Some Considerations on Emotions and Political Practice," *Hypatia,* 1988, vol. 3, no. 2, pp. 31–47.

REFERENCES

Eisler, R. (1990). "The Gaia Tradition and the Partnership Future: An Ecofeminist Manifesto," in I. Diamond and G. F. Orenstein (eds.). *Reweaving the World: The Emergence of Ecofeminism.* San Francisco: Sierra Club Books.

Griffin, S. (1978). *Woman and Nature: The Roaring Inside Her.* New York: Harper & Row.

Kheel, M. (1990). "Ecofeminism and Deep Ecology: Reflections on Identity and Difference," in I. Diamond and G. F. Orenstein (eds.). *Reweaving the*

World: The Emergence of Ecofeminism. San Francisco: Sierra Club Books.

Plumwood, V. (1991). "Nature, Self, and Gender: Feminism, Environmental Philosophy, and the Critique of Rationalism," *Hypatia* 6, 1: 3–27.

Salleh, A. K. (1984). "Deeper than Deep Ecology: The Eco-Feminist Connection," *Environmental Ethics* 6, 4: 339–45.

Shiva, V. (1990). "Development as a New Project of Western Patriarchy," in I. Diamond and G. F. Orenstein (eds.). *Reweaving the World: The Emergence of Ecofeminism.* San Francisco: Sierra Club Books.

Swimme, B. (1990). "How to Cure a Frontal Lobotomy," in I. Diamond and G. F. Orenstein (eds.). *Reweaving the World: The Emergence of Ecofeminism.* San Francisco: Sierra Club Books.

Taylor, P. W. (1986). *Respect for Nature: A Theory of Environmental Ethics.* Princeton, NJ: Princeton University Press.

Warren, K. J. (1990). "The Power and the Promise of Ecological Feminism," *Environmental Ethics* 12, 2: 125–46.

Warren, K. J. (1992). "Taking Empirical Data Seriously: An Ecofeminist Philosophical Perspective," in *Human Values and the Environment* (conference proceedings). Institute for Environmental Studies, University of Wisconsin, Madison: Wisconsin Academy of Sciences, Arts and Letters.

DISCUSSION TOPICS

1. Davion argues that ecofeminists must critically examine the roles women currently play in patriarchal societies. She rejects Ariel Salleh's claim that "women's lived experiences" provide a genuine alternative to patriarchy. Do you agree more with Davion or Salleh? Explain your position.

2. What response might be given to Davion's position that there is no basis for describing goddess-worshiping cultures as feminine?

3. According to Davion not all felt connections with nature are healthy. Give some examples of what might be unhealthy connections.

4. How might a follower of the deep ecology movement (Chapter 8) respond to Plumwood's critique?

CLASS EXERCISES

1. Have students write down their associations with the terms *masculine, feminine,* and *nature.* Which terms overlap the most? The least? Have the students share these results in small groups, with one student then summarizing the results in a report to the class.
2. Organize a debate on the topic Resolved: Women are closer to nonhuman animals and the earth than are men. (See the description of classroom debates in the appendix.)

FOR FURTHER READING

Adams, Carol J., ed. *Ecofeminism and the Sacred.* New York: Continuum, 1993. What does ecofeminism look like in Christian, Buddhist, Jewish, and Hindu forms? Native American and African spiritualities are also discussed.

Adams, Carol J., and Josephine Donovan, eds. *Animals and Women: Feminist Theoretical Explorations.* Durham, N.C.: Duke University Press, 1995. A collection of pioneering essays, presenting original material from scholars in a variety of fields, including an early article by Virginia Woolf.

Biehl, Janet. *Rethinking Ecofeminist Politics.* Boston: South End Press, 1991. A critique of ecofeminism by a social ecologist. Biehl argues that ecofeminism is a regressive force, particularly in its embrace of goddess worship, its emphasis on metaphors and myths, and its glorification of the early Neolithic. Ecofeminism situates women outside of Western culture as essentially "natural."

Bigwood, Carol. *Earth Muse: Feminism, Nature, and Art.* Philadelphia: Temple University Press, 1993. Postmodern art-philosophy, relying on insights from Heidegger, Merleau-Ponty, and Derrida as well as ecofeminism and accompanied by meditations on great artworks. A demanding book.

Colard, Andree, with Joyce Contrucci. *Rape of the Wild: Man's Violence against Animals and the Earth.* Bloomington: Indiana University Press, 1989. A powerful and eloquent statement of the patriarchal connection between the violation of nature, animals, and women. Includes animal experimentation, hunting, and space exploration.

Dexter, Miriam Robbins. *Whence the Goddesses: A Source Book.* New York: Pergamon Press, 1990. A clearly written, scholarly study of ancient female- and male-centered theologies, the assimilation of eight groups of Neolithic European and Near Eastern goddesses, and a discussion of the functions of the female in male-centered society. Extensive notes in original languages.

Diamond, Irene, and Gloria Feman Orenstein. *Reweaving the World: The Emergence of Ecofeminism.* San Francisco: Sierra Club Books, 1990. A valuable collection of essays expressive of the many facets of ecofeminism.

Gaard, Greta, ed. *Ecofeminism: Women, Animals, Nature.* Philadelphia: Temple University Press, 1993. An outstanding collection of articles, reflecting on ecofeminism from a number of perspectives, including theoretical, historical, political, and cultural.

———. *Ecological Politics: Ecofeminism and the Greens.* Philadelphia: Temple University Press, 1998.

Griffin, Susan. *Woman and Nature: The Roaring inside Her.* New York: Harper & Row. 1980. A pioneering, lyrical, and immensely powerful account that juxtaposes patriarchal judgments about the nature of matter and the nature of women.

Hallen, Patsy. "Making Peace with the Environment: Why Ecology Needs Feminism." *Trumpeter* 4 (1987): 3–14. A wide-ranging, clearly written argument for the feminist reconstruction of society, including natural science.

Hogan, Linda, and Brenda Peterson, eds. *The Sweet Breathing of Plants: Women Writing on the Green World.* New York: North Point Press, 2001. A rich and diverse anthology.

Hypatia: A Journal of Feminist Philosophy 6 (1991). Special Issue on Ecological Feminism, ed. Karen J. Warren. The first collection of explicitly philosophical essays on ecological feminism.

Keller, Evelyn Fox. *A Feeling for the Organism: The Life and Work of Barbara McClintock.* San Francisco: W. H. Freeman, 1983. A perceptive study of a scientist, often cited by ecofeminists, whose exceptional work in plant genetics and cytology has incorporated respect and love for plants.

Matthews, Freya. *The Ecological Self.* Savage, Md.: Barnes and Noble, 1991. Matthews presents a metaphysical vision of the "geometrodynamical universe" as a self.

Merchant, Carolyn. *The Death of Nature: Women, Ecology and Scientific Revolution.* San Francisco: Harper & Row, 1989. A masterly study of how during 1500 to 1700 the organic conception of the cosmos with a "living female earth at its center" gave way to a mechanistic model, with a dead and passive nature. Merchant argues that concepts of nature and women are historical and social constructions. Contains extensive notes.

———. *Earthcare: Women and the Environment.* New York: Routledge, 1995. A collection of well-written essays on goddesses, environmental history, and ecofeminist practices in America, Sweden, and Australia.

Orenstein, Gloria Feman. *The Reflowering of the Goddess.* New York: Pergamon Press, 1990. An integration of art, literature, history, and spirituality. Extensive bibliography.

Plant, Judith, ed. *Healing the Wounds: The Promise of Ecofeminism.* Philadelphia: New Society Publishers, 1989. A collection of accessible essays and some poetry from a spectrum of ecofeminists.

Ruether, Rosemary. *New Woman/New Earth: Sexist Ideologies and Human Liberation.* New York: Seabury Press, 1975. A historical critique of patriarchy and a sketch of an egalitarian society by a prominent Christian theologian.

Spretnak, Charlene. *Lost Goddesses of Early Greece: A Collection of Pre-Hellenic Myths.* Boston: Beacon Press, 1981.

Warren, Karen J., ed. *Ecological Feminism.* New York: Routledge, Chapman & Hall, 1994. Important essays dealing with connections to deep ecology, human population, animal rights, epistemology, and peace politics.

———. *Ecological Feminist Philosophies.* Bloomington: Indiana University Press, 1996. An expanded version of the 1991 *Hypatia* special issue, with a useful introduction by Warren.

CHAPTER TEN

Environmental Ethics in Society

In this chapter we identify and evaluate issues that arise when environmental problems are addressed by society. These issues have complex economic, legal, and political dimensions. We first address the developing discipline of biotechnology.

ASSESSING BIOTECHNOLOGY

Biotechnology is an umbrella term, defined differently by various organizations. We use the term in the narrow sense, to mean the deliberate manipulation of the DNA molecules of living organisms or their products for the production of knowledge, goods, and services. Thus biotechnology includes genetic engineering and cloning. The readings in this chapter consider biotechnology from several different approaches. Andrew Dobson, in "Biocentrism and Genetic Engineering," argues for an open-minded approach to genetic engineering, but one that recognizes that human interests are not the only ones of moral significance. Concern for individual animals as well as attention to the value of species must be included in any evaluation of genetic engineering.

In "Ecological Risks and Benefits of Transgenic Plants," Gabor Lövei notes that little scientific assessment concerning the risks and benefits of transgenic plants from an ecological perspective has been done to date. (*Transgenic plants* are plants modified to contain DNA from an external source.) In "The Ecological Critique of Agricultural Biotechnology," political philosopher Mark Sagoff points out that if we mean by *nature* what is spontaneous and wild, biotechnology does in fact mean the end of nature. John Meyer addresses philosophical and legal issues concerning the patenting of genetically modified living organisms in "Rights to Life? On Nature, Property and Biotechnology." He concludes that currently there is no sound theoretical foundation for such patents.

PROPERTY

Private ownership, public ownership, or something in between — questions of ownership are foremost for many people. Garrett Hardin, in his classic "The Tragedy of the Commons," argues that disaster results when individuals make use of a commonly held resource on the basis of their own rational self-interest. Thus some kind of coercion is required to prevent such disaster.

This "tragedy," as Hardin calls it, is an example of a social trap. A social trap occurs when individuals base their decisions on what they believe will benefit them personally in the short term. These decisions produce circumstances that work to everyone's detriment, including their own. The existence of social traps challenges Adam Smith's idea of the "invisible hand," according to which, if each pursues his or her own prosperity, all will benefit.

Larry Lohmann's observations in "Visitors to the Commons" indicate that such social traps do not necessarily occur in Southern countries such as Thailand, because land use decisions are not made according to the self-interest of private owners. Rather, village communities exercise effective control over resource use.

In "Taking the Land Rights Movement Seriously," Kirk Emerson describes the arguments used to support the land rights movement. She argues that private property and individual freedom can be compatible with governmental regulation in the name of public welfare.

ECONOMICS

Economic questions are often significant concerns in environmental issues. We discuss a few of the key ideas below.

Homo Economicus

The term *Homo economicus* is used to refer to economic man, an abstract concept of the man or woman who is concerned only with his or her own satisfaction (personal utility) and indifferent to where that satisfaction comes from. This idea is related to Norton's notion of strong anthropocentrism, according to which any goals pursued by humans can be valued with little or no critical analysis. (See the introduction to Chapter 8.) Many environmental theorists maintain that the assumptions underlying this abstraction result in deeply flawed environmental policies. For example, Herman Daly and John Cobb, Jr. argue that the concept is empirically false

and also dangerous in encouraging the uninhibited pursuit of personal gain.[1] Terry Anderson and Donald Leal, however, maintain in the excerpt from *Free Market Environmentalism Today* that the concept is an indispensable assumption of free market environmentalism.

Personal Preferences as Normative

Many economists argue that normative evaluation of an individual's desires by others is unacceptable. Only the Pareto-efficiency criterion is used: By this criterion an action is considered economically efficient if no one is harmed while at least one person benefits.[2] Whether an individual benefits is left to the sole judgment of that individual. The source of value is found in subjective individual wants, not in the needs of other human beings or other species. While this subjective treatment of the individual's wants is often criticized, Anderson and Leal argue that allowing the voluntary exchange of property rights between consenting owners promotes individual liberty.

Sustainable Resource Use and Preventing Irreversible Losses

Defining sustainable use of a natural resource is a fundamental issue in environmental economics. Sustainable use is often defined as the level of use at which the benefits of a resource are maximized without jeopardizing the potential for similar benefits in the future. Unfortunately, many environmental consequences of contemporary development projects are either completely irreversible or reversible only over a very long time. Examples include species extinctions, groundwater contamination, fossil fuel depletion, loss of traditional knowledge of indigenous tribal people as they are acculturated, soil erosion,

---

[1]Herman E. Daly and John B. Cobb, Jr., *For the Common Good: Redirecting the Economy Toward Community, the Environment, and a Sustainable Future* (Boston: Beacon Press, 1989), pp. 85–96.

[2]K. Terry Turner, David Pearce, and Ian Bateman, *Environmental Economics: An Elementary Introduction* (Baltimore: Johns Hopkins University Press, 1993), p. 96.

human-induced climatic changes, and removal of coral reefs and certain forest types. Such irreversible losses traditionally are not considered in cost-benefit analyses.

Sustainability also refers to a key concept in steady-state economics, an approach associated with Herman E. Daly's work and that of others beginning in the 1970s. Steady-state economics stresses the limits to resource use based on the carrying capacity of the earth. This view also affirms a view of human beings as capable of stewardship and kinship with both future generations and nonhuman life.[3] Mainstream economists, however, such as James Robin, Robert Solow, and William Nordhaus, typically state that nature sets no limits to economic growth. They maintain that the earth's carrying capacity is a function of the state of human knowledge and technology.[4]

Externalities

Externalities are "spillover effects of someone's production or consumption that affect the well-being of other producers and consumers."[5] These effects are not directly reflected in market transactions; externalities are sometimes referred to as the problem of "missing markets." Such externalities can include pollution, soil erosion, and losses or gains in wildlife habitat. The free-market or neoclassical strategy for abating environmental problems is that of improving markets by figuring out ways to internalize externalities.

---

[3]Herman E. Daly, *Steady-State Economics* (Washington, D.C.: Island Press, 1991), pp. 14–49. Steady-state economists see the economy as a subsystem of the environment; the economy lives by importing low-entropy matter-energy (raw materials) and exporting high-entropy matter-energy (waste). Since the environment is finite, so must the economy be.

[4]For a thoughtful critique of both positions, together with extensive references, see Mark Sagoff, "Carrying Capacity and Ecological Economics," *Bioscience* 45, no. 9 (October 1995): 610–20. While Sagoff is sympathetic to ecological economics, he argues that the concept of carrying capacity fails to show that economic growth is unsustainable. Nevertheless, he warns against equating economic growth with moral desirability.

[5]Eric L. Hyman and Bruce Stiftel, *Combining Facts and Values in Environmental Impact Assessment: Theories and Techniques* (Boulder, CO: Westview Press, 1988), p. 64.

Nonmonetized Values

Comparing economic values with values that cannot be easily given a monetary value is often a controversial issue. Some economists argue that the concept of economic value can encompass any instrumental value.[6] According to this approach, nonmonetized values (values not easily converted into monetary terms) can be converted to monetary terms by "contingent valuation" surveys, which assess the individual's willingness to pay (how much a person is willing to pay to obtain or retain a resource) or willingness to be reimbursed (how much a person would require to be reimbursed for the loss or degradation of a resource). Such assessments assume the applicability of the *Homo economicus* model.

Economists sometimes assign shadow, or surrogate, prices to goods or services that have no market price or create and assign exchangeable property rights (such as pollution or depletion quotas), which are then priced in markets as they are traded. Christopher Stone's essay recommends the use of shadow pricing in order to allow incorporation of natural objects into the legal system.

Ascribing intrinsic value to natural entities may further complicate economic considerations, because such ascription often greatly enhances value or involves intangible value. For example, "existence value" is the value that individuals may attach to the mere knowledge that rare and diverse species, unique natural environments, or other "goods" exist, even if these individuals do not contemplate ever using or benefiting from them. In his second selection, "At the Monument to General Meade," Mark Sagoff stresses the impossibility of ever capturing intrinsic value in the concept of a measurable "existence value."

New Types of Economic Measurement

In "Genuine Progress Indicator (GPI) Accounting," Mark Anielski and Colin Soskolne present the Genuine Progress Indicator (GPI), a new form of economic measurement that includes the health and well-being of human beings and the environment.

---

[6]Stephen E. Edwards, "In Defense of Environmental Economics," *Environmental Ethics* 9 (1987): 73–85.

According to their analysis, while the Gross National Product in the United States rose steadily from 1950 to 1999, human and environmental well-being has been declining since the mid-1970s when measured by the Genuine Progress Indicator.

Scientists Alexander James, Kevin Gaston, and Andrew Balmford, in "Can We Afford to Conserve Biodiversity?" estimate that the cost of maintaining global biodiversity represents only a fraction of existing environmentally harmful governmental subsidies to resource users. If only ten percent of environmentally harmful subsidies were eliminated, a substantial proportion of biodiversity would be preserved for current and future generations.

LEGAL RIGHTS AS REFORMATIVE

Legal rights are conventional (based on social institutions) and hence can develop in ways that may reform social awareness. In "Should Trees Have Standing?" Christopher Stone urges the extension of legal rights to include natural objects in order to reform human perceptions of the importance of the natural world. Such inclusion requires not only shadow pricing but the use of legal guardianships to represent the interests of natural objects. Sagoff's "At the Monument to General Meade" demonstrates the limitations of environmental economics and the importance of environmental laws in stating general moral principles and setting overall goals reflecting choices made through public deliberation.

POLICY

In "Fragile Freedoms," Bryan Norton argues for an environmental policy that values nature in a total context, including human cultural history. The criteria of ecological health must include human activities, and environmentalists must do a better job of educating the public so that social policy will reflect ecological values.

Mikael Stenmark, in "The Relevance of Environmental Ethical Theories for Policy Making," identifies some obstacles in the path of developing the environmental policy to which Norton points. Stenmark argues that the differences in basic values between anthropocentric, biocentric, and ecocentric thinkers result in divergent policies regarding human population, wilderness preservation, and wildlife management.

MANAGEMENT

Cheryl Davis, manager of the Water Supply and Treatment Division of the San Francisco Public Utilities Commission, explains in "Environmental Ethical Issues in Water Operations and Land Management," the many ethical dilemmas encountered in the work of water utilities. She urges water professionals to see themselves as stewards of a beautiful and complex environment rather than as simply managers of water as a commodity.

POLITICS

The Australian philosopher John Dryzek has analyzed environmental politics into six "discourses" (shared ways of apprehending the world) in an excerpt from *The Politics of the Earth*. A number of authors in this book express one or the other of these discourses. While all of the discourses challenge industrialism, they are often in conflict with each other. One of Dryzek's goals is to promote interchange between discourses as societies evolve toward renewed democratic politics.

With regard to political activism, in "Leopold as an Advocate," Sara Vickerman points out that Aldo Leopold affirmed that society will continue to need "a militant minority of wilderness-minded citizens." He was willing to advocate for the land ethic, supported holistic rather than narrowly specialized education for scientists, and proposed committees composed of people with diverse public interests. Vickerman cites contemporary citizen management committees as descendants of these proposals.

Biocentrism and Genetic Engineering

Andrew Dobson

Andrew Dobson is a professor in the Department of Ecology and Evolutionary Biology at Princeton University. In the following reading, excerpted from an article published in Environmental Values *in 1995, Dobson argues that genetic engineering is a genuinely new technology that is of ethical significance for biocentrists. Dobson believes that we should not take a rigidly prohibitive view of genetic engineering; we should weigh the claims of benefits and harms within the specific fields of application. Human interests are not the only ones of moral significance. Concern for individual animals is appropriate, as is concern for the value of species.*

. . . Biocentric holism I take to be a position that holds that value resides in "wholes" of living entities besides human beings — for instance, in species.[1] I do not plan to argue for this holism, but rather to accept that some environmental philosophers do argue for it, and to assess its status in the particular context of genetic engineering.[2]

In the spirit of instruction, and however basic it might seem, I want to begin by distinguishing three terms which are worth keeping apart: biotechnology, genetic selection, and genetic engineering. This is important because people often jump all too readily to the conclusion that genetic engineering is simply an advance on techniques of which we already have ethical experience, and that therefore no new ethical thinking needs to be done. My contention has two aspects: first, that genetic engineering is so sufficiently different from other techniques as to demand new thinking; and second, that biocentric and ecocentric holism introduce a new ethical dimension anyway.

Biotechnology could be taken to be the general term of reference for all three of these practices, but it is best to reserve it for the exploitation of the catalytic power of enzymes in, for instance, the preparation of food and drink. This technology has been used for thousands of years, and there is good evidence that the Sumerians and Babylonians used yeasts to make beer 8000 years ago, and that the Egyptians learned to make leavened bread with brewers' yeast about 6000 years ago. This is the kind of thing that tempts people to say — wrongly I believe — that genetic engineering is nothing new, and that therefore we need think no harder about endorsing its practice than we need think about the ethical implications for yeast of beer-making.

Slightly closer to the terrain of genetic engineering proper lies genetic selection. Again, genetic selection of plants and animals has been going on for longer than most people realise. Corn, for example, is quite unlike its nearest wild relatives teosinte and *Tripsacum,* and is a 10,000 year-old invention brought about by selecting seed for propagation and then interbreeding plants. Corn is entirely dependent on human beings for its survival because it cannot propagate itself, and it is an early example of genetic selection in the plant world.[3] Similarly, animals became the subjects of genetic selection as soon as their domestication became a fact of human social life — probably in the Neolithic period.

The selective breeding of plants and animals does not amount to genetic engineering however, and while there may be ethical issues at stake in genetic selection, I suggest that genetic engineering throws up new ones and it is these that will be the subject of what follows. While it is clear that biotechnology (as I have described it above) and genetic selection both have long histories, genetic engineering (sometimes referred to as recombinant technology) has a relatively short one, beginning around the 1970s. I want to refer to two definitions of genetic engineering, and to show why the differences are instructive in ethical terms.

First, Stephanie Yanchinski writes that, "Simply put, genetic engineering means isolating the gene of one organism and inserting it into another."[4] This definition stresses the *techniques* involved in genetic engineering and suggests that the gulf between it and genetic selection is a large one in that neither "isolation" nor "insertion" can be said to be taking place when breeding new strains of pea (for example). It is also important to note that there is also a difference of degree, if not wholly of kind, between the gene transfer (whether confined to the present generation or handed down to subsequent ones) of which Yanchinski writes and that which takes place when genes are transferred "in nature" — either by "gene jumping," by speciation, or by the introgression of genes between species caused by infertile hybrids breeding successfully with either or both of the parent species. The difference in degree is a result both of the accuracy of the isolation and transfer, and of the element of human premeditation that informs it.

Second, a draft definition prepared by the European Commission describes a genetically modified organism as one "in which the genetic material is altered in a way that passes the natural barriers of mating and recombination."[5] In contrast to Yanchinski's definition this one underscores the *nature* of the changes that take place. There are, of course, those who will argue that no such "natural barriers" exist, in that while fertile breeding between hybrids may not be possible, breeding between hybrids and one or other of the parental species is possible. This objection in fact concedes the point that there is a "natural barrier" (hybrids cannot breed), but makes the useful observation that drawing rigid biological distinctions is unwise. I think, in any case and for the moment, that these two definitions are sufficiently accurate and suggestive to sustain the following point: that the *techniques* to which Yanchinski refers make the *nature* of the changes to which the European Commission refers new to our general — and therefore to our ethical — experience. We are able to do things we have never done before in ways which are themselves new.

I am aware of standing out on something of a limb here. Alan Holland, for example, has written that, "In truth, a genetic engineer with a lawyer's nose for precedent can find precedent enough in our present practices."[6] I do not think this is right. In my view genetic engineering and genetic selection are only similar in the same sense that walking and space travel are both forms of locomotion. As Bill McKibben has written, "Mendel could cross two peas, but he couldn't cross a pea with a pine, much less with a pig, much less with a person."[7] I agree, therefore, with Michael Fox when he writes that, "A common assertion by animal production technolo-

gists is that genetic engineering is simply an extension of the age-old practices of selective breeding and cross-breeding (or hybridization). [But] whatever analogy exists between the old practices and the new is shattered by the fact that in traditional breeding practices genes cannot be exchanged between unrelated species, whereas, in many transgenic manipulations, they can."[8] On this reading, interference with old species and the ability to create new ones is what creates new ethical dilemmas.

This introduces a different variation on the theme that genetic engineering is really nothing new. Its opponents often object to it in the vague sense that it is "unnatural." When articulated, this turns out to mean that transgeneticism effectively amounts to the creation of animals and plants that are not to be found in nature. Others will refer, though, to the phenomenon of natural speciation whose mechanics are explained by the Darwinian theory of evolution. Both are, of course, right. On the one hand, speciation clearly does take place — if it didn't it is hard to see how evolution could take place at all. On the other, the *kind* of creation brought about by genetic engineering is of a sort that nature is hardly likely to come up with — the "shoat" (sheep/goat), for example.[9] The question is: does the kind of change that results from genetic engineering matter ethically? I shall suggest that from a biocentric point of view, it does. . . .

One radical environmental ethicist has drawn a direct link between an animal's *telos* and its genetic makeup, thereby making genetic engineering problematic in a very obvious way. Holmes Rolston III writes that we should regard what *is* as a standard for what we *ought* to do, and in terms of organisms, "what is" is given in the genetic code. He suggests that "[T]his information is a modern equivalent of what Aristotle called formal and final causes; it gives the organism a *telos,* or end, a kind of (nonfelt) goal. Organisms have ends, although not always ends in view."[10] He further argues that the genetic set that gives an organism its *telos* is also a normative set: what genetically is is what genetically ought to be. Evidently genetic engineering turns out to be, on this reading, a problematic form of meddling in what is at the heart of what is morally considerable in organisms. It needs to be pointed out that Rolston's position, taken at face value, leads to some uncomfortable conclusions, not the least of which is that "damaged" genetic codes (such as that of the human sufferer of cystic fibrosis) should be left alone. It would seem prudent to add an "in principle" clause to anything fundamentalist Rolston might have to say so as to preserve his general intention yet make way for reasonable judgements in specific cases.

Rolston also gives us a lead into the fundamental biocentric and holistic theme concerning the relationship between environmental ethics and genetic engineering: the role of species. Rolston says bluntly that "A species exists; a species ought to exist,"[11] and that this means that, "The species too has its integrity, its individuality, its right to life."[12] Taken at face value again this implies that transgenetic experiments are morally indefensible in that they interfere, by definition, with the integrity of species. It might be objected — against Rolston — that interference with individual members of a species cannot amount to interference with the species itself because there will always be examples of the unengineered species in existence. If the identities of species A1 (unengineered) and species A2 (engineered) are seen as discrete then the objection probably holds, but if their identities are defined (at least partly) in a relational sense, then the "creation" of species A2 affects the identity of species A1. In this sense, the interference with individual members of A1 that led to the creation of A2 amounts to interference with the species A1.

At this point, of course, the question of whether discrete species actually exist becomes crucial. It has been argued that arguments from integrity have no basis in biological fact: "If one accepts Darwin's theory on the origin of species it becomes very difficult to argue that natural kinds and individuals have an integrity which artificial kinds and individuals lack."[13] At the same time (and assuming that something like a species can be said to exist) it will be objected that more is required for a species' integrity to be destroyed than the transference of one or two genes. And if no more *is* required than this, then surely species are continually destroyed in an entirely "natural" way through the phenomenon of "jumping genes"?

Is Rolston forced to concede, then, that species do not exist? In the discrete, Platonic, sense maybe he is — but then he might still refer to the European Commission's definition of a genetically engineered organism cited earlier. From the point of view of this definition, natural barriers to mating and reproduction exist in that hybrids cannot breed successfully with one another. The attenuated and admittedly porous sense of "species" to which this gives rise is strong enough at least to sustain an "amber traffic light" notion [of caution]. From this point of view barriers to mating — even if overcome by hybrids breeding with either one or both of the parental species — have moral significance in that we are invited to pause and wonder whether what is difficult "in nature" should be made easy by technology. I think, in other words, that too much can be made by both sides of the question of the existence of species. Those like Rolston who say, uncompromisingly, that they do exist are likely to fall foul of biologists who argue that the biological evidence says otherwise. But these biologists, in uncompromising turn, are in danger of missing the very real ethical concerns that biocentrics have raised by attending only to the letter, and not to the spirit, of their message.

Where has this got us to? Biocentric views of genetic engineering derive from two main sources. First, genetic engineering is held to constitute a practice that expresses a human will to domination of the non-human natural world. This they will say, is inappropriate in the context of a global environmental crisis part of whose cause, at least, is the very habits and practices of which genetic engineering is such a sophisticated example. Second, biocentrics find value in beings and collections of beings whom we do not normally regard as members of the moral community. From this point of view, and to the extent that genetic engineering interferes with the moral considerability of an individual's *telos,* or with a species, it is held in *prima facie* suspicion by biocentrics.[14]

There seem to be two principal ways to go from here. First, this *prima facie* suspicion can be turned into wholesale opposition to all forms of genetic engineering, on the grounds that its practice is immoral from the perspectives outlined above. Such a view, though, has two possible defects. The first is that the biological descriptions upon which the moral case are based are themselves questionable. There are biologists who will claim that the notion that species are morally considerable cannot be true because species do not, as such, exist.

The second is that such wholesale rejection pays too little mind to the potentially beneficial consequences of some forms of genetic engineering, and I would like to explore this objection in rather more detail. On this reading, a case-by-case examination is appropriate in which the guideline questions would be *what* is being done to *whom* (or to what), and *why*. Biocentrics might merely demand in this context that the moral considerability of species (to the extent that it is believed that there is such a thing) be taken into account as a further factor in the decision-making process. They would probably be happy, in this case, with a stewardship-type formulation such as that suggested by Alan Holland . . . : that genetic engineering should be conducted "in a manner compatible with the continuing existence of the biosphere viewed as a community."

This consequentialist dimension seems an appropriate one for biocentrics to take into account: the fields of application of genetic engineering are many and varied, and it is unhelpful to take an uncompromisingly prohibitive view of its practice. In the context of medicine, for example, the uses to which genetic engineering can be put are multiple, and the list can sometimes read as a succession of nails being banged into the coffin of those who would seek to restrict genetic engineering experimentation. How could anyone refuse to endorse something with such potential for improving human health? Applications range from the production of larger quantities of insulin than would be available without genetic engineering, through the manufacture of vaccines for (for example) malaria, dengue fever and leprosy, to the possible treatment of genetically based human disorders.

As far as agriculture is concerned, genetic engineering has sometimes been hailed as the cutting edge of the second "green revolution": the application of scientific and industrial techniques to the problem of growing more food, more effectively in ever smaller spaces. In this case, genetic manipula-tion takes the place of artificial pesticides, herbicides, fungicides and fertilisers. There is, for example, the possibility of creating cereal crops with built-in herbicide or pesticide resistance, or of developing plants that are capable of "fixing" airborne nitrogen, thus doing away with the need to use ever greater quantities of nitrogen-rich artificial fertiliser which have uncertain but potentially environmentally damaging effects if used over long periods of time.[15]

Not only plants but animals, too, can "benefit" from the snip of genetic scissors. Techniques of genetic selection can be improved so as to produce woolier sheep,[16] and genetic engineers can of course create new animals, such as pigs carrying a human growth hormone so as to make them leaner and heavier. Animals carrying new genes in this way are said to be "transgenic,"[17] and it is worthwhile observing that fattening pigs in this way amounts to a crossing of the natural barrier as defined by the European Commission, in that if we take this natural barrier to be the species then its crossing constitutes the creation of a new species.

Again, much of the opposition to genetic engineering comes from the environmental movement, while its supporters will point out the irony of this given that genetic engineering has the potential to deal with environmental problems. Most obviously, micro-organisms with the ability to degrade toxic waste can be cultured and then put to work on the dispersal of (for example) oil slicks. Similarly, environmentalists' concerns over water scarcity could be made redundant with the creation of drought-resistant plants. More generally, genetic engineering could be read as undermining many of the positions environmentalists adopt on environmental protection because whatever we do to the environment can be rectified or modified by genetic manipulation. In this respect genetic engineering turns out to be the ultimate "technological fix": "Environmentalists . . . may lose important utilitarian or prudential arguments for protecting natural ecosystems [with advances in genetic engineering]. These arguments become harder and harder to defend as we find cheap technological substitutes for nature's gifts."[18]

Determining the legitimacy of genetic engineering, then, becomes a question of weighing up the claims of moral agents and objects within these various fields of application. In these contexts most people will agree on the legitimacy of the genetic engineering of microbes with a view to dispersing oil slicks, on the grounds that the value of microbes and of the ecosystems into which they are delivered[19] are outweighed by the good that will be done. Likewise, we might reach the conclusion that genetic engineering can be carried out on an animal without altering its *telos* in unacceptable ways, and for sufficiently good reason. An example of this would be the work carried out by Ian Wilmut, John Clark and Paul Simons in Edinburgh with a view to producing proteins required for the treatment of haemophilia. The clotting factors are normally made in the liver, but the Edinburgh team sought to have them produced in sheep's milk so that they could be harvested from the mammary glands. If we take the team's report that the transgenic sheep are "perfectly healthy"[20] at face value, then concern at the violation of species boundaries might be overridden by the knowledge that the animal's *telos* is more or less intact (female sheep are supposed to produce milk) and that the aim of treatment is a worthy one. On the other hand most people shudder when they learn that pigs made fatter and leaner by the introduction of a growth hormone typically suffer from arthritis, lack of co-ordination in the back legs and high levels of stress.[21] Biocentrics (among others) may argue here that the suffering of individual pigs, the altering of their *telos* and interference with the integrity of a species are too high a price to pay for leaner meat.

The examples of genetic engineering are legion, and in my view any ethical committee formed with a view to recommending principles for legislation would be bound to look at a large number of them. The point of this article has been to show that a biocentric perspective should now be represented on any such committee so that the question of the value of species forms a part of the moral equation. The point would be to argue that human interest is not the only interest of moral significance, and that adding in concern for (some) individual animals does not take fully enough into account the range of ethical positions now on offer. Despite the views of its detractors, biocentrism need not lead to unhelpful forms of irrationalism. It is perfectly possible to advance rational arguments both voicing concern for the general implication of genetic engineering in respect of human relations with the non-human natural world, and on behalf of the putative values of species.

It would be naive, though, to expect such issues to be satisfactorily settled by philosophers alone. Even assuming that guidelines can be agreed upon and enacted as legislation, unscrupulous operators will take their business to places where there either is no legislation, or no means to enforce it. In the same way that the principles of free trade dictate that pollution can be exported to where it can be most cheaply disposed of, so genetic engineers will move their laboratories to countries with less restrictive practices.[22] They may even feel that it is worth running criminal risks to garner the profits that can be made, as the Wistar Institute, a private research organization in Philadelphia, is reported to have done by running rabies experiments — strictly regulated in the USA — in Argentina: "The organization did not tell the Argentine authorities about the field trial, still less seek their approval."[23]

So research in genetic engineering is as likely to be driven and regulated by the demands of the capitalist market as it is by good intentions and philosophical principles. There is no guarantee that once it had been decided that the violation of the integrity of the species caused by gene transfer between plants is overridden by the potential benefits to human beings, that a disease-resistant kiwi-fruit would not be engineered ahead of a disease-resistant staple crop for the Third World. It is a real worry that research will chase the interests of the rich and powerful rather than those of the poor and needy. The poor and needy are often poor and needy because they have no voice to express their demands. The environment is the most silent political subject of them all, and environmental ethicists choose to speak on its behalf. The question is whether anyone is listening — genetic engineers included.

NOTES

1. I shall discuss later whether species can be said to exist.
2. Rolston (1992) is an example of a biocentric holist.
3. Dixon, 1985, p.46

4. Yanchinski, 1987, p.46
5. The Royal Commission on Environmental Pollution, 1989, p.9
6. Holland, 1990, p.169
7. McKibben, 1990, p.134
8. Fox, 1990, p.34
9. The "shoat" is called a "geep" in the United States of America. Perhaps, as an anonymous referee of this article pointed out, it is just a different color.
10. Rolston, 1992, p.79
11. Ibid, p.83
12. Ibid, p.85
13. Holland, 1990, p.169
14. It is worth pointing out that not only genetic engineering is potentially morally culpable in these terms. From the point of view I have been describing traditional breeding techniques could also come under scrutiny. The differences between the two are, though, considerable and a detailed comparison of them is beyond the remit of this paper. The most important distinction here, though, is that traditional breeding techniques are confined to potentially "natural" combinations of the species' gene pool whereas engineering techniques are not.
15. See, for example, Postgate, 1990, p.57
16. "In Australia, feeding sheep with a diet containing genetically engineered alfalfa which has an increased content of cysteine, has led to a 5% increase in production of wool, worth Australian $300 million in a single year," Chakrabarti and Bhargava, 1990, p.83
17. Wilmut et al., [1988,] p.56
18. Sagoff, 1988, p.29
19. Assuming that rigorous impact assessments have been carried out.
20. Wilmut et. al., 1988, p.57
21. MacKenzie, 1988, p.29 and Wilmut et. al., 1988, p.58
22. This is already happening in respect of German companies, for instance, where the bureaucratic workload required to comply with laws regulating genetic engineering safety is encouraging companies to relocate in countries where laws are more lax. See Toro, 1992, p.6
23. Connor, 1988, p.66

REFERENCES

Borman, F. and Kellert, S. (eds.) 1992. Ecology, Economics, Ethics. New Haven and London: Yale University Press.

Chakrabarti, C. and Bhargava, P. 1990. "Chemicals Through Biotechnology: Facts, Hopes, Dreams and Doubts," *Impact of Science on Society:* 157.

Connor, S. 1988. "Genes on the Loose," *New Scientist,* 26 May.

Dixon, B. 1985. "Genes: Out of the Laboratory, into the Unknown," *New Scientist,* 24 October.

Fox, M. 1990. "Transgenic Animals: Ethical and Animal Welfare Concerns," in Wheale and McNally, 1990.

Holland, A. 1990. "The Biotic Community: A Philosophical Critique of Genetic Engineering," in Wheale and McNally, 1990.

MacKenzie, D. 1988. "Science Milked for All It's Worth," *New Scientist,* 24 March.

McKibben, B. 1990. *The End of Nature.* Harmondsworth: Penguin.

Postgate, J. 1990. "Fixing the Nitrogen Fixers," *New Scientist,* 3 February.

Rolston, Holmes, III 1992. "Environmental Ethics: Values in and Duties to the Natural World," in Borman and Kellert (eds), 1992.

The Royal Commission on Environmental Pollution 1989. *The Release of Genetically Engineered Organisms into the Environment.* London: HMSO.

Sagoff, M. 1988. "Biotechnology and the Environment: What Is at Risk," *Agriculture and Human Values,* Summer.

Toro, T. 1992. ". . . While Germans Flee Paperwork," *New Scientist,* 8 August.

Wheale, P. and McNally, R. 1990. *The Bio-Revolution: Cornucopia or Pandora's Box?* London: Pluto Press.

Wilmut, I.; Clark, J. and Simons, P. 1988. "A Revolution in Animal Breeding," *New Scientist,* 7 July.

Yanchinski, S. 1987. "Boom and Bust in the Rio Business," *New Scientist,* 22 January.

DISCUSSION TOPICS

1. Do you agree with Dobson that genetic engineering is different from selective breeding over the centuries? Explain your reasoning.
2. What reasons does Dobson provide for the ethical importance of the question of whether discrete species exist? In your view, how morally important are species?

3. Dobson argues that biocentrists should not oppose all forms of genetic engineering. Evaluate his argument.

4. In what ways might genetic engineering undermine environmentalists' arguments for environmental protection?

5. Dobson points out that research in genetic engineering is driven by demands of the capitalist market as well as by moral philosophy. What, if any, restrictions or regulations should be placed on genetic engineering based on moral grounds? Justify your perspective.

Ecological Risks and Benefits of Transgenic Plants

Gabor L. Lövei

Gabor L. Lövei is in the Department of Crop Protection of the Danish Institute of Agricultural Sciences, Tjele. In this article from New Zealand Plant Protection *(2001), Lovei demonstrates the complexity of the effects of transgenic plants. He advocates an ecological framework for assessment, including effects on nontarget organisms, natural enemies, pollinators, soil organisms, and biodiversity. While there are potential ecological benefits, he argues that none of these benefits have been sufficiently documented.*

INTRODUCTION

There is intense public interest accompanying the technology of genetic manipulations. Possibly not since nuclear physics produced the atomic bomb has an area of science fallen under such a sharp searching light by society. Different groups of the society are active in the field, spending an enormous amount of energy in different activities according to their roles, aims and perceptions. Much of this energy, however, goes up in heat; much less light has been generated. When attempting to add to the already profuse (but often data-poor, see Domingo 2000) literature related to the topic of transgenic or-

ganisms, it may be useful to precisely determine the scope of this review. Several important aspects of the effects of transgenic plants have been discussed and studied. An important consideration is *ethical:* do we have the right, or are we "doing the proper thing" when engaged in genetic manipulations (Carr & Levidow 1997)? The technology should also be evaluated in *economic* terms: are there real benefits from using this technology? There are concerns relating to the *safety* of transgenic food *for human consumption* (Domingo 2000; Ewen & Pusztai 1999). Gene spread and resistance management are also major concerns (Gould 1998). These are important aspects of the topic, but lie outside the scope of the current review. This review only discusses potential risks and benefits of transgenic plants that can affect ecosystem services.

THE CURRENT SITUATION WITH FIELD-GROWN TRANSGENIC CROPS

The first transgenic crops were commercially planted in 1995. By 2000, a total of 44.2 million ha of transgenic plants were grown in 13 countries (James 2001). While this is only an 11% increase over the area in 1999 (much smaller than in earlier years), the spread of this technology has so far been very rapid. In 2000, the majority (84%) of this increase occurred in the developing countries. Worldwide, most transgenic crops are grown in developed countries (76% of total area) and 24% in developing countries. Four countries, the U.S.A., Argentina, Canada and China, grew 99% of the global total of transgenic crops in 2000.

Most of this area is divided among four crops, soybean (58%), maize (23%), cotton (12%) and oilseed rape (7%). The area devoted to transgenic soybean and cotton increased since 1999, but that of maize and oilseed rape decreased (James 2001).

While a wide array of traits has been inserted into many species of plants, there are only a few in commercial cultivation, mostly herbicide resistance and insect resistance. Seventy-four percent of all transgenic crops in 2000 were herbicide resistant, 19% insect tolerant and further 7% contained both these traits. Herbicide-resistant soybean was the most widely planted transgenic crop (59% of the global area devoted to transgenic crops), with insect-resistant maize a distant second (15% of global area). Since 1999, the area devoted to herbicide tolerant plants has increased, while that of insect-resistant (Bt-) crops has decreased. The global share of transgenic crops is already considerable; 36% of all soybean, 16% of cotton, 11% of oilseed rape and 7% of maize was transgenic in 2000 (James 2001).

The regulations required for commercialisation and field growing of transgenic plants are diverse; in many countries they do not even exist. The latest directive of the European Union requires an environmental impact assessment and post-release monitoring, but specifies no methods. Generally, there is a lack of precise, justified legal framework that hinders assessment, potential commercial application and evaluation of this technology. This is not surprising, given the novelty of transgenic plants, and the state of research into their environmental effects. When the industry developing transgenic plants has been required to assess the potential environmental consequences of their products, the results have not been impressive (Purrington & Bergelson 1995). There is clearly a need for a conceptual framework and more involvement of ecologists.

AN ECOLOGICAL FRAMEWORK FOR ENVIRONMENTAL RISK ASSESSMENT

We should not forget that agricultural fields are also part of the "ecological theatre" in which the "evolutionary play" (sensu Hutchinson 1965) is continuously being played. When transgenic plants are planted in the field, they will inevitably come into contact with many other species that together perform several ecological processes operating in agricultural fields. Listed below are a few significant "actors" in this "ecological theatre" that the transgenic plant will come into "ecological contact" with.

- Other plants, whether conspecifics or individuals of other species. This creates the question of invasiveness and gene spread.

- Herbivores that feed on plants above or below ground. The effects on non-target herbivores (and biodiversity) must be considered.

- Natural enemies of these organisms. What are the consequences for natural pest control?

- Pollinators that visit their flowers. What are the potential consequences for pollinating insects?

- Symbionts that live in the root zone, such as mycorrhizae or nitrogen-fixing bacteria.

- Detritivores and decomposers that feed on dead plant parts. How does this affect the soil ecological processes maintaining soil fertility, nutrient cycling and plant growth?

Gene Escape/Invasiveness

Gene escape has been recognised as a potentially significant hazard (Wolfenbarger & Phifer 2000). For many crops, outcrossing and hybridisation with wild relatives is possible (Elstrand et al. 1999). The ecological consequences of this could be serious if the new trait changes fitness parameters or invasiveness of the modified plants.

Invasiveness is recognised as a major threat in New Zealand, but invasions are also a global concern (Vitousek et al. 1997a; Lövei 1997). Data related to fitness or invasiveness of genetically modified plants are scarce. Stewart et al. (1997) found that oilseed rape containing the *Bt*-toxin gene acquires a fitness advantage under insect herbivory. In a long-term study of survival in the wild and invasiveness of herbicide-resistant crop plants in different areas of the British Isles, no genetically modified plant line survived longer than 4 years when planted in natural habitats (Crawley et al. 2001).

However, invasion success is scale-related, and it is rather difficult to predict the consequences of wide-scale planting of transgenic crops from limited scale studies.

Effects on Non-Target Organisms

Phytophagous organisms that were not targeted may still be affected by insect-resistant plants. For example, transgenic maize pollen, deposited on milkweed leaves could cause larval mortality of the monarch butterfly (*Danais plexippus*) (Losey et al. 1999), which is a species of important nature conservation focus in the U.S.A. This study spawned a number of others, indicating that natural pollen concentrations can still cause significant mortality (Hansen Jesse & Obrycki 2000). Not all butterfly species seem to be under such risk. Larvae of the black swallowtail (*Papilio polyxenes*) are not sensitive to transgenic maize pollen (Wraight et al. 2000).

Effects on Natural Enemies

Insect-resistant plants are aimed at reducing the densities of certain phytophagous insects. These insects, however, also serve as prey for a range of natural enemies. An important potential effect of transgenic plants is the consequences of changing the occurrence and density of prey for natural enemies. If the density of prey is reduced, a direct flow-on effect could be a reduced density of their natural enemies. Transgenic potato controlling the Colorado potato beetle is probably responsible for a documented decrease of its specialist predatory ground beetle (Riddick et al. 1998).

Predatory and parasitoid insects are also sensitive to prey quality, and prey quality can be influenced by host plants, giving rise to tri-trophic interactions (Price et al. 1980). Several such examples have been found using transgenic plants or their experimental equivalents. For example, the parasitoid wasp *Eulophus pennicornis* had reduced parasitisation on tomato fruitworm (*Lacanobia oleracea*) hosts from plants with the cowpea trypsin inhibitor (Bell et al. 2001). Parasitoids can also react at a behavioural level to a host originating on transgenic plants (Schuler et al. 1999).

Adults of the coccinellid *A. bipunctata,* when fed on aphids raised on transgenic potato (expressing the snowdrop lectin), were negatively affected. Adult female (but not male) longevity was reduced, egg laying and egg viability decreased (Birch et al. 1999). Interestingly, larvae of the same coccinellid did not seem to suffer the same consequences (Down et al. 2000).

In experiments conducted in New Zealand, Jørgensen & Lövei (1999) found that adult ground beetles consumed less of their caterpillar prey when this prey was raised on proteinase inhibitor-containing diet vs normal diet. This effect persisted longer than the actual exposure to the manipulated prey and was age-dependent (Jørgensen & Lövei 1999). Proteinase inhibitors seem to affect herbivore suitability as prey for this predator.

Effects on Pollinators

Plants that are pollinated by animals provide more than 25% of the world's food. Pollinating organisms in the temperate regions are mostly insects, namely bees and wasps (Buchmann & Nabham 1996). They can be agents of pollen spread and exposed to any transgenic product that is expressed in pollen or nectar. Bees and bumble bees can be affected by transgenic products (Malone et al. 2001) and their systematic study needs to be incorporated into the environmental risk assessment of transgenic plants to make sure that this essential ecosystem service is not damaged (Lövei et al. 2001).

Effects on Soil Organisms and Decomposers

In root exudates of transgenic Bt-maize, the Bt-toxin was detected at concentrations that can kill insects (Saxena et al. 2000). The long-term consequences of this are not yet known. The study of soil organisms and processes is generally less advanced, reflecting the relative emphasis on above vs belowground ecological processes (Brown & Gange 1990). In one of the most detailed studies published to date, Griffiths et al. (2000) found transient effects and significant changes in soil protozoan populations in soil under genetically engineered potato lines. As soil fertility maintenance is a biological process, tests of the effects of GM plants on soil processes are very important.

Many of these actors participate in ecological processes that are useful and necessary for agricultural production. These processes are termed "ecosystem services" (Costanza et al. 1997). Until very recently an unappreciated "endless resource," the global monetary value of these ecosystem services was estimated to surpass the combined Gross Domestic Product of the Earth's nations (Costanza et al. 1997).

I suggest that this framework of "ecosystem services" would be useful in order to conceptualise the environmental risk assessment of transgenic plants.

Effects on Biodiversity

Intensive agriculture, especially in the Northern Hemisphere, is a significant environmental management factor, and much of those countries' biological diversity is maintained in a cultivated landscape (Krebs et al. 1999). Altering the current management regime has potentially significant consequences for biological diversity in such countries.

Herbicide-resistant crops are expected to allow more efficient weed control. Concerns have been raised, especially in the United Kingdom, that this will have negative consequences for countryside biological diversity, with fewer surviving flowering plants to provide resources for organisms ranging from invertebrates to birds. The possible effects of such a scenario were approximated by modelling (Watkinson et al. 2000). These authors used a weed (*Chenopodium album*) and a songbird (skylark, *Alauda arvensis*) model in a landscape context to predict the effects of herbicide-resistant sugarbeet on biological diversity in general. Their work points to potentially significant negative effects on seed-eating birds.

Similar concerns prompted the U.K. government to ban commercial growing of transgenic plants and initiate a 4-year farm-scale field trial to study what effect herbicide-resistant transgenic plants will have on biodiversity (Firbank et al. 1999). Studies published so far on the effects of transgenic plants on agricultural biodiversity are rather imperfect (Hilbeck et al. 2000).

Agricultural biodiversity in New Zealand is generally low, and non-native species often form the majority of species found in cultivated habitats (Lövei 1991). There seems to be a limited interplay between native and non-native habitats in New Zealand. Current political thinking about biodiversity in New Zealand is concentrated on native organisms. Consequently, changes in cultivated land due to transgenic crops are expected to create problems for biodiversity only if invasiveness is affected.

POTENTIAL ECOLOGICAL BENEFITS

The evaluation of the environmental impact of transgenic organisms often centres on the risks attached to them. This is justified, as any new, large-scale technology does have risks and unforeseen consequences. However, a number of arguments have suggested a positive environmental impact from large-scale production of transgenic plants (Wolfenbarger & Phifer 2000).

Reduced Environmental Impact from Pesticides

Transgenic crops may decrease the use of environmentally harmful chemicals to control weeds and pests. This can happen in several different ways:

certain pesticides are no longer used, the frequency of treatments is reduced, or the area treated is reduced (Wolfenbarger & Phifer 2000).

For example, reduced frequency of treatments can bring a net decrease in pesticide pollution if paralleled with a decrease in the total amount of pesticide and herbicide used. Conflicting claims have been made about the effect of herbicide-tolerant crops in the U.S.A. (Ferber 1999; Carpenter & Gianessi 2000). In the absence of published documentation where the assumptions and the validity of the arguments can be checked, no conclusions can be drawn (Wolfenbarger & Phifer 2000).

Increased Yield

If crop yields increased, less cultivated area would be needed to produce the total amount of food required by people. This could result in a lower pressure on land not yet under cultivation and could allow more land to be left under protection. The potential environmental benefits of this type may be greatest in developing countries where most of the agricultural production increase was due to new areas taken into cultivation.

Soil Conservation

Herbicide-tolerant crops may allow farmers to abandon the use of soil-incorporated pre-emergent herbicides. This shift to post-emergent weed control may increase the no-till and conservation tillage practices, decreasing soil erosion, water loss, and increasing soil organic matter (Cannell & Hawes 1994).

Phytoremediation

Genetically modified plants and micro-organisms can be used for *in situ* remediation of soil and water pollution. Transgenic plants can sequester heavy metals from soils (Gleba et al. 1999) or detoxify pollutants (Bizily et al. 2000). This has not yet been used widely, so its environmental impact has not been studied.

CONCLUSION

In conclusion, I suggest that the evaluation of the environmental effects of transgenic plants should include the study of beneficial ecological interactions.

The significance of conceptualising this as the study on "ecosystem services" is more than semantic, as it links this question to one of the most important intellectual concepts of current ecology. This was borne by the necessity to convey the realisation that human impacts on ecosystems are global and profound (Vitousek et al. 1997b), and we need to use a unified conceptual approach to interpret them. If transgenic technology causes significant harm to these ecological services, we are heading the wrong way. There is too little resilience left in the natural ecosystems to absorb continued abuse.

However, assessing the impact of this technology does not have to be conducted with the mindset of "averting damage." The arguments regarding possible benefits of transgenic plants are plausible, but so far all of them are insufficiently documented (Wolfenbarger & Phifer 2000). They need to be incorporated into the environmental impact of this technology. It is important to stress that the total environmental impact should be measured against current practice, and not against an idealised but non-existing agricultural cultivation system.

This may all seem entirely logical and unnecessary to emphasise. However, this view is not universal. The international think-tank CGIAR (Consultative Group on International Agricultural Research) lists the "environmental risk" of transgenic plants (Serageldin & Persley 2000) in terms of:

- gene flow & containment
- weediness
- trait effect
- genetic and phenotypic variability
- expression of genetic material from pathogens
- worker safety

From this seemingly exhaustive list (it even considers "worker safety"), *all* ecosystem services are missing. There is no mention of natural pest control, soil fertility maintenance, pollination or symbiosis as ecological functions that need to be considered when assessing the potential environmental impacts of this technology.

This may represent an exception, but the short-sightedness of this influential forum makes it important to spell out clearly that for GMO environmental risk assessment, an ecological approach is necessary. Further, ecology as a science has the conceptual framework and the methods that allow us to ask meaningful questions and produce answers pertinent to the environmental impact of gene technology.

REFERENCES

Bell, H.A.; Fitches, E.C.; Down, R.E.; Ford, L.; Marris, G.C.; Edwards, J.P.; Gatehouse, J.A.; Gatehouse, A.M.R. 2001: Effect of cowpea trypsin inhibitor (CpTI) on the growth and development of the tomato moth *Lacanobia oleracae* (Lepidoptera: Noctuidae) and on the success of the gregarious ectoparasitoid *Eulophus pennicornis* (Hymenoptera: Eulophidae). *Pest Mgt Sci. 57:* 57–65.

Birch, A.N.E.; Geoghean, I.E.; Majerus, M.E.N.; McNicol, J.W.; Hackett, C.A.; Gatehouse, A.M.R.; Gatehouse, J.A. 1999: Tri-trophic interactions involving pest aphid, predatory 2-spot ladybirds and transgenic potatoes expressing snowdrop lectin for aphid resistance. *Mol. Breed. 5:* 75–83.

Bizily, S.P.; Rugh, C.L.; Meagher, R.B. 2000: Phytodetoxification of hazardous organomercurials by genetically engineered plants. *Nat. Biotechnol. 18:* 213–217.

Brown, V.K.; Gange, A.C. 1990: Insect herbivory below ground. *Adv. Ecol. Res. 20:* 1–58.

Buchmann, S.L.; Nabham, G.P. 1996: The forgotten pollinators. Island Press, Washington, D.C. 292 p.

Cannell, R.Q.; Hawes, J.D. 1994: Trends in tillage practices in relation to sustainable crop production with special reference to temperate climates. *Soil Till. Res. 30:* 245–282.

Carpenter, J.; Gianessi, L. 2000: Herbicide use on Roundup ready crops. *Science 287:* 803–804.

Carr, S.; Levidow, L. 1997: How biotechnology regulation separates ethics from risk. *Outlook on Agric. 26:* 145–150.

Costanza, R., et al. 1997. The value of the world's ecosystem services and natural capital. *Nature 387:* 253–260.

Crawley, M.J.; Brown, S.L.; Hails, R.S.; Kohn, D.D.; Rees, M. 2001: Transgenic crops in natural habitats. *Nature 409:* 682–683.

Domingo, J.L. 2000: Health risks of GM foods: many opinions but few data. *Science 288:* 1748–1749.

Down, R.E.; Ford, L.; Woodhouse, S.D.; Raemaekers, R.J.M.; Leitch, B.; Gatehouse, J.A.; Gatehouse, A.M.R. 2000: Snowdrop lectin (GNA) has no acute toxic effects on a beneficial insect predator, the 2-spot ladybird (*Adalia bipunctata* L.). *J. Ins. Physiol. 46:* 379–391.

Elstrand, N.C.; Prentice, H.C.; Hancock, J.F. 1999: Gene flow and introgression from domesticated plants into their wild relatives. *Ann. Rev. Ecol. Syst. 30:* 539–563.

Ewen, S.W.B.; Pusztai, A. 1999: Effects of diets containing genetically modified potatoes expressing *Galanthus nivalis* lectin on rat small intestine. *Lancet 354:* 1353–1354.

Ferber, D. 1999: GM crops in the cross hair. *Science 286:* 1662–1666.

Firbank, L.G.; Dewar, A.M.; Hill, M.O.; May, M.J.; Perry, J.N.; Rothery, P.; Squire, G.R.; Woiwod, I.P. 1999: Farm-scale evaluation of GM crops explained. *Nature 399:* 727–728.

Gleba, D.; Borisjuk, N.V.; Borisjuk, L.G.; Kneer, R.; Poulev, A.; Sarzhinskaya, M.; Dushenkov, S.; Logendra, S.; Gleba, Y.Y.; Raskin, I. 1999: Use of plant roots for phytoremediation and molecular farming. *Proc. Natl. Acad. Sci. U.S.A. 96:* 5973–5977.

Gould, F. 1998: Sustainability of transgenic insecticidal cultivars: integrating pest genetics and ecology. *Ann. Rev. Entomol. 43:* 701–726.

Griffiths, B.S.; Geoghean, I.E.; Robertson, W.M. 2000: Testing genetically engineered potato, producing the lectins GNA and ConA, on non-target soil organisms and processes. *J. Appl. Ecol. 37:* 159–170.

Hansen Jesse, L.C.; Obrycki, J.J. 2000: Field deposition of Bt transgenic corn pollen: lethal effects on the monarch butterfly. *Oecologia 125:* 241–248.

Hilbeck, A.; Meier, M.S.; Raps, A. 2000: Review on non-target organisms and Bt-plants. Ecostrat Gmbh, Zurich. 77 p.

Hutchinson, G.E. 1965: The ecological theatre and the evolutionary play. Yale Univ. Press, New Haven, U.S.A.

James, C. 2001: Global review of commercialized transgenic crops: 2000. ISAAA Briefs No. 21: Preview. ISAAA, Ithaca, NY.

Jørgensen, H.B.; Lövei, G.L. 1999: Tritrophic effects on predator feeding: consumption by the carabid *Harpalus affinis* of *Heliothis armigera* caterpillars fed on proteinase-inhibitor-containing diet. *Entomol. Exp. Appl. 93:* 113–116.

Krebs, J.R.; Wilson, J.D.; Bradbury, R.B.; Siriwardena, G.M. 1999: The second silent spring? *Nature 400:* 611–612.

Losey, J.E.; Raynor, L.S.; Carter, M.E. 1999: Transgenic pollen harms monarch larvae. *Nature 399:* 214.

Lövei, G.L. 1991: The ground-dwelling predatory fauna in an organic and an abandoned kiwifruit orchard. *In:* Popay, L. ed. *Proceedings of the N.Z. Inst. Agric. Sci. & N.Z. Hort. Soc. Symp. on Sustainable Agriculture and Organic Food Production.* Pp. 9–14.

Lövei, G.L. 1997: Global change through invasion. *Nature 388:* 627–628.

Lövei, G.L.; Felkl, G.; Broodsgaard, H.B.; Hansen, L.M. 2001: Environmental risks of insect-tolerant transgenic plants. *18th Danish Plant Prot. Conf., DJF Rapport nr. 41:* 171–176.

Malone, L.A.; Burgess, E.P.J.; Gatehouse, H.S.; Voisey, C.R.; Tregida, E.L.; Philip, B.A. 2001: Effects of ingestion of a *Bacillus thuringiensis* toxin and a trypsin inhibitor on honey bee flight activity and longevity. *Apidologie 32:* 57–68.

Purrington, C.B.; Bergelson, J. 1995: Assessing weediness of transgenic crops: industry plays plant ecologist. *Trends Ecol. Evol. 10:* 340–342.

Price, P.W.; Bouton, C.E.; Gross, P.; Bruce, A.M.; Thompson, J.N.; Weis, A.E. 1980: Interactions among three trophic levels: influence of plants on interactions between insect herbivores and natural enemies. *Ann. Rev. Entomol. 11:* 41–65.

Riddick, E.W.; Dively, G.; Barbosa, P. 1998: Effect of a seed-mix deployment of Cry3A-transgenic and nontransgenic potato on the abundance of *Lebia grandis* (Coleoptera : Carabidae) and Coleomegilla maculata (Coleoptera : Coccinellidae). *Annals Entomol. Soc. America 91:* 647–653.

Saxena, D.; Flores, S.; Stotzky, G. 2000: Insecticidal toxin in root exudates from *Bt* corn. *Nature 402:* 480.

Schuler, T.H.; Potting, R.P.J.; Denholm, I.; Poppy, G.M. 1999: Parasitoid behaviour and *Bt* plants. *Nature 400:* 825–826.

Serageldin, I.; Persley, G.J. 2000. Promethean science: agricultural biotechnology, the environment, and the poor. Consultative Group on International Agricultural Research, Washington, D.C. 41 p.

Stewart, C.N. jr.; All, J.N.; Raymer, P.L.; Ramachadran, S. 1997: Increased fitness of transgenic insecticidal rapeseed under insect selection pressure. *Mol. Ecol. 6:* 773–779.

Vitousek, P.M.; D'Antonio, C.M.; Loope, L.L.; Rejmanek, M.; Westbrooks, R. 1997a: Introduced species: a significant component of human-caused global change. *N.Z. J. Ecol. 21:* 1–16.

Vitousek, P.M.; Mooney, H.A.; Lubchenco, J.; Melillo, J.M. 1997b: Human domination of Earth's ecosystems. *Science 277:* 494–499.

Watkinson, A.R.; Freckleton, R.P.; Robinson, R.A.; Sutherland, W.J. 2000: Predictions of biodiversity response to genetically modified herbicide-tolerant crops. *Science 289:* 1554–1557.

Wolfenbarger, L.L.; Phifer, P.R. 2000: The ecological risks and benefits of genetically engineered plants. *Science 290:* 2088–2093.

Wraight, C.L.; Zangerl, A.R.; Carroll, M.J.; Berenbaum, M.R. 2000: Absence of toxicity of *Bacillus thuringiensis* pollen to black swallowtails under field conditions. *Proc. Natl. Acad. Sci. U.S.A. 97:* 7700–7703.

DISCUSSION TOPICS

1. Given the potential environmental effects of transgenic plants, what kind of regulation do you think should be in place? Give your reasoning.

2. Enumerate the "actors" in the "ecological theatre" that Lövei describes. Which actors may he have omitted?

3. Give three specific risks from transgenic plants identified by Lövei. Which of these risks do you believe have not been thoroughly researched? Why do you believe this is the case?

4. Describe some of the potential ecological benefits of transgenic organisms that Lövei mentions. Which do you believe to be most important? Explain your position.

5. Lövei uses the concept of "ecosystem services." What is the relationship of this concept to his evaluation of transgenic plants?

The Ecological Critique of Agricultural Biotechnology

Mark Sagoff

Mark Sagoff is a researcher at the Institute for Philosophy and Public Policy in the School of Public Affairs at the University of Maryland, College Park. He has been a Pew Scholar in Conservation and the Environment, a Wilson Center Scholar, and a Fellow of the American Association for the Advancement of Science. His book The Economy of the Earth *was published in 1988. The following selection is excerpted from "Biotechnology and Agriculture: The Common Wisdom and Its Critics" (2001). Sagoff briefly analyzes definitions of* biodiversity *and* nature. *Depending on the definition used, he notes that it can be said either that biotechnology can greatly increase biodiversity or that biotechnology diminishes biodiversity and in fact means the end of nature in the sense of what is spontaneous and wild.*

Those who raise doubts about the application of GMOs in agriculture question not necessarily its economic but its ecological consequences. In this spirit, the Cartagena Protocol on Biosafety (Protocol) cites the potential adverse effects on biological diversity as a reason for adopting a "precautionary approach" in regulating genetic technologies in agriculture.[1] The Protocol is a supplementary agreement to the Convention on Biological Diversity, which endorsed efforts "to regulate, manage or control the risks associated with the use and release of living modified organisms resulting from biotechnology which are likely to have adverse environmental impacts that could affect the conservation and sustainable use of biological diversity."[2]

One critic has said that genetic engineering spearheads a "human siege on the natural environment."[3] That is to say, it mounts a final attack upon wild, natural ecosystems and organisms now comparatively unaffected by human activity. Activist Jeremy Rifkin has argued that "virtually every genetically engineered organism released into the environment poses a potential threat to the ecosystem."[4] Greenpeace International likewise has declared that genetically modified crops "threaten biodiversity, wildlife and truly sustainable forms of agriculture."[5]

It is difficult to assess these concerns because they refer to a wide variety of problems. One must concede that agriculture in general—with or without GMOs—damages biodiversity and the environment by replacing complex, diverse ecosystems with amber waves of grain. Insofar as biotechnology further industrializes agriculture—turning more landscapes into monocultures—it is likely to threaten what Jeremy Rifkin calls the ecosystem. The problem, however, lies not in biotechnology as such but in the ability of human beings, unlike the lilies of the field, to survive in the wild. We have to engage in agriculture because we cannot subsist on the free bounty of ecosystems.

The relation between biotechnology and biodiversity is complicated but depends largely on how one defines "biodiversity." If one means, "the variety of morphology, behavior, physiology, and biochemistry in living things,"[6] then biotechnology can contribute immensely, one might say infinitely, to biodiversity. This is true because by virtue of genetic manipulation, recombination, mutation, and Heaven knows what else, biologists can concoct all sorts of living things never before seen on earth — and perhaps recreate species that have gone extinct. The prospects are unlimited.

Take rice, for example. By using conventional methods of forced mutation and artificial selection, breeders have produced from about twenty wild species in the genus *Oryza* the far more than 100,000 cultivars of rice that exist in the world today.[7] The international Rice Research Institute located in the Philippines alone has stored about 85,000 cultivated landraces in its long-term *ex situ* facility. Over 1,700 useful new varieties of rice have been created by artificial selection (that is, forced evolution) since the early 1960s.[8] If explorers had discovered in the wild a strain of rice that contained Vitamin A or one that was rich in iron, environmentalists would have hailed the discovery as proof that society should protect wild lands for their economic benefits. One might on the same logic hail the value of genetic engineering that actually makes such wonders available.

If one means by "biodiversity" just those plants and animals that arise in the wild, however, the relation between biotechnology and biodiversity is different. Agriculture depends on the cultivation of very few of these species and those it uses have by now been so altered by artificial selection that they bear very little relation to their wild forebears.[9] "Using a variety of tools over the past few decades, plant breeders have radically transformed our crop plants by altering their architecture (such as the development of dwarf wheat and rice), shortening growing seasons, developing greater resistance to diseases and pests (all crops), and developing big-

ger seeds and fruits."[10] Thus the vast variety of agricultural crops would not have existed without human intervention, e.g., forced mutation and artificial selection. It is unclear how much wild nature contributes. Wild progenitors of some crops have long been extinct; the last wild ancestor of dairy and beef cattle disappeared in about 1746 in Poland. Nevertheless, genetic engineering allows us to contemplate all sorts of new varieties, for example, beef cattle with lower fat or cholesterol.

Farmers cultivate very few of the roughly 600,000 known plants available to them.[11] "Of an estimated 80,000 types of plants we know to be edible," a U.S. Department of the Interior document says, "only about 150 are extensively cultivated."[12] About twenty species, none of which is in any way endangered, provide ninety percent of the food the world takes from plants. If agriculture basically depends on just twenty species — out of, say, the more than twenty million that some biologists reckon the world contains — the importance of biodiversity to agriculture can be overstated. Of course, genetic engineers, breeders, and other plant technologists will manipulate the genomes of the major food crops to improve their economic and nutritional properties. Genetic engineering increases the genetic diversity of these plants by allowing scientists to recombine their genetic materials with genes from virtually any other living thing. This source variety — genetic recombination in the laboratory — can produce more novel kinds of plants and animals than one might want to think about.

There is little call for new species for cultivation — just for improvements in old ones. Corporations find it difficult to create demand for a new product, such as paw-paws, even though they are delicious. Any new food has to take "shelf space" or "market-share" from one that is now purchased. It is hard enough to get people to eat their broccoli and lima beans. It is harder still to develop consumer demand for new foods. This may be the reason the Kraft Corporation, for example, does not prospect in remote places for rare and unusual plants and animals to add to the menu. Biotechnology will do a lot more than bioprospecting to improve the human diet.

If one means by "biodiversity" the variety of life, genetic engineering can add immensely and immeasurably to biodiversity. If the term refers only to wild things, that is, to Nature untouched by human hands, biotechnology can only diminish and never augment biodiversity. In that case, "biodiversity" refers to Nature as the opposite of "artifact" or "technology." As ecologist Michael Soule points out, "there's a lot of overlap between *nature* and *biodiversity*."[13] Three biologists summarize, "'Maintenance of biodiversity' can be thought of as' another way to say 'maintenance of *everything*.'"[14]

Terms like "biodiversity," "ecosystem," and "sustainability" appear to have no clear scientific meaning, measurement, or reference. Rather, they are supposed to move public debate from a concern with endangered species to nature in all its variety.[15] This was clearly the intention of those who coined the term "biodiversity." Historian David Takacs writes that Walter Rosen, a program officer at the National Research Council, used the National Academy's imprimatur to hold a conference that expanded the boundaries of biology to include advocacy and launched the term *biodiversity*.[16]

Ecologist Dan Janzen commented, "We needed a word that would . . . serve as a little flag for Congress."[17] The term "biodiversity," as Kevin Gaston notes, embodies "concepts not only of the variety of life, but additionally of the importance of that variety, of the crisis represented by its loss, and of the need for conservation action."[18] No one can assess the relation between agricultural biotechnology and biodiversity, ecosystems, sustainability, etc., without a firmer definition of these concepts. Perhaps they all refer to the same thing: Nature or the natural world unaffected by human activity.

V. NATURE'S SERVICES

The terms "nature" and "natural" may refer to two very different ideas. First, these terms may refer to everything in the universe, that is, everything to which the laws of physics apply. In this context, the "natural" constitutes the opposite of the "supernatural." On this conception of the "natural," human beings are as much part of nature as any other creature and nothing we can do can upset the laws, rules, patterns, or principles that govern or organize natural systems. The philosopher John Stuart Mill explains:

To bid people conform to the laws of nature when they have no power but what the laws of nature give them—when it is a physical impossibility for them to do the smallest thing otherwise than through some law of nature, is an absurdity. The thing they need to be told is, what particular law of nature they should make use of in a particular case.[19]

If one thinks of "nature" in the sense of everything that obeys the rules of physics and chemistry, then one can understand the success of hydrology, agronomy, sanitation engineering, biochemistry, microbiology, etc., in helping society to organize nature for human purposes. Corporate giants such as Weyerhaeuser, Georgia Pacific, Monsanto, Cargill, and ConAgra hire thousands of bioindustrial engineers who manage vast agricultural, silvicultural, and aquacultural operations. The systems they create rely on the very principles that nature obeys. There is no doubt that these systems feed, clothe, and comfort us; they clearly provide goods and services upon which we all depend.

If one thinks of nature—the ecosystem, biodiversity, or the sustainable—as that which human beings have not affected, then it seems clear that biotechnology may contaminate what little remains of it. The loss of the natural—the end of nature, the death of nature—presents a terrible aesthetic, moral, cultural, and spiritual loss. Poets, artists, and religious leaders have shown us this. What is not as clear, however, is that the human domestication of nature—replacing prairies with plantations, savannas with suburbs, forests with factories, arcadias with arcades, and dells with delis—however horrible aesthetically, has been detrimental economically. Indeed, the *Great Transformation*, as Karl Polanyi[20] titled it, while baleful and baneful from a cultural perspective, seems to have served the economic or utilitarian needs of humanity rather well.

Is the loss of nature—the disappearance of what is spontaneous and wild—a problem from an instrumental, economic, or prudential point of view? Ecologist Hal Mooney and others argue that "conditions and processes characterizing natural ecosystems supply humanity with an array of free services upon which society depends."[21] Gretchen Daily and others likewise warn "that natural ecosystems . . .

perform fundamental life-support services without which human civilizations would cease to thrive."[22]

I want to leave you with the question whether this is true. Hunter-gatherer societies may survive in undeveloped nature in this sense. We cannot and need not do so. In the United States, nature in that Romantic sense disappeared more than a century ago with the closing of the frontier. A "natural eco-system" can hardly be found between Maine and Mexico. It persists as an icon of the Romantic or the ecological imagination. The television program "Survivor" gives an inkling of the extent to which the natural ecosystem will sustain bourgeois humanity, i.e., not at all. Philosophers like Spinoza and Hobbes described the state of nature as a war of each against all, a horrendous tyranny of tooth and claw, in which organisms exercise every right that power allows and appetite suggests. Nature has been shorn of its terror mainly because it has been supplanted and subdued by technology.

I suspect that biotechnology in agriculture spells the end of nature in the deepest conceptual sense — Nature as God's Creation — since it allows humans to invent living things.[23] It divests us of our innocent belief that nature will care for us as it does the lilies of the field. From a scientific perspective, nature includes GMOs and everything that conforms to the laws of chemistry and physics. Evolution is now artificial. This may mean that everything is artificial. Having eaten of the Tree of Knowledge, we now turn to the Tree of Life. Nature as distinct from artifice will survive in the Romantic and religious imagination — in poetry, art, theology, sitcoms, ecological theory, and so on. Realistically speaking, however, Nature is now what we must do without.

NOTES

1. Cartagena Protocol on Biosafety to the Convention on Biological Diversity, Jan. 29, 2000, 39 I.L.M. 1027 (2000).
2. United Nations Conference on Environment and Development: Convention on Biological Diversity, June 5, 1992, art. 8, 31 I.L.M. 818, 825 (1992).
3. Karen M. Graziano, Comment, "Biosafety Protocol: Recommendations to Ensure the Safety of the Environment," 7 *Colo. J. Int'l Envtl. L. & Pol'y* 179, 185 (1996).
4. Jeremy Rifkin, "The Biotech Century," *E. Mag.,* May–June 1998, at 36, 38.
5. Greenpeace Int'l, "Genetically Engineered Food: 7. Public Concern," at http://www.greenpeace.org/~geneng/reports/food/intrfo07.htm (last visited Dec. 15, 2001).
6. James Mallet, "The Genetics of Biological Diversity: From Varieties to Species," in *Biodiversity: Biology of Numbers & Difference* 13, 13 (Kevin J. Gaston ed., 1996).
7. Robert E. Evenson & Douglas Gollin, "Genetic Resources, International Organizations, and Improvement in Rice Varieties," 45 *Econ. Dev. & Cultural Change* 471, 471–73 (1997).
8. *Id.*
9. See Jack R. Harlan, *Crops & Man* 117–33 (2d ed. 1992).
10. Channapatna S. Prakash, "The Genetically Modified Crop Debate in the Context of Agricultural Evolution," 126 *Plant Physiology,* May 2001, at 8, 10, available at http://www.plantphysiol.org/cgi/reprint/126/1/8.pdf.
11. See David R. Given, *Principles & Practice of Plant Conservation* 1 (1994); see also Edward O. Wilson, *The Diversity of Life* 287–88 (1992).
12. U.S. Dep't of Interior, Nat'l Park Serv., Biological Diversity, "Nature's Harvest," at http://www.nature.nps.gov/wv/biodiv.htm (last modified Apr. 13, 1999).
13. David Takacs, *The Idea of Biodiversity: Philosophies of Paradise* 79 (1996).
14. Gregory H. Aplet et al., "The Relevance of Conservation Biology to Natural Resource Management," *Conservation Biology* 298, 299 (1992).
15. See Reed F. Noss, "From Endangered Species to Biodiversity," in *Balancing on the Brink of Extinction: The Endangered Species Act & Lessons for the Future* 227 (Kathryn A. Kohmed, 1991); see also Dennis D. Murphy, "Invertebrate Conservation," in *Balancing on the Brink of Extinction, supra,* at 181.
16. See Takacs, *supra* note 13, at 34–39.

17. Elizabeth Pennisi, "Biodiversity Rides a Popular Wave," *Scientist,* Apr. 15, 1991, at 8–11.
18. *Biodiversity: A Biology of Numbers & Differences* 5 (Kevin J. Gaston ed., 1996).
19. John Stuart Mill, "Nature," in *Three Essays on Religion* 3, 16 (Greenwood Press, 1969) (1874).
20. Karl Polanyi, *The Great Transformation: The Political & Economic Origins of Our Time* (2001).
21. Harold A. Mooney et al., "Biodiversity and Ecosystem Functioning: Basic Principles," in *Global Biodiversity Assessment* 275, 282 (Vernon Hilton Heywood & R. T. Watson eds., 1995).
22. Gretchen C. Daily, et al., "Ecosystem Services: Benefits Supplied to Human Societies by Natural Ecosystems." *Ecology* (1997), at http://www.wvhighlands.org/VoiceJun99/EcoServices.JS.June99Voice.txt.htm.
23. Mildred K. Cho et al., "Ethical Considerations in Synthesizing a Minimal Genome," 286 *Science* 2087, 2090 (1999).

DISCUSSION TOPICS

1. In your view, should we retain the term *biodiversity*? Why or why not?
2. Which of the two meanings of *nature* identified by Sagoff do you believe to be more appropriate? Explain your position. Do you have another definition for nature? If so, how does it differ from those discussed by Sagoff?
3. Explain what Sagoff might mean by the statement that "the loss of the natural . . . presents a terrible aesthetic, moral, cultural, and spiritual loss." Evaluate his statement.
4. Sagoff maintains that now "everything is artificial." If this is the case, should there be any ethical guidelines regarding the development of biotechnology? If this is not the case, what role might ethical guidelines play?
5. Sagoff doubts whether natural ecosystems perform fundamental life-support services. Do you agree with his view? Explain why or why not.

READING 54

Rights to Life? On Nature, Property and Biotechnology

John M. Meyer

John M. Meyer is assistant professor of government and politics at Humboldt State University and coordinator of the Master's Program in Environment and Community. His first book, Political Nature, *was published in 2001. The following article is excerpted from the* Journal of Political Philosophy *(2000). Meyer evaluates the claim that genetically engineered life-forms may be patented as products of human labor and creativity, a line of reasoning based on the well-known labor theory of John Locke. He argues that the philosophical justification for life patents collapses due to its reliance upon Locke's illusory distinction between nature and artifice.*

LIFE PATENTS IN THE U.S.

While silent on many subjects of contemporary political significance, the U.S. Constitution explicitly grants to Congress the power "[t]o promote the progress of science and useful arts, by securing for limited times to authors and inventors the exclusive right to their respective writings and discoveries"[1] This provision was codified in the U.S. Patent Act, originally authored by Jefferson in 1793. It declares that:

> [w]hoever invents or discovers any new and useful process, machine, manufacture, or composition of matter, or any new and useful improvement thereof, may obtain a patent therefor, subject to the conditions and requirements of this title.[2]

If a patent is granted, then the possessor of that patent obtains a largely unrestricted private property right over the patented subject for twenty years from the time of application.[3]

The first question to be addressed in light of this formulation is whether a plant, animal, or microorganism whose genetic code has been altered through a process of bioengineering could qualify as a patentable subject under this code. In the past, varieties of life developed by farmers and breeders were quite explicitly regarded as *not* meeting the standards required by the patent act. In other words, in order to establish if it is legally possible to own a life form, one must first answer the question of whether the process of genetic engineering leads to varieties of micro-organisms, plants, and animals that are properly viewed as a "machine, manufacture, or composition of matter."

In the key 1980 case of *Diamond v. Chakrabarty,* the U.S. Supreme Court ruled for the first time that genetically engineered life forms *do* meet the patent act standards.[4] Rejecting the contrary interpretation of the patent office, the Court ruled that the distinction relevant to the case was "between products of nature, whether living or not, and human-made inventions."[5] More particularly, the Court ruled that the micro-organism whose genetic structure had been altered by Chakrabarty was evidently "not nature's handiwork, but his own; accordingly it is patentable subject matter."[6] Thus the basis for ownership rights over genetically engineered life forms is precisely the claim that such forms are "not nature's handiwork" and are human inventions. With this claim as its centerpiece, the ruling both affirms the industry arguments . . . and reinforces the understanding of naturalness upon which critics attack genetically engineered products as inventions. Upon this logic, there is little distinction to be made between a genetically altered micro-organism and a plant, animal, or even human being, whose genetic structure has been modified in some manner. As Leon Kass observed shortly after the *Chakrabarty* decision, "The principle used in *Chakrabarty* says that there is nothing *in the nature of a being,* no, not even in the human patenter himself, that makes him immune to being patented."[7] Indeed, just a few years later the U.S. Patent Office itself reached the same conclusion (although not — yet? — extending the logic to human being), stating that it "now considers nonnaturally occurring non-human multicellular living organisms, including animals, to be patentable subject matter"[8] . . .

. . . In the end, it is the claim that genetically engineered life forms are the product of human labor and creativity — that they are not "manifestations

of . . . nature" — that is the most relevant. Patents, moreover, are typically characterized by their proponents as a form of intellectual property *right*. The relevant claim is not "we should be rewarded a patent because transgenic species are useful" but is instead "we deserve patent rights because we created this transgenic product, just as other inventors deserve patent rights to their creations." The notion that such a right exists, and that it naturally belongs to the person who creates something new by mixing their (intellectual) labor with nature, is a notion that can be readily identified as having roots in the political philosophy of John Locke.

GENETIC ENGINEERING AND THE LABOR THEORY OF PROPERTY

Locke, of course, is well known for his labor theory of property, detailed in chapter five "Of Property," in his *Second Treatise of Government.* Beginning with the contention that in its natural condition all the world belongs "to Mankind in common," Locke goes on to argue that each of us necessarily has property in our own person, and hence in our own labor. From this observation, he most famously concludes that:

> Whatsoever then he removes out of the State that Nature hath provided, and left it in, he hath mixed his Labour with, and joyned to it something that is his own, and thereby makes it his *Property.* It being by him removed from the common state Nature placed it in, it hath by this *labour* something annexed to it, that excludes the common right of other Men. For this *Labour* being the unquestionable Property of the Labourer, no man but he can have a right to what that is once joyned to, at least where there is enough, and as good left in common for others.[9]

The mixing of human labor with nature is thus central to Locke's understanding of the creation of property. For Locke, this mixing process is presented as one in which physical labor is combined with physical nature to create some sort of real or tangible property. Recently, a number of theorists have drawn upon this Lockean argument to offer a defense of intellectual property rights. These are not, of course, either real or tangible in the sense of, say, a field that one has plowed, or a house that one has built. While patents for genetically engineered life forms are most usually characterized as a type of intellectual property right, I will argue here that property rights claims to such life forms do not wholly fit either the model of real property or of intellectual property. As a result, while life patents are often regarded as a simple extension of a labor theory of property, the granting of such patents should also be recognized as challenging this theory in a manner rarely noted.

A. Physical Property/Intellectual Property/Biotechnology Property

When focused upon physical property, as Locke was, the labor theory seems to offer relatively clear guidelines for the delineation of property rights. In the absence of conflicting claims or provisos, my labor in building *this* house, or in cultivating *that* field, is the basis for my claim to an ownership right in it. Clearly, my ownership of the house I build does not give me any claim to other houses, nor to houses in general. Equally clearly, ownership of the field that I cultivate in no way entitles me to any other field. If it is forty acres upon which I labored, then it is that particular forty acres that I own and no other; these acres can be clearly delineated by a surveyor's map. Locke did, however, offer or suggest several important caveats to these property rights, the significance of which has been the subject of enormous debate among interpreters of his texts.[10] Perhaps the most notable of these apparent caveats is the requirement that any property right leave "enough, and as good . . . in common for others." Certainly if this requirement is applied to land itself, then the scarcity of available land would often result in limitations upon the creation of property rights in our world. Conversely, if C. B. MacPherson and others are correct in arguing that such physical scarcity is obviated for Locke by the emergence of capitalist economic growth, then this limitation would be far less relevant.[11] Even so, however, the application of a Lockean labor theory of property to physical or tangible subjects seems likely to confront some sort of conditions of scarcity — and hence conditions in which there is not "enough, and as good" remaining — at some point.[12]

Interestingly, although Locke's attention was focused upon physical property, his labor theory may fit most comfortably with the delineation of intangible forms of property — of which intellectual property is a leading exemplar. Here, there does not appear to be any likelihood of encountering physical limits that might serve to trigger the "enough, and as good" proviso. While the physical world may operate according to "zero-sum" rules in which more property for me means less for you, such rules seem inapplicable to the sort of creative and inventive endeavors that lead to the development of intellectual property. . . .

The ease with which Locke's labor theory can be and has been applied to intellectual property, combined with the recurring characterization of biotechnology patents as a form of intellectual property right, makes it easy to see why Locke's approach resonates with the arguments advanced by defenders of the biotechnology industry. The extension of a labor theory of property into this new field is not, however, as seamless as it might at first appear. After all, while we have seen that the justification of life patents relies heavily upon the claim that genetically engineered life forms are the product of creative human labor, this labor necessarily is mixed with existing physical nature. The parallel here is much greater with Locke's characterizations of the creation of *physical* property rights (where the transformation of nature is central) rather than with intellectual property rights (where a role for nature is said to be nonexistent). Just as my claim to my field rests on the fact that I mixed my labor with it in the process of cultivation, and hence transformed the pre-existing nature of the field, so does Chakrabarty's legal claim to his microorganism rest on the contention that its nature has been transformed through his actions as a genetic engineer.[13] As noted, for the creator or inventor whose idea can appropriately be defined as intellectual property, "nature" plays at most an incidental role. By contrast, the "natural" characteristics of the organism before it had been altered remain inescapably important to Chakrabarty; neither he nor any subsequent bioengineers have been able to so much as fully describe — to say nothing of actually creating — the basis for even a relatively simple life form. . . .

The parallel between a physical property right as Locke described it and a life patent is that in both cases human labor is inherently intertwined with some aspect of the natural world. Yet at the same time, a life patent *is* a claim to an *idea* itself — like an intellectual property right — not to one particular physical manifestation of that idea. While the farmer who cultivates forty acres may claim a property right to those particular acres and no others, the genetic engineer who manipulates the genetic structure of cotton, or of a mouse, can seek a patent that applies to *all* the cotton or *all* the mice of that type, breed, or germline, including all future generations. Indeed, there have been even more extreme instances where a patent for *any* genetically engineered variety of a species was granted to a single corporation.[14] The patents being sought — and secured — by the biotechnology industry are thus to forms of life themselves. . . .

The biotechnology industry has continually sought — both in the U.S. and internationally — what can be best understood as classically liberal rights to the property that they claim to have created, in the sense that the rights amount to essentially unrestricted private ownership and control (albeit for a fixed number of years).[15] From this angle, it is quite crucial for those seeking life patents to emphasize the discontinuity between contemporary genetic engineering, on the one hand, and earlier practices of plant and animal breeding, on the other. The claim to patent biotechnological products requires that they first be affirmed to be human inventions, hence fundamentally non-natural — an assertion central to the *Chakrabarty* decision. It is the *dis*continuity between biotechnology and non-patentable products of breeding that enables the argument for a *continuity* between biotechnology and (first) the subjects of liberal intellectual property rights claims, and (second) the subjects of liberal physical property rights claims. Yet life patents cannot properly be understood as a mere extension of Locke's argument about labor as the basis for the creation of property.

B. The Erasure of Lockean "Nature"

We might obtain insight into why the labor theory fails to offer coherent support for life patents by revisiting the troubling question of what is or is not "natural" about genetically engineered life forms. While the biotechnology industry must emphasize the non-naturalness of these life forms for the pur-

poses of patentability, it also highlights the contrary claim that there is no meaningful distinction between its products and those that are not genetically engineered.[16] Here, the claim that a tomato grown from a patented, transgenic seed is just as natural as one grown from any other seed becomes vital to efforts to win consumer acceptance, to fight proposed laws to label such produce as genetically engineered, and to allow it to qualify even for the now-coveted designation as "organic." The industry can make both of these divergent claims with at least some degree of effectiveness because the contemporary development of biotechnology is serving to erase the last vestiges of a familiar but ambiguous boundary between nature and artifice. To consider what that familiar boundary looked like, and how biotechnology is erasing it while the industry is still appealing to it, we can once again turn to a consideration of Locke.

By advancing his labor theory of property, Locke clearly endorsed and justified the transformation of pre-existing nature through human labor. It is perhaps an obvious point, but not all of nature can be transformed for Locke. For the labor theory of property to retain its coherence, nature must also remain "out there" — distinct from the property or economic goods into which some manifestations of it may be transformed through human labor. Locke relies upon a firm boundary between nature and artifice in order to identify the appropriate holders of property rights. If, in fact, all of nature was recognized as transformed through human labor, then a labor theory would be unable to offer further guidance as to the delineation of property rights. Any labor that I engage in would be mixed with something that had already been transformed from its natural state. As a consequence, my labor would necessarily be mixed with someone else's property. A Lockean government may be able to delineate ownership rights in such circumstances, but his labor theory alone could not. While Locke's theory may be able to cope with the scarcity of nature in particular, limited, senses (that is, a shortage of land), it is unable to make sense of a condition in which the very existence of the natural as a category is itself called into question.

The centrality of the boundary between nature and artifice is also made clear in Locke's *First Treatise*. Here, he characterizes life itself as a creation of

God, hence rejecting any pretensions that humans might have to claim an ability to create life. "To give life . . . is to frame and make a living Creature, fashion the parts, and mould and suit them to their uses, and having proportion'd and fitted them together, to put into them a living Soul."[17] For example, parents can in no way claim to have given life to their children, Locke argues, but are merely "the occasions of their being."[18] This appeal to God as the source of that which is natural is characteristic of Locke, and serves as a basis for his delineation of nature from the often hubristic pretensions of humans. Nature is raw material for Locke, but it is more than that; it is simultaneously an unalterable manifestation of God's creation and so of God's law. A consideration of the relationship between these two Lockean understandings of nature is in order here.

For Locke, human exploitation of the natural world for purposes of sustenance and utility is not only permitted by God, it is in fact "the Will of [our] Maker." Having implanted within us "reason" and "natural Inclination" that prompt us to make use of the natural world, God is best understood as having "directed" us to exercise mastery over nature. "And thus [Locke asserts] Man's *Property* in the Creatures, was founded upon the right he had, to make use of those things, that were necessary or useful to his Being."[19] It is important to note that it is "reason" and "natural Inclination" that serves for Locke as the primary basis for concluding that God wishes for us to master nature — he does not rely upon biblical revelation to establish this point. Natural law, understood by Locke as discoverable by reason, offers support and justification for our labor upon the natural world, and for the propertization of the products of that labor. The labor theory of property thus does not exist in a vacuum. For Locke, labor upon nature is the key to the creation of property *because* it is commanded by God and we are able to know this because of our reasoned access to the Natural Law.[20] The natural law context is thus crucial to an understanding of why Locke believed that we ought to be mixing our labor with nature *and* why he believed that by doing so, the resultant product becomes the property of the laborer. The boundary between nature and artifice — so central

to Locke's theory of property — is itself justified as natural in this manner. In the absence of such a natural law justification, neither the designation of private property, nor the particular delineation of artifice from nature, are self-evident.

Given Locke's theoretical need for a nature untouched by human labor, it is unsurprising that he sought to identify one empirically. "[I]n the beginning," Locke posits, "all the World was *America.*"[21] America, when and where it existed unmodified by European influences, is characterized by Locke as the state of nature itself. Locke's frequent references to American Indians in his writing, and in particular the recurring references and comparisons in chapter five ("Of Property") of the *Second Treatise,* offer important insight into the problematic character of the nature–artifice boundary as he conceived of it. As James Tully has argued convincingly, Locke elaborates his concept of property in explicit contrast to American Indian forms of land tenure and resource usage.[22] Locke refers, for example, to the "uncultivated waste of America left to Nature, without any improvement, tillage or husbandry,"[23] and offers support for his claim that virtually the entirety of the value of things is the product of labor the example that "the [native] *Americans* . . . whom Nature having furnished as liberally as any other people . . . yet for want of improving it by labour, have not one hundreth part of the Conveniencies we enjoy."[24] Moreover, because Locke presents his own conception of the boundary between nature and artifice as natural (in accordance with natural law), he is unable to so much as acknowledge that the American Indians truly had a form of land tenure or property holding. Instead, these forms became conflated with nature itself. As Tully argues:

> The planning, coordination, skills, and activities involved in native hunting, gathering, trapping, fishing, and non-sedentary agriculture, which took thousands of years to develop and take a lifetime for each generation to acquire and pass on, are not counted as labour at all, except for the very last individual step (such as picking or killing), but are glossed as "unassisted nature" and "spontaneous provisions" when Locke makes his comparisons.[25]

We should not be surprised that Tully is able to offer numerous examples of writings by American colonists that adhere closely to both the arguments and the very terminology employed by Locke in his chapter on property as a justification for the disposition of American Indian lands.[26]

While this utilization of the labor theory of property is clearly of significance for discussions of aboriginal rights, its most immediate importance here is that it highlights the illusory character of the "nature" upon which Locke's labor theory depends for its own coherence. The point is not simply that American Indians had long engaged in some practices that could qualify, by Locke's own definition, as labor if he had been aware of them. More significant is that *all* their practices mix with "nature" in some sense. No matter how primeval an example of native people Locke might have appealed to; no matter how unfamiliar their forms of land use; the nature–artifice boundary that Locke employs would be nonetheless incoherent as a basis for distinguishing the activities of such peoples from those of (that is, European) societies reliant upon ideas of private property that more closely approximate Locke's own.[27]

The point that I wish to make here is key not only to an interpretation of Locke, but also to our understanding of contemporary biotechnology. It is important, then, that it not be misunderstood. I do not wish to argue that Locke's nature–artifice dichotomy fails by denying the possibility of "unassisted nature," as some contemporary postmodernist authors have done.[28] Instead, I wish to make what I believe is a more powerful, yet more limited, argument—that this nature–artifice dichotomy cannot be utilized to distinguish between various types of human practices or human societies, as Locke clearly attempted to do in his comparisons between Europe and America. An acceptance of this argument should prompt us to reconsider both sides of Locke's comparisons. Not only is it the case that American Indians engaged in a wide variety of forms of human labor and artifice to which Locke's theory blinded him, it is also the case that the cultured European societies were far more dependent upon "nature" than the various proportions that Locke offers at different points in his property chapter—1/10th, 1/100th,

1/1000th—suggest.[29] It is more appropriate to say that these societies were always far more *inter*dependent *with* nature and as a result that the independent contributions of "unassisted nature" and human labor cannot be delineated in anything like the clear-cut manner that Locke consistently presumes.

The labor theory today constrains its adherents from acknowledging the key roles played by both the ongoing human contributions to the development and maintenance of the biological diversity of the planet and the natural contributions to the life forms that result from the laboratories of genetic engineers. This is particularly evident with respect to the crucial contributions of the people in the so-called Third World to the gene pool.

Contrary to its legal pretensions to have created life, contemporary biotechnology actually relies heavily upon the identification and utilization of genes and genetic traits from the existing diversity of species on the planet. Genetic—hence biological—diversity is key because it is necessary for bioengineers to find unusual, distinctive, and desired genetic characteristics in order to modify familiar organisms to perform in different ways. As it happens, the preponderance of the world's genetic stock is traceable to a number of particular regions, almost all of which are located in what is now the so-called Third World.[30] The question of ownership and control of this gene pool is thus not only one of intra-societal standards of property and justice, but also one of power, property, and distributive justice between nations of the "North" and "South." Of course, these sorts of distributive concerns predate the development of contemporary forms of biotechnology and many such concerns are not distinctive to this development.[31] Nonetheless, biotechnology patents have added significantly to these distributive concerns. Previously, as one analyst explains:

> . . . plant breeding was largely conducted by the public sector, whether that be a U.S. University or one of the breeding centers of the Consultative Group on International Agricultural Research (CGIAR), and developing countries did not grant patent rights for pharmaceutical products [therefore] money did not change hands south to north and concerns were limited.[32]

Just as Locke's view of America as a state of nature prevented him from acknowledging the labor of its native inhabitants, so does the conclusion that genetically engineered species are distinctively products of human art — inventions — obscure the vital role of everyone from Third World farmers to Mendelian plant breeders in the development and maintenance of the current diversity of genetic material on the planet. Consider, for example, genetically engineered seeds for food crops. Corn, soybeans, potatoes, and tomatoes are a few crops for which genetically engineered varieties have now been patented. We have seen that explicit in the U.S. Supreme Court's *Chakrabarty* decision is the position that such patents are based upon the distinction that these varieties are inventions, in contrast to non-engineered "natural" varieties. Yet there is simply no product of "unassisted nature," to use the Lockean phrase, that reasonably resembles the corn, soybean, potatoes, or tomatoes that we consume. There are few food crops that we would recognize as such "in nature." Instead, these crops exist only because of a long history of cultivation and modification by generations of farmers. Much of this has taken place through everyday farming techniques. For millennia, farmers have typically saved the best and hardiest specimens of their crops for the seeds to replant again the next year. By doing so, the crop is yearly being refined and evolved for the particular qualities of taste and other cultural preferences valued by those who consume the crop, as well as for the particular soils, climate, and pests that exist where the crop is grown. Without these longstanding practices, the food crops that we consume today simply would not exist. This is an inescapable part of agriculture as it has been practiced through the ages. Whether or not it is done intentionally and with a strategic understanding of its effect seems to be of secondary importance at best.[33]

All of this belies the false presumption that our food crops are readily traceable to any sort of seed that exists apart from human participation. As geneticist Ruth McNally explains, "These [seeds] are not raw materials in the sense that they are lying around. They are the product of stewardship and selection and replanting in the case of crops. They also come with knowledge attached."[34] The central point is also well summarized by Vandana Shiva:

No technological artifact or industrial commodity is formed out of nothing; no industrial process takes place where nothing was before. Nature and its creativity as well as people's social labor are consumed at every level of industrial production as raw material or energy. *The biotech seed that is treated as creation to be protected by patents could not exist without the farmer's seed.*[35]

. . .

THE CONTROL AND DIRECTION OF BIOTECHNOLOGICAL DEVELOPMENT

The court rulings and policy decisions that have allowed for the patenting of biotechnology products as inventions established a fundamental dividing line between all previous forms of human cultivation of species and these of the contemporary genetic engineer. The line is presented as a division between life forms in which nature predominates versus those in which the creative, human contribution is central. Ultimately, however, it serves as a division between forms of development and cultivation in which communal, public, or government-funded activity and control is at the forefront, and forms in which private, corporate-funded and controlled activity takes a leading role. This is the case largely because corporate involvement can emerge only if and when there is a structure in place that offers assurance that the profits from an innovation can be successfully captured by a private entity — as patents (especially when they are enforced internationally) clearly are intended to do. Several years ago, a cautious observer of this change concluded that it has resulted in what he termed the "creeping propertization" of the scientific community.[36] Yet what then appeared to be "creeping" can now only be understood as a gallop. At the University of California-Berkeley, for example, the biotechnology corporation Novartis recently committed U.S. $50 million in exchange for complete access to the research of all the faculty, graduate students, and post-doctoral fellows in the Department of Plant and Microbial Biology.[37]

The effects of this propertization or commodification of science, seeds, and the gene pool itself are far-reaching. Many are optimistic, of course, that the primary effect will be the acceleration of research and development in biotechnology, with the end result of beneficent cures to diseases, expanded food production for a growing population, and the overall progress of humankind. Attractive though such a scenario might appear, we at the dawn of the twenty-first century have all too much basis for skepticism about such enthusiastic visions of the link between scientific advances and human progress. Among the less attractive, but seemingly more certain short-term consequences are: an increased concentration of wealth and control among owners of life patents — overwhelmingly in the developed nations of Western Europe, Japan, Australasia, and the U.S. — and an exclusive preoccupation with research that might lead to commercially profitable applications.[38]

There are many potential avenues of biotechnological research that *might* be pursued. Given the increasingly concentrated nexus of control by multinational corporations with interests in agricultural chemicals, however, it may not be surprising that a recent OECD report found that the most common trait tested for in agricultural biotechnology research was tolerance to herbicides.[39] Developing this tolerance enables companies such as Monsanto to produce patented seeds resistant to the formulation of pesticides that they already manufacture (for example, "Roundup Ready" soybeans). That *pesticide* resistance should become a greater focus of research efforts than *pest* resistance represents in a rather bald manner the particular direction in which the development of biotechnology is being oriented by the private ownership of genetic resources, and so of life itself.

CONCLUSION

From a point of view critical — or even merely questioning — of contemporary biotechnological developments, a defense of the "integrity of nature," and a characterization of genetically engineered life as unnatural can easily appear to be both a compelling and effective approach to the subject. Despite the initial rhetorical attraction, however, I hope to have shown this approach to be

both incorrect and ultimately self-defeating. The characterization of genetically engineered life as unnatural relies upon a particular understanding of the boundary between nature and artifice, an understanding entirely consistent with the biotechnology industry's claim that this life is a patentable human invention. If we leave this boundary unchallenged, then we have seen that transgenic life forms resist the many concerted efforts to locate them on the side of artifice. This undermines a crucial basis for the extension of Lockean property rights claims to transgenic life.

For those who question the conceptual basis for life patents, or whose focus is limited to the peculiarly urgent challenges posed by the rapid developments in the field of genetic engineering, the above effort may prove sufficient. Yet close consideration of biotechnological practices and products makes it increasingly difficult to ignore broader problems inherent in this division between nature and artifice. This understanding of the nature–artifice boundary obscures the intimate and ongoing human connection with the forms of life that are placed on the natural side of this boundary. While both sides of the biotechnology question appeal to this boundary to advance their arguments, the development of biotechnology itself serves as a final challenge to its coherence. The consequence is to call into question a wide array of arguments rooted in a Lockean labor theory of property.[40]

By refocusing attention upon the control and direction of biotechnological development, we can begin to see that the key questions are now, as they have always been, centered around the sorts of *values* that guide our inescapable interactions with the non-human world. They are about the manner in which we delineate the appropriate limits of market mentality, of private property, and even of human action itself in the face of these values. It is, of course, these sorts of limits that those who appeal to the standard of "nature" wish to highlight. Yet only a direct confrontation with these questions can even hope to have the desired effect. Such a confrontation cannot offer us a determination as to whether genetic engineering *per se* is good or evil. It can, however, allow us to discuss questions of who controls its development, what criteria are employed, whether limits are imposed, and how the distributive consequences will — or will not be — addressed.

NOTES

1. *U.S. Constitution,* Art. I, Sec. 8.
2. *35 U.S.C.* Sec. 101.
3. It used to be 17 years from approval, but was revised to bring U.S. law in line with GATT provisions.
4. *Diamond v. Chakrabarty,* 447 U.S. 303. See Kass, "Patenting life," [*Commentary,* Dec. 1981] for very helpful reflections on this case. It is important to recognize — as I will develop below — that agricultural products have been the result of selective breeding and development efforts for virtually the entire history of agriculture. For the past century, moreover, these practices have often been guided by sophisticated techniques based upon Mendelian genetics. Yet the products of such breeding programs were always unpatentable under U.S. (and other) law, because of their status as life forms, and/or the conviction that they were natural. Although limited property rights protection for plant breeders was adopted by the U.S. Congress in 1930 and 1970, these acts served as much to distinguish these products from traditionally patentable subjects as it did to protect them.
5. *Diamond v. Chakrabarty,* p. 313.
6. Ibid., p. 310.
7. Kass, "Patenting life," p. 56.
8. Quoted in Mark Sagoff, "Animals as inventions: biotechnology and intellectual property rights," *Institute for Philosophy and Public Policy,* vol. 16, no. 1 (Winter 1996) http://epn.org/ippp/sagoff1.html, p. 4. As Sagoff notes, this ruling also opened the door to the patenting of many organisms bred through conventional means.
9. John Locke, *Second Treatise of Government,* ch. five, sec. 27; in *Two Treatises of Government,* ed. Peter Laslett (Cambridge: Cambridge University Press, 1988; originally published 1689), at p. 288.

10. For two of the most relevant — and contrasting — interpretations of the qualifications upon property rights that Locke may have offered, see: C. B. MacPherson, *The Political Theory of Possessive Individualism* (Oxford: Oxford University Press, 1962), pp. 203–20; and James Tully, *A Discourse on Property* (Cambridge: Cambridge University Press, 1980) and *An Approach to Political Philosophy: Locke in Contexts* (Cambridge: Cambridge University Press, 1993), ch. 3.
11. MacPherson, *Possessive Individualism,* pp. 203–20.
12. In *Ecology and the Politics of Scarcity Revisited* (New York: W. H. Freeman, 1992), pp. 190–2, William Ophuls stresses this point. However, one need not accept as strong a version of the "limits to growth" thesis as Ophuls does in order to accept this argument. Most of the rebuttals to the limits to growth thesis are based upon the contention that human ingenuity will lead to innovations that can avoid meaningful scarcity; see e.g. Julian Simon, *The Ultimate Resource* (Princeton, N.J.: Princeton University Press, 1982). These innovations are said to be based upon ideas that would allow us to avoid particular limits, often through a substitution of resources or alteration of technique. Such claims do little to challenge the more limited common sense observation that land and other physical resources are ultimately finite. Instead they make their case by contesting the significance of this notion of finitude.
13. Note that the focus of the Supreme Court decision was not whether Chakrabarty had a right to patent the *process* by which he engineered the organism. A process patent had already been granted, and was relatively uncontroversial. The question was whether he also had a right to patent the *product* that resulted from this process.
14. In one case, the patent to the company, Agracetus, intended to cover "all cotton seeds and plants which contain a recombinant gene construction (i.e., are genetically engineered)" was retroactively rejected upon review. Agracetus appealed. See [Fred] Powledge, "Who owns rice and beans?" [*BioScience* 45 (1995):] pp. 440–1.

15. The question of whether this classically liberal conception of private property rights is truly the one held by Locke need not detain us. What I believe is undeniable is that Locke's labor theory offers a basis for this liberal view, although his provisos may, as interpreters such as James Tully have argued, go a long way toward restricting this liberal conception. See Tully, *Locke in Contexts,* p. 120.

16. Vandana Shiva, *Biopiracy: The Plunder of Nature and Knowledge* (Boston: South End Press, 1997), p. 23.

17. Locke, *First Treatise,* ch. 5, sec. 53, p. 179.

18. Ibid., ch. 5, sec. 54, p. 179. Mark Sagoff highlights this passage in "Animals as inventions," p. 1, and notes the significant parallel between Locke's argument and that of critics of biotechnology's pretensions to have created life (cf. quotation cited in note 14).

19. Locke, *First Treatise,* ch. 9, sec. 86, p. 205 and *Second Treatise,* ch. 5, sec. 35, p. 292. See also Matthew H. Kramer, *John Locke and the Origins of Private Property* (Cambridge: Cambridge University Press, 1997), p. 95.

20. See Peter Drahos, *A Philosophy of Intellectual Property* (Aldershot, UK: Dartmouth, 1996), p. 44.

21. Locke, *Second Treatise,* ch. 5, sec. 49, p. 301.

22. Tully, "Rediscovering America: the two treatises and aboriginal rights," in *Locke in Contexts,* p. 138.

23. Locke, *Second Treatise,* ch. 5, sec. 37, p. 294.

24. Ibid., ch. 5, sec. 41, pp. 296–7.

25. Tully, "Rediscovering America," p. 156.

26. Ibid., pp. 149–50.

27. Cf. Bhikhu Parekh, "Liberalism and colonialism: a critique of Locke and Mill," *The Decolonization of Imagination,* ed. Jan Nederveen Pieterse and Bhikhu Parekh (London: Zed Books, 1995), pp. 89–91.

28. For a comprehensive survey and discussion of these, see Harlan Wilson, "Postmodernism, authority, and green political theory," paper presented at Annual Meeting of the American Political Science Association, San Francisco, August 29–September 1, 1996.

29. Locke, *Second Treatise,* ch. 5, sec. 40, p. 296; sec. 43, p. 298.

30. These are the so-called "Vavilov centers of genetic diversity." As Jack Kloppenburg notes, "Of crops of economic importance, only sunflowers, blueberries, cranberries, pecans, and the Jerusalem artichoke originated in what is now the United States and Canada. An all-American meal would be somewhat limited. Northern Europe's original genetic poverty is only slightly less striking; oats, rye, currants, and raspberries constitute the complement of major crops indigenous to that region." Jack Ralph Kloppenburg, *First the Seed: The Political Economy of Plant Biotechnology, 1492–2000* (Cambridge: Cambridge University Press, 1988), pp. 46–9.

31. Nigel Dower, "Biotechnology and the Third World," http://www.abdn.ac.uk/cpts/a4.htm.

32. Lesser, *Institutional Mechanisms Supporting Trade in Genetic Materials* [Geneva: UNEP, 1994], p. 5.

33. Nonetheless, many have done so with intention. "Third World farmers have been found to employ taxonomic systems, encourage introgression, use selection, make efforts to see that varieties are adapted, multiply seeds, field test, record data and even name their varieties." Cary Fowler, "Biotechnology, patents and the Third World," *Biopolitics: A Feminist and Ecological Reader on Biotechnology,* ed. Vandana Shiva and Ingunn Moser (London: Zed, 1995), pp. 221–2.

34. Quoted in Lisa Sykes, "Plant rights," *Geographical Magazine,* May 1997, p. 12.

35. Shiva, *Biopiracy,* p. 62 (emphasis added). Of course, during the twentieth century, these practices of the world's farmers have also been supplemented by the more methodical efforts of plant breeders acting in accordance with Mendelian principles. In the U.S., researchers at land-grant universities and other public offices have long carried out much of this work. More recently, as Jack Kloppenburg documents in *First the Seed,* the growth of commercial seed companies, the hybridization of crops, the "green revolution," and other trends

have dramatically changed many earlier farming practices.

36. Robert P. Merges, "Property rights theory and the commons: the case of scientific research" *Social Philosophy and Policy,* 13 (Summer 1996), p. 147.
37. Charles W. Petit, "Germinating access; Berkeley department's big deal with firm aimed at speeding genetic finds to market," *U.S. News and World Report,* October 26, 1998, p. 60.
38. Henk Hobbelink, "Biotechnology and the future of agriculture," *Biopolitics,* ed. Shiva and Moser, p. 227.
39. Ibid.
40. This need not lead to a wholesale dismissal of other elements in Locke's theory. When emphasizing consent as the basis for legitimate government, Locke seems to move some distance from the absolutist property claims encouraged by the labor theory itself. Perhaps, as some have argued, a genuinely Lockean government would have the resources needed to examine the relationship between biotechnology practices and the public good. Tully, *A Discourse on Property,* suggests such a view of Locke; Susan Liebell has developed this argument in an explicitly environmental context: "Political theory and environmental public policy: revisiting liberal theories of property," paper presented at the 1999 annual meeting of the American Political Science Association, Atlanta, September 1999.

DISCUSSION TOPICS

1. Assess the view that genetically engineered organisms are unnatural. Explain the definition of *unnatural* you are using in your answer.
2. Explain Locke's theory of property when applied to physical property. Why does his theory fit more comfortably with intellectual property? How does a life patent differ from a physical and an intellectual property right?
3. Evaluate Meyer's point that the biotechnology industry appeals to the boundary between nature and artifice and at the same time erases it.

4. According to Meyer, why was Locke unable to recognize the form of property holding found in American Indian cultures? What is the significance of Locke's inability to recognize such forms of land use?
5. Evaluate Meyer's view that the crucial distinction in biotechnological development is not nature versus human invention but communal, public control versus private, corporate-funded control.

The Tragedy of the Commons

Garrett Hardin

Garrett Hardin is emeritus professor of human ecology, University of California, Santa Barbara.

Hardin argues that in a commons—a publicly owned resource—general public good does not follow from everyone serving their own interest, in contrast to Adam Smith's theories.

The solution recommended by Hardin is some mutually agreed-upon public coercion, such as taxation. Even if imperfect, such a system would be preferable to the status quo in which selfish individuals can damage many others.

. . . *The Wealth of Nations* (1776) popularized the "invisible hand," the idea that an individual who "intends only his own gain," is, as it were, "led by an invisible hand to promote . . . the public interest."[1] Adam Smith did not assert that this was invariably true, and perhaps neither did any of his followers. But he contributed to a dominant tendency of thought that has ever since interfered with positive action based on rational analysis, namely, the tendency to assume that decisions reached individually will, in fact, be the best decisions for an entire society. If this assumption is correct it justifies the continuance of our present policy of laissez-faire in reproduction. If it is correct we can assume that men will control their individual fecundity so as to produce the optimum population. If the assumption is not correct, we need to reexamine our individual freedoms to see which ones are defensible.

TRAGEDY OF FREEDOM IN A COMMONS

The rebuttal to the invisible hand in population control is to be found in a scenario first sketched in a little-known pamphlet[2] in 1833 by a mathematical amateur named William Forster Lloyd (1794–1852). We may well call it "the tragedy of the commons," using the word "tragedy" as the philosopher Whitehead used it:[3] "The essence of dramatic tragedy is not unhappiness. It resides in the solemnity of the remorseless working of things." He then goes on to say, "This inevitableness of destiny can only be illustrated in terms of human life by incidents which in fact involve unhappiness. For it is only by them that the futility of escape can be made evident in the drama."

The tragedy of the commons develops in this way. Picture a pasture open to all. It is to be expected that each herdsman will try to keep as many cattle as possible on the commons. Such an arrangement may work reasonably satisfactorily for centuries because tribal wars, poaching, and disease keep the numbers of both man and beast well below the carrying capacity of the land. Finally, however, comes the day of reckoning, that is, the day when the long-desired goal of social stability becomes a reality. At this point, the inherent logic of the commons remorselessly generates tragedy.

As a rational being, each herdsman seeks to maximize his gain. Explicitly or implicitly, more or less consciously, he asks, "What is the utility *to me* of adding one more animal to my herd?" This utility has one negative and one positive component.

(1) The positive component is a function of the increment of one animal. Since the herdsman receives all the proceeds from the sale of the additional animal, the positive utility is nearly +1.

(2) The negative component is a function of the additional overgrazing created by one more animal. Since, however, the effects of overgrazing are shared by all the herdsmen, the negative utility for any particular decision-making herdsman is only a fraction of −1.

Adding together the component partial utilities, the rational herdsman concludes that the only sensible course for him to pursue is to add another animal to his herd. And another; and another. . . . But this is the conclusion reached by each and every rational herdsman sharing a commons. Therein is the tragedy. Each man is locked into a system that compels him to increase his herd without limit—in a world that is limited. Ruin is the destination toward which all men rush, each pursuing his own best interest in a society that believes in the freedom of the commons. Freedom in a commons brings ruin to all.

Some would say that this is a platitude. Would that it were! In a sense, it was learned thousands of years ago, but natural selection favors the forces of psychological denial.[4] The individual benefits as an individual from his ability to deny the truth even though society as a whole, of which he is a part, suffers. . . .

In an approximate way, the logic of the commons has been understood for a long time, perhaps since the discovery of agriculture or the invention of private property in real estate. But it is understood mostly only in special cases which are not sufficiently generalized. Even at this late date, cattlemen leasing national land on the western ranges demonstrate no more than an ambivalent understanding, in constantly pressuring federal authorities to increase the head count to the point where overgrazing produces erosion and weed-dominance. Likewise, the oceans of the world continue to suffer from the survival of the philosophy of the commons. Maritime nations still respond automatically to the shibboleth of the "freedom of the seas." Professing to believe in the "inexhaustible resources of the oceans," they bring species after species of fish and whales closer to extinction.[5]

The National Parks present another instance of the working out of the tragedy of the commons. At present, they are open to all, without limit. The parks themselves are limited in extent—there is only one Yosemite Valley—whereas population seems to grow without limit. The values that visitors seek in the parks are steadily eroded. Plainly, we must soon cease to treat the parks as commons or they will be of no value to anyone.

What shall we do? We have several options. We might sell them off as private property. We might keep them as public property, but allocate the right to enter them. The allocation might be on the basis of wealth, by the use of an auction system. It might be on the basis of merit, as defined by some agreed-upon standards. It might be by lottery. Or it might be on a first-come, first-served basis, administered to long queues. These, I think, are all the reasonable possibilities. They are all objectionable. But we must choose — or acquiesce in the destruction of the commons that we call our National Parks.

POLLUTION

In a reverse way, the tragedy of the commons reappears in problems of pollution. Here it is not a question of taking something out of the commons, but of putting something in — sewage, or chemical, radioactive, and peat wastes into water; noxious and dangerous fumes into the air; and distracting and unpleasant advertising signs into the line of sight. The calculations of utility are much the same as before. The rational man finds that his share of the cost of the wastes he discharges into the commons is less than the cost of purifying his wastes before releasing them. Since this is true for everyone, we are locked into a system of "fouling our own nest," so long as we behave only as independent, rational, free-enterprisers.

The tragedy of the commons as a food basket is averted by private property, or something formally like it. But the air and waters surrounding us cannot readily be fenced, and so the tragedy of the commons as a cesspool must be prevented by different means, by coercive laws or taxing devices that make it cheaper for the polluter to treat his pollutants than to discharge them untreated. We have not progressed as far with the solution of this problem as we have with the first. Indeed, our particular concept of private property, which deters us from exhausting the positive resources of the earth, favors pollution. The owner of a factory on the bank of a stream — whose property extends to the middle of the stream — often has difficulty seeing why it is not his natural right to muddy the waters flowing past his door. The law, always behind the times, requires elaborate stitching and fitting to adapt it to this newly perceived aspect of the commons.

The pollution problem is a consequence of population. It did not much matter how a lonely American frontiersman disposed of his waste. "Flowing water purifies itself every 10 miles" my grandfather used to say, and the myth was near enough to the truth when he was a boy, for there were not too many people. But as population became denser, the natural chemical and biological recycling processes became overloaded, calling for a redefinition of property rights. . . .

MUTUAL COERCION MUTUALLY AGREED UPON

The social arrangements that produce responsibility are arrangements that create coercion, of some sort. . . . The only kind of coercion I recommend is mutual coercion, mutually agreed upon by the majority of the people affected.

To say that we mutually agree to coercion is not to say that we are required to enjoy it, or even to pretend we enjoy it. Who enjoys taxes? We all grumble about them. But we accept compulsory taxes because we recognize that voluntary taxes would favor the conscienceless. We institute and (grumblingly) support taxes and other coercive devices to escape the horror of the commons. . . .

RECOGNITION OF NECESSITY

Perhaps the simplest summary of this analysis of man's population problems is this: the commons, if justifiable at all, is justifiable only under conditions of low-population density. As the human population has increased, the commons has had to be abandoned in one aspect after another.

First we abandoned the commons of food gathering, enclosing farm land and restricting pastures and hunting and fishing areas. These restrictions are still not complete throughout the world.

Somewhat later we saw that the commons as a place for waste disposal would also have to be abandoned. Restrictions on the disposal of domestic sewage are widely accepted in the Western world; we are still struggling to close the commons of pollution by automobiles, factories, insecticide sprayers, fertilizing operations, and atomic energy installations. . . . Every new enclosure of the commons involves the infringement of somebody's personal liberty.

. . . But what does "freedom" mean? When men mutually agreed to pass laws against robbing, mankind became more free, not less so. Individuals locked into the logic of the commons are free only to bring on universal ruin: once they see the necessity of mutual coercion, they become free to pursue other goals. I believe it was Hegel who said, "Freedom is the recognition of necessity."

The most important aspect of necessity that we must now recognize, is the necessity of abandoning the commons in breeding. No technical solution can rescue us from the misery of overpopulation. Freedom to breed will bring ruin to all. At the moment, to avoid hard decisions many of us are tempted to propagandize for conscience and responsible parenthood. The temptation must be resisted, because an appeal to independently acting consciences selects for the disappearance of all conscience in the long run, and an increase in anxiety in the short.

The only way we can preserve and nurture other and more precious freedoms is by relinquishing the freedom to breed, and that very soon. "Freedom is the recognition of necessity" — and it is the role of education to reveal to all the necessity of abandoning the freedom to breed. Only so, can we put an end to this aspect of the tragedy of the commons.

NOTES

1. A. Smith, *The Wealth of Nations* (New York: Modern Library, 1937), p. 423.
2. W. F. Lloyd, *Two Lectures on the Checks to Population* (Oxford: University Press, 1833), reprinted (in part) in *Population, Evolution and Birth Control,* ed. G. Hardin (San Francisco: Freeman, 1964), p. 37.
3. A. N. Whitehead, *Science and the Modern World* (New York: Mentor, 1948), p. 17.
4. G. Hardin, ed., *Population, Evolution and Birth Control* (San Francisco: Freeman, 1964), p. 56.
5. S. McVav, *Scientific American* 216, no. 8 (1966): 13.

DISCUSSION TOPICS

1. Identify a commons in your geographical area. Is this commons falling into the pattern described by Hardin? Explain.
2. What other forms of mutual coercion besides taxation might reduce individual exploitation of a commons?
3. Do you agree with Hardin that the freedom to breed will bring ruin to all? Explain your reasoning.

READING 56

Visitors to the Commons: Approaching Thailand's "Environmental" Struggles from a Western Starting Point

Larry Lohmann

Larry Lohmann spent most of the 1980s in Thailand. He is co-editor (with Ricardo Carrere) of Pulping the South *(1996) and (with Marcus Colchester) of* The Struggle of the Land and the Fate of the Forest *(1996). In this essay, from* Ecological Resistance Movements *(1995, edited by B. Taylor), Lohmann argues for the inapplicability of Western dichotomies, such as legal versus illegal action and jobs versus environment, to Southern countries such as Thailand. He notes that instead of governments and private owners controlling the land, as is the case in Western countries, each village community exercises its own type of stewardship.*

WESTERN DICHOTOMIES

Whatever motivates Western discussions of Thai "environmentalism," and whatever they are used for, they are inevitably couched in language which owes a good deal to Western concepts and Western experience. This is only natural. All interpretations must begin somewhere, and people brought up in highly industrialized societies, including the writer of this chapter and most of its readers, can only start, like everyone else, with the frameworks and models which they know and which have proved useful in familiar contexts. As philosopher Hilary Putnam inquires wryly in another context, "We should use some-body *else's* conceptual scheme?" (cf. Taylor 1985).

To Western industrialists and environmentalists alike, a number of dichotomies seem almost inevitable in any description of environmental action. These include the following. Society is dominated either by the *state* or by the *market*. Land management, to avoid anarchy, must be either *public* or *private*. Attitudes toward nature are either *anthropocentric* or *ecocentric*. Actions tend to be inspired either by *religious and moral* or by *self-interested* motives. Policies can favor either *jobs* or *environment*, and environmental action can be either *pragmatic* or *radical*. Countries are either *overpopulated* or *underpopulated*. Environmental action is based on putting ecological *theory* (which may include religion, objectives, techniques, or science) into *practice* through first laying out a plan or set of laws and then implementing them. This action can be either *legal* or *illegal, militant* or *non-militant*.

Not all Western environmentalists, of course, take all of these dichotomies for granted. But most will unreflectively assume the validity of at least a few of them. Thus it is not uncommon for North American environmentalists to presume without thinking that their counterparts in Thailand must be faced with the job of "reconciling livelihood and environment," or to suppose that the task for environmentalists in a country without strong central authority like Laos is one of helping the government and the private sector establish firmer control over how land, forests, and water are used. Other American environmentalists may find it natural to assume that (say) the divisions in India's Chipko movement are parallel to the anthropocentric/ecocentric distinction familiar in Western industrialized societies, or that the major religions originating in India express moral sentiments which are "shared by the philosophy now called 'deep ecology'" (Taylor 1992). The presupposition, in short, is likely to be that the societies, cultures, and individuals of less industrialized nations, as well as their environmental movements, are in many important respects similar to their counterparts in the West.

There is nothing inherently wrong with this assumption. Indeed, as mentioned above, as a first move in dialogue with members of other societies it may be unavoidable. The application to Southern countries of the dichotomies that I have mentioned, however, can provoke resistance among those whom they are supposed to describe (MacIntyre 1988:385). This has proved to be the case in Thailand as well as elsewhere in the south. Western activists who lecture their Thai counterparts on the need to take a "scientific" or a "market" approach to environmental problems, for example, or to "apply Buddhism" to them, or to "take overpopulation seriously," or to "stop being so confrontational with the state," or to act as Westerners' lieutenants in initiatives to change international institutions, may find themselves quietly dismissed by many of their Thai counterparts as contemptuous, ignorant, or politically naïve. Cooperative between the two sides may suffer as a result.

Western environmentalists who are interested in understanding and building solidarity with Thai social movements, by contrast, will learn to recognize and take seriously Thai hesitations about, or objections to, being described by the dichotomies I have mentioned. They will not treat these dichotomies as universal, and will thus not automatically assume that Thai "environmentalism" must be (for example) either anthropocentric or ecocentric, or either militant or non-militant. Nor will they insist that resistance to the use of these dichotomies must be due to disagreements over semantics, stubbornness, or inability to see the light. Rather, they will devote time to learning where and when to drop or modify these dichotomies. In the process they may be able to find out how to cooperate with their Thai counterparts in a more practically effective way.

In what follows, I will consider briefly why Thai activists might find certain of the Western dichotomies I have mentioned to be of limited use to them, and in what directions a more acceptable approach might lie.

DICHOTOMIES OF LIMITED RELEVANCE

Some Western dichotomies used to describe Thai "environmentalism" are based on assumptions which, while not necessarily false, seem to me nevertheless to be less than crucial to many Thai movements, to impose systems of thought which many Thai activists might find unfruitful, or to imply criteria of success and failure which many Thai analysts may not share.

The distinction between legal and illegal action, for example, is probably on the whole less important for movements in Thailand than for those in the United States or in European countries. This is due largely to the fact that, in Thailand, orally mediated customary norms involving personalized structures of authority and obligation often carry greater moral weight than written statutes. In some cases in which a community feels that its informally recognized rights to land or water have been ignored, it will take action regardless of the law, often in some confidence of a sympathetic public reaction. By the same token, it may strongly censor actions which are not formally illegal. Judges may meanwhile try to head off acrimonious litigation through avuncular efforts at informal compromise, and official study commissions may be appointed never to be heard from again. Many high officials and notables, for their part, regularly and openly flout the laws whether they are building tourist resorts in protected areas, polluting rivers, or dealing in drugs. Perhaps the best index of the significance (or lack of it) of the legal/illegal distinction in Thai "environmental" politics is the fact that approximately 11 million rural residents, or between 15 and 20 percent of the country's people, are officially classified as "illegal squatters" because they are living on land which has been gazetted as National Reserve Forest. While this legal fact is often dragged out as a pretext for threatening or evicting particular communities whose land is coveted by the plantation industry or the Royal Forest Department, no one has yet suggested putting the 11 million in jail.

The Western militant/non-militant distinction is also misleading when applied to contemporary Thailand. Since the beginning of the 1980s, no Thai movement which outsiders would call "environmental" has identified itself by means of a word which could be translated as "militant." This is not because such movements never display what Westerners would call "militant tactics." They do — often as a last-ditch and politically double-edged response to persistent trickery or brutal ploys on the part of the police, the army, or other bureaucracies. Indeed, Western observers misled by stereotypes of "Oriental passivity" are often dazed at the extent of openly defiant public action in Thailand in defense of land, as farmers rip out eucalyptus saplings in commercial plantations, lie down in front of bulldozers to prevent a village in a national park from being destroyed, or organize mass marches on Bangkok to protest eviction plans. But in a context in which flexibility, community feeling, and popular legitimacy are at a premium, such movements do not and cannot tie themselves to a strategic notion as rigid, abstract, and morally suspect as "militancy." During the country's current water shortage and the resulting opportunistic information blitz by the government about the supposed necessity for high-tech river management, even mere slogans such as "no more dams" can discredit the activists who adopt them because of their unreasonable militant ring in the ears of the Thai public.

The widespread Western presupposition that environmental action consists in first identifying on a theoretical basis "what has to be done" and then "getting others to understand and join in" has also, I think, proved an obstacle to Westerners' attempts to come to grips with Thai movements. Such an academic, top-down conception ignores the fact that much environmental knowledge and action, in Thailand as elsewhere, is locally specific, dependent on a constant, fluid interplay between theory and practice, and embedded in the democratically evolving practices of ordinary people. It also ignores the fact that no neutral conceptual framework or physical forum exists in which all sides can agree on "what has to be done." In disputes about Thai forests, for example, any particular conceptual or physical arena — "science," parliament, a subdistrict council meeting, the national Forestry Sector Master Plan, the Royal Forest Department, the main national forestry faculty, or a seminar arranged by environmental organizations — will favor some interest groups over others. Indeed, such arenas are typically chosen precisely so that certain groups can get an advantage over others. To insist that a discussion on forests be conducted exclusively in the terms of academic science, for example, tends to disadvantage and disempower ordinary villagers. This is not only because they may have difficulty arguing using its terminology, and because to appeal to science is to delegitimize local (often unwritten) knowledge, but also because dividing the world among forestry, limnology, agronomy, geology, demography, and so forth automatically encourages a centralized, bureaucratic approach at odds with local subsistence interests. In particular, it directs attention to a fuzzy picture of the aggregate production of discrete, countrywide sectors (forestry, agriculture, mining) instead of to a sharply focused picture of the highly localized, integrated forest conservation–irrigation–pasturage–rice farming–fruit growing systems to which many villagers are accustomed and in which distinctions between sectors are difficult to make (Lohmann 1996). By the same token, the frequently heard Western suggestion that social movements protesting dams or plantations have an obligation, before they take action, to propose "alternatives" which meet conditions Westerners consider important—such as satisfying national or international electricity or pulp demand—is misplaced when addressed to villagers and other activists in Thailand who do not recognize the validity or importance of those conditions.

The related notion that environmental action is to be evaluated according to how well it achieves some narrow, preset theoretical or technical goal also violates the sense of many Thai activists of what is important. The Nam Choan dam struggle is considered successful, for example, not only because it stopped a dam, but also because it helped build new political alliances and democratizing strategies among varied groups which have been crucial in other "environmental" battles since. Similarly, the simplistic claim frequently made by Western observers that the 1989 logging ban has failed because some illegal logging still takes place, or because Thai sawmills and furniture factories are now being fed with timber from Burma, ignores the way in which the ban has legitimated the political struggle which led up to it, provided a precedent for bans in other countries, and supplied local villagers with a court of appeal which it will be difficult for private firms or the government to undermine in the future.

So far, I have discussed dichotomies whose significance for Thai "environmental" activism is merely

dubious. Other dichotomies—between state and market, public and private, jobs and environment, pragmatism and radicalism, and anthropocentrism and ecocentrism—are based on assumptions which, in Thailand, seem quite straightforwardly false. To ask Thai activists Are you pragmatic or radical? Anthropocentric or ecocentric? In favor of free enterprise or in favor of government intervention? is thus often to put them in the position of the defendant in the hoary joke who is asked by the prosecuting attorney, And when did you stop beating your wife? Instead of answering the question, defendant and activists are each likely to want to challenge the premises which underlie it. It is with this last sort of dichotomy that I will be mainly concerned in the rest of this chapter.

RESISTING THE STATE-MARKET AND PUBLIC-PRIVATE DICHOTOMIES

Western and Japanese aid agencies, when they come to Thailand, typically presuppose that the main actors who will be able to implement solutions to the country's environmental problems are the government and the private sector (Lohmann 1991a; cf. Ferguson 1990). Thus a Forestry Master Plan for Thailand financed by FINNIDA, the Finnish bilateral aid agency, suggests that deforestation can be checked only by dividing forests into essentially two categories: those which are managed for commercial production, and those which are off limits to human interference. Although the plan recognizes some rights of rural communities to use forests for subsistence goods, the communities are envisaged essentially as temporary lieutenants of commercial interests, first to be "organized and instructed" by government and corporate representatives, then to be gradually moved to the cities as they are assimilated into the market system and lose their land to commercial interests (Jaakko Pöyry Oy 1993). Similarly, the proposed Global Environmental Facility program for conserving the Thung Yai Naresuan Wildlife Sanctuary near the Burmese border (the site of the defeated Nam Choan dam) assumes almost automatically that, if the sanctuary is to be protected, thousands of residents belonging to the Karen ethnic group must be evicted from it in order to ensure that it comes under the total control of government forest rangers (MIDAS et al. 1993). In the same vein, Caroline Sargent, a forester with the British-based International Institute for Environment and Development, laments in a recent book that the 1989 logging ban brought about a state of affairs in which there were "no longer loggers to defend the forests and prevent encroachment on forest land which was held under concession — and thus the natural forest continues to diminish" (Sargent and Bass 1992:20). This focus on, and faith in, the resource management of the public and private sectors is not confined to members of the international environmental establishment. Even unofficial environmentalist visitors to Thailand often make a beeline for bureaucracies or policy think tanks such as the National Environment Board, Thai Development Research Institute, or Royal Forestry Department on the assumption that, even given the failures of such institutions in the past, that is where the action is and where the new, more successful plans which will save the country's environment will originate.

Many Thai villagers and activists find such assumptions questionable. They point out that while in many Western countries it may be the case that stewardship of land, water, and forests rests overwhelmingly either with governments or with individual private owners and companies integrated into a monetized and centralized modern market system, this is not the case in much of Thailand. Here, a third type of authority, that of the village community exercising its own type of stewardship over common land, forests, and water, is also important; and it is the undermining of this authority by state or market that typically results in disorder and degradation (*The Ecologist* 1993).

One example of such commons regimes is the *mŭang făăi* rice irrigation/forest conservation system used in most regions of northern Thailand (Chatchawan and Lohmann, 1991). In this system the local community builds (and periodically adjusts and rebuilds) a small reservoir and canal system to conduct water from a hill forest through rice fields in the valley below. Both the forest and the canal system are preserved and maintained as a unit by the community as a way of ensuring a minimum rice crop for everyone each year, through a complex sys-

tem of organization of labor and time which relies on constant face-to-face discussion, homegrown materials, and local enforcement and mutual adjustments. Such commons can be found throughout Thailand, ranging from various kinds of community forests, which provide free vegetables, fruit, game, fodder, bamboo, and firewood as well as burial grounds, to communal pastures used for grazing cows and buffaloes, to coastal fisheries (Pinkaew and Rajesh 1992; Sanitsuda 1990).

Such commons regimes cannot be run from afar by the state since their maintenance requires highly flexible, democratic responses to local circumstances and needs and is finely dependent on local knowledge, materials, personalities, and senses of responsibility (Apffel-Marglin and Marglin 1990; Apffel-Marglin and Marglin 1994). Nor can they be run by a private corporation, since they are oriented toward community subsistence and cooperation rather than the profit maximization of individuals considered apart from the community. Here it is instructive to look at the answer which a Karen villager in a remote part of Chiang Mai recently gave to a foreign consultant who put a hypothetical choice to him about how to manage a local pine forest — used by the villagers for many years mainly for subsistence — for commercial gain. Two of the choices the consultant suggested were, first, for individual families to be assigned rights to separate forest plots, and second, for government officials to oversee the management of the forest as a whole. The villager rejected the consultant's entire approach. First, he objected to the manner in which the choice was put to him. If such matters were to be considered, he said, they could only be considered as a community, not through approaches to people like him as individuals. Second, he said, putting the forest in the hands of discrete individuals would destroy community cooperation and thus the forest itself. Putting the forest in the hands of government officials would lead to power imbalances, corruption, and again the destruction of the forest. The way to preserve the forest, the villager maintained, was to leave it defined by the local people's customary relationship to it.

Indeed, commons regimes such as *mŭang făăi*, as Thai activists and villagers point out, have generally proved to be more effective in Thailand in protecting

what Westerners call the "environment" than either
the state or the private sector. The Royal Forest and
Irrigation Departments, for example, prodded by
foreign agencies, timber firms, and the export economy, have presided over nearly a century of inefficient water use and degradation of forests and
land—degradation which accelerated precipitously
after 1960 as state control was extended over more
and more of the countryside. *Pace* Caroline Sargent,
timber concessionaires never "defended the forests
and prevented encroachment." Few, if any, ever observed regulations calling for rotational cutting or
prevention of clearance. (In Indonesia, similarly, a
study by a Jakarta-based environmental organization
found that no more than 22 of 578 timber concessionaires followed state forestry rules (Durning 1994).)
State promotion of commercial agriculture for export, meanwhile, has resulted in the clearance of tens
of thousands of square kilometers of forests for up-
land crops such as corn, cassava, and pineapple in
the space of a few decades. Even the state's policy
of demarcating protected areas, in effect since the
1960s, has often resulted in degradation, when villagers are evicted from protected areas to which they
are well-adapted and forced to pursue more ecologically destructive careers elsewhere. *Mŭăng făăi,* on
the other hand—to take only one example of commons regime—has resulted in the preservation of
forests in most areas of northern Thailand, as well as
a consistently frugal and sustainable use of available
water, for upwards of seven hundred years. Small
wonder, then, that it strikes many activists and researchers who are acquainted with the facts on the
ground as ludicrous that power over forests and land
is so seldom entrusted to village communities and is
instead turned over to the government and its concessionaires, often following the advice of international agencies, as being the "only shows in town."

Much of what might be labeled by outsiders as
"environmentalist" resistance, too, has been led not
by government officials nor by urban-based intellectuals, but by commoners with firsthand experience of what is happening to their land and commons. When, for example, in the 1970s and 1980s,
farmers began to block logging roads and march on
local government offices in protest against timber
concessions which the Royal Forest Department

had given out to local companies, their objective
was not to save rare bird species nor halt global
warming nor gain commercial profit from the forests
themselves, but rather to safeguard part of the commons they relied on for water, vegetables, mush-
rooms, medicine, firewood, and game. The attempt
of Ubon Ratchatanee villagers to stop the Pak Mun
dam, similarly, was rooted partly in fears, later
proved justified, that the project would result in a
decline in household fish catches in the Mun River
(Project for Ecological Recovery 1993). None of
this is to suggest that the state has not taken positive
steps to safeguard land, forests, and water. The logging ban is one example, and a recent decision to
curb roadbuilding in protected areas another. But
when such steps have been taken, they have invariably followed and not preceded popular action.

RESISTING THE JOBS-ENVIRONMENT AND PRAGMATISM-RADICALISM DICHOTOMIES

It is not surprising that Thai villagers and activists find
the jobs-environment and pragmatism-radicalism
dichotomies which seem common sense to many
Northern environmentalists to be often inappropriate
or incomprehensible when applied to Thailand. They
point out that to a majority of Thais, secure livelihood depends not, as it does to a majority in North
America or Europe, on the availability of permanent
paid employment in the industrial, service, or state
sectors, but rather on the sustained availability of
local land, water, and forests to rural communities.
In Thailand, the commercial forces which are damaging the "environment" are thus also destroying, in
a sense, "jobs." For every temporary construction
job created by dam construction, for example, several farming and fishing livelihoods may be permanently lost. Similarly, even if northeastern farmers
wanted jobs on the plantations which threaten to
replace their farms, they would not be able to find
nearly enough of them year-round to make up for
the subsistence losses plantations entail (Lohmann
1991b). For rural Thais, then, there is not necessarily anything "pragmatic" about acquiescing in a development project which advertises itself as "creating" a handful of jobs. Rather, such projects are

likely to appear, as they often in fact are, dangerously idealistic, radical, and utopian, uninformed by history and by the facts on the ground and, for local people, no substitute for the solid guarantee of secure land and water. In Thailand, in short, pragmatism and what an outsider would call "environmentalism" very often coincide. The struggle for livelihood very often *is* a struggle for the "environment."

One leader of a Muslim fishing community in south Thailand was recently entertaining some environmentalist visitors who were curious about why the villagers, after years of providing labor for a local charcoal factory which was cutting the coastal mangrove forests, decided to try to halt the logging and establish community forest zones off limits to the factory. The community leader explained that, since the mangroves served as nursery grounds for fish, the logging had resulted in declining catches by the village's fisherpeople, and that the villagers had finally decided that this had to be stopped. After a few years of efforts at limiting the charcoal factory's depredations, catches were again rising, and the community's future looked more secure. "I'm not interested in wildlife conservation," the village leader concluded, "but the sea is my rice bowl [*mau khâaw*]."

RESISTING THE ANTHROPOCENTRIC-ECOCENTRIC DICHOTOMY

Rural people in Thailand, including those who have been most prominent in fighting to preserve the "environment," have typically looked at forests, streams, and wild animals largely in the light of their connection to agriculture, fishing, hunting, and gathering. Although wilderness, like community forests, has been a source of certain spiritual values (Tambiah, 1984), to some extent rural people have even shared the traditional attitude of Thai elites that the wilderness is a menace until it is, by being cleared, brought within the sphere of a polity dominated by the royal city or *muang* (Stott 1991).

Such attitudes can make visiting Western deep ecologists slightly uneasy. While they applaud Thai villagers' activism in defense of local forests and streams and are intrigued by the Buddhist tradition of respect for the rights of animals and indeed all

living things (Yenchai 1989), they cannot help but look down their noses a bit at what they see as an essentially "instrumental" attitude toward nature. Thai farmers, they feel, are regrettably "anthropocentric," and their preoccupation with agriculture and ambivalence toward "wild nature" suggest a lack of appreciation of the intrinsic value of plants and animals. Even if they agree with Guha (1989) that deep ecology "is of very little use in understanding the dynamics of environmental degradation" and of equally little use in explaining the real-life motivations of the most powerful local social movements aimed at halting that degradation, they still worry that Thai activists lack sufficient reverence for untouched nature and awareness of the importance of wilderness areas. This remains so even when they are reminded of the mixed practical record of the American model of wilderness preservation in Thailand.

Thai villagers and activists are unlikely to be completely unsympathetic to the deep ecologists' concerns. At the same time, however, it would be easy for them to point out that the attitude of (say) *mŭăng fǎǎi* villagers toward forests, streams, rice, and animals, when more closely examined, is not comfortably categorized as either anthropocentric or ecocentric.

That attitude is highly practical. The villagers assuredly do not leave forests, streams, animals, or rice alone, nor contemplate them from afar in the manner of middle-class backpackers pondering the peaks of the Sierra Nevada, nor devote their energies to ensuring that they survive after the end of civilization. Instead, they alter and use them for the necessities of life.

It does not follow, however, that *mŭăng fǎǎi* villagers treat forests, streams, animals, or rice as instruments. Nor does it follow from the fact that the villagers use and alter these things that they place humans at the center of the universe (cf. Collier 1994). Rather, forests, streams, animals, and rice are valued for themselves, treated as things which have intrinsic value and in some sense even as persons who can benefit humans but who if abused will also punish them. At annual meetings of the committees responsible for maintenance of *mŭăng fǎǎi* systems, for example, farmers offer food to the spirits of the irrigation system and the forest and to the lords of the water and ask through an incantation that water be plentiful and the harvest good during the coming year, that the water users be happy and untroubled by disease, and the *mŭăng făăi* repairs take place without injury to anyone. Taking care to inform the spirits of what they intend to do, the villagers simultaneously beg pardon for their actions, reflecting their submission to, respect for, and friendship with nature, rather than an attempt to master it. There is even a spirit of the rice. *Mŭăng făăi* farmers, in short, do not treat nature as a means to an end which is separated from nature, any more than Westerners, when they have a conversation with their friends to try to change their minds, treat those friends as a means to their own ends. *Mŭăng făăi* thus offers a counterexample to the presuppositions of many deep ecologists (which are also presuppositions of industrialists and neoclassical economists) that all practical reasoning and action must be instrumental, and that recognizing something's intrinsic value entails leaving it alone.

Insofar as they have avoided concrete experience of the specific human-environment and self-interest–community interests dichotomies which the West has created in recent centuries, Thai villagers cannot be expected to be much moved by deep ecologists' rather strained suggestions about how to paper over these constructed gaps with abstract "feelings of kinship with everything else in the universe" or an abstract view of "nonhuman life as intrinsically valuable." Indeed bringing *mŭăng făăi* into juxtaposition with deep ecology helps show just how much the latter — despite its pretences of being connected to all sorts of Eastern and native American thought — is in fact a historical artefact of the middle class in industrialized societies and remains addressed to the concerns of that group.

For deep ecologists to become more self-conscious about this historical boundedness could be a positive step toward political solidarity (cf. Lohmann 1991b; Haraway 1989; Sellars 1963). It could enable them to recognize that the ambivalence they may feel toward the type of activism they find in Thailand is largely a result of mistakenly reading the pattern of Western industrial agriculture — which *is* instrumentalist — into commons regimes such as *mŭăng făăi*. Once such regimes are seen

more on their own terms, and the Western obsession with dividing attitudes into anthropocentric and ecocentric is left behind, some of this ambivalence could well vanish.

CONCLUSION

In trying to describe certain Thai social movements from a Western point of view, and mainly for Western readers, this chapter has, of necessity, started from a conceptual framework which Westerners are likely to share. But because one of its motivations is to foster intercultural dialogue between movements — to ask not only What are Thai environmental movements all about? But also According to whom? — it has also tried to make this Western framework itself into a subject for scrutiny and criticism and to suggest that it be located carefully within its own history and culture. This has not been done from a Thai point of view: nor has it been done using the words that Thai activists would use. Rather, it has been done from the point of view of a Westerner looking forward to seeing closer practical engagement between Western and Thai social activists.

REFERENCES

Apffel-Marglin, Frederique, and Stephen A. Marglin, eds. 1990. *Dominating Knowledge.* Oxford: Oxford University Press.

Apffel-Marglin, Frederique, and Stephen A. Marglin. 1994. *Decolonizing Knowledge.* Oxford: Oxford University Press.

Chatchawan, Tongdeelert, and Larry Lohmann. 1991. "The Traditional Muang Faai Irrigation System of Northern Thailand." *The Ecologist* 21.2: 101–6.

Collier, Andrew. 1994. "Value, Rationality and the Environment." *Radical Philosophy* 66: 3–9.

Durning, Alan. 1994. "Redesigning the Forest Economy." In *State of the World*, ed. Lester R. Brown. New York: W. W. Norton.

The Ecologist. 1993. "Whose Common Future?" London: Earthscan, 1993. Reprint. Philadelphia, PA: New Society.

Ferguson, James. 1990. *The Anti-Politics Machine: "Development," Depoliticization and Bureaucratic Power in Lesotho.* Cambridge: Cambridge University Press.

Guha, Ramachandra. 1989. "Radical American Environmentalism and Wilderness Preservation: A Third World Critique." *Environmental Ethics* 11 (Spring): 71–83.

Haraway, Donna. 1989. *Primate Visions: Gender, Race and Nature in the World of Modern Science.* London: Routledge.

Jaakko Pöyry Oy. 1993. "Thai Forestry Sector Master Plan," Final Draft. 6 Vols. Helsinki: FINNIDA.

Lohmann, Larry. 1991a. "Peasants, Plantations and Pulp: The Politics of Eucalyptus in Thailand." *Bulletin of Concerned Asian Scholars* 23.4: 3–17.

———. 1991b. "Who Defends Biological Diversity? Conservation Strategies and the Case of Thailand." In *Biodiversity: Social and Ecological Perspectives,* ed. Vandana Shiva. Penang, London, and New Jersey: World Rainforest Movement and Zed Books.

———. 1996. "Land, Power and Forest Colonization in Thailand." In *The Struggle for Land and the Fate of the Forests,* ed. Marcus Colchester and Larry Lohmann. London and New Jersey: Zed Books.

MacIntyre, Alasdair. 1988. *Whose Justice? Which Rationality?* London: Duckworth.

MIDAS Agronomics Co., Ltd., and Centre de Cooperation Internationale en Recherche Agronomique pour le Developpement. 1993. "Conservation Forest Area Protection, Management and Development Project: Pre-Investment Study Draft Final Report." Washington: Global Environment Facility.

Pinkaew, Leungaramsri, and Noel Rajesh (eds.). 1992. *The Future of People and Forests in Thailand After the Logging Ban.* Bangkok: Project for Ecological Recovery.

Project for Ecological Recovery. 1993. Survey Report for the Pak Mun Area. Bangkok: Project for Ecological Recovery.

Sanitsuda Ekachai. 1990. *Behind the Smile: Voices of Thailand.* Bangkok: Bangkok Development Support Committee.

Sargent, Caroline, and Stephen Bass, eds. 1992. *Plantation Politics: Forest Plantation in Development.* London: Earthscan.

Sellars, Wilfrid. 1963. *Science, Perception and Reality.* London: Routledge and Kegan Paul.

Stott, Philip. 1991. "Mu'ang and Pa: Elite Views of Nature in a Changing Thailand." In *Thai Constructions of Knowledge,* ed. Manas Chitkasem and Andrew Turton, 142–54. London: University of London.

Tambiah, Stanley Jeyaraja. 1984. *The Buddhist Saints of the Forest and the Cult of Amulets.* Cambridge: Cambridge University Press.

Taylor, Charles. 1985. "Interpretation and Ethnocentricity": In *Interpretation and Human Sciences.* Cambridge: Cambridge University Press.

Taylor, Dorceta. 1992. "Can the Environmental Movement Attract and Maintain the Support of Minorities?" In *Race and the Incidence of Environmental Hazards: A Time for Discourse,* ed. Bunyan Bryant and Paul Mohai, 28–54. Boulder: Westview Press.

Yenchai Laohavanich. 1989. "A Thai Buddhist View of Nature." In *Culture and Environment in Thailand,* ed. Michael Shari. Bangkok: Siam Society.

DISCUSSION TOPICS

1. Lohmann emphasizes a number of advantages of the commons regimes in Thailand over state management or private ownership of resources. Which advantages seem most important to you? Are there weaknesses that Lohmann does not discuss?

2. Lohmann argues that in Thailand the commercial forces damaging the environment are also destroying jobs. Explain his reasoning.

3. According to Lohmann, why do rural people in Thailand resist the dichotomy between anthropocentrism and ecocentrism? How does their view of forests, streams, animals, and rice contrast with that of deep ecologists?

READING 57

Taking the Land Rights Movement Seriously

Kirk Emerson

Kirk Emerson is director of the U.S. Institutes for Environmental Conflict Resolution. In the following essay, drawn from A Wolf in the Garden *(1996, edited by P. Brick and R. M. Cawley), she looks beyond arguments about rights to the underlying disagreements over property itself. Emerson discusses five key rationales present in the rhetoric of the land rights movement, with the aim of using these controversial rationales as a motivation for American political culture to connect public and private rights and responsibilities.*

What distinguishes the land rights movement, in all its complexity and across its many constituents, I suggest, is a latticework of interconnected, complementary understandings of property in land. Behind the rhetoric of property-rights talk are substantive conceptions of property that include its value, how rights in property are to be governed, property ownership, the stability of the rules that define property, and the autonomy afforded by private property. I am intentionally *not* framing the debate exclusively around rights. As Dennis Coyle notes, "The language of rights permeates controversies over the uses of land."[1] Behind those rights claims, however, are more substantive and foundational conceptions about property that need to be unraveled and looked at. In the next section of this chapter, I discuss the rationales that incorporate these conceptions of property and help us further articulate the dimensions of the land rights movement.

DEFINING RATIONALES

In order to take the land rights movement seriously and engage in more substantive and productive deliberation, we need a more discriminating understanding of the rationales that guide this complex coalition. By rationales, I mean the basic arguments or fundamental reasoning about property expressed by and motivating its adherents. These rationales provide the outside boundaries of the land rights movement as well as differentiate among the various personal, political, and ideological interests that compose the movement. Together these arguments also lend some insight to the origins of the movement, its likely staying power, and its connections to other ongoing political and policy debates.

I have identified five rationales from my readings of the movement's own membership materials and background papers, legal argumentation in regulatory takings cases, legislative proposals for state and federal property rights protection, as well as both critical and supportive commentary on the movement. These rationales include equity claims, new populist principles, privatization arguments, market transaction reasoning, and libertarian assertions. Each of these rationales represents a facet of the land rights movement and is articulated by key actors and associations who draw predominantly on that line of argumentation.

These are not meant to be mutually exclusive rationales. Rather they tend to be mutually consistent and reinforcing (like intersecting spheres in a Venn diagram). However, these rationales are sufficiently distinct to enable a useful classification of the central claims and priority principles. It is important to note that several groups endorse many, if not most, of these rationales of the land rights movement. Nonetheless, one need not embrace all of these principles, and certainly not in their extreme forms, to identify oneself as a supporter of the land rights movement. (That is what makes membership counts an irrelevant measure of the movement's strength.) I see the land rights movement as a coalescence of political activists, policy entrepreneurs, patrons, organizers and organized groups, as well as unorganized supporters, all sharing complementary, mutually reinforcing rationales. That is one of the sources of the movement's strength—an associational commitment that incorporates expected material benefits with the sharing of compatible conceptions of property.

The equity rational represents concerns for fairness and justice that are raised when private landowners bear unanticipated or burdensome costs due to public regulation or direct condemnation. The demands for compensation spring from this rationale. Equity concerns are also expressed when private users of public lands are restricted in ways that are perceived as unfair and unjustified. These equity concerns are perhaps the most compelling and most intractable of the movement's rationales. They require weighing the relative values of property with respect to different competing interests—private owners, public agencies, and the public at large. Three major equity arguments stand out, most of them well developed within the legal reasoning presented in regulatory takings claims.

The most familiar of these is the argument that some individual property owners are bearing a disproportionate regulatory burden imposed for the positive benefit of the rest of society. The constitutional restriction on eminent domain in the Just Compensation Clause is the foundational principle here. The private value of the property is being diminished, it is argued, well beyond the positive public value being preserved for hard-to-quantify, broadly enjoyed, often delayed or future benefits. It is one thing to be restricted from creating a nuisance or jeopardizing public health or safety; private value should not include an unrecognized right to harm others. It is quite another thing, it is argued, to pay excessive costs for what are perceived as public uses or benefits for which just compensation should be paid. Unfortunately, the line distinguishing public harm from public benefit, as Justice Scalia admitted in his 1992 *Lucas v. South Carolina Coastal Council* opinion, is not well drawn, particularly with respect to wetlands and biodiversity values. Nor is the composition and source of "private" value straightforward. Fair market value, for example, is not necessarily the exclusive product of private investment.

Much, if not most, of the unresolved doctrinal issues over regulatory takings have to do with sorting out these values in land (many, potentially indeterminate) in order to balance fairly majoritarian interests with individual rights. Whether or not to compensate, how much to compensate, or on what basis to compensate property owners for their lost property value in exchange for protection of public value remain open questions.

A second equity argument challenges the justification for direct condemnation or regulation of private land that does not serve a valid public purpose or is not legally authorized by statute or by the Constitution. For example, Peggy Reigle's group, Fairness to Landowners Committee (claiming 8,800 property-owning members in thirty states) fights the legitimacy of wetlands regulations and promotes more restrictive field definitions and less protective standards. Here the declared public value in private land is questioned. If there is no legitimate public value, then it is unfair and unreasonable to diminish the private property value. This argument most often takes the form of substantive due process claims against "arbitrary and capricious" public decision making. A companion claim is expressed by private users of public lands who defend their "vested rights" or use privileges by denying the legitimacy of the federal government's exercise of the Property or Supremacy Clauses of the Constitution.

A third, closely connected set of equity claims is about the efficacy of governmental actions; are the regulations really going to achieve the intended public purpose? If not, it is argued, then they place an unfair and unjustifiable burden on property owners who must forgo private value in exchange for unrealized, if not unrealizable, public gains. This was the line of reasoning pursued in the 1987 *Nollan v. California Coastal Commission* ruling, in which the "essential nexus" doctrine for exactions originated and again in the 1994 *Dolan v. City of Tigard* decision's "rough proportionality" test. Despite one's reading of these Supreme Court rulings, the demand for efficacious regulation is certainly a justifiable concern for property owners and taxpayers alike.

This equity rationale then motivates a distinct set of issues around the multiple values of property and the "calculus of fairness" for resolving competing claims over those values.[2] This presents one critical area for deliberation with property rights advocates. Much of the current discourse on these issues has been conducted through the courts and in legal briefs. Several conservative legal foundations and defense funds field litigators, join law suits, and provide amicus briefs on cases that are driven by these equity claims.[3] Legal scholars debate these issues in law review articles and law school symposia.[4] As the efforts increase to provide legislative remedies for losses in private property value, the debate is shifting to the political and public arena as well. However, the issues are being cast more as "rights talk" than equity claims.[5]

A second major line of reasoning within the land rights movement is the new populism rationale, which raises questions about the governance of property. Who should be making decisions ultimately affecting the property of the common man and woman and their local communities? The neopopulist response is that competent, accountable, and decent government should stay close to home. Bureaucrats and legislators back in Washington, D.C., do not have the knowledge or commitment to plan or regulate or adjudicate local or state land

and natural resource issues. Only decentralized and limited government can foster responsible self-determining individuals and communities. These are the perennial arguments of supporters for rejuvenated federalism and stronger states rights. But they have been emboldened by reactions to the cumulative reach of a growing number of federal regulations for environmental cleanup and natural resource protection, worker safety, and consumer protection that now extend into the affairs of individual proprietors, small farms and businesses, school boards, and property owners. Enforcement of these regulations has also been considerably strengthened; now violators can be criminally liable for unauthorized polluting activities or property damage. The new populists are responding to these multiple intrusions into "their" lives and onto their lands.

What is perceived as the arrogance of federal bureaucrats abusing their powers of office, be they from the Bureau of Land Management, the Fish and Wildlife Service, the Army Corps of Engineers, or the Environmental Protection Agency, is a major source of neopopulist anger. This has been a continuing theme for inholders (private property owners living in or adjacent to publicly owned and managed lands) who are often subject to direct condemnation, or prolonged threats of condemnation, and to stringent development standards or restrictions.[6] Nasty behavior, lack of notice, exclusion from public discussion or timely involvement, and below-market compensation offers are recurrent complaints. Most critically, these property owners contend they have no political recourse, since unelected bureaucrats from federal or state agencies are often the final decision makers over the disposition of their property.

These neopopulist arguments can be found in the self-presentation of essentially all the local and national property rights groups. The Alliance for America describes its membership as follows:

> We are farmers, cattlemen, private landowners, fishermen, miners, loggers, teachers, carpenters, truck drivers, and a thousand more . . . the people, families and communities that make America the greatest nation on earth. This nation, however, seems to no longer be one whose government is of, by, and

for the people, but one which is of, by, and for the unelected bureaucrats and regulators. Today government and environmental regulations, some of which seem to be based on tea leaf readings and Tarot card predictions, have made criminals of ordinary citizens doing ordinary things. It is time for the common sense people of this land to wake up and take back the control of their lives and futures.[7]

For additional examples, see Pendley's catalogue in *It Takes a Hero,* or the *Land Rights Letter* (where one column, entitled "Reluctant Warriors," features profiles on regular people who have made the movement a success).[8]

Admittedly the populist rhetoric is self-conscious and has been exploited by the political and policy entrepreneurs of the land rights movement. Nonetheless, the new populism rationale represents deeply felt values and the extension of a long-standing political tradition in this country. Classic questions about representation, accountability, the regulatory role of government generally, and the limit of federal authority specifically, are central to deliberation along this line of reasoning.

The privatization rationale focuses on the ownership of property through two lines of argumentation. The first is the standard efficient management argument: that private ownership of land is a necessary, if not sufficient, condition for the most efficient and environmentally sound stewardship practices. This is coupled with an entitlement argument that supports private rights to public lands. The core of the wise use movement's case rests on these twin claims, rallying support from ranchers, miners, loggers, oil drillers, and those dependent on the resource extraction industries. The second entitlement claim is particularly important when squaring the seeming contradiction between support for private ownership with protection of public subsidies for low mining fees and grazing permits. However, since the twentieth-century federal land retention policies are not recognized as valid by many wise users or by those in the newly dubbed "county ordinance movement," such nominal fees are seen as interferences with vested or promised rights, not as undeserved subsidies. The escalating protests and civil disobedience in eastern Nevada over new grazing restrictions by the U.S. Bureau of Land Management and the U.S. Forest Service demonstrate this entitlement perspective.[9]

The documentation and economic reasoning behind this privatization rationale have been elaborated on by free-market environmentalists and new-resource economists out of the Political Economy Research Center (PERC).[10] Their intellectual heritage of economic liberalism reaches way back to John Locke and Adam Smith and is intertwined with the conservation lineage from Pinchot. Wise, multiple-use principles for management of natural resources, it is argued, can be carried out by those who know the land, know the resources, and have the greatest incentives to manage for long-term productivity. Indeed, the incentive structure of this rational-actor model is the central logic. Public regulations, for example, such as those in the Endangered Species Act, can provide perverse incentives to private property owners to defy their stewardship principles and destroy listed species on their property rather than come under the jurisdiction of the ESA.[11] Admittedly the wise use groups' interests go beyond this privatization rationale and incorporate many of the other lines of reasoning being presented, but their originating rationale resides with the privatization argument. At the very least, the wise users give the most direct expression of and priority to privatization interests. This makes sense, of course, given the western provenance of these groups, where more than a third of the land is federally owned.[12]

Dueling anecdotes of egregious mismanagement of both public and private lands abound. These are familiar and persistent indictments. The dichotomous assumption behind the rationale that there are only two forms of ownership in land, public and private, and both are absolute, is the real culprit here.[13] It becomes particularly dysfunctional when applied by either side to the challenges of ecosystem management, where legal boundaries between private and public lands are rarely coincident with natural system delineations. Rather than confront this directly, unfortunately, the battles are fought over legalistic interpretations of congressional intent and administrative discretion, and such arcane doctrines as *noscitur a sociis* (where words are known by the company they keep), as in the 1994 *Sweet Home v. Babbitt* ruling by the D.C. Circuit Court of Appeals. . . .

The market transaction rationale, although closely akin to the privatization argument, emphasizes property's role in the productive workings of the economy as a whole. The rules that govern property in land, it is argued, must be clearly and consistently applied so that expectations about the future use of land can be realized. Stable, predictable property rights and values reduce transaction costs, minimize risk, and encourage investment. Unanticipated changes or burdensome regulations concerning the institutions of property, its administration, protection, and adjudication, will discourage private risk taking and the productive use of resources.

This market transaction rationale originates in Ronald Coase's seminal work on social cost theory and has been extended by political economists and transaction costs analysts as well as by legal scholars of the law and economics tradition. One extreme extension of this reasoning has been developed by Richard Epstein at the University of Chicago. Epstein has played a pivotal intellectual role in raising the takings issue to its current prominence. Many of his colleagues and students form the cadre of policy entrepreneurs and public interest litigators who have pushed for revisions in the judicial takings doctrine and new statutory limits on regulatory impacts on property values.[14]

The private business interests supporting this rationale are those with speculative interests to protect; owners of undeveloped land, the real estate industry, and the home builders' associations. Rule changes, such as the redefinition of regulated wetlands or local rezoning (particularly down zoning), or lengthy, uncertain permit approval processes, in the long run, it is argued, hinder risk-taking investments necessary for economic development. This rationale comes across in the strategy to correct the takings dilemma through statutory rather than judicial means. What we now see in Congress and in statehouses around the country are proposals for bright-line rules that would reduce the risk of investment in land and provide insurance against future rule changes that cannot be ensured from the muddled judicial doctrine on takings. One thing [that] did become clear in the *Lucas* decision was that even Justice Scalia, writing for the majority, could not adequately define a total taking, let alone a partial taking (cases where less than 100 percent of all productive use of the land is taken by regulation). Indeed, Scalia's efforts at a categorical ruling for total taking were compromised by upholding the nuisance exceptions based on background principles in state property and common law. Categorical rules can be accomplished more bluntly, at least in theory, by statute.

The libertarian rationale is evoked quite simply by Professor Epstein's philosophy that all regulation is theft.[15] I distinguish this last rationale in its emphasis on private property as an essential element of personal autonomy. The right to exclude is consonant with freedom, as Bruce Yandle explains, "The ability to exclude, to select who may enter and use a resource, is powerful evidence of freedom and liberty.[16] Expressed in the NIMBY syndrome, adherents to the libertarian rationale want exclusive control not only over their backyards but their back pockets as well. Compulsory shelling out for the public interest is an infringement on individual liberty and any lost property value from governmental regulation ought to be compensated. The libertarian rationale offers the natural rights argument for private property and recognizes few, if any, justifiable constraints on individual freedom.

It is from this rationale that property rights are defended as co-equal with civil and political rights and in need of the same diligent constitutional protections.[17] Erasing the "double standard" will restore "fundamental rights, rights that are crucial to individual freedom and democracy.[18] This "double standard" for judicial review originated with a famous footnote by Justice Harlan Stone in a 1938 ruling by the Supreme Court, *United States v. Carolene Products*. Deference was given to regulatory impositions on property that passed a simple "rational basis" test, while closer scrutiny was given to governmental actions that might jeopardize free speech and criminal procedure rights, political rights such as voting, and the rights of "discrete, insular minorities." In a recent, well-documented study of judicial treatment of land-use regulation, Coyle states, "In its zeal to justify an expanding regulatory state, the land use establishment . . . has undermined the freedom critical to the American polity and has supported the dilution of the Constitution beyond the bounds of credible interpretation.[19]

The more radical libertarian extension of this rationale is expressed by the "freedom fighters" of the movement, given to the most radical rhetoric and emotional "rights talk." While Robert Nozick articulates best the modern libertarian philosophy, those drawn to this rationale in the movement tend to cite our revolutionary Founding Fathers as their main inspiration and refer to the land rights movement as a revolt.[20] The most radical activists and organizers of the movement tend to argue the extreme libertarian rationale, including the radical recreationists, hunters and bikers who defend their right to ride the desert free and clear.

This libertarian argument is particularly challenging to objectify into a domain for critical deliberation. It is one thing to acknowledge the opposition to, say, a rails-to-trails program that could diminish privacy and present security concerns for private homeowners; it is another to understand the withdrawal from civic engagement or any responsibility for a collective public interest. Through the lens of this rationale, however, regulations are seen as unjustifiable constraints on individual freedom: the "negative" freedom from governmental intrusion. The forgotten half of the equation, as opponents have countered, are those governmental measures that enable the "positive" freedom to pursue one's own course, to have educational opportunities that enable informed choices, to live in a safe civil society, to have some stable expectations about the behavior of one's neighbors or the quality of the air one breathes. Deliberation about libertarian premises is essential to reengage individual rights with collective responsibility.

OPPORTUNITIES FOR DELIBERATION

If there is any consolation to be found in the rise of the land rights movement, it is in the opportunities that have been created for public deliberation about property and its role in connecting, not just delimiting, public and private rights and responsibilities. This is unfinished business not only for the environmental movement, but also for our American political culture. Some might say unresolvable business, and hence the pendulum swing from reform to conservation, or from collective welfare to robust economic liberalism. If we are to moderate that arc of action-reaction, which it is in the interests of environmental integrity to do, then we need to take hold of this new opportunity for deliberation.

In some regards, I am arguing for an approach not unlike Cass Sunstein's articulate defense of regulation and reconstruction of the activist state in *After the Rights Revolution.*[21] Let me illustrate with just a few of the opportunities for deliberation presenting themselves right now in the growing public debate. The new populism rationale, described above, provides the underpinning for policy proposals to limit the reach of regulation at its source, that is, by reducing the authorized scope of what constitutes a legitimate governmental action. One of the ways this is being approached is by redefining and narrowing the justification for regulations to only those situations that would prevent "imminent and identifiable 1) hazard to public health and safety or 2) damage to specific property other than the property whose use is limited" (the current language in H.R. 925). A more subtle companion approach is to excise the word "welfare," from the heretofore standard rubric of "health, safety and welfare," as the general domain for the exercise of traditional police powers of the state. This omission occurs, for example, in the model assessment bills that specify guidelines that state attorneys general would convey to state agencies for required reviews of the "constitutional takings implications" of proposed regulations.[22]

Dropping the term "welfare" from the scope of affirmative duties of government has more than symbolic significance and, of course, represents the essence of the current deregulatory fervor. Land-use planning and zoning, for example, are based on public welfare reasoning. Ironically, the protection of property values was an original justification for separating land uses through zoning and has been understood and interpreted as a legitimate public welfare goal of government.[23] If the nuisance definitions of state courts or the "imminent and identifiable hazard" language of statutes become the sole basis for governmental regulation, innumerable public protections that people have come to expect from state and local government may well be withdrawn.

Engaging with the new populist argumentation on this requires discussion of the role of government in the definition and protection of property. Rather than quietly substituting environmental protection into the equation (we now hear on occasion "health, safety, and environmental protection"), we need to address the legacy and meaning of welfare more directly. Before banishing "public welfare" to the politically incorrect ashpile along with the "L" word, let's discuss more fully the sources of value in property and the role of government in providing that value. Are the majority of people really willing to write off all provision of public amenities such as natural corridor protection or historic preservation or future public resources, such as those provided by a diverse species gene pool? Do we simply abandon all prospective welfare duties because contemporary budget exigencies now prohibit them?

Ideas are now beginning to emerge that address some of these questions, particularly with respect to determining value. For example, the concept of "givings" or "makings" of value by government-financed infrastructure or insurance that enhances private property values is revealing the complexity of what constitutes property value. Local zoning restrictions add potential value in future use provisions for not only your property but neighboring property as well. Discussions on the fluidity of property value are now starting; how are fair market values obtained, what is their margin of error, how stable are they, how dependent are they on other factors, like changing interest rates and market dynamics? Federal, state, and local governments actually play several roles that affect property value, not just that of regulator. At the same time, the government is not the only determinant of influence on property values.

As a final example of an opportunity for deliberation, a major equity-based policy proposal is the categorical definition of a compensable taking as a specific percentage reduction in property value. Traditionally, judicial determinations of whether or not a taking has occurred are based on a case-specific, contextual balancing of the nature of the governmental action with the economic burden on the property owner and his or her investment-backed expectations.[24] The categorical proposal provides a predetermined cap on lost property value, which, if exceeded and proved to be due to the effect of the regulation, would be automatically compensable. The earliest proposals of this sort appeared in 1991 model language sponsored by the American Legislative Exchange Council for state takings bills and recommended 50 percent reduction as the limit of regulatory impacts. On its face, that sounds reasonable. Looked at another way, property owners would willingly or at least legally sustain losses of up to 50 percent in fair market value due to governmental intrusions before a statutory taking would be triggered. That sounds rather generous. Why not lower the limit to, say, 35 percent or 25 percent? The official bargaining position of the Congressional Republican's Contract with America began at 10 percent, then moved to 33⅓, then returned to 10.

The problem is that there is no rational basis for choosing one categorical cap over another — 10 percent or 80 percent. Did 10 percent sound fair, or was it the most politically palatable, or merely beyond the average margin of error for most real estate appraisals? At issue is the problem of imposing a uniform decision rule for complicated phenomena, such as property in land, that derive value and ownership from multiple sources and conditions. It looks simple on its face, but a raft of administrative rules will be needed to determine which cases meet the cut off. How do we determine what 10 percent is and of what base? And what happens to those who lose only 9.5 percent? This legislation turns a muddled judicial doctrine into a bureaucratic nightmare. Nonetheless, there are legitimate equity issues here and by attending more closely to the property values at issue, perhaps the complexity of such calculations can return us to a more reasonable balancing approach, not unlike, perhaps, but more definitive than, the court's contextual balancing of public purpose and private burdens.

In sum, to take the land rights movement seriously requires an acknowledgment of the various rationales behind the rhetoric and an understanding of their relation to different conceptions of property in land and to specific policy initiatives. Opportunities now exist for public deliberation around all of these rationales. If not taken, we risk a descent into a pathogenic environmental politics (to extend David Truman's phrase), where lines are drawn and never crossed. This should prompt public regulators and environmentalists to reevaluate and reaffirm their own underlying rationales and refresh the public's understanding of the "essential nexus" between private interests and public responsibility.

CASES CITED

Agins v. City of Tiburon, 447 U.S. 255 (1980).

Dolan v. City of Tigard, No. 93-518. U.S. Supreme Court (1994).

Lucas v. South Carolina Coastal Council, 112 S.Ct. 2886 (1992).

Nollan v. California Coastal Commission, 483 U.S. 825 (1987).

Penn Central Transportation v. New York City, 438 U.S. 104 (1978).

Sweet Home Chapter of Communities for a Great Oregon v. Babbitt, 17 F.3d 1463 (D.C. Cir. 1994).

United States v. Carolene Products Co., 304 U.S. 144 (1938).

Village of Euclid v. Ambler Realty, 272 U.S. 365 (1926).

NOTES

1. Dennis J. Coyle, *Property Rights and the Constitution Shaping Society through Land Use Regulation* (Albany: SUNY Press, 1993), 6.
2. Mark L. Pollot, *Grand Theft and Petit Larceny* (San Francisco: Pacific Research Institute for Public Policy, 1993).
3. The Pacific Legal Foundation (PLF), for example, has filed amicus briefs for virtually every takings case that has reached the Supreme Court since 1981, and successfully brought the Nollan appeal before the Court. It should be noted that on the other side, environmental organizations as well as other national professional and public interest associations also file supportive briefs, for example, American Planning Association and the National Trust for Historic Preservation.
4. For particularly insightful critiques of the Lucas decision, see the special issue published by the *Stanford Law Review* (vol. 45, May 1993) with articles by Richard Epstein, Joseph Sax, Richard Lazarus and William Fisher. As another example, a three day symposium,

"Regulatory Takings and Resources: What Are the Constitutional Limits," was sponsored in summer 1994 by the Natural Resources Law Center and the Byron R. White Center for American Constitutional Study, University of Colorado School of Law.

5. The House debate on March 2–3 over H.R. 925 may be the first nationally televised public exchange on these and other property rights concerns. The fall 1994 referendum in Arizona on Proposition 300 provided a forum for state deliberation, but the equity issue was not highlighted as such.

6. The *Land Rights Letter* in the east and the National Inholders Association (now named the American Land Rights Association) have been the most prominent national networks for inholders and other property owners faced with unwanted federal government action.

7. Alliance for America, *Information Sheet,* P.O. Box 449, Caroga Lake, N.Y. 12032 (1994).

8. William Perry Pendley, *It Takes a Hero* (Bellevue: The Free Enterprise Press, 1994).

9. Tom Kenworthy, "Dueling with the Forest Service," *Washington National Weekly Edition* (27 February–5 March 1995), 31.

10. See Terry L. Anderson and Donald R. Leal, *Free Market Environmentalism* (San Francisco: Pacific Institute for Public Policy Research, 1991), and John Baden and Richard Stroup, *Natural Resources: Bureaucratic Myths and Environmental Management* (San Francisco: Pacific Institute for Public Policy Research, 1983).

11. A frequently cited example is of the Riverside, California, fires in 1993 where the property owners who defied the prohibition against disking their fields to protect an endangered gnatcatcher saved their homes and any remaining habitat by building firebreaks. In the Hill Country in Texas, potential restrictions on treecutting to save the golden-cheeked warbler and the black-capped vireo nesting habitat have led some property owners (including Ross Perot it is claimed) to clearcut trees prematurely. As Richard Stroup has explained, the ESA has created a "Shoot, shovel, and shutup" response on the part of potentially affected property owners.

12. Over 25 percent of the land in twelve western states is owned by the federal government. In five of the states (Alaska, California, Idaho, Nevada, and Utah) federally owned land comprises over 60 percent of the states' acreage.

13. See Lyton K. Caldwell and Kristin Shrader-Frechette, *Policy for Land, Law, and Ethics* (Lanham, Md.: Rowman & Littlefield, 1993).

14. See Mark Pollot, *Grand Theft and Petit Larceny* (San Francisco: Pacific Research Institute for Public Policy, 1993); Roger Clegg, Michael DeBow, Jerry Ellig and Nancie G. Marzulla, *Regulatory Takings: Restoring Private Property Rights* (Washington, D.C.: National Legal Center for the Public Interest); Hertha L. Lund, *Property Rights Legislation in the States: A Review* (Bozeman: Political Economy Research Center [PERC] 1994); Bruce Yandle, "Regulatory Takings, Farmers, Ranchers and the Fifth Amendment" (Clemson: Center for Policy Studies Property Rights Project, 1994); and Paul Heyne, "Economics, Ethics and Ecology," in *Taking the Environment Seriously,* edited by Roger E. Meiners and Bruce Yandle (Lanham, Md.: Rowman & Littlefield, 1993), 25–50.

15. Richard A. Epstein, *Takings, Private Property, and the Power of Eminent Domain* (Cambridge: Harvard University Press, 1985).

16. Bruce Yandle, "Property Rights, Bootleggers, Baptists, and the Spotted Owls" (Presentation to the South Carolina Agricultural Council, Cayce: 23 April 1993), 11.

17. Chief Justice Rehnquist opined in the Tigard ruling, "We see no reason why the Takings Clause of the Fifth Amendment, as much a part of the Bill of Rights as the First Amendment or the Fourth Amendment, should be relegated to the status of a poor relation."

18. Coyle, *Property Rights and the Constitution Shaping Society through Land Use Regulation,* 13.

19. Ibid; see also Stanley Brubaker, "Up (Sort of) from Footnote Four: In the Matter of Property Rights," *Public Interest Law Review* (1993): 97–126

20. Robert Nozick, *Anarchy, State, and Utopia* (New York: Basic Books, 1974).

21. Cass R. Sunstein, *After the Rights Revolution: Reconceiving the Regulatory State* (Cambridge: Harvard University Press, 1990).

22. "Welfare" has been deleted from the recently defeated Arizona statute. For example, "State agencies whose governmental actions are specifically to protect public health and safety are ordinarily given broader latitude by courts before their actions are considered takings. However the mere assertion of a public health and safety purpose is insufficient to avoid a taking." They must, it goes on, constitute real and substantial threats to public health and safety; significantly advance but be no greater than necessary to achieve the public health and safety purpose, etc. Not only is welfare not included here, but public health and safety actions are expressly limited. From Title 37. Arizona Revised Statutes, Article 2.1, Section 37-221(b)(4).

23. See: *Village of Euclid v. Ambler Realty*, 272 U.S. 365 (1926).

24. See: *Penn Central Transportation v. New York City*, 438 U.S. 104 (1978), and *Agins v. City of Tiburon*, 447 U.S. 255 (1980).

DISCUSSION TOPICS

1. Which of the three equity arguments described by Emerson do you find most convincing? Explain your reasoning.

2. Many in the land rights movements are populists, who believe that government should be decentralized and limited. Do you agree with this view? Why or why not?

3. The wise use movement argues on the basis of entitlement that fees for the use of public lands are interferences with the rights of private ownership. What is your evaluation of this position?

4. Assess the libertarian rationale that all regulation is theft because private property is an essential element of personal freedom.

5. Emerson points out that libertarians often forget those governmental measures that contribute to individual freedom. Explain and evaluate her reasoning.

6. Assess Emerson's opposition to using a specific percentage reduction in property value as an automatic requirement for compensation to the property owner.

READING 58

From *Free Market Environmentalism Today*

Terry L. Anderson and Donald R. Leal

Terry L. Anderson is executive director of the Political Economy Research Center (PERC) and professor of economics at Montana State University at Bozeman. He is the author or editor of twenty books. Donald R. Leal is a senior associate at PERC, Bozeman, Montana. His current research includes the study of federal and state management of public forests. In the following passage, drawn from the revised edition of Free Market Environmentalism Today *(2001), they challenge the common belief that governmental control is necessary to avoid environmental degradation. The key to free market environmentalism lies in well-defined property rights to natural resources; the role of government is to enforce these rights.*

. . . At the heart of free market environmentalism is a system of well-specified property rights to natural and environmental resources. Whether these rights are held by individuals, corporations, nonprofit environmental groups, or communal groups, a discipline is imposed on resource users because the wealth of the property owner is at stake if bad decisions are made. Moreover, if private owners can sell their rights to use resources, the owners must not only consider their own values, they must also consider what others are willing to pay. In the market setting, it is the potential for gains from trade that encourages cooperation. Both the discipline of private ownership and the potential for gains from trade stand in sharp contrast to the political setting. When resources are controlled politically, the costs of misuse are more diffused and the potential for cooperation is minimized because the rights are essentially up for grabs.

Perhaps the best example of how these characteristics of private ownership can enhance environmental quality comes from the Nature Conservancy, the largest environmental group in the United States that depends on private landownership. When the conservancy obtains title to a parcel of land, it uses a formal system for evaluating whether the property has significant ecological value. Consider the case in which the Wisconsin Nature Conservancy was given title to beachfront property on St. Croix, Virgin Islands. One might think that the Nature Conservancy would go to great lengths to prevent development of oceanside property in the Caribbean. But, indeed, it actually traded the property for a much larger tract in Wisconsin and allowed selective beachfront development to occur under some protective covenants.

Why would an environmental group let this happen? The answer, in a word, is tradeoffs. As owner of the beach, the Wisconsin Nature Conservancy had to ask what would be gained and what would be sacrificed if development was prevented. The gain was obviously beachfront protection. The sacrifice may not be obvious to the casual observer, but it was obvious to the organization. At the time, the Wisconsin Nature Conservancy was actively trying to complete protection of a watershed in southern Wisconsin. It did not have the money to buy the last parcel of land needed to complete the protection, but it saw an opportunity to trade St. Croix beachfront for the rocky hillside. As owner of the St. Croix property, the Nature Conservancy faced the cost of just saying no or reaping the benefit of an entrepreneurial trade. The discipline and the incentives of private ownership forced the conservancy to make careful decisions and allowed it to accomplish its goal of saving a watershed. As a result, the Nature Conservancy's wealth in the form of environmental amenities was enhanced.

The emphasis of free market environmentalism on private ownership and decentralized decision making should not be taken to mean that there is no role for government. On the contrary, government has an integral role to play in the definition and enforcement of property rights. In the absence of the rule of law, the incentives inherent in private ownership disappear and with them goes the potential for environmental stewardship. With clearly specified titles obtained from land recording systems, strict liability rules, and adjudication of disputed property rights in the courts, market processes can encourage owners to carefully weigh costs and benefits and to look to the future.

Free market environmentalism conflicts with traditional environmentalism in its visions regarding human nature, knowledge, and processes. A consideration of these visions helps explain why some people accept this way of thinking as an alternative to bureaucratic control and why others reject it as a contradiction in terms.

Human nature: Free market environmentalism views man as self-interested. This self-interest may be enlightened to the extent that people are capable of setting aside their own well-being for close relatives and friends or that they may be conditioned by moral principles. But beyond this, good intentions will not suffice to produce good results. Developing an environmental ethic may be desirable, but it is unlikely to change basic human nature. Instead of intentions, good resource stewardship depends on how well social institutions harness self-interest through individual incentives.

Knowledge: In addition to incentives, good resource stewardship depends on the information available to individuals who make decisions about resource use. Free market environmentalism views this information as being time- and place-specific rather than general and concentrated in the hands of experts. Whether we are considering interactions among humans or interactions between humans and nature, the information necessary for good management varies significantly from time to time and from place to place. Certainly there is some knowledge that is general and concentrated in the minds of experts, such as the laws of physics or principles of ecology, but the complexity of ecosystems makes them impossible to model and therefore to manage from afar. Given that this type of time- and place-specific information cannot be gathered in a single mind or groups of minds that can account for the multiple interconnections of ecosystems, decentralized management guided by the incentives of private ownership becomes an alternative to centralized political control.

Process or solutions: These visions of human nature and knowledge combine to make free market environmentalism a study of process rather than a prescription for solutions. If man can rise above self-interest and if knowledge can be concentrated, then the possibility for solutions through political control is feasible. But if there are self-interested individuals with diffuse knowledge, then processes must generate a multitude of solutions conditioned by the costs and benefits faced by individual decision makers. By linking wealth to good stewardship through private ownership, the market process generates many entrepreneurial experiments; and those that are successful will be copied, while those that are failures will not. The question is not whether the right solution will always be achieved, but whether good decisions are rewarded and bad ones penalized.

These three elements of free market environmentalism—self-interest, information, and process—also characterize the interaction of organisms in nature. Since Charles Darwin's revolutionary study of evolution, most scientific approaches have implicitly assumed that self-interest generally dominates behavior for higher as well as lower forms of life. Individual members of a species may act in altruistic ways and may cooperate with other species, but species survival depends on adjustments to changing parameters in ways that enhance the probability of individual and species survival. To assume that man is not self-interested or that he can rise above self-interest requires heroic assumptions about *Homo sapiens* vis-à-vis other species.

Ecology also emphasizes the importance of time- and place-specific information in nature. Because the parameters to which species respond vary considerably within ecosystems, each member of a species must respond to time- and place-specific characteristics with the knowledge that each possesses. These parameters can vary widely, so it is imperative for survival that responses utilize the diffuse knowledge. Of course, the higher the level of communication among members of a species, the easier it is to accumulate and concentrate time- and place-specific knowledge. But a giant leap of faith is necessary if humans are to be able to accumulate and

assimilate the necessary knowledge to manage the economy or the environment. Evidence from Eastern Europe underscores the problems that can arise with centralized management of either the economy or the environment.[1]

Continuing the analogy between ecology and free market environmentalism is instructive for thinking about the implications for policy. When a niche in a ecosystem is left open, a species will profit from filling that niche and will set in motion a multitude of other adjustments. If an elk herd grows because there is abundant forage, there will be additional food for predator species such as bears and wolves. Their numbers will expand as they take advantage of this profit opportunity. Individual elk will suffer from predation as elk numbers will be controlled. Plant species will survive and other vertebrates such as beavers will be able to survive. This is a process that no central planner could replicate because there is no best solution for filling niches and because each species is reacting to time- and place-specific information.

Comparing free market environmentalism with ecosystems serves to emphasize how market processes can be compatible with good resource stewardship and environmental quality. As survival rewards species that successfully fill a niche, increased wealth rewards owners who efficiently manage their resources. Profits link self-interest with good resource management by attracting entrepreneurs to open niches. If bad decisions are being made, then a niche will be open. Whether an entrepreneur sees the opportunity and acts on it will depend on his or her ability to assess unique information and act on that assessment. As with an ecosystem, however, the diffuse nature of this information makes it impossible for a central planner to determine which niches are open and how they should be filled. If the information or incentives are distorted because property rights are incomplete or because decision makers receive distorted information through political intervention, then the market process will not necessarily generate good stewardship.

Visions of what makes good environmental policy will change only if we realize that our current visions are not consistent with reality. We must ask ourselves whether well-intentioned individuals armed with sufficient information dominate the political decisions that affect natural resources and the environment. Forest policy analyst and environmentalist Randal O'Toole answered this question in the context of the U.S. Forest Service.

> While the environmental movement has changed more than the Forest Service, I would modestly guess that I have changed more than most environmental leaders. . . . In 1980, I blamed all the deficiencies in the markets on greed and big business and thought that government should correct these deficiencies with new laws, regulatory agencies, rational planning, and trade and production restrictions. When that didn't work, I continued to blame the failure on greed and big business.
>
> About 1980, someone suggested to me that maybe government didn't solve environmental or other social problems any better than markets. That idea seemed absurd. After all, this is a democracy, a government of the people, and what the people want they should be able to get. Any suggestion that government doesn't work was incomprehensible.
>
> But then I was immersed in the planning processes of one government agency for ten years (sort of like taking a Berlitz course in bureau-speaking). I learned that the decisions made by government officials often ignored the economic and other analyses done by planners. So much for rational planning. Their decisions also often went counter to important laws and regulations. So much for a democratic government.
>
> Yet, I came to realize that the decisions were all predictable, based mainly on their effects on forest budgets. . . .
>
> I gradually developed a new view of the world that recognized the flaws of government as well as the flaws in markets. Reforms should solve problems by creating a system of checks and balances on both processes. . . . The key is to give decision makers the incentives to manage resources properly.[2]

This book provides a "Berlitz course" in free market environmentalism that challenges entrenched visions. Because free market environmentalism depends on clearly specified property rights and accompanying price signals, it works better for some resources than for others. Markets can allocate land, water, and energy better than they can water quality or the global atmosphere. As we shall see, even on

the western frontier, free market environmentalism was at work as cattlemen and farmers developed property rights to land and water and avoided the tragedy of the commons. In contrast, since one-third of the nation was set aside in the late nineteenth century for federal management, special interest politics has resulted in fiscal and environmental mismanagement. But even in the case of public lands, the implications of free market environmentalism are being utilized to improve incentives for federal managers by allowing them to charge user fees and to keep those fees for reinvestment in improving those lands. Similarly, in the case of water allocation, markets are improving efficiency and increasing instream flows for fish, wildlife, and recreation.

If land and water allocation are easy problems for free market environmentalism, pollution concerns challenge the paradigm. Again, however, the focus on property rights, with the accompanying right to be free from trespass by pollutants, provides a way of thinking how polluters can be held accountable. If it is possible to identify who is releasing pollutants into the soil, water, or air and to determine what the impacts of those pollutants are, then broad regulations can be replaced with negotiations between those who are harmed and those who are causing the pollution. In this way, property rights allow those who want cleaner land, water, or air to charge those who want to use it for waste disposal and hence make polluters accountable for costs they create. . . .

. . . British economist A. C. Pigou . . . argued that because not all costs are taken into account by private decision makers, political intervention is necessary to correct what he saw as failures of the market.[3] Hence, in the case of a paper mill disposing of its wastes by dumping them into the air or water, the mill is imposing unwanted costs on the rest of society, costs for which the mill owners are not held accountable. With these costs unaccounted for by polluters, private decision makers will overuse the water and air for waste disposal, and people who want to use these resources for other purposes (e.g., swimming or breathing) will bear the costs.

To counter this market failure and maximize the value derived from natural resources, Pigou called for taxes or regulations on polluters imposed through a political process. In his words,

No "invisible hand" can be relied on to produce a good arrangement of the whole from a combination of separate treatments of the parts. It is therefore necessary that an authority of wider reach should intervene to tackle the collective problems of beauty, of air and light, as those other collective problems of gas and water have been tackled.[4]

Pigou believed that this authority should be given "to the appropriate department of central Government to order them (the polluters) to take action.[5]

Following the teaching of Pigou, economists and policy analysts have approached natural resource and environmental policy with the presumption that markets are responsible for resource misallocation and environmental degradation and that political processes can correct these problems. . . .

The purpose of this book is to challenge this traditional way of thinking and to provide a more realistic way of thinking about natural resource and environmental policy, thinking based on markets and property rights. This alternative recognizes and emphasizes the importance of incentives and of the costs of coordinating human actions. Rather than assuming that people are always altruistic, it presumes that self-interest prevails and asks how that self-interest can be harnessed to produce environmental goods that people demand. It does not assume that the costs of obtaining information or coordinating activities are zero or that there is perfect competition among producers. To the contrary, free market environmentalism focuses on how the costs of coordinating human actions (transaction costs, as economists label them) limit our ability to attain human goals through political processes and how markets can help overcome these costs. . . .

We emphasize from the outset that this way of thinking assumes that the environment's only value derives from human perceptions. Under this anthropocentric conception, the environment itself has no intrinsic value. People cannot manage natural resources for the sake of animals, plants, or other organisms because there is no Dr. Doolittle to "talk to the animals" and find out what is best for them. As long as humans have the power to alter the environment, they will do so based on human values—the only values that are ascertainable.

INCENTIVES AND TRANSACTION COSTS

In rethinking natural resource and environmental policy, two facts must be recognized. First, we cannot ignore the important role of incentives in guiding human behavior. No matter how well intended resource managers are, incentives affect their behavior. Like it or not, individuals will undertake more of an activity if the benefits of that activity are increased or if the costs reduced. This holds as much for bureaucrats and politicians as it does for profit-maximizing owners of firms or for citizens. Everyone accepts that managers in the private sector would dump production wastes into a nearby stream if they did not have to pay for the cost of their actions. Too often, however, we fail to recognize that the same elements work in the political arena. If a politician is not personally accountable for allowing oil development on federal lands or for the environmental impact of building dams on naturally flowing rivers, we can expect too much oil development or too many dams. Moreover, when the beneficiaries—call them special interest groups—of these policies do not have to pay the full cost, they will demand more of them from their political representatives.

Once incentive effects are recognized, we can no longer rely on good intentions to generate good resource stewardship and environmental quality. Even if the superintendent of a national park believes that grizzly bear habitat is more valuable than additional campsites, his good intentions will not necessarily result in the creation of more grizzly bear habitat. Hence, Grant Village, a tourist facility in the southern part of Yellowstone National Park, was built in the middle of prime grizzly bear habitat because politics, not science, dominated the decision.[6] In a political setting where commercial interests have more influence over a bureaucrat's budget, his peace and quiet, or his future promotions, good intentions by the bureaucrat will have to override political incentives if grizzly bear habitat is to prevail. Although possible in some cases, there is ample evidence that good intentions are not enough.

If a private resource owner believes that grizzly bear habitat is more valuable and can capture that value through a market transaction, then politics will not matter. Moreover, if those demanding the preservation of grizzly habitat are willing to pay more than those who demand campsites, then incentives and information reinforce each other. . . .

. . . [F]ree market environmentalism focuses our attention on the costs of coordinating human activities. The scribblings of Nobel laureate Ronald Coase brought the importance of transaction costs into the forefront of policy analysis.[7] Coase's important point was that transaction costs in the marketplace and in the political arena explain why individuals may not always be able to resolve their competing uses of resources and the environment. He explained that, in a world of zero transaction costs, markets would work perfectly because producers and consumers would know all. Producers would always supply consumers with what they want, and consumers would always be able to hold producers accountable for any costs created by production. In the political arena, zero transaction costs would also yield perfect results because citizens would have no problem communicating their demands to politicians or knowing whether their demands were being met.

Of course, transaction costs are not zero in the real world. Producers do not always know what consumers want. Consumers do not always get what they expect. And people who use resources or dispose of garbage in the environment are not always held accountable for their actions. It is this lack of accountability that explains almost all concerns about natural resource stewardship and environmental quality.

Consider what happens when two people engage in a trade where one offers meat raised on private land in exchange for fish caught in the open ocean. The supplier of meat must consider the impact of his grazing cattle on the future productivity of the land. If he grazes too many cattle this year, there will be less grass next year, and possibly no grass at all. The fish supplier, on the other hand, faces a very different set of costs. Catching fish this year means those fish will not have an opportunity to grow larger and to reproduce, but in the open ocean a fish left for tomorrow will be caught by another fisher. Hence, each fisher ignores the future value of the fishery and overharvests today. After all, a fish not taken will be caught by someone else. Indeed, tak-

ing a fish today imposes costs on all fishers tomorrow because fish will be smaller and will not be reproducing, but these costs are spread among all fishers, while the benefits redound to the individual.

This problem is known as the tragedy of the commons.[8] If access to a valuable resource such as an ocean fishery is unrestricted, people entering the commons to capture its value will ultimately destroy it. Even if each individual recognizes that open access leads to resource destruction, there is no incentive for him to refrain from harvesting the fish. If he does not take it, someone else will, and therein lies the tragedy. . . .

The tragedy of the commons can also result in not enough production of a good thing if people can free ride on the actions of others. For example, if one individual or group sets aside land for biodiversity, the benefits of that biodiversity may redound to many people who did nothing to help provide it. As long as third parties can enjoy environmental amenities without paying for them, there is the potential for a free ride and therefore the possibility that the amenities will be underproduced. In other words, if third-party costs result in too much pollution, third-party benefits (free riding) result in too little production of environmental amenities.

All of these tragedies raise two questions: who has what rights and what are the costs associated with defining and enforcing those rights? Where rights are clearly defined and easily enforced, as in the case of surface land, there is no tragedy because entry is limited by the owner's fence. If party A dumps his garbage on party B's land, party B can enforce his right against trespass. On the other hand, where rights are not well defined or easily enforced, as with the right to clean air, trespass is much more difficult to prevent. It is much more difficult to identify who owns the fish, the water, or the air than it is to specify who owns the land, making enforcement against trespass a much tougher task. If the value of preserving wilderness is derived mainly by those who wish to hike in that wilderness, then the landowner can install pay booths at entrances and collect payment for the services he is providing. If the value is derived mainly by people who enjoy sitting in their offices thinking about the existence of wilderness, however, it will be more difficult for the owner/provider of wilderness to collect for his efforts.

Reenter transaction costs. If it were costless to organize to restrict entry into the commons, the tragedy would never occur. It does occur, however, because organizing to restrict entry is costly. People will not always know the impact of their actions until it is too late and the commons is overexploited. Even if they do recognize the potential for tragedy, the costs of organizing can be high. Bargaining to agree on who will fish and when and forming binding agreements to restrict fishing will be costly especially to the extent that detection of violators is difficult. . . .

MARKETS AND POLITICS COMPARED

Though there is a myriad of processes for coordinating human interaction in order to benefit from potential gains from trade (for example, families, clubs, or totalitarian states) and to prevent the tragedy of the commons, we compare and contrast transaction costs in the context of two—market processes and political processes. The important point is that although the information and contracting costs outlined above are endemic to both coordination processes, costs and benefits faced by decision makers differ systematically between the two and thus affect incentives and outcomes.

Information Costs

First, consider information costs. In a world of scarce resources, private and political resource managers must obtain information about the relative values of alternative uses of everything from land to wildlife to air. When one resource use rivals another, tradeoffs must be made, and resource managers can only make these tradeoffs based on the information they receive, or on their own personal values. For example, if timber managers believe lumber is more valuable than wildlife habitat, they will cut trees. Timber managers may know how fast trees grow under different soil and climate conditions, but they cannot know the value of that growth without incurring some cost of surveying how consumers value the wood.

In the marketplace, prices provide an objective measure of subjective preferences and are therefore an important source of information about subjective values. Because each of us places different value on environmental amenities, there must be some way of quantifying and aggregating those values. Some see a forest as a place for quiet hikes, while others see it as a place for snowmobiling. Some see a rain forest as a jungle that, when cleared, can grow crops, while others see it as a source of biodiversity. Psychology can tell us a little about how these values are formed and influenced by peers, parents, advertising, genetics, and so on, but ultimately they are subjective to each individual.

Once individuals undertake market trades to achieve their desires, their bids provide an objective measure of these subjective values because bidders must give up one thing of value to obtain another. In the case of timberlands, private and public timber managers can obtain relatively comprehensive information on the value of wood from a lumberyard, where people offer money, which could be used to purchase other goods and services, for the wood products they value more highly. In the absence of markets for wildlife habitat or hiking trails, however, obtaining values is more costly. Nonetheless, private timber managers in a company such as International Paper obtain information on the value of wildlife amenities through an active market for hunting, camping, and other recreation on their private lands. When leasing its land for these activities, the company faces a tradeoff between timber harvesting, which produces revenue from wood products, and recreational land uses, which produce revenue from not cutting trees. Decisions on land use are driven by the differences in potential profit between the two activities.

Prices also allow a measure of efficiency through profits and losses. If a shareholder wants to know how well the management of his firm is performing, he can at least consult the profit and loss statement. This may not be a perfect measure of performance, but continual losses suggest that actual results differ from desired results. This can indicate to the shareholder that he should consider alternate managers who can produce the product at a lower cost or that he should reconsider the market for the product. Unlike the political sector, where the output of government is not priced and where agency performance is not measured by the bottom line, profits and losses in the private sector provide concise information with which owners can measure the performance of their agents.

In the public sector, on the other hand, there are few market prices and no profits to motivate decisions. Loggers compete in auctions for timber sales and thus provide some objective measure of market values, but recreational users of public lands generally pay little or nothing for the services they receive. Hence information on recreational values must be revealed through the political process. Special interest groups may articulate their demands through voting, campaign contributions, and letter-writing campaigns, to mention a few. In this process, lumber companies might argue that timber harvesting is the most important use of public land, while environmental groups will argue that wilderness values should trump all other values, including logging.

Hence free market environmentalism identifies systematic differences in the way information about subjective values is communicated in markets and politics. In the marketplace, prices lower information costs by converting subjective values into objective measures. In a democratic political process, the main counterpart to prices for signaling values is voting. Voting is a signal that, at best, communicates the subjective values of the median voter and, especially given that voter turnout is often low and representative of organized interest groups, communicates the subjective values of special interest groups. While information costs are positive in both processes, prices offer a low-cost mechanism for articulating subjective values, and connect the person paying the price with the actual cost of the product or service. . . .

. . . [T]he key to getting the incentives right through free market environmentalism is to establish property rights that are well defined, enforced, and transferable. Consider each of these elements.

The physical attributes of the resources must be defined in a clear and concise manner if individuals are to reap the benefits of their good actions and are to be held accountable for their bad actions. The rectangular survey system, for example, allows us to define ownership rights over land and clarifies some disputes over ownership. This system may also help us define ownership to the airspace over land, but more questions arise here because of the fluidity of air and the infinite vertical third dimension above ground. If property rights to resources cannot be defined, they obviously cannot be exchanged for other property rights.

Property rights must also be defendable. A rectangular survey may define surface rights to land, but conflicts are inevitable if there is no way to defend the boundaries and prevent other incompatible uses. Barbed wire provided an inexpensive way to defend property rights on the western frontier; locks and chains do the same for parked bicycles. But enforcing one's rights to peace and quiet by "fencing out" sound waves is more difficult, as is keeping other people's hazardous wastes out of a groundwater supply. Whenever the use of property cannot be monitored or enforced, conflicts are inevitable and trades are impossible.

Finally, property rights must be transferable. In contrast to the costs of measuring and monitoring resource uses, which are mainly determined by the physical nature of the property and technology, the ability to exchange is determined largely by the legal environment. Although well-defined and enforced rights allow the owner to enjoy the benefits of using his property, legal restrictions on the sale of that property hinder the potential for trade gains. Suppose that a group of fishers values water for fish habitat more highly than farmers value the same water for irrigation. If the fishers are prohibited from renting or purchasing the water from the farmers, then gains from trade will not be realized and potential wealth will not be created. The farmer will, therefore, have less incentive to leave the water in the stream.

In sum, free market environmentalism requires well-specified rights to take actions with respect to specific resources. If such rights cannot be measured, monitored, and marketed, then there is little possibility for exchange. Garbage disposal through the air, for example, is more of a problem than solid waste disposal in the ground because property rights to the atmosphere are not as easily defined and enforced as are ones involving the Earth's surface. Private ownership of land works quite well for timber production, but measuring, monitoring, and marketing the land for endangered species habitat requires entrepreneurial imagination—especially if the species migrate over large areas. . . .

ADDRESSING THE CRITICS

There are three main critiques of free market environmentalism: free market environmentalism considers only economic values and ignores environmental values; free market environmentalism pays too little attention to the distribution of rights; and free market environmentalism's focus on markets and politics ignores other important allocative institutions.[9]

Which Values: Economic or Environmental?

Because free market environmentalism focuses on human values, it is criticized by those who argue that saving the environment is a moral issue, not an economic one. Philosopher Mark Sagoff puts it this way:

> Lange's Metalmark, a beautiful and endangered butterfly, inhabits sand dunes near Los Angeles for the use of which developers are willing to pay more than $100,000 per acre. Keeping the land from development would not be efficient from a microeconomic point of view, since developers would easily outbid environmentalists. Environmentalists are likely to argue, however, that preserving the butterfly is the right thing morally, legally, and politically—even if it is not economically efficient.[10]

Assuming that property rights to the land in question are well defined and that the environmental values can be captured, Sagoff is correct.[11] Free market environmentalism argues that the willingness of developers to outbid environmentalists tells us which values are higher. This is not to say that moral values have no place in decisions or that moral suasion is not a valuable tool for influencing human behavior. Sagoff further asserts that "environmentalists are concerned about saving magnificent landscapes and species, keeping the air and water clean, and in general getting humanity to tread more lightly on the Earth. They are not concerned . . . about satisfying

preferences on a willing-to-pay basis."[12] Turning moral values into political issues and arguing that it is a matter of treading more lightly on the Earth, however, becomes another form of rent seeking, wherein people with one set of moral values get what they want at the expense of others.

Whose Rights?

The second criticism of free market environmentalism is that it pays too little attention to the distribution of rights. The issue here is who has claims over resources and therefore who must pay whom.[13] To the extent that those wanting to save magnificent landscapes and species must pay landowners for those landscapes and habitats, distribution will be important. It is entirely possible that people with environmental preferences will not have enough wealth to act on their preferences. It is here that environmentalists like to take a page from Marx and suggest that "what is important is not the choices people *do* make but the choices people *would* make if they were free of their corrupt bourgeois ideology."[14] By this reasoning, it is easy to say that environmentalists would be willing to pay more if only they had the resources. Of course, this is not verifiable through voluntary trading and thus opens the door for political redistribution.

A related argument is that the distribution of wealth favors people with nonenvironmental preferences over those with environmental preferences.[15] In the case of public lands, making people pay for use of national parks or forests is unfair because it precludes poor people from using the parks. In the case of private land, big corporations already have the rights to use the land, and poor environmentalists cannot afford to purchase these rights from them. In response, there is the empirical question of whether poor people do, in fact, use environmental amenities such as national parks at their current low price. If they do not, what is the justification for subsidizing the environmental amenity for use by the wealthy? Second, because poor people do not have access to many amenities, there may be an argument for redistributing income in their favor, but the redistribution does not have to come in the form of in-kind services from national parks. If they had more income, they could decide how to spend it without subsidizing wealthy park visitors. Finally, is it the case that environmentalists who demand environmental goods and services are poor compared to the rest of the population? A growing body of evidence suggests that the demand for environmental quality is highly sensitive to income and that members of environmental groups have quite high incomes, thus this argument seems tenuous.[16]

Is the Choice between Only Markets and Politics?

As described above, market processes and political processes are but two alternatives for addressing natural resource use and environmental quality. Even within each of these there are gradations between individual resource owners, corporate owners, town governments, and national governments. It is becoming better recognized that between markets and government are community organizations that can play a role in resource allocation.[17] These might be communities of fishers who regulate access to a fishery[18] or tribal members who restrict access to a grazing common.[19] In either case, how well the institutional arrangement works will depend on its ability to generate information on values and provide incentives for individuals to act on those values. Thought of in this way, free market environmentalism is less about markets and government and more about how various management institutions determine environmental values and how decision makers respond to that information.

CONCLUSION

Which institutional process is more likely to move resources from lower- to higher-valued alternatives is ultimately an empirical question. Traditional natural resource economics has generally concluded that markets do not do very well and that the political process can do better . . .

. . . Traditional economic analysis stresses the potential for market failure in the natural resource and environmental arena on the grounds that externalities are pervasive. Free market environmentalism explicitly recognizes that this problem arises because it is costly to define, enforce, and trade rights

in both the private and political sectors. In fact, the symmetry of the externality argument requires that specific attention be paid to politics as the art of diffusing costs and concentrating benefits. Assuming that turning to the political sector can solve externality problems in the environment ignores the likelihood that government will externalize costs. Just as pollution externalities can generate too much dirty air, political externalities can generate too much water storage, clear-cutting, wilderness, or water quality.

Free market environmentalism emphasizes the importance of market processes in getting more human value from any given stock of resources. Only when rights are well defined, enforced, and transferable will self-interested individuals confront the tradeoffs inherent in a world of scarcity. . . .

NOTES

1. Mikhail S. Bernstam, "Comparative Trends in Resource Use and Pollution in Market and Socialist Economies," in *The State of Humanity,* ed. Julian Simon (Cambridge, MA: Blackwell Publishers, 1995), 503–22.
2. Randal O'Toole, "Learning the Lessons of the 1980s," *Forest Watch* 10 (January–February 1990): 6.
3. A. C. Pigou, *The Economics of Welfare* (London, England: Macmillan, 1920).
4. Ibid., 195.
5. Ibid.
6. Alston Chase, *Playing God in Yellowstone* (Boston: Atlantic Monthly Press, 1986).
7. Ronald Coase, "The Problem of Social Cost," *Journal of Law and Economics* 3 (October 1960): 1–44.
8. Garret Hardin, "The Tragedy of the Commons," *Science* 162 (December 1968).
9. For several articles critiquing free market environmentalism, see Mark Sagoff, "Free Market Versus Libertarian Environmentalism," *Critical Review* 6 (spring/summer 1992): 211–30.
10. Sagoff, "Free Market," 214.
11. The free market environmentalism argument is premised on the existence of property rights.

It can always be argued that externalities exist and therefore that market exchanges won't work, but this is an efficiency argument, not a moral argument.

12. Sagoff, "Free Market," 218.
13. Coase, "The Problem of Social Cost."
14. Sagoff, "Free Market," 218.
15. Peter S. Menell, "Institutional Fantasylands: From Scientific Management to Free Market Environmentalism," *Harvard Journal of Law and Public Policy* 15 (1992): 489, 509.
16. Jane S. Shaw, "Environmental Regulation: How It Evolved and Where It Is Headed," *Real Estate Issues* 1 (1996): 6.
17. Elinor Ostrom, *Governing the Commons: The Evolution of Institutions for Collective Action* (New York: Cambridge University Press, 1990).
18. Donald R. Leal, "Community-Run Fisheries: Avoiding the Tragedy of the Commons," *PERC Policy Series* No. PS-7 (Bozeman, MT: Political Economy Research Center, September 1996).
19. Terry L. Anderson, "Conservation—Native American Style," *PERC Policy Series* No. PS-6 (Bozeman, MT: Political Economy Research Center, July 1996).

DISCUSSION TOPICS

1. Anderson and Leal discuss the visions of human nature, knowledge, and processes that inform free market environmentalism. Do you agree with these visions? Why or why not?
2. Give an example of an environmental problem in your community in which third parties involuntarily bear some of the cost of the transaction. Can you propose a solution based on new kinds of private property rights?
3. Can the value of everything be expressed in a price? Why or why not?
4. Should we develop private property rights in endangered species? In portions of the human genome? Explain your reasoning.

READING 59

At the Monument to General Meade, or on the Difference between Beliefs and Benefits

Mark Sagoff

Mark Sagoff is senior research scholar in the School of Public Affairs at the University of Maryland, College Park. The following selection is excerpted from an article published in Arizona Law Review *in 2001. Using the example of Gettysburg National Military Park, Sagoff demonstrates that, according to environmental economics (as found, for example, in the preceding article by Anderson and Leal), resources should go to those willing to pay the most for them. For Sagoff, this approach is fundamentally mistaken. Public deliberation about values does and should decide social policy about entities that possess intrinsic value, such as endangered species and old-growth forests.*

When you visit Gettysburg National Military Park, you can take a tour that follows the course of the three-day battle. The route ends at the National Cemetery, where, four months after the fighting, Abraham Lincoln gave the 270-word speech that marked the emergence of the United States as one nation.[1] The tour will not cover all of the battlefield, however, because much of it lies outside the park. Various retail outlets and restaurants, including a Hardee's and a Howard Johnson's, stand where General Pickett, at two o'clock on a July afternoon in 1863, marched 15,000 Confederate soldiers to their deaths. The Peach Orchard and Wheatfield, where General Longstreet attacked, is now the site of a Stuckey's family restaurant.[2] The Cavalry Heights Trailer Park graces fields where General George Custer turned back the final charge of the Confederate cavalry.[3] Over his restaurant, Colonel Sanders, purveyor of fried chicken, smiles with neon jowls upon the monument to George Meade, the victorious Union general.[4] Above this historic servicescape looms a 310-foot commercial observation tower many Civil War buffs consider to be "a wicked blight on the battlefield vista."[5]

One spring day, on my way to give a seminar on "economics and the environment" at Gettysburg College, I drove quickly past the battlefield where 23,000 Union and 28,000 Confederate soldiers fell in three days. I felt guilty speeding by the somber fields, but I had to teach at two o'clock. I checked my watch. I did not want to be late. How do you keep your appointments and still find time to pay homage to history? . . .

I. ARE BATTLEFIELDS SCARCE RESOURCES?

I began the seminar at Gettysburg College by describing a Park Service plan, then under discussion, to build new facilities to absorb the tide of visitors—an increase of 400,000 to 1.7 million annually—that welled up in response to "Gettysburg," a 1993 movie based on Michael Shaara's blockbuster novel, *The Killer Angels.* [6] Working with a private developer, the Park Service proposed to construct a new $40 million visitor center, including a 500-seat family food court, a 450-seat theater, and a 150-seat "upscale casual" restaurant with "white tablecloth" service, gift shops, parking lots, and a bus terminal not far from the place where Lincoln delivered the Gettysburg Address.[7] Several senators, including Senate Majority Leader Trent Lott (R-Miss.), objected that the project "commercializes the very ground and principle we strive to preserve.[8] . . .

. . . [T]he upscale tourist mall envisioned by the initial Park Service plan seemed, at least to Senator Lott, to elevate commercialism into a principle for managing Gettysburg. Rather than stand by the principle of commercialism or consumer sovereignty, however, the Park Service scaled back its plan.[9] . . .

Since the seminar took place in mid-afternoon—siesta time in civilized societies—I had to engage the students. I did so by proposing a thesis so outrageous and appalling that the students would attack me and it. I told the class that the value of any environment—or of any of its uses—depends on what people now and in the future are willing to pay for it. Accordingly, the Park Service should have stuck with its original plan or, even better, it should have auctioned the battlefield to the highest bidder, for example, to Disney Enterprises.[10]

I asked the students to bear with me long enough to consider my proposal in relation to the subject of the seminar, the theory of environmental economics. This theory defends consumer sovereignty as a principle for environmental policy. More specifically, this theory asserts that the goal of environmental policy is to maximize social welfare at least when equity issues—matters involving the distribution of benefits among individuals—are not pressing.[11] Welfare, in turn, is defined and measured by consumer willingness to pay ("WTP") for goods and services. According to this theory, environmental policy should allocate goods and services efficiently, that is, to those willing to pay the most for them and who, in that sense, will benefit from their enjoyment, possession, or use.

In the United States, unlike Europe, I explained, battlefields are scarce resources which, like any scarce environmental asset, should be allocated efficiently. To be sure, the Park Service tries to accommodate tourists. The problem, though, is that the Park Service does not exploit heritage values as efficiently as a competitive market would. At present, Gettysburg is woefully underutilized, or so I argued. Even Dollywood, Dolly Parton's theme park in rural east Tennessee, attracts more visitors every year.[12] The Park Service does not even try to allocate the resources efficiently. It pursues goals that are not economic but ethical; it seeks to educate the public and honor "the valor and sacrifices of those men who fought and died on that ground for their beliefs."[13]

A young lady in the class blurted out, "But that's what the Park Service should do." She acknowledged that the Park Service has to provide visitor services. It should do so, she said, only to the extent that it will not "detract from what they did here," to paraphrase President Lincoln.[14] This young lady thought that the history of the place, rather than what people are willing to pay for alternative uses of it, determined its value. She understood the significance of "what they did here" in moral and historical, rather than economic, terms. The value of hallowed ground or of any object with intrinsic value has nothing to do with market behavior or with WTP, she said.

I explicated her concern the following way. A private developer, I explained, might not realize in gate receipts at Gettysburg the WTP of those individuals, like herself, who wished to protect an area for ethical or aesthetic reasons. I promised to describe to the class the contingent valuation ("CV") method economists have developed to determine how much individuals are willing to pay for policies consistent with their disinterested moral beliefs. Using this method, the Park Service could take her preference and therefore her welfare into account. It could then identify the policy that maximizes benefits over costs for all concerned, whether that concern is based on consumer desire or on ethical commitment.

This reply, I am afraid, did little more than taunt the student. In stating her opinion, she said, she implied nothing about her own well-being. She described what she thought society ought to do, not what would make her better off. The student did not see how scientific management, by measuring costs and benefits, served democracy. The Park Service, she added, had no responsibility, legal or moral, to maximize "satisfactions," including hers. Rather, it had an obligation to keep faith with those who died on that ground for their beliefs. No CV survey, no amount of WTP, she said, could add to or detract from the value of Gettysburg. No action we take could alter, though it may honor or dishonor, what the soldiers did there; no cost-benefit study, however scientific, could change our obligation to those who gave their lives that this nation might live.

II. CONSERVATION REVISITED

To prepare for the seminar, I had asked the students to read "Conservation Reconsidered,"[15] an essay economist John V. Krutilla published in 1967 in response to neoclassical economists, who studied the effects of technological advance on economic growth. Neoclassical macroeconomists like James Tobin,[16] Robert Solow, and William Nordhaus[17] argued that technological progress would always make more abundant materials do the work of less abundant ones — for example, the way kerosene substituted for whale oil in providing household illumination.[18] Solow, a Nobel laureate in economics, wrote that "[h]igher and rising prices of exhaustible resources lead competing producers to substitute other materials that are more plentiful and therefore cheaper."[19] These economists adopted a model of economic growth that

contained two factors: capital (including technology) and the labor to apply it.[20] This model differed from that of classical economists, such as Ricardo and Malthus, because "resources, the third member of the classical triad, have generally been dropped."[21]

In this essay, Krutilla cited studies to show that advancing technology has "compensated quite adequately for the depletion of the higher quality natural resource stocks."[22] He observed that "the traditional concerns of conservation economics — the husbanding of natural resource stocks for the use of future generations — may now be outmoded by advances in technology."[23] Krutilla, along with other environmental economists in the 1970s, rejected the view that the resource base imposes limits on growth.[24] . . .

The neoclassical model of growth, insofar as it takes natural resources for granted, did not sit well with environmentalists, many of whom rejected neoclassical thinking and joined the maverick discipline of ecological economics, which emphasizes traditional Malthusian concerns about resource depletion.[25] . . .

Krutilla and other mainstream environmental economists, to find fertile fields for research, moved the focus of their science from macroeconomic to microeconomic analysis.[26] Microeconomists study the behavior of individuals and firms as they trade in competitive markets. When markets fail to properly bring buyers together with sellers, prices at which goods and services change hands may fail to reflect the full WTP for them and the full costs involved in producing them. Microeconomists identify ways to correct market failure and to make prices better reflect marginal supply and demand.[27]

Pollution is the standard example. If the production of a good, say, an automobile, imposes costs, for example, dirty air, on members of society for which they are not compensated, these individuals unwillingly subsidize the production or consumption of that item. This subsidy distorts markets because it encourages the overproduction of some things (e.g., cars) and the underproduction of other things (e.g., clean air) relative to what people want to buy. The production and use of cars imposes social costs, costs on society, that are not reflected in the private costs, prices people pay, to own and drive those cars. This gap between social and private costs, economists reason, justifies regulation.

As early as 1920, welfare economist A. C. Pigou distinguished between "private" and "social" costs and characterized pollution as an unpriced "externality" or social cost of production.[28] Pigou had also proposed the solution: the solution: to tax the difference between private costs, those reflected in prices, and social costs, those people bear without compensation, so that the prices charged for polluting goods would reflect the full costs, including the pollution costs, that go into providing them.[29]

. . . The microeconomic analysis of pollution in terms of a divergence between private and social costs, however, has had little if any effect on public policy. Pollution control law relies for its justification on common law principles of nuisance, not on a Pigouvian concept of market failure. Public law regulates pollution, in other words, not as an "externality" to be controlled to the extent that the benefits outweigh the costs, but as an invasion, trespass, or tort.[30]

Krutilla and his colleagues saw a way, however, to apply the Pigouvian analysis of market failure far, far beyond the problems of pollution. These economists knew that people often make sacrifices, e.g., by paying dues, to support causes and to vindicate convictions concerning the natural world. These beliefs or commitments surely involve values; values, in the context of economic theory, suggest costs or benefits and, therefore WTP, that market prices may not fully capture.[31] This WTP, if entered into a social cost-benefit analysis, could serve environmentalism by justifying regulation. . . .

III. MORAL COMMITMENT AS MARKET DEMAND

. . .

Krutilla argued that if people value natural objects because they are natural, then technological advance cannot provide substitutes for them. Among the permanently scarce phenomena of nature, Krutilla cited familiar examples including "the Grand Canyon, a threatened species, or an entire ecosystem or biotic community essential to the survival of the threatened species."[32] On this basis, Krutilla and many colleagues reinvented environmental economics as a "new conservation"[33] that addresses the failure of markets to respond to the "existence" or "nonuse" value of natural objects people want to preserve

but may not intend to experience, much less use or consume.

Krutilla was correct, of course, in observing that people often are willing to pay to preserve natural objects such as endangered species. Among them, for example, is Tom Finger, a Mennonite, who said, "we're eliminating God's creatures. All these nonhuman creatures . . . have a certain intrinsic worth because they are part of God's creation."[34] People who believe species have an intrinsic worth may be willing to pay to protect them. Does this suggest that endangered species are scarce resources? Do those who believe extinction is wrong suffer a loss, a kind of social cost, when species vanish? Does endangered species habitat have an economic value that market prices fail to reflect? . . .

Krutilla's analysis suggests an argument to show that a private firm should manage Dollywood but not Gettysburg, even if the principle of consumer sovereignty applies to both. At Dollywood, the owners can capture in gate and table receipts total WTP for the goods and services the resort provides. Owners who respond to market signals supply just those goods and services the public most wants to buy. The managers of Dollywood, moreover, cover all the costs in labor, materials, etc., of their business. The prices they charge, then, will reflect the full social costs involved in producing what they sell.

At Gettysburg, it is different. Patriotic Americans, many of whom may never visit the area, may be willing to pay to restore the battlefield or to save it from commercial exploitation. Private, for-profit owners of Gettysburg would have no incentive to take this WTP into account, however, because they cannot capture it in gate and table receipts. . . .

This kind of economic argument may appeal to environmentalists because it opposes the privatization of places, such as Gettysburg, that possess intrinsic value. This argument seems especially appealing because it rejects privatization for economic reasons—the very sorts of reasons that might be thought to justify it. Since this Pigouvian analysis leads to comfortable conclusions, environmentalists might embrace it. Why not agree with respect to all environmental assets, whether in places like Dollywood or in places like Gettysburg? After all, the cost-benefit analysis, once it factors in the WTP of environmentalists, surely will come out in favor of protecting the environment.

The problem is this: to buy into this argument, one must accept the idea that the same goal or principle — net benefits maximization — applies to both Dollywood and Gettysburg.[35] Critics of economic theory may contend, however, that the approach to valuation appropriate at Daydream Ridge in Dollywood is not appropriate at Cemetery Ridge in Gettysburg. At Daydream Ridge, the goal is to satisfy consumer demand. At Cemetery Ridge, the goal is to pay homage to those who died that this nation might live.

To say that the nation has a duty to pay homage to those from whom it received the last full measure of devotion is to state a moral fact. You can find other moral facts stated, for example, in the Ten Commandments.[36] The imperative "Thou shalt not murder" should not be understood as a policy preference for which Moses and other like-minded reformers were willing to pay. Rather, like every statement of moral fact, it presents a hypothesis about what we stand for — what we maintain as true and expect others to believe — insofar as we identify ourselves as a moral and rational community.

Our Constitution puts certain questions, for example, religious belief, beyond the reach of democracy. Other moral questions, over military intervention in conflicts abroad, for example, invite reasoned deliberation in appropriate legislative councils. Environmental controversies, once the issues of resource scarcity are removed from the agenda, turn on the discovery and acceptance of moral and aesthetic judgments as facts. The belief that society should respect the sanctity of Cemetery Ridge states a moral fact so uncontroversial nobody would doubt it. This tells us nothing, however, about a scarcity of battlefields, an inelasticity of hallowed ground, market failure, or the divergence of social and private costs. It suggests only that the principle of consumer sovereignty that economists apply to evaluate management decisions at Dollywood does not apply at Gettysburg or, indeed, wherever the intrinsic value of an environment is at stake.[37]

IV. ARE BELIEFS BENEFITS?

By construing intrinsic or existence value as a kind of demand that market prices fail to reflect, Krutilla and other environmental economists envisioned a brilliant strategy to respond to the quandary in which neoclassical economic theory had placed them.[38] They kept their credentials as mainstream economists by accepting the neoclassical macroeconomic model with respect to resources the economy uses. Yet they also "greened" their science by attributing a general scarcity to "non-use" resources such as wilderness, species, scenic rivers, historical landmarks, and so on, that people believe society has a duty to preserve. Indeed, by applying the divergence-of-private-and-social-cost argument not just to pollution but also to every plant, animal, or place that anyone may care about for ethical or cultural reasons, economic theory performed a great service to environmentalists. Environmentalists now could represent their moral, religious, or cultural beliefs that WTP market prices failed to reflect.[39] At last, they could claim that economic science was on their side.[40]

By transforming moral or cultural judgments about the environment into preferences for which people are willing to pay, Krutilla and his colleagues in the early 1970s achieved a great deal. First, they created a complex research agenda centering on the measurement of benefits associated with non-use or existence value.[41] Since 1970, indeed, research in environmental economics, both theoretical and empirical, has been preoccupied with measuring the economic benefits people are supposed to enjoy as a result of environmental policies consistent with their moral and religious beliefs.[42]

Second, Krutilla and his colleagues created a division of labor between policy scientists and policy consumers.[43] As policy scientists, economists lay down the goals and principles of environmental policy — indeed of all social policy — on the basis of their own theory and without any political deliberation, consultation, or process.[44] Economists Edith Stokey and Richard Zeckhauser, for example, assert that "public policy should promote the welfare of society."[45] A. Myrick Freeman III explains, "The basic premises of welfare economics are that the purpose of economic activity is to increase the well-being of the individuals who make up the society."[46] In a widely used textbook, Eban Goodstein states, "Economic analysts are concerned with human welfare or well-being. From the economic perspective, the environment should be protected for the material benefit of humanity and not for strictly moral or ethical reasons."[47]

As policy consumers, citizens make judgments about what is good for them.[48] Economists reiterate that "each individual is the best judge of how well off he or she is in a given situation."[49] Henry Ford is reputed to have said that people could have automobiles "in any color so long as it's black."[50] From the standpoint of economic theory, individuals can make any social judgment they wish, as long as it concerns the extent to which policy outcomes harm or benefit them.[51]

Economists may offer a ceremonial bow in the direction of markets, but this is quickly followed by a story of market failure followed by a call for centralized management based on cost-benefit analysis.[52] Experts, i.e., economists themselves, must teach society how to allocate resources scientifically, since markets cannot cope with environmental public goods. In markets, individuals make choices and thus function as agents of change. In microeconomic theory, in contrast, individuals function not as agents but primarily as sites or locations where WTP may be found.

Third, as the methodology for benefits estimation developed, it typically assigned very high shadow prices to existence values, and this appealed to environmentalists. An endangered butterfly, for example, may be worth millions if every American is willing to pay a dime for its survival. Public interest groups, who associated economists with the enemy, now saw that economic science could be their friend.[53] Environmentalists, who might have complained that industry groups had "numbers," could now come up with numbers, too.[54] And since WTP adds up quickly when aggregated over all members of society, environmentalists could be sure that the numbers would come out "right."

V. IS EXISTENCE VALUE A KIND OF ECONOMIC VALUE?

To establish a connection between existence value and economic value, economists have to explain in what sense people benefit from the existence of goods they may neither experience nor use. To be sure, individuals are willing to pay to protect endangered species, rain forests, and other wonders of na-

ture they may never expect to see. That they are willing to pay for them, however, does not show that they expect to benefit from them. Generally speaking, just because a person's preferences are all his own, it does not follow that the satisfaction of all or any of those preferences necessarily improves his welfare or well-being. The students in my class were quite willing to contribute to a fund to protect hallowed ground at Gettysburg. They did so, however, largely from a sense of moral obligation and not in any way or manner because they thought they would be better off personally if the battlefield were preserved. . . .

VI. CONTINGENT VALUATION

During the past thirty years, economists have worked hard to develop a method, known as contingent valuation ("CV"), to assess the "existence" or "non-use" values of natural phenomena.[55] The CV method, as one authority writes, "is based on asking an individual to state his or her willingness to pay to bring about an environmental improvement, such as improved visibility from lessened air pollution, the protection of an endangered species, or the preservation of a wilderness area."[56] The authors of a textbook write that the CV method "asks people what they are willing to pay for an environmental benefit. . . ."[57] They see this method as "uniquely suited to address non-use values."[58]

Contrary to what this textbook asserts, the CV questionnaire never asks people what they are willing to pay for an environmental *benefit*. It asks respondents to state their WTP for a particular policy outcome, for example, the protection of a rare butterfly. Economists interpret the stated WTP for the environmental improvement as if it were WTP for a personal benefit the respondent expects it to afford her or him. Yet a person who believes that society ought to protect a species of butterfly may have no expectation at all that he or she will benefit as a result. . . .

Respondents to CV questions express disinterested views about policy rather than judgments about what will benefit them. Reviewing several CV protocols, economists concluded that "responses to CV questions concerning environmental preservation are dominated by citizen judgments concerning desirable social goals rather than by consumer preferences."[59] . . .

We should not confuse WTP to protect a battle-field, species, or wilderness with WTP for some sort of benefit. Battlefields and benefits constitute different goods which can be provided and should be measured separately. If economists cared to measure the economic value, i.e., the benefits, of alternative outcomes, the CV questionnaire should ask respondents to state their WTP for the welfare change they associate [with] an environmental policy. Here is an imaginary protocol I suggested to the class:

Many people believe society should respect the "hallowed ground" at Gettysburg for moral, cultural, or other disinterested reasons. This questionnaire asks you to set aside all such disinterested values; it asks you not to consider what is right or wrong or good or bad from a social point of view. In responding to this survey, consider only the benefit you believe you will experience, i.e., the personal satisfaction, if the battlefield is preserved. Please state your WTP simply for the welfare change you expect, not your WTP for the protection of the battlefield itself.

Since CV questionnaires in fact ask nothing about benefits, responses to them tell us nothing relevant to economic valuation. Yet CV methodology, which economists have been developing for decades, has become the principal technique policy-makers use to measure "nonmarket benefits based primarily on existence value" of assets such as old-growth forests and endangered species.

As philosopher Ronald Dworkin points out, many of us recognize an obligation to places and objects that reflects a moral judgment about what society should do, not a subjective expectation about what may benefit us.[60] He writes that many of us seek to protect objects or events—which could include endangered species, for example—for reasons that have nothing to do with our well-being. Many of us "think we should admire and protect them because they are important in themselves, and not just if or because we or others want or enjoy them."[61] The idea of intrinsic worth depends on deeply held moral convictions and religious beliefs that underlie social policies for the environment, education, public health, and so on. Dworkin observes:

Much of what we think about knowledge, experience, art, and nature, for example, presupposes that in different ways these are valuable in themselves and not just for their utility or for the pleasure or satisfaction they bring us. The idea of intrinsic value is commonplace, and it has a central place in our shared scheme of values and opinions.[62]

Beliefs are not benefits. If economists believe that society should allocate resources to maximize welfare, they do not necessarily think this because they will be better off as a result. They are not simply trying to increase demand for their services. Similarly, as the evidence cited above suggests, people who believe that society should protect endangered species, old-growth forests, and other places with intrinsic value do not necessarily think that this will improve their well-being.[63] A person who wants the Park Service to respect hallowed ground may consider that policy justified by the historical qualities of the battlefield and not by the welfare consequences for her. It is hard to understand, then, how CV measures the non-market benefits of environmental goods.[64] If responses to CV surveys are based on moral beliefs or commitments, there would seem to be no relevant benefits to measure.

. . .

The central argument of environmental economics, then, comes to this: An allocation of resources to those willing to pay the most for them maximizes net benefits; net benefits, in turn, are measured in terms of the amount people are willing to pay for those resources. The central contention of environmental economics is logically equivalent to the claim that resources should go to those willing to pay the most for them, because they are willing to pay the most for those resources. In this tautology, the terms "welfare" or "well-being" simply drop out. These terms function only as stand-ins or as proxies for WTP and cannot logically be distinguished from it. The measuring rod of money—or WTP—correlates with and measures nothing but itself.

Environmental economics fails as a normative science because it cannot tell us why or in what sense an efficient allocation is better than a less efficient one. Lacking all normative content, terms like "utility," "well-being," or "welfare" fail to move environmental economics from the "is" of WTP to the "ought" of value or valuation.

VIII. NAKED PREFERENCES

A young man in the class wondered aloud if this critique of environmental economics had gone too far. The CV method, after all, attributes enormous economic value to so-called "useless" species and to remote places that few people may visit. Instead of rejecting this technique, he suggested, we should be grateful for it. "To the extent that people are willing to pay for existence value—whether the protection of species and habitats, the functioning of ecosystems, or the dignity of Gettysburg—these intangibles are appropriately included in the overall calculus of benefit," he said. He added that the CV method, because it aggregates WTP for policy preferences, provides valuable information to policymakers. This is true whether preferences reflect judgments about personal benefit or judgments about the goals or values of society.

The student suggested, then, that even if WTP and economic value are logically equivalent, environmental economics retains its usefulness as a policy science. He conceded that references to "welfare" or "well-being" could be dismissed as window-dressing. All that matters is WTP itself as an expression of preference. Preferences still matter whether or not they are based on self-interest or on moral or political judgment.

This view expresses what many economists believe. "The modern theory of social choice," writes W. Michael Hanemann, "considers it immaterial whether preferences reflect selfish interest or moral judgment."[65] This view goes back at least to Kenneth Arrow's observation: "It is not assumed here that an individual's attitude toward different social states is determined exclusively by commodity bundles which accrue to his lot under each. . . . [T]he individual orders all social states by whatever standards he deems relevant."[66]

Let us drop the reference to welfare or well-being, then, from the fundamental thesis of environmental economics. We are left, then, with the idea that preferences, as weighed or ranked by WTP, should be satisfied insofar as the resource base allows. "In this framework, preferences are treated as

data of the most fundamental kind," writes economist Alan Randall.[67] "Value, in the economic sense, is ultimately derived from individual preferences."[68]

What sort of value can be derived from preferences? If we no longer refer to welfare or well-being, it is hard to understand why the satisfaction of preferences, weighed by WTP, matters. Plainly, individuals should have the greatest freedom possible, consistent with the like freedom of others, to try to satisfy their preferences, promote their beliefs, and vindicate their values both in markets and through democratic political processes. The statement that people should be free to pursue their own goals through social institutions that are equitable and open expresses a piety nobody denies.

The thesis that social policy should aim at satisfying people's preferences, in contrast, expresses a dogma of welfare economics for which no good argument can be given. Having a preference may give the individual a reason to try to satisfy it, and he or she should have the greatest freedom to do so consistent with the like freedom of others. Absent a reference to a meaningful social goal such as welfare or well-being, however, what reason does society have to try to satisfy that preference? . . .

Democracy relies on deliberative discourse in public to evaluate policy options. The point of political deliberation in a democracy is to separate, on the basis of argument and evidence, more reasonable from less reasonable policy proposals. The Park Service held public meetings (but did not commission CV studies) to reevaluate its plan for Gettysburg. It sought out the opinions of those who knew the history of the place. As a result, it located the new facility in an area where no soldier had fallen.[69] The outcome of political and moral deliberation depends less on the addition of individual utilities than on the force of the better argument about the public interest.[70]

IX. DESIGNING FOR DILEMMAS

. . .

Environmental agencies may find it difficult . . . to embrace an approach to regulation that relies on collaboration and deliberation rather than centralized science-based decision making. The statutes under which these agencies operate, such as the

Clean Air Act, tend to be so vague, so aspirational, and so precatory that they offer little or no guidance to an agency that has to answer the hard questions, such as how safe or clean or natural is enough. The agency, in the absence of a meaningful mandate, has to find some way to give its decisions legitimacy. It therefore cloaks its ethical determinations in the language of science. Environmental professionals, in their eagerness to speak truth to power, may encourage this reliance on their disciplines.

The problem, however, is that science has no moral truth to speak; it cannot say how safe, clean, or natural is safe, clean, or natural enough. Nevertheless, agencies defend moral and political decisions with arguments to the effect that, "The science made me do it."[71] Environmental agencies, though they must adopt regulations that are ethical at some level, rarely, if ever, offer a moral argument or principle for Congress to review and citizens to consider and debate. Instead, agencies tend to use the best available science to answer moral and political questions the science cannot possibly answer. And the environmental sciences — strained in this way well beyond their limits — lose credibility as a result.[72]

X. RETREAT FROM GETTYSBURG

After the seminar, I chose a route out of Gettysburg that avoided the battlefield and, with it, the ghosts of the past. But my path was full of portents of the future. At a 110-acre site southeast of the battleground, which had served as a staging area for Union troops, I saw equipment gathered to construct the massive mall the Park Service decided not to build. The developer, the Boyle Group of Malvern, Pennsylvania, according to its promotional literature, promises to erect an "authentic village" containing seventy outlet stores, an eighty-room country inn, and a large restaurant. According to the flyer, visitors to Gettysburg will find the village a refuge from the drudgery of touring the battlefield and learning its history. "History is about the only thing these millions of tourists take home," the promo states. "That's because there is no serious shopping in Gettysburg."[73]

Society can count on firms such as the Boyle Group to provide shopping as serious as anyone

could want at Gettysburg and everywhere else. The nation does not have to elevate shopping and, with it, the allocation of goods and services to those willing to pay the most for them, to the status of legislation. Environmental laws state general moral principles or set overall goals that reflect choices we have made together. These principles and goals do not include the empty and futile redundancy of environmental economics — the rule that society should allocate resources to those willing to pay the most for them because they are willing to pay the most for those resources.

An agency, such as the Park Service, may engage in public deliberation to determine which rule to apply in the circumstances. The principle economists tout, net benefits maximization, is rarely if ever relevant or appropriate. At Gettysburg, the principle speaks for itself. "What gives meaning to the place is the land on which the battle was fought and the men who died there," as longtime Gettysburg preservationist Robert Moore has said. "Keeping the place the same holy place, that's what's important."[74]

NOTES

1. Abraham Lincoln, "The Gettysburg Address" (1863), reprinted in *Lincoln on Democracy* at 307 (Mario M. Cuomo & Harold Holzer eds., 1990).
2. See George Will, "A Conflict over Hallowed Ground," *New Orleans Times-Picayune,* June 11, 1998, at B7. For a brief description of the events, see Lisa Reuter, "Gettysburg: The World Did Long Remember," *Columbus Dispatch,* Dec. 5, 1999, at 1G ("At the wheat field alone, 6000 men fell in 2½ hours. One soldier would later write, 'Men were falling like leaves in autumn; my teeth chatter now when I think of it.' So many bodies covered the field, remembered another, that a person could walk across it without touching the ground.").
3. See Rupert Cornwell, "Out of the West; Developers March on Killing Fields," *Independent* (London), Dec. 18, 1991, at 10 (43,000 deaths in total).
4. The Kentucky Fried Chicken restaurant has long occupied the area near the monument and

by now may have its own authenticity. Kentucky nominally never left the Union.

5. Will, *supra* note 2, at B7.

6. See Michael Shaara, *The Killer Angels: A Novel* (1974). For details about the effect on the visitor load, see Will *supra* note 2, at B7.

7. For a description of the Park Service plan and its history, see Edward T. Pound, "The Battle over Gettysburg," *USA Today,* Sept. 26, 1997, at 4A.

8. Stephen Barr, "Hill General Retreats on Gettysburg Plan," *Wash. Post,* Oct. 2, 1998, at A25. See also Ben White, "Lawmaker Criticizes Plan for Gettysburg," *Wash. Post,* Feb. 12, 1999, at A33.

9. See Brett Lieberman, "Park Service Unveils Revised Gettysburg Plan," *Plain Dealer* (Cleveland), June 19, 1999, at 14A.

10. In fact, such a proposal is not as far-fetched as it sounds. See Heather Dewar, "Corporate Cash Eyed for Parks, Bill Puts Sponsorships at $10 Million Apiece," *Denver Post,* June 8, 1996, at A1; "Parks May Get "Official" Sponsors, Senate Measure Would Lure Corporate Bucks," *St. Louis Post-Dispatch,* June 9, 1996, at 1A. This plan was much derided. See, *e.g.,* Joshua Reichert, "Commercializing Our National Parks a Bad Joke," *Houston Chron.,* Sept. 23, 1996, at 19.

11. From the perspective of welfare economics, a regulation is rational — it promotes the welfare of society — only if it confers on members of society benefits in excess of costs. Since the benefits and costs may well accrue to different individuals, welfare economists recognize two fundamental values in terms of which regulatory policy may be justified. The first is economic *efficiency,* which is to say, the extent to which total benefits of the policy exceed total costs. The second goal is *equity,* which is to say, the extent to which the distribution of costs and benefits is equitable or fair. For a presentation of this view, see generally Arthur M. Okun, *Equality and Efficiency: The Big Tradeoff* (1975). He writes, "This concept of efficiency implies that more is better, insofar as the 'more' consists in items people want to buy." *Id.* at 2.

12. Dollywood attracts about 2 million patrons annually and is open only during the warmer months. See "Dollywood" (visited Mar. 26, 2000) <http://company.monster.com/dolly/>.

13. [APCWS Position on Proposed Gettysburg Development Plan (statement by Denis P. Galvin, Deputy Director, National Park Service, Feb. 24, 1998) (visited Mar. 26, 2000) <http://users.erols.com/va-udc/nps.html>.]

14. See Lincoln, *supra* note 1.

15. John V. Krutilla, "Conservation Reconsidered," 57 *Am. Econ. Rev.* 777 (1967).

16. See, *e.g.,* William D. Nordhaus & James Tobin, "Is Economic Growth Obsolete?" 5 *Econ. Growth* 1 (1972).

17. See generally William D. Nordhaus, *Invention, Growth, and Welfare: A Theoretical Treatment of Technological Change* (1969).

18. See Daniel Yergin, *The Prize: The Epic Quest for Oil, Money, and Power* 22 (1992).

19. Robert M. Solow, "Is the End of the World at Hand?" in *The Economic Growth Controversy* 39, 53 (Andrew Weintraub et al. eds., 1973) [hereinafter Solow, "End of the World"]. Solow sought to establish that technological change, rather than the resource base, is essential to economic production. See, *e.g.,* Robert M. Solow, "A Contribution to the Theory of Economic Growth," 70 *Q.J. Econ.* 65 (1956); Robert M. Solow, "Technical Change and the Aggregate Production Function," 39 *Rev. Econ. & Stat.* 312 (1957).

20. Solow argued that if the future is like the past, raw materials will continually become more plentiful. See Solow, "End of the World," *supra* note 19, at 49.

21. Nordhaus & Tobin, *supra* note 16, at 14. Many mainstream economists accept Solow's argument. As analyst Peter Drucker has written, "[w]here there is effective management, that is, application of knowledge, we can always obtain the other resources." Peter Drucker, *Post Capitalist Society* 45 (1993). Others have argued that our technical ability to substitute resources for one another is so great that "the particular resources with which one starts increasingly become a matter of indifference. The reservation of particular resources for

later use, therefore, may contribute little to the welfare of future generations." Harold J. Barnett & Chandler Morse, *Scarcity and Growth: The Economics of Natural Resource Availability* 11 (1963).

22. Krutilla, *supra* note 15, at 777.

23. *Id.* at 778.

24. See *id.* at 784. See also, *e.g.,* V. Kerry Smith, "The Effect of Technological Change on Different Uses of Environmental Resources," in *Natural Environments: Studies in Theoretical and Applied Analysis* 54, 54–87 (John V. Krutilla ed., 1972). Smith wrote, "advances in scientific knowledge and a mastery of techniques have been sufficiently pervasive and rapid to allow for an ever expanding supply of natural resource commodities at constant or falling supply prices." *Id.* at 54.

25. See, *e.g.,* Robert Costanza et al., "Goals, Agenda, and Policy Recommendations for Ecological Economics," in *Ecological Economics: The Science and Management of Sustainability* 1, 8 (Robert Costanza ed., 1991) (arguing that we have "entered a new era" in which "the limiting factor in development is no longer manmade capital but remaining natural capital").

26. See, *e.g.,* Edwin Mansfield, *Microeconomics: Theory and Applications* (2d ed. 1976). Mansfield writes that economics is divided "into two parts: microeconomics and macroeconomics. Microeconomics deals with the economic behavior of individual units like consumers, firms, and resource owners; while macroeconomics deals with the behavior of economic aggregates like gross national product and the level of unemployment." *Id.* at 2.

27. See generally *The Theory of Market Failure: A Critical Examination* (Tyler Cowen ed., 1988).

28. See A. C. Pigou, *The Economics of Welfare* 172–203 (4th ed. 1932).

29. See *id.*

30. Since pollution is clearly a form of coercion rather than of exchange, to ask how much pollution society should permit is to ask how far one individual may use the person or property of another without his or her consent. Nothing in our law, shared ethical intuitions, or cultural history supports or even tolerates the utilitarian principle that one person can trespass upon another—indeed, should do so—whenever the benefits to society exceed the costs. See, *e.g., United States v. Kin-Buc, Inc.,* 532 F. Supp. 699, 702–03 (D.N.J. 1982) (holding that the Clean Air Act preempts federal common law claims of nuisance for air pollution). See also William C. Porter, "The Role of Private Nuisance Law in the Control of Air Pollution," 10 *Ariz. L. Rev.* 107, 108–17 (1968).

The non-utilitarian basis of pollution control law is so obvious that, as Maureen Cropper and Wallace Oates observe, "the cornerstones of federal environmental policy in the United States," such as the Clean Air and Clean Water Acts, "*explicitly* prohibited the weighing of benefits against costs in the setting of environmental standards." Maureen L. Cropper & Wallace E. Oates, "Environmental Economics: A Survey," 30 *J. Econ. Lit.* 675, 675 (1992) (emphasis in original).

31. For an illustrative example of this sort of reasoning, see E. B. Barbier et al., "Economic Value of Biodiversity," in *Global Biodiversity Assessment* 823, 829 (V. H. Heywood ed., 1995) ("Moral or ethical concerns, like tastes and preferences, can be translated into a willingness to commit resources to conserve biodiversity.").

32. Krutilla *supra* note 15 at 778.

33. *Id.* at 783.

34. Carlyle Murphy, "A Spiritual Lens on the Environment; Increasingly, Caring for Creation Is Viewed as a Religious Mandate," *Wash. Post,* Feb. 3, 1998, at A1.

35. "Market-determined prices," some economists claim, "are the only reliable, legally significant measures of value. . . . [T]he value of a natural resource is the sum of the value of all of its associated marketable commodities, such as timber, minerals, animals, and recreational use fees." Daniel S. Levy & David Friedman, "The Revenge of the Redwoods? Reconsidering Property Rights and the Economic Allocation of Natural Resources," 61 *U. Chi. L. Rev.* 493, 500–01 (1994) (discussing the possibility of WTP estimates for existence values).

36. See Exodus 20:3–17.

37. Gettysburg here serves as an example of any moral decision that confronts society. Economists have applied the WTP criterion to adjudicate the most important moral decisions that confront society. For example, economists have argued that the decision to wage war in Vietnam represented not a moral failure or political failure, but a market failure. The decision to carry on the war failed to reflect the WTP demonstrators revealed, for example, in the travel costs they paid to protest against it. See generally Charles J. Cicchetti et al., "On the Economics of Mass Demonstrations: A Case Study of the November 1969 March on Washington," 61 *Am. Econ. Rev.* 179 (1971).

    Whatever the question, from segregation in housing to certain kinds of slavery, practices people oppose for moral reasons may also be characterized as objectionable for economic reasons, once the WTP of those opponents is factored into the cost-benefit analysis. See generally Duncan Kennedy, "Cost-Benefit Analysis of Entitlement Problems: A Critique," 33 *Stan. L. Rev.* 387 (1981).

    Microeconomists sometimes seem to hold that WTP can adjudicate all questions of truth, beauty, and justice. The use of WTP or utility "to measure preferences can be applied quite generally," three economists explain. "Utility or preference exists for any activity in which choice is involved, although the choices may themselves involve truth, justice, or beauty, just as easily as the consumption of goods and services." Jonathan A. Lesser et al., *Environmental Economics and Policy* 42 (1997).

38. That is, the quandary involved in finding a subject matter for environmental economics to study when mainstream economics had determined that natural resources could be taken for granted.

39. The high-water mark of this approach to environmental evaluation may be found in Robert Costanza et al., "The Value of the World's Ecosystem Services and Natural Capital," 387 *Nature* 253 (1997) (estimating the economic benefits of the world's ecosystem services and natural capital at $33 trillion per year).

40. See, *e.g.,* Pete Morton, "The Economic Benefits of Wilderness: Theory and Practice," 76 *Denv. U. L. Rev.* 465, 465 (1999) ("While steadfastly acknowledging that the economic benefits of wilderness will never be fully quantified, without at least qualitatively describing and understanding these benefits, politicians and public land managers will continue to make policy decisions that short-change wilderness in public land management decisions."). Some environmentalists question the use of contingent valuation largely for technical reasons. See, *e.g.,* Kristin M. Jakobsson & Andrew K. Dragun, *Contingent Valuation and Endangered Species* 78–82 (1996).

41. For examples of this research agenda, see *Valuing Natural Assets: The Economics of Natural Resource Damage Assessments* (Raymond J. Kopp & V. Kerry Smith eds., 1993).

42. For a good review of the literature, see generally A. Myrick Freeman III, *The Benefits of Environmental Improvement: Theory and Practice* (1979).

43. See Krutilla, *supra* note 15 at 779 n.7 (describing environmentalists as having subjective reactions to, rather than objective opinions about, the loss of a species or the disfiguring of an environment).

44. For a general statement and defense of the position of welfare economics in environmental policy, see Daniel C. Esty, "Toward Optimal Environmental Governance," 74 *N.Y.U. L. Rev.* 1495 (1999). See also Louis Kaplow & Steven Shavell, "Property Rules Versus Liability Rules: An Economic Analysis," 109 *Harv. L. Rev.* 715, 725 (1996) (taking the cost-benefit balance to define ideal regulation).

45. Edith Stokey & Richard Zeckhauser, *A Primer for Policy Analysis* 277 (1978).

46. A. Myrick Freeman III, *The Measurement of Environmental Resource Values* 6 (1993).

47. Eban S. Goodstein, *Economics and the Environment* 24 (2d ed. 1999).

48. Commentators generally refer to this idea as the principle of consumer sovereignty. For a general statement of how this principle fits within the foundations of economic theory, see Martha Nussbaum, "Flawed Foundations: The

Philosophical Critique of (a Particular Type of) Economics," 64 *U. Chi. L. Rev.* 1197, 1197–98 (1997).

49. Freeman, *supra* note 46, at 6.

50. For a discussion of Ford's beliefs see Roland Marchand, *Advertising the American Dream: Making Way for Modernity, 1920–1940,* at 118, 156–58 (1985).

51. Following social choice theory, economists apply the principle of consumer sovereignty to all views but their own — in other words, they regard everyone else as having wants rather than ideas. For the classic statement of this position, see Joseph Schumpeter, "On the Concept of Social Value," 23 *Q.J. Econ.* 213, 214–17 (1909).

52. See, *e.g.,* Allen V. Kneese & Blair T. Bower, "Introduction," in *Environmental Quality Analysis: Theory and Method in the Social Sciences* 3–4 (Allen V. Kneese & Blair T. Bower eds., 1972).

53. See Kennedy, *supra* note 37, at 401–21.

54. Critics of Krutilla's approach charged that it came primarily "from economists desperately eager to play a more significant role in environmental policy and environmental groups seeking to gain the support of conservatives." Fred L. Smith, Jr., "A Free-Market Environmental Program," 11 *Cato J.* 457, 468 n.15 (1992).

55. For commentaries, see generally John F. Daum, "Some Legal and Regulatory Aspects of Contingent Valuation," in *Contingent Valuation: A Critical Assessment* [389 (J. A. Hausman ed., 1993)]; William H. Desvousges et al., "Measuring Natural Resource Damages with Contingent Valuation: Tests of Validity and Reliability," in *Contingent Valuation: A Critical Assessment, supra,* at 91.

56. James R. Kahn, *The Economic Approach to Environmental and Natural Resources* 102 (2d ed. 1998).

57. Lesser et al., *supra* note 37, at 282.

58. *Id.*

59. R. Blamey et al., "Respondents to Contingent Valuation Surveys: Consumers or Citizens?" 39 *Australian J. Agric. Econ.* 263, 285 (1995).

60. See Ronald Dworkin, *Life's Dominion: An Argument About Abortion, Euthanasia, and Individual Freedom* 69–77 (1993).

61. *Id.* at 71–72. See also *id.* at 75–77 (discussing the preservation of animal species).

62. *Id.* at 69–70.

63. Experiments show again and again that responses to CV questionnaires express what the individual believes to be good in general or good for society and not — as the CV methods seek to determine — what individuals believe is good for *them.* See, *e.g.,* Thomas H. Stevens et al., "Measuring the Existence Value of Wildlife: What Do CVM Estimates Really Show?" 67 *Land. Econ.* 390 (1991); Thomas H. Stevens et al., "Measuring the Existence Value of Wildlife: Reply," 69 *Land Econ.* 309 (1993).

64. Some economists agree and write: "[I]t may be inappropriate to use the [contingent valuation methodology] as an input to [benefit cost analysis] studies, unless means can be found to extract information on consumer preferences from data predominantly generated by citizen judgments." Blamey et al., *supra* note 59, at 285.

65. W. Michael Hanemann, "Contingent Valuation and Economics," in *Environmental Valuation: New Perspectives* 79, 105 (K. G. Willis & J. T. Corkindale eds., 1995).

66. Kenneth J. Arrow, *Social Choice and Individual Values* 17 (2d ed. 1963).

67. Alan Randall, *Resource Economics: An Economic Approach to Natural Resource and Environmental Policy* 156 (1981).

68. *Id.*

69. See Elizabeth Stead Kaszubski, Letter to the Editor, "Park Plan Honors 'Hallowed Ground'," *USA Today,* June 24, 1999, at 14A (describing the events that transpired at the spot where the Park Service proposed to build its new Visitors' Center).

70. See generally Jürgen Habermas, *Justification and Application: Remarks on Discourse Ethics* (Ciaran Cronin trans., 1993).

71. As Judge Williams remarked in *American Trucking,* "[I]t seems bizarre that a statute intended to improve human health would, as EPA claimed at argument, lock the agency into looking at only one half of a substance's health effects in determining the maximum level for that substance." *American Trucking*

Ass'n v. EPA, 175 F.3d 1027, 1052 (D.C. Cir. 1999), modified on reh'g, 195 F.3d 4 (D.C. Cir. 1999), petition for cert. filed, Feb. 28, 2000 (No. 99-1442). The point here is that the EPA, by citing the "knee-of-the-curve" or any other moral basis for its decision, could meet the requirements that Judge Williams and democratic theory impose on them. Utterly mired in the progressive tradition, however, the EPA will not concede that it makes moral or political judgments but will hide these judgments behind a smokescreen of environmental science. Even the threat by the D.C. Circuit panel—that the EPA's interpretation of the statute might be voided for over-delegation unless the agency acknowledges the ethical judgments it makes and must make—is unlikely to dislodge the agency from its scientism.

72. For commentary, see Sheila Jasanoff, *The Fifth Branch* 1 (1990) (arguing that appeals to science should not "take the politics out of policymaking"); Bruce Bimber & David H. Guston, "Politics by the Same Means: Government and Science in the United States," in *Handbook of Science and Technology Studies* 554, 559 (Sheila Jasanoff et al., 1995); Sheila Jasanoff, "Research Subpoenas and the Sociology of Knowledge," *Law & Contemp. Probs.,* Summer 1996, at 95, 98–100 (describing the deleterious effect of the expectations of law on the community of scientists).
73. Pound, *supra* note 7, at 4A.
74. *Id.* (quoting Robert Moore).

DISCUSSION TOPICS

1. Should the Park Service have auctioned the battlefield to the highest bidder? Why or why not? Explain your answer.
2. Sagoff defines environmental economics as the theory that the goal of environmental policy is to maximize social welfare, defined as consumer willingness to pay (WTP) for goods and services. Do you agree that this is the appropriate goal for environmental policy? Provide reasons for your view.
3. Do you agree with economists such as Solow that technological progress means that resources will never be scarce? Apply your answer to automobile transportation.
4. Explain the concept of "existence" or "nonuse" value of natural objects. Why does Sagoff believe that environmentalists should not use this concept?
5. Sagoff says that "science has no moral truth to speak." Do you agree? Why or why not?

READING 60

Genuine Progress Indicator (GPI) Accounting: Relating Ecological Integrity to Human Health and Well-Being

Mark Anielski and Colin L. Soskolne

Mark Anielski is director of sustainability measurement at the Pembina Institute for Appropriate Development, in Vancouver and Toronto, Canada. Colin L. Soskolne is professor of epidemiology and graduate coordinator in the Department of Human Health Sciences at the University of Alberta. *The following selection is from* Just Ecological Integrity: The Ethics of Maintaining Planetary Life *(2002). Anielski and Soskolne argue that current economic measurements such as the Gross National Product (GNP) focus exclusively on monetary measures of well-being and ignore the physical condition and welfare of human beings and the environment. They propose a more comprehensive measurement, the Genuine Progress Indicator.*

FUNDAMENTAL FLAWS IN MEASURING ECONOMIC PROGRESS

Paradoxically, the word "economy" comes from the Greek oikonomia, meaning the careful management or stewardship of the household. "Ecology" is comprised of the words "oikos" (household) and "logia" (knowledge or logic). Anielski (2000) argues that modern economics has lost its soul by focusing almost exclusively on monetary (chrematistic) measures of well-being to the exclusion of measuring the physical condition and welfare of individuals, households, communities and the environment.

For example, the United Nation's System of National Accounts (UNSNA) and the GDP, derived from the national accounts, simply account for the monetary value of the goods and services produced in an economy while ignoring the physical realities of the "living capital" (human, social, natural) which contributed to this production (Anielski 2000).

Indeed, Simon Küznets (1965), the original architect of the USA's GDP and System of National Accounts and 1971 winner of the Nobel Prize in economics, warned the US Congress that: "The welfare of a nation can scarcely be inferred from a measurement of national income as defined (by the GDP). Goals for more growth should specify of what and for what." Robert Kennedy once remarked that the "Gross National Product (GNP or GDP) measures everything, in short, except that which makes life worthwhile" (Kennedy [1993] 1968).

The GDP ignores, for example, the value of many important activities, such as unpaid work (housework, parenting, eldercare, volunteerism) and the value of ecosystem services in providing society with clean air, water and waste assimilation. Neither does the GDP distinguish between expenditures in the economy that contribute to genuine improvements in human, social and environmental "health" or well-being, and those that were made to mitigate or repair damage to or erosion of human health (e.g., disease), social cohesion (e.g., crime) or [ecological integrity] EI. Indeed, the greater the level of production and the more money changing hands, the greater the GDP grows.

The GDP also does not distinguish between health care expenditures that contribute to improved human health and those made to mitigate against disease, injury or other human health outcomes that are impacted by various determinants of health (socio-economic, environmental, genetic, and others). When decision-makers use the GDP and other economic variables to guide decision-making, they are diagnosing the health of the patient "economy" through a very narrow lens.

GENUINE PROGRESS INDICATOR WELL-BEING ACCOUNTING

In order to measure the total health and well-being of the economy, society and the environment, a more comprehensive system of accounting for the physical conditions of total well-being or total wealth is needed. The Genuine Progress Indicator (GPI) System of Sustainable Well-being Accounts has been developed by Anielski et al. (2001) to address this challenge, providing a more holistic diagnostic tool for measuring the overall health and well-being of nations. The new GPI accounting system has been applied for the first time to the province of Alberta, Canada (Anielski et al. 2001).

GPI accounting takes an inter-disciplinary, integrated approach to assessing the condition of overall well-being and thus is ideally suited to measuring the overall conditions of and risks to human health, social cohesion, and EI. However, GPI accounts do not provide a definitive answer to discerning where epidemiological and EI thresholds may exist. Rather, they provide evidence of long-term trends in the condition of all "living capital."

GPI accounts allow decision-makers to diagnose the total health and well-being at the individual, household, societal (community) and the environmental scale. GPI accounts provide meaningful indicators of the condition and sustainability of "living capital" (human, social, and natural-environmental) and produced capital (manufactured and financial).

One of the strengths of the GPI accounting system is that it takes a traditional accounting approach. Using both physical and qualitative inventories or assessments of all capital, and monetary values of production, the data can be presented in the form of a GPI balance sheet and net sustainable income statement. The GPI balance sheet, for example, shows the current and historical physical conditions of all assets and liabilities related to human, social, natural and produced capital. The GPI balance sheet provides an early warning system of emerging risks to sustainable well-being. The GPI income statement accounts for the full costs and benefits associated with economic production (GDP)

TABLE 1

THE ALBERTA GENUINE PROGRESS INDICATORS OF SUSTAINABLE WELL-BEING

GPI Economic Well-Being Indicators	GPI Social-Human Well-Being Indicators	GPI Environmental Well-Being Indicators
Economic growth	Poverty	Oil and gas reserve life
Economic diversity	Income Distribution	Oilsands reserve life
Trade	Unemployment	Energy use intensity
Disposable income	Underemployment	Agriculture sustainability
Weekly wage rate	Paid work time	Timber sustainability
Personal expenditures	Household work	Forest fragmentation
Transportation expenditures	Parenting and eldercare	(ecological integrity)
Taxes	Free time	Fish and wildlife
Savings rate	Volunteerism	Parks and wilderness
Household debt	Commuting time	Wetland
Public infrastructure	Life expectancy	Peatland
Household infrastructure	Premature mortality	Water quality
	Infant mortality	Air quality related emissions
	Obesity	Greenhouse gas emissions
	Suicide	Carbon budget deficit
	Drug use	Hazardous waste
	Auto crashes	Landfill waste
	Divorce	Ecological footprint
	Crime	
	Problem gambling	
	Voter participation	
	Educational attainment	

in an economy. These include accounting for the total costs and benefits associated with consuming human, social and natural-environmental capital in the production of goods and services. The structure of the GPI income statement is drawn from the original USA GPI model by Cobb, Halstead and Rowe (1995) at Redefining Progress and updated by Anielski and Rowe (1999) for measuring sustainable economic welfare.

From the data contained in the GPI accounts, indicators of well-being (genuine progress indicators) can show longitudinal trends. For example, the Alberta GPI accounts developed by Anielski et al. (2001) include some 51 indicators of well-being (Table 1). The breadth of the database and the GPI's open architecture lends itself to analyzing the interrelationships of variables that determine human health and ecological well-being outcomes. For example, changes in human health conditions can be compared with trends in the condition of ecosys-

tems, natural resource stocks or socio-economic conditions. The accounts can also be used to show liabilities or risks to well-being that may be emerging in areas of social cohesion (e.g., poverty, income inequality), ecosystem fragmentation, toxic waste production and other risk factors.

GPI Accounts yield a longitudinal time series of: 1) the physical-qualitative inventory of stocks and flows of living and produced capital, and; 2) monetary accounts or full cost-benefit accounts related to the consumption of living and produced capital. From this inventory, any number or combination of indicators and composite indicators of genuine well-being, sustainability, or quality of life can be derived. These could include indicators of EI.

There are limitations to the GPI accounts, including lack of data and incompatible data time-series. Nor do the indicators themselves reveal causality between a driver or multiple drivers and health or ecological outcomes. The indicators provide only a

FIGURE 1

USA GDP GROWTH (PER CAPITA) VERSUS GPI (PER CAPITA), 1950 TO 1999

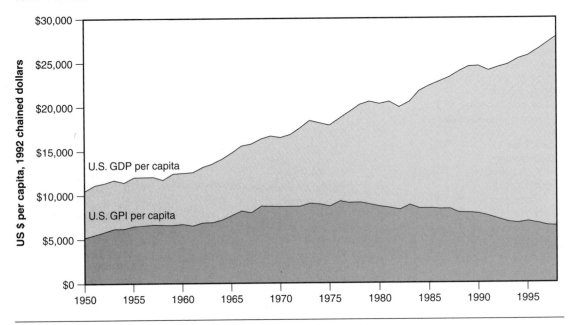

Source: Data derived from spreadsheets from the U.S. Genuine Progress Indicator (GPI) for 1999. Redefining Progress, Oakland, CA

rough portrait of overall well-being. GPI accounts do, however, allow decision-makers to assess the tradeoffs, relationships and common trends between variables. For example, the GDP can be compared with trends in human health (e.g., disease, premature mortality, suicide), environmental degradation, natural resource depletion and social costs (e.g., crime).

LIVING CAPITAL DECLINES WHILE THE ECONOMY BOOMS

The Alberta GPI accounts by Anielski et al. (2001) show that economic growth (GDP) from 1961 to 1999 has been mirrored by a dramatic loss of EI (fragmentation) of Alberta's forests. The Alberta GPI accounts also reveal declines in the stock and quality of other natural capital including forests, agricultural soils, and ground water and wildlife habitat. . . .

The USA GPI results for 1999 show that USA GDP per capita rose steadily from 1950 to 1999, yet

the GPI, a wider account of economic well-being, rose with GDP up until the mid-1970s, then has declined since its peak (Figure 1). The key determinants of this decline in sustainable economic well-being (GPI) are rising income inequality, declining stocks of non-renewable energy resources (oil and gas), loss of wetlands and old-growth forest ecosystems, and the growing environmental costs associated with greenhouse gas emissions and the accumulated costs of ozone-depleting substances (e.g., CFCs). In addition, there have been rising levels of the cost of crime, family breakdown and a net loss of quality leisure time.

EVIDENCE OF DECLINING LIVING CAPITAL

Using the detailed cost and benefit analysis contained in the 1999 USA GPI accounting system of data spreadsheets (Anielski and Rowe 1999) and analysis by Anielski (2000), a comprehensive "report" card of the changes (trends) in key indicators of well-being in the USA was developed (see Table 2 [pages 544–545]). This total "well-being diagnostic report card" shows where the USA is better or worse off in 1999, relative to 1950, or after almost 50 years of economic progress. Of the 28 indicators examined, 7 showed improvements, 18 showed declines, and 3 showed no discernable change. While many of the proxies for the condition of human, social, and environmental capital are based on monetary estimates of costs or benefits, they nevertheless provide a common denominator for comparison with monetary metrics of economic prosperity. Ideally, we would like to compare real physical or qualitative conditions in these "living capital" assets and identify emerging "liabilities" to sustainable well-being.

The results are sobering. Virtually every indicator of human, social and environmental well-being has declined in the USA since 1950. Yet, virtually every measure of financial and economic prosperity (GDP and stock markets) has shown dramatic increases. For example, the market value of all stocks traded on USA stock exchanges has increased 6,060 percent (in current dollars per capita) from 1950 to 1999. The USA GDP per capita increased 1,529 percent (in current dollars). And, levels of financial debt (personal, business and government debt) have risen 3,262 percent (current dollars per capita) since 1950, to in excess of US\$ 26 trillion, eclipsing all other market values, including the GDP and stock markets.

Some of the more important declines in living capital include the growing disparity between the incomes of the rich and poor in the USA that may lead to the erosion of social cohesion. Such signs of poverty are likely to have long-term human health impacts. The social fabric of households and communities also appears to be fraying as evidenced by increases in divorce and family breakdown as well as by high levels of crime and the world's second highest level of incarceration rates after Russia.

The USA's GPI results also suggest rising ecological liabilities or deficits, with the loss of wetlands and old-growth forest ecosystems, as well as the increasing ecological liability associated with the extraction and burning of fossil fuels. Agricultural sustainability may also be a question with soil erosion impacts. Ozone depletion caused by accumulated Chlorofluorohydrocarbons (CFCs) in the atmosphere also poses a long-term human health risk. The only exceptions to declining ecological health have been improvements in air quality that began following the introduction of stringent environmental standards in the 1970s.

While the results suggest declining stocks and flows of living capital, they do not necessarily provide definitive evidence that these losses in EI are having any measurable impact on long-term human health. In fact, the continual increase in USA life expectancy suggests that the *meta* measure of human health is improving. Neither does the evidence provide any sense of where potential unsustainable thresholds might exist for ecological or human health given the continuation of the trends we observe. The problem is that the indicators of both human health and ecosystem health conditions may simply not be sensitive enough to emerging risks to sustainable well-being and thus need to be refined and expanded. This is where epidemiological studies and detailed EI studies could assist in shedding light on why declining living capital is relevant to long-term well-being. For example, more detailed analysis of the incidence of disease by age-sex cohorts, associated with various ecosystem regions across the USA, could provide useful information about these complex relationships.

Another perspective on living capital conditions is to compare other international indicators of human development, social health and ecological health relative to the GPI, the GDP and other measures of economic well-being (see Table 2 and Figure 2). Figure 2 compares the key monetary expression of economic well-being (the GDP per capita) with several indices of social, human, and ecological well-being indicators. By converting raw data to an index we can compare trends in the GDP per capita against the UN Human Development Index (for the USA), the GPI per capita (converted to an index), the Index for Social Health (Miringoff and Miringoff 1999), the Living Planet Index (World Wildlife Fund 2001) and a measure of the USA EF [ecological footprint] deficit.

The results show that while the USA's GDP has continued to increase over the past 50 years, virtually every measure of human, societal and en-

FIGURE 2

**LIVING CAPITAL INDICATORS VERSUS ECONOMIC GROWTH (GDP):
THE USA GPI, GDP, INDEX FOR SOCIAL HEALTH, WWF LIVING
PLANET INDEX, AND UN HUMAN DEVELOPMENT INDEX (U.S.)
1950 TO 1999, 1975 AS BENCHMARK YEAR.**

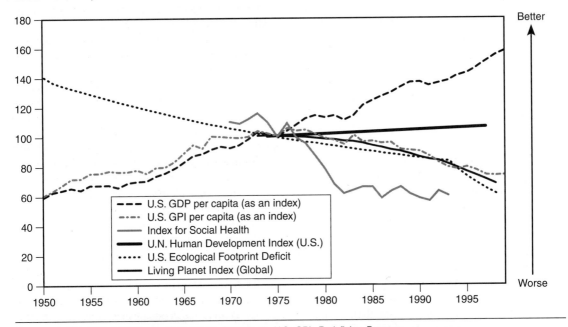

Sources: 1. US GDP: U.S. Bureau of Economic Analysis. 2. U.S. GPI: Redefining Progress
(www.rprogress.org). 3. Index for Social Health: Miringoff (found in Zeesman and Brink (1997)). 4.
UN HDI: U.N. Human Development Report 1999. 5. U.S. Ecological Footprint derived from source:
Wackernagel & Rees, "Our Ecological Footprint" and www.rprogress.org. 6. Living Planet Index:
World Wildlife Fund.

vironmental well-being has declined. The only exception is the UNDP Human Development Index
(HDI) that has risen slightly. However, this is not
surprising given that the HDI is composed of only
five key indicators which include GDP per capita
and life expectancy, both of which have increased.
Again, while the GDP, stock markets and debt have
risen substantially in 50 years, three composite indices of living capital all show declines.

Anielski (2000) shows that since 1970, USA financial wealth indicators grew dramatically. For example, a composite index of USA stock market values and total credit market debt reached heights
of 1,688 basis points by 1999 from the 1970 benchmark year of 100 basis points; an increase of some

16.9 times the 1970 value. At the same time, the Index of Social Health (ISH) had fallen by almost half
(55%) by 1993, compared to 1970. The global Living Planet Index, a broad measure of global ecological health, fell 68 percent by 1995 since 1970. So,
as financial assets have shown torrid growth, real or
living capital has been eroding.

The World Wildlife Fund's (2001) LPI—a composite index of the health of the world's forests, fresh
waters and oceans—shows that between 1970 and
1999, the world's ecosystems have declined by 33
percent. This ranged from declines of 12 percent for
forests, 50 percent for fresh waters, and 35 percent
for oceans (World Wildlife Fund 2001). Their study
also found that human pressure on nature has

increased about 50 percent over the study period and concluded that "the natural wealth of the world's forests, freshwater ecosystems, oceans and coasts has declined rapidly, particularly in freshwater and marine ecosystems." The authors concluded that sometime in the 1970s, humanity passed the point at which it lived within the global regenerative capacity of the earth. These findings are supported by the independent work of Loucks et al. (1999) and Karr and Chu (1999) who found that between 1982 and 1997, in the ecosystems that they have monitored, there has been an approximately 50 percent decline in their ecological and biological integrity, respectively.

The conclusion that the earth's carrying capacity has been breached is based on the EF analysis of humanity by each nation. The EF analysis is used as the basis for calculating the overshoot of global ecosystem carrying capacity. The EF is a measure of the land area, resources and ecosystem services (e.g., to assimilate waste) required to meet current levels of human consumption of food, materials and energy. While some historical EF data points are available for the USA, the LPI for the USA is not. We have assumed that the global LPI can serve as a proxy for EI for the USA, given the significant EF that Americans impose on both North American and also on global ecosystems from their lifestyles. Future analysis should consider an LPI or similar index for the USA that could be compared with other USA indicators of economic, social, and human development and environmental well-being.

The UN Human Development Index (HDI) for the USA (using only the five data points: 1975, 1980, 1985, 1990, and 1997 and interpolating between years) suggests rising quality of life in the USA since 1975. However, this may be misleading because the HDI includes only GDP per capita (as a proxy for income and economic prosperity), life expectancy, literacy and educational attainment. Since both GDP and life expectancy have risen for the USA and most nations along with rising levels of educational attainment, it is not surprising that this narrow measure of human well-being is improving.

The Miringoff and Miringoff (1999) Index of Social Health (ISH), which includes a composite index of 17 social and human health indicators, has shown a steady decline since the benchmark year of

1971, including indicators such as suicide rates, teen pregnancy, income inequality, life expectancy and other intuitive social and human health indicators. Many of these are also used in the GPI Accounting framework. . . .

The GPI Accounting framework provides an important starting point towards a more holistic and unified analytic framework for assessing the physical, qualitative, and monetary conditions or expressions of living capital. . . .

The examples of GPI accounting presented in this paper provide a glimpse of what is possible for future well-being accounting. Even more detailed and comprehensive GPI accounts of well-being are desirable, accounts capable of demonstrating the full impact on human health and well-being of ecological degradation. Only then will epidemiology be able to fulfill its role as the science for rational policy formulation in this critical area.

REFERENCES

Anielski, Mark, Mary Griffiths, David Pollock, Amy Taylor, Jeff Wilson, and Sara Wilson. 2001. *Alberta Sustainability Trends 2000: The Genuine Progress Indicators Report 1961 to 1999.* The Pembina Institute for Appropriate Development. <www.pembina. org> (22 May 2001).

Anielski, Mark. 2000. "Fertile Obfuscation: Making Money Whilst Eroding Living Capital." Paper presented to the 34th Annual Conference of the Canadian Economics Association, University of British Columbia, Vancouver, BC <www.pembina.org> (22 May 2001).

Anielski, Mark and Jonathan Rowe. 1999, *The Genuine Progress Indicator—1998 Update.* San Francisco, CA: Redefining Progress. <www.rprogress.org> (22 May 2001).

Cobb, Clifford, Ted Halstead, and Jonathan Rowe. 1995. *The Genuine Progress Indicator: Summary of Data and Methodology.* San Francisco, CA: Redefining Progress.

Karr, J. R. and E. W. Chu. 1999. *Restoring Life in Running Waters: Better Biological Monitoring.* Washington, DC: Island Press.

Kennedy, Robert. 1993. "Recapturing America's Moral Vision," March 18, 1968 in *RFK: Collected Speeches.* Viking Press.

TABLE 2

IS THE UNITED STATES (U.S.) BETTER OFF OR WORSE OFF IN 1999 COMPARED TO 1950?

	Better Off or Worse Off Than in 1950?	% Change in Cost/Value Per Capita Since 1950 (or benchmark year)	Absolute Quantitative Change
What We Want More of . . .			
Longer life (life expectancy)	▲ Better	Up 8.5% since 1970	Average life expectancy has increased 6.0 years between 1970 and 1997
More sustainable and genuine progress (GPI)	▼ Worse	Down 29% since 1978 peak	
Higher quality of life (UN Human Development Index and Index for Social Health, Miringoff)	▲▼ Better and Worse	U.S. HDI improved 7.2% between 1975 and 1999; the ISH declined 45% between 1970 and 1993	
More economic growth (GDP)	▲ Better	Up 164% (1992 $) Up 1,529% (current $)	
More U.S. stock market growth (total stock market capitalization value)	▲ Better	Up 6,060% (current $)	
More personal consumption (expenditures)	▲ Better	Up 181%	
Higher quality and more household durables	▼ Worse	Down 245%	
More leisure and family time	▼ Worse	Down 1,428%	19% less leisure time per worker; 58% increase in hours of TV viewing per household
More productive farm land	▼ Worse	Down 248%	
More volunteerism	▲ Better	Up 128%	169% increase in average hours volunteered per cap.
More renewable energy use	▲ Better		3% of total energy consumption from less than 2/10th of 1% in 1950
What We Want Less of . . .			
Less debt (total market credit)	▼ Worse	Up 3,262% (current dollars per capita)	20,410% increase in margin debt
Less foreign borrowing	▼ Worse	Up 400% (since 1983 peak of net foreign lending)	
Less inequality (income and wealth)	▼ Worse	Up 18% (since 1968 low)	In 1995 the richest 0.5% of families claimed 28% of net worth, almost as much as the bottom 90% of the population (32%)

TABLE 2

	Better Off or Worse Off Than in 1950?	% Change in Cost/Value Per Capita Since 1950 (or benchmark year)	Absolute Quantitative Change
What We Want Less of . . . (continued)			
Less poverty	▲ Better	Down 17.5%	In 1969 13.7% of U.S. citizens lived in poverty; in 2000 11.3% lived in poverty
Less family breakdown	▼ Worse	Up 121%	195% increase in number of divorces; 238% increase in number of kids impacted by divorce
Less hours of work	▼ Worse		7% more hours worked per annum per worker
Less commuting time	▼ Worse	Up 89%	30% increase in times commuting to work
Less underemployment	▼ Worse	Up 375%	125% increase in the number of constrained hours per worker
Less automobile accidents	▼ Worse	Up 200%	
Smaller ecological footprint	▼ Worse	Up 152%	The U.S. has the third-highest EF in the world; each American consumes over 5 times the global carrying capacity
Less depletion of nonrenewable resources	▼ Worse	Up 389%	14% increase in nonrenewable energy produced per capita from U.S. sources
Less long-term environmental damage	▼ Worse	Up 142%	73% increase in barrels of oil equivalent of nonrenewable energy consumed per capita
No net loss of wetlands	▼ Worse	Up 358%	6% decrease in the area of total wetlands
No net loss of old growth forests	▼ Worse	Up 6%	69% less old-growth forest
Less ozone depletion	▼ Worse	Up 5,109%	9,247% increase in global CFC production
Less air pollution	▲ Better	Down 67%	42% improvement in ambient air quality; but emissions of CO are down 13%, NO_2 up 132%, VOCs down 9%, SO_2 down 15% and particulate matter up 83%
Less water pollution	▼ Worse	Up 33%	
Less noise pollution	▼ Worse	Up 43%	

Source: The analysis is based on Anielski 2000.

Küznets, Simon. 1965. "Economic Growth and Structure" in *Towards a Theory of Economic Growth.* New York: W. W. Norton and Co.

Loucks, O., O. H. Ereksen, J. W. Bol, R. F. Gorman, P. C. Johnson, and T. C. Krehbiel. 1999. *Sustainability Perspectives for Resources and Business.* Lewis Publishers.

Miringoff, Marc and Marque-Luisa Miringoff. 1999. *The Social Health of the Nation.* New York: Oxford University Press.

World Wildlife Fund. 2001. *The Living Planet Report 2000.* <www.wwf.org> (22 May 2001).

DISCUSSION TOPICS

1. Do you believe that policy makers should use the GPI instead of the GNP (GDP)? Why or why not?
2. Which indicators of social, human, and ecological well-being do you believe to be most important? Justify your view.
3. Anielski and Soskolne maintain that as financial assets have grown, real or living capital in the United States has been eroding. Identify any factors in U.S. life omitted by their indicators that might give a more positive picture.

READING 61

Can We Afford to Conserve Biodiversity?

Alexander James, Kevin J. Gaston, and Andrew Balmford

Alexander James is professor of land economy at the University of Cambridge. Kevin J. Gaston is professor of biodiversity and macroecology at the University of Sheffield, England. He is editor of the journal Functional Ecology. *Andrew Balmford is senior lecturer in the Department of Zoology at the University of Cambridge. In the following excerpt from their article published in* Bioscience *in 2001, they estimate the cost of maintaining biodiversity and argue that these costs are considerably less than current government expenditures on environmentally harmful subsidies.*

Recent studies have highlighted the potentially enormous economic losses due to the degradation of biological diversity (Heywood 1995, Daily 1997). Environmental goods and services provided by natural biological systems have been valued at between $2.9 trillion and $33 trillion annually (Costanza et al. 1997, Pimentel et al. 1997). Although some of these goods and services may depend more on biomass than on biological diversity per se (Myers 1996, Hector et al. 1999, Tilman 1999), it seems very likely that biodiversity itself is worth several trillion dollars a year.

In contrast, the costs of maintaining biodiversity have received rather less comment, and few reliable figures are available (Pimentel et al. 1997). Estimates range from $680 million to $42 billion (UNEP 1992), clustering around $20 billion (IUCN/UNEP/WWF 1991, WCMC 1992, WRI/IUCN/UNEP 1992). However, the data and assumptions underlying these estimates are generally unclear. To improve the empirical basis and precision of these estimates, we set out a sequence of steps for global biodiversity conservation and computed their costs based on new data and published figures. Our estimates of the costs of global conservation, while high, are considerably less than government expenditures on environmentally harmful subsidies.

Our estimates focus on area-based conservation (explicitly ignoring activities such as conservation education) and address two separate components of global biodiversity cost: conservation within an ecologically representative reserve network and conservation within the wider matrix of landscapes, including agriculture, forestry, freshwater, and marine systems. We assume that a reserve network would comprise the core of global biodiversity conservation activities, whereas conservation within the wider matrix of landscapes would integrate conservation measures with mainstream economic activities. We regard both approaches as essential to effective conservation, and we suggest that the overall level of conservation achieved in this two-tiered strategy would be largely sufficient to maintain the flow of benefits from global biodiversity into the future.

We estimated the cost of conservation within a global reserve network in five steps. First, we surveyed current expenditure on protected areas globally and, second, made an estimate of the funding shortfalls in the existing reserve system. Third, we projected the cost of purchasing land to expand this network for ecological representation; fourth, we added the cost of managing these new areas effectively in the future. Fifth, we estimated the scale of compensation required to meet the opportunity costs incurred by local people living in or near reserves. The sum of these five steps equals, very roughly, the annual cost of biodiversity conservation within a global reserve system.

Funding required in the wider matrix of landscapes includes the cost of conservation activities in the agriculture, forestry, freshwater, coastal, and marine sectors. These activities include implementing conservation laws and regulations, as well as incentives, subsidies, and other measures designed to encourage sustainable use of biodiversity. Because data are insufficient for making these estimates, we relied primarily on published figures, as noted below. The estimates of biodiversity conservation costs in the wider matrix are very crude; nevertheless, they provide an indication of the magnitude of funds required for biodiversity remediation in the human-dominated landscape.

We close this article with a discussion of the feasibility of implementing such a global conservation program. We note that government expenditures on subsidies that encourage environmentally harmful practices are many times greater than the fiscal requirements for adequate global biodiversity conservation. These subsidies include government financial support for the agriculture sector, forestry, fishing, mining, and freshwater use. Reducing these expenditures by as little as 10% would contribute to sustainability of resource use throughout the wider matrix of landscapes, reduce environmental remediation costs, and provide funding for a global biodiversity conservation program.

We recognize that, as a first attempt at structuring and costing out a global biodiversity program, our estimates are necessarily crude and incomplete. However, in making our calculations and assumptions explicit, our intention is that these ballpark figures will be revised as better data become available. By demonstrating that the cost of effective biodiversity conservation represents only a fraction of existing government subsidies to resource users, and an even smaller fraction of the value of biodiversity, we hope to dispel the myth that effective conservation is unaffordable. . . .

HOW TO AFFORD A GLOBAL CONSERVATION PROGRAM

In total, the annual funding requirement of approximately $317 billion for global biodiversity conservation dwarfs the gross national product of many nations (WRI/UNEP/UNDP/World Bank 1998). However, conservation in reserves could be achieved for about 1%, and conservation in the wider matrix for about 10%, of the annual value of natural ecosystems (Pimentel et al. 1997). Using less conservative estimates of ecosystem value (Costanza et al. 1997), the figures are 0.1% and 1%, respectively. The annual premium for global biodiversity conservation is thus minuscule relative to the value of the assets being insured.

Equally important, the total costs of conservation are small when contrasted with the scale of "perverse" subsidies—the environmentally harmful payments already being made to support agricultural production, energy use, road transportation, water consumption, and commercial fisheries. These governmental measures keep resource prices for producers and consumers below market levels, thereby encouraging resource overexploitation and attendant environmental problems. Environmentally perverse subsidies total between $950 billion (van Beers and de Moor 1999) and $1450 billion per year globally (Myers 1998). The $950 billion estimate attributes $325 billion to the agriculture sector, $225 billion to automobile users, $205 billion to energy users, $60 billion to water users, $55 billion to manufacturing industries, $35 billion to forestry, $25 billion to mining, and $20 billion to fisheries (van Beers and de Moor 1999).

A globally representative and adequately managed nature reserve system could be accomplished for about 2% of the annual expenditure on such environmentally harmful subsidies. A truly comprehensive global conservation program that addresses conservation issues in all the major natural resource sectors could be established for only one-third of the cost of these subsidies. The entire bill for conservation could be readily met by redirecting a small fraction of these subsidies; moreover, because they inflate land prices, a reduction in perverse subsidies would directly reduce the conservation bill. The challenge therefore lies in redirecting patterns of government expenditure to favor environmental sustainability, not in artificially lowering the cost of resource use for producers and consumers.

However, these environmentally harmful subsidies are not necessarily concentrated where conservation needs are greatest. Only about one-quarter of perverse subsidies are located in the developing countries, and most of these are attributable to the transitional countries of Russia and the CIS (van Beers and de Moor 1999). In fact, the study by van Beers and de Moor (1999) identified less than 10% ($100 billion) of global perverse subsidies in the developing countries outside the former Soviet Union (although in certain sectors, such as forestry, perverse subsidies in developing countries may be considerably higher than estimated). Given their far greater scope for cutting environmentally harmful subsidies, it seems reasonable to expect the developed countries to assist the developing world with meeting the costs of a global biodiversity conservation program.

The Convention on Biological Diversity provides both a mechanism for such a redistribution of funds and the legal basis for the removal of environmentally perverse subsidies. Parties to the convention are required to identify processes and categories of activities that have significant adverse impacts on the conservation and sustainable use of biodiversity and to regulate or manage these activities with a view to ensuring adequate in situ conservation. Subsidization of resource use must be considered one of the most important categories of environmentally harmful activities undertaken by governments, given the scale of public resources involved. In addition, the convention requires developed country parties to provide additional financial resources for biodiversity conservation to the developing countries; a mechanism for distributing these funds, the Global Environmental Facility (GEF), has already been established.

Since its founding in 1992, much of GEF's biodiversity investment of over $1 billion has been directed to protected areas. Implementation of the global biodiversity program outlined in this article would require a major increase in the administrative capacity of GEF. For instance, the protected

areas component alone would require a multiplication of GEF's biodiversity resources. The program would also require a significant strengthening of national conservation and park management agencies throughout the developing world, a challenge that is potentially even more difficult. Private sector institutions could also be involved in the implementation of a global conservation program. For example, privately held land conservancies already contribute to biodiversity conservation goals in many countries (Adelman 1994, WCMC 1996). These and other private sector activities could be explicitly acknowledged and incorporated into the global conservation program.

CONCLUSIONS

Numerous documents have outlined strategies and priorities for global biodiversity conservation (IUCN/UNEP/WWF 1991, UNEP 1992, WCMC 1992, WRI/IUCN/UNEP 1992), but none has presented detailed cost estimates. Although this shortcoming is understandable in light of the paucity of hard data, the ill-defined nature of the costs has undermined efforts to galvanize support for a global conservation program. Better information on the actual costs of achieving specific conservation objectives may help international conservation efforts, particularly since these costs may not be as high as policymakers suspect.

The analyses presented in this article, which couple WCMC's database on protected area budgets with data from the gray literature, suggest that current expenditures on reserves run at about $6.0 billion per year. We project that improving protection, expanding the network in line with IUCN guidelines, and implementing an innovative plan for meeting the opportunity costs of local communities could all be achieved for an annual increase in expenditure of $12.0 billion to $21.0 billion. The cost of biodiversity conservation in the wider matrix remains an area for which data are almost nonexistent. Our preliminary review suggests that these costs may well be 10 times higher than those of protected areas, which puts into perspective the remarkable conservation bargain presented by parks and reserves. While all of the estimates presented in this article are at best approximate, they are based on a more transparent and data-driven set of calculations than any figures. We hope that the estimates set out here will be refined as more data on the costs of effective reserve management, and accommodation of biodiversity beyond reserves, become available.

Lack of understanding of the costs of biodiversity conservation has contributed to the impression that global conservation strategies are unrealistically expensive, when in fact they are not. A small shift in government expenditures toward environmental sustainability could preserve a substantial proportion of global biodiversity for current and future generations. What is needed now is for parties to the Convention on Biological Diversity to take the first step toward reducing environmentally harmful subsidies while linking this progress to funding global biodiversity conservation. Effective conservation lies well within our means.

REFERENCES CITED

Adelman CL 1994. The economics and the role of privately owned lands used for nature tourism, education, and conservation. In Munasinghe M, McNeely JA, eds. Protected Area Economics and Policy. Washington (DC): World Bank.

Costanza R, et al; 1997. The value of the world's ecosystem services and natural capital. Nature 387: 253–260.

Daily GC, ed. 1997. Nature's Services: Societal Dependence on Natural Ecosystems. Washington (DC): Island Press.

Hector A, et al. 1999. Plant diversity and productivity experiments in European grasslands. Science 286: 1123–1127.

Heywood VH, ed. 1995. Global Biodiversity Assessment. Cambridge (UK): Cambridge University Press.

[IUCN/UNEP/WWF] World Conservation Union/ United Nations Environment Programme/World Wide Fund for Nature. 1991. Caring for the Earth. A Strategy for Sustainable Living. Gland (Switzerland): IUCN/UNEP/WWF.

Myers N 1996. Environmental services of biodiversity. Proceedings of the National Academy of Sciences 93: 2764–2769.

———. 1998. Lifting the veil on perverse subsidies. Nature 392: 327–328.

Pimental D, et al. 1997. Economic and environmental benefits of biodiversity. BioScience 47: 747–757.

Tilman D 1999. Diversity and production in European grasslands. Science 286: 1099–1100.

[UNEP] United Nations Environment Programme. 1992. Biodiversity Country Studies: Executive Summary. New York: UNEP.

van Beers CP, de Moor APG. 1999. Addicted to Subsidies. The Hague (Netherlands): Institute for Research on Public Expenditure.

[WCMC] World Conservation Monitoring Centre. 1992. Global Biodiversity: Status of the Earth's Living Resources. London: Chapman & Hall.

———. 1996. Private Protected Areas: A Preliminary Study of Private Initiatives to Conserve Biodiversity in Selected African Countries. Cambridge (UK): World Conservation Monitoring Center.

[WRI/IUCN/UNEP] World Resources Institute/World Conservation Union/United Nations Environment Programme. 1992. Global Biodiversity Strategy. Washington (DC), Gland (Switzerland), and New York: WRI/IUCN/UNEP.

[WRI/UNEP/UNDP/World Bank] World Resources Institute/United Nations Environment Programme/ United Nations Development Programme/World Bank. 1998. World Resources 1998–99. New York: Oxford University Press.

DISCUSSION TOPICS

1. What is the two-tiered strategy that James, Gaston, and Balmford believe to be essential? Do you agree with this claim? Why or why not?

2. The authors identify perverse subsidies that support agricultural production, energy use, road transportation, water consumption, and commercial fisheries. Such subsidies keep resource prices for producers and consumers below market levels. Are there any government subsidies that you believe distort market prices? Explain your reasoning.

3. What expanded role do the authors suggest for the Global Environmental Facility, as established by the Convention on Biological Diversity? Do you think this expanded role is a good idea? Why or why not?

4. The authors argue that global conservation strategies are well within the economic means of the global community. Assuming that the estimates by the authors are correct, what is the importance of this finding in your view?

From *Should Trees Have Standing? Toward Legal Rights for Natural Objects*

Christopher D. Stone

Christopher D. Stone is professor of law at the University of Southern California in Los Angeles. The publication of "Should Trees Have Standing?" *in 1972 was an important influence on the development of the field of environmental ethics. Stone is author of* Earth and Other Ethics: The Case for Moral Pluralism *(1987) and* Should Trees Have Standing? and Other Essays on Law, Morals, and the Environment *(1997).*

Stone proposes giving legal rights to natural objects. He summarizes what it means for something to have legal standing and proposes an extension of the legal guardianship model.

. . . Throughout legal history, each successive extension of rights to some new entity has been . . . a bit unthinkable. We are inclined to suppose the rightlessness of rightless "things" to be a decree of Nature, not a legal convention acting in support of some status quo. It is thus that we defer considering the choices involved in all their moral, social, and economic dimensions. . . . The fact is, that each time there is a movement to confer rights onto some new "entity," the proposal is bound to sound odd or frightening or laughable.[1] This is partly because until the rightless thing receives its rights, we cannot see it as anything but a *thing* for the use of "us" — those who are holding rights at the time.[2] . . .

The reason for this little discourse on the unthinkable, the reader must know by now, if only from the title of the paper. I am quite seriously proposing that we give legal rights to forests, oceans, rivers and other so-called natural objects in the environment — indeed, to the natural environment as a whole.[3]

As strange as such a notion may sound, it is neither fanciful nor devoid of operational content. In fact, I do not think it would be a misdescription of recent developments in the law to say that we are already on the verge of assigning some such rights, although we have not faced up to what we are doing in those particular terms.[4] We should do so now, and begin to explore the implications such a notion would hold.

TOWARD RIGHTS FOR THE ENVIRONMENT

Now, to say that the natural environment should have rights is not to say anything as silly as that no one should be allowed to cut down a tree. We say human beings have rights, but — at least as of the time of this writing — they can be executed.[5] Corporations have rights, but they cannot plead the fifth amendment;[6] *In re Gault* gave 15-year-olds certain rights in juvenile proceedings, but it did not give them the right to vote. Thus, to say that the environment should have rights is not to say that it should have every right we can imagine, or even the same body of rights as human beings have. Nor is it to say that everything in the environment should have the same rights as every other thing in the environment.

What the granting of rights does involve has two sides to it. The first involves what might be called the legal-operational aspects; the second, the psychic and socio-psychic aspects. I shall deal with these aspects in turn.

THE LEGAL-OPERATIONAL ASPECTS

What It Means to Be a Holder of Legal Rights

There is, so far as I know, no generally accepted standard for how one ought to use the term "legal rights." Let me indicate how I shall be using it in this piece.

First and most obviously, if the term is to have any content at all, an entity cannot be said to hold a legal right unless and until *some public authoritative body* is prepared to give *some amount of review* to actions that are colorably inconsistent with that "right." For example, if a student can be expelled from a university and cannot get any public official, even a judge or administrative agent at the lowest level, either (i) to require the university to justify its actions (if only to the extent of filling out an affidavit alleging that the expulsion "was not wholly arbitrary and capricious") or (ii) to compel the university to accord the student some procedural safeguards (a hearing, right to counsel, right to have notice of charges), then the minimum requirements for saying that the student has a legal right to his education do not exist.[7]

But for a thing to be *a holder of legal rights,* something more is needed than that some authoritative body will review the actions and processes of those who threaten it. As I shall use the term, "holder of legal rights," each of three additional criteria must be satisfied. All three, one will observe, go toward making a thing *count* jurally — to have a legally recognized worth and dignity in its own right, and not merely to serve as a means to benefit "us" (whoever the contemporary group of rights-holders may be). They are, first, that the thing can institute legal actions *at its behest;* second, that in determining the granting of legal relief, the court must take *injury to it* into account; and, third, that relief must run to the *benefit of it. . . .*

Toward Having Standing in Its Own Right

It is not inevitable, nor is it wise, that natural objects should have no rights to seek redress in their own behalf. It is no answer to say that streams and forests cannot have standing because streams and forests cannot speak. Corporations cannot speak either; nor can states, estates, infants, incompetents, municipalities or universities. Lawyers speak for them, as they customarily do for the ordinary citizen with legal problems. One ought, I think, to handle the legal problems of natural objects as one does the problems of legal incompetents — human beings who have become vegetable. If a human being shows signs of becoming senile and has affairs that he is de jure incompetent to manage, those concerned with his well-being make such a showing to the court, and someone is designated by the court with the authority to manage the incompetent's affairs. The guardian[8] (or "conservator"[9] or "committee"[10] — the terminology varies) then represents the incompetent in his legal affairs. Courts make similar appointments when a corporation has become "incompetent" — they appoint a trustee in bankruptcy or reorganization to oversee its affairs and speak for it in court when that becomes necessary.

On a parity of reasoning, we should have a system in which, when a friend of a natural object perceives it to be endangered, he can apply to a court for the creation of a guardianship.[11] Perhaps we already have the machinery to do so. California law, for example, defines an incompetent as "any person, whether insane or not, who by reason of old age, disease, weakness of mind, or other cause, is unable, unassisted, properly to manage and take care of himself or his property, and by reason thereof is likely to be deceived or imposed upon by artful or designing persons."[12] Of course, to urge a court that an endangered river is "a person" under this provision will call for lawyers as bold and imaginative as those who convinced the Supreme Court that a railroad corporation was a "person" under the fourteenth amendment, a constitutional provision theretofore generally thought of as designed to secure the rights of freemen.[13] (As this article was going to press, Professor Byrn of Fordham petitioned the New York Supreme Court to appoint him legal guardian for an unrelated foetus scheduled for abortion so as to enable him to bring a class action on behalf of all foetuses similarly situated in New York City's 18 municipal hospitals. Judge Holtzman granted the petition of guardianship.[14]) If such an argument based on present statutes should fail, special environmental legislation could be enacted along traditional guardianship lines. Such provisions could provide for guardianship both in the instance of public natural objects and also, perhaps with slightly different standards, in the instance of natural objects on "private" land.[15]

The potential "friends" that such a statutory scheme would require will hardly be lacking. The Sierra Club, Environmental Defense Fund, Friends of the Earth, Natural Resources Defense Counsel, and the Izaak Walton League are just some of the many groups which have manifested unflagging dedication to the environment and which are becoming increasingly capable of marshalling the requisite technical experts and lawyers. If, for example, the Environmental Defense Fund should have reason to believe that some company's strip mining operations might be irreparably destroying the ecological balance of large tracts of land, it could, under this procedure, apply to the court in which the lands were situated to be appointed guardian.[16] As guardian, it might be given rights of inspection (or visitation) to determine and bring to the court's attention a fuller finding on the land's condition. If there were indications that under the substantive law some redress might be available on the land's behalf, then the guardian would be entitled to raise the land's rights in the land's name, i.e., without having to make the roundabout and often unavailing demonstration, discussed below, that the "rights" of the club's members were being invaded. Guardians would also be looked to for a host of other protective tasks, e.g., monitoring effluents (and/or monitoring the monitors), and representing their "wards" at legislative and administrative hearings on such matters as the setting of state water quality standards. Procedures exist, and can be strengthened, to move a court for the removal and substitution of guardians, for conflicts of interest or for other reasons,[17] as well as for the termination of the guardianship.[18]

The guardianship approach, however, is apt to raise two objections, neither of which seems to me to have much force. The first is that a committee or guardian could not judge the needs of the river or forest in its charge; indeed, the very concept of "needs," it might be said, could be used here only in the most metaphorical way. The second objection is that such a system would not be much different from what we now have: is not the Department of Interior already such a guardian for public lands, and do not most states have legislation empowering their attorneys general to seek relief—in a sort of *parens patriae* way—for such injuries as a guardian might concern himself with?

As for the first objection, natural objects can communicate their wants (needs) to us, and in ways that are not terribly ambiguous. I am sure I can judge with more certainty and meaningfulness whether and when my lawn wants (needs) water, than the Attorney General can judge whether and when the United States wants (needs) to take an appeal from an adverse judgment by a lower court. The lawn tells me that it wants water by a certain dryness of the blades and soil—immediately obvious to the touch—the appearance of bald spots, yellowing, and a lack of springiness after being walked on; how does "the United States" communicate to the Attorney General? For similar reasons, the guardian-attorney for

a smog-endangered stand of pines could venture with more confidence that his client wants the smog stopped, than the directors of a corporation can assert that "the corporation" wants dividends declared. We make decisions on behalf of, and in the purported interests of, others every day; these "others" are often creatures whose wants are far less verifiable, and even far more metaphysical in conception, than the wants of rivers, trees, and land.[19]

As for the second objection, one can indeed find evidence that the Department of Interior was conceived as a sort of guardian of the public lands.[20] But there are two points to keep in mind. First, insofar as the Department already is an adequate guardian it is only with respect to the federal public lands as per Article IV, section 3 of the Constitution.[21] Its guardianship includes neither local public lands nor private lands. Second, to judge from the environmentalist literature and from the cases environmental action groups have been bringing, the Department is itself one of the bogeys of the environmental movement. (One thinks of the uneasy peace between the Indians and the Bureau of Indian Affairs.) Whether the various charges be right or wrong, one cannot help but observe that the Department has been charged with several institutional goals (never an easy burden), and is currently looked to for action by quite a variety of interest groups, only one of which is the environmentalists. In this context, a guardian outside the institution becomes especially valuable. Besides, what a person wants, fully to secure his rights, is the ability to retain independent counsel even when, and perhaps especially when, the government is acting "for him" in a beneficent way. I have no reason to doubt, for example, that the Social Security System is being managed "for me"; but I would not want to abdicate my right to challenge its actions as they affect me, should the need arise.[22] I would not ask more trust of national forests, vis-à-vis the Department of Interior. The same considerations apply in the instance of local agencies, such as regional water pollution boards, whose members' expertise in pollution matters is often all too credible.[23]

. . . The guardian would urge before the court injuries not presently cognizable—the death of eagles and inedible crabs, the suffering of sea lions, the loss from the face of the earth of species of commercially valueless birds, the disappearance of a wilderness area. One might, of course, speak of the damages involved as "damages" to us humans, and indeed, the widespread growth of environmental groups shows that human beings do feel these losses. But they are not, at present, economically measurable losses: how can they have a monetary value for the guardian to prove in court?

The answer for me is simple. Wherever it carves out "property" rights, the legal system is engaged in the process of *creating* monetary worth. One's literary works would have minimal monetary value if anyone could copy them at will. Their economic value to the author is a product of the law of copyright; the person who copies a copyrighted book has to bear a cost to the copyright-holder because the law says he must. Similarly, it is through the law of torts that we have made a "right" of — and guaranteed an economically meaningful value to — privacy. (The value we place on gold — a yellow inanimate dirt — is not simply a function of supply and demand — wilderness areas are scarce and pretty too — but results from the actions of the legal systems of the world, which have institutionalized that value; they have even done a remarkable job of stabilizing the price.) I am proposing we do the same with eagles and wilderness areas as we do with copyrighted works, patented inventions, and privacy: *make* the violation of rights in them to be a cost by declaring the "pirating" of them to be the invasion of a property interest.[24] If we do so, the net social costs the polluter would be confronted with would include not only the extended homocentric costs of his pollution (explained above) but also costs to the environment per se.

How, though, would these costs be calculated? When we protect an invention, we can at least speak of a fair market value for it, by reference to which damages can be computed. But the lost environmental "values" of which we are now speaking are by definition over and above those that the market is prepared to bid for: they are priceless.

One possible measure of damages, suggested earlier, would be the cost of making the environment whole, just as, when a man is injured in an automobile accident, we impose upon the responsible party the injured man's medical expenses. Comparable expenses to a polluted river would be the costs of dredging, restocking with fish, and so forth. It is on the basis of such costs as these, I assume, that we get the figure of $1 billion as the cost of saving Lake Erie.[25] As an ideal, I think this is a good guide applicable in many environmental situations. It is by no means free from difficulties, however.

One problem with computing damages on the basis of making the environment whole is that, if understood most literally, it is tantamount to asking for a "freeze" on environmental quality, even at the costs (and there will be costs) of preserving "useless" objects.[26] Such a "freeze" is not inconceivable to me as a general goal, especially considering that, even by the most immediately discernible homocentric interests, in so many areas we ought to be cleaning up and not merely preserving the environmental status quo. In fact, there is presently strong sentiment in the Congress for a total elimination of all river pollutants by 1985,[27] notwithstanding that such a decision would impose quite large direct and indirect costs on us all. Here one is inclined to recall the instructions of Judge Hays, in remanding Consolidated Edison's Storm King application to the Federal Power Commission in *Scenic Hudson:*

> The Commission's renewed proceedings must include as a basic concern the preservation of natural beauty and of natural historic shrines, keeping in mind that, in our affluent society, the cost of a project is only one of several factors to be considered.[28]

Nevertheless, whatever the merits of such a goal in principle, there are many cases in which the social price tag of putting it into effect are going to seem too high to accept. Consider, for example, an oceanside nuclear generator that could produce low cost electricity for a million homes at a savings of $1 a year per home, spare us the air pollution that comes of burning fossil fuels, but which through a slight heating effect threatened to kill off a rare species of temperature-sensitive sea urchins; suppose further that technological improvements adequate to reduce the temperature to present environmental quality would expend the entire $1,000,000 in anticipated fuel savings. Are we prepared to tax ourselves $1,000,000 a year on behalf of the sea urchins? In comparable problems under the present law of damages, we work out practicable compromises by abandoning restoration costs and calling upon fair market value. For example, if an automobile is so severely damaged that the cost of bringing the car to its original state by repair is greater than the fair market value, we would allow the responsible tortfeasor to pay the fair market value only. Or if a human being suffers the loss of an arm (as we might conceive of the ocean having irreparably lost the sea urchins), we can fall back on the capitalization of reduced earning power (and pain and suffering) to measure the damages. But what is the fair market value of sea urchins? How can we capitalize their loss to the ocean, independent of any commercial value they may have to someone else?

One answer is that the problem can sometimes be sidestepped quite satisfactorily. In the sea urchin example, one compromise solution would be to impose on the nuclear generator the costs of making the ocean whole somewhere else, in some other way, e.g., re-establishing a sea urchin colony elsewhere, or making a somehow comparable contribution.[29] In the debate over the laying of the trans-Alaskan pipeline, the builders are apparently prepared to meet conservationists' objections half-way by re-establishing wildlife away from the pipeline, so far as is feasible.[30]

But even if damage calculations have to be made, one ought to recognize that the measurement of damages is rarely a simple report of economic facts about "the market," whether we are valuing the loss of a foot, a foetus, or a work of fine art. Decisions of this sort are always hard, but not impossible. We have increasingly taken (human) pain and suffering into account in reckoning damages, not because we think we can ascertain them as objective "facts" about the universe, but because, even in view of all the room for disagreement, we come up with a better society by making rude estimates of them than by ignoring them.[31] We can make such estimates in regard to environmental losses fully aware that what we are really doing is making implicit normative judgments (as with pain and suffering)—laying down rules as to what the society is going to "value" rather than reporting market evaluations. In making such normative estimates decision-makers would

not go wrong if they estimated on the "high side," putting the burden of trimming the figure down on the immediate human interests present. All burdens of proof should reflect common experience; our experience in environmental matters has been a continual discovery that our acts have caused more long-range damage than we were able to appreciate at the outset. . . .

The strongest case can be made from the perspective of human advantage for conferring rights on the environment. Scientists have been warning of the crises the earth and all humans on it face if we do not change our ways—radically—and these crises make the lost "recreational use" of rivers seem absolutely trivial. The earth's very atmosphere is threatened with frightening possibilities: absorption of sunlight, upon which the entire life cycle depends, may be diminished; the oceans may warm (increasing the "greenhouse effect" of the atmosphere), melting the polar ice caps, and destroying our great coastal cities; the portion of the atmosphere that shields us from dangerous radiation may be destroyed. Testifying before Congress, sea explorer Jacques Cousteau predicted that the oceans (to which we dreamily look to feed our booming populations) are headed toward their own death: "The cycle of life is intricately tied up with the cycle of water . . . the water system has to remain alive if we are to remain alive on earth."[32] We are depleting our energy and our food sources at a rate that takes little account of the needs even of humans now living.

These problems will not be solved easily; they very likely can be solved, if at all, only through a willingness to suspend the rate of increase in the standard of living (by present values) of the earth's "advanced" nations, and by stabilizing the total human population. For some of us this will involve forfeiting material comforts; for others it will involve abandoning the hope someday to obtain comforts long envied. For all of us it will involve giving up the right to have as many offspring as we might wish. Such a program is not impossible of realization, however. Many of our so-called material comforts are not only in excess of, but are probably in opposition to, basic biological needs. Further, the "cost" to the advanced nations is not as large as would appear from Gross National Product figures.

GNP reflects social gain (of a sort) without discounting for the social *cost* of that gain, e.g., the losses through depletion of resources, pollution, and so forth. As has well been shown, as societies become more and more "advanced," their real marginal gains become less and less for each additional dollar of GNP.[33] Thus, to give up "human progress" would not be as costly as might appear on first blush.

Nonetheless, such far-reaching social changes are going to involve us in a serious reconsideration of our consciousness toward the environment. . . . What is it within us that gives us this need not just to satisfy basic biological wants, but to extend our wills over things, to objectify them, to make them ours, to manipulate them, to keep them at a psychic distance? Can it all be explained on "rational" bases? Should we not be suspect of such needs within us, cautious as to why we wish to gratify them? When I first read that passage of Hegel, I immediately thought not only of the emotional contrast with Spinoza, but of the passage in Carson McCullers' *A Tree, A Rock, A Cloud,* in which an old derelict has collared a 12-year-old boy in a streetcar cafe. The old man asks whether the boy knows "how love should be begun":

The old man leaned closer and whispered:
"A tree. A rock. A cloud."

"The weather was like this in Portland," he said. "At the time my science was begun. I meditated and I started very cautious. I would pick up something from the street and take it home with me. I bought a goldfish and I concentrated on the goldfish and I loved it. I graduated from one thing to another. Day by day I was getting this technique. . . .

. . . For six years now I have gone around by myself and built up my science. And now I am a master. Son, I can love anything. No longer do I have to think about it even. I see a street full of people and a beautiful light comes in me. I watch a bird in the sky. Or I meet a traveler on the road. Everything, Son. And anybody. All stranger and all loved! Do you realize what a science like mine can mean?[34]

To be able to get away from the view that Nature is a collection of useful senseless objects is, as Mc-

Cullers' "madman" suggests, deeply involved in the development of our abilities to love — or, if that is putting it too strongly, to be able to reach a heightened awareness of our own and others' capacities in their mutual interplay. To do so, we have to give up some psychic investment in our sense of separateness and specialness in the universe. And this, in turn, is hard giving indeed, because it involves us in a flight backwards, into earlier stages of civilization and childhood in which we had to trust (and perhaps fear) our environment, for we had not then the power to master it. Yet, in doing so, we — as persons — gradually free ourselves of needs for supportive illusions.

. . . What is needed is a myth that can fit our growing body of knowledge of geophysics, biology and the cosmos. In this vein, I do not think it too remote that we may come to regard the Earth, as some have suggested, as one organism, of which Mankind is a functional part — the mind, perhaps: different from the rest of nature, but different as a man's brain is from his lungs. . . .

To shift from such a lofty fancy as the planetarization of consciousness to the operation of our municipal legal system is to come down to earth hard. Before the forces that are at work, our highest court is but a frail and feeble — a distinctly human — institution. Yet, the Court may be at its best not in its work of handing down decrees, but at the very task that is called for: of summoning up from the human spirit the kindest and most generous and worthy ideas that abound there, giving them shape and reality and legitimacy.[35] Witness the school desegregation cases which, more importantly than to integrate the schools (assuming they did), awakened us to moral needs which, when made visible, could not be denied. And so here, too, in the case of the environment, the Supreme Court may find itself in a position to award "rights" in a way that will contribute to a change in popular consciousness. It would be a modest move, to be sure, but one in furtherance of a large goal: the future of the planet as we know it.

How far we are from such a state of affairs, where the law treats "environmental objects" as holders of legal rights, I cannot say. But there is certainly intriguing language in one of Justice Black's last dissents, regarding the Texas Highway Department's plan to run a six-lane expressway through a San Antonio Park.[36] Complaining of the Court's refusal to stay the plan, Black observed that "after today's decision, the people of San Antonio and the birds and animals that make their home in the park will share their quiet retreat with an ugly, smelly stream of traffic. . . . Trees, shrubs, and flowers will be mown down."[37] Elsewhere he speaks of the "burial of public parks," of segments of a highway which "devour parkland," and of the park's heartland.[38] Was he, at the end of his great career, on the verge of saying — just saying — that "nature has 'rights' on its own account"? Would it be so hard to do?

NOTES

1. Recently, a group of prison inmates in Suffolk County tamed a mouse that they discovered, giving him the name Morris. Discovering Morris, a jailer flushed him down the toilet. The prisoners brought a proceeding against the Warden complaining, *inter alia,* that Morris was subjected to discriminatory discharge and was otherwise unequally treated. The action was unsuccessful, on grounds that the inmates themselves were "guilty of imprisoning Morris without a charge, without a trial, and without bail," and that other mice at the prison were not treated more favorably. "As to the true victim the Court can only offer again the sympathy first proffered to his ancestors by Robert Burns. . . ." The Judge proceeded to quote from Burns' "To a Mouse." *Morabito v. Cyrta,* 9 CRIM. L. REP. 2472 (N.Y. Sup. Ct. Suffolk Co., Aug. 26, 1971).

    The whole matter seems humorous, of course. But what we need to know more of is the function of humor in the unfolding of a culture, and the ways in which it is involved with the social growing pains to which it is testimony. Why do people make jokes about the Women's Liberation Movement? Is it not on account of — rather than in spite of — the underlying validity of the protests, and the uneasy awareness that a recognition of them is inevitable? A. Koestler rightly begins his study of the human mind, *Act of Creation* (1964), with an analysis of humor, entitled "The Logic of Laughter." And *cf.* Freud, *Jokes and the Unconscious,* 8 Standard Edition of the Complete Psychological Works of Sigmund Freud (J. Strachey transl. 1905). (Query too: What is the relationship between the conferring of proper *names,* e.g., Morris, and the conferring of social and legal *rights?*)

2. Thus it was that the Founding Fathers could speak of the inalienable rights of all men, and yet maintain a society that was, by modern standards, without the most basic rights for Blacks, Indians, children and women. There was no hypocrisy; emotionally, no one *felt* that these other things were men.

3. In this article I essentially limit myself to a discussion of non-animal but natural objects. I trust that the reader will be able to discern where the analysis is appropriate to advancing our understanding of what would be involved in giving "rights" to other objects not presently endowed with rights — for example, not only animals (some of which already have rights in some senses) but also humanoids, computers, and so forth. *Cf.* the National Register for Historic Places, 16 U.S.C. § 470 (1970), discussed in *Ely v. Velde,* 321 F. Supp. 1088 (E.D. Va. 1971).

4. The statement in text is not quite true; *cf.* Murphy, *Has Nature Any Right to Life?,* 22 Hast. L.J. 467 (1971). An Irish court, passing upon the validity of a testamentary trust to the benefit of someone's dogs, observed in dictum that "'lives' means lives of human beings, not of animals or trees in California." *Kelly v. Dillon,* 1932 Ir. R. 255, 261. (The intended gift over on the death of the last surviving dog was held void for remoteness, the court refusing "to enter into the question of a dog's expectation of life," although prepared to observe that "in point of fact neighbor's [sic] dogs and cats are unpleasantly long-lived." *Id.* at 260–61.)

5. Four cases dealing with the Constitutionality of the death penalty under the eighth and fourteenth amendments are pending before the United States Supreme Court. *Branch v. Texas,* 447 S.W.2d 932 (Tex. 1969), *cert. granted,* 91 S. Ct. 2287 (1970); *Aikens v. California,* 70 Cal. 2d 369, 74 Cal. Rptr. 882, 450 P.2d 258

(1969), *cert. granted,* 91 S. Ct. 2280 (1970); *Furman v. Georgia,* 225 Ga. 253, 167 S.E.2d 628 (1969), *cert. granted,* 91 S. Ct. 2282 (1970); *Jackson v. Georgia,* 225 Ga. 790, 171 S.E.2d 501 (1969), *cert. granted,* 91 S. Ct. 2287 (1970).

6. See *George Campbell Painting Corp. v. Reid,* 392 U.S. 286 (1968); *Oklahoma Press Pub. Co. v. Walling,* 327 U.S. 186 (1946); *Baltimore & O.R.R. v. ICC,* 221 U.S. 612 (1911); *Wilson v. United States,* 221 U.S. 361 (1911); *Hale v. Henkel,* 201 U.S. 43 (1906).

7. See *Dixon v. Alabama State Bd. of Educ.,* 294 F.2d 150 (5th Cir.), *cert. denied,* 368 U.S. 930 (1961).

8. *See, e.g.,* Cal. Prob. Code §§ 1460–62 (West Supp. 1971).

9. Cal. Prob. Code § 1751 (West Supp. 1971) provides for the appointment of a "conservator."

10. In New York the Supreme Court and county courts outside New York City have jurisdiction to appoint a committee of the person and/or a committee of the property for a person "incompetent to manage himself or his affairs." N.Y. Mental Hygiene Law § 100 (McKinney 1971).

11. This is a situation in which the ontological problems discussed in note 3 *supra* become acute. One can conceive a situation in which a guardian would be appointed by a county court with respect to a stream, bring a suit against alleged polluters, and lose. Suppose now that a federal court were to appoint a guardian with respect to the larger river system of which the stream were a part, and that the federally appointed guardian subsequently were to bring suit against the same defendants in state court, now on behalf of the river, rather than the stream. (Is it possible to bring a still subsequent suit, if the one above fails, on behalf of the entire hydrologic cycle, by a guardian appointed by an international court?)

    While such problems are difficult, they are not impossible to solve. For one thing, pretrial hearings and rights of intervention can go far toward their amelioration. Further, courts have been dealing with the matter of potentially inconsistent judgments for years, as when one state appears on the verge of handing down a divorce decree inconsistent with the judgment of another state's courts. *Kempson v. Kempson,* 58 N.J. Eg. 94, 43 A. 97 (Ch. Ct. 1899). Courts could, and of course would, retain some natural objects in the *res nullius* classification to help stave off the problem. Then, too, where (as is always the case) several "objects" are interrelated, several guardians could all be involved, with procedures for removal to the appropriate court — probably that of the guardian of the most encompassing "ward" to be acutely threatened. And in some cases subsequent suit by the guardian of the more encompassing ward, not guilty of laches, might be appropriate. The problems are at least no more complex than the corresponding problems that the law has dealt with for years in the class action area.

12. Cal. Prob. Code § 1460 (West Supp. 1971). The N.Y. Mental Hygiene Law (McKinney 1971) provides for jurisdiction "over the custody of a person and his property if he is incompetent to manage himself or his affairs by reason of age, drunkenness, mental illness or other cause."

13. *Santa Clara County v. Southern Pac. R.R.,* 118 U.S. 394 (1886). Justice Black would have denied corporations the rights of "persons" under the fourteenth amendment. See *Connecticut Gen. Life Ins. Co. v. Johnson,* 303 U.S. 77, 87 (1938) (Black, J. dissenting): "Corporations have neither race nor color."

14. *In re Byrn, L.A. Times,* Dec. 5, 1971, § 1, at 16 col. 1. A preliminary injunction was subsequently granted, and defendant's cross-motion to vacate the guardianship was denied. Civ. 13113/71 (Sup. Ct. Queens Co., Jan. 4, 1972) (Smith, J.). Appeals are pending. Granting a guardianship in these circumstances would seem to be a more radical advance in the law than granting a guardianship over communal natural objects like lakes. In the former case there is a traditionally recognized guardian for the object — the mother — and her decision has been in favor of aborting the foetus.

15. The laws regarding the various communal resources had to develop along their own lines, not only because so many different persons'

"rights" to consumption and usage were continually and contemporaneously involved, but also because no one had to bear the costs of his consumption of public resources in the way in which the owner of resources on private land has to bear the costs of what he does. For example, if the landowner strips his land of trees, and puts nothing in their stead, he confronts the costs of what he has done in the form of reduced value of his land; but the river polluter's actions are costless, so far as he is concerned — except insofar as the legal system can somehow force him to internalize them. The result has been that the private landowner's power over natural objects on his land is far less restrained by law (as opposed to economics) than his power over the public resources that he can get his hands on. If this state of affairs is to be changed, the standard for interceding in the interests of natural objects on traditionally recognized "private" land might well parallel the rules that guide courts in the matter of people's children whose upbringing (or lack thereof) poses social threat. The courts can, for example, make a child "a dependent of the court" where the child's "home is an unfit place for him by reason of neglect, cruelty, or depravity of either of his parents." Cal. Welf. & Inst. Code § 600(b) (West 1966). *See also id.* at § 601: any child "who from any cause is in danger of leading an idle, dissolute, lewd, or immoral life [may be adjudged] a ward of the court."

16. *See note supra.* The present way of handling such problems on "private" property is to try to enact legislation of general application under the police power, *see Pennsylvania Coal Co. v. Mahon,* 260 U.S. 393 (1922), rather than to institute civil litigation which, though a piecemeal process, can be tailored to individual situations.

17. Cal. Prob. Code § 1580 (West Supp. 1971) lists specific causes for which a guardian may, after notice and a hearing, be removed.
    Despite these protections, the problems of overseeing the guardian is particularly acute where, as here, there are no immediately identifiable human beneficiaries whose self-

interests will encourage them to keep a close watch on the guardian. To ameliorate this problem, a page might well be borrowed from the law of ordinary charitable trusts, which are commonly placed under the supervision of the Attorney General. *See* Cal. Corp. Code §§ 9505, 10207 (West 1955).

18. *See* Cal. Prob. Code §§ 1472, 1590 (West 1956 and Supp. 1971).

19. Here, too, we are dogged by the ontological problem discussed in note 3 *supra.* It is easier to say that the smog-endangered stand of pines "wants" the smog stopped (assuming that to be a jurally significant entity) than it is to venture that the mountain, or the planet earth, or the cosmos, is concerned about whether the pines stand or fall. The more encompassing the entity of concern, the less certain we can be in venturing judgments as to the "wants" of any particular substance, quality, or species within the universe. Does the cosmos care if we humans persist or not? "Heaven and earth . . . regard all things as insignificant, as though they were playthings made of straw." Lao-Tzu, Tao Teh King 13 (D. Goddard transl. 1919).

20. *See Knight v. United States Land Ass'n,* 142 U.S. 161, 181 (1891).

21. Clause 2 gives Congress the power "to dispose of and make all needful Rules and Regulations respecting the Territory or other Property belonging to the United States."

22. *See Flemming v. Nestor,* 363 U.S. 603 (1960).

23. *See* the *L.A. Times* editorial *Water: Public vs. Polluters* criticizing: ". . . the ridiculous built-in conflict of interests on Regional Water Quality Control Board. By law, five of the seven seats are given to spokesmen for industrial, governmental, agricultural or utility users. Only one representative of the public at large is authorized, along with a delegate from fish and game interests." Feb. 12, 1969, Part II, at 8, cols. 1–2.

24. Of course, in the instance of copyright and patent protection, the creation of the "property right" can be more directly justified on homocentric grounds.

25. *See* Schrag, "Life on a Dying Lake," in *The Politics of Neglect* 167, at 173 (R. Meek & J. Straayer, eds., 1971).

26. One ought to observe, too, that in terms of real effect on marginal welfare, the poor quite possibly will bear the brunt of the compromises. They may lack the wherewithal to get out to the countryside — and probably want an increase in material goods more acutely than those who now have riches.

27. On November 2, 1971, the Senate, by a vote of 86–0, passed and sent to the House the proposed Federal Water Pollution Control Act Amendments of 1971, 117 Cong. Reg. S17464 (daily ed. Nov. 2, 1971). Sections 101(a) and (a)(1) of the bill declare it to be "national policy that, consistent with the provisions of this Act — (1) the discharge of pollutants into the navigable waters be eliminated by 1985." S.2770, 92d Cong., 1st Sess., 117 Cong. Rec. S17464 (daily ed. Nov. 2, 1971).

28. 354 F.2d 608, 624 (2d Cir. 1965).

29. Again, there is a problem involving what we conceive to be the injured entity. *See* notes 3, 19 *supra.*

30. *N.Y. Times,* Jan. 14, 1971, § 1, col. 2, and at 74, col. 7.

31. Courts have not been reluctant to award damages for the destruction of heirlooms, literary manuscripts or other property having no ascertainable market value. In *Willard v. Valley Gas Fuel Co.,* 171 Cal. 9, 151 Pac. 286 (1915), it was held that the measure of damages for the negligent destruction of a rare old book written by one of plaintiff's ancestors was the amount which would compensate the owner for all detriment including sentimental loss proximately caused by such destruction. The court, at 171 Cal. 15, 151 Pac. 289, quoted approvingly from *Southern Express Co. v. Owens,* 146 Ala. 412, 426, 41 S. 752 (1906).

32. J. Cousteau, "The Oceans: No Time to Lose," *L.A. Times,* Oct. 24, 1971, § (opinion), at 1, col. 4.

33. *See* J. Harte & R. Socolow, *Patient Earth* (1971).

34. C. McCullers, *The Ballad of the Sad Cafe and Other Stories* 150–51 (1958).

35. C. D. Stone, "Existential Humanism and the Law," in *Existential Humanistic Psychology* 151 (1971).

36. *San Antonio Conservation Soc'y v. Texas Highway Dep't, cert. denied,* 400 U.S. 968 (1970) (Black, J. dissenting to denial of certiorari).

37. *Id.* at 969.

38. *Id.* at 971.

DISCUSSION TOPICS

1. On what basis does Stone argue for the extension of legal rights to natural objects?

2. What disadvantages do Stone's proposals have?

3. In a critique of Stone's proposed extension to natural objects of the guardianship of legal incompetents model, John Rodman has written: "Is this, then, the new enlightenment — to see nonhuman animals as imbeciles, wilderness as a human vegetable?"* How might Stone defend himself against this criticism?

---

*John Rodman, "The Liberation of Nature?" *Inquiry* 20 (1977): 83–145.

READING 63

Fragile Freedoms

Bryan G. Norton

Bryan Norton is professor of philosophy in the School of Public Policy at Georgia Institute of Technology in Atlanta. His most recent book is Searching for Sustainability *(2002). The following selection is from* Toward Unity among Environmentalists *(1991). Using sand dollars as an example, Norton argues for an anthropocentric view that values nature in a total context, including our own cultural history. Environmentalists must develop a criterion of ecological health that includes human activities and educate the public in seeing nature in this larger context. We can protect the "incredible creativity" of nature.*

DOLLARS AND SAND DOLLARS

The poignancy of the dilemma facing advocates of environmental protection was dramatized for me in an encounter with a little girl. It was a sleepy, summer-beach Saturday and I was walking on a sandbar just off my favorite remnant of unspoiled beach on the north tip of Longboat Key, Florida. The little girl clambered up the ledge onto the sandbar, trying not to lose a dozen fresh sand dollars she cradled against her pushed-out and Danskinned stomach. I guessed she was about eight.

Thirty yards away, in knee-deep water, her mother and older sister were strip mining sand dollars—they walked back and forth through the colony, systematically scuffing their feet just under the soft sand on the bottom of the lagoon and bending over to retrieve each disk as it was dislodged. Their treasure was held until collected by the eight-year-old transporter, whose feet were too small to serve as plowshares. Gathering the sand dollars at the point of excavation, she relayed them to the sandbar where a considerable pile was accumulating near the family's beached powerboat.

Many months earlier, I had noted how the fickle current through Longboat Inlet had begun to dump sand in a large crescent spit out into the Gulf of Mexico, forming a waist-deep lagoon. Next came a profusion of shore birds and the colony of sand dollars that multiplied in the protected water, and then came the little girl and her family in their powerboat.

I was startled by the level of industrial organization; even the little girl executed her task with square-jawed efficiency. I engaged her as she emerged onto the sandbar. "You know, they're alive," I said.

"We can put 'em in Clorox at home and they'll turn white."

I asked whether they needed so many. She said, "My Momma makes 'em outta things."

I persisted: "How many does she need to make things?"

"We can get a nickel apiece for the extras at the craft store." I sighed and walked away. Our brief conversation had ended in ideological impasse. . . .

FRAGILE FREEDOMS

. . . When I saw the little girl with so many sand dollars, I was struck speechless because the languages readily available to an environmentalist were inadequate. Once it is admitted that sand dollars can be exchanged for nickels, the language of economic aggregation encourages the application of a maximization criterion. On that language, the little girl's utilitarian logic was unassailable: More is better. But the traditional language of morality, developed and honed over centuries and millennia to articulate rules for interpersonal behavior among human individuals, was equally inadequate: An extension of the language of individual rights and interests to apply to this interspecific situation would encourage a total prohibition on exploitation—and thus would deny the obvious fact that humans must sometimes exploit elements of nature in order to live and enjoy.

Our search for a way between the horns of the environmentalists' dilemma has led to an emphasis on the *context* of human actions. The family's strip-mining operation, on this view, is wrong primarily because it was inappropriate to its context. The exploitative activity turned the beach into the first stage of a trinket factory; building sandcastles and learning about nature had lost out to an economic perspective. That little remnant of beach was saved for little girls, but for little girls to learn to love and respect their natural context, not for them to learn to exploit its products.

I wish now that I had used the incident as an opportunity (with her parents' consent, of course) to teach the little girl some ecology and natural history. I'll bet I could have interested her in the way that sand dollars make a living. I could turn over a sand dollar so that the little girl could see and feel the kneading of the hundreds of little sucker-feet by which sand dollars pull themselves through the sand while passing some of the particles through their bodies, digesting diatoms from the particles as they pass through and are then flushed out.

I'll bet the little girl would have been fascinated to see that the sand dollar has a pentagonal structure analogous to our head, arms, and legs, but that the sand dollar's nervous system is undifferentiated. Therefore the behavioral repertoire of sand dollars is far more limited than our own. Sand dollars' life in predator-rich lagoons encouraged them to invest in external armour rather than mobility.

This approach, turning the beach into a natural laboratory rather than a trinket factory, is in keeping with the environmentalists' long-standing commitment to the educability of the American public. They believe that if enough people adopt the ecological viewpoint, their approach to environmental policy will win out and their common-denominator goals will be achieved. The natural history approach to the situation on the beach is, in other words, to follow Thoreau, Muir, and Leopold in putting faith in the power of observation and experience to transform worldviews. Here, it is possible to say, is the single greatest failure of the environmental movement. While groups have been quite successful in educating their own members through slick membership magazines, they have made less headway in educating the general population. For example, few schools teach conservation in any systematic way, and most science texts do no more than mention conservation in passing.

But I should not, as part of my lesson, insist that the little girl value the sand dollars *in their own right.* That would be like taking the little girl to a symphony concert and trying to teach her to value one note or to an art museum and teaching her to value one brush stroke. We must value nature from our point of view *in a total context,* which includes our cultural history and our natural history. Nature must be valued, from the ecological-evolutionary viewpoint of environmentalists, in its full contemporary complexity and in its largest temporal dynamic.

And this crucial lesson of our dependence on the larger systems of nature can be learned from sand dollars — for sand dollars, just like humans, act within an ecological context. The success of their activities depends on a relatively stable context to which they have adapted. The freedom and creativity of sand dollars is a *constrained* freedom, freedom to adapt to a limiting context. We differ from

sand dollars in having a repertoire of behaviors almost infinitely more complex than theirs. But our freedom and creativity is no less than theirs a constrained freedom.

The freedom to collect sand dollars, to catch rockfish and bluefish, and to propel ourselves about the countryside by burning petroleum are all fragile freedoms. They are freedoms that depend on the relatively stable environmental context in which they have evolved. If I could, then, have used the incident on the beach to teach the little girl that sand dollars embody an ancient wisdom from which we can learn, and also to illustrate for her the way in which our activities — just like the activities of sand dollars — are possible, and gain meaning and value, only in a larger context, I would have progressed a good way toward the goal of getting the little girl to put most of the sand dollars back. The strip-mining activities of the family were not wrong in the absolute terms of interpersonal morality; they were inappropriate on a beach set aside for relaxation and enjoyment of nature.

The family's reaction, upon finding sand dollars in the lagoon, was to treat them as an economic resource. But the power boat gave me a clue that they did not really need the nickels, and the little girl's dogged efforts convinced me that she was the loser on the beach. Trips to the beach should be explorations of a larger world than the limited sphere of economic activity in which the little girl will no doubt spend most of the rest of her life. Like Muir and Leopold I should have emphasized the ecstatic aspect of observation and natural history studies. I could have avoided the environmentalists' dilemma by encouraging the little girl to see the world through a lens larger than a cash register. Then, she might have killed some sand dollars to study them, but she would still have *respected* sand dollars as living things with a story to tell. I hope she would also have realized, then, that sand dollars are more valuable alive than dead.

Moralists among environmental ethicists have erred in looking for a value in living things that is *independent* of human valuing. They have therefore forgotten a most elementary point about valuing anything. Valuing always occurs from the viewpoint of a conscious valuer. Since I doubt that sand dollars are conscious, I doubt they are loci of value-expression. To recognize that only the humans are valuing agents at the beach, however, need not enforce the conclusion that the sand dollar will be valued only from the narrow perspective of human economics. If the little girl can learn to value sand dollars in a larger perspective, an ecological context in which sand dollars are fellow travelers in a huge, creative adventure, she will have taken the first tentative steps toward thinking like a lagoon.

Charter captains see restrictions on the taking of bluefish as unjustified infringements of their freedoms. That, as Leopold recognized, represents a failure of *perception,* not value. The captains, used to apparently unlimited bounty from nature, are unable to think like the bay. Environmentalism will succeed if it educates the public so that all citizens are capable of seeing environmental problems at the interface of two systems — the slow-changing systems of nature that change in ecological and evolutionary time and the relatively fast-changing systems of human economics. To the extent that individual freedoms to take bluefish or rockfish depend on the complex, usually slow-changing, systems of nature, they are fragile freedoms. They depend upon, and gain meaning and value within the larger, natural context in which they are pursued.

Does the fragility of freedoms to use nature entail onerous restrictions? Have we, after all, arrived at the depressing conclusion that the future — if environmentalists are correct in seeing the world contextually — will be one of increasing constraints on individual freedoms? Will we, in a world of growing populations and increasing scarcity, be driven to ever more oppressive restrictions on individual freedoms?

I think not. This depressing conclusion follows only if we accept the contextualist worldview incompletely. It is not arrogant to value things from one's own conscious perspective, and to that extent a degree of anthropocentrism is a foregone conclusion. The hard questions will concern which actual activities will be discouraged or limited, and in those arguments environmentalists, anthropocentrists, and ecocentrists alike will support a broadly scientific, ecological, and contextual viewpoint. Most values, from the ecological perspective, depend on saving the ecological systems that are the context of human cultural and economic activities.

Most environmental ethicists have, to date, assumed that we must, to escape arrogance, posit value as independent of human valuing or human valuers. This value has proven to offer little guidance in action and has raised innumerable and intractable questions in the metaphysics of morals. The moral premise of this book is that there exist limits on human treatment of nature — thereby rejecting the implication that humans may do anything they please to their natural context — while leaving the original idea of anthropocentrism — that all value will be perceived from the viewpoint of conscious beings — intact.

To accept the contextualist viewpoint encouraged by an ecological worldview is to recognize that the creative force is outside us. We do not create either energy or biomass — we are derivative beings, who value and choose within a complicated system to which we adapt. Even as we learn more and more about the cunning and creativity of nature, we learn simultaneously that we are finite beings who are free only in the sense that we are free to react creatively and differentially to ever-changing situations outside us, a system that extends beyond our bodies in both time and space.

As Muir and the ecological thinkers who succeeded him emphasized our role as a part of a larger whole, they did not *introduce* the idea that our freedoms are fragile — that idea is clearly implied in the story of the fall from grace and the expulsion from the Garden of Eden. Freedom has always been understood as occurring within constraints. The new idea that must guide environmental ethics is not that our freedoms are limited, but that an important element of those limits exists in nature itself, not in the commandments of a disembodied God or the rights of our fellow humans. The rules governing our treatment of nature are guided neither by the authority of God nor by a priori, precultural moral norms such as rights of natural objects. Environmentalists have been forced to recognize that we must struggle to articulate limits on acceptable behavior by learning more and more about how we affect, and are affected by, our environmental context. The land ethic is nothing more than the latter half of our culture's search for a good life in a good environment. Ecology, the transformative science, prefers an organic metaphor; environmentalists believe that the organic analogy of nature as creative—which is illustrated throughout natural history studies—provides a better metaphor for understanding our adaptive role in larger environments.

In this sense, environmentalists must reject the arrogance involved in the suggestion that humans can do as they please with regard to nature. They must also admit that the creativity of nature is the Great Mystery. If we destroy without understanding, we commit the greatest arrogance, for it is understanding the sweep of millennia, the ability of nature to create more and more elaborate life forms from the deaths of countless individuals, that will ultimately explain our own existence, our correct place. The search for the self-moved mover has only since Darwin become a question in biology. But it was the prophetic Muir who recognized most clearly that science and theology would eventually merge once again as they did in Genesis I. The linchpin of the modern environmental movement is the belief that the study of nature has this ecstatic aspect; the ability to inspire wonder at our "partness" and at the whole of which we are a part is simply the ability to inspire a shift to a new perspective in which nature is an object of contemplation, not exploitation. If that change were to occur, environmentalists believe, there would be more support for contextually sensitive policies.

But still we are left with the disturbing question: How onerous must the restrictions be on future human activities? The answer to this question, I think, must be "It depends." It depends on how we conceive those restrictions. If we, as at present, conceive nature as a machine capable of producing unlimited amounts of a small number of economically useful items, we will view nature and our opportunities statically. If charter captains, who once could offer their clients unlimited catches of bluefish, insist on that freedom indefinitely, they will destroy that freedom. Bluefish catches will eventually be limited by rules and regulations or by natural declines in bluefish stocks. The outlook for human freedom from this static viewpoint looks bleak.

But consider an analogy. Whaling is in the process of fading away as an economically feasible activity. Whale stocks are so depleted that the search becomes ever more expensive. Technology has found substitutes for all but the most esoteric uses of whale oil. Environmentalists therefore insist that whaling is no longer an appropriate activity, even if there are governments that will prop up the dying industry with economic subsidies. If environmentalists and others succeed in the desperate effort to save populations of the great whales, however, there will be a whole new, nonconsumptive, and dynamic industry, whale watching, that will take its place. Children of future generations will pay, it can be assumed, to watch a great whale swim playfully under their boat and breach a few yards away. The fragile freedom to kill whales will be replaced with a more secure freedom, a freedom consonant with the life history of these great, but not reproductively prolific, creatures.

And this suggests the proper answer to charter boat captains who are justifiably wary of catch restrictions given the present attitudes of charter renters. The charter captains have an obligation to educate as well as profit from their customers. The whale-watching case suggests how salable a natural spectacle is. Participation in a bluefish run should be reward enough—and it would be if fishermen carried away information and understanding as well as a couple of bluefish. Charter captains should teach themselves some marine ecology and pass it on as part of their explanations of why, next year, we're going to release all bluefish but three per fisherman. This is the proper response to a demand for bluefish that cannot be met indefinitely: educate the public and have them pay for it as part of the skills of a competent charter captain. If charter captains will not educate their fishermen, who will?

The writer Annie Dillard expresses a sense of awe, a dogged persistence in seeing and wondering at it all. Nowhere is this sense of wonder—which was, after all, what was missing from the little girl's afternoon at the beach—stronger than in her graphic description of nature's profligacy, a chapter called "Fecundity," in *Pilgrim at Tinker Creek.* She describes aphids, which lay a million eggs to achieve a few adults.[1]

Dillard is saying something very profound, and it holds the key to being content with fragile freedoms. The recognition that our freedoms are fragile is, in a sense, no more than an admission of our own finitude. That, by way of bad news, is nothing new. But Dillard's illustration of the incredible, virtually infinite creativity of nature is the good news. Our freedom and creativity may appear limited when looked at from a conservative viewpoint that insists on pressing fragile freedoms, such as the freedom to take bluefish, rockfish, or whales to their limit. But the same insight should encourage us to recognize that we have the ability to learn, through science, the limitations of populations of rockfish and whales to reproduce, and to encourage alternative, more adaptive human behaviors before an element of nature's productive fabric is destroyed.

And here we see the potentially true nobility of the human species. Unlike the other forces of nature, which react unconsciously to their surroundings, mainly through the weeding out of unfit individuals, we are conscious beings who can adapt consciously to our changing environment. If we can progress beyond the environmentalists' dilemma, which encourages us to understand and value nature either in the limited context of human economics or in the limited context of human ethics, and value nature from *our* point of view, but in its full and glorious context, there is yet hope for the human species.

Conservation biology must now move rapidly to propose a positive criterion of ecological health for natural systems, a criterion that places value neither on simply exploiting the atomistic elements of nature nor on isolating nature and separating human activities from it. But conservationists should not propose their criterion imperiously; they should work with nature interpreters in parks, on television, and in books to involve the public in the search for a land ethic. It should be a positive criterion for the ecological health of systems that recognizes that some human activities are compatible with the ongoing health of the energy pyramid, and others will positively enhance it. The good news for us and future generations of humans is that we, as conscious beings with scientific tools, can occupy a synoptic viewpoint from which we can understand, and protect, the incredible creativity of nature. Our success will depend on how quickly we develop such a positive criterion and how quickly this criterion can become a basis for private actions and public policies. And that, of course, will depend on how successful envi-

ronmentalists are in encouraging contextual thinking and educating the public in the ecological, systematic viewpoint on nature. It is the firm commitment to the dynamic aspect of human valuing—its reactivity to changing situations—that marks the ecological/ evolutionary perspective: humans must understand and value from a realistic perspective by recognizing their role in the larger ecological context.

NOTE

1. Annie Dillard, *Pilgrim at Tinker Creek* (New York: Harper and Row, 1974), p. 175

DISCUSSION TOPICS

1. According to Norton, why is the strip-mining of the sand dollars wrong? Do you agree with his view? Why or why not?
2. Norton believes that people can be educated to appreciate natural history. In your own experience in elementary and secondary school, how was conservation addressed? What kind of conservation education (if any) should be standard in public education?
3. According to Norton, in what sense is driving a gasoline-powered car a "fragile freedom"? Do you agree? Explain your reasoning.
4. Compare Norton's and Callicott's view that valuing requires a conscious valuer to Rolston's vision of nonconscious organisms as holding (rather than beholding) value.
5. According to Norton, what is the "new idea which must guide environmental ethics"?

READING 64

The Relevance of Environmental Ethical Theories for Policy Making

Mikael Stenmark

Mikael Stenmark teaches philosophy of religion and environmental ethics in the Department of Theology, Uppsala University, Sweden. His most recent book is

Environmental Ethics and Policy-Making *(2002). The following essay was published in the journal* Environmental Ethics *in 2002. Stenmark tests Bryan Norton's "convergence hypothesis" that "environmentalists are evolving toward a consensus in policy even though they remain divided regarding basic values." Stenmark concludes that Norton's hypothesis is incorrect, because differences in basic values do generate divergent policies in three important areas.*

I. INTRODUCTION

An issue of great importance is whether differences in ethical theory have any relevance for the practical issues of environmental management and policy making. Bryan G. Norton has been one of the key advocates of the view that the difference in value commitments has little relevance when it comes to concrete decisions about growth, pollution control, biological diversity, and so on. In his book, *Toward Unity among Environmentalists,* he offers an extended argument for this conclusion. The central hypothesis of the book is that "environmentalists are evolving toward a consensus in policy even though they remain divided regarding basic values."[1] He calls this hypothesis the "convergence hypothesis." Norton tries to vindicate this hypothesis by taking us through four regions of the current policy debate (issues of growth, pollution control, biological diversity, and land use policy). His conclusion is, if generalized, that

> introducing the idea that other species have intrinsic value, that humans should be "fair" to all other species, provides no operationally recognizable constraints on human behavior that are not already implicit in the generalized, cross-temporal obligations to protect a healthy, complex, and autonomously functioning system for the benefit of future generations of humans.[2]

Many nonanthropocentrists disagree, however, claiming that divergence in basic values makes all the difference when it comes to environmental policy making. Paul Taylor, for example, writes, "It makes a practical difference in the way we treat the natural environment whether we accept an anthropocentric or a biocentric system of ethics."[3] Like-

wise, Holmes Rolston, III is convinced that "A model in which nature has no value apart from human preferences will imply different conduct from one where nature projects all values. . . ."[4] Finally, J. Baird Callicott's direct reply to Norton is that "Norton's 'convergence hypothesis' . . . is dead wrong."[5]

Who is right? Can Norton's convergence hypothesis be sustained or is Callicott right that it is dead wrong? More specifically, what differences (if any) could or should divergence in basic values make for environmental management and policy making? My aim in this article is to offer an answer to this issue, which I call the *theory-policy issue.* I try to show that there are good reasons to reject Norton's position if it is taken to imply that the value differences between anthropocentrists and nonanthropocentrists are of little relevance at the level of policy making. I also try to state more explicitly what these differences amount to on the policy level.

The article is arranged as follows. First, I distinguish between some of the main versions of anthropocentrism and nonanthropocentrism. Second, I identify the different goals that the advocates of these ethical theories set up for environmental policy making. Third, I discuss three important policy areas (human population, wilderness preservation and wildlife management) and show that differences in basic values generate divergent policies.

II. VERSIONS OF ANTHROPOCENTRISM AND NONANTHROPOCENTRISM

Anthropocentrism and nonanthropocentrism come in a variety of different forms. It is therefore necessary that we stipulate what versions of them we intend to compare. Let us also try to find formulations that make the step from ethical theory to policy fairly easy. We can then specify *anthropocentrism* as the view that people's behavior toward nature should ultimately be evaluated solely on the basis of how it affects human beings, whereas *nonanthropocentrism* is the idea that people's behavior toward nature should be evaluated also on the basis of how it affects other living beings or ecosystems. The reason the anthropocentrists give for why we should take into account only humans is that they maintain that humans are the only ones who have intrinsic value or moral standing. Correspondingly, the reason nonanthropocentrists give for taking into account not merely humans is that they claim that other living things or natural objects also have intrinsic value or moral standing.

Furthermore, two important versions of anthropocentrism need to be distinguished. *Traditional anthropocentrism* is the position that people's behavior toward nature should be evaluated solely on the basis of how they affect now living human beings, whereas *intergenerational anthropocentrism* is the view that people's behavior toward nature should be evaluated on the basis of how they affect both present and future human generations. (Norton's claim is thus, more exactly, that nonanthropocentrism provides no operationally recognizable constraints on human behavior that are not already implicit in intergenerational anthropocentrism.) But two versions of nonanthropocentrism must also be distinguished. *Biocentrism* is the view that people's behavior toward nature should be evaluated on the basis of how they affect living beings (including humans) and only them. Hence, at least some living things besides humans have intrinsic value or moral standing, but since species or ecosystems are not, *per se,* living things they lack such a value or standing. Ecocentrists, on the other hand, deny this view. Thus, *ecocentrism* (or the land ethic) is the view that people's behavior toward nature should be evaluated also on the basis of how they affect species and ecosystems and not merely living beings.

These views show that anthropocentrists, biocentrists, and ecocentrists disagree, first, about which natural things have intrinsic value or moral standing. They offer different answers to the question concerning the kinds of things in nature we can treat morally rightly or wrongly and thus must take into account in our moral evaluations. I call this disagreement the *moral standing issue.* However, we need more information to be able to detect whether these ethical theories support different environmental policies. Second, to state the point differently, environmentalists disagree about whether the natural things we can treat morally rightly or wrongly have the same moral standing or equal moral worth. They offer different answers to the question of what degree of *moral significance* the objects of moral standing have. These differences are possible because

moral standing does not entail equal moral significance. I call this issue the *moral significance issue.* Callicott, for example, claims:

> The land ethic manifestly does not accord equal moral worth to each and every member of the biotic community; the moral worth of individuals (including, take note, human individuals) is relative, to be assessed in accordance with the particular relation of each to the collective entity which Leopold called "land."[6]

Taylor, on the other hand, maintains that "every species counts as having the same value in the sense that, regardless of what species a living thing belongs to, it is deemed to be prima facie deserving of equal concern and consideration on the part of moral agents."[7] Callicott's ethic is thus an example of a value-differentiated nonanthropocentrism, whereas Taylor's is an example of a value-undifferentiated nonanthropocentrism. Accordingly, we can expect that an ecocentrism that contains the idea that the moral significance of human beings is much higher than that of species and ecosystems will be much closer to intergenerational anthropocentrism when it comes to policy issues, than a form of ecocentrism that treats human beings as plain members and citizens of the biotic community and thus maintains that the moral significance of species and ecosystems is higher than that of human beings.

The problem is that the options — when it comes to the question about moral significance — are almost innumerable, although we know, for instance, that ecocentrists typically accord a higher moral worth to biological wholes than biocentrists do, who tend to emphasize biological individuals. However, it will do for our purpose to differentiate between a weak and a strong version of biocentrism and ecocentrism. What I take to be characteristic of the *strong version* is that its advocates accord almost equal, equal, or higher moral significance to some other nonhuman natural things, which are taken to have moral standing. Thus, Callicott's statement, "In every case the effect upon ecological systems is the decisive factor in the determination of the ethical quality of actions," illustrates strong ecocentrism.[8] Examples of strong biocentrism include

Regan's view that "all animals are equal, when the notion of 'animal' and 'equality' are properly understood, 'animal' referring to all (terrestrial, at least) moral agents and patients, and 'equality' referring to their equal possession of inherent value"[9] and Taylor's view that contains a "total rejection of the idea that human beings are superior to other living things [including plants]."[10]

What is common for the *weak version,* on the other hand, is that its defenders accord in general (though not always) a higher moral significance to humans than the other natural things, which are taken to have moral standing. On these grounds, Rolston is an example of an advocate of weak ecocentrism. In contrast to Callicott, who takes the effect of decisions upon ecological systems to be the decisive factor, Rolston writes, "*an* important ethical constraint in environmental decisions is concern for the integrity, stability and beauty of biotic communities."[11] In other words, the effect upon ecological systems is important, but not necessarily the most important constraint on human behavior. He thinks, for instance, that it "has been necessary in the course of human history to sacrifice most of the wildlands, converting them to rural and urban settlements, and this is both good and ecological."[12] A Swedish professor of ethics, Carl-Henric Grenholm, has recently defended a weak version of biocentrism. He claims that "a human being has a unique moral standing. His or her intrinsic value carries greater weight than the intrinsic value of other living creatures. . . . In a conflict between the well-being of humans and that of animals, the well-being of humans have in general a greater weight than that of animals."[13]

Notice also that we can, in a similar way, distinguish between weak and strong versions of intergenerational anthropocentrism. We can say that those anthropocentrists who maintain that future human generations have almost equal, equal, or higher moral significance than now living human generations, are defenders of strong intergenerational anthropocentrism, whereas those who deny this defend the weak version. Thus, Andrew C. Kadak's statement that "no generation should (needlessly), now or in the future, deprive its successors of the opportunity to enjoy a quality of life equivalent to its

own," is an example of the strong version.[14] A defender of the weak version is arguably James P. Sterba because he writes that "a right to life applied to future generations would be a right of a person whom we can definitely expect to exist to receive the goods and resources necessary to satisfy their basic needs or to noninterference with their attempts to acquire the goods and resources necessary to satisfy their basic needs."[15] Thus, the weak and the strong version offer different principles of intergenerational equity.

III. THE GOAL OF ENVIRONMENTAL MANAGEMENT AND POLICY MAKING

The question I am trying to find an answer to is whether differences in basic values have an impact on the choice of environmental policies. This question can now be restated as follows: *is it the case that nonanthropocentrism (either in its strong or weak biocentric version or in its strong or weak ecocentric version) supports different environmental policies than intergenerational anthropocentrism does?*

A problem we immediately face is that while we can find a number of documents where the policies of intergenerational anthropocentrism are explicitly stated, such as the World Commission's *Our Common Future* and UN's *Agenda 21,* similar documents expressing the policies of biocentrism and ecocentrism are harder to find. What we typically have to settle for are the examples philosophers sometimes give of what practical implications they attribute to their biocentric or ecocentric theories. Let us, however, proceed in this way and, with the help of the distinctions drawn in the last section, see if we can systematize their account and perhaps also derive additional practical consequences from their basic value commitments.

Let us first, however, focus on the *goal* of environmental policy making. According to the World Commission, the purpose of environmental protection and management is "to begin managing environmental resources to ensure both sustainable human progress and human survival."[16] We can read in the chairman's foreword that the report's "message is directed toward people, whose well-being is the ultimate goal of all environmental and development policies."[17] This statement fits nicely with what is also stated in the first principle of the Rio Declaration, namely, "Human beings are at the centre of concerns for sustainable development." The goal of intergenerational anthropocentric policy making is, thus, *to ensure that the natural resources are used in an efficient and a farsighted way so that the needs of present and future human generations can be satisfied.* The goal is to create an ecologically sustainable development.

What is the purpose of environmental protection according to biocentrists? This purpose is seldom stated explicitly, but we get a good hint when, for instance, Regan writes, "the overarching goal of wildlife management should not be to insure maximum sustainable yield: it should be to protect wild animals from those who would violate their rights."[18] Contrary to what the World Commission claims, it is not merely the well-being of humans, but also of animals (and Taylor would add, plants) which is the ultimate goal of all environmental and development policies. The objective is to formulate a policy program that is also fair to other living things. The goal of biocentric policy making would then be *to ensure that humans in their treatment of nature do not violate the rights of other living things to be left alone and to flourish.*

It is perhaps not so difficult to formulate what ecocentrists think is the purpose of environmental protection and management, if we recall Aldo Leopold's famous words, "A thing is right when it tends to preserve the integrity, stability, and beauty of the biotic community. It is wrong when it tends otherwise."[19] Hence, the goal of ecocentric policy making seems to be *to ensure that humans in their use of nature do not violate the integrity and stability of the biotic community and its individual members.* That is, in Rolston's terminology, to ensure that we do not get engaged in "superkilling."[20] A decisive or, at least, an important factor to take into account in formulating a policy program is then the effect the policies have on the health and flourishing of species and ecosystems. Wetlands, rain forests, and endangered species are at the center of concern, and they are of concern whether or not it benefits the human community.

In other words, the goals for environmental policy making that anthropocentrists, biocentrists, and ecocentrists envision are not the same. But what about the *means?* Is it the case that the specific policies which are required to reach these different goals are nevertheless the same? I next try to show that anthropocentrism, biocentrism, and ecocentrism support divergent policies to a significant extent, which perhaps is not surprising once we become aware that the advocates of these views offer different accounts of what the goal of environmental protection and management should be.

IV. HUMAN POPULATION POLICIES

In many parts of the world, the population is growing at rates that cannot be sustained by available environmental resources and in such a way that the productive potential of the ecosystems is threatened both in the short and the long run. Urgent steps are therefore needed to limit extreme rates of population growth. The World Commission agrees on this point, but also notes that the issue is not just the size of the population, but how the number of people relates to available resources. An additional person in an industrial country consumes far more and places far greater pressure on natural resources than an additional person in the third world. Therefore, the World Commission argues that governments need to develop long-term population policies, because "sustainable development can only be pursued if population size and growth are in harmony with the changing productive potential of the ecosystem."[21] Furthermore, the "critical issues are the balance between population size and available resources and the rate of population growth in relation to the capacity of the economy to provide for the basic needs of the population, not just today but for generations."[22] That is to say, our responsibility toward other people and future human generations requires, what we can call, a "stabilization policy": *we must ensure that the size of the population stabilizes at a level compatible with the productive capacity of the supporting ecosystems.* Not until it is stabilized can the objective of "ensuring a sustainable level of population" be achieved.[23]

What a sustainable level of population in more absolute numbers is is merely suggested. It is perhaps that the global population stabilizes at 7.7 billion by 2060 (p. 102). This level would occur if the replacement level were reached in 2010 (that is, when slightly over two children on average per couple are born). But the issue is, of course, for the anthropocentrists, always related to how much we can improve agricultural productivity and efficiency within the framework set by the carrying capacity of the supporting ecosystems. The "challenge" is "to keep pace with demand, while retaining the essential ecological integrity of production systems. . . ."[24]

What about the nonanthropocentrists? Can we find any hints about what population policies they advocate? Yes, I believe we can. I also think that there are good reasons to believe that they typically differ from the intergenerational anthropocentric ones. Rolston maintains, for instance, that "conserving the Earth is more important than having *more* people." It is even "more important than the needs, or even the welfare, of *existing* people."[25] Arne Naess tells us that one of the key principles of deep ecology is that "The flourishing of human life and cultures is compatible with a substantial decrease of the human population. The flourishing of nonhuman life requires such a decrease."[26] Furthermore, Naess writes as a response to an answer given by a United Nations study (to the question "Given the present world-wide industrial and agricultural capacity, technological development, and resource exploitation, how many people could be supported on Earth today with the standard of living of the average American?") that

> The authors think that 500 million would not result in a uniform, stagnant world and refer to the seventeenth century. Agreed, but the question raised refers only to humans. How about other living beings? If their life quality is not to be lowered through human dominance, for instance agriculture, are not 500 million too many? Or: are cultural diversity, development of the sciences and arts, and of course basic needs of humans not served by, let us say, 100 million?[27]

Likewise, Callicott suggests that as "omnivores, the population of human beings should, perhaps, be roughly twice that of bears, allowing for differences of size. A global population of more than four billion persons and showing no signs of an orderly decline . . . is at present a global disaster . . . for the biotic community."[28]

I do not think, however, that nonanthropocentrists give a homogeneous answer to the question of what an optimal human population would be. In part, their answer is related to an issue within human ethics: should we maximize the number of people with minimal standard of living or should we limit the number of people and strive to have a high standard of living? It also depends on whether we have in mind the weak or the strong versions of biocentrism and ecocentrism. Nevertheless, in all the examples just given, other living things are assumed to have such a high moral significance that a self-limitation of the human population is to taken to be morally mandatory. These nonanthropocentrists support, in contrast to the World Commission, a "limitation population policy": *We must ensure that the size of the population is reduced to a level that is compatible with a respect for other living things and/or the integrity of species and ecosystems.* Many of them even think that a substantial decrease of the size of the human population is morally required. It is less clear, however, what strategies the nonanthropocentrists think we should use to implement the limitation policy. I do not think that most nonanthropocentrists share William Aiken's radical view that "massive human diebacks would be good. It is our duty to cause them. It is our species' duty, relative to the whole, to eliminate 90 percent of our numbers."[29] At least not if *eliminate* means shooting people. Rather, I think, Irvine and Ponton list a number of more reasonable options available to the nonanthropocentrists. They write:

> There could be payments for periods of non-pregnancy and non-birth (a kind of no claims bonus); tax benefits for families with fewer than two children; sterilization bonuses; withdrawal of maternity and similar benefits after a second child; larger pensions for people with fewer than two children; free, easily available family planning; more funds for research into means of contraception, especially for men; an end to fertility research and treatment; a more realistic approach to abortion; the banning of surrogate motherhood and similar

practices; and the promotion of equal opportunities for women in all areas of life.[30]

Nonanthropocentrists, nevertheless, need to be more explicit about how they think that we should implement the limitation policy. However, and this is what is relevant for my argument, it is clear that nonanthropocentrism and intergenerational anthropocentrism support different population policies.

V. WILDLIFE PRESERVATION POLICIES

An issue closely related to the population problem concerns how much of nature ought to be left wild or unexplored. If the population is allowed to continue to grow, then those areas of nature that at present are not used by humans must be transformed into agricultural landscapes to satisfy people's needs.

According to the authors of *Our Common Future* and *Agenda 21,* the question of the size of the wilderness is understood as an issue about the conservation of living natural resources. The objective is to conserve "a representative sample of Earth's ecosystems," which is "an indispensable prerequisite for sustainable development" and they add, "our failure to do so will not be forgiven by future generations."[31] They write that now nearly four percent of the Earth's land area is protected, but add that probably the total expanse of protected areas needs to be at least tripled.[32] This expansion would amount to, *in toto,* roughly twelve percent. It is not clear, however, if they think that it is a *duty* we have toward future generations to protect areas of roughly this size. They at least maintain that we have a duty toward future generations not to exploit all areas of wilderness. But let us assume that a representative sample of Earth's ecosystems would amount to twelve percent of all the land on the planet and that it is our duty to future generations to ensure that such areas are set aside and protected.

Can we find a consensus in policy on this issue even though differences in basic values remain between anthropocentrists and nonanthropocentrists? To some extent, as I show below, the answer is yes. Rolston, who has been classified as a weak ecocentrist, writes, "I do not say that there is no further cultural development needed, only that we do not need

further cultural development that sacrifices nature for culture, that enlarges the sphere of culture at the price of diminishing the sphere of nature."[33] He thinks that we have a duty to protect the wilderness that remains (although this is a duty toward ecosystems and not to future people). Hence, the weak ecocentric "wilderness preservation policy" is *to ensure that the remaining areas of wilderness stay wild and non-exploited.*

What nevertheless makes it difficult to compare Rolston and the World Commission is that Rolston estimates that ninety to ninety-five percent of the land is already modified by humans, whereas the commission obviously thinks that at least fifteen percent (if not more) still remains wild.[34] However, since Rolston takes the objective to be to ensure that the remaining areas of wilderness stay wild, the wilderness preservation policy suggested by the commission seems to converge with Rolston's, namely, that *we must ensure that roughly twelve percent of the landscape remains wild.* No difference in the short run would, therefore, exist between intergenerational anthropocentrism and weak ecocentrism.

Nevertheless, in the long run they do diverge. The justification of this wilderness preservation policy given by the commission is that species and natural ecosystems make many important contributions to human welfare; in particular, they contain useful genetic material.[35] But, of course, these wilderness areas can only provide important genetic material for future generations if *they* (in contrast to us) are allowed to *use* these areas. Nothing, it seems, would therefore require that this twelve percent of the landscape remain wild or untouched also in the future. Rolston, on the other hand, thinks enough is enough. Any further exploitation of the wilderness would only further upset an already unbalanced situation.[36] Independently of whatever use present or future generations may make of these wilderness areas, they ought to be left—now and forever—alone. Thus, the intergenerational anthropocentric wilderness policy is actually that we must ensure that twelve percent of the landscape remains wild *for future human generations to use,* whereas the weak ecocentric wilderness policy is that we must ensure that twelve percent of the landscape remains wild *for plants and animals to use.*

Is it reasonable to think that advocates of strong ecocentrism would be satisfied with this wilderness preservation policy? Hardly, because for Callicott the effect upon ecological systems is the decisive factor in the determination of the ethical quality of actions. It is the well-being of the biotic community, and not of the human community, that ought to be at the center of concern for environmental policy making. It is, therefore, likely that a strong ecocentric ethic would imply that humans should live in such a way that much less of the natural ecosystems would be modified for human purposes, than is actually the case. Thus, Bill Devall and George Sessions write that "we should live with minimum rather than maximum impact on other species and on the Earth in general"[37] and Callicott tells us, "The land ethic . . . requires a shrinkage, if at all possible, of the domestic sphere."[38]

But is shrinkage of the domestic sphere possible or, phrased differently, can we successfully restore cultivated land if we wanted to? Rolston argues that it is possible to restore, for instance, a prairie that has been not too badly overgrazed:

> Revegetating after strip mining cannot properly be called rehabilitation . . . because there is in fact nothing left to rehabilitate. But one can rehabilitate a prairie that has been not too badly overgrazed. Overgrazing allows many introduced weeds to outcompete the natives; perhaps all one has to do is pull the weeds and let nature do the rest. . . . Overgrazing allows some native plants to outcompete other natives, those that once reproduced in the shade of the taller grasses. So perhaps, after the taller grasses return, one will have to dig some holes, put in some seeds that have been gathered from elsewhere, cover them up, go home, and let nature do the rest. . . . The naturalness returns.[39]

Let us, therefore grant that nature can, once we put the parts back in place, heal itself. Thus, shrinkage of the domestic sphere seems to be possible and, according to strong ecocentrism, also a part of our duty toward ecosystems and other species. However, depending on what degree of moral significance that is given to natural ecosystems and other species in contrast to human beings, strong ecocentrists may disagree about exactly how much already "occupied land" we ought to return to the other members of the biotic community.

Nevertheless, we can certainly assume that their basic values lead them to an environmental protection program that not only contains the wildlife preservation policy but also a restoration policy. A "wildlife restoration policy" which states that *we should rehabilitate those (or, at least, parts of those) areas of the land that can still be restored to pristine nature.* We ought to back off from these occupied areas for the sake of the wildlife, so that they can once more live there and the land can heal itself. Notice also that this policy may not necessarily require extensive human intervention in the ecosystems because the ecocentrists also endorse the population limitation policy, which is typically taken to imply a significant reduction of the number of human beings in the future. Thus, nature itself can be assumed to take care of most of the rehabilitation work.

VI. WILDLIFE MANAGEMENT POLICIES

Let us move on to a third and final area for environmental policy making, namely, wildlife management, and on this issue compare principally biocentrism and anthropocentrism. The focus of biocentrists is not so much on biological wholes such as wetlands and rain forests, as on the individual inhabitants of the land. According to a strong biocentrist such as Regan, environmental policy making is about defending "wild animals in the possession of their rights, providing them with the opportunity to live their own life, by their own lights, as best they can. . . ."[40] Hence, wildlife management should be designed to protect wild animals against humans. We ought to let wildlife be and let the members of these other species carve out their own destiny. Likewise, Taylor explains that the biocentric rule of noninterference "means that we must not try to manipulate, control, modify, or 'manage' natural ecosystems or otherwise intervene in their normal functioning."[41] If, for instance, it is the case that the extinction of the members of a species population is due to entirely natural causes, we are morally prohibited from trying to stop the natural sequence of events from taking place in order to save it, even if that species would provide us with important genetic material.

This prohibition means that the general directive for wildlife management consists of a "hands off policy": *we must ensure that wildlife is left alone and that human interventions in it are severely restricted.* Furthermore, strong biocentrism generates a "hunting and fishing policy" that tells us to *to ensure that hunting, trapping and fishing are severely restricted or even prohibited.* Regan maintains that what hunters "do is wrong because they are parties to a practice that treats animals as if they were a naturally recurring renewable resource."[42] Taylor writes that besides "breaking the Rule of Fidelity, hunting, trapping, and fishing also, of course, involve gross violations of the Rules of Nonmaleficence and Noninterference."[43]

But these strong biocentric policies seem to come in direct conflict with intergenerational anthropocentrism, as it is developed in *Our Common Future* and *Agenda 21.* No argument can be found in these documents, for a comprehensive hands off policy. Rather, the objective is to begin "managing environmental resources to ensure both sustainable human progress and human survival."[44] We must promote a more efficient, long-term natural resource use. In other words, in this particular case, we must learn to use animals and plants in a more efficient and long-range way. If, for instance, a species population is threatened by natural extinction and we know that it can provide present or future generations with important genetic material, then we should try to save this species (unless the costs are unbearably high).

Thus, the whole idea of managing environmental resources to ensure both sustainable human progress and human survival is the very opposite to Regan's idea. The commission's viewpoint is that we must have a program for wildlife management that takes into account the idea that animals *are* naturally recurring renewable resources. We therefore need policies that regulate hunting, trapping, and fishing is such a way that no animal species (or at least those with high instrumental value) are threatened by extinction. The challenge is to do so, while at the same [time] making sure that these practices become more efficient in feeding the growing population. What is needed is a hunting and fishing practice that is more

efficient and ecologically sustainable. The World Commission writes: "Landings (of fish) have increased by 1 million tons per year over the past few years; by the end of the century, a catch of around 100 million tons should be possible."[45] The problem is, however, that the catch is well short of the projected demand and there are indications that freshwater fish stocks are fully exploited and damaged by pollution. One piece of advice the commission gives to solve this problem is to suggest a further development of aquaculture or fish farming, because it "can help meet future [human] needs."[46] The intergenerational anthropocentric hunting and fishing policy is, therefore, not to prohibit or severely limit hunting, trapping and fishing, but *to ensure the improvement of these activities,* both when it comes to efficiency and ecological sustainability. Once again, differences in basic values lead to different policies.

VII. CONCLUSION

I have addressed the issue of whether differences in ethical theory have any relevance for the practical issues of environmental management and policy making. I have called this issue the theory-policy issue. Norton's answer, expressed as a convergence hypothesis, is that environmentalists are evolving toward a consensus in policy even though they remain divided regarding basic values. I have tried to show that there are good reasons for rejecting Norton's position, at least, if it is taken to imply that the value differences between intergenerational anthropocentrists and nonanthropocentrists are of little relevance when it comes to policy making. I have done so, first, by distinguishing between different forms of anthropocentrism and nonanthropocentrism, second, by contrasting the different goals that anthropocentrists, biocentrists, and ecocentrists set up for environmental policy making, and, lastly, by identifying three important policy areas (population growth, wilderness preservation and wildlife management) where differences in basic values generate divergent policies.

NOTES

1. Bryan, G. Norton, *Toward Unity among Environmentalists* (Oxford: Oxford University Press, 1991), p. 86.

2. Ibid., pp. 226–27.

3. Paul Taylor, *Respect for Nature: A Theory of Environmental Ethics* (Princeton: Princeton University Press, 1986), p. 12.

4. Holmes Rolston, III, *Environmental Ethics* (Philadelphia: Temple University Press, 1988), p. 230.

5. J. Baird Callicott, "Environmental Philosophy Is Environmental Activism: The Most Radical and Effective Kind," in Don E. Marietta, Jr. and Lester Embree, eds., *Environmental Philosophy and Environmental Activism* (Boston: Rowman and Littlefield, 1995), p. 22.

6. J. Baird Callicott, "Animal Liberation: A Triangular Affair," in J. Baird Callicott, *In Defense of the Land Ethic* (Albany: State University of New York Press, 1989), p. 28.

7. Taylor, *Respect for Nature,* p. 155.

8. Callicott, "Animal Liberation: A Triangular Affair," p. 21.

9. Tom Regan, *The Case for Animal Rights* (Berkeley: University of California Press, 1983), p. 240.

10. Taylor, *Respect for Nature,* p. 129.

11. Holmes Rolston, III, *Conserving Natural Value* (New York: Columbia University Press, 1994), p. 82 (emphasis added).

12. Rolston, *Environmental Ethics,* p. 226.

13. Carl-Henric Grenholm, "Etik och djurförsök" ["Ethics and Animal Experimentation"], *Årsbok 1997 för Föreningen lärare i Religionskunskap,* pp. 93–94 (my translation).

14. Andrew C. Kadak, "An Intergenerational Approach to High-Level Waste Disposal," *Nuclear News,* July 1997, p. 50.

15. James P. Sterba, "The Welfare Rights of Distant People and Future Generations: Moral Side-Constraints on Social Policy," *Social Theory and Practice* 7 (1981): 107.

16. The World Commission on Environment and Development, *Our Common Future* (Oxford: Oxford University Press, 1987), p. 1.

17. World Commission, *Our Common Future,* p. xiv.

18. Regan, *The Case for Animal Rights,* p. 357.

19. Aldo Leopold, *A Sand County Almanac and Sketches Here and There* (London: Oxford University Press, 1949), pp. 224–25.

20. Rolston, *Environmental Ethics,* p. 144.

21. World Commission, *Our Common Future,* p. 9.

22. Ibid., p. 105.

23. Ibid., p. 49.

24. Ibid., p. 144.

25. Rolston, *Conserving Natural Value,* p. 233.

26. Arne Naess, *Ecology, Community and Lifestyle* (Cambridge: Cambridge University Press, 1989), p. 29.

27. Ibid., pp. 140–41.

28. Callicott, "Animal Liberation: A Triangular Affair," p. 27.

29. William Aiken quoted in J. Baird Callicott, "The Conceptual Foundations of the Land Ethic," in Callicott, *In Defense of the Land Ethic,* p. 92.

30. Sandy Irvine and Alec Ponton, *A Green Manifesto: Policies for a Green Future* (London: Macdonald Optima, 1988), p. 23.

31. World Commission, *Our Common Future,* p. 166.

32. Ibid., pp. 147 and 166.

33. Holmes Rolston, III, "Winning and Losing in Environmental Ethics," in Frederick Ferré and Peter Hartel, eds., *Ethics and Environmental Policy* (Athens: University of Georgia Press, 1994), p. 231.

34. See Rolston, *Conserving Natural Value,* p. 68.

35. World Commission, *Our Common Future,* pp. 13 and 147.

36. Rolston, *Conserving Natural Value,* p. 27.

37. Bill Devall and George Sessions, "Deep Ecology," in Donald VanDeVeer and Christine Pierce, eds., *The Environmental Ethics and Policy Book* (Belmont, Calif.: Wadsworth, 1994), p. 217.

38. Callicott, "Animal Liberation: A Triangular Affair," p. 34.

39. Rolston, *Conserving Natural Value,* p. 91.

40. Regan, *The Case for Animal Rights,* p. 357.

41. Taylor, *Respect for Nature,* p. 175.

42. Regan, *The Case for Animal Rights,* p. 356.

43. Taylor, *Respect for Nature,* p. 183.

44. World Commission, *Our Common Future,* p. 1.

45. Ibid., p. 137.

46. Ibid., p. 138.

DISCUSSION TOPICS

1. According to Stenmark, how do anthropocentrists, biocentrists, and ecocentrists differ regarding the moral standing issue? Which approach do you believe to be most correct?
2. Stenmark distinguishes "strong biocentrism" from "weak biocentrism" and "strong ecocentrism" from "weak ecocentrism." Explain the differences.
3. Explain how the goals of policy making differ whether one is an anthropocentrist, a biocentrist, or an ecocentrist.
4. According to Stenmark, what differences exist between the policies of anthropocentric, biocentric, and ecocentric thinkers regarding population, wildlife preservation, and wildlife management? Which policies do you believe are correct? Explain your reasoning.

Environmental Ethical Issues in Water Operations and Land Management

Cheryl Davis

Cheryl Davis is manager of the Water Supply and Treatment Division of the San Francisco Public Utilities Commission. She is the editor of Navigating Rough Waters: Ethical Issues in the Water Industry *(2001), from which this essay is drawn. Davis explains the many ethical dilemmas encountered in the work of water utilities. She urges water professionals to go beyond seeing themselves as passive suppliers of water as a commodity and to see themselves as stewards of a beautiful and complex environment.*

WHERE LAND AND WATER MEET

Water utility management of both water and land reflects the historical priorities of the water industry: reliability in water supply and water quality. Sextus Julius Frontinus, the Water Commissioner

of the City of Rome during the first century A.D., was proud to be responsible for a duty so crucial to the safety of his fellow citizens. In the book he wrote about Rome's water supply, he talked about design of transmission pipes, equity in billing, and the importance of drawing water from a pure source to protect public health. One thing he did not talk about was any flora or fauna the Romans may have disrupted in the course or building those long aqueducts.[1] . . .

While a basic hope of any environmentalist is to "tread lightly" on the earth and minimize environmental impacts, a basic reality of water systems is that construction, maintenance, and repair of facilities that store, convey and treat water inevitably impact the environment. It is a struggle to find ways to do this basic job with a minimum of damage. The purpose of this paper is to discuss the ethical issues encountered by water utilities as they go about their tasks of water collection, storage, transmission, and treatment, using the specific example of the San Francisco Public Utilities Commission (SFPUC).

The Commission currently provides water to four counties in the Bay Area, and owns over 60,000 acres of land within those counties. Approximately 85% of the Commission's water supply comes from the Hetch Hetchy system, located over 150 miles away in the Sierra Nevada Mountains. Those watersheds are owned and managed by the National Park Service. However, the SFPUC also operates five reservoirs in the San Francisco Bay Area—two in the East Bay and three on the Peninsula south of San Francisco. This paper focuses on the management of Bay Area watershed lands, and the operation of the portion of the regional water system that transports both Hetch Hetchy and local water.

WATER OPERATIONS V. ENVIRONMENTAL PROTECTION?

Some of our pipelines go though wetlands and other environmentally sensitive areas, which poses specific challenges for the operation of the system. For instance, where our transmission pipelines cross wetlands they are supported by crossbars. In the early 1990's these crossbars were so badly decayed that whole sections of these major transmission lines were inadequately supported. We were concerned that one of the pipelines might topple off a trestle and cause hydraulic mining of these wetlands. However, before we could begin the needed repair we had to obtain the necessary permits from the resource agencies, including the California Department of Fish and Game and the US Corps of Engineers. We didn't object to the restrictions they put on the work—that it could only be performed at certain times of the year, for example, to avoid the mating season of the clapper rail—but the regulators seemed to work in glacial time, a pace more appropriate for academic research or even spiritual meditation than water operations. Given the risk associated with potential failure of a large pipeline operating at high pressure, our interpretation of "doing the right thing" included moving forward on the project at a reasonable speed. Where inaction is dangerous, even pace can become an ethical issue.

Structural changes are often required to make water operations compatible with responsible environmental protection. To avoid the danger of uncontrolled flooding during the El Niño storms of 1998, we deliberately released water into a stream below one of our dams, increasing its reserve capacity. As we operated the valve that released water into the creek on a daily basis for an extended period of time, it became clear that the water gushing out of the dam was seriously eroding the hillside across the stream from the valve. The erosion, loss of vegetation, and the potential effects of turbidity on fish in the stream concerned us. However, our over-riding concern was the need to manage releases in a way that minimized the risk of flooding a hospital and homes that had been built into the floodplain of the stream. At the end of the rainy season, we repaired the damage to the embankment and got consultation on how to protect the hillside better in the future. Based on technical consultation, we installed riprap to armor the hillside and adopted a new protocol for operation of the discharge valve.

Environmental problems can also occur where operations result in the inadvertent creation of habitat, as we discovered when we attempted to restore the height of the same dam. Because of a seismic reliability issue, we had for a period of time been operating the dam without the stoplogs which allowed us to raise the level of the reservoir. We had become concerned that the roadway bridge running across

the top of the dam might not be supported by the wooden stoplogs in the event of an earthquake, causing an uncontrolled release. While planning and designing a permanent structural replacement for the stoplogs, we operated the reservoir at lower levels, unintentionally creating habitat for several endangered species. The top of the dam, a cement structure that does not appear particularly enticing, became a seasonal nursery for the red-legged frog. The terrain exposed by lowered levels of the reservoir became habitat for the San Francisco garter snake. The planned construction project to restore the storage capacity of the dam has been significantly delayed by the need to address the potential loss of habitat for these species. . . .

Routine operations can even be impacted in urban areas where the native wildlife and vegetation are long gone. We recently received notification that burrowing owls had been sighted in the right-of-way where our pipelines run though a heavily populated area. The burrowing owl is a bird that makes its nest in burrows abandoned by ground squirrels, and it has been listed as a "Species of Special Concern" by the California Department of Fish and Game. In one case, a local government along the right-of-way has asked that we mow our right-of-way rather than disc it for weed abatement, since mowing minimizes the likelihood that visiting owls will take up residence in vacant burrows.

We have found it vital to provide operations and maintenance staff (e.g., plumbers, laborers, and carpenters) with training on how to recognize wetlands and rare and endangered vegetation species. This kind of information is not normally covered in the training and apprenticeship programs of either engineering or craft staff who work for utilities. A utility which wishes to minimize the environmental damage caused by both its construction and maintenance projects must provide staff with the training and direction needed to avoid unintentional harm.

THE CHALLENGE OF RESTORATION

In management of watershed lands, there is a high correlation between management practices that protect water quality and practices that are environmentally sound. Sometimes, when circumstances allow, we even have the opportunity to enhance wildlife by removing dams or changing water operations for the benefit of the environment. When the San Francisco Water Department acquired water rights and facilities from Spring Valley Water Company in 1930, it acquired dams that are not needed for our operations today. These dams remain barriers to fish navigation on a creek which is one of the few viable fish passageways still emptying into the South Bay, and their removal would go a long way towards helping restore this slice of the environment to its "pre-development" condition. However, like most utilities, we are hard-pressed to keep up with the cost of the basics of water delivery (reliability and quality), so it is extraordinarily difficult for us to fund environmental restoration projects that have no impact on either. We hope to obtain funds from the State or federal level to support this project based on its environmental benefits. . . .

APPROPRIATE USES FOR WATERSHED LANDS

Another challenge facing water utilities is protecting the diverse biotic communities under their supervision from the constant pressure of incompatible use. A prime example facing the SFPUC is the Alameda Watershed in the East Bay, which provides habitat for a variety of wildlife. Grassland communities cover more than 50% of the watershed and woodlands cover about 22%. Other habitats include freshwater marshes, where streams discharge into reservoirs, and brush, scrub, and chaparral communities in the flatter, drier, or steeper lands. Ridgelands and open water make the area an attractive winter foraging and resting habitat for migrating and resident bird species, drawing birds of prey, waterfowl, and perching birds. In total, the watershed contains more than 17 types of wildlife habitat that support a range of animals, including tule elk, black-tailed deer, coyote, mountain lions, and bald eagles.

Because the portion of the watershed which is owned by the SFPUC has been subjected to limited public, commercial, and residential use, the Alameda watershed is a haven for a variety of rare, threatened, or endangered species. These include plants (e.g., the Santa Clara thorn mint and Oakland star-tulip), invertebrates (e.g., the Bay checkerspot butterfly), amphibians (e.g., the California tiger sala-

mander), reptiles (e.g., the Alameda whipsnake and Western pond turtle), birds (e.g., the American white pelican and the bald eagle), and mammals (e.g., the San Joaquin kit fox and the American badger). These are species that have lost much of their habitat in other parts of the Bay Area due to increasing urbanization and development.[2]

The tule elk are part of a herd that wandered onto our land after the Department of Fish & Game placed them on Mount Hamilton. Tule elk used to be considered an endangered species, but the herd is growing so rapidly that in time its size could become a problem. The mountain lion population is growing to the extent it's keeping down the deer population and sometimes threatening hikers. The feral hog population got so large and was so hard on both the land and our water that we had to hire a contractor to trap and shoot them. We allow no sport hunting on our watershed, but poaching is an ongoing problem.

The two most controversial issues in the East Bay are quarries and grazing. Gravel quarries generate revenue for us, and dig holes that we can use in the future for water storage. The question is whether to expand quarrying operations, how much and where? In the geographical area where this issue was most contentious, the property had been in agricultural production at various levels over the years, so the issue was not industrial transformation of a wilderness area. However, wildlife did frequent this relatively undeveloped site, and it was close to a small East Bay town. Opponents of the quarry cited the noise and dust associated with quarry operations as a cause of concern. Some raised the issue of environmental justice, arguing that the new quarry site would degrade the quality of life in their town and perhaps the health of their children. Lengthy discussions were held, and the Commission expressed desire to design the site to minimize adverse impacts. But the plan had been approved by Alameda County, which certified the environmental review, and the SFPUC decided to proceed with the quarry expansion. Given the significant needs of the regional water system for upgrade and repair of its facilities, the Commission considered the increased revenue a valuable source of funding for infrastructure improvements. Since the quarries would contribute to water supply reliability for 2.4 million customers by providing additional water storage and funding that could be applied toward capital improvements, environmental issues had to be balanced against water supply needs.

The second major issue has been grazing. Despite its current population growth and a corresponding boom in residential and commercial construction, the East Bay was historically dominated by agriculture and cattle ranching. At one time the Water Department was guilty of allowing its property to be over-grazed to a level that was environmentally unsound and contributed to erosion. Over time the Department has improved its management practices so that herd sizes are limited, their location is rotated in response to the condition of the vegetation, and riparian areas are increasingly protected. Since mammals in general and calves in particular have been identified as a source of Cryptosporidium, we also limit the times of year cows can be on our watershed, to avoid contaminated runoff coming into our reservoir during calving season. At one point during our planning process the Commission seriously considered eliminating cattle grazing from that portion of the watershed that we own. However, cows help us with fire management, and the Commission's current program is to (1) continue a tightly monitored and managed grazing program, and (2) encourage other ranchers in our watershed to manage their herds the same way.

While the Commission's reservations about cattle grazing were related to water quality concerns, environmental concerns have also been raised by groups which see this land use as antithetical to biodiversity. Since the area we now lease to cattle ranchers has been used for grazing since the Spaniards first settled the area, restoration of the "original" ecology of the area would not be a realistic goal. Instead our intent is to manage grazing so that it is consistent with the re-introduction of native species into the area. This view has been reinforced by conversations we have had with staff of one of the major environmental land acquisition/protection organizations. Their experience with purchasing property previously used for cattle grazing and simply ceasing such use was that (to their surprise) biodiversity actually decreased due to accelerated invasion by exotic species. We have had the same experience. For example, we fenced the Jacob's Valley area to enhance wildlife habitat around the pond by keeping cattle out. Large amounts of dried vegetation accumulated on the ground after livestock were excluded, which adversely affected the plant composition of the area. For the sake of improved vegetation management, we then decided (with our lessee, a regional park) to implement grazing in that area on a high intensity/short duration basis. While we are not planning to take any watershed lands which are currently in a near-wilderness state and convert them to cattle grazing use, we are continuing cattle grazing in areas where it is a historical use. In order to protect water quality and the environmental values associated with riparian zones, we are making increased investments in fencing and water facilities which have been designed to keep cattle from entering (and degrading) riparian corridors. By enhancing riparian corridor management, we hope to attain biodiversity and water quality while continuing a prudent level of cattle grazing.

THE DILEMMA OF PUBLIC ACCESS

Even more than the East Bay, our Peninsula Watershed is famous for its biodiversity. The watershed was originally protected by Spring Valley Water Company, which purchased the land to construct local reservoirs. Their management of the property reflected their desire to protect the quality of the water in these reservoirs. The San Francisco Water Department, when it acquired these lands and reservoirs, also limited public access, creating an oasis of near-wilderness in an urban setting. The Peninsula Watershed contains a wide range of natural habitats, from coniferous and riparian forests to rare serpentine grasslands. Many of these habitats were once abundant through the hills of the Bay Area, but today only remnants remain. Today the Peninsula Watershed is the largest contiguous piece of land left intact on the Peninsula. The Watershed is home to an enormous array of plants and animals, including almost 800 species of plants and trees, 50 species of mammals, 165 species of birds, 30 species of reptiles and amphibians, many species of fish, and hundreds of species of insects. The Watershed is designated as a State Fish and Game Refuge, and its remarkable plant and animal life have earned it recognition by UNESCO as an International Biosphere

Reserve. Today the Peninsula Watershed supports the highest concentration of rare, threatened, and endangered species in the Bay Area. These rare, threatened, and endangered species include plants (e.g., San Mateo thorn-mint and San Mateo tree lupine); invertebrates (e.g., the Mission blue butterfly and San Francisco fork-tailed damsel fly); amphibians and reptiles (e.g., San Francisco garter snake and Western spadefoot toad); birds (such as the marbled murrelet and American peregrine falcon); mammals (e.g., the mountain lion and the pallid bat); and fish (steelhead trout).

There has been considerable pressure to open the watershed to greater public access, reflecting the fact that high-density development in the Bay Area has limited open space recreational opportunities. For example, creation of a new golf course on the Peninsula Watershed had the strong support of many residents of San Mateo County. Under this proposal, land that had been largely undisturbed to date, including land that is home to rare and endangered plants associated with serpentine soil, could have been turned into turf. We already have one golf course on our property right next to our reservoir, and this recreational use would have been expanded. This proposed use was highly controversial. The new golf course was not included in the first version of the Peninsula Watershed Plan selected by the Commission for environmental review, because of the Commission's concerns about possible water quality and environmental impacts. San Mateo County and golf course advocates were successful in convincing the Commission that the benefits of the new golf course would outweigh potential impacts, so the new golf course was added to the proposed plan. Subsequently, the San Francisco Board of Supervisors (which has a higher level of authority in our form of government than the San Francisco Public Utilities Commission) reconsidered the issue and took the new course back out of the plan.

Perhaps our most contentious land use issue has been the alignment of the Bay Area Ridge Trail. Environmental and recreation advocates on the one hand and the water utility on the other had different opinions about the appropriate alignment of the trail (i.e., how deep it should go into our protected watershed area and how close to our reservoirs). An even more fundamental disagreement arose between all

parties about the nature of the access: whether permits should be required, how difficult they would be to obtain, and how closely supervised the permitted access might be. We knew from our own experience that recreationalists enjoyed the 27 miles of Peninsula trails that have been open to the public for years. We also knew that the level of noise, litter, and environmental degradation had been higher on our peripheral trails (where we have allowed free public access) than on trails where access was allowed only with group permits.

As we studied the issue, we made on-site visits to utilities with a variety of watershed management practices in terms of public access. We found some utilities which were highly restrictive in that regard; Seattle and Portland, for example, do not currently filter their water and have highly protected watersheds. Both the Portland Water Bureau and Seattle Public Utilities seemed pleased with the extent to which their restrictive policies have protected both water quality and species diversity. Some of our counterparts in the Bay Area, however, permit a much higher level of public access, allowing unrestricted access from dawn to dusk for hikers, bicyclists (including mountain bikers), and equestrians. By comparison, their staff reported increasing public use of approved trails, as well as unauthorized development of "outlaw trails" by mountain bikers, with associated degradation of environmental values. However, public enjoyment of recreational access was such that the water officials did not consider diminishment of such access a realistic option. . . .

In recent years, there has been increasing concern about protecting wildlife not only for the enjoyment of our human heirs, but also because of its inherent value. There has been dissension among recreationalists about the degree of environmental degradation associated with different recreational uses. In our watershed planning process there were mountain bikers who decried the trail of waste left by equestrians. There were hikers and equestrians who accused mountain bikers of being much more likely than they to depart from approved trails, causing erosion and habitat destruction. Some reported that in their clean-up work in public parks, they had discovered considerable garbage, litter, and evidence of potentially dangerous campfires, associated with the off-trail recreational activities of other hikers.

While hiking use of approved trails by hikers has generally been considered an environmentally benign use, even this level of use has, more recently, been questioned. For example, the hiking shoe of even the most conscientious environmentalist can carry the seed or spore of an exotic species. In an article entitled, "Don't Even Leave Footprints: Rethinking the Impact in Recreation," Mike Vandeman cites recent research on the effects of recreation suggesting that even "passive" recreation like hiking may be harmful to wildlife. An encounter with a human may increase energy needs, elevate heart rate, or trigger hormonal responses that modify the animal's behavior and physiology for an extended period. The energy expended in fleeing, or the feeding time lost, may be a significant cost for an animal that survives on a tight food/energy budget and that requires additional energy to reproduce.[3] . . .

Land acquisition has been part of the watershed management strategy of many utilities, and has been adopted as policy by the San Francisco Public Utilities Commission. The purpose of such land purchases or conservation easements is to avoid residential or commercial development of watershed lands. Such development can increase vulnerability to water quality risks (e.g., pesticides, herbicides, sewer leakage, and industrial wastes). Land acquisition can also protect utility lands from trespass and poaching by property-owners or their guests. Land acquisition by utilities creates the possibility of partnering with groups such as The Nature Conservancy which have an interest in protecting open space for environmental purposes. While the organizational "personality" of the water industry might well be characterized as the performer who works well invisibly and alone, effective action in the land acquisition area will probably require improved ability to "play well with others."

CONCLUSION

The challenges of our time force us to confront our fears and move beyond the venues where we have comfortably operated in the past. Water industry professionals, as a group, like to avoid direct involvement with land use policy, preferring to remain politically "neutral." But, however hard we try to keep our distance from controversial subjects like land development and population growth, the reality is that we are ultimately impacted by them and can hardly avoid them. Take water conservation— a program which is well supported by the general population and considered environmentally sound. Conservation has not only resulted in a per capita reduction of demand but had also produced the peripheral effect of enabling the larger community to grow to an unsustainable degree. Practically speaking, a hardened demand leaves fewer options for coping with the next drought. Furthermore, the general population tends not to support initiatives to expand water supply if it appears that the additional supplies (e.g., conserved water, recycled water projects) will only be used to fuel further growth. Water utilities may dismiss these concerns as tangential, preferring to see themselves as passive suppliers of community demand. But in failing to require developers to conserve water sources by limiting vegetation, building high-density units or using recycled water, utilities endanger their own ability to meet their constituents' needs in the long run. . . .

One might note that the Roman Emperor Aurelius, who wrote his *Meditations* while engaged in military campaigns against the barbarians, apparently tempered his own compassion with other goals that he and his compatriots considered non-negotiable. So do we all. Marcus Aurelius pointed out that it would be easier for us to be kind to fellow human beings if we saw ourselves as part of the human community, and therefore serving ourselves when we served others.[4] Similarly, it may be easier for us to function effectively as water professionals in a world full of environmental regulations, if we perceive ourselves as ultimate beneficiaries of environmental stewardship. This does not mean that we should forget our water suppy or water quality obligations, or subordinate them to every interpretation of law made by any given regulator at a specific moment in time. It does mean, in my opinion, that we will be more successful water managers if we go beyond tunnel vision, and view the world around us with some tenderness. It is an opportunity to see ourselves not simply as cogs in a machine that produces a commodity called water, but as participants in a complicated, interactive game that is intriguing, uncharted, often frustrating, and a little bit fun.

NOTES

1. Sextus Julius Frontinus, *The Water Supply of the City of Rome.* Tr. by Clemens Herschel. New England Water Works Assn., Boston, 1973, pp. 27–73.
2. San Francisco Public Utilities Commission, *Alameda Watershed: Managing Water Quality and Natural Resources for the Future.* Public Affairs Management, San Francisco, 2000.
3. Vandeman, Michael J., "Don't Even Leave Footprints: Rethinking the Impacts of Recreation, in *Sierra Club Yodeler,* Sierra Club, Vol. 63, No. 8, August 2000.
4. Marcus Aurelius, *Meditations.* Barnes & Noble, New York, 1996, p. 107.

DISCUSSION TOPICS

1. Explain the effects of water conservation. What steps does Davis suggest utility managers take to conserve water?
2. Imagine that you are an employee of a water utility. In theory, how would you rank the following goals? Justify your ranking.
   a. low water rates
   b. public recreational access
   c. wildlife enhancement
   d. water quality
   e. maintenance of pipelines
   f. conservation of endangered species
   g. stream quality for fish
   h. dam removal
   i. revenue from grazing and quarries
   j. biodiversity
   k. land acquisition

READING 66

From *The Politics of the Earth*

John S. Dryzek

John S. Dryzek is in the Social and Political Theory Program of the Research School of Social Sciences, Australian National University, Canberra. His most recent book is Deliberative Democracy and Beyond *(2002). The following selection is from* The Politics of the Earth, *which was published in 1997. Dryzek analyzes six types of political discourses concerning the environment, suggesting that such comparative analysis can contribute to an understanding of what has to change in liberal capitalism—the system that dominates the world and is mostly insensitive to environmental concerns.*

CLASSIFYING THE MAIN ENVIRONMENTAL DISCOURSES[1]

Environmental discourse begins in industrial society, and so has to position itself in the context of the long-dominant discourse of industrial society, which we can call industrialism. Industrialism may be characterized in terms of its overarching commitment to growth in the quantity of goods and services produced and to the material well-being which that growth brings. Industrial societies have of course featured many competing ideologies, such as liberalism, conservatism, socialism, Marxism, and fascism. But whatever their differences, all these ideologies are committed to industrialism. Indeed, from an environmental perspective they can all look like variations on the theme of industrialism. This commonality might surprise their adherents, who are far more conscious of their ideological differences than of their industrialist commonalities. But all these ideologies long ignored or suppressed environmental concern. If what we now call environmental issues were thought about at all, it was often in terms of inputs to industrial processes. For example, rational use of such inputs was the main concern of the Conservation Movement founded at the beginning of the twentieth century in the United States, whose key figure was Gifford Pinchot.[2] This movement did not want to preserve the environment for aesthetic reasons, or for the sake of human health. Instead, the Conservation Movement sought only to ensure that resources such as minerals, timber, and fish were used wisely and not squandered, so that there would always be plenty of them to support a growing industrial economy.

Environmental discourse cannot therefore simply take the terms of industrialism as given, but must depart from these terms. This departure can be reformist or it can be radical; and this distinction forms one dimension for categorizing environmental discourses.

A second dimension would take note of the fact that departures from industrialism can be either prosaic or imaginative. Prosaic departures take the political-economic chessboard set by industrial society as pretty much given. On that chessboard, environmental problems are seen mainly in terms of troubles encountered by the established industrial political economy. They require action, but they do not point to a new kind of society. The action in question can be quite dramatic and radical. As we will see, there are those who believe that economic growth must be reined in, if not brought to a halt entirely, in order to respond effectively to environmental problems. But the measures endorsed or proposed by these people are essentially those which have been defined by and in industrialism. For example, those who would curb economic growth normally propose that this be done by strong central administration informed by scientific expertise — a quintessentially industrialist instrument.

In contrast, imaginative departures seek to redefine the chessboard. Notably, environmental problems are seen as opportunities rather than troubles. Imaginative redefinition of the chessboard may dissolve old dilemmas, treating environmental concerns not in opposition to economic ones, but potentially in harmony. The environment is brought into the heart of society and its cultural, moral, and economic systems, rather than being seen as a source of difficulties standing outside these systems. The thinking is imaginative, but the degree of change sought can be small and reformist, or large and radical. As we shall see, imaginative reformist ways of rendering the basic political-economic structure bequeathed by industrial society capable of coping with environmental issues may be found. On the other hand, imaginative radical changes can also be envisaged, requiring wholesale transformation of this political-economic structure. Combining these two dimensions — reformist versus radical and prosaic versus imaginative — produces four cells, as indicated in Table 1.

TABLE 1		
CLASSIFYING ENVIRONMENTAL DISCOURSES		
	Reformist	Radical
Prosaic	Problem Solving	Survivalism
Imaginative	Sustainability	Green Radicalism

Environmental Problem Solving is defined by taking the political-economic *status quo* as given but in need of adjustment to cope with environmental problems, especially via public policy. Such adjustment might take the form of extension of the pragmatic problem-solving capacities of liberal democratic governments by facilitating a variety of environmentalist inputs to them; or of markets, by putting price tags on environmental harms and benefits; or of the administrative state, by institutionalizing environmental concern and expertise in its operating procedures. Within the overall discourse of environmental problem solving there may be substantial disagreement as to which of these forms is appropriate. So, for example, a debate between proponents of administrative regulation and market-type incentive mechanisms for pollution control has been under way since the 1970s, and shows few signs of letting up.

Survivalism is the discourse popularized in the early 1970s by the efforts of the Club of Rome . . . and others, still retaining many believers. The basic idea is that continued economic and population growth will eventually hit limits set by the Earth's stock of natural resources and the capacity of its ecosystems to support human agricultural and industrial activity. The limits discourse is radical because it seeks a wholesale redistribution of power within the industrial political economy, and a wholesale reorientation away from perpetual economic growth. It is prosaic because it can see solutions only in terms of the options set by industrialism, notably, greater control of existing systems by administrators, scientists, and other responsible élites.

Sustainability begins in earnest in the 1980s, and is defined by imaginative attempts to dissolve the conflicts between environmental and economic values that energize the discourses of problem solving and limits. The concepts of growth and development are redefined in ways which render obsolete the simple projections of the limits discourse. There is still no consensus on the exact meaning of sustainability; but sustainability is the axis around which discussion occurs, and limits are nowhere to be seen. Without the imagery of apocalypse that defines the limits discourse, there is no inbuilt radicalism to the discourse. The era of sustainability begins in earnest with the publication of the Brundtland Report in 1987 (World Commission on Environment and Development, 1987). More recently, ideas about ecological modernization, seeing economic growth and environmental protection as essentially complementary, have arisen in Europe.

Green Radicalism is both radical and imaginative. Its adherents reject the basic structure of industrial society and the way the environment is conceptualized therein in favor of a variety of quite different alternative interpretations of humans, their society, and their place in the world. Given its radicalism and imagination, it is not surprising that green radicalism features deep intramural divisions—to which I shall attend. In the United States, social ecologists with a pastoral vision and a concern for social justice debate with deep ecologists, who prefer landscapes without humans. In Germany, Green *Fundis* eventually lost a struggle with Green *Realos* over tactical questions about action in the streets versus action in parliament. Everywhere, green romantics disagree with green rationalists, proponents of the rights of individual creatures disagree with more holistic thinkers, and advocates of green lifestyles disagree with those who prefer to stress green politics. These debates are lively and persistent; but the disputants have far more in common with each other in terms of basic dispositions, assumptions, and capabilities than they do with either industrialism or with the three competing discourses of environmental concern just introduced.

These, then, are the four basic environmental discourses. . . . All four reject industrialism; but all four engage with the discourse of industrialism—if only to distance themselves from it. And this is why their engagement with industrialism and its defenders is often more pronounced than their engagement with each other.

QUESTIONS TO ASK ABOUT DISCOURSES

So far I have identified the four basic discourses in fairly general terms. But in order to see why and how these discourses have developed, and to what effect, it is necessary to pin down their content more precisely. . . . To this end, let me now develop a set of questions for the analysis of discourses.[3]

Discourses enable stories to be told; in fact, the title of a discourse can be an abbreviated story line (the concept of environmental story lines is employed by Hajer, 1995). To refer back to the four discourses just enumerated, limits or survivalism connotes a story about the need to curb ever-growing human demands on the life-support capacities of natural systems. Problem solving connotes a different story—indeed, can subsume a number of different stories—about the unpleasant side-effects of particular economic activities requiring piecemeal remedies. Each discourse constructs stories from the following elements:

1. Basic Entities Whose Existence Is Recognized or Constructed

Technically, this is what is meant by the "ontology" of a discourse. Different discourses see different things in the world. Some discourses recognize the existence of ecosystems, others have no concept of natural systems at all, seeing nature only in terms of brute matter. At least one other entertains the idea that the global ecosystem is a self-correcting entity with something like intelligence. This is the idea of Gaia, which I will address in my analysis of Green radicalism. Some discourses organize their analyses around rational, egoistic human beings; others deal with a variety of human motivations; others still recognize human beings only in their aggregates such as states and populations. Most believe it is fruitful to deal with "humans" as a category, a few that it is necessary to break down on the basis of gender. Some assume governments and their actions matter; others believe it is the human spirit that is crucial.

2. Assumptions about Natural Relationships

All discourses embody notions of what is natural in the relationships between different entities. Some see competition, be it between human beings in markets or between creatures locked in Darwinian struggle, as natural. Others see cooperation as the essence of both human social systems and natural systems. Hierarchies based on gender, expertise, political power, species, ecological sensibility, intellect, legal status, race, and wealth are variously assumed in different discourses; as are their corresponding equalities.

3. Agents and Their Motives

Story lines require actors, or agents. These actors can be individuals or collectivities. They are mostly human, but can be nonhuman. In one discourse we may find benign and public-spirited expert administrators. Another discourse might portray the same people as selfish bureaucrats. Still others might ignore the presence of government officials altogether. Many other kinds of agents and motives put in appearances. They include enlightened élites, rational consumers, ignorant and short-sighted populations, virtuous ordinary citizens, a Gaia that may be tough and forgiving or fragile and punishing, among others.

4. Key Metaphors and Other Rhetorical Devices

Most story lines, in the environmental arena no less than elsewhere, depend crucially on metaphor. Key metaphors that have figured in environmental discourse include:

- spaceships (the idea of "spaceship earth");
- the grazing commons of a medieval village ("the tragedy of the commons");
- machines (nature is like a machine that can be reassembled to better meet human needs);
- organisms (nature is a complex organism that grows and develops);
- human intelligence (ascribed to non-human entities such as ecosystems);
- war (against nature);
- goddesses (treating nature in benign female form, and not just as Mother Nature).

Metaphors are rhetorical devices, deployed to convince listeners or readers by putting a situation in a particular light. Many other devices are available to perform the same tasks. These include appeal to widely accepted practices or institutions, such as established rights, freedoms, constitutions, and cultural traditions. For example, the rights of species, animals, or natural objects can be justified through reference to the long-established array of individual human rights in liberal societies. Appeals can be made to deeper pasts, such as pastoral or even primeval idylls, as a way to criticize the industrial present. The negative and discredited can be accentuated as well as the positive and treasured. For example, it is possible to collect horror stories about government mistakes on environmental issues, and sprinkle these horror stories into arguments. On the other hand, some discourses collect and accentuate success stories.

This completes my checklist of items for the scrutiny and analysis of discourses. . . . Beyond capturing the essence of the various discourses and their subdivisions, it is of course important to determine what difference each of them makes. I have already asserted that the language we use in addressing environmental affairs does make a difference, but this needs to be demonstrated for particular discourses, rather than just asserted as a general point.

THE DIFFERENCES THAT DISCOURSES MAKE

With this need to demonstrate the implications of different discourses in mind, I will take a look at the history as well as the content of each discourse. As I noted earlier, this history can generally be traced back to some aspect of industrialism—if only as a rejection of that aspect. With time, environmental discourses develop, crystallize, bifurcate, and (perhaps someday) dissolve. A crucial part of this history consists of the kind of politics surrounding, shaping, and shaped by the discourse. In some cases the politics might be that of a social movement or political party; in other cases, that of governmental commissions and intergovernmental negotiations; in others, that of administrative control; in others, élite bargaining; in others, rationalistic policy design. Sometimes there will be little in the way of politics at all, as, for example, in the case of "lifestyle" greens. Sometimes the politics may be local, sometimes national, sometimes transnational, sometimes global.

The impact of a discourse can often be felt in the policies of governments or intergovernmental bodies, and in institutional structure. For example, the flurry of environmental legislation enacted in many industrialized countries around 1970 mostly reflected a discourse of administrative rationalism (a sub-category of what I have defined as problem solving). Since 1970, problem-solving discourse has also been embodied in a number of institutional innovations that extend the openness and reach of liberal democratic control of environmental affairs (in the form of devices such as public inquiries and various procedures for consensual dispute resolution). Beyond affecting institutions, discourses can become embodied in institutions. When this happens, discourses constitute the informal understandings that provide the context for social interaction, on a par with formal institutional rules. Or to put it slightly differently, discourses can constitute institutional software while formal rules constitute institutional hardware. Sometimes, though, discourses do not have direct effects on the policies or institutions of governments, but take effect elsewhere. For example, green radicalism has helped some individuals and communities to distance themselves from both government and corporate capitalism in putative attempts to create an alternative political economy relying on self-sufficiency.

To assess more fully the worth and impact of a discourse requires attention to its critics as well as its adherents. Sometimes adherents of different discourses will ignore and dismiss rather than engage one another. Nevertheless, some dispute does indeed occur across the boundaries of different discourses. Most frequently, this occurs between the environmental discourse in question and the older discourse of industrialism. Given that each of the four categories of discourse I have identified has its roots in either modification or conscious rejection of industrialism, this is not too surprising. Occasionally, debate is engaged between the problem solving, limits, sustainability, and green radical discourses. If such engagement is infrequent, that is mostly a matter of these four discourses viewing issues and problems in such different ways that little interchange

across their boundaries can occur. One goal of this book is to promote such interchange.

Attention to the arguments of critics will facilitate identification of flaws in the discourse. Such identification will also be helped by attention to experience of the practical implications of the discourse, in politics, policies, institutions, and beyond. The tools of discourse analysis which I have enumerated enable further critical analysis of the promise and peril attached to each discourse in its contribution to environmental debate, analysis, and action. It may even turn out that there are some complementarities between different discourses, rather than simple rivalry. . . .

THE USES OF DISCOURSE ANALYSIS

As should be clear by now, my intent is to advance analysis in environmental affairs by promoting critical comparative scrutiny of competing discourses of environmental concern. This intent distances me from some others who have developed and deployed discourse analysis.

The concept of discourse in the sense I am using it owes much to the efforts of Michel Foucault (for example, 1980), who revealed the content and history of discourses about illness, sex, madness, criminality, government, and so forth. Foucauldians are generally committed to the idea that individuals are for the most part subject to the discourses in which they move, and so seldom able to step back and make comparative assessments and choices across different discourses. It should be evident that I disagree. Discourses are powerful, but they are not impenetrable (as Foucault and his readers have themselves inadvertently demonstrated in their own exposé of the history of various discourses; they at least have escaped from the prison of particular discourses!). Foucault and his followers also often portray discourses in hegemonic terms, meaning that one single discourse is typically dominant in any time and place, conditioning not just agreement but also the terms of dispute. In contrast, I believe that variety is as likely as hegemony. The environmental arena reveals that for long the discourse of industrialism was indeed hegemonic, to the extent that "the environment" was hardly conceptualized prior to the 1960s. However, this hegemony eventually began to disintegrate, yielding the range of environmental discourses now observable. While in its totality environmentalism does challenge industrialism, it does not constitute a unified counter discourse to industrialism. Rather, environmentalism is composed of a variety of discourses, sometimes complementing one another, but often competing. . . .

GLOBAL LIMITS AND THEIR DENIAL
[Survivalism and the Promethean Reaction]

Environmental issues can be as local as the dog droppings on the grass in front of my house, or as global as the greenhouse effect. When environmental issues made their first dramatic leap to the top of the political agenda in so many countries in the late 1960s, it was the global issue which really captured the public attention. Not coincidentally, this was also the first time the Earth was photographed from space, and a beautiful, fragile place it looked. For the first time in human history the Earth could be conceptualized readily as a finite planet, and for the first time a true politics of planet Earth became conceivable. Environmental problems were soon cast in terms of threats to the capacity of this planet to support life — especially human life.

The threats in question involved degradation of the global environment through pollution, and exhaustion of the Earth's natural resources (fossil fuels, minerals, fisheries, forests, and croplands). Urgency came from population explosion and economic growth. Exponential growth in both human numbers and their level of economic activity meant that there was no time to lose, for humanity seemed to be heading for the limits at an ever-increasing pace. Hitting these limits would mean global environmental disasters, accompanied by a crash in human populations.

This discourse of limits and survival was given a major boost by the Club of Rome, an international organization composed of industrialists, politicians, and academics. The Club's most famous product was a set of computer-generated projections of the global future published in 1972 in the international best seller *The Limits to Growth.* These projections showed in quite precise graphical terms that if humanity continued on its profligate course then it had at the very most a century before disaster would

strike on a scale unparalleled in human history. Not surprisingly, there were many calls for radical action to stop this headlong rush to destruction; though the survivalists' political repertoire turned out to consist mainly of some tried-and-tested practices, especially strong governmental control.

Survivalism met with an immediate counterattack from defenders of the established industrial economy, whose taken-for-granted order of things survivalism had challenged. These defenders argued that humans are characterized by unlimited ingenuity, symbolized in Greek mythology by the progress made possible by the theft of fire from the gods by Prometheus. Platometheans asserted that the Earth was in truth unlimited; that as soon as one resource threatened to run out, ingenious people would develop a substitute. This had always happened in the past, and it would continue to happen in the future. The Promethean reaction gathered speed in the 1980s, for it fit quite well with the ideological climate of the Reagan years in the United States.

The dispute between the two camps continues, and neither shows any [sign] of conceding. Yet it matters crucially which side is right. If the Prometheans are correct, then not only is survivalism wrong, but environmentalism of any kind simply loses its urgency. So: who is right? . . .

SOLVING ENVIRONMENTAL PROBLEMS
[Administrative Rationalism, Democratic Pragmatism, and Economic Rationalism]

The clash of survivalists and Prometheans . . . is full of drama, and the stakes involved appear to be massive — nothing less than the fate of the Earth. Yet if we look for specific changes in institutions, policies, and practices directly traceable to these discourses, we are likely to be disappointed. Prometheans would say that the whole point is that nothing much needs changing, though there are in fact a large number of public policy practices they would like to see eliminated, involving some fairly radical changes. In practice, we find more limited policy responses in an environmental context. Governments have not engaged in draconian population control or sought an end to economic growth. Instead, they have opened their doors to environmental lobbyists, passed laws to conserve resources or ameliorate pollution, and created bureaucracies to implement these laws.

I turn then to a less apocalyptic discourse that has had obvious consequences in terms of the way societies, and especially governments, have gone about characterizing and attacking environmental problems. The discourses of environmental problem solving recognize the existence of ecological problems, but treat them as tractable within the basic framework of the political economy of industrial society, as belonging in a well-defined box of their own. The basic story line is that of problem solving rather than heroic struggle. Human interactions with the environment generate a range of problems (rather than one big problem like overshoot of limits threatening social collapse), to which human problem-solving devices need to be turned. Now, different varieties of this discourse reveal different conceptions about how best to organize human problem solving, especially when social problem solving is at issue, which requires the coordination of large numbers of individuals. The three main ways human beings have found to coordinate such efforts are by bureaucracy, democracy, and markets. Corresponding to these three coordination mechanisms are the three discourses which I will address [later]: administrative rationalism, democratic pragmatism, and economic rationalism. However much partisans of these three variations may disagree with each other, they share the basic story line of problem solving as I have just defined it; and their differences with survivalists, Prometheans, sustainable developers, and green radicals are striking. Of the three, I will deal with administrative rationalism first because it captures the dominant governmental response to the initial onset of environmental crisis. Democratic pragmatism soon emerges as a corrective to administration. And economic rationalism builds on its advances in all areas of political life to generate alternatives to and remedies for the pathologies it identifies in both administration and liberal democratic governance.

GREEN RADICALISM [Green Romanticism and Green Rationalism]

As befits its imaginative and radical leanings, the world of green discourse is a diverse and lively place, home to a wide variety of ideologies, parties, movements, groups, and thinkers. Found here are Green parties and their factions, animal liberationists, bioregionalists, ecofeminists, deep ecologists, social ecologists, eco-Marxists, eco-socialists, eco-anarchists, eco-communalists, ecological Christians, Buddhists, Taoists, and pagans, environmental justice advocates, green economists, critical theorists, post-modernists, and many others. This sheer variety notwithstanding, I believe green radicalism can be usefully divided into just two major categories: one romantic, and one rationalistic. . . .

The key difference between the two main strands of green radicalism has a very deep history, rooted in different reactions to the Enlightenment. Enlightenment is the name for the eighteenth-century movement which renounced religion, myth, and traditional social order in the name of reason. Reason in turn meant liberal politics and human rights of the sort established in the English, American, and French Revolutions of 1689, 1776, and 1789 respectively. Reason also meant that modern science became the route to secure knowledge, which enabled in turn the growth of modern technology. The defining feature of modern society is that it embodies the principles of the Enlightenment.

Just like the romantics of the eighteenth and nineteenth centuries, green romanticism rejects core Enlightenment principles. Green romanticism seeks to change and save the world by changing the way individuals approach and experience the world, in particular through cultivation of more empathetic and less manipulative orientations toward nature and other people. It is heir to the older romantic rejection of the Enlightenment's emphasis on rationality and progress.

Green rationalism, in contrast, embraces rather than rejects key aspects of Enlightenment. This embrace of Enlightenment and modernity is rarely if ever wholehearted. Green rationalists recognize that some aspects of Enlightenment are indeed complicit in the destruction of nature and the production of injustice. They agree with romantics that modern science and technology wielded in human arrogance have meant massive environmental destruction, along with profound human costs. But Enlightenment also means equality, rights, open dialogue, and critical questioning of established practices. Green rationalism builds upon this more attractive side of Enlightenment and modernity. . . .

ECOLOGICAL DEMOCRACY

. . .

What can be said by way of conclusion about how the various discourses have survived the questions asked of them here, and their comparison with other discourses? First, the discourses are not always and inevitably competitors. There are some complementarities. For example, a "weak" form of ecological modernization is quite compatible with administrative rationalism and economic rationalism. And green radicalism is happy to subscribe to many of the ideas about global limits developed by survivalists — though not to survivalists' political analysis and prescription. Equally clearly, there can be plenty of tension between discourses. Survivalists have core disagreements with Prometheans, sustainable development, and ecological modernization. Economic rationalists are never going to agree with administrative rationalists, democratic pragmatists, or green radicals about the best way of ordering environmental affairs.

One way of easing the tensions somewhat is to note that different discourses may be applicable to different kinds of problems. In essence, survivalism and Promethean discourse are about global issues. Whatever position one reaches in the dispute between them, it would be possible to follow any one of the three problem-solving discourses at the local level (though Prometheans might say that even such local efforts are often unnecessary). Other compatibilities might be found: for example, one might be a green romantic when it comes to lifestyle, but a democratic pragmatist when it comes to policy.

Such potential compatibilities notwithstanding, it remains the case that most of the discourses analyzed offer a comprehensive account of and orientation to environmental affairs at all levels, from the global to the local, and across different issue areas (pollution, resource depletion, wilderness protection, and so forth). This comprehensiveness certainly applies to Promethean discourse, administrative rationalism, democratic pragmatism, economic rationalism, sustainable development, green romanticism,

and green radicalism. It is less applicable to survivalism, which concerns itself only with global affairs, and ecological modernization, which has so far addressed only how industrial economies might be restructured, with little application to non-industrial societies or global analysis.

With these competing comprehensive visions and the need to identify productive compatibilities in mind, I would argue by way of approaching a conclusion that an intelligent approach to environmental issues demands two things. The first is a dynamic, structural-level analysis of the liberal capitalist political economy, where it might be headed, and what realistically can be done to alter this trajectory to more ecologically benign ends. For a confident and globally organized liberal capitalism mostly insensitive to environmental concerns is the dominant political fact of our times. Without such an analysis, we are reduced to wishful thinking about how things might be different. Of the discourses surveyed, ungrounded wishful thinking about a different world characterizes survivalism, economic rationalism, and green romanticism — though of course they wish for very different things! Only two of the discourses provide a coherent analysis of the kind needed: Promethean discourse and ecological modernization.

Prometheans believe that the current trajectory of liberal capitalism is unproblematical, and that all we need do is leave it alone to provide abundance for humanity, in the future as in the past. Ecological modernizers, in contrast, recognize that *laissez-faire* liberal capitalism is environmentally destructive. Thus they seek an ecological restructuring of capitalism that respects the constraints imposed by this economic system on political action, and which is consistent with the basic imperatives of the system. If one accepts the Promethean viewpoint, then the matter ends. On the other hand, if one rejects that viewpoint . . . then the second quality demanded by an intelligent approach to environmental affairs comes into play.

This second quality is the capacity to facilitate and engage in social learning in an ecological context. Environmental issues feature high degrees of uncertainty and complexity, which are magnified as ecological systems interact with social, economic, and political systems. Thus we need institutions and discourses which are capable of learning—not least about their own shortcomings. Survivalism, Promethean discourse, administrative rationalism, economic rationalism, and green romanticism provide few such resources, and exhibit little or no awareness of their own limits. In contrast, resources for this learning project are provided by democratic pragmatism, sustainable development, ecological modernization, and green rationalism. In each case, though, our appropriation from the discourse must be selective.

From democratic pragmatism come discursive procedures for the resolution of disputes through cooperative problem solving. Such procedures, including policy dialogue, environmental mediation, regulatory negotiation, and societal dialogues, are often limited in their scope and constrained by the structural context in which they operate. Critics of them rightly note that they can involve co-optation and neutralization of troublemakers by powerful state and corporate officials. The key, then, is [to] try to break these shackles, moving such experiments in the direction of what I have described elsewhere as discursive designs, which arguably transgress the boundaries of democratic pragmatism by pointing to a more radical participatory democracy. Discursive designs involve collective decision making through authentic democratic discussion, open to all interests, under which political power, money, and strategizing do not determine outcomes (see Dryzek, 1990*b:* 29–56). That such radicalization is possible is shown by the rightly celebrated Berger Inquiry.... That such radicalization is problematical is shown by the frequency of Berger's celebration in the literature as an exemplary case. But a careful search would reveal an ever-growing number of cases, some of which I have mentioned under democratic pragmatism and green rationalism.

From sustainable development comes the possibility of a decentered approach to the pursuit of sustainability. While at first glance the sheer variety of available definitions of sustainable development seems like a defect of this discourse, from the perspective of social learning it is a distinct advantage, for it does not rule out a variety of experiments in what sustainability can mean in different contexts, including the global context. A decentered approach to sustainability meshes quite nicely with

discursive designs, which could find roles as the steering institutions and reflective components of experiments in sustainability (as Torgerson, 1994; 1995 also recognizes).

From ecological modernization comes the possibility of a "strong" or "reflexive" version of the discourse, the essence of which goes beyond the retooling of the economy with waste reduction and profitability in mind. Ecological modernization so radicalized can involve institutional change in the direction of democratic experimentation, and open-ended exploration of what ecological modernization itself might mean. The very idea of reflexive development is that it is self-monitoring and critically aware of itself, thus conducive to social learning. Again, this fits quite nicely with a decentered approach to sustainability and discursive designs.

From green rationalism come the reasons why democratic pragmatism, sustainable development, and ecological modernization need to be radicalized to begin with. Green rationalism can bring to them a sense of urgency which survivalism shares but finds more difficult to disseminate, given that survivalism's imagery of certainty leaves little space for search and experimentation. Moreover, survivalism's flirtation with authoritarianism alienates democratic pragmatists, sustainable developers, and ecological modernizers alike. Green romanticism for its part is not easily connected with radicalized versions of these three discourses, given that its adherents are uninterested in institutions, or institutional experimentation. Green rationalism can also remind us that oppositional politics in social movements can play a key role in social learning, which does not have to be tied to conventional politics (and may indeed proceed more readily outside the realm of conventional politics). Green rationalists can further bring to bear plenty of ideas about how political and economic institutions might look in an ecological future beyond industrial society. Linking these ideas to the other three discourses is a way of grounding such ideas in a more realistic analysis of how the future can actually unfold, as opposed to wishful thinking about how it should unfold.

The common thread that can be developed here is a renewed democratic politics, an ecological democracy.[4] But would such a politics indeed promote ecological values? One affirmative answer comes from democratic pragmatism: the kinds of values that can survive authentic democratic debate are those oriented to the interests of the community as a whole, rather than selfish interests within the community (or outside it). Foremost among such community interests is the integrity of the ecological base upon which the community depends. From green rationalism comes a reminder to democratic pragmatism that existing liberal democracies typically frustrate such processes: the influence of power, money, and strategy need to be unmasked and countered, as does the degree to which human communities have lost any sense of their ecological foundations.

For democracy, if it is about anything, is about authentic communication. Overcoming the impediments that distort such communication is crucial. One such impediment, ignored in the history of democratic theory but now exposed by the rise of green thinking, concerns communication with the non-human world. It would be absurd to think of that world as having preferences, or able to "vote," which is why most models of democracy are of limited applicability in a green context. But the non-human world can communicate, and human decision processes can be structured so as to listen to its communications more or less well. Large bureaucracies operating according to standard procedures insensitive to local ecological contexts fail this test; bioregional authorities governed by citizens with a thorough knowledge of local circumstances are likely to do much better.

Ecological democracy blurs the boundary between human social systems and natural systems. There is an additional sense in which ecological democracy is democracy without boundaries. Ecological problems and issues transcend established governmental jurisdictions, such that democratic exercises may need to be constituted in order to fit the size and scope of particular issues. When established authority in governmental jurisdictions is recalcitrant, then such fora may need to be constituted as oppositional democratic spheres. The impact of non-governmental organizations in international politics . . . can be understood in these terms. When it comes to politics above local action, the appropriate organizational form may often be the network, as developed by the environmental justice movement. . . .

This sort of democracy without boundaries is clearly very different from the institutions established by and in industrial society which still dominate today's world. Yet discourses, including environmental ones, help to constitute and re-constitute the world just as surely as do formal institutions or material economic forces. And in this discursive realm as we have seen, the beginnings of ecological democracy are already present. Environmentalism already flourishes in opposition to industrialism; but much remains to be done if industrial society is ever to give way to ecological society.

NOTES

1. Dryzek defines "discourse" as a "shared way of apprehending the world" (*The Politics of the Earth*, p. 8).
2. True, a few romantics such as John Muir extolled wilderness — but they did so in rejection of industrial society.
3. This checklist extends and modifies a scheme I developed in Dryzek (1988) in a nonenvironmental context.
4. More extensive discussion of ecological democracy may be found in some of my other writings (Dryzek, 1987; 1990*a;* 1992*c;* 1996*c;* 1996*d*).

REFERENCES

Berger, Thomas (1977), *Northern Frontier, Northern Homeland: Report of the MacKenzie Valley Pipeline Inquiry.* Toronto: James Lorimer.

Dryzek, John S. (1987), *Rational Ecology: Environment and Political Economy.* New York: Basil Blackwell.

———. (1988), "The Mismeasure of Political Man," *Journal of Politics,* 50: 705–25.

———. (1990a), "Green Reason: Communicative Ethics for the Biosphere," *Environmental Ethics,* 12: 195–210.

———. (1990b), *Discursive Democracy: Politics, Policy, and Political Science.* New York: Cambridge University Press.

———. (1992c), "Ecology and Discursive Democracy: Beyond Liberal Capitalism and the Administrative State," *Capitalism, Nature, Socialism,* 3 (2): 18–42.

————. (1996c), "Political and Ecological Communication," pp. 13–30 in F. Matthews (ed.), *Ecology and Democracy*. London: Frank Cass.

————. (1996d), "Strategies of Ecological Democratization," pp. 108–23 in William M. Lafferty and James Meadowcroft (eds.), *Democracy and the Environment: Problems and Prospects*. Cheltenham: Edward Elgar.

Foucault, Michel (1980), *Power/Knowledge: Selected Interviews and Other Writings, 1972–1977*. Brighton: Harvester.

Hajer, Maarten A. (1995), *The Politics of Environmental Discourse: Ecological Modernization and the Policy Process*. Oxford: Oxford University Press.

Torgerson, Douglas (1994), "Strategy and Ideology in Environmentalism: A Decentered Approach to Sustainability," *Industrial and Environmental Crisis Quarterly*, 8: 295–321.

————. (1995), "The Uncertain Quest for Sustainability: Public Discourse and the Politics of Environmentalism," pp. 3–20 in Frank Fischer and Michael Black (eds.), *Greening Environmental Policy: The Politics of a Sustainable Future*. Liverpool: Paul Chapman.

World Commission on Environment and Development (1987), *Our Common Future*. Oxford: Oxford University Press.

DISCUSSION TOPICS

1. Which of the six environmental discourses described by Dryzek do you believe to be most correct? Which of the discourses appeals to you the least? Explain your reasoning.

2. Analyze the favorite discourse you chose in question 1 according to "Questions to Ask about Discourses." Does the outcome of this analysis change your evaluation of your chosen discourse?

3. Dryzek aims at an ecological democracy, which, he believes, requires authentic communication. What are some ways that such communication could be fostered, in your view?

4. Dryzek envisions a "democracy without boundaries," in the form of networking. Given the state of the international world, do you think such a democracy is viable? Why or why not?

Leopold as an Advocate

Sara Vickerman

Sara Vickerman is director of the West Coast office of Defenders of Wildlife, a national nonprofit organization. She received the U.S. Department of the Interior's highest conservation award for her work on the Oregon Biodiversity Project. This essay was published in the Wildlife Society Bulletin *in 1998.*

Vickerman identifies some key ideas and observations of Aldo Leopold that have not yet been incorporated into conservation. She proposes a number of ways in which people might better connect with the land.

Close examination of most programs of natural resource agencies reveals cultures and administrative systems shackled by their utilitarian histories and often dominated by economic concerns. In his insightful article, "Recurring Environmental Policy Nightmares," University of Michigan professor Steven Yaffee identified several tendencies of natural resource agencies that contribute to ineffective decision making: piecemeal solutions to cross-cutting problems, fragmentation of interests and values, fragmentation of responsibilities, and fragmentation of information and knowledge (Yaffee 1997).

With few exceptions, state fish and wildlife agencies remain heavily dependent on license revenues from hunters and fishermen. Although many state fish and wildlife agency biologists are among the most articulate spokespersons for ecological concepts and good land management, agencies have been slow to shift emphasis from the production of game and fish to a more natural approach favoring wild stocks. To a certain extent, we remain in the trap described by [Aldo] Leopold 50 years ago in which intensive management of game and fish lowers the unit value by making it artificial. In the Pacific Northwest, reliance on hatcheries to replace wild stocks of salmon has been the primary focus of "mitigation" efforts. Although people are beginning to challenge this practice, for many species and sub-species of fish it is already too late.

Revenue from consumptive uses is declining. Yet the public is demanding greater attention to biodiversity conservation, recovery of endangered species, and watershed management. A few states (notably Missouri and, more recently, Arkansas) have secured general fund revenues. Most, however, have found it difficult to persuade lawmakers to allocate general fund revenues to conserve their state's natural heritage. Ecosystem components are still forced into programmatic boxes and treated as if they were separate entities in the real world. For example, in Oregon, the Oregon Department of Fish and Wildlife manages fish and wildlife, except for predators and endangered plants, which come under the purview of the Oregon Department of Agriculture. Invertebrates, unwanted by any agency, ended up in the privately funded Oregon Natural Heritage Program. Until recently, fish biologists and wildlife biologists were housed separately. Water quality and quantity are handled by different agencies.

CONSERVATION EDUCATION

In general, substantive actions and investments in natural resources seem driven by one crisis after another, often by the listing of an endangered species or a human health concern. Despite resistance to heavy-handed federal regulations, the threat of enforcement under the Endangered Species Act, Clean Water Act, or other federal statutes is often necessary to motivate states, local government, industry, and private citizens. As a result, society keeps treating symptoms without ever really solving problems. Scientists collect voluminous information on highly specialized environmental issues, but often the results get lost in the debate. Leopold called for a reversal of specialization; "instead of learning more and more about less and less, we must learn more and more about the biotic landscape. . . . Harmony with the land is like harmony with a friend; you cannot cherish his right hand and chop off his left" (Leopold 1949:189).

Our institutions of higher learning seem to struggle with the challenge of integrating studies and dis-ciplines as they did in Leopold's day, when he noted that "much higher education seems to deliberately avoid ecological concepts." *Conservation Biology* editor Gary Meffe wrote that "there are serious deficiencies in academia's response to the biodiversity crisis, and those deficiencies can be traced partly to the narrow visions of the university departments and the disciplines they represent" (Meffe 1998:259). Science, however, demands a level of precision impossible to achieve in the natural world, and few scientists want to risk criticism from peers by straying outside academic boundaries. Leopold was ridiculed by some and praised by others for his capacity to understand and his willingness to explain natural phenomena beyond quantitative technical details. Few scientists today seem willing to search for linkages between elements of the natural world, and those who do may either gain considerable respect or lose credibility with peers and certain constituencies. Although I consider advocacy for natural resources and the integrity of ecosystems to be a legitimate and worthwhile pursuit for scientists and resource professionals (on and off of the job), many of my colleagues do not. For that reason alone, important ecological concepts are not effectively communicated to a general public that is increasingly disconnected from the natural world. . . .

Who bears the responsibility for informing private landowners, suburban gardeners, and others whose daily activities have a profound and often adverse impact on nature about the need for a land ethic? Leopold lamented that the whole structure of biological education was aimed at perpetuating the "professional monopoly on research" (Leopold 1949:221). By protecting privileged academic positions, and by couching ecological knowledge in seemingly inaccessible language, has education failed to engage people who might otherwise care deeply about nature and take responsibility for protecting ecological values? . . .

PREDATORS

Despite the progress we have made in advancing the concepts of biodiversity and ecosystem management within the resource profession, we have barely made a dent in the attitudes and behaviors of most

Americans. Loss of biodiversity and degradation of ecosystems continue at a pace and level that would surely horrify Leopold. On the brighter side, however, Leopold would be proud of the greater acceptance among the public and professionals of the restoration of predators. He would undoubtedly be especially gratified to know that wolves (*Canis lupis*) howl once again in Yellowstone National Park. But he would be disappointed to find that the Farm Bureau remains intolerant of predators and persists in its attempts to have the newly established wolf population removed.

Predator politics have long been polarized, and perhaps they always will be. However, we may have learned something from our own experiences and from Leopold. In a 1936 essay about protecting rare animals, Leopold proposed that government agencies form a committee of diverse public interests to define the needs of endangered species. He saw this collaborative arrangement as one that would foster trust and action (Leopold 1949).

Defenders of Wildlife has heeded Leopold's wisdom, and, where feasible, has either facilitated or participated in such collaborative approaches to conservation. In Idaho and Montana, Defenders helped develop the idea for a citizen management committee to oversee the reintroduction of grizzly bears (*Ursus arctos*). The proposal has been severely criticized by the industry and environmental adversaries, but remains one of the most promising examples of people working together to accomplish ecologically and culturally significant goals. If Leopold were alive today, I have no doubt that he would be a champion of the concept of citizen management committees. There is some truth to the adage that "with age comes wisdom." Much later in his life, Leopold concluded that the central goal of conservation must be not only to enhance how people relate to the land, but also how people relate to each other.

ROLE OF GOVERNMENT AND THE PRIVATE SECTOR

This, unfortunately, is a lesson that, if learned at all, is learned over time. Twenty years ago, I came to this profession like so many other young people, as a crusader. My commitment and passion motivated me, but sometimes I was so convinced that my viewpoint was right that I failed to take the time to listen to and understand other positions and values. Over time, I have taken Leopold's words to heart and adopted a more thoughtful and strategic approach that engages people with different viewpoints in constructive dialogue to find creative, win-win solutions. Today, when I encounter people whose enthusiasm and passion backfires, I wonder how long it will take for them to gain some tolerance and humility. I can only hope they will also someday benefit from Leopold's timeless wisdom. The process of exploring new options with people encourages acceptance of different viewpoints and makes it difficult, if not impossible, to demonize people. The inevitable result of a more collaborative approach is building trust and respect among people who, year after year, find themselves around the same table. Trust and respect are essential in any relationship and a necessary prerequisite to influence.

In Oregon, Defenders has facilitated a collaborative program in which dozens of diverse interests — from academia, government, and the private sector — have worked together to develop a statewide strategy to conserve biodiversity and healthy ecosystems. The strategy recognizes that biodiversity conservation is not possible through the establishment of reserves alone and it must extend to public and private land managers. This is not a novel concept. Leopold in fact recognized it when he wrote that government couldn't possibly own or control all lands of ecological value. "If the private land owner were ecologically minded, he would be proud to be the custodian of a reasonable portion of such areas, which add diversity and beauty to his farm and community." Leopold wondered at what point government conservation, like the mastodon, would be handicapped by its own dimensions (Leopold 1949:249). He concluded that a land ethic, or some other force that assigns more responsibility to the private landowner, was needed.

In my own efforts to promote a land ethic, I have struggled with the challenge of how society can offer "stewardship incentives" to landowners. My conclusions are tentative, but I recognize that although economic forces often determine what happens on the land, many people, nevertheless, are motivated by factors other than financial gain. Yet, as a society, we must do a better job of encouraging and rewarding good land stewards until Leopold's land ethic becomes a dominant cultural value. We must persevere until people accept in their hearts that "a thing is right when it tends to preserve the integrity, stability, and beauty of the biotic community," and ". . . wrong when it tends otherwise" (Leopold 1949:262).

Getting beyond narrow special interests and adversarial politics seems to be an important ingredient in the recipe for a more thoughtful approach to land management. Building better linkages between public and private interests, between science and policy, and between rural and urban communities seems critical to the success of any conservation program. Finding ways to enlist the broader public in conservation research and action on the ground also seems essential, if challenging. As Leopold noted, in our attempts to make conservation easy, we have made it trivial. . . .

When I re-read *A Sand County Almanac,* I wanted more than anything to have a few hundred hectares of my own to restore to ecological health. But in a sense it is too late for that. Most of us will never own a few hundred acres or even a single acre. We are too many and our demands on the land are too great to permit our population to sprawl across the landscape, dividing it into ever-smaller parcels at the expense of the last remaining open space. Somehow, we must find a way for people to connect with the land and learn to enjoy and appreciate its wild inhabitants without devouring them completely. I doubt that people who have no connection to the land will ever have much of a land ethic.

OUTDOOR RECREATION

Which brings me to a final subject considered by Leopold in *A Sand County Almanac* — outdoor recreation. Leopold had strong opinions on the subject. An avid hunter, he considered hunting central to the making of a good conservationist. He noted the political importance of hunters to conservation by pointing out that "a national game

policy could not be built on the assumption that 'America consisted of 120 million ornithologists'" (Lorbiecki 1996:113). But he seemed to hold "tourists" in contempt. In 1915, he described campers on the rim of the Grand Canyon as if they were the scourge of the West. "Electric signs jutted out from the canyon rims. Store peddlers trumpeted their wares. Piles of uncontrolled garbage stained the trails and campsites. Untreated sewage ran into the river. The tourists had a death grip on the site" (Lorbiecki 1996:68). While this description is not entirely unheard of today, "ecotourism" has come a long way since 1915. People are better educated and agencies are better educators. Entire industries have grown up around tourism, and the better ones combine fun and relaxation with learning and responsibility.

We need to offer people quality opportunities in natural settings where they can learn about nature and even make a contribution to restoration. Educators, resource agencies, conservation organizations, community groups, ecotourism enterprises, civic organizations, and industry groups can all participate in efforts to provide meaningful outdoor experiences. Such experiences are enhanced by the involvement of skilled and enthusiastic naturalists who inspire people and help them discover the magic and mystery of nature. People also need a greater stake in the outcome of their activities. What if people were given a chance to sign a "stewardship agreement" in which they could make a long-term commitment to restore a particular parcel of land? Watching the land recover and the wildlife return would provide an intrinsic reward and a sense of pride. This is a different kind of outdoor recreation that gives citizens the chance to learn and give something back to the land and to wildlife.

What is the future for conservation advocacy in the century to come? Surely society will still need "a militant minority of wilderness-minded citizens" to be "on watch throughout the nation and vigilantly available for action," as Leopold wrote (Leopold 1949:279). But we need more. We need to give more people a chance to connect with the land and with wild creatures, to ignite a fire within them that causes them to act on behalf of the natural world.

Those who are not influenced by militant advocacy, and perhaps are even offended by it, must be reached by other, more subtle and effective means. Some will be engaged through direct experiences with the natural world, as I have proposed. Some will be drawn to develop collaborative, community-based solutions by participating in working groups or watershed councils. Others will be persuaded by good science or convincing economic arguments. Still others will begin to change when neighbors complain about their gullied farm or about manure running into a nearby stream, when social pressure begins to invoke a land ethic. And, yes, some will accept change only to avoid prosecution.

Although he would certainly be dismayed by the growth of the human population and disheartened by the losses of biodiversity that have taken place in the last 50 years, Leopold would find reasons for optimism. His beloved Forest Service has turned the corner, embracing ecological concepts. National laws work to protect species and habitats. International agreements address biodiversity and sustainable forestry. When fishing interests demand the destruction of terns, cormorants, and seals to protect hatchery fish, they are met with public opposition and cautious agency responses that suggest recognition of the ecological complexities involved. A national campaign is under way to finance "wildlife diversity" programs to elevate the conservation status of species long ignored by fish and game agencies — and by society.

Yet much remains to be done. Our educational institutions, resource agencies, and conservation organizations must adopt more holistic, integrated, and interdisciplinary approaches. More naturalists and extension agents are needed to help people understand nature and to inspire them to get involved with protecting and restoring damaged lands. A greater commitment is needed from private industry to sustain the ecosystems upon which we all depend, not because it is demanded by the federal government, but simply because it is the right thing to do. A greater commitment is needed from us all, for we are all in this together. "All ethics so far evolved rest upon a single premise," Leopold asserted, "that the individual is a member of a community of interdependent parts. His instincts prompt him to compete for his place in the community, but his ethical sense prompts him also to co-operate. . . . ."

LITERATURE CITED

Leopold, A. [1949. A sand county almanac and sketches here and there]. Oxford University Press. New York, New York.

Lorbiecki, M. 1996. Aldo Leopold: a fierce green fire. Falcon Press. Helena, Montana.

Meffe, G. K. 1998. Softening the boundaries. Conservation Biology 12:259–260.

Yaffee, S. L. 1997. Why environmental policy nightmares recur. Conservation Biology 11:328–337.

DISCUSSION TOPICS

1. Vickerman identifies a number of obstacles to holistic decision making concerning natural resources. What are the most significant obstacles, in your view, and why?

2. How might conservation education best be integrated into the institutions of higher learning?

3. Vickerman states that Leopold was ridiculed by some for his willingness to advocate for the integrity of ecosystems. To what degree do you believe that scientists should be advocates? Explain your view.

4. According to Vickerman, if Leopold were alive today he would strongly support citizen management committees. What environmental issues in your region might benefit from the formation of such a committee?

5. Vickerman explains how private landowners as well as non-landowners might be encouraged to be better land stewards. Which of these ideas seem most workable?

6. Leopold stated that society will continue to need "a militant minority of wilderness-minded citizens" to be on watch and willing to act. Evaluate his statement.

7. Vickerman believes that many different strategies are needed in order to promote the development of a land ethic. What strategies do you believe are most effective and why?

CLASS EXERCISES

1. Develop a debate concerning the following point: Resolved: Living organisms should not be patented.
2. Suppose the class is a community that has depended on the logging of a redwood forest by private timber companies. There is now a national movement to preserve some of this forest (parts of which are a thousand years old) for future generations. Should the decision be made by the timber companies, public resource agencies (U.S. Forest Service), the majority vote of the local community, or by Congress? Identify the pros and cons for each group having the decision.
3. Ask students to indicate whether they feel empowered and significant as citizens. Have students separate into groups based on their answers. Ask those who do feel empowered to describe to others the reasons for their feelings. Ask those who do not feel empowered what would have to change for them to feel that their choices were significant in forming public policy.

FOR FURTHER READING

Anderson, Elizabeth. *Value in Ethics and Economics.* Cambridge, Mass.: Harvard University Press, 1993. A strong critique of current economic concepts of value. Anderson argues for an "expressive" theory of practical reason.

Attfield, Robin, and Barry Wilkins, eds. *International Justice and the Third World: Studies in the Philosophy of Development.* London and New York: Routledge, 1992. The essay by Attfield, "Environmentalism and Development," is particularly clear and stimulating. Extensive bibliography.

Azariah, Jayapaul, Hilda Azariah, and Darryl R. J. Macer, eds. *Bioethics in India.* Christchurch, New Zealand: Eubios Ethics Institute, 1998. A useful collection of over 100 mostly short papers providing a broad coverage of bioethics.

Bormann, F. Herbert, and Stephen R. Kellert, eds. *Ecology, Economics, Ethics: The Broken Circle.*

New Haven, Conn.: Yale University Press, 1991. Essays on species, agriculture, values, market mechanisms, and ethics.

Cafaro, Philip. "For a Grounded Conception of Wilderness and More Wilderness on the Ground." *Ethics and the Environment* 6, 1 (2001): 1–17. Argues against Cronon and Callicott for increased wilderness preservation.

Callicott, J. Baird. "The Wilderness Idea Revisited: The Sustainable Development Alternative." *Environmental Professional* 13 (1991): 235–47. An important article in which Callicott argues for an integration of human economic activities with biological conservation. He maintains that the popular idea of wilderness perpetuates the man-nature split, is ethnocentric, and ignores the dynamism of natural processes. He provides several examples of mutually enhancing human/nature symbioses. Extensive references.

Cater, Erlet, and Gwen Lowman, eds. *Ecotourism: A Sustainable Option?* Chicester, England: John Wiley & Sons, 1994. Articles assessing ecotourism in a number of countries; a sustainable balance between costs and benefit is the goal.

Coleman, Daniel A. *Ecopolitics: Building a Green Society.* New Brunswick, N.J.: Rutgers University Press, 1994. A clearly written argument for participatory and economic democracy.

Costanza, R. "Visions, Values, Valuation and the Need for an Ecological Economics." *Bioscience* 51, 6 (2001): 459–68.

Coufal, James E., and Charles M. Spuches. *Environmental Ethics in Practice: Developing a Personal Ethic.* Albany, N.Y.: Research Foundation of SUNY, 1995. Materials for upper-division, graduate, and continuing education courses, focusing on natural resource management. Contains many overhead masters and brief case studies, as well as codes of ethics of natural resource organizations. Extensive bibliography.

De-Shalit, Avner. *The Environment: Between Theory and Practice.* Oxford: Oxford University Press, 2000. Essays on the relationship between liberalism and environmentalism.

Edwards, Steven F. "Ethical Preferences and the Assessment of Existence Values: Does the Neoclassical Model Fit?" *Northeastern Journal of Agricultural and Resource Economics* 15 (1986): 145–50. Recommends that contingent valuation surveys collect data on underlying motives as well as monetary valuation in order to distinguish between egoists and altruists.

Environmental Values. A journal published in England, which began publication in 1992. Contains interdisciplinary articles.

Farmer, John. *Green Shift: Towards a Green Sensibility in Architecture.* Oxford: Butterworth-Heinemann, 1996. Commissioned by the World Wildlife Fund; an interdisciplinary, holistic overview of the history of modern architecture as seen from a green standpoint.

Georgescu-Roegen, Nicholas. *The Entrophy Law and the Economic Process.* Cambridge, Mass.: Harvard University Press, 1971. A highly influential book arguing that economics must take seriously the fact that human activity is limited by the low stock of entrophy on the globe.

Goodland, Robert, and Valerie Edmundson, eds. *Environmental Assessment and Development.* Washington, D.C.: World Bank, 1994. Multidisciplinary case studies of environmental assessment and management in industrial and developing countries.

Guerrier, Yonne, Nicholas Alexander, Jonathan Chase, and Martin O'Brien, eds. *Values and the Environment: A Social Science Perspective.* Chicester, England: John Wiley & Sons, 1995. Contains a range of responses to the current debate about environmental change, deriving from a 1993 conference on Values and the Environment at the University of Surrey.

Hale, Monica, ed. *Ecology in Education.* Cambridge: Cambridge University Press, 1993. School landscapes and urban environments.

Hardin, Garrett, and John Baden, eds. *Managing the Commons.* San Francisco: W. H. Freeman, 1977. An anthology concerned with cultural changes needed to ensure human survival.

Hardner, Jared, and Richard Rice. "Rethinking Green Consumerism." *Scientific American* (May 2002): 89–95. Describes replacing emphasis on green products with the opportunity to purchase biodiversity preservation directly.

Heaf, David, and Johannes Wirz. *Genetic Engineering and the Intrinsic Value and Integrity of Animals and Plants.* Dornach, Switzerland: *If*gene, 2002. A valuable collection of workshop proceedings.

Hempel, Lamont C. *Environmental Governance: The Global Challenge.* Washington, D.C.: Island Press, 1996. Makes a persuasive case that global changes in ecology and political economy are beginning to foster greater reliance on supranational, regional, and local levels of governance. Nation-states are losing some power.

Hubbard, Harold M. "The Real Cost of Energy." *Scientific American* 264 (1991): 36–42. Argues for various strategies of incorporating all the costs of energy into the market.

Inner Voice. A bimonthly paper published by the Association of Forest Service Employees for Environmental Ethics (P.O. Box 11615, Eugene, Oregon 97440). Contains informative and well-written articles.

Journal of Economic Perspectives 8, no. 4 (Fall 1994). A special issue on environmental economics.

King, Donna Lee. *Doing Their Share to Save the Planet: Children and Environmental Crisis.* New Brunswick, N.J.: Rutgers University Press, 1995. A valuable book that discusses children's art and what it means to children to be green, based on childrens' comments. Good bibliography.

Klyza, Christopher McGrory. *Who Controls Public Lands?* Chapel Hill: University of North Carolina, 1996. Clear, useful historical discussion of public lands and competing ideas of the public interest. Extensive references.

Lassen, J., K. H. Madsen, and P. Sandoe. "Ethics and Genetic Engineering—Lessons to Be Learned from GM Foods." *Bioprocess and Biosystems Engineering* 24 (2002): 263–71. Scientific experts must develop respect for the values and concerns of the general public.

Light, Andrew, and Eric S. Higgs. "The Politics of Ecological Restoration." *Environmental Ethics* 18, 3 (1996): 227–47. Argues that restoration should be democratic rather than commodified as in the United States or nationalized as in Canada.

Luke, Timothy W. *Ecocritique: Contesting the Politics of Nature, Economy and Culture.* Minneapolis: University of Minnesota Press, 1997. Includes a criticism of deep ecology as political philosophy.

Merchant, Carolyn, ed. *Ecology: Key Concepts in Critical Theory.* Atlantic Highlands, N.J.: Humanities Press, 1994. A well-researched, well-selected anthology of readings on critical theory (such as Marxism, anarchism, socialism, feminism, gay/lesbian liberation, national liberation movements).

Midgley, Mary. "Biotechnology and Monstrosity: Why We Should Pay Attention to the 'Yuk Factor'." *Hastings Center Report* 30, 5 (2000): 7–15. Feeling is an essential part of our moral life.

Ostrom, Elinor. *Governing the Commons: The Evolution of Institutions for Collective Action.* Cambridge: Cambridge University Press, 1990. Ostrom has studied collective action by individuals using common-pool resources (CPR) for over thirty years. The book provides descriptions of both successful and unsuccessful CPR arrangements.

Pearce, David W., and Jeremy J. Warford. *World without End: Economics, Environment, and Sustainable Development.* New York: Oxford University Press, 1993. Based on extensive material from the World Bank, emphasizing policies appropriate for developing countries.

Platt, Rutherford H. *Land Use and Society: Geography, Law, and Public Policy.* Washington, D.C.: Island Press, 1996. The influence of law on the human use of land. Includes a review of Supreme Court decisions regarding the takings issue.

Reitz, Elizabeth J., Lee A. Newson, and Sylvia J. Scudder, eds. *Case Studies in Environmental Archaeology.* New York: Plenum, 1996. Multidisciplinary, using ethnographic and biological case studies; includes sites from North America, the Caribbean, and South America.

Rolston, Holmes, III. "The Wilderness Idea Reaffirmed." *Environmental Professional* 13 (1991): 1–9. Rolston argues that Callicott's account of human beings as entirely natural is incorrect. Rolston maintains that wilderness has intrinsic value and should be protected from human utilization.

———. "Enforcing Environmental Ethics," in *Social and Political Philosophy,* ed. James P. Sterba. London: Routledge, 2001. Calls for civic law to protect natural value.

Rolston, Holmes, III, and James Coufal. "A Forest Ethic and Multivalue Forest Management." *Journal of Forestry* 89, 4 (1991): 35–40. Provides ten categories of values: life support; economic, scientific, recreational, and aesthetic use; wildlife; biotic diversity; natural history; spiritual; and intrinsic.

Rudig, Wolfgang, ed. *Green Politics Three.* Edinburgh: Edinburgh University Press, 1995. Addresses many of the problems facing green organizations, both theoretical and empirical.

Sagoff, Mark. *The Economy of the Earth: Philosophy, Law, and the Environment.* Cambridge: Cambridge University Press, 1988. A collection of important essays arguing against market failure as the basis of social regulation and in favor of the thesis that social regulation expresses what we believe as a nation.

———. "On the Value of Natural Ecosystems: The Catskills Parable." *Politics and the Life Sciences* 21, 1 (2002): 16–21.

Snape, William J., III, ed. *Biodiversity and the Law.* Washington, D.C.: Island Press, 1996. Excellent, particularly a discussion of legal protection of wildlife.

Steingraber, Sandra. *Having Faith: An Ecologist's Journey to Motherhood.* Cambridge, Mass.: Perseus, 2001. Hope for a future based on political implementation of biological realities. Steingraber is an ecologist and a poet.

Theobald, William, ed. *Global Tourism: The Next Decade.* Oxford: Butterworth-Heinemann, 1994. International tourism is growing at a tremendous rate. This book contains twenty-nine essays and is a fine introduction to a range of issues, including ecotourism.

Thomashow, Mitchell. *Ecological Identity: Becoming a Reflective Environmentalist.* Cambridge, Mass.: MIT Press, 1995. Thomashow has taught for years in an innovative environmental studies program. Provides practical exercises for developing a sense of ecological identity.

Underwood, Daniel A., and Paul G. King. "On the Ideological Foundations of Environmental Policy." *Ecological Economics* 1 (1989): 315–34. Contrasts steady-state and neoclassical economic schools of thought and argues that steady-state economic theory is in accord with scientific knowledge.

Varner, Gary E. "The Takings Issue and the Human-Nature Dichotomy." *Human Ecology Review* 3, 1 (1996): 12–15. The wise-use movement separates humans from the ecosystems on which they depend.

Wann, David. *Deep Design: Pathways to a Livable Future.* Washington, D.C.: Island Press, 1996. An inspiring book that argues that we need to design in a way which integrates efficiency, recycling, and biological and cultural knowledge.

Western, David, and Michael R. Wright. *Natural Connections: Perspectives in Community-Based Conservation.* Washington, D.C.: Island Press, 1994. Case studies of community-Based conservation, demonstrating their success in enhancing biodiversity.

Westing, Arthur H. "Core Values for Sustainable Development." *Environmental Conservation* 23, 3 (1996): 218–25. Challenges all concerned individuals to actively participate in the political process.

von Weizsacker, Ernst U. *Earth Politics.* London: Zed Books, 1994. Calls for carbon taxes and new models of wealth.

Zaslowsky, Dyan, and T. H. Watkin, *These American Lands: Parks, Wilderness, and the Public Lands.* Washington, D.C.: Island Press, 1994. A highly useful compilation of essays, including national wildlife refuges and wild and scenic rivers. Excellent appendixes.

CASE STUDIES

We present a series of case studies to stimulate thought and discussion on significant environmental problems. In the following case studies, we recognize that the amount of information is well below what would be needed to make a fully informed decision. We also recognize that in our effort to keep the background descriptions brief, those involved with these issues might dispute some of the details presented (or omitted). Nevertheless, we present these issues as important starting points for discussions on the kinds of real problems facing resource managers, scientists, environmental philosophers and activists, and the many other members of the public concerned with environmental issues.

A. ENDANGERED SPECIES: THE NENE[1]

The nene (Hawaiian goose) is the state bird of Hawaii and is one of at least twenty-nine threatened and endangered bird species on Hawaii.[2] Much of the original decline of the nene resulted from overhunting, the conversion of former goose habitat to agriculture, and introduction of the rat and mongoose to the islands. Despite a fifty-year recovery effort, the nene is still on the edge of extinction, and there are no known self-sustaining populations living on the island. Is it worth continuing the effort to establish the nene? On the negative side is the observation that much of the original and prime nene habitat has been lost from the islands. Further, nene now seem to capitalize on nonnative (exotic) plants. Virtually all other goose populations in North America are managed by providing food (e.g., grasses, forbs, and agricultural crops); this normal kind of waterfowl management is unacceptable to Hawaiian agencies that are calling for the removal of exotic plants. Finally, there are at least twelve bird species even more critically endangered than the nene; these birds are less well known, but the islands' biodiversity would benefit from recovery efforts for these species too. In contrast, supporters of the nene argue that no species should be abandoned and that the fifty years of effort have generated important lessons about endangered species

[1]The authors thank Dr. Jeff M. Black, Humboldt State University, for inspiration on this case study, and for providing key information on topics involved in this discussion. Additional sources of information on this topic include Jeff M. Black, "The Nene Recovery Initiative: Research against Extinction," *Ibis* 135 (1995): S153–60; P. C. Banko, J. M. Black, and W. C. Banko, "Hawaiian Goose (Nene) (*Branta sandvichensis*)," in *The Birds of North America*, A. Poole and F. Gill, eds. (Philadelphia: The Birds of North America, 1999).

[2]J. Michael Scott and Sheila Conant, "Recovery and Management Introduction." *Studies in Avian Biology* 22 (2001): 306–7.

recovery efforts. Stopping efforts at this point with such a high-profile species could seriously undermine future endangered species efforts for the nene and perhaps other endangered species as well.

What additional information do you believe is necessary to make a more informed decision? What further efforts should be expended on the nene, and how should those efforts be ranked in comparison to other endangered birds? Give reasons for your position.

B. THE KLAMATH RIVER: FARMERS, FISHERS, NATIVE AMERICANS, AND SALMON

In September 2002, an estimated 33,000 fish, including chinook salmon, coho, and steelhead, died directly and indirectly from the effects of reduced water flow in the Klamath River (California and Oregon); the coho are an endangered species. Several interest groups were involved. Farmers in the Klamath Basin depend on water from the Klamath River for their crops, and those settling in the region in the 1800s were promised water by the government for their crops. When farmers complained that low diversions from the Klamath to their fields in 2001 had caused over $200 million in losses, the Bureau of Reclamation developed a ten-year plan for Klamath water use to help ensure adequate water to the farmers, while still attempting to provide adequate water for the Klamath fisheries. The National Marine Fisheries Service argued that, as written, the plan would place the coho in jeopardy and conflict with the Endangered Species Act. Coastal salmon fishers also challenged the Bureau's ten-year plan as potentially devastating to the commercially valuable Klamath River salmon runs. Further, long-standing treaties with Native Americans of the Klamath region promised them fish, including suckers (some of which are endangered and culturally important) and salmon. In essence, these groups argued that there was not enough water to maintain a healthy fisheries and still meet the water needs of the farming community.

Numerous options have been discussed. For example, some argue that the farmers should be allowed to go bankrupt if circumstances dictate, since it is an accepted risk of engaging in commerce that any business venture and even entire types of businesses may face dissolution as societies evolve. Others argue that the region should be seen as not having enough water to support adequate fisheries and meet treaty responsibilities and most or all farmlands should be "bought out" by the government, even if some farm families prefer to continue. Still others cite contributions of farmers to society's food needs and believe earlier commitments by the government to provide water to farmers must be honored. Some have even said that endangered fish of little commercial value should not be used as an excuse to question the contributions of productive farm communities to human society.

What, if any, responsibilities do you believe society has to support the farmers in the Klamath region? Based on the amount of information you have, what would be your first choice on how this situation should be resolved? Give reasons for your position. What further information would assist you in making a more confident decision?

C. MAKAH INDIAN TRIBE AND WHALE HUNTING

In 1855 the U.S. government made a treaty guaranteeing whaling rights to the Makah, a tribe currently comprising about 1800 Native Americans in Washington State. When the gray whale was considered endangered (due to non-Indian whalers), the Makah tribe did no whaling over a seventy-year period. However, after the gray whale population was delisted (1994) from the Endangered Species Act, the Makah requested permission to hunt again, emphasizing the significance of traditional whaling to their culture. The International Whaling Commission approved a 1998–2002 quota to the Makah, which allowed a total kill of up to twenty whales or a wounding of up to thirty-three whales in these five years, whichever came first. The Makah tribe had to employ traditional methods of harvest, including use of a canoe and hand-thrown harpoon. However, to ensure humaneness of the kill, the tribe used a 50-caliber gun, of which a single shot can quickly kill a whale. Whale products could be used only for established cultural purposes; no commercial use of whale products was allowed. One whale was killed in May 1999.

Several groups opposed reinstitution of these hunts. The Sea Shepherd Society strongly opposed Makah hunting by actively attempting to interfere with the Makah boats during the successful May 1999 hunt. The Cetacean Society International opposed the hunts through public and private communications with the Makah tribe and peaceful protest rallies. A lawsuit filed by the Fund for Animals, the Humane Society of the United States, and others contended that the Makah whaling would endanger public safety and harm gray whales in Washington's Strait of Juan de Fuca. Based on this lawsuit, a Federal Appeals Court ruled in December 2002 that the Makah Tribe could not resume hunts until after the National Marine Fisheries Service created an environmental impact statement — a more extensive document than the environmental assessment conducted earlier.

Some of the values addressed by various interest groups include a desire to honor cultural traditions of native peoples; concern for suffering of sentient and highly intelligent creatures; concern that these hunts serve as precedents for justifying additional whale hunts by other native cultural groups or countries (e.g., Norway, Japan); the observation that availability of nonwhale sources of food for contemporary native peoples makes whale hunting obsolete; a desire to honor treaties established years ago and often ignored since their establishment; and concern for public safety.

What additional values do you believe should be addressed in this case study? Rank the relative importance of these values, as you believe they pertain to this case. Give your reasoning. What outcome do you believe to be most just in the case of Makah whaling? Justify your position

D. SCIENCE AND ADVOCACY

Scientists have long recognized a tension between maintaining a scientific objectivity in addressing controversial issues and taking responsibility as citizens to advocate for values they believe to be appropriate based on their experience with these controversial issues. Most scientists can agree that science in general is not value free, but assessing their degree of responsibility as advocates regularly generates considerable discussion among scientists and resource managers. A 1996 issue of *Conservation Biology* (10 (3): 904–20) includes a number of articles addressing the role and responsibility of scientists to openly assert their values.

Barry and Oelschlaeger[3] argue that some scientific disciplines, such as conservation biology, are inescapably normative and that advocacy for the preservation of biodiversity is part of the scientific practice of conservation biology. Further, to pretend, for example, that the acquisition of "positive knowledge" alone will avert mass extinctions is misguided.

In contrast, Tracy and Brussard[4] assert that because science requires an open-minded approach willing to accept new models of what is known and supported by new data and analysis, it is difficult for any scientist to zealously advocate singular solutions to environmental problems except under very simple circumstances. They conclude that objective scientists cannot ordinarily be zealous activists, and zealous activists cannot be constrained by objective science as a sole source of knowledge.

Do you believe that these ideas can be resolved and are just a difference in degree along a continuum? Or, do you see an essential difference in perspectives among these sets of authors? Give your reasoning.

Consider the assertion made by many ecologists and conservation biologists that the earth is entering a period of mass extinction similar to, or even more serious than, the one occurring during the Cretaceous Period. Apply the ideas of each set of authors to how they would interpret the proper approach for scientists to take. How do your own values align with these perspectives? Justify your position.

E. ARE WE ON A LIFEBOAT?

In 1974 Garrett Hardin published an essay entitled "Living on a Lifeboat," in which he presented a metaphor for life on earth.[5] Each rich nation is a

---

[3]Dwight Barry and Max Oelschlaeger. "A Science for Survival: Values and Conservation Biology." *Conservation Biology* 10 (3) (1996): 905–11.

[4]C. Richard Tracy and Peter F. Brussard. "The Importance of Science in Conservation Biology." *Conservation Biology* 10 (3) (1996): 918–19.

[5]Garrett Hardin, "Living on a Lifeboat," *Bioscience* 24 (1974).

lifeboat full of comparatively rich people, and the poor of the world are in other, much more crowded lifeboats. Often the poor fall out of their lifeboats and swim for a while, hoping to be admitted to a rich lifeboat or benefit from its bounty. What should the passengers on the rich lifeboat do?

Hardin's answer turns on the biological concept of the carrying capacity of the land. He recommends that those in rich lifeboats admit no more to their boat in order to preserve the small safety factor that protects against the boat being swamped and everyone drowning.

He states that the rate of reproduction in rich countries as contrasted with poor countries means that the lifeboat metaphor will become even more appropriate in the future. Poor countries will exceed the carrying capacity of their environment to an ever more extreme degree. If rich countries share food with poor countries, they will simply be encouraging incompetent governments who fail to plan ahead and whose people fail to control their own reproductive rate. Rich countries should not share food in a world of irresponsible reproduction.

Hardin also argues that immigration simply moves people to the food, speeding up the destruction of the environment in rich countries. The main selfish interest in unimpeded immigration is the interest of employers in cheap labor, and this interest should not be socially supported. The unselfish interest in sharing the bounty with the poor will result in the ruin of the environment for one's grandchildren.

Since the time Hardin wrote his article in the early 1970s, population growth has continued. The global human population in 1974 was 4 billion; by 2003 it was 6.3 billion (U.S. Census Bureau). World population will reach 7 billion between 2011 and 2015 and is predicted by the U.N. Population Division to reach 9 billion by 2050. Average annual population growth worldwide, after surging in the 1960s, has continued to decline, so that worldwide population may stabilize at around 9 billion. Almost all population growth is taking place in the less developed regions of the world.[6] Studies have shown that declining fertility rates correlate with improved population planning programs and increased services to women, such as educational opportunities.[7]

1. To what degree do you believe that world population figures should be a cause for concern? To what degree do you believe that the future of your grandchildren or the future of wildlife will be affected by population growth?
2. What actions should be taken by our government and/or by individuals in response to population growth, or is it better to take no action?
3. Is the lifeboat metaphor an accurate one for the relationship between rich and poor nations? Why or why not?
4. In your view, is the abundance of food the key element in determining the reproductive rate of a country? If not, what other factors are relevant?
5. Does the predicted stabilization in world population at 9 billion diminish your concerns about population growth?

---

[6]U.N. Population Fund, 2003. Retrieved from http://www.unfpa.org/.

[7]Population Action International, 2003. Retrieved from http://www.populationaction.org/resources/publications/educating_girls/ggap_fin/.

APPENDIX

Class Exercises

Three approaches have commonly been used to increase participation of students in class discussions: small-group discussions, debates, and conflict resolution exercises.

A. SMALL-GROUP DISCUSSIONS

The students divide themselves into groups of three or five each. A question is posed or a problem is presented on which they are asked to present their considered opinions. Some of the discussion topics presented in the case studies could be used. After approximately ten minutes of discussion, a spokesperson from each group presents the group's assessment, with at least one cogent reason to support the group position. Each group normally has two to four minutes to summarize its position. The instructor keeps a summary of various answers and opinions on the board and summarizes them with the class at the end of the exercise. With each new exercise, students are encouraged to change groups.

B. DEBATES

A controversial issue is presented to the class, and all students are allowed to choose the side they wish to represent. Unequal groups can be balanced by asking for volunteers to change sides. The issue is then debated by standardized debating procedures, as presented by Dominic Infante.[1] We recommend the following schedule:

Introduction
    Advocates for proposal   (10 minutes)
    Opponents to proposal   (10 minutes)
Rebuttal
    Opponents to proposal   (10 minutes)
    Advocates for proposal   (10 minutes)
Summary
    Opponents to proposal   (7 minutes)
    Advocates for proposal   (7 minutes)

A five-minute break is normally allowed between introduction and rebuttal, and rebuttal and summary. If necessary to accommodate a 50-minute

---

[1]Dominic A. Infante. *Arguing Constructively.* Prospect Heights, IL: Waveland Press, 1988, pp. 33–126.

class period, the summary arguments and judges' decisions can be completed during a second class period.

Based on our experiences, we recommend the following:

1. To be most effective, each team in the debate has no more than seven students; a larger class would benefit by having additional debates rather than larger teams.
2. Before the first debate, one class period should be devoted to presenting debating principles and strategies to the students, such as outlined in Infante (1988).
3. One class period is set aside for the respective teams to prepare their positions. This gives everyone an opportunity to work together at a time that all have available.
4. We recommend that the debate be judged by an independent panel of five students from the class, who are not part of either team. The student judges develop their own scoring criteria and procedures, which they share with the competing teams before the debate. Although the criteria used to judge have varied, some used by our students include currency and adequacy of the evidence; scientific reliability of the sources of evidence; relevance of the arguments used; appearance (voice and posture) of the advocates during their presentation; consistency and logic of ideas used; degree to which emotional appeal is used or avoided; clarity with which underlying assumptions are directly addressed; and overall persuasiveness.

One variation of this exercise is that after choosing positions, all students are required to switch sides and advocate the opposing view. Despite their initial resistance, students almost uniformly have agreed at the end of the exercise that they learned as much or more than if they had simply argued the position they originally chose.

C. CONFLICT RESOLUTION EXERCISES

In cooperation with Dr. Elizabeth (Betsy) Watson, a professor of sociology and also director of the Institute for the Study of Dispute Resolution (ISADR), Humboldt State University, we have incorporated conflict resolution exercises into our courses. Dr. Watson has completed development of a module of basic dispute resolution definitions, concepts, skills, and bibliographic information designed to be used by college instructors who wish to include such material in their curricula. Entitled *Putting Dispute Resolution into Your Course Curriculum,* it includes worksheets for overhead transparencies, role plays, strategies for skill building, and an extensive annotated bibliography. A copy of the module can be obtained directly from Dr. Watson, Department of Sociology, Humboldt State University, Arcata, California, 95521. Some additional references for conflict resolutions are listed below, courtesy of Dr. Watson.

REFERENCES

Adler, Peter S., et al. *Managing Scientific and Technical Information in Environmental Cases.* Pasadena, Calif.: Western Justice Center Foundation, 2000.

Carpenter, Susan L. *Managing Public Disputes: A Practical Guide to Handling Conflict and Reaching Agreements.* San Francisco: Jossey-Bass, 1991.

Fisher, Roger, William Ury, and Bruce Patton. *Getting to Yes.* Boston: Houghton Mifflin, 1991.

Gray, Barbara. *Collaborating: Finding Common Ground for Multiparty Problems.* San Francisco: Jossey-Bass, 1989.

Maser, Chris. *Resolving Environmental Conflict: Towards Sustainable Community Development.* Tallahassee, Fla.: St. Lucie Press, 1996.

Moore, Christopher W. *The Mediation Process: Practical Strategies for Resolving Conflict.* San Francisco: Jossey-Bass, 1986.

Schwerin, Edward W. *Mediation, Citizen Empowerment, and Transformational Politics.* Westport, Conn.: Praeger, 1995.

ACKNOWLEDGMENTS

INTRODUCTION

Merwin, W. S. 1993. Unchopping a Tree, pp. 479–481. In *A Forest of Voices,* 2nd ed., Chris Anderson and Lex Runciman, eds. Mayfield Publishing, Mountain View, California. Reproduced with permission from The McGraw-Hill Companies, Inc.

CHAPTER ONE

Woodward, James, and David Goodstein. 1996. Conduct, Misconduct and the Structure of Science. *American Scientist* 84: 479–90. By permission of *American Scientist,* magazine of Sigma Xi, The Scientific Research Society.

Freyfogle, Eric T., and Julianne Lutz Newton. 2002. Putting Science in Its Place. *Conservation Biology* 16: 863–73. Used by permission of Blackwell Science, Inc.

Fjelland, Ragnar. 2002. Facing the Problem of Uncertainty. *Journal of Agriculture and Environmental Ethics* 15:155–69. With kind permission of Kluwer Academic Publishers.

Zuk, Marlene. 1993. Feminism and the Study of Behavior. *BioScience* 43: 774–78. Copyright © 1993 by American Institute of Biological Sciences. Reproduced with permission of American Institute of Biological Sciences in the format Textbook via Copyright Clearance Center.

Wilson, Edward O. 1987. The Little Things That Run the World. *Conservation Biology* 1: 344–46. Used by permission of Blackwell Science, Inc.

CHAPTER TWO

Rachels, James. 2003. A Short Introduction to Moral Philosophy. From *The Right Thing to Do,* 3rd ed., McGraw-Hill, New York. Reproduced with permission from The McGraw-Hill Companies, Inc.

Rachels, James. 2003. Some Basic Points about Arguments. From *The Right Thing to Do,* 3rd ed., McGraw-Hill, New York. Reproduced with permission from The McGraw-Hill Companies, Inc.

Rolston, Holmes III. 1991. Environmental Ethics: Values in and Duties to the Natural World. In *Ecology, Economics, Ethics: The Broken Circle,* F. Herbert Bormann and Stephen R. Kellert, eds. Yale University Press, New Haven, Connecticut. Copyright 1991. By permission of Yale University Press.

Peterson, Anna. 1999. Environmental Ethics and the Social Construction of Nature. *Environmental Ethics* 21.4: 339–57. Reprinted with permission of Anna Peterson.

Cheney, Jim, and Anthony Weston. 1999. Environmental Ethics as Environmental Etiquette. *Environmental Ethics* 21.2: 115–34. Reprinted with permission of Jim Cheney and Anthony Weston.

Wenz, Peter S. Just Garbage: Environmental Injustice. From *Faces of Environmental Racism: Confronting Issues of Global Justice,* Laura Westra and Peter S. Wenz, eds. Rowman & Littlefield, Lanham, Maryland. Copyright © 1995 by Rowman & Littlefield Publishing Group, Inc. Reproduced with permission of Rowman & Littlefield Publishing Group, Inc. in the format Textbook via Copyright Clearance Center.

CHAPTER THREE

Thoreau, Henry David. 1980. Walking (originally published 1862). In *The Natural History Essays.* Peregrine Smith, Inc., Salt Lake City. By permission of Gibbs Smith, Publisher.

Muir, John. 1913 (originally published 1894). A Near View of the High Sierras. In *The Mountains of California.* Century Company, New York.

Callicott, J. Baird. 1992. The Land Aesthetic. Unpublished version from author. By permission of J. Baird Callicott. Revised version published in *Renewable Resources Journal* 10.4: 12–17.

Nabhan, Gary Paul. 1994. The Far Outside. In *Place of the Wild,* David Clark Burks, ed. Island Press, Washington, D.C.

Abram, David. 1996. A More-Than-Human World. In *An Invitation to Environmental Philosophy,* Anthony Weston, ed. Oxford University Press, New York. Copyright 1998 by Oxford University Press, Inc. Used by Permission of Oxford University Press, Inc.

CHAPTER FOUR

Hughes, J. Donald. 1975. The Ancient Roots of Our Ecological Crisis. In *Ecology in Ancient Civilizations,* pp. 147–56. University of New Mexico Press, Albuquerque. By permission of the author.

Hargrove, Eugene C. 1980. Anglo-American Land Use Attitudes. *Environmental Ethics* 2: 121–48. Copyright © 1980 by Center for Environmental Philosophy. Reproduced with permission of Center for Environmental Philosophy in the format Textbook via Copyright Clearance Center.

Callicott, J. Baird. 1990. Whither Conservation Ethics? *Conservation Biology* 4: 15–20. Used by permission of Blackwell Science, Inc.

Taylor, Alan. 1998. "Wasty Ways": Stories of American Settlement. *Environmental History* 3.3: 291–310. Copyright © 1999 by Forest History Society. Reproduced with permission of Forest History Society in the format Textbook via Copyright Clearance Center.

Evernden, Neil. 1989. Nature in Industrial Society. In *Cultural Politics in Contemporary America,* Ian Angus and Sut Jhally, eds., pp. 151–64. Routledge, New York. Copyright 1989 from *Cultural Politics in Contemporary America* by I. Angus and S. Jhally. Reproduced by permission of Routledge, Inc., part of The Taylor & Francis Group.

Cafaro, Philip. 2002. Rachel Carson's Environmental Ethics. *Worldview* 6: 58–80. By permission of Brill Academic Publishers.

CHAPTER FIVE

White, Lynn, Jr. 1967. The Historical Roots of Our Ecologic Crisis. *Science* 155: 1203–7. Copyright 1967 American Association for the Advancement of Science.

Troster, Lawrence. 1991–92. Created in the Image of God: Humanity and Divinity in an Age of Environmentalism. Reprinted with permission from *Conservative Judaism* 44: 14–24, © 1992 by the Rabbinical Assembly.

Rolston, Holmes III. 1993. Environmental Ethics: Some Challenges for Christians. The Annual Society of Christian Ethics, Harlan Beckley, ed., pp. 163–86. Georgetown University Press, Washington, D.C. By permission of Georgetown University Press

Izzi Deen (Samarrai), Mawil Y. 1990. Islamic Environmental Ethics, Law, and Society. In *Ethics of Environment and Development: Global Challenge, International Response,* J. Ronald Engel and Joan Gibb Engel, eds., pp. 189–98. University of Arizona Press, Tucson. © 1990. Reproduced by permission of John Wiley & Sons Limited.

LaDuke, Winona. 2000. Voices from White Earth. In *A Forest of Voices: Conversations in Ecology,* 2nd ed., Chris Anderson and Lex Runciman, eds., pp. 435–64. Mayfield Publishing, Mountain View, California. Reproduced by permission of The McGraw-Hill Companies, Inc.

Hanh, Thich Nhat. 1993. The Sun My Heart. In *Love in Action: Writings on Nonviolent Social Change,* pp. 127–38. Parallax Press, Berkeley. By permission of Parallax Press.

Guha, Ramachandra, and Juan Martinez-Alier. 1997. The Environmentalism of the Poor. In *Varieties of Environmentalism: Essays North and South,* pp. 3–21. Earthscan, London. Copyright © and by permission of Kogan Page Publishers, London.

CHAPTER SIX

Descartes, René. Animals Are Machines. Selection I (Discourse on Method) in *Philosophical Works of Descartes* 1: 115–18, Haldine, E. S. and G. R. T. Ross, translators, Cambridge University Press, 1968. Reprinted with permission of Cambridge University Press. Selections II and III from *Descartes Philosophical Letters,* A. Kenny, translator and editor, University of Minnesota Press, Minneapolis, 1970. By permission of the University of Minnesota Press.

Skidmore, James. 2001. Duties to Animals: The Failure of Kant's Moral Theory. *Journal of Value Inquiry* 35: 541–59. With kind permission of Kluwer Academic Publishers.

Murdy, William. H. 1975. Anthropocentrism: A Modern View. *Science* 187: 1168–72. Copyright 1975 American Association for the Advancement of Science.

Gould, Stephen Jay. 1990. The Golden Rule: A Proper Scale for Our Environmental Crisis. Reprinted from *Natural History,* September: 24–30. Copyright © Natural History Magazine, Inc., 1996.

Turner, Frederick. 1994. The Invented Landscape. In *Beyond Preservation: Restoring and Inventing Landscapes,* A. Dwight Baldwin, Jr., Judith DeLuce, and Carl Pletsch, eds., pp. 35–66. University of Minnesota, Minneapolis. Copyright © 1994 by University of Minnesota Press. Reproduced with permission of University of Minnesota Press in the format Textbook via Copyright Clearance Center.

CHAPTER SEVEN

Regan, Tom. 1983. From *The Case for Animal Rights,* pp. 245, 248, 280, 353–63. University of California Press, Berkeley, California. © 1983 University of California. Reprinted with the permission of University of California Press.

Singer, Peter. 1993. Equality for Animals? In *Practical Ethics,* 2nd ed., pp. 48–54, 60–62, 68–71. Cambridge University Press, Cambridge, England. © Cambridge University Press 1993. Reprinted with the permission of University of California Press.

Singer, Peter. 1991. Environmental Values. In *The Environmental Challenge,* pp. 3–24. Longman Cheshire, Melbourne. Pearson Education, Australia.

Jamieson, Dale. 1998. Animal Liberation Is an Environmental Ethic. *Environmental Values* 7: 41–57. © 1998 White Horse Press. Reprinted with the permission of White Horse Press.

Taylor, Paul W. 1986. From *Respect for Nature: A Theory of Environmental Ethics,* Princeton University Press, Princeton, New Jersey. Copyright 1986 by Princeton University Press. Reprinted by permission of Princeton University Press.

Varner, Gary. 2002. Biocentric Individualism. In *Environmental Ethics: What Really Matters, What Really Works,* Daniel Schmidtz and Elizabeth Willott, eds., pp. 108–20. Oxford University Press, New York. Copyright © 2002 by Oxford University Press, Inc. Used by permission of Oxford University Press, Inc.

CHAPTER EIGHT

Leopold, Aldo. 1966. The Land Ethic. In *A Sand County Almanac: And Sketches Here and There,* pp. 201–26. Oxford University Press, New York. Copyright © 1949, 1968, 1977 by Oxford University Press, Inc. Used by permission of Oxford University Press, Inc.

Callicott, J. Baird. 1990. Whither Conservation Ethics? *Conservation Biology* 4: 15–20. Used by permission of Blackwell Science, Inc.

Callicott, J. Baird. 1992. Aldo Leopold's Concept of Ecosystem Health. In *Ecosystem Health: New Goals for Environmental Management,* Robert Costanza, Bryan G. Norton, and Benjamin Haskell, eds., Island Press, Washington, D.C. Copyright © 1992 Island Press. Reprinted by permission of Island Press, Washington, D.C. and Covelo, California.

Rolston, Holmes III. 2000. The Land Ethic at the Turn of the Millennium. *Biodiversity and Conservation* 9: 1045–58. With kind permission of Kluwer Academic Publishers.

Devall, Bill. 2001. The Deep, Long-Range Ecology Movement: 1960–2000 — A Review. *Ethics & the Environment* 6: 18–41. Used by permission of Indiana University Press.

CHAPTER NINE

Warren, Karen. 2000. Quilting Ecofeminist Philosophy. *Ecofeminist Philosophy: A Western Perspective on What It Is and Why It Matters.* Rowman and

Littlefield, Lanham, Maryland. Copyright © 2000 by Rowman & Littlefield Publishing Group, Inc. Reproduced with permission of Rowman & Littlefield Publishing Group, Inc. in the format Textbook via Copyright Clearance Center.

Shiva, Vandana, and Maria Mies. 1993. Introduction to *Ecofeminism*, Maria Mies, ed. Zed Books, London. © 1993 London. Reprinted by permission of Zed Books.

Spretnak, Charlene. 1991. From *States of Grace: The Recovery of Meaning in the Postmodern Age,* pp. 102–13, 127–30, 133–38. HarperCollins, New York. Copyright (1991) by Charlene Spretnak. Reprinted by permission of HarperCollins Publishers, Inc.

Hill, Julia "Butterfly." 2001. From *The Legacy of Luna: The Story of a Tree, a Woman, and the Struggle to Save the Redwoods.* HarperCollins, San Francisco. © 2001 HarperCollins Publishers. Used by permission.

Davion, Victoria. 1994. Is Ecofeminism Feminist? In *Ecological Feminism*, Karen Warren, ed., pp. 8–28. Routledge, New York. © 1994. Reprinted with permission of Victoria Davion.

CHAPTER TEN

Dobson, Andrew. 1995. Biocentrism and Genetic Engineering. *Environmental Values* 4: 227–39. © 1995 White Horse Press. Reprinted with the permission of White Horse Press.

Lövei, Gabor L. 2001. Ecological Risks and Benefits of Transgenic Plants. *New Zealand Plant Protection* 54: 93–100. Reprinted with permission of G. L. Lövei.

Sagoff, Mark. 2001. The Ecological Critique of Agricultural Biotechnology. *Indiana Journal of Global Legal Studies* 9.3. Used by permission of Indiana University Press and Mark Sagoff.

Meyer, John. 2000. Rights to Life? On Nature, Property, and Biotechnology. *Journal of Political Philosophy* 8.2: 154–75. Used by permission of Blackwell Publishing.

Hardin, Garrett. 1968. Tragedy of the Commons. *Science* 162: 1243–48. Copyright 1968 American Association for the Advancement of Science. By permission of Garrett Hardin and *Science.*

Lohmann, Larry. 1995. Visitors to the Commons: Approaching Thailand's "Environmental" Struggles from a Western Starting Point. Reprinted by permission from *Ecological Resistance Movements: The Global Emergence of Radical and Popular Environmentalism,* Bron Raymond Taylor, ed., pp. 109–26. State University of New York Press, Albany. All rights reserved.

Emerson, Kirk. 1997. Taking the Land Rights Movement Seriously. In *A Wolf in the Garden: The Land Rights Movement and the New Environmental Debate,* Philip D. Brick and R. McGreggor Cawley, eds., pp. 115–33. Rowman and Littlefield, Lanham, Maryland. Copyright © 1997 Rowman & Littlefield Publishing Group, Inc. Reproduced with permission of Rowman & Littlefield Publishing Group, Inc. in the format Textbook via Copyright Clearance Center.

Anderson, L. Terry, and Donald R. Leal. 2001. *Free Market Environmentalism Today,* 2nd edition. St. Martins Press, New York.

Sagoff, Mark. 2000. At the Monument to General Meade, or on the Difference between Beliefs and Benefits. *Arizona Law Review* 42.2: 433–62. Copyright © 2000 by the Arizona Board of Regents. Reprinted by permission.

Anielski, Mark, and Colin L. Soskolne. 2002. Genuine Progress Indicator (GPI) Accounting: Relating Ecological Integrity to Human Health and Well-Being. In *Just Ecological Integrity: The Ethics of Maintaining Planetary Life,* Peter Miller and Laura Westra, eds., pp. 83–97. Rowman and Littlefield, Lanham, Maryland. Copyright © 2002 Rowman & Littlefield Publishing Group, Inc. Reproduced with permission of Rowman & Littlefield Publishing Group, Inc. in the format Textbook via Copyright Clearance Center.

James, Alexander, Kevin J. Gaston, and Andrew Balmford. 2001. Can We Afford to Conserve Biodiversity? *BioScience* 51.1: 43–52. Copyright © 2001 by American Institute of Biological Sciences. Reproduced with permission of American Institute of Biological Sciences in the format Textbook via Copyright Clearance Center.

Stone, Christopher D. 1996. From *Should Trees Have Standing? and Other Essays on Law, Morals, and the Environment,* Oceana Publications, Dobbs Ferry, New York. © 1996 Oceana Publications, Inc. Reprinted with permission of Oceana Publications, Inc.

Norton, Bryan G. 1991. Fragile Freedoms. In *Toward Unity among Environmentalists,* pp. 249–55. Oxford University Press, New York. Copyright © 1994, 1991 by Oxford University Press, Inc. Used by permission of Oxford University Press, Inc.

Stenmark, Mikael. 2002. The Relevance of Environmental Ethical Theories for Policy Making. *Environmental Ethics* 24.2: 135–48. Used by permission of M. Stenmark.

Davis, Cheryl. 2001. Environmental Ethical Issues in Water Operations and Land Management. In *Navigating Rough Waters: Ethical Issues in the Water Industry,* Cheryl K. Davis and Robert E. McGinn, eds., 179–96. American Water Works Association, Denver, Colorado. Reprinted by permission. Copyright © 2001 American Water Works Association.

Dryzek, John S. 1997. Ecological Democracy. In *The Politics of the Earth: Environmental Discourses.* Oxford University Press, New York. Copyright © 1997 by Oxford University Press, Inc. Used by permission of Oxford University Press, Inc.

Vickerman, Sara. 1998. Leopold as Advocate. *Wildlife Society Bulletin* 26.4: 751–56. Copyright 1998 by Wildlife Society. Reproduced with permission of Wildlife Society in the format Textbook via Copyright Clearance Center.